W9-CHP-847

# Handbook of Social Work Practice with Vulnerable Populations

▼

# HANDBOOK OF SOCIAL WORK PRACTICE WITH VULNERABLE POPULATIONS

▼

Edited by Alex Gitterman

COLUMBIA UNIVERSITY PRESS
*New York*

Columbia University Press

New York    Chichester, West Sussex

Copyright © 1991 Columbia University Press

All rights reserved

Casebound editions of Columbia University Press books are
printed on permanent and durable acid-free paper.

Book design by Jennifer Dossin

Printed in the United States of America

c  10 9 8 7 6 5 4

*In memory of my friends and colleagues
Professors Sherman Barr, Mary Funnyē Goldson, Charles Grosser,
Melvin Herman, William Schwartz, and Hyman Weiner.
They were people of vision and action.*

# Contents

▼

Acknowledgments     ix

Contributors     xi

Introduction: Social Work Practice with
Vulnerable Populations     1
*Alex Gitterman*

## PART I *Vulnerable Life Conditions*

1. AIDS     35
   *George S. Getzel*

2. Alcoholism and Other Drug Addictions     65
   *Meredith Hanson*

3. Borderline Personality     101
   *Harriette C. Johnson and Dennis E. Goguen*

4. Chronic Physical Illness and Disability     137
   *Rita Beck Black and Joan O. Weiss*

5. Depression     165
   *Joanne E. Turnbull*

6. Eating Problems     205
   *Barbara von Bulow*

7. Learning Disabilities     234
   *Naomi Pines Gitterman*

8. Mental Retardation 265
*Dale M. Brantley and Patsy A. Gemmill*

9. Schizophrenia 286
*Susan Matorin*

PART II *Vulnerable Life Circumstances and Events*

10. Adolescent Pregnancy 319
*Bruce Armstrong*

11. Child Abuse and Neglect 345
*Lynn Videka-Sherman*

12. Children in Foster Care 382
*Brenda G. McGowan and Emily Stutz*

13. Crime Victims 416
*Rosemary C. Masters*

14. Death of a Child 446
*Barbara Oberhofer Dane*

15. Domestic Violence 471
*Bonnie E. Carlson*

16. Elderly in Need of Long-Term Care 503
*Toby Berman-Rossi*

17. Family Caregivers of the Frail Elderly 549
*Ronald W. Toseland and Gregory Smith*

18. Homeless People 584
*Stephen Holloway*

19. Immigrants and Refugees 618
*Diane Drachman and Angela Shen-Ryan*

20. Imprisonment 647
*Barbara Grodd and Barbara Simon*

21. Suicide and Suicidal Behavior 677
*André Ivanoff*

22. Workers in Job Jeopardy 710
*Beth Silverman, Barbara Simon, and Richard Woodrow*

Author Index 749

Subject Index 767

# Acknowledgments

▼

I wish to express my deep appreciation to the contributors for their willingness to prepare a chapter for the *Handbook*. They accepted and carried out a difficult and comprehensive assignment.

I am very appreciative of their willingness to follow a demanding outline, their openness to editorial suggestions, their acceptance of the need to rewrite drafts, and their good spirit about my constant calling to "inquire" about their progress. I hope you will be as pleased as I am with their significant accomplishments and contributions to the profession's literature.

I would also like to thank my friend and colleague Professor Irving Miller for many helpful suggestions, demands for intellectual rigor, warm support, and social vision.

A special thanks to my daughter, Sharon, for her frequent computer and spelling consultations.

Finally, I would like to thank James Raimes, Senior Editor, Columbia University Press, for his interest in and commitment to this project.

A.G.

# Contributors

▼

**Bruce Armstrong, D.S.W.**
Columbia University School of Public Health, Center for
Population and Public Health, Director, Adolescent Social
Support Services

**Toby Berman-Rossi, D.S.W.**
Assistant Professor, Columbia University School of Social Work

**Rita Beck Black, D.S.W.**
Associate Professor, Columbia University School of Social Work

**Dale M. Brantley, M.S.W.**
Director of Social Services, Chauncey Sparks Center for
Developmental and Learning Disorders, University of Alabama
at Birmingham

**Barbara von Bulow, Ph.D.**
Associate Director, Columbia Presbyterian Psychiatric Associates

**Bonnie E. Carlson, Ph.D.**
Associate Professor, School of Social Welfare, Nelson A.
Rockefeller College of Public Affairs and Policy, The University at
Albany, State University of New York

**Barbara Oberhofer Dane, D.S.W.**
Associate Professor, New York University School of Social Work

**Diane Drachman, D.S.W.**
Associate Professor, University of Connecticut School of
Social Work

**George S. Getzel, D.S.W.**
Professor, Hunter College School of Social Work

**Patsy A. Gemmill, M.S.W.**
Social Worker, Chauncey Sparks Center for Developmental and
Learning Disorders, University of Alabama at Birmingham

**Alex Gitterman, Ed.D.**
Professor, Columbia University School of Social Work

**Naomi Pines Gitterman, M.S.W.**
Assistant Dean and Director of Educational Site, Columbia
University School of Social Work

**Dennis E. Goguen, M.S.W.**
Recent graduate, University of Connecticut School of Social Work

**Barbara Grodd, M.S.W.**
Director of Substance Abuse Services, Montefiore Medical Center/
Rikers Island Health Services

**Meredith Hanson, D.S.W.**
Assistant Professor, Columbia University School of Social Work

**Stephen Holloway, Ph.D.**
Dean, Barry University School of Social Work

**André Ivanoff, Ph.D.**
Assistant Professor, Columbia University School of Social Work

**Harriette C. Johnson, Ph.D.**
Professor, University of Connecticut School of
Social Work

**Rosemary C. Masters, J.D., M.S.W.**
Private practice

**Susan Matorin, M.S.W.**
Director of Social Work, Payne Whitney Clinic of the
New York Hospital

**Brenda G. McGowan, D.S.W.**
Professor, Columbia University School of Social Work

**Angela Shen-Ryan, D.S.W.**
Assistant Professor, Hunter College School of Social Work

**Beth Silverman, D.S.W.**
Assistant Professor, Columbia University School of Social Work

**Barbara Simon, Ph.D.**
Associate Professor, Columbia University School of Social Work

**Gregory Smith, Ed.D.**
Research Associate, Ringel Institute of Gerontology, School of
Social Welfare, Nelson A. Rockefeller College of Public Affairs and
Policy, The University at Albany, State University of New York

**Emily Stutz, M.S.W.**
Social worker, Center for Family Life in Sunset Park, Brooklyn,
New York

**Ronald W. Toseland, Ph.D.**
Associate Professor, School of Social Welfare, Nelson A.
Rockefeller College of Public Affairs and Policy, The University at
Albany, State University of New York

**Joanne E. Turnbull, Ph.D.**
Associate Professor, Columbia University School of Social Work

**Lynn Videka-Sherman, Ph.D.**
Dean and Associate Professor, School of Social Welfare, Nelson A.
Rockefeller College of Public Affairs and Policy, The University at
Albany, State University of New York

**Joan O. Weiss, M.S.W.**
Coordinator, Alliance of Genetic Support Groups and Consultant
in Social Work to the John Hopkins Center for Medical Genetics

**Richard Woodrow, D.S.W.**
Associate Director, Department of Social Work, Mt. Sinai
Medical Center

# Handbook of Social Work Practice with Vulnerable Populations

▼

# INTRODUCTION

# Social Work Practice with Vulnerable Populations

## ALEX GITTERMAN

Through my teaching and practice experiences, I have become acutely aware of the increasing degradation and distress faced by large sectors of the client population served by social workers. Students and professionals confront daily the crushing impact of such problems as mental illness, substance abuse, disability and death, teenage pregnancy, and child neglect and abuse. Clients suffer from the debilitating effects of such life circumstances as homelessness, violence, family disintegration, and unemployment. The miseries and human suffering encountered by social workers in the 1980s and 1990s are different in degree and kind from those encountered in the '50s, '60s and the '70s. AIDS and homelessness are examples of new devastating social phenomena.

Social workers in practice today deal with profoundly vulnerable populations, overwhelmed by oppressive lives, and by circumstances and events they are powerless to control. The problems are often intractable because they are chronic and persistent, or acute and unexpected. When community and family supports are weak or unavailable and when internal resources are impaired, these populations are vulnerable to physical, cognitive, emotional, and social deterioration. While, historically, the profession of social work has assumed the task of providing social services to disadvantaged and vulnerable populations, this task has become significantly more difficult to fulfill. For the stubborn truth is that problems have been increasing, while resources to mitigate them decrease. Those with less

1

get less! Given these bitter realities, heroism is required and has actually been shown by social workers in their efforts to provide meaningful services.

Many schools of social work have redesigned their curricula to respond to changes in social realities and conditions. Many have assumed a broad ecosystems perspective to reflect the complex relations between people and their environments. This perspective provides the bases for conceptualizing and teaching various professional roles and behaviors (e.g., advocate, educator, facilitator) and integrated methods (e.g., individual, family, group, community practice). Several widely used social work texts conceptualize and illustrate this perspective. Though providing generic and generalist knowledge and skills, they waver in the specialized knowledge required to help the most severely vulnerable and powerless populations.

What does the social worker need *to know* and to be able *to do* to provide resourceful programmatic and individualized clinical services to such populations? *The Handbook of Social Work Practice with Vulnerable Populations* explores these questions, according to two distinctive sets of issues. Part I, "Vulnerable Life Conditions," examines social work practice with vulnerable populations who have to cope with chronic life conditions that have dynamic genetic, biochemical, and physiological bases. Chapters on AIDS, alcoholism and other drug addictions, borderline personality, chronic physical illness and disability, depression, eating problems, learning disabilities, mental retardation, and schizophrenia, all explore the theoretical, empirical, demographic, programmatic, and clinical issues with which social workers need to be familiar to provide relevant and empowering services.

Part II, "Vulnerable Life Circumstances and Events," examines social work practice with populations that often confront desperate life circumstances such as homelessness and very stressful life events such as the death of a child. Chapters on adolescent pregnancy, child abuse, children in foster care, crime victims, the death of a child, domestic violence, elderly in need of long-term care, family caregivers of the frail elderly, homelessness, immigration, imprisonment, suicide, and workers in job jeopardy similarly explore the theoretical, empirical, demographic, programmatic, and clinical issues.

## PROBLEM DOMAIN

All chapters follow the same outline. After a brief introduction about the respective population, the contributors analyze the theoretical and empirical problem domain of the life condition, circumstance, or event. In certain "personality conditions" such as chronic depression, schizophrenia, and borderline personality, and in certain addictions such as alcoholism, growing evidence suggests potent predisposing genetic, biochemical factors. Researchers' studies have, for example, analyzed the life careers of identical twins separated at birth and have used other tracking designs to find significant genetic links to alcoholism (Cloninger, Bohm, and Sigvardsson 1981, 1983, 1987, 1988; Goodwin et al. 1973), borderline personality (Andulonis et al. 1981;), depression (Gershon 1983; Mendelwicz and Rainer 1977; Wender et al. 1986), and schizophrenia (Feldman, Stiffman, and Jung 1987; Kety 1988).

These conditions have in common certain genetic and neurochemical predispositions. In alcoholism, for example, serotonin, a synthesized molecule in the brain, has been associated with depression. Experiments with rats have shown that when levels of serotonin were decreased, the result was a marked increase in alcohol consumption. In contrast, raising the levels of serotonin resulted in a pronounced reduction of alcohol intake (Zhukov, Varkof, and Burov 1987). Based on a review of research, Wallace (1989) identified two different types of alcoholics: (1) the "hyperaroused," who may suffer from too high a level of serotonin and seek out alcohol to sedate and blot out stimulation overload, and (2) the "anhedonic," who may suffer from too low a level of serotonin and seek alcohol to arouse and to compensate for stimulation under load. The brain also manufactures natural substances, opoids, that have pain-killing properties. Blum and Topel (1986) found that the less this substance was present in mice, the more they consumed alcohol. Thus, genetically induced chemical imbalances appear to be associated with various life conditions.

With AIDS, our vulnerability to parasitic relations with microorganisms from within and without is ominous. The biological reality of AIDS demonstrates how defenseless our immune systems can be to parasitic and toxic environments. In other life conditions such as anorexia and bulimia, the genetic links have not yet been discovered. Thus far personality and family dynamic explanations have frequently been offered for these conditions. We should not, however, be surprised if, in the near future, genetic and biochemical predisposing conditions are discovered. In obesity, however, there is clear evidence of genetic influence (Foch and McClearn 1980).

Chronic physical illnesses and disabilities, learning disabilities, and mental retardation reflect problems in physiological and neurological functions. Mental retardation often has genetic determinants (Abuelo 1983; Dickerson 1981). Similarly, a possible genetic basis for

Alzheimer's disease (Schmeck 1987a) and cancer has also been identified (Schmeck 1987c, 1987b). Even though many of the presented life conditions have genetic determinants, they may not be inherited. Certain toxic environmental agents can damage and disrupt normal genetic processes. For example, a woman who abuses alcohol may give birth to an infant with fetal alcohol syndrome, which is often characterized by mental retardation, facial deformity, etc. Radiation, as another example, can cause infertility and birth defects (Rauch 1988). Whatever the cause, physiological and cognitive impairments severely curtail human activities. People with these life conditions often suffer for protracted and indefinite time periods. Their neurological and physiological disabilities create limitations and burdens of varying severity.

Genetic, biochemical, and neurological loading and a predisposition to a condition do not, however, imply that a person will necessarily acquire it or, if it is acquired, will be debilitated by the particular condition. The resources and the gaps in the person's environment (i. e., family, relatives, friends, work mates, neighbors, community, organizations, and spiritual life) transact with individual constitutional resources and limits. On one end of the continuum, high genetic and organic loading may push certain people toward alcoholism, depression, borderline personality, or schizophrenia regardless of how protective and supportive the environment (although a supportive environment can certainly cushion the consequences). Similarly, a youngster born mentally retarded or severely physically disabled has to function within the constraints of these neurophysiological impairments. While supportive environments can provide instrumental and expressive resources, they cannot eliminate the disability itself. On the other end of the continuum, severely impoverished and invalidating environments may push certain people toward alcoholism or depression no matter how well those people are constitutionally endowed. With limited, or even without, genetic predispositions, a youngster repeatedly exposed to malnourishment and physical and emotional abuse may succumb to these harsh environmental assaults and develop alcoholism or depression. Studies of psychiatric epidemiology have demonstrated that the lower the social class, the higher the rates of mental illness and the greater the severity of the mental illness (Hollingshead and Redlich 1958; Strole and Fischer 1977).

Family, community, and society dysfunctions provide the most frequent theoretical explanations for the distressing life circumstances and events presented in the *Handbook*. Unplanned pregnancies, for example, are associated with poverty, repeated academic failures, and pervasive lack of opportunities and with consequent hopelessness and despair. Community and family norms reinforce or mitigate the personal impact of poverty. In domestic violence, the female as victim of her male partner is the principal problem. A pattern of control over the female maintained by physical, emotional, and sexual abuse is associated with violence and battering. On a more general level, sexism and sex-role socialization surely contribute to, if they do not induce, domestic violence. Boys observing their fathers abuse their mothers are more likely than not to be violent toward their own wives (Gelles and Straus 1988). Clearly, domestic violence is learned behavior that has to be unlearned.

No citizen, regardless of class or social status, is safe from crime. Women, children, and the elderly, especially those living in poor communities, are at highest risk of victimization by crime. They simply are easier prey. The perpetrators tend to be caught in a cycle of family poverty, illiteracy, drugs, racism, child abuse, and family violence. When they are incarcerated, they usually return to their community further damaged, hardened, and embittered. They often become socialized to a lifetime of crime and intermittent incarceration. In poor communities, both the victim and the perpetrator are trapped in the mire of despair. Similarly, underemployment and unemployment, the elimination of low-income housing, sharply curtailed benefit programs, and unplanned-for and unprovided-for deinstitutionalization have all conspired to create an unconscionable large number of adults and children deprived of shelter, a basic human need.

When people find themselves in such distressing life circumstances, some feel and become helpless, hopeless victims. They live on the margin, struggling for day-to-day survival. Others somehow miraculously manage deeply adverse situations as survivors, not as victims. Various theories are used to explain what differentiates a victim from a survivor. No single theory seems capable of providing a comprehensive explanation. We do know, however, that people's social functioning and adaptations reflect the interplay and degree of congruence and compatibility between body, mind, and environment. Sometimes people's exchanges with their environments are mutually fulfilling. The congruence and compatibility between people and their environments provide the context for realization of potential. At other times, these exchanges lead to isolation and alienation. A poor fit limits realization of potential. How people perceive their personal and environmental resources and limitations, their personal attributions and social constructions, also has a profound impact. Thus, two people with similar personal and environmental attributes may subjectively perceive their personal and environmental resources differently and may consequently function at differing levels. And finally, there is the simple element of chance: good fortune and misfortune. For example, many people who survived the Holocaust were at the right place at the right time. While our efforts to be scientific may cause us to shy away from the idea of chance, it may well enhance our understanding of and feeling for the human experience.

## SOCIETAL CONTEXT

After discussing the problem domain of the distressing life condition, circumstance, or event, the authors examine how institutions cushion, exacerbate, or "cause" the problems in question. When institutions provide resources and supports, they are critical buffers, helping people cope with life transitions, environments, and interpersonal problems (Germain and Gitterman 1980a). By providing emotional, instrumental, informational, and appraisal supports, societal structures influence the worldviews and self-concepts of people and fortify them against physiological, psychological, and social harm (Gottlieb 1988). In contrast, when these resources and supports are unavailable or insufficient, people are apt to feel helpless and hopeless, and to lack skill in interpersonal and environmental coping.

Poverty and its consequences are directly responsible for many of the most difficult life situations. The rich continue to become richer; the poor become poorer. From 1979 to 1987, the poorest fifth of our citizens, more than 40 million, had their standard of living decline by 9 percent, while the living standard of the top fifth increased by 19 percent. When income is adjusted for inflation and family size, the poorest fifth suffered a 1 percent decrease from 1973 to 1979 and a further decrease of 10 percent from 1979 to 1989. The adjusted income of the top fifth, in contrast, swelled by 7 percent and then 16 percent more during comparable years (Passell 1989). Essentially, the gap between the poor and the wealthy has widened.[1]

There has been a dramatic increase in single-parent families, mostly headed by women; almost half live below the poverty line. As a consequence, large numbers of children live in poverty:

> In 1984, more than ⅕ of America's 62 million children under 18 lived in poverty: nearly one of every two black children, two of every five Hispanic children, and one in every six white children, fall at or below the poverty level. . . . Today our youngest children, those under the age of six, are more likely to be poor than any other group. (DMCH 1986:3–4)

Since 1979, the number of children living in poverty has increased by over 30 percent (NASW 1987:1). During the same period, benefits have not changed significantly (except for greater difficulty in access and eligibility). Over 60 percent of the poor are ineligible for Medicaid. A consequence of the large numbers of single-parent families living in severe poverty is the dramatic increase of children entering the foster care system. In New York City, for example, a 40 percent increase was projected from 1985 to 1989 (SSC 1989).

The environment of the poor is particularly harsh. Because of their economic position, they are unable to command needed goods and services. Good education, preventive health care, jobs, housing, safe communities, neighborhood amenities, and geographic and social mobility are unavailable to or extremely limited for the poor. They are not able to compete for societal resources and their leverage on social institutions is extremely limited. They suffer prolonged unemployment. For example, changes in our economy have resulted in a large and growing number of young black males hopelessly locked into a life of unemployment. A dramatic economic transformation, intensified by our country's long history of racism and discrimination, has left the black family extremely vulnerable. Even by the 1960s, the national rate of unemployed black men between the ages of 18 and 24 was five times as high as that of white males of the same age (Clark 1965:34). While the previously slave-exploiting agricultural economy required relatively unskilled labor, our increasingly automated and service economy requires skilled labor. Hence the current economy now has little need of the unskilled black male. Wilhelm and Powell suggested: "He is not so much unwanted as unnecessary; not so much abused as ignored. The dominant whites no longer need to exploit him. If he disappears tomorrow he would hardly be missed. As automation proceeds it is easier and easier to disregard him . . . thus, he moves to the automated urbanity of 'nobodiness' " (1964:4).

Lack of employment opportunities institutionalizes poverty. A devastating cycle of physical, psychological, and social consequences follows. Among the economically disadvantaged, morbidity and mortality rates are strikingly higher than those of the economically more fortunate. Lacking access to adequate health care, the 40 million people living below the poverty line have, for example, a relative cancer survival rate of 10 percent to 15 percent below the rate of those living above the poverty line (Cimons 1989:1). Blacks have higher rates of virtually all cancers than whites. Black men below the age of 45 are ten times more likely to die of hypertension than whites and have a 45 percent higher rate of lung cancer. The diabetes rate is 33 percent higher among blacks than among whites. Blacks have twice the level of infant mortality. They also account for more than 25 percent of the diagnosed AIDS cases even though they represent only

13 percent of the population (Lee 1989:1). Beyond inadequate preventive services and health care, high rates of cancer, substance abuse, and hypertension among poor blacks have been directly linked to numerous self-defeating behaviors (e.g., poor eating habits, drugs and alcohol abuse). A number of theories link low self-esteem to living in an intensely racist society. For example, a study using computer technology found links between a black person's school failure, lowered self-esteem, and cardiovascular overreactivity (Lee 1989:11).

Violence is endemic to and epidemic in our society. In 1989, over 30,000 people died of gunshot wounds. In a two-year period, 1987–1989, more Americans died of gunshot wounds than died in the Vietnam war. Only automobile accidents (approximately 49,000 a year) account for more deaths (Maggnuson 1989:31). It was estimated by the President's Task Force on Criminal Justice (1982) that a murder occurs every twenty-three minutes and that a woman is raped every six minutes. Moreover, a United States Department of Justice publication (1986) reported that 28 people out of every 1,000 over the age of 12 are victimized by violent crimes. Guns also account for a significant proportion of suicides. In 1986, for example, 64 percent of men who committed suicide shot themselves (Maggnuson 1989:61). In spite of these grim data, the gun lobby has successfully stifled gun control legislation.

In addition to being at risk in their own communities, women and children are at risk of violence in their own homes. Approximately 1.6 million women each year are victimized by domestic violence (Gelles and Straus 1988). Since 1981, child maltreatment has risen dramatically, approximately 66 percent (U.S. HHS 1988). The cumulative impact of the exposure to violence is devastating. An increasing number of inner-city children, for example, suffer from low self-esteem and a posttraumatic stress syndrome similar to that seen in Vietnam veterans (Lee 1989). These children have been exposed to violent attacks on and the murder of their parents, friends, relatives, and neighbors. They are further traumatized by domestic violence and child abuse. These experiences have long-lasting physical, psychological, and social effects.

Mass media and advertising contribute to social problems. Violence, drugs, flashy cars, and impulsive and degrading sexual encounters are too often romanticized. Adolescents are exposed to sexually provocative depictions. The media encourage youth to be sexually active. Since the majority of poor children live in single-parent households, unsupervised apartments are more likely to be available to them than to more affluent youth. In fact, the most common location for first sexual intercourse is in one's own or the partner's home (Hayes 1987).

The mass media portray women as sexual objects whose primary functions are to be glamorous, beautiful, and thin. Stunning professional female models and actresses beguile women with products they need to improve their beauty. Advertisements imply that women should cook but not eat. Being thin becomes a preoccupation and a form of self-assumed tyranny. These messages trigger self-doubts and feelings of inferiority. Serious eating problems, such as anorexia nervosa and bulimia, may also result.

The social context defines our caseloads. We need to be sensitive to its pervasive impact on our clients' lives. Most psychological theories underemphasize the power of this reality. To the extent that we remain wedded to these theories as the sole explainers of people's problems, we limit our understanding and our potential to be helpful.

## RISKS AND NEEDS OF POPULATIONS

Each contributor identifies the populations and subpopulations most vulnerable to the various problems presented in the *Handbook*. As the social context discussion observes, *poverty and a lack of social supports* are the most potent risk indicators in many distressing life circumstances and events. Poor people are simply most likely to become homeless, victimized by crime, abused and violated, imprisoned, pregnant in adolescence, jobless, etc. For illustrative purposes, the domain of violence is instructive. Poverty breeds violence. Child abuse has been associated with lower socioeconomic status, unemployment, lack of education, childbearing at an early age, alcohol and drug abuse, and spousal violence (Hampton and Newberger 1985; Olsen and Holmes 1986). Similarly, neighborhoods that have a large amount of reported child abuse tend to be very poor, with inadequate housing and a low level of neighborhood interaction (Skinner and Castle 1969). Abusing parents have been found to have fewer social supports than nonabusing parents (Milner and Wemberly 1980). Abusing parents also seem to have histories of having been abused as children themselves. Poverty is also the most powerful correlate with wife battering. Most studies suggest that low-income men are more likely to engage in family violence and abuse than middle- and high-income men. Similarly, men who observed their fathers batter their mothers are more likely to batter their wives. Alcohol and drug abuse, work stress and unemployment, and inadequate social support increase the potential for domestic violence.

The pervasiveness of violence in our nation has already been discussed. However, it is important to note that the poor are the primary victims of violent crimes. In fact, the person who earns less than $7,500 a year is 2.5 times more likely to be the victim of violent crime than the person earning more than $50,000 (U.S. Dept. of Justice 1986:3–5). Jails and prisons are overcrowded with poor people who either are awaiting trial or have been found guilty of crime. By 1986, more than 2.6 million adults were in the penal system. (U.S. Dept. of Justice 1988). Almost half (45 percent) of the jail inmates were unemployed at the time they were arraigned, and a large proportion were functionally illiterate and high school dropouts (Wilson and Herrnstein, 1985; U.S. Dept. of Justice 1988). Black citizens are six times more likely to be incarcerated than whites, and by the age of 64, 18 percent of black men have served some time compared to only 3 percent of the white male population (U.S. Dept. of Justice 1988).

Poverty is also related to adolescent pregnancy. Poor adolescents appear to be sexually active at a younger age and less likely to use birth control than their more affluent counterparts (Pittman and Adams 1988). Adolescent mothers are more likely to drop out of school and not to complete a high school degree than are females who delay childbearing (Marsiglio and Mott 1985). These young people become caught in hopeless poverty. Also, their children are more likely to have physical, emotional, and social problems. A similar pattern is evident with addictions to certain drugs, particularly crack. As poor inner-city communities become poorer and as they become more alienated, escape into crack becomes a viable option, and as the drug users become addicted, a "career" in unemployment, violence, and criminality becomes a virtual inevitability.

As previously discussed, there has been a sharp increase in the numbers of children living in poverty. This is most evident in the increase in homeless families (now constituting about 20 percent of all the homeless). In New York City, fewer than 1,000 families were identified as homeless before 1982; three years later, in 1985, there were 4,000 families with 8,000 children (Harvard Medical School 1987). Even more distressing is the estimate that between 250,000 and 500,000 young people are homeless nationwide (Harvard Medical School 1987).

The consequences of childhood poverty are manifold and manifest. Poor children learn early in life that they have limited control over their lives, that things happen to and are done to them. They develop a "learned helplessness" and internalize feelings of powerlessness

(Seiligman 1975). Poor children are at greater risk than others of suffering various acute illnesses and specific health problems. At every age, poor children are at a relatively higher risk of death (DMCH 1986). They are more likely than others to be exposed to violence, malnutrition, poor education, family disruption and disorder, and institutionalization or incarceration of parents, and consequently, they are more likely than other children to respond with antisocial behavior, addiction, and depression.

*Ethnicity* is a significant differentiating risk factor in what life has in store. Morbidity and the related death rates are much higher for blacks and Hispanics than for whites for cancer, diabetes, hypertension, drug-related AIDS in females and children, and, of course, infant mortality. Birth rates among black and Hispanic adolescents are significantly higher than among white adolescents. By age eighteen, 14 percent of Hispanic and 26 percent of black adolescents have given birth, compared to 7 percent of white adolescents (Pittman and Adams 1988). Suicide, however, appears to be more frequent among whites; in fact, they are twice as likely as blacks to commit suicide, with males over age 80 having the highest reported rates (NCHS 1988).

*Sex* differences are another factor in most types of depression. Women have significantly higher rates than do men (Boyd and Weissman 1981). Women confronting stressful life circumstances and life events are particularly vulnerable to depression. For example, they are almost always the caregivers for frail elderly parents, and the process of caregiving is almost always a source of considerable stress (Horowitz 1985). It also typically interferes with and attenuates their own employment schedules and other family obligations (Stone, Cafferata, and Sangl 1987). The majority of persons living in nursing homes are childless, never-married, often socially isolated women (Kane 1987). Finally, anorexia nervosa, bulimia, and related eating disorders are virtually the exclusive domain of women. Ballerinas, female models, and female athletes are at higher risk than others. Professional female dance students, for example, were found in a study to have a prevalence rate of anorexia nervosa seven times higher than females in the rest of the population (Garner and Garfinkel 1985). Women are at greater risk of injury in domestic conflict than are men. Their risk increases if either or both partners grew up in families of batterers, and also if the man is an alcoholic, is a drug abuser, or is unemployed, and if both are socially isolated.

Adolescent males (aged 16–19) are victims of violent crimes at a rate nearly three times the national average for the total population (U.S. Justice 1986:3). Men also appear to commit almost all of the crimes. Ninety-three to ninety-six percent of all jail and prison inmates are men (U.S. Justice 1988). In prisons, older and developmentally disabled and physically weaker men tend to be at greatest risk of sexual assault and harassment. Men are also more likely to commit violence against themselves; i.e., their suicide rate is nearly four times higher than that of women (NCHS 1988).

*Age* itself is also a differentiating factor in the troubles people have. Adolescents and young adults in our society are particularly at risk of many of the unfavorable life situations discussed in this *Handbook*. For example, they have higher rates of drug abuse and related problems than other age groups (Lukoff 1980). Young adult males have been found to drink more and to have more alcohol-related problems than any other age group (Cahalan and Room 1974). Although 15–29-year-olds comprise 27 percent of the overall population, 66 percent of all jail and prison inmates are in that age group (U.S. Justice 1988). Adolescence and young adulthood are also associated with the development of eating problems (Garfinkel and Garner 1982). And as we grow older, decline in physical capacities (i.e., arthritis, hypertension, hearing and visual loss, and other impairments) can be expected. We can also expect to become poorer, especially in the 75 and older age group (U.S. HHS 1985–86).

Many life conditions seem to have entrenched careers in the *family*. Alcoholism and some drug addictions often have long family histories. Persons whose parents have had a history of addiction have an increased chance of becoming addicted as well (Goodwin 1988). Family histories seem to predispose the members to major depression (Weissman, Kidd, and Prusoff 1982). It has been shown that children of depressed parents tend to be vulnerable to both major depression and substance abuse (Weissman et al. 1987); also, siblings of drug users are more likely than not to use and abuse drugs (Vance 1977). Similarly, children of one schizophrenic parent have a 7–19 percent higher probability of developing psychosis than the population generally, and a 29 percent greater probability if both parents are schizophrenic (Meyer-Kimling 1977).

## PROGRAMS AND SOCIAL WORK SERVICES

Each contributor examines programs and social work services developed to deal with the population's problems. Since each author examines specific programs, services, and modalities, the discussion here is limited to selected ideas about primary-prevention programs.

What do we do with our knowledge about populations vulnerable to various pernicious life conditions, circumstances, and events? Funding sources have placed an increasing emphasis on the public health concept of primary prevention, the main objective of which is to anticipate and forestall some undesirable event or condition that may otherwise occur and spread (Gitterman 1988a).[2] Primary prevention has two distinct strategies: 1) *specific protection,* an explicit intervention for disease prevention in which a population at risk is identified and something is done with the population to strengthen its resistance, and 2) *health promotion,* an intervention for improving the quality of life and raising the general-health and mental-health level of a population. Social workers have inherited from the past a third prevention strategy: 3) *environmental change,* doing something about the social conditions that foster the problems. At present, this tradition, if not ignored, is certainly neglected. Funding and, consequently, professional interests are both engaged primarily in the "specific protection" aspect of prevention.

This direction can be a problem. By emphasizing "specific protection," our efforts may promise much more than they can deliver. Childhood poverty, for example, is deeply embedded in our social structure. The high levels of actual unemployment, the decreases in public entitlements, inflation, and increases in adolescent pregnancy and out-of-wedlock births all conspire to enlarge the dimensions of childhood poverty. These children's problems are becoming more intractable, and dangerous. In this context, the premise of specific-protection prevention (i.e., intervening before a problem has "struck") must be reexamined. If we identify poverty as the major problem, the prevention of social ills becomes elusive, if not illusory.

As other examples, domestic-violence and child-abuse prevention programs are being implemented within the context of a violent society. Our society promotes and tolerates violence, and few prevention programs deal with the cultural propensity toward violence. Programs that teach targeted adolescents to avoid pregnancy by saying "no" or that advise parents who may abuse their child to manage their angry feelings, however useful and pertinent, cannot deal with the multidimensional pathways to social problems. In fact, most new immigrant groups have shown high rates of "social pathology," but as they achieved economic security, the social pathology rates have declined. These social pathologies are analogous to a high fever: "specific protection" interventions—for example, aspirin—may momentarily reduce the fever, but they disguise the problem. Social pathologies are outcomes of complex ecological chains, which include attributes of the individual's genetic and biopsychosocial makeup, the structure of the family, social networks, community, school, work-place, religious organizations, health system, recreational resources, general culture, subculture, social class, and the overall polity.

Another problem with specific-protection strategies is difficulty in identifying the subpopulations at risk. Certain life problems, for example, have been associated with pathogenic family processes. The problem is what to do about these findings: A boy observing his father batter his mother does not, of course, inevitably become a wife batterer himself. Based on his experiences, he may become determined not to batter his wife. Similarly, boys growing up in nonbattering families may, due to unemployment or addictions, become batterers. What can we do about aggregate data? Can we attribute to the individual the characteristics of the group, thus stigmatizing and defining them as being "at risk"? To draw a parallel, a colleague was asked to study alcohol abuse in a police department. He found that Irish policeofficers were particularly at risk of becoming alcoholics. It is obvious from a logical (if not a political) point of view that action, if any, can be taken only in relation to health promotion for the total police population. When identifying a subpopulation as being at "risk" and as needing specific-protection interventions, rather than using a universal "health-promotion" approach, we are in danger of adding to the burdens of that population. Moreover, by seeking and accepting restrictively defined prevention funding, we are, in effect, promising to reduce or eliminate problems such as child abuse, drug addiction, and teenage pregnancy. And when these modestly funded specific-protection programs are unable to mitigate what are probably the consequences of structurally ingrained poverty, we diminish our professional credibility.

The second strategy, health promotion, is a viable alternative. It attempts to improve quality of life and to foster optimal health in the total population. It focuses on "wellness" and on maintaining health rather than on treating "sickness" and restoring health. Services based on a developmental approach scheme emphasize access to health education, recreation, and socialization activities, and to cultural programs. In effect, the health-promotion approach offers many pathways to well-being. Examples include genetic counseling, marital counseling, pregnancy planning, pre- and postnatal care, obstetrical care, well-baby clinics, preschool programs and enrichment programs, parental involvement in school programs, and sex education. These programs attempt to promote social competence, cognitive and emotional coping, and achievement. Maximizing early positive experiences and minimizing negative experiences are more likely to have long-lasting effects. Thus, in social planning for universal services, programs need to be designed to strengthen major social institutions: the family, the school, the world of work, and the community. When these institutions are strengthened, general health is promoted.

Our programs also ought to reflect more involvement in the third strategy: environmental change. We need to revitalize the community organization tradition in our practice. Community organization is essential both for instrumental accomplishments (e.g., voter registration) and for the sake of the experience of challenging imbalances in power relations. Participation and action can absorb hopelessness, despair, and apathy. Experiencing and developing the belief that one can take the initiative to achieve some control of one's environment is a powerful element in promoting physical and mental health.

## DIFFERENTIAL CLINICAL ASSESSMENTS AND INTERVENTIONS

Most social workers provide direct clinical services to individuals, families, and groups. We attempt to help clients adapt to and cope with the tasks and struggles in day-to-day living. In their transactions with their environment, disturbances and disruptions often occur. People experience stress when they perceive an imbalance between the external demands placed on them and their self-defined ability to meet the demands with their own internal and environmental resources. These transactional disturbances create *problems in living* in three interrelated areas: life transitions, environmental pressures, and maladaptive interpersonal process (Gitterman and Germain 1976; Germain and Gitterman 1980a).

### *Life Transitions*

Whether a person has to adapt to depression or schizophrenia, to homelessness or foster care status, transitions in life impose new demands, require new responses, and are, therefore, often deeply distressing. All such transitions require some changes, some flexibility, and some creativity in dealing with the environment, processing information, and solving problems, and relating to others. Gradual life changes usually provide an opportunity for planning and preparation, and consequently the attendant stress is more manageable than when the change is sudden and unexpected. For some clients, change represents major threats to environmental survival and to self-image. For others, change represents an opportunity for environmental and self-enhancement. But for most people, all change has its difficulties.

## *Environmental Pressures*

While social and physical environments can support or obstruct the tasks of daily living, the environment itself is a source of severe stress. A society riven by prejudice against people of color, women, homosexuals, and old people provides unequal opportunities for its citizens. Many clients are dealt a "stacked deck." If they are impaired physically, cognitively, and emotionally, this "deal" can be insurmountable. Organizations (schools, hospitals, etc.) established to provide essential services may, in fact, block access and impose harsh and restrictive policies and procedures. Social networks (i.e., relatives, friends, work mates, and neighbors) may be scarce and unavailable, so that clients are, in effect, socially isolated. The characteristics of physical and spatial arrangements (e.g., density, crowding, safety, and privacy) may be unsuitable and may generate a great deal of distress.

## *Maladaptive Interpersonal Processes*

In dealing with life transitions or unresponsive environments, families and groups may experience intensified stress because of difficult interpersonal relationships and communication patterns. Inconsistent mutual expectations, exploitative relationships, and blocks in communication are examples of problems in interpersonal communication for individual members and for the family or the group itself. Similar problems may also emerge between workers and their clients. Workers may add to the client's burden by defining his or her behavior as resistant or unmotivated rather than as reflecting a transactional difficulty between them (Gitterman 1983, 1989).

How overwhelming and disabling clients experience their daily problems in living to be and how effectively they manage the associated life tasks will depend largely on the degree of fit between their personal and environmental resources, the timing and effectiveness of professional interventions, and, as previously suggested, sometimes chance. Workers have to be able to assess the particular client's abilities to deal with his or her problems in living, especially the degree of fit between his or her personal and environmental resources. Professional judgments have to be based on reasoned inferences and reasonable premises. To achieve such judgments, workers *collect data.* All inferences have to be based on and supported by data. Mutually agreed-upon definitions of the most pressing problems and mutually agreed-upon goals and methods of working on them (i.e., the contract) determine the direction and the content of the data to be sought.

Workers can readily become overwhelmed by a mass of data and therefore need to be able to *organize* the data, as they are being collected. The problems-in-living formulation provides a useful schema for partializing and grouping data about clients' problems. Besides providing a useful schema for problem identification, the problems-in-living formulation also serves as an assessment framework throughout the helping process. To illustrate: A worker is trying to help an adolescent mother mourning her decision to surrender her infant for purposes of adoption. In the fifth session, she agitatedly complains about her loneliness and isolation. The worker must decide whether the client is requesting help for further exploration of her grief (i.e., life transition); whether she is asking for help with her feelings of isolation from her teenage friends and family and with reconnecting herself to these natural support systems; whether the client is requesting help in constructing new environmental support systems; or, finally, whether she is complaining obliquely about the worker's inattentiveness and, therefore, subtly pressing for attention to their own interpersonal transactions. Organizing the data by problems-in-living themes helps the worker select, as the work with the client moves along, the appropriate intervention. A system for organizing data lends focus and direction to clinical interventions.

If all the relevant inferences are to be developed, the collected and classified data have to be *analyzed and synthesized.* Workers have to develop inferences based on the following: 1) an identification and definition of the clients' problems in living; 2) the meaning that these problems have for the clients; 3) the clients' strengths for and limitations in dealing with and working on their problems in living; 4) social and physical environmental supports and obstacles in maintaining and resolving the clients' problems in living; and 5) the degree of fit between the clients' (individual, family or group) and the environments' resources and deficits. Developing inferred propositions requires two disciplined forms of reasoning: inductive and deductive. *Inductive* reasoning is the intellectual process of moving from the data to generalizations based on them. As professionals, we have to conscientiously distinguish data from inferences and always to be tentative about the validity of our generalizations. *Deductive* reasoning is the intellectual process of applying the generalizations (i.e., practice knowledge and research findings) to the specific case situation. The disciplined use of informing knowledge is an important aid in determining practice focus and direction. As professionals, we have to be careful that our need for certainty, constancy, and stability does not compromise our curiosity and our ability to individualize clients.

Through disciplined forms of reasoning as well as spontaneous intuition, workers assess the degree of fit between the client and the environment and their respective demands, resources, and limitations. When an imbalance exists between a perceived demand and a perceived ability to meet the demand through the available internal and external resources, people have problems and experience stress. How severe the stress and the problems will be when a frail elderly person is discharged from a hospital after surviving a stroke and being confined to a wheelchair will depend on the degree of the physiological impairment and damage, amount of the person's physical strength and resiliency, and the person's inner resources (e.g., motivation, outlook on life, coping skills, interpretation of illness). Also extremely important are the family and extended-network caregivers in their ability and willingness to provide emotional and instrumental supports. Moreover, access to such resources as medical staff, homemakers, nursing, physical rehabilitation, and speech therapy, as well as financial entitlements, medical insurance, and financial status and ability to purchase services will have a significant impact on the final prognosis. Finally, the flexibility of the physical environment (e.g., building entrance door, corridors, furniture) will also affect recovery. Figure 1 shows the combined impact of a client's internal resources and limitations and environmental resources and limitations. While the figure may be a bit too pat and an oversimplified a view of reality, it does offer a representation of the fit between personal and environmental resources.

FIGURE 1. Person–Environment Fit.

*Environmental Resources\**

|  |  | Low | High |
|---|---|---|---|
|  | *Low* | − − | − + |
| *Personal Resources* |  | A | B |
|  | *High* | + − | + + |
|  |  | C | D |

\*"Low" indicates limited resources; "High" indicates significant resources.

In situations of low internal and low environmental resources (A), the client is at most serious risk. The poor person–environment fit suggests potential disorientation, deterioration, and disintegration. These situations require immediate attention and an active worker with sufficient time to become a critical resource for what may become an extended period. Situations of high inner and environmental resources (D) suggest a good person–environment fit and an optimistic prognosis. In these situations, the worker's activities may be limited to uncomplicated referrals, suggestions, and support. In situations of low inner resources and high environmental resources (B) and high inner and low environmental resources (C), less definitive statements can be made. When inner resources are low, the worker is usually required to be active in using his or her technical problem-solving competence and energy. Finding and connecting the client with the available network and community resources to compensate for biopsychosocial deficits are essential professional activities. When environmental resources are low, the worker usually assists the client in asserting his or her needs, seeking alternative resources, or constructing new ones.

Figure 1 provides a diagrammatic overview of the fit between client and environmental resources and deficits, offering general guidelines for different practice directions. To be useful, an assessment must be more refined than an overview. One can never, however, collect all of the available data and can never have all of the available knowledge. All professionals must act in the context of varying degrees of ambiguity. Every worker faces an array of cues, messages, and themes, sometimes perplexing and at other times overwhelming. At every and any moment, the worker has to decide which ones to respond to and which to table or defer. There is little time to think about and plan the "correct" intervention. Yet, within the context of uncertainty, the worker must act with sureness. What is being suggested here is a way to think about clients and their situations, a way to organize and analyze data, and a way to systematize practice.

The view that help in social work consists in helping people with their problems in living provides the social worker with a clear and distinctive professional function: to improve the transactions between people and their environment and to facilitate a better match (i.e., a better degree of fit) between their needs and the environmental resources. This conception of professional practice asks us 1) to help people deal with their problems in living, and 2) to design services and environmental resources and to work with constituencies to promote health and to gain entitlements.

To help clients meet the demands of life transitions, workers should be professionally competent in various roles.[3] The *enabler* role encourages clients to engage their own intellectual, emotional, and social resources to deal with their life transitions. The *educator* role teaches clients the skills for problem solving and stress management. (This role will be elaborated later.) The *facilitator* role supports clients in making decisions and in taking action in their own behalf.

To help clients deal with environmental pressures, workers define the environment as a critical arena for professional assessments and interventions. When organizational and network resources are available, but clients are unable or unwilling to use them, the roles of facilitator, teacher, and enabler come into play. When the environmental problems are not due to the clients' inabilities to use available resources, the worker also needs to be competent in other roles. The *coordinator*, for example, links clients to the available resources. When the problem is distorted transactions between clients and their social environments, the *mediator* helps clients and organizational and social-network members to connect with each other effectively. At times, workers' mediating efforts fail, and *advocate* action is taken to help clients receive the needed services and entitlements. In observing and documenting the needs of numerous clients with similar concerns and needs, the *organizer* role is needed to put together communities, informal networks, and self-help or task groups to achieve the desired outcomes and to combat social and emotional isolation.

To help families and groups deal with problem relationships and communication processes, workers must act in the roles previously discussed and must be, as well, *internal mediators*. Workers help families and groups to identify and work on their maladaptive communication patterns. With weaker and more vulnerable members (e.g., a battered wife or children), workers may also be *internal advocates*, lending clients strength and offsetting power imbalances.

These roles must be carried out in a mutual, reciprocal, and respectful manner. The life model repeatedly emphasizes the importance of shifting client-worker roles from subordinate recipient and superordinate expert—roles that are too often assumed in a "professional" relationship—to roles based on collaboration (Germain and Gitterman 1980a). By reducing social distance and power differences, the worker helps to support clients' competencies and strengths. When, and only when, social workers eliminate the existing power differential in their relationships with clients can these relationships empower clients rather than reinforce continued powerlessness (Gitterman 1983, 1989).

For illustrative purposes, the role of the social worker as educator will be discussed more fully. This role has received too little attention in the literature and is particularly appropriate in helping to empower clients coping with the life situations presented in this *Handbook*.

Many client populations described here have multiple problems and experience severe stress. They often lack the requisite skills to face and solve their problems in living and to cope with the associated stress. Successful coping calls for an ability to 1) identify and evaluate life stresses; 2) deal with the attendant emotions; and 3) delineate and choose among alternative responses in problem resolution (Lazurus and Laumier 1987). The social worker can become a critical teacher of such skills.

In teaching coping skills, the worker needs to attend to the different ways people learn. Some people learn primarily by doing ("enactive" learners). Others learn primarily by summarizing, visualizing, and organizing perceptions into patterns and images ("iconic" learners). Still others learn primarily by abstracting and conceptualizing ("symbolic" learners) (Brunner 1966). Workers need teaching methods that will accommodate the particular learning style of the client rather than the worker's own particular way of learning. The following teaching methods are feasible (Germain and Gitterman 1980b):

1. *Discussion method.* The worker uses discussion to help clients learn coping behaviors. By focusing discussion on, for example, the meanings of the surgery to the client, the worker can explore mistaken perceptions, reasoning, and beliefs, and can help clients to understand the relevant health issues and the overall features of the impending surgery, and to restructure some of the unhelpful thought processes. The role of discussion leader includes several core strategies: a) posing questions to stimulate clients' reflective out-loud thinking; b) making comments to support and encourage client examination and evaluation of alternative coping responses; and c) maintaining a flexible focus to provide the client sufficient "space" to examine, explore, and try new behaviors. If discussion is to be truly helpful, the worker needs to be clear about what is being taught and sensitive to what is being caught. The worker cannot readily teach a client how to ask questions and how to listen to what the physician is saying without also asking questions and listening attentively to the client's responses. Consensus about the focus of discussion improves the client's participation and the mutuality of agreement on the tasks to be accomplished.

2. *Didactic method.* An informal and brief exposition of issues and ideas can increase clients' problem-solving abilities. Workers need to share ideas simply and without jargon. Some formulations may also help clients to look at their situations in new ways. Berne's analysis

of people's transactions, for example, and of the games people play can help the worker in confronting an alcoholic's relationship and communication patterns (Berne 1961, 1964; Steiner 1971). By analyzing the subtleties of explicit and implicit communication patterns with significant others, the worker can help an alcoholic client and a significant other to understand their dysfunctional transactional ego states (i.e., child, adult, parent) and various ulterior games (e.g., "Yes . . . but," "Kick Me," and "Now I've Got You, You S.O.B."). Recognizing nonadaptive transactions and game patterns can be very illuminating.

Another important formulation is assertiveness training. It can be very useful, for example, in helping a foster child negotiate with his foster and biological parents. An assertive behavior sequence contains four steps that help the client complain effectively and feel more empowered and less helpless: (a) describe the behavior; (b) express the associated feeling; (c) request a specified change; and (d) identify the positive consequence (Lange and Jakobowski 1976). For example, the following is an assertiveness sequence: "Mom when you run in and out of my room without knocking (the described behavior), I begin to feel that I have no privacy, get upset, and have trouble doing my homework (the associated feelings and thoughts). Please knock on my door before you come in (the requested specified change). I will be less upset and more able to concentrate on my homework (the identified positive consequence)."

As a final example of a formulation, workers can teach clients the specific steps in problem solving: (a) delay immediate, impulsive action (i.e., "stop and think," "hold it"); (b) formulate and define problems (i.e., search for alternative definitions); (c) develop strategies to deal with the problem (i.e., general direction and specific tactics); (d) evaluate strategies (i.e., feasibility, possible and unexpected outcomes); and (e) select and carry out specific actions.

Knowledge lends clients some power (D'Zurrilo and Goldfried 1971). These various cognitive tools provide clients with greater control over problems and their consequences.

3. *Visual methods.* Graphic presentations that allow the client to visualize and organize perceptions can illuminate heretofore unidentified patterns of relationships and behavior. Egograms reveal communication styles between people; genograms elucidate and trace the family tree, covering several generations (Dussy 1977; Hartman 1979). Charts and lists can be used to sort out ambivalent thoughts and feelings. Diagrams, such as forced-field analysis, are useful in assessing environmental supports and restraints (Brager and Holloway 1978). Similarly, ecomaps describe the complexity of the client's transac-

tions with the environment, and social-network maps examine social relationships and links (Hartman 1978; Swenson 1979). Finally, the sociogram depicts friendship patterns in a group. For clients who are visual learners and thinkers, these graphic representations enhance understanding and problem-solving abilities.

4. *Action methods.* Action can speak more effectively than prescriptive instruction. Role playing can usefully prepare a hospitalized anorectic for a conversation with her "intimidating" physician. Role modeling and coaching demonstrate effective communication skills; role reversal permits the patient to examine the physician's experience and reactions as well. By mirroring the patient in a role play, the worker demonstrates how the patient will be perceived by the other person. And, finally, in role re-creation and dramatization, the patient examines and analyzes her actual meeting with the physician. Family sculpture dramatizes interpersonal patterns in families. By sculpting, family members consider and reflect on their interpersonal roles. In work with developmentally disabled children and severely impaired adults, games and activities facilitate comfort in interaction. For some, it is much easier to talk while doing than just to talk. We tend to underestimate how well activities can be used in learning how to manage problems and stress. Managing stress can also be learned by relaxation exercises as well as by systematic desensitization, in which an anxiety hierarchy is constructed and is reciprocally inhibited by relaxation (Benson 1975). Thus, through various action methods, clients can learn to cope more effectively.

In addition to these more general educational methods, there are very specific educational skills.[4] Some clients described in the *Handbook* find it difficult to manage and solve their problems because they simply lack basic information or are handicapped by misinformation. Others may have difficulty because they are unaware of unproductive, possibly self-destructive patterns of behavior. They remain mired in helplessness. Still others may have difficulty because they cannot discover alternatives and take action. They are too overwhelmed by their oppressive disappointments to accomplish daily tasks. These clients do have the inherent and potential life skills to cope with their problems and the associated stresses, but they are immobilized by a particular life event (e.g., the death of a child or the institutionalization of a parent) and are unable to use coping strategies for this particular life change. In these situations, the social worker guides the problem-solving aspects of coping, selecting from a repertoire of educational interventions to influence and support the client's own coping strategies and skills. Such interventions include:

1. *Providing relevant information.* Elaborating and clarifying skills

enables clients to unfold their concerns. The information flows principally from client to worker; the clients, however, need and expect relevant information in return. When this expectation is not met, they often feel frustrated (Mayers and Timms 1969). Informing clients of their entitlements, the stages of bereavement, or community resources provides them with the essential tools for improved coping.

2. *Clarifying misinformation.* Misinformation about physical, emotional, and social functioning creates problems in living. At times, distress is caused or exacerbated by misinformation. For example, adolescents who believe that crack is nonaddicting "until you use it a few times" or that rhythm and withdrawal birth-control methods will prevent pregnancy are courting disaster and disappointment. Misinformation must be replaced by accurate information.

3. *Offering advice.* People often expect advice about what to do when they seek or accept social work services. Studies suggest that clients are frequently more satisfied when advice is offered and less satisfied when too little advice is given (Maluccio 1979). Advice may be offered to encourage a client to try a new behavior (e.g., "If you feel your boyfriend is too rough with you, tell him firmly that he is hurting you and that he should immediately let go of your arm"). Advice may also be offered to discourage a client's self-defeating behavior (e.g., "If you continue to pull out your IV, the AIDS antibodies will not enter your system and the nurses will have to bind your arms"). Depending on the severity of the problem and the client's level of functioning, the worker determines how direct the advice should be, in a range from "suggesting" to "urging" to "warning" to "insisting." The more direct advice is usually most helpful to anxious and impaired clients. In offering advice, the worker has to be familiar with the client and the situation, being careful not to impose her or his own values and coping style. The advice should reflect what a client is actually requesting, rather than the worker's need to demonstrate helpfulness.

4. *Offering interpretations.* In helping clients to explain and explore their concerns, a worker may offer an "informed" interpretation. In offering an interpretation, the worker shares the meanings and inferences that he or she attributes to the client's feelings, behavior, and situation. By patterning the available data, the worker may provide a new frame of reference for a client to consider (e.g., "I sense that a lot of your concern about being a diabetic, about the injections and the special diet, is being expressed in disappointment and annoyance with your family. This is understandable"). Timing is an essential element in how interpretations are received. The worker must have sufficient data and must sense the client's trust before venturing an

interpretation. Premature insights distance clients from workers. Of course, the worker's interpretation may be incorrect, but even if it is correct, the client may not be ready to integrate it. Some writers have suggested that an interpretation should not be given unless it is virtually irrefutable.

5. *Providing feedback.* People are usually unaware of how they are perceived by others, in both their strengths and their limitations. By sharing his or her own reactions to a client, the worker provides invaluable feedback, rarely available from friends and family. When it is offered out of an objective caring and concern rather than out of frustration and anger, it is more likely to be receive and believed. A worker may decide to share a feeling at a particular moment (e.g., "Right now, I am feeling overwhelmed. When I try to say something you cut me off. I feel you are running right by me, pushing me away"). The worker uses her or his reactions to examine the client's experiences and transactional patterns. To be most helpful, the worker's reaction is presented in concrete, behavioral terms and is expressed calmly and empathically.

6. *Inviting feedback.* Direct interventions should be followed by a request for the client's reactions (e.g., "What's your reaction to what I have suggested?"). Sometimes a client will say immediately, without prompting, whether the advice or interpretation is helpful or unhelpful. At other times, the response will be more indirect (e.g., "I *guess* you're right" or "Yes, *but* . . ."). The worker should be aware of hesitation, lack of clarity, and negative reactions. Even if the advice or interpretation is perceived as unhelpful, the client's feedback will stimulate further work. Without client feedback, the worker may sound "smart" or may, in fact, be insightful, but the work may not be deepened.

7. *Specifying action tasks.* Clients are helped to mobilize and use their coping skills so that they can deal effectively with their familial and social environments. To do so, they often need assistance in specifying action, i.e., what to do next. For example, consider a frail elderly person who has decided that she can no longer live alone. She is, however, concerned about her children's reactions. The worker might, at the appropriate time, say, "Let's decide *when* and *where* you want to tell the children, *how* you want to tell them, and *what* you want to tell them." The more active and specific the task formulation, the more likely it is to be put into action. Similarly, research suggests that the more clients are involved in specifying and selecting their tasks, the more likely they will be to make progress (Reed 1978).

8. *Preparing and planning for task completion.* Not only do clients need to be involved in specifying the actions to be taken, they need

help to prepare and plan for such actions. Actual assignments (e.g., "During the week, how about if each one of you writes down what you think the children should be told about your husband's suicide attempt") and role play (e.g., "I'll be your children; let's rehearse what you will try to say to me") are usually helpful and practical in preparing clients to carry out agreed-upon tasks. Such concrete methods also prepare clients to anticipate and handle related situations, e.g., when children remain silent, refuse to listen, or ask difficult questions. When preparation planning is completed, it is usually helpful to summarize and review the specific agreed-upon strategies.

## CASE ILLUSTRATION

Each contributor follows the "differential clinical assessments and interventions" section with a specific case presentation to illustrate and typify the problems and situations confronted by the client population. The focus of the case illustration is on the worker's professional behaviors and skills, i.e. what the worker actually does to help. Contributors were asked to pay special attention to this section and to try to capture the art and science of social work helping.

As our profession has been pushed into a preoccupation with accountability, one of the consequences has been a preoccupation with practice outcomes and a tendency to evaluate professional competence and skills primarily on the basis of outcomes specified beforehand. The client's progress or lack of progress is attributed to the worker's skills or lack of skills. This attribution is absurd, if not dangerous, because it leads logically to working only with motivated clients and clients without serious environmental problems. Moreover, evaluating professional competence solely on the basis of outcomes also ignores and negates the reality of what happens in the helping process: a worker trying to be helpful and a client deciding whether and how to use help from this particular person at this particular time.[5] The worker's behaviors may be skillful and the client may not progress (or may even regress); the worker's behaviors may be unskillful and the client may progress. We can properly hold professionals accountable for professional skills and an informed use of the relevant knowledge, but not for unattainable outcomes. It has been said that clients benefit because, in spite of, and without our help. Lawyers who lose their cases may be justly praised for their fine work in a lost cause, and doctors often do well but some of their patients still die. In all cases, the question is whether they did the right thing in the circumstances, considering the available options.

Similarly, in social work, the behavior of helping has to be evaluated in its own terms and must be distinguished from the client's use of the help.

How can the general public and specific client populations have confidence in a profession that is unclear and uncertain about its methodology (Ellis 1984)? How will professional social workers be able to demonstrate their competence without committing themselves to the acquisition of established and newly emerging skills? As professionals, we are and become what we do. Being competent is our most reliable means of survival. Although society does not fully appreciate what our profession does and what social workers accomplish day in and day out, this *Handbook* tries to capture and convey our profession's vision and our practitioners' professional competence, spirit, and, in many situations, heroism.

This essay attempts to introduce the reader to the content of the *Handbook* and to social work practice with vulnerable populations. In Part I, "Vulnerable Life Conditions," each contributor deals with etiology. A complex ecological chain emerges that links genetic, family, and environmental forces. Alcoholism, chronic heart disease, diabetes, learning disability, manic-depression, mental retardation, and schizophrenia all appear to share genetic predispositions. Inherited levels of cholesterol, other blood fats, and structural defects, for example, set the conditions for heart disease. A family tradition of cooking in fats and grease increases the risk. Living in a society in which fast-food chains serve high-fat hamburgers and potatoes fried in lard, smoking by youth is pervasive, and ice cream is a favorite dessert also acts on the genetically vulnerable individual. A similar chain exists for many of the life conditions described in this *Handbook:* a genetic predisposition; a society and culture that either provide insufficient supports and environmental controls or encourage unhealthy behaviors; and dysfunctional family and individual behaviors. In problem life conditions, all the factors in the ecological chain are usually present in some degree. However, extreme family and environmental factors such as excessive family stress and work stress can also precipitate a serious difficulty even though there is little genetic basis for it.

Poverty has a pervasive impact on most distressing life circumstances and undesired events. In virtually every chapter, the authors poignantly describe the all-encompassing consequences of poverty. When there is prejudice and discrimination, when family and social-network ties are weak, and when individuals have the added burdens of physical, intellectual, or emotional impairments, the impact of poverty is particularly devastating. Poor people with AIDS, homeless people, unemployed black adolescents, and isolated elderly people—all are at a severe high risk of not being able to survive in our environment.

It is precisely the people in greatest need and at the highest risk to whom some in social work have responded with great personal commitment and zeal, as well as professional creativity and competence. With extremely limited resources, these social workers struggle daily to provide the necessary services. They refuse to abandon social agencies; they refuse to desert these most vulnerable populations; and instead, they continue to develop programs, to provide individualized services, and to offer hope. This *Handbook* is a tribute to these professionals, and we hope it does them justice.

## ENDNOTES

1. Martin Luther King, Jr., once made the mordant observation that our society has socialism for the rich and rugged individualism for the poor.
2. This discussion is based on a prior publication (Gitterman 1988a).
3. This discussion is based on a prior publication. (Germain and Gitterman 1980a).
4. This discussion is based on a prior publication by the author (Gitterman 1988b).
5. I wish to acknowledge the contribution of William Schwartz to my ideas about the nature of professional skills.

## REFERENCES

Abuelo, D. N. 1983. "Genetic Disorders." In J. L. Matson and J. A. Mulick, eds., *Handbook of Mental Retardation*, pp. 105–126. New York: Plenum.
Andrulonis, P., C. Glueck, C. Stroebel, N. Vogel, A. Shapiro, and D. Aldridge. 1981. "Organic Brain Dysfunction and the Borderline Syndrome." *Psychiatric Clinics of North America* 4(1):47–66.
Benson, R. 1975. *The Relaxation Response.* New York; William Morrow.
Berne, E. 1961. *Transactional Analysis in Psychotherapy.* New York: Ballantine.
Berne, E. 1964. *Games People Play: The Psychology of Human Relation.* New York: Grove.
Blum, K. and H. Topel. 1986. "Opiod Peptides and Alcoholism: Genetic Deficiencies and Chemical Management." *Functional Neurology* 1:71–83.
Boyd, J. and M. Weissman. 1981. "Epidemiology of Affective Disorder." *Archives of General Psychiatry* 38:1039–1046.
Brager, G. and S. Holloway. 1978. *Changing Human Service Organizations: Politics and Practice*, pp. 104–128. New York: Free Press.
Brunner, J. 1966. *Toward a Theory of Instruction* pp. 1–21. Cambridge: Harvard University Press.

Cahalan, D. and R. Room. (1974). *Problem Drinking Among American Men.* New Brunswick, N.J.: Rutgers Center for Alcohol Studies.

Clark, K. 1965. *Dark Ghetto,* New York: Harper & Row.

Cloninger, R. 1983. "Genetic and Environmental Factors in the Development of Alcoholism." *Journal of Psychiatric Treatment and Evaluation* 5:487–496.

Cloninger, R. 1987. "Neurogenetic Adaptive Mechanisms in Alcoholism." *Science* 236:410–16.

Cloninger, R., M. Bohman, and S. Sigvardsson. 1981. "Inheritance of Alcohol Abuse." *Archives of General Psychiatry* 38(86):1–68.

Cloninger, R., S. Sigvardsson, and M. Bohman. 1988. "Childhood Personality Predicts Alcohol Abuse in Young Adults." *Alcoholism: Clinical and Experimental Research* 5:494–505.

Dickerson, M. U. 1981. *Social Work Practice with the Mentally Retarded.* New York: Free Press.

DMCH (Division of Maternal and Child Health). 1986. *Information Bulletin: Youth 2000.* Washington, D.C.: U.S. Department of Health and Human Services.

Dussy, J. (1977). *Egograms.* New York: Harper & Row.

D'Zurrila, T. and M. Goldfried. 1971. "Problem-Solving and Behavior Modification." *Journal of Abnormal Psychology* 78:107–126.

Ellis, A. 1984. "Must Most Psychotherapists Remain as Incomplete as They Are Now?" In J. Hariman, ed., *Does Psychotherapy Really Help People?* pp. 24–36. Springfield, Ill.: Charles C Thomas.

Feldman, R., A. Stiffman, and K. Jung. 1987. *Children at Risk.* New Brunswick, N.J.: Rutgers University Press.

Foch, T. and G. McClearn. 1980. "Genetics, Body Weight, and Obesity." In A. Strunkard, ed., *Obesity,* pp. 48–71. Philadelphia: W. B. Saunders.

Garfinkel, P. and D. Garner. 1982. *Anorexia Nervosa: A Multidimensional Perspective.* New York: Brunner/Mazel.

Garner, D. and P. Garfinkel 1985. *Handbook of Psychotherapy for Anorexia Nervosa and Bulimia.* New York: Guilford.

Gelles R. J. and M. A. Straus. 1988. *Intimate Violence: The Definitive Study of the Causes and Consequences of Abuse in the American Family.* New York: Simon & Shuster.

Germain, C. and A. Gitterman. 1980a. *The Life Model of Social Work Practice.* New York: Columbia University Press.

Germain, C. and A. Gitterman. 1980b. *The Life Model of Social Work Practice: Teachers Guide.* New York: Columbia University Press.

Gershon, E. 1983. "The Genetics of Affective Disorders." In L. Grinspoon, ed., *Psychiatry Update: The American Psychiatric Association Annual Review,* vol. 2, Part 5, p. 434. Washington, D.C.: American Psychiatric Press.

Gitterman, A. 1983. "Uses of Resistance: A Transactional View." *Social Work* (March/April), 28:127–131.

Gitterman, A. 1988a. "Social Work Looks Forward." In Gerald St. Denis, ed., *Implementing a Forward Plan: A Public Health Social Work Challenge (Proceedings),* pp. 3–14. Pittsburgh: University of Pittsburgh Graduate School of Public Health.

Gitterman, A. 1988b. "The Social Worker as Educator." *Health Care Practice Today: The Social Worker as Educator,* pp. 13–22. New York: Columbia University,

Gitterman, A. 1989. "Testing Professional Authority and Boundaries." *Social Casework* (March), 70:165–171.

Gitterman, A. and C. Germain. 1976. "Social Work Practice: A Life Model." *Social Service Review* (December), 50:601–610.

Goodwin, D. 1988. *Is Alcoholism Hereditary?* New York: Ballantine.

**30** *Alex Gitterman*

Goodwin, D. Schulsinger, F., Hermansen, L., Guzi S. and G. Winokur 1973. "Alcohol Problems in Adoptees Raised Apart from Alcoholic Biological Parents." *Archives of General Psychiatry* 28:238–243.

Gottlieb, B., ed. 1988. *Marshalling Social Support: Formats, Processes and Effects.* Newbury Park, Calif.: Sage.

Hampton, R. and E. Newberger. 1985. "Child Abuse Incidence and Reporting by Hospitals: Significance of Severity, Class and Race." *American Journal of Public Health* 75:56–60.

Hartman, A. 1978. "Diagrammatic Assessment of Family Relationships." *Social Casework* (October), 59:465–476.

Hartman, A. 1979. *Finding Families: An Ecological Approach to Family Assessment in Adoption*, pp. 33–64. Beverly Hills, Calif.: Sage.

Harvard Medical School. 1987. *Mental Health Letter* (January). Boston: Harvard Medical School.

Hayes, C. 1987. *Risking the Future: Adolescent Sexuality, Pregnancy, and Childbearing.* Washington, D.C.: National Academy Press.

Herrnstein, J. and J. Wilson. 1985. "Made or Born?" *The New York Times Magazine* (August), 4:31–33.

Hollingshead, A. and F. Redlich. 1958. *Social Class and Mental Illness.* New York: John Wiley.

Horowitz, A. 1985. "Family Caregiving to the Frail Elderly." In C. Eisdorfer, M. Lawton and G. Maddox, eds, *Annual Review of Gerontology and Geriatrics*, vol. 5, pp. 194–246. New York: Springer.

Kane, R. 1987. "Long-Term Care." *Encyclopedia of Social Work*, pp. 59–72. Silver Spring, Md.: National Association of Social Workers.

Kety, S. 1988. "Schizophrenic Illnesses in the Families of Schizophrenic Adoptees: Findings from the Danish National Sample." *Schizophrenia Bulletin* 14:217–222.

Lange, A. and P. Jakobowski. 1976. *Responsible Assertive Behavior.* Champaign, Ill.: Research Press.

Lazarus, R. and B. Laumier. 1978. "Stress-Related Transactions Between Person and Environment." In L. Pervin and M. Lewis, eds., *Perspectives in International Psychology*, New York: Plenum.

Leary, W. 1989. "U.S. Needs Data on Drug and Sex Habits to Halt Aids, Study Says." *New York Times* (February 9), p. A25.

Lee, F. 1989. "Doctors See Gap in Blacks' Health Having a Link to Low Self-Esteem." *New York Times* (July 17), p. A11.

Lukoff, I. 1980. "Toward a Sociology of Drug Use." In D. Lettieri, M. Sayers, and H. Pearson, eds., *Theories on Drug Use: Selected Contemporary Perspectives*, pp. 201–211. Research Monograph 30. Rockville, Md.: National Institute on Drug Abuse.

Maggnuson, E. 1989. "7 Deadly Days." *Time* (July 17), 30–61.

Maluccio, A. 1979. *Learning from Clients.* New York: Free Press.

Marsiglio, W. and F. Mott. 1986. "The Impact of Sex Education on Sexual Activity, Contraceptive Use, and Premarital Pregnancy Among American Teenagers." *Family Planning Perspectives* 18:151–161.

Mayer, J. and N. Timms. 1969, "Clash in Perspectives Between Worker and Client." *Social Casework* (January), 50:32–40.

Mendlewicz, J. and J. Rainer. 1977. "Adoption Study Supporting Genetic Transmission in Manic-Depressive Illness." *Nature* 268:327.

Meyer-Kimmling, E. 1977. "Issues Pertaining to Prevention and Intervention of Genetic Disorders Affecting Human Behavior." In G. Albee and J. Jaffe, eds., *The Issues: An Overview of Primary Prevention.* pp. 68–91. Hanover, N.H.: University Press.

Milner, J. and R. Wemberly. 1980. "Prediction and Explanation of Child Abuse." *Journal of Clinical Psychology* 36:875–884.

NASW (National Association of Social Workers) 1987. *NASW News Letter* (March). Albany: New York State Chapter.

NCHS (National Center for Health Statistics). 1988. *Vital Statistics of the United States, 1986. Vol. 2: Mortality, Part A* [DHSS Publication No. (PHS) 88–1122.] Washington, D.C.: GPO.

Olsen, L. and W. Holmes. 1986. "Youth at Risk: Adolescents and Maltreatment." *Children and Youth Services Review* 8:13–35.

Pasell, P. 1989. "Forces in Society, and Reaganism, Helped Dig Deeper Hole for the Poor," *New York Times* (July 16), pp. 1, 20.

Pittman, K. and G. Adams. 1988. *Teenage Pregnancy: An Advocate's Guide to Numbers*. Washington, D.C.: Children's Defense Fund.

Rauch, J. 1988. "Social Work and the Genetics Revolution: Genetic Services." *Social Work* 33:389–397.

Reed, W. 1978. *The Task Centered System*. New York: Columbia University Press.

Schmeck, H. M., Jr. 1987a. "Genetic Abnormality Seen as Link with Alzheimer's." *New York Times* (March 13), p. A14.

Schmeck, H. M., Jr. 1987b. "Scientists Link an Activated Gene to Lung Cancer." *New York Times* (October 8), p. A28.

Schmeck, H. M., Jr. 1987c. "Young Science of Cancer Genes Begins to Yield Practical Application," *New York Times*, (October 6), pp. C1, C4.

Seligman, M. 1975. *Helplessness*. San Francisco: Freeman.

Skinner, A. and R. Castle. 1969. *78 Battered Children*. London: National Society for the Prevention of Cruelty to Children. SSC (Special Services for Children). 1989. "Foster Care Expansion Plan for Fiscal Year 1989." New York: SSC.

Steiner, C. M. 1971. *Games Alcoholics Play*. New York: Grove.

Stone, R., G. Cafferata, and J. Sangl. 1987. "Caregivers of the Frail Elderly: A National Profile." *The Gerontologist* 27:616–626.

Strole, L. and A. Fischer. 1977. *Mental Health in the Metropolis*. New York: Harper Torchbooks.

Swenson, C. 1979. "Networks, Mutual Aid, and the Life Model." In C. Germain, ed., *Social Work Practice: People and Environments*, pp. 213–238. New York: Columbia University Press.

United States. (1982). *President's Task Force on Victims of Crime: Final Report*. Washington, D.C.: GPO.

U.S. HHS (U.S. Department of Health and Human Services). 1985–86. *Aging in America: Trends and Projections*. Washington, D.C.: GPO.

U.S. HHS (U.S. Department of Health and Human Services). 1988. *Study Findings: Study of National Incidence and Prevalence of Child Abuse and Neglect*. Washington, D.C.: GPO.

U.S. Department of Justice. Bureau of Justice Statistics. 1986. *Criminal Victimization in the United States*. Washington, D.C.: GPO.

U.S. Department of Justice. Bureau of Justice Statistics. 1988. *Census of Local Jails*. Washington, D.C.: GPO.

Vance, E. 1977. "A Typology of Risks and the Disabilities of Low Status." In G. Albee and J. Jaffe, eds., *The Issues: An Overview of Primary Prevention*, pp. 207–237. Hanover, N.H.: University Press of New England.

Wallace, J. 1989. "Biopsychosocial Model of Alcoholism." *Social Casework* (June), 70:325–332.

Weissman, M. D. Gammon, John K., Merikangas, V. Warner, B. Prusoff, and D. Scholemskins. 1987. "Children of Depressed Parents." *Archives of General Psychiatry* 44:847–853.

Weissman, M., K. Kidd, and B. Prusoff. 1982. "Variability in Rates of Affective Disorders in Relatives of Depressed and Normal Probands." *Archives of General Psychiatry* 39:1397–1403.

Wender, P., Kety, S., Rosenthal, D., Schulsinger, F., Ortman, J., and I. Lunde. 1986. "Psychiatric Disorders in the Biological and Adoptive Families of Adopted Individuals with Affective Disorders." *Archives of General Psychiatry* 43:923–929.

Wilhelm, S. and E. Powell. 1964. "Who Needs the Negro?" *Trans-Action* (September/October), 1:3–6.

Zhukov, U., A. Varkof, and Y. Burov. 1987. "Effect of Destruction of the Brain Serotoninergic System on Alcohol Intake by Rats at Early Stages of Experimental Alcoholism." *Biogenic Amines* 4(3):201–204).

# I
# VULNERABLE LIFE CONDITIONS

▼

# 1

# AIDS

▼

## GEORGE S. GETZEL

Acquired immune deficiency syndrome (AIDS) is a bad dream that will not go away. After hesitation and apathy from different levels of government (Cahill 1984; Altman 1986; Shilts 1987; Kramer 1989), the health care system, and the general public, AIDS has become a haunting specter in our culture, as well as this country and the world's most significant public health problem, forecast to continue into the next century (Nichols 1987; Mann et. al. 1989; Sontag 1988). Without a doubt, the growing AIDS epidemic will radically alter the ways in which health care and human services are delivered (Fineberg 1988; Ron and Rogers 1989). The pressures on these service systems will grow as large numbers of people with AIDS overwhelm already over-burdened service facilities in large epicenters of the epidemic in cities, and even in rural areas where sick former residents come home to die near kith and kin (Rounds 1988).

Because of their major presence in community and health care organizations,* social workers have played a pioneering role in pro-viding an array of services to persons with AIDS and their families since the beginning of the epidemic (Lopez and Getzel 1984; Caputo 1985; Greenly 1986; Leukefeld and Fimbres 1987. Social work profes-sionals have made contributions to policy developments occurring in New York City, San Francisco, and Los Angeles, as well as in the state and federal governments. Although as a profession, social work per-haps minimizes its history of contributions to different fields of hu-

This essay is lovingly dedicated to the memories of Richard Gambe and Diego Lopez, friends and collaborators, who pioneered services to people with AIDS, and who died during the pandemic.

**35**

man endeavor, individual social workers have made early and significant contributions to public awareness about AIDS and the need for community-based and institutional resources for AIDS prevention activities and for direct services to persons who are ill or incapacitated (Ryan 1987; Palacios-Jimenez and Shernoff 1986; Lopez and Getzel 1987; Sonsel, Paradise, and Stroup 1988).

## PROBLEM DOMAIN

Since much of system thinking, such as the concept of homeostasis, as well as ecological concepts, originates from biology (Cannon 1939; Buckley 1967), a biopsychosocial system framework is particularly applicable to the variables associated with AIDS in social work practice.

René Dubos (1959) wrote that modern persons tend to deny their organismic nature and their place in biological evolution, largely because of the widespread elimination of many life-threatening infectious diseases that, in past centuries, killed infants, children, and large portions of the populations of towns and cities. Clean water systems separated from sewage outlets, fresh food, housing regulations, and mass innoculation for childhood diseases are largely responsible for human longevity and the revolution in life expectations. A likely early death has been superseded by concerns about chronic disease in old age in modern industrial and postindustrial societies.

The emergence of AIDS has made us aware that human beings are indeed organisms of exquisite complexity and are subject to parasitic and symbiotic relations with microorganisms from within and without (Bateson and Goldsby 1988). Microorganisms can disable, disfigure, and kill a larger organism when their numbers reach a sufficient level, if they are not stopped by the organism's resistance to their increase.

In the highly sophisticated and technologically advanced countries, human beings can falsely believe that they are beyond the grasp of a variety of microorganisms, such as tubercle bacilli and streptococci, as well as a multiplicity of viruses capable of bringing on life-threatening diseases and horrific symptoms. The biological reality, however disconcerting it may be, is that the tissues of the human organism are awash with a variety of bacteria, protozoa, invertebrates, and viruses that are contained because of the multilevel defenses of the immune system.

Unless the balance of microorganisms radically shifts in the host, it is perfectly possible for an individual to live his or her life oblivious of their existence. Biologists are beginning to explore the possible benefits of microorganisms, as well as their harm when resistance to them falters. An investigation of public health measures through the centuries points to social activities such as sanitation and changed behaviors such as hand washing by doctors and midwives that have altered the environments of people and the balance of life-threatening microorganisms (Dubos 1965).

Pestilences like war have caused great social changes, not only by dramatically decreasing population size, but also by challenging cultural expectations (Risse 1988; Rosenberg 1989; Sontag 1988). Camus (1952) noted that plagues and war surprise us because each assumes a size exceeding expectations and forces us to confront mass deaths, which are met with initial denial and slowness to react.

The life model developed by Germaine and Gitterman (1980) uses an ecological system perspective that can be applied to the complexities of AIDS as a biological entity interacting with different psychological, social, and cultural dimensions. AIDS touches and influences the whole fabric of society and its cultural assumptions. Clearly, AIDS points to the Darwinian struggle for survival as human beings begin to engage in a life-and-death struggle to fit into a natural world that is also inhabited by the human immunodeficiency virus (HIV) associated with AIDS. Human beings' failure on the biological, psychological, social, and cultural levels to understand and to adapt to their new place in the natural world is a matter of individual and collective life and death.

Bateson and Goldsby (1988) noted that HIV has created a new niche for itself in the natural world, supported not only by the individual human organism, but by the behavior that transmits HIV to other human organisms. Thus, the extent to which the individual human organism has favorable internal and external environments determines the individual's health and life chances, and specifically whether he or she will become infected with HIV and go on to develop AIDS. While epidemics start by growing exponentially, changes in the infected organism or in the organism's environment slow down the rate of infection. AIDS reveals how vulnerable human beings are in their biological relations with microorganisms, and for that matter with their fellow human organisms in maintaining bodily integrity and well-being.

AIDS is a worldwide natural event. Modern transportation links populations all over the world, and in time, material, ideas, and microorganisms are diffused throughout different nations and cultures with significant, and sometimes catastrophic, consequences. The resources needed to maintain the health of men, women, and children may not be available, and individuals, families, and whole communities may break down under the crisis of the worldwide AIDS pandemic.

The AIDS pandemic taxes the available resources and may call for a redistribution of material resources and expertise in the interest of the whole of the human community—to halt the spread of disease and to care for those infected and affected. AIDS also points out that the human species is highly interdependent: they inhabit a finite planet and must discover ways to ensure their mutual security and well-being.

Social work practice with people with AIDS demands a constant review of the emerging knowledge about the nature of the disease, its treatment, and the social and cultural impact on persons infected and ill, as well as on all those who interact with them over time. Medical discoveries related to HIV will have far-reaching effects on medical treatments, strongly affecting the longevity and quality of life, not to mention the hopes and expectations, of persons with life-threatening conditions. The ever-changing character of the AIDS epidemic requires constant updating of knowledge and systematic reflection on the interaction of biological, psychological, social, economic, political, and cultural factors. The biopsychosocial systems framework that has evolved in social work practice in health care is a useful heuristic for handling the complexity of the data emerging on AIDS and HIV infection; conversely, this tragic epidemic may be an example par excellence of the usefulness of this framework.

## SOCIETAL CONTEXT

AIDS evokes powerful psychosocial responses in persons at the point of diagnosis (and often earlier), and in all those intimates and service providers with whom they interact. Such responses reflect current and changing societal values and assume greater magnitude as more individuals, families, and communities have direct experiences with persons with AIDS.

The meaning of AIDS on a societal and cultural level is constantly delineated and reinterpreted in the mass media, particularly as the number of persons who become ill and die grows larger. The economic costs of providing expensive, if not scarce, health and social services at the state and local levels of government to people with AIDS are gaining more attention as a political concern. Those who do not have AIDS and who perceive themselves as being in no danger of becoming HIV-infected may challenge the use of resources for people with AIDS because of their high economic and social costs. In short, compassionate concern may decrease because of self-interest and a protectionist outlook in the general population.

Powerlessness and stigma are inextricable aspects of AIDS on a societal level. Ironically, because of their prior stigmatized and isolated condition, gay and bisexual men as well as intravenous drug users and their sexual partners and newborns have had the heaviest concentrations of HIV infection.

The societal prejudice against homosexual persons now has a powerful biological analogue in the form of AIDS, which reinforces the existing enmity toward them and severely limits their civil rights and opportunities to live full and productive lives. The homophobia experienced by gay people is frequently internalized, adding to the pain that vulnerable persons feel, even before they develop HIV-related symptoms or a formal AIDS diagnosis.

The largest proportion of intravenous drug users are the inner-city poor, black, and Hispanic adults whose health, security and life chances are greatly diminished even before they are HIV-infected. Poor-quality medical services, lack of access to care, and community distrust and suspicion effectively deprive inner-city people of required preventive, acute, and long-term health care. Prejudice toward addicts on the part of providers and the public is accompanied by racial, ethnic, and class hostilities.

An abiding and very serious question asked by inner-city community leaders and concerned advocates for AIDS services is whether inner-city populations are being written off as expendable because they cannot be served easily and because they come with so many enmeshed problems, such as homelessness and poverty. Most HIV-infected women are from poor, inner-city, minority backgrounds, and they frequently have infected infants and children. The directing of resources of all kinds to this population, as to gay and bisexual men, has been initially indifferent and typically slow in response.

On a societal level, AIDS challenges the historically new concept of what constitutes a fair share of life by devastating young adults with an exotic array of chronic, life-threatening diseases and with early deaths. AIDS links a death-dealing disease to sexual activities, with far-reaching effects on sexual attitudes and behavior. Sexual freedom and expression are now fraught with danger, microscopic mysteries, and mortality.

## RISKS AND NEEDS OF POPULATION

With each year, the basic understanding of the magnitude and the international scope of the AIDS pandemic grows. The World Health Organization estimates that there are as many as 5 million persons infected with HIV, a number that is growing throughout the world (Mann et al. 1989). The HIV infection seen today probably started eight or ten years ago and is only now appearing in symptoms or opportunistic infections.

Two strains of retrovirus, HIV I and the less virulent HIV II, have been located throughout the inhabited world; they follow different patterns. Pattern I, which is found in the United States, Canada, Mexico, Western Europe, Australia, and New Zealand, probably began in the late 1970s and occurs among gay and bisexual men and urban intravenous drug users. Women tend to be infected by men in a ratio of from 10 to 15:1 more than men are infected by women. Consequently, women and their infants are a smaller proportion of the population infected where Pattern I prevails.

Pattern II, occurring in central, eastern, and southern Africa and in Latin American countries in the Caribbean, also started in the late 1970s but is characterized by bilateral transmission between men and women, and consequently by a greater proportion of infected infants. Male homosexual transmission is a minor source of infection in Pattern II.

Pattern III prevails in Eastern Europe, North Africa, Asia, and parts of the Pacific and seems to have occurred in the early 1980s through contact with travelers from elsewhere and through unscreened infected transfused blood. More recently, male homosexual and intravenous drug activities have been found to be a limited source of infection in these parts of the world.

It is estimated that 1.5 million persons in the United States are HIV-infected (Heyward and Curran 1989). According to the Centers for Disease Control (CDC), from 1981 to the end of 1988 there were more than 81,000 cumulative cases (CDC 1988). Of the cumulative diagnosed cases, 62 percent have been identified as homosexual and bisexual males; 19 percent as intravenous drug users (IVDUs); 8 percent as both male homosexuals or bisexuals and IVDUs; 4 percent as adults who were infected through heterosexual contact; and the remaining 7 percent as persons who received infected blood or blood products or as infants infected before or during birth. Of the total cumulative cases of A.I.D.S., approximately 9 percent have been identified as women, of whom 52 percent had histories as IVDUs; 29

percent were infected through heterosexual contact; and the remaining 18 percent were infected through blood, blood products, or undetermined sources. Children under the age of 13 made up 1 percent of the cumulative cases of AIDS, 78 percent having been infected before or during birth and the remaining 12 percent having been infected through blood, blood products, or undetermined sources.

Of the total cummulative cases of women with AIDS, at the end of 1988, more than 80 percent were black and Hispanic, and over 90 percent of all the children were black and Hispanic, from inner-city areas where the sources of infection were intravenous drug users. Whole families have become sick and died in poor neighborhoods in New York City, New Jersey, and Miami (Williams 1989; Leary 1989).

Of the more than 81,000 cumulatively diagnosed AIDS cases at the end of 1988, 56 percent of the persons diagnosed between January and June 1987 were dead from complications of AIDS by the end of December 1988, and 86 percent of all persons diagnosed between January and June 1985 had died by end of 1988. There is evidence that women die more quickly after diagnosis than men; IVDUs often die less than a year after diagnosis. Many IVDUs are believed to die from the debilitating symptoms of HIV infection before a major opportunistic infection occurs that would permit a formal diagnosis of AIDS (Joseph 1989). In areas of high prevalence of drug use, AIDS cases related to IV use have become the majority of newly diagnosed cases (NYCDH 1989).

The epidemiological evidence, to date, gives overwhelming support to the proposition that AIDS cannot be transmitted through casual contract, such as touching, kissing, and using the same toilet; it can be transmitted only through the exchange of blood, semen, vaginal fluid, and mother's milk. Studies of persons sharing the same households indicate that transmission occurs only between those individuals engaged in sexual activities and IV drug use and to infants born of infected mothers (Friedland 1989).

Social workers dealing with AIDS must understand the biology of HIV infection and must be able to translate this understanding for clients both in AIDS prevention activities and in practice with persons who have AIDS-related symptoms and infections. Social workers will increasingly be called on to speak to a wide range of individuals and groups about AIDS and the transmission of HIV. Therefore, all AIDS education for social workers must begin with an understanding of HIV biology and must go on to considerations of the person, dyadic relations, the family, the community, and the larger social systems. In simple, unadorned language with apt analogies designed for specific audiences, social workers must start discussions about HIV transmission and prevention. Social workers must be prepared to react to simple ignorance as well as to highly intellectualized arguments that reveal persons' denial of the actual modes of AIDS transmission and the real threats to their lives.

AIDS, an underlying disease of the immune system, must be understood as a metadisease process, a generator of otherwise rare opportunistic infections such as *Pneumocystis carinii* pneumonia (PCP), cytomegaloviral infections, toxoplasmosis, and rare cancers such Kaposi's sarcoma and non-Hodgkin's lymphomas. AIDS is a disease associated with the catastrophic collapse of bodily immunity and with the presence of HIV infection. HIV is transmitted only through the intimate exchange of body fluids, specifically semen, vaginal fluid, blood, and mother's milk. The activities identified with a high risk of the transmission of HIV are anal, oral, and vaginal sex; the use of infected blood or blood proucts; the sharing of infected drug paraphernalia; and breast feeding; HIV is also transmitted from mother to fetus in the uterus or during birth (Mass 1987; Gallo and Montagnier 1989; Heyward and Curran 1989).

Not all persons who have contact with HIV become infected, nor do all persons infected develop HIV symptoms (such as night sweats, swollen glands, weight loss, and rashes) or full-blown AIDS with the appearance of an opportunistic infection. Because of the dangers of spreading infection to others and exacerbating existing infections, it is vital for all persons with or without current HIV infection to be aware of the modes of transmission; to practice safer sex through the use of rubber latex condoms during anal, oral, and vaginal sex; and to avoid the sharing of intravenous drug paraphernalia.

In the course of their direct practice with individuals, families, and groups, social workers have frequent opportunities to assist clients to examine the activities that place them at risk of infection. Social workers must develop comfort in discussing sexual practices and drug use, so that they can help clients make behavioral changes to avoid infection. Neither the induction of fear nor calls for abstinence are sufficient to encourage new, life-saving behaviors. Social workers have created exciting approaches to teaching safer sex behaviors by positive techniques such as eroticizing the use of condoms with both gay and nongay men and women (Shernoff 1988; Getzel and Mahony 1988).

Scientific knowledge about HIV and the cellular processes of infection grows daily as research proceeds in the United States and throughout the world. Because of its specific attraction to T4 helper lymphocytes (blood cells), HIV infects them, replicates, and thus overwhelms the individual's overall immune capacity. The growth of opportunistic infections and cancers may proceed rapidly or over a long period of time. There is strong evidence that HIV has a long latency period before replicating. Scientists are investigating the conditions or cofactors associated with the development of specific symptoms and opportunistic infections related to the flaring up of HIV infection.

HIV infection can be readily detected by the use of antibody tests and emerging new test strategies. These tests have been useful in the mass screening of blood in hospitals and blood banks. The use of antibody testing for individuals presents serious practical, clinical, and ethical questions. The tests check for the presence of HIV antibodies, which the body produces six weeks to three months or longer after infection has occurred. There is clearly a possibility of a false-negative test finding; it is therefore recommended that persons abstain from high-risk activities and be tested again within six months (Nichols 1987; Redfield and Burke 1989; Fineberg 1988; Walters 1988).

The test is a diagnostic tool, and negative test findings are not a signal that a person is immune from infection. There is a strong danger of magical thinking that turns the test into a stimulus for unsafe activities. Consequently, there is a profound need for pretest counseling about what the test is and is not, as well as for an exploration of the meaning of both a negative and a positive test finding. Skilled posttest counseling by a social worker or other qualified health professional is vital to reinforce safer sex guidelines and to handle the often strong emotional responses of those hearing about a positive test finding. It is not uncommon for a person with a positive test finding to become depressed or even suicidal. Other reactions may be a fear of informing intimates and rage at those who are perceived as the source of the infection.

In certain jurisdictions, important practical and ethical issues arise about the counselor's legal requirement to report positive test findings to government officials, to the tested person's intimates, and to other agencies (Bayer 1989; Dickens 1988). The reporting requirements should be known in advance by the client. Anonymous testing sites, where available, provide the opportunity to assist in teaching AIDS prevention activities and to helping the client get the necessary health care. To the extent possible, test findings should be kept confidential. Some states protect test findings legally, a most difficult task in many health care agencies. The revealing of a positive test finding or an AIDS diagnosis frequently causes the loss of a job and benefits, breaches of civil liberties, and incidents of violence (Senack 1987; Dickens 1988).

Medical treatment for persons with HIV infection and AIDS has changed radically since the beginning of the epidemic in 1981. Changes in the treatment of HIV infection and opportunistic diseases are occurring rapidly because of the introduction of new treatment procedures and drugs. Such developments significantly affect the quality of life of ill persons.

Until fairly recently, the treatment of AIDS and HIV-related symptoms focused exclusively on the treatment of opportunistic infections and the provision of palliative relief, but with the development of antiviral medications such as Azidodeoxythimidine (AZT) and preventive treatments such as aerosol pentamidine for PCP infections, significant increases in longevity and improvements in quality of life appear to have occurred (Kolata 1989). Yet the bulk of medical interventions in and outside hospitals still focuses on the direct treatment of opportunistic infections and not on the underlying HIV infection. The treatment of opportunistic infections often involves the use of highly toxic drugs and radiation, which may have strong side effects, and may entail painful procedures that leave stigmata. Treatment benefits, when they occur, are often of short duration, only to be followed by the onset of yet another opportunistic event as bodily immunity continues to fail (Price et al. 1988; Friedland 1989).

## PROGRAMS AND SOCIAL WORK SERVICES

Since the early 1980s, there have been many social-work programmatic efforts in response to the AIDS epidemic in the United States. Social workers have participated in the development of *community-based programs* for persons with AIDS and their loved ones under gay auspices, first in the establishment of the Gay Men's Health Crisis in New York City in 1982 (Lopez and Getzel 1984), followed by the Los Angeles AIDS Project and the Shanti Project in San Francisco. These innovative programs operate through the large-scale use of nonprofessionals and professionals as volunteers providing an array of personal services to help people with AIDs and their loved ones to handle the multiple crises often associated with diagnosis and the subsequent biopsychosocial crises precipitated by illness, hospitalizations, financial difficulties, legal and employment problems, familial conflicts, and entitlement concerns. Hundreds of community-based programs for people with AIDS initially started by the gay and lesbian community now serve thousands of gay and nongay persons throughout North America and parts of Europe.

Social workers with other professionals have been particularly influential in the development of and leadership in volunteer *crisis intervention teams*, whose members are available to provide emotional support and advocacy activities to people with AIDS and their loved ones at critical periods of stress in the psychosocial sequence of the disease (Lopez and Getzel 1987).

Volunteer crisis workers should undergo careful recruitment and require ongoing supervision and training. Another widespread innovative program uses volunteers as "buddies" who do light houshold chores for disabled people with AIDS as well as provide social contact to break down social isolation.

Community-based programs offer *support groups* for people with AIDS, which are generally run by social workers and other professional volunteers. Membership in these groups may be open-ended and as needed, or closed-ended and long-term (Gambe and Getzel 1989). Support groups for family members and care partners are also quite common. Innovative couples' groups for both gay and nongay couples are sometimes used, as well as groups that focus on bereavement adjustment and that are generally time-limited.

*Educational* or more *didatic-oriented group programs* are increasingly used to teach safer sex by cognitive-behavioral techniques. Support groups for persons who are HIV positive, but who are otherwise asymptomatic, that focus on more healthful living and on social support are becoming more widespread as testing for the virus is related to experimental treatments to ward off HIV symptoms and an AIDS diagnosis. Social workers and other health care professionals may conduct such groups in community health programs or at HIV testing sites. The special problems of women who are HIV-infected, of children who have siblings with AIDS, and of survivors of multiple losses due to AIDS may be addressed through special focused groups that universalize their difficult situations with peer support.

*Family counseling* with persons from a variety of backgrounds, conducted by social workers, has proved promising (Walker 1988). Increasingly, social workers in private practice and agency work are seeing the direct and indirect influence of AIDS and HIV infection in their caseloads. For example, agencies serving the visually disabled are being asked to work with persons with AIDS blinded by different opportunistic infections and cancers. Long-term-care facilities and home care programs are being pressed into service for multiply disabled persons with AIDS, including individuals with AIDS dementia. Hospice programs tailored to the particular needs of people with AIDS are beginning to be established.

A primary setting for social work intervention remains the *acute care hospital* during the health crises of persons with AIDS. Whether dispersed or in a designated area, persons with AIDS and their families require focused crisis intervention and even short-term groups.

Increasingly, *case management work* by social workers is an area of importance because of the growth of outpatient care provision. Sensitive work with persons with AIDS is necessary as they become more disabled and disoriented. Homelessness and poverty among inner-city hospital AIDS patients require intensive case management and the elimination of routine bureaucratic red tape. Social workers frequently become strong advocates for entitlements and prompt responses from large public agencies, especially when their clients are in crisis and are under the stresses of life-threatening conditions. A high degree of interprofessional cooperation is not unusual in hospital programs designed for AIDS patients.

Support networks of social workers have also developed in different parts of the country to allow exchanges of information as well as to provide professional recognition and emotional support. The National Association of Social Workers (NASW) has developed policy statements on AIDS and has designated it a primary policy priority. The New York City Chapter of the NASW (1986) developed a widely circulated series of guidelines for social work practice for all professionals, designating their ethical responsibilities during the AIDS pandemic. Social workers have also given expert testimony to local, state, and federal panels on AIDS and HIV infection.

## DIFFERENTIAL CLINICAL ASSESSMENTS AND INTERVENTIONS

Clinical work with persons with AIDS must be particularly sensitive to the diversity of the people infected and affected in each case. Individuals, families, communities, and regions reflect different patterns and variations that significantly influence diagnoses, assessments, and interventions. The following case illustrations point to the complexity of understanding needed to work with persons with AIDS and HIV infection:

> Peter is currently hospitalized in a room filled with cards and flowers. This is his third hospitalization in four months. He is a white 24-year-old gay man and the first college-educated member of his working-class suburban family. Recently, he was excited by becoming a computer programmer; then his life chances were diminished by the diagnoses of Kaposi's sarcoma and AIDS. Remarkably, he has survived successive infections of meningitis and toxoplasmosis encephalitis. His friends and his former lover

have been available to help him in the hospital and at home. Within a month of diagnosis, Peter told his parents both that he was gay and that he had AIDS. To Peter's relief, his parents and sister, unlike some of his friends, have not abandoned him.

Martha is a Hispanic female, aged 40, and is a recovering narcotic addict with a history of drug abuse from the age of 14 to 35. She had one child when she was 20 years old; at 6 months of age, the child was removed from her by the department of child welfare. After her second child was shot to death in a gunfight, Martha joined Narcotics Anonymous and has been drug-free for five years. She joined a AIDS support group shortly after being diagnosed six months ago. Martha, a leader in the group, says the group helps her fight intense bouts of depression.

Warren is a white 35-year-old bisexual man who is married and has no children. His wife does not know about his AIDS diagnosis; he is frightened that she is HIV-infected. Warren has been able to continue working but spends all his available time reading medical journals; he tells his social worker at the clinic that he will "beat" AIDS. Warren has been asymptomatic since discovering Kaposi's sarcoma lesions on his chest a year and a half ago.

Jane is a 30-year-old middle-class woman who was exposed to HIV through a six-year relationship with a boyfriend, a recovering intravenous drug user who recently died. She was diagnosed with PCP after giving birth to a daughter. Jane recently expressed a wish to commit suicide rather than be a burden to her parents. She is overwhelmed by the possibility that her baby will die of AIDS.

Allan is an 8-year-old hemophiliac who became HIV-positive from infected blood products used for their clotting substance. Allan's older brother, also a hemophiliac, died a year ago from AIDS. Allan is currently unaware that his father, a hemophiliac, is HIV-positive, while his mother is not. Recently, his parents have been fighting and have discussed a trial separation.

Of particular importance in the differential diagnosis and assessment of persons with AIDS and HIV infection are AIDS pathogenesis, transmission, and medical treatment, as well as the influence of neurological impairment (Buckingham and Van Gorp 1988) and HIV symptoms and AIDS as life-threatening events on individuals directly and indirectly affected by the disease (Lopez and Getzel 1984).

Each person with HIV infection has a unique history, specific life experiences, social supports, and other resources. In considering how to serve this population, social workers should pay particular attention to the following assessment criteria and treatment foci:

Christ, Weiner, and Moynihan (1986) indicated that at diagnosis, an individual generally goes through profound and far-reaching emotional responses to the *psychosocial* consequences of the illness. In turn, all persons intimately related to the diagnosed person may experience similar strong emotional reactions. The social worker must understand the intensity of the coping efforts that underlie the strong and sometimes confusing reactions of individuals and their families.

Psychosocial issues are expressed at the dyadic relational level between a person with AIDS (PWA) and providers of health and human service and within the family system (Getzel 1987). A person with symptoms associated with HIV or an AIDS diagnosis goes through strong responses during his or her periods of illness. Anxiety about being diagnosed may precede the development of any symptom of an opportunistic infection. Persistent respiratory infections, skin rashes, and transitory fever may occasion sleeplessness, psychosomatic symptoms, and obsessive thinking.

Panicky reactions build if a person develops night sweats, swollen glands, weight loss, and other HIV related symptoms before the presence of an AIDS diagnosis. Paradoxically, once the PWA develops an opportunistic infection and finally receives a formal AIDS diagnosis, he or she may be emotionally relieved for a time. A PWA often feels, "At least I can now stop worrying that I'm going to get AIDS."

Pre- or postdiagnosis preoccupation with becoming ill results in social isolation. Affected individuals may see themselves as possessed by the disease—controlled at every turn by thoughts about illness— and subtly and not so subtly reminded by others that they have a potentially progressive fatal condition. Therefore, it is not unusual for PWAs to see themselves as toxic, stigmatized outcasts worthy of others' rejections.

Susan Sontag wrote, "Any illness that is treated as a mystery and acutely enough to be feared will be felt to be morally, if not literally contagious" (1977:5–6). The association of AIDS with homosexuality and substance abuse has contributed to the public's fears and the legitimation of prejudice and aversion. Unfortunately, many PWAs also assume these powerful negative images of themselves, which are too frequently reinforced by the actual withdrawal of kin, friends, and others who become fearful of becoming ill or tainted by their contact with AIDS.

Family members' and friends' vulnerabilities are heightened, if they share PWAs' lifestyles, age, interests, and personal habits. Aversive and rejecting behavior by providers of health and human service is particularly potent in feeding depression, diminishing self-esteem, and engendering rage in already stressed and burdened PWAs.

Mounting social isolation contributes to PWAs' feeling withdrawn, depressed, emotionally worthless, physically fatigued, and sexually void. PWAs may experience shame at being exposed as gay or as drug users or as sexually linked with these populations. Tragically, some PWAs may associate AIDS with a personal attribute and not with past activities. Defensively, these PWAs may bargain to go straight or to swear off the use of drugs, if they might be cured. This kind of magical thinking and self-condemnation becomes a dead-end approach by PWAs to overcome the crises of diagnosis, illness, and disabilities.

Social workers must carefully assess the positive coping elements in PWAs' emotional expression during crisis periods. During crises, PWAs' characteristic methods of coping with feeling states and problem solving falter. An emotional rollercoaster ride of anger, guilt, rage, sadness, and fear represents PWAs' early efforts to cope with each bit of medical information, new symptoms, and functional losses.

Social workers are most helpful when they assist PWAs to understand their reactions at a specific time. For example, sadness and depression reflect, in part, authentic grieving over actual bodily and functional losses. As PWAs are able to give themselves time and space to grieve, they can approach other aspects of personal mortality. The prospect of dying from AIDS often opens up memories of the deaths of family members and friends. PWAs may feel guilty about the burdens that they believe their illness is placing on loved ones for their care. Consequently, PWAs may be reticent to ask for help from others.

PWAs' anger and rage are reflections of the injustices of falling ill and being rejected by others. Anger can be positive, if it can be channeled into being more assertive with physicians and other providers of health and social services when it becomes clear that treatment is inappropriate.

Becoming a thoughtful and responsive consumer of help results from social workers' legitimating PWAs' sometimes diffuse anger and sense of impotence when approaching the staffs of hospitals and social agencies. Far too often, PWAs feel powerless as they face making new and greater demands for care. If PWAs can gain a sense of control over their care, they are apt to experience enhanced responses and practical assistance from the medical establishment, social agencies, employers, and others.

Finally, in the face of ultimate questions of life and death, PWAs show remarkable capacities for hope. Even though PWAs occasionally intimate as well as actually speak about suicide, expressions of hope are ubiquitous. In many situations, denial of being ill or of having a foreshortened existence is a necessary and useful coping strategy. Hope is supported when PWAs live as fully as they can. Just as PWAs should be allowed to deny aspects of their illness, they should be free to express concerns about dying and death, which often come up in the discussion of wills, funeral arrangements, and living wills that control quality of life while dying.

Social workers and other professionals serving people with HIV infection and AIDS—and, for that matter, responding to a variety of other problems and conditions—should draw a broad operational definition of *family*, so that it includes all relatives, life companions, and friends who demonstrate a long-term commitment to caring for the person in need (Walker 1987; Chackhes 1987; Stulberg and Buckingham 1988).

Social workers should identify a PWA's functional family as the network that provides some measure of emotional support, guidance, material resources, and help with practical, everyday routines and chores. Members of the family network play an important role in determining how PWAs receive needed health care, social services, legal assistance, and other services, particularly during crisis periods and at points of incapacitation.

The family network undergoes changing patterns of closeness and social support to a PWA as he or she experiences the crises associated with HIV and AIDS. A PWA may be overwhelmed at the prospect of revealing a diagnosis to unsuspecting relatives for fear of emotional rejection and abandonment. The pressure on the PWA is heightened if family members will also discover the "secret" of homosexuality or drug use. While such fears cannot be dismissed, it is also not uncommon for relatives and friends to move closer after such revelations, paradoxically surprising the wary PWA.

The decision to inform a family of an AIDS diagnosis must always be the PWA's; the social worker can be the most helpful in assisting the PWA to find the appropriate time and way to share the diagnosis with particular family members and friends. Family dynamics as well as cultural and ethnic styles may be factors in how and with whom information is first shared. Clearly, there are political consequences in and outside the family network when an AIDS diagnosis is revealed.

Very often, the social worker's balanced, nonjudgmental, and accepting attitude toward a PWA, during good times and bad, serves as an antidote to recurrent feelings of isolation, diminished self-esteem, and suspicion. One of the most powerful and effective tools for helping a PWA to break down isolation and to regain a sense of normality and trust is the PWA support group, which universalizes experiences and provides true understanding and a safe environment. (Gambe and Getzel 1989; Getzel and Mahony 1989; Child and Getzel 1989).

AIDS may prompt family members to try to resolve longstanding concerns related to sexuality, drug use, and other significant historical issues in the kinship network. A PWA and a family member may share guilt and recriminations, holding themselves or others responsible for the irreversible tragedies each perceives. Gay couples may experience a breakdown in their relationship and in their capacity for trust and intimacy. Family members may be ashamed to share their feelings with friends who are perceived as too judgmental about the subject of AIDS.

Fear of HIV contagion is especially upsetting to members of the family network who fear casual contact or who are justifiably concerned about sexual, intravenous-needle, or fetal transmission. Therefore, in the course of their work with family members, social workers must assess the risks of transmission and the wisdom of HIV antibody testing in the immediate and long-term interests of the members of the kinship network (Honey 1988). Social workers have an important role in the direct teaching of families about AIDS transmission and prevention and about safer sex practices.

If spouses and life companions of PWAs are HIV-positive or believe themselves to be infected, they may fear developing symptoms or opportunistic infections. Powerful feelings of anxiety, helplessness, and even anger toward PWAs may make it difficult for spouses and life companions to acknowledge self-concerns, especially if they are providing significant caregiving. They may have recurrent fatalistic fantasies and fears of becoming ill alongside the PWA. Even if a spouse or life companion is HIV-negative, he or she may experience survivor's guilt and feelings of personal unworthiness. If a child is infected, the emotional burdens for the mother and others in the family are catastrophic.

Social workers should be aware of the ethical questions entailed in sharing information about HIV infection and AIDS. Legal requirements for reporting test results to a person's sexual partners exist in certain jurisdictions, as well as rules for strict confidentiality about sharing test findings and diagnoses. The reporting requirements should be known in advance by clients (Bayer 1989; Dickens 1988; Senak 1987).

Families of intravenous drug users may have several members who are infected and ill at different times or all at once; over time, the family network may collapse functionally and physically from within. Such families require humane and continuous survival services and ongoing grief and bereavement counseling. Child welfare services become very important (Anderson 1986). Before care can be provided and formal diagnoses made, poverty, racism, and cultural barriers must be overcome by community-based-service providers and inner-city hospitals staff who often discover HIV-infected men, women, and children who have long been ill and are severely debilitated. Intravenous drug users' survival strategies frequently entail subterfuge, criminality, and suspicion, which continue in their relationships with AIDS service providers, who in turn become antagonistic adversaries (Caputo 1985; Lewert 1988).

The burdens of family caregivers deepen with successive health crises. PWAs' concerns about becoming increasingly dependent on others may be expressed in strong emotional reactions to family members. Stresses from the indignities of illness and from historic conflicts within the family network are bound to overwhelm even the most even-tempered PWAs from time to time. Support groups for family caregivers provide valuable opportunities to discuss practical concerns and emotional issues with others who are having similar experiences.

When conflicts erupt in the family network, it is important that social workers assume a mediating function. The well-being of the PWAs must always be of paramount concern. When PWAs face life-threatening health crises, family members may wish to discuss such contingencies as living wills, powers of attorney, funeral arrangements, and estate planning. If these arrangements are made carefully in advance, they help families avoid excessive conflict during periods of stress. Discussion of these practical concerns of living and dying allows anticipatory grief expressions and some partial acceptance of the prospective losses.

Many persons now appear to be living longer with AIDS. An immediate death from opportunistic infections may be less likely because of more sophisticated medical treatments and the effectiveness of antiviral medications. As PWAs live longer with AIDS, they make plans against a backdrop of incertitude. Life cycle events like baptisms, weddings, bar mitzvahs, and holiday rituals assume greater importance because they break down social isolation and allow opportunities to participate in activities that represent continuity and contribution to others. PWAs often desire ways to identify their legacies to loved ones as they review the meaning of their lives during or after life-threatening episodes.

Family members and PWAs exhibit considerable variation in their capacity to discuss illness directly, regardless of how ominous circumstances become. Caregivers may need help to accept respite from the increasing anxiety and pressures that occur during the course of the disease. Often, a PWA is relieved of guilt if the burdens of caregiving are lightened for a primary-caregiving family member.

Family members continue to struggle with AIDS after PWAs die. The need for remembrance, validation, and continued expressions of grief is natural and predictable. Loved ones may benefit from bereavement groups geared to the special needs of "survivors" of AIDS. There are no simple formulas for adjusting to the loss of so many people cut off in the prime of their lives by devastating illnesses. Family members who care for PWAs may find volunteer work in AIDS service organization a meaningful way to memorialize relatives and friends, and to participate anew in life's sorrows and joys.

## CASE ILLUSTRATION

It is in the specific case that the human face of AIDS is revealed. Understanding human responses to AIDS is important, not only in indicating how the mechanics of diagnosis and intervention may be accomplished, but in sensitizing the clinician to the pathos of PWAs, who often must face, in addition to the indignities of disease, societal stigma and isolation. In preparation for AIDS work, practitioners may benefit from an examination of the emerging literature of firsthand encounters with AIDS (Monette 1988; Dreuilhe 1988; Peabody 1986; Whitmore 1988) or accounts by practitioners (Snow 1987; Greenly 1986).

In the following case description of Jeff, a 55-year-old gay man, a large community-based agency under gay auspices, serving gay and nongay persons, provided a range of services, beginning shortly after his diagnosis and until his eventual death from complications of AIDS, twenty-six months later.

Jeff sought help from a community-based AIDS service agency. He attended an entitlement group meeting to familiarize himself with the insurance and benefits that he might need, Jeff joined a PWA support group. He later made use of the agency's crisis intervention services and of a "buddy" to assist with household tasks that he could no longer handle as he became more physically incapacitated. Jeff participated in the support group until shortly before his death, and toward the end of his life, close family and friends were approached by the social worker leading the support group in Jeff's behalf.

In Jeff's case, a number of interpersonal themes and practice issues developed during the provision of comprehensive social work services. The onset of Jeff's AIDS diagnosis began in January, when he noticed two enlarging purple lesions on his right forearm. Jeff said he knew the diagnosis before he went to the doctor and accepted it with depressed resignation. The June before, Jeff's 41-year-old lover, Marc, had committed suicide when he came down with the HIV-related symptoms of swollen glands, herpes rashes, and weight loss. Jeff went into shock and a profound depression after he found Marc's body. Despite the support and assurances of friends, Jeff could not stop blaming himself for not stopping Marc's suicide. Some of Jeff's guilt and obsessive thinking dissipated by itself after he discovered his lesions, an experience that he shared with his private therapist and his therapy group. However, Jeff felt that his private therapist and the therapy group members could no longer understand him since he had "crossed over the border to AIDS."

His sense of isolation and uniqueness grew stronger and resulted in Jeff's mounting interest in learning how other gay men managed their AIDS diagnosis. With Jeff's growing sense of isolation and apartness came a passive wish to be at peace in a dreamlike death that would reunite him with his beloved Marc. Ordinarily, Jeff was a remarkably active and highly ordered person who took relish in making lists of things to do and was proud of his accomplishments. Jeff's dreams of passively easing into death, however peaceful and beautiful, frightened him, sometimes waking him in a panic at night.

Working as a highly successful accountant, Jeff was bored, but his job did manage to divert his thoughts. Jeff was glad that he had excellent private health insurance "once the other shoe dropped." Jeff revealed his diagnosis only to his trusted secretary, since he had never indicated to his fellow workers that he was gay. Jeff said that he felt slightly pressured in dissembling his diagnosis with other workers to whom he was close.

Although he had weekly contact with his younger brother, a successful married businessman with three grown children, and his 84-year-old widowed father, Jeff had never told them that he was gay and now had AIDS. Jeff maintained that only his 23-year-old niece, who lived nearby and to whom he was very close, knew that he was gay and diagnosed. Jeff was very fearful that his brother, knowing the truth, would reject him and felt that his father should not know because the elderly man was forgetful and rather distant from his sons.

Jeff's life was split into the public world of work and a private world where he had many gay and "straight" friends who shared his appetite for ballet, opera, and travel. He was a very generous and thoughtful friend. Jeff's many friends gave him support after Marc's death and during the period of diagnosis

In the practice excerpts that follow, the sequential phases of intervention in working with Jeff are identified and illustrated.

In the first phase, the social worker engages and assesses the condition of the PWA. The person with AIDS often receives quick relief by hearing similar reactions to diagnosis and hospitalization from peers in a support group. The beginning phase of intervention is also characterized by approach–avoidance responses prompted by a PWA's unconscious sense of dependency and the loss of control that is associated with simply reaching for help. AIDS itself is emblematic of the loss of bodily control. Therefore, it is vital that the social worker strive mightily to give PWAs a sense of control by allowing them to define their needs at their own pace and in their own terms.

The interventive approach is, therefore, nonconfrontational and typically permits a PWA to ritually tell and retell his or her survival story beginning with diagnosis and/or hospitalization. The social worker points out commonalities of the experience and acknowledges explicit and implicit painful affects, including shame, guilt, loneliness, rage, and sadness. Although many group members may be locked into their own emotional world, the group offers nonthreatening acceptance and, at first, a recognition of shared experiences.

During Jeff's first session in a newly formed support group, the members introduced themselves by telling about the nature and time of their diagnoses. Michael recounted his hospitalization with PCP and his surprise at his religious fundamentalist parents' rejection of him. His sense of hurt and rejection was clearly shared by the group members, who appeared quietly sympathetic and upset. This story was soon followed by Al's; Al told how his lover, himself sick with AIDS, had discovered Al unconscious after a suicide attempt. Al said that after becoming conscious in the hospital, he did not know whether to be angry or pleased that his lover had sought emergency assistance. The social worker acknowledged to the group members that AIDS would often challenge them to think about the quality of life that was acceptable and suggested this as a possible subject for the group members to discuss together.

Next, Jeff noted that he had not known what to expect from an AIDS support group, and that he was surprised by how open the members appeared to be. He told the group that after he was diagnosed, he just assumed that he would die in a few months and was somewhat sorry that death had not come quickly. Jeff said that if it were not for his friends and the ballet, he did not know how he would survive. Eyes welling up with tears, Jeff briefly told the others about his beloved Marc. The social worker acknowledged the strong attachment that Jeff still had for his dead lover.

Two months later, the topic for group members was the consequences of telling family and friends about their diagnosis. Two members used the group as a source of guidance and support to inform their parents that they had AIDS. Jeff felt group pressure to do the same, which he resisted by giving a long monologue explaining how, at one time, he had been close to his brother and now was uncertain of his brother's love because of the antipathy he sensed from his brother's wife. Jeff wanted the support of his brother but wondered if it would ever be possible. With strong, stifled emotion, he lamented the occurrence of his mother's death when he was 19; Jeff maintained that she would have accepted him unconditionally and would have cared for him now. The group was quiet for a time. Then the social worker noted that he himself felt some of the weight of Jeff's continuing grief over the death of his mother and Jeff's hurt about his isolation from his family, especially his brother and his father. The group quickly changed the subject to promising treatments for PCP.

In the second phase, assisting and supporting the PWA's autonomy, the social worker provides continuing acceptance of and concern for PWAs by helping them, as a group, identify and explore complex psychosocial problems. The social worker establishes a relationship with each PWA that maximizes the individual's autonomy. The social worker must avoid the temptation to preempt the PWA's self-determination out of anxiety arising from a perception that the PWA's condition is deteriorating.

Six months later, Jeff complained that he did not have much energy in the morning and did not feel like going in to work some days. When the group members suggested the possibility of his staying home once in awhile, Jeff bristled, saying that it was nearly impossible for him to stay out because it might become a tempting habit. In the next few sessions, Jeff and other group members discussed the virtues of stopping work and going on disability benefits. Jeff was concerned that early retirement would throw him into a depression if he did not structure each day. Jeff ruefully admitted that going to doctors and taking medication had almost become a second career, and that he might have to consider going on disability in the immediate future. Jeff's remarks were prompted by two group members' decision to file for disability benefits.

In the third phase, challenging the helping relationship and the meaning of AIDS, the PWA's growing trust of the social worker may paradoxically, allow him or her to challenge the authenticity of their relationship. This is yet another step in the client's efforts to maintain autonomy in the face of uncontrollable bodily changes. A PWA's unexpressed rage at family and friends and others with better life prospects (including the social worker) may be expressed metaphorically or in strong emotional responses directed at others. PWAs are quick to pick up cues of the social worker's and others' survival guilt, death fears, and sadness.

After a year in the support group, Jeff announced, with muted affect, that he would be leaving the group. The group and the social worker expressed their surprise, since Jeff had been such an active member, often taking on a leadership role by getting information about new experimental medical treatments. With submerged hostility, Jeff told the group that he really needed a more sophisticated group of people, since his problems were more complicated than those of some of the newer members of the group. The group members grew restive and seemed unable to express their obvious shock, hurt, and rage at Jeff. The social worker noted that, although he could not speak for the rest of the group, it seemed clear that Jeff was also angry at him, which Jeff loudly denied. The social worker stated that it was always a group member's right to leave a group, but that in this case, he felt Jeff was flying away from the group and, perhaps, not examining some of his concerns about his health and about what Jeff described as "incomplete answers" from his trusted physician. A few group members said that they wished Jeff would not leave the group.

The following week, Jeff told the group that he would stay; he expressed growing anxiety about bouts of diarrhea that had resulted in his defecating twice in his bed. Tests indicated that he had a cytomegalovirus (CMV) in his colon and might need an experimental medication, which he was reading about in medical newsletters. The social worker and the group members commiserated with him and noted how upsetting these new developments were for him and for them.

After the group meeting, Jeff asked if the social worker had been offended by his request to leave the group; he said that his diarrhea had got the better of him, and that he had meant to speak to the social worker sooner. The social worker indicated that it was perfectly appropriate for Jeff to get angry at him from time to time, and that he and Jeff should find ways of speaking to one another at these times, in or outside the group.

The fourth phase is supporting a PWA in recognizing a fore-shortened life and yet-living fully. With the succession of symptoms, a PWA begins to acknowledge directly the cumulative declines in functioning due to the disease process. Intimations of death are expressed metaphorically or as a contingency to be planned for and thus controlled. Events in the past assume saliency as future planning is fraught with uncertainties. A social worker should assist the PWA to recognize the actual functional consequences of AIDS without encouraging either a morbid preoccupation with or a denial of the implications of specific health concerns.

Of critical significance is the social worker's powerful emotional identification with a declining PWA, which may propel the social worker to assume either premature fatalistic or magical solutions to the tragic elements of the downward AIDS trajectory. Through an ongoing life-review process, a PWA seeks modes of mastery through active use of the past to make sense of the present and an uncertain future. Relationships with family members and longtime friends are examined in light of the realities of shifting life chances.

Jeff, fifteen months after diagnosis, was becoming increasingly sad because of the diarrhea resulting from the CMV colitis; the prescribed treatment would require medication through a catheter surgically implanted in his chest. Edward, who already had a catheter, reassured Jeff that once it was implanted, he would forget it was there. Jeff wondered if that would be so in his case, since he was so vain and would no longer want to take his shirt off or go swimming. Jeff said with deep resignation that it was not a sexual concern in his case, since he had largely lost interest after his lover's death. Peter said that was too bad, since intimate contact with his lover made him feel better about himself, even with disfiguring lesions.

Later in the session, Jeff said that he guessed he was going through "the beginning of the beginning" and began a long monologue about how he had started to accept the possibility that he would not survive AIDS and, consequently, had recently written letters to friends to be opened at his death, saying to them things that he was unable to say while he was alive. The group grew very quiet. Finally, Allan said that Jeff's actions were very sobering, and that he admired Jeff's courage because he could not tolerate the idea of death. Peter said that the group was getting too morbid, and that they should talk about living, not death. The social worker engaged the members in a discussion of what they saw as the group's purpose. After heated discussion, the members decided that concerns about death could not be avoided, and that they would determine together when the discussion of death became too overwhelming.

After agonizing over the prospect of the implant, a year and a half after joining the group, Jeff felt a stronger need to get closer to his family, particularly his younger brother, to whom he had been very close in childhood. They had grown further apart after the death of his mother, described as the only person who really understood him. The group and the social worker helped Jeff to come to the decision to tell his brother both that he was gay and that he had AIDS. At one point the social worker and Jeff actually role-played the worst possible scenario: his brother's complete rejection of him. Jeff actually did speak to his brother and was shocked when his brother broke down in tears and embraced him. In telling the group and thanking them for their support, Jeff wept and said that he regretted he had not told his brother sooner.

The fifth phase is monitoring and supporting PWAs during episodic crises. As PWAs grow more seriously ill, they naturally become more dependent on others for care and emotional validation. The social worker assists PWAs to become more observant of their changing health status, and to acknowledge the need to accept help from others.

After twenty months in the group, Jeff discovered in a short period that he had become rundown, that he had disseminated tuberculosis, and that his vision had become impaired by the pressure of lymphatic cancer tissue against his left eye. He approached these "verdicts" with an emotional equilibrium that surprised both him and the group members. Jeff's mode of coping was to become highly rational and instrumental, a mode that was abetted by his close relationship with his doctor and their mutual respect. Jeff helped other group members become more assertive with their physicians, particularly if they were concerned about not being fully apprised of their condition.

In a group session, Jeff puzzled over his friends' falling over themselves to spend time with him during three recent hospitalizations. He seemed both to enjoy their solicitous behavior and to be bothered by their concern. Allan asked Jeff why he had so much trouble accepting his friends' love. Jeff said that since his lover's suicide, he had grown suspicious of his friends' kindnesses to him; he felt unworthy of everyone's love except that of the 2-year-old child of some friends. Jeff said that he knew her love was true and spontaneous; he intended to leave the child a large life insurance policy to attend college. This would be his legacy. The social worker indicated that Jeff's kindnesses to the child and others might be the reason people were there for him in his time of need.

The sixth phase is supporting intimacy and more active grief work by a PWA. As a PWA experiences more a precipitous decline, especially in mental status and mobility, more sustained discussion of loss and separation occurs in the group. Members often grow closer in their efforts to gain increased support and emotional validation. Planning for death and searching for the personal meaning of lives completed occur in the group.

For the next three months, through deaths and relocations, Jeff and two of the other founding members of the group remained together. Jeff came late to a session, apologizing to a very sympathetic group. He related a series of incidents of forgetfulness, wondering if this was the onset of HIV dementia. Other group members talked openly and long of their constant fears of becoming demented. The social worker stated that just as they might talk freely about physical symptoms, the mental ones were also a legitimate topic.

In another session, Jeff shared a dreamlike vision of being in two worlds: this one and a heavenly one. He had a clear image of his mother with his dead lover and with an old cat that he had had to put to sleep because it was too ill to be cared for during his recent hospitalization. He warmly shared memories of his mother and the remote father with whom he could never share his being gay. Group members were very moved by these images, which seemed to provide Jeff some measure of peace in the face of death.

In the seventh phase, the social worker assumes a more direct role in caring for and advocating in behalf of a PWA. The PWA may not be able to discuss concerns. Caregivers become vital for their assistance at obvious points of intervention. The social worker supports and advocates for appropriate and dignified care during the often upsetting last days of life.

Two years after joining the group, Jeff became housebound and more disoriented. He was cared for by a home-health-care team, friends, and family. Just before Jeff's death, during a home visit, his elderly father indicated to friends and the social worker that he had known Jeff was gay for more than twenty years but had never talked about it because, as a father, he did not want to embarrass his son. Jeff heard his father's statement of acceptance, however belated, before his death, and he smiled broadly. Jeff died three weeks later, and the social worker and some group members joined a hundred other friends and family at a memorial service. Subsequently, his friends made a quilt in his memory to be added to the thousands of others made to memorialize persons who have died in the pandemic.

It is not hyperbole to say that the measure of our society and the profession of social work will be made in how we respond to the AIDS pandemic in this country and throughout the world. Every aspect of our knowledge and our values will be challenged by the multilevel complexity of the efforts at prevention, treatment, and social reconstruction called for by the HIV infection and AIDS. Camus (1954) concluded in *The Plague* that in times of pestilence, there will hopefully be more to admire in humankind than to despise. In social solidarity, social workers, with other professionals and an educated citizenry, can and must act humanely and intelligently in the days and years ahead, as together, we face the complexity and challenges of the pandemic.

## REFERENCES

Altman, Dennis. 1986. *AIDS in the Mind of America*. New York: Anchor Book Press.
Anderson, Gary B. 1986. *Children and AIDS: The Challenge for Children Welfare*. Washington, D.C.: Child Welfare League of America.
Bateson, Mary Catherine and Richard Goldsby. 1988. *Thinking AIDS: The Social Response to the Biological Threat*. Reading, Mass.: Addison-Wesley.
Bayer, Ronald. 1989. *Private Act, Social Consequences: AIDS and The Politics of Public Health*. New York: Free Press.
Buckingham, Stephan L. and Wilfred G. Van Gorp. 1988. "AIDS-Dementia Complex: Implications for Practice." *Social Casework* 69:371–375.
Buckley, Walter. 1967. *Sociology of Modern Systems Theory*. Englewood Cliffs, N.J.: Prentice Hall.
Cahill, Kevin M. 1984. "Preface: The Evolution of an Epidemic." In Kevin M. Cahill, ed., *The AIDS Epidemic*, (pp. 2–6). New York: St. Martin's Press.

Camus, Albert. 1952. *The Plague.* New York: Knopf.

Cannon, Walter B. 1939. *The Wisdom of the Body.* New York: Norton.

Caputo, Larry. 1985. "Dual Diagnosis: AIDS and Addiction." *Social Work* 30:62–73.

CDC (Centers for Disease Control). 1988. *Acquired Immunodeficiency Disease Syndrome Weekly Surveillance Report.* (December 26). Atlanta, Ga: CDC.

Chackhes, Esther. 1987. "Women and Children with AIDS." In Carl G. Leukefeld and Manuel Fimbres eds., *Responding to AIDS*, pp.51–64. Washington, D.C.: National Association of Social Workers.

Child, Rachel and George S. Getzel. 1989. "Group Work with Inner City People with AIDS." *Social Work with Groups.* 12(4):65–80.

Christ, Grace, Lori Weiner, and Rosemary Moynihan. 1986. "Psychosocial Issues in AIDS." *Psychiatric Annals* 16:173–179.

Dickens, Bernard M. 1988. "Legal Rights and Duties in the AIDS epidemic." *Science* 239:580–586.

Dreuilhe, Emmanuel. 1988. *Mortal Embrace.* New York: Hill and Wang.

Dubos, René. 1959. *Mirage of Heath: Utopias, Progress and Bological Change.* New York: Harper & Row.

Dubos, René. 1965. *Man Adapting.* New Haven; Conn.: Yale University Press.

Fineberg, Harvey V. 1988. "Education to Prevent AIDS: Prospects and Obstacles." *Science* 239:592–596.

Fox, Daniel M., Patricia Day, and Rudolf Klein. 1989. "The Power of Professionalism: Policies in Britain, Sweden and the United States." *Daedalus* 118:93–112.

Friedland, Gerald H. 1989 "Clinical Care in the AIDS Epidemic." *Daedalus* 118:59–83.

Gallo, Robert C. and Luc Montagnier. 1989. "The AIDS Epidemic." *The Science of AIDS: Readings from Scientific American.* pp.1–12. New York: W. H. Freeman.

Gambe, Richard and George S. Getzel. 1989. "Group Work with Gay Men with AIDS." *Social Casework.* 70:172–179.

Germaine, Carel B. and Alex Gitterman. 1980. *The Life Model of Social Work Practice.* New York: Columbia University Press.

Getzel, George S. 1987. *Psychosocial Considerations in Respect to AIDS.* New York: Gay Men's Health Crisis.

Getzel, George S. and Kevin Mahony. 1988. "Education for Life During the AIDS Pandemic." *Social Casework* 69:393–396.

Getzel, George S. and Kevin Mahony. 1989. " Facing Human Finitude: Group Work People with AIDS." *Social Work with Groups:* 2:95–107.

Greenly, Mike. 1986. *Chronicle.* New York: Irvington.

Heyward, William and James W. Curran. 1989. *The Science of AIDS: Readings from the Scientific American.* New York: W. H. Freeman.

Honey, Ellen 1988. "AIDS and the Inner City: Critical Issues." *Social Casework* 69:365–370.

Joseph, Stanley. 1989. *Report of the Expert Panel on HIV Seroprevalence Estimates and AIDS Case Projection Methodologies, February, 1989.* New York: New York City Department of Health.

Kolata, Gina. 1988. "Better Drugs and Skills Prolonging Many Lives." *New York Times.* (February 7), p. B6.

Kramer, Larry. 1989. *Reports from the Holocaust: The Making of an AIDS Activist.* New York: St. Martin's Press.

Leary, Warren. 1989. "U.S. Needs Data on Drug and Sex Habits to Halt AIDS, Study Says." *New York Times.* (February 9), p. A25.

Leukefeld, Carl G. and Manuel Fimbres. 1987. *Responding to AIDS.* Washington D.C.: National Association of Social Workers.

Lewert, George. 1988. "Children and AIDS." *Social Casework* 69:348–354.

Lopez, Diego J. and George S. Getzel. 1984. "Helping Gay Patients in Crisis." *Social Casework* 65:387–394.

Lopez, Diego J. and George S. Getzel. 1987. "Strategies for Volunteers Caring for Persons with AIDS." *Social Casework* 68:47–53.

Mann, Jonathan M., James Chinn, Peter Pilot, and Thomas Quinn. 1989. "The International Epidemiology of AIDS." In *The Science of AIDS: Readings from the Scientific American.* pp. 51–61. New York: W. H. Freeman.

Mass, Lawrence. 1987 *Medical Facts About AIDS.* New York: Gay Men's Health Crisis.

Monette, Paul. 1988. *Borrowed Time: An AIDS Memoir.* San Diego: Harcourt Brace Jovanovich.

New York City Chapter of the National Association of Social Workers. 1986. *Guidelines for Social Work Practice with People with AIDS and HIV Infection.* New York. N.A.S.W. AIDS Task Force.

NYCD (New York City Department of Health). 1989. *AIDS Surveillance Update March 29, 1989.* New York: New York City Department of Health.

Nichols, Eve K. 1987. *Mobilizing Against AIDS: The Unfinished Story of a Virus.* Cambridge: Harvard University Press.

Palacios-Jimenez, Luis and Michael Shernoff. 1986. *Eroticizing Safer Sex.* New York: Gay Men's Health Crisis.

Peabody, Barbara. 1986. *The Screaming Room: A Mother's Journal of Her Son's Struggle with AIDS.* San Francisco: Old Oak Press.

Price, Richard W., Bruce Brew, John Sidtis, Marc Rosenblum, Andrienne C. Scheck, and Paul Cleary. 1988. "The Brain in AIDS: Central Nervous System, HIV I and AIDS Dementia Complex," *Science* 239:586–592.

Redfield, Robert R. and Donald S. Burke. 1989. "HIV Infection: Clinical Picture." In *The Science of AIDS: Readings from the Scientific American.* pp. 63–733. New York: W. H. Freeman.

Risse, Guenter B. 1988. "Epidemics and History: Ecological Perspectives and Social Responses." in Fee, Elizabeth and Daniel M. Fox, eds., *AIDS: The Burdens of History*, pp. 33–66. University of California Press.

Ron, Aran and David E. Rogers. 1989. "AIDS in the United States: Patient Care and Politics." *Daedalus* 118:41–58.

Rosenberg, Charles E. 1989. "What Is an Epidemic? AIDS in Historical Perspective." *Daedalus* 118:1–17.

Rounds, Kathleen A. 1988. "Responding to AIDS: Rural Community Strategies." *Social Casework* 69:360–364.

Ryan, Caitlin C. 1987. "Statement of Challenge." In Carl G. Leukefeld and Manuel Fimbres, eds., *Responding to AIDS*, Washington D.C.: National Association of Social Workers, pp. 1–6.

Ryan, Caitlin C. and Mona J. Rowe. 1988. "AIDS: Legal and Ethical Issues." *Social Casework* 69:324–333.

Senak, Mark. 1987. *Legal Answers to AIDS.* New York: Gay Men's Health Crisis.

Shernoff, Michael. 1988. "Integrating Safer-Sex Counseling Into Social Work Practice." *Social Casework* 69:334–339.

Shilts, Randy. 1987. *And the Band Played On: Politics, People and the AIDS Epidemic.* New York: St. Martin's Press.

Snow, John. 1987. *Mortal Fear: Meditations on Death and AIDS.* Cambridge, Mass.: Cowley.

Sonsel, George E., Frank Paradise, and Stephen Stroup. 1988. "Case-Management Practice in an AIDS Service Organization." *Social Casework* 69:388–392.

Sontag, Susan. 1977. *Illness as Metaphor.* New York: Random House.

Sontag, Susan. 1988. *AIDS and Its Metaphors.* New York: Farrar, Straus & Giroux.

Stulberg, Ian and Stephan L. Buckingham. 1988. "Parallel Issues for AIDS Patients, Families, and Others." *Social Casework* 69:355–359.

Walker, Gillian. 1987. "AIDS and Family Therapy, Part II." *Family Therapy Today* 2:1–6.

Walters, LeRoy. 1988. "Ethical Issues in the Prevention and Treatment of HIV Infection and AIDS." *Science* 239:597–603.

Whitmore, George. 1988. *Someone Was Here*. New York: New American Library.

Williams, Lena. 1980. "Inner City: Under Siege Fighting AIDS in Newark." *New York Times* (February 6), p. 1.

# 2

# Alcoholism and Other Drug Addictions

▼

## MEREDITH HANSON

Knowingly or unknowingly, all social workers encounter the problems and needs of clients suffering from the effects of alcoholism and other drug addictions. Addictions (including alcoholism) are among the most common and serious social and health problems experienced in modern society. Persons from all walks of life are affected; the personal and social costs are monumental.

In a major epidemiological study funded by the National Institute of Mental Health, alcoholism was the most prevalent core (or major) psychiatric diagnosis, while drug abuse or dependence was the third most frequently reported disorder among approximately 20,000 respondents aged 18 and older. The lifetime prevalence rate for alcoholism was 13.7 percent, and the lifetime prevalence rate for drug abuse or dependence was 5.9 percent (Helzer and Przybeck 1988). So frequent were the addictive disorders, that some investigators asserted that without them, the number of persons experiencing at least one of the surveyed mental disorders would have declined by between one third and one fifth (Robins et al. 1984).

In addition to findings such as these, other reports suggest that drug addiction—in particular cocaine and crack abuse—is responsible for breakdowns in the emergency mental health systems of large urban centers (e.g., Barbanel 1988b), for many difficulties that exist in shelters for the homeless (e.g., Barbanel 1988a), and for the rise in family violence (e.g., Lee 1989). Combining alcohol and other drugs is probably the most frequent cause of drug-related medical emergencies in the United States (DAWN 1980). Both drug and alcohol abuse are associated with increased risk for acquired immune deficiency

**65**

syndrome (AIDS) (Ginzburg 1984; Molgaard et al. 1988). Finally, it is estimated that alcohol and other drug abuse cost American business and industry nearly $100 billion per year in lost productivity (Walsh and Gust 1986). Clearly, addictions pose major problems in society. Virtually no one seeking professional assistance is free from their effects—direct or indirect.

As clinicians struggle with the dilemmas that accompany addictions, they discover few clear explanations for the problems and few effective intervention strategies. Over the years, the characteristics of drug abusers have changed. Also, definitions, explanations, and treatments of choice for addictions have evolved. This chapter will review some of these changes, and it will suggest practice approaches that not only have promise for effectiveness but also are consistent with social work's focus and value base.

## PROBLEM DOMAIN

How a problem or need is defined determines, in large part, what is done about it (Germain and Gitterman 1980). This is especially true of the addictions, since no universally accepted definition of alcoholism and other drug addictions exists. Although the modern disease concept dominates the field of alcoholism (Jellinek 1960; Kissin 1983), many competing explanations for alcoholism and other addictions have been proposed (e.g., Pattison, Sobell, and Sobell 1977; Orford 1985; Peele 1985, 1988; Fingarette 1988). One source estimated that there are over 100 separate definitions for alcoholism alone (Rogers and McMillin 1988). Over the years, definitions of addictions have varied greatly, from formulations based on the presence or absence of physiological disease to views placing greater emphasis on the moral, legal, social, and/or psychological characteristics of the addict and society.

In many respects, definitions of addictions are metaphors—images that shape reality not only for addicts but also for society. For example, defining addictions in moral terms places them in the legal arena. Addicts become people who are at best "weak-willed" and at worst "criminal." They are stigmatized as persons suffering from character defects, who must be controlled and from whom society must be protected.

Historically, most addiction control efforts have been morally based. In colonial times heavy drinking was the norm, and alcohol misuse was considered a matter of personal choice (Levine 1978). Alcohol was the "good creature of God"; the drunkard was "from the Devil" (Austin 1978; Lender and Martin 1982). Efforts to control excessive drinking were confined primarily to criminal sanctions, including corporal punishment, incarceration, and public censure (Boche 1981; Lender and Martin 1982).

When drug addiction was defined as a problem in the latter part of the nineteenth century, it, too, was addressed legally and morally. Images of crazed, out-of-control dope fiends emerged. Opium smoking was identified with racial stereotypes, and it was considered a "willful indulgence" (Morgan 1981). Like alcohol-control efforts, the attempts made to control drug use were legal. With the passage of laws like the Harrison Act of 1914, drug use became effectively illegal (Musto 1973; Brill 1981; Brecher 1986), and society was "protected" from a potent danger.

There is some evidence that a major consequence of the moral-legal approach to addictions was a change in the characteristics of the addict population. For example, in the early twentieth century, when opium was legal and opium-based medicines could be purchased over-the-counter, the typical addict was an elderly, white, middle-class woman who was addicted to laudanum, an opium derivative (Ray 1983). When drug use became illegal, drug use patterns changed and, at present, the typical opiate (e.g., heroin) addict is more likely to be a male member of a deviant subculture and a person who is alienated from many aspects of conventional society. In short, a consequence of moral-legal definitions may be the emergence of a social group that is less accessible to treatment.

Although addictions are still considered moral matters by some persons, the most commonly accepted definitions appearing in the professional literature assert that they are diseases, that they are symptoms of underlying emotional conflicts, that they are learned behaviors, and/or that they reflect social dysfunction:

## Genetic/Disease Models

Disease models suggest that addictions are caused by some combination of preexisting physiological deficiency, heritable genetic traits, and/or metabolic changes resulting from drug use (Jellinek 1960; Dole and Nyswanger 1967; Cloninger 1987). Most of the models do not stress excessive drug use per se but focus on "loss of control" over drug use, which is the central feature of the disease (Jellinek 1952). Loss of control means that addicts cannot predict reliably when they will stop their drug use once an episode starts, nor can they control the amount they will consume during an episode. The inability to control drug use is not due to lack of willpower or psychological inadequacies. Rather, it results from physiological characteristics that cause addicts to react differently than nonaddicts to both drug ingestion and drug withdrawal. Once an addiction has been established, according to disease theorists, addicts are qualitatively different from nonaddicts, and they cannot resume drug use without reinstating the addiction. The essence of addiction is the uncontrollable, continued use of drugs, including alcohol, despite the presence of adverse consequences.

Intervention approaches that are based on disease models of addictions assert that addicts must establish lifelong abstinence from drugs in order to remain free from the effects of addictions. Without abstinence, addictions will progress, and addicts' conditions will deteriorate. Intervention strategies, therefore, are designed to educate addicts about the adverse consequences of addictions; to help them overcome psychological defenses, like denial, that interfere with recovery; to support their efforts at maintaining abstinence; and, in some cases, to block the effects of the illicit drug with another drug (e.g., methadone).

## Symptom Models

Drawing on psychoanalytic theories of personality, symptom models suggest that drug use is a manifestation of unconscious emotional conflict. Some psychodynamic theorists have asserted that addicts experience narcissistic defects of self (Kohut 1977) or that they have poor self-esteem because of "tense depression" (Rado 1933). Others have argued that addictions result from unconscious power motivations (McClelland et al. 1972). For addicts, drug addictions are "compromise solutions" that allow them to satisfy primitive dependency needs while maintaining a facade of adult autonomy (e.g., McCord and McCord 1960). Within this framework, drug addictions are defined as symptoms that both shape and are shaped by the addict's personality.

Viewing addictions as symptoms, or manifestations of an addictive personality, leads to intervention approaches that focus on the underlying emotional conflicts that maintain drug use. It is believed that stressing drug use without considering the basic unconscious conflicts or personality patterns that produced it will lead to therapeutic failure. Therefore, therapeutic strategies are designed to help addicts gain an insight into their addictions that will promote emotional integration and growth.

## *Learning Models*

Definitions of addictions based on learning theory assert that addictions are learned behaviors maintained by antecedent and consequent events (Miller and Mastria 1977). Over the years, a number of different explanations for drug use have been included within the learning framework. For example, early learning theorists argued that addictive behaviors persist because of the tension reduction qualities of drugs (Cappell and Greeley 1987). Other theorists have emphasized the role of social learning and modeling in the development of drug use (Bandura 1969). Still others have stressed the role of cognitions and expectancies (Marlatt and Gordon 1985). Central to all the approaches is the role of learning in the addiction process. Addictions, it is argued, are learned in the same way that any other behavior is learned. To understand why an addict uses drugs, one must discover the antecedent stimuli that elicit drug use, the mediating events that impinge on it, and/or the consequent effects that maintain it.

Interventions based on learning models emphasize the drug user's behavior and the contemporaneous factors that affect it. It is assumed that breaking the addiction cycle involves disrupting the reinforcement patterns that support addictive behavior. Examples of techniques used to interrupt drug use behavioral patterns and to develop alternative behaviors are aversive conditioning, contingency management, cognitive restructuring, and skills development.

## *Social Models*

Some theorists have explained addictions as functions of social arrangements and have argued that they are caused by conditions producing alienation, frustration, and despair (Biernacki 1986), or by the existence of subcultures that support deviant and alternative lifestyles such as drug use (Goode 1972; Johnson 1973). Some social theorists have argued that addictions may be the result of a disengagement from conventional values and norms (e.g., Lukoff 1980). Others have asserted that social and cultural arrangements legitimize and influence the behavioral patterns associated with alcohol and drug use (e.g., MacAndrew and Edgerton 1969; Fine, Akabas, and Bellinger 1982). Still others have declared that addicts are "double failures" who have been unable to reach culturally approved goals by either legitimate or illegitimate means (Cloward and Ohlin 1960).

Common to each of these arguments is the belief that social factors are the critical variables in addiction patterns.

Interventions based on social models of addictions assume that to eliminate them, one must change the social conditions that produce them. Examples of intervention strategies that are consistent with this assumption are vocational training and job development programs designed to give addicts access to the legitimate opportunity structure, therapeutic communities that remove addicts from prodrug subcultures and place them in antidrug environments, and worksite prevention programs aimed at organizational factors that normalize drug use.

The preceding definitions are representative of the many addiction theories that have been developed. Each has strengths and limitations. Disease definitions have called attention to critical biological features of addictions, including lost (or impaired) control over drug use, and they have legitimized addiction treatment; psychological approaches have highlighted intrapsychic and personal aspects of addictions; social explanations have revealed environmental and interpersonal factors. All the approaches err, however, to the extent that they oversimplify the addiction process and underemphasize its multifaceted nature. Each definition is a necessary but insufficient view of reality (Goluke, Landeen, and Meadows 1983). If they are used in isolation from each other, they are likely to result in poor communication across disciplines, incomplete assessments of addiction problems, and ineffective intervention strategies.

Taken together, the definitions illustrate that alcoholism and other drug addictions are biopsychosocial conditions (Kissin and Hanson 1982; Galizio and Maisto 1985). As the addiction process unfolds, factors from multiple domains—the psychological, the physiological, and the sociocultural—interact sequentially and simultaneously to influence not only the emergence of addictions, but also their maintenance and interruption. To understand and to intervene with addictions, clinicians must be sensitive to these factors and to the way they interrelate.

## SOCIETAL CONTEXT

The United States has been described as a "drug-saturated society" (Akers 1985). The types of drugs available are innumerable. Most drug use, however, consists of the acceptable use of legitimate substances. For any discussion of addictions to remain in perspective, it must be remembered that drug abuse and alcoholism occur in societal contexts that are generally drug-oriented.

The chief contribution of the societal context to drug use and abuse may be that it facilitates exposure to favorable attitudes toward and opportunities and pressures to use drugs. The societal context and setting in which alcohol and other drug use occurs give it meaning not only to users (or abusers) but also to social control agents (e.g., Zinberg 1984). The sociocultural context is the most powerful factor influencing not only whether people use drugs, but also the drugs they choose.

Research with Vietnam veterans who used heroin in Vietnam revealed that "rather than equalizing the drug experience of men from different social and behavioral backgrounds, easy access [to drugs] seemed to increase their pre-existing differences" (Robins 1978:195). In other words, a facilitating context exaggerated, rather than reduced, the preexisting tendencies that these men had to use drugs. Other research suggests that for individuals to use or abuse drugs in the absence of a favorable context, they must experience greater personal psychopathology (Kaufman 1974).

Drug use is a learned behavior. Regardless of an individual's predisposing vulnerability to drug addiction, to become a drug user, one must learn 1) to use the drugs; 2) to recognize the drugs' effects and attribute them to the drugs; and 3) to define the effects as positive (e.g., Becker 1953; Akers 1985). For the most part this learning occurs in a social context in which people learn drug-related norms and observe drug use by significant others. Like other social behavior, learning to use drugs is the result of a continuous, reciprocal interaction among people and a facilitating environment.

Cultural approval and social structure increase the accessibility of specific drugs; cultural ritual and social structure regulate their use (e.g., MacAndrew and Edgerton 1969; Burns 1980). Favorable attitudes toward drugs like alcohol can emerge early in childhood, by the age of 6 (Jahoda and Cramond 1972). Such attitudes can interact with parental and peer norms and behaviors to influence adolescents' definitions of alcohol use and the probability that they will become heavy drinkers (Zucker 1979).

In a study of drug and alcohol use among 3,000 adolescents in grades 7 through 12, social learning factors—such as *differential association* (differential exposure to drug-using peers and adults and to favorable drug use norms), *definitions* (definitions favorable to drug use), *differential reinforcement* (variations in rewards and punishments for use), and *imitation* (differential exposure to admired models who used drugs)—were correlated highly with the use and abuse of alcohol and marijuana (Akers et al. 1979). Variations in the same factors were related to both the continuation of drug use and its cessation (Lanza-Kaduce et al. 1984).

Generally, cultural and societal values are communicated to individuals through their interactions with meaningful persons, like parents and peers. The relative influence of parents and peers on drug use varies as adolescents grow older. One study suggested that peer models become more important relative to adult models as teenagers mature (Huba and Bentler 1980). Another report revealed that, while parental influences remained stable through high school, peer influence increased (Margulies, Kessler, and Kandel 1977). A third study reported that the drinking of young adolescents was affected directly by parental norms, while that of middle adolescents was a response to peer pressures. By late adolescence, parental and peer norms were equally influential (Biddle, Bank, and Marlin 1980).

These studies and others (e.g., Jessor and Jessor 1977) clearly demonstrate that drug use is learned in a favorable social context, with friends, parents, and other role models influencing an individual's decision to use drugs. Social factors interact with personal and demographic attributes to affect the onset of drug use; they continue to interact reciprocally to influence its continuance and cessation.

Even though all drug use is learned in social contexts, drug abuse seems to pose a greater threat to persons from society's more disadvantaged groups (Cahalan 1982; Wylie 1989). To understand this fact, one must examine the functions of drug use and how they interact with the societal context. Among the reasons that people use drugs are to gain peer acceptance (e.g., Akers 1985), to cope with stress (e.g., Gottheil et al. 1987), to escape overpowering threats and pressures (Cahalan 1970), and to get high (e.g., Zuckerman 1972). Individual motivations to use drugs emerge in societal contexts that not only provide access to drugs and definitions favorable to drug use, but also present people with a range of environmental demands with which they must cope.

Adaptive functioning is a transactional process in which people respond to environmental demands that are mediated by social and personal resources. It is well documented that a supportive social environment, or social network, is associated positively with healthier adaptive functioning (e.g., Cohen and Syme 1985). Persons from the most disadvantaged social groups are likely to experience environmental demands that are greater than or equal to the demands experienced by other people. However, they often lack a "social margin," the relationships and resources needed to survive in society (Segal, Baumohl, and Johnson 1977). For example, inner-city black communities are growing poorer and becoming more alienated and isolated from the conventional opportunity structure (Wilson 1987). In such settings with increasing demands, ready access to drugs, and favorable definitions for drug use, drug use and abuse become viable options for many individuals. Given the inaccessibility of legitimate opportunities, persons at high risk for drug use (i.e., those with favorable attitudes and other vulnerabilities) are more likely to use or abuse drugs. As use continues, they are likely to become enmeshed in cultures of drug use that foster greater drug use and that alienate them further from conventional sources of support.

## RISKS AND NEEDS OF POPULATION

Until the 1940s, most drug problems were localized in specific geographic areas, each of which experienced difficulties with particular drugs (Arif and Westermeyer 1988). For example, heroin abuse tended to be a major problem in parts of Asia and North America, while cocaine posed more serious difficulties in Latin American and South American countries. Further, in most cases, affluent social groups were the first to encounter drug problems. However, as mass culture "homogenized" the world and as technological and communication advances made it smaller, differences in drug abuse patterns changed to the point where many drug problems are worldwide now.

As observed earlier, although drug use and abuse extend to all strata of society, the problems associated with drug abuse and the risks of becoming addicted are not equally distributed among society's members (e.g., Wallace 1987; Maddahian, Newcomb, and Bentler 1988; Tarter 1988). Among the most critical factors associated with increased risk for drug abuse are disadvantaged socioeconomic status and association patterns (which were discussed in the previous section), age, sex, ethnicity, and a family history of alcoholism and/or other drug abuse.

### *Age*

Surveys of drug use and abuse patterns have revealed one unambiguous finding: Drug and alcohol use are associated with youth. For all drugs, young adults have greater rates of use and more problems related to use than do older persons (Kandel 1978; Lukoff 1980; Clark and Midanik 1982; Robins and Przybeck 1985). A national survey of drinking practices among men found that the youngest respondents (those aged 21–24) not only drank at greater rates, but that they experienced the highest rates of alcohol-related problems, including loss of control, interpersonal conflicts, legal problems, and financial difficulties (Cahalan and Room 1974). Analyses of alcohol use patterns among women (e.g., Herd 1988), surveys of use and abuse patterns for specific illicit drugs such as cocaine (e.g., Abelson and Miller 1985; Washton and Gold 1987), and reviews of American drug use patterns in general (e.g., Schuster 1987) have shown similar results. In one report, it was concluded that the period of greatest risk for starting illicit drug use ends by the mid-20s and that persons who start drug use at a later age not only experience less drug involvement but are also more likely to cease drug use (Kandel 1978). As persons grow older, they "mature out" of drug use; that is, as they age, most people reduce and discontinue drug use (e.g., Winick 1962; Cahalan 1970).

### Sex

Other individual characteristics and demographic variables are less strongly associated with drug use and abuse than is age. Men are more likely than women to drink and to use illicit drugs (e.g., Clark and Midanik 1982; Schuster 1987); women are more likely to abuse prescription drugs (Gomberg 1986). In the youngest age groups, however, gender differences are less marked.

Men and women also experience different risk factors for addictions. Women drug abusers are less "visible" than men (Sandmaier 1980; Gomberg 1986). Because of "male-oriented" clinical and research practices, as well as women's drug abuse patterns (e.g., women are more likely to abuse prescribed drugs and to abuse drugs alone at home), clinicians are often insensitive to the signs of addiction in their women clients. Alcoholic women experience depression more often than alcoholic men, who are more apt to experience other mental disorders, such as antisocial personality disorders (e.g., Winokur et al. 1970, 1971; Leigh 1985). Women alcoholics also seem more likely than men to have alcoholic relatives (Cotton 1979; McKenna and Pickens 1983; Midanik 1983). As women gain sexual, social, and economic equality, however, they are becoming more visible, and gender differences seem to be lessening (e.g., Kaestner et al. 1986).

### Ethnicity

Analyses of the drug use patterns of blacks, whites, and Hispanics reveal that blacks and whites use drugs like marijuana and cocaine at similar rates and at heavier rates than Hispanics (Schuster 1987), while blacks are overrepresented among opiate users (Akers 1985). Hispanic adults are more likely than black and white adults to be heavy drinkers and to experience alcohol-related problems (Clark and Midanik 1982). Blacks, especially black women, are more likely to be nondrinkers (Clark and Midanik 1982; Herd 1988). Among Hispanic groups, Mexican-Americans have attitudes more favorable to alcohol consumption, are more likely to drink, and are more likely to experience drinking-related problems than are Puerto Ricans and Cuban-Americans (Caetano 1988).

For other people of color, extensive research is lacking. However, native Americans appear to have serious alcohol problems, especially among urban dwellers (Weibel 1982). In addition, although some research indicates that heavy drinking among Korean- and Japanese-American men is as prevalent as that among other American men (Chi, Lubben, and Kitano 1989), it is generally believed that Asian-Americans consume alcohol and other drugs at lower rates than other groups. Researchers speculate, however, that as Asian-Americans encounter more friends who use drugs, gain greater access to drugs, and become more acculturated to American lifestyles their drug-related problems will increase (Sue, Zane, and Ito 1979; Maddahian, Newcomb, and Bentler 1986).

Although it is evident that different ethnic groups develop different cultural norms and attitudes about drug use, it is not clear to what extent ethnic and racial differences in drug abuse actually reflect economic and social conditions. Some research indicates that ethnic differences disappear as social factors, like association patterns, are considered (e.g., Maddahian, Newcomb, and Bentler 1986). The same reports and other literature reveal, however, that ethnic factors continue to operate when income and lifestyle variables are considered (e.g., Maddahian, Newcomb, and Bentler 1986; Herd 1988). In general, the available evidence indicates that the social and ethnic groups with the greatest proportions of drug users are not necessarily the groups with the highest proportion of people who abuse drugs and experience drug-related problems (e.g., Cahalan 1982).

## Family History of Alcoholism and/or Other Drug Abuse

Alcoholism (e.g., Cotton 1979; Bohman, Cloninger, and Sigvardsson 1981; Cloninger, Bohman, and Sigvardsson 1981; Harford, Haack, and Spiegler 1987–88; Goodwin 1988) and, more recently, other drug addictions (e.g., Scherer 1973; Fawzy, Coombs, and Gerber 1983; Meller et al. 1988) have been described as family "diseases" (or "problems") that are transmitted intergenerationally. Persons whose parents were alcoholic have an increased risk for alcoholism (Cotton 1979; Goodwin 1988), other drug addictions (Cadoret et al. 1986) and other social-emotional difficulties (e.g., Wallace 1987; Berkowitz and Perkins 1988; Woodside 1988). Parental alcoholism also is associated with higher rates of alcoholism among opiate addicts (Kosten, Rounsaville, and Kleber 1985). Finally, parents' abuse of other drugs (e.g., hashish, marijuana, and prescription drugs) is predictive of the abuse of the same drugs by their children (Scherer 1973; Fawzy, Coombs, and Gerber 1983).

Although the evidence strongly suggests that a genetic vulnerability to alcoholism may exist, the evidence is less conclusive for other drugs. Further, in the case of a genetic transmission of an alcoholism vulnerability, neither the alcoholism-specific nature of the transmitted gene (Reich 1987/1988) nor the manner in which genetic and environmental factors interact (McClearn 1983) is clear. Despite an increased risk for alcoholism among children of alcoholics, not only do most children of alcoholics *not* develop alcoholism, but most alcoholics do *not* have alcoholic parents. Further research is needed (1) to clarify the implications and nature of genetic vulnerability for alcoholism and other drug addictions; and (2) to identify the differential risk factors for persons living in different (and the same) societal contexts.

In addition to having differing risks of becoming addicted, clients from different risk groups have specific service needs. For example, members of disadvantaged social and economic groups, who are isolated and alienated from conventional opportunity structures and who have ready access to a wide variety of addictive drugs, require assistance in establishing links with conventional and nondrug sources of support. Public-health education initiatives are unlikely to have a major impact if they are not paired with other educational and clinical efforts designed to aid disadvantaged addicts in developing the personal and social resources necessary to alter their addictive lifestyles.

Young persons also need specialized services. It is well documented that younger persons do not remain in traditional addiction facilities (Baekeland and Lundwall 1975; Hanson 1988). Services for young adults and youth must be sensitive to their developmental stage (e.g., adolescence), to the tasks accompanying that stage (e.g., identity struggles and transitions to adult roles), and to the particular vulnerabilities for drug abuse that they experience (e.g. more rapid intoxication because of lower body weights, higher rates of driving while intoxicated or impaired, and parental drug addiction or alcoholism). Because of the effect of peer and family pressures on the lives of younger addicts, clinical efforts that use social interventions (therapeutic communities, group counseling, and family therapy), as well as education seem particularly useful (Kinney and Leaton 1987).

Finally, women drug abusers require services that meet their unique needs. Generally, although women are underrepresented in treatment centers, once they enter treatment they have success rates that are equal to, and in some cases surpass, those of men (e.g., Straussner 1985). Services for women, however, must address issues that are difficult for them. For example, 1) because of their higher rates of prescription drug abuse, women must be made aware of the cross-addiction potential that many prescription drugs have with other drugs such as alcohol; 2) because of the risk of fetal alcohol or drug syndromes (i.e., children born with drug withdrawal symptoms and experiencing other congenital defects related to a woman's drug or alcohol use during pregnancy), pregnant women (and women wishing to become pregnant) must be alerted to the potential dangers of alcohol and drug use, especially during the early months of pregnancy (Blume 1987); and 3) because of the impact of unstable familial and marital relationships on women addicts (e.g., Wilsnack, Wilsnack, and Klassen 1984), attempts to engage them in family and marital counseling may also be beneficial.

In summary, the differential risk factors and treatment needs of persons with addiction problems illustrate that alcoholics and other drug addicts comprise a heterogeneous population. Consequently, "standard packages of care" that are not individualized to respond to the specific treatment needs of different clients will result in ineffective services (e.g., Glaser 1980). To respond most effectively to the needs of such a heterogenous population, clinicians must have available a wide variety of treatment modalities and techniques.

## PROGRAMS AND SOCIAL WORK SERVICES

A diversified service-delivery system has emerged to meet the needs of people experiencing problems related to alcohol and other drugs. Alcoholics Anonymous (AA) and other *self-help groups* like Narcotics Anonymous (NA) and Pills Anonymous (PA), while not part of the formal service-delivery system, have reached the largest number of drug abusers. In general, AA, NA, and other self-help groups are not treatment systems. Rather, they are fellowships that provide unconditional support and acceptance to any person suffering from addictions. Consequently, they are integral adjuncts to most formal intervention systems. Several hybrids of AA have formed to meet the needs of children, other family members, and associates of drug abusers (e.g., Al Anon and Adult Children of Alcoholics).

Although self-help groups have undoubtedly reached the largest number of persons experiencing drug-related problems, there are no definitive evaluations of their effectiveness (Miller and Hester 1986). In addition, like any other service option, AA and other self-help groups are not useful for all clients. According to some clinicians, self-help group members have a great belief in their group's traditions and values. "If these are not compatible with a client's thinking or belief system, it is probably unwise to coerce him or her to conform to this mode of thought. Such coercion often results in resistance and treatment failure" (Lewis, Dana, and Blevins 1988:151). Because of the potential support clients can receive from self-help groups, however, it is important to encourage them to attend some group meetings. If after attending several meetings they find them to be unhelpful, continued participation should not be mandated.

Besides self-help groups, an extensive professional service-delivery system exists for people with addiction problems. Clinicians who encounter alcoholics and other drug abusers are employed in two broad types of settings: *specialized, hospital-based and free-standing addiction facilities* and *nonspecialized agencies*. Agency setting and mandate set the parameters for clinical response. Consequently, the tasks and responsibilities of clinicians employed in nonspecialized agencies differ from those of clinicians working in specialized addiction services.

In *nonspecialized agencies*, like hospitals, employee assistance programs, and family service agencies, the major clinical roles are identification and referral. Clinicians employed in these settings are in positions where addiction problems can be identified early (sometimes before clients are aware of their severity) and assistance can be provided before the clients' conditions worsen. Thus, the primary clinical tasks become 1) making preliminary determinations that possible addiction problems exist; 2) performing "triage" (i.e., ascertaining clients' needs and locating the available resources); and 3) linking clients with the most appropriate levels of care (Pattison 1982). Because of their position in nonspecialized agencies, clinicians also have opportunities for helping clients become reintegrated with natural support groups as they recover from their addiction.

Clinicians employed in *specialized addiction facilities* may work in any of the following settings: detoxification units, inpatient rehabilitation or residential facilities, halfway houses and therapeutic communities, or outpatient settings. Although their clinical assignments vary by setting, the basic tasks of clinicians working in these settings are to help clients overcome their addiction and establish a drug-free existence.

*Detoxification units* were established to assist drug-dependent clients in "detoxifying" (withdrawing) from physically addictive drugs, while preventing the development of the drugs' unique withdrawal syndromes (Balis 1989b). Detoxification occurs in medical settings for people with severe drug dependence; it may be accomplished in nonmedical facilities if their physiological dependence is less marked.

*Inpatient rehabilitation* and *residential treatment facilities* were developed to meet the needs of clients who do not need drug detoxification, but who require brief care (thirty to ninety days) in a protected environment. The primary goals of these facilities are 1) to remove clients from environments in which they are at risk of using drugs; 2) to help them develop an understanding of their addiction; and 3) to prepare them and their social support networks for their return.

Persons whose social networks are more damaged and who are more enmeshed in drug-abusing lifestyles are often referred to *halfway houses* or *therapeutic communities*, where they are involved in intensive social therapy that lasts for a year or more. Although the intervention techniques differ (e.g., therapeutic communities, which were developed for opiate addicts, rely more on forceful confrontation and encounters), the goals of these modalities are to rehabilitate and resocialize alcoholics and other drug addicts by fostering a sense of mutual aid and peer support. This goal is accomplished by isolating clients from the external environment and creating highly structured systems in which they can undergo "identity transformations" from drug abusers to drug-free persons (e.g., Yablonsky 1965).

Alcoholics and other drug abusers are assisted most often and most extensively in *outpatient settings*. Outpatient services are most appropriate for persons who are not physically dependent on addictive drugs and who have personal and social resources that can be mobilized to help them overcome their addiction. The main value of outpatient intervention is that clients are able to face their addiction in the context within which it arose. Most outpatient treatment is long-term; therefore, clients can establish stepwise recovery plans in which they set and attain short- and long-term goals in multiple areas of life functioning. Since time constraints and setting demands are more flexible than in other modalities, outpatient interventions are individualized more easily than are other interventions.

A variety of intervention methods is available to clinicians employed in the different specialized addiction facilities. Core interventions include group counseling, individual therapy, family therapy, chemotherapy (e.g., methadone maintenance and disulfiram treatment), and referral to self-help groups. These interventions may be used (or initiated) in all of the settings. Other interventions—detoxification, vocational and educational assistance, referral for financial and other entitlements, and medical and psychiatric care—are supplementary in that they are not needed by all clients.

Core interventions are designed to address the basic addiction problems that all clients face: 1) altering addictive life-styles; 2) developing more effective coping skills; and 3) establishing social networks that are supportive of abstinent behavior. Supplementary services are designed to address specific issues that are not common to all clients. The sequence and timing of interventions are determined by the nature and the severity of the clients' needs. Generally, the "natural sequence" of assistance, in order of urgency, is 1) detoxifying the client; 2) meeting emergent social, medical, and emotional needs; 3) providing core interventions aimed at the addictive lifestyle; and 4) delivering additional services (e.g., vocational rehabilitation) that will strengthen a client's general adaptive capacity (e.g., Kissin 1977).

The superiority of any specific treatment modality or method has not been clearly established. As noted earlier, self-help groups reach the largest number of people; yet, no definitive effectiveness studies have been reported on them. Similarly, group methods are preferred by many clinicians (Levine and Gallogoly 1985); however, they, also, have not been demonstrated to be more effective than other intervention techniques (e.g., Anderson 1982; Solomon 1982). Finally, experts disagree on the utility of specific interventions like methadone maintenance (e.g., Lukoff 1977; Sells 1979).

Treatment outcome studies consistently reveal that client characteristics, such as age, sex, history of drug abuse, socioeconomic status, family history of drug abuse, and prior treatment history, are correlated strongly with treatment success (e.g., Emrick and Hansen 1983; Longabaugh and Lewis 1988). In many cases, they are more strongly related to beneficial outcomes than are the types of services the clients receive (e.g., Lukoff 1977; Ferber et al. 1985; Marotta and Hale 1986).

Because support for the effectiveness of clinical services is inconclusive and because differing risk factors exist among drug abusers, it is necessary to assess carefully each client's needs and assets and to tailor services to match those needs and assets (Gottheil, McLellan, and Druley 1982; Pattison 1985). As indicated earlier, alcoholism and other drug addictions can be conceptualized as attempts by individuals to cope with environmental pressures in settings where they receive considerable encouragement and support for drug use. Given this situation, the effectiveness of clinical services will be increased if they are individualized to 1) help clients develop alternative coping skills, like assertive behavior and self-management techniques, to replace addictive behavioral patterns, and 2) involve social support networks in the therapeutic process (e.g., Chaney, O'Leary, and Marlatt 1978; Stanton et al. 1982; McCrady 1985, 1986; Miller and Hester 1986). When the professional response is individualized and is made meaningful to clients' life situations, clients are empowered to overcome addictive patterns and to develop adaptive, alternative lifestyles.

## DIFFERENTIAL CLINICAL ASSESSMENTS AND INTERVENTIONS

Since addictions affect multiple areas of life health (Maisto and McCollam 1980), assessment and intervention strategies must be multidimensional. To be useful, they must be informed by a conceptual framework that draws attention to the physiological, intrapersonal, and environmental forces that interact in the addiction process. Such a framework is the biopsychosocial perspective of addictions (e.g., Kissin and Hanson 1982; Galizio and Maisto 1985; Donovan 1988). In its essence, this perspective reflects "systems thinking" in that it assumes that:

> specific diseases [or human conditions] represent the complex *interaction* of specific environment stresses . . . *and* the organism in question (including its genetic and experiential history) and that biological and behavioral stresses always interact with each other to produce particular constellations of signs and symptoms in particular individuals. (Schwartz 1982:1042)

From this perspective, addictions can be viewed in the following manner: Addictions consist of the use of mood-altering substances, characterized by impaired control over their consumption and continuous or persistent use despite negative consequences which ensue in one or more areas of life functioning. While some persons may be at greater risk for becoming addicted (e.g., they may inherit a biological vulnerability), addictive behavior generally is socially acquired and maintained by multiple individual and social consequences. If addictive behavior persists, its negative consequences will become more severe for most individuals.

This view of addictions is consistent with a social work orientation. It requires clinicians to focus on the person–situation context and to assess drug abuse as a function of a dynamic tension existing within that context. Assessment becomes the process of determining not only the nature and causes of client problems (Lewis, Dana, and Blevins 1988) but also the characteristics of the impinging systems.

Differential clinical assessments and interventions for addictions occur in a general therapeutic context in which clinicians align themselves with the real possibilities for change in their clients and the environment. In the process, efforts are made that encourage and support "movement along these 'natural' pathways of recovery" (Edwards 1982:198). Many alcoholics and other drug addicts feel tremendous personal guilt and shame (e.g., Bean 1981; Fossum and Mason 1986). Also, their drug abuse draws them away from conventional sources of social support. Therefore, special attention must be given to establishing rapport. It is essential to determine the circumstances under which the clients have entered treatment, their current interests, their motivation to engage in being helped, and the potential benefits of therapeutic involvement. Early in the intervention process, clinical efforts must focus on mobilizing the client's resolve to recover (Miller 1983).

Clients seek, or are referred for, assistance at different stages of dealing with their addictions (Prochaska and DiClemente 1984; Marlatt 1988). Many persons are coerced into counseling (e.g., they may be in job jeopardy, or they may be referred on driving-while-intoxicated charges), and they may not define their drug use as a problem. Others are more willing to question their drug use and are prepared to take steps to change it. Consequently, as part of the engagement process, clinicians must assess clients' motivations and their readiness to address their drug use. Strategies that link therapeutic involvement with clients' concerns and that develop clients' awareness of potential adverse consequences if they do not enter counseling are particularly useful (Johnson 1986; King 1986). Linking assessment with work status and with family consequences is an effective engagement strategy for drug abusers.

Once clients have been engaged in being helped, it is necessary to assess the severity of their addiction. Several standardized drug-dependence scales are available to aid in this determination (e.g., Selzer 1971; Skinner 1982; Skinner and Horn 1984). Important diagnostic signs include the client's general drug use patterns, including the quantity and frequency of drug use; the presence of specific drug withdrawal symptoms (see the DSM-III-R for a detailed discussion of these symptoms; APA 1987); personality and behavioral changes associated with drug use; environmental supports for drug use; and physical signs and symptoms of drug-related problems and addiction (e.g., tremors, bruises, liver disease, needle marks, hepatitis, blood-shot eyes, rhinorrhea, and laboratory findings indicating the presence of drugs in the body).

The diagnostic classification system for addictions that is used most frequently at present comes from the revised third edition of the *Diagnostic and Statistical Manual of Mental Disorders, (DSM-III-R);* (APA 1987). The *DSM-III-R*, which draws on research from organizations such as the World Health Organization (Edwards, Arif, and Hodgson 1981), places addictions in two broad categories: "Psychoactive Substance-Induced Organic Mental Disorders," which are organic mental syndromes, like withdrawal states, amnestic disorders, dementia, and intoxication caused by the direct effects of psychoactive drugs on the central nervous system, and "Psychoactive Substance Use Disorders," maladaptive drug-dependent and drug-abusing behaviors resulting from the use of psychoactive drugs: "In most cases the diagnosis of . . . Organic Mental Disorders [is] made in people who also have a Psychoactive Substance Use Disorder" (APA 1987:123).

The behavioral changes accompanying the persistent use of alcohol and other drugs are generally defined as undesirable by most societal groups. By *DSM-III-R* criteria, maladaptive drug use is classified as either psychoactive substance dependence or a "residual diagnosis" of psychoactive substance abuse. The diagnostic criteria for *psychoactive substance dependence* include the presence of at least three of the following for a period of one or more months: the use of drugs in greater amounts or for longer periods than the person intended; craving for drugs; unsuccessful efforts to reduce or eliminate drug use; stereotypical drug-taking behaviors; frequent intoxication or withdrawal symptoms that interfere with major role obligations; important social, occupational, or recreational activities given up or reduced because of drug use; continued use despite perceived drug-induced problems; marked tolerance (i.e., a need for greater amounts of the drug to produce the desired effects or diminished effect with continued use of the same amounts); characteristic withdrawal symptoms; drug use to avoid withdrawal (some drugs, like hallucinogens, phencyclidine, and marijuana, may not produce withdrawal).

When individuals have maladaptive drug-use patterns that do not meet the criteria for drug dependence, they may be diagnosed as manifesting *psychoactive substance abuse.* This diagnosis generally applies to people who have started drug use recently or who use drugs like marijuana that do not produce physiological withdrawal. Examples of persons who might be diagnosed as psychoactive substance abusers are college students who binge on marijuana every few weekends and individuals who repeatedly drive while intoxicated but who experience no other symptoms of a drug disorder (APA 1987).

Clients with addictions of differing severity need different types of helping efforts. For example, if they are experiencing drug withdrawal symptoms, detoxification must be a part of any intervention plan (Balis 1989a). Contingent on the severity of the withdrawal symptoms, the clients' previous attempts to establish sobriety, and the availability of personal and social resources, detoxification may occur in either inpatient or outpatient settings. Clients with less severe drug abuse and more social supports may benefit from less intrusive forms of service. Clients who are experimenting with drug use may benefit from prevention programs aimed at educating them about the potential dangers of drug abuse and/or teaching them responsible drinking practices.

In addition to assessing the severity of clients' addictions and their motivations for treatment, clinicians must attempt to understand clients and their drug use *in their own terms*. It cannot be assumed that the act of seeking addiction treatment indicates that an individual has an addiction problem. To clarify clients' status, clinicians must evaluate their current and past functioning, including their current drug use, any prior difficulties with drugs, and any attempts to seek help (Miller and Marlatt 1984). Also, clinicians must undertake a "review of systems" to reveal assets and liabilities in areas such as physical condition, social supports, emotional functioning, interpersonal relationships, leisure-time activities, occupational functioning, and economic self-sufficiency.

Assessment proceeds with highly detailed microanalyses of high-risk drug use situations (Annis and Davis 1988). Since drug use and abuse occur in some situations and not in others, it is critical to assess the characteristics of the situations in which use and abuse occur. For example, one study found that over two thirds of all alcoholic relapses occurred in three types of situations: those evoking *negative emotional states*, like anger, anxiety, and depression; those involving *interpersonal conflict;* and situations containing *social pressures* to drink. Heroin relapse followed the same pattern. However, while alcoholic relapses were associated most strongly with negative emotional states, social pressures were the strongest determinants of heroin relapses (Cummings, Gordon, and Marlatt 1980). These findings have been replicated in other studies, which have found that younger drinkers relapsed in a wider range of situations and that men were more likely than women to drink in response to social pressures (Annis and Davis 1988).

Critical to the analysis of high-risk drug use situations is the assessment of clients' *perceived self-efficacy*, that is, their expectations about their capacity to cope effectively with situational demands and tasks (Bandura 1977; Marlatt and Gordon 1985). Research has demonstrated that drug use and abuse involve a process in which people with differing vulnerabilities to drug abuse enter high-risk drug use situations (sometimes unintentionally) and encounter pressures to use drugs. If they perceive that they can cope with the pressures without using drugs, the likelihood that they will resist drug use is increased. If, however, they perceive that they are unable to cope with the situational demands without drug use, the probability that they will use and abuse drugs is increased (Marlatt and Gordon 1985).

Emerging logically from the microanalyses of drug use situations, differential interventions become situational in nature. Clients must learn that drug use and abuse are a process. That is, the potential for drug use is established *before* the clients use drugs. "Apparently irrelevant decisions" (Marlatt and Gordon 1985) may place them in high-risk drug use situations. For example, without consciously planning to drink, individuals may decide to go to parties where they will encounter social pressures to drink. If they have not prepared for these pressures, they may feel ill equipped to respond to them and may give in to pressures to drink. Consequently, clients must learn problem-analysis and decision-making skills; they must heighten their sensitivity to situations in which they are likely to use drugs; they must be alert to the adverse consequences of drug use; and they must develop alternative coping skills for use in those situations (e.g., assertion skills and drink-refusal responses).

Because many drug abusers' control over drug use has been impaired (i.e., they can not control the quantity of drugs they consume or determine the conditions under which they will use drugs), their sense of mastery is damaged. If drug use and abuse are defined as attempts to adapt to life stresses (Shiffman and Wills 1985; Davis 1987), effective intervention strategies must empower clients to restore their sense of mastery. Skills development strategies aimed at developing the clients' personal resources, like social skills training, stress management inoculation, and self-control training, and social systems interventions, like family-oriented treatment, work site services, and community reinforcement programs, are particularly effective clinical strategies for helping clients improve their abilities to cope without drug use (Miller and Hester 1986). The skills development strategies help the clients distinguish their impaired control over drug use from their ability to master drug use situations; the social systems approaches make the environment more responsive to drug-free behavior.

Because addictions are socially acquired and maintained adaptive responses, it is critical that clinicians attend to the clients' social support networks. Some network members may be "codependents," who unknowingly conspire with clients to enable them to continue their addiction (Cermak 1986). Others may control powerful contingencies, like continued employment and friendship, which will mobilize clients toward abstinence and recovery. The presence of these network forces must be uncovered early in treatment so that they can be altered and used to promote treatment participation and a positive therapeutic outcome.

The presence of supportive social networks is associated strongly with both continuation in treatment and eventual recovery (Baekeland and Lundwall 1977; Ogborne 1978). Social network members (family, friends, and coworkers) who are supportive of abstinence can enhance intervention (Galanter 1986). Network members like employers who ignore poor work performance that results from drug use can impede recovery. When supportive networks are strengthened and network members are involved in the intervention process and when network practices that encourage or permit drug abuse are altered, the likelihood of a client's eventual recovery increases.

For some clients, no viable drug-free social systems exist. For these persons, abstinence and recovery depend on their ability to disengage from pro-drug-use social networks and to establish links with new social support networks. A study of opiate users, for example, found that persons who stopped drug use changed their social network interaction patterns so that they had fewer contacts with opiate users and more links with positive, non-drug-using role models (Hawkins and Fraser 1983). As this study illustrates, effective social network intervention requires not only that pro-drug-use patterns be disrupted but also that anti-drug-use (or non-drug-use) contacts be established. When no viable drug-free networks exist in clients' natural environment, they must be linked to new support systems like self-help groups (e.g., Alcoholics Anonymous or Narcotics Anonymous) and other social organizations (e.g., religious groups and outpatient socialization groups) that discourage drug use and support drug-free lifestyles.

In summary, differential clinical assessments and interventions with alcoholics and other drug addicts require clinicians to be sensitive to the multiple factors that affect addiction and recovery. The clinical strategies discussed above lead to clinical responses that empower clients and provide them with choices for coping with the unique environmental demands they encounter. In the assessment of the severity and meaning of clients' addictive patterns, a situational perspective must be maintained. Interventions, in turn, will be effective if 1) they help clients develop alternative coping skills to handle environmental demands, and 2) they establish environmental supports for abstinence and recovery. Because addictions are chronic, recovery must be ongoing. Sobriety is the first step in this process. To help clients prevent relapse and to continue recovery, clinicians must encourage them to alter prodrug lifestyles, to remain cognizant of drug use cues, and to nurture non-drug-using social support networks, including self-help groups (Alcoholics Anonymous and Narcotics Anonymous), family, friends, and coworkers.

## CASE ILLUSTRATION

The following case illustrates the process of differential assessment, contracting, and clinical intervention for addictions. As a case illustration, it is not a "recipe" for social work practice; rather, it highlights useful practice principles. Attempting to develop "standardized" clinical responses based on single examples is contrary to the principles espoused in this book. Effective clinical services require that interventions be individualized and matched with clients' resources and needs.

Bernard was a separated, black, 52-year-old bus mechanic, employed by the metropolitan transit authority of a large urban center. He had been on the same job for twenty-five years. He lived alone in a small apartment in a working-class section of the city. When he enrolled in the alcohol clinic, he had been suspended from work for three months because of excessive absenteeism and poor work performance, secondary to alcohol abuse. He had been advised that he could apply for reinstatement in six months. He supported himself with savings and with income he earned as a handyman in his apartment building.

Bernard had been detoxified from alcohol at least three times in ten years; he had never attended outpatient treatment. He was referred to the alcohol clinic this time following his most recent alcohol detoxification. His *DSM-III-R* diagnosis on admission to the hospital for detoxification was "Uncomplicated Alcohol Withdrawal"; on discharge, it was "Alcohol Dependence." He dated the onset of his drinking problems to fifteen years earlier, when his wife left him. He claimed to have been abstinent for five days on admission to the alcohol clinic.

A "review of systems" uncovered the following additional information: he had no physical problems; he was slightly depressed but manifested no symptoms of major mental disorder; he tended to handle problems rigidly and reactively; he was not introspective, responding, "That's the way things are" and "I guess I'm alcoholic," when asked about his difficulties at work; he had no girlfriend but maintained contact with his ex-wife; his leisure time was spent watching sporting events on television and drinking with coworkers ("after work only!").

An assessment of his drug use revealed that he had never used illicit drugs. He denied drinking "that much," stating that he preferred beer and "rarely" drank more than a six pack. Since his self-report contradicted other facts (e.g., his job suspension and a recent hospitalization for detoxification), the clinician administered several standardized scales to help Bernard (and the clinician) become more aware of the nature and severity of his drinking pattern. His score on the Alcohol Dependence Scale (ADS) was 23 indicating a "substantial level of alcohol dependence" (Skinner and Horn 1984). Specifically, his responses indicated that, among other symptoms, in the past year he had experienced alcohol-induced tremors, he frequently drank more than he intended, he had auditory hallucinations secondary to alcohol use, and he had experienced alcohol amnestic states (blackouts).

A situational assessment of his drinking pattern revealed further that during the past year Bernard had been most likely to drink heavily after conflicts with others—especially on the job and with his supervisor. A hierarchy of situational risks suggested that, after interpersonal conflict, the next riskiest situations were those in which he encountered social pressures to drink (e.g., parties with his coworkers).

Preparatory to developing a service plan with Bernard, the clinician also completed a Situational Confidence Questioinnaire (SCQ) with him (Annis and Davis 1988). To help clients develop a sense of mastery and self-efficacy, it is important to plan tasks with them that are neither too difficult nor too easy. The SCQ is a clinical tool that can be used for this purpose; it provides information about specific drinking situations and clients' perceived confidence levels in those situations. The results of Bernard's SCQ indicated that he felt least confident in his ability to handle interpersonal conflict, especially at work. He was moderately confident about his ability to resist social pressures to drink, however. Thus, intervention focusing on social pressures should logically precede and set the stage for interventions involving interpersonal conflict.

The clinician presented to Bernard the results of the assessments—the "review of systems," the ADS score, the situational assessments, the SCQ findings, and his current work status—and asked him for his interpretation. Bernard responded, "I guess I have a problem. I'll handle it; I'll stop drinking. I'll use willpower and stop!" Rather than confronting Bernard's interpretation and possibly increasing his resistance, the clinician sided with him and suggested that they develop a plan that would strengthen Bernard's strategies. The clinician pointed out that some situations were more difficult than others for Bernard to handle, and that Bernard could develop skills for coping with the difficult situations and avoiding relapse. When Bernard agreed to "try," the following objectives were established with him:

1. He would increase his awareness of drinking cues, and he would identify correctly situations in which he was at risk of drinking.
2. He would take disulfiram, a drug that produces aversive physical reactions when people who take it drink alcohol. (Disulfiram is an added deterrent to drinking.)
3. He would develop skills for handling interpersonal encounters—first, general social encounters, then temptations to drink, and finally, interpersonal conflict.
4. When he had improved his sense of mastery and competence in other social situations, he would focus on work-related situations such as his coworkers' pressures to drink and arguments with his supervisor.
5. Before Bernard returned to work, the employee assistance program (EAP) counselor would be contacted, and a plan for reintegration into the work setting would be developed.

To attain these objectives Bernard contracted with the clinician to participate in weekly group and individual counseling at the alcohol clinic to improve his coping skills; he agreed to attend Alcoholics Anonymous (AA) meetings in the community to establish a new social support network. Because he planned to return to work in six months, a six-month time frame was established for the contract.

Typical of the group therapy sessions Bernard attended were the following (individual meetings were used to supplement group meetings and to develop the issues arising in the groups): The group's purpose was to encourage members to identify and practice alternate ways of handling problem situations. The techniques used included role plays, modeling, coaching, positive feedback, support, and practicing new skills in "real life" (Chaney, O'Leary, and Marlatt 1978). Since Bernard found himself "at a loss for words" in most social encounters, in early group meetings he learned how to relax and prepare himself for the encounters. He also observed other members model social encounters without drinking; then he role-played the situations himself. For example, at simulated parties, he practiced making "small talk" about sports and television shows (interests of his), as well as local politics. Group members gave him positive feedback and encouragement, and his confidence in social situations improved.

Because a typical family gathering, at which there was generally a fair amount of drinking, was coming up, it was important to help Bernard develop means of handling social pressures to drink. The group offered strategies such as avoiding the gathering, leaving early if the pressure became too great, politely declining drinks, and carrying a glass of ginger ale (people are less apt to push drinks if someone is drinking already). The different options were role-played in the group. In addition, in individual counseling, Bernard agreed to invite his older brother to a session. At the session, he self-disclosed his alcohol problem and enlisted the brother's support to help him resist temptations to drink at the family gathering. After attending the affair and not drinking, Bernard reported the results to the group, noting, "You guys helped a lot; it was the first reunion I've attended since I was an adult that I didn't get drunk at." He was congratulated by the group members, whose own resolve for sobriety seemed to be strengthened by the experience.

As Bernard improved his sense of self-efficacy in general social situations, he felt more capable of addressing work-related demands. Using techniques similar to those described above, he developed a repertoire of coping options for dealing with his coworkers and with criticism from his supervisor.

The final step in preparing Bernard for his return to work was to contact the EAP counselor. Because many supervisors and coworkers are unaware of the seriousness of alcoholism and the fact that recovery continues when an employee returns to work, it is important to prepare all parties so that the employee's reintegration into the workplace will be successful. In meetings between the EAP counselor, Bernard, and the alcohol clinic's clinician, a work reentry contract (Morse 1988) was developed. As part of the contract, it was agreed that 1) Bernard would continue to take disulfiram for at least the first three months after his return to work; 2) he would continue to attend AA meetings and the alcohol clinic (in the evenings); 3) the alcohol clinic's clinician would help him reenter the hospital if he relapsed; 4) the EAP counselor would be his buffer at work and would arrange for a meeting with Bernard, his supervisor, and his union representative to clarify job expectations and to encourage the supervisor to be open and candid with Bernard about his work performance; and 5) all parties would remain in close communication and meet again in three months to evaluate Bernard's reintegration into the work setting.

Bernard remained in treatment at the alcohol clinic for one year and faced no new difficulties in his recovery. A two-year follow-up revealed that he still attended AA, had been sober for over three years, and had passed a civil service examination for supervising mechanic.

This case illustration highlights some of the important features in social work practice with alcoholism and other drug addictions. Clinical assessments and interventions were individualized to meet the client's life circumstances. Total health intervention helped to deemphasize the "alcoholic" label (stigma), to overcome the client's denial, and to make the assistance offered meaningful to his experience. Because Bernard's alcohol-related problems were linked to his desire to return to work, he was mobilized to address them. Once he was engaged in counseling he became responsive to interventions that related to life areas other than work.

Once differential, situational assessments were completed, a treatment contract that established a stepwise hierarchy of high-risk drinking situations and coping strategies was developed. The intervention plan centered on developing both general coping skills (e.g., interpersonal skills and conflict resolution skills) and alcohol-specific coping skills (e.g., drink refusal skills). For recovery to progress, both categories of skills had to develop, since the general coping skills provided the context in which the alcohol-specific skills could emerge (Shiffman and Wills 1985).

Finally, as the client improved his sense of self-efficacy, mastery, and competence, environmental interventions were effected. Alternative support networks (e.g., AA) were established, existing supports (e.g., his brother) were strengthened, and problem systems (e.g., the work setting) were prepared to support the client's recovery.

A multidimensional intervention strategy that included the client's total life health 1) helped him to develop the skills needed to meet life demands and 2) helped create support networks that would be more responsive to his efforts at adaptive functioning. As a consequence, two years after formal services had ended the client's recovery was continuing, and he was coping successfully with situational demands.

This paper has provided an introduction to social work practice with persons experiencing problems related to alcoholism and other drug addictions. Addictions were described as biopsychosocial conditions that are influenced by multiple factors and that affect all areas of life functioning. To understand addictions and to help people who encounter drug-related difficulties, social workers must adopt a dual focus: the client and the social and environmental context. Such a stance increases the likelihood that they will 1) understand the clients and their problems in their own terms; 2) accurately assess the nature and severity of their problems, as well as the characteristics of impinging systems; and 3) develop meaningful intervention strategies that will help clients to alter addictive lifestyles and to develop social supports for sobriety.

Addictions are major life difficulties that affect persons from all social groups. Their detrimental impact on people and society is immense. Clients who use the services of any social work setting may be affected by the consequences of alcoholism and other drug addictions. Therefore, it is imperative that social workers become sensitive to a population at risk and that they respond to help the affected individuals develop adaptive, drug-free functioning.

## REFERENCES

Abelson, Herbert I. and J. D. Miller. 1985. "A Decade of Trends in Cocaine Use in the Household Population." In Nicholas J. Kozel and Edgar H. Adams, eds., *Cocaine Use in America: Epidemiologic and Clinical Perspectives.* Research Monograph 61, pp. 35–49. Rockville, Md.: National Institute on Drug Abuse.

Akers, Ronald L. 1985. *Deviant Behavior: A Social Learning Approach*, 3d ed. Belmont, Calif.: Wadsworth.

Akers, Ronald L., Marvin D. Krohn, Lonn Lanza-Kaduce, and Marcia Radosevich. 1979. "Social Learning and Deviant Behavior: A Specific Test of a General Theory." *American Sociological Review* (August), 44:636–655.

APA (American Psychiatric Association). 1987. *Diagnostic and Statistical Manual of Mental Disorders*, 3d ed., rev. Washington, D.C.: APA.

Anderson, Sandra C. 1982. "Group Therapy with Alcoholic Clients: A Review." *Advances in Alcohol and Substance Abuse* 2(2):23–40.

Annis, Helen M. and Christine S. Davis. 1988. "Assessment of Expectancies." In Dennis M. Donovan and G. Alan Marlatt, eds., *Assessment of Addictive Behaviors*, pp. 84–111. New York: Guilford.

Arif, Awni and Joseph Westermeyer, eds. 1988. *Manual of Drug and Alcohol Abuse.* New York: Plenum.

Austin, Gregory A. 1978. *Perspectives on the History of Psychoactive Substance Use.* Research Issues 24. Rockville, Md.: National Institute on Drug Abuse.

Baekeland, Frederick and Lawrence Lundwall. 1975. "Dropping Out of Treatment: A Critical Review." *Psychological Bulletin* 82(5):738–783.

Baekeland, Frederick and Lawrence K. Lundwall. 1977. "Engaging the Alcoholic in Treatment and Keeping Him There." In Benjamin Kissin and Henri Beglei-ter, eds., *The Biology of Alcoholism. Vol. 5: Treatment and Rehabilitation of the Chronic Alcoholic*, pp. 161–195. New York: Plenum.

Balis, George U. 1989a. "Psychoactive Substance Use Disorders." In William H. Reid, ed., *The Treatment of Psychiatric Disorders: Revised for the DSM-III-R*, pp. 133–160. New York: Brunner/Mazel.

Balis, George U. 1989b. "Withdrawal and Intoxication." In William H. Reid, ed., *The Treatment of Psychiatric Disorders: Revised for the DSM-III-R*, pp. 112–129. New York: Brunner/Mazel.

Bandura, Albert. 1969. *Principles of Behavior Modification.* New York: Holt, Rinehart, & Winston.

Bandura, Albert. 1977. "Self-Efficacy: Toward a Unifying Theory of Behavioral Change." *Psychological Review* 84(2):191–215.

Barbanel, Josh. 1988a. "Crack Use Pervades Life in a Shelter." *New York Times* (February 18), pp. A1, B3.

Barbanel, Josh. 1988b. "System to Treat Mental Patients is Overburdened." *New York Times* (February 22), pp. A1, B6

Bean, Margaret H. 1981. "Denial and Psychological Complications of Alcoholism." In Margaret H. Bean and Norman E. Zinberg, eds., *Dynamic Approaches to the Understanding and Treatment of Alcoholism*, pp. 55–96. New York: Free Press.

Becker, Howard S. 1953. "Becoming a Marihuana User." *American Journal of Sociology* 59:235–242.

Berkowitz, Alan and H. Wesley Perkins. 1988. "Personality Characteristics of Chil-dren of Alcoholics." *Journal of Consulting and Clinical Psychology* 56(2):206–209.

Biddle, Bruce J., Barbara J. Bank, and Marjorie M. Marlin. 1980. "Social Determi-nants of Adolescent Drinking." *Journal of Studies on Alcohol* 41(3):215–241.

Biernacki, Patrick. 1986. *Pathways from Heroin: Recovery without Treatment.* Phila-delphia: Temple University Press.

Blume, Sheila B. 1987. "Public Policy Issues Relevant to Children of Alcoholics." *Advances in Alcohol and Substance Abuse* 6(4):5–15.

Boche, H. Leonard. 1981. "Alcohol and Drug Abuse Services." In Neil Gilbert and Harry Specht, eds., *Handbook of Social Services*, pp. 202–214. Englewood Cliffs, N.J.: Prentice-Hall.

Bohman, Michael, C. Robert Cloninger, and Soren Sigvardsson. 1981. "Maternal Inheritance of Alcohol Abuse." *Archives of General Psychiatry* 38(9):965–969.

Brecher, Edward M. 1986. "Drug Laws and Drug Law Enforcement: A Review and Evaluation Based on 111-Years of Experience." *Drugs and Society* 1(1):1–27.

Brill, Leon. 1981. *The Clinical Treatment of Substance Abusers.* New York: Free Press.

Burns, Thomas F. 1980. "Getting Rowdy with the Boys." *Journal of Drug Issues* (Spring), 10:273–286.

Cadoret, Remi J., Ed Troughton, Thomas W. O'Gorman, and Ellen Heywood. 1986. "An Adoption Study of Genetic and Environmental Factors in Drug Abuse." *Archives of General Psychiatry* 43(12):1131–1136.

Caetano, Raul. 1988. "Alcohol Use Among Hispanic Groups in the United States." *American Journal of Drug and Alcohol Abuse* 14(3):293–308.

Cahalan, Don. 1970. *Problem Drinkers: A National Survey.* San Francisco: Jossey-Bass.

Cahalan, Don. 1982. "Epidemiology: Alcohol Use in American Society." In Edith Lisansky Gomberg, Helene Raskin White, and John A. Carpenter, eds., *Alcohol, Science and Society Revisited*, pp. 96–118. Ann Arbor: University of Michigan Press.

Cahalan, Don and Robin Room. 1974. *Problem Drinking Among American Men.* New Brunswick, N.J.: Rutgers Center of Alcohol Studies.

Cappell, Howard and Janet Greeley. 1987. "Alcohol and Tension Reduction: An Update on Research and Theory." In Howard T. Blane and Kenneth E. Leonard, eds., *Psychological Theories of Drinking and Alcoholism*, pp. 15–54. New York: Guilford.

Cermak, Timmen L. 1986. *Diagnosing and Treating Co-Dependence.* Minneapolis: Johnson Institute Books.

Chaney, Edmund F., Michael R. O'Leary, and G. Alan Marlatt. 1978. "Skill Training with Alcoholics." *Journal of Consulting and Clinical Psychology* 46(5):1092–1104.

Chi, Iris, James E. Lubben, and Harry H. L. Kitano. 1989. "Differences in Drinking Behavior Among Three Asian-American Groups." *Journal of Studies on Alcohol* 50(1):15–23.

Clark, Walter B. and Lorraine Midanik. 1982. "Alcohol Use and Alcohol Problems Among U.S. Adults: Results of the 1979 National Survey." In National Institute on Alcohol Abuse and Alcoholism, *Alcohol Consumption and Related Problems.* Alcohol and Health Monograph 1, pp. 3–52. Rockville, Md.: NIAAA.

Cloninger, C. Robert. 1987. "Neurogenetic Adaptive Mechanisms in Alcoholism." *Science* (April 24), 235:410–416.

Cloninger, C. Robert, Michael Bohman, and Soren Sigvardsson. 1981. "Inheritance of Alcohol Abuse." *Archives of General Psychiatry* 38(8):861–868.

Cloward, Richard A. and Lloyd E. Ohlin. 1960. *Delinquency and Opportunity.* New York: Free Press.

Cohen, Sheldon and S. Leonard Syme, eds. 1985. *Social Support and Health.* New York: Academic Press.

Cotton, Nancy S. 1979. "The Familial Incidence of Alcoholism." *Journal of Studies on Alcohol* 40(1):89–116.

Cummings, Claudette, Judith R. Gordon, and G. Alan Marlatt. 1980. "Relapse: Prevention and Prediction." In William R. Miller, ed., *The Addictive Behaviors: Treatment of Alcoholism, Drug Abuse, and Obesity*, pp. 291–321. New York: Pergamon.

Davis, Donald I. 1987. *Alcoholism Treatment: An Integrative Family and Individual Approach.* New York: Gardner Press.

Dole, Vincent P. and Marie Nyswanger. 1967. "Heroin Addiction—A Metabolic Disease." *Archives of Internal Medicine* 120:19–24.

Donovan, Dennis M. 1988. "Assessment of Addictive Behaviors: Implications of an Emerging Biopsychosocial Model." In Dennis M. Donovan and G. Alan Marlatt, eds., *Assessment of Addictive Behaviors*, pp. 3–48, New York: Guilford.

Dawn (Drug Abuse Warning Network). 1980. *1979 DAWN Annual Report.* Rockville, Md.: National Institute on Drug Abuse.

Edwards, Griffith. 1982. *The Treatment of Drinking Problems: A Guide for the Helping Professions.* New York: McGraw-Hill.

Edwards, Griffith, Awni Arif, and Ray Hodgson. 1981. "Nomenclature and Classification of Drug- and Alcohol-Related Problems: A WHO Memorandum." *Bulletin of the World Health Organization* 59(2):225–242.

Emrick, Chad D. and Joel Hansen. 1983. "Assertions Regarding Effectiveness of Treatment for Alcoholism: Fact or Fantasy?" *American Psychologist* 38(10):1078–1088.

Fawzy, Fawzy I., Robert H. Coombs, and Barry Gerber. 1983. "Generational Continuity in the Use of Substances: The Impact of Parental Substance Use on Adolescent Substance Use." *Addictive Behaviors* 8(2):109–114.

Ferber, Jane, Marilyn Oswald, Jane Ungemack, and Murray Schane. 1985. "The Day Hospital as Entry Point to a Network of Long-Term Services: Program Evaluation." *Hospital and Community Psychiatry* 36(12):1297–1301.

Fine, Michelle, Sheila H. Akabas, and Susan Bellinger. 1982. "Cultures of Drinking: A Workplace Perspective." *Social Work* (September) 27:436–440.

Fingarette, Herbert. 1988. *Heavy Drinking: The Myth of Alcoholism as a Disease.* Berkeley: University of California Press.

Fossum, Merle A. and Marilyn J. Mason. 1986. *Facing Shame: Families in Recovery.* New York: Norton.

Galanter, Marc. 1986. "Social Network Intervention for Cocaine Dependency." *Advances in Alcohol and Substance Abuse* 6(2):159–175.

Galizio, Mark and Stephen A. Maisto. 1985. "Toward a Biopsychosocial Theory of Substance Abuse." In Mark Galizio and Stephen A. Maisto, eds., *Determinants of Substance Abuse: Biological, Psychological, and Environmental Factors*, pp. 425–429. New York: Plenum.

Germain, Carel B. And Alex Gitterman, 1980. *The Life Model of Social Work Practice.* New York: Columbia University Press.

Ginzburg, Harold M. 1984. "Intravenous Drug Users and the Acquired Immune Deficiency Syndrome." *Public Health Reports* 99(2):206–212.

Glaser, Frederick B. 1980. "Anybody Got a Match? Treatment Research and the Matching Hypothesis." In Griffith Edwards and Marcus Grant, eds., *Alcoholism Treatment in Transition*, pp. 178–196. Baltimore: University Park Press.

Goluke, Ulrich, Robert Landeen, and Dennis Meadows. 1983. "A Comprehensive Theory of the Pathogenesis of Alcoholism." In Benjamin Kissin and Henri Begleiter, eds., *The Biology of Alcoholism, Vol. 6: The Pathogenesis of Alcoholism: Psychosocial Factors*, pp. 605–675. New York: Plenum.

Gomberg, Edith S. Lisansky. 1986. "Women: Alcohol and Other Drugs." *Drugs and Society* 1(1):75–109.

Goode, Erich. 1972. *Drugs in American Society.* New York: Knopf.

Goodwin, Donald W. 1988. *Is Alcoholism Hereditary?*, 2d ed. New York: Ballantine.

Gottheil, Edward A., Keith A. Druley, Steven Pashko, and Stephen P. Weinstein, eds. 1987. *Stress and Addiction.* New York: Brunner / Mazel.

Gottheil, Edward, A. Thomas McLellan, and Keith A. Druley, eds. 1982. *Matching Patient Needs and Treatment Methods in Alcoholism and Drug Abuse.* Springfield, Ill.: Charles C Thomas.

Hanson, Meredith. 1988. "Involving Clients in Alcoholism Outpatient Treatment: Implications for Social Work Practice." *Alcoholism Treatment Quarterly* 5(3/4):209–220.

Harford, Thomas C., Mary R. Haack, and Danielle L. Spiegler. 1987–88. "Positive Family History for Alcoholism." *Alcohol Health and Research World* 12(2):104–107.

Hawkins, J. David and Mark W. Fraser. 1983. "Social Support Networks in Treating Drug Abuse." In James K. Whittaker and James Garbarino, eds., *Social Support Networks: Informal Helping in the Human Services*, pp. 355–380. Hawthorne, N.Y.: Aldine.

Helzer, John E. and Thomas R. Przybeck. 1988. "The Co-Occurrence of Alcoholism with other Psychiatric Disorders in the General Population and Its Impact on Treatment." *Journal of Studies on Alcohol* 49(3):219–224.

Herd, Denise. 1988. "Drinking by Black and White Women: Results from a National Survey." *Social Problems* 35(5):493–505.

Huba, G. J. and P. M. Bentler. 1980. "The Role of Peer and Adult Models for Drug

Taking at Different Stages in Adolescence." *Journal of Youth and Adolescence* 9(5):449–465.

Jahoda, G. and J. Crammond. 1972. *Children and Alcohol*. London: HMSO.

Jellinek, E. M. 1952. "Phases of Alcohol Addiction." *Quarterly Journal of Studies on Alcohol* 13(4):673–684.

Jellinek, E. M. 1960. *The Disease Concept of Alcoholism*. New Haven, Conn.: College and University Press.

Jessor, Richard and Shirley L. Jessor. 1977. *Problem Behavior and Psychosocial Development: A Longitudinal Study of Youth*. New York: Academic Press.

Johnson, Bruce D. 1973. *Marijuana Users and Drug Subcultures*. New York: Wiley.

Johnson, Vernon E. 1986. *Intervention: How to Help Someone Who Doesn't Want Help*. Minneapolis: Johnson Institute Books.

Kaestner, Elisabeth, Blanche Frank, Rozanne Marel, and James Schmeidler. 1986. "Substance Use Among Females in New York State: Catching Up with the Males." *Advances in Alcohol and Substance Abuse* 5(3):29–49.

Kandel, Denise B. 1978. "Convergences in Prospective Longitudinal Surveys of Drug Use in Normal Populations." In Denise B. Kandel, ed., *Longitudinal Research on Drug Use*, pp. 3–38. New York: Halsted.

Kaufman, Edward. 1974. "The Psychodynamics of Opiate Dependence: A New Look." *American Journal of Drug and Alcohol Abuse* 1(3):349–370.

King, Barbara L. 1986. "Decision Making in the Intervention Process." *Alcoholism Treatment Quarterly* 3(3):5–22.

Kinney, Jean and Gwen Leaton. 1987. *Loosening the Grip: A Handbook of Alcohol Information*, 3d ed. St. Louis: Times Mirror / Mosby.

Kissin, Benjamin. 1977. "Theory and Practice in the Treatment of Alcoholism." In Benjamin Kissin and Henri Begleiter, eds., *The Biology of Alcoholism; Vol. 5: Treatment and Rehabilitation of the Chronic Alcoholic*, pp. 1–51. New York: Plenum.

Kissin, Benjamin. 1983. "The Disease Concept of Alcoholism." In Reginald G. Smart, Frederick B. Glaser, Yedy Israel, Harold Kalant, Robert Popham, and Wolfgang Schmidt, eds., *Research Advances in Alcohol and Drug Abuse Problems*, Vol. 7, pp. 93–126. New York: Plenum.

Kissin, Benjamin and Meredith Hanson. 1982. "The Bio-psychosocial Perspective in Alcoholism." In Joel Solomon, ed., *Alcoholism and Clinical Psychiatry*, pp. 1–19. New York: Plenum.

Kohut, Heinz. 1977. "Preface." In Jack D. Blaine and Demetrios A. Julius, eds., *Psychodynamics of Drug Dependence*. Research Monograph 12, pp. vii–ix. Rockville, Md.: National Institute on Drug Abuse.

Kosten, Thomas R., Bruce J. Rounsaville, and Herbert D. Kleber. 1985. "Parental Alcoholism in Opioid Addicts." *Journal of Nervous and Mental Disease* 173(8):461–469.

Lanza-Kaduce, Lonn, Ronald L. Akers, Marvin D. Krohn, and Marcia Radosevich. 1984. "Cessation of Alcohol and Drug Use Among Adolescents: A Social Learning Model." *Deviant Behavior* 5:79–96.

Lee, Felicia R. 1989. "Destroyers of Families, Crack Besieges a Court." *New York Times* (February 9) pp. A1, B9.

Leigh, Gillian. 1985. "Psychosocial Factors in the Etiology of Substance Abuse." In Thomas E. Bratter and Gary G. Forrest, eds., *Alcoholism and Substance Abuse: Strategies for Clinical Intervention*, pp. 3–48. New York: Free Press.

Lender, Mark E. and James K. Martin. 1982. *Drinking in America: A History*. New York: Free Press.

Levine, Baruch and Virginia Gallogoly. 1985. *Group Therapy with Alcoholics: Outpatient and Inpatient Approaches*. Beverly Hills, Calif.: Sage.

Levine, Harry Gene. 1978. "The Discovery of Addiction: Changing Conceptions of

Habitual Drunkenness in America." *Journal of Studies on Alcohol* 39(1):143–174.

Lewis, Judith A., Robert Q. Dana, and Gregory A. Blevins. 1988. *Substance Abuse Counseling.* Pacific Grove, Calif.: Brooks / Cole.

Longabaugh, Richard and David C. Lewis. 1988. "Key Issues in Treatment Outcome Studies." *Alcohol Health and Research World* 12(3):168–175.

Lukoff, Irving F. 1977. "Consequences of Use: Heroin and Other Narcotics." In Joan D. Rittenhouse, ed., *The Epidemiology of Heroin and Other Narcotics.* Research Monograph 16, pp. 195–227. Rockville, Md.: National Institute on Drug Abuse.

Lukoff, Irving F. 1980. "Toward a Sociology of Drug Use." In Dan J. Lettieri, Mollie Sayers, and Helen W. Pearson, eds., *Theories on Drug Abuse: Selected Contemporary Perspectives.* Research Monograph 30, pp. 201–211. Rockville, Md.: National Institute on Drug Abuse.

MacAndrew, Charles and Robert D. Edgerton. 1969. *Drunken Comportment.* Chicago: Aldine.

Maddahian, Ebrahim, Michael D. Newcomb, and P. M. Bentler. 1986. "Adolescents' Substance Use: Impact of Ethnicity, Income, and Availability." *Advances in Alcohol and Substance Abuse* 5(3):63–78.

Maddahian, Ebrahim, Michael D. Newcomb, and P. M. Bentler. 1988. "Risk Factors for Substance Use: Ethnic Differences Among Adolescents." *Journal Of Substance Abuse* 1(1):11–23.

Maisto, Stephen A. and Janice B. McCollam. 1980. "The Use of Multiple Measures of Life Health to Assess Alcohol Treatment: A Review and Critique." In Linda C. Sobell, Mark B. Sobell and Elliott Ward, eds., *Evaluating Alcohol and Drug Abuse Treatment Effectiveness: Recent Advances,* pp. 15–76. New York: Pergamon.

Margulies, Rebecca Z., Ronald C. Kessler, and Denise B. Kandel. 1977. "A Longitudinal Study of Onset of Drinking Among High School Students." *Journal of Studies on Alcohol* 38(5):897–912.

Marlatt, G. Alan. 1988. "Matching Clients to Treatment: Treatment Models and Stages of Change." In Dennis M. Donovan and G. Alan Marlatt, eds., *Assessment of Addictive Behaviors,* pp. 474–483. New York: Guilford.

Marlatt, G. Alan and Judith R. Gordon, eds. 1985. *Relapse Prevention: Maintenance Strategies in the Treatment of Addictive Behaviors.* New York: Guilford.

Marotta, J. and R. Hale. 1986. "Marital Variables and Treatment Completion." Paper presented at the National Council on Alcoholism Forum, San Francisco.

McClearn, Gerald E. 1983. "Commonalities in Substance Use: A Genetic Perspective." In Peter K. Levison, Dean R. Gerstein, and Deborah Maloff, eds., *Commonalities in Substance Use and Habitual Behavior,* pp. 323–341. Lexington, Mass.: Lexington Books.

McClelland, David C., William N. Davis, Rudolf Kalin, and Eric Wanner. 1972. *The Drinking Man: Alcohol and Human Motivation.* New York: Free Press.

McCord, William and Joan McCord. 1960. *Origins of Alcoholism.* Stanford, Calif.: University of Stanford Press.

McCrady, Barbara S. 1985. "Alcoholism." In David H. Barlow, ed., *Clinical Handbook of Psychological Disorders,* pp. 245–298. New York: Guilford.

McCrady, Barbara S. 1986. "The Family in the Change Process." In William R. Miller and Nick Heather, eds., *Treating Addictive Behavior: Processes of Change,* pp. 305–318. New York: Plenum.

McKenna, Thomas and Roy Pickens. 1983. "Personality Characteristics of Alcoholic Children of Alcoholics." *Journal of Studies on Alcohol* 44(4):688–700.

Meller, William H., Richard Rinehart, Remi J. Cadoret, and Ed Troughton. 1988.

"Specific Familial Transmission in Substance Abuse." *International Journal of the Addictions* 23(10):1029–1039.

Midanik, Lorraine. 1983. "Familial Alcoholism and Problem Drinking in a National Drinking Practices Survey." *Addictive Behaviors* 8(3):133–141.

Miller, Peter M. and Marie Mastria. 1977. *Alternatives to Alcohol Abuse: A Social Learning Model.* Champaign, Ill.: Research Press.

Miller, William R. 1983. "Motivational Interviewing with Problem Drinkers." *Behavioural Psychotherapy* 11:147–172.

Miller, William R. and Reid K. Hester. 1986. "The Effectiveness of Alcoholism Treatment: What Research Reveals." In William R. Miller and Nick Heather, eds., *Treating Addictive Behaviors: Processes of Change,* pp. 121–174. New York: Plenum.

Miller, William R. and G. Alan Marlatt. 1984. *Manual for the Comprehensive Drinker Profile.* Odessa, Fla.: Psychological Assessment Resources.

Molgaard, Craig A., Chester Nakamura, Melbourne Hovell, and John P. Elder. 1988. "Assessing Alcoholism as a Risk Factor for Acquired Immunodeficiency Syndrome (AIDS)." *Social Science and Medicine* 27(11):1147–1152.

Morgan, H. Wayne. 1981. *Drugs in America: A Social History, 1800–1980.* Syracuse, N.Y.: Syracuse University Press.

Morse, Gary A. 1988. "Work Reentry Contracting." *Professional Counselor* 3(2):47–48.

Musto, David F. 1973. *The American Disease: Origins of Narcotic Control.* New Haven, Conn.: Yale University Press.

Ogborne, Alan C. 1978. "Patient Characteristics as Predictors of Treatment Outcomes for Alcohol and Drug Abusers." In Yedy Israel, Frederick B. Glaser, Harold Kalant, Robert E. Popham, Wolfgang Schmidt, and Reginald G. Smart, eds., *Research Advances in Alcohol and Drug Problems,* Vol. 4, pp. 177–223. New York: Plenum.

Orford, Jim. 1985. *Excessive Appetites: A Psychological View of Addictions.* New York: John Wiley.

Pattison, E. Mansell. 1982. "Decision Strategies in the Path of Alcoholism Treatment." In William M. Hay and Peter E. Nathan, eds., *Clinical Case Studies in the Behavioral Treatment of Alcoholism,* pp. 251–274, New York: Plenum.

Pattison, E. Mansell. 1985. "The Selection of Treatment Modalities for the Alcoholic Patient." In Jack H. Mendelson and Nancy K. Mello, eds., *The Diagnosis and Treatment of Alcoholism,* pp. 189–294. New York: McGraw-Hill.

Pattison, E. Mansell, Mark B. Sobell, and Linda C. Sobell. 1977. *Emerging Concepts of Alcohol Dependence.* New York: Springer.

Peele, Stanton. 1985. *The Meaning of Addiction.* Lexington, Mass.: Lexington Books.

Peele, Stanton, ed. 1988. *Visions of Addiction.* Lexington, Mass.: Lexington Books.

Prochaska, James O. and Carlo C. DiClemente. 1984. *The Transtheoretical Approach: Crossing Traditional Boundaries of Therapy.* Homewood, Ill.: Dow Jones-Irwin.

Rado, Sandor. 1933. "The Psychoanalysis of Pharmacothymia (Drug Addiction)." *Psychoanalytic Quarterly* 2:1–23.

Ray, Oakley. 1983. *Drugs, Society and Human Behavior.* St. Louis: C. V. Mosby.

Reich, Theodore. 1987–88. "Beyond the Gene: Research Directions in Family Transmission of Susceptibility to Alcoholism." *Alcohol Health and Research World* 12(2):104–107.

Robins, Lee N. 1978. "The Interaction of Setting and Predisposition in Explaining Novel Behavior: Drug Initiations Before, In, and After Vietnam." In Denise B. Kandel, ed., *Longitudinal Research on Drug Use,* pp. 179–196. New York: Halsted.

Robins, Lee N., John Helzer, Myrna M. Weissman, Helen Orvaschel, Ernest Gruenberg, Jack Burke, Jr., and Darrel Regier. 1984. "Lifetime Prevalence of Specific

Psychiatric Disorders in Three Sites." *Archives of General Psychiatry* 41(10):949–958.

Robins, Lee N. and Thomas R. Przybeck. 1985. "Age of Onset of Drug Use as a Factor in Drug and Other Disorders." In Coryl L. Jones and Robert J. Battjes, eds., *Etiology of Drug Abuse: Implications for Prevention.* Research Monograph 56, pp. 178–192. Rockville, Md.: National Institute on Drug Abuse.

Rogers, Ronald L. and Chandler Scott McMillin. 1988. *Don't Help: A Guide to Working with the Alcoholic.* Seattle: Madrona.

Sandmaier, Marian. 1980. *The Invisible Alcoholics: Women and Alcohol Abuse in America.* New York: McGraw-Hill.

Scherer, Shawn E. 1973. "Self-Report Parent and Child Drug Use." *British Journal of Addiction* 68(4):363–364.

Schuster, Charles R. 1987. "The United States' Drug Abuse Scene: An Overview." *Clinical Chemistry* 33(11B):7B–12B.

Schwartz, Gary E. 1982. "Testing the Biopsychosocial Model: The Ultimate Challenge Facing Behavioral Medicine." *Journal of Consulting and Clinical Psychology* 50(6):1040–1053.

Segal, Steven P., Jim Baumohl, and Elsie Johnson. 1977. "Falling Through the Cracks: Mental Disorder and Social Margin in a Young Vagrant Population." *Social Problems* (February), 24:387–400.

Sells, S. B. 1979. "Treatment Effectiveness." In Robert I. Dupont, Avram Goldstein, and Jonn O'Donnell, eds., *Handbook on Drug Abuse,* pp. 105–118. Rockville, Md.: National Institute on Drug Abuse.

Selzer, Melvin L. 1971. "The Michigan Alcoholism Screening Test: The Quest for a New Diagnostic Instrument." *American Journal of Psychiatry* 127(12):1653–1658.

Shiffman, Saul and Thomas Ashby Wills, eds. 1985. *Coping and Substance Use.* Orlando, Fla.: Academic Press.

Skinner, Harvey A. 1982. "The Drug Abuse Screening Test." *Addictive Behaviors* 7:363–371.

Skinner, Harvey A. and John L. Horn 1984. *Alcohol Dependence Scale (ADS): User's Guide.* Toronto: Addiction Research Foundation.

Solomon, Susan D. 1982. "Individual Versus Group Therapy: Current Status in the Treatment of Alcoholism." *Advances in Alcohol and Substance Abuse* 2(1):69–86.

Stanton, M. Duncan, Thomas C. Todd, eds. 1982. *The Family Therapy of Drug Abuse and Addiction.* New York: Guilford.

Straussner, Shulamith Lala Ashenberg. 1985. "Alcoholism in Women: Current Knowledge and Implications for Treatment." *Alcoholism Treatment Quarterly* 2(1):61–77.

Sue, S., N. Zane, and J. Ito. 1979. "Reported Alcohol Drinking Patterns Among Asian and Caucasian Americans." *Journal of Cross-Cultural Psychology* 10:41–56.

Tarter, Ralph E. 1988. "Are There Inherited Behavioral Traits That Predispose to Substance Abuse?" *Journal of Consulting and Clinical Psychology* 56(2):189–196.

Wallace, John. 1987. "Children of Alcoholics: A Population at Risk." *Alcoholism Treatment Quarterly* 4(3):13–30.

Walsh, J. Michael and Steven W. Gust, eds. 1986. *Interdisciplinary Approaches to the Problem of Drug Abuse in the Workplace: Consensus Summary.* Rockville, Md.: National Institute on Drug Abuse.

Washton, Arnold M. and Mark S. Gold. 1987. "Recent Trends in Cocaine Abuse as Seen from the '800-Cocaine' Hotline." In Arnold M. Washton and Mark S. Gold, eds., *Cocaine: A Clinician's Handbook,* pp. 10–22. New York: Guilford.

Weibel, Joan Crofut. 1982. "American Indians, Urbanization, and Alcohol: A Developing Urban Indian Drinking Ethos." In National Institute on Alcohol Abuse and Alcoholism, *Special Population Issues*. Alcohol and Health Monograph 4, pp. 331–358. Rockville, Md.: NIAAA.

Wilsnack, Richard W., Sharon C. Wilsnack, and Albert D. Klassen. 1984. "Women's Drinking and Drinking Problems: Patterns from a 1981 National Survey." *American Journal of Public Health* 74:1231–1238.

Wilson, William Julius. 1987. *The Truly Disadvantaged: The Inner City, the Underclass, and Public Policy*. Chicago: University of Chicago Press.

Winick, Charles. 1962. "Maturing Out of Narcotic Addiction." *Bulletin on Narcotics* 14(1):1–7.

Winokur, George, Remi Cadoret, Joe Dorzab, and Max Baker. 1971. "Depressive Disease: A Genetic Study." *Archives of General Psychiatry* 24(2):135–144.

Winokur, George, Theodore Reich, John Rimmer, and Ferris N. Pitts. 1970. "Alcoholism. III: Diagnosis and Familial Psychiatric Illness in 259 Alcoholic Probands." *Archives of General Psychiatry* 23(2):104–111.

Woodside, Migs. 1988. "Research on Children of Alcoholics: Past and Future." *British Journal of Addiction* 83(7):785–792.

Wylie, Mary S. 1989. "The Crack Epidemic." *The Family Therapy Networker* 13(1):14–15.

Yablonsky, Lewis. 1965. *Synanon: The Tunnel Back*. Baltimore: Penguin.

Zinberg, Norman E. 1984. *Drug, Set, and Setting: The Basis of Controlled Intoxicant Use*. New Haven, Conn.: Yale University Press.

Zucker, Robert A. 1979. "Developmental Aspects of Drinking Through Young Adult Years." In Howard T. Blane and Morris E. Chafetz, eds., *Youth, Alcohol, and Social Policy*, pp. 91–146, New York: Plenum.

Zuckerman, M. 1972. "Drug Use as One Manifestation of a 'Sensation-Seeking' Trait." In W. Keup, ed., *Drug Abuse: Current Concepts and Research*, pp. 154–163. Springfield, Ill.: Charles C Thomas.

# 3

# Borderline Personality

▼

## HARRIETTE C. JOHNSON
## DENNIS E. GOGUEN

Persons with characteristics that qualify them to be considered "borderline" are a very heterogeneous group (Johnson 1988). In fact, several of the vulnerable populations discussed in this book include significant numbers of people who meet criteria for a *DSM-III-R* (APA 1987) diagnosis of "Borderline Personality Disorder" and/or "Borderline Personality Organization" (these criteria are discussed later in the chapter). Borderlines often suffer from the life conditions of addiction, depression, eating disorders, and learning disabilities and experience adolescent pregnancy, child abuse, family violence, and suicide. Since each of these topics is the subject of a separate review, this paper will focus on the particular characteristics typical of persons referred to as *borderline* that cut across many vulnerable population groups.

Borderlines are widely regarded as being difficult and frustrating to work with (Stone 1987; Waldinger 1987) because of characteristics such as intense hostile-dependent feelings toward the practitioner, overidealization of the worker alternating with rageful disappointment, suicidal or otherwise violent behaviors, impulsivity and recklessness, transient lapses into psychosis, and the tendency to terminate counseling abruptly and prematurely when painful issues arise (Waldinger 1987; Stone 1986).

## PROBLEM DOMAIN

Borderline personality attracted wide attention among social workers during the 1980s and has been the subject of numerous articles in social work journals (Freed 1980; Palombo 1983; Goldstein 1983; Baker 1984; Eckrich 1985; Graziano 1986; Hodis 1986; Johnson 1988). The literature attests to the fact that virtually every social work setting includes clientele who meet the diagnostic criteria for the borderline personality. These clients often present themselves to social workers in the community in relation to manifestations such as substance abuse, suicidal attempts and gestures, family violence, eating disorders, and other problems of self-control. Yet there is a considerable lack of clarity about what a "borderline" really is. As Akiskal and colleagues pointed out (1986:566), borderline conditions embrace the entire gamut of psychopathology.

The concept of the *border* invokes a spatial metaphor. The notion of a *border* between different spaces can refer to *levels of functioning*, with the upper border being in proximity to neurosis and "normality," and the lower border in proximity to psychosis, or it can refer to *regions of overlap* with "parallel" diagnoses such as affective disorder, some of the other *DSM-III* (APA 1980) personality disorders, and subtle impairments of the central nervous system. In other words, the *border* concept applies both to quantitative measures (i.e., the severity of the conditions and how "sick" a person is) and to qualitative measures (i.e., the nature of the sickness and the other conditions that it resembles or overlaps).

Among practitioners, there is a fair degree of consensus on clinical description. Many observers agree on what the "typical" borderline looks like: he or (more commonly) she shows impulsivity, intense emotion, self-destructive behavior, shallowness or fragility in relationships, mechanisms of splitting and projection, and preservation of reality testing. He or she often abuses alcohol or drugs and also has other self-control problems related to food, sex, or money. He or she may have brief transient psychotic experiences when under great stress or in reaction to drugs or alcohol. Most borderline scholars also agree that the borderline state is a long-term condition whose amelioration requires some kind of counseling over an extended period of time.

The areas of major disagreement between clinicians involve the following questions: 1) Should borderline personality be defined as a syndrome or as a cluster of symptoms (APA 1980; Gunderson 1984; Grinker 1968) or as a personality structure or organization (Kernberg

1984)? 2) Are persons who meet the criteria for the *DSM-III* "Borderline Personality Disorder" or for Kernberg's "Borderline Personality Organization" a single identifiable group, or do they actually suffer from a variety of underlying disorders that bear only a superficial resemblance to each other (Grinker, Werble and Drye, 1986; Stone 1986; Klein 1977)? 3) To what extent is borderline pathology the result of biological factors, maternal behavior, or life stresses (Stone 1986), and how relevant is the answer to that question (Palombo 1983)? And 4) What kinds of treatment are most effective: expressive psychotherapy, supportive psychotherapy combined with environmental interventions, family therapy, behavioral management, medication with or without psychotherapy, education, or some combination of these approaches (Kernberg 1984; Goldstein 1983; Stone 1986)?

The most widely used diagnostic criteria at the present time are those listed in the category "Borderline Personality Disorder" (BPD), one of eleven personality disorders in the *DSM-III-R* (APA 1987). According to the *DSM-III-R* criteria, a person qualifies as having a borderline personality disorder if he or she manifests at least five of eight characteristics: unstable and intense relationships characterized by overidealization and devaluation; impulsivity in at least two of six listed areas (spending, sex, substance use, shoplifting, reckless driving and binge eating); affective instability; inappropriate intense anger; recurrent suicidal threats or self-mutilating behavior; identity disturbance; chronic feelings of emptiness and boredom; and frantic efforts to avoid abandonment.

Kernberg's "Borderline Personality Organization," on the other hand, is a much broader and more inclusive term that comprises all major forms of character pathology and was estimated by Gunderson (1984:11) to exist in 25 to 30 percent of the general population, or, according to Kernberg's own more modest estimate, about 15 percent.

Kernberg (1967 1984) observed that a fairly large group of psychopathological constellations had in common a specific and stable form of pathological ego structure. He emphasized the personality structure rather than a description of characteristics. According to Kernberg, the hallmarks of "Borderline Personality Organization" are 1) "ego weakness" (manifested in poor tolerance of anxiety, impulsivity, and lack of "sublimatory channels" through work, school, or hobbies; 2) manifestations of primary-process thinking as revealed by projective tests; 3) the use of primitive defenses (splitting, projective identification, and denial); and 4) the preservation of good reality testing. These characteristics appear not only in the *DSM-III* "Borderline Personality Disorder," but also in varying degrees in such *DSM-III* disorders as cyclothymic, histrionic, narcissistic, and antisocial personalities. Some of these characteristics are also major features of attention deficit disorder and organic brain disorder.

The preponderance of the evidence now supports the view that the borderline personality, by any definition, represents a common or similar clinical picture that is the outcome of a *heterogeneous developmental course*. Almost all observers agree that both biological and environmental factors, in interaction with each other, play an etiological role. They differ about which aspects, biological or environmental, are most important, and about which treatment approaches are most effective. Theories of etiology include at least two psychogenic views (a developmental psychoanalytic / object relations theory and a family systems perspective), as well as systems interactional theories that view borderline pathology as a manifestation of complex interaction between biological, social, and cultural forces.

Another view, explicated by self psychology, distinguishes between *objective* assessment (all of the etiological positions just mentioned fall into this category) and *subjective* experience, the meaning that the individual attaches to internal and external events. This meaning itself becomes a motivating force or a cause of behavior or symptoms (Palombo 1983), that is, an etiological force interacting with "objective" etiological factors to produce the clinical outcome of the borderline state.

According to Palombo, the question of whether borderline states have their origin in biological or environmental factors is irrelevant to the issue that clinicians face. Palombo (1983:330) observed that the borderline feels a sense of internal disruption and perceives the world as chaotic, overwhelming, and ungratifying. This subjective experience occurs regardless of the degree to which the origins are biological or environmental. The clinician's task is "to help bring some order into the lives of our patients, to reexamine the meaning of what they have lived through, and to establish a sense of coherence in their identities" (Palombo 1983:337).

This paper does not disagree with this definition of the task; it attempts to show that knowledge of objective etiological factors is in fact relevant to the accomplishment of that task, for at least three reasons. First, when biological factors are important in etiology, as Palombo agreed they often are, the therapeutic task of helping the client to make sense of his or her world requires a knowledge and understanding of biological as well as intrapsychic and interpersonal factors. Second, some of the borderline conditions shown by research to have a probable basis in biological factors have been found to be responsive to medication, but the type of medication that is helpful differs significantly, depending on the nature of the presumed biological substrate. Third, when the family of the borderline is involved in treatment, the focus of family therapy differs radically, depending on the therapist's preferred "objective" theory of etiology.

Although certainty about etiology is seldom possible, educated guesses based on existing research an clinical data can, we believe, lead to more effective treatment than relying exclusively on therapeutic encounters that dismiss etiology as either unknowable or irrelevant.

## *Psychogenic Views: Object Relations Theory*

Object relations theory, according to Kernberg (1984), transcends any particular psychoanalytic "school" and represents a general development of psychoanalytic thinking to which contributions have been made by authors of very different orientations. The theory focuses on the *internalization of interpersonal relations*. An individual's intrapsychic structures derive from previous internalized relations with others, which then operate in present interpersonal relations.

Most object relations theorists believe that different pathologies arise from a poor resolution of the conflicts characteristic of certain stages of development.

According to object relations theory, the defense of *splitting*, characteristic of normal children in the separation-individuation phase (6–36 months), reappears in the adult borderline as a pathological mechanism that is one of the hallmarks of the borderline personality structure. Splitting consists of dissociating or actively keeping apart mental representations with opposite affective "valences" (i.e., opposite emotional charges, either positive or negative). Splitting is manifested in the borderline adult by dramatic shifts in affect toward others, whom he or she loves at one moment and hates the next.

The belief that the developing child "fixates" at different levels and later, as a pathological adult, "regresses" to points of earlier fixation is central to object relations theory and to psychodynamic stage theories in general. It assumes that development is a continuous process. Progression through each stage requires the prior successful negotiation of the previous stage, and deficits carried over from each stage accrue in later stages. Kagan (1984) challenged this view, positing instead that the human psyche, like the human body, develops adaptational capacities related to the particular needs of the person at a given time, discarding some structures that are no longer useful.

Virtually all contemporary object relations theorists except Masterson and Rinsley acknowledge that constitutional factors play at least some role in the etiology of the borderline personality. Mahler (1971:435) attributed differences in the ability of infants to trust, in part, to differential endowment. Otto Kernberg (1984) made reference to possible mechanisms of particular systems within the brain that may be involved in the development of psychopathology. Paulina Kernberg referred to the frequent presence of neuropsychological deficits in borderline children (Pine 1986). Grotstein (1987) viewed borderline states as the outcome of interaction between constitutional disorders of emotional regulation (arousal and attention), psychological mechanisms used to cope with these disorders, and environmental responses.

However, despite acknowledgements that biology is important, the theoretical paradigms of Mahler and the Kernbergs are built on psychosocial interaction and do not incorporate biological variables explicitly. Their interest in the biological determinants of the borderline syndrome, therefore, appears desultory.

Masterson (1981) denied any role for biology; he believes that maternal behavior is the sole cause of the borderline personality. According to Masterson, mothers, themselves borderlines, create borderline children by rewarding clinging behavior and punishing thrusts toward independence, specifically during the rapprochement subphase of individuation-separation.

Whether or not object relations theorists attribute any etiological role to biological factors, most believe that decisive events leading to a borderline outcome take place in the first three years of life in the child's relationship with the primary caretaker. Family systems theorists attribute more importance to ongoing family interaction.

## Psychogenic Views: The Family Systems Perspective

The second major subtype of psychogenic view is the family systems perspective. The family therapy literature does not have a well-developed theory of the borderline, in contrast to its extensive treatment of the pathogenesis of schizophrenia. However, purists among family theorists, such as Jay Haley (1980), regard all psychopathology in individuals as artifacts of family system dysfunction. According to this view, borderline pathology is really a symptom of dysfunctional family interaction and not an individual pathology at all. Some structural family therapists, noting "unclear boundaries, inappropriate coalitions, and inappropriate roles" in the families of borderlines

(Baker 1984:322), attempt some amalgamation of the object-relations and the family-systems theoretical formulations.

A review of the literature on the families of borderlines found that all reports ascribed the later development of borderline pathology to early abuse and neglect and poor nurturance in early mother–child interaction. While there was disagreement among the authors on which parental characteristics contributed most significantly to borderline symptoms, all noted that within these families, the expression of emotion was intense and dramatic (Gunderson and Englund 1981:167).

According to Gunderson and Englund (1981), none of this literature meets any criteria for scientific credibility. Almost all the reports were based on unclear diagnostic criteria for the use of the term *borderline,* unstated sample sizes and unarticulated biases, and unsystematic data collection. In no study were families of borderlines compared with families of nonborderlines, nor did the literature deal either with siblings or with characteristics of the families as a whole, limiting itself instead to the patient and his or her parents. Since the families of borderlines were not compared with families of nonborderlines, the possibility remains that families whose children are not borderline also manifest characteristics observed in these families of borderlines. The omission of siblings and families as a whole from these family studies raises further questions about the validity of these studies.

Gunderson and Englund (1981) likened these accounts of the families of borderlines to the (now discredited) theory of the schizophrenogenic mother. No evidence is supplied to support the assertions of badness in these parents (and particularly the mothers). Gunderson and Englund (1981:166) suggested that the tendency of borderlines as well as their therapists to see the borderlines' mothers as "bad" may be a function of the splitting mechanisms used so frequently by borderlines; they may, in reconstructing their past, project negative behaviors or affects onto their mothers that did not in fact exist.

Palombo observed that the borderline person has experienced the world as hostile and chaotic and believes that his or her caretakers have failed to provide a benign environment.

> Regardless of whether or not the parents did fail, [they] were in all likelihood helpless to provide such an environment for the child. . . . The most benign, responsive, caring parents may in that sense be utter failures from the perspective of the child because his needs were not adequately attended to. Conversely, neglectful parents raising a competent, well-endowed child might be experienced as loving and responsible. . . .

[The borderline individual] could, and often does, pin the blame for his suffering on those around him; from his perspective, they are the causes of it. Since [the parents] are perceived as powerful and mighty, they cannot be absolved of the blame for permitting his suffering to occur. Myths are then created about the terrible things that parents did to the child . . . even though in reality the parents may have struggled mightily to provide for the child. (1983:335–336)

An implication of this view is that "average" or "normal" mothering is insufficient to prevent emotional difficulties in vulnerable children. Conversely, the appearance of borderline pathology, in and of itself, in no way indicates the absence of "normal" mothering. The future borderline may have special idiosyncratic needs that are different from the needs of so-called normal children. Only when it has become possible to identify a child's vulnerability at an early age, and to discern the special needs of these children, will professionals be able to guide parents effectively to provide the special, different kind of environment that may help minimize later manifestations of borderline pathology.

However, even the most sensitive parenting cannot inoculate children from pathogenic life stresses. Typical in the histories of borderlines are losses of loved persons, disruption and uprooting related to life circumstances such as geographical moves, and, not uncommonly, a history of incest (Stone 1986; Esman 1987). A borderline outcome may be the cumulative result of life stresses (Goldstein 1983), with or without early inadequacies in parenting.

## Systems / Interactional Theories

Interactional views, which hold that constitutional hypersensitivity, or even actual minimal brain damage, combined with adverse circumstances of many possible kinds (not just unsatisfactory early mother–child relationships), lead to the clinical presentation of borderline pathology, form a second category of etiological theory. Within psychiatry, there is a growing movement toward systems interpretations of psychopathology that recognize the limitations of etiological theory focusing solely on a single category of variables (Grinker 1968; Gunderson 1984; Andrulonis et al. 1981). Within social work, Goldstein (1983) has emphasized the role of external stresses in the etiology of borderline conditions.

Interactionist views ascribe pathology to biological, interpersonal, and environmental factors in reciprocal interaction with each other. Different factors may predominate in different individuals. During the 1970s and 1980s, views that emphasize constitutional factors gained support from the work of various researchers, notably Liebowitz and Klein (1981), Andrulonis et al. (1981), Ballak (1979), Cohen and Young (1977), and Quitkin, Rifkin, and Klein (1976).

An important impetus for the exploration of biological factors has been the recognition that many of the characteristics of borderlines are similar to those found in other psychiatric populations. Overlapping is frequent with three groups of disorders: affective disorders, schizotypal disorders, and brain damage or dysfunction.

*Depression* is a major component of many borderline states, and most borderline scholars agree that a large number of people meeting the criteria for borderline personality disorder are on the border of major affective disorder (Gunderson 1984; Klein 1977; Stone 1986). A strongly positive family history of a serious affective disorder is found in many of the borderline affective disorders, and borderlines often have symptoms also characteristic of bipolar, cyclothymic, and some unipolar affective disorders. Klein (1977), Stone (1988), and others have reported significant improvement on antidepressant medication of the subgroup of borderlines in whom affective components are prominent. Another subgroup, phobic-anxious persons meeting the criteria for borderline personality, also respond to imipramine and other antidepressants, suggesting an underlying neurobiological similarity of phobic-anxious states to affective disorders.

Klein asserted that although different borderlines may resemble each other superficially, their underlying neurobiological substrates often differ significantly. Treatment planning, therefore, requires knowledge about these underlying differences. Within the group who border on affective disorder, Klein identified several subgroups, such as the hysteroid dysphoric, the emotionally unstable character, and the phobic-anxious, each of which responds to different medications. Klein's typology, too lengthy to include here, offers the clinician specific guidelines with respect to choosing appropriate interventions.

*Schizotypal* characteristics such as peculiar ideation, unusual perceptual experiences, (ideas of reference), paranoid thoughts, magical thinking, odd or unkempt appearance, constricted relatedness, and social anxiety (APA 1987) are sometimes found in persons also meeting the criteria for borderline personality disorder, qualifying them for a dual diagnosis of schizotypal and borderline personality disorders (Schulz et al. 1988).

In a recent study by Schulz and colleagues (1988), distinctions between borderlines with an underlying schizophrenia spectrum disorder and those with an underlying affective disorder were demonstrated. Among sixteen borderlines given amphetamine (a chemical that enhances the action of the neurotransmitter dopamine), borderlines who also carried a diagnosis of schizotypal personality disorder worsened to the point of becoming (temporarily) actively psychotic, whereas borderlines without this additional diagnosis improved on amphetamine. The latter group had substantial increases in energy and an improved outlook and sense of well-being. These results were consistent with the view that persons with borderline characteristics have different underlying biological substrates and differing responses to medications of various kinds.

Based on their research with hospitalized borderlines, Andrulonis and colleagues (1981) estimated that about one third of hospitalized persons diagnosed as borderline have underlying *neurological deficits* of various types. In an ongoing research project at the Institute of Living in Hartford, Connecticut, specific etiological factors for certain subcategories of borderline patients were identified. The project involved ninety-one hospitalized patients fulfilling the DSM-III criteria (APA 1980) for the borderline syndrome. Of the ninety-one patients, 38 percent had a history of organicity: 27 percent had had *minimal brain dysfunction* (MBD) or *learning disability*, and 11 percent had had *brain trauma, encephalitis*, or *epilepsy*. The differences by gender were highly significant, with 53 percent of the males having a positive history for MBD or learning disability and only 13.5 percent of the females having such a history. The females more frequently fell within the group on the border of major affective disorder.

Childhood MBD or attention deficit disorder often continues into adulthood. Adults with minimal brain dysfunction may show characteristics that typify the borderline personality, such as impulsivity, irritability, poor frustration tolerance, aggressive outbursts and temper tantrums, readiness to anger, drug and alcohol abuse, suicidal gestures, distractibility, mood swings, anhedonia (diminished ability to experience pleasure), impoverishment of creative activity ("sublimatory capacity" in Kernberg's terminology 1967), antisocial behavior, and feelings of emptiness and loneliness. The need for continuous stimulation often seen in these individuals arises from their attempt to escape the pain of feelings of emptiness and even depersonalization (Bellak 1979; Hartocollis 1977). Electroencephalographic abnormalities may be correlated with symptoms of impulsivity, emotionality, depersonalization, and dyscontrol, probably arising from dysfunction of the limbic system of the brain, a part of the brain that influences aggression, emotionality, and sexual activity (Bellak 1979).

Some of these symptoms—impulsivity, outbursts and temper tantrums, distractibility, and emotional overreactivity—often respond to stimulant medications such as methylphenidate (Ritalin) in adults whose borderline characteristics arise from MBD (Wender, Reimherr, and Wood 1981). Wender and colleagues found that 60 percent of adults with MBD responded to methylphenidate with a reduction in impulsivity and hot-temperedness and an increase in concentration, calmness, and energy. Stimulant medication has an alerting effect that may help the individual to organize the multiple incoming stimuli, internal and external, that he or she has experienced as chaotic, and thus to reduce anxiety and increase confidence and a sense of mastery. As yet, it is not known with certainty why stimulants reduce disinhibition, but it is hypothesized that defective inhibitory mechanisms in the brain are activated in response to stimulant medication, which thus enhances impulse control (Johnson 1980).

Andrulonis and others have postulated a major role for the temporal-lobe–limbic system in the etiology of a range of episodic behavioral disturbances. Some individuals with episodic outbursts show abnormal electroencephalographic findings. Others do not, because more than one half of the brain is inaccessible to routine electroencephalographic investigation. Many show clinical improvement in response to anticonvulsant medication (Andrulonis 1981: 50–51).

There are no reports in the literature of the effects of the above definitions of and explanations for borderline personality on the larger community, on service providers, or on service users. We can give impressions only. It appears that the label *borderline personality* is not widely known in the community at large, in contrast to *schizophrenia* or *manic-depression*, which are part of popular parlance. Service providers, however, have embraced the diagnosis of borderline personality disorder as a way to identify groups of clients whom they find particularly unpredictable, frustrating, or unlikable. It is not clear how the individuals themselves labeled *borderline* are affected by definitions and explanations of the condition.

## SOCIETAL CONTEXT

The kinds of problems in living experienced by borderline persons are as varied as those experienced by the entire population. It follows that the kind and quality of the supports that are available in a range of social and physical environments have a major impact on the functioning of borderline persons. As yet, there are no data to show that supportive environments enhance the functioning of borderlines in contrast to unsupportive environments, so once again, we must speculate in the absence of evidence. We assume (without evidence) that social and environmental supports can enhance the quality of life for borderline persons and, by alleviating stress, can improve the goodness of fit between their needs and the environment's resources.

Unless independently wealthy, borderlines need employment or public assistance to survive. Thus, the availability of jobs, the willingness of employers to tolerate behaviors that deviate from the norm, the degree of access to public income-support systems, the level of grants in the borderline person's geographic area, and the dignity with which public assistance workers treat applicants are just a few examples of conditions in the environment that can either support or frustrate the borderline person. A job market that has more jobs than workers is more likely to absorb persons who sometimes behave erratically than a market in which there are more workers than jobs. A public assistance system responsive to client needs is more likely to give borderline clients sufficient support to prevent desperate, impulsive acts, than is a punitive, restrictive, or demeaning system.

Borderlines are often in contact with health, mental health, or correctional facilities because of their proclivity toward substance abuse, suicidal threats and attempts, shoplifting, reckless driving, and problems of impulse control such as binge eating and spending. It is reasonable to assume that the kind and quality of health and mental health services and the nature of correctional services are critically important for borderlines. The reader is referred to chapters on addictions, depression, eating disorders, family violence, and suicide for discussions of the specific social and environmental contexts for each of these problems in living.

## RISKS AND NEEDS OF POPULATION

The major risks for borderlines are the consequences of addiction, impulsive acting out, and an intense, volatile demanding quality in interpersonal relations. Loss of jobs, dissolution of important relationships, alienation from family and friends, and, in some cases, suicide are among these consequences. There are not data to indicate the exact prevalence of persons meeting the *DSM-III-R* criteria for borderline personality nor for Kernberg's borderline personality organization, but they are believed to be common (APA 1987:347; Gunderson 1984:11). Nor is there any information on prevalence by social class, race, or religion. According to the *DSM-III-R* (APA 1987:347), the disorder is more common in females, and Stone (1986) estimated this ratio to be between 2:1 and 3:1 females to males.

It is difficult to specify what are the most significant psychosocial needs of this population because the range of needs varies so greatly from one person to another. Like everyone, borderlines need a steady source of income, safe housing, affordable health care, and a network of psychosocial supports, including family, friends, and helpers. Their particular characteristics, however, sometimes makes it difficult to sustain employment or to avoid alienating other people in their social network. Unstable, intense interpersonal relationships, often characterized by alternating idealization and devaluation and intermittent periods of intense anger (APA 1987:346–347), may prevent them from sustaining long-term supportive relationships. In a therapeutic context, they are notoriously difficult to engage in psychotherapy and often flee from treatment early in the process (Waldinger 1987). They often arouse negative feelings in practitioners because they may assault the worker verbally, act out in self-destructive ways that create anxiety in the practitioner, and frustrate the worker by terminating services abruptly (Stone 1987; Waldinger 1987). A major need for such people is to have persons in their social environment, including social workers, who are able and willing to "weather the storm," i.e., remain committed to the borderline despite hostility or self-destructive, impulsive acts. This issue is discussed further in the section on interventions.

## PROGRAMS AND SOCIAL WORK SERVICES

As noted above, borderlines enter the social service delivery system through many different access routes, depending on the type of problem that is the most salient aspect of the individual case. They may be brought to an emergency room because of a suicidal gesture or attempt; they may enter through the correctional system because of a driving-while-intoxicated citation, disturbing the peace, family violence, or petty larceny. They may receive services at alcohol or drug abuse treatment centers, shelters for the homeless, or eating-disorder clinics. More severe cases are often seen in psychiatric inpatient services, but large numbers of less severely impaired borderlines are seen in private and public outpatient mental health services.

Obviously, social work programs that serve borderlines are almost as varied as the profession itself. The kinds of programs that deal with borderlines are described in other chapters. The only types of services that are specifically geared to working with borderlines as a distinct entity are inpatient and outpatient mental health facilities. All programs, no matter what their target populations, however, need knowledge about the borderline in order to modify their population-specific programs to respond to the special characteristics and needs of borderlines. That is, they must be able to assess who among their clients are borderlines, and to modify their approaches to these clients to respond to needs that differ from those of, say, other alcoholics, bulimics, or spouse abusers. In the following section, on clinical assessment and interventions, these idiosyncratic needs are spelled out in more detail.

## DIFFERENTIAL CLINICAL ASSESSMENTS AND INTERVENTIONS

In order to intervene effectively with clients showing borderline characteristics, social workers need to be able to identify these characteristics and also to be aware of the current stage of knowledge about the origins of the borderline state. Borderlines have constitutional and psychological deficits that interfere with their ability to cope with problems in living and that also interfere with social workers' efforts to help them solve problems in living. Unless workers understand these deficits, they are likely to become frustrated and angered by perverse and uncooperative behavior coming from clients who appear, at first meeting, to be rational.

These interventions fall into at least six categories: medication, intervening with the environment, helping the client to solve problems, family and client education, and group and individual counseling. Whether an individual is on the border of affective disorder, schizotypal disorder, or brain damage or dysfunction, the same principle applies. *Medication* is often helpful in alleviating psychic pain and restoring a capacity for psychosocial functioning. In many cases, well-targeted medication is the sine qua non of effective treatment, a necessary condition for meaningful psychotherapy (Stone 1980:285–287; Frances and Soloff 1988).

Widely diverse pharmacological treatments have been found to be helpful, depending on whether the proximate border is affective disorder, schizotypal disorder, or neurological impairment, and within these broad areas, different subtypes are responsive to different medications (Goldberg et al. 1986; Soloff et al. 1986; Stone 1986; Klein 1977; Andrulonis et al. 1981). Although social workers are not qualified to prescribe, they need to become familiar with the therapeutic options. Such knowledge can maximize their ability to intervene effectively by referring for medication evaluation in addition to helping with the psychosocial aspects of disturbed functioning.

In recent years, several controlled studies of the effects of different medications have led to some general indicators for choosing medications to treat borderline conditions (Schulz et al. 1988; Cowdry and Gardner 1988; Soloff et al. 1986; Goldberg et al. 1986; Frances and Soloff 1988; Links and Steiner 1988; Egan 1988). We summarize these indicators here in order to familiarize social workers with them. Clearly, workers must study this material in more depth in order to be able to discuss the options with prescribing physicians. Medications are referred to by their generic names (lower case), and illustrative commercial names are given in parentheses (upper case).

1. When schizotypal symptoms are prominent, low-dose neuroleptics such a trifluoperazine (Stelazine), haloperidol (Haldol), thiothixene (Navane), or perphenazine (Trilafon) are most effective in alleviating disturbed thinking. They also alleviate some of the depressive symptoms that these clients experience. Tricyclic antidepressants such as amitriptyline (Elavil) may worsen psychoticlike symptoms in such clients. However, when neuroleptics fail to alleviate severe depression in a schizotypal borderline, concurrent treatment with an MAOI (monoamine oxidase inhibitor) may be helpful.

2. Minor tranquilizers such as the benzodiazepines (e.g., Valium) are contraindicated as they tend to increase behavioral dyscontrol and impulsive acting out. As yet, there are no controlled studies on the use of the popular minor tranquilizer Xanax.

3. When attention deficit disorder underlies borderline disorder, stimulant medications such as methylphenidate (Ritalin) should be tried.

4. When residual attention deficit disorder is combined with depression, imipramine (Tofranil) can be used, as it is effective in both conditions.

5. For depression without schizotypal symptoms, MAOIs such as phenelzine (Nardil) and tricyclic antidepressants such as imipramine and amitriptyline are effective. In addition to sadness and suicidal thoughts or behavior, common symptoms of depression in borderlines are a multiplicity of physical complaints, oversleeping and overeating, lack of energy, and sensitivity to rejection. This pattern is most responsive to MAOIs (Frances and Soloff 1988). MAOIs are considered the drug of choice when panic disorders, agoraphobia, hysteriod dysphoria, or atypical depression are prominent (for a discussion of these conditions, see Liebowitz and Klein 1981). However, when schizotypal symptoms are also present, as noted above, antidepressants may exacerbate the schizotypal symptoms.

6. An anticonvulsant and mood stabilizer, carbamazepine (Tegretol), has been effective in controlling impulsivity, hypomania, or behavioral dyscontrol. Its effectiveness may suggest some underlying seizure phenomena. Since impulsivity and behavioral dyscontrol also

occur because of attention deficit disorder or as an attempt to escape the pain of depression, the origin of the dyscontrol and the choice of medication are seldom clear-cut.

7. Aggression has been reduced with lithium carbonate (a mood stabilizer), haloperidol, and propranolol (a beta blocker).

8. In general, the symptom decompensations of borderline clients are reactive, stress-related, and transient. A period of three to twelve weeks of full pharmacological treatment is usually sufficient except for schizotypal borderlines, who may require up to four months (Frances and Soloff 1988). Because of the danger of tardive dyskinesia, low-dose neuroleptics should not be used as long-term maintenance therapy for borderlines.

Social workers have often opposed the use of medication except as a last resort, an attitude that predisposes them to discourage clients from using it. Yet the evidence is compelling that medication can be extremely helpful in many cases. Caution and careful monitoring are, of course, necessary, and social workers need sufficient knowledge to carry out the monitoring function. Equally important, of course, is enabling the client to articulate the meaning that the use of medication has for him or her.

But social workers' generalized prejudice against medication, arising from a combination of ignorance, knowledge of instances of medication abuse, and ideological indoctrination against treating "symptoms" instead of "causes," may have the unfortunate result of depriving some clients of an important source of help.

In addition to sensitizing the worker to the possible use of medication, understanding the biological aspects of an individual client's borderline disturbance, in the authors' view, is a crucial issue in the helping process. The question "Why am I this way?" is a salient preoccupation of most clients, even if they do not articulate the question. Palombo referred to the borderline client's "maddening sense of inadequacy at coping with an imperfectly understood environment" (1983:331). The clinician can help the client understand his or her environment (internal as well as external) by giving information.

When the client has a history of MBD, head injury, or other neurological impairment, it is helpful to be able to say, "You know, your MBD (head injury, epilepsy, etc.) seems to have the effect of making you fly off the handle easily (get distracted, say things you're sorry about, look for excitement all the time)." Once the worker has helped the client identify a biological basis for weak impulse control or stimulus-seeking needs, as a *real* factor in his or her difficulties, the helping issues surrounding this information—the questions "Am I a hopeless case?" and "What's the best way of handling this deficit?"—can be explored.

When there is no history of neurological insult, but a tendency toward major affective disorder is apparent in the client and (possibly) in family members as well, the workers can point out that the client seems to have a constitutional proclivity for depression (and/or mania) that interacts with stressful life events. For more sophisticated clients, it is often useful to suggest reading that can help them understand their own vulnerabilities and that outline the service options, including medication.

Virtually all the empirical work that has been done on practice with borderlines comes from the psychiatric literature. Social work articles on borderlines are anecdotal and prescriptive; none involve systematic data collection and analysis. Thus, the question "How does a practitioner work with borderlines to solve problems of living?" (as opposed to giving psychotherapeutic treatment) cannot yet be addressed with confidence. In principle, we agree with social work writers who stress the importance of concrete services and emphasize the need to alleviate *environmental* stresses. However, there are no data either to confirm or to refute the assertion that social work interventions geared to enhancing client–environment goodness-of-fit can diminish the development of borderline personality in childhood or relieve its severity in adulthood. Presumably, ameliorating housing problems or helping a client gain access to better health improves the client's quality of life even if his or her borderline traits remain unchanged. Therefore, we advocate maximum efforts by social workers to enhance the responsiveness of the client's environment through referral, brokering, case advocacy, and social action in substantive areas such as employment, housing, addiction, health, and mental health.

To the extent that the upheavals and traumas in the lives of borderline persons reflect constitutional and psychological deficits in personality, it may be difficult, however, to work with borderlines in a problem-solving role vis-à-vis their situational and environmental stresses when the borderline's intense emotional needs, idealization-devaluation, and fear of abandonment become transferred to the social work helper. When road blocks to progress are encountered because of the client's borderline state rather than because of barriers in the environment, individual treatment is usually necessary.

Whatever the type of biological substrates involved in borderline conditions, *education* is an important intervention for borderlines and for members of their families. Psychoeducational strategies in both individual and family counseling with persons suffering from psychosis and their families have proved highly effective (Rohrbaugh 1983; Anderson et al. 1986; Anderson, Reiss, and Hogarty 1986). To be able to fulfill the educative function with the borderline, the clinician must have knowledge about specific biological factors, not just a global belief that biology is important.

Knowledge about biological contributions to borderline pathology has important conceptual as well as ethical implications in work with families. Family therapies whose stated purpose is to "restructure" family relationships (Minuchin 1974; Haley 1980) fail to recognize that the so-called identified patient—in this case, the borderline individual—often has a genuine deficit that sets off a chain reaction of unhelpful responses between family members. Biologically based deficits can directly cause lack of impulse control, poor frustration tolerance, intense affective needs, irritability and emotional explosiveness, and other psychological and behavioral manifestations. Family conflicts, tension, and recriminations and a repertoire of behaviors developed to try to cope with such manifestations in the "identified patient" are often mistakenly viewed as pathogenic rather than responsive. It is not easy to respond in the most therapeutically desirable manner to such characteristics, nor would workers, in similar circumstances, necessarily do any better than the members of the families of borderlines that they help. To focus exclusively on negative interactional sequences, while overlooking or denying outright the role of a biologically based deficit that has generated or has decisively contributed to those interactions in the first place, is to "blame the victim" (Johnson 1986, 1987).

While families often need to develop more constructive patterns of relating to each other, therapeutic methods that start with educating the family and the symptomatic individual about possible biological, interpersonal, and environmental contributors remove the onus of blame and convey the worker's conviction that families want to help and are competent to do so, given appropriate information and guidance (Anderson 1983; Schulz et al. 1985).

Once the worker has established an ambience of respect for and acceptance of the family in this manner, his or her assessment in relation to needed behavior change is more readily accepted. It is important to emphasize, however, that getting families to change their behavior *is not the goal of psychoeducation.* The goal is to help families cope more effectively with the overwhelming stress of having a mentally ill family member. In the treatment of schizophrenia, psychoeducational family therapy has shown far more impressive outcomes than any other family therapy (Rohrbaugh 1983; Hogarty and Anderson 1986). Its success warrants an extension of the method to family therapy with borderlines to demonstrate whether psychoeducation shows similar effectiveness in preventing treatment dropout and reducing hospitalization (Schulz et al. 1985).

Grunebaum and Friedman (1989) have provided clinicians with sensitive and detailed recommendations for building collaborative relationships with the families of mentally ill persons. Several tasks are involved:

1. Practitioners must ensure that families will have a chance to be heard and to relate their own account of the primary client's illness, his or her life, and the life of the family.
2. Workers must impart information about the nature of the condition, its prognosis, and the treatment methods. When they do not know the prognosis or the treatment that is most likely to help, they should be honest and say so.
3. They must help families with feelings engendered by the family member's illness and hospitalization (if it has occurred) and the treatment effects.
4. Workers must identify which of three patterns or combinations of patterns families are using to cope: denial, intrusiveness and overcontrol, or giving up their own lives and concentrating entirely on the ill member. These coping patterns reflect depression about the patient's future as well as lack of knowledge about how to help a mentally ill person. Therefore, families need to be encouraged to grieve, and to attend "caring and sharing" meetings with other families, and they should be given information and/or skills training in more effective ways to cope. In most states, chapters of the National Alliance for the Mentally Ill have been formed. Although their members so far have been predominantly the families of persons with schizophrenia, families of borderlines, especially those with prolonged and/or repeated hospitalizations, may find participation in a local chapter of the Alliance helpful.
5. Finally, families need help in facing the ethical and existential dilemmas of how to balance the needs of the ill member with their own and other family members' needs.

As yet, no data are available that give clear indications to practitioners of the most effective ways to help borderline clients *solve problems in living*. For reasons discussed earlier in the chapter, borderlines sometimes sabotage efforts by practitioners to engage them in problem solving because of their compelling emotional needs, surfacing as "transference." Seeking gratification of these intense emotional needs may seem more important to the borderline client than solving nitty-gritty, day-to-day problems. Thus, the worker's agenda (helping the client solve the day-to-day problems that interfere with the client's well-being) may be at odds with the client's agenda (to elicit emotional support for narcissistic, dependent, or power needs or to obtain relief from the pain of feelings of emptiness and meaninglessness).

A recent addition to the problem-solving approaches to borderlines, "dialectical behavior therapy," has shown considerable promise in reducing self-destructive behavior and inducing borderlines to remain in treatment (Linehan et al. 1989). This variant of behavior therapy is "dialectical" because it deals with multiple tensions, notably the necessity of accepting clients *as they are* while attempting to try to *teach them to change* (Linehan 1987:272). The counseling approach is behavioral because it focuses on skills training, collaborative problem-solving, contingency clarification and management, and the observable present (Linehan 1987:272). It is directive and intervention-oriented.

In this approach, the worker frequently expresses sympathy for the client's intense pain and sense of desperation (creating a "validating environment") while conveying a matter-of-fact attitude about current and previous self-destructive behaviors (Linehan, 1987:272). The worker actively reframes suicidal and other dysfunctional behaviors as part of the client's learned problem-solving repertoire and tries to focus the counseling process on active problem-solving. In both individual and group counseling, workers actively teach emotion regulation, interpersonal effectiveness, distress tolerance, and self-management skills. They openly reinforce the desired behaviors to promote progress, make clear the limits of their own availability and ability to be of help, and try to maintain contingencies that shape adaptive behaviors and extinguish self-destructive behaviors. The counseling process emphasizes building and maintaining a positive, interpersonal, collaborative relationship in which the worker's role is consultant to the client.

Because of continual crises, it is sometimes difficult to follow a behavioral intervention plan within the context of individual counseling, especially if this plan involves teaching skills that are not obviously related to the current crisis and that do not promise immediate relief. Therefore, behaviorally oriented workers have developed psychoeducational group-counseling modules to teach specific behavioral, cognitive, and emotional skills (Linehan 1987:270).

The literature on the *group counseling* of borderlines is extremely limited and is based entirely on clinician observations. As yet, no controlled studies have been reported (Blum and Marzial 1988). Most psychodynamic writers believe that groups should contain no more than one or two borderlines because their behaviors may prevent the development of group cohesion (Horwitz 1987). In addition, writers agree that borderlines usually require individual counseling along with group counseling to help the client tolerate the stresses arising in the group experience, such as feelings of deprivation or narcissistic injuries (Horwitz 1987). Behaviorally oriented theorists do not appear to advocate such restrictions, presumably because the psychoeducational format emphasizing the *teaching* of behavioral, cognitive, and emotional skills (Linehan 1987) diminishes process-related problems inherent in unstructured psychodynamic group therapy.

Psychodynamic writers have observed several indications for counseling borderlines in groups. First, borderlines sometimes cannot tolerate a close, intense one-to-one relationship (Grobman 1980; Roth 1980). Second, borderlines have a tendency to develop intense feelings toward and distorted views of an individual therapist or worker (called *transference regression* in the psychoanalytic literature) (Horwitz 1987; Kibel 1978), a process less likely to occur in group settings. Third, they may be emotionally fragile, with an intense hunger for emotional support, a sense of loneliness, difficulty in feeling a sense of belonging, and rapid, intense fluctuations in self-esteem (Grobman 1980; Glatzer 1972; Kernberg 1975). Writers have observed that that group reduces loneliness, enhances a sense of belonging, and encourages the individual client to assume a helping role with peers, which conveys a sense of competence and enhances self-esteem (Horwitz 1987). Fourth, the group experience may help overcome the borderline's extreme self-involvement. Altruistic concern for fellow sufferers often develops after a client experiences an empathic response from a group (Macaskall 1982).

Contraindications for group counseling may include lack of accomplishment in life as compared with other group members (so that group participation would diminish self-esteem even further); overwhelming affect and anxiety due to the lack of a stimulus barrier; or suspiciousness and heavy reliance on pathological splitting (Horwitz 1987). In addition, extremely narcissistic individuals may place a heavy burden on group members, as well as on the group leader, because of lack of empathy for peers, feelings of entitlement, and expectations of admiration (Yalom 1975; Horwitz 1987d).

Yet, observers believe that the characteristics of borderlines that make them difficult to work with within groups are also the characteristics for which group treatment can be especially helpful. If the client has enough compensating characteristics to become successfully integrated into a group, such as likableness, a sense of humor, perseverance, and an ability to appreciate others, then the problems created by having the borderline in a group may be offset by benefits to the borderline person (Horwitz 1987). Group theorists have noted that cohesive groups can civilize and socialize members and can thus diminish egocentrism, demandingness, social isolation, or otherwise socially unacceptable behavior (Horwitz 1987).

Fairly often, social workers function in intensive *counseling* with borderlines. In a review of the literature on the therapeutic approaches and techniques used with borderlines, Waldinger (1987) summarized some basic tenets of safe and effective intensive counseling of the borderline person, with which most borderline theorists agree. These are reported here as guidelines for social workers who engage with borderlines in any kind of ongoing counseling process:

1. Client–worker contacts should be structured and predictable. The practitioner should establish regular appointment times, begin and end on time, and make all expectations about attendance and fee paying very clear from the outset. When either client or practitioner deviates from these rules, these deviations should be actively addressed.

2. The practitioner should assume an active role in the sessions by making frequent comments, since worker activity anchors the client in reality and minimizes the severity of the transference distortions to which borderline persons are prone in unstructured situations.

3. The worker must be able to withstand the borderline person's verbal assaults without either retaliating or withdrawing. The client's hostility toward the worker should not be buried but should be examined as a part of a more general pattern of relating to others.

4. The worker must repeatedly point out the adverse results of the client's self-destructive behavior such as drug use, risky sexual behavior, manipulativeness, and inappropriate rageful outbursts. The worker should focus on the results, not the client's motives for these behaviors. The reason is that borderline persons have a high investment in remaining unaware of the self-destructive nature of their actions because these actions also gratify certain wishes and allay anxiety.

5. The worker should help clients establish a connection between their actions and their feeling states at the time they engage in these actions. Action for borderlines is a defense against painful feelings. In order to develop autonomy and self-control, clients must be helped to see that they communicate through action and that this action serves a defensive purpose. Self-destructive acts have a variety of meanings. Suicidal behaviors, for example, may arise from a desire for revenge, a wish to coerce another person, or, paradoxically, a wish to feel alive

(rather than to die) by cutting through feelings of emptiness and meaninglessness (Egan 1988). Focusing on real or imagined physical illnesses may also serve the purpose of helping the borderline feel "real."

6. The worker must set limits on behavior that threatens the safety of the client or the worker, as well as on behavior that is used to avoid dealing with issues arising in the helping process.

7. Interpretation and clarification should focus on the here and now, not on the past.

8. The worker must carefully examine his or her own feelings toward the borderline client. Because borderlines can be so frustrating and irritating, workers need to monitor their own reactions to help themselves avoid acting out (Waldinger 1987:268).

In addition to these recommendations, for which there is consensus among most borderline scholars, major areas of controversy also exist. One fundamental disagreement pertains to the importance of interpretation versus creating a "holding environment" (Waldinger 1987). Kernberg (1975) and Masterson (1981) believe that the worker should interpret the client's behavior and feelings early in the helping process. Kernberg believes that borderline clients can respond to the actual content of interpretive comments early in treatment if these comments are properly framed. Since the client distorts the worker's comments through such mechanisms as splitting, denial, projection, and projective identification, the worker must first try to bring these distortions to light so that the client is able to hear the actual meaning of the worker's comments rather than distort them. For example, a client who projects his or her own sadistic feelings onto others may hear every interpretation by the worker as an attack and may therefore be unable to benefit from the content. Such misperceptions must be clarified before the client can use the actual content.

Masterson (1981) also believes that the borderline can use interpretation early in counseling, but he has emphasized the need to begin by clarifying, over and over, the self-destructive nature of the client's behavior rather than focusing on the tendency to distort the worker's comments in the therapy hour (Waldinger 1987). Gunderson (1984) holds a third view, i.e., that the borderline's ability to understand and make use of the content of interpretations varies from one session to another, depending on how anxious the client is and how supported he or she feels by the worker at any given moment. Current stresses, such as an impending loss, can cause the client to lose the ability at that moment to respond to interpretation (Waldinger 1987).

Among writers who believe that the sine qua non of successful counseling is to create a "holding environment" early in the helping process (Buie and Adler 1982; Volkan 1986; Chessick 1982) rather than to interpret, borderline pathology is believed to be due to a deficit in the ability to hold or soothe oneself arising from early developmental failure. This view contrasts with that of Kernberg and Masterson, who see the goal of treating borderlines as the undoing of a malformed structure rather than as the remediation of a deficit (Waldinger 1987). According to the deficit view, the worker must be a "holding self-object" (a term taken from Kohut's self psychology, 1984), i.e., must perform the holding and soothing functions for borderlines that they cannot perform for themselves (Waldinger 1987). Healing comes about not through interpretation, but through the act of being a "stable, consistent, caring, nonpunitive person who survives the patient's rage and destructive impulses and continues to serve this holding function" (Waldinger 1987:270). According to this view, experiential factors are more important than the content of interpretations. Buie and Adler (1982) believe that the therapist must function *in reality* as a stable holding person by offering such supports as hospitalizing the client if necessary, giving extra appointments, allowing phone calls between sessions, giving vacation addresses, and even sending postcards to the client while away on vacation (Waldinger 1987:270).

What becomes of borderlines? Do they continue to be volatile, self-destructive, impulsive, addictive people living on the brink of calamity? To what extent does treatment diminish these tendencies, and what kind(s) of treatment are most effective?

Evidence that illuminates these issues comes from the subset of borderlines who have spent time in psychiatric hospitals, via the method of long-term follow-up studies (McGlashan 1986; Stone 1987), and from a recent study of comparative treatment effects on an outpatient population (Linehan et al. 1989). The Chestnut Lodge follow-up study (McGlashan 1986) provides data on long-term outcomes. Eighty-one persons meeting the criteria for borderline personality disorder during the hospitalization period were followed up an average of 15 years after discharge (range 2–32 years). Slightly more than half (43 of 81) were rated "good" or "recovered" on global ratings of functioning; 17 (about one fifth) were rated "poor" or "marginal"; and the remainder fell in between. Having a high IQ was strongly related to better outcome, in contrast to populations of schizophrenics, for whom IQ is not a predictor of outcome. A second strong predictor was the presence or absence of affective instability, defined as marked shifts within brief time periods (hours up to a few days) from normal mood to depression, irritability, or anxiety. A third predictor was the length of time spent in other hospitals before admission to Chestnut Lodge, a measure of the chronicity of the illness. In contrast to the findings for schizophrenia outcomes, premorbid work and social functioning (how the client functioned before becoming ill) were not predictors of outcome.

The New York State Psychiatric Institute study (Stone 1987) supplied data about long-term outcome as well as some indications about treatment effectiveness: 254 borderline patients were evaluated ten to twenty-three years after discharge. Most had shown serious self-destructive tendencies at the time of admission. Among this group two fifths were rated on follow-up as recovered, with a score greater than 70 on the Global Assessment of functioning Scale (GAS; APA 1987:12). The recovery process had often required five to ten years. Two thirds had at least a good outcome (GAS > 60). For all patients, supportive interventions were important and were often sufficient to bring about significant improvement. Only about one third of the hospitalized borderlines turned out to be truly amenable to insight-oriented ("expressive") psychotherapy. Among this group, dramatic benefits took place only for those who were culturally and otherwise disposed to work within the framework of intensive analytically oriented therapy, i.e., who had been reared in an atmosphere conducive to the development of introspection and psychological-mindedness. They were generally liked by others, motivated, focused, and free of the more overwhelming impulsivity and substance craving and had not come from "grotesquely destructive" early environments (Stone 1987:240). Many patients improved but gravitated toward different treatment strategies and different types of therapists following discharge. Both introspective and nonintrospective patients were equally represented among the group with the best outcomes (GAS > 80).

The effects of therapy could not be compared systematically with effects of no treatment. However, several borderline patients left the New York State Psychiatric Institute against medical advice soon after the three months required for inclusion in the study. Many recovered with no intensive therapy and no aftercare. In these cases, recovery was ascribed to effective containment during the critical self-destructive phase and the clients' innate powers of recuperation, related to personal assets such as courage, perseverance, and industriousness. Some became alcoholics, had several difficult years, then joined AA, and improved steadily.

Among the few outcome studies on the effectiveness of psychological interventions in reducing suicidal behaviors, two studies of brief (two- to ten-week) inpatient treatments with random assignment found behavior therapy more effective than insight therapy in reducing repeat parasuicidal (self-destructive) behaviors following discharge

(Bartman 1976; Liberman and Eckman 1981). In another randomized study comparing dialectical behavior therapy with other treatments in the community, the subjects were women with multiple parasuicidal episodes who met the criteria for borderline personality disorder. At each assessment point during treatment (four months, eight months, and twelve months), dialectical behavior therapy was found to be more effective than other treatments in reducing the incidence of parasuicidal episodes, as well as in preventing dropout from treatment (Linehan et al. 1987).

Overall conclusions about borderlines impaired enough to be hospitalized are that one half to two thirds have a good prognosis in the long run (not immediately after discharge). Supportive counseling is important for all, and intensive psychotherapy is beneficial to a small subset with high intelligence and motivation who are culturally disposed to a psychological orientation, and who are not severely impaired. Behavioral strategies are promising as methods for reducing suicidal acting out and for improving continuance in outpatient treatment.

These conclusions have important implications for social work practice with borderlines. Most of our clients do not meet the "elitist" criteria predictive of a favorable response to intensive psychodynamic treatment. The majority would appear to need a "holding environment" in which the worker provides support, structure, education, predictability, limit setting and an ability to "weather the storm" (Waldinger 1987) of the borderline's frequently erratic and vacillating behavior. Those clients who do have characteristics that indicate a likely favorable response to intensive insight-oriented therapy should be helped to obtain such treatment if the worker is unable to provide it. Both Stone and Waldinger have emphasized that different types of clients do best with different kinds of treatment and different types of therapists.

## CASE ILLUSTRATION

Marie was seen by the worker in a state hospital over a period of eight years, during which she experienced more than twenty hospitalizations. When first seen by the worker, she had just been admitted for having taken a drug overdose. She reported having heard voices telling her to kill herself, as well as episodes of racing thoughts and anxiety. Before this admission, she had had previous hospitalizations for similar behavior.

Marie had been referred to the state hospital by a community clinic following an attempt harm herself with an overdose. She was 18 years old at the time of admission, was obese (200 pounds, 5 feet 1½ inches) and was the oldest of three siblings in an intact family. Marie was described as argumentative, combative, and needing constant supervision to guard against repeated attempts to harm herself, which included having ingested the family dog's worm pills. Educationally, she was having difficulty but had succeeded in making it to her senior year in high school. School personnel noted that Marie had few peer friendships and was prone to causing arguments and fights.

Her early years were reported to have been uneventful. During pubescence, she reported having been "sexually abused" by a known offender in town and had been referred to a youth guidance and mental health center, but the charges had not been substantiated. Her father described himself as a disciplinarian but felt that his attempts at discipline were going nowhere. The mother admitted to being more lenient but could understand her husband's feelings. They acknowledged some marital discord in response to Marie's behavior. Her siblings were reportedly concerned and somewhat frightened by their sister's behavior. Despite their feelings of helplessness and hopelessness, her family was very concerned about Marie's plight. They expressed feelings of guilt and anger about her being in a state hospital, feelings that intensified as Marie's illness continued over many years.

During the initial weeks after admission, Marie demonstrated aggressive and suicidal behavior, requiring both chemical and physical restraint to prevent her from harming herself. Her judgment and insight appeared to be very poor. The service plan focused on trying to prevent her from physically harming herself by constant monitoring, suicide precautions, medication (thioridazine [Mellaril] and loxapine [Loxitane]), encouragement from staff to seek them out when she was feeling upset, and referral to a community agency under contract to the hospital to provide individual and family counseling to hospitalized adolescents.

Marie was initially diagnosed as having schizophrenia, but the diagnosis was subsequently changed to borderline personality disorder. During the course of this hospitalization (seven months), it became apparent to the staff that Marie had more control over her behavior than she admitted. Her behavior often seemed to be calculated; for example, she would wait to act out until she would be the center of attention or knew she would be stopped. The staff felt that her behavior had a histrionic and manipulative quality. She also "split" the staff and her parents.

For example, she changed her behavior between shifts, so that the staff on one shift would see her as "doing good" (i.e., being helpful to them or managing her outbursts), while the staff on the next shift would see her as "doing poorly" (i.e., being self-centered, antagonistic, and unwilling to use the prescribed interventions). The consequence of this behavior was disputes among the staff about how she should be helped, generating an atmosphere of turmoil and instability. Similarly, with her parents, she would blame her father for her difficulties, while imploring her mother to rescue her. The parents then argued about where she should live and what was the most effective way to manage her behavior.

A worker was assigned to Marie as case manager. Initially, he focused on gathering information, coordinating the interdisciplinary team, and case-managing the services that were in place. He convened conferences with providers and family to share information and to try to arrive at at plan for discharge. Although all staff agreed that Marie's prognosis was poor, she was able to finish her high school requirements while in the hospital, evidence that she was able to respond to structure and to maintain focused activities without intrusive auditory hallucinations. It became apparent that separation and individuation issues were a major focus of her difficulty. The staff agreed that she didn't want to "grow up" or to be responsible for her own behavior. Each time she felt that she was being pressured to take responsibility, she acted out. For example, on occasion, she would request to go home for a visit and would do everything necessary (i.e., follow the prescribed hospital service plan) to earn this privilege. After plans were coordinated and shortly before she was to depart, she would "act out," through a suicide gesture or striking-out behavior, thereby sabotaging the plan and requiring her visit to be canceled. Then she became angry at the staff for taking her pass away and tearfully apologetic to her parents for having acted this way. She would blame her voices for this behavior rather than accepting responsibility for her actions. These instances also demonstrated attempts to split the staff and her parents, the result being disagreement about the best environment for her to live in.

As time went on, the providers, as well as her family, became concerned about how comfortable she had become in the hospital. It was decided to refer her to a newly opening halfway house, where she could live with three other clients. The residence was based on the psychiatric rehabilitation model, which develops daily living skills provides support and structure, and facilitates participation in a sheltered workshop and individual and medication therapies. Much coordination was required at this time, in addition to filing for medical and financial assistance and referring Marie to a community clinic.

During the transition into the halfway house, Marie again sabotaged the plan. Over a five-month period, she returned to the hospital four times following suicide attempts, including running in front of traffic, attempting to overdose on another patient's medication and then on Tylenol, threatening to drink ammonia, and spraying Lysol into her mouth. Each attempt had been precipitated by voices telling her to harm herself. Various medications were tried, including Mellaril, Loxitane, and Valium.

In retrospect, it seems clear that the stress of leaving the hospital and moving into a community residential situation exceeded Marie's coping skills and abilities. Marie returned to the hospital for another ten months. Again, she adjusted well to the hospital but occasionally become threatening, argumentative, or hyperactively impulsive. For example, she would lash out at a staff member or another resident with no apparent provocation. A pattern of hypochondriacal complaints also emerged.

While hospitalized, Marie resumed involvement with the community adolescent agency, where she received individual counseling twice weekly; had a structured day schedule, including employment in the agency as an office trainee; and participated in a peer support group and family work with a different worker. At the hospital, she received medication, attended weekly community meetings, and, at this time, began to form a significant alliance with the worker. As she became trusting of him, she began to reveal more of herself. It became apparent that her crises were linked to her desire to be taken care of, her wish to be the center of attention, and her hope never to have to take responsibility for her actions. She avoided responsibility by blaming those around her, her voices, or past events. As her style of coping had now become clear to him, she and the worker spent time exploring these coping patterns. The worker knew what resources were available and pointed out what was and was not acceptable. In addition, because of Marie's characteristic manipulating and splitting behaviors, he was often called on to act as a mediator between the day and evening hospital staff, between the hospital staff and Marie's parents, and between hospital and outside providers. During these times, he would try to point out Marie's patterns of behavior, i.e., how she was setting up confrontations between factions. He suggested that the team react objectively rather than subjectively. However, this goal was not easy to achieve.

As time passed, Marie's state remained relatively unchanged. The providers as well as Marie's family suggested that she try being at home for a while. Having received education about the nature and course of Marie's illness, and being prepared with a structured schedule of Marie's day, the family was feeling better about her attempting to live with them again.

During the next couple of years, the worker saw little of Marie but was kept abreast of her status. In addition, she began to call him periodically to inform him how she was, to complain, or just to talk. During this time, the community psychiatrist who was treating her observed a cyclical pattern to her manic, impulsive behavior. He suspected an underlying bipolar disorder and initiated a trial of lithium carbonate, which seemed to smooth out the extremes of her behavior and to stabilize her mood. Marie continued to live with her family.

She again had a crisis when the adolescent program she had been attending ended. There, Marie had formed significant relationships with several people. She and her family decided that she should again move into a structured halfway house, which she did. During this time, she maintained contact with the worker. He continued to focus on her successful coping skills and tried to help her build on each success. Sometimes, she would call in panic, but she was becoming more able to calm herself and to solve problems, with his assistance. She was becoming more able to recognize stress-inducing events, but she still lacked the ability to anticipate them, nor did she trust her skill to deal with them. On a positive note, she indicated to the worker that she did not want to return to the state hospital. She viewed herself as more capable than most of the patients there. The worker was encouraged by this assertion but warned Marie to think about potential sources of stress, so as not to become overwhelmed when stressful situations arose and then to react with suicidal behavior.

After two years, Marie again return to the hospital following an incident in which voices told her to harm herself. She had been living in the halfway house, attending a day treatment program, receiving medication and individual counseling at a community mental health center, and working in a volunteer job at a laundry at a local hospital. On the occasion when she heard these voices, a staff person at the community residence, to whom she had formed a strong attachment, had just left for another job. Instead of acting on the commands of her voices, Marie called the worker, who suggested that she be evaluated at the hospital. The circumstances of this hospitalization, then, showed that Marie was making progress. Instead of acting out impulsively, she had reached for help in a more positive way.

This hospitalization was very brief. Following a conference with all the providers, Marie was discharged. She was receiving lithium carbonate, thioridazine (Mellaril), and desipramine (Norpramine), a tricyclic antidepressant. She reported feeling well on this regimen. She remained out the hospital for a year while maintaining telephone contact with the worker. He continued to offer support and encouragement. Over the next few years, Marie alternated between living in a room of her own, a community residence, a small apartment in her parents' hometown, and, from time to time, the hospital. She continued to receive medications including lithium and Xanax. Periodically, conferences among all providers were convened, and the various services and agencies, together with Marie's parents, succeeded in following a coordinated plan and presenting a united front to Marie.

As part of her discharge planning, the social worker and Marie discussed her present situation and began to problem-solve around how she could maintain herself in the community. We planned that she would be responsible for securing Supplemental Security Income by making contact with her field representative, and that the worker would provide whatever information was needed by the Social Security office. She opted to discontinue the sheltered workshop and the day treatment program, as she preferred to volunteer at a local bookstore, whose owner knew her and was willing to train her and work with her. This plan was agreed to by all providers, Marie, and her parents. She was also encouraged to resume her phone calls to the worker, which had ceased when she had run out of money. They worked out an arrangement whereby the worker could call her instead.

Very brief hospitalizations occurred from time to time. Two other medications were tried: trifluoperazine (Stelazine), a neuroleptic, and doxepin (Sinequan), a tricyclic antidepressant. Marie maintained telephone contact with the worker. As they spoke, he was increasingly impressed by her emerging coping skills and her ability to use her therapist positively. She informed the worker what the therapist was assisting her with relaxation therapy to control her bouts of panic. He was teaching her to recognize situations that made her panicky and had also given her tapes so that she could practice exercises at home. Marie vowed to the worker that she was never going to the state hospital again. She was increasingly convinced that she would be able to stay out of the hospital. During this time, they reviewed the gains that she had made, the strategies that had helped her cope, and potential new solutions to problems. The worker always tried to educate her about where her issues came from, whether they were developmental (not wanting to separate and grow up), interpersonal (conflicts with others), or environmental (reactions to losses).

When the worker was concerned about her mood, he checked on her safety. At other times, he contacted her therapist to inform him of the content of their conversation. Through this communication, he learned that Marie had in effect set up a telephone support network that included her therapist, a social worker at the community hospital, and him. On one occasion, he had the opportunity to see these people and was encouraged by discovering that we were all providing Marie with similar growth-promoting opportunities.

Marie's occasional hospitalizations occurred in reaction to environmentally induced stresses, such a conflict with a roommate, the loss of some significant person at one of the facilities with which she was involved, and rejection by a boyfriend. She became increasingly able to see that her voices were not real and that her pattern of parasuicidal (self-harming) behavior was a response to a precipitating stress.

After many years, an electroencephalogram was performed, and Marie was found to have neurological abnormalities (slow alpha activity at the frontal leads and suppression of activity at the occipital leads, combined with paroxysmal activity at the frontal leads). She was subsquently put on dilantin (an anticonvulsant) and continued to take lithium.

The worker hasn't seen Marie for a couple of years because he no longer works at the state hospital. She has remained out of the hospital for increasing periods of time, has greatly reduced the incidence of self-destructive behavior, and has used her support network effectively. Marie will probably continue to need a range of services for the foreseeable future. Although her adjustment must be described as marginal, it is far better than it was in the early years of her contact with the worker.

# REFERENCES

Abramowitz, I. A. and R. D. Coursey. 1989. "Impact of an Educational Support Group on Family Participants Who Take Care of Their Schizophrenic Relative." *Journal of Consulting and Clinical Psychology* 57(2):232–236.

Akiskal, H. S., S. E. Chen, G. C. Davis, V. R. Puzantian, M. Kashgarian, and J. M. Bolinger. 1986. "Borderline: An Adjective in Search of a Noun." In M. Stone, ed., *Essential Papers on Borderline Disorders*. New York: New York University Press, pp. 549–568.

APA (American Psychiatric Association). 1980. *Diagnostic and Statistical Manual of Mental Disorders (DSM-III)*, 3rd ed. Washington, D.C.: APA.

APA (American Psychiatric Association). 1987. *Diagnostic and Statistical Manual of Mental Disorders (DSM-III-R)*, 3d ed., rev. Washington, D.C.: APA.

Anderson, C. M. 1983. "A Psychoeducational Program for Families of Patients with Schizophrenia." In W. McFarlane, ed., *Family Therapy in Schizophrenia*, pp. 99–116. New York: Guilford.

Anderson, C. M., S. Griffin, A. Rossi, I. Pagonis, D. P. Holder, and R. Treiber. 1986. "A Comparative Study of the Impact of Education vs. Process Groups for Families of Patients with Affective Disorder." *Family Process* 25:185–205.

Anderson, C. M., D. J. Reiss, and G. E. Hogarty. 1986. *Schizophrenia and the Family: A Practitioner's Guide to Psychoeducation and Management*. New York: Guilford.

Andrulonis, P. A., B. C. Glueck, C. F. Stroebel, N. G. Vogel, A. L. Shapiro, and D. M. Aldridge. 1981. "Organic Brain Dysfunction and the Borderline Syndrome." *Psychiatric Clinics of North America* 4(1):47–66.

Baker, P. K. S. 1984. "A Comprehensive Model of Practice for Borderline Adolescents." *Clinical Social Work Journal* 12(4):320–331.

Bartman, E. R. 1976. "Assertive Training with Hospitalized Suicide Attempters." Unpublished doctoral dissertation, Catholic University of America, Washington, D.C.

Bellak, L. P., ed. 1979. *Psychiatric Aspects of Minimal Brain Dysfunction in Adults*. New York: Grune & Stratton.

Berger, P. A. 1987. "Pharmacological Treatment for Borderline Personality Disorder." *Bulletin of the Menninger Clinic* 51(3):277–284.

Blum, H. M. and E. Marziali. 1988. "Time-Limited Group Psychotherapy for Borderline Patients." *Canadian Journal of Psychiatry* 33(5):364–369.

Brown, Valdeane. 1989. "Borderline Adults in Treatment." Workshop, American Health Care Institute, East Hartford, Conn., April 11.

Buie, D. and G. Adler. 1982. "The Definitive Treatment of the Borderline Patient." *International Journal of Psychoanalysis and Psychotherapy* 9:51–87.

Chessick, R. D. 1982. "Intensive Psychotherapy of a Borderline Patient." *Archives of General Psychiatry* 39:413–419.

Cohen, D. J. and J. G. Young. 1977. "Neurochemistry and Child Psychiatry." *Journal of the American Academy of Child Psychiatry* 16:353–411.

Cowdry, R. W. and D. L. Gardner. 1988. "Pharmacotherapy of Borderline Personality Disorder." *Archives of General Psychiatry* 45(2):111–119.

Eckrich, S. 1985. "Identification and Treatment of Borderline Personality Disorder." *Social Work* 30(2):166–171.

Egan, J. H. 1988. "Treatment of Borderline Conditions in Adolescence." *Journal of Clinical Psychiatry* (Supplement, September), 49(9):32–35.

Esman, A. 1987. "The Borderline Adolescent." Talk given at the Linden Hill School, Hawthorne, New York, January 14.

Falloon, I. R. H., J. L., Boyd, C. W. McGill, M. Williamson, J. Razani, H. B. Moss,

**134** *Harriette C. Johnson and Dennis E. Goguen*

A. M. Gilderman, and G. M. Simpson. 1985. "Family Management in the Prevention of Morbidity of Schizophrenia." *Archives of General Psychiatry* (September), 42:887–896.

Frances, A. J., J. F. Clarkin, M. Gilmore, S. W. Hurt, and R. Brown. 1984. "Reliability of Criteria for Borderline Personality Disorder: A Comparison of DSM III and the Diagnostic Interview for Borderline Patients." *American Journal of Psychiatry* 141(9):1080–1084.

Frances, A. J. and P. H. Soloff. 1988. "Treating the Borderline Patient with Low-Dose Neuroleptics." *Hospital and Community Psychiatry* 39(3):246–246.

Freed, A. O. 1980. "The Borderline Personality." *Social Casework* 61(9):548:558.

Gardner, D. L., P. B. Lucas, and R. W. Cowdry. 1987. "Soft Sign Neurological Abnormalities in Borderline Personality Disorder and Normal Controls." *Journal of Nervous and Mental Diseases* 175:177–180.

Glatzer, H. T. 1972. "Treatment of Oral Character Neurosis in Group Psychotherapy." In C. J. Sager and H. S. Kaplan, eds., *Progress in Group and Family Therapy*, pp. 54–65. New York: Brunner/Mazel.

Goldberg, S. C., S. C. Schulz, P. M. Schulz, R. J. Resnick, R. M. Hamer, and R. O. Friedel. 1986. "Borderline and Schizotypal Personality Disorders Treated with Low-Dose Thiothixene vs. Placebo." *Archives of General Psychiatry* 43:680–686.

Goldstein, E. G. 1983. "Clinical and Ecological Approaches to the Borderline Client." *Social Casework* 64(6):353–362.

Graziano, R. 1986. "Making the Most of Your Time: Clinical Social Work with a Borderline Patient." *Clinical Social Work Journal* 14:262–275.

Grinker, R., B. Werble, and R. C. Drye. 1986. "The Grinker Study." In M. Stone, ed., *Essential Papers on Borderline Disorders* New York: New York University Press pp. 320–356.

Grobman, J. 1980. "The Borderline Patient in Group Psychotherapy: A Case Report." *International Journal of Group Psychotherapy* 30:299–318.

Grotstein, J. S. 1987. "The Borderline as a Disorder of Self-Regulation." In J. S. Grotstein, M. F. Solomon, and J. A. Lang, eds., *The Borderline Patient*, vol. 1, pp. 347–383. Hillsdale, N.J.: Analytic Press.

Grunebaum, H. and H. Friedman. 1988. "Building Collaborative Relationships with Families of the Mentally Ill." *Hospital and Community Psychiatry* 39(11):1183–1187.

Gunderson, J. G. 1984. *Borderline Personality Disorder.* Washington, D.C.: American Psychiatric Press.

Gunderson, J. G. and D. W. Englund. 1981. "Characterizing the Families of Borderlines." *Psychiatric Clinics of North America* 4(1):159–168.

Gunderson, J. G. and M. T. Singer. 1975. "Defining Borderline Patients: An Overview." *American Journal of Psychiatry* 132:1–10.

Haley, J. 1980. *Leaving Home.* New York: McGraw-Hill.

Hartocollis, P. 1977. *Borderline Personality Disorders.* New York: International Universities Press.

Hodis, L. 1986. "The Borderline Patient: Theoretical and Treatment Considerations from a Developmental Approach." *Clinical Social Work Journal* 14(1):66–78.

Horwitz, L. 1987. "Indications for Group Psychotherapy with Borderline and Narcissistic Patients." *Bulletin of the Menninger Clinic* 51(3):248–260.

Johnson, H. C. 1980. *Human Behavior and the Social Environment: New Perspectives,* Vol. 1: *Behavior, Psychopathology, and the Brain.* New York: Curriculum Concepts.

Johnson, H. C. 1986. "Emerging Concerns in Family Therapy." *Social Work* 31(4):299–306.

Johnson, H. C. 1987. "Biologically Based Deficit in the Identified Patient: Indications for Psychoeducational Strategies." *Journal of Marital and Family Therapy* 13(4):337–348.

Johnson, H. C. 1988. "Where Is the Border? Issues in the Diagnosis and Treatment of the Borderline." *Clinical Social Work Journal* 16(3):243–260.

Kagan, J. 1984. *The Nature of the Child*. New York: Basic Books.

Kernberg, O. 1967. "Borderline Personality Organization." *Journal of the American Psychoanalytic Association* 15:641–685.

Kernberg, O. 1975. *Borderline Conditions and Pathological Narcissism*. New York: Jason Aronson.

Kernberg, O. 1984. *Severe Personality Disorders*. New Haven, Conn.: Yale University Press.

Kety, S. S., D. Rosenthal, P. H. Wender, and F. Schulsinger. 1968. "The Types and Prevalence of Mental Illness in the Biological and Adoptive Families of Adopted Schizophrenics." In D. Rosenthal and S. S. Kety, eds., *The Transmission of Schizophrenia*, pp. 357–384, Pergamon Press. Reprinted in M. Stone, ed., *Essential Papers on Borderline Disorders*. New York: New York University Press.

Kibel, H. D. 1978. "The Rationale for the Use of Group Psychotherapy for Borderline Patients on a Short-Term Unit." *International Journal of Group Psychotherapy* 28:339–358.

Klein, D. F. 1977. "Psychopharmacological Treatment and Delineation of Borderline Disorders." In P. Hartocollis, ed., *Borderline Personality Disorders*, pp. 365–383. New York: International Universities Press.

Kohut, H. 1978. *The Search for the Self*, vols. 1 and 2. New York: International Universities Press.

Liberman, R. P. and T. Eckman. 1981. "Behavior Therapy vs. Insight-Oriented Therapy for Repeated Suicide Attempters." *Archives of General Psychiatry* 38:1126–1130.

Liebowitz, M. R. and D. F. Klein. 1981. "Interrelationship of Hysteroid Dysphoric and Borderline Personality." *Psychiatric Clinics of North America* 4:67–88

Linehan, M. M. 1987. "Dialectical Behavior Therapy for Borderline Personality Disorder." *Bulletin of the Menninger Clinic* 51(3):261–276.

Linehan, M. M., H. E. Armstrong, A. Suarez, and D. J. Allman. 1987. "Dialectical Behavior Therapy with Chronic Parasuicidal Women Meeting Criteria for Borderline Personality Disorder." Unpublished manuscript.

Links, P. S. and M. Steiner. 1988. "Psychopharmacologic Management of Patients with Borderline Personality Disorder." *Canadian Journal of Psychiatry* 33(5):355–359.

Macaskill, N. D. 1982. "Therapeutic Factors in Group Therapy with Borderline Patients." *International Journal of Group Psychotherapy* 32:61–73.

Mahler, M. S. 1971. "A Study of the Separation–Individuation Process." In R. S. Eissler, A. Freud, M. Kris, S. Lustman, A. Solnit eds., *The Psychoanalytic Study of the Child*, pp. 403–424. New Haven, Conn.: Yale University Press.

Masterson, J. F. 1981. *The Narcissistic and Borderline Disorders: An Integrated Approach*. New York: Brunner/Mazel.

McGlashan, T. H. 1986. "The Chestnut Lodge Follow-Up Study, 3:. Long-Term Outcome of Borderline Personalities." *Archives of General Psychiatry* 43:20–30.

Minuchin, S. 1974. *Families and Family Therapy*. Cambridge: Harvard University Press.

Palombo, J. 1983. "Borderline Conditions: A Perspective from Self Psychology." *Clinical Social Work Journal* 11(4):323–338.

Pine, F. 1986. "On the Development of the Borderline-Child-to-Be." *American Journal of Orthopsychiatry* 56(3):450–457.

Quitkin, F. and D. F. Klein. 1969. "To Behavioral Syndromes in Young Adults

Related to Possible Minimal Brain Dysfunction." *Journal of Psychiatric Research* 7:131–142.

Quitkin, F., A. Rifkin, and D. F. Klein. 1976. "Neurologic Soft Signs in Schizophrenia and Character Disorders." *Archives of General Psychiatry* 33:845–853.

Rochford, J. H., T. Detre, G. Tucker, M. Harrow (1970). "Neuropsychological Impairments in Functional Psychiatric Disease." *Archives of General Psychiatry* 22:114–119.

Rohrbaugh, M. 1983. "Swimming Against the Mainstream: Schizophrenia Research." *Family Therapy Networker* (July/August),:28–31, 62.

Schulz, P. M., S. C. Schulz, R. Hamer, R. J. Resnick, R. O. Friedel, and S. C. Goldberg. 1985. "The Impact of Borderline and Schizotypal Personality Disorders on Patients and Their Families." *Hospital and Community Psychiatry* 36(8):879–881.

Schulz, S. C., J. Cornelius, P. M. Schulz, and P. H. Soloff. 1988. "The Amphetamine Challenge Test in Patients with Borderline Disorder." *American Journal of Psychiatry* 145(7):809–814.

Schulz, S. C. and S. C. Goldberg. 1984. "Is Borderline Personality Disorder an Illness?" *Psychopharmacology Bulletin* 20(3):554–560.

Searles, H. F. 1979. "The Countertransference with the Borderline Patient." In J. LeBoit and A. Capponi, eds. *Advances in Psychotherapy with the Borderline Patient.* pp. 309–346. Northvale, N.J.: J. Aronson.

Shelley, E. M. and A. Riester. 1972. "Syndrome of Minimal Brain Damage in Adults." *Diseases of the Nervous System* 33:335–338.

Soloff, P. H., A. George, S. Nathan, P. M. Schulz, R. F. Ulrich, and J. Perel. 1986. "Progress in Pharmacotherapy of Borderline Disorders." *Archives of General Psychiatry* 43:691–697.

Soloff, P. H. and J. W. Millward. 1983. "Psychiatric Disorders in the Families of Borderline Patients." *Archives of General Psychiatry* 40:37–44.

Spitzer, R. L., J. Endicott, and M. Gibbon. 1979. "Crossing the Border Into Borderline Personality and Borderline Schizophrenia: The Development of Criteria." *Archives of General Psychiatry* 36:17–24.

Stone, M. H. 1980. *The Borderline Syndrome: Constitution, Personality, and Adaptation.* New York: McGraw-Hill.

Stone, M. H. 1986. *Essential Papers on Borderline Disorders: One Hundred Years at the Border.* New York: New York University Press.

Stone, M. H. 1987. "Psychotherapy of Borderline Patients in Light of Long-Term Follow-Up." *Bulletin of the Menninger Clinic* 51(3):231–247.

Volkan, V. D. 1986. "Six Phases of Psychoanalytic Psychotherapy of Borderline Patients." In J. S. Grotstein, M. Solomon, and J. A. Lang, eds., *The Borderline Patient,* New York: Analytic Press.

Waldinger, R. J. 1987. "Intensive Psychodynamic Therapy with Borderline Patients: An Overview." *American Journal of Psychiatry* 144(3):267–274.

Wender, P. H., F. W. Reimherr, and D. R. Wood. 1981. "Attention Deficit Disorder ('Minimal Brain Dysfunction') in Adults: A Replication Study of Diagnosis and Drug Treatment." *Archives of General Psychiatry* 38(4):449–456.

Yalom, I. D. 1975. *The Theory and Practice of Group Psychotherapy,* 2d ed. New York: Basic Books.

# 4

# Chronic Physical Illness and Disability

▼

## RITA BECK BLACK
## JOAN O. WEISS

At first glance, a paper on chronic physical illnesses and disabilities appears to include such a broad array of assessment and intervention issues as to prevent any focused consideration of practice details. After all, the large number and types of chronic illnesses result in many different physical difficulties and medical prognoses. For example, what commonalities exist between the challenges faced by the family with a young child recently diagnosed with severe asthma, the older woman recovering from a stroke, the teenager who faces paralysis following a car accident, and the middle-aged executive facing lifelong changes after a heart attack?

Although such variations in physical events and psychosocial contexts demand different knowledge and skills from social work, medical, and other professionals, persons with chronic illnesses and disabilities also share a number of profoundly important similarities as they live with their physical limitations and abilities in our society. This paper considers this common core of psychosocial experience and the principles it suggests for social workers who wish to work with chronically ill and disabled individuals and their families as they face the challenges posed by their medical status and the meaning they attribute to it over time.

## PROBLEM DOMAIN

A thorough examination of the "problems" that arise in chronic illness calls for a dual focus on both the medical and the sociological definitions of illness and disability. A purely medical, physiological perspective is suggested by a frequently used definition of a chronic illness as one that lasts more than three months in a year or that leads to continuous hospitalization for at least one month in a year (Hobbs, Perrin, and Ireys 1985; Pless and Pinkerton 1975). Similarly, many national health statistics on chronic illness and disabilities refer to the number of days that activity is limited or the number of days lost from school or work.

The shared implications of many chronic illnesses and disabilities are reflected in the broader definition of *handicapped individual* found in the Rehabilitation Act of 1973, P.L. 93–112, as amended by P.L. 95–602, Section 7:

1. any person whose physical or mental impairment substantially limits one or more of the person's major life activities;
2. has a record of such impairment; or
3. is regarded as having such an impairment.

The Rehabilitation Act affirms that handicaps are sequelae of chronic illnesses and disabilities and emphasizes the contribution of societal perceptions to producing handicaps. Definitions are broadened further by the stipulation that chronic illnesses result in different burdens of varying severity. For example, Hobbs, Perrin, and Ireys (1985) argued that a chronic illness can be considered "severe" when it results in serious physical difficulties, major financial burdens, serious emotional or psychological problems for the affected individual, or major disruptions in family life.

As the focus of attention shifts away from the biological nature of a chronic health problem, one moves into the realm of the *social construction* of disability. Scholars and activists in the disability rights movement (Bowe 1980; DeJong 1979; Fine and Asch 1988; Gliedman and Roth 1980) have pointed out that people with chronic illnesses and disabilities share the sociological situation of discrimination in our society and therefore should be viewed as an oppressed minority group. This oppression takes such forms as outright prejudice, job discrimination, and misconceptions that exaggerate the true limitations of a given handicap (Gliedman and Roth 1980).

Fine and Asch (1988) deepened this sociological analysis by pointing out the parallels between feminism and the disability rights movement. Just as feminist researchers have "unhooked notions of gender from those of sex," so too have disability activists insisted that *"disability* (the *biological* condition) be conceptually disentangled from the *handicap* (the *social* ramifications of the condition" (p. 5, italics in text). Much as women's biological status as females has been used to assume certain inherent limitations in what they can accomplish, so too has disease status been generalized to characterize the disabled person (Hobbs, Perrin, and Ireys 1985) Thus, the child with cystic fibrosis is referred to as a *cystic* or the adult with epilepsy becomes an *epileptic.* Such overgeneralization of illness status "limits, in a profound but subtle fashion, the future one might envision for the [person]" (Hobbs, Perrin, and Ireys 1985:55).

This view of disability as a social construction represents an inherently ecological perspective, one that views "handicaps" as being the result of an interaction between people and their environments. The ecosystems perspective of social work practice (Meyer 1976, 1983; Germain and Gitterman 1980) is congruent with this outlook in its call for a professional stance that considers the individual and family in transaction with their immediate and larger society. For the practitioner, this means recognition that, to the extent that disabled persons and their families share society's discriminatory views of handicapped persons, they are likely to experience greater personal difficulty and to feel less hopefulness about the future. Similarly, professionals, who have grown up with those same societal prejudices around them, may categorize clients and develop treatment strategies based on unexamined assumptions about the limitations imposed by specific physical problems.

## SOCIETAL CONTEXT

Even the briefest review of the societal context of chronic illness and disability confirms the lack of a coherent public policy to guide service delivery for this population (Fox 1986; Hobbs, Perrin, and Ireys 1985; Walkover 1988). Despite the prevalence of chronic conditions, the health care system has had difficulty shifting away from its earlier focus on the treatment of infectious diseases and acute illnesses. Ironically, recent pressures to help people with AIDS, who need a comprehensive range of medical and social supports, have highlighted the deficiencies in current services for the chronically ill (Fox 1986).

The patchwork nature of society's response to the disabled is reflected in the variety of legislative initiatives and funding sources (Hobbs, Perrin, and Ireys 1985). Early attention to children's needs came in Title V of the Social Security Act of 1935, which provided assistance to children through Crippled Children's Services programs in the states and territories and through other categorical programs such as those for hemophilia and pediatric pulmonary conditions. The 1970s saw the passage of the Developmentally Disabled Assistance and Bill of Rights Act of 1975 (P.L. 94–142), which provides assistance to children with a wide range of chronic conditions, and the Education for All Handicapped Children's Act of 1975, which provides federal subsidies to improve educational opportunities. An increased recognition of the importance of early intervention resulted in the recent passage of P.L. 99–457, which supports educational services for children with special needs starting at birth. In addition, funds are available to some health-impaired children through Medicaid and the Supplemental Security Program, both under the Social Security Act.

Of particular significance to adults with disabilities was the passage of Section 504 of the 1973 Rehabilitation Act, which bars employment discrimination on the basis of disability in federally funded programs. The 1974 amendments to that act also developed a comprehensive definition of disability (cited in the previous section above) that considers the handicapping potential of society's stigmatizing views of certain disabilities.

The major cash transfer programs for disabled adults are Disability Insurance (DI) and Supplemental Security Income (SSI). Disability insurance helps those who have been workers with Social Security coverage and entitles the recipient to Medicare coverage after two years on DI. Supplemental Security Income focuses on low-income children and adults with no work experience or too little to be eligible for DI and provides medical coverage under Medicaid (Mudrick 1988). Smaller numbers of disabled adults receive benefits under Aid for Families with Dependent Children (AFDC; for low-income families in which there is a disabled parent), veterans' pensions, and workers compensation (for workers injured on the job).

Although the preceding review of legislation and funding confirms the gains that have been made on behalf of the rights of seriously health-impaired children and adults, significant barriers in health care, education, employment, and income support continue to impede their attempts to participate in our society to the fullest extent of their abilities.

In particular, the lack of comprehensive services in the health care system remains an important source of distress for many in this population. Hobbs, Perrin, and Ireys (1985:166–167) identified the following continuing problems that arise out of the narrow, disease-specific focus of services for the chronically ill. First, the concentration of services for chronic illnesses within specialty centers in larger cities limits access to quality services for many. Second, the services that are available vary tremendously from one disease to another. For example, the presence of an interested specialist or a particular comprehensive clinic can mean a dramatically higher level of services for one disorder than for another in the same locale. And third, communication among providers and coordination of services are often missing, although essential, ingredients.

Although educational opportunities for some children with chronic illnesses and disabilities were expanded with the passage of the special-education initiatives of the 1970s, many chronically ill children are not easily or appropriately served by special-education programs. Since special education itself is often stigmatizing, many parents and children resist this designation. Regular education programs are appropriate for many health-impaired children with additions or modifications to health services in the regular school setting. However, the decline in the numbers of school health nurses and related services represents a barrier to mainstream education for many children with chronic health conditions (Hobbs, Perrin, and Ireys 1985).

For the disabled adult attempting to participate in the labor force, antidiscrimination laws have provided leverage for combating the more obvious and extreme prejudicial barriers. More difficult to counter are the handicapping effects of inadequate special-education programs, architectural and transportation barriers, job structures that allow few opportunities for part-time or flexible work hours, or salary and benefits inadequate to cover such extra expenses as medical care, home attendants, or specialized transportation assistance.

Programs that replace wages when a worker becomes disabled or that provide income for those not in the labor force form a patchwork of supports, none of which bases eligibility solely on the nature and the severity of physical disability (Mudrick 1988). Instead, eligibility rests on such non-illness-related criteria as required periods of work covered by Social Security, veteran's status, or poverty. Under these programs, disabled women in particular are less likely to achieve eligibility because household work does not qualify as gainful employment and women's more frequent patterns of part-time participation in the labor force often disqualify them from Social Security coverage (Mudrick 1988).

## RISKS AND NEEDS OF POPULATION

Although estimates of the incidence of chronic illnesses and disabilities (their frequency) and their prevalence (the number of those affected by the disorders at a given time) vary with the definitions used for illness and disability, the relative contribution of severe and chronic illnesses to mortality and morbidity has increased over the last several decades (Fox 1986; Hobbs, Perrin, and Ireys 1985; Manton, Patrick, and Johnson 1987).

The prevention of many infectious childhood diseases and improved technology for the care of newborns and young infants has allowed survival in the face of even serious health problems and disabling conditions. After reviewing a wide range of surveys reporting on childhood illness, Hobbs, Perrin, and Ireys (1985) concluded that perhaps 10 to 15 percent of children in the United States have some chronic health impairment, and that perhaps 1 percent of those problems are so severe that the health care system is unlikely to serve them more than moderately well. Any definition of severe chronic illness that includes severe burdens on physical, monetary, psychological, and family functioning leads to an estimate of perhaps 1 million children with serious chronic illness out of 7.5 million under 18 years with chronic health conditions. If one considers the broader impact on the family of each child with a chronic illness, the number of those affected rises even higher.

As adults grow older, they face increasing chances of experiencing chronic illness or disability in themselves or in a close, family member (Kermis 1986). For example, while less than 4 percent of children under age 17 are limited in activity as a result of a chronic health condition, the comparable figure for adults 45 to 64 is 25 percent (National Center for Health Statistics 1979, as cited in Hobbs, Perrin, and Ireys 1985). In 1975, it was estimated that 60 percent of the health costs in the United States resulted from chronic disease (Rice 1979), and there has been increasing recognition that the majority of patient services in the health care system now go to those with chronic illnesses (Fox 1986).

For those citizens who are poor, who lack education, and who are from racial minority groups, the risks of chronic illness and disability are even higher. Inadequate or no prenatal care increases the risk of mortality or later difficulties for a baby, yet prenatal care is least likely to be obtained by poor women who are unmarried, especially those who are young, who are not well educated, who live in rural areas, or who are Hispanic (Brown 1988). Poor children are more likely to have more illnesses and more severe illness than their non-poor counterparts (Starfield 1982).

Racial differentials in health status are also evident in comparisons of the percentage of persons with limitations in activity due to chronic conditions: blacks outnumber whites by a ratio of 1.4 among those 45 to 64 years of age (National Center for Health Statistics 1985, as cited in Andersen, Mullner, and Cornelius 1987).

As discussed in the previous section, counts of the number of disability days or the number of people with activity limitations due to chronic conditions tell little about the many aspects of individual and family functioning placed at risk by chronic health problems. For children, the opportunity to achieve the maximum level of educational attainment may be jeopardized by numerous sick days, inadequate special-education arrangements, and incorrect assumptions about the limitations imposed by their illness (Hobbs, Perrin, and Ireys 1985). Adults often face similar difficulties as career choices are limited, job advancement is curtailed, or the opportunity for productive work is foreclosed. As noted earlier, these limitations may result from environmental rather than medical difficulties. Prejudice, ignorance, and a lack of flexibility in arranging work schedules frequently combine to cut off options for disabled individuals (Bowe 1980; Kleinfield 1979; Pettyjohn 1988).

Family harmony is placed at risk as parents struggle to integrate a disabled child into the family system (Hobbs, Perrin, and Ireys 1985; Rolland 1988) or as spouses attempt to readjust roles and responsibilities in response to a decline in physical capabilities (Corbin and Strauss 1988). Siblings are also at risk of inadvertent neglect by overburdened parents, of teasing and exclusion by peers, and of limitations on personal options posed by the financial strains placed on the family system by the illness (Hobbs, Perrin, and Ireys 1985). Certainly, when the chronic illness occurs in a family already burdened by poverty, poor education, or racial discrimination, the risks of distress and lowered functioning are heightened.

## PROGRAMS AND SOCIAL WORK SERVICES

The previous review of the definitions, risks, and societal contexts of chronic illnesses and disabilities highlights the multifaceted nature of the service needs of this client population. As a result, these clients and families often work with a broad, and sometimes bewildering, array of medical, social work, and other helping professionals, the exact composition of the array varying with the context of service delivery. Those settings in which social workers provide most of their assistance to the chronically ill and disabled include health settings, schools, and community settings.

In health settings, social workers frequently function as members of *multidisciplinary teams* that serve persons with chronic and disabling health problems in specialty programs devoted to similar clusters of illnesses (e.g., renal, orthopedic, or gastrointestinal clinics). In this context, social workers often become a resource to which families turn for guidance in their negotiations with other health professionals, for referral to community resources, and for personal support at times of medical crises or changes in the course of the illness. Unfortunately, families' access to social workers in health settings may be limited by the size of the social work staff. Many smaller hospitals do not employ social workers, and even the larger programs in academic medical centers often employ only one social worker to cover a large and busy clinic. The hospital-based social worker may also face difficulties in providing referrals and coordinating services for families from a wide geographic area. Communities differ widely in available services, and the fragmentation of programs can frustrate efforts to develop a coherent service package for many clients.

*Rehabilitation programs* also exist as part of the health sector but specialize in remediating disabilities and teaching alternative approaches to managing the tasks of daily living. The social worker functions not only as a member of a distinct discipline but also as a member of the interdisciplinary team that is at the core of rehabilitation services (Russell 1988). Treatment plans in rehabilitation extend into the community and often include the involvement of close family and friends. Social workers, with their knowledge of family functioning and community resources, are particularly equipped to make important contributions on rehabilitation teams (Russell 1988).

*School social workers* become involved with affected children and their families either as providers of services to augment regular classroom programs or as members of interdisciplinary teams mandated to serve children in need of special-education services. They often act as pivotal resources, orchestrating ongoing communications between school personnel, health professionals, the child, and the parents. The professional tasks vary from providing direct mental health assistance to advocating for policies that prevent inappropriate special-education designations for intellectually able but physically handicapped youngsters.

Similarly, social workers can be found in the range of *community programs* and *voluntary agencies* that provide services for disabled persons. Social services that can benefit clients and families with chronic health problems include 1) those that support and reinforce the caretaking abilities of the client or parent, e.g., family or mental health counseling, and anticipatory child guidance; 2) those that supplement care, e.g., respite care, homemakers, and transportation; and 3) those that provide substitute care, e.g., foster and adoption services, and long-term care facilities (Hobbs, Perrin, and Ireys 1977). Social workers employed in these non-illness-specific social service settings are critical providers of services for this population but are often hampered in their efforts by the same fragmentation of programs and limited resources that frustrate the social worker in health settings. The special needs of certain families with very rare disorders or those whose illness requires very specialized service arrangements also tend to lose urgency in programs designed to serve broad populations (Hobbs, Perrin, and Ireys 1977).

*Disease-oriented voluntary organizations* and *self-help groups* are another important component of community services. Many of the larger organizations include social workers on their professional staff and engage in active efforts to influence policymakers and legislators on behalf of their constituencies. Social workers sometimes serve as facilitators of *mutual aid groups* sponsored by these organizations. The sibling support group described later in this chapter is an excellent example of such a group. Self-help groups offer their members potentially important help by providing a sense of cohesiveness or belonging; a universalizing sense that one's problems are not unique; the opportunity to help others; a sharing of common values and beliefs; and an exchange of information (Borman 1985). Social workers' involvement with self-help groups also includes referrals to the groups, service on their professional advisory committees, service as consultants to the groups, and initiating or helping in the development of new groups (Silverman 1980). Exciting opportunities exist for social workers to collaborate with these independent groups in developing more responsive clinical services and advocating for legal and social changes to improve opportunities for children and adults with chronic illnesses and disabilities (Black and Weiss 1989).

## DIFFERENTIAL CLINICAL ASSESSMENTS AND INTERVENTIONS

As social workers assist patients and their families in moving toward an integration of chronic illness into their lives, they direct their practice efforts toward increasing mastery and empowering clients. In this context, empowerment becomes the continuous development of new competence simultaneous with the ongoing or advancing course of the illness (Coelho, Hamburg, and Adams 1974). These principles translate into a practice stance that emphasizes collaborative relationships with clients, brief episodes of service at critical points in the course of the illness, and primary attention directed to maximizing clients' skills in problem solving and in making use of the people in their illness-related and non-illness-related social networks. The following concepts are helpful in assessing clients' needs and in developing interventions designed to empower clients and their families.

Corbin and Straus' (1985) concept of the *trajectory of a chronic illness* highlights both the physical unfolding of an illness or disability and the changing nature of the "work" generated by disorders over time. The evolving "shape" of a trajectory is influenced by an interplay of the illness itself, the reactions of the involved participants, and the personal and environmental contingencies that arise and affect the trajectory. Trajectories may show stable or unstable patterns, upward or downward progressions, and acute and comeback periods, all denoting the need for different types of management work by the affected persons and their loved ones.

The identification of phases helps to specify the personal and professional tasks that must be done at various points on the illness trajectory. For those whose illness has a more gradual onset or an ambiguous symptomatology, there may be a prolonged process of seeking for the meaning of symptoms, a "diagnostic quest" (Corbin and Strauss 1988). The longer process of living with a chronic illness (Rolland 1988) includes an initial crisis phase that begins before diagnosis and may extend into the early period of adjustment. The second, chronic phase is the "long haul" period of the illness trajectory, whose characteristics are determined by the severity of the illness and the extent to which it is progressive, relapsing, or constant in nature. The terminal phase occurs when death looms as an inevitable event that dominates family life.

It also is helpful to think about the stages through which clients may pass as they acquire illness-related coping skills. Matson and Brooks (1977) described the process of adjusting to a chronic illness as often starting with an initial period of denial. Patients and family members may attempt initially to conceal the symptoms, seek out authorities to deny the illness, refuse offers of help, and cling to previous activities and values. As minimal acceptance of the diagnosis develops over time, the second stage, resistance, may emerge. Here the client says "It won't get me down!" and searches actively for cures and treatment. As patients attempt to gain some control over their disease, they may become active in support programs and may seek out other patients. However, help may still be accepted with some reluctance. The third stage, affirmation, is often a time of self-confrontation and grieving for the loss of the former self (or the loved one). A key task becomes learning to accept help without feeling devalued. Work also begins on rearranging one's priorities in life. The final stage, integration, is exemplified by the comment, "I know it's part of my life, but I don't think much about it." This is a stage that often not only takes a long time to achieve but may also require remastery after setbacks, remissions, or other changes in the illness trajectory. However, the positive coping of this stage is evident when patients and families deal with the tasks presented by the illness and use help when necessary, while also spending energy and thought on matters other than the disability.

Thus, for social workers, a first step in assessment is consideration of the past and the projected shape of the client's illness trajectory. The complexity of such assessments becomes evident when one recognizes that both physical and emotional issues influence the impact of an illness (Corbin and Strauss 1988). Information on the likely physical course of an illness is critical, but it is inadequate to predict a trajectory for specific clients. For example, some persons manage to maintain a sense of personal integrity and self-worth despite a stormy and erratic illness course. Others express despair and hopelessness in the face of physical prognoses that suggest considerable stability and rehabilitative potential. Consideration of the developmental stage of the affected person and the family must also enter into trajectory predictions.

Thus, a background knowledge of 1) the coping tasks generated by the physical symptoms and the course of the illness, 2) the recency of the onset of the illness or disability and its prognosis, 3) the developmental stage of the client, and 4) the frequently seen phases of personal coping (Matson and Brooks 1977) allows social workers to begin work with some general predictions about the practical, emotional, and family tasks that will need to be addressed. In addition, as social workers enter into this assessment process, they also ask questions about the experiences of that family since the first emergence of the presenting health problem and their experiences with other difficulties: What kinds of experiences have they already lived through? What have been their physical, emotional, and family struggles? Has the family faced other significant stressors in the past or concurrently with the disability? What strategies have they used to cope with these difficulties and which have worked for them? Answers to such questions begin to help the social worker form a picture of the illness work in which this family have been engaged and the contributions they already have made to shaping their own and their loved one's illness trajectories (Corbin and Strauss 1988).

The active involvement of client and family in this assessment process enhances mastery by providing them with an opportunity both to teach and to learn about the illness and the work it entails for them. Information is shared, and competencies as well as deficiencies in coping resources and skills are brought forward for discussion.

Since identity is so often linked to one's body and its capacity for action, body failure and the inability to perform the usual tasks may be experienced as a "loss of self" (Corbin and Strauss 1988). Thus, recognition of the centrality of one's self-image and the meanings attached to body failure guide the social worker in assessing the *personal interpretations or appraisals* of the illness made by the affected individual and the family. We use the term *appraisal* here in order to emphasize an active process of "searching, sifting, and evaluating cues" (Hatfield 1987:67; Lazarus, Averill, and Opton 1974) in one's changing situation.

Personal appraisals of the impact of an illness also develop from experiences with attempted *coping efforts*. In a very real sense, self-esteem grows out of actual success in coping with problems (Hatfield 1987) and requires the trio of adequate information, satisfactory internal conditions, and the autonomy and skills sufficient for choosing and altering coping strategies (Coelho, Hamburg, and Adams 1974; Black, Dornan, and Allegrante 1986). The maintenance of positive self-esteem may be a formidable task in the face of the social and environmental obstacles encountered by persons with chronic illnesses as they attempt to find friends, to obtain proper schooling, and to enter into satisfying employment.

An assessment of the nature and sources of clients' self-appraisals requires a consideration of the combined impact of psychological and social factors in the experience of chronic illness (Corbin and Strauss 1988) and will suggest interventions that emphasize different elements of the trio of information, internal conditions, and skills. For example, in a recently disabled young woman, depressive feelings and lack of follow-through on recommended therapies may reflect a basic sense of identity confusion. As a result of her diminished physical ability to act on the environment, she feels worthless. In addition, she is just entering adulthood and is still struggling to achieve a clear sense of who she is as an adult woman. Interventions for this client are likely to include supportive counseling that provides a safe haven for sharing intense feelings of despair about her altered feminity. In addition, the social worker and the client might identify ways in which she can begin to take charge of her illness management and regain some sense of competency. Entirely different issues influence the single father of a child with a serious, chronic illness. When questioned about his sad affect and unkempt appearance, he, like the young woman, might describe feeling depressed and lacking the energy to deal with many of his responsibilities. However, those feelings might be found to result only partly from feelings of personal confusion or grief over his son's illness. Of more immediate importance might be his accumulated fatigue and frustration because of the daily physical care requirements of his child and his limited financial resources to pay for outside help. This assessment would suggest that the first intervention priorities would be to provide him with current information on low-cost respite-care services and to rehearse with him strategies for assertively negotiating for those services. Support might also be offered to encourage him in identifying recreational outlets with other adults.

Although consideration of potential sources of support or strain from a client's *social network* is a standard element of all social work assessments, this task takes on a special meaning for families facing chronic illnesses and disabilities. Their natural or non-illness-related network of relatives and friends may offer crucial understanding and practical assistance at critical points in the illness trajectory. However, contacts with even close friends and relatives may dwindle as the patient and the family pour all their available energies into illness-related activities and concerns, or social interactions may become strained as a result of unspoken or awkward questions about the disabled person (Terkelsen 1987).

When assessing areas of potential support or strain in a client's social network, it is important to consider the personal importance to the client of persons in the network and to set intervention priorities accordingly. For example, the grandparent who lives nearby and is a frequent visitor in the household may be a critical member of the family's network. That grandparent's apparent denial of a child's illness or criticism of the parents' approaches to giving care might be significant sources of strain. Here, the social worker might decide to intervene with one or all of three approaches: 1) helping the parents' rehearse strategies for discussing the illness with their parents: 2) providing the grandparents with published information about the illness; and 3) offering the grandparents opportunities to discuss directly with the social worker their own concerns about the child.

When a client or family lacks significant contacts with a non-illness-related circle of friends, assessment includes a realistic consideration of the practical drains on the family's time and energies as well as the possibility that they are having difficulty moving toward a balance of illness-related and non-illness-related involvements. Thus, interventions might vary from helping a family obtain home care assistance to supporting their efforts to develop new social interests. Sometimes, the social worker helps just by lending support and approval that allow a family to do a "less-than-perfect" job in their illness-related work.

Persons with chronic illnesses also acquire a second, illness-related network comprised of 1) the professionals who provide them with services and 2) other persons with disabilities and their families (Terkelsen 1987). Since chronic illnesses and disabilities require at least episodic collaborations with professionals for optimum illness management, an assessment of the quality of the available and perceived support from professional caregivers becomes an important task for the social worker. Clients may encounter difficulties because of their own limited skills in expressing their concerns and asserting their needs. On the other hand, some professionals provide more comprehensive and individualized attention to their clients. Social work interventions to enhance clients' skills in personal advocacy may be in order in either situation.

Social work practitioners also give emphasis to determining whether clients have a sufficient opportunity to develop supportive contacts with other disabled persons or their caregivers. In effect, these peers represent an alternative form of "neighborhood," based on need rather than geography (Terkelsen 1987:149). Professionally led support groups are one vehicle for bringing together people with shared concerns, particularly those who face more complicated coping issues because of situational or personality factors. Appropriate self-help groups also should be considered an important referral not only because they provide opportunities for members to meet others on a common ground but also because of the opportunities they provide for autonomous functioning and leadership outside the confines of professional guidance.

## CASE ILLUSTRATION

This case concerns a young girl who was born with a disabling genetic condition, achondroplasia. It is the most common form of dwarfism and also results in a prominent head, disproportionate limbs and certain orthopedic problems, an altered gait, and slower developmental milestones. Intelligence is not affected. Although achondroplasia is genetic, when neither parent of an affected child has the disorder the child's illness results from a new mutation. The parents thus carry no increased risk of having additional offspring with the disorder, but the person with achondroplasia has a 50 percent chance of passing the disorder on to her or his children.

The primary social worker in this case was involved with the family over a period of two decades. Her place of employment was the genetics clinic of a major teaching hospital. The family was seen in this clinic for initial diagnostic evaluations and then periodically throughout the client's childhood for ongoing monitoring and referral to other specialists. This social worker also organized and led support groups for parents of children of short stature. She and the parents in these groups eventually went on to host a national symposium for other families and professionals. In addition, the social worker was a consultant to a national voluntary organization for people of short stature. In her work with that organization, she was instrumental in developing some of the support groups that were used by family members in the case that follows.

This is the story of Jessica, but it also illustrates the issues faced over the life cycle by many individuals with disabilities and their families. It shows how personal appraisals of the meaning of a disorder and developmental tasks change over time and vary among different family members. Jessica's experiences also tell us about the challenging hills and the relatively quiet plateaus that are part of life with many chronic disorders. We see how the social worker makes ongoing assessments of the changing needs of a client and the family and uses those assessments in determining the magnitude and types of professional assistance needed at a given stage in the illness trajectory. Often, as in Jessica's case, important sources of help are those who have similar disabilities or family members who share similar challenges in living with a loved one who is chronically ill or disabled. Ever-present themes for both the ill person and the family include finding a balance between illness- and non-illness-related concerns and interests, and maintaining a maximum level of independence while also acknowledging realistic needs to seek out and accept appropriate help.

Jessica, the youngest of three children, was born to Arthur, an accountant, and Sally, a part-time legal secretary, when they were in their late 30s. They were both second-generation Americans, with no private income other than what they earned. They were members of the Unitarian church but attended irregularly.

Jessica's brother, Adam, was 8 at the time of her birth, and Michael was 5. Both boys were developing normally, and Sally's third pregnancy had gone just as smoothly as the previous two.

She had had prenatal testing (amniocentesis) in her second trimester because of her age, and the test results had not revealed any particular problems with the fetus. In fact, both Arthur and Sally were thrilled to learn that their baby was female. Their bonding with Jessica was affirmed in that second trimester as they began to imagine a beautiful little girl who looked like her mother.

Sally was awake but groggy when Jessica was born. She later recalled that there was a lot of whispering among the medical staff in the delivery room and that they rushed off with the baby for "cleaning up" before Sally could see her. When she was more fully alert and Arthur was with her, Sally asked to see the doctor. When the pediatrician finally appeared, he told them immediately that they had an achondroplastic, dwarfed daughter and that they should consider placing her for adoption. "Otherwise," he exclaimed, "you will be beset by her illnesses and will have to pay for repeated surgery. Besides, she will undoubtedly be retarded, and everyone will laugh at her because she will walk like a duck. She will be considered a freak by society and will probably end up in the circus." Unfortunately, this physician had let his personal biases block any acknowledgment of his profound lack of factual information about this disorder.

Arthur and Sally were in a state of shock, too numb to be angry at the doctor who was telling them what to do. At first, Arthur did not admit, even to himself, that he prayed that first night that Jessica would die. He was not feeling strong enough to handle a lifetime of crises, of repeated illnesses and surgeries, much less having a child who would be considered a freak. He only wanted the little girl that he had dreamed about. Sally, on the other hand, thought that the doctor must be wrong. She demanded to see her baby.

Jessica appeared to have a large head, and her arms and legs were tiny, but she looked beautiful to Sally. Still, the nurse seemed reluctant to spend as much time with Sally as with the other mothers on the floor, who also appeared to be uncomfortable talking with Sally about her baby. When Sally asked questions about Jessica, the nurse did not answer them directly.

Because of the nature of Jessica's condition, the genetics unit was notified, and the social worker was asked to speak to the parents before discharge from the hospital. The worker was also informed that Sally seemed to be withdrawing from caring for Jessica. Unfortunately, the delay meant that the social worker entered only after those painful first days of miscommunication between the parents and health professionals. Her preparatory discussions with the pediatrician and the nurses had alerted her to the staff's ignorance about achondroplasia and their stigmatizing reactions to this family. Thus, in her first contacts with Arthur and Sally, the social worker had to strike a balance in attending to their multiple needs: 1) to obtain correct facts about the disorder: 2) to share their initial reactions of grief, disappointment, and fear about the future; and 3) to obtain practical suggestions about the next steps they needed to take after returning home.

The social worker acted on the first and third items quite quickly and simply. She immediately provided the family with material written for parents on achondroplasia. She then did a little advocacy within the hospital system to speed up the scheduling of a predischarge session with a doctor who specialized in this disorder. Appointments with the genetics clinic were also scheduled before discharge. The social worker and the parents worked together on the emotional side of the parents' reactions and needs in the hospital, and this work carried over into the parents' clinic contacts in the next few months.

The social worker began by asking about not only what they had been told about their child but also how they had been told, whether they were together when they received the diagnosis, and what they had understood. These questions helped them to begin with the social worker, and the parents moved quickly from these immediate experiences into their disappointments and fears over not having the child they had been expecting. They wondered what they might have done to cause the defect. What the social worker offered at this early stage was a safe haven for discussion of these difficult issues and validation of the appropriateness of the parents' strong feelings.

The worker began to anticipate with the parents what they might face in their relations with other family members, such as their young sons and Jessica's grandparents. Together, they considered how different family members might react to the social stigma associated with Jessica's disability and to consider how strategies used successfully in previous family crises might be adapted to the current situation.

Jessica's brothers seemed too young to comprehend the implications of Jessica's disorder. She seemed like any crying newborn to them. The grandparents proved more of a challenge, however. Jessica's maternal grandparents had come to visit her in the hospital two days after she was born. Her grandfather had worked as a truckdriver when he came to American from Poland; his wife had taken care of the home and their two children. They had longed for a granddaughter and were overjoyed to learn that their dreams had come true. When they learned about Jessica's problems, they immediately exclaimed, "What have we done?"

Arthur had a good relationship with his parents and called them immediately. However, they were unable to believe that anything could be wrong with their first granddaughter and reinforced Sally and Arthur's initial tendencies to deny any imperfection in the baby. Arthur's mother, in fact, began to crochet a large 2-year-size outfit for her granddaughter, saying, "She'll grow into it, dear—you'll see!"

In discussions with Sally and Arthur and the few brief contacts that could be arranged with the grandparents, the social worker tried to help all parties develop greater understanding of their feelings and needs. Grandparents may be in the process of retirement and looking to their children and grandchildren to carry on their own dreams. They may hope for a bond with estranged children; they may want a grandchild to make up for their own and their children's shortcomings; they just may want reassurance that their own positive values and character traits will continue in future generations. Thus, grandparents may find it difficult to confront the birth of a grandchild who faces a life of stigmatizing disability.

Many parents may still be seeking their own parents' support and approval. If they are trying to impress their parents with their capabilities, they may be devastated when their child is born with or develops a serious illness or disability. Parents who are uncertain about being accepted by their own parents may find it difficult even to tell the grandparents about the child's disorder. They may tell the social worker that they do not want the grandparents to be brought into the hospital or to be part of the important process of history taking.

Stresses between parents also may arise as mothers and fathers struggle to absorb the narcissistic blow each experiences to her or his self-esteem. Differences in the parents' coping styles can become an additional source of stress; a father's increase in work hours, which is his own desparate effort to relieve his pain, may be interpreted instead by the mother as his not caring. Sexual relations may be disrupted, particularly when the parents fear that they may have a second impaired child.

Sally and Arthur seemed to have had a solid marriage before Jessica's birth and were able to share their initial feelings fairly well. The social worker had noted, however, that Arthur's early comments suggested hesitation and uncertainty about this baby, whereas Jessica's initial reaction tended toward denial of any serious problems. After a few weeks at home, Sally did reach out to the worker with concerns about Arthur's seeming ambivalence about Jessica and her own increasing feelings of isolation. Indeed, Sally herself was becoming more aware each day that Jessica did not look like their sons, that she appeared "different." The social worker told Sally that her concerns were important and not uncommon among families in the early phase of learning about their child's disability. She suggested that it might be the right time for Sally and Arthur to meet another couple who had gone through this experience with their own dwarfed daughter, now 8 years old. The social worker was acquainted with this couple through her work with the organization for people of short stature. She also knew that they had been trained by a social worker to be peer helpers and had been quite successful in outreach efforts to other parents in similar situations.

Sally and Arthur flooded the other couple with questions: Would Jessica be able to go to a regular public school? Would she date, marry, get a job, be happy? Although the other parents certainly could not begin to answer all these questions, they provided reassurance, based on their own experience, that Sally, Arthur, Jessica, and the boys could cope and even thrive. Although the social worker had already told Arthur and Sally about the support organization, she suspected that they were not ready to meet many adult dwarfs, even those who were doing well. Contact with these trained peer-support parents provided an alternative and gentler first step for Arthur and Sally. Not long afterward, Arthur also joined a fathers' group sponsored by the organization. The men met regularly for six months, and the group provided them with an accepting environment where they could express feelings without having to worry about hurting their wives.

During Jessica's preschool years, the social worker's periodic contacts with Arthur and Sally centered principally on their acknowledged difficulties in letting Jessica have appropriate amounts of independence. As Sally put it, "It is all too easy to do for Jessica instead of demanding that she do for herself." Unlike children with a developmental disability whose cognitive and social development are below those for their chronological age, Jessica had delays that were limited to her physical development. She deserved the same intellectual and social challenges as her same-aged peers.

Unfortunately, the worker's efforts proved less than a total success during these early years. Although Arthur and Sally came to an intellectual understanding of Jessica's need to develop a sense of independence, they often retreated from the painful gaze of strangers in the shopping center and the blunt questions of other children. They were overprotective of Jessica, not allowing her to go to preschool or to cross the street, even if Adam, her older brother, held her hand. They spoke for Jessica when friends addressed questions to her. They did not let her make decisions about what play dress to wear, for fear she would make herself look even more different than other little girls her age. Arthur and Sally were not ready to develop the middleground approaches that the social worker suggested they might look for in helping Jessica assume greater autonomy. The worker watched in frustration as Jessica developed a slight speech impediment and became painfully shy.

When Jessica began first grade it became obvious that behind her veil of timidity was a superior intellect. However, she also became more acutely aware of her short stature and disabilities. She became more socially withdrawn as classmates asked why she was so small for her age and why she "walked funny." Her short legs prevented her from keeping up with the group during games in the schoolyard, and her difficulties with fine motor skills impeded her initial efforts to learn to write.

The social worker suspected that Arthur and Sally were going to find it very difficult on their own to provide Jessica with the support she needed to handle the teasing, the cruel looks, and the ignorance of other children and her teachers. The worker also knew that they were likely to communicate their own anxious feelings about the beginning of school to Jessica. Fortunately, the worker was able to involve Arthur and Sally in a group she was leading for parents of children with disabilities who were of a similar age. These parents helped each other face their anxieties about their children being hurt in school and shared alternative ways for intervening constructively without taking away their children's budding independence.

The social worker also helped the parents consider what they should tell their children's teachers and prinicipals about their children's physical condition and how much they could do for themselves. The parents thus felt empowered to talk to the school officials about how to meet the special needs of their child without lowering expectations for performance (for Jessica, this meant things as simple as obtaining a footstool to allow her to reach the blackboard and providing her with an extra set of schoolbooks to leave at home); how to plan ahead for the extra stresses that arise at the start of the school year or after transfers; and how to help the other children in the class correct misconceptions about chronic illness and disabilities by "share-and-tell" sessions in which the disabled child participates. When parents faced a particularly difficult situation, the social worker was available to accompany them to meetings at the school and to take a more active advocacy role when asked by the parents.

Jessica's social difficulties with her peers continued throughout her early school years, and in many ways, she remained a rather unhappy little girl. As happens so often with chronically ill children whose lives are surrounded by adults, Jessica related better to grown-ups and remained a loner among her peers. However, the school setting allowed her to express her considerable intellectual abilities, and Jessica excelled in her academic work.

The social worker's own relationship with Jessica deepened over these elementary-school years. Jessica shared with the worker her ambition to become a lawyer. Together, she and the social worker considered how Jessica could share these and other feelings with her parents and become more assertive with them. The social worker also supported Jessica's growing interest in the organization for people of short stature and encouraged her to attend one of their support-group meetings that her parents knew about in their area.

Jessica went on to become an active participant in the organization's groups for children of short stature. She appeared to feel more secure with her new friends, with whom she shared so many concerns. Together, these young people struggled to find suitable clothing that did not make them look younger and, some years later, to learn how to drive a car with mechanical aids. Jessica was able to share with other young people like herself her fears and memories of the lengthy hospital stays, the surgical procedures, and the leg braces that were all too frequent intrusions on her life throughout childhood and adolescence.

Arthur and Sally were often discouraged and felt more stress and emotional pain than Jessica ever knew. The social worker listened to them and supported them through difficult periods, and also as they became more able to express loving encouragement of Jessica's greater independence. In fact, Jessica's own growing self-confidence and increasing academic honors were important in helping her parents to develop the confidence they needed to support her. They became more involved in her school's Parent-Teacher Association (PTA) and eventually became leaders of discussion groups for other parents in the organization for people of short stature.

Jessica's two brothers reacted in different ways to their sister's disability. When Adam was an 18-year-old college freshman (and Jessica was 10), he began to express resentment of the attention given to Jessica during his home visits on vacations. He angrily reported that he sometimes could not even find his parents because they were so immersed in support-organization or PTA activities "for Jessica." He began to run around with a group of freshmen who drank heavily, and his grades deteriorated markedly. The social worker helped Sally and Arthur during this period to consider Adam's needs from them as parents. He was their first child and needed tangible reassurances of their love and their involvement in his life.

Michael, who was five years older than Jessica, seemed quite fond of his sister. He literally fought on the playground with anyone who called her names like "shrimp" or "midget." He became her protector and defender. But he also grew tired of having to explain to his friends what it meant to have achondroplasia; why Jessica had to spend so much time away from school in the hospital; and why she returned so often with casts on her legs. He was embarrassed by the label inflicted on them all: "Oh, you know the Steins—they're the family with the dwarfed girl!"

The social worker supported Michael in his decision to join a group for siblings that was sponsored by the support organization and that met regularly in the area. Here, he found enormous relief in learning that his reactions to his sister's dwarfism were shared by many in the group.

Unaffected siblings may have a variety of responses. They may worry about their own vulnerability to developing the same chronic illness. They may be angry at their affected sibling for burdening their parents and disrupting their lives. They may be resentful that the parents have had to devote so much time and effort to the needs of the affected child. To gain their parents' attention, these siblings may choose either to withdraw and sulk or to act out with behavior problems. They may feel ashamed of and embarrassed by the appearance or the behavior of their brother or sister, and they may grieve for the normal sibling they might have had. They may begin to worry about who will take care of the affected sibling when their parents die. And as they get older, they often become concerned about potential risks to their own children.

Who ever wants to relive their teen years? For adolescents with a chronic health impairment those teen years seem endless. They must cope not only with their changing hormonal system but also with looking or feeling different than their peers. Many are romantic and desolate at the same time, longing to find romance (or just acceptance) but experiencing sudden rejection and loneliness as former friends begin dating and leaving them behind. Sexual development is often delayed for young persons with chronic disorders like dwarfism, and they may become concerned about their lack of sexual achievement compared to their peers. Even age-appropriate sexual development and interests may lead to disappointments as other teens avoid dating anyone who does not fit easily into the familiar mold. It is not unusual for a teenager with a chronic health problem to graduate from high school without ever having dated.

Jessica was not spared these challenges. Although she had made a large number of friends, adolescence brought increasing awareness of her physical differences and disabilities. The social worker's interventions during these years focused on 1) helping Jessica and her parents understand the developmental tasks they were encountering: 2) supporting the parents in letting Jessica openly verbalize her feelings of sadness and frustration rather than pushing them aside with premature efforts to boost her morale; 3) encouraging Jessica, with her parents' assistance, to enter organized activities, such as a coed church group or school club, where she could remain with healthy peers of her own age who had similar interests; and 4) encouraging her active involvement in the teen groups sponsored by the support organization, where she could continue her contacts with other teens of short stature.

Jessica thus embarked on adolescence aided by a range of positive supports. She was enjoying the coed activities, becoming more active in the short stature organization, and excelling in school. However, her growing self-esteem took a hard beating when the need for additional surgery suddenly arose. The emerging adult side of her knew that if she did not have the surgery now, she might end up in a wheelchair by high school. But the adolescent 13-year-old longed to have a normal life and to continue as before with her friends.

Her parents joined her in this ambivalence. At first, they pressed for the surgery, then shifted to supporting Jessica's reluctance to having more surgery at this time of personal growth. They became annoyed by the surgeon's emphasis on the timeliness of the surgery. The social worker was called in again, but this time by the surgeon, who asked for her assistance in helping the parents to understand the implications of postponing the procedure.

The social worker's goal in the discussions that followed with Jessica and her parents was for them to consider the facts carefully, while maintaining Jessica's right to have her say in the final decision. In individual meetings with the social worker, Jessica struggled to come to terms with her anger at her parents for not being powerful enough to prevent the surgery. She also voiced her apprehensions that her friends would not be there for her when she returned from the hospital in a body cast.

Jessica finally acquiesced, but with great apprehension, as reflected in this excerpt from a poem she composed before the surgery.

*Reflections of a Tormented Person*

I am so depressed, my surgery is coming near.
The closer it comes, the greater grows the fear;
The fear that I won't get out of bed,
And be mentally and emotionally dead.
I want so much to stay in school, right here.

Jessica had had surgical procedures at least six times in her childhood, but this one was the most traumatic for her. With the enhanced cognitive capacities of an adolescent, she now could look on serious medical procedures with a new realization of their potentially dangerous consequences. As for many teenagers who have serious health problems, hospitalization for Jessica also represented total aloneness and tremendous fear of bodily harm and distortion. In the following two poems, she reflected on her ambivalent feelings toward her surgeon and her hospital experiences after the surgery:

*My Doctor*

It scares me that he has my life in his hand,
Not to mention my ability to stand.

But I need help and he can offer it.
Although sometimes I'd rather quit,
Without him, I may not be able to walk on the land.

*"The Hospital"*

The hospital is a terrible place to be in,
Especially without friends or kin.
The nurses are really cruel;
The doctors are obnoxious as a rule.
The way the personnel treat the patients is a sin.

The nurses totally ignore the patients' calls;
Instead they socialize in the halls.
This is bad when a patient is in pain,
And she is about to go insane.
Our confidence in them, they slowly maul.

It looks as if I'll have to go back once more,
Although they may have to take me screaming to
    the door;
To go through it again, that's not fair.
Sometimes I feel as if no one does care;
But I have to go and enter the Nurse–Patient war.

This episode of surgery required that Jessica remain in the hospital for six weeks. When she was discharged, she was treated initially as a celebrity, arriving at school in her body cast. But Jessica was aware that her friends had gone on with their lives without her, and once again, she began to feel lonely and different. However, this time, Jessica herself had the strength to come to the social worker for support. She also gradually rejoined the activities in her local support group, where other young people shared and understood some of her feelings.

Jessica's intellectual accomplishments and her growing sense of positive identity helped her gain acceptance to a prestigious university. She was fortunate to find this an enlightened institution that reached out to accommodate her needs for environmental modifications in her dormitory room, classrooms, and laboratories. Although she continued to maintain some contacts with the organization for people of short stature, her growing sphere of non-illness-related interests and friends began to take up much more of her free time.

The social worker's contacts with Jessica and her family have appropriately diminished in recent years. Jessica now assumes the major responsibility in advocating for her rights to equal opportunities. However, she did engage the social worker's assistance when her initial applications to law school met with inexplicable rejections. Her strong academic record and her volunteer experiences seemed to suggest an easy acceptance. Jessica was angered by what appeared to be discrimination because of her disability, and she chose to challenge these rebuffs with a new round of applications and a demand for interviews. She asked the social worker to contribute a letter on her behalf.

Jessica's efforts brought success. She is now in law school, where she plans to specialize in legal advocacy for the disabled. She believes that her own painful experiences in coping with a chronic condition will help her assist others in similar situations. She and the social worker have talked about whether her career choice moves her too much again into her illness-related world. She understands that she may be vulnerable to overidentifying with her clients and will need to plan for ways to maintain her own separate interests. Only time will tell how she will work out a balance between her professional and personal lives, but she has the skills she needs to achieve this goal. She also knows where to get professional assistance should she need it.

The case of Jessica and her family reads as a success story. Her disability will continue to challenge them all but they have been fortunate in having access to a wide array of services and in encountering environments that responded relatively flexibly to requests for modification. Unfortunately, many other clients with chronic illnesses and disabilities encounter greater obstacles to successful coping. Not all have parents and siblings who become strong sources of support. Many children and adults with disabilities come from single-parent households in which personal and financial resources are frequently stretched beyond the breaking point. Health insurance that covers the necessary surgeries and treatments may be inadequate or nonexistent. Rights to an appropriate education and equal employment opportunities may exist as a legal principle that finds only limited application in everyday life. One's residence may be in an older urban area where architectural barriers prove almost insurmountable or in an isolated rural area where transportation seems an impossibility.

As discussed in this essay, the population that is described as chronically ill or disabled is large and diverse. This diversity is mirrored in the variety of settings in which social workers serve this population and in the array of interventions that we use. Moreover, society's responses to the people in this population have a fundamental impact on their daily lives and on the development of their potential. Thus, social work priorities begin with, but cannot remain limited to, relieving immediate distress and maximizing coping in the affected individuals and their families. Our professional responsibilities extend also to advocacy efforts to improve access to education and employment, to increase health care resources, and to change social prejudices against physical and mental differences.

## REFERENCES

Andersen, R. M., R. M. Mullner, and L. J. Cornelius. 1987. "Black-White Differences in Health Status: Methods or Substance?" *Milbank Quarterly* (Supplement 1) 65:72–99.

Black, R. B., D. H. Dornan, and J. P. Allegrante. 1986 "Challenges in Developing Health Promotion Services for the Chronically Ill." *Social Work* 31:287–293.

Black, R. B. and J. O. Weiss. 1989. "Genetic Support Groups and Social Workers as Partners." *Health and Social Work*, in press.

Bowe, F. 1980. *Rehabilitating America: Toward Independence for Disabled and Elderly People*. New York: Harper & Row.

Brown, S. S., ed. 1988. *Prenatal Care: Reaching Mothers, Reaching Infants*. Washington, D.C.: National Academy Press.

Coelho, G. V., D. A. Hamburg, and J. E. Adams, eds. 1974. *Coping and Adaptation*. New York: Basic Books.

Corbin, J. M. and A. Strauss. 1988. *Unending Work and Care*. San Francisco: Jossey-Bass.

DeJong, G. 1979. "Independent Living: From Social Movement to Analytic Paradigm." *Archives of Physical Medicine and Rehabilitation* 60:435–446.

Feldman, D. J. 1974. "Chronic Disabling Illness: A Holistic View." *Journal of Chronic Disease* 27:287–291.

Fine, M. and A. Asch, eds. 1988. *Women with Disabilities: Essays in Psychology, Culture, and Politics*. Philadelphia: Temple University Press.

Fox, D. M. 1986. "AIDS and the American Health Polity: The History and Prospects of a Crisis of Authority." *Milbank Quarterly* (Supplement 1); 64:7–33.

Germain, C. and A. Gitterman. 1980. *The Life Model of Social Work Practice*. New York: Columbia University Press.

Gliedman, J. and W. Roth. 1980. *The Unexpected Minority*. New York: Harcourt Brace Jovanovich.

Hatfield, A. B. 1987. "Coping and Adaptation: A Conceptual Framework for Understanding Families." In A. B. Hatfield and H. P. Lefley, eds., *Families of the Mentally Ill: Coping and Adaptation*, pp. 60–84 New York: Guilford.

Hobbs, N., J. M. Perrin, and H. T. Ireys. 1985. *Chronically Ill Children and Their Families*. San Francisco: Jossey-Bass.

Kermis, M. D. 1986 *Mental Health in Late Life: The Adaptive Process*. Boston: Jones & Bartlett.

Kleinfield, S. 1979. *The Hidden Minority*. Boston: Little Brown.

Lazarus, R. S., J. R. Averill, and E. M. Opton. 1974. "The Psychology of Coping: Issues of Research and Assessment." In G. V. Coelho, D. A. Hamburg, and J. E. Adams, eds. *Coping and Adaptation*, pp. 249–315 New York: Basic Books.

Manton, K. G., C. H. Patrick, and K. W. Johnson. 1987. "Health Differentials Between Blacks and Whites: Recent Trends in Mortality and Morbidity." *Milbank Quarterly* (Supplement 1), 65:129–199.

Matson, R. R. and N. A. Brooks. 1977. "Adjusting to Multiple Sclerosis: An Exploratory Study." *Social Science and Medicine* 11:245–250.

Meyer, C. 1976. *Social Work Practice: The Changing Landscape*, 2d ed. New York: Free Press.

Meyer, C., ed. 1983. *Clinical Social Work in the Eco-Systems Perspective*. New York: Columbia University Press.

Mudrick, N. R. 1988. "Disabled Women and Public Policies for Income Support." In M. Fine and A. Asch, eds., *Women with Disabilities: Essays in Psychology, Culture, and Politics*, pp. 245–268 Philadelphia: Temple University.

NCHS (National Center for Health Statistics). 1985. *Current Estimates from the National Health Interview Survey*. Series 10 (160). Hyattsville, Md.: Department of Health and Human Services.

Pless, I. B. and P. Pinkerton. 1975. *Chronic Childhood Disorder—Promoting Patterns of Adjustment*. London: Henry Kimpton.

Rice, D. P. 1979. "Scope and Impact of Chronic Diseases in the U.S." In *Public Policy and Chronic Disease*. (DHEW Publication No. (PHS) 79-1986). Washington, D.C.: GPO.

Rolland, J. S. 1988. "A Conceptual Model of Chronic and Life-Threatening Illness and Its Impact on Families." In C. S. Chilman, E. W. Nunnally, and F. M. Cox, eds., *Chronic Illness and Disability*, pp. 17–68 Newbury Park, Calif.: Sage.

Russell, M. B. 1988. "Clinical Social Work." In J. Goodgold, ed., *Rehabilitation Medicine*, pp. 942–950 St. Louis: C. V. Mosby.

Starfield, B. "Family Income, Ill Health, and Medical Care of U.S. Children." *Journal of Public Health Policy* 3:244–259.

Strauss, A. L. and B. G. Glaser. 1975. *Chronic Illness and the Quality of Life*. Saint Louis: C. V. Mosby.

Terkelsen, K. G. 1987. "The Meaning of Mental Illness to the Family." In A. B. Hatfield and H. P. Lefley, eds., *Families of the Mentally Ill: Coping and Adaptation*, pp. 128–150 New York: Guilford.

Walkover, M. 1988. "Social Policies: Understanding Their Impact on Families with Impaired Members." In C. S. Chilman, E. W. Nunnally, and F. M. Cox, eds., *Chronic Illness and Disability*, pp. 220–247 Newbury Park, Calif.: Sage.

# 5

# Depression

▼

JOANNE E. TURNBULL

Depression is so common in our society that it is often referred to as the "common cold" of mental illness. It is also a complicated problem that is difficult to comprehend, assess, and treat effectively. Because it is so common in our society, social workers come across depression in their work with clients regardless of their field of practice. Consequently, social workers have to be able to recognize depression in their clients. To that end, this paper describes social work practice as it relates to depression.

Depression is heterogeneous; that is, there is not one type but several types of depression. Many scholarly references on depression do not distinguish between a mood state, a cluster of symptoms, or a clinical syndrome, but most agree that a core cluster of depressive symptoms cuts across all types of depression, regardless of severity. These symptoms include low mood, reduced ability to experience pleasure, pessimism, slowed speech and action, and a variety of physical complaints.

Although the popular notion of depression is limited to mood disturbance, the symptoms of depression can be grouped into four dimensions. In the cognitive dimension are memory deficits and distorted thinking, including beliefs of hopelessness and helplessness. In the motivational dimension are feelings of apathy, fatigue, and inactivity. In the affective dimension are feeling sad, blue, and depressed and being unable to enjoy activities that are usually pleasurable; many depressed people also feel irritable, anxious, angry, and hostile and direct these feelings especially toward those close to them. In the vegetative or somatic dimension are appetite, sleep, and psychomotor disturbances.

In addition to mood state and symptoms, the term *depression* also refers to a classification of affective disorders that describes several different problems. Major affective disorder includes both manic-depressive illness (bipolar disorder) and major depressive disorder. Manic-depressive illness is characterized by extreme fluctuations in mood that cycle from high (mania) to low (depression). At one extreme, the mood state is elevated or irritable and accompanied by hyperactivity, fast and pressured speech, an overabundance of ideas that do not connect coherently, inflated self-esteem, a decreased need for sleep, distractibility, and an unawareness of the consequences of one's actions. Manic-depressive illness is rare and afflicts only 1 percent of the population (Boyd and Weissman 1981). Hypomania consists of symptoms similar to mania, but not as severe.

At the other extreme is the much more common major depressive disorder (also called *unipolar depressive disorder*). It is characterized by an enduring low mood, loss of interest or pleasure in usual activities, and other symptoms associated with depression, such as appetite and sleep disturbance, feelings of guilt and worthlessness, decreased energy, concentration and memory disturbance, and suicidal thoughts or attempts. At some time in their lives, 8 to 12 percent of men and 20 to 26 percent of women meet the criteria for major depressive disorder (Boyd and Weissman 1981; Hirschfield and Cross 1982). Major depressive disorder can be differentiated into subtypes based on the presence or absence of a cluster of severe symptoms that are known as *endogenous* or *melancholic features*.

Minor depressive disorders are even more pervasive and also include subtypes. *Dysthymia* refers to chronic, persistent, low-level symptoms of depression that may or may not occur in coexistence with major depressive disorder (Weissman and Klerman 1977). Other names for minor depressive disorder are *neurotic depression* (or *neurotic depressive disorder*) and *chronic* and *intermittent depressive disorder*. The essential feature is a chronic mood disturbance accompanied by the other symptoms associated with depression, which are not of sufficent severity or length to meet the criteria for a major depressive episode. Cyclothymia is a chronic minor depressive disorder of at least two years' duration that mimics manic-depressive illness. The symptoms are milder and the episodes are shorter, so that a diagnosis of manic-depressive illness is not warranted.

Finally, *reactive depression, disappointment reaction*, and *bereavement reaction* are terms that refer to a sudden change from normal to low mood following frustration or loss. Although symptoms of depression, such as blue mood, poor appetite, weight loss, and insomnia, may be present, reactive depression is a universal phenomenon and not a mental illness.

Figure 5.1 displays the different classifications of depression along with the various subtypes and different names used for them. The different theoretical models underlying each classification and related treatment modalities are also presented and may be used for reference throughout the paper.

Because the different types of depression share so many symptoms, the continuity hypothesis has emerged, which suggests that the clinical syndrome of depression is only an exaggeration of normal low mood, although they may have very different causes (Beck 1967). Alternatively, the discontinuity hypothesis, noting the distinct sets of symptoms that occur in specific types of serious affective disorder, states that low mood and clinical syndromes are distinct entities.

## PROBLEM DOMAIN

Several theoretical models have been formulated to explore the intrapsychic, cognitive-behavioral, and social aspects of depression. Each approach has implications for the formulation of clinical interventions.

### Psychodynamic Formulations

*Psychodynamic* conceptualizations were the earliest to provide a causal framework for depression. The role of repressed hostility is the central explanatory variable. Basically, depression is viewed as anger that is first projected onto one's parents and is later generalized to the wider interpersonal environment. In the process, the anger becomes detached from its roots in hostility, is turned inward on the self, and is experienced as a deep sense of inferiority (Abraham 1911/1986; Freud 1896/1962).

Additions to the basic theory include the notion that depression is based on early childhood trauma that translates into a vulnerability to feeling helpless in the face of specific frustrations in adulthood (Bibring 1953), and the idea that adult patterns of interpersonal relationships are forged in early family life in an emotional climate that is characterized by conformity. As a result, a narrow range of relationships, characterized by dependency and sensitivity to disapproval and rejection, is developed (Cohen et al. 1954).

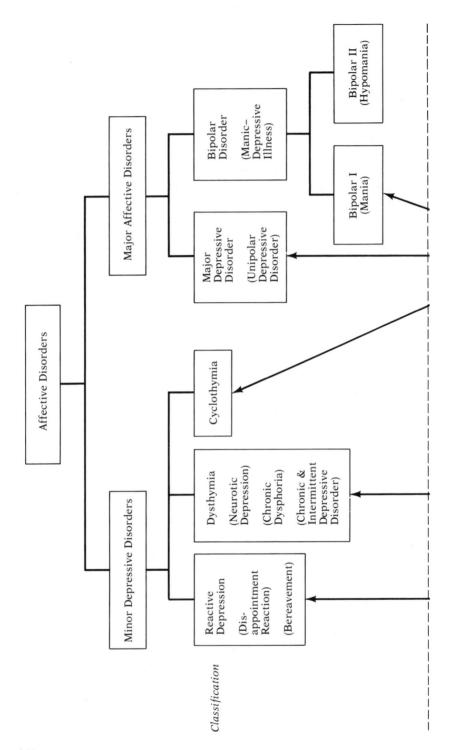

Classification

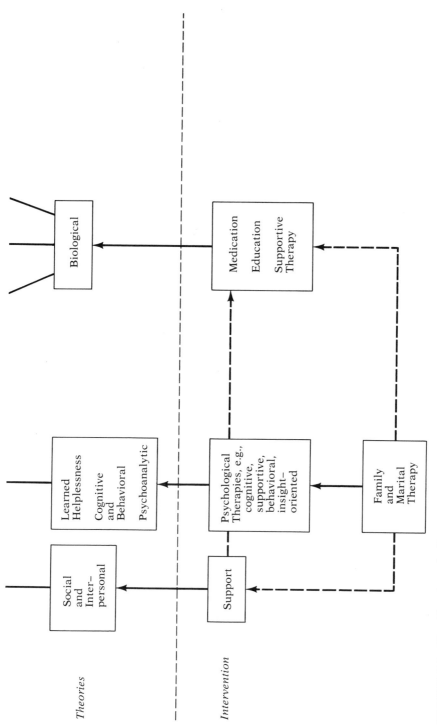

FIGURE 5.1. Classification of Affective Disorders and Related Theories and Interventions.

169

## Behavioral and Cognitive Formulations

The *behavioral perspective* conceptualizes depression in terms of observable behaviors that operate under the influence of antecedent events (controlling stimuli) and subsequent events (reinforcement contingencies) in the environment. Depression is viewed as a low rate of behavior and a concurrent low mood that is a function of the total amount of positive reinforcement available for any available response (Ferster 1971; Lewinsohn 1986). Not only must the reinforcement be available, but the person must also respond to the reinforcement. The rate of response-contingent reinforcement available depends on three factors: 1) events that are reinforcing to a person; 2) reinforcing events that are available in the immediate environment; and 3) the ability of the person to receive the reinforcement. The events that precipitate depression affect one or more of these factors.

*Cognitive theories* of depression emerged from the behavioral perspective and assume that cognition determines affect; that is, affective, motivational, and behavioral deficits are secondary to negative cognitions (Blaney 1977). Beck (1967) theorized that the root of depression is a "negative cognitive triad" that consists of a gloomy view of oneself, the world, and the future. Beck also introduced the notions of negative cognitive schemata and selective abstraction. Negative schemata are enduring, organized negative representations of past experience that act as filters and distort incoming information from the environment. *Selective abstraction* refers to an exclusive focus on the negative aspects of one's life. Taken together, these processes cause the depressed individual to exaggerate negative experiences, and to characterize themselves in negative all-or-nothing terms.

The *learned-helplessness model* of depression integrates the behavioral and cognitive models. Originally, the model applied observations from animal laboratory experiments to the human condition. Dogs exposed to repeated shocks from which they cannot escape (Overmier and Seligman 1967) eventually sit passively and receive the shock; when placed in a new situation in which they are able to escape the shock, they fail to do so. The analogue of learned helplessness in humans is a perceived lack of connection between one's own efforts and outcomes in the environment. Following multiple, uncontrollable events, a stable, generalized belief forms that the environment is uncontrollable and independent of one's efforts. This belief inhibits active coping responses in new situations. A perception of response-reinforcement independence is acquired as the individual comes to believe that responding is ineffective (Seligman 1975). The depressed individual does not then engage in actions that will challenge his or her perception of environmental control.

*Attribution theory* has been integrated into the original learned-helplessness model and is called the *reformulated model*. The reformulated model hypothesizes that depressed persons not only come to expect that future outcomes will be uncontrollable but also ask themselves why they are helpless to control the outcomes. The answer to the question, called a *causal attribution*, determines how enduring or chronic the helplessness will be, and whether or not the helplessness will be generalized to other situations and will influence self-esteem. The key rests in the tendency to interpret negative events in internal, global, stable terms. Internal attributions ("I am responsible") for events result in self-blame, while attributions to global factors ("not just in this situation, but in all situations") and attributions to stable factors ("not just this time, but every time") lead to a chronic sense of helplessness that is manifested in depression.

## *Interpersonal and Social Approaches*

Interpersonal relationships may have an impact on the development and maintenance of depression. *Family systems models* of depression are based on the hypothesis that the interaction of the depressed person with intimate others, particularly the spouse, exerts a powerful effect in the direction of triggering and maintaining the depression. A circular process of mutual causality is postulated, in which the depressed person and family members collude inadvertently to create and maintain a stable system that resists change.

Theoretically, the depressed person engages others in the intimate environment in such a way that support is lost (Coyne 1976.) Initial communications of hopelessness, helplessness, and irritability by the depressed person are answered with direct reassurances. The depressed person must decide whether the reassurances that he or she is worthy and acceptable are sincere or are empty responses to repeated attempts of elicit reassurances. Accelerated efforts to elicit feedback in order to answer this question have profound negative effects on interpersonal relationships.

With time, depressive symptoms gain an aversive and powerful ability to arouse guilt in others, and to inhibit direct expressions of annoyance and hostility. Instead of direct expressions, manipulative attempts at nongenuine reassurance and support are made to reduce the aversive behavior of the depressed person, accompanied by simultaneous rejection and avoidance of the depressed person. As he or she becomes aware of the reaction of others, the depressed person displays more symptoms of distress, which stimulate the depressive social process further. Hostility toward others or a self-defeating desire for attention may cause the depressed person to become uncooperative. Family members withdraw further as they find themselves unable to answer the person's pleas, the result is even more desperation on the part of the depressed person.

Social factors outside the family may also contribute to depression. The *social causation hypothesis* suggests that lower social status (lower education, income, and occupational levels) causes depression because individuals in this life condition experience more environmental stressors, such as unemployment, financial setbacks, and poor health (Liem and Liem 1978). Conversely, the *social selection hypothesis* postulates that those of lower social status are more vulnerable to the effects of stress and are hence more likely to be depressed because they lack supportive social and personal resources (Myers, Lindenthal, and Pepper 1975) and less effective coping strategies (Kessler 1979). Less is known about the ways in which other environmental factors (i.e., crowding, urban traffic congestion, airport noise, and social conditions such as economic factors, racial prejudice, and sexism) contribute to depression, but it is known that the physical features and the organizational characteristics of a community influence the amount and quality of environmental resources, which in turn have a relationship to depression (Moos and Mitchell 1982).

## Biological Theories

The *biological* aspects of depression focus on genetics, endocrinology, and neurophysiology. Research documents that affective disorders are familial, that is, that there is a genetic component in the transmission of depression from one generation to another. Depression is more likely to occur among close relatives of those with the disorder than among unrelated persons (Wender et al. 1986; Gershon 1983). Different rates of depression are observed in identical and fraternal twins: identical or monozygotic twins have much higher rates of depression than do fraternal or dizygotic twins (Bertelsen 1979). High rates of depression have been found among the offspring of depressed parents who have been adopted by families without a history of depression (Mendelwicz and Rainer 1977). Finally, studies of depression among the Amish have linked depression to a specific gene (Egeland 1983).

Other biological theories focus on deficiencies in the neurodendocrine system and on the functioning of neurotransmitters. The biogenic amine hypothesis, for example, states that depression is associated with a functional deficit in one or more neurotransmitter amines at critical synapses in the central nervous system, and that these amines work in complex interaction with other neurotransmitter or neuromodulator systems, such as the cholinergic and endorphin systems (Schildkraut, Green, and Mooney 1985).

## *Current Theory: The Biopsychosocial Model*

Current theories recognize that simple conceptual models are inadequate to explain depression. Rather, multidimensional models, such as the *biopsychosocial* model, are required to grasp thoroughly the complex nature of the problem and to develop effective treatment methods. The theory underlying the biopsychosocial model calls for an integration of biological, psychological, and social factors to explain both the onset and the maintenance of depression. As figure 5.2 indicates, the conceptual framework of the biopsychosocial model requires the interaction of biological, psychological, and social factors to produce depression.

While the biopsychosocial model is generally accepted, there is disagreement over the importance of each individual factor, although many agree that the relative contribution of biological, psychological, and social factors may vary depending on the subtype of depression. There is also disagreement about whether these factors act as precipitating or predisposing factors. A precipitating factor is an event or circumstance that can be identified as occurring closely enough in time to the onset of an episode of depression so that it may be presumed to play a causal role. In contrast, a predisposing factor can be defined as a circumstance or condition that makes one vulnerable to a depression; it may have occurred in the distant past. For example, an undesirable life event, such as the death of a loved one, is a social factor that may precipitate a time-limited experience of low mood. An inherited genetic vulnerability is a biological factor that predisposes one to major depressive disorder. Similarly, a passive coping style that stems from a childhood of deprivation and neglect is a psychological factor that may predispose one to neurotic depression.

Consensual definitions of depression and uniform ways of measuring it have only begun to emerge. Until recently, multiple definitions have pervaded the literature and have confused the field. For example, the term *depression* is used to describe low mood, a set of symptoms, and a serious major affective disorder without differentiating between them. Another problem is that some studies have included subjects who have a clearly defined affective disorder (Epstein, Baldwin, and Bishop 1983; Miller et al. 1986), while other studies appear to have subjects with only dysphoric symptoms or unhappiness (Weissman, Paykel, and Klerman 1972), yet the findings are discussed as if no differences existed. Most studies, moreover, make no effort to distinguish between the subtypes of depression. The duration of the affective episodes and the previous number of episodes are rarely documented (Ruestow et al. 1978). Assessment varies widely; many different scales are used, and some are without demonstrated reliability and validity. Outcome measures of social role functioning are confounded because they are also measures of depressive symptoms. Most study designs have been cross-sectional, and the subjects have been studied after the onset of depression, so that it is not

BIOLOGICAL

- Somatic Factors — medical illness or condition; drug reaction
- Other Psychiatric Illness
- Genetic Predisposition

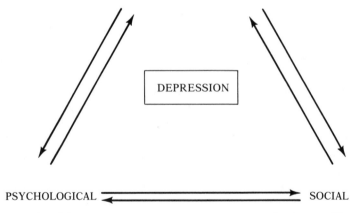

PSYCHOLOGICAL　　　　　　　　　　　　　　　　　　SOCIAL

- Learned Helplessness
  - early object loss
  - chronic deprivation, neglect
  - socialization

- Inadequate Material Resources
- Inadequate Social Support
- Conflicted Interpersonal Relationships
- Aversive Life Event
  - object loss, bereavement
  - loss of job status

FIGURE 5.2. Biopsychosocial model of depression.

possible to know whether the depression was the cause or the effect of the reported problems.

These definitional problems contribute to the serious difficulties that exist in recognizing depression and to disagreement over treatment methods. At any one time, one fifth of the adult population will have significant depressive symptoms, and most will remain undiagnosed and untreated (NIMH/NIH 1985; Weissman and Myers 1981). Many people suffering from depression are unable to articulate the true nature of their problem and so seek help for problems other than depression. For example, depressed people frequently seek help for marital problems (Overall, Henry, and Woodward 1974), and a practitioner who is unfamiliar with the symptoms and subtypes of depression will be unable to recognize the problem. Further, service providers wedded to a narrow theoretical orientation may misdiagnose and mistreat depression. For example, a psychiatrist with a biological orientation may inappropriately prescribe medication to a patient, ignoring the needed psychosocial intervention. Conversely, a social worker with a family systems orientation may work on marital problems in an effort to alleviate serious depressive symptoms that warrant biological intervention.

Serious societal consequences result from a failure to identify and help with depression appropriately. Of those with a lifetime history of a depressive disorder, 24 percent attempt suicide (Regier et al. 1988), and 15 percent eventually succeed (Munoz 1987). High social and economic costs are associated with episodes of depression. For example, father–daughter incest has been linked to undiagnosed depression in the mother (Herman and Hirschman 1981). Dysthymia, which may not be severe enough to meet the diagnostic criteria for depression, results in impaired social-role functioning and the inappropriate use of health and psychiatric services and of psychotropic drugs (Weissman et al. 1988). Depression has been estimated to cost $16.5 billion per year, $3 billion being in treatment costs and the remainder in indirect costs, such as lost work productivity (Munoz 1987). Other costs to society, individuals, and families are more difficult to estimate but are no less real.

In most cases, the family touched by major depression experiences profound burdens and disrupted family life. Most people who have major depression are, or have been, married, so that spouses and children bear the emotional burden of coping with their illness. Not surprisingly, the children of depressed parents are more likely to have psychological and social difficulties than the children of parents with no disorder or even than children of parents with other psychiatric disorders (Beardslee et al. 1988; Weiner and Rice 1988).

In recent years, following deinstitutionalization, the failure of community resources to adequately meet the needs of the mentally ill has led to an increasing interest in mobilizing "natural" helping networks such as the family. Accordingly, it is important to evaluate how families respond to the needs of the depressed family member and how families are affected by depression, and to identify the family features associated with depression so that effective intervention strategies can be formulated.

## SOCIETAL CONTEXT

Epidemiological studies describe trends that indicate that mild depression may be increasing and striking at an earlier age (Hagnell 1982; Klerman 1988). Better methods of identifying depression may account for some of the increase, but they do not explain it entirely. Social factors such as changes in family structure, higher divorce rates, and increased family mobility with a concomitant loss of the extended-family system may be contributing to these trends. These indicators often represent disrupted attachments and deficient social supports. Earlier onset may be fueled by increased social and competitive pressures, and by earlier exposure to alcohol and drugs among young people. Thus, stresses inherent in contemporary society seem to be related to certain types of depression and have turned theoretical and empirical attention to the social factors that may influence depression.

Social support may protect one against the onset of certain types of minor depression and may be associated with a good outcome in biologically based affective disorders (Henderson 1984; O'Connell et al. 1985). Alternatively, lack of social support or negative social support may make one vulnerable to depression. Social support can be broken down into two types: instrumental and expressive. Instrumental support is practical help and membership in community groups. Expressive social support is characterized by access to and use of intimate, confiding relationships. Companionship, emotional support, guidance and advice, and material aid and services, as well as a sense of identity and social role expectations, are all components of the construct of social support (Billings and Moos 1986).

Questions regarding the nature of the relationship between social support and depression include 1) whether social support directly protects one against depression (Tennant 1985) or act as a buffer against depression in the face of stressful life events (Brown and Harris 1986); 2) whether this effect varies according to such factors as the type and severity of the depression and access to treatment (Billings and Moos 1981; Wilcox 1981); and 3) whether lack of social support is a cause or an effect of depression.

Evidence that depression goes hand in hand with marital distress (Pearlin and Lieberman 1977) suggest that the primary adult relationship is a critical social context for depression. Depressive symptoms are strongly associated with marital conflict in community samples (Ilfield 1977), and there is an even stronger relationship in treatment samples (Rounsaville et al. 1979), irrespective of subtype (Birtchnell and Kennard 1983). The lifetime incidence of divorce and marital instability is higher among subjects in community samples who meet the criteria for a diagnosis of affective disorder than for subjects with other psychiatric diagnoses (Turnbull under review), and divorce rates are significantly higher still if both members of a couple are depressed (Merikangas, Bromet, and Spiker 1983).

Marital relationships are the most impaired aspects of social functioning among depressed people (Hinchcliffe, et al. 1975, 1978). These marriages are characterized by disengagement, submission and dependency, guilt, resentment, and sexual problems (Weissman, Paykel, and Siegel 1971; Weissman and Siegel 1972). Couples with a depressed member exhibit less facilitative, supportive behavior and are dissimilar in their overall behavior from couples without a depressed member. They have negative and uneven communication styles, which lack responsiveness and contain disruptions and emotional outbursts (Biglan et al. 1985; Hops et al. 1987).

Marital difficulties persist after recovery from the depressive episode (Hops et al. 1987; Paykel 1978; Paykel and Weissman 1979; Rounsaville, Prussoff, and Weismann 1980), a finding suggesting that marital difficulties are not artifacts of the depression. Rather, the social context of marital distress may play an important role in the onset and maintenance of depression. Intimacy seems to be the critical factor (Waring and Patton 1984), as these interpersonal difficulties do not extend to other relationships (Hautzinger, Linden, and Hoffman 1982; Linden, Hautzinger, and Hoffman 1983). The level of perceived marital intimacy predicted improvement in depressed patients at one-month follow-up; depressed patients with the lowest levels of marital intimacy failed to improve (Waring and Patton 1984).

The actions of the nondepressed spouse are implicated by studies showing that the nondepressed spouse makes negative evaluations of both the depressed partner and the relationship, rarely agrees with the depressed partner's statements, and adds negative statements about the partner to offers of help (Hinchcliffe et al. 1975, 1977, 1978a, 1978b). The spouse is implicated further by the concept of *expressed emotion*, which is a measure of the number of critical remarks and the level of overinvolvement expressed spontaneously by a relative during a discussion of the depressed person and his or her problem during the acute phase of the illness. The remarks are strong predictors of a future recurrence of depression (Vaughan and Leff 1976; Hooley, Orley, and Teasdale 1986).

Research on expressed emotion has been attacked because it ignores the possibility that the purported negative comments may be an appropriate representation of the strain of living with a depressed person, while positive comments may reflect masochism, sainthood, or depression in a family member; neglect or rejection; or appropriate detachment (Kanter, Lamb, and Loeper 1987). Advocacy groups composed of members of the families of chronically mentally ill patients have objected to the blaming of relatives inherent in linking a family member's distress to the level of family tensions. Because it emphasizes pathological family qualities, the notion that family interactions play a role in the maintenance of depression exacerbates the sense of guilt and shame that most relatives already experience.

Finally, the phenomenon of assortative mating must be considered as it affects the marital context of depression. The term *assortative mating* refers to the tendency of individuals with affective disorders to marry each other (Merikangas, Bromet, and Spiker 1983). The social adjustment of depressed subjects with normal spouses is only slightly worse than in the normal population, but depressed subjects with depressed spouses have far greater social adjustment difficulties and their divorce rate is significantly greater that that of couples with a well spouse. The caveat is that depression in the spouse of a depressed person may not always represent major depressive disorder; rather, depressive symptoms or minor depressive disorder may be a consequence of the chronic strain associated with living with a severely ill spouse.

## RISKS AND NEEDS OF POPULATION

The prevalence figures for depression depend on definition, measurement, and population subgroups. Depressive symptons, which range from 13 to 20 percent, are much more common than diagnosable depressive disorders, which range from 3 to 8 percent (Boyd and Weissman 1981; Weissman and Boyd 1983). Major depression is found in 3 percent of the population in a given six-month period and jumps to 5.8 percent for a lifetime (Regier et al. 1988; Myers et al. 1984). The prevalence of depressive disorders varies dramatically among sociodemographic groups, finding indicating that certain segments of the population are at high risk. The rate of clinically significant affective disorder for women is double the rate for men. The separated and divorced are 2.5 times more likely than the married to suffer from an episode of depression (Regier et al. 1988; Weissman et al. 1988).

The age of risk for depression increases from childhood to middle age, peaks in middle age, and then declines somewhat in later life (Eagles and Whalley 1985; Lewinsohn et al. 1986). Persons aged 25 to 44 are at the highest risk. Compared to the onset of disorders in other diagnostic groups, the onset of affective disorder is relatively late (Lewinsohn et al. 1986; Baron, Mendelwicz, and Klotz 1981), so that subjects with affective disorder remain single, separate, and divorce at rates that are comparable to those for well controls (Dunner et al. 1976); most subjects have separated from their family of origin and have married. The age of risk varies among subtypes. For bipolar illness, the average age of onset is the late 20s, which is younger than the age for unipolar depression, which tends to occur in the middle to late 30s.

*Risk* or *vulnerability factors* are characteristics that are associated with an increased chance of having a particular problem. Many risk factors have been associated with minor depressive disorders: being female, young, poor, unemployed, separated, divorced, or unhappily married; experiencing stressful life events; and having low educational and occupational status or physical illness (Brown and Harris 1978; Radloff 1986).

It is often difficult to assess whether a certain variable is a risk factor for depression, the consequence of depression, or some combination. Many vulnerability factors interact with each other to further increase the likelihood of depression. For example, social class both exposes one to and protects one from certain stressors. It also influences access to treatment. When sex and social class are controlled for, rates of depression among blacks and whites do not seem to differ, but race and ethnicity may act as risk factors indirectly. Blacks, for example, are underrepresented among those diagnosed as manic and are overrepresented among those diagnosed as schizophrenic (Marquez, Taintor, and Schwartz 1985); there is some evidence that bipolar disorders are overrepresented in the higher social classes, particularly among professionals (Weissman and Myers 1978). These figures may represent misdiagnosis due to cultural differences in the expression of symptoms and problems in access to treatment.

Major depressive disorder shows no preference for economic and educational status or race. The risk factors for major depressive disorder include being female and having a family history of depression.

Major depressive disorder has been found to be twice as frequent in urban areas (Blazer et al 1985). There is virtually no knowledge on the relationship between religion and affective disorder (Larsen et al. 1986).

For most types of depression, women have rates that are two to three times those reported by men (Boyd and Weissman 1981), the highest rates occurring for women in the 25–44-year-old age group (Weissman 1987). Women in specific life circumstances are particularly vulnerable. Working-class women and women with young children in the home, no outside employment, and no intimate relationship with the opposite sex are at high risk of developing depression in the face of stressful life events (Brown and Harris 1978). Theories have been formulated to test hypotheses about female socialization and role functioning in an effort to discover what makes women so vulnerable to depression. Empirical studies have examined socialization, social and vocational roles, and biological events such as childbirth and menopause (Aneshensel, Frerichs, and Clark 1981; Belle 1982; Gove, Hughes, and Style 1983; Gove 1972; Parry and Shapiro 1986; Pearlin and Lieberman 1977; Thoits 1983).

Family history doubles or triples the risk of major depression. For endogenous depression and bipolar disorder, a family history of depression is the strongest risk factor (Weissman, Kidd, and Prusoff 1982; Egeland, Gerhard, and Pauls 1987). The rate of major depression in the relatives of depressed patients, whether outpatient or hospitalized, is triple that in the general population regardless of the criteria used to measure depression (Weissman, Kidd, and Prusoff 1982). Children of depressed parents have an increased risk of both major depression and substance abuse (Weissman et al. 1987). Assortative mating, the tendency for depressed people to marry each other, increases the risk of depression to offspring. The risk is twice as high if both parents are depressed as it is if only one parent is depressed (Merikangas et al. 1988).

Negative life events seem to be precipitating factors, although minor ones, that trigger certain types of depression (Hirschfeld and Cross 1982). The emotional, cognitive, and social problems that accompany depression make it difficult to interpret the relationship between depression and life events; because of their difficulties, some people may have a role in bringing about a stressful life event. For example, depression may cause a person to experience relationship difficulties, and relationship difficulties may cause depression. Reporting bias must also be considered. Because of the cognitive distortions that accompany depression, individuals tend to recall only negative events and therefore may report more of them (Lewinsohn and

Rosenbaum 1987). Other aspects of life events that must be considered are severity, perception of threat, timing, chronicity, and personal context and meaning.

Depressed people report more stressful life events in the period immediately preceding an episode that do people in the general population (Brown, Harris, and Peto 1973), but the importance of life events in the onset of depression may vary among subtypes. The vulnerability hypothesis postulates that factors associated with vulnerability, such as low self-esteem or lack of social supports, are also associated with an increased risk for depression when stressful life events occur (Brown, Bifulco, and Harris 1987). Accordingly, when vulnerable individuals are exposed to uncontrollable events, they may be more likely to experience minor depression. In biologically based affective disorders, the role of life events may be more important at the beginning of the illness than it is later in the course of the illness. The kindling hypothesis, for example, states that people with bipolar disorder become more sensitized to the recurrences of affective episodes as the physiological processes involved become more easily initiated, so that an initial episode may be precipitated by an aversive event, but those that follow require increasingly less provocation and may take on a life of their own and start without provocation (Post, Rubinow, and Ballenger 1986).

While recent life events may be precipitating factors in depression, traumatic events in the early environment are considered predisposing factors that render one vulnerable to depression in adulthood. For instance, separation from a parent during early childhood may be a predisposing factor for nonendogenous adult depression (Paykel 1982; Roy 1987), but the effect is not a strong one. Qualitative aspects of the loss, such as the nature of the loss (whether it was due to illness, marital separation, or death), its timing (the developmental stage when the loss occurred), the nature of the attachment, and the quality of the home life following the loss (adequate care and family stability), are critical elements that may influence the outcome (Tennant 1982; Rutter 1985; Bifulco, Brown, and Harris 1987; Breier et al. 1988).

The link between childhood experiences and vulnerability to adult depression is hypothesized to be a downward spiral of negative circumstances that stem from the loss and from which it is difficult to escape (Harris, Brown, and Bifulco 1987). For example, the loss of one's mother may be accompanied by subsequent neglect, which may impair or arrest personality development and may result in inadequate coping mechanisms and difficulty in forming close, lasting relationships. These factors, in turn, make it more difficult to adapt to losses and stresses as an adult (Ragan and McGlashan 1986). The quality of early parenting has been implicated in adult depression (Gotlib et al. 1988), particularly in women. Depressed women often report that their mothers were simultaneously overprotective and unaware of their needs as separate individuals (Parker, Tupling, and Brown 1979). Other early environmental factors that may be important are physical abuse (Crowell, George, and Blazer, under review) and parental alchol abuse (VanValkenberg et al. 1977).

## PROGRAMS AND SOCIAL WORK SERVICES

Programmatic social work responses to depression can occur at three levels: at the interpersonal level, at the organizational and policy level, and through social work education. Based on theories of and research on depression, clinical programs have been developed that go beyond traditional psychotherapy. These programs tend to be readily available in clinical settings, especially those that specialize in the treatment of depression, but they have also been modified and distributed to the general public through books on self-treatment. Based on cognitive and behavioral theories, these approaches use self-control techniques, relaxation training, pleasant activities, social skills, and cognitive restructuring (Burns 1980; Lewinsohn et al. 1978). Many social workers are incorporating these techniques into their clinical work with clients. Self-help groups exist both in clinical settings and in the community, and social workers can offer their skills as resource consultants.

New approaches are sensitive to the burden shouldered by families and emphasize effective coping (Noh and Turner 1987; Jacob et al. 1987). When mental illness strikes a family, that family becomes intimately and indefinitely involved with the mental health system so that they must learn to gain access to and interact effectively with the appropriate services. New approaches consider families "consumers" of mental health services. As such, they are viewed as equals on the treatment team and may be involved in treatment-planning decisions (von Bulow et al. 1987; Spiegel and Wissler 1987). They may even be used to train professionals in family issues related to the care of the mentally ill. In this model, social workers offer consultation as it is needed on such issues as community resources, interpersonal problems, and crisis intervention.

In hospitals, training programs and administrative changes are being implemented to increase cooperation between staff and patients' families (Bernheim and Switalski 1988). Psychoeducational groups and workshops for families maximize family strengths to enable significant others to become useful, long-term resources for their loved ones (Jacob et al. 1987). Families are taught how to recognize the early warning signs of depression so that appropriate treatment can be sought quickly in an effort to ward off serious episodes. Families can be oriented to the complex issues that surround hospitalization, and the support of others struggling with similar issues is also provided (Turnbull et al. 1990). Families are empowered through self-help groups that counteract the devastating effects of mental illness and feelings of guilt (Battaglino 1987). Skills-training programs for parents afford an opportunity for preventive work with offspring. For the families of those with unremitting depression, day and respite programs similar to those designed for families of the elderly are appropriate. To date, these programs are less available than clinical programs. Social workers can take a role in starting up these groups and programs where a need exists and can also serve as facilitators. They may also be advocates for these groups and may serve as resources.

On the organization and policy level, educational programs are under way. Government-funded training programs and promotional materials are increasing public and professional awareness (Regier et al. 1988), and television programs are informing the public through educational programs on depression and other mental health problems. Such interventions are critical in decreasing the stigma associated with depression and, in turn in facilitating the search for appropriate help. Despite these positive trends, social workers need to develop more public education programs that deal with the psychosocial aspects of these problems and to conduct workshops in their communities for the public and for professionals in other disciplines.

Grass-roots, university-based, and state-supported family support programs have emerged as important social and political movements (Zigler and Black 1989; Weiss 1989). Social workers should be actively involved in these organizations and should support other social actions that are directly or indirectly related to depression. These include feminist programs that empower women and families and lead to mastery coping, such as child care programs that enable women to work and to obtain training programs.

Social work education is becoming increasingly systematic in teaching students to recognize and assess depression. Our academic institutions need to take more responsibility for conducting research into the manifestations of depression among vulnerable subgroups of the population such as the poor and, from this research, to design effective interventions and programs.

## DIFFERENTIAL CLINICAL ASSESSMENTS
## AND INTERVENTIONS

The assessment of depression is complex because depression is difficult to recognize and there are several subtypes. A systematic evaluation of current symptoms and the clinical features associated with depression (the age when the first depression occurred, its duration, and the number of episodes) helps one to identify the correct subtype of depression and to estimate the amount of disruption caused by depression. The documentation of family history of psychiatric illness and an evaluation of psychosocial functioning are also essential.

The practitioner must first distinguish between low mood that is a normal part of everyday living and a mood disturbance that is serious enough to warrant more vigorous intervention. Judging is difficult because many of the symptoms are identical. All depression, for example, consists of dysphoric mood. Although it is sometimes misused as a synonym for *depression, dysphoria* is a descriptive term that refers to the universal experience of low mood; it is a symptom of depression and not depression per se. Other symptoms that may be present regardless of depressive subtype are pessimism, feelings of guilt or worthlessness, concentration and thinking difficulties, and decreased energy.

An increased need for sleep, increased appetite, and weight gain are usually associated with milder forms of depression (Turnbull, Kessler, and Landis, in preparation), and thoughts of suicide or suicide attempts are usually associated with severe depression. A major depressive episode with melancholic or endogenous features is distinguished from other types of depression by a cluster of specific symptoms: 1) anhedonia, which is a loss of pleasure in activities that are normally experienced as pleasurable; 2) a lack of reactivity to usually pleasurable or aversive stimuli; and 3) physiological disturbances related to sleep, appetite, and sexual and psychomotor functioning.

Endogenous depression is also characterized by two other clinical phenomena. The first is diurnal variation. Literally translated as "daily change," this term refers to a regular worsening of mood at a particular point in the day, usually the morning, with gradual, although minimal, improvement as the day goes on. The other distinguishing feature is distinct quality of mood, which is a subjective perception that the depressed mood is qualitatively different from the sad feelings associated with loss. The clinical presentation of distinct quality of mood is semantic, conveyed by graphic descriptive metaphors such as "a wet blanket," "a steel curtain," "a concrete block," or a "gray veil."

The most widely used diagnostic scheme in the United States today is the revised third edition of the *Diagnostic and Statistical Manual of Mental Disorders (DSM-III-R);* (APA 1980). Although the *DSM-III-R* provides a clear taxonomy for different subtypes of depression, it offers little insight into the causal factors that guide the selection of interventions. Any depression of sufficient duration that includes certain symptoms common to all depressions can be classified as a major depression, regardless of severity. The diagnosis is descriptive, and there is no attempt to link the observed symptoms to underlying theoretical constructs. Further, the criteria are such that several subjects may receive the same diagnosis without sharing any symptoms.

The *DSM-III-R* criteria for manic-depressive illness center on one or more distinct periods of an elevated or irritable mood, which must be prominent, must persist for at least one week, and must include at least three of the following symptoms: increased activity or restlessness, talkativeness, racing thoughts, inflated self-esteem, decreased need for sleep, distractibility, and excessive involvement in risky activities without recognition of negative consequences, e.g., buying sprees, sexual indiscretions, or reckless driving. The criteria for major depressive disorder according to the *DSM-IIIR* include the presence of at least five symptoms (e.g., depressed mood, diminished interest or pleasure, weight loss or gain, increased or decreased sleep, psychomotor agitation or retardation, fatigue or loss of energy, feelings of worthlessness or inappropriate guilt, indecisiveness, inability to concentrate, recurrent thoughts of death or suicide) for the same two-week period. These symptoms must result in decreased functioning, and at least one symptom must be either depressed mood or loss of interest or pleasure (APA 1980).

The limitations of the *DSM-III-R* compel the practitioner to go beyond a catalog of symptoms to consider the pattern of the symptoms, their severity, and their duration in order to formulate effective interventions for depression. Accordingly, the most useful way to conceptualize depression may be according to symptom pattern and course, rather than by diagnostic category (Klein 1974; Van Valkenburg et al. 1977); such classifications have emerged from efforts to group depression into homogeneous symptom clusters for research studies.

The first group includes *reactive depression,* disappointment reaction, and bereavement. In the most general sense, these terms refer to a sudden change from normal to low mood that is experienced following frustration or loss. None of these terms refer to mental illness. A universal phenomenon, reactive depression can be distinguished from other types of depression by a preoccupation with the lost object rather than preoccupation with one's own worthlessness, and by feelings of guilt that are not pervasive and amorphous but associated with specific regrets in relation to the circumstances before or surrounding the loss. There is usually no family history of mental illness and no gender difference in rates of occurrence. Interests and reactivity to external stimuli are retained.

Grief can be distinguished from the other types of reactive depression and requires a specialized form of intervention involving guided imagery and the construction of an identity without the deceased (Melges 1982). In normal bereavement, the depressive symptoms persist intermittently throughout the first year following the loss. Therefore, unresolved grief is identified by depressive symptoms that started shortly after the loss of a significant person whose image still preoccupies the bereaved's mind more than a year after the loss. In addition, unresolved grief may involve one or more of the following factors: yearning for and overidentification with the lost object, blocked affect, anger and ambivalence, previous unresolved losses, and the lack of a support group (Melges 1982).

The appropriate treatment for all reactive depression, including normal bereavement, consists of passage of time, the opportunity for ventilation, and social support. Without these factors, reactive depressions may evolve into a chronic depression, particularly if multiple threatening life events are involved. Unresolved grief may lead to more serious depressive disorders, psychiatric disorders, health problems, and substance abuse.

The *minor depressive disorders* are dysthmia, chronic dysphoria, and neurotic depression. This classification typically describes habitually unhappy people whose problems with depression start early in life (Van Valkenburg et al. 1983). Minor depressive disorders occur most often among women who report a high incidence of alcoholism among their relatives (Torgersen 1986). Environmental factors seem to play a more significant role than genetic factors (Spring and Rothgery 1984). These individuals retain the ability to experience pleasure, but they describe a core life experience composed of severe psychological distress, unhappiness, and apathy. Their subjective experience is so painful that their capacity for pleasure and their maintenance of interests must be determined by others' observations, rather than self-report. The symptoms represent a transient phase of a more enduring lifelong proclivity toward unhappiness.

Clients with minor depressive disorders often exhibit "helpless and hopeless" behaviors analogous to those contained in the theory of learned helplessness (Beck 1967). These clients often self-medicate in an effort to relieve painful affective symptoms and are likely to receive a diagnosis of borderline personality disorder. While this diagnosis may be appropriate for certain clients (Vaglum and Vaglum 1985), appropriate treatment may result in a total cessation of the behaviors that suggest the diagnosis.

Chronic dysphoria is often not responsive to insight-oriented psychotherapy but is often responsive to cognitive psychotherapy (Kovacs, Rush, and Beck 1981), as well as intervention that includes significant others. Many intervention plans fail to address the issues that promote depressive symptomatology, especially in women. Critical issues for depressed clients include socialized dependency and helplessness, sexuality, low self-esteem, cultural expectations in terms of parenting, guilt, and a traditional sex-role orientation (Schwab-Bakman et al. 1981). These characteristics are all components of the construct of passivity, a primary characteristic of depression. Interventions designed to counteract passivity and to promote competence and mastery are appropriate. Exemplary interventions include assertiveness training, job training, training to rectify skill deficits, and support groups.

*Major depressive disorders,* especially those with melancholic features, require biological intervention. Endogenomorphic or "biological" depression tends to occur late in life with equal rates among men and women. The family histories of people who suffer from this type of depression reveal high rates of depression in relatives but no alcoholism or other psychiatric problems (Zimmerman, Coryell, and Pfohl 1986; James and Chapman 1975). Melancholic depression is noted for recurrence or periodicity. Marked by a distinct beginning and ending, episodes of depression are separated by periods of remission and improved functioning. When not in an episode, people with this type of depression may experience minor depression (Keller and Shapiro 1981). Whether or not they suffer from minor depressive disorder, people with biological depression may experience reactive depression like everyone else.

Endogenous depression is never amenable to psychotherapy alone and requires an adequate trial of antidepressant medication as adjunctive therapy. A word of caution is in order regarding the use of antidepressant medication with people whose depressive symptoms suggest an underlying learned helplessness. Endogenous depression is a rare phenomenon affecting only 1 percent of all people with depression (Boyd and Weissman 1982). Thus, most depressive disorders are minor depressive disorders, and whether medication is used or not, the relevant issues should always be addressed. Depression that stems from the belief that actions and outcomes are independent will only be reinforced by the notion that an external force (i.e., medication), and not one's own actions, is involved in relieving depression. Medication should be prescribed with great caution, following a meticulous assessment.

People with endogenous depression benefit from supportive therapy, which includes straightforward educational information about depressive symptoms and what to expect during the course of an episode. Clients may also benefit from cognitive psychotherapy, and family members may benefit from therapeutic involvement to alleviate their anxiety about their own mental stability and guilt over their inability to control the client's cognitive malfunctioning. Denial of the nature or the severity of the problem requires confrontation. Many social workers are unfamiliar with endogenous depression and attempt psychotherapy aimed at dynamic conflicts during an episode. For clients whose depressive symptoms include severe cognitive deficits, such as memory loss and an inability to engage in abstract thinking, the experience is frustrating at best and cruel at worst. Typically, clients blame themselves for their inability to benefit from a therapeutic intervention that leaves them with increased feeling of worthlessness and hopelessness. They may even become desperate, because they continue to feel bad despite attempts to clarify conflicts, to rectify problems in interpersonal relationships, and to formulate new goals for themselves.

Because depression is complex, a thorough psychosocial and family history that documents the family incidence of depression and alcoholism is essential. Even when clients are articulate, it is a task to draw a history from a person whose memory is impaired and whose speech is decreased and is marked by long pauses between words and sentences. Therefore, the history should be gathered not only from the client, but also from significant others who have observed the client's behavior. This expanded assessment approach provides an opportunity to develop an alliance with familiy members and increases the likelihood that objective, reliable data about the client's depression will be gathered.

Based on the assumption that different family histories represent different types of illness, the subtypes of depression have been classified according to a family history of psychiatric illness reported in first-degree relatives (Winokur and Morrison 1973; Winokur 1974). The diagnosis pure depressive disorder, which is applied to 25 to 33 percent of all depressed subjects, includes subjects who have first-degree family members who are depressed but have no other psychiatric illness (Lowry, Van Valkenburg, and Winokur 1978; Schlesser, Winokur, and Sherman 1979). Theoretically, this type of depression has a biological basis and is more serious than the other types; it is analogous to major depressive disorder with melancholic features. A second type, depressive spectrum disorder, is analogous to minor depressive disorders. It includes individuals who have a first-degree family member who is alcoholic or antisocial, and who may or may not have a family member with depression. This category includes 25 percent of all depressed subjects. Primarily female, subjects with depressive spectrum disorder have more ill relatives (Winokur et al. 1978; Van Valkenburg and Winokur 1979). The third category, sporadic depressive disorder, is believed to characterize a heterogeneous group that consists of several subtypes (Schlesser, Winokur, and Sherman 1979). This group contains the majority of depressed subjects who report no close family members with psychiatric illness.

An evaluation of psychosocial functioning is essential. An acute episode of depression can be conceptualized as a crisis that commands all of the individual's coping resources and leaves little energy for personal growth. As in any crisis, regression may occur during episodes of depression, and functioning may improve after the depressive symptoms have abated. For clients who have had a long course of depressive illness marked by multiple severe episodes, it is not uncommon for the developmental tasks to be those of an earlier life stage rather than those indicated by chronological age. In this instance, the client may be fixated at the developmental stage operating when the first episode of depression occurred. Intervention planning should maximize the periods between episodes as opportunities for completing developmental tasks, advancing psychosocial functioning, and moving to a more advanced developmental stage.

Secondary depression is depression that begins after another problem. Secondary depression is common. In the broadest sense, reactive depression is secondary depression since it follows an event but the term *secondary depression* usually refers to comorbidity. Comorbidity is any distinct additional clinical entity that has existed or that may occur during the clinical course of an existing illness (Feinstein 1970). Depression is the most frequent diagnosis to occur in conjunction with another psychiatric problem (Reich 1985; Hyler and Frances 1985). Secondary depression is a common condition among patients receiving medical care (Saltz and Magruder-Habib 1985). Estimates of the prevalence of depression among patients with medical illness range from 13 to 43 percent (Zung 1982; Friedman and Bennet 1977), depending on the particular patient population under study and the screening method used; approximately 50 percent of these depressions are not diagnosed by the physician (Nielsen and Williams 1980). Approximately one third of the 2 million women who suffer from alcohol problems in the United States experience depression in addition to alcohol dependence (Turnbull 1988; Schuckit 1983; Weissman, Meyers, and Harding 1980). The term *secondary* refers to time sequence and does not imply causality.

Successful intervention for all depression, regardless of subtype, is marked by the alleviation of depressive symptomatology. For all clients, a hierarchical intervention model that establishes goals in the order of their urgency is necessary. The first goal is always the resolution of depressive symptoms. While symptoms resolve, intensive support and provision of hope are critical to alleviate painful affective symptoms and to counteract helplessness and hopelessness. It is also a time to educate both clients and significant others regarding the symptoms of depression so that these are attributed to the illness and not to stable personality traits. After the depression is alleviated, subsequent goals can address intrapsychic and interpersonal domains.

Effective short-term therapies focused on symptom reduction include cognitive therapy (Beck 1979), behavioral therapy (Ferster 1971; Lewinsohn, Sullivan, and Grosscup 1980; Bellack, Herson, and Himmelhoch 1983), and interpersonal therapy (Klerman, Weissman, and Rounsaville 1984). Increasingly, these models are replacing the open-ended, long-term psychodynamic approaches to depression. Conjoint marital therapy models based on these theories have been developed, tested, and shown to be as effective as individual psychotherapy (Beach and O'Leary 1986; Dobsen and Jacobson 1988). A conjoint family therapy approach that shifts the focus away from the patient's symptoms and onto a discussion of marital and family relationships results in improved participation in therapy and family role performance for the depressed client with marital problems (Klerman, Weissman and Rounsaville 1984). The targets for intervention may include marital conflict, expressed emotion, skill deficits such as failure to volunteer support, and increases in expressiveness and marital intimacy (Biglan et al. 1985; Hops et al. 1987).

It is possible for a person to be so depressed or for a partner's negative attitudes and ideas about the hopelessness of the depressed person to be so overwhelming that marital therapy is impossible. For severe depression, especially when medication is necessary, it may be wise to delay marital therapy until the symptoms are alleviated sufficiently so that the depressed person can participate actively (Friedman 1975). Marital and family approaches have the added benefits of affording an opportunity to assess and intervene with the spouse, who may also be suffering from depressive symptoms, and to lessen blame and sick-role identification for the depressed person, who is vulnerable to feeling worthless, guilty, and inappropriately responsible for problems.

When hospitalization is necessary, brief inpatient family interventions that include the goals of accepting and understanding the illness and the possible precipitating stressors, as well as of elucidating and forming strategies to deal with stressful family interactions, may improve family coping with depression and may result in greater compliance with and willingness to accept professional help (Glick 1985). Family interventions can concentrate on interrupting negative sequences of interaction between depressed patients and their significant others. Family members can be encouraged to avoid overinvolvement so that they will foster the depressed person's autonomy and will avoid burnout (Anderson et al. 1986). Multiple family groups can decrease stigmatization and isolation and improve communication. These groups use a psychoeducational approach that consists of information given to family members regarding the impact of depression and mania on family life, with specific suggestions for coping. The importance of clear and simple communication, and realistic feedback is emphasized (Anderson et al. 1986).

It can be difficult to work with depressed clients. The practitioner often feels drained after an extended interaction and may feel frustrated by the seeming lack of effort on the part of the client. These feeling may be alleviated by consultation with other professionals, a mixed caseload that includes problems other than depression, and a firm sense of where one's responsibilities begin and end.

The following case illustration is used to highlight several of the important clinical issues that emerge in working with depressed clients.

## CASE ILLUSTRATION

Catherine G. is a 33-year-old nurse who was referred three days after the birth of her daughter. She was referred for a suspected postpartum depression. The social worker immediately suspected major depressive disorder based on symptoms such as slowed movements and a flat expression. The interview, which was difficult to conduct because of the client's slowed speech and memory difficulties, revealed multiple psychosocial stressors, including several major life events. Catherine was married to man who suffered from debilitating lung disease. Both Catherine and her husband worked in the field of developmental disabilities and had planned to adopt a handicapped child. These plans were interrupted by the unplanned pregnancy. Catherine's mother had died eight weeks before the baby was born. Catherine had undergone a tubal ligation immediately following the birth in accordance with her husband's wishes.

An evaluation indicated that Catherine was suffering from major depressive disorder with melancholic features. Her depressive symptoms responded to a course of antidepressant medication within a few weeks. She had to stop nursing her baby when she began the medication, and once the symptoms lifted, she stopped the medication to resume nursing. Unfortunately, the symptoms reemerged, and she had to stop nursing in order to begin medication again. Within four months of her mother's death, Catherine's father remarried suddenly. The social work involvement during this time consisted of evaluation, support, and education about major depressive disorder. The supportive work included the provision of hope in the face of overwhelming hopelessness, as well as continual reminders that painful symptoms such as hopelessness would remit as the depression lifted. Catherine also needed continual reminders that symptoms such as feelings of worthlessness were components of depression and not of her character.

Catherine's significant past psychosocial history included a brief hospitalization as a teenager. She remembered only feeling blamed and refusing to talk to her parents during this time. She had been raped by her gynecologist when in her early 20s but had not reported the rape. Although she had worked with a variety of mental health professionals intermittently for ten years, her problem had never been assessed as a depression with a biological basis. The therapy had tended to focus on her passive-aggressive behavior and her hostility, and one therapist had told her that she "chose to be depressed" when therapy failed to alleviate her symptoms. She worked as a filing clerk until her mid-20s, when she decided on a career in nursing and eventually obtained a graduate degree.

Catherine's family history revealed many female relatives with histories consistent with depression, as well as an overly close mother–daughter relationship. The mother seemed to have been overinvolved, yet unaware of her daughter's needs. For example, Catherine had been named after her mother's favorite doll and had been discouraged from dating or other peer activities as a teenager. The parents had an unhappy marriage and the father traveled extensively in his work. The mother had confided her longstanding marital difficulties, including her father's numerous infidelities, to her daughter.

Once the symptoms of depression were under control, Catherine asked to work with the social worker on issues related to long-term feelings of helplessness and job and marital difficulties. She expressed a desire to understand why she had become an adult who lacked confidence and fulfillment, and she wanted to put the recent events, such as death of her mother and her depression, behind her. The working relationship lasted three years. For some periods, the work was intermittent because of financial problems. At other times, when things were going well, the work would cease and contact would be on an as-needed basis. The majority of the three years consisted of sustained work every week that intensified during episodes of severe depression.

Following the initial episode, Catherine's depressive symptoms decreased, but she continued to experience low self-confidence, little interest in sex, and lack of energy. She also had fleeting thoughts of suicide. An initial attempt at insight-oriented psychotherapy proved minimally useful. She talked of experiencing anger interpersed with sadness and was able to describe several strengths, such as determination, insightfulness, and motivation. She was passive in response to interpretations, and while she would superficially agree when ways to improve her situation were pointed out to her, she was unable to formulate independent solutions to her problems or to grapple actively with issues.

Because of Catherine's job termination, coupled with her husband's low-paying job, the family began experiencing severe financial difficulties. They moved into a small basement apartment in a poor neighborhood, and the dampness in the apartment set off serious asthmatic problems in the baby. With many disagreements over money management and sex, the couple experienced increased emotional distance.

Things improved as some of the stresses abated. Catherine's obtaining another job relieved the financial strain somewhat. At this point, the intervention plan was modified to incorporate mutually agreed-upon cognitive strategies. Negative cognitive schemata and the use of selective abstraction were actively challenged. Catherine began to be more assertive in her marriage. At her insistence, the couple obtained credit counseling despite her husband's strong resistance. She began to explore the possibilty of having her unwanted tubal ligation reversed. Her marital dissatisfaction increased, and over time, a see-saw marital pattern was revealed: When Catherine's depression lifted, her husband's chronic illness would invariably worsen. Eventually, he began to have an affair with a woman at work, which prompted Catherine's first and only suicide attempt.

Within three years, Catherine experienced two additional episodes of severe depression and was hospitalized briefly only once. Each episode responded to a course of antidepressant medication, and after the second episode, she refused to stop the medication. Eventually, she began to experience severe cardiac side effects from her medication. Numerous changes and reductions in medication ensued. Despite the serious complications, Catherine resisted stopping the medication for fear that the deep depression would return. She came to believe that the depression was entirely controlled by the antidepressant medication. The worker–client relationship ended when the social worker moved from the area. During termination, Catherine was unable to express any feelings of anger or loss, saying only that there was nothing she could do about the move.

This case clearly demonstrates the complex coexistence of several types of depression. In addition to an assessment of biological depression, the social work intervention occurred in stages to deal with the psychosocial issues presented by each of the types of depression. Support was critical during episodes of severe depression, to fill in temporarily for the deficits caused by the severe depressive symptoms and to help the client deal with the multiple uncontrollable life events that were operating.

Support continued between episodes, and other issues were addressed. Glimmers of appropriate mastery behavior can be seen in Catherine's psychosocial history (her return to school) and in the current work (her active handling of the financial situation and her exploration of reversing the unwanted tubal ligation).

Socialization into a passive orientation to life is relevant to this case and is not uncommon in many women in our society. It is relevant here. Inappropriate intrusiveness like that exhibited by Catherine's mother is often found in the histories of depressed women (Parker, Tupling, and Brown 1979). We can surmise that the inappropriate disclosure of her father's behavior did little to foster a vision of healthy, reciprocal relationships between men and women. We can also hypothesize that the developmental stage of separation and individuation that usually occurs in late adolescence was hampered by depression and hospitalization, and that the rape only reinforced Catherine's feeling of not being in control of her life. Not surprisingly, insight-oriented therapy was not the treatment of choice, as evidenced by her response to medication and cognitive strategies.

The worker–client relationship in this case reflects typical relationships between depressed clients and significant others. An alliance is easily established during the most severe episode of depression but is characterized by extreme dependency. The alliance must be renegotiated when the depression lifts, or the worker will join the larger environment by sending a message that the client perceives as saying that the client is not capable of taking control of his or her own life. An underlying current of hostility can also be read in this vignette. The inability to express feelings of anger or loss is evident in the client's attitude toward termination.

This paper has described the theories, the social factors, and the risk factors associated with depression. Assessment and intervention issues have also been described. A great deal of clinical "knowledge" about depression is based on the fallacy that it is a homogeneous phenomenon. It is not. Clear definitions of depression and a clarification of the distinguishing features of the different types of depression will enhance treatment for social workers' clients, but we need to learn more. Most information about depression has been gleaned from middle-class samples, and very little information exists about the poor. More research is needed to verify the subtypes of depression and to explore effective treatment strategies and programs for these subtypes.

The prevalence of depression, the extensive suffering it causes, and the effective clinical interventions available stand in tragic contrast to the lack of appropriate care received by those who need it. Today, 80 to 90 percent of persons with a major depressive disorder can be helped successfully, but only one person in three with depression ever seeks treatment (Regier et al. 1988).

Depression is the most treatable of any of the major psychiatric disturbances, but it goes unrecognized and untreated because it is misunderstood. Public attitudes toward depression need to be changed so that there is greater acceptance of depression as a serious health problem, rather than a moral weakness. Social workers can help to alleviate or prevent problems with depression that is a reaction to social problems among vulnerable people by taking an active role in educating other professionals to recognize depression. The training that social workers receive in the dynamics of human behavior makes them especially suited to alert the professionals in other disciplines to the need to identify and obtain treatment for depressed clients outside psychiatric settings. Social workers can also work to increase public knowledge about the symptoms of depression and the availability of effective interventions, and to develop new programs to meet the needs of the depressed.

Social workers are in a unique position to assume a critical role in ensuring that clients will be identified early and will be provided appropriate care. Social workers have the perspective, the training, and the expertise to identify the emotional distress associated with social problems, especially as it varies with the particular social problem presented, and with the characteristics of the client. With their unique person–environment perspective, social workers are able to understand depression as a symptom of distress that accompanies child abuse, sexual abuse, family violence, and substance abuse. Early recognition and proper care of depressed clients may help prevent other, more serious social problems.

## REFERENCES

Abraham, K. 1911/1986. "I. Notes on Psychoanalytical Investigation and Treatment of Manic-depressive Insanity and Allied Conditions (1911)." In J. Coyne, ed., *Essential Papers on Depression*, pp. 23–31. New York: New York University Press.

APA (American Psychiatric Association). 1980. *Diagnostic and Statistical Manual of Mental Disorders (DSM-III)*, 3d ed. Washington, D.C.: APA pp. 217–223.

Anderson, C., S. Griffin, A. Rossi, I. Pagonis, D. Holder. 1986. "A Comparative Study of the Impact of Education vs. Process Groups for Families of Patients with Affective Disorders." *Family Process* 25:185–205.

Aneshensel, C., R. Fredrichs, and V. Clark. 1981. "Family Roles and Sex Differences in Depression." *Journal of Health and Social Behavior* 22:379–393.

Baron, M., J. Mendelwicz, and J. Klotz. 1981. "Age of Onset and Genetic Transmission in Affective Disorders." *Acta Psychiatrica Scandinavica* 64:373–380.

Battaglino, L. 1987. "Family Empowerment Through Self-Help Groups." In A. Hatfield, ed., *Families of the Mentally Ill: Meeting the Challenges*, 43–51. New Directions for Mental Health Services, No. 34. San Francisco: Jossey-Bass.

Beach, S. and K. O'Leary. 1986. "The Treatment of Depression Occurring in the Context of Marital Discord." *Behavioral Therapy* 17:43–49.

Beardslee, W., M. Keller, P. Lavori, G. Klerman, D. Dorer, and H. Samuelson. 1988. "Psychiatric Disorder in Adolescent Offspring of Parents with Affective Disorder in a Non-Referred Sample." *Journal of Affective Disorders* 15 (3):313–322.

Beck, A. 1967. *Depression: Clinical, Experimental, and Theoretical Aspects*. New York: Harper & Row.

Beck, A., A. Rush, B. Shaw, G. Emary. 1979. *Cognitive Therapy of Depression*. New York: Guilford.

Behar, D., G. Winokur, C. Van Valkenburg, and M. Lowry. 1980. "Familial Subtypes of Depression: A Clinical View." *Journal of Clinical Psychiatry* 41:52–56.

Bellack, A., M. Herson, and J. Himmelhoch. 1983. "A Comparison of Social-Skills Training, Pharmacotherapy and Psychotherapy for Depression." *Behavioral Research Therapy* 21:101–107.

Belle, D. 1982. "The Stress of Caring: Women as Providers of Social Support." In L. Goldberger and S. Breznitz, eds., *Handbook of Stress*. pp. 496–505. New York: Free Press.

Bernheim, K. and T. Switalski. 1988. "Mental Health Staff and Patient's Relatives: How They View Each Other." *Hospital and Community Psychiatry* (January) 39(1):63–68.

Bertelsen, A. 1979. "A Danish Twin Study of Manic-Depressive Disorders." In M. Shou and E. Stromgren, eds., *Origin, Prevention and Treatment of Affective Disorder*, pp. 227–239. London: Academic Press.

Bibring, E. 1953. "The Mechanism of Depression." In P. Greenacre, ed., *Affective Disorders*, pp. 48–64. New York: International Universities Press.

Bifulco, A., G. Brown, and T. Harris. 1987. "Childhood Loss of Parent, Lack of Adequate Parental Care and Adult Depression: A Replication." *Journal of Affective Disorders* 12:115–128.

Biglan, A., H. Hops, L. Sherman, L. Friedmen, J. Arthur, V. Osteen. 1985. "Problem-Solving Interactions of Depressed Women and Their Husbands." *Behavior Therapy* 16: 431–451.

Billings, A. and R. Moos. 1986. "Psychosocial Theory and Research on Depression: An Integrative Framework and Review." In J. Coyne, ed., *Essential Papers on Depression*, pp. 331–366. New York: New York University Press.

Billings, A. and R. Moos. 1982. "Social Support and Functioning Among Community and Clinical Groups: A Panel Model." *Journal of Behavioral Medicine*, 5:295–311.

Birtchnell, J. and J. Kennard. 1983. "Marriage and Mental Illness." *British Journal of Psychiatry* 142:193–198.

Blaney, P. 1977. "Contemporary Theories of Depression: Critique and Comparison." *Journal of Abnormal Psychology* 86:203–223.

Blazer, D., L. George, R. Landerman, M. Perrybacke, M. Melville, M. Woodbury, K. Marton, K. Jordon, B. Locke. 1985. "Psychiatric Disorders: A Rural/Urban Comparison." *Archives of General Psychiatry* 42:651–656.

Bowlby, J. 1977. "The Making and Breaking of Affectional Bonds." *British Journal of Psychiatry* 136:201–210.

Boyd, J. and M. Weissman. 1981. "Epidemiology of Affective Disorder." *Archives of General Psychiatry* 38:1039–1046.

Boyd, J. and M. Weissman. 1983. "Epidemiology of Affective Disorder: A Reexamination and Future Directions." *Archives of General Psychiatry* 38:1039–1046.

Breier, A., J. Kelsoe, P. Kirwin, S. Bellar, O. Walkowitz, D. Pickar. 1988. "Early Parental Loss and Development of Adult Psychopathology." *Archives of General Psychiatry* 45:987–993.

Brown, G., A. Bifulco, and T. Harris. 1987. "Life Events, Vulnerability and the Onset of Depression: Some Refinements." *British Journal of Psychiatry* 150:30–42.

Brown, G. and T. Harris. 1978. *The Social Origins of Depression*. London: Tavistock.

Brown, G. and T. Harris. 1986. "Stressor, Vulnerability and Depression: A Question of Replication." *Psychological Medicine* 16:739–774.

Brown, G., T. Harris, and J. Peto. 1973. "Life Events and Psychiatric Disorders, 2: Nature of Causal Link." *Psychological Medicine* (London), 3:159–176.

Bulow, B., J. Sweeney, M. Shear, R. Friedman, C. Plowe. 1987. "Family Satisfaction with Psychiatric Evaluations." *Health and Social Work* (Fall) pp. 290–295.

Burns, D. 1980. *Feeling Good: The New Mood Therapy*. New York: Signet.

Cadoret, R. 1978. "Evidence of Genetic Inheritance of Primary Affective Disorder in Adoptees." *American Journal of Psychiatry* 135: 463–466.

Clayton, P., R. Hirschfeld, and B. Larkin. 1974. *Personal Resources Inventory (PRI)*. Rockville, Md: National Institute of Mental Health.

Cohen, M., G. Baker, R. Cohen, F. Fromm-Reichmen, E. Weigert. 1954. "An Intensive Study of Twelve Cases of Manic-Depressive Psychosis." *Psychiatry* 17:103–137.

Cole, C. and J. Coyne 1977. "Situational Specificity of Laboratory Induced Learned Helplessness." *Journal of Abnormal Psychology* 86:615–623.

Coyne, J. 1976. "Toward an Interactional Description of Depression." *Psychiatry* 39:28–40.

Crowell, B., L. George, and D. Blazer. Submitted for publication. "Psychiatric and Social Outcomes of Child Abuse."

Dobson, K., N. Jacobson. and J. Victor. 1988. "Cognitive Therapy and Behavorial Marital Therapy: Towards an Integration." In J. Clarkin, G. Haas, and I. Glick eds., *Deffective Disorders and the Family*, pp. 51–88. New York: Guilford.

Dunner, D., J. Fleiss, G. Addonizio, and R. Fieve. 1976. "Assortative Mating in Primary Affective Disorder." *Biological Psychiatry* 2:43–51.

Eagles, J. and L. Whalley. 1985. "Aging and Affective Disorders: The Age at First Onset of Affective Disorders in Scotland, 1969–1978." *British Journal of Psychiatry* 147:180–187.

Egeland, J., D. Gerhard, D. Pauls, J. Sussex, K. Kidd, C. Allen, A. Hostetter, D. Housman. 1987. "Bipolar Affective Disorder Linked to DNA Markers on Chromosome II." *Nature* 325:783–787.

Egeland, J. and A. Hostetter. 1983. "Amish Study, 1: Affective Disorders Among the Amish, 1976–1980." *American Journal of Psychiatry* 140:56.

Epstein, N., L. Baldwin, and D. Bishop. 1983. "The McMaster Family Assessment Device." *Journal of Marriage and Family Therapy* 9:171–180.

Ferster, C. 1971. "A Functional Analysis of Depression." *American Psychologist* 10:857–870.

Finestein, A. 1970. "The Pre-Therapeutic Classifications of Co-Morbidity in Chronic Disease." *Journal of Chronic Disease* 23:455–468.

Freud, S. 1896/1986. "Mourning and Melancholia." *Standard Edition of the Collected Works of Sigmund Freud.* London: Hogarth. In J. Coyne, Ed., *Essential Papers on Depression*, pp. 48–63. New York: New York University Press.

Friedman, A. 1975. "Interaction of Drug Therapy with Marital Therapy in Depressive Patients." *Archives of General Psychiatry* 32:619–637.

Friedman, J. and P. Bennet. 1977. "Depression and Hypertension." *Psychosomatic Medicine* 39:134–142.

Gershon, E. 1983. "The Genetics of Affective Disorders." In L. Grinspoon, ed., *Psychiatry Update: The American Psychiatric Association Annual Review*, vol. 2, part 5, p. 434. Washington, D.C.: American Psychiatric Press.

Gilbert, P. 1984. *Depression: From Psychology to Brain State.* Hillsdale, N.J.: Erlbaum.

Glick, I., J. Clarkin, J. Spencer, G. Haas, A. Levis, J. Pryser, N. OrMare, M. Good-Ellis, E. Harris, V. Vestelle. 1985. "A Controlled Evaluation of Inpatient Family Intervention." *Archives of General Psychiatry* 42:882–886.

Gotlib, I., J. Mount, N. Cordy, and V. Whiffen. 1988. "Depression and Perceptions of Early Parenting: A Longitudinal Investigation." *British Journal of Psychiatry* 152:24–27.

Gove. W. 1972. "The Relationship Between Sex Roles, Marital Status and Mental Illness." *Social Forces* 51:34–44.

Gove, W., M. Hughes, and C. Style. 1983. "Does Marriage Have Positive Effects on the Psychological Well-Being of the Individual?" *Journal of Health and Social Behavior* 24:122–131.

Hagnell, O., J. Lanke, B. Rorsman, and L. Ojesjo. 1982. "Are We Entering an Age of Melancholy? Depressive Illnesses in a Prospective Epidemiological Study Over 25 Years: The Lundby Study, Sweden." *Psychological Medicine* 12:279–289.

Hautzinger, M., M. Linden, and N. Hoffman. 1982. "Distressed Couples with and Without a Depressed Partner: An Analysis of Their Verbal Interaction." *Journal of Behavior Therapy and Experimental Psychiatry* 13:307–314.

Henderson, A. 1984. "Interpreting the Evidence for Social Support." *American Journal of Psychiatry* 19:49–52.

Herman, J. and L. Hirschman. 1981. "Families at Risk for Father-Daughter Incest." *American Journal of Psychiatry* 138(7):967–970.

Hinchcliffe, M., D. Hooper, F. Roberts, P. Vaughn. 1975. "A Study of the Interaction Between Depressed Patients and Their Spouses." *British Journal of Psychiatry* 126:164–172.

Hinchcliffe, M., D. Hooper, F. Roberts, P. Vaughn. 1978. "The Melancholy Marriage: An Inquiry into the Interaction of Depression, 4: Disruptions." *British Journal of Medical Psychology* 51:15–24.

Hinchcliffe, M., P. Vaughan, D. Hooper, et al. 1978. "The Melancholy Marriage: An Inquiry into the Interaction of Depression, 3: Responsiveness." *British Journal of Medical Psychology* 51:1–13.

Hinchcliffe, M., P. Vaughan, D. Hooper, F. Roberts. 1977. "The Melancholy Marriage: An Inquiry into the Interaction of Depression, 2: Expressiveness." *British Journal of Medical Psychology* 50:125–142.

Hirschfeld, R. and C. Cross. 1982. "Epidemiology of Affective Disorders." *Archives of General Psychiatry* 39:35–46.

Hooley, J. 1986. "Expressed Emotion and Depression: Interactions Between Patients and High-Versus Low-Expressed Emotion Spouses." *Journal of Abnormal Psychology* 95:237–246.

Hooley, J., J. Orley, and J. Teasdale. 1986. "Levels of Expressed Emotion and Relapse in Depressed Patients." *British Journal of Psychiatry* 148:642–647.

Hooper, D., F. Roberts, M. Hinchcliffe, P. Vaughn. 1977. "The Melancholy Marriage: An Inquiry into the Interaction of Depression, 1: Introduction." *British Journal of Medical Psychology* 50:113–124.

Hooper, D., P. Vaughn, M. Hinchcliffe, F. Roberts. 1978. "The Melancholy Marriage: An Inquiry into the Interaction of Depression, 5: Power." *British Journal of Medical Psychology* 51:387–398.

Hops, H., A. Biglan, L. Sherman, J. Arthur, L. Friedman, V. Osteer. 1987. "Home Observations of Family Interactions of Depressed Women." *Journal of Consulting and Clinical Psychology* 55:341–346.

House, J. 1981. *Work Stress and Social Support.* Reading, Mass.: Addison-Wesley.

Hyler, S. and A. Frances. 1985. "Clinical Implications of Axis I and Axis II Interactions." *Comprehensive Psychiatry* 26(4):345–351.

Ilfield, F. 1977. "Current Social Stressors and Symptoms of Depression." *American Journal of Psychiatry* 134:161–166.

Jacob, M., E. Frank, D. Kupfer, and L. Carpenter. 1987. "Recurrent Depression: An Assessment of Family Burden and Family Attitudes." *Journal of Clinical Psychiatry* (October) 48(10):395–400.

Jacob, M., E. Frank, D. Kupfer, C. Cornes, L. Carpenter. 1987. "A Psychoeducational Workshop for Depressed Patients, Family, and Friends: Description and Evaluation." *Hospital and Community Psychiatry* (September) 38(9):968–972.

James, N. and C. Chapman. 1975. "A Genetic Study of Bipolar Affective Disorder." *British Journal of Psychology* 126:449–456.

Kahn, J., J. Coyne, and G. Margolin. 1985. "Depression and Marital Conflict: The Social Construction of Despair." *Journal of Social and Personal Relationships.* 2:447–462.

Kanter, J., H. Lamb, and C. Loeper. 1987. "Expressed Emotion in Families: A Critical Review." *Hospital and Community Psychiatry* 38:374–380.

Keller, M. and R. Shapiro. 1982. "Double Depression: Superimposition of Acute

Depressive Episodes on Chronic Depressive Disorders." *American Journal of Psychiatry* 139:438–442.

Kessler, R. 1979. "A Strategy for Studying Differential Vulnerability to the Psychological Consequences of Stress." *Journal of Health and Social Behavior* 20:100–108.

Klein, D. 1974. "Endogenomorphic Depression." *Archives of General Psychiatry* (October) 31:447–454.

Klerman, G. 1988. "The Current Age of Youthful Melancholia: Evidence for Increase in Depression Among Adolescents and Young Adults." *British Journal of Psychiatry* 152:4–14.

Klerman, G., M. Weissman, B. Rounsaville, E. Chevron. 1984. *Interpersonal Psychotherapy of Depression*. New York: Basic Books.

Kovacs M., A. Rush, and A. Beck. 1981. "Depressed Outpatients Treated with Cognitive Therapy or Pharmacotherapy: A One-Year Follow-Up." *Archives of General Psychiatry* (January) 38:33–39.

Kuipers, L. 1979. "Expressed Emotion: A Review." *British Journal of Social and Clinical Psychology* 18:237–243.

Larson, D., E. Pattison, D. Blazer, A. Omrar, B. Kaplan. 1986. "Systematic Analysis of Research on Religious Variables in Four Psychiatric Journals, 1978–1982." *American Journal of Psychiatry* 143:329–334.

Lewinsohn, P. 1986. "A Behavioral Approach to Depression." In J. Coyne ed., *Essential Papers on Depression*. pp. 150–180 New York: New York University Press.

Lewinsohn, P., E. Duncan, A. Stanton, and M. Hautzinger. 1986. "Age at First Onset for Nonbipolar Depression." *Journal of Abnormal Psychology* 94:378–383.

Lewinsohn, P., R. Munoz, M. Youngren, and A. Zeiss. 1978. *Control Your Depression*. Englewood Cliffs, N.J.: Prentice-Hall.

Lewinsohn, P. and M. Rosenbaum. 1987. "Recall of Parental Behavior by Acute Depressives, Remitted Depressives, and Nondepressives." *Journal of Personality and Social Psychology* 52:611–619.

Lewinsohn, P., J. Sullivan, and S. Grosscup. 1980. "Changing Reinforcing Events: An Approach to the Treatment of Depression." *Psychotherapy: Theory, Research and Practice* 17:322–334.

Liem, R. and J. Liem. 1978. "Social Class and Mental Illness Reconsidered: The Role of Economic Stress and Social Support." *Journal of Health and Social Behavior* 19:139–156.

Linden, M., M. Hautzinger, and N. Hoffman. 1983. "Discriminant Analysis of Depressive Interactions." *Behavior Modification* 7:403–422.

Lowry, M., C. Van Valkenburg, and G. Winokur. 1978. "Baseline Characteristics of Pure Depressive Disease." *Neuropsychological Biology* 4:333–343.

Marquez, C., Z. Taintor, and M. Schwartz. 1985. "Diagnosis of Manic-Depressive Illness in Blacks." *Comprehensive Psychiatry* 26:337–341.

Melges, F. 1982. *Time and the Inner Future*. New York: Wiley Interscience.

Mendlewicz, J. and J. Rainer. 1977. "Adoption Study Supporting Genetic Transmission in Manic-Depressive Illness." *Nature* 268:327.

Merikangas, K., E. Bromet, and D. Spiker. 1983. "Assortative Mating, Social Adjustment, and Course of Illness in Primary Affective Disorder." *Archives of General Psychiatry* 40:795–800.

Merikangas, K., M. Weissman, B. Prusoff, and K. John. 1988. "Assortative Mating and Affective Disorders: Psychopathology in Offspring." *Psychiatry* 51:48–57.

Miller, I., R. Kabacoff, G. Keitner, N. Epstein, D. Bishop. 1986. "Family Functioning in the Families of Psychiatric Patients." *Comprehensive Psychiatry* 27:302–312.

Moos, R. and R. Mitchell. 1982. "Social Network Resources and Adaptations: A

Conceptual Framework." In T. Wills, ed., *Basic Processes in Helping Relationships*, pp. 213–231 New York: Academic Press.

Munoz, R. 1987. "Depression Prevention Research: Conceptual and Practical Considerations." In R. Munoz, ed., *Depression Prevention: Research Directions*, p. 4 Washington, D.C.: Hemisphere Publishing Corporation.

Myers, J., J. Lindenthal, and M. Pepper. 1975. "Life events, Social Integration and Psychiatric Symptomatology." *Journal of Health and Social Behavior* 16:421–427.

Myers, J., M. Weissman, G. Tischler, C. Holzer, P. Leaf, H. Orveschel, J. Anthony, J. Boyd, J. Burke, M. Kramet, R. Stoltgman. 1984. "Six-Month Prevalence of Psychiatric Disorders in Three Communities, 1980–1982." *Archives of General Psychiatry* 41:959–967.

Myers, J., M. Weissman, G. Tischler, C. Holzer, P. Leaf, H. Orveschel, J. Anthony, J. Boyd, J. Burke, M. Kramet, R. Stoltgman. 1985. "Six-Month Prevalence of Psychiatric Disorders in Three Communities, 1980 to 1982." *Archives of General Psychiatry* 42:651–656.

NIMH/NIH National Institute of Mental Health/National Institute of Health Mood Disorders: Pharmacological Prevention of Recurrences Consensus Development Panel. 1985. "Mood Disorders: Pharmacologic Prevention of Recurrences." *American Journal of Psychiatry* 142:469–476.

Nielsen, A. and T. Williams. 1980. "Depression in Ambulatory Medical Patients: Prevalence by Self Report Questionnaire and Recognition by Nonpsychiatric Physicians." *Archives of General Psychiatry* 37:999–1004.

Noh, S. and R. Turner. 1987. "Living with Psychiatric Patients: Implications for the Mental Health of Family Members." *Social Science and Medicine* 25(3):263–271.

O'Connell, R., J. Mayo, L. Eng, J. Jones, R. Gabel. 1985. "Social Support and Long-Term Lithium Outcome." *British Journal of Psychiatry* 147:272–275.

Overall, J., B. Henry, and A. Woodward. 1974. "Dependence of Marital Problems on Parental Family History." *Journal of Abnormal Psychology* 83:446–450.

Overmier, J. and M. Seligman. 1967. "Effects of Inescapable Shock Upon Subsequent Escape and Avoidance Responding." *Journal of Comparative and Physiological Psychology* 63:23–33.

Parker, G., H. Tupling, and L. Brown. 1979. "A Parental Bonding Instrument." *British Journal of Psychology* 52:1–10.

Parry, G. and D. Shapiro. 1986. "Social Support and Life Events in Working Class Women." *Archives of General Psychiatry* 43:315–323.

Paykel, E. 1978. "Recent Life Events in the Development of Depressive Disorders." In R. Depue, ed., *The Psychobiology of Depressive Disorders: Implications for the Effects of Stress*, pp. 245–262. New York: Academic Press.

Paykel, E. 1982. "Life Events and Early Environment." In E. Paykel, ed., *Handbook of Affective Disorders*, pp. 146–161. New York: Guilford.

Paykel, E., J. Myers, M. Dienelt, G. Klerman, J. Linduthal, M. Pepper. 1969. "Life Events and Depression: A Controlled Study." *Archives of General Psychiatry* 21:753–760.

Paykel, E. and M. Weissman. 1979. "Social Adjustment and Depression: A Longitudinal Study." *Archives of General Psychiatry* 28:659–663.

Pearlin, L. and M. Lieberman. 1979. "Social Sources of Emotional Distress." In R. Simmons, ed., *Research in Community and Mental Health*, pp. 217–248. Greenwich, Conn.: JAI.

Post, R., D. Rubinow, and J. Ballenger. 1986. "Conditioning and Sensitization in the Longitudinal Course of Affective Illness." *British Journal of Psychiatry* 149:191–201.

Radloff, L. 1986. "Risk Factors for Depression: What Do We Learn from Them"? In

J. Coyne, ed., *Essential Papers on Depression*, pp. 403–419. New York: New York University Press.

Ragan, P. and T. McGlashan. 1986. "Childhood Parental Death and Adult Psychopathology." *American Journal of Psychiatry* 143:153–157.

Regier, D., J. Boyd, J. Burke, D. Roe, J. Myers, M. Kramet, L. Robins, L. George, M. Karao, B. Locke. 1988. "One-Month Prevalence of Mental Disorders in the US—Based on FIve Epidemiologic Catchment Area Sites." *Archives of General Psychiatry* 45(11):977–986.

Regier, D., R. Hirschfeld, F. Goodwin, J. Burke, J. Lazar, L. Judd. 1988. "The NIMH Depression Awareness, Recognition, and Treatment Program: Structure, Aims, and Scientific Bias." *American Journal of Psychiatry* 145(11):1351–1357.

Reich, J. 1985. "The Relationship Between Antisocial Behavior and Affective Illness." *Comprehensive Psychiatry* 26(3):296–303.

Robins, L., J. Helzer, M. Weissman, H. Orvaschlof, E. Gruerberg, J. Burke, D. Regier. 1984. "Lifetime Prevalence of Specific Psychiatric Disorders in Three Sites." *Archives of General Psychiatry* 41:949–958.

Rounsaville, B., B. Prusoff, and M. Weissman. 1980. "The Course of Marital Disputes in Depressed Women: A 48-Month Follow-Up Study." *Comprehensive Psychiatry* 21:111–118.

Rounsaville, B., M. Weissman, B. Prusoff, R. Harcay-Baron. 1979. "Marital Disputes and Treatment Outcome in Depressed Women." *Comprehensive Psychiatry* 20:483–490.

Roy, A. 1987. "Five Risk Factors for Depression." *British Journal of Psychiatry* 150:536–541.

Ruestow, P., D. Dunner, B. Bleecker, R. Fieve. 1978. "Marital Adjustment in Primary Affective Disorder." *Comprehensive Psychiatry* 19:565–571.

Rutter, M. 1985. "Resilience in the Face of Adversity: Protective Factors and Resistance to Psychiatric Disorders." *British Journal of Psychiatry* 145:1–10.

Saltz, C. and K. Magruder-Habib. 1985. "Recognizing Depression in Patients Receiving Medical Care." *Health and Social Work* 10 (1):15–22.

Schildkraut, J., A. Green, and J. Mooney. 1985. "Affective Disorders: Biochemical Aspects." In H. Kaplan and B. Sadock, eds., *Comprehensive Textbook of Psychiatry*, Fourth Edition, Volume 1, pp. 769–777. Baltimore: Williams & Wilkins.

Schlesser, M., G. Winokur, and B. Sherman. 1979. "Genetic Subtypes of Unipolar Primary Depressive Illness Distinguished by Hypothalamic-Pituitary-Adrenal Axis Activity." *Lancet* 1:739–741.

Schuckit, M. 1983. "Alcoholic Patients with Secondary Depression." *American Journal of Psychiatry* (June), 140:711–714.

Schwab-Bakman, N., H. Appelt, F. Rist. 1981. "Sex-Role Identification in Women Alcoholics and Depressives." *Journal of Studies on Alcohol* (July) 42:654–660.

Seligman, M. 1975. *Helplessness: On Depression, Development, and Death.* San Francisco: Freeman.

Smith, E. and E. North. 1988. "Familial Subtypes of Depression: A Longitudinal Perspective." *Journal of Affective Disorders* 14:145–154.

Spiegel, D. and T. Wissler. 1987. "Using Family Consultation as Psychiatric Aftercare for Schizophrenic Patients." *Hospital and Community Psychiatry* (October) 38(10):1096–1099.

Spring, G. and J. Rothgery. 1984. "The Link Between Alcoholism and Affective Disorders." *Hospital and Community Psychiatry* 35:820–823.

Tanner, J., M. Weissman, and B. Prusoff. 1975. "Social Adjustment and Clinical Relapse in Depressed Outpatients." *Comprehensive Psychiatry* 16:547–556.

Tennant, C. 1985. "Female Vulnerability to Depression." *Psychological Medicine* 15:733–737.

Tennant, C., P. Bebbington, and J. Hurry. 1982. "Social Experiences in Childhood and Adult Psychiatric Morbidity: A Multiple Regression Analysis." *Psychological Medicine* 12:321–327.

Thoits, P. 1983. "Multiple Identities and Psychological Well-Being: A Reformulation and Test of the Social Isolation Hypothesis." *American Sociological Review* 48(2):174–187.

Torgerson, S. 1986. "Genetic Factors in Moderately Severe and Mild Affective Disorders." *Archives of General Psychiatry* 43:222–226.

Turnbull, J., M. Galinsky, D. Meglin, W. Wilner. 1990. "Empowering Families in Inpatient Psychiatry Setting." Paper presented at the Annual Meeting of the National Association of Social Workers, San Francisco, October.

Turnbull, J. 1988. "Primary and Secondary Alcoholic Women." *Social Casework: The Journal of Contemporary Social Work* (May), 69(5):290–297.

Turnbull, J., L. George, R. Landerman. Submitted for publication. "Social Outcomes Related to Age of Onset of Categories of Psychiatric Disorder."

Turnbull, J., R. Kessler, and K. Landis. In preparation. "Grade of Membership Analysis of Depressive Symptoms from the SADS in a Community Sample."

Vaglum, S. and P. Vaglum. 1985. "Boderline and Other Mental Disorders in Alcoholic Female Psychiatric Patients: A Case Control Study." *Psychopathology* (January) 18:50–60.

VanValkenburg, C., H. Akiskal, and V. Puzantian. 1983. "Depression Spectrum Disease or Character Spectrum Disorder: A Clinical Study of Major Depressives with Familial Alcoholism or Sociopathy." *Comprehensive Psychiatry* 24:589–595.

Van Valkenburg, C., M. Lowry, G. Winokur, and R. Cadoret. 1977. "Depression Spectrum Disease Versus Pure Depressive Disease." *Journal of Nervous and Mental Disorders* 165:341–347.

VanValkenburg, C. and G. Winokur. 1979. "Depressive Spectrum Disease." *Psychiatric Clinics of North America* 2:269–482.

Vaughn, C. and J. Leff. 1976a. "The Influence of Family and Social Factors on the Course of Psychiatric Illness." *British Journal of Psychiatry* 129:125–137.

Vaughn, C. and J. Leff. 1976b. "The Measurement of Expressed Emotion in the Families of Psychiatric Patients." *British Journal of Social and Clinical Psychology* 15:157–165.

Waring, E. and D. Patton. 1984. "Maritial Intimacy and Depression." *British Journal of Psychiatry* 145:641–644.

Watson, S., R. Richard, R. Ciaranello, J. Barchas. 1980. "Interaction of Opiate Peptide and Noradrenalin Systems: Light Microscopic Studies." *Peptides* 1:23–30.

Weiner, Z. and J. Rice. 1988. "School-Aged Children of Depressed Parents: A Blind and Controlled Study." *Journal of Affective Disorders* 15(3):291–302.

Weiss, H. 1989. "State Family Support and Education Programs: Lessons from the Pioneers." *American Journal of Orthopsychiatry* (January) 59(1):32–48.

Weissman, M., K. Kidd, and B. Prusoff. 1982. "Variability in Rates of Affective Disorders in Relatives of Depressed and Normal Probands." *Archives of General Psychiatry* 39:1397–1403.

Weissman, M. and G. Klerman. 1977. "Sex Differences in the Epidemiology of Depression." *Archives of General Psychiatry* 34:98–111.

Weissman, M., G. Klerman, and E. Paykel. 1971. "Clinical Evaluation of Hostility in Depression." *American Journal of Psychiatry* 128:261–266.

Weissman, M., P. Leaf, M. Bruce, and L. Florio. 1988. "The Epidemiology of Dysthymia in Five Communities: Rates, Risks, Co-Morbidity, and Treatment." *American Journal of Psychiatry* (July), 145:815–819.

Weissman, M., P. Leaf, G. Tischler, D. Blazer, M. Karne, M. Bruce, L. Florio. 1988.

"Affective Disorders in Five United States Communities." *Psychological Medicine* 18:141–153.

Weissman, M., J. Meyers, and P. Harding. 1980. "Prevalence and Psychiatric Heterogeneity of Alcoholism in a United States Urban Community." *Journal of Studies on Alcohol* (July) 41:672–681.

Weissman, M. and J. Myers. 1978. "Rates and Risks of Depressive Symptoms in a United States Urban Community." *Acta Psychiatrica Scandinavica* 57:219–231.

Weissman, M., and J. Myers. 1981. "Depression and Its Treatment in a U.S. Urban Community, 1975–1976." *Archives of General Psychiatry* 38:417–426.

Weissman M., E. Paykel, and G. Klerman. 1972. "The Depressed Woman as Mother." *Social Psychiatry* 7:98–108.

Weissman, M., E. Paykel, R. Siegel, G. Klerman. 1971. "The Social Role Performance of Depressed Women: Comparisons with a Normal Group." *American Journal of Orthopsychiatry* 41:390–405.

Weissman, M. and R. Siegel. 1972. "The Depressed Woman and Her Rebellious Adolescent." *Social Casework* 53:563–570.

Weissman, M., G. Gammer, K. John, K. Merikanges, V. Warner, B. Prusoff, D. Sholorskes. 1987. "Children of Depressed Parents." *Archives of General Psychiatry* 44:847–853.

Wender, P., S. Kety, D. Rosenthal, F. Schuliaget, J. Ortmann, J. Lunde. 1986. "Psychiatric Disorders in the Biological and Adoptive Families of Adopted Individuals with Affective Disorders." *Archives of General Psychiatry* 43:923–929.

Whybrow, P., H. Akiskal, and W. McKinney. 1984. *Mood Disorder: Toward a New Psychobiology.* New York: Plenum.

Wilcox, B. 1981. "Social Support, Life Stress, and Psychological Adjustment: A Test of the Buffering Hypothesis." *American Journal of Community Psychology* 9:371–386.

Winokur, G. 1972. "Depression Spectrum Disease: Description and Family Study." *Comprehensive Psychiatry* (January), 13:3–8.

Winokur, G. 1985. "The Validity of Neurotic-Reactive Depression." *Archives of General Psychiatry* 42:1116–1122.

Winokur, G., D. Behar, D., C. Van Valkenburg, and M. Lowry. 1978. "Is a Familial Definition of Depression Both Feasible and Valid?" *Journal of Nervous and Mental Disease* 166:764–768.

Winokur, G., R. Cadoret, M. Baker, and J. Dorzab. 1974. "Depression Spectrum Disease Versus Pure Depressive Disease: Some Further Data." *British Journal of Psychiatry* 127:75–77.

Winokur, G. and J. Morrison. 1973. "The Iowa 500: Follow-Up of 225 Depressives." *British Journal of Psychiatry* 1223:543–548.

Zigler, E. and K. Black. 1989. "America's Family Support Movement: Strengths and Limitations." *American Journal of Orthopsychiatry* (January), 59(1):6–19.

Zimmerman, M., W. Coryell, and B. Pfohl. 1986. "Validity of Familial Subtypes of Primary Unipolar Depression: Clinical, Demographic, and Psychosocial Correlates." *Archives of General Psychiatry* 43:1090–1096.

Zimmerman, M., W. Coryell, and B. Pfohl, D. Stargl. 1986. "The Validity of Four Definitions of Endogenous Depression, 2: Clinical, Demographic, Familial and Psychosocial Correlates." *Archives of General Psychiatry* 43:234–244.

Zuckerman, M. and B. Lubin. 1965. *Manual for the Multiple Affect Checklist.* San Diego: Educational and Industrial Testing Service.

Zung, W. 1982. "The Puzzle of Depression Diagnoses: A Binomial Solution." In J. Cavenar and K. Brodie, eds., *Critical Problems in Psychiatry*, pp.157–179. Philadelphia: Lippincott.

# 6

# Eating Problems

▼

## BARBARA VAN BULOW

Eating problems such as anorexia nervosa and obesity have long been of interest to social work clinicians. More recently, with the growth in bulimia, mental health workers have been increasingly interested in this disorder. An eating disorder can present as a sole problem or as one of many difficulties. These eating problems are encountered by social workers in medical settings, psychiatric clinics, and family agencies, as well as in private practice. Therefore, it is important for social workers to have a comprehensive theoretical understanding of eating disorders and to be able to devise appropriate plans for helping these clients.

## PROBLEM DOMAIN

Eating disorders can be divided into three diagnostic categories: anorexia nervosa, bulimia nervosa, and obesity. Sometimes, these diagnoses occur simultaneously in one client (e.g., an anorexia nervosa client may also purge). At other times, they follow each other (e.g., a bulimic woman may stop purging and become obese). A careful assessment is essential because the eating problem may be a specific illness or one symptom within a larger constellation of symptoms, or it may occur along with other illness in a single client. Depression is an illness in which an eating problem is a prominent symptom but not an exclusive one. Most individuals with a severe depression become anorexic and lose weight; in contrast, patients with a mild to moderate depression often have an increased appetite, which can lead to weight gain or bulimia. However, those suffering from depression also have other symptoms, such as anhedonia, depressed mood, sleep disorder, and loss of concentration. For depressed clients, counseling is insufficient if it focuses only on the eating problem. In addition, an eating disorder can coexist with substance abuse. Some excessive eaters, such as obese and bulimic individuals, may also drink excessive amount of alcohol. An increased appetite is know to occur with marijuana intoxication and nicotine withdrawal. Other clients may try to curb their excessive intake of food by using cocaine, which is known to decrease appetite, and therefore, they develop an additional problem. In these examples, counseling must be geared to both the eating problem and the substance abuse.

The term anorexia is defined literally as "loss of appetite." However, usually those with anorexia nervosa have not lost their appetite; rather, they expend enormous energy in curbing their intake of food. Anorexics are extremely thin, often to the point of emaciation, yet they do not perceive that they are underweight. The *DSM-III* (APA 1980) and the *DSM-III-R* (APA 1987) provide a common language in which mental health clinicians and researchers can communicate about psychological disorders. The diagnostic criteria for anorexia nervosa in the *DSM-III-R* include body weight 15 percent below that expected, intense fear of gaining weight or becoming fat, amenorrhea, and a disturbance in the way in which one's body weight, size, or shape is experienced.

Bulimia, an eating disorder rarely mentioned (a decade ago,) has recently received increasing attention in both the professional and the popular literature, although there is some confusion in the literature because the diagnosis is still evolving. The diagnosis of bulimia in the *DSM-III-R* is different from the diagnosis of bulimia nervosa in the *DSM-III*. The *DSM-III* (1980) diagnosis of bulimia stressed recurrent eating binges, the feeling of being out of control of eating, and self-depreciation after a binge. However, the diagnosis did not necessitate vomiting and/or purging behavior and did not require a preoccupation with body shape and weight. The revised diagnosis of bulimia nervosa in the *DSM-III-R* (1987) includes recurrent episodes of binge eating, a feeling of lack of control over the eating behavior, an average of two binge-eating episodes a week, persistent overconcern with body shape and weight, and the use of self-induced vomiting, laxatives or diuretics, strict dieting or fasting, or vigorous exercise in order to prevent weight gain.

The diagnoses of anorexia nervosa and bulimia had little in common as they were delineated in the *DSM-III*. However, the changes in the *DSM-III-R* have illuminated the common psychopathological feature in these two diagnostic categories: overconcern with shape and weight. The commonality in diagnostic criteria is underlined by the change of *bulimia* to *bulimia nervosa*.

Obesity is a medical diagnostic entity and is listed in the *ICD-9* (U.S. HHS 1980) as a subcategory under "278 Obesity and Other Hyperalimentation." Obesity is generally defined as weighing at least 20 percent above a standard weight such as that established by the Metropolitan Life Insurance tables. The *DSM-III* and the *DSM-III-R* do not list obesity as a psychiatric diagnosis because obese people do not have in common a characteristic cluster of psychological symptoms. In addition, many studies of psychopathology associated with obesity have not found the obese to differ from normals (Halmi 1980). However, other studies have shown an increased level of depression, especially in the obese who binge, as opposed to the obese who chronically overeat slightly (Prather and Williamson 1988).

Social workers have to be able to assess eating problems in their clients. Anorexia nervosa can be a life-threatening disease, and clinicians have to know when referral to a medical doctor is essential. Even though clients with bulimia nervosa are usually within a normal weight range, this illness can also be life-threatening because of electrolyte imbalance and cardiac complications. Bulimia nervosa patients tend to be secretive about the extent of their psychopathology because of enormous shame. Therefore, referral for a medical evaluation needs to be very carefully handled. Finally, even if the obese client does not have psychopathology, the social worker needs to be knowledgeable about intervention models for the obese, as continued obesity is a serious health hazard. If depression accompanies the obesity, the social worker should know about broad-spectrum programs that address depression as well as emphasize behavior modification and exercise.

There are different theoretical orientations that attempt to explain eating disorders and why these eating problems are found predominantly in females. A sociocultural explanation suggests that in this century, girls in our culture gain self-esteem and social acceptance for their physical appearance, whereas boys are valued for intellectual and physical prowess and success. Since the late 1960s, the standard of physical beauty for women has been changing, and there has been an increasing emphasis on lean, almost boyish figures. Unfortunately for women, female physiology runs counter to this standard, as women have more body fat than men, a lower metabolic rate, and a tendency to gain weight with each pregnancy and difficulty in losing it after childbirth.

The psychoanalytic explanation for anorexia nervosa and bulimia nervosa emphasizes that the adolescent girls' fear of fat (i.e., of developing a rounded, feminine figure) has to do with concern about adult female sexuality and pregnancy (Wilson, Hogan, and Mintz 1983). Briefly summarized the object relations point of view is that an unempathic, unresponsive mother results in the child's having an ego structure inadequate to the tasks of automony and self-regulation as well as little capacity to monitor hunger and a resulting tendency to act out conflicts over independence and self-control via the body and food intake (Bruch 1973). The process of separation-individuation is hypothesized to persist much longer in women (Beattie 1988). There is far more blurring of boundaries and identification for mothers with female children than for mothers with male children. Mothers also see their daughters as narcissistic extensions of themselves, and project onto their daughters their own hopes, fears, and fantasies about femininity. At puberty, the girl's ambivalent struggle for autonomy from the mother is intense as she tries to attain psychosocial maturation. The mother, on the other hand, is often threatened by her daughter's growing sexual attractiveness and, at the same time, is heavily invested in her social success.

In her studies of anorexic and obese patients, Bruch (1973) described their psychological disturbances, differentiating three areas of disordered experiences: distrubances in body image; disturbances in the perception of affective and visceral sensations, including inaccuracy in the way hunger is experienced; and an overall "sense of ineffectiveness." This sense of ineffectiveness is characterized by passivity, a sense of helplessness, difficulty in mastering bodily functions, and the conviction of being unable to change anything about one's life. These patients experience themselves as not being in control of their behavior, needs, and impulses, as not owning their own bodies, and as not having a center of gravity within themselves. Instead, they feel that they are under the influence and direction of external forces.

Preillness features in anorexia nervosa patients, including misperceptions of bodily sensations and cognitive and emotional disturbances in regard to body image, result from early interactional patterns that were unresponsive to the child's independent needs (Bruch 1978). Often, it is alarm over bodily changes during puberty that precipitates the desire for slimness. Normal developmental changes are interpreted as being fat. "Whatever the outward criticism of the body, the deeper anxiety is that, with adult size, more independent behavior is expected. Many have said that anorexics are expressing a fear of adulthood. They are actually afraid of becoming teenagers" (Bruch 1978:61–62). Palmer, and Kalucy (1976), have speculated that the body image distortion of anorexic patients is based on a desire to avoid biological maturity and the resulting demands of adulthood.

The dynamics of the anorexia nervosa patient can also be understood from an object relations perspective (Selvini-Palazzoli 1978). People suffering from anorexia nervosa may view their bodies as threatening forces that must be kept in check. From this perspective, the anorexic equates her body with the incorporated object (i.e. the mother) in its negative, overwhelming aspects. The anorexic experiences her body as all powerful, indestructible, growing, and threatening. The findings of Halmi and colleagues (1981) also support a developmental concept of body image. Their study shows that the accuracy of self-estimation increases as adolescent girls become older.

Some family theorists believe that family dynamics can result in anorexia nervosa. According to Minuchin's theory, (1980), families of patients with anorexia nervosa demonstrate rigidity, enmeshment, overprotectiveness, and failure to resolve conflict. Initially, Selvini-Palazolli (1978) theorized that the seeds for anorexia nervosa lay in the mother–daughter relationship. However, over time, she shifted her focus to the whole family's interactions. Both Minuchin (1980) and Selvini-Palazzoli (1978) have postulate a systems model in which certain family relationships contribute to the development of anorexia nervosa and, in turn, in which the illness maintains the family's hemeostasis.

Some studies have evaluated the psychodynamics of bulimic patients' families. Strober (1981) reported that affective disorder, alcoholism, and drug abuse in the first- and second-degree relatives of 35 bulimics were all more prevalent than in the relatives of 35 anorexics or in the general population. In terms of parental personality characteristics, fathers of bulimics were more impulsive and excitable, had lower frustration tolerance, and were more dissatisfied with their familial relations. Mothers scored higher on depression, hostility, and dissatisfaction with family relationships. Ordman and Kirschenbaum (1986) compared the families of bulimics with the families of normal controls and found more conflict and less cohesion in the bulimic families. Humprey's (1986) finding were similar to Ordman's; in addition, she found that the bulimic-anorexic families were less involved and less supportive. There are not more overweight family members in bulimic's families; however, the families of severe bulimics are highly anxious about weight, and derogatory of overweight people (Wold 1985).

Some theorists have examined the genetic factors in the predisposition to eating problems. For anorexia nervosa, there are few data about genetic factors. Mother–child concordance for anorexia nervosa is rare, although, there are many reports of more than one case in a single family (Garfinkel and Garner 1982). However, anorexia in more than one female in a family may be due to environmental factors, rather than genetic factors. In regard to bulimia nervosa, the emergence of large numbers of sufferers is so recent that the incidence of bulimia in both mother and child is rare. There are no studies of anorexics or bulimics that indicate genetic factors, such as studies of adopted offspring or genetic markers or evaluations of twins reared apart. However, bulimics do tend to have a family history of psychological problems, as the incidence of affective illness and/or alcoholism in the parents of bulimics is high (Pyle, Mitchell, and Eckert 1981; Fairburn and Cooper 1984). Finally, with regard to obesity, there appears to be clear evidence that genes can influence body weight and obesity; however, weight appears to be quite malleable by the environment (Foch and McClearn 1980). Twin studies have demonstrated high concordance of weights, in contrast to adoptive studies, which have shown an absence of correlations in weight between adopted children and their adoptive parents and siblings. The magnitude of the genetic contribution varies with age and sex and with the criteria used for obesity.

Bulimia nervosa and anorexia nervosa can be understood theoretically as modern-day versions of obsessive-compulsive neuroses. Social and educational factors influence the development of particular symptomatology. What is common to all anorexic and bulimic women is a constant preoccupation with food and a persistent pursuit of thinness and an ideal body size. Certain foods become forbidden and highly valued negatively and thus both strongly feared and strongly desired (Rothenberg 1986). For clients with eating disorders, the emphasis on body image and body dissatisfaction may divert attention from other stressful areas and may become a defense against dealing with other problems in life.

In discussing obesity, it is necessary to distinguish between juvenile-onset obesity and adult-onset obesity. In their work on weight reduction in obese patients, Glucksman and Hirsh (1969) found striking body image differences between severely obese persons with juvenile-onset obesity and those with adult-onset obesity. The onset of obesity during adolescence seems to be an extremely crucial factor in terms of that individual's self-concept and evaluation of body image. Obesity is an extremely visible physical deviation not unlike any other type of physical handicap. The ramifications of this handicap include teasing by peers and family and an inadequate opportunity to learn appropriate social skills. Thus, the obese youngster develops an extremely poor body image and self-concept (Leon 1982).

## SOCIETAL CONTEXT

In the Western world, there are intense and conflicting messages about weight and eating (Saunders 1985). On one hand, we are constantly bombarded with food in television commercials and in magazine advertisements, and there are a multitude of food stores and restaurants. On the other hand, there is intense pressure to be thin exemplified by the diets in every magazine, numerous health clubs and spas, and clothes and shoes for every sport. These intense and conflicting social pressures lead women to be enormously concerned about weight and eating behavior. Most people with eating disorders are women. A majority of women report feeling fat although only a minority of women are actually overweight. For many women, dieting has become a way of life. A survey by Nielson found that 56 percent of female respondents between the ages of 24 and 54 were currently on a diet (Silberstein, Striegel-Moore, and Rodin 1987). In addition to this enormous concern with weight and dieting, women also experience enormous shame in relation to their bodies. This shame derives from the woman's perception that her actual body does not match her internalized ideal body shape. Many females try to adhere to society's dictates of a fashionably slim body by episodes of severe dieting that leads to anorexia nervosa or to food cravings and episodic binge eating, i.e., bulimia nervosa.

Cultural and societal standards of appropriate body shape are major determinants of the perception and evaluation of one's body. A woman's ideal body image is not her individual creation but the product of a societal prescription. Beauty ideals are highly culture-bound and change with time. In America, there is a preoccupation with thinness and a negative evaluation placed on being fat. There is an inverse relationship between low body weight and high social class in Western society; the reverse is true in less developed societies. However, the longer immigrants have been in Western countries, the less obese they tend to be (Furnham and Alibhai 1983).

Because of the pressure in Western culture to be thin, there is a particular cultural emphasis by women on themselves to be thin. Fallon and Rozin (1985) studied 248 male and 227 female undergraduates and found that the men were satisfied with their figures and that the women's perceptions put pressure on them to lose weight.

Secord and Jouard (1953) studied idealized female figures and satisfaction or dissatisfaction with the body. They found that women's satisfaction with aspects of their bodies varied with the magnitude of the deviation of their measured size from what they considered the ideal size. The ideal figure in our culture is quite slender but with a full bust. Since this standard is difficult to attain, this ideal is indirectly responsible for much insecurity and anxiety in women.

The mass media's idealization of a slim female figure has a major impact on women (Orbach 1985). Body insecurity is almost bred into women, both at the level of mass culture and in the family's dynamics. Few mothers have been able to feel secure in the natural shape of their bodies and to convey this confidence to their daughters; instead, they express a discomfort with their own bodies and a desire to have their bodies and the bodies of their daughters reflect the contemporary norm, no matter how difficult, if not impossible, this standard may be to achieve. For an overwhelming number of women in our society, being a woman means feeling too fat. Many women are not naturally as thin as the culture dictates is attractive; thus, women are preoccupied with weight because of shame at not reaching this internalized ideal. The psychological consequences of this preoccupation include decreased self-esteem, distorted body image, and feelings of helplessness and frustration in regard to dieting.

One of the precipitants of the increasing incidence of anorexia nervosa and bulimia nervosa is the apparent shift in cultural preference toward thinner women (Garner et al. 1980). In an effort to document this shift, Garner and colleagues collected data from *Playboy*, the Miss America Pageant, population norms, and the number of diet articles in women's popular magazines. The results of this survey confirmed a shift toward an ideal of a thinner female figure over the twenty years from 1959 to 1979, particularly between 1969 and 1979. Furthermore, since 1970, the Miss America Pageant winners have been thinner than the average size of the other contestants, a finding that suggests that the thinnest woman is considered the most beautiful. However, over this same period, women's average weights actually increased. Therefore, paradoxically, as women's actual weights went up, the idealized female figure became thinner. Schwartz, Thompson, and Johnson (1982) were also interested in the interplay between social-cultural forces and eating disorders. They speculated that sociocultural pressures affect the shape of psychological symptoms. Pointing to the dramatic increase in eating disorders, the authors added sociocultural factors to the previously suggested etiological causes of eating problems, such as mother–child interaction, family system problems, and organic causes.

Being overweight has profound psychological effects. Adolescent and adult patients who sought treatment for overweight were found to accept the dominant values of society, viewing obesity—and hence, their own bodies—as undesirable and, in extreme cases, as repulsive (Leon 1982). These overweight patients often feel that their bodies are grotesque and loathsome and exhibit low self-esteem and a negative self-concept. Obese girls have been found to display personality characteristics strikingly similar to those recognized by social anthropologists as typical of ethnic and racial minorities subjected to intense discrimination; these characteristics include passivity, obsessive concern about appearance, the expectation of rejection, and progressive withdrawal. Patients who were obese during adolescence developed an attitude toward weight that caused them to judge people in terms of adiposity; they expressed contempt for fat people and admiration for thin people (Stunkard and Mendelson 1967). All the patients' disappointments were attributed to this handicap of obesity. The feelings of a 12-year-old child on a diet about his body image were expressed in a poem that ended, "Happy when skinny/and sad when fat" (Bruch 1981:47).

## RISKS AND NEEDS OF POPULATION

Anorexia nervosa is growing in incidence in the West (Bruch 1978). This increased incidence appears to be real, rather than apparent, and not to be related to changes in diagnostic or hospitalization practices. The incidence of bulimia nervosa has dramatically increased in the past ten to twenty years (Garner and Garfinkel 1985). It is unclear how much of this increase is due to the revelation of a previous shameful secret, how much is due to women's copying other women, and how much is due to societal and familial pressures. Although obesity does not appear to have increased in incidence recently, public censure of obesity has not lessened; indeed, there appears to be more emphasis than ever on maintaining a normal weight for health reasons.

Most epidemiological studies report that 90 to 95 percent of anorexic nervosa subjects are female, and this percentage has not changed over time: there are very few documented cases of males who are truly diagnosed as having anorexia nervosa. Also, anorexia nervosa tends to occur predominantly in women from an upper socioeconomic background and to be mainly a disease of Western society. However, Garner and Garfinkel (1985) found a progressive rise in the proportion of patients from the lower social classes. Between 1970 and 1975, 70.6

percent of their patients fell into Hollingshead's Social Classes I and II whereas, between 1976 and 1981, only 52 percent of their anorexia nervosa patients were from Classes I and II. Women whose profession requires that they control their weight, such as ballerinas, models, and athletes, are at higher risk of developing anorexia nervosa. Garner and colleagues (1980) found the prevelance of anorexia nervosa among professional dance students to be seven times what might be expected in young females in the general population. In non-Western societies, anorexia nervosa is reported to be growing in incidence in Japan but is relatively rare elsewhere.

Historically, Anorexia nervosa usually develops during adolescence or the early 20s. Recently, there appears to be a significant increase in onset in young adulthood over an earlier age of onset (Garner and Garfinkel 1982). The actual incidence of anorexia nervosa is not clear as one study found 1 severe case in every 100 adolescent girls (Crisp, Palmer, and Kaluey 1976) and another study reported that 10 percent of the surveyed adolescents showed some anorexic behavior (Garfinkel and Garner 1982). Although anorexic nervosa was historically almost exclusively an illness of Caucasian women, more recently there have been a few reports of cases of non-Caucasian women with anorexia. Hsu (1987) reported on seven black patients (one was male), who represented 4 percent of their patient population within a forty-two-month period. Four suffered from anorexia and three from bulimia. Siber (1986) wrote about seven black and Hispanic female adolescent anorexia nervosa patients, who represented 5 percent of their patient population during a twelve-year period. Both of these studies caution that the prevailing stereotype of the victim of anorexia nervosa as a white upper-middle-class female may prevent the early diagnosis of nonwhite clients.

Some researchers have attempted to document the incidence of bulimia nervosa and to describe the course and symptoms of this disorder (Fairburn and Cooper 1982; Halmi 1983). The incidence of bulimia in the community has been reported to be as high as 13 percent (Halmi 1983). Bulimic women have been found to aspire to a thinner ideal body than normal controls. Also, women who are heavier than their peers tend to develop bulimia because the gap between the ideal body and the actual body is intensified by a thinner than average ideal and a heavier then average self. (Johnson et al. 1982). Bulimia often begins when a woman goes on a diet. This food deprivation is followed by bingeing and subsequent purging by vomiting, laxative or diuretic abuse, excessive exercise, or starving. Bulimics are intensely afraid of gaining weight and are acutely sensitive to small fluctuations in weight. In addition, bulimic women appear to be significantly more ashamed of their weight than other women, as bulimic women accept and internalize most deeply the societal norms of attractiveness and thinness (Silberstein, Striegel-Moore, and Rodin 1987).

Five major studies have been done to delineate the characteristics of bulimic individuals (Fairburn and Cooper 1982, 1984; Johnson et al. 1982; Pyle, Mitchell, and Eckert 1981; Russell 1979). The results of these studies were compared by Bulow and DeChillo (1987). The average age of onset of bulimia is between 18 and 20 years, and the victims generally suffer with the illness for four or five years before seeking treatment. About half of these bulimic individuals binge daily, and more than 80 percent vomit or else purge in other ways. A history of anorexia nervosa was noted for only 6 percent in the Johnson et al. study, in contrast to 57 percent in Russell's study. The majority of bulimics have an acceptable weight for their height. Menstrual irregularities (including amenorrhea) occur in one third to three fourths of bulimic women. Most bulimics have depressive symptomatology, and many report suicidal plans or acts. These women are also noted to have high levels of anxiety, interpersonal sensitivity, and impulsivity as measured by general personality inventories such as the Minnesota Multiphasic Personality Inventory (MMPI) or the General Health Questionnaire (GHQ) in Great Britain. It appears that the onset of bulimia occurs after voluntary restrictive dieting, or following a period of emotional upset (Johnson et al. 1982; Pyle 1981).

Family history data are limited; however, families have been implicated in the etiology of bulimia because of the psychodynamic interactions in the family and/or a genetic loading for psychopathology. Pyle and colleagues (1981) noted that there seemed to be a high incidence of alcoholism and weight problems in the families of bulimic subjects. Half of their subjects reported alcoholism in at least one first-degree relative, and 68 percent reported obesity in one or more first-degree relative. Similarly, Fairburn and Cooper (1984) noted that 29 percent of their subjects reported that a first-degree relative had received treatment from a psychiatrist, usually for a depressive disorder, and more than half the patients (59 percent) had a relative who had been advised by a doctor to lose weight. Igoin-Apfelbaum (1985) studied bulimics' family background and found a significantly higher percentage of broken homes than in the study's control population. He also found that a significant proportion of the intact families were hiding massive internal tensions.

Social environment differences have important implications for the development and maintenance of obesity. There is a marked inverse relationship between socioeconomic status and the prevalence of obesity, particularly in women; obesity in men is much less class-linked. Although obesity occurs in every social class, it is predominantly a disease of the lower classes. Stunkard (1980) surveyed midtown Manhattan and found that obesity was more prevalent among downwardly mobile people than among those who had remained in the social class of their parents. The predominance of obesity in lower-class women was 30 percent, while 16 percent of middle-class women and only 5 percent of upper-class women were obese. Religous affiliation was another social factor linked to obesity. Jews demonstrated the greatest prevalence of obesity, followed by Roman Catholics and then Protestants. The relationship between obesity and Protestant religious affiliation was that Baptists had the largest proportion of obesity, followed by Methodists, Lutherans, and Episcopalians. Ethnic factors were also demonstrated, as the percentage of obesity in first-generation Americans from Czechoslovakia, Hungary, and Italy were much more likely to be obese than first-generation Americans from England or fourth-generation Americans. Black women tended to be heavier than white women at all age levels; however, when the economic levels were the same, there were no significant racial differences (Allon 1982).

During midadolescence, heterosexual associations begin. However, obese girls in particular may find great difficulties in dating and developing romantic relationships; therefore, they may show an overall immaturity. Obese adolescent girls are often overly dependent on the family, have separation anxiety about leaving their mothers, and are greatly interested in sex, but only on the fantasy level. Both male and female adolescents who are obese are often the butt of comments and are often excluded from peer-group activities; thus, their social development is stunted. Some obese adolescents use their excessive weight consciously or unconsciously as a protection against sexual involvement, which they feel incapable of handling. A small percentage of obese adolescent girls go to the opposite extreme and become sexually promiscuous in their search for acceptance.

Obesity is a serious handicap in the social life of a child and even more for a teenager. Fat children are often the butt of their peers and become miserable and reclusive. In obese adolescents, the preoccupation with weight and appearance may become so intense that it overshadows all other feelings and actions, as everything is experienced in terms of "weight" and "figure." Many of the personality features of obese people—their shyness and oversensitivity, their easy discouragement in the face of difficulties or when confronted with the slightest rejection, and their tendency toward depression—may be considered to be related to their constant concern with their obese appearance and the impression they make on others (Bruch 1949, 1975).

Obesity can provide a defense against dealing with the "real" problems of life (Kornhaber and Kornhaber 1975). Adults who want to lose weight must be able to reexperience all the tumultuous feelings of the adolescent period that they buried in an obese body. These adults may have delayed a social life and professional advancement because of the vow, "First I must lose weight, then I shall . . ."

Almost all investigators have found problems in normal-weight families in which there is an obese child whom the parents have urged or demanded to lost weight. The obese child has often been ridiculed or rejected or had become the scapegoat of parents and siblings. Obese children are often used as an object by one or the other parent to satisfy the parent's own needs (Wolman 1982). In addition, obese children are frequently the opposite sex of that wished for by the parent or a disappointment in some other way (Bruch 1973). This wish for an opposite-sex child can lead to the child's being confused in sexual identification. Adolescents were able to move toward a more normal weight when the family did not demonstrate excessive anxiety about the overweight; in families in which there was constant preoccupation with weight, the child became increasingly overweight and psychologically less well adjusted (Daniel 1982). Disturbances in the families of obese children are frequently characterized by poor sociability among family members and much sibling fighting (Daniel 1982).

Three factors predispose an obese individual to the development of a disturbed body image: the onset of obesity before adulthood, the presence of a neurotic behavior pattern, and censure by significant family members (Stunkard and Mendelson 1967). The disturbance in relation to body image is generally not affected by weight reductions and is improved only by long-term psychotherapy. The impaired body image does not usually occur in families in which other people are large and fat, and when overweight is associated with strength and health. Therefore, a probable cause of the disturbed body image is censure or rejection by parents or significant others because of the obesity.

## PROGRAMS AND SOCIAL WORK SERVICES

Social workers encounter eating problems in their clients in a variety of settings. Medical social workers see eating problems in both outpatient and inpatient settings because of medical difficulties caused by the bodily abuse of massive food intake and restriction. Anorexia and bulimia nervosa clients may have gastrointestinal difficulties, esophageal tears, dermatological problems, cardiac complications, etc. Obese clients run an increased risk of diabetes, hypertension, and cardiac problems. Family agencies have clients whose predominant difficulty is family interaction around a female member's food intake or lack of it. Social workers in psychiatric settings will probably be involved with both anorexia nervosa and bulimia nervosa clients. Finally, social workers in private practice may have a young woman in treatment who reveals her bulimic behavior only after a long period of counseling.

Many options are available to social workers who want to help clients with eating disorders. These options can be used singly or in combination after a thorough clinical assessment. In assessing an individual's eating disorder, developmental problems, psychodynamics, and environmental context, the social worker should maintain an ecological perspective. This perspective views individual psychopathology as being due to a lack of fit between the individual's needs and the environmental resources and supports (Germain and Gitterman 1980; Goldstein 1984). Therefore, a clinician needs to assess the family and social supports of clients with eating disorders in order to determine which of the many programmatic possibilities are most suited to the client and which programs will respond best to the environment. This ecological assessment requires a nonlinear view of causality and an understanding of the meaning of the eating problems to both the client and the environment.

All of the following possibilities have been effectively used with clients with primary eating problems: individual psychodynamic counseling, group work, family work, medication, and hospitalization. Each treatment option is discussed in depth as it applies to the different eating disorders.

*Individual counseling* is the most frequently recommended helping modality for anorexia nervosa and bulimia nervosa patients. Sometimes, individual counseling is the only modality chosen; at other times, it is the major component of a plan that includes hospitalization and/or medication. The helping approach also needs to be defined: the psychoanalytic approach focuses on internal dynamics; the behavioral approach concentrates on symptoms; and a life model emphasizes interpersonal, life-transitional, and environmental task resolution. Unfortunately, despite the widespread use of individual counseling, very little research has been done on either substantiating the effectiveness of the different approaches or delineating which elements of individual work are most helpful.

For anorexia nervosa clients, Bruch (1982), an analyst and a well-known authority on eating disorders, recommended an active therapist who conducts counseling as a "fact-finding mission" rather than a traditional interpretive analytic approach. However, some analysts still recommend intense psychoanalysis to deal with underlying conflicts regarding identity and object relations (Wilson, Hogan, and Mintz 1983). Other theorists use cognitive techniques to deal with the intellectual problems that seem to be quite common among anorexia nervosa clients, such as dichotomous thinking and overgeneralization. Behaviorists recommend behavioral techniques such as eating diaries to deal with eating pathology in terms of behavioral manifestations. Life-model-oriented social workers intervene in the dysfunctional transactions between the client and the environment.

Women with bulimia nervosa rival anorexic clients in being difficult to help. The illness is viewed by its sufferers as being a "secret sin," and merely getting the client to acknowledge the problem is an enormously difficult task. Also, bulimics frequently want "instant cures" and have unrealistic expectations about being able to stop the bingeing and purging cycle in a short time. Fairburn (1981) reported on a cognitive-behavioral approach for bulimics in which the treatment was divided into three phases and generally extended from four to six months. He emphasized increased self-control with the use of eating diaries, specific strategies for avoiding overeating, and the development of an understanding of the events that lead to a bulimic episode. In contrast to this cognitive-behavioral approach, Wilson, Hogan, and Mintz (1983) advocated a psychoanalytically oriented treatment that focuses on the underlying conflicts rather than on the overt symptoms, with an emphasis on the patient's understanding of internalized object representations and, ultimately, on an analysis of the triadic oedipal conflict. Lowenkopf (1983) used supportive psychotherapy or exploratory therapy or a combination of supportive therapy with psychotropic medication, depending on the severity of bulimic episodes.

Even though anorexia nervosa and bulimia nervosa clients are extremely difficult to help in individual counseling, perhaps the most difficult clients of all problem eaters are the obese. Obese people tend to be vague and nonspecific in counseling when asked about their eating habits, probably for many reasons, including shame and guilt, not thinking the quantity eaten is too much, and fear that the food on which they are psychologically dependent will be taken away. As Bruch stated, "The basic attitude toward life of a fat person is passive and demanding and he expects to have everything done for him. His ideal of treatment is something, anything, that will melt his fat away without effort on his part" (1949: 236).

Psychodynamically oriented psychotherapy with the obese focuses on obesity as a somatic manifestation of a problem in personality development. Obesity symbolizes the strength and the security that the passive-dependent obese person lacks. Anxiety is masked by chronic overeating. Focusing on these dynamic issues, however, is only moderately successful in encouraging weight reduction in the mildly obese and is not at all successful with the morbidly obese. Individual counseling of the obese that combines a respectful tolerance of initial overeating with the use of some behavioral techniques may be more successful in helping clients to lose weight gradually. In a review article on practice effectiveness, Tomlinson (1984) commented that the obese appear to respond better, at least in the short run, to behavioral techniques. Weekly eating diaries, the development of a moderate diet based on the individual's needs, and counseling that facilitates an understanding of feelings may be successful over a long period of time.

*Group work* has increasingly been recommended as the modality of choice for eating disorders, either singly or in combination with other modalities. As in individual counseling, the approaches vary from psychoanalytically oriented to cognitive and behavorial work. From an ecological perspective, a disturbance in eating behavior may develop because of a lack of fit between an individual's ego capacity and self-identity and the expectations, stresses, and rewards of the environment. The pressure put on women by Western society to have a beautiful body is excessive and unrealistic. Therefore, acceptance by a group of peers can be enormously reassuring and ego-enhancing. In addition, practical advice is often given by other group members and the social worker about how to change eating patterns.

Anorexia nervosa clients seem to do less well in group work than do their bulimic sisters. Anorexia nervosa sufferers are often anxious and withdrawn and have extreme difficulty indentifying and expressing their feelings. Although superficially socially competent, anorexics are limited in their ability to establish and maintain social relationships. Their self-esteem is quite low, and they have a limited frustration tolerance of any comment that may be experienced as even the mildest criticism. Anorexics often respond to the anxiety stirred up by the group with a competitive desire to be the thinnest group member and, therefore, unfortunately to lose more weight. However, in spite of all the pitfalls listed above, when the group modality is successful it offers the anorexic meaningful social interactions and a unique experience of social acceptance. The selection of the members is crucial for a successful anorexia nervosa group; the clients must not be at a stage of extreme starvation and should have moved beyond denial to wanting help (Hall 1985).

Group work has also been successful in helping bulimic clients. Generally, theses groups consist exclusively of bulimic clients rather than clients with mixed diagnoses because of the envy bulimics experience about anorexic behavior and the fear anorexics have that, like the bulimics, they will lose control of eating. Again, the particular approach varies: some groups use a formats short-term behavioral format, other approaches use psychodynamic understanding for long-term groups, and still others use a group format with behavioral, cognitive, and psychodynamic components (Boskind-White and White 1983; Stevens and Salisbury 1984; Johnson, Connors, and Stuckey 1983, Roy-Byrne, Lee-Benner, and Yager 1984).

Group work is perhaps the single most useful modality for helping the obese. Most obese people do not demonstrate psychopathology beyond the single symptom of overeating; therefore, it is this symptom that needs to be addressed. In this way, obese clients are similar to alcoholics, who have to stop drinking before they can deal with other possible problem areas. A group format can offer emotional support for the trials of dieting and a weekly check on progress. In addition, specific approaches including diets can be suggested that may be helpful.

The mutual-aid or self-help group tradition has been enormously useful for many years in addition to, or instead of, professionally run individual, family, or group sessions (Gitterman and Schulman 1986: Katz and Bender 1976). This alliance of individuals who need each other to work on a common problem can be very successful with clients who have eating disorders. Anorexics, bulimics, and obese people often respond positively to self-help programs such as Weight Watchers or Overeaters Anonymous, in addition to or instead of professionally led group sessions. Weight Watchers is an enormously successful organization that combines sound dietary recommendations with group support in an environment similar to a religious pep rally. The philosophy of Overeaters Anonymous (OA) is similar to that of Alcoholics Anonymous in that both are "Twelve-Step" programs with the major goal of achieving abstinence (Malenbaum 1988). Abstinence in OA is defined as freedom from compulsive overeating and eating only three meals a day with no snacks. Some OA meetings are specifically focused on anorexic and bulimic women. Many obese people do not seek help through the mental health profession and go instead to Weight Watchers, OA, or Take Off Pounds Sensibly (TOPS). Stuart and Mitchell (1980) suggested that the current treatment of choice for the mildly to moderately obese is self-help groups that incorporate behavioral self-management techniques.

*Family work* is often recommended for clients with eating disorders, particularly if they are young and still living at home. A disturbed eating pattern is the obvious symptom of all three problems discussed: anorexia nervosa, bulimia nervosa, and obesity. However, underlying this symptom in all three conditions are a paralyzing sense of ineffectiveness, a lack of control over one's body, and an inability to discriminate hunger from other states. These deficits in automony and initiative have originated in the mislabeling of feelings and moods from early childhood. Family work can therefore often facilitate appropriate developmental growth so that these clients will acquire a sense of competence and autonomy.

For anorexia nervosa clients, family counseling is often not only useful, but essential. Anorexia nervosa suffers have difficulties with independence, with not feeling in control of their bodies, and with being overprotected. These issues of separation-individuation can sometimes most effectively be dealt with by involvement of the entire family. The focus of therapy with anorexia nervosa families is to challenge the enmeshment within the family as it interferes with the developmental growth of the anorexic.

Family work is also often used with bulimia nervosa clients, especially those who are living with or near their families. Often bulimia nervosa clients (unlike many anorexics) have succeeded in separating physically from their families of origin. However, often their internal life is dominated by demands for perfection that developed because of family dynamics. Also, they are frequently emotionally too intensely involved with the families of origin, and they have great difficulty establishing an independent adult sexual relationship. Bulimic women experience performance demands by their families, are compelled to meet those demands, and, as a result, feel hugely overburdened (Jones 1985). An ecological perspective can facilitate the clinician's evaluation of how the client's family and environment have affected the client in the past and how the bulimic symptoms distort and interfere with current object relations and environmental interactions (Yudkovitz 1983). In Mintz's (1982) treatment of young women with bulimia nervosa, the primary therapy modality was individual sessions, with cojoint family sessions as needed.

Family work is discussed much less frequently as a modality of treatment for obese clients unless the client is an obese child or adolescent. Obese adolescents, according to Daniel (1982), often suffer from disruptive family relationships that delay psychosocial maturation. Family therapy can facilitate the psychological development of these adolescents. Obese children tend to lose more weight when they are accepted by their families, not severely censured. Family therapy can promote acceptance of the child rather than harsh criticism because of the obesity.

Many *medications* have been tried with anorexia nervosa patients, including major tranquilizers, minor tranquilizers, antidepressants, lithium, anticonvulsants, insulin, and appetite stimulants. However, while some medications may prove to be helpful to some anorexics, there is no consensus in the field about the efficacy of any of these medications. There is a consensus, however, that none of these medications should be used as the sole or primary mode of treatment.

Women who have bulimia nervosa, in contrast, have been shown to be much more responsive to medications, particularly antidepressants. Bulimia may be closely related to the affective disorders, as evidenced by depressive symptomatology and a family history of affective disease. Several studies have reported significant results with different types of antidepressants. Pope and colleagues (1983) recommended tricyclic antidepressants, whereas Walsh's group (1982) demonstrated the usefulness of monoamine oxidase inhibitors (MAOIs). More recently, a new medication, Prozac, has been used successfully, although there are still no published articles about Prozac's effectiveness. Obese clients, like anorexics, have not generally demonstrated postive response to medications.

*Hospitalization* should be recommended to an anorexia nervosa client only if her physical condition has become medically precarious. When hospitalization is proposed to an anorexic client, the focus should be on the symptoms of food preoccupation, irritability, and social isolation rather than on the need for weight gain. It is also important to keep an ecological perspective and to deal constructively with family and environmental supports.

Professionals disagree about the value of hospitalization for bulimic clients. Many therapists agree with Mintz (1983) that hospitalization should be reserved for patients who are in danger of dying or becoming severely medically ill, or who are suicidal or psychotic. In contrast, using the British criteria for bulimia nervosa, Russell (1979) recommended hospital admission for most patients to interrupt the vicious cycle of overeating, self-induced vomiting, other kinds of purging, and weight loss.

Hospitalization may be used as a last resort for the obese who are massively overweight, i.e. those who weigh 100 percent over normal weight. In the controlled environment of an inpatient medical unit, these obese persons do lose weight. However, follow-up studies demonstrate that most of these clients, unfortunately, regain their lost pounds over a period of months or years.

## DIFFERENTIAL CLINICAL ASSESSMENTS AND INTERVENTIONS

A comprehensive initial evaluation is essential to the appropriate counseling of clients with eating disorders. The degree of pathology in these clients is quite variable; therefore, a broad perspective is required. The evaluation process should take into account current symptomatology, including the duration and frequency of the symptoms; psychodynamics; and the degree of fit between personal and environmental resources. The client's level of object relations and degree of family pathology should be reviewed. In addition, the presence or absence of concurrent psychopathology, such as depressive symptoms or other impulse-control problems (alcohol or drugs), should be assessed. Medical evaluations are important if physical health is being jeopardized or if psychotropic medication may be indicated.

Obviously, the first consideration in the assessment of the client with anorexia nervosa is how precarious her physical condition is and whether medical intervention is necessary. The most common reason for hospitalization is weight loss. If the client is 25 percent below normal weight for her height or if weight loss is rapid (four to five pounds a week or more), hospitalization is usually indicated. Symptoms that result from weight loss include the lowering of vital signs, physical weakness, coldness, and difficulty in concentrating. The other possible indications for hospitalizaton include severe depression and/or strong suicidal ideation.

If the weight loss can be contained and the depressive symptomatology is not severe, outpatient counseling is indicated. Then, the question becomes what form of intervention would be most helpful. Individual counseling is almost always prescribed, either solely or in conjunction with other modalities of treatment. All anorexics initially need support, realistic encouragement, and a sense that the clinician empathizes with their struggle against fat. Cognitive-behavorial techniques are often used to facilitate weight gain. An assessment of whether more dynamic counseling would be useful should be based on the client's age, capacity for insight, and psychological maturity.

As discussed earlier, it is important to evaluate not only the client, but also the family and environmental supports. Family sessions are often vitally important in altering family dynamics and facilitating change. Families of anorexics are suffering also and have a mixture of feelings, including guilt, anger, and a sense of being overwhelmed by the illness.

The assessment of the bulimic client is similar to that of the anorexic in that many factors need to be considered, including psychiatric impairment, the actual symptomatology, psychodynamics, the family, and the broader environment. Hospitalization is rarely indicated for bulimic clients unless they are severely depressed and suicidal. The other indications for inpatient care include being incapacitated by the bulimic symptoms or being addicted to other substances.

There are major differences among bulimic clients in regard to symptomatology. The frequency of binge–purge episodes varies from many times per day to less than one time per week. Bulimics vary in how they define a binge, from consuming many thousands of calories to eating one cookie. Purging behavior also demonstrates great variability, from vomiting to laxatives or diuretic abuse to excessive exercise or a combination of these. Some women have developed major physical and dental problems, whereas others do not experience such complications. All bulimics with active symptoms should have regular medical and dental checkups to assess the development of complications. The client's degree of competence and ability to function effectively in the world fluctuate widely, as does the degree of social involvement or social isolation. Some women have been able to separate from their families, whereas others are enmeshed in a pathological family system. The psychodynamic pattern of these clients includes lack of self-esteem, distorted body image, and a paralyzing sense of ineffectiveness. Underlying conflicts over dependency-independency and passivity-assertiveness are prominent. These women often feel lonely and isolated from their peers. Bulimia is a "secret sin" and the sufferers live in terror of being found out.

The clinician assesses all of the above factors to determine what modality should be recommended (individual, group, or family counseling; medication; or hospitalization) and what focus the intervention should take (cognitive, behavioral, or dynamic). For example, if a client, has frequent binge–purge episodes, a combination program may be suggested, consisting of individual and group sessions and medications. Initially, cognitive-behavorial techniques may be used to get the symptoms under control, followed by dynamic interventions to uncover underlying conflicts. When clients live at home or when family enmeshment is found, family meetings are essential.

The initial assessment of the obese client entails a consideration of whether there is a concomitant psychopathology such as depresson or alcohol abuse. Hospitalization is rarely indicated unless the client is markedly obese to the point of medical danger. An ecological perspective is particularly crucial for obese clients because family dynamics and social supports may have the most impact on ameliorating the obesity. Individual psychodynamic counseling seems to be quite unsuccessful in helping clients to reduce, while behavioral interventions seem to be somewhat more successful. Family sessions are necessary for symptomatic alteration when the client is a child. Ideally, when the child is an adolescent, the family sessions are supplemented by group work because of the importance of peer support at this transitional stage. Finally, for adult obese clients, group sessions are frequently indicated, possibly to include both professionally run group sessions and self-help groups such as Weight Watchers or Overeaters Anonymous.

## CASE ILLUSTRATION

As noted above, many different modality forms of counseling have been recommended for clients with eating problems. The clinician is left with the difficult decisions of which type of intervention is best suited to the client, and which intervention, if any, should be pursued for the family and the environment.

Rose is a 41-year-old single white registered nurse. Born to white working-class parents, Rose is the fifth child in a family of six siblings; her next older sister is exactly one year older and her younger sister is approximately two years younger. The sibling order is as follows: the oldest child is male, the next oldest is female, the third child is male, and the last three are all female. According to family mythology, the sibling order would have been "perfect" if only Rose were a male. During Rose's early childhood, her mother was physically and emotionally drained by the demands of her many children. Rose's father worked hard in his occupation as a printer; however, every night, as soon as he arrived home from work, he began to drink alcohol until he put himself to sleep. Eventually, when the patient was 16, he died of physical problems resulting from alcoholism. As soon as her youngest daughter finished high school, Rose's mother moved to North Carolina, where two of the mother's sisters live. As evident from this history, Rose received very little early nurturance, and she feels that she had virtually to raise herself. Her reputation in the family is that of the "good daughter" who caused no problems.

An evaluation of Rose revealed the following. Her employment record is excellent. She is a very conscientious worker who functions responsibly and competently. The hospital where she is currently employed is only the second facility in which she has worked. The first hospital was in the neighborhood where she lives, and her mother took her to that personnel office. After the first hospital closed, the client obtained employment with a hospital where her older sister worked. Rose still lives in the family's apartment, which is in a middle-class neighborhood in Brooklyn. At the time of the initial evaluation, she was involved in a overly dependent relationship with a man addicted to marijuana. This man had been living with her in her apartment for the past 2½ years although they were no longer sexually active. In contrast to Rose, with her excellent work history, her boyfriend was only episodically employed as a construction worker. In addition to Rose's obvious obesity (her height is five feet eight inches; her weight was 225 pounds), she was drinking excessive amounts of alcohol and smoking 1½ to 2 packs of cigarettes a day. Rose was phobic of crowds and was reluctant to use public transportation or go to restaurants, movies, etc. Rose's presenting complaint was not her obesity, excessive alcohol intake, or cigarette smoking, but her phobias and sexual frustration. Rose was similar to many obese clients in that she had a mixture of negative feelings about dealing with her obesity. This reluctance to discuss weight and food consisted primarily of both a feeling of helplessness about losing weight and a fear that I would deprive her of food, which she required for both physical and psychological sustenance.

In this case, obesity was obviously not the only problem that needed to be addressed. Thus far, fortunately, Rose had not developed medical complications from her excessive orality (food, alcohol, and cigarettes). However, it is important for such a client to have periodic medical checkups.

The initial treatment recommendation for Rose was for individual counseling, supplemented by couple sessions for Rose and her boyfriend and, as soon as she was ready, self-help groups (such as AA or Weight Watchers). However, because of Rose's fear of groups and crowds, she refused to go to a self-help program, and her boyfriend refused couple sessions. The initial focus of treatment was Rose's alcohol abuse and her relationship. These two aspects of her life were intertwined, as every evening, Rose and her boyfriend got "high" together, he on marijuana, and she on alcohol. Rose's weight when she began the relationship had been much less (around 180 pounds). She was in conflict about this relationship as she was quite dependent and fearful of change and had difficulty recognizing that she deserved a good relationship. At the same time, she was angry about the lack of sexual activity and this man's financial instability and marijuana abuse.

The therapeutic efforts initially centered on the client's recognizing her anxiety about change and on her beginning to accept that she has a right to be treated well. Like many obese clients, Rose was very passive and concerned about pleasing others instead of recognizing her own needs. Gradually, Rose was able to confront her boyfriend, and as he was not able or willing to change, she eventually asked him to move out. After the relationship ended, Rose's alcohol intake decreased considerably, and she was more able to control her alcohol consumption. With the use of behavioral techniques, Rose's phobias decreased and she began being able to go to restaurants, movies, the theater, etc.

Only after the above symptoms were under control could the focus in counseling shift to Rose's weight problem, which was the most intractable symptom of all. Gradually, her self-confidence and self-esteem improved because of her conquering her phobias, which allowed her to increase her social activities, and because she had extricated herself from her destructive relationship. For the first time since counseling had begun, she was able to look at herself in the mirror. She had her hair cut in a stylish new fashion, started wearing subtle makeup, bought a few new clothes, and began to talk about her negative feelings about her body and her feelings of helplessness and hopelessness about dieting and food intake. Interestingly, as Rose was revealing her attitude about her external appearance, she also became much more aware of her inner psychic experiences. She was able to recognize how she denied painful feelings by consuming food or alcohol or by smoking.

Reluctantly, Rose finally agreed to fill out and share daily eating diaries which recorded her food, alcohol, and cigarette intake. She felt great shame about what these diaries revealed and was fearful that I would try to control her intake of various substances. What was evident in these diaries was that, for Rose, food and alcohol increased and decreased simultaneously, not as a substitute for each other. Also evident from the diaries was her unhealthy choice of food, consisting of heavy fat and cholestorol content. Eating diaries are a very effective therapeutic device with problem eaters because the diaries record patterns of behavior and assist in the discussion of therapeutic goals and guidelines.

With Rose, the first eating objective was to reduce her intake of fats, not the quantity of food. Next, calories were discussed, and a modified reducing diet was devised by Rose, not by the therapist. Simultaneous with the discussion of food was a consistent focus on feelings and inner psychological experiences. These feelings included being deprived of usual oral outlets, a desire for as well as a fear of sexual activity, and emotional reactions to her body. Gradually, Rose achieved more moderate food intake, a healthier diet, and more frequent exercise, all of which contributed to a slow weight loss. Rose has reached and is maintaining a weight of 165–170 pounds, which is appropriate for her height and body build. Although this weight is higher than society's ideal, Rose is comfortable and pleased with it.

Many obese people, even after they have lost weight, continue to be preoccupied with being thinner, spend their lives struggling with dieting, and therefore yo-yo up and down in weight.

Eating disorders are a challenge for social workers, who need to educate themselves about these problems and about the appropriate treatment options. All clients who have anorexia nervosa, bulimia nervosa, or obesity are not the same. Social workers should assess clients' symptom constellation as well as their current and past functioning in interpersonal relationships and employment. An ecological assessment examines the goodness of fit between clients and their environmental resources. Other factors to be considered are the availability of various modalities and the client's ability to pay for the different treatment options. Self-help groups may be useful additions to counseling.

A complete evaluation leads to more appropriate treatment choices with better outcome. These choices should be continually reassessed, and the counseling plan should be modified or augmented according to the client's and the family's needs. Until controlled studies compare the different treatment modalities for eating problems, clinicians must rely on a comprehensive diagnostic evaluation as well as on the experience of other clinicians to determine an appropriate counseling plan.

# REFERENCES

Allon, N. 1982. "The Stigma of Overweight in Everyday Life." In B. Wolman, ed., *Psychological Aspects of Obesity: A Handbook*, pp. 130–174. New York: Van Nostrand Reinhold.

APA (American Psychiatric Association). 1980. *Diagnostic and Statistical Manual of Mental Disorders (DSM-III)*, 3d ed. Washington, D.C.: APA.

APA (American Psychiatric Association). 1987. *Diagnostic and Statistical Manual of Mental Disorders (DSM-III-R)*, 3d ed. Washington, D.C.: APA.

Andersen, A., C. Morse, and K. Santmyer. 1985. "Inpatient Treatment for Anorexia Nervosa." In D. Garner and P. Garfinkel, eds., *Handbook of Psychotherapy for Anorexia Nervosa and Bulimia*, pp. 311–343. New York: Guilford.

Beattie, H. 1988. "Eating Disorders and the Mother–Daughter Relationship." *International Journal of Eating Disorders* 7:453–460.

Boskind-White, M. and W. White. 1983. *Bulimarexia*. New York; London: W. W. Norton.

Bruch, H. 1949. "Psychological Aspects of Obesity." In P. Mullahy, ed., *A Study of Interpersonal Relations*, pp. 223–238. New York: Hermitage Press.

Bruch, H. 1973. *Eating Disorders*. New York: Basic Books.

Bruch, H. 1975. "The Importance of Overweight." In P. Collipp, ed., *Childhood Obesity*, pp. 75–81. Acton, Mass.: Publishing Sciences Group.

Bruch, H. 1978. *The Golden Cage*. Cambridge: Harvard University Press.

Bruch, H. 1981. "Developmental Considerations Of Anorexia Nervosa and Obesity." *Canadian Journal of Psychiatry* 26:212–16.

Bruch, H. 1982. "Anorexia Nervosa: Therapy and Theory." *American Journal of Psychiatry* 139:1531–1538.

Bulow, B. and N. DeChillo. 1987. "Treatment Alternatives for Bulimia Patients." *Social Casework* 68:477–484.

Crisp, A., R. Palmer, and R. Kalucy. 1976. "How Common Is Anorexia Nervosa? A Prevalence Study." *British Journal of Psychiatry* 218:549–554.

Daniel, W. 1982. "Obesity in Adolescence." In B. Wolman, ed., *Psychological Aspects of Obesity*, pp. 104–117. New York: Van Nostrand Reinhold.

Fairburn, C. 1981. "A Cognitive Behavioural Approach to the Treatment of Bulimia." *Psychological Medicine* 11:707–711.

Fairburn, C. and P. Cooper. 1982. "Self-Induced Vomiting and Bulimia Nervosa: An Undetected Problem." *British Medical Journal* 284:1153–1155.

Fairburn, C. and P. Cooper. 1984. "The Clinical Features of Bulimia Nervosa." *British Journal of Psychiatry* 144:238–246.

Fairburn, C. and D. Garner. 1986. "The Diagnosis of Bulimia Nervosa." *International Journal of Eating Disorders* 5:403–419.

Fallon, A. and P. Rozin. 1985. "Sex Differences in Perceptions of Desirable Body Shape." *Journal of Abnormal Psychology* 94:102–105.

Foch, T. and G. McClearn. 1980. "Genetics, Body Weight, and Obesity." In A. Stunkard ed., *Obesity*, pp. 48–71. Philadelphia: W. B. Saunders.

Furnham. A. and N. Alibhai. 1983. "Cross-Cultural Differences in the Perception of Female Body Shapes." *Psychological Medicine* 13:829–837.

Garfinkel, P. and D. Garner. 1982. *Anorexia Nervosa: A Multidimensional Perspective*. New York: Brunner/Mazel.

Garner, D. and P. Garfinkel. 1985. *Handbook of Psychotherapy for Anorexia Nervosa and Bulimia*. New York: Guilford.

Garner, D., P. Garfinkel, D. Schwartz, and M. Thompson. 1980. "Cultural Expectations of Thinness in Women." *Psychological Reports* 47:483–491.

Germain, C. and A. Gitterman. 1980. *The Life Model of Social Work Practice.* New York: Columbia University Press.

Gitterman, A. and L. Shulman. 1986. *Mutual Aid Groups and the Life Cycle.* Itasca, III.: Peacock.

Glucksman, M. H. and J. Hirsch. 1969. "The Response of Obese Patients to Weight Reduction." *Psychosomatic Medicine.* 31:1–7.

Goldstein, E. 1984. *Ego Psychology and Social Work Practice.* New York: Free Press.

Hall, A. 1985. "Group Therapy for Anorexia Nervosa." In D. Garner and P. Garfinkel, eds., *Handbook of Psychotherapy for Anorexia Nervosa and Bulimia,* pp. 213–239. New York: Guilford.

Halmi, K. 1980. "Psychiatric Diagnosis of Morbidly Obese Gastric Bypass Patients." *American Journal of Psychiatry* 137:470–472.

Halmi, K. 1983. "The State of Research in Anorexia Nervosa and Bulimia." *Psychiatric Development* 3:247–262.

Halmi, K., J. Falk, and E. Schwartz. 1981. "Binge-Eating and Vomiting: A Survey of a College Population." *Psychological Medicine* 11:697–706.

Hsu, L. 1987. "Are the Eating Disorders Becoming More Common in Blacks?" *International Journal of Eating Disorders* 6:113–124.

Humphrey, L. 1986. "Family Relations in Bulimic-Anorexic and Nondistressed Families." *International Journal of Eating Disorders* 5:223–232.

Igoin-Apfelbaum, L. 1985. "Characteristics of Family Background in Bulimia." *Psychotherapy and Psychosomatics* 43:161–167.

Johnson, C., M. Connors, and M. Stuckey. 1983. "Short-Term Group Treatment of Bulimia." *International Journal of Eating Disorders* 2:199–208.

Johnson, C., M. Stuckey, L. Lewis, and D. Schwartz. 1982. "Bulimia: A Descriptive Survey of 316 Cases." *International Journal of Eating Disorders* 2:3–16.

Jones, D. 1985. "Bulimia: A False Self Identity." *Clinical Social Work Journal* 13:305–316.

Jourard, S. and P. Secord. 1955. "Body-Cathexis and the Ideal Female Figure." *Journal of Abnormal and Social Psychology* 10:243–246.

Katz, A. and E. Bender. 1976. *The Strength in Us.* New York: New Viewpoints.

Kornhaber, R. and E. Kornhaber. 1975. "Obesity in Adolescents: Contributing Psychopathological Features and Their Treatment." In P. Collipp, ed., *Childhood Obesity,* pp. 109–115. Acton, Mass.: Publishing Sciences Group.

Leon, G. 1982. "Personality and Behavior Correlates of Obesity." In B. Wolman, ed., *Psychological Aspects of Obesity,* pp. 15–29. New York: Van Nostrand Reinhold.

Lowenkopf, E. 1983. "Bulimia: Concept and Therapy." *Comprehensive Psychiatry* 24:546–554.

Malenbaum, R., D. Herzog, S. Eistenthal, and G. Wysbak. 1988. "Overeaters Anonymous: Impact on Bulimia." *International Journal of Eating Disorders* 7:139–143.

Mintz, N. 1982. "Bulimia: A New Perspective." *Clinical Social Work Journal* 10:289–302.

Mintz, I. 1983. "An Analytic Approach to Hospital and Nursing Care." In C. Wilson, ed., *Fear of Being Fat,* pp. 315–324. New York: Jason Aronson.

Minuchin, S., B. Rosman, and L. Baker. 1980. *Psychosomatic Families: Anorexia Nervosa in Context.* Cambridge: Harvard University Press.

Orbach, S. 1985. "Accepting the Symptom: A Feminist Psychoanalytic Treatment of Anorexia Nervosa." In D. Garner and P. Garfinkel, eds., *Handbook of Psychotherapy for Anorexia Nervosa and Bulimia,* pp. 83–104. New York: Guilford.

Ordman, A. and D. Kirschenbaum. 1986. "Bulimia: Assessment of Eating , Psychological Adjustment, and Familial Characteristics." *International Journal of Eating Disorders* 5:865–878.

Pope, H., J. Hudson, J. Jones, and D. Yurgelun-Todd. 1983. "Bulimia Treated with Imipramine: A Placebo-Controlled Double-Blind Study." *American Journal of Psychiatry* 140:554–558.

Prather, R., and D. Williamson. 1988. "Psychopathology Associated with Bulimia, Binge Eating, and Obesity." *International Journal of Eating Disorders* 7:177–184.

Pyle, R., J. Mitchell, and E. Eckert. 1981. "Bulimia: A Report of 34 Cases." *Journal of Clinical Psychiatry* 42:60–64.

Rodin, J., L. Silberstein, and R. Striegel-Moore. 1985. "Women and Weight: A Normative Discontent." In T. Sonderegger, ed., *Psychology and Gender. Nebraska Symposium on Motivation, 1984*, pp. 267–307. Lincoln: University of Nebraska Press.

Rothenbrg, A. 1986. "Eating Disorder as Modern Obsessive-Compulsive Syndrome." *Psychiatry* 49:45–53.

Roy-Byrne, P., K. Lee-Benner, and J. Yager. 1984. "Group Therapy for Bulimia." *International Journal of Eating Disorders* 3:97–116.

Russell, G. 1979. "Bulimia Nervosa: An Ominous Variant of Anorexia Nervosa." *Psychological Medicine* 9:429–448.

Saunders, R. 1985. "Bulimia: An Expanded Definition." *Social Casework: The Journal of Contemporary Social Work* 66:603–610.

Schwartz, D., M. Thompson, and C. Johnson. 1982. "Anorexia Nervosa and Bulimia: The Socio-Cultural Context." *International Journal of Eating Disorders* 1:20–36.

Secord, P. and S. Jourard. 1953. "The Appraisal of Body-Cathexis: Body-Cathexis and the Self." *Journal of Consulting Psychology* 17:343–347.

Selvini-Palazzoli, M. 1978. *Self-Starvation*. New York: Jason Aronoson.

Silber, T. 1986. "Anorexia Nervosa in Black and Hispanics." *International Journal of Eating Disorders* 5:121–128.

Silberstein, L., R. Striegel-Moore, and J. Rodin. 1987. "Feeling Fat: A Woman's Shame." In H. Lewis, ed., *The Role of Shame in Symptom Formation*, pp. Hillsdale, N.J.: Erlbaum.

Stevens, E. and J. Salisbury. 1984. "Group Therapy for Bulimic Adults." *American Journal of Orthopsychiatry* 54:156–161.

Strober, M. 1981. "The Relationship of Personality Characteristics to Body Image Disturbances in Juvenile Anorexia Nervosa: A Multivariate Analysis." *Psychosomatic Medicine* 43:323–330.

Stuart, R. and C. Mitchell. 1980. "Self-Help Groups in the Control of Body Weight." In A. Stunkard, ed., *Obesity*, pp. 345–354. Philadelphia: W. B. Saunders.

Stunkard, A. 1980. *Obesity* Philadelphia: W. B. Saunders.

Stunkard, A. and V. Burt. 1967. "Obesity and the Body Image, 2: Age at Onset of Disturbances in the Body Image." *American Journal of Psychiatry* 123:1443–1447.

Stunkard, A. and M. Mendelson. 1967. "Obesity and the Body Image, 1: Characteristics of Disturbances in the Body Image of Some Obese Persons." *American Journal of Psychiatry* 123:1296–1300.

Thomlison, R. 1984. "Something Works: Evidence from Practice Effectiveness Studies." *Social Work* 29:51–56.

U.S. HHS (U.S. Department of Health and Human Services). 1980. *International Classification of Diseases (ICD-9)*, 9th revision Washington, D.C.: GPO.

Walsh, B., J. Steward, L. Wright, W. Harrison, S. Roose, and A. Glassman. 1982. "Treatment of Bulimia with Monoamine Oxidase Inhibitors." *American Journal of Psychiatry* 139:1629–1630.

White, W. and M. Boskind-White. 1981. "An Experiential-Behavioral Approach to the Treatment of Bulimarexia." *Psychotherapy: Theory, Research and Practice* 18:501–507.

Wilson, C., C. Hogan, and I. Mintz. 1983. *Fear of Being Fat.* New York: Jason Aronson.

Wold, P. 1985. "Family Attitudes Toward Weight in Bulimia and in Affective Disorder—A Pilot Study." *The Psychiatric Journal of the University of Ottawa* 10:162–164.

Wolman, B. 1982. *Psychological Aspects of Obesity: A Handbook.* New York: Van Nostrand Reinhold.

Yudkovitz, E. 1983. "Bulimia: Growing Awareness of an Eating Disorder." *Social Work* 28:472–478.

# 7

## Learning Disabilities

▼

### NAOMI PINES GITTERMAN

When we refer to someone as learning-disabled, what do we mean? Many people would answer that the term *learning disabilities* refers to children with some specific cognitive deficits.

This is what much of the public believes about learning-disabled people. This is also what many in our profession currently believe. Yet, such perceptions are now dated and too narrow. Work on the subject during the past three decades has brought out a wealth of new information, documented by research that has led to a significantly expanded perspective and to changing definitions of the term *learning disabilities*.

A review of the literature suggests that social work has left much of the development of an understanding of the learning-disabled and interventions to assist this population to our colleagues in such allied professions as education, psychology, and the health field. Yet, we need to pay attention. For the prevalence of learning disabilities among all ages is wide and represents possibly the most common disorder of children seen in mental health settings (Small 1982; Gross and Wilson 1974; Silver 1987). These clients are referred to social agencies or are seeking help with a wide range of behavioral problems affecting their social interactions and their ability to effectively carry out certain expected developmental tasks. We need to understand the possible etiologies of their problems if we are to effectively develop strategies to address their needs.

234

# PROBLEM DOMAIN

It was not until the 1960s that the concept of *learning disabilities,* a term originated by an educator, Samuel Kirk (1962), became known to professionals and the general public. During this same period, Clements (1966) introduced into the psychiatric literature a syndrome he called *minimal brain dysfunction,* and these two terms have since been used interchangeably. The following year, Johnson and Myklebust broadened this definition to refer to children "as having a psychoneurological learning disability, meaning that behavior has been disturbed as a result of a dysfunction of the brain and that the problem is one of altered processes, not of a generalized incapacity to learn" (1964:8.) To understand the development of these concepts, one needs to trace two sometimes parallel and interrelated areas of study: *how people learn,* and *what determines behavior.* In accepting the meaning and implication of these concepts, people began to reexamine some of their earlier beliefs.

Our thinking about childhood development in the first half of this century was dominated by the introduction of psychoanalytic thought. Clinicians viewed problems in children as originating in the experiences or unresolved conflict of early childhood, and parents, especially the mother, were viewed as critical influences (Gross and Wilson 1974). For example, difficulties in learning, as well as behavioral problems, were widely thought to be the result of some underlying emotional problem.

The professional literature prior to the 1960s was replete with descriptions of learning and behavioral problems of children that did not fit into existing classifications and were not responsive to the usual interventions based on such classifications (Ochroch 1981). In the 1930s and '40s, a few pioneers were exploring other avenues of explanation and began to produce research and new hypotheses based on clinical observations of patients with neurological disorders. Increasingly, evidence was provided about the relationship between brain processes and various cognitive or behavioral disorders. In 1937, Orton, a neuropathologist, became interested in the relationship between cerebral dominance and language disabilities and developed a theory about how differences in specific aspects of brain functioning affected a child's capacity to read (Lerner 1971). Several years later, in 1942, Kurt Goldstein's research revealed that people with brain injuries exhibited certain disordered behaviors, such as distractibility, that persisted even after healing (McCarthy and McCarthy 1969).

Straus and Lehtinen's classic work, *Psychopathology and Education of the Brain-Injured Child* (1947), marked the beginning of learning disabilities as a field of study (Lerner 1971). In their work, Straus and Lehtinen carried out close observations of children with similar patterns of behavior who had been categorized with such diagnoses as mentally retarded or emotionally disturbed. They theorized that these behavior and learning problems were the result of brain injury and were not emotionally based or caused by psychogenic factors. Their definition of the brain-injured child included the following:

> The brain injured child is the child who before, during, or after birth has received an injury to or suffered an infection to the brain. As a result of such organic impairment, defects of the neuromotor system may be present or absent; however, such a child may show disturbances in perception, thinking and emotional behavior, either separately or in combination. (Strauss and Lehtinen 1947:4)

Similarities in certain behavior manifestations between children with brain damage and a large group of children with problems of behavior and learning led to the concept of *minimal brain dysfunction*. This latter group gave evidence not of "hard" neurological impairments, such as motor weakness, but of "soft" signs, such as clumsiness. Compelling evidence for the existence of minimal brain dysfunction can be shown by the similarity between children with these symptoms and those with organic brain disorders, and in the response of this population to medication (Gross and Wilson 1974).

There have been changes in the nomenclature and, more important, in the definitions and working hypotheses in the field of learning disabilities since the advent of Gross and Wilson's book. During this process, we have had to incorporate new knowledge, question old beliefs, and look at the effects of new educational, physiological, and therapeutic interventions on identified populations.

Certainly, the discovery of antipsychotic drugs in the 1950s and their impact on mental illness led to a resurgence of interest in the brain and its effect on behavior. Internal processes or the external environment could no longer be seen as the sole factor in the etiology of behavior. This discovery played a major role in dispelling long-held myths. We now realized that behavioral symptoms can be, at least in great part, organically based.

Perhaps the first example, and among the best known, has been the discovery that autism is a behavioral disorder based on some dysfunction in the brain and is not the result of a psychological disturbance (Gross and Wilson 1974; Johnson 1980). Similarly, over the years, the symptom of hyperkenesis has been demonstrated often to result from some abnormality in brain function (Gross and Wilson 1974).

In the 1960s, Thomas, Chess, and Birch (1963, 1968) introduced the concept that temperament is an inborn trait. In their pioneer research, they showed how a child's temperament affects family relationships. Their findings were very influential in demonstrating the reciprocity between nature and nurture.

In the 1980s, a whole new body of research was developed, through long-term studies of twins and adopted children, that validates the idea that the core of determinants of many behaviors and personality traits are genetically determined, for example, social potency, e.g., shyness and extroversion; stress reactions, e.g., vulnerability; and aggression and control. (Franklin 1989; Pines 1982; Goleman 1986). Our common understanding that physical attributes and intellectual potential are affected by heredity must now be enlarged to include many personality characteristics.

Thus, as we enter the final decade of this twentieth century, our understanding of learning has been expanded and refined to reflect the concept that all areas of leaning development and dysfunction are affected by complicated, yet subtle, brain processes. Findings demonstrate the impact of genetics and brain function on a great range of behaviors, formerly considered to be based solely on psychological, cultural, or environmental influences. Such understandings have a profound impact on how we define the disorders and syndromes of learning and behavior, as well as the options for intervening effectively.

The definition of *learning disability*, or *minimal brain dysfunction*, has been affected over the years by newly emerging information and by differences of professional orientation and opinion. Following Kirk's original definition of the term *learning disabilities*, the National Advisory Committee on Handicapped Children formulated the following definition in 1967:

> Children with special learning disabilities exhibit a disorder in one or more of the basic psychological processes involved in understanding or using spoken or written languages. These may be manifested in disorders of listening, thinking, talking, reading, writing, spelling, or arithmetic. . . . They do not include learning problems which are due primarily to visual, hearing, or motor handicaps, to mental retardation, emotional disturbance, or to environmental disadvantage. (Lerner 1971:4)

This definition was widely quoted and became the basis for landmark legislation called P.L. 94–142, that resulted in the establishment of educational programs for handicapped children and the training of professionals in this arena of service. This law provided a systematic methodology for the identification, assessment, and education of children with handicaps and was followed in later years by important amendments. The significance of this legislation has been considerable. Yet, the definition quickly created certain theoretical and service delivery problems. The National Joint Committee on Learning Disabilities was joined by others in its position that the federal definition did not convey the heterogeneity of learning disorders; that it incorrectly limited the application of the definition to children; and it did not clearly state the etiology of learning disabilities, but merely made a listing of terms (NJCLD 1987).

The vast changes in this field can be seen if one compares the proposed new federal definition for the term *learning disabilities*. It refers to "a heterogeneous group of disorders, presumed to be due to central nervous system dysfunction and manifested by significant difficulties in the acquisition and use of listening, speaking, reading, or mathematical abilities, or of social skills" (ICLD 1987) This definition is particularly significant because it acknowledges that many classified as learning-disabled have significant difficulties in establishing and maintaining satisfying peer and adult relationships (Gershon and Elliot 1989).

Also, in common usage today is the *DSM-III-R* (APA 1987), which uses two major diagnostic categories to describe commonly identified features of this syndrome. The first is "Attention Deficit Hyperactivity Disorder." It refers to developmentally inappropriate degrees of inattention, impulsiveness, and hyperactivity or undifferentiated attention-deficit disorder, where signs of impulsiveness and hyperactivity are not present. The other diagnostic classification is "Specific Developmental Disorders." This refers to the inadequate development of specific academic, language, and motor skills. In this context, attentional disorders have been separated from cognitive deficits, although in the diagnoses of many people, the two areas of dysfunction coexist.

The cause of learning disabilities is not known. There are various hypotheses about its origin, including the probability that in any one person, there may well be multiple origins. What we can also surmise is that the cause in one person probably differs from the cause in another, which may explain why there are many variations in this syndrome (Silver 1979; Small 1982).

Beginning with the assumption that understanding the etiology of a problem will assist in the selection of appropriate interventions, the practitioner may need to establish the probability of a specific etiology or to rule out, at least, those that are unlikely. Over forty different causative factors of learning disabilities have been reported on in the literature of the last two decades. The following paragraphs discuss the major etiologies.

At some time, a learning-disabled person may have experienced some *brain damage.* Such injuries may have occurred during gestation, the period of prenatal development, the birth process, or the early years of life. Such injuries may have been caused by disease, by exposure to lead or other toxic substances, by trauma, by ingestion of drugs or medication by the mother, or by anesthesia. Depending on the location, the extent of the damage, and the time period in the life cycle, an individual may suffer severe damage or a minimal form of subtle brain dysfunction.

*Maturational lag* is another possible cause, which is defined as some delay in the development of the central nervous system (Silver 1979). Another common explanation relates to some *biochemical or physiological dysfunction.* This hypothesis suggests that there may be some deficiency or altered homeostasis in the metabolic functioning of the body. For instance, some allergic conditions are associated with specific behavioral manifestations. An example of this problem can be found in Feingold's work (1974), in which it was found that an *allergic reaction* to food additives can result in specific learning or behavioral problems.

As already indicated, *genetic transmission* is commonly identified as a probable etiology, although in some families with such histories, it is not a determinant. There is a school of thought that certain *dysfunctions of the eye*, especially in its ability to effectively gather visual information, can lead to dyslexia and are correctable by special eye exercises (Small 1982; Friedman 1981). Other examples of possible causes are *low birth weight, environmental pollutants, radiation exposure of the mother or child*, and *cortical dysfunction.*

The clinical picture of the person with learning disabilities is not homogeneous. Though each person's functioning reflects a different combination of characteristics, they all fall into the same, broad unitary syndrome. *Learning disabilities can effect cognitive, social, emotional, and physical development and functioning.* Some common general characteristics are an uneven growth pattern, which results in areas of maturational lag; average or above-average intelligence; and discrepancies between achievement and potential. This syndrome can effect a person's capacity to meet academic and life tasks.

## SOCIETAL CONTEXT

The advent of federal legislation for people with handicaps, and in particular the learning-disabled, was associated with two major phenomena. In the 1960s, America learned about equal rights for minorities, and legislation for racial and ethnic minorities paved the way to a consideration of the needs of other minority groups. But for learning-disabled people to be perceived as a group with special needs, they had to be so identified. As already indicated, the labeling of this population and the growing understanding of the ways in which learning-disabled people were disadvantaged, especially in the educational system, enabled legislators and professionals to articulate the special needs of this population. Lobbying efforts seemed especially effective, because children from middle-class families composed a sizable portion of this group. Their parents were effective in initiating efforts for legal recognition and resources.

There have been two profoundly important pieces of federal legislation supporting the rights and need for services of the learning-disabled. In 1973, Congress passed Section 504 of the Rehabilitation Act, prohibiting discrimination on the basis of physical or mental handicap in any federally assisted program or activity. The intent of this act was to effect fundamental changes in the attitudes of institutions and individuals toward handicapped persons. People with a diagnosis of specific learning disabilities fell into the federal definition if their impairment was severe enough to limit one or more major life functions. This legislation provided assurances that no handicapped child would be excluded from a public education because of a disability, that these children would be educated with nonhandicapped students to the extent possible, and that their parents or guardians could object to evaluation or placement decisions. In addition to supporting the rights of children in the educational system, the legislation also mandated that postsecondary institutions could not discriminate against applicants or students because of a handicap. The law further stipulated that employers could not refuse to hire or promote solely because of a worker's disability and that health and welfare services must provide equal access to services to persons with disabilities (U.S. HEW 1978)

Then, in November of 1975, Congress adopted P.L. 94-142, the Education for All Handicapped Children Act, and it became effective in October 1977. The spirit of this law was to assure handicapped children a free and appropriate education, and it set forth procedures to ensure that all parts of the law would be implemented. The legislation introduced important concepts, including a mandate that children be educated in the least restrictive environment; that they be provided with individual educational plans (*IEPs*); that decisions on evaluation and placement be made by a committee composed of representative educators, professionals from related disciplines, and parents; and that due process provisions allow parents to challenge the school system's decisions or inaction (Smith 1979). Subsequent amendments—namely, the Education of Handicapped Act of 1986—extended services to handicapped infants and preschool children (NCCIP 1989).

The opportunities generated by this act are extraordinary, but the funds to support such options are often extremely high for local and state governments to carry. The federal government's good intentions far exceeded its fiscal generosity. One finds local communities, large cities, and small villages torn between serving the needs of their children, some of whom are severely handicapped by physical disabilities, by retardation, by autism, etc, and, at the same time, trying to keep local taxes from spiraling further. Taxpayers' pleas compete with the pleas of desperate parents. Committees on the handicapped are mandated to make sound educational decisions in behalf of children, yet anyone observing such a group in action becomes aware that fiscal concerns loom large in the background. Similarly, many communities cannot keep pace with the growing needs of their handicapped population. Four years after the passage of P.L. 94-142, the New York City school system was under court order to accommodate handicapped youngsters. Yet, 12,684 eligible children were placed on waiting lists. This situation resulted from both a shortage of qualified teachers and the resistance of many administrators who were struggling to use their limited resources to serve many unmet needs in their schools (Kleiman 1981).

Other issues were raised about the mandate of this legislation. The notion of the *least restrictive environment* implied that moving toward mainstreaming was the preferred option, especially for learning-disabled children. Clearly, the legislation enabled many formerly forgotten or "hidden" children to return to neighborhood schools to learn and socialize with peers, yet for others it was not the panacea. Assignment to regular classes meant that many would not have the opportunity for more individually designed learning and would be singled out by classmates as being "stupid." Others could not keep up socially, lacking either the skills or the self-confidence (Johnson 1981; Diamond 1979). Placing children in regular classes with resource room supports or in self-contained special-education classrooms is only a beginning. Again, some unprepared or overburdened staff, with limited resources, have not been able to carry out the goals set for each child.

Persons with learning disabilities often have an invisible handicap. Their problems are less blatantly observable than those of a person with mental retardation or pervasive developmental disabilities. The very definition that a learning-disabled person must have average or above-average intelligence may further camouflage specific limitations. It is not difficult in our society to find those who feel that learning problems are precipitated by unmotivated or lazy students or serve as a symptom of some psychological "block." They are unsympathetic to people identified as learning-disabled, feeling that if only they tried harder or were not obtaining secondary gain, they could overcome whatever cognitive or behavioral problem they have. The situation is even more difficult for learning-disabled adults, because learning disabilities were originally deemed to be a problem of children, which they would eventually outgrow. The research of the past two decades amply demonstrates that the characteristics of learning-disabled youngsters persist into adulthood and that learning disabilities often exist, some in changed form, throughout the life span (Buchanan and Wolf 1986; Adelman and Taylor 1986). Legislation has largely been geared toward youth. While some laws provide for vocational education for adults with learning disabilities, the other needs of these adults, such as support in independent living and training, receive less attention. Finally, professional training and funding reflect society's unifacted concern with academic and employment issues. Society does not seem to understand the primacy of the area of social needs of the learning-disabled and the ways in which such deficits affect total life functioning. This lack of understanding takes its toll on all levels, from the kind of expectations we have for the learning-disabled to the kinds of services and resources we make available to them.

## RISKS AND NEEDS OF POPULATION

It is a complicated task to determine the number of persons affected by learning disabilities from the demographic data used to describe such persons. Prevalence varies, in great part, by the definition used. The criteria for inclusionary and exclusionary measures have changed over the years and also differ depending on the perspective or source used. School-based reports are most easily obtainable, yet these exclude youngsters who are learning-disabled but whose major deficits may not be in the academic sphere; of course, these reports exclude adults. The United States Department of Education reported in 1987 that almost 5 percent of all school-aged children received special-education services (ICLD 1987). Other studies have reported higher numbers, ranging from 10 to 15 percent (ICLD 1987; Silver 1987). During that same year, the Interagency Committee on Learning Disabilities reported to Congress that it believed that 5 to 10 percent of the population in this country was affected by learning disabilities. It further reported that the prevalence was slightly higher among *socioeconomically disadvantaged* populations, and at least twice as common in *males as in females*. Studies to date are not adequate, largely because of the problems in achieving a consensus about definition, so that current estimates tend to be conservative guesses, and the numbers of people affected may well be considerably greater than estimated.

Genetic factors may be important predictors for people with certain types of learning problems. Twin and foster-child rearing studies further support a genetic etiology. In as many as 40 percent of learning-disabled children, *family histories* of learning disabilities were discerned (Silver 1987). Reports also show that children of *low birth weight* are at risk for learning problems, as are those with *seizure disorders* (ICLD 1987).

The incidence of learning disabilities in *delinquent populations* is considerably higher than in the general population. Estimates of prevalence range from 26 percent to 73 percent (Larson 1988). There are several hypotheses that attempt to explain the link between learning disability and delinquency, such as vulnerability to peer group pressure and school failure (Berman 1974). Current investigators postulate that ineffective problem-solving skills increase the risk for delinquency in learning-disabled youth (Larson 1988). Certainly, people who have problems with impulsivity and who lack social judgment skills have an increased propensity for engaging in antisocial behaviors.

## PROGRAMS AND SOCIAL WORK SERVICES

Social workers have not been in the forefront in identifying or addressing the needs of this population. Over the past three decades, educators have played a prominent role in advocating for and developing services to meet academic needs. Public schools offer an array of options for learning-disabled children, though there is a significant gap between the actual need and the available services. Private schools have also been established, which broaden options for parents with the economic means to make their own choices for their children and for overburdened school districts to provide support to children referred to private resources. Libraries for teachers abound with literature on theories and specialized techniques for teaching these youngsters. Educators are even in the vanguard of the learning disability movement in devising and offering social-skill-training programs.

Psychiatrists and neurologists have carried out extensive and important research in this field, as well as offering both assessment and intervention services, especially medication. The community has often turned to psychologists to administer testing to children and adults, to make learning and psychological assessments, and to determine the nature and extent of learning and behavioral deficits and strengths. Both psychiatrists and psychologists have been major providers of therapeutic services and also work alongside those in other disciplines, such as speech therapists, in serving this population's needs.

Social workers in child guidance clinics, mental health and family agencies, and school systems are receiving very sizable numbers of referrals and are working with people of all ages who are learning-disabled. Similarly, child welfare and criminal justice settings serve youth or adults who struggle with many problems, including learning disabilities. Clients with this diagnosis come to social agencies primarily because their social and behavioral problems have led to difficulty in some aspect of their life functioning. Parents may also seek help with their reactions to their learning-disabled child, for assistance in acting in their child's behalf, or for help in dealing with child development or management issues. In these agencies and community institutions, social workers are offering multimethod interventions ranging from evaluation, to consultation, to counseling, to advocacy.

In response to clients' needs and requests, various other programs are available. Beyond academic programs, there are special camps or recreational and social programs for learning-disabled youth and young adults. Such settings feature structured programs in which learning-disabled people with either social or motoric deficits may function with needed supports and in less competitive environments conducive to growth. Parents of learning-disabled children and adolescents may wish to join educationally oriented or mutual aid groups to enhance their understanding of their child's difficulties, to obtain new child-rearing skills, or to gain the support of others in similar situations (Gitterman 1979). Many parents or learning-disabled adults have also made active use of information and referral centers.

Middle-class parents have been effective in spearheading movements for their children. They have joined together in local and national associations to lobby for legislation, funds and services. They are active presenters at professional conferences and join boards and school committees to enlighten the community and to advocate for resources. In lower socioeconomic communities, progress is slower, probably because parents besieged with so many life problems generally have not mobilized themselves in such organized efforts. Yet, the numbers of learning-disabled are great and their needs are naggingly persistent. There are never enough services, and as professionals, we are still neophytes in developing our technology for helping the learning-disabled.

## DIFFERENTIAL CLINICAL ASSESSMENTS AND INTERVENTIONS

In order to obtain a total and accurate picture, carrying out an assessment of a person with learning disabilities often involves contributions from other disciplines, including neurologists, psychiatrists, speech therapists, psychologists, and remedial specialists. Each discipline, if appropriate, will administer its own set of tests to illuminate areas of strength and the nature of the problem. A social worker can make an overall assessment, which, among other things, usually includes history taking. One important aspect involves documentation of exactly how the persons's functioning deviates from what is normally expected, with an emphasis on information about language, motor, cognitive, and social development, including delays in reaching developmental milestones and inconsistencies in performance (Collard 1981). Methods of determining possible etiologies would include an exploration of such areas as genetic factors, nutritional and allergy problems, mixed dominance, and prenatal, birth, and medical history. Evaluations would include interviewing the person, the family, and significant collateral contacts, such as a teacher or a recreation counselor. Observations may be carried out in the office, the home, and/or the school. It would be particularly important to see the person in his or her social environment and to understand and assess the impact on the person's functioning of the supports or stress factors, chaos or structure, cultural norms, performance expectations, and degree of acceptance or rejection in the environment. If the client is a child or adolescent, it is also important for the social worker to understand the meaning of the disability for the parent and siblings and the family environment, pressures, and resources.

In making an assessment, a professional needs to inquire into the following areas of functioning where evidence of deficits or delays may exist.

An early sign of learning disabilities may emerge in the area of *language development*. A disorder exists when there is a qualitative difference in some aspect of language behavior from expected normal development, based on a child's chronological age. Language disorders encompass many different kinds of disruptions in the content, form, and use of language (Bloom 1978). Sometimes, children do not express themselves well conceptually because they lack the verbal acuity, or because they think in more concrete terms. Children may also not express themselves well grammatically and cannot, for example, produce full sentences or use the correct parts of speech. Sometimes, a child speaks in an immature manner.

A frequent signal of learning disabilities is a delay in language development, e.g., children who do not begin to speak until the age of 3 years or later. Children may also experience difficulty in articulation and do not produce sounds correctly. This can be the result of a motoric problem in which the mouth, tongue, and lips do not function well together in producing certain sounds. Language provides a person with a means to communicate and to interact socially with others, so that significant deficiencies can have a profound impact on a child's social development. If the disorder is readily apparent, it can also be a form of acute, public embarrassment.

Problems in *motor coordination* may be another early sign in the learning disability syndrome. While some learning-disabled children have histories of reaching early milestones in motor development and possess strong athletic skills, many more have histories of awkwardness or clumsiness. Children may have difficulties with gross motor coordination, such as running or hopping; with small motor dexterity, such as cutting with scissors, tieing shoelaces, or handwriting; or in both areas. Others have problems with balance. These deviations usually show up as "soft" neurological signs, rather than as "hard" classical neurological symptoms (Wender 1971).

*Visual perception* plays an important part in learning. Problems in visual perception may take one or more forms. Some people have difficulty with spatial relations, that is, how objects are viewed together in space and how one organizes oneself in space. For example, people may have trouble reading or doing arithmetic because of how they view letters or numbers and their relationship to space, or they may have difficulty discriminating left from right, or they may feel disoriented or dizzy when placed in an open-spaced environment (Lerner 1971; Silver 1979). People may have difficulty with depth perception, in which distance is misjudged, so that a person may miss a step in climbing stairs, bump into things, or fall down while trying to sit. Visual discrimination problems often occur when people reverse letters (eg. *d* and *b*) or words (e.g., *saw* and *was*) or see symbols in reverse, as in mirror reading. They may copy incorrectly, become confused by visual directions, or experience visual motor problems, as in trying to track and catch a ball. Visual perception problems often lead to difficulties in reading, due to some limitation in the ability to decode correctly.

Some people's problems occur more in the area of *auditory perception*. They have no problem with hearing acuity but may have difficulty in distinguishing subtle differences in sound, distinguishing significant sounds to pay attention to, or in integrating different phonic sounds. Other difficulties occur when people experience auditory lag, so they cannot process quickly what they hear and the speaker must speak more slowly; or they may have trouble with auditory sequencing, not being able to remember the order of things given in oral directions.

A particularly serious dysfunction is *memory disability*, that is, problems with either integrating, storing, or having to retrieve information from memory. The two primary forms of memory are short-term and long-term, and the problems may occur in the visual or the auditory sphere. Short-term memory refers to information that needs to be retained for only a short time, while a person is using it. In long-term memory, knowledge is retained and is available for retrieval when required. For instance, a person may look up and remember a number long enough to dial it on the telephone; this requires only short-term memory. When a person learns that telephone number and can retrieve it at will many hours or days later, then it has become a part of long-term memory. With constant repetition, a person usually learns to store things in long-term memory. When this process fails, learning is seriously affected and impaired.

A pervasive problem that many learning-disabled people experience is *disorganization*, which takes many forms and affects many areas of daily functioning and learning. People are bombarded constantly with all kinds of sensory stimuli coming from the environment. The learning-disabled are often overwhelmed by the stimuli. They cannot easily process, integrate, and act on the stimuli appropriately or effectively.

Two major areas of *behavioral characteristics* are viewed as part of the learning disability syndrome: 1) *problems in attention* and 2) *social immaturity or problems in social competence*. The *DSM-III* (APA 1980) classifies the first group as "Attention Deficit Disorders" (ADD), but describes this disorder as existing as a distinct entity or as being attendant to specific learning disabilities. The diagnosis of attention disorders refers to *hyperactivity*, which is physiologically based rather than anxiety-based; that is, evidence of hyperactivity can be traced to early childhood. Frequently, though not always, children with this disorder were very active from birth, being frequently in motion, often colicky, and not always east to cuddle. Their movements can be described as jittery, their cries as piercing, and their meals as fraught with difficulty (Kavanagh and Truss 1988). Such children leave their parents exhausted, with the house looking very much like a combat zone. Hyperactive children are described as "always on the go," as if "driven by a motor" (Kavanagh and Truss 1988); have difficulty sitting still; fidget excessively, and run around or climb on things excessively. Some children are more appropriately classified as distractible, meaning that some external stimuli are affecting their behavior, and they are distracted from attending to the task at hand. To differentiate between these two sets of behavior, hyperactive people act as if they are internally driven into motion, while distractible people are excessively disturbed, for example, by the noise of a pencil dropping in the rear of the room while a teacher is speaking in the front. A much less observed symptom that the leaning-disabled sometimes have is the reverse problem, known as hypoactivity, in which there is lethargy.

Other people have what is described as *problems with inattention*, for they lack the capacity for sustained attention or have a short attention span. They do not seem always to listen or to finish what they start. Sometimes, they are described as daydreaming. Problems with impulsivity, or what is sometimes call *poor impulse control*, is a common manifestation in many learning-disabled people (Wender 1971). Evidence of such behaviors is seen in a person's tendency to act before thinking, to experience difficulty in delaying gratification, and generally to have a low frustration tolerance. Such people become quickly upset when things or other people fail to react as anticipated or hoped. Impulsive people may also experience problems in disorganization or in staying with one activity for any length of time. Impulsivity often results in unplanned or socially inappropriate responses.

Children with problems in attention, especially hyperactivity, experience difficulty during infancy and in the preschool years, but it is at the beginning of the school years that the problems are markedly apparent. Virtually every aspect of the child's environment is affected: school, peers and home (Kavanagh and Truss 1988). It was initially thought that problems in inattention greatly subside in the early years of adolescence with the change in hormones. However, studies in recent years reflect some dissipation of gross motor symptoms but a persistence into adulthood of many of the other attentional problems (Kavanagh and Truss 1988).

Cognitive problems and problems in attention often coexist in one person. Estimates of this co-occurrence vary considerably from 80 to 90 percent to as low as 10 percent, with many studies falling in the middle (Kavanagh and Truss 1988). ADD is considerably more common in boys than in girls. Boys with ADD exhibit more physical aggression and loss of control, and girls with ADD exhibit greater cognitive impariments and social lability.

For many years, the definitions of *learning disability* or *minimal brain dysfunction* did not include the identification of social behaviors or social adjustment. Yet, throughout this period, studies increasingly demonstrated the evidence of various patterns of *social immaturity* endemic to the learning-disability syndrome. They concluded that many learning-disabled persons present with primary interactional learning disabilities (Gerson and Elliot 1989; Jackson, Enright, and Murdock 1987; Kavanagh and Truss 1987; Kronick 1978, 1981; Lerner 1971; Ritter 1989). And in terms of total life functioning, social ineptitude tends to be far more disabling than most cognitive deficits (Kronick 1978).

Previously, some characterized the social problems observed as secondary problems resulting from children's difficulties and frustration in coping with cognitive and other previously identified deficits. Yet, the new federal definition, coupled with the new research, suggests that, indeed, social skill problems are an integral part of the learning disability syndrome and are the result of some physiological determinant or delay. This finding fits in with all that we are now learning about the effect of genetics and brain function on many behaviors.

Characteristically, socially immature people exhibit difficulty in some of the following areas. They lack acuity in social perception and tend to misread or ignore the cues of others. They may have real problems in exercising social judgment, namely, in how they choose to handle social situations, so that their behavior often appears immature or inappropriate. Such lack of sophistication also results in difficulties in social problem-solving. Many experience problems in social interactions, especially with peers, on age-appropriate levels. Their desire to make friends is clearly apparent, but their social behaviors are often awkward, lacking in social competence and appropriateness. The picture looks different at different age levels, but almost always, it is not what would be expected at a specific age. For instance, in young children, there may be extroversion; excessive hugging and kissing; inviting friends too quickly, such as asking a stranger on the street to visit their home; or joining in games without considering possible rejection and the impact on others. They may blurt out what they think without the expected social prohibitions (for example, "You look fat" or "Your house is messy"). Children with such problems may have inappropriate expectations of others so that the judgments they make may be met with annoyance. For example, if an 8-year-old learning-disabled boy is playing with a 3-year-old girl and she takes his ball away, the boy acts as if the 3-year-old were his peer, grabs the ball back, and does not take into account the age difference.

As children grow older, they learn and integate various age-appropriate interactions; however, these are offset by frequent lapses into less age-appropriate behaviors. Initiating and sustaining friendships and making mature social judgments may still prove to be a problem. By adolescence, the peer group takes on greater importance, but learning-disabled children are often excluded by peers because they lack peer-valued attributes (Kronick 1981). Thus, the gap for social opportunities for learning and interaction is widened. The behaviors of learning-disabled adolescents, and adults as well, is varied and colored by the accumulation of other life experiences. Yet, one can factor out certain traits that seem to be characteristic of the learning-disabled person. They may miss the point of what is being said, they may overreact, or they may make inappropriate remarks or actions or poorly timed responses. They may need to be in control, which grows out of their need to organize other people and situations because of their own sense of internal disorganization. They may sometimes, incorrectly, project blame. They may be simultaneously and acutely aware of the messages of others to them but may have difficulty knowing how to respond effectively. They may seem stubborn, or they may need time alone to pull themselves together and to withdraw from bombarding and overwhelming stimuli. For some, poor judgment may result in antisocial acts (Smith 1980). The form these behavioral symptoms take is varied, but the common denominator is usually eagerness for interaction, coupled with qualities of social ineptness.

There are three other behavioral traits that one sees in many learning-disabled people. The first is what is called *emotional lability*, meaning strong vulnerability. Excessively labile people may be hurt out of proportion to what one might anticipate and may react with a corresponding degree of pain. It may be as simple as how one responds to a belonging being broken or misplaced, or to losing in a game or to teasing. The second is *perseveration*, meaning that a person seems to "get stuck." The learning-disabled do not easily pull themselves out of a situation to look at options, and they create a mental set, a script of expectations that may not come to fruition. One common and sad example is the child who gets into a physical fight and cannot stop. Finally, there is the problem of *slower adaptive mechanisms*, meaning that people cannot deal with unexpected changes easily and need more time to integrate changes that are nonroutine or unexpected. A change may be small (e.g., a new textbook); it may be an unanticipated visitor, a trip to a new place, or almost any change in known ritual, plan, structure, or interaction.

It is not uncommon for the learning-disabled to experience *secondary emotional problems*, which grow out of many years of experiencing frustration and failure, and to which they react in many ways. They may develop such symptoms as withdrawal or hypochondria, or they may resort to clowning to divert attention from their problems. In one way or another, most struggle with a poor sense of self-esteem (Silver 1979).

Still, the learning-disabled bring to their lives some very special qualities. They may display a hearty enthusiasm, spontaneity, or adverturousness (Smith 1980). Particularly impressive is the courage, resilience, and persistence that many ultimately apply over and over again in facing difficult life tasks. Clearly, one is often captivated by the uniqueness of their personalities and their ability to draw on their resources.

In work with this population, interventions are dictated by the implications of an assessment for learning disabilities. For some children whose difficulties are predominantly cognitive, academic remediation is undoubtedly very important. Specific suggestions should be made, including the kind of class structure needed and the specific remediation techniques that will help the person to learn the required skills or to find appropriate compensatory measures. Such options abound, but to offer a simple example, a child with problems in handwriting may learn to write more effectively if he can learn to draw in sand or fingerpaint, may copy over dots more readily than trying to copy from a picture, or may need wide lines rather then open spaces as a guide.

Speech therapists have been effective in helping children with a range of language problems, and early intervention, especially, reaps important success. In the field of medicine, the use of medication has had a profound impact in alleviating such symptoms as hyperactivity. While the use of medication, especially on children, has been controversial, medication that has been carefully monitored to reduce possible side effects has achieved significant results (Gross and Wilson 1974). Research findings indicate that 60 to 90 percent of hyperactive children can focus their attention better and can refrain physically and mentally from responding to diversions when taking stimulant mediations (Smith 1986). Therefore, there is a decrease in motor activity and an increase in attention span (Silver 1979). These medications do not affect specific learning deficits but modify the child's activity level, so that the child becomes more available to learning and the use of other interventions and experiences increased acceptance from adults and peers. Wender (1971) argued that substituting psychotherapy for medication could be viewed as malpractice, a harmful withholding from a child of needed treatment. He suggested that psychological help is popular, but that for pragmatists, the question is not what is popular, but what works.

Social workers may assume various roles in working with learning-disabled clients and their families. They may serve as coordinators, helping the client or the family to locate appropriate resources for evaluation and future planning and to think through decisions and needed actions. Social workers often function in the role of consultants, providing information and suggestions, usually to parents, about learning disabilities and ways in which they can understand and be helpful to their child. Learning-disabled clients and their families are often referred to or seek help from social workers for counseling services because of some interpersonal, developmental, and/or environmental problems. Finally, social workers serve as advocates or mediators and help to empower clients to act in their own behalf or in support of a family member.

Having a learning disability often means experiencing some difficulties throughout the life span. Therefore, help may have to be obtained to cope with tasks at different points in the life cycle, during crises as well as for longer periods of time. If one traces the path a learning-disabled person takes, it is not uncommon to see him or her moving in and out of different kinds of helping relationships.

The first encounter usually occurs when the problems are initially identified. Parents often become aware during the infant, toddler, or, certainly, the latency years that their child's development is different from that of her or his peers. By the time the parent seeks help, they already suspect that something is wrong. They may even imagine that the problem is worse than it is (Faerstein 1986). On another level, parents go through different stages as they assimilate their observations and try to cope with their emerging anxieties. Parents may begin by denying the problem, trying to minimize what they observe or are told. This stage may be followed by anger, as parents question, "Why me?" These emotions are coupled with feelings of helplessness or frustration. If this anger is directed inward, they become depressed, and for some, there is attendant guilt. They worry about something they may have inadvertently done that created the problem. If the anger is directed outward, the parents may begin to blame others, including their child. They then move into a time of grieving, as they slowly give up their hopes and dreams for a certain "kind of child."

During this period, they are especially vulnerable to panaceas. From this point, they gradually begin to move toward greater acceptance, and in many cases, they begin, then, to take the needed action (Silver 1979).

Unlike parental grieving at the birth to a child with a visible handicap, such as a physical deformity, the process of mourning for a child with a marginal and less observable handicap is prolonged (Killner and Crane 1979). The parents' reactions are staggered and not clear-cut, as they may move from panic, to anger, to grief, in any given situation or period of time. How parents react has implications for professional intervention.

The period of denial has many ramifications. For many parents, denial may serve an important function, as they need time to prepare to accept the painful reality and its implications Therefore, professionals who provide evaluative interpretations may need to give parents several weeks to assimilate what they have heard, before they meet with the parents again to plan. Still, during the time of denial, a child is often left vulnerable. The child knows something is wrong, that she or he is different, but feels, "If my parents can't accept me for who I am, how will others? I must hide my problems."

Parents need guidance and support through the lengthy grieving process, as well as help in separating when they are irrationally angry from when their rightful expectations are not being met by other professionals. How often one hears of the frustrations of perceptive parents who have brought their concerns about their child to a pediatrician, only to be told they are being impatient and overanxious. Parents need to be relieved of their guilt. Raising a learning-disabled child will have an effect on the family. Parents need to know they did not cause the problem, for if they feel so, they will then feel they can "cure" the problem. Social workers can be most helpful when they recognize the legitimate pain that raising a child with problems may cause, as well as the sadness parents must experience as their child struggles to cope.

Raising a child who has special problems means that parents often need assistance in specifying expectations and in learning effective techniques for helping their child gain mastery in their environment. For example, parents need to learn how to break down everyday tasks for a child who is less adept and easily overwhelmed. Learning how to put on a pullover sweater can be demonstrated to a child step by step, as can learning to brush one's teeth, or learning how to order and buy an item in a store. For those who cannot master certain tasks, alternatives need to be considered. Zippers and buckles are more easily handled than buttons and laces. Youth who adapt to new or unanticipated situations more slowly need anticipatory guidance and more time. A child who is going on a class trip needs help in thinking about what to expect and how to handle any problems, for instance, what to do if he or she gets lost. Parents tend to end up in power struggles when children insist unrealistically that an event will happen a certain way. Rather than argue, parents are more effective when they say, "That's what you wish, but that is not what may happen."

Youngsters with problems in social competence need parental assistance at many levels. They lack natural ease in relationships, and efforts at engaging and sustaining contacts can be awkward and therefore labored. When children are young, parents can take the initiative in structuring social opportunities for their child. They can play a more active role in helping their child to connect appropriately and to engage in successful play. As their child grows older, role modeling, direct advice, and active problem-solving help youngsters learn needed social skills. Since learning-disabled children are often taken advantage of or rejected, without provocation, they need help in dealing with peer reaction. Efforts to strengthen social skills take on special relevance in view of a recent study showing that learning-disabled youth have demonstrated their ability to improve their social-perceptual skills, so that by late adolescence, they are closing the maturational gap (Jackson, Enright, and Murdock 1987).

Children with problems in attention may need medication. In addition, providing structured and predictable environments, setting clear boundaries, and minimizing distractions lend important sources of support to these children. Parents need to learn to handle disciplinary issues effectively, and to evade futile power struggles and attacks on their child (Johnson 1989). For example, impulsivity in children can best be addressed by helping them develop awareness and then creating an extra moment between impulse and action, which provides youngsters with time to stop and think so they can alter their response.

Learning-disabled adolescents do not achieve autonomy at the same rate as their peers and therefore have prolonged and wider dependence on adults (Margalit and Shulman 1986). They are also more vulnerable to stress and experience greater anxiety as they confront difficult tasks. The dilemma for parents and educators is to find the appropriate balance between providing help and offering increasing supports toward achieving independence.

Learning-disabled people face certain common tasks with which they often need help. It is the social worker who can, and indeed should, address these tasks with them. By the time children develop a sense of awareness about themselves in relation to peers or siblings, they may well realize that in certain subtle ways, they are different from others. It may be apparent in the difficulties they experience in mastering academic expectations (e.g., reading); in the way they behave (e.g., hyperactivity), or in the way they are perceived socially by their peers or their family (e.g., they may be ignored). The child begins to worry and thinks, "Why me? What's wrong anyway? What can be done? Will I fail? Why don't I have friends?" Those are the kinds of questions that a professional or a parent needs to help children with, clarifying that what they are having trouble with (e.g., sitting still or writing well) is not their fault, and helping them to specify strengths and weaknesses and to avert gross negative generalizations, e.g., "I am dumb." Learning-disabled youth are often teased by their peers, and they need specific ideas on how to respond. For example, people make fun of them because they may attend a different school or class, or they may be taunted because they perform poorly in athletics. Expecting youngsters to ignore these comments is not realistic. Rather, they need to learn to respond with straightforward answers, such as "I know I am not good at sports."

The therapeutic context for work with learning-disabled youngsters should have both structure and predictability. Children need a sense of organization, for open-ended sessions will evoke greater anxiety and loss of control. It is often necessary to depart from traditional psychotherapeutic strictures, for with the learning-disabled, the worker must take a more active role. This population responds best to a strong, positive working alliance, one in which the worker moves patiently and very supportively with the client while interceding to develop receptivity in the environment.

By the time of adolescence, problems may intensify, and family, teachers, and peers may be less patient. Adolescents may be angry about the demands made on them that they can not meet. Those who lack social or communication skills feel a deepened inadequacy and loneliness because they are not part of the teenage group. Adolescents who have poor impulse control and lack social judgment may be exploited by peers and may become easy targets for involvement in antisocial acts. Parents and other adults have become worn out, are less tolerant, and express such feelings as, "It's time to shape up already. Aren't you ever going to grow up?" So, the cycle of conflict, already present in this phase of life, may greatly intensify.

Learning-disabled adults have been a less visible and identified population. As noted before, it was originally assumed that people outgrew these problems by the time they reached adulthood. We now know that this outcome is not necessarily to be expected. We see adults discovering, for the first time, that they are learning-disabled.

We also see learning-disabled adults struggling in the job market, being discriminated against because of their handicaps, or losing employment because they do not adapt well to more sophisticated workplace demands (Brown 1979).

The learning-disabled are born into a wide range of families, some functioning more or less effectively than others. Having a learning disability can not be attributed to a problem within the family; rather, families may need help in coping with their reactions to existing difficulties and stress. A social worker may need to reinforce and support the family's efforts to improve behavioral management, to enhance avenues of communication, to define realistic expectations of each other, and to tolerate periods of ambiguity and frustration in the context of long-term progress (Zeigler and Holden 1988). Marital stress may be precipitated by the birth of a learning-disabled child (Featherstone 1980). Parents may find themselves not able to draw strength from their relationship; rather, they may be divided by their own fears, their anger, their disappointments, and their impotence. Differences in decision making while raising a disabled child may result in additional marital discord. Lastly, families carry extra emotional and physical burdens in living with a learning-disabled member and need assistance in locating and using resources for support within the community (Schilling 1988).

It is often helpful to focus on and offer service to the siblings of learning-disabled children and to understand their reactions. Some siblings experience guilt because they function more effectively than the learning disabled child, especially if the sibling is actually younger. More frequently, however, brothers and sisters experience acute embarrassment in having to explain to their own peers their sibling's differences in behavior or achievement. They may bear the brunt of teasing. Some siblings long for a "real" brother or sister with whom they could share more, one who would more closely reflect their own feelings and experiences. Finally, siblings resent what they may experience as a double standard in their families when there are two levels of expectations, one for the learning-disabled child and another for the siblings (Kronick 1973). These siblings need help in sorting through their own reactions, opening up communication within the family, and finally, developing strategies to deal with their peers' reactions.

A person's disability touches every family member, throughout the life cycle. We are only beginning to learn about how emerging issues affect family members as the learning-disabled person carries out his or her roles as child, spouse, and then parent.

# CASE ILLUSTRATION

The kinds of problems for which the learning-disabled and their families seek help from social workers may occur at various points in their lifetime. The tasks that they face, often coupled with an unresponsive environment, may produce situations that warrant crisis intervention, short-term consultation, or longer term counseling. The following case was selected because it provides the opportunity to learn about a learning-disabled child and her parents who obtained services intermittently over the period of a decade and a half.

This is a story of Cindy (now age 16), her brothers, Barry and David (aged 21 and 23), and her parents, Mr. and Mrs. Stone. This is a middle-class, Unitarian family who live in southern Connecticut. Mr. Stone is a journalist and a devoted and caring father. Mrs. Stone is an early childhood educator, who works parttime and has a deep investment in the well-being of her children. The sons are bright, competent, and highly engaging young men who have fared very well in both their academic and their social lives.

Mrs. Stone's first two pregnancies were normal. She was 35 years old and pregnant with Cindy when she developed a serious respiratory infection, for which she took antibiotic drugs. She remained healthy for the remainder of her pregnancy, and Cindy was born, at full term, by forceps delivery. Cindy appeared to be a healthy, quiet, content infant whose sole problem, at that time, was some colic, which she experienced for several months after the introduction of whole milk into her diet. Mrs. Stone became concerned about Cindy's physical development when Cindy reached 9 months and still had difficulty sitting without support. Mrs. Stone's worries remained dormant, until she began to realize that Cindy continued to reach other physical developmental milestones at a slower pace than almost all of her peers. Mrs. Stone's efforts to bring her questions to the pediatrician were met by overreassuring statements that some children develop more slowly than others, but Cindy would soon catch up.

Mrs. Stone tried to get her husband to listen to and acknowledge her fears that Cindy was not developing normally, but he offered reasons for any differences and cited areas in which Cindy performed at the norm. Feeling alone in her growing anxiety, even panicked by the gloomy picture she fantasized and foresaw for her child, Mrs. Stone became depressed. She was obsessed with thoughts about Cindy, impatient with the ambiguity of not knowing what was wrong, and distraught with her own impotence. She went to a local mental health clinic for help. The social worker played an instrumental role in alleviating the symptoms of depression but was not able, understandably, to offer Mrs. Stone the assurances she repeatedly sought that her child would eventually achieve the capacity for normal functioning. The social worker offered to meet with Mr. and Mrs. Stone jointly. She gently helped Mr. Stone to hear his wife's concerns and to move past his own denial.

Cindy began to walk at about 18 months, and Mr. and Mrs. Stone went through a period of relief and renewed hope. However, after several months, it became apparent that Cindy's receptive speech was limited, and that she understood less than other children her age, who were already speaking words, if not sentences. Although a seemingly self-content child, Cindy often played in an isolated way away from her peers. Family and friends began to notice and comment on Cindy's lack of ability to speak. Again, Mr. and Mrs. Stone became alarmed and concerned and contacted a pediatric neurologist for an evaluation. The physician pointed out uneven areas of development, ruled out retardation or autism, hypothesized what was then called *minimal brain dysfunction*, and recommended speech therapy to address Cindy's delayed language development.

Cindy attended a local speech therapy clinic and made rapid strides in gaining language. Some difficulties in articulation persisted because of problems in the proper placement of her tongue in mouth coordination.

Cindy entered nursery school at the age of 4, and her delays in certain areas of emotional and social development became readily apparent. The noise level and the active environment of preschoolers were overwhelming to Cindy, who sometimes sought refuge by herself or under a blanket. Other times, she tried to engage with her classmates, but her judgments on how to enter play and her ongoing social interaction skills were inept. She was easily upset by changes in routines, and her excessive vulnerability led to outbursts of crying if someone, for example, sat in her chair by mistake.

During this time, her parents sought professional guidance in order to understand Cindy's behavior, to learn the needed new parenting skills, and to make future educational plans. For many months, they met monthly with the social worker and provided her with examples of Cindy's behavior. She helped create a framework for understanding Cindy and frequently pointed to areas of strength and effective efforts that Cindy was making to cope with a sometimes overwhelming or rejecting environment. Through these interventions, the social worker helped to alleviate some parental anxiety, offered new perspectives on Cindy's functioning and progress, and helped the Stones to learn to influence Cindy's school experience. One poignant example occurred when Mrs. Stone described a recent meeting with the nursery-school teacher. This teacher was critical of Cindy, saying she had entered the room of an adjoining class to play, and that many of the children had begun to yell at and ridicule Cindy. The envisaged pain of this scene caused Mrs. Stone to dissolve in sudden tears. The social worker softly asked Mrs. Stone, "What did you say when the teacher told you this story?" Mrs. Stone replied, "I said nothing. I felt she was telling me how my daughter misbehaved." The social worker commented, "But this was a 4-year-old, not acting in malice. You should have said to the teacher, 'And what did you do?'" This important lesson that parents don't have to accept someone else's definition of a problem, and that parents have the right to expect their child to be appropriately represented and protected, became a model that the Stones used over and over again in their negotiations with the programs in which Cindy was enrolled.

Cindy entered kindergarten in a small school when she was almost 6, so she could have an extra year of developmental time. Although she lacked competence in both social interaction and motor agility (especially graphomotor skills), her cognitive abilities were within the norm, and she was even precocious in reading. This was surprising because an aunt and a cousin had histories of dyslexia. Cindy's behavior was seen as immature, rather than deviant, and she was not well organized. Still, Cindy was an appealing youngster, had a quick sense of humor, and related well to adults. Her perceptiveness, coupled with her unusual resilience and persistence, served as important strengths as she faced daily problems. Throughout her latency years, she progressed in most areas, especially in speech and academic work. Her continuing difficulty in social functioning remained a source of frustration to her and of concern and sadness to her family.

As Cindy entered adolescence, she appeared dissatisfied, if not somewhat depressed, by the disparity between her aspirations and what she could actually expect for herself. Her parents tried to locate a counseling group for learning-disabled children, where she might obtain professional help in acquiring skills and feedback in this social context, but they were not successful. So, they returned to a social worker to seek additional help for themselves and now also for Cindy. Mr. and Mrs. Stone moved to a deeper level in sharing their worries, especially about whether Cindy could move toward greater independence in functioning. They were also helped to reflect on how their frustrations were inadvertently being communicated to Cindy, and how they might try to respond positively to her new efforts to communicate and interact.

Cindy was immediately receptive to the social worker's active, interested style and the kind of support, patience, and acceptance she experienced in their work together. Cindy has been meeting weekly with the social worker for the past two years. They have explored many themes, including Cindy's feelings of being different and her search for who she is, as she straddles two worlds, the world of normal children and the world of the learning-disabled. By the age of 14, Cindy had developed some problems secondary to her differences in development. Primary among them was her lack of self-esteem, which increasingly affected her expectations for herself and her communications with others. It became so marked that she sometimes walked with her head down to avert any possible peer rejection. Cindy has made slow, but consistently positive strides. The use of a dual educative and therapeutic focus on coping skills as she faced interactional tasks in her family, school, and the social arena has given her new confidence and mastery. She has also gained self-awareness, so she can "catch herself" when acting in dysfunctional ways, such as, "I guess I am nervous about getting a new coat because I am so used to the old one." She can anticipate problems and plan accordingly, e.g., finding ways to organize her school assignments. She has also learned to move from initial rigidity to greater flexibility in handling everyday situations. Finally, Cindy has been helped to handle the multiple demands of high school. At this time, Cindy has been able to taper off contacts with the social worker, to assume some greater responsibility for autonomous functioning, and to advocate for her own needs. Cindy may need to return for help when she prepares for her college entrance year.

Several salient issues emerge. The first is that the learning disability syndrome (also referred to as minimal brain dysfunction) is extremely common. These terms serve as umbrella categories covering certain dysfunctions in cognitive, language, physical, and/or behavioral functioning. Initially, this syndrome was seen as affecting only children, but it is now a documented problem that persists, sometimes in changing form, into adolescence and adulthood. In this relatively young, and still growing, field, there is ambiguity and lack of agreement about the definition and etiology of learning disabilities. Recent research attests to the effectiveness of a range of new interventive techniques and particularly highlights the usefulness of medication, counseling, psychoeducational techniques, and environmental supports. Certainly, early identification, assessment, planning, and intervention have reaped important gains in ameliorating the effects of this dysfunction and its secondary problems.

The challenge for social workers lies ahead. We have inadvertently played a major role in working with people with learning disabilities because this population abounds in our social agencies and institutions. Yet, we have not been in the forefront of service and have relied on old and improper diagnostic categories and models of psychotherapeutic "treatment" that have not necessarily been helpful.

Our expertise in work with individuals, families, and groups, and in helping clients with their problems in the context of their environment certainly bodes well for our assuming increasing leadership in services to the learning-disabled. Within our own range of social work settings, we have the unique opportunity to reach out, to innovate a practice technology, and, in collaboration with other disciplines, to offer much needed help to this population. We also need to join with other professionals in developing programs, influencing legislators, and educating the public about what life is like for the learning-disabled and how to support them in our society.

## REFERENCES

Adelman, Howard S. and Linda Taylor. 1986. "Moving the Field Ahead: New Paths, New Paradigms." *Journal of Learning Disabilities* 19(12):602–607.

APA (American Psychiatric Association). 1980. Diagnostic and Statistical Manual of Mental Disorders (DSM-III), 3d ed. Washington, D.C.: APA.

APA (American Psychiatric Association). 1987. *Diagnostic and Statistical Manual of Mental Disorders (DSM-III-R), 3d ed.*, rev. Washington D.C.: APA.

Berman, Allen. 1974. "Delinquents Are Disabled." In Betty Lou Kratoville, ed, *Youth in Trouble*, pp. 86–96. San Rafael, Calif.: Academy Therapy Publications.

Bloom, Lois and Margaret Lahey. 1978. *Language Development and Language Disorders*. New York: Wiley.

Brown, Dale. 1979. "Learning Disabled Adults Face the World of Work." *Learning Disability: Not Just a Problem Children Outgrow*. President's Committee on Employment of the Handicapped. Washington, D.C.: *U.S. Government Printing Office.*

Buchanan, Mary and Joan S. Wolf. 1986. "A Comprehensive Study of Learning Disabled Adults." *Journal of Learning Disabilities* 19(1):34–38.

Clements, Sam. 1966. *Minimal Brain Dysfunction in Children.* National Institute of Neurological Diseases and Blindness, Monograph No. 3. Washington D.C.: U.S. Department of Health, Education, and Welfare.

Collard, Jean. 1981. "The MBD Child: The Art of Definitive History Taking for Diagnostic Clarification." In Ruth Ochroch, ed., *The Diagnosis and Treatment of Minimal Brain Dysfunction*, New York: Human Services Press, pp. 46–62.

Diamond, Barbara. 1979. "Myths of Mainstreaming." *Journal of Learning Disabilities* 12(4):246–250.

Faerstein, Leslie Morrison. "Coping and Defense Mechanisms of Mothers of Learning Disabled Children." *Journal of Learning Disabilities* 19(1):8–11.

Featherstone, Helen. 1980. *A Difference in the Family.* New York: Basic Books.

Feingold, Ben. 1974. *Why Your Child Is Hyperactive.* New York: Random House.

Franklin, Deborah. 1989. "What a Child Is Given." *The New York Times Magazine* (September 3, pp. 36–41, 49.

Friedman, Harold N. 1981. "The Rationale for Optometric Intervention in Learning Disabilities." In Ruth Orchorch, ed., *The Diagnosis and Treatment of Minimal Brain Dysfunction*, pp. 160–164. New York: Human Services Press.

Gershon, Frank M. and Stephen N. Elliot. 1989. "Social Skills Deficits as a Primary Learning Disability." *Journal of Learning Disabilities* 22(2):120–124.

Gitterman, Naomi Pines. 1979. "Group Services for Learning Disabled Children and Their Parents." *Social Casework* 60(4):217–226.

Goldstein, Kurt. 1942. *After Effects of Brain Injuries in War.* New York: Grune and Stratton.

Goleman, Daniel. 1986. "Major Personality Study Finds That Traits Are Mostly Inherited." *New York Times*, December 2, C1.

Gross, Mortimer D. and William C. Wilson. 1974. *Minimal Brain Dysfunction.* New York: Brunner/Mazel.

ICLD (Interagency Committee on Learning Disabilities). 1987. *Learning Disabilities: A Report to the U.S. Congress.* U.S. Dept of Health and Human Services, U.S. Government Printing Office.

Jackson, Sara C., Robert D. Enright, and Jane Y. Murdock. 1987. "Social Perception Problems in Learning Disabled Youth: Developmental Lag Versus Perceptual Deficit." *Journal of Learning Disabilities* 20(6):361–364.

Johnson, Doris J. and Helmer R. Myklebust. 1964. *Learning Disabilities: Educational Principles and Practices.* New York: Grune & Stratton.

Johnson, Harriette C. 1980. *Human Behavior and Social Environment New Perspectives*, Vol. 1: *Behavior Psychopathology, and the Brain.* New York: Curriculum Concepts.

Johnson, Harriette C. 1989. "Behavior Disorders." In Francis Turner, ed., *Child Psychopathology*, pp. 73–139. New York: Free Press.

Johnson, Sharon, 1981. "Dissent on Mainstreaming." *New York Times*, Spring Survey on Education (April 26) p. 16.

Kavanagh, James F. and Tom J. Truss, 1988. *Learning Disabilities: Proceedings of the National Conference.* Parkton, Md: York Press.

Killner, Selma K. and Rochelle Crane. 1979. "A Parental Dilemma: The Child with a Marginal Handicap." *Social Casework* 60(1):30–35.

Kirk, Samuel. 1962. *Educating Exceptional Children.* Boston: Houghton Mifflin.

Kleiman, Dena. 1981. "Many Disabled Still Not Placed by City Schools." *New York Times* (August 31), p. A1.

Kronick, Doreen. 1973. *A Word or Two About Learning Disabilities.* San Rafael, Calif.: Academic Therapy Publications.

Kronick, Doreen. 1978. "An Examination of Psychosocial Aspects of Learning Disabled Adolescents." *Learning Disability Quarterly* (Fall), 1:86–92.

Kronick, Doreen. 1981. *Social Development of Learning Disabled Persons.* San Francisco: Jossey-Bass.

Larson, Katherine A. 1988. "A Research Review and Alternative Hypothesis Explaining the Link Between Learning Disability and Delinquency." *Journal of Learning Disabilities* 21(6):357–261.

Lerner, Janet W. 1971. *Children with Learning Disabilities.* Boston: Houghton Mifflin.

Margalit, Malka and Shmuel Shulman. 1986. "Autonomy Perceptions and Anxiety Expressions of Learning Disabled Adolescents." *Journal of Learning Disabilities* 19(5):291–293.

McCarthy, James J. and Joan F. McCarthy. *Learning Disabilities.* Boston: Allyn & Bacon.

Orton, Samuel T. 1937. *Reading, Writing and Speech Problems in Children.* New York: Norton.

NCCIP (National Center for Clinical Infants Programs). 1989. *The Intent and Spirit of P.L. 99–457.* Washington, D.C.: NCCIP. U.S. Government Printing Office.

NJCLD (National Joint Committee on Learning Disabilities), 1987. "Learning Disabilities: Issues on Definition." *Journal of Learning Disabilities* 20(2):107–108.

Ochroch, Ruth, ed. 1981. *The Diagnosis and Treatment of Minimal Brain Dysfunction.* New York: Human Services Press.

Pines, Maya. 1982. "Behavior and Heredity: Links for Specific Traits Are Growing Stronger." *New York Times* (June 29), p. C1.

Ritter, David R. 1989. "Social Competency and Problem Behavior of Adolescent Girls with Learning Disabilities." *Journal of Learning Disabilities* 27(7):460–464.

Rudel, Rita with Jane M. Holmes, and Joan Rudel Pardes. 1988. *Assessment of Developmental Learning Disorders.* New York: Basic Books.

Schilling, Robert F. 1988. "Helping Families with Developmentally Disabled Members." In C. S. Chilman, E. M. Nunnely, and F. M. Cox, eds., *Chronic Illness and Disability.* Vol 2., Newbury Park, Calif.: Sage, pp. 171–192.

Silver, Larry B. 1987. "The 'Magic Cure': A Review of the Current Controversial Approaches for Treating Learning Disabilities." *Journal of Learning Disabilities* 20(8):498–504.

Silver, Larry B. 1979. "The Minimal Brain Dysfunction Syndrome." In Joseph Noshpitz, ed., *The Basic Handbook of Child Psychiatry*, pp.416–439. New York: Basic Books.

Small, Leonard. 1982. *The Minimal Brain Dysfunctions.* New York: Free Press.

Smith, Corinne Roth. 1986. "The Future of the LD Field: Intervention Approaches." *Journal of Learning Disabilities* 19(8):461–468.

Smith, Sally L. 1980. *No Easy Answers: The Learning Disabled Child at Home and at School.* New York: Bantam Books.

Strauss, Alfred and Laura Lehtinen. 1947. *Psychopathology and Education of the Brain Injured Child.* New York: Grune & Stratton.

Thomas, A., S. Chess, and A. Birch. 1963. *Behavioral Individuality in Early Childhood.* New York: New York University Press.

Thomas, A., S. Chess, and A. Birch. 1968. *Temperament and Behavior Disorders in Children.* New York: New York University Press.

U.S. HEW (U.S. Department of Health, Education and Welfare) 1978. *Section 504 of the Rehabilitation Act of 1973. Handicapped Persons: Rights Under Federal Law.* Washington. D.C.: GPO.

Wender, Paul H. 1971. *Minimal Brain Dysfunction in Children.* New York: Wiley-Interscience.

Wilchesky, Marc and Tom Reynolds. 1968. "The Socially Deficient LD Child in Context: A Systems Approach to Assessment and Treatment." *Journal of Learning Disabilities* 19(7):411–415.

Ziegler, Robert and Lynn Holden. 1988. "Family Therapy for Learning Disabled and Attention-Deficit Disordered Children." *American Journal of Orthopsychiatry* 58(2):196–210.

# 8

## Mental Retardation

▼

### DALE M. BRANTLEY
### PATSY A. GEMMILL

Mental retardation is an area of increasing involvement for social work. Knowing that mental retardation produces an inherently stressful impact and that it requires, in many cases, lifelong support from a variety of clinical and educational specialties is fundamental to understanding the role of social work in the field of mental retardation. Traditionally, social work has been concerned primarily with the impact that mental disorders have on the lives of people in terms of personal and family distress. This is a valid concern, but successful social work intervention in the field of mental retardation must include a broader knowledge base concerning mental retardation, its causes, and its consequences.

## PROBLEM DOMAIN

Many times, people with mental retardation do not fit neatly into any one classification; in fact, wide variations in the type and degree of handicaps are found from person to person. Some are profoundly mentally retarded with several associated handicaps and require lifelong protective care; others are only mildly affected and achieve and maintain productive, independent lives.

The definition of mental retardation, as formulated by the Ameri-

Portions of this essay were taken from *Understanding Mental Retardation*, by Dale Brantley, 1988, courtesy of Charles C Thomas, Publisher, Springfield, Illinois.

**265**

can Association on Mental Deficiency, is a widely used system of classification and is generally accepted by health professionals throughout the world. According to this definition, an individual is considered mentally retarded if he or she has "significant sub-average general intellectual functioning resulting in or associated with concurrent impairments in adaptive behavior and manifested during the developmental period" (Grossman 1983:11). The first part of the definition refers to subaverage intelligence, or an IQ level of 70 or below obtained on an individually administered standardized test designed to measure intellectual functioning. In addition to intellectual limitations, there must be evidence of delays, defects, or deficits in acquiring personal independence and social responsibility expected for age and cultural group as determined by clinical assessment and, usually, standardized scales (Grossman 1983). The final part of the definition considers the age at which the mental retardation is manifested. To fall within the definition, mental retardation must be present during the developmental years, which is the time between conception and 18 years of age. For example, a 2-year-old who suffered brain damage as the result of an accident would have a diagnosis of mental retardation; a 19-year-old who was brain-damaged by the same accident would have a diagnosis of brain damage.

Mental retardation is separated into four levels: mild, moderate, severe, and profound. Table 8.1 shows the levels of retardation with the corresponding IQ values (Grossman 1983).

IQ scores are obtained by using standardized tests for certain age groups. The Bayley Scales of Infant Development is an example of a test used to evaluate children who are from 1 month to 2 1/2 years of age. Since this test depends on nonverbal items, the test results should be used with caution. The Stanford-Binet Intelligence Scale is frequently used to test children as well as adults. However, the Wechsler Intelligence Scale for Children–Revised (WISC-R) is preferred for older children because it contains a number of subtests of language ability

TABLE 8.1. Levels of Retardation According to IQ Range
(American Association on Mental Deficiency)

| Term | IQ Range for Level |
|---|---|
| Mild mental retardation | 55 to 69 |
| Moderate mental retardation | 40 to 54 |
| Severe mental retardation | 25 to 39 |
| Profound mental retardation | Below 24 |
| Unspecified | |

and performance and consequently allows the examiner to determine the child's strengths and weaknesses.

It is well to remember that intellectual development is influenced by many factors: heredity, culture, and environment, to name three. Scores on IQ tests do not reflect motivation, creativity, mechanical ability, and many other aspects of brain functioning, which may explain why some people who are otherwise mentally retarded perform adequately in their daily lives.

The great majority of the mentally retarded are *mildly* affected and are "educable." Many of these individuals appear to be normal, with no physical or other manifestations of mental retardation. As young children, they may not reach certain developmental milestones on time, but mental retardation per se may not be suspected until the early school years, when they fail to achieve academically at a normal pace. A two-year delay in academic performance can be expected, with grade achievement rarely surpassing the sixth-grade level. However, the mildly retarded have the potential to acquire independent living skills and to develop certain vocational skills. While many individuals who are mildly retarded show good social adjustment, some do not; personality or behavioral problems may limit their ability to adjust socially. Nevertheless, the majority remain in the open community working as semiskilled or unskilled workers and, in general, maintain fairly normal lives without ever being identified as mentally retarded.

Individuals who are *moderately* retarded fit into what is called the *trainable category* and comprise about 10 percent of the mental retardation population (Chinn, Drew, and Logan 1975). In addition to their intellectual limitations, they often have other handicaps, including speech and language disorders, visual impairment, neurological problems, poor dental hygiene, poor dietary habits, and other health-related problems. With special help, they can acquire a limited number of basic competency and self-help skills. Some demonstrate limited potential for developing vocational and occupational skills and function satisfactorily under close supervision in a sheltered work situation.

The *profoundly* and *severely* retarded comprise about 3 percent of all mentally retarded individuals (Chinn, Drew and Logan 1975). Many of them have little or no potential for independent living and require lifelong supervised care. Frequently, they, too, are multihandicapped with central nervous system abnormalities, musculoskeletal problems, sensory defects, and other health-related problems. Individuals who are severely and profoundly mentally retarded are likely to be diagnosed at birth or shortly thereafter because of apparent handicaps or stigmata that are present, usually in conjunction with other types of pathology.

Mental retardation is not a phenomenon with a single cause; more than 200 causes have been identified. However, the etiological classification of mental retardation is complicated by the fact that the etiology is unknown in a large percentage of the cases; that percentage may be as high as 75 percent. Most tables of etiological classification of mental retardation show two major categories: genetic and acquired (Milunsky 1975).

*Genetic disorders* account for about 5 to 10 percent of all cases of mental retardation (Litch, 1978). Some geneticists report a higher percentage, and each year more disorders of mental retardation are being identified as having a genetic etiology. Among the genetic disorders of mental retardation, chromosomal abnormalities are the most common. One example is Down syndrome, which is a well-known and easily recognizable disorder. The fact that there is a preponderance of males who are mentally retarded (approximately 60 percent males to 40 percent females) can be explained partially by genetic influences or what is called *X-linked mental retardation*. In fact, fragile X syndrome is thought to be the second most common chromosomal cause of mental retardation in males (Hagerman, McBogg, and Hagerman 1983). Most metabolic disorders, such as phenylketonuria, galactosemia, homocystinuria, and maple syrup urine disease, have a genetic etiology, but individually, these disorders are rarely seen. Though the frequency of these disorders may seem small compared to other mental retardation syndromes, they nevertheless can be devastating and crippling when they do occur. Usually, genetic disorders come to the attention of health professionals early in the life of an affected child, either because they are identified at birth or because families suspect something is wrong and spontaneously seek diagnosis and treatment.

*Acquired causes* of mental retardation involve nonheritable, environmental somatic factors that can occur in utero, perinatally, or postnatally. As with genetic etiology, acquired causes of mental retardation can result in multiple and severe handicaps, but in the majority of the cases of mental retardation of this type, no identifiable physical characteristics are apparent. Furthermore, in contrast to cases involving more severe forms of mental retardation, most affected individuals in this category are usually not identified by their families; in fact, diagnosis is not likely until the early school years. If the diagnosis is eventually made, the cause may well be ascribed to psychosocial reasons. Without any clear-cut clinical evidence, the etiology is listed simply as unknown.

Infections, drugs, malformations, and prenatal injuries are just a few examples of early influences on embryonic development that can result in mental retardation along with physical and/or sensory anomalies. For example, several viruses and infectious organisms do more damage to the unborn child than they do to the mother. Cytomegalovirus (CMV) infections occurring during pregnancy can result in a number of birth defects in the child, including mental retardation. Another example of an infection occurring during pregnancy that can cause birth defects and mental retardation is toxoplasmosis, which is an intracellular parasite, not a virus. (The incidence of toxoplasmosis infections during pregnancy could be reduced if pregnant women did not handle cats or cat litter and avoided eating rare meats.) Occurring early in pregnancy, this type of infection can result in birth defects similar to the defects found in CMV. Other types of prenatal infections that can produce mental retardation are congenital syphilis, hepatitis, herpes simplex, and congenital rubella, although rubella is now controllable because serological testing and immunization are now available.

Drugs and toxic substances can result in complications during pregnancy, including bleeding, stillbirths, and premature delivery. The deleterious effects of alcohol and smoking on the unborn fetus are now being brought to the attention of the public. Also, health professionals now are beginning to report that the use of cocaine during pregnancy has serious health consequences for the developing fetus and can leave the infant with permanent physical and mental damage.

Evidence is increasing that maternal malnutrition during pregnancy can cause mental retardation in the infant. An expectant mother who has thyroid deficiency or diabetes is at risk of having a mentally retarded child. Toxemia (high blood pressure, excessive weight gain, and fluid retention) is most harmful to the infant in the later months of pregnancy, and if the condition is not promptly treated, brain damage can result. Of course, other hazards can prevent the mother from protecting and adequately nourishing the infant during pregnancy, but fortunately, some disorders associated with mental retardation have been eliminated or almost eliminated through dietary management, antibiotics, vaccines, mass immunizations, and other types of health intervention.

During the perinatal period, the infant is vulnerable to birth injuries and other complications that can result in lifelong handicapping conditions. Asphyxia, or lack of oxygen at the time of birth, is considered a major cause of birth defects, including mental retardation and cerebral palsy (Apgar and Beck 1974). Any complication that cuts off the infant's supply of oxygen during the birth process increases the risk of brain damage.

Very small, premature babies with birth weights less than 2 1/2 pounds are at risk for delayed development (Drillien 1961; Parmelee and Haber 1973). Women at risk for premature and low-birth-weight babies include teenage mothers, women more than 35 years of age, women with certain health problems (fe.g., diabetes or epilepsy), and women with histories of genetic diseases, as well as women who are poor, obese, and poorly nourished.

Pregnancy among teenagers has serious health consequences for both the mother and the child. Young and physically immature mothers are at high risk for producing infants with developmental disabilities. These mothers have more obstetrical problems than women in the "safe" childbearing range, and they tend to wait beyond the first trimester to seek prenatal care. They have high rates of toxemia, prolonged labor, premature delivery, and small-for-date infants. In general, they have a greater incidence of maternal complications and of fetal abnormalities, all of which are extremely high-risk factors for mental retardation (Haynes 1980; Williams 1982).

Many other perinatal problems are associated with mental retardation. They include placental anomalies, birth trauma, fetal malnutrition, postmaturity, hypoglycemia, hyperbilirubinemia, and multiple birth (twins, triplets, etc.).

The early years of life represent a crucial time for the developing infant. Fortunately, most infants, after a successful gestation, are born free of complications and enter life as normal, healthy individuals. Nevertheless, certain conditions or influences can lead to serious and permanent disabilities, including mental retardation. Early-childhood diseases, accidents, malnutrition, toxic substances, intracranial tumors, special sensory handicaps, asphyxia, and environmental and social problems are frequently mentioned as mechanisms that can cause mental retardation during the postnatal period.

Studies are now showing that children with AIDS have a wide variety of neurological and developmental abnormalities (Belman et al. 1984). The causes of these abnormalities are thought to be related to prolonged hospitalizations, recurrent infections, and nutritional problems affecting the central nervous system.

There are several other causes of mental retardation during the postnatal period: infections (e.g., encephalitis and meningitis), intoxications (e.g., lead poisoning), head trauma (e.g., accidents), special sensory handicaps (e.g., deafness or blindness), and asphyxia (e.g., near-drowning).

Much, however, is still unknown about the causes of mental retardation. For the practicing social worker, a basic understanding of what is generally known about the etiology of mental retardation must be the first step in providing services and in helping to prevent the occurrence of such a disorder.

## SOCIETAL CONTEXT

In the American culture, intelligence and competition are considered of prime importance and are strongly sanctioned. This is still a society with lingering attitudes of rugged individualism. The mentally retarded person, who cannot achieve the level of independence expected of average adults, is less likely to experience the quality of life anticipated by people possessed of normal intelligence capacity and competitiveness. However, the cultural emphasis on quality of life has intensified in the last generation as the birthrate has fallen. The mentally retarded individual must now fit into a society that has increased expectations of and for its members.

In a legislative attempt to ensure appropriate education for all handicapped children, Public Law 94-142, the Education for All Handicapped Children Act, was passed by Congress and signed into law by President Ford in November 1975. In this legislation, the term *handicapped children* refers to children between the ages of 3 and 18 who are eligible for "special education and related services."

The new law also established certain rights for parents of handicapped children. These fall generally into three areas: the individualized education plan (IEP), confidentiality of information, and due-process procedures. Individual states may add specific rights, but none can decrease the basic rights established by the federal law.

The relationship between poverty and mental retardation has long been recognized, especially by the social work profession. In fact, socioeconomic conditions, according to some sources, may account for as much as 75 percent of all mental retardation (Stark, 1983). Malnutrition, unhealthy living conditions, poor child care, family emotional problems, and the inability to afford medical care are a few factors that contribute to the disproportionate frequency of mental retardation found among the poor. Frequently, the impaired learning ability of some children is blamed on sensory deprivation or the lack of stimuli in the home.

## RISKS AND NEEDS OF POPULATION

Most researchers have found that the prevalence of severe mental retardation (IQ < 50) is 3 to 4 per 1,000. Since the data are more commonly obtained from case registers or agencies for mental retardation than from total population screening, this may be an underestimate of the actual prevalence of severe mental retardation. Moderate retardation prevails at about the rate of 2 people in every 1,000, and profound mental retardation has a reported prevalence of approximately 0.4 per 1,000. The prevalence of mild mental retardation among the population is the highest rate, with an estimate of 3.7 to 5.9 per 1,000. The wide disparity of figures reflects the problems of ascertainment complicated by diagnostic practices that change over time and vary from region to region.

The reported prevalence of mental retardation tends to increase until about age 20, after which it decreases from 5 to 7 per 1,000 to approximately 4 per 1,000. A rate of about 2 per 1,000 for children under 5 years of age probably reflects underreporting for this age group. In most surveys conducted, the highest reports by chronological age occur between the ages of 10 and 20 years. Since some individuals are identified as mentally retarded only in an academic setting, and since most individuals who are over 20 or are very young are not participating in an academic program, it is probable that the actual prevalence of mental retardation does not change with age. It is the number of unidentified cases that increases.

Mental retardation is more prevalent among males than females; researchers report a male-to-female ratio of 1.6 to 1.0. One explanation for the sex difference in mild retardation may be that males are more likely to be *labeled* mentally retarded. Such findings are better explained in terms of sex-role expectations than in terms of physiological differences (Fishbach and Hull 1982). However, there is evidence that males are overrepresented in mental retardation of biological (particularly genetic) origins, which suggests that X-linked mental retardation may account for the higher proportion of males reported with mental retardation.

Another important consideration when examining demographic data is the frequency and type of disorders that are commonly found in mental retardation. A large percentage of the people who have mental retardation also have additional developmental or functional disorders. Cerebral palsy or seizure disorders are diagnosed in up to 30 percent of the mentally retarded population. Other common impairments include speech and language deficits, behavioral and psychiatric problems, and sensorimotor disturbances. The level of retardation has an inverse relationship to the number of associated disorders, so that the lower the level of IQ, the greater the number of associated disorders, and vice versa.

Nevertheless, it is important to keep in mind that the true causal factors in nearly half of all cases of mental retardation remain undetermined. What is known is that there are fewer chromosomal problems and more unknown etiologies in mild mental retardation than in the moderate, severe, and profound categories. The most common causal factor in severe mental retardation is Down syndrome, which accounts for up to 40 percent of the cases in this category (Elwood and Darragh 1981). Other prenatal factors, such as single-gene disorders, multifactoral-polygenetic causes, and environmental effects, also predominate in the etiology of severe mental retardation.

Some of the causal factors accounting for another substantial portion of cases with diagnosed etiologies are postnatal traumas and/or neglect and perinatal hypoxia. Although the research on etiology reflects a biological bias, more recent studies highlight psychosocial variables. Fetal alcohol syndrome now rivals Down syndrome as a major single prenatal factor. Perinatal problems seem to correlate with a variety of maternal social variables, and postnatal etiology is much more prevalent in urban than in rural areas, a finding that indicates the greater risk of accidents, child abuse, and serious infection in cities.

Also, the effects of inadequate mothering and intellectually limited parents are now receiving attention as a risk factor in causing mental retardation (Kaminer and Cohen 1983). However, further studies are needed to determine the prevalence of the problem. Data indicate that, whatever the reason, children born and raised in poverty are more likely to be diagnosed as mentally retarded than are children from middle- and upper-class backgrounds.

Child abuse and neglect are serious and pervasive problems, more than 1 million cases being reported each year. Contrary to popular belief, the problem of child abuse is not confined to the poor but is found throughout the socioeconomic scale. One of the many negative effects of the maltreatment of children is the likelihood of mental retardation. Severe and prolonged malnutrition, for example, if present during the first year of life, may result in permanent damage to the brain and the central nervous system (Scrimshaw 1969). Additionally, the battered child with head injuries is likely to suffer severe and permanent brain damage. Whether preexisting retardation is a causative agent for abuse is not clear because studies have shown that children who are different (i.e., the hyperactive, the handicapped, and the mentally retarded) are at greater risk for abuse than the so-called normal child (Lieber and Baker 1976). Evidence is mounting that abuse and neglect are causative agents in mental retardation (Runyan and Gould 1985).

Families of children with mental retardation are especially vulnerable to stress. For example, the parents of mentally retarded children have a higher divorce and suicide rate than parents in the population as a whole. These parents are also more likely to commit child abuse. Increased tension in the family resulting from the child's handicap, plus the child's reduced ability to perform acceptably, often results in harsh and punitive parental behavior.

These families face increased financial demands as a result of the child's needs for special equipment, medical care, and interventive services and programs. In addition to the increased financial obligations, the parents have less freedom and social mobility, producing a marked degree of social isolation. Common manifestations of stress on the parents are fatigue, depression, anger, guilt, and anxiety.

As mentally retarded children grow older, they become more difficult to manage, physically as well as behaviorally. Differences between delayed children and their age-group peers become more obvious. The degree of parental stress is also affected by such characteristics as the degree of dependency, the physical incapacitation, and the personality characteristics of the child. Children with mental retardation, like all other children, display the entire range of personality traits from recalcitrance to obeisance. Other factors that tend to increase parental stress are a child with a slower rate of progress, less social responsiveness, and more stereotypical behavior patterns, and the number of additional, unusual caregiving demands.

In addition to the influence of child-based factors on severity of stress, parental characteristics also play a significant role in the perception of stress in general and the ability to cope with the situation. Socioeconomic class, intelligence, verbal skills, past experience, age, occupation, and income modify the parents' perception of stress. The parents' belief regarding the cause of their child's handicapping condition affects their behavior toward the child:

> The nature and intensity of some parent affective reactions may be linked to their belief that somehow they caused the child's handicap. Other parents, however, might believe that something else caused the child's handicap or that it was an accident or an act of God. (Lavelle and Keogh 1980:4)

In general, fathers of mentally retarded children experience more depression, lowered self-esteem, and lack of gratification from the parent–child relationship than mothers (Cummings and Rie 1976). They have greater difficulty coping with the child and appear to be more vulnerable to the social stigma than the mothers. Other paternal concerns include supporting their wives, who carry the daily burden of caregiving. This concern highlights a great need for fathers to be more involved in programs for their children and to be provided with opportunities for the expression of frustration, anger, and a sense of loss.

Perhaps the most critical factor influencing stress are the socioeconomic status of the family and the family structure itself. Mothers in economically disadvantaged families must expend much of their time and energy just to maintain an intact household, with little left to give the children. Lower-class families are often less receptive to intervention programs for their children than are middle-class families. Single-parent families and families with siblings also present family structures that can be more stress-producing.

When parents are faced with the initial diagnosis of the child's mental retardation, they experience something very akin to *sudden grief*. In the beginning, they enter a crisis period of high anxiety and shock, usually followed by denial, anger, and rationalization. During the early phases, the parents are motivated to address the problem directly, whereas later on, the defenses of denial and rationalization appear to protect them against further vulnerability. It is likely that directive counseling during the early stages is helpful in developing new coping techniques. Supportive work can be initiated when the parents become more receptive.

Parents of mentally retarded children can be expected to experience chronic, recurrent grief. Periodic bouts of sadness, feelings of loss, and disappointment are normal for these parents. Support services should be available to them on a long-term basis. The high stress level and recurring grief that these families experience require the social worker to use skill and sensitivity. The families' realistic response to their life circumstance can all too easily be misdiagnosed as resistance and emotional disturbance. What the worker must keep in mind is that these parents struggle with a continuing problem and work through a major assault on their ego integrity every day. Social workers can become demoralized by the continual depression of the parents. A careful distinction must be made between situational depression and a depressive disorder to avoid setting unrealistic goals.

The danger of unrealistic goal-setting (and consequent ineffective and/or damaging intervention) is critical when working with mentally retarded clients and their families. The social worker, the family, and the child (or adult) must know what it is realistically possible to achieve. A standard of normality *for that particular person* must be identified in order to set realistic and achievable goals.

## PROGRAMS AND SOCIAL WORK SERVICES

In an attempt to address some of these socioeconomic factors, various programs, subsidies, and federal regulations have expanded, developed, or been defined. Department of Health and Human Services (HSS) regulations prohibit discrimination against handicapped persons in employment practices. Since many mentally retarded people can learn to perform routine job functions, these people can now hope to secure employment and a measure of financial autonomy not likely before H.H.S.'s antidiscrimination provisions.

Mentally retarded people who have little or no income, and whose retardation is sufficient to prevent them from earning substantial wages, are provided monthly cash payments from the federal government. These payments are called *Supplemental Security Income,* or SSI. In addition to providing basic income, this subsidy also qualifies the recipients for the Medicaid program. which pays for the health care costs of low-income mentally retarded persons.

Early infant stimulation programs are available through agencies such as centers for the developmentally disabled. Preschools for 3–6-year-olds are available through Head Start, churches, and local or regional organizations. Parent training, nutritional counseling, food subsidies, and respite care are other services available to the mentally retarded and their families. However, these services are very limited all across the nation. The cost of starting and maintaining such services is high at a time when public concern about and awareness of these problems are limited as well as blunted by other pressing social problems and their taxpayer costs.

The social work effort to bring support and assistance to the mentally retarded and their families is diverse, providing an umbrella of services from family counseling to networks of social and professional assistance. Social workers are involved in most of the medical, educational, residential, public aid, and social integration programs and services currently in operation for mentally retarded children and adults and their families. The training of new professionals to work with this client population as well as to do research is also an area of social work involvement with the problems of retardation.

Social work and social workers are an element of most programs, services, and agencies that address the problems and needs of the mentally retarded population. Although the forward progress made in this service area during the '60s and '70s suffered funding cutbacks during the '80s, the social work focus in services for the mentally retarded has continued to increase. Now social workers are involved in all aspects of services, from prenatal and genetic counseling to residential placement for the elderly with mental retardation.

*Early-intervention programs* for children suspected of being at risk for mental retardation, as well as for children with other or additional handicaps, are available in many areas for the provision of early diagnostic, special-education, and treatment services to these children from birth to 3 years of age. Here, the emphasis is typically on sensori-motor activities. Sometimes, services are available in centers, and sometimes, they are provided in the home (usually the latter is done in conjunction with parent training).

*Family-training programs* focus primarily on teaching the parents or the caregiver the skills necessary to continue special intervention in the absence of developmental specialists. Family training is available for all age groups, depending on the family's needs and desires and the conditions of the child's handicap.

*Preschool programs* continue where the early-intervention program stops. The 3-year-old participates in the preschool program until school age. These programs address the development of language, motor skills, self-help ability, and cognitive and social skills. Services are most often available in centers, although in-center services are supplemented with home-based and family-trained services as necessary.

*Respite care services* provide temporary relief from continuous care of the child for the natural or foster families of mentally retarded children. Specialized family care programs are designed to help children with intensive needs to remain in family settings when at all possible. These programs offer physical and occupational therapy and if needed, habilitation training.

*Family support services* include social and emotional supportive counseling, assistance in obtaining generic and special services, the provision of teaching, and the provision of incidental information. Service coordination, time management principles, advocacy, and assistance in maintaining special services are provided by other professionals or agencies.

*Schools, sheltered workshops, state vocational rehabilitation services, and residential facilities* all use the services of social workers. However, much still needs to be done in the areas of policy and procedure. For example, eligibility, intake criteria, and procedures must be determined to ensure that the families and children most in need will receive services. Procedures are needed for family service planning that promote family independence and include families in the planning process. A range of services that families can choose from to tailor support service to their actual needs and desired level of autonomy is hoped for. Identification of the specific elements of family support service that are most helpful to families should be carried out, as well as exit criteria and procedures for transition to other services, such as adult community service. Staff qualifications and training are necessary to ensure effective service provision. Funding sources, including the most efficient use of federal funding, must be investigated for the provision of support services.

Another difficulty in work with mentally retarded children is the lack of an integrated referral and monitoring feedback system for the client and the service provider. This kind of system would especially assist the social worker in child protective service agencies in working with abused mentally retarded children. The effectiveness of programs could be more quickly assessed, and duplication of services could be eliminated.

## DIFFERENTIAL ASSESSMENTS
## AND INTERVENTIONS

There are three elements about which the social worker must arrive at some conclusion in working with the mentally retarded individual and his or her family. First, it must be decided whether there is a specific goal to achieve, difficulty to overcome, or both. Second, the strengths and weaknesses of the person, the family, and the situation in *their unique dynamic combination* must be considered. Third, goals must be agreed on, and the means for reaching them must be clarified. This process is the differential diagnostic method practiced by medicine and education, as well as by social work.

The identity of the "client" is determined following the collection of relevant data. Depending on agency focus, the client is the mentally retarded individual and/or the family and/or the environment. In assessing whether a mentally retarded individual can be best cared for in the familial home or in an institution, for instance, the social worker must consider different factors depending on client focus.

Whether a mentally retarded person will do better at home or in an institution is a decision based on whether the parents want to keep the person at home, whether they can accept the person as he or she is, whether the person can reach his or her fullest developmental potential within the cultural and material limitations of the particular home, and whether the family is capable of training the patient and maintaining constant supervision over many years. If these questions are, in general, determined in the affirmative, the best decision *may* be home-based care, since more affection and individual attention are possible within the home environment. However, the best decision is always the most *viable* alternative.

When the *family* is the client, the family must be considered as a whole, with normal family life and interrelationships being a goal. Homes and families are geared to average children. The mentally retarded child is not the average child and requires many adjustments by the family.

The mentally retarded child may need so much care that the primary caregiver cannot have a normal life nor give the necessary care and attention to other members of the family. In some families, the retarded child may cause quarreling or serious conflict between the parents or between the parents and the normal siblings. Sometimes, the emotional effect on family members is marked and severe. The family's financial stress, emotional strength, size, and living-space limitations must also be considered in terms of the impact of a child's mental retardation on the family. If home life cannot be maintained at a level that provides for normal satisfaction and growth for *each* member of the family, it may not be advisable to maintain the mentally retarded child in the home.

*Institutionalization* is seldom the client focus. However, in cases where the child may be a danger to herself or himself or to others, institutional care may be chosen in the best interests of the child and the community. In many cases, though, the retarded child is docile and harmless and may serve to draw a family closer together in the common effort to help a weaker member. With proper care, affection, and training, the home-based mentally retarded child can contribute to the common welfare of the community.

Once the assessment of needs is made, a service plan must be decided on. Again, the information gained during assessment must be used and weighed in choosing how to effect positive change. If we use the previous example of home care vs. institutional care, when the assessment indicates that the child will do best in institutional care, the choice of intervention has only begun. Now the social worker must assist the family in deciding what institution will be the most satisfactory intervention—state school or private—and help them process the feelings that are associated with the decision.

Although the public image of the state schools is generally negative, there are some things available in these facilities that are of considerable advantage to the mentally retarded child or adult. Usually, the state schools have medical and nursing services on the premises. Planned recreation programs, specialized training, and farm, domestic, or shop training provide practice to the older residents that may lead to employment someday. The child's having many companions with the same handicap encourages socialization.

The state schools offer permanence, security, and skilled care for life to those who need it. For others, the schools may maintain "halfway houses" or group homes as stepping-stones to living in the community.

However, the drawback of state school admission is the serious overcrowding experienced in most state-supported schools. The shortage of personnel is usually so serious that the individual may not receive all the benefits that the facility was designed to give. In such a rehab, the law of survival of the fittest often prevails. In other words, when resources are limited or curtailed, the level of functionality correlates with the resources accessed.

On the other hand, private institutions can give more individual attention than the public institution. They lack the extensive facilities of the state schools, though. And there are greater differences in private schools for the retarded than in state schools. Some give good all-around training, and others offer only good custodial care. For the child with severe mental retardation and multiple handicaps, lifelong custodial care may be the appropriate intervention. The moderately retarded child may be served best in a program that emphasizes training and some independence planning.

Another factor that goes into deciding on the appropriate intervention is the family financial picture. Private residential care is extremely expensive. Many families cannot pay for such care and still provide for their own basic needs. So it is quite obvious that an accurate assessment, as well as the best choice and application of intervention, must be based on a dynamic of interacting personal, familial, and community variables.

In addition to the dynamic nature of social work assessment, it is essential to schedule the mentally retarded individual and their families for periodic reassessment. Mothers become incapacitated sometimes. Fathers may lose their jobs. Significant siblings or relatives may become seriously ill or die. The onset of puberty or menopause affects the retarded individual. Needs change from life stage to life stage and with every crisis as the retarded person and the family get older. Reassessment can take place at regular intervals but should most certainly be carried out during those developmental stages most likely to be stressful. Social work with the mentally retarded and their families cannot be a one-shot affair; it should be a lifelong process.

Karnes and Teska (1980) summarized the necessary characteristics of professionals who work with the parents of handicapped children in general. These characteristics most assuredly apply to workers with the parents of mentally retarded children. The list includes an ability to be emotionally supportive; to give accurate, understandable information; to access the help of other parents; and to provide the appropriate programs. Goods and services which do not seem as critical to adequate social support can be seen as actions and attitudes that convey to the person a sense of being cared for, valued, and included in a group that exchanges communication and obligation.

Typically, social support is traditionally provided by extended-family members as well as by friends and individuals in the helping professions. Some families are blessed with supportive, concerned relatives and friends. Others are more socially isolated. In the latter case, social support may be derived solely from contact with helping professionals. It is this group that is most likely to show signs of too much stress.

## CASE ILLUSTRATION

Bobby, a 7-year-old child, had experienced fetal distress during delivery and was delivered by an emergency cesarean section. The only abnormality reported in his birth record was an unusually large fontanel. During his short lifetime, he had been examined by numerous different specialists for a number of problems, including delayed physical growth and delayed speech and language development. He was in the process of being evaluated by a geneticist, with a tentative diagnosis of Kenny syndrome. However, he had some features of the Russell-Silver syndrome. Further genetic studies were scheduled.

Bobby was referred to a diagnostic and evaluation center for developmental and learning disorders for a comprehensive interdisciplinary development evaluation. The center offered very limited service programs. Therefore, the social casework provided involved little long-term follow up. In this setting, the social worker was responsible for obtaining an in-depth psychosocial history and an assessment of family dynamics, strengths, and weaknesses, and for locating the available, appropriate resources for the family and supportive counsel during the parent conference portion of the total evaluation. Since the in-person contact with the child and family was for one time only, the social work follow-up consisted of phone calls to the family to discover whether they had been able to obtain the resources or to follow up on the recommendations over the succeeding several months. Follow-up calls also focused on determining the effectiveness of the services and programs accessed by the family.

When Bobby was seen at the center, he had never been in a special program and was repeating the first year of kindergarten for the third time because the mother did not feel that he was ready for the first grade. He had a moderate conductive hearing loss, vision problems corrected by prescription glasses, and minor orthopedic problems.

During the social work interview, it became apparent that there was a great degree of conflict between the parents. The conflict had begun to surface when the child was very young and his mother, suspecting something was wrong, had begun taking him to various specialists. Bobby was the youngest of three children and the only son. His mother could not have any more children and believed the father had turned away from the family because he could not accept the idea that his only son was less than perfect. The father, however, insisted that he accepted Bobby "as he is." Furthermore, the father pointed out that he was not neglecting the other children and using up the family savings by driving Bobby from city to city, seeking new expert opinions on the child's condition, as the mother was.

Further discussion disclosed other pertinent data regarding the family. The mother had been married once before the current marriage. The eldest of Bobby's sisters was the product of the first marriage. However, the mother, although a lifelong Catholic and morally opposed to divorce, had obtained a divorce from the first husband and had remarried as soon as legally possible. The second husband had adopted the older girl immediately, with her father's consent.

The mother admitted to strong feelings of guilt and ambivalence about the contracting of a second marriage while the first husband was alive. Subsequently, he died in an automobile accident, but she reported only a minimal reduction of guilt feelings. She may have been manifesting these feelings during her pregnancy with Bobby. She told of feeling strong certainty, after the pregnancy was confirmed, that her unborn child had "something terrible wrong with him" and discussing her concern with her mother.

From an early age, Bobby's mother had begun to take him to specialists to determine exactly "what was wrong" with him. So far, no comprehensive diagnosis had been determined. The mother spent a large part of her off-duty hours taking him for evaluations and examinations all across the state.

The mother, a registered nurse, worked the night shift at a local hospital. The father, a pharmacist, worked a ten-hour day, six days a week. The two daughters, 9 and 15, were expected to function more independently than most children of those ages. It was very clear that the parents were distanced, with the mother enmeshed with Bobby. The two girls were experiencing some degree of emotional abandonment, and Bobby's behavior at home was increasingly anxious and demanding.

The interdisciplinary evaluation resulted in determining that Bobby did indeed have a partial hearing loss as well as a limited range of motion in his right leg and foot. It was also found that Bobby scored 69 on his intelligence tests. Although such a score indicated that Bobby had mild mental retardation, the psychologists felt that he might actually score higher if the conflict in the home were resolved and if a reduction in Bobby's marked anxiety resulted.

It was clear that Bobby needed to be in an appropriate educational setting. A recommendation was made, and consultation with his school arranged for admission to a class for the educable mentally retarded. Retesting his IQ was recommended after one year. He also required some physical therapy follow-up to correct a limited range of motion in his right leg and foot, and a referral to a physical therapist was made. The school was cautioned to take the partial hearing loss into consideration in seating Bobby in class. In addition, family counseling was discussed with the parents as a recommendation. At first, the father refused to consider such an intervention, insisting that the mother needed help. When she agreed that she did and was willing to seek out a worker, the father changed his mind. Referrals were made to two family counselors in their city.

In follow-up three months later, the mother reported that the whole family was actively involved in the counseling sessions. She did not feel that any problems had been solved, but she felt hopeful. She had recently requested transfer to a day shift, and her husband had arranged to work a five-day week. Best of all, Bobby seemed well adapted at school and was not scheduled to see any more "experts."

Social workers who work with mentally retarded persons and their families face a challenge of combining psychosocial and systems expertise with complex and ever-changing biophysiological information. This is especially true when the problems faced by the clients are complex and require multiple medical specialists to diagnose and prescribe treatment, and when the problems are chronic. For the student or practitioner unfamiliar with the field of mental retardation, a working knowledge of mental retardation, including definitions, causes, prevention strategies, and implications for social work research, is essential.

Persons with mental retardation require a diversity of services, and social work's major role is the provision and coordination of the services. A combination of technical knowledge from other fields and traditional social work skill is necessary for successful intervention in this field. Some social work practice has been greatly enhanced by the interdisciplinary training, service, and research activities of the more than forty university-affiliated programs for the developmentally delayed across the United States. These programs have provided an opportunity for many social workers to acquire a working knowledge from other fields and the ability to integrate this knowledge with traditional social work to meet the multiple needs of the mentally retarded and their families.

Significant progress has been made in the field of mental retardation, but much remains to be done. Perhaps the major task facing social workers and all professionals concerned with mental retardation is to perpetuate the concept of prevention, a concept introduced in the early '60s. In the past, social work has responded to many challenges. Today's challenge in the field of mental retardation is consistent with the basic philosophy of social work: to promote a more positive lifestyle for our fellow human beings who comprise this segment of society.

## REFERENCES

Apgar, V. and J. Beck. 1974. *Is My Baby All Right?* New York: Trident Press.

Belman, A. L., B. Novick, M. H. Ultmann, A. Spiro, D. S. Horoupian, and H. Cohen. 1984. "Neurological Complications in Children with Acquired Immune Deficiency Syndrome" (Abstract). *Annals of Neurology* 16:414.

Chinn, P. C., C. J. Drew, and D. R. Logan. 1975. *Mental Retardation: A Life Cycle Approach.* St. Louis: C. V. Mosby.

Cummings, B. H. and H. Rie, 1976. "Effects of the Child's Deficiency on the Mother: A Study of Mothers of Mentally Retarded, Chronically Ill, and Neurotic Children." *American Journal of Orthopsychiatry* 35:595–608.

Drillien, C. 1961. "A Longitudinal Study of the Growth and Development of Prematurely and Maturely Born Children." *Archives of Diseases in Childhood* 36:1–22

Elwood, J. H. and P. M. Darragh, 1981. "Severe Mental Handicap in Northern Ireland." *Journal of Mental Deficiency Research* 25:147–155.

Fishbach, M. and J. T. Hull. 1982. "Mental Retardation in the Province of Manitoba." *Canada's Mental Health* 30:16–19.

Grossman, H. J., 1983. *Classification in Mental Retardation.* Washington, D.C.: American Association on Mental Deficiencies.

Hagerman, R. J., P. McBogg, and P. J. Hagerman. 1983. "The Fragile X Syndrome: History, Diagnosis and Treatment." *Developmental and Behavioral Pediatrics* 4:122–130.

Haynes, U. 1980. *Risk Factors: A Developmental Approach to Case Findings Among Infants and Young Children.* U.S. Department of Health and Human Services, Public Health Service, Health Services Administration, Bureau of Community Health Services, Office for Maternal and Child Health. Washington, D.C.: GPO.

Kaminer, R. K. and H. J. Cohen. 1983. "Intellectually Limited Mothers." In E. M. Eklund, ed., *Developmental Handicaps: Prevention and Treatment,* vol. 2, *Maternal and Child Health/Crippled Children's Programs* (cooperative project between University Affiliated Facilities and State MCH/CC). Silver Spring, Md.: American Association of University Affiliated Programs for Persons with Developmental Disabilities.

Karnes, M. and J. Teska. 1980. "Toward Successful Parent Involvement in Programs for Handicapped Children." In J. Gallagher, ed., *New Directions for Exceptional Children,* vol. 4, p. 16. San Francisco: Jossey-Bass.

Lavelle, N. and B. Keogh. 1980 "Expectations and Attributions of Parents of Handicapped Children." In J. Gallagher, ed., *New Directions for Exceptional Children,* vol. 4, p. 4. San Francisco: Jossey-Bass.

Lieber, L. L. and J. M. Baker. 1976. "Parents Anonymous: Self-Help Treatment for Child Abusing Parents." Paper presented to the International Congress on Child Abuse and Neglect. Geneva, Switzerland, September.

Litch, S. 1978. *Towards the Prevention of Mental Retardation in the Next Generation.* Fort Wayne, Ind.: Fort Wayne Printing.

Milunsky, A. 1975. *The Prevention of Genetic Disease and Mental Retardation.* Philadelphia: W. B. Saunders.

Parmelee, A. H. and A. Haber. 1973. "Who Is the 'Risk Infant'?" *Clinical Obstetrics and Gynecology* 16:376.

Price-Bonham, S. and S. Addison. 1978. "Families and Mentally Retarded Children: Emphasis on the Father." *The Family Coordinator* 3:221–230.

Runyan, D. K. and C. L. Gould. 1985. "Foster Care for Maltreatment, 2: Impact on School Performance." *Pediatrics* 76(5):841–847.

Scrimshaw, N. S. 1969. "Early Malnutrition and Central Nervous System Function." *Merrill-Palmer Quarterly* 15:375–387.

Stark, J. 1983. "The Search for Cures of Mental Retardation." In F. Menolascino, R. Neman, and J. Stark,eds. *Curative Aspects of Mental Retardation,* pp. 1–9. Baltimore: Paul H. Brookes.

Williams, D. M. 1982. "Coordinating Comprehensive Child Health Services." In D. Brantley and S. Wright, eds., *Coordinating Comprehensive Child Health Services: Service, Training, and Applied Research Perspectives,* p. 499.

Zirpoli, T. J. 1986. "Child Abuse and Children with Handicaps." *Remedial and Special Education* 7 (2):39–48.

# 9

# Schizophrenia

▼

## SUSAN MATORIN

In 1964 *I Never Promised You A Rose Garden* provided for many students of clinical practice the benchmark description of one young woman's struggle with schizophrenia (Green 1964). Nearly twenty years later, students read *Is There No Place on Earth for Me?* (Sheehan 1982). Client anguish pervades both accounts. In the former, a clinician's therapeutic skill, courage, and persistence enable a psychotic woman to confront life. In the latter, however, a harsh and fragmented mental-health-care delivery system and an unsupported family add to a young woman's psychotic chaos and destine her for a lifetime of arid institutionalization.

How has our definition and understanding of the illness of schizophrenia changed in this twenty-year time span? What are the psychosocial needs of persons and their families who struggle with this disease? What quality interventions are available to them, both on an individual and programmatic level? What unique tools are essential to intervene therapeutically with this vulnerable population? What is our profession's contribution to the overall effort? As current definitions of schizophrenia have shifted to encompass a biopsychosocial perspective, the profession of social work has unique contributions to offer in assessments, interventions, programmatic policy, and research. It is unfortunate that much of the profession's contribution in this area has been subsumed under the psychiatric literature, rather than fully reflected in the social work literature. Disciplines and their literatures tend to remain isolated from one another, and cross-fertil-

The author wishes to acknowledge Mr. William Goerin for his contribution to the case illustration.

**286**

ization occurs less often than is desirable. Thus, the social work voice is perhaps dimmer than it should be.

## PROBLEM DOMAIN

In the following excerpt, an articulate client describes her painful struggle with schizophrenia. Her poignant account offers the reader a vivid description of the crippling and confusing symptoms of this disease, as well as the obstacles the client confronts in obtaining humane services:

When my first episode of schizophrenia occurred, I was 21, a senior in college. . . . I was making good grades, assistant vice president of my chapter in my sorority, president of the Spanish club, and very popular. Everything in my life was just perfect. I had a boyfriend whom I liked a lot, a part-time job tutoring Spanish, and was about to run for the Ms. Senior pageant.

All of a sudden things weren't going so well. I began to lose control of my life and, most of all, myself. I couldn't concentrate on my schoolwork, I couldn't sleep, and when I did sleep, I had dreams about dying. I was afraid to go to class, imagined that people were talking about me, and on top of that I heard voices. . . . I was afraid to go outside and when I looked out of the window, it seemed that everyone outside was yelling "kill her, kill her." My sister forced me to go to school. I would go out of the house until I knew she had gone to work; then I would return home. Things continued to get worse. I imagined that I had a foul body odor and I sometimes took up to six showers a day. . . . I tried to tell my sister about it, but she didn't understand. She suggested that I see a psychiatrist, but I was afraid to go out of the house to see him.

One day I decided that I couldn't take this trauma anymore, so I took an overdose of 35 Darvon pills. At the same moment, a voice inside me said, "what did you do that for? Now you won't go to heaven." At that instant I realized that I really didn't want to die, I wanted to live, and I was afraid. . . . I just couldn't accept a psychiatrist. I thought that psychiatrists were only for crazy people, and I definitely didn't think I was crazy yet. . . .

I stayed in the hospital for 1 week. It wasn't too bad. First I was interviewed, then given medication (Trilafon). . . . I had a nice doctor, but he didn't tell me that I had schizophrenia—only that I had an "identity crisis." I was then transferred to another hospital. I did not care for my doctor. He told me that I was imagining things and constantly changed my medication. . . . At this stage of my recovery I was no longer imagining things, but I feared large crowds of people and therefore avoided going shopping, dancing, or riding buses. . . . It took me 7 months to recover. By the way, this particular doctor diagnosed my case as an "anxiety-depression reaction." In the meantime my family was very supportive of me.

In April, I decided that I was well and didn't need medication anymore (not knowing that I had schizophrenia and that it was incurable), and I also stopped going to the doctor. I got a job, from which I was terminated after a week. I became hypersensitive and nervous without realizing it. My friends and family said I was behaving strangely, but I took no notice. I went out dancing practically every night to make up for the time lost while being afraid. . . .

I had decided to complete my senior year. After all, I only had 1 measly year toward my Bachelor of Arts degree in Spanish, and I wanted to complete my education at the college where my education began. My parents, however, suggested that I finish in Pittsburgh, in case anything else might occur. I didn't listen, and somehow thought they were plotting against me. Next, I found myself in Atlanta and sick once again. I was taken to another psychiatric hospital. This time things were twice as bad as the first. I no longer heard voices, but the things I saw and dreamed about were far more traumatic. I recall at one point thinking I was Jesus Christ and that I was placed on this earth to bear everyone's sins.

My stay in that particular hospital was absolutely terrible. Each time I saw things I was placed in seclusion. They constantly used me as a guinea pig to discover which medicine would best suit my needs. However, I met many people (patients), some of whom became very close friends. I remained in the hospital 1 month and was finally prescribed Loxitane, which I am presently taking.

After I was released, I became an outpatient. My doctor is very good and I respect her a lot. She's really a great person. It took me 6 months to recover. Again I was afraid of crowds of people, and I avoided them whenever I could.

Now I have been taking Loxitane for almost 2 years with considerable results. All of the symptoms seem to have vanished. I have my own apartment, I am back in college, president of my chapter of my sorority, and, above all, more confident and happier than I have ever been in my life. I reflect back on the pains of the past and consider them a learning experience. I foresee the future as a bright challenge. My doctor once asked me what do I think taking medicine means and I replied, "not being sick." Today I take my medicine daily, just as a person with high blood pressure or a diabetic does. It doesn't bother me. Today I am really free! (O'Neal 1984:109–110)

This poignant first-person account illustrates a number of issues specific to schizophrenia. The client describes a prior history of high functioning, an early age of onset of difficulties (late adolescence/ young adulthood), and a number of symptoms: poor concentration, social withdrawal, auditory hallucinations, delusions, and deterioration in functioning. In her efforts to receive care, she had to confront her own denial and anguish about her condition and to solicit the support of her family. She experienced the confusion of diagnoses on the part of a number of doctors who treated her, a variety of medications, and numerous treatment options, including the most restrictive (use of a seclusion room in a psychiatric hospital). With acceptance of the chronic nature of her illness and a positive therapeutic alliance, she worked toward a more hopeful recovery.

The increased visibility of the homeless mentally ill in urban areas has confused and frightened persons attempting to better understand the illness of schizophrenia and the outcome possibilities. Schizophrenia is now understood as a *spectrum* of neuropsychiatric disorders or a cluster of clinical subgroups with a number of potential outcomes for those who suffer (Kaplan 1988). On a phenomenological level, persons with this disease present with severe and persistent disordered thinking, gross distortions of reality, often hallucinations and/ or delusions, flattened emotional expressivity, and a deterioration of social functioning. Because schizophrenia does not present with one unique symptom, there has been difficulty in arriving at a precise and consistent definition. Such a definition is essential for treatment and research. Originally, Kraepelin defined schizophrenia narrowly (McGlashan 1989). Early age of onset, cognitive impairment, and deterioration in functioning were the main features. In 1911, Bleuler broadened the definition to include flat affect (McGlashan 1989). In more recent years, considerable effort has been devoted to objectifying clinical observations so as to better distinguish this disorder from the many others that present with similar symptomatology (Gress 1989). Currently, in addition to a six-month presentation of the "positive" symptoms noted above before affixing a diagnosis, there has been increased attention to "negative" symptoms: loss of drive (anhedonia), nonfluent speech, social isolation and withdrawal, difficulties in holding a job or attending school, and troubled interpersonal relationships (Andreasen 1988). These negative symptoms have been both more recalcitrant to intervention and more disturbing to society.

Because schizophrenia is now understood as a cluster of neuropsychiatric disorders with varying outcomes, it is essential to base its definitions on as broad a data base as possible. In this way, one avoids reductionism and affixing a diagnostic label prematurely. To this end, age of onset, family history, length of dysfunction, course of illness, and response to treatment are essential sources of information and complement data gathered from available structured-interview instruments. With an increased knowledge base from a number of disciplines, schizophrenia is now understood on a diathesis–stress model, that is, one in which *environmental stressors* affect a *genetically vulnerable* person, so as to alter that individual's *neurobiological mechanisms.* The result is the cluster of *clinical syndromes* we describe as schizophrenia. This thinking—rooted in a biopsychosocial framework and thus richly compatible with social work knowledge and contributions—represents a considerable departure from previous etiological theories. A brief review will illustrate how current thinking has shifted in focus. Especially in the area of family work, this shift has the considerable implications for current practice to be addressed at a later point.

The behavior now subsumed under schizophrenia has intrigued investigators searching for an understanding of this complex disorder. Before the new explosion of neuropsychiatric data available to us, theoreticians put forth a number of explanations in an effort to explain the confusing cluster of symptoms we now describe as schizophrenia (Kaplan 1989). In the eighteenth century, the presence of delusionary content in the disease often resulted in religious explanations of the disorder. The prevalence of persons with this disease in urban areas led some to adopt a sociological explanation, which posited that the harsh environmental stressors more common in poor urban areas caused the illness.

For a considerable period of time, theoreticians also focused on individual characteristics of the illness. Developmental theoreticians examined disturbances in self–object differentiation in an effort to understand the impairment of ego functions so apparent in clients with schizophrenia. Such theoreticians speculated that individuals overwhelmed by aggressive affect "regressed" to a poor level of ego integration under stress. Such thinking highlighted the role of early psychic trauma in the formation of and distortion of the child's defenses against separation anxiety. "Getting under the skin" of the patient to elucidate the psychotic experience was a prevalent approach during this phase.

Simultaneously, with the focus on individual personality development—and here, of course, America's fascination with the work of Sigmund Freud heavily influenced theory development—theoreticians scrutinized the family context, the soil in which the child's personality is nurtured or not. As a result, for a considerable period of time, theoreticians examined the communication styles and the family relationships of persons with schizophrenia in an effort to better understand the origins of this disease. A number of intellectually interesting theories emerged—often, however, on a "soft" research data base without an adequate comparison with control samples (Howells and Guirguis 1985). Such theories focused on the faulty communication patterns of families with a schizophrenic member and hypothesized that such families contribute to or cause the disorder by conveying mixed or double messages to a vulnerable child. In addition, theoreticians described the family's efforts to discourage individuality and separation, overt marital discord or thinly disguised efforts to conceal such discord under the pretense of harmony, and parental projection of emotional insecurities onto children—all as family conditions that might produce children with schizophrenia. Such theorizing alienated families in their search for mental health services.

Most of the research, while well intended, was predicated on a weak scientific data base. Continued problems in defining the illness in a unitary manner across studies, and the absence of comparisons with normals bring the "findings" into serious question. At this point, most of the above family explanations of causation have been discarded. Vestiges remain, however, and it is not uncommon to find mental health professionals who continue to analytically scrutinize parent–child relationships when working with a schizophrenic family member, and who lapse into a posture of blame. As will be discussed later a recognition of the burden, stress, and crises experienced by such families has redirected assessment and intervention.

There is one area of familial context that continues to draw research attention, and that is the issue of expressed family emotion. It has now been demonstrated that the exposure of a patient with schizophrenia to family with pervasively high critical interaction can aggravate relapse (Leff et al. 1982). Such findings are based on more solidly designed work, using control groups, than previous investigations and have led to very fruitful interventions. There are families, however, who feel negatively labeled rather than empathically understood and who are understandably put off by this continued attention to "family life," especially given the paucity of research about psycho-social supports (Hatfield, Spaniol, Zipple 1987).

Several sources of data now exist to strengthen the view that this syndrome has genetic roots:

1. The higher risk of developing the illness if a relative is similarly ill.
2. The incidence of concordance in identical twins.
3. The increased prevalence of the illness in children adopted away from *biologically* ill parents. (Cloninger 1989; Kety 1988)

As noted at the outset, some uniformity of definition of the illness is essential both to expand treatment options and to put studies of whatever aspect—phenomenology, familial context, brain, etc.—on a more solid scientific footing.

It should be noted, however, that efforts to refine definitions and to strengthen the biological base for understanding the syndrome are controversial (Cohen 1989). Some would argue that diagnostic labels rob patients of their uniqueness and humanity and place clients at risk to be labeled, with social and legal bias. Alternatively, a reluctance to refine definitions and objectify labels may deprive a client of new treatments and renewed hope.

Newer definitions of the syndrome have forced providers to reexamine their relationships with the families who must cope with this illness. As psychoanalytic theorizing has been replaced by newly available knowledge about stress and burden, providers have had to revise their relationships with families and forge partnerships more akin to working with the family of a medically ill member. Most service providers now offer support and information to families rather than analytically oriented family therapy. Newer definitions of this condition have encouraged families to form self-help organizations to press for research and services and to advocate for vulnerable clients who often cannot do so for themselves. Recent research developments in psychopharmacology and in the education and support of families to create a more supportive "holding" environment have enhanced our sense of hopefulness in working with these vulnerable clients.

## SOCIETAL CONTEXT

The increased visibility of the mentally ill on our streets, many of whom suffer from schizophrenia, speaks to the societal failure to provide humane care on a continuum of intervention options for this vulnerable group. At the current time, society commits "sins" of omission and commission in the care of persons with schizophrenia: omissions of policies and programs that work; commission of stresses that aggravate the disease. As noted earlier, while social explanations of the disease have largely been discarded, there remains considerable evidence that environmental stressors greatly increase the possibility of an exacerbation of symptoms (Kaplan 1988). The higher incidence of the illness in urban areas and the observation that less developed countries more easily reintegrate persons with this illness support this hypothesis. Especially in urban areas, the harsh living conditions, the limited options for low-stress employment, and the bureaucratic obstacles to obtaining disability entitlements and continuity of psychosocial care—all converge to stress the person vulnerable to developing this disorder. Those familiar with the early community-based care of schizophrenic patients in Gheel, Belgium, can contrast that with the current fragmented care usually available in our urban areas (Bellak 1958). The isolation of single-room-occupancy hotels, the absence of links among systems of care, the red tape involved in obtaining benefits, and the sparsity of model programs are environmental conditions that generate stress for the vulnerable client with a predisposition to this disorder.

With changing definitions of the condition come troubling questions about the optimal setting in which to provide help. The profession of social work, with its emphasis on the value of client self-determination and its interest in family intervention, should be at the center of the controversy about what is the least restrictive setting in which to care for clients with the disorder.

The move toward deinstitutionalization and the concomitant sluggish efforts to provide quality community-based care have resulted in scores of clients with schizophrenia, especially in urban settings, living in shelters or on the street without adequate services (Moynihan 1989). This group of homeless mentally ill—one third to two thirds estimated to suffer from schizophrenia—have received media attention because of their heightened visibility in the community. The negative symptoms described above, often recalcitrant to current or poorly applied interventions, result in social morbidity that is especially troublesome and costly to the larger community. It has been estimated that 50 percent of psychiatric beds in the United States are occupied by persons with schizophrenia (Karno 1989). Treatments, decreased productivity, and additions to the public assistance rolls represent considerable societal costs, estimated at 2 percent of the gross national product. Interestingly, while the costs to society are estimated to be far greater than those of all cancers combined, only $14 a year per patient (vs. $300 per cancer patient) are spent on research. While the latest research initiatives underscore the need to develop a gradation of protective services, the reality for many persons who suffer is highly fragmented systems of care (Carpenter 1988).

Biopsychosocial definitions require biopsychosocial solutions. Since the current description of the syndrome encompasses several possible courses and outcomes, communities should optimally provide different programs that allow for this, e.g., restrictive facilities when the client most needs a haven and the community needs protection from severe psychopathology, as well as more low-stress free-choice options to facilitate stabilization and maintenance in the community.

The identification of supports for clients vulnerable to this disorder is a more difficult task. While quality model programs do exist (they are discussed later in the chapter), access to them and availability on a larger scale are limited for most clients. The recent initiative to help clients to obtain back disability benefits so as to secure more adequate living conditions is one positive large-scale move. This is one example of what can be done on a programmatic level to decrease one very real source of stress for those with the illness. A recent innovation in family intervention—capitalizing on a partnership so as to solicit familial support and reduce the family's burden—is another initiative to reduce stress and increase social supports.

## RISKS AND NEEDS OF POPULATION

It is known that schizophrenia affects 1 percent of the population, cutting across all classes and both genders (Kaplan 1988). Each year 200,000 new cases are reported; two thirds of patients with this illness require hospitalization. For reasons that are not entirely known, the age of onset is slightly higher for women (25–35 vs. 15–25 in males). There are no racial differences. Of those with schizophrenia, 50 percent attempt suicide; 10 percent succeed. In addition, schizophrenics have a higher but unexplained mortality rate.

As noted earlier, advanced research methodology now allows for an understanding of genetic risk. It has been well established that monozygotic twins are at far greater risk of developing the disorder than dizygotic twins or siblings, and that first-degree relatives are ten times at risk. Investigators have directed considerable attention to the risk for the children of a schizophrenic parent. A number of studies have compared children of schizophrenic parents with children of those in other diagnostic categories as well as with normal controls on a variety of behavioral parameters. While there is some evidence that children of a schizophrenic parent function less well than those of depressed parents, the findings are equivocal.

Epidemiological studies that have followed larger cohorts over the risk period have yielded more valuable data. For example, in a ten-year follow-up in Denmark of 207 children of schizophrenic mothers vs. 104 controls, 9 percent of the risk sample developed schizophrenia, and an additional 32 percent exhibited other disorders vs. 1 percent of the control group. The risk if one parent is schizophrenic is approximate 11.6 percent, 7 to 19 percent higher than for the general population; with two ill parents, the risk jumps to 36 percent (Feldman, Stiffman, and Jung 1987). Studies of children of schizophrenics adopted away at birth have revealed behavioral difficulties validating genetic vulnerability. However, recent findings suggest that the quality of parent–child interactions may be a more important risk variable than a specific clinical diagnosis. Thus, children at genetic risk may be more vulnerable because of faulty social interactions resulting from parental illness than because of the illness per se. Intervening variables such as marital discord, conflicts over child rearing, and irritability may be more deleterious to such children than simply the presence of schizophrenic illness in one parent.

Siociodemographic risk factors are considerably more complicated to tease out. Some factors (social class) are mutable and thus subject to the influence of the insidious onset of the illness. Thus, what may at first appear to be a cause of risk may be more accurately a reflection of functioning related to the disease. Schizophrenia is described in all cultures and all classes at a fairly consistent rate. One puzzling finding of well-designed cross-cultural studies is the increased risk for the illness of residents of the Irish Republic and a peninsula of Yugoslavia.

As noted earlier, there is a disproportionate incidence in dense urban areas. The finding has intrigued investigators. Some have suggested that poorer quality prenatal care, greater environmental hazards, and diminished resources may explain the higher incidence of schizophrenia in inner-city slums. The fragmented service picture and the plethora of environmental stressors may further explain this disparity. Alternatively, investigators have looked at sample mobility within and across generations and have hypothesized that persons with schizophrenia are less mobile on socioeconomic parameters than their parents and also accomplish less within the life course. Such studies suggest achievement diminished by illness, resulting in a selection and drift process whereby less functional persons migrate toward or remain in harsher life circumstances (Eaton 1986). It has been further noted that the illness presents as less severe and chronic in nonindustrialized countries. One explanation for this observation is that family structures may be more benign: the failures of the schizophrenic to function adequately may be less obvious and may invite less stigma. In industrialized cultures, technology may ensure that genetically vulnerable infants will survive more easily. Such hypotheses, while intriguing, are complicated to study and remain largely hypothetical. They are, however, valuable in directing attention to possible genetic risk factors that may interact with vulnerability to produce illness.

What are the psychosocial needs of this population? What buffers risk of illness and relapse? Persons with schizophrenia can be remarkably articulate about their social needs. Listening to them provides insights that can guide our profession in policy and program initiatives. It can also highlight our failures in providing quality service. A 40-year-old woman employed as a medical records transcriber poignantly described her twenty-year struggle with schizophrenia (Leete 1987). She began by identifying the predisposition linked to a family history of the disease; then she described the onset of her symptoms in late adolescence and her first psychotic episode in college. Her critique of her treatment experiences highlights a number of significant needs common to such clients: multiple hospitalizations, some of considerable length, and medication and individual and group therapies, which enabled this woman to stabilize, complete school, and marry. With improvement, this client, like many we work with, discontinued medication and therapeutic contact. Her distrust and denial delayed treatment significantly. When the symptoms recurred in the absence of a sustaining therapeutic alliance, this young woman's distrust was fueled by restrictive and humiliating hospital experiences and her ensuing power struggles with authoritarian mental health professionals.

Placement in a residential halfway house—a safe, accepting, low-stress community-based arena in which she could learn social skills and become a partner in the treatment—marked a turning point. This woman was now able to accept and learn about her illness, and to construct a life around her disability. The program enabled this client to work through her misgivings about medication, to identify stress, to educate herself better about the disease, and to develop coping strategies in a predictable setting that did not mirror the inner chaos experienced by those with schizophrenia. Throughout her description, this articulate client identified the concept of hope as crucial to her survival.

If we read between the lines, it would appear that a major risk for this vulnerable group is difficulty in obtaining quality mental health services. Ideally, such services should be offered on a continuum: the most restrictive inpatient care should be reserved for those periods of acute exacerbation in which a client may engage in self-destructive behavior. Such facilities should be humane in tone rather than custodial and authoritarian. Less restrictive care should embrace state-of-the art pharmacology and the opportunity for a therapeutic alliance. Individually and/or in small groups, the client can work through distrust and denial, can learn to accept the need for ongoing treatment, and can identify the environmental stressors that may trigger symptoms (Bachrach 1989). The family, if available, should be included so that their support can be solicited and their knowledge of the illness enhanced. Throughout, the thread of hope should be prominent so as to diffuse the lonely isolation and anguish to which such clients have been relegated by the nature of their illness.

The prevalence of fragmented options and the absence of replicated model programs are indicative of the chasm between a knowledge of what works and planning on a policy level. The absence of such an overriding, cohesive humane public policy has been well described (Pepper 1987). In addition to difficulty in locating quality care, persons with this disorder are at significant risk of being offered *narrow* treatment options based on pervasive hopelessness and some confusion about the possible outcomes. A review of a number of long-term studies challenges widely held notions about the inevitability of a deteriorating course (Harding 1987). In a variety of studies spanning a twenty-year follow-up, a significant proportion of patients (one third to two thirds) achieved improved functioning and capacity to return to normal role functions. Impressions of a chronic outcome and the intractability of negative symptoms in this subgroup are heavily confounded by a number of intervening variables, among them the deleterious effects of institutionalization, absence of expectations of recovery on the part of therapeutic personnel, limited economic options, and a lack of rehabilitation services. Optimism about the natural outcome for this subgroup has been seriously damaged by failure to tease out these factors. Persons with the disorder are thus at considerable risk of being mislabeled in a misleading way, of being viewed as "permanently disabled," and of being deprived of helpful interventions. In parallel, incorrect notions of the course of the disorder significantly influence policy and program.

## PROGRAMS AND SOCIAL WORK SERVICES

Historically, our profession focused its initial efforts on individual casework with persons with schizophrenia, as well as some rehabilitation initiatives. In recent years, the profession has dramatically shifted toward greater participation in program initiatives, research, and new partnerships with families. As a result, many of the current programs have developed from the profession's expertise. Unfortunately, not all of our efforts have been widely reflected in the profession's literature, nor does our literature accurately reflect the very major contributions of our profession in state of the art service delivery. Initially, caseworkers using an individual relationship counseled patients hospitalized for an acute exacerbation (Bellak 1958). The method was ego-supportive; the goal was to reconnect the client to reality and to bolster ego functions. Nelson's writings (1975), for example, address ways in which the worker can manage the therapeutic relationship and enhance coping skills. Simultaneously, others in the field were establishing links with the community to ease the patient's posthospital transition; experimenting with locating and supervising foster families who would provide a supportive environment to which the patient might return; and setting up sheltered workshops to provide patients with less stressful vocational settings.

With shorter hospital stays and the move toward deinstitutionalization in the 1970s, we have directed our attention to the supports available for caregivers. The profession has spearheaded exciting research, with a significant impact on programming. Most prominent is the work of Anderson and Hogarty (Anderson, Reiss, and Hogarty 1986), who demonstrated the value of social-role therapy, in conjunction with psychopharmacology, in reducing relapse. Their design of a *psychoeducation model* for the families of such patients and their research on its efficacy in reducing relapse, as well as the elaboration of a behavioral model for the family management of schizophrenia, represent the new approaches of group and family practice (Faloon 1984). These models are compatible with our profession's values, interest in the ecological perspective of practice, crisis theory, and stress management (Iodice 1987).

As noted earlier, the initial interventions with families of persons with schizophrenia were rooted in individual analytic approaches rather than in programmatic models. Rising out of earlier etiological hypotheses about causation, at first family intervention scrutinized relationships, especially that of the parent—often the mother—and ill "child," and patterns of communication. More recently, as such hypotheses of causation have been discarded and replaced, the profession has shifted toward a greater appreciation of the crisis imposed by this illness, the burden on families who must cope with it, and the need for a programmatic response rather than an exclusively individual therapeutic intervention (Beels 1982). A number of studies have documented the stress that families experience in negotiating service delivery systems for their ill relative, not the least of which is the often faulty partnership with mental health professionals (Francell, Conn, and Gray 1988). Much of this distrust and antagonism arises out of earlier interventions, which left families feeling blamed for their relative's illness rather than assisted. The profession has now forged a new partnership, more collegial in tone, and has designed workshops in which families can both learn in detail about the illness and develop coping strategies.

Anderson, Reiss and Hogarty (1986) designed such workshops to begin in the inpatient phase of hospitalization. Didactic knowledge is imparted in a concise, nontechnical manner in a frank discussion of the prognostic possibilities; the need for medication and structured aftercare is emphasized. Problem-solving skills, practical coping techniques, and resources are shared. Model programs now incorporate this psychoeducational component as a central feature. In recognition that families may be coping with different stages of the illness and may have greater or less capacity to absorb and use the knowledge garnered in a workshop, the programming now available offers a continuum of groups to families from the crisis-oriented to those focused on skill acquisition (Ferres 1987).

The *group modality* provides an especially fertile climate for the family sharing of burden and grief and may be as beneficial as the actual knowledge about the illness communicated. Professionals experienced in conducting such workshops have been impressed by the responsivity of family participants and their overtly expressed gratitude for the opportunity to be listened to and to talk to professionals as partners rather than as patients themselves. There is some early indication that families who participate in workshops are more easily engaged to participate in research studies, which are sorely needed.

One area, familial expressed emotion, has attracted considerable research attention and programmatic response on the part of professionals but is less enthusiastically embraced by families themselves. This interest developed out of some very important studies that suggested a strong correlation between relapse in persons with schizophrenia and frequent contact with relatives in a climate of intense critical communication and emotional overinvolvement (Brown, Birley, and Wing 1972). Subsequent research has illustrated that family intervention (in conjunction with medication) that reduces such contact also reduces the risk of relapse (Leff 1982).

These fruitful findings have resulted in attention to a *behavioral model* of family intervention in which families are reeducated to view the patient's disruptive behavior as illness-driven rather than as personality driven (Faloon 1984). Very specific toxic communications—critical and intense—are reframed more positively so as to reduce the stress on the vulnerable patient. This type of intervention has also been successfully used in a home visit model. While it remains to be clarified which specific family model is preferable, it is now clear that any family intervention in conjunction with medication reduces relapse (Leff 1986).

As can occur with any new and exciting venture, the psychoeducational model is not without its critics. In an attempt to undo years of pathology attribution to family members, mental health professionals have embraced the psychoeducational model, sometimes in a reductionist manner. Those who suggest that families of schizophrenics function on a continuum and may require different programming may invoke a tense response, both from the families and from some members of the current mental health community. Psychoeducational programs rely primarily on behavioral measures to gauge success and, by doing so, limit treatment offerings to families who might benefit from an exploration of conflicts, guilt, and developmental-life-cycle issues that may impinge on patient recovery (Hunter 1988). Programs that attend to the concept of expressed emotion as a factor in relapse and to interventions that address and correct deficiencies in the parental management of the identified patient broaden the available repertoire.

Families and some mental health professionals continue to press for an even stronger alliance than the shift in program has embraced. Pepper (1987) urged clinicians to join with family self-help groups to advocate for urgently needed research and resource development. Bernheim (1988) described a project in New York State in which families actively advise, consult, and define policy around their institutional involvement with their hospitalized relative in treatment. Recognizing the distrust that many families have of us, this program has experimented with a "buddy system" in which a relative more seasoned in negotiating the mental-health-care maze paves the way for the novice.

Again, the many *community-based programs* available to persons with schizophrenia as an alternative to hospitalization have been largely initiated and described by the psychiatric profession. Social work, however, has particularly contributed in the area of grass-roots *self-help groups* and mutual aid organizations. Such mutual aid groups, either for clients or for families, may or may not benefit from professional input and have the following goals: 1) the provision of a social context for clients isolated by this illness and 2) an opportunity, despite illness, to build on ego assets, to improve community adjustments, and to locate resources. Participation is reciprocal, the growth of a supportive network key, and reaching out to new members an ongoing enterprise. Such organizations provide a link at points of crisis as well as a resource for ongoing friendship. Central is the concept of the empowerment of the members. Social work programming in this area has provided key support for this invaluable resource for clients, the format of which may be somewhat threatening to more traditional service delivery structures (Salem 1988). Our profession's conceptual interest in the fit of person to niche makes our support of such natural groups especially compatible.

## DIFFERENTIAL CLINICAL ASSESSMENTS AND INTERVENTIONS

The tilt toward neurophysiological explanations of schizophrenia and the concurrent development of new drugs open considerable vistas for professional practice with individual clients and their families, in groups and on a resource level. Now more than ever, assessments of the fit between the person (with the deficit) and the environment (a potential stressor) are crucial to sound interventions (Ivker 1987). Whatever the setting, a thorough assessment by a psychiatrist competent in psychopharmacology is essential for diagnostic clarity and to delineate those symptoms and behaviors that may be better controlled by medication. Misdiagnosis leads to mistreatment. Because a number of symptoms of schizophrenia mimic those of manic-depressive illness, diagnostic rigor is essential to appropriate treatment (Pope 1978). Moreover, such consultation ensures attention to medication side effects, which may, if undetected and untreated, alarm and frighten clients and deter them from seeking help and/or maintaining themselves on a dose level that will contain the symptoms. Social workers have to be knowledgable about the commonly used medications and their side effects, both to support a regime that will maintain the client in the community and to educate families about the value of treatment compliance (Matorin 1984). Practitioners have to work through their own questions, reservations, and biases about the role of pharmacology, so that clients will not be needlessly deprived of pharmacological interventions that can alleviate their crippling symptoms and improve their quality of life.

In addition to the above, many clients can benefit from an individual supportive relationship. Workers have to avoid becoming reductionistically focused on the overt symptom picture—often bizarre and frightening when the client is in a state of psychotic exacerbation—and forgetting the person behind the diagnostic label. Clients with schizophrenia have dreams, hopes, fears, and personalities in spite of their disease. With the tilt toward the biological treatments of late, the role of individual casework has been underplayed. While the earlier theoretical explanations of schizophrenia have been discarded in conceptualizations of the illness, interest in the individuality and uniqueness of the person should be preserved, and individual counseling should be offered as an intervention. A relationship with a skilled and caring professional offers the client an opportunity to work though painful feelings of humiliation and grief about coping with this disability (Turkelson 1985; Ruocchio 1989; "Can We Talk" 1986). In addition, an individual relationship helps the client work toward realistic goals and learn to identify environmental stressors that may trigger a decompensation. Recent renewed interest in a *case management role* for social workers has unfortunately focused more on the maintenance and management aspects than on the clinical components (Harris 1987; Walsh 1989). Within the context of a case management relationship, the worker has an opportunity, using himself or herself as a model, to teach coping skills as the client negotiates the environment. Individualizing a plan with a client so as to enable that person to negotiate a web of health and social supports requires a clinical relationship that can provide real opportunities for identification, growth, and mastery.

Our profession is uniquely qualified to examine the fit between the person with schizophrenia and his or her living and vocational circumstances. Such an examination may reveal the presence or absence of support and may delineate stressors that can be minimized with intervention. For example, if the client has no available family, how isolated are the living circumstances? Is the client sufficiently stable to maintain the activities of daily life? Are structured daytime activities necessary to enhance coping skills? Is there a link between systems that the client must negotiate so that potentially problem behaviors are identified early, before the client jeopardizes whatever community supports he or she may have? Here, the role for our profession in clinical case management is highly relevant. Many persons with schizophrenia have fragile egos, are easily stressed, and are vulnerable to overstimulation, distortion, and withdrawal. With the support of a skilled manager, they can be stabilized and connected to resources so as to manage the environment better. Matching a client's needs to the maximally helpful day program requires clinical skill; knowledge of the client's ego capacities, deficits, and tolerance of stimulation; and the characteristics of specific programs. Within such programs, professionals can maximally use the group method in organizing and leading patient groups tailored to the functional capacities of patients to interact with others. Such groups enhance opportunities to develop social skills, decrease painful isolation, and improve ego capacities. A number of the new models of family intervention draw heavily on group method skills both in conducting didactically oriented workshops as well as in consulting with self-help organizations.

The most dramatic shifts in family work have occurred in the area of schizophrenia. New neurophysiological explanations of the disorder have altered family practice: practitioners now attend primarily to the burden of living with and caring for a relative with schizophrenia. With the exception of important findings about the toxic impact of expressed emotion on relapse potential, in general practitioners assume a less analytic posture toward family relationships and attempt to establish a partnership that is less alienating. Such partnerships are highly compatible with the value that our profession places on client self-determination. Family work taps skills in crisis work, education, grief work, and, at times, behavioral interventions and advocacy.

Many families experience their first contacts with mental health professionals around the crisis of a hospitalization. The anxiety engendered may sharply color the ways in which families present themselves and may mask coping capacities and courage. Simultaneously, in a number of settings, not all professionals have uniformly reeducated themselves about newer models, so that families will continue to interact with some who attribute to them the causation of the disorder. In a recent paper, Walsh (1989) delineated the essential features of the relationship with a schizophrenic client and her or his family that are a prerequisite to any assessment. Among them are an honest examination of one's own countertransference biases in working with persons with this disorder, as well as the absolute capacity to listen to and fully appreciate the stresses with which such families cope. Reviewing with the family their previous therapeutic contacts with mental health professionals—often disappointing ones—is a helpful intervention. Such relationship-building skills are crucial before an assessment of client–family "fit."

Beel's (1975) description of the possible "career" tracks of persons with schizophrenia serves as a very helpful guide for assessments in family work. Is this a first psychotic episode in a young person attempting to leave home? Is this a client who has failed to follow through on a treatment plan and who has relapsed? Is this a client on a more chronic course of disability who will need ongoing lifetime supportive care? The family's questions will vary depending on the stage they are at in coping with the disorder. The need and ability to hear didactic information about the illness and its course and prognosis will vary depending on where the family is on this continuum. The defense of denial and the concept of timing in providing information must be assessed. Providing information prematurely, in a piecemeal fashion, in the absence of a relationship in which the family feels nonjudged and understood can be destructive. The demonstrated success of psychoeducational workshops is predicated in part on cognitive mastery occurring in the context of a supportive arena of sharing with other families in pain. The referral of a family to such a program, however, requires the worker to assess the stage that the family is at in coping with this disorder. In addition to didactically oriented workshops, workers have also organized resource libraries within institutions to encourage family access to a wealth of lay materials now available on living with schizophrenia (Michaelson 1984). Such materials should not be read in a vacuum; rather, they should be incorporated in the therapeutic framework so as to dispel the potential for distortions.

It is now fashionable practice to embrace the psychoeducational model. Practitioners need to recognize the limitations of this approach and the necessity of other interventions on a continuum. It is essential to tease out those families who may benefit from some counseling and grief work on an individual basis. First-person accounts by relatives reveal anguish, burden, and failed dreams in coping with this disorder (Lauguetot 1988; Brodoff 1988). Some of this can be shared in group settings during information giving; for other families, however, such feelings drive and influence behaviors that are not helpful to the person with schizophrenia and need to be worked through more specifically. Even Anderson's Reiss, Hogarty (1986) psychoeducational model outlines individual work with families during the initial hospitalization phase without the presence of the patient. This approach allows an opportunity to ventilate frustration and grief without the potential for scapegoating an already vulnerable client.

Similarly, the worker needs to reevaluate notions of dependency and the concept of enmeshment in the light of relatives struggling with a chronic illness. Given the vagaries and inadequacies of the mental-health-care service-delivery system, it seems especially punitive to critique families analytically for picking up the pieces of our public policy failures. Clients who need ongoing support and who experience particular stress around separation from the family necessitate an assessment of the family's involvement that takes this need into account. Here, a structural assessment that examines how the organization and leadership of the family can encourage the patient to remain in treatment and achieve a maximum level of functioning can be useful. A family member perceived as "intrusive" can be more accurately assessed as being overburdened with care-taking functions, and a plan should be designed to reorganize the family so as to correct this arrangement. Here, the contributions of Minuchin (1977) and Haley (1980) are helpful in directing our attention to the necessity for leadership in managing a psychiatrically ill member. The parental splits described by Haley as often being indicative of a dysfunctional family become especially pronounced in the absence of sufficient guidelines for managing an ill member. Clinical interventions to strengthen the parental coalition around expectations that the ill member will follow a medication and treatment regimen can both support a family struggling to manage this disorder and contribute to the stabilization of the client. Contracting and specificity in helping families confront very disruptive behaviors by an ill member can be especially useful components of a behavioral intervention for that subgroup of families in which the worker has assessed the presence of high expressed emotion.

Here, it is essential that workers retain objectivity, familiarize themselves with the research about expressed emotions, and not be swayed by the currently fashionable tendency to exempt families entirely from any responsibility for aggravating the patient's condition. Whether arising out of disturbed personality structure or the stress of simply coping with an ill relative, family members' highly charged negative interactions with a vulnerable client are destructive. For such families, education and support are insufficient to the task. On occasion, behavioral approaches conducted in the home hone in on specifically toxic interactions and teach families to reframe negative critical comments and behaviors more constructively. These interventions, in conjunction with sound psychopharmacology, have been shown to reduce relapse. Such an intervention is best accomplished when family burden is appreciated and behaviors are acknowledged as misguided efforts to cope rather than as being purposely destructive. The worker equipped to assess families on a continuum and to use intervention models flexibly to best ameliorate the person–family fit contributes greatly to the stabilization of a vulnerable client in the community.

For those families who must cope with a lifelong course of illness, a referral to a support group can be an especially helpful intervention. The disturbing and embarrassing behavior of a psychiatrically ill family member can result in family isolation from friends and community. Insensitive and ignorant media depictions of psychiatrically ill clients result in considerable stigma for them as well as for their families. Surveys indicate that such families have not found mental health professionals especially helpful in coping with stigma (Wahl 1989). The National Alliance of the Mentally Ill (and its affiliate groups) provides support, decreased isolation, and practical assistance for thousands of struggling families. Such self-help organizations provide a focal point for advocacy and political pressure for research and service, and thus a highly constructive outlet for the distress of families. Here again, as with any referral, timing is essential.

In summary, the clinical worker skilled in the assessment of client–environmental fit is in a maximally optimal position to design a service package that takes into account the client's stage of disorder, the burden to the family, and the client's need for low-stress, structured care in the least restrictive setting possible. The worker operating from a biopsychosocial perspective can link the vulnerable client with competent psychopharmacology resources, can educate the family and titrate their involvement to achieve maximum support, and can locate disability benefits and structured resources for social and vocational skill acquisition, capitalizing on the concept of continuity of care. Throughout, the concept of an individual relationship—a therapeutic alliance—is retained so that hope thrives.

## CASE ILLUSTRATION

Ms. Amalfi, a 20-year-old white woman of Italian origin, was admitted to a short-term unit of a psychiatric hospital two weeks after stepping off the deck of her parent's home and sustaining a fractured leg. The patient had run on the broken leg after the jump, greatly aggravating the injury.

Ms. Amalfi, the third of four siblings, lives with her parents: Mr. Amalfi is a bus driver; Mrs. Amalfi is a sales clerk. Ms. Amalfi has two older brothers and one younger brother. Her next older brother moved out of the home 1½ years before her admission. Ms. Amalfi dropped out of the tenth grade and has since worked intermittently at clerical jobs. Although she was able to obtain work, she was usually fired after a short time. The patient presented as a tall, attractive young woman with a leg in a cast.

Given the short-term nature of the setting, the worker immediately met with the family both to address the impact of the hospitalization crisis on them and to reach diagnostic clarity by reviewing the events that had happened before the admission. No clear precipitant emerged in this exploration; however, it became clear that the patient had experienced a significant deterioration in functioning over the past year and a half. This was evidenced by her inability to hold a job, religious preoccupations of delusionary proportion, her lability of mood, her increasingly withdrawn and isolative behavior, and auditory hallucinations commanding her to hurt herself. It was in response to one such command that Ms. Amalfi had injured her leg.

Before the above behavioral changes, the family described Ms. Amalfi as a vibrant, happy, talkative teenager—flirtatious with boys. The family also shared with the worker important information about past and current family issues. First, Ms. Amalfi's maternal grandmother was described as suffering "the same illness," untreated; the mother's side of the family was, in general, described as being "loners" in the family mythology. Second, the Amalfis revealed considerable marital dysfuntion. Mr. Amalfi gave a history of significant alcohol abuse and "womanizing"; the couple had not had sex for the past seven years. Third, the father had converted to the Pentecostal Christian religion from Catholicism fifteen years earlier after suffering a depression. He and his sons were heavily involved in that religion.

Like many clients with this disorder, in the nine months prior to hospitalization Ms. Amalfi had sporadically seen a psychiatrist on an individual outpatient basis, and antipsychotic medications had been prescribed.

In the hospital, the worker observed highly isolative behavior of the patient, who refused to attend any therapeutic activities prescribed for her and remained in bed instead. Mrs. Amalfi's daily visits had to be curtailed when it became apparent to the staff that her emotional involvement and constant presence in her daughter's room aggravated the withdrawal. During family meetings, the worker noted both the patient's close relationship with her brother who had moved out of the home and considerable physically demonstrative contact between father and daughter. It also became clear to the worker that Ms. Amalfi's illness had served to bring the family together, particularly her parents. Their concern about her difficulties had deflected attention from their own marital discord.

This vignette illustrates both the rich complexity of a "real" case and a number of important practice points to bear in mind in work with such clients. Like many clients with whom we work, Ms. Amalfi had exhibited disturbing behaviors for a considerable time before hospitalization. Because of her family's difficulty in recognizing quite serious behavioral changes, their toleration of her low functioning, and their inability to take action, we would speculate that their capacity to function as a family was at the dysfunctional end of the continuum.

Using a *genogram and a time line*, the worker can identify a family history that will clarify a confusing diagnostic picture, as well as note a possible stressor—in this case, the older brother's move out of the family home. In addition, a genogram would highlight this young woman's developmental stage (young adulthood) and her sex—the only daughter among four children. The worker could then hypothesize that the young woman, who was predisposed to the disorder by family history, had been stressed by the life cycle issue of separation (school-work-independence), the "loss" of her favored sibling, and, as a daughter, perhaps being more caught in the parental marital fray than were her brothers. The worker's astute observations during visiting hours of this young woman's intense involvement with her parents would support a hypothesis that the family system, as currently organized, did not encourage the patient's independent functioning. Similarly, the worker noted the ethnicity of this family and the deep religious roots—both working to reinforce the patient's ties to, rather than separation from, the family. Thus, the notion of dependency needed to be evaluated not only in terms of Ms. Amalfi's inability to function autonomously, but especially in the context of the ethnic and religious rules by which this family operated.

Last, the worker noted that Ms. Amalfi was ultimately hospitalized, the most restrictive but safest option, because of spotty outpatient care. Ms. Amalfi saw a doctor erratically and did not take medications as prescribed; her family was not involved in her treatment, although she was living with them and was a great source of concern.

Because Ms. Amalfi lived with her family and the departure of a brother was a factor in her illness, the worker decided to meet with the entire unit, initially without the patient. His goals of intervention were 1) to acknowledge the family anguish and confusion about Ms. Amalfi's illness and especially the alarming events just before admission, as well as Mrs. Amalfi's burden in coping with an ill mother as well; 2) to garner crucial data about the patient's functioning and family history, which could help the team clarify the diagnosis; 3) once the diagnosis had been established, to provide education about the illness, the medication and its side effects, the necessity of after-care, relapse, prognosis, etc; and 4) to provide information about disability benefits, given the likelihood Ms. Amalfi would be unable to return to work in the near future.

The hospital team decided to give medication by injection because of Ms. Amalfi's previously poor history of compliance, as well as to recommend a young-adult day-hospital referral to counteract her isolative behavior and to provide a structured low-stress setting because of her previous inability to hold a job. To implement this plan, it was essential that the worker appreciate the religious and ethnic culture of this family. These family rules would influence their capacity to support a treatment plan, any piece of which might signal the patient's separation from this close family unit and might engender anxiety on everyones' part. The worker strategically enlisted the active support of Ms. Amalfi's brothers, both for the overall plan and to diffuse parental involvement with Ms. Amalfi, who, in the parents' presence, behaved more regressively. The involvement of the brothers also served to strengthen Ms. Amalfi's alliance with the healthy peer subgroup in the family. With this foundation, the Amalfis were able to accept a referral to a specialized family program in which they could continue to identify behaviors that were harmful to their daughter's functioning and could learn to manage her more effectively through specific problem-solving techniques. Last, as sometimes occurs in an atmosphere of acceptance and practical assistance, the Amalfis began to seek help for themselves, expressing a desire to "heal the wounds" of marital discord and Mr. Amalfi's years of infidelity.

The following exchange, occurring midway in the patient's hospitalization, illustrates the worker's attunement to psychiatric symptoms exacerbated by stress, family dynamics that may impede independent functioning, and the use of psychoeductional techniques in work with the families of severely ill clients. Condensation does not allow for a full apreciation of the art and science of this work!:

> The patient sat, as always, between her parents, but closer to her father. The sons sat on the other side of the mother. Throughout the meeting, Ms. Amalfi was in physical contact with her father (hand-holding, occasionally kissing, verbally expessive of their love for one another). I asked everyone how they were. They responded well. Ms. Amalfi, however, seemed to be somewhat disorganized and anxious. Her affect was flat and inappropriate when she stated, "Everything is fine." She would stare at me or her parents and throughout was only able to repeat (mir-

ror) what others had just stated. I asked how the interview at the day hospital had been. Ms. Amalfi stared at me for a moment and said, "What?" Again, I asked how the day program interview had gone. She said, "OK." I asked what about it was OK. She said she didn't know. Then there was silence. I asked if she had any thoughts now, after her first interview. She said, "No." I asked if we could start at the beginning and find out some things about the experience.

Here, the worker—undaunted by this impaired client's inability to communicate—attempted to patiently explore her plans to begin to leave the hospital and to follow through on essential aftercare, a referral to a structured day program. As is true in the case of many such clients, the family stepped in to communicate for the client, aprising the worker of her considerable anxiety about this transition:

Mrs. Amalfi shifted in her chair uncomfortably and stated that her daughter had been staring since the weekend. When I asked Mrs. Amalfi what she meant, she replied, "She's been quiet on her visits and seems to be doing worse." I asked if Mrs. Amalfi had noticed anything specific. She said that the patient seemed "lost." She had inquired if her daughter was hearing voices, and the daughter had replied, "Yes." I asked if anything special had happened that day. Mrs. Amalfi said no, they had been to dinner, and the patient had appeared to have a nice time. When I asked what had been discussed at dinner, the mother replied, "Her coming home and the day program."

I turned to the patient and again asked how she felt about going to the day program. She stared and said she that wanted to go, that it "seemed fine." She looked at her father and held onto his hand. Mr. Amalfi encouraged her to tell me about the program. Ms. Amalfi looked at her father and then at me and said, "It was fine. I really want to go. I am better. I'm 100 percent better. I want to go home." The father, again in an infantilizing tone, said, "You know we all want the best for you and are working hard to help you." She stared at him and then said, "I love you." He responded, "I love you too, but you have to tell the staff when you are hearing voices, OK?" She just stared as if through him and said, "OK."

I asked Ms. Amalfi if she was still hearing voices. She replied, "All the time." The dialogue was slow and prodding, at times like "pulling teeth." Mr. Amalfi interjected, again in an infantilizing tone, "Didn't you feel you could tell daddy?" Although she said yes, she was becoming a bit agitated. He then lectured her on the difference between hearing voices and being close to God.

At this point, the worker faced a clinical decision tree. On the one hand, having taken note of the father's infantilizing tone with the client and the intensity of their interaction he could interpret Mr. Amalfi's difficulty in allowing the client to speak for herself, his intense involvement with his daughter (often to the exclusion of the other family members), and his religious preoccupations. Given this patient's withdrawal, this was a tempting option. Alternatively, the worker could choose not to challenge the religious belief system, but to educate the family about their daughter's anxiety in making the transition to a day hospital setting.

The worker chose the second option. Supportively, he acknowledged the family's fear about the patient's symptom exacerbation while placing the behavior in the context of a response to a new stress. Simultaneously, he enlisted the support of her siblings to accompany her to the next appointment. This intervention reinforced materials about the illness that had been presented to the family in a psychoeducational workshop, and it strategically diffused the intensity of the father–daughter relationship by reinforcing her contact with her siblings. The worker's patience with a withdrawn client and recognition of his own visceral discomfort with the quasi-seductive quality of the father–daughter interaction enabled him to keep on the track of his central goal: helping the client and the family to follow through on an aftercare plan designed to reduce the risk of relapse. This posture, in contrast to one that would interpret the psychopathology, strengthened the therapeutic alliance with the family, reducing their defensiveness and opening the way for later behavioral interventions that would directly address the parents' infantilizing tone with their daughter.

This vignette illustrates the worker's practice: knowledge and skill laced with an appreciation of the unique characteristics of this family. The worker so equipped maximizes the support of a vulnerable client by a better informed and better educated family. Thus, this worker greatly increased the probability that this client, so supported, would be more likely to follow through on essential components of the aftercare plan (the medication and the day program), and he thus reduced the risk of relapse. He did not urge premature separation, which would have threatened a delicate family–client balance; instead, he identified the family organization, dynamics, and alliances that were impeding rather than enhancing the client's capacity for more independent functioning. A well-thought-out referral to a structured day program, assistance in obtaining benefits, and direction to a specialized behavioral program for ongoing family intervention completed the package.

This worker, by virtue of his expertise in person–environment fit, fleshed out what a well-intentioned but individually oriented psychiatrist had been unable to provide for this young woman. With particular sensitivity, this worker began with a recognition of anguish and burden and was able to provide the family with crucial psychoeducational materials; he then shifted to behavioral management and marital work that would ensure a more hopeful outcome for Ms. Amalfi. It should be noted that Ms. Amalfi had the good fortune to have the support of a close-knit, caring family and access to quality social work in a teaching hospital in her struggle with this illness.

It is a maximally opportune time for the profession of social work to assume a leadership role in work with schizophrenic clients and their families. Newer etiological theories and revised notions of chronicity highlight the necessity of honing in on person–environment fit to reduce stress and maximize resources for these vulnerable clients (Winterstein 1986; Jiminez 1988). Our profession's skill in this type of biopsychosocial assessment and our capacity to intervene clinically with individuals and groups particularly equip us to work effectively with this population. Our belief in client self-determination is especially compatible with enabling the schizophrenic client to live in the least restrictive setting possible, and to work with families as partners and advocates to correct a failed mental health policy. In addition to a clinical role, social work practitioners, by virtue of their knowledge of person–environment fit, are in an optimal position to design programs that allow for the ingredient of continuity of care—the backbone of quality care for these clients. Our leadership in program design taps our advocacy expertise as we join with families to press for humane policies that will mitigate the environmental stresses that aggravate this disorder—not the least of which is a harsh and fragmented health-care-delivery system.

Out of this practice arise numerous research questions and rich opportunities for social work participation. For example, which subgroups of families can benefit from which models of intervention? Which features of the psychoeducational model maximize the cognitive mastery of didactic material? What factors enhance treatment compliance? What are the ingredients of an optimal worker–family collaboration? Greater involvement in these and other questions would place our profession on the cutting edge of schizophrenia research and would infuse that field with insights from our unique areas of expertise. The trend toward the medicalization of psychiatry and the recent findings in neurophysiology have much to offer clients and their families—only, however, if practice and research in psychosocial interventions keep pace with equal vigor (Ivker 1987). Social work has the values, the knowledge base, and the clinical skill to assume leadership both in generating these research data and in influencing policy.

Finally, the profession must exert leadership from within in the educational sphere. In order to counter the allure of private practice and the potential drift from public-health-related fields of practice, social work educators must underscore for students the rich opportunities for professional developement in work with the mentally ill (Lefley 1988), as well as the revised notions of chronicity and the diverse knowledge and skills needed to intervene therapeutically. The National Institute of Mental Health aims to train clinical neurobiologists, that is, individuals who combine excellence in care with a grounding in science. Our mission should be to educate clinicians who can provide both quality care and programmatic vision.

## REFERENCES

Anderson, Carol, Douglas Reiss, and Gerald Hogarty. 1986. *Schizophrenia and the Family*. New York: Guilford.

Andreasen, N. 1988. "Clinical Phenomenology, Panel Recommendation, National Plan for Schizophrenia Research." *Schizophrenia Bulletin* 14(3):345–363.

Bachrach Leona, L. 1989. "The Legacy of Model Programs." *Hospital and Community Psychiatry*. 40(3):234–236.

Beels, C. 1975. "Family and Social Management of Schizophrenia." *Schizophrenia Bulletin* 13:97–118.

Beels Christian, C. and William McFarlane. 1982. "Family Treatments of Schizophrenia: Background and State of the Art." *Hospital and Community Psychiatry* 33(7):541–549.

Bellak, L. 1958. *Schizophrenia—A Review of the Syndrome*. New York: Logos Press.

Bernheim Kayla, F., and Tim Switalski. 1988. "The Buffalo Family Support Project: Promoting Institutional Change to Meet Families Needs." *Hospital and Community Psychiatry* 39(6):663–665.

Brodoff Ami, S. 1988. "Schizophrenia Through a Sister's Eyes: The Burden of Invisible Baggage." *Schizophrenia Bulletin* 14(1):113–116.

Brown, G. W., J. L. T. Birley, and J. K. Wing, 1972. "Influence of Family Life on the Course of Schizophrenic Disorders: A Replication." *British Journal of Psychiatry* 121:241–258.

"Can We Talk." 1986. "The Schizophrenic Patient in Psychotherapy." *American Journal of Psychiatry* 143(1):68.

Carpenter, William. 1988. "Treatment, Service, and Environmental Factors, Panel

Recommendation, National Plan for Schizophrenia Research." *Schizophrenia Bulletin* 14(3):427–437.

Clonninger, R. S. T. 1989. "Schizophrenia: Genetic Etiological Factors." In Kaplan and Sadock (eds.). *Comprehensive Text Book of Psychiatry*, pp. 699–705. Baltimore: Williams and Wilkins.

Cohen, David. 1989. "Biological Basis of Schizophrenia: The Evidence Reconsidered." *Social Work* 34(3):255–257.

De Chillo, Neal. 1989. "Collaboration Between Social Workers and the Families of the Mentally Ill." Unpublished doctoral dissertation, Fordham University, New York.

Eaton, W. William. 1986. "The Epidemiology of Schizophrenia." In Graham D. Burrows and Trevor R. Norman, eds., *Handbook of Studies on Schizophrenia*, part 1: *Epidemiology, Aetiology and Clinical Features*, pp. 11–27. Amsterdam: Elsevier.

Faloon, Ian and Christine McGill. 1984. *Family Care of Schizophrenia*. New York: Guilford.

Feldman, Ronald, Arlene Rubin Stiffman, and Kenneth G. Jung. 1987. *Children at Risk*. New Brunswick, N.J.: Rutgers University Press.

Ferres, P., and C. Marshall. 1987. "A Model Project for Families of the Mentally Ill." *Social Work* 32(2):110–114.

Francell, Griffin Clair, Victoria S. Conn, and D. Patricia Gray. 1988. "Families' Perceptions of Burden of Care for Chronic Mentally Ill Relatives." *Hospital and Community Psychiatry* 39(12):1296–1300.

Goeren, William. 1989. Unpublished Manuscript New York: Columbia University School of Social Work.

Grebb, Jack and Robert Cancro. 1989. "Schizophrenia: Clinical Features." In Kaplan and Sadock, eds. *Comprehensive Text Book of Psychiatry*, pp. 757–777. Baltimore: Williams and Wilkins.

Green, Hanah 1964. *I Never Promised You a Rose Garden*. New York: Signet.

Hafner, Heinz and Wolfram Ander Heiden. 1989. "Effectiveness and Cost of Community Care for Schizophrenic Patients." *Hospital and Community Psychiatry* 40(1):59–63.

Haley, Jay. 1980. *Leaving Home: The Therapy of Disturbed Young People*. New York: McGraw-Hill.

Harding, Courtenay M., Joseph Zubin, and John S. Strauss. 1987. "Chronicity in Schizophrenia: Fact, Partial Fact, or Artifact?" *Hospital and Community Psychiatry* 38(5):477–486.

Harris, Maxine and Helen C. Bergman. 1987. "Case Management with the Chronically Mentally Ill: A Clinical Perspective." *American Journal of Ortho-Psychiatry* 57(2):296–302.

Hatfield, Agnes B., Leroy Spaniol, and Anthony M. Zipple. 1987. "Expressed Emotion: A Family Perspective." *Schizophrenia Bulletin* 13:221–226.

Howells, John G. and Waguih Guirguis. 1985. *The Family and Schizophrenia*. New York: International Universities Press.

Hunter, D. 1988. "Family Therapy in Trouble: Psychoeducation as Solution and Problem." *Family Process* 27:327–338.

Iodice, Jody D. and John S. Wodarski. 1987. "Aftercare Treatment for Schizophrenics Living at Home." *Social Work* 32(2):123–128.

Ivker, Barry and William Sze. 1987. "Social Work and the Psychiatric Nosology of Schizophrenia." *Social Casework* 68(3):131–139.

Jimenez, Mary A. 1980. "Chronicity in Mental Disorders: Evolution of a Concept." *Social Casework* 69(10):627–633.

Kaplan, Harold I. and Benjamin J. Sadock. eds. 1989. "Schizophrenia." *Compre-*

*hensive Text Book of Psychiatry,* pp. 699–806. Baltimore: Williams and Wilkins.

Karno, Marvin and Grayson S. Marquist. 1989. "Schizophrenia: *Epidemiology.* In Kaplan and Sadock eds., *Comprehensive Text Book of Psychiatry,* pp. 699–705. Baltimore: Williams and Wilkins.

Kety, Seymour S. 1988. "Schizophrenic Illness in the Families of Schizophrenic Adoptees: Findings from the Danish National Sample." *Schizophrenia Bulletin* 14(2):217–222.

Lauguetot, Roxanne. 1988. "Being Mother and Daughter." *Schizophrenia Bulletin* 14(2):337–341.

Leete, Esso. 1987. "The Treatment of Schizophrenia: A Patient's Perspective." *Hospital and Community Psychiatry* 38(5):486–491.

Leff, Julian and Norman Rubinstein. 1986. "Family Therapy." In Graham Burrows, Trevor Norman, and Gertrude Stein (eds.), *Hand Book of Studies on Schizophrenia,* pp. 101–113. New York: Elsevier Science Publishers.

Leff, Julian, Liz Kuipers, Ruth Berkowitz, Rose Marie Faberlain-Vries and David Sturgeon. 1982. "A Controlled Trial of Social Intervention in the Families of Schizophrenic Patients." *British Journal of Psychiatry* 141:121–134.

Lefley, Harriet and David Cutler. 1988. "Training Professionals to Work with the Chronically Mentally Ill." *Community Mental Health Journal* 24(4):253–257.

Matorin, Susan and Neal De Chillo. 1984. "Psychopharmacology: Guidelines for Social Workers." *Social Casework* 65(10):579–589.

McGlashan Thomas H. 1989. "Schizophrenia: Psychodynamic Theories." In Kaplan and Sadock, eds., *Comprehensive Text Book of Psychiatry,* pp. 745–757. Baltimore: Williams and Wilkins.

Michaelson, Arlene, Laura Nitzberg, and Phyllis Rubinton. 1984. "Mental Health Resources Library: A Consumer Guide to the Literature." *The Psychiatric Hospital* 15(3):133–139.

Minuchin, Salvador. 1977. *Families and Family Therapy.* Cambridge: Harvard University Press.

Moynihan, Daniel. 1989. "Letters to the Editor." *New York Times* (May 22).

Nelson, Judith C. 1975a. "Treatment Issues in Schizophrenia." *Social Casework* 56(3):145–151.

Nelson, Judith C. 1975b. "Treatment Planning in Schizophrenia." *Social Casework* 56(2):67–73.

O'Neal, Jeanine M. 1984. "First Person Account." *Schizophrenia Bulletin* 10(1):109–110.

Pepper, Bert. 1987. "A Public Policy for the Long-Term Mentally Ill: A Positive Alternative to Reinstitutionalization." *American Journal of Orthopsychiatry* 57(3):452–457.

Pope, H. and J. Lipinski. 1978. "Diagnosis in Schizophrenia and Manic-Depressive Illnesses." *Archives of General Psychiatry* 35:811–828.

Ruocchio, Patricia J. 1989. "How Psychotherapy Can Help the Schizophrenic Patient." *Hospital and Community Psychiatry* 40(2):188–190.

Salem, Deborah A., Edward Seidman, and Julian Rappaport. 1988. "Community Treatment of the Mentally Ill: The Promise of Mutual-Help Organizations." *Social Work* 33(5):403–408.

Sheehan, L. 1982. *Is There No Place on Earth for Me?* Boston: Houghton Mifflin.

Taylor, Edward. 1987. "The Biological Basis of Schizophrenia." *Social Casework* 32(3):115–121.

Taylor, Edward. 1989. "Schizophrenia: Fire in the Brain." *Social Casework* 34(3):258–260.

Turkelson, Kenneth. 1985. "On the Humiliations of Recovering from Chronic Psychosis." Paper presented at American Psychiatric Association Annual Meeting.

Wahl, Otto F. and Charles R. Harman. 1989. "Family Views of Stigma." *Schizophrenia Bulletin* 15:131–139.

Walsh, Joseph. 1989. "Engaging the Family of the Schizophrenic Client." *Social Casework* 70(2):106–113.

Wintersteen, Richard T. 1986. "Rehabilitating the Chronically Mentally Ill: Social Work's Claim to Leadership." *Social Work* 31(5):332–337.

# II
# VULNERABLE LIFE CIRCUMSTANCES AND EVENTS

▼

# 10

## Adolescent Pregnancy

▼

### BRUCE ARMSTRONG

Adolescents have had premarital intercourse and borne children outside of marriage throughout American history. Steadily increasing proportions of sexually active teens and dramatic transformations in family and labor market structures during the past twenty years, however, have left young Americans increasingly vulnerable to the negative health, social, and economic effects of early, unplanned pregnancy. Moreover, AIDS now poses the risk of devastating consequences for sexually active youth and their children.

With more than a million teenage pregnancies occurring each year (the vast majority unintended), the United States has a higher adolescent fertility rate than most other developed countries (Westoff, Calot, and Foster 1983). More than half of the nearly 500,000 teens who give birth each year are unmarried, and about one quarter have had a prior birth. It is not surprising, therefore, that the 1987 outlay in Aid to Families with Dependent Children (AFDC), Medicaid, and Food Stamps for families in which mothers had their first child as a teenager was about $19 billion. (U.S. HHS 1987).

The social, educational, and economic consequences of early pregnancy and childbearing have been abundantly documented (Hayes 1987). Adolescent parents, for example, are likely to leave school earlier and to have far lower lifetime earnings than peers who delay childbearing. Poor and minority youth are particularly vulnerable to early pregnancy and the stresses of being a young parent. Because of these severe personal and public costs, adolescent pregnancy and parenthood have come to be regarded as problems not only for teenagers, their children, and families, but for American society. A very

**319**

private event has been transformed into a significant social issue that poses numerous policy and service delivery dilemmas.

## PROBLEM DOMAIN

Adolescence and parenthood are significant turning points in the life cycle. Even when the adolescent passage is on course and parenthood is perceived as a positive event, the demand for adaptation to the new tasks of both roles generates stress. When parenthood occurs simultaneously with the normative crisis of adolescence, there is great potential for a severe lack of fit between a young person's readiness to assume a parental role and the social environment's ability and/or willingness to respond.

There are many different views on why American teenagers do not avoid pregnancy more successfully, why many embark on the challenging career of parenting while so young, and why they experience difficulties raising their children. Some explanations of teenagers' sexual risk-taking behavior emphasize the nature of adolescence itself. Adolescents are simply viewed as too impulsive or irresponsible to avoid pregnancy. Such attitudes are implied by staff complaints that teens find the time to have sex but not to keep clinic appointments. Unfortunately, such perceptions are likely to contribute to tense exchanges when visits are finally made.

A more benevolent approach recognizes that while physical maturation occurs at increasingly younger ages, the social, emotional, and cognitive changes of adolescence occur over time. During these transitional years, many youth are vulnerable to unintended pregnancy because thinking skills that facilitate contraceptive and parenting behaviors are not yet developed. Unprotected intercourse, for example, may be a manifestation of the adolescent's "personal fable," i.e., a sense of unique invulnerability to the consequences experienced by others (Elkind 1974). Awareness of such egocentric thinking blocks the tendency to critically evaluate youth and may instead suggest interventions to bolster their capacity to make and implement thoughtful decisions.

Poverty, poor basic skills, and academic failure leading to demoralization also play a part in unplanned teenage pregnancy. Most poor adolescents with low basic skills do not "plan" to get pregnant. Limited expectations of positive life options, however, may diminish motivation to actively avoid pregnancy. When pregnancy occurs, parenthood may be perceived as having few costs since future opportunities seem limited.

Environmental factors rather than individual capacities and motivations offer yet another explanation for the problems related to adolescent sexual behavior and pregnancy. While norms conveyed through the media depict sex as spontaneous and romantic, and as having few costs (e.g., contracting AIDS or other sexually transmitted diseases), American social and political attitudes toward adolescent sexuality are ambivalent at best. An international study comparing the United States to other industrialized nations, for example, suggests that America's less tolerant attitude towards teens' sexual behavior may contribute to the difficulty youth have acknowledging activity and obtaining services. Several comparison countries with lower fertility rates have made it easier for all teens to access contraception by not limiting subsidized services to economically disadvantaged youth. In these countries, pregnancy (not adolescents' sexual activity) is the problem being addressed, and preventing unplanned pregnancy (not eliminating premarital sex) is the goal (Jones et al. 1985).

Groups such as the National Urban League have responded to the saturation of sexual content in the media by attempting to influence industry executives to present more balanced programming. Others, however, contend that the provocative nature of the media demands that teens be given direct messages about alternative behaviors. "Just Say No" approaches to sex education are proposed as more appropriate than those that "assume" that teens will become sexually active. Parents are encouraged to establish themselves as barriers between their children and early sexual activity by conveying the clear message that abstinence is the preferred behavior.

Problems associated with adolescent pregnancy have generally been viewed as a concern only of women. Relatively little research has been available to help policymakers or service providers understand male reproductive behavior, and few programs have been crafted with males' unique needs in mind. Difficulty documenting their activity and the fact that many do indeed deny responsibility have contributed to this neglect. In recent years, however, research has challenged the notion that most adolescent males are uncaring and uninvolved (Sullivan 1985). Complex living arrangements and delayed coresidence, for example, may mask a young father's participation. Involvement may also go unnoticed and unrewarded, as when a partner is escorted to a family planning clinic or small "in-kind" contributions such as Pampers and baby-sitting are made.

Failure to adequately include males has been costly since the male often plays a key role in a couple's decision to use contraception. Moreover, the most commonly used methods in early sexual encounters are condoms and withdrawal. Missing opportunities to involve young men is even more disturbing given the growing concern over the spread of AIDS and the important part condoms play in preventing its transmission.

## SOCIETAL CONTEXT

As noted, adolescents are continuously exposed to sexually provocative materials. Afternoon and prime-time "soaps" feature extramarital affairs but fail to mention contraception. Rock videos are filled with sexual content, and VCR technology has brought X-rated movies into the home. Youth are encouraged to be sexually active by the media and are advised to abstain by the church, school, and family but are rarely helped by adults to sift through these conflicting messages.

While Americans generally support sex education in schools, only about 60 percent of females and 52 percent of males take a formal course by age 19, according to data from the 1984 National Longitudinal Survey of Work Experience of Youth (Marsiglio and Mott 1986). Less than half of all teens receive information about contraception. Moreover, sex education in the schools is often brief and is offered after many have already begun having intercourse. Students are left with additional knowledge, but without the behavioral or critical thinking skills needed to make informed decisions about sexual activity.

Dramatic changes in both the labor market and family structures during the past several years have intensified the problems encountered by young parents. Millions of adequately paying industrial jobs that required little education and few skills have been replaced by lower paying jobs in retail and service industries. When manufacturing layoffs have occurred, workers with the least seniority (often young minority males) have been terminated first. As a result, disproportionate numbers of young black and Hispanic males are unemployed or working at poverty wages. Discouraged and feeling they have little chance of supporting a family, many young men are reluctant to become involved fathers. Given their meager earnings, couples may decide against marriage to avoid losing AFDC benefits.

Such societal changes and personal decisions have had a serious impact on young families. The rate of nonmarital childbearing among teens has risen steadily. Black adolescent mothers are several times more likely to be unmarried at first birth than their white peers. Real median incomes declined by almost a third for all young families between 1973 and 1986, but by about one half for young black families (CDF 1988c).

Poor youth are several times more likely to have below-average basic skills than their more affluent peers, and the interaction of poverty and poor skills (regardless of race) greatly increases the likelihood that youth will drop out of school and experience single parenthood. Youth living in poor neighborhoods also have less proof of the link between educational success and good jobs. They see fewer working families, have little exposure to neighbors owning or employed in local business, and have weaker connections to job networks that can be the first step out of poverty (CDF 1988b). When the adults do work, it is often in low-wage jobs that do little to inspire enthusiasm.

Schools in poor neighborhoods are frequently overcrowded, in poor repair, and lacking in safe, organized, and constructive after-school activities. Few meet the criteria of successful after-school programs suggested by Kerewsky and Lefstein (1982): diverse activities, time for reflection, meaningful active participation, and positive interaction with adults and peers. Even when programs exist, participation may be discouraged by parents who fear their children's being out alone in unsafe neighborhoods.

Economically disadvantaged neighborhoods are likely to have a substantial proportion of single-parent households. The diminished availability of extended-family support, coupled with increasing numbers of parents who work outside the home, leave many youth with lengthy periods of unsupervised time after school. It is not surprising, therefore, that first sexual intercourse usually occurs in a partner's home, one's own, or that of a relative or friend (Zelnik 1983).

Young parents need a wide array of social, health, and educational services to cope effectively with the stress of caring for young children. Critically needed services, however, are often unavailable to the teens who need them most. Affordable and safe child care, for example, enables youth to stay in or return to school, attend general equivalency diploma (GED) programs, or to participate in vocational training, yet the United States is one of few industrialized nations without a comprehensive child care policy. While new legislation in Congress fosters hope that more adequate services will be developed, federally funded child care programs currently serve a small portion of the several million children under 6 who are poor.

Teen parents and their children are one of the fastest growing groups of homeless people in the United States, yet a grossly inadequate supply of low-cost housing poses a grave risk to young families. As a result, pregnant and parenting teens must often live in temporary and even dangerous settings. While many remain at home or move in with partners, others live in transitional shelters, on their own in substandard conditions, or doubled up in friends' or relatives' apartments. Many move constantly, traveling from friend, to relative, to street or shelter, and then repeating the cycle. Even when resources exist, policies may interfere with teens' receiving services, as when AFDC housing allowances fall far below real market rents.

## RISKS AND NEEDS OF POPULATION

Over the past two decades, teen pregnancy rates have increased, while birthrates have declined (Hayes 1987). Part of the growth in pregnancy rates is explained by the sharp rise in sexual activity among teens. By age 20, for example, about 80 percent of males and 70 percent of females are sexually active, i.e., have had intercourse at least once (Hayes 1987). While the average age of first intercourse has been reported to be 16.2 for females and 15.7 for males (Zelnik and Shah 1983), urban youth are known to initiate sexual activity even younger (Clark, Zabin, and Hardy 1984). Black youth are more likely to be sexually active than whites or Hispanics, but the sharpest increase in the rate of sexual activity in recent years has been among white teenagers.

Many adolescents, especially those who have recently initiated intercourse, are at high risk for unplanned pregnancy because of inconsistent or no use of contraception. A national survey conducted in 1979, for example, revealed that 39 percent of sexually active unmarried females between 15 and 19 reported only occasionally using contraception, and 27 percent said they never used any (Zelnik and Kantner 1980). Less than half of all sexually active teens use a contraception at first intercourse (Zelnik and Shah 1983). When contraception is used, methods with high failure rates (e.g., withdrawal) are often the choice. Since the median delay between first intercourse and approaching a clinic is about one year (Zabin and Clark 1981), it is not surprising that about half of all first premarital teenage pregnancies occur within six months of becoming active (Zabin, Kantner, and Zelnik 1979). Younger teens are particularly vulnerable, as indicated by rising pregnancy rates for girls 14 and under (ACOG 1988).

Adolescent pregnancy is a problem for American youth from rural and urban areas, of all socioeconomic levels, and from all racial and ethnic groups. Black and Hispanic youth, however, while not accounting for the majority of births to American teens, have higher birthrates than white teens. By age 18, 14 percent of Hispanic and 26 percent of black teens have experienced a birth, compared with 7 percent of whites (Pittman and Adams 1988). Moreover, 87 percent of the births to 15–19-year-old black females were outside of marriage in 1982, compared to 36 percent of births to white teens (NCHS 1984). This steadily increasing number of unmarried youth giving birth is of tremendous concern, as three quarters of all single mothers under 25 have incomes below poverty level (U.S. Commerce 1983).

Recent analyses of data have shown that much of the racial and ethnic difference in early pregnancy and childbearing can be attributed to minority youth's being poorer and having lower basic skills. Regardless of race, for example, about 20 percent of women 16 to 19 years old living in poor families and having below-average academic skills became a parent in 1981. In contrast, only 3 to 5 percent of black, white, and Hispanic 16–19-year-olds with good basic skills and living in families above the poverty line became mothers (Pittman and Adams 1988).

Many of the problems youth experience, once they are parents, are related to rapid subsequent births, early school-leaving, and poverty. In one study, about 20 percent of young women who had their first child between 15 and 19 had a repeat birth within one year (Koenig and Zelnik 1982). Poor teens are more likely than their affluent peers to experience a rapid subsequent birth (Mott 1986). Whereas only about half of all teens who have a child before age 18 complete high school, Hispanic teens are at particularly high risk. Only 27 percent of these youth graduated high school, compared with 66 percent of black and 55 percent of white teen mothers (Pittman and Adams 1988). Partly because of their reduced schooling, lifetime earnings for women who start their families as teens are about half of what is earned by those who delay having children until after 20 (CDF 1988a).

Forced to cope with limited incomes, teen parents and their children are vulnerable to increased stress from difficulty in accessing adequate child care and other necessary services. Babies born to young teens are several times more likely to be of low birth weight than the babies of older mothers. Low-birth-weight babies are much more likely to die during the first year of life and are also more vulnerable to other impairments, such as seizure disorders and learning disabilities. Many of the health problems associated with young maternal age are largely attributed to poor nutrition during pregnancy and delays in initiating prenatal care. Only a third of 15-year-olds began prenatal care during the first trimester, for example, compared with 60 percent of 18–19-year-olds (Brindis and Mitchell 1987).

Problems related to adolescent pregnancy and parenting are compounded for youth who are runaways and for those with extensive histories of foster placement. Abandoned, moved about, and surviving alone on the streets, these youth are often left with little sense of past or future. When homeless or living in crowded hotels, they have increased daily exposure to violence and drugs. These youth may also be vulnerable to AIDS and other sexually transmitted infections from exchanging sex for needed resources. Babies are at increased risk of being born at low birth weight and of experiencing medical problems due to maternal drug involvement.

For a number of reasons, youth with long histories of foster placement are less likely to have received sexuality and contraceptive information, and thus they are at higher risk for early sexual activity and pregnancy. Reluctant to trust because of their years of shifting caretakers or because of a fear that their babies will be taken from them, these youth may be even more likely to delay approaching social or health agencies for contraceptive or prenatal care.

## PROGRAMS AND SOCIAL WORK SERVICES

Social workers play important roles in *hospital, school, residential,* and *community-based programs* designed to prevent adolescent pregnancy and to bolster the parenting capacity of teens who have children. Hospital inpatient and outpatient obstetrical-gynecological social work staff provide clients with psychosocial screening, assessment, and intervention. The services include, for example, counseling around interpersonal problems and decision dilemmas (e.g., choosing to continue or terminate an unplanned pregnancy), helping with environmental problems such as inadequate housing, and facilitating referrals to such services as day care and home health care.

Recognizing the reluctance of teens to approach formal agencies for preventive health care, workers at one urban hospital broadcast services by systematically visiting youth on neighborhood streets and playgrounds as well as at after-school programs. They engage interested adult leaders as "gatekeepers" to their clinic. Utilizing medical students as actual workers, local youth groups have athletic events videotaped and shown at the hospital. (Youth are informed that reproductive health services will also be offered.)

At the clinic, social workers and medical students conduct individual and group sessions aimed at modifying beliefs about reproductive health behaviors and their consequences. Males role-play a woman's pelvic exam and meet pregnant teens who tell of their concerns about childbirth and raising children. Positive adult role models make "cameo" appearances to convey beliefs about the benefit of delaying childbearing. Staff attempt to match the clinic environment to the needs and interests of adolescents. To reduce the tension in crowded waiting rooms, for example, a VCR plays sports and music videos. "Rap groups" broadcast community resources, such as how to locate sponsors of summer employment. Young parents learn about procedures for obtaining entitlements and for filing complaints against landlords who refuse to install window guards.

Social workers also play vital roles in school health programs. In some cases, workers from community-based organizations are "outposted" to school sites. Through individual and group counseling, they attempt to bolster the capacity of teens to make informed choices about sexual activity, e.g., helping youth who do not want to become pregnant delay the onset of intercourse or to use contraception. In other instances, workers are part of a multidisciplinary staff in school-based clinics. Services include crisis intervention, short-term individual and family counseling, consultations with school personnel, and referrals to community agencies. One particularly important task is aggressively tracking sexually active youth. Psychoeducational groups increase the number of students served and capitalize on the importance of the peer group. Because it is recognized that knowledge alone is not sufficient to influence behavior, trigger films, role playing, and problem-solving vignettes are used to help students identify options, anticipate costs and benefits, clarify values, and formulate action plans such as visiting a family-planning clinic.

Since motivation to delay parenthood is enhanced when adolescents believe they have a future, interventions that bolster the employment prospects of youth are particularly important. In one school-based program, social workers collaborate with educators and public health staff in arranging work experiences for youth at risk of dropping out. In addition to experiential learning, youth meet in small groups to reflect on their activities, interact with adults from a variety of professions, and go on field trips to police stations, banks, and other neighborhood work sites. Through such activities, students are stimulated to expand their vision of future choices and are challenged to weigh the effects of early parenthood on achieving their vocational objectives.

Social workers in residential programs for young parents and their children arrange for comprehensive and coordinated services that match the multiple and shifting needs of these clients. In transitional shelters, workers help parents obtain scarce permanent housing by assisting in housing searches and coaching mothers on how to interview for government- or agency-sponsored apartments. Through individual and group interventions, mothers receive emotional support as well as training in parenting and independent living skills. Workers arrange for assessment and placement in educational or vocational programs and facilitate referrals to medical, day care, and recreational services. Aftercare case management is provided to ease transitions to more permanent settings.

Adolescent parents are also served in a variety of community-based agencies. Comprehensive parenting programs provide on-site child care while young mothers and fathers receive intensive instruction leading to their GED. The young parents participate in individual counseling as well as group activities that bolster their home management skills and enable them to obtain concrete resources such as Medicaid. In addition to learning parenting skills (e.g., alternate ways of soothing a crying child), young parents are helped to work through unresolved issues emanating from past frustrations with their own early-childhood caretakers. When parents are unable to attend classroom and group activities because of other more pressing needs, staff adapt by advocating for them at court hearings, by brokering for them at face-to-face and public housing interviews, and by accompanying them as they attempt to access health and employment services.

For numerous reasons (e.g., organizational policy, insufficient staffing, and safety concerns), few programs venture out to young parents' homes to engage them in services. Recognizing that many teen parents are isolated or overwhelmed by numerous demands, however, some family agencies use home visits as a primary service modality. Through aggressive outreach, parents are helped to access entitlements, to negotiate complex bureaucracies, and to experience less social isolation. In one agency, home and office visits are alternated as the teen grows to trust the worker. Respite care is provided through a developmental playroom so that young mothers can use other agency services and can have time for themselves. Recreational outings and activity groups (e.g., sewing classes) cultivate skills while enhancing social contact with peers. Parenting groups bolster young mothers' and fathers' capacity to respond to their children. In addition to encouraging mutual aid and support, workers negotiate confrontations, as when peers challenge a young mother to weigh the potential costs of continuing a relationship with a drug-dealing boyfriend.

The training and supervisory activities of social workers enhance the quality and expand the resources available to sexually active and parenting teens. Medical students are trained by social workers to deliver reproductive health counseling at an urban clinic. Foster grandparents in a support program for young mothers are supervised by a social worker and are used as home visitors who share their skills and life wisdom to bolster clients' parenting competence. At a municipal health agency, a social worker directs a multidisciplinary staff that provides parenting education in schools, shelters, and community agencies, as well as a formal training program for professionals working with pregnant and parenting teens.

## DIFFERENTIAL CLINICAL ASSESSMENTS AND INTERVENTIONS

There is no one cause of teenage pregnancy or of the problems encountered by young parents. Adolescents are not a homogeneous group, nor is America a homogeneous society. While coming from an economically disadvantaged family can contribute to hopelessness, for example, many poor youth successfully avoid pregnancy. Social workers, therefore, are challenged to make careful assessments of where a poor fit exists between what adolescents need to prevent pregnancy or to raise children and how their environment responds to those needs. When effective assessments are achieved, interventions can be more accurately targeted at bolstering individuals' adaptive capacities, changing environments, or both.

Reproductive and parenting behaviors are products of constantly changing interactions between people and their sociocultural environment. Events take place in the "life space," i.e., an open system with interrelated parts that include youth, family and friendship networks, service agencies, neighborhood environments, etc. Unprotected intercourse, for example, may be a manifestation of an imbalance between teenagers' needs (e.g., for accurate information), adaptive capacities (e.g., communication skills), and the need-meeting qualities of their real and imagined environments (e.g., the perceived prevalence of peers' sexual activity).

Assessment entails gathering and making sense of information about such factors as 1) key actors' perceptions of the "problem" (e.g., whether the pregnancy was planned); 2) the capacities available to resolve needs (e.g., how developed the mother's ability is to structure time); and 3) the adequacy of environmental resources (e.g., whether the grandparents can help with child care). Connections between the system's components are also assessed (e.g., whether the mother and father are willing and able to be resources to each other).

Apart from demographic factors such as age, socioeconomic status, and family intactness, other important considerations in assessing the risk for unplanned pregnancy are the adolescent's 1) knowledge of reproductive facts; 2) capacity to plan and communicate clearly; 3) educational achievement and expectation; 4) personal beliefs and attitudes, as well as perceptions of peer, family, and community norms about reproductive behaviors (e.g., premarital sex); 5) patterns of sexual activity; and 6) nature of relationship with partner(s). The availability (real and perceived) of informational and contraceptive services also needs to be considered.

In order to make and implement informed decisions, adolescents need accurate reproductive information (e.g., about pregnancy risk) as well as cognitive and interpersonal skills. While youth may be motivated to avoid pregnancy, inaccurate facts leave many vulnerable to an unwanted conception (e.g., "Since I had VD, I thought I was infertile"; "She was a virgin so I didn't use a condom"; "Don't worry, we always avoid intercourse during my period"). Moreover, the undeveloped abstract-thinking skills of younger teens limit their ability to plan ahead for intercourse (e.g., "I didn't have a condom because we didn't expect to do anything").

Youth who are failing in school and who have below-average academic skills and low expectations for future academic achievement are more likely to be sexually active at an early age and not to use contraception. As noted before, these youth usually do not consciously plan to conceive, but they may be insufficiently motivated to take the necessary steps to avoid pregnancy. When conception occurs, early parenthood is perceived as having few real "costs" since positive future life options are vague or are judged to be unattainable.

Adolescents' beliefs and attitudes about sex-related issues influence their subsequent behavior. The belief, for example, that "Everyone has sex but me" can have an impact during a developmental period when the value of peer group acceptance is so strong. Ambivalence about intercourse, on the other hand, may contribute to a teen's delay in obtaining contraception (e.g., "Using the pill makes me look 'easy'") and is often the explanation underlying the often-heard response that "It just happened." Discussion of contraception and the use of barrier methods like condoms may be avoided because of the anticipated consequences of those behaviors (e.g., "He'll be insulted if I ask him to use one").

Family and community norms and expectations, in turn, influence peer group and personal beliefs. While an environment that easily tolerates premarital sexual activity does not "cause" youth to have intercourse, such behavior is not discouraged either. In a similar way, early childbearing may be reinforced by traditional cultural expectations that a woman's place is at home with children, not pursuing higher educational goals.

Patterns of sexual activity and the nature of the relationship with a partner also affect reproductive decision-making. Since the sexual activity of very young adolescents is often sporadic, for example, planning ahead and using contraception can be difficult. While "steady" dating seems to be associated with the early onset of intercourse, youth in committed relationships are also more likely to use contraception, as communication becomes easier and perceptions of the partner's reactions become clearer.

During times of scarce resources, it is easy for a serious mismatch to occur when adolescents approach formal agencies for help. Free and confidential family-planning care may not be available. Clinics that target teens may not be used because there are no evening hours, or because there are few bilingual staff in areas with large populations of newly arrived immigrants. The uninviting attitude of overwhelmed receptionists may discourage youth from taking advantage of free contraceptive services. Perceptions of services can also affect their use, as when youth view a school clinic as a place to go only for help with "problems." Resistance to following through on referrals to a community health clinic may arise from beliefs that parents will be informed, or from exaggerated perceptions of the distance from the school to the clinic.

In helping adolescent parents adapt to their new role and avoid a rapid subsequent pregnancy, many of the same knowledge and motivational issues just discussed need to be assessed. An additional key element to be determined is the adolescent's attitude toward pregnancy and child rearing. Some studies, for example, have suggested that youth who want to become pregnant are likely to have a second child sooner than those whose pregnancy is unplanned. On the other hand, a positive attitude toward parenthood is an important asset in coping with the stress of raising a child. Resentment at having social activity or educational goals curtailed should be explored so that suppressed anger is not displaced onto the child.

The availability and adequacy of family support (e.g., child care and personal guidance) need to be determined since such assistance buffers many of the social, economic, and emotional stresses of early parenthood and increases the likelihood of a mother's returning to school (Rosen et al. 1988) and making use of family planning (Auerbach et al. 1985). Family involvement can also generate stress, as when the grandparents function as "gatekeepers" between a young couple. Paternal grandparents, for example, may blame their son's partner for interfering with his future. Maternal grandparents (overemphasizing the male role of "breadwinner") may reprimand a young father for his inability to provide fully for his child. Even when the teen parent is able to live at home, tension can be substantial because of overcrowding or a grandparent's inability to resolve her disappointment with her child. Partner involvement can also alleviate or intensify the stress of parenting. A young father's "in-kind" contribution of baby-sitting, for example, can help supply some of the respite a mother needs. On the other hand, young mothers who had been making great strides toward establishing independent living have been known to withdraw from programs abruptly, to fail to follow through on scheduled appointments (e.g., AFDC face-to-face interviews), and to become less responsive to their child because of increased or renewed contact with less stable partners.

Assessment may determine that helping activities should be targeted, not directly at young parents, but at service providers or organizational policies and procedures. Difficulty experienced by young mothers in a maternity residence, for example, may be exacerbated by the unrealistic expectations of caretakers, who forget that parenthood does not automatically bestow adult capacities on teenagers. Poor relations with clients may, on the other hand, be a manifestation of the staff's resentment at being excluded from agency decision-making or case-planning.

To bolster adolescents' reproductive knowledge as well as to enhance their cognitive and interpersonal abilities, activities such as "life skills" counseling (Schinke and Gilchrist 1984) may be implemented. Through such interventions, teens are helped to make more informed health decisions by personalizing information (e.g., "I can get pregnant") and using communication skills (e.g., making requests and refusals) and higher order thinking skills (e.g., generating multiple solutions). Such training in anticipation of decision dilemmas increases the likelihood that new information will be used when stressful situations arise.

Adolescents' capacity to obtain needed services can also be bolstered if they are prepared for encounters with providers and are encouraged to persist when they meet with adversity. Explicitly instructing pregnant youth about shifting Medicaid regulations, helping them gather necessary documents, and role-playing interviews with eligibility workers enable adolescents to negotiate better for themselves. Simply filling information gaps often resolves discrepancies. Young mothers who receive public assistance, for example, may be unaware that they can receive supplemental entitlements for child care in a baby-sitter's home if such care allows them to go to high school or to complete their GED.

Since all components of an open system are related, change in one area can bring about change elsewhere. Linking a grandmother to a peer support group and thus reducing her sense of isolation may help diffuse some of the friction that arises over child-rearing practices at home. Helping a young father sustain contact in the face of peer pressure to avoid involvement can positively affect both mother and child. Advocating with school personnel for an expeditious transfer to a smaller alternative high school may be a critical first step in preventing a young mother from becoming demoralized, dropping out, and experiencing the economic consequences that such a choice is likely to bring.

Worker roles and helping responses need to be multifaceted. At a community agency for young parents, social workers help clients who are having difficulty with GED studies by tutoring them during part of a counseling session. When advocacy is needed at a court appearance, workers shift focus. Such flexibility is also demonstrated by the school social worker's decision to conduct "life space" interviewing in the gym and hallways to increase the efficiency of outreach to students at risk for early pregnancy. By venturing out of the clinic and adapting the nature of interviews, the worker was able to contact more clients, make quicker risk assessments (e.g., relying on withdrawal as birth control), and promptly discuss options to reduce risk.

Because the needs of adolescents are numerous and the psychological and social distance from service providers is often great, interventions need to use a variety of helpers. To reduce the perception that a family-planning clinic was far away, for example, a school social worker had students make a narrated videotape and slide show of the walk to the clinic and used them in classroom presentations. An older sister who realized the importance of prenatal care was encouraged to accompany her pregnant sister to appointments. At a program for young fathers, a social worker had the more involved clients assertively reach out by phone to those whose attendance had been decreasing.

## CASE ILLUSTRATION

Maria was 16 years old and six months pregnant when the worker first met her. She was the second of five children, and her family lived in a poor urban neighborhood. Her mother was a seamstress, and her father had recently returned home after several years in jail. Maria had a history of grade retention and academic and school behavior problems. Although a talented artist, she had dropped out during ninth grade because she felt she was "going nowhere fast." Maria knew of her boyfriend's involvement with drugs but had stayed with him because "he made me feel good." Maria hadn't seen him since he learned of her pregnancy, and she was certain he had left the country.

Maria was first examined in an emergency room when she was three months pregnant. Three months later, she came to the worker's clinic seeking prenatal care. She presented as a nervous young woman wearing a baggy jacket zippered up to her chin. She had delayed coming to the clinic because "I wasn't sick." She had not used birth control since experiencing nausea two years earlier while on the pill, and she was unsure of her fertility since friends had told her that a prior infection had "blocked" her tubes.

Maria said her boyfriend's behavior was "just like all men." Her father had always been in and out of her life. While he rarely used physical punishment with his children, he often hit Maria's mother. She described her mother as a "weak" woman and their relationship as one of chronic conflict. Maria was certain she would be a better parent to her child.

Maria had been living home until a week before her clinic visit. Home had been tolerable until her father's return and the resumption of violent fights between her parents. Maria said she looked forward to "getting my own place" and having "a baby of my own to love." Since she had always taken care of her younger siblings after school, she believed she could care for an infant.

Maria's main support was her older sister Joanna, and her mood was noticeably elevated when Joanna was present. Joanna had two young children and lived with her unemployed boyfriend. Because she was uncertain of his reaction to Maria's staying with them, the worker suggested that contingency plans be considered. Maria said there was no place else to go and made it clear she would never move back home. Joanna, however, felt certain that their aunt would take Maria in if necessary. The worker asked Maria to call when plans were finalized, and she expressed confidence that other arrangements were possible if these did not work out.

Maria wanted the baby to be born at the worker's hospital but did not know how she'd pay for it. The worker calmed her by assuring Maria that she would help obtain Medicaid. When Joanna offered to fill out the application forms, the worker suggested that it would be better if Maria did so, but that Joanna should stay nearby. The worker reviewed the documentation that was needed and told Maria and Joanna where the office was located and how interviews were usually conducted. She suggested that all documents be copied and encouraged Maria to call from the Medicaid office if she had any difficulty. The worker alerted Maria that because the social work receptionist had to manage several calls at a time, she was sometimes curt on the phone. The worker briefly demonstrated what to say to maximize the chance of Maria's reaching her.

Maria accepted the worker's referral to an agency that would do home visits, help her obtain entitlements, and file applications for public housing. Maria said that the only other services she wanted was prenatal care and instruction about childbirth. The worker gave information on childbirth classes and promised to look for Maria during the classes. Two days later, Joanna called to say that her boyfriend had agreed to Maria's staying in the apartment and that temporary Medicaid authorization had been obtained. The worker again offered to help prepare for the baby. Joanna said they did not have a crib, so the worker informed her of a local thrift shop that sold used furniture. When the worker asked if Maria would come to the phone, she refused since her favorite "soap" was on TV.

Two weeks later, the sisters came to the worker's office after Maria's first prenatal exam. Joanna sat while Maria lingered in the doorway. Joanna said that the doctor was concerned about Maria's anemia and had suggested dietary changes. Maria said nothing but produced a list of recommended foods. The worker expressed pleasure that Maria was taking positive steps to prepare for the baby's coming. She asked if she could send Maria a recipe that was high in iron and was told she could "if you want to."

Maria made two other prenatal visits during the remainder of her pregnancy, each time accompanied by Joanna. After the sisters had missed an appointment, the worker called but Maria again did not want to talk. Joanna explained that because her 3-year-old was sick, she had been unable to bring Maria. Responding to the worker's interest in her child, Joanna asked if she had any information on Head Start programs. The worker gave information about a center that had just opened, alerted Joanna about the need to act quickly and be persistent, and offered to write a letter in support of her application.

During one childbirth class, the worker noticed that while many of the participants were reluctant to practice breathing exercises, Maria and Joanna were actively involved. After class, the worker commented on how well Maria was doing and prompted her to speculate on what it would be like to live with the baby at home. How, for example, did she think Joanna's children might react? These overtures failed to elicit much response from Maria, who curtly remarked that things would be "all right."

When Maria's baby, Nicky, was born, Joanna called the worker as she had promised. Although she was tired and amazed by the events of the previous evening, Maria told the worker how her breathing had helped to make the birth easier. She appeared to be proud that she had accomplished her childbirth "tasks" so well, and the worker commented that all her practice seemed to have paid off. The worker visited once more before Maria's discharge and had Maria recall their prior discussions about her need for rest and about how she might feel if people paid attention to the baby, not her. On leaving the hospital, the worker gave Maria a small gift of coloring pencils and encouraged her to keep up with her sketching.

A few weeks after the birth, Joanna called to inform the worker of Maria and Nicky's progress. Maria got on the phone and said thing were "OK," but that feeding Nicky was annoying because he "wouldn't cooperate." Despite previous instructions, she was giving him solids "so he'd stop crying." The worker reminded her that it was not yet time to introduce solids and suggested that she call pediatrics to talk with one of the nurses. Joanna got back on the phone and complained that Maria was watching too much TV and not spending enough time with Nicky. The worker reminded Joanna of Maria's need for respite and asked her to recall what it was like when she had had her first baby. It was agreed that she would encourage Maria to go out more, but that she would also keep after her to care for her baby better.

At Maria's postpartum visit to the hospital two weeks later, she came by to show Nicky to the worker. The worker took a picture of her and another with her son and promised to send copies. As they walked the hallway, the worker asked about birth control. Maria said she had been given oral contraceptives but wasn't sure she'd use them because of her past experience. The worker noted that the doctor had prescribed a lower dosage and suggested taking the pill with her meal to reduce nausea. When asked about returning to school, Maria said that she was beginning to feel lonely at home but didn't want to leave the baby. The worker affirmed that this was a special time but encouraged Maria to attend the teen parent group. She offered to mail brochures about educational programs in preparation for Maria's eventual return. Maria agreed to reopen the discussion in three months.

Over the next few months, Maria sporadically attended the parents' group at the hospital. When present, she remained quiet but seemed to enjoy the supportive atmosphere. She listened attentively to lecturettes on normal infant development, etc. When the group practiced skills such as how to massage and bathe a baby, she became intensely engaged and even demonstrated techniques for others. She was pleased by the feedback given by the child development worker. Maria developed a relationship with one member and exchanged numbers so they could go out together and alternate baby-sitting.

During subsequent phone and face-to-face contacts (which usually occurred in hallways after group), the worker pointedly commented on the behavioral competencies Maria was exhibiting. She noted that Maria was an excellent listener, and that the group members seemed to appreciate her support. When asked if any of the issues discussed seemed relevant to her situation, Maria said she was surprised that others also had conflicts with their parents, and that so many were angry at not being able to go out. She was puzzled that they all could love their babies and, at the same time, be angry at them because of their actions.

The worker periodically asked about school, reminding Maria that she had expressed interest in going back when Nicky was older. Maria said she liked the special program for teen parents at a nearby youth agency because it was small, had a nursery, and offered GED tutoring. She agreed to call there and arrange a visit, but she asked the worker (who knew the program's director) to write her a referral letter.

A few days later, Maria called to say she had missed her appointment because the baby had kept her up all night. When asked what she planned to do next, Maria said she felt awkward calling back because she had not canceled her visit and was afraid the staff would be angry with her. She also "felt bad" that she had embarrassed the worker by not following through. The worker thanked her for her concern but offered reassurance that Maria had not made an irreparable mistake.

Several weeks later, Maria connected to the agency's parents' program. She stopped attending the hospital support group but saw the worker when she had family-planning visits. Maria's recurring fear of Nicky's rejecting her efforts to be a "good mother" were noticed in her restricting his attempts to walk and explore his surroundings. The worker shared this observation and encouraged Maria to discuss her discomfort during groups at the parenting program. Otherwise, it appeared that the baby was developing normally, and that Maria was growing comfortable in her dual role of mother and student.

When the worker first met Maria, she was already a demoralized young woman. A history of behavior problems, school failure, and grade retention had contributed to her distaste for formal education. Since few in her environment demonstrated confidence in her, she set low expectations for herself. She had a dim vision of future options, and neither family or neighborhood provided much inspiration to look beyond the safety of what was known.

Maria had been prematurely pushed into a caretaking role with her younger siblings because of her mother's need to work and the absence of extended-family support. Denied contact with peers and opportunities for self-expression in the area in which she excelled (art), Maria was filled with resentment. Her need for nurturing and her difficulty believing she deserved better led her to settle for what her boyfriend had to offer.

Several factors leading up to and affecting the resolution of Maria's difficulties were related to her developmental level. Like many adolescents, she did not use contraception and delayed initiating prenatal care until late in her pregnancy. While due in part to ambivalence about being pregnant, such procrastination also arises from adolescents' belief that they are immune to the consequences experienced by others.

Adolescence is a time of giving up childlike dependency, but the desire for independence is usually marked by ambivalence. Especially if dependency needs are not satisfied during age-appropriate periods, the offer of a supportive relationship at a vulnerable time intensifies a wish to be close and a fear of again being frustrated. Maria's hesitation with the worker was fueled by her repeated earlier disappointments. The worker recognized her need to maintain distance and was not put off by her negativism. The worker slowly earned Maria's trust by consistently following through on small commitments (e.g., mailing program brochures), and by first addressing the issues that Maria found pressing, i.e., obtaining Medicaid. Through letters and telephone calls, the worker gave Maria the opportunity to push away if she got too close (e.g., asking her if it was all right to send the recipe), while leaving an opportunity for contact that demanded little effort (e.g., presenting her dropping by the prenatal groups as part of her daily routine).

The worker's first interventions were targeted at enhancing Maria's capacity to locate and obtain concrete services. Because of her lack of experience in seeking help, Maria was overwhelmed by the idea of accessing resources on her own. The worker helped keep Maria's fears within manageable limits by gently reassuring her that there was time, and that she and Joanna would help, and by breaking down tasks into smaller steps. For example, Maria was taken step by step through the Medicaid application process and was prompted to think of contingencies (e.g., calling the worker) if difficulties arose. By modeling how to reach her by phone, the worker bolstered Maria's problem-solving skills while conveying her belief in Maria's capacity to master her situation.

No one person or helping system could meet Maria's multiple needs. The worker mobilized several helpers before and after Nicky's birth. Joanna functioned in a special way as Maria's "auxiliary ego," helping her think through problems, generate alternatives, and follow through on plans. The worker strengthened their collaboration by informing Joanna of resources that ultimately enabled her to be more helpful to Maria. Joanna became the transitional link between her sister and the worker until Maria was capable of increased relatedness on her own. In enlisting Joanna's support, however, the worker was careful not to undermine Maria's growing desire for autonomy. For example, the worker blocked Joanna's eager offer to fill out the Medicaid forms. Telephone numbers and other written information were handed directly to Maria, and when calls were made, the worker promptly asked that Maria come to the phone.

Linking Maria to a service that provided supportive home visits demonstrated the worker's awareness that interagency collaboration was essential in meeting Maria's many needs. Since her initial interest was in securing concrete services, not counseling, Maria was open to such a referral. While the waiting lists were substantial, beginning the process of applying for public housing increased the chance of eventually securing subsidized shelter and enhanced Maria's sense of taking charge of her life. The worker was prepared to be as active as necessary in ensuring that appropriate connections would be made, e.g., writing advocacy letters. At each transition, she attempted to verify that services had been obtained and were accurately matched to Maria's needs.

The group provided Maria with some of the support, guidance, and motivation typically supplied by well-functioning families. Though her attendance was sporadic, Maria was able to address some of the conflicting needs that arose from her dual status as parent and adolescent. Hearing others in similar circumstances ventilate their frustrations partly satisfied her need for affiliation with peers, and her isolation was reduced. Learning new facts and skills and being rewarded for successful performance of tasks bolstered Maria's sense of competence in her role as a parent.

As is often the case, the young mothers became their own best teachers. They shared knowledge of resources as well as insights into how to cut through bureaucratic barriers, and thus they enhanced each other's capacity to master parental tasks. The structure and process of this task-focused group allowed Maria to control the pace and extent of her involvement with the worker. No demands were made to attend each meeting. Since others were present, contact with the worker was less threatening. While Maria rarely spoke, she heard others describe their struggles. Maria's cautious acknowledgment that the members sometimes spoke for her demonstrated her growing self-awareness and her developing trust in the worker.

While every individual needs to feel competent, Maria's need was even more acute because of her history of academic failure and of rejection in parental and sexual relationships. To bolster her tenuous esteem, the worker selectively attended to Maria's smallest successes. Skillful performance of tasks in the group were emphasized and verbally rewarded. When the appointment at the alternative school was missed, the worker purposefully thanked Maria for calling to explain and for her concern that she had tarnished the worker's reputation. Even the small gift after the baby's birth was targeted at reinforcing an area where Maria stood apart from the rest.

The worker consistently engaged Maria in anticipatory planning, prompting her to consider next steps and potential problems. She helped Maria discriminate between the fantasy and reality of a baby by having her project ahead to whom she might call on if she became frazzled. Such anticipatory guidance provided "emotional innoculation" for the moments when Maria realized that Nicky did not provide, but demand, love, and when it became apparent that her social life would be curtailed.

Maria's dependency needs were temporarily met during her pregnancy. Once she was at home, much of the attention shifted to the baby. Her fantasy of how a baby would satisfy her need for love was abruptly dashed by the reality of having to care for Nicky. Moreover, Maria's unresolved adolescent developmental tasks sometimes clashed with the demands of parenting and affected her responses. Nicky's crying and attempts to walk were perceived as signs of his rejecting her maternal efforts, and as a statement of her inadequacy. Her frustration at his expressions of discomfort and her attempts to quiet him by prematurely feeding him solids illustrate that to be an effective parent, knowledge is not enough.

While the worker was certain that Maria's future would be enhanced by a return to school, Maria was not ready to resume an activity that had been a cause of demoralization. She was enjoying her time with Nicky, believed it was right for her to be close to him during his first months, and felt that she was doing a reasonably good job of parenting. Maria's desire for time with the baby was acknowledged, and her assertion of this need was seen as a healthy sign of a growing ability in independent decision-making.

At the same time, Maria's reluctance to resume school reflected her doubt that things would ever be different. She was not sure that the potential benefits of education outweighed the known benefits of parenting. Because she was concerned that Maria would become fearful of ever returning, the worker found a "middle ground" by providing written materials about options and time-limited goals, and by intermittently raising the topic. She encouraged Joanna to talk about school and coached her on how to help Maria choose the program that was the right "fit" by weighing options on parameters such as size, location, and the type of credential earned.

The worker balanced counseling, advocacy, and referral tasks to match Maria's shifting needs. Since her hesitation was seen as a manifestation of the adolescent's normal ambivalence about admitting the need for help, the worker was not put off by her initial unresponsiveness. The worker's interventions highlight the need to allow such clients to maintain distance and still to reconnect on their own terms.

Like most adolescent parents, Maria had to experience empathy and nurturance before empathizing with and nurturing her child. Since her needs were multiple, the worker was challenged to mobilize numerous supports, including herself, Maria's family and friends, and other professionals. The worker was aware of the community's resources, was skilled at negotiating a good fit between Maria and the referrals, and reduced the distance between her and the needed services. Since the most stressful problems encountered by young parents occur once the baby is home, Maria's case emphasizes the importance of continuous contact that goes far beyond birth. The worker demonstrated the need to aggressively track and sustain contact with the adolescent to counter the problems and reversals that are inevitable, and to ensure that services will be not only located but used.

It is important to recognize that most sexually active youth successfully avoid pregnancy and that most young parents competently care for their children. The severe consequences of early parenthood, however, are a cause for grave public concern and demand a substantial response by social workers. Early parenthood brings the "psychosocial moratorium" of adolescence—i.e., that period of commitment-free "delay granted to somebody who is not ready to meet an obligation" (Erikson 1968: p. 157)—to an abrupt halt. Prematurely assuming the massive responsibilities of raising a child too often cuts short educational pursuits and the development of critically needed basic skills. Lacking "employability" skills and adequate social supports, young parents are at a disadvantage when forced to compete with their better prepared peers and often suffer serious long-term economic hardships. As a result, the stage is set for their children to continue a cycle of economic dependency, unfulfilled dreams, and underachievement.

Just as there is no one "cause" of unintended pregnancy, there is no one simple solution. Multiple strategies need to be crafted so that teens will obtain accurate information about sexuality, will develop the cognitive and interpersonal capacities that facilitate well-considered behaviors, and will have access to health and parenting support services. Adolescents also need to first acquire solid basic skills that open up possibilities for decent-paying employment with a real opportunity for advancement. Above all, they need to cultivate a "rationale" for delaying parenthood based on a hopeful sense that future options are available and within reach. Given the high personal and public costs involved, it is imperative that social workers continue to contribute actively and creatively to both the prevention of unwanted pregnancy and the promotion of competent child-rearing by adolescent parents.

## REFERENCES

ACOG (American College of Obstetricians and Gynecologists). 1988. *Adolescent Pregnancy Fact Sheet.* Washington, D.C.: ACOG.

Auerbach, Stephanie K., Betsey Nathan, Donna O'Hare, and Milagros Benedicto. 1985. "Impact of Ethnicity." *Society* (November/December), pp. 38–40.

Brindis, Claire and Faith Mitchell. 1987. "Pew Memorial Trust Policy Synthesis: 3." *Health Services Research.* (August), p. 3.

CDF (Children's Defense Fund). 1988a. *A Call to Action to Make Our Nation Safe for Children: A Briefing Book on the Status of America's Children in 1988.* Washington D.C.: CDF.

CDF (Children's Defense Fund). 1988b. *A Children's Defense Fund Budget FY 1989: An Analysis of Our Nation's Investment in Children.* Washington, D.C.: CDF.

CDF (Children's Defense Fund). 1988c. *Reports* (May). Washington, D.C.: CDF.

Clark, Sam, Laurie Zabin, and Janet Hardy. 1984. "Sex, Contraception, and Parenthood: Experience and Attitudes Among Urban Black Young Men." *Family Planning Perspectives* (March/April), *16*:77-82.

Elkind, David. 1974. *Children and Adolescents: Interpretive Essays on Jean Piaget.* New York: Oxford University Press.

Erikson, Erik H. 1968. *Identity, Youth and Crisis.* New York: W. W. Norton.

Hayes, Cheryl. 1987. *Risking the Future: Adolescent Sexuality, Pregnancy, and Childbearing;* vol. 1. Washington D.C.: National Academy Press.

Jones, Elise, Jacqueline Forrest, Noreen Goldman, Stanley Henshaw, Richard Lincoln, Jeannie Rosoff, Charles Westoff, and Deidre Wulf. 1985. "Teenage Pregnancies in Developed Countries: Determinants and Policy Implications." *Family Planning Perspectives*, 17:53–62.

Kerewsky, William and Leah Lefstein. 1982. "Young Adolescents and Their Communities: A Shared Responsibility." In Leah Lefstein, William Kerewsky, Elliot Medrich, and Carol Frank, eds., *3:00 to 6:00 P.M.: Young Adolescents at Home and in the Community*, pp. 5–22. Carrboro: University of North Carolina Press.

Koenig, Michael and Melvin Zelnik. 1982. "Repeat Pregnancies Among Metropolitan Area Teenagers." *Family Planning Perspectives* (November/December), 14:341–344.

Marsiglio, William and Frank Mott. 1986. "The Impact of Sex Education on Sexual Activity, Contraceptive Use, and Premarital Pregnancy Among American Teenagers." *Family Planning Perspectives* 18:151–161.

Mott, Frank. 1986. "The Pace of Repeated Childbearing Among Young American Mothers." *Family Planning Perspectives* (January/February), 1:5–12.

NCHS (National Center for Health Statistics). 1984. *Advance Report of Final Natality Statistics, 1982.* Monthly Vital Statistics Report 33(6). Hyattsville, Md.: U.S. Department of Health and Human Services.

Pittman, Karen and Gina Adams. 1988. *Teenage Pregnancy: An Advocate's Guide to the Numbers.* Adolescent Pregnancy Prevention Clearinghouse (January/March). Washington D.C.: Children's Defense Fund.

Rosen, Jacqueline, Joelle Sander, Theresa Rogers, with Maryl Cannon. 1988. *Teenage Parents and Their Families: Findings and Guidelines from a Collaborative Effort to Promote Family Competence.* New York: Bank Street College of Education.

Schinke, Stephen and Lewayne Gilchrist. 1984. *Life Skills Counseling with Adolescents.* Baltimore: University Park Press.

Sullivan, Mercer. 1985. *Teen Fathers in the Inner City: An Exploratory Ethnographic Study.* New York: Vera Institute of Justice.

U.S. Commerce (U.S. Department of Commerce, Bureau of the Census). 1983. *Characteristics of the Population Below the Poverty Level.* Current Population Reports, No. 147. Washington D.C.: GPO.

U.S. HHS (U.S. Department of Health and Human Services, Family Support Administration. 1987. *Teen Pregnancy Prevention.* Share Fact Sheet #7. Rockville, Md.: The Share Resource Center on Teen Pregnancy Prevention, Family Support Administration, U.S. Department of Health and Human Services.

Westoff, Charles, Gerard Calot, and Andrew Foster. 1983. "Teenage Fertility in Developed Nations." *Family Planning Perspectives* 15:105–110.

Zabin, Laurie and Sam Clark. 1981. "Why They Delay: A Study of Teenage Family Planning Clinic Patients." *Family Planning Perspectives* (September/October), 13: 205–216.

Zabin, Laurie, John Kantner, and Melvin Zelnik. 1979. "The Risk of Adolescent Pregnancy in the First Months of Intercourse." *Family Planning Perspectives* 11:215–222.

Zelnik, Melvin. 1983. "Sexual Activity Among Adolescents: Perspective of a Decade." In E. R. McAnarey, ed., *Premature Adolescent Pregnancy and Parenthood.* New York. Grune & Stratton.

Zelnik, Melvin and John Kantner. 1980. "Sexual Activity, Contraceptive Use and Pregnancy Among Metropolitan Area Teenagers." *Family Planning Perspectives* (September/October), 12:230–237.

Zelnik, Melvin and Faridah Shah. 1983. "First Intercourse Among Young Americans." *Family Planning Perspectives* 15:64–72.

# 11

## Child Abuse and Neglect

▼

### LYNN VIDEKA-SHERMAN

Child maltreatment is a heterogeneous grouping of types of inadequate care or protection that results in actual or potential harm to the child. Child maltreatment encompasses acts of commission and omission. Each state has laws that define child maltreatment for that jurisdiction. While most state laws are modeled after the federal legislation, (P.L. 93-247, Child Abuse Prevention and Treatment Act), the states' definitions of child maltreatment vary. In addition to laws regarding the reporting of child maltreatment, the states legislate family laws that specify the conditions under which the state agencies and courts can intervene in family life in order to protect the child. The states also legislate criminal statutes that address acts of violence without distinguishing between intra- and extrafamilial occurrence.

### PROBLEM DOMAIN

Most definitions of child maltreatment encompass three components: 1) the occurrence of at least one identifiable instance of adult behavior toward a child under 18 years of age; 2) physical or psychological harm or endangerment to the child that results from this behavior; and 3) a clear causal link between the adult behavior in question and the harm resulting to the child (Faller and Russo 1981).

Child maltreatment is usually further classified into six forms: physical or emotional abuse; physical, emotional, or educational neglect; and sexual abuse. For the purposes of defining types of child maltreatment, the 1988 National Incidence Study definitions are used

345

(U.S. HHS 1988). *Abuse* connotes an act of commission that results in harm to the child. It includes intentional injury such as burns, bruises, fractures, contusions, lacerations, or other injuries resulting from physical assault. Emotional abuse results from verbal assault or chronic scapegoating by the parenting person. Verbal assaults include conveying to the child that he or she is no good, worthless, evil, or hated. Emotional abuse also includes confinement, threats, and withholding life necessities such as sleep or food.

Sexual abuse is a specific form of physical abuse. In this form of abuse, injury to the child results from sexual contact by a caretaking person. Sexual contact includes intercourse, touching, and fondling. Other acts that use children as sexual objects are also included in the definition of child sexual abuse, such as child pornography and subjecting children to viewing sexual acts committed by adults.

Physical child neglect usually results from a parental act of omission; the parent fails to provide for a child's basic needs, making that child actually suffer or be susceptible to harm or injury. The most common type of child neglect is inadequate supervision, that is, leaving the child unattended or unsupervised. Other forms of physical child neglect include failure to thrive (growth failure due to inadequate nurturance); failing to provide basic physical needs such as shelter, clothing, health care, and food; abandonment; and expulsion of the child from the home. Educational neglect includes failing to enroll the child in school, permitting chronic truancy, or not attending to special educational needs of the child. Emotional neglect includes inadequate nurturance or affection, chronic domestic violence, and permitting alcohol or substance abuse by a child.

Difficulties abound in the definition of the various forms of child maltreatment. To complicate matters further, different forms of child maltreatment may coexist. For example, in 1984, 16 percent of all reports of child maltreatment were for both child abuse and neglect (AHA 1986).

The National Center on Child Abuse and Neglect is mandated to conduct studies of child maltreatment incidence. Two sets of studies have been funded by this federal agency. The first is the study of official child protective services (CPS) reports by the American Humane Association (AHA). The most recent CPS reporting study was for the year 1984 (AHA 1986). The second set of studies is the National Incidence Study (NIS) conducted by the National Center on Child Abuse and Neglect (NCCAN). The second NIS was conducted in 1988 (U.S. HHS 1988). A third study of child abuse incidence is part of a larger study of violence in American families (Straus, Gelles, and Steinmetz 1980; Straus and Gelles 1987; Wauchope and Straus 1987).

This study was funded by the National Institute of Mental Health. These three incidence studies differ in the information they yield. The AHA study focuses exclusively on CPS reports. The NIS focuses on both CPS reports and child maltreatment not known to CPS but known to community agencies such as police courts, health and social service agencies, and schools and day care centers. The Gelles and Straus studies focus on reports of violence by parents themselves. The Gelles and Straus studies also differ from the other two incidence studies in three additional ways. They used a different and more inclusive measure of family violence than the AHA or the NIS. They studied violence or abuse toward children, but not neglect or sexual abuse. They also restricted their study to intrafamilial violence, while the AHA and NCCAN studies include maltreatment by all perpetrators. The data discussed in this section have been excerpted from these three studies. All data on incidence are limited because of sampling biases (Widom 1989).

Reports of child maltreatment have been increasing since 1976. In 1976, 669,000 CPS reports were made. In 1984, 1,727,000 reports were made, a 258 percent increase in eight years (AHA 1986). The NIS found a 66 percent increase in maltreatment from 1980 to 1988 (U.S. HHS 1988). Most experts believe that heightened public awareness of child maltreatment explains much of the increase.

Of all the CPS reports, 50 percent are made by professionals; the other 50 percent are made by friends, neighbors, relatives, or the abusing parent themselves. About 42 percent of the reports made are substantiated by a child-protective-service investigation. Nonprofessionals make more unsubstantiated reports than professionals. Unsubstantiated reports are a growing problem for the child-protective system. Thousands of families are victimized by mandated investigations because of reports of child maltreatment. The National Center for Child Abuse and Neglect has funded studies to determine the causes and to suggest methods to decrease the number of unsubstantiated child maltreatment reports. Information about these can be obtained from the Clearinghouse on Child Abuse and Neglect Information.[1]

Characteristics of families reported to child protective agencies in 1984 were compiled by the American Humane Association (1986). Of the reported perpetrators, 89 percent were the child's primary caretaker. The average age of victimized children was 7.2 years. Children under age 5 and racial minorities were disproportionately reported as victims of maltreatment.

Male children accounted for 48 percent of all reports; females, for 52 percent. The racial composition of the reported families was 67 percent white, 21 percent black, 10 percent Hispanic, and 3 percent other (AHA 1986). The NIS found no statistical relationship between the incidence of maltreatment and the child's race or ethnicity (U.S. HHS 1988). The average age of the reported child's caretaker was 31.9 years. Of the reported families, 37 percent were single-parent female-headed households, and 48 percent were receiving public assistance (AHA 1986). The NIS also found low income to be a risk factor in all forms of maltreatment (U.S. HHS 1988). Wauchope and Straus (1987) found a higher incidence of physical punishment and abuse in blue-collar than in white-collar families. But when they looked only at the families in which abuse had occurred, they found a greater frequency of abuse incidents in white-collar families.

Deprivation of necessities (child neglect) accounted for 55 percent to 63 percent of child maltreatment (AHA 1986; U.S. HHS 1988). Although there has been a decreasing trend in reporting deprivation of necessities, it is still the most common form of maltreatment (AHA 1986). Minor physical injury accounted for 18 percent of maltreatment and major physical injury for 3 percent. Sexual maltreatment accounted for 13 percent of all maltreatment. Of all cases, 18 percent of maltreated children were placed in out-of-home settings.

Awareness of and interest in child maltreatment began after World War II, when social work was heavily influenced by psychodynamic approaches to practice. Given this historical context, it is not surprising that initial theoretical formulations of child maltreatment and intervention sprang from psychoanalytic thinking. This theoretical approach focused largely on the intrapsychic deficits of the maltreating parent. The recommended treatment was long-term ego-supportive psychotherapy with the parent (usually the mother).

As knowledge about child maltreatment grew during the 1960s and 1970s, there was little empirical validation of the psychodynamically influenced approach. Research on the association between poverty and child maltreatment led to different theoretical formulations, including family systems theories of the multiproblem family (Minuchin et al. 1983; Wood and Geismar 1989) and sociological perspectives that emphasize the relationships between the tolerance of violence in our society, the lack of resources among poor families, the public scrutiny of poor families, and the occurrence of child maltreatment. Family systems and sociological perspectives are important theoretical influences because they broaden intervention approaches to maltreating families from the individual psychopathology approach to approaches that formally acknowledge the family and social system factors that lead to and perpetuate child maltreatment in our society.

Recent research on social learning theory has elucidated the behavioral interactions that are likely to be associated with abuse and, to a lesser extent, with neglect and sexual abuse. This research describes the "cycle of coercion" between abusive parents and their children. It illustrates family interaction characteristics that are linked to the occurrence of maltreatment. This theoretical perspective is useful to the practitioner because it targets very specific child management and family interaction patterns that are changeable. While much of the research on the interaction in maltreating families and the research on parental social skill deficits and child maltreatment can also be explained from an object relations perspective, the intervention approaches stemming from the two theoretical perspectives are very different (Videka-Sherman in press). The object relations approach emphasizes client change and growth through the therapeutic relationship in a long-term psychotherapeutic approach to treatment. The social learning approach emphasizes the client's ability to learn social skills without requiring major shifts in the parents' own psychological development. One recent comparative study shows no differences in outcomes between the two approaches (Azar 1987). The efficacy of the social learning approach has been researched more thoroughly than the object relations approach or any other psychodynamic approach (Videka-Sherman 1989).

The most current theoretical approach is a pluralistic blend of the theories outlined above. Sometimes termed the *ecological approach to maltreatment* (Belsky 1980), this theoretical orientation encompasses a family and social system emphasis in understanding and intervening for child maltreatment. It has influenced intervention by acknowledging that environmental supports must be a mainstay of any effective intervention for child maltreatment. The ecological approach has set the stage for an emphasis on the prevention of child maltreatment.

Recent research reflects a renewed emphasis on individual parent and child need in interaction in the evolution of maltreatment. Zuravin's (1986) research on depression and child neglect suggests that many neglectful mothers are also depressed and that these depressed women are underserved by child maltreatment programs and by formal mental health services. They may be underserved by traditional mental health services because they are not amenable to talking therapies. Polansky and his associates (1981) described neglectful mothers as typically verbally inaccessible.

This growing body of research, although of varying quality, has influenced the communities involved with child maltreatment in several ways. Research on child maltreatment has been both a reflection of and an influence on our society's concern about child maltreatment. Research has served to increase public attention to and concern and knowledge about child maltreatment. Increased reporting of all forms of child maltreatment is evidence of this raised societal consciousness.

The field is far from a consensus on the necessary and sufficient causes of child maltreatment, let alone effective ways to prevent or to intervene in this social problem. The complexity of the phenomena of child maltreatment and the unlikelihood that we are soon to arrive at a simple and accurate theoretical formulation of the problem and effective intervention for it have led to a mixed bag of research that is limited by methodological inadequacies. Much of the research is retrospective; much of the intervention research is uncontrolled. These limitations have led to confusion regarding effective intervention for child maltreatment.

Despite the association between different indicators of economic hardship and child maltreatment, there is relatively little research on sociocultural influences on maltreating parents' behavior. Gil (1971), Straus and Gelles (1983), Gelles and Strauss (1987), and others (Parke and Collmer 1975; Zigler 1978) have argued that the approval of violence in our society provides a tolerant societal context for all forms of family violence, including child maltreatment. Few prevention programs address our cultural propensity toward violence. As Belsky stated:

> It is doubtful that maltreatment can be eliminated so long as parents rear their offspring in a society in which violence is rampant, corporal punishment is condoned as a child-rearing technique, and parenthood itself is construed in terms of ownership. (1980:329)

There are also serious biases in the literature on child maltreatment that should be acknowledged. Most of the research on maltreating families has focused almost exclusively on the mothers of maltreated children, although the findings are often discussed in terms of parents. The focus on mothers alone has resulted in less knowledge about the male partner's role in abusive and neglectful family situations. The focus on mothers has also perpetuated the victimization of women in the definition and investigation of and the intervention in child maltreatment.

Another limitation in our knowledge about child maltreatment is that child neglect has been seriously understudied. The available research shows that neglectful families are different from abusive families. We know far too little about the specific processes of child neglect and their ramifications for the child and family. We know even less about effective intervention for this group. Most intervention programs do not distinguish between abusive and neglectful families, although experienced clinicians claim that there are fundamental differences between them.

## SOCIETAL CONTEXTS

There is considerable agreement that social and physical environments generate stresses that can lead to child abuse and neglect. A number of studies have found that social support is negatively associated with the occurrence of child maltreatment. Families who maltreat their children have less support available to them in their own interpersonal networks (Giovannoni and Billingsly 1970; Light 1973; Polansky et al. 1979; Altmeier et al. 1979; Starr 1982; Milner and Wemberly 1980). Some research is showing that these families may be less supported, not because they have fewer resources available, but because these parents seek out support less frequently and less effectively than other families.

Dumas and Wahler (1985) and Wahler and Hann (1984) have shown that poor social skills characterize the "insular" parent's interaction with others in the community and lead to social isolation. In a study of parental relationship histories and child development, Pianta, Egeland, and Hyatt (1986) showed that parents who have a history of unstable relationships with adult partners have disruptive and inconsistent relationships with their children, that lead to disturbances in the child's relationship skills, which are first evident in toddlerhood and become pronounced by school age.

Other studies have associated neighborhood variables with an elevated incidence of abuse or neglect. Neighborhoods that have a high number of child maltreatment reports tend to be very poor, to have poor housing, and to have low levels of neighbor interaction (Skinner and Castle 1969). Other studies have shown that maltreating parents perceive greater stress in their lives, including the parenting role, although the absolute level of stress in their lives may not exceed normative levels (Conger, Burgess, and Barret 1979; Starr 1982; Rosenberg and Rappucci 1983; Egeland, Breitenbucher, and Rosenberg 1980). These studies suggest that social stresses play a role in the evolution of child maltreatment but that stresses are most meaningfully considered in interaction with the parents' coping skills and capacity.

## RISKS AND NEEDS OF THE POPULATION

In addition to research on the social risks, four sets of variables have been associated with abusing or neglecting parenting: epidemiological or "marker" variables, parental variables, child variables, and parent–child interactional variables. For a detailed review of this literature, see Wolfe (1987).

A host of *sociodemographic marker variables* has been associated with child abuse in empirical investigations: lower socioeconomic status, unemployment, lack of education, childbearing at a younger age, alcohol and drug abuse, health problems, and spousal violence (Hampton and Newberger 1985; Garbarino and Gilliam 1980; Olsen and Holmes 1986; Wauchope and Straus 1987; Smith, Hanson, and Noble 1974; Pelton 1978; AHA 1986).

These variables are identified as "marker" variables because they are based on correlational studies. These correlates of abuse and neglect have been helpful in constructing profiles of the problems encountered by maltreating families. Studies of marker variables do not predict the occurrence of maltreatment with sufficient accuracy for clinical use. For example, the vast majority of impoverished families provide adequate or better care for their children. Most maltreating families exhibit some but not all of these characteristics. Therefore, these "markers" provide a descriptive picture that is limited.

Some research has shown that *maltreating parents* have had personal histories of violence in their own lives (Kempe and Helfer 1972; Spinetta and Rigler 1972), leading to the widely held belief that there is *"intergenerational transmission"* of the predisposition to maltreat one's children. Other studies have evidenced psychopathological symptoms, such as poor impulse control, psychological immaturity, and low frustration tolerance, along with difficulty in expressing anger (Elmer 1963; Green 1976; Kempe et al. 1962; Steele and Pollock 1968). Polansky et al. (1981) found two sets of personality characteristics that distinguished neglectful from nonneglectful mothers. These were the "apathy-futility syndrome" and "infantilism." Other studies can be found that fail to demonstrate the relationships just described. The mixed picture of findings indicates that precise psychological factors that lead to child maltreatment probably do not exist in isolation from the family and social system contexts in which they operate.

Recent studies use a social learning approach employing constructs such as behaviors, beliefs, and cognitions. They find the predictors of maltreatment to be high levels of anger and low levels of frustration tolerance, inappropriate expectations for the child's behavior, and greater perceived stresses in the parenting role and in life in general (Azar et al. 1984; Bauer and Twentyman 1985; Frodi and Lamb 1980; Lahey et al. 1984; Mash, Johnston, and Kovitz 1983; Milner and Wemberly 1980; Spinetta 1978; Sussman et al. 1985; Wolfe et al. 1983; Wolfe and Mask 1985). Both sets of studies point to maltreating parents as feeling more stressed and as having fewer coping resources to meet the challenges of parenthood. Of the most importance are the observed deficits in communication and relationship skills among these parents. These characteristics will be discussed further in the family interaction section.

Several studies have documented that *maltreated children have had more health and developmental problems* in utero and after birth than their nonmaltreated counterparts (Elmer and Gregg 1967; Fontana 1971; Starr, 1982). Other studies have shown that temperament differences are associated with lower parent socialization efforts. Stevens-Long (1973) found that parents responded more punitively to children with high activity levels than to those with lower activity levels. Patterson (1982) found more parental punitiveness toward aggressive and disruptive children than toward less aggressive ones. These studies point to child factors as well as parental factors in the development of a maltreating relationship.

The most current thinking is that *parent, child, and social factors* operate to create family situations in which children's health and development are threatened. This view has spawned research on the relationship between family interaction patterns and child maltreatment. This research is useful to social work clinicians since it illuminates the family processes associated with maltreatment. This research provides the foundation for many of the newest approaches to social work intervention. The thrust of this body of research is that maltreating families interact differently than nonmaltreating families. Some of this research goes further and distinguishes the family interaction patterns in abusive families from those in neglectful families.

Disturbances in parent–child attachment have been shown to predict later child abuse and neglect (Crittenden 1985; Egeland and Sroufe 1981; Schneider-Rosen and Cicchetti 1984). Some attachment disturbances have been associated with the children who have special needs as discussed above. Other studies have compared family interaction in abusive, neglectful, and normative families (Burgess and Conger 1978; Lahey et al. 1984; Oldershaw, Walter and Hall 1986; Lorber, Felton, and Reid 1984). These studies have found that both the neglectful and the abusive families interacted less than the control families. The neglectful families interacted least of all. Both the abusive and the neglectful families exhibited fewer positive interactions between parents and children than the control families. Both types of maltreating families exhibited higher ratios of negative or aversive interactions in total amount of interactions. Less positive interaction and disproportionately high rates of negative or coercive interaction characterized family communication in the maltreating families. These interaction patterns were not restricted to the maltreating incidents but may have led to parental behaviors that were harmful to the children.

Related studies conducted by Patterson (1982) identify a cycle of coercive interaction patterns that occur in families. The process by which hostile interchanges escalate between parent and child is illustrated in these studies. It begins with the parents' giving a direction to the child. In nondistressed families, the children comply with parental directions about 86 percent of the time. In abusive families, the children comply with parental directives only 46 percent of the time. Lack of compliance is met initially with weak or inconsistent parental attempts to get the child to comply, such as scolding or threats. These attempts are usually followed by ongoing child noncompliance and escalating anger and hostile responses on both the parents' and the childs' parts. These interchanges may culminate in physical aggression on the child by the parent. This "cycle of coercion" can lead to an abusive episode.

There is a consensus that being maltreated has *severe negative consequences for most children*. In correlational studies, maltreated children have been shown to have lower IQs than their nonabused counterparts, perform worse at school, have more behavior problems, and have poorer peer relationships (Egeland and Sroufe 1981; Egeland 1986; Wolfe 1987; Hoffman, Plotkin, and Twentyman 1984). The negative consequences of child maltreatment include developmental deficits in all domains of child development. A history of abuse and neglect has been associated with delinquent behavior during adolescence and with criminal behavior in adulthood. (Tarter et al. 1984; Loeber, Weisman, and Reid 1983). Another disturbing finding is that the experience of being maltreated is associated with deficits in social relationships with peers and with nurturing adults such as teachers (Main and George 1985). Especially distressing is the observed lack of empathy for others and the tendency to respond with fear, attack, or anger to others in distress. Another study found abused children more depressed and hopeless and exhibiting lower levels of self-esteem than matched nonmaltreated children (Kazdin et al. 1985). Although some of these studies have been correlational or retrospective, some more recent controlled, longitudinal studies have yielded similar findings (Egeland 1986).

There is not a perfect correspondence between the experience of maltreatment as a child and damaged adaptive capacities as an adult. Many believe that there are resilient children among those who are victims of maltreatment (Garmezy 1983; Rutter 1983). It is difficult to pinpoint the resources that enable some children to emerge undamaged from maltreatment. Some research points to the role of constitutional factors. Resilient children appear to be brighter than their more vulnerable peers. They seem to be more likable and appealing. Another protective factor is the presence of a nurturing adult during childhood. This adult may be a nonabusing parent, an extended-family member, a friend, or a teacher. While these studies introduce some important ideas in terms of protective factors that can mitigate the damaging effects of maltreatment, they do not provide clear clues to constructing protective factors in any given child's life.

## PROGRAMS AND SOCIAL WORK SERVICES

In order to provide some depth to the discussion, the focus will be on community-based services to the families of abused and neglected children. The reader is referred to other sources for discussions of out-of-home placement services (Kadushin 1980). Several excellent discussions of sexual abuse intervention are also available elsewhere (Sgroi 1988; McFarlane 1986; Finkelhor 1986).

Intervention in child maltreatment is usually multidisciplinary, involving social workers, physicians, nurses, psychologists, and educators. There is a growing presence of paraprofessional services to this population. While it may be impossible to tease out what is uniquely social work in this service response, it is clear that social workers have had and should continue to take a lead role in knowledge development and service provision to abused and neglected families.

The public health model of service provision describes preventive measures for maltreated children and their families. There are three levels of preventive services for maltreated children and their families. *Primary prevention* is the provision of parenting support services to the entire population of families, without regard to maltreatment status or risk of maltreatment. Examples of primary prevention programs include parenting classes held for members of a health maintenance organization and school-based sexual-abuse-prevention programs. *Secondary prevention* is the provision of parenting support services to families who are considered at risk for child abuse and neglect. Examples of secondary prevention programs include providing parenting support services to impoverished primiparous teen mothers and encouraging a mother who is afraid that she will become abusive toward her toddler to join Parents Anonymous, a self-help organization for abusive or potentially abusive parents. *Tertiary prevention* is the provision of helping services to families in which abuse or neglect has already occurred. Tertiary services are aimed at preventing the recurrence of abuse or neglect.

## Primary Prevention

Many parent and family educational services provided by social workers in health care, schools and family agency settings are for the primary prevention of child maltreatment. Much social work practice in maternal and child is, in effect, primary prevention of child maltreatment. Public education campaigns about child maltreatment are primary prevention efforts. Unfortunately, these are seldom evaluated for their effectiveness. While many social workers may "know in their gut" that such family support programs prevent child abuse and neglect, there is little documented evidence to support such an assertion.

In a review of evaluations of services meant to reduce child abuse and neglect, this author found only two controlled studies of primary prevention for child maltreatment. Both were sex-abuse-prevention programs. Some believe that until we have clearly articulated national policies that support families (such as family leave, a family allowance, and a day care policy), we will not have coherent primary prevention of child maltreatment. Others assert that until our society gives up its penchant for violence, primary prevention of child maltreatment is impossible (Gil 1980; Gelles and Straus 1983). Feminist thinkers believe that the elimination of child maltreatment is impossible until we replace the patriarchal societal view with an egalitarian, humanistic one.

The life-cycle family-support program is one conceptual model of primary prevention (Zigler and Black 1989; Weiss 1989; Price et al. 1989). Family support programs provide direct social, educational and recreational services to families (Weissbourd and Kagan 1988:21).

## Secondary Prevention

Most of what has been labeled *child maltreatment prevention* is actually secondary prevention, or services to families at risk of abusing or neglecting their children. Interest in the secondary prevention of child maltreatment has grown as the field has learned more through research about the long-term negative consequences for abused and neglected children. The success of early intervention programs for children such as Head Start (Berrueta-Clement et al. 1984) has also bolstered interest in prevention services. Savings in terms of the future social costs of delinquency, unemployment, and crime can be translated into societal savings.

Recently many efforts have been directed at preventing child abuse and neglect. Some have had a noticeable success. In one program, nurse home visitors made weekly home visits to the homes of poor first-time-pregnant single women (Olds et al. 1986). The nurses provided health teaching concerning pregnancy, labor, delivery, and infant development and care. They also provided assistance for the mother to obtain concrete resources such as health care, legal assistance, and education for herself. They specifically helped the woman access assistance and support from her own social network by involving friends and relatives in the home visits and by encouraging them to be involved with the woman. Home visitation occurred from the second trimester of pregnancy through the second birthday of the child.

This randomized study found that nurse home visitation resulted in positive benefits, especially evident from the time that the children were 1 to 2 years of age. The benefits were greatest for the highest risk group, that is, very poor teen mothers with initially limited social supports and little sense of control over their own lives. Among the observed benefits was that nurse-visited families were reported less frequently for child abuse or neglect during the child's first two years of life ($p < .07$; Olds et al. 1986:72). Nurse-visited mothers also reported that their babies had happier moods and cried less frequently. They also reported less conflict with their babies, although they also reported that their babies had more feeding problems, and they reported greater concern about the infant's behavior. Nurse-home-visited babies evidenced higher developmental quotients and were seen less often in the emergency room than control babies. The Olds program is currently being replicated by social-work-trained and supervised paraprofessionals (Sherman 1989).

In another experimentally tested child-maltreatment-prevention program, Uohara (1978) found that home visitor services resulted in lowered scores on a child abuse risk scale and less actual abuse or neglect compared to the control group. Professionally trained and supervised paraprofessional home visitors provided emotional support; parent–child interaction training; assistance in obtaining other community supports, such as health care, financial services, or housing; and a "time-out" nursery that provided time away from child care for the mothers and a nurturing environment for the infants.

Gray et al. (1977) found that high-risk families who had received intervention did not maltreat their children during the child's first seventeen months of life, although maltreatment did occur among nontreated high-risk families in this randomized study. The preventive intervention included intensive pediatric care (weekly visits or telephone contacts between pediatrician and family) and weekly public-health-nurse or lay-health-home-aide visits.

Certain key features distinguish successful child-maltreatment-prevention programs. They provide services early in the family life cycle. Prenatal programs appear promising in their potential to deter child maltreatment. Effective programs minimize stigma by delivering services through health care settings or community centers. Effective programs involve parents and children in interaction as opposed to providing services to the parent alone. Most include a parent education component highlighting the parental role in child development. Parent education is discussed in greater detail below. Play and positive interaction are emphasized.

Secondary prevention programs look promising. Long-term outcome information is needed. This has been suggested as a funding priority for future research on child maltreatment (Finkelhor 1988). Since many families served in prevention programs live with limited financial, educational, and other social resources, they may need support throughout the life cycle.

## Tertiary Prevention

Most child-maltreatment-intervention research focuses on tertiary prevention, or the rehabilitation of maltreating families. Before the findings of these practice studies are discussed, the reader should be aware of the limitations of this research. Specifically, behavioral approaches to intervention account for a large proportion of the evaluations of intervention effectiveness (Videka-Sherman 1989). Programs have typically not distinguished between abusive and neglectful families. When they have, research is startlingly absent on child neglect intervention (Videka-Sherman in press). Samples in controlled studies include clients who have agreed both to intervention and to be studied. Therefore, their generalizability to the population of maltreating families is limited. Finally, there are no long-term follow-ups of intervention effectiveness, and there is little replication of findings across studies.

Like research on the origins of child maltreatment, most of the research on child maltreatment intervention focuses on physical abuse. In a recent review of 124 published and unpublished child-maltreatment-intervention research reports, 30 percent were found not to distinguish between abusive and neglectful families. Presumably, these programs provided the same services to both. Another 23 percent of the studies focused on services to abusive families. Another 23 percent studied services for sexual abuse. Only five studies that targeted neglectful families were located. In addition to the overrepresentation of studies of physical child abuse, an analysis of controlled studies showed that programs for abusive families were more successful than programs for mixed (abuse *and* neglect) families (Videka-Sherman 1989). This finding suggests one of two explanations: either neglecting families are more difficult to change and this lowered the success rate of the combined programs, *or* abusive and neglectful families need different interventions. With these limitations in mind, let us proceed to examine what we have learned about effective intervention for child maltreatment.

In further examining the most successful interventions for abusive families, it is clear that *parent education and training* are core components. Parent education is the topic of several current books on child abuse intervention (Kelly 1986; Wolfe et al. 1981; Goldstein, Keller, and Erne 1985; Polster and Dangel 1984). Parent training most often includes the following components:

1. Teaching parents to notice and reward positive child behaviors.
2. Teaching parents alternatives to the use of verbal or physical punishment. The alternatives that are usually focused on include withdrawing attention for misbehavior, giving positive directives on what the child should do, and using time-out for child misbehavior.

Many successful intervention programs for abusive parents include in-session practice or homework for the family between sessions. Having the family practice new skills is critical to enhancing their acquisition.

Also included in effective tertiary prevention programs are services designed to enhance parents' coping skills. These include stress management and relaxation training and social skills or communication skills training. Although mentioned less frequently as a "core" intervention component, concrete supports such as transportation, child care, and assistance with financial, housing, and legal needs are also provided.

One example of this approach is the program reported by Wolfe, Sandler, and Kaufman (1981). Group training of abusive parents took place over eight weekly two-hour sessions. The training included instruction in human development and child management, practice in solving child behavior problems by the use of videotaped anecdotes to which parents devised a response based on what they had learned, and deep muscle relaxation as a response to stress. In addition to group sessions, home visits were made weekly to help families apply the skills they had learned. Compared to the control group, the intervention parents evidenced better child management skills.

In another study, Cadol (1976) mounted a randomized clinical trial of a multimodal intervention including well- and sick-child health care; concrete environmental assistance with food, housing, finances, and legal needs; marital, financial, and family-planning counseling; anticipatory planning to head off crises; teaching and modeling of problem-solving skills; assertiveness training; child-care-skill development; infant stimulation taught to parents; and crisis availability. Treated children were superior to nontreated children in physical development and improved more in motor and mental development, although this difference did not reach statistical significance.

Barth et al. (1983) tested the effectiveness of a time-limited cognitive-behavioral group intervention for abusing programs. The treatment included parent skills training as described above, as well as self-control training (which included recognizing stress, relaxation and alternative thoughts and actions as a response to stress, and self-rewards for effective coping). Role playing and practice were emphasized. Although this study was limited by the inclusion of a nonequivalent control group of nonabusive families from a well-baby clinic, the authors found that the treated parents reported less anger and less negative affect than the control families. The experimental families also performed better than the controls in role plays of parent–child interactions.

Using a different theoretical approach, Levant (1981) tested an ego-psychology-based intervention called *content therapy*. In content therapy, parents are encouraged to acknowledge the hostility that they experience, to gain perspective on their overreactions, and to develop alternative methods of managing their hostility. The intervention also included an emphasis on the conscious and current experience of the client and the provision of supportive services. Levant found that after treatment, the parents in the experimental group were better able to cope with their hostility, but that the behavior of their children was rated worse than that of the control group's children. These authors suggested that abused children need treatment as well as their parents. Another interpretation is that parents need enhancement of parenting skills as well as of skills in dealing with their own hostility.

These studies suggest that a tripartite approach is useful in intervening with abusive parents. Programs should include interventions that enhance parenting skills, that bolster parents' coping skills, and that provide assistance with economic and other tangible needs.

There are no controlled evaluations of interventions for neglectful families. The National Center on Child Abuse and Neglect has recently funded several demonstration intervention programs for neglectful families, but the results have not yet been published. There are programs that serve both abusive and neglectful families. Some of these programs have reported that the majority of the families they have served have been neglectful rather than abusive. These programs are our best source of information on treating child neglect. Neglectful families are probably more difficult to change than abusive families, as suggested by the relatively low effect sizes for programs that serve both abusive and neglectful families.

The first is a program reported by Laughlin and Weiss (1981). This program served severe cases of neglect or abuse that had a poor prognosis for the client's engagement in any type of service. In a quasi-experimental evaluation that is flawed because there is no information regarding the experimental and control groups' equivalence, Laughlin and Weiss found that the experimental families became engaged 85 percent of the time, as compared to the 25 percent engagement rate for the control families (who had been referred to ordinary community services). Children were removed from the homes of 22 percent of the study families, compared to 37 percent in the control group. Maltreatment recurred in 11 percent of the study cases and in 27 percent of the control cases. Intervention was delivered in an informal "family center" setting by a team of MSWs, an early-childhood-education specialist, and two paraprofessionals. The intervention included an extensive outreach component, in which concrete problems were given primary attention. Conversations were focused by staff away from child maltreatment allegations. Contacts were kept brief and informal. The staff tried to find ways to notice and compliment good family functioning and achievements. Transportation was provided for the clients to and from the family center. A host of services for the children included a crisis nursery, a nursery school, and child enrichment activities between staff, parent, and child. These included the provision of play materials as well as instruction and modeling for parents in how to use them. The mothers were trained in child development and child management as they served as parent aides in the nursery. The family counseling was designed to be counterisolating. Socialization and group activities were emphasized. Laughlin and Weiss noted that "Most of the clients were so depressed that they lacked the ability to have a good time" (1981:109). To counter this sad reality, the staff planned "fun" activities and engaged the parents in an active role by setting up client planning committees.

In another series of single-subject design studies, Lutzker and his associates described Project 12-Ways (Tertinger, Greene, and Lutzker 1984; Barone, Greene, and Lutzker 1986; Campbell, et al. 1983; Lutzker, 1984). Project 12-Ways is a multimodal program primarily serving neglectful families in rural Illinois. The services provided directly by Project 12-Ways are listed in table 11.1. All services are provided with a backdrop of environmental supports coordinated with other agencies such as homemakers, mental health workers, public health nurses, and pediatric health services.

Effective interventions for neglectful families require different ele-

---

TABLE 11.1. Services Provided by Project 12-Ways

- Parent skills training
- Stress management training
- Assertiveness training
- Self-control training
- Weight reduction and smoking cessation training (reported to be the program's most popular components with clients)
- Referral for alcoholism treatment
- Job-finding service
- Money management training
- Prenatal preventive services to unwed mothers
- Family leisure-time-activity training
- Marital counseling
- Direct services to older children, including self-care skills (dressing, toileting, and communication skills), and active involvement with schools and recreational settings
- Home safety training to reduce the number of nonintentional injuries

SOURCE: Lutzker (1984).

ments than intervention with abusive families. Specifically, they seem to require a slower pace and longer term intervention than the child management skills and stress management approaches used for abusive families. They require a longer relationship-developing period with the families and must provide some services that the family wants.

## DIFFERENTIAL CLINICAL ASSESSMENTS AND INTERVENTIONS

The assessment of service needs should reflect the ecological perspective that is most effective in explaining the occurrence of child maltreatment. Assessments must reflect individual client, family, and community strengths as well as problems. Assessments should also include resources for alleviating the problems.

It is always important to include the client's perceptions and relevant others' perceptions of problems as well as the social worker's perceptions. Since the problems experienced by many maltreating families are so pervasive and complex, a complete assessment can be daunting, adding to the client's and the practitioner's sense of futility. Throughout the assessment process, the practitioner should partialize or triage the problems experienced by the family. In order to build client morale for change, complex problems must be broken down into simpler components that are important for child and family well-being, but that are also solvable.

As research on the origins of child maltreatment shows, maltreating parents usually experience stress in many spheres of their lives. Effective intervention should include services to the maltreating parent. These services should be based on a careful assessment of the parent's needs. Parental assessment includes *sources of stress* in the parent's life. Potential sources of stress include financial strain, unemployment, inadequate housing, the presence of children with special needs, or health or emotional problems of the parent. It is important that the social worker assess the parent's perception of stress as well as the existence of observable stressors such as unemployment or an exceptionally difficult child, since some research has shown that maltreating parents may perceive themselves to be under greater stress whether or not they actually encounter more stressors than normaltreating families. Table 11.2 lists some stressors commonly found in maltreating families.

The social worker should also assess parents' *coping skills* in order to deal with the stress in their lives. Specific coping skills include the ability to modulate emotions and to think before acting. These skills may be especially pertinent for abusive parents, who have difficulty with anger control. Another coping resource is the parent's child management and relationship skills. It is also important to assess the parent's morale and worldview.

Another arena of coping skills is *life management skills*. These include a host of skills such as household management, financial management, basic employment skills, grooming, and self-care.

A thorough assessment of the children's needs is an essential part of a child maltreatment assessment. Since the most successful intervention programs also include services to the child, it is essential that the child be included in the assessment process.

The assessment of the child should begin with a basic *physical assessment*. This includes basic observations of the child's health, grooming, and presentation. It should also include height, weight, and head circumference measurement (for infants). Growth charts that define normal limits for children of different ages are available from any pediatric text, such as Nelson (1983). If the child has not received a medical examination within the time frame recommended by the American Academy of Pediatrics, such an exam should also be scheduled.

The social worker should also screen the child or have the child

TABLE 11.2. Stressors Commonly Found in Maltreating Families

*Environmental Stresses*

Unemployment
Financial difficulties
Isolation and lack of social support
Impoverished neighborhood
Low levels of neighbor interaction

*Family Stresses*

Early childbearing
Alcohol or substance abuse
Health problems of parent or child
Spousal violence
History of victimization
Complicated pregnancy
Temperamentally "difficult" child
Disruption of parent–child attachment

screened for *social and cognitive development*. There are a number of developmental assessment tools that can be used by social workers. These include the Denver Developmental Screening Test (Frankburg, Dodds, Fondal 1968), the Bayley Scales of Infant Development (Bayley 1969), the Kent Infant Development Scale (KIDS; Reuter and Bickett 1985), and the Minnesota Child Development Inventories (MCDI; Ireton and Thwing 1974). Each scale has advantages and disadvantages.

In addition to assessing the developmental level of the child, the social worker should assess school-aged child functioning and coping in the two main extrafamilial roles for children: *school performance* and *peer relationships*. School performance includes both academic performance and behavior control. Peer relationships include the child's ability to make and keep friendships. Most maltreated children have difficulties in both these spheres.

Finally, *basic life skills* should also be assessed for children who are at preschool age and older. These skills include dressing, toileting and grooming themselves.

An assessment of family relationships and interaction is important since many of the newest and most promising interventions focus on family-level phenomena. Family assessment should include an assessment of the *marital relationship*, if relevant, or the *parents' relationship history*. This provides important information about the marriage as a source of stress or support in the family. It also provides important information about the parents' relationship style and skills. A number of standardized assessment scales are relevant to the marital relationship. These include the Locke-Wallace Marital Adjustment Test (Locke and Wallace 1959), the Dyadic Adjustment Scale (Spanier 1976), and the Index of Marital Satisfaction (Hudson 1982).

Family assessment should include practitioners' observations of actual family interaction as well as family members' perceptions of the quality of family interaction. *Family interaction* includes the amount of interaction, the methods used to deal with conflict or child noncompliance, and the tone of interaction (positive, negative, or neutral). Standardized assessment tools are available to assess family interaction (Burgess et al. 1981). While most social work agencies do not have the resources to gather systematic data with independent trained observers, the observation scheme can be a useful guide to the practitioner who is conducting a qualitative assessment. There are also a number of tools that assess family members' perceptions of the quality of family life. These include the McMaster Family Assessment Device (Epstein, Baldwin, and Bishop 1983) and the Hudson Scale of Family Satisfaction (Hudson 1982).

Another set of family measures centers on the *quality of the home environment* (the level of nurturance and stimulation). These include the HOME (Home Observation for Measurement of the Environment) scale (Caldwell and Bradley 1984) and the Environmental Hazards Scale (Lutzker 1984), which assesses the safety of the home environment.

Standardized assessment tools that measure the likelihood of abuse or neglect are available. The Child Abuse Potential Inventory (CAPI) is a self-administered seventy-seven-item, seven-dimension scale that has been shown to predict physical child abuse and, with less accuracy, child neglect (Milner 1986). There are also two validated scales for assessing the level of child neglect: the Childhood Level of Living Scale (Polansky 1981) and the Child Neglect Severity Scale (Edgington 1980). These standardized assessment tools are clinically useful because they allow the practitioner to demonstrate the degree of maltreatment potential. If used repeatedly, they can also demonstrate the progress made in intervention.

It is imperative for social work practitioners to assess the community sources of strain for the maltreating family as well as the community resources for these families. Community assessment should include the *family's position in the community*, that is, how well known they are, how many friends and family live nearby, and whether the family is scapegoated by or isolated from other community members. *Community resources* should also be assessed, including helping norms in the community, informal helpers available (family and friends), and formal help available.

A number of treatment issues are not addressed in any discussion of programmatic responses to child maltreatment. This gap is due to the differences between the idiographic thinking of the clinician (maximizing the potential of success of the individual client) and the programmatic approach (built on maximizing positive group responses to intervention). Programs cannot take into account all the individual circumstances that the clinician considers when working with a family. Idiographic treatment issues are considered in this section. This subject is best understood as being how to make "successful" programs work for a particular client.

Maltreating parents, especially neglectful parents, are notoriously difficult to engage in the helping process. To engage maltreating families, the social worker must find some common ground between societal expectations for the parents and the parents' own values and beliefs (Laughlin and Weiss 1981). The social worker brokers societal parenting norms and the family's norms.

Setting specific and realistic intervention goals with the client enables rather than impedes the engagement process. Clearly specifying client and practitioner responsibilities is important. The more clients know about the intervention process, the goals to be worked toward, and what is expected of them, the more successful the intervention will be. Social workers should do all they can to demystify the intervention process. This is especially important for clients with limited verbal or other cognitive skills.

A *contract* includes an explicit statement of goals, processes, and social worker and client responsibilities in the intervention process. In their pioneering study of children in foster care, Stein, Gambrill, and Wiltse (1974) found that written contracts enhanced parents' completion of the tasks necessary for reuniting children with their natural families. Contracting is a tool that demystifies the intervention process for maltreating families and for social workers. The contract serves as a guide and a reference point. It is easy to lose focus with maltreating families since they typically experience so many crises. The contract sets a course with these families. It can be used to move back on course when diverting forces, such as a new crisis, come in to play.

Whether a contract should be written or verbal is debated. Wolfe et al. (1981a) believe that contracts should be written. Written contracts are explicit and are always available for reference in the event of lapsed memories or misunderstandings. Contracts can also be used with school-age children. Wolfe et al. (1981a) gave two examples of model contracts for maltreating families.

One reason that social workers have traditionally felt frustrated by maltreating families is that they allowed intervention to amble along in a relatively unstructured manner, letting the client's problems and concerns emerge over (sometimes long periods of) time. While engagement may take time, especially for neglectful families, no evidence indicates that it is productive to let the client–practitioner relationship go along in an unstructured and unguided manner. This approach is especially inappropriate for clients who are cognitively limited since it obfuscates the purpose and progress of the intervention.

*Structure and clarity of purpose* are essential in working effectively with maltreating families. Structure and purpose may minimize social worker discouragement and burnout, which is a reflection of the families' own discouragement about their lives.

We know little about the necessary *duration of services* to prevent the occurrence or recurrence of child maltreatment in families. Short-term programs with limited goals, such as the parent-training programs, are effective in reaching those goals. How these small accomplishments relate to the long-term picture of risk of child maltreatment is unknown. Many families are referred for services over and over again. Are these families failures because they need more services? Why must their situations regress to the point where their children are again in danger of being harmed in order for them to receive assistance? Are open-ended, long-term supportive services always necessary? These are thorny questions for which we do not have clear answers. The concept of family support programs available in a preventive, nonstigmatizing manner throughout the life cycle holds great appeal as a way to mount resources to respond to the ongoing stresses and dilemmas in the lives of vulnerable families.

A maltreating family's needs typically exceed the services that any single agency can provide. Therefore, community liaison work or *case management* is necessary. It is increasingly common for public welfare agencies to have legal and monitoring responsibilities for maltreating families, but for actual supportive or change services to be provided by a multitude of private agencies, such as family service centers, schools, and child development centers. Coordination of such services is essential for effective and efficient services for maltreating families and their children. In some cases, MSWs or BSWs find themselves the agents of this coordination task. In other cases, a person other than a trained social worker manages the multiple services provided to the family. The social worker may find himself or herself a member of the team. Coordination requires regular communication and case planning by the many agencies serving the family.

*Ethical issues* abound for social workers in child abuse and neglect. Value conflicts between families identified as maltreating and the social worker are not uncommon.

For example, one family was repeatedly referred for physical child neglect due to unsanitary conditions in the home. It was later discovered that chronic truancy was also a problem. The family was indicted for child neglect. When the social worker assigned the case visited the home, she was taken aback by the stench and dirt, including animal excrement, in the home. Although the situation appeared to be an obvious health hazard, none of the family members, children or adults, were sick or had a history of illness. Several of the school-aged children had been diagnosed as borderline mentally retarded. No one in the family placed a positive value on schooling. Should the social worker attempt to modify the values of the parents or the school-aged children? Would this case move forward in intervention without a values shift? Probably not. What were the comparative harms of allowing the children to continue to grow up in an environment so deviant from mainstream American values and of removing them from their family to live in one or a series of foster homes? No one in this family defined any family or lifestyle problems. Even the horrified social worker noticed some harmony and warmth among family members.

This is just one example of the ethical dilemmas faced by social workers in this field. Social workers in child abuse and neglect are on the front line of the conflict between societal values and social work's commitment to individualism and self-determination. We often use the concept of harm to another as a justification for limiting the rights of an individual, but harm is a fuzzy concept. We usually make choices that involve some benefits and some harm. Identifying the best choice is often difficult.

Some individuals raise the issue that impoverished families differ from mainstream middle-class American society in their basic family values. Polansky et al. (1981) found no support for this assertion. They found that poor rural white families and inner-city black families held values and beliefs and knowledge that were indistinguishable from white middle-class values and beliefs about family life, child care, and child development. There is little literature to guide social workers working with families who have been defined as maltreating or at risk for maltreating their children and who affiliate with a cultural group different from the social worker's. There is a growing literature on social work practice with ethnicly and racially diverse populations (Devore and Schlesinger 1981; Brown and Oliver 1985a; Brown and Oliver, 1985b). Unfortunately, there has been little direct application of this work to abusive and neglectful families.

## CASE ILLUSTRATION

The Bartholomews were referred to child protective services by a call from the county-health-department nurse who had been assigned to provide follow-up health care for a severe and stubborn ear infection in their 6-month-old son. The public health nurse stated that the family had been remiss in seeking health care for Jason in several episodes of ear infections. The health care professionals involved in this case asserted that Jason would suffer hearing damage if this lack of health care continued.

Child-protective-service investigation found that the Bartholomews had indeed failed to seek regular health care for Jason. He had not begun to receive communicable illness innoculations and had been brought to the emergency room twice for severe middle-ear infections that had shown signs of being present for several weeks without medical care. The Bartholomews had also failed to give Jason prescribed medication for the ear infections and had failed to keep follow-up medical appointments. The incident that had prompted the public health nurse's call was that the Bartholomews had failed to keep their latest follow-up ear check for Jason and had refused to open the door when the public health nurse arrived at their home. The Bartholomews also refused to admit the child-protective-service investigator. She had to return to their home with a police escort before the Bartholomews would permit her to enter.

Child protective services determined that the Bartholomew family had medically neglected Jason. The case was referred to a child-maltreatment-intervention program in a local family-service agency. Although the agency was private, its child maltreatment program was funded under contract from the state department of social services. The state's child-protective-services caseworker, who was not trained with a social work degree, was designated as the case manager for the Bartholomews. Her role was to coordinate the services of several agencies, including pediatric health care, early intervention for at-risk children and counseling services to the family.

Mr. and Mrs. Bartholomew were both mentally retarded at the high-functioning level. Neither had completed high school. Neither had held a job for longer than two weeks. Peggy Bartholomew, 20 years old, had never attempted employment. Larry, 21 years old, had worked as a mechanic's assistant in three automotive repair garages. He had never held these jobs for longer than two weeks. The reason for the loss of these jobs was that he didn't show up for work. The family was supported by public assistance. Larry wanted to apply for Supplemental Security Insurance (SSI).

When the social worker first attempted to contact the Bartholomews, they locked the door and drew the shades as they had done for the public health nurses and the child-protective-services worker in the past. The social worker eventually gained entry by making regular biweekly visits to the home, which were announced by letters sent four days before the scheduled visit. The social worker also talked to the Bartholomews through the open windows (through the drawn shades). The family court judge had made it clear to the Bartholomews that they must allow human service providers entry; otherwise, they would run the risk of Jason's being placed in a foster home. The court directive was effective in persuading, or perhaps coercing, the Bartholomews to allow the social worker to enter. It did not work the same magic in enabling the Bartholomews to build a collaborative relationship with their social worker. They refused to talk to her for her first several visits to their home.

In the first three months of the relationship, the social worker worked carefully to gain the trust of the Bartholomews. She began each visit by repeating her purpose for visiting them. This purpose was to help them do what was necessary to ensure that Jason would receive good care. If Jason was assessed as being well-cared-for, he would not be removed from their home. The Bartholomews were already certain that they cared well for Jason—they loved him so. They were, although grudgingly at first, willing to do whatever was necessary to avoid the threat of his removal.

After two months, Peggy Bartholomew felt comfortable enough with her social worker to begin to talk to her. It was at this point that the social worker learned the Bartholomews story, at least from Peggy's point of view. All Peggy Bartholomew had ever wanted to be was a mother. She adored her son and was highly invested in him and in her role as a mother. To be investigated for child maltreatment was a devastating blow to her. She was extremely afraid of losing her son, yet had no idea of why this threat had been made to her. Couldn't people tell that she loved her baby very much?

While the social worker had no doubt about Peggy and Larry's investment in and attachment to Jason, she also noticed some serious deficits in the home with regard to conditions for Larry's growth and development. Many of these stemmed from Peggy and Larry's lack of cognitive skills and the deprivations of their own upbringing. Foremost among these deficits was something that the social worker observed at each of these first visits. The Bartholomews always kept Jason in his crib in a dark room with no toys or other objects near. The Bartholomews had only two toys for Jason, which had been given to him as baby presents. They did not have money to buy toys for him, and frankly, they never even thought to do so. They did not see the need for toys and other sensory stimulation for Jason.

The social worker was also concerned because Peggy and Larry became easily unnerved when Jason cried, which was infrequently since he was a placid baby. When he cried, they tried to feed and diaper him. If that did not calm him, they put him in his crib and closed the door to his room, so that his crying was less disturbing to them. This didn't happen often, but it did happen when Jason had ear infections.

Finally, fitting with the observations made above, the Bartholomews did not know much about infant or child development. Nor did they even know there were gaps in what they knew or expected about children. They did not anticipate Jason's blossoming development.

The social worker assessed that Larry and Peggy had a good deal of motivation to be the best parents that they could. They were isolated in the community and were fearful of the power of community agencies to determine their lives. They experienced extreme threat when any community agencies became involved with their family, and they responded by trying to ignore or block out that agency. While the Bartholomews had every intention of being good parents, they had limited knowledge of infant behavior or appropriate parenting and had limited skills for coping with Jason's crying.

The social worker prioritized two goals in working with the Bartholomews. First, she wanted to ensure Jason's well-being and optimal development by educating his parents about normal infant development and parents' role in it. Specifically, she wanted to bolster their skills in providing a stimulating environment for Jason and in constructively responding to his crying. Second, the social worker aimed to help the Bartholomews develop better skills for interacting with the human service system, especially the child-health-care system. The social worker tried to engage the Bartholomews in goal setting; they were only minimally interested. They were, however, agreeable to the goals outlined above. A verbal contract was made.

The social worker referred Peggy and Larry to a parenting-skills group sponsored by a local family-service agency, but Peggy and Larry did not attend the group, despite their verbal agreement to do so. After several attempts to get them to the group, the social worker decided to adapt the group content to individual sessions between herself and the Bartholomews. The social worker instructed Larry and Peggy about the importance of stimulation and play for a developing infant. She brought bright-colored toys to the house. Even more important, she played with Jason and Peggy and Larry and the toys. Neither Peggy nor Larry knew how to play. They felt awkward talking to Jason or holding up toys for him to respond to. Over a period of several months, Peggy and Larry gained a degree of comfort in playing with and talking to Jason. They allowed the toys to remain in his bed. They set Jason on a blanket, surrounded by his toys. After several months, the social worker noticed that Peggy seemed to begin to enjoy Jason's reactions to his toys. The Bartholomews continued to find it awkward to talk to Jason as they were caring for him. Although they knew it was good to do so, they just didn't talk much, even between themselves.

To further support the parenting skills that the Bartholomews were acquiring, the county health department assigned a visiting nurse to visit the Bartholomews to provide a structured infant-stimulation program with Jason. This service also provided an arena in which the Bartholomews could develop better skills in relating to health care professionals. At first, the Bartholomews refused to let the nurse in the house. The social worker conferred with the case manager and the nurse. She gave suggestions about how to approach the Bartholomews in an unthreatening way. The social worker also worked with the Bartholomews to explain why the nurse was visiting, to discuss the negative consequences of their not allowing her in, and to give them ideas for how they could respond to her and to modulate their own anxiety when she visited. The social worker and the Bartholomews practiced their interactions with the nurse. Eventually, Peggy and Larry let her in, although they claimed that they still "did not like her snotty attitude."

The nurse and the social worker both explained to the Bartholomews how important regular health care was for Jason. They stood by while Peggy called the health care center and made a 9- and 12-month well-baby appointment for Jason. They rehearsed with the Bartholomews their questions and concerns to be shared with the pediatric nurse practitioner (PNP). The question that was of greatest concern to Peggy (and that she *was* able to ask at Jason's 9-month check-up) was, "Is he developing normally?" She did ask the PNP this question and felt very good at hearing the response that, "He certainly is. You're doing a good job."

The Bartholomews and Jason progressed well over the next nine months. At this time, the social worker was changing jobs. Child-protective services decided that it was time to terminate services to the Bartholomews. Peggy and Jim were upset about their social worker's leaving. They stated that they were afraid that the nurse would start bothering them again. As the termination date neared, they intermittently refused to let the infant-stimulation-program nurse in the house, although they did attend well-baby appointments independently and felt a good rapport with their nurse practitioner. Jason was developmentally assessed and found to be within normal limits on all indicators except language.

The Bartholomew family illustrates several important points about social work intervention with maltreating families. This case also illustrates how prevention can be integrated into work with a family that is currently being served for existing maltreatment.

One issue illustrated by the Bartholomew family is the importance of engagement in order for any services to be effective. Initially, the Bartholomews deeply distrusted human service providers. Through careful and consistent repetition of her purpose in contacting them and through her persistent and nonthreatening demeanor, the social worker was gradually able to gain Peggy's trust. The court mandate for services was used by the social worker to enhance Peggy and Larry's motivation to become involved with social work services. As with many maltreating families, without court mandates the likelihood that the Bartholomews would ever have let the social worker into their home and their lives is slim.

Contracting and using a structured approach to intervention was useful with this family. Because of their limited cognitive and communication skills and their suspicious stance toward human service providers, concreteness reduced the ambiguity and threat of the intervention situation. Structure enhanced the working relationship with the Bartholomews.

Coordination of services was necessary in order to serve the Bartholomews effectively. Case management is one approach to providing such service coordination. In addition to referrals and recommendations for services (these are discussed below), it is imperative for professionals to work together to enhance the family's receptivity to intervention. A case manager, one human service professional who is responsible for accessing and coordinating services for the family, should be designated. If the social worker is not the case manager, she or he should still take a leading role in educating other professionals about how to effectively approach and engage the family. This may take a great deal of tact and good interpersonal skills.

The family needed and received information and training about child care. Equally important was secondary prevention of future neglect of Jason. As Jason moves into toddlerhood, he will voice his autonomy through normal opposition and motoric expression. The Bartholomews may become overwhelmed and unable to adequately socialize Jason. Parenting-skills training will probably be an ongoing need for the Bartholomews.

The Bartholomews' social isolation intensifies their risk of future maltreatment. Although they made progress in relating to health care professionals, they continued to be isolated from family, friends, and neighbors.

Social work as a profession has had a historical mission to provide assistance to abused and neglected children and their families. There are few service populations that are as central to the mission of our profession as this one. There are also few populations that are as difficult to serve, particularly in the ethos of short-term episodes of service.

## ENDNOTE

1. The address for the Clearinghouse on Child Abuse and Neglect Information is P.O. Box 1182, Washington, D.C. 20013. The phone number is (301) 251-5157.

## REFERENCES

Altmeier, William A., Susan S. O'Connor, K. B. Sherrock, and E. Tucker. 1979. "Outcome of Abuse During Childhood Among Pregnant Low Income Women." *Child Abuse and Neglect* 10:319–330.

AHA (American Humane Association). 1986. *Trends in Child Abuse and Neglect: A National Perspective.* Denver Colo. AHA.

Azar, Sandra, D. R. Robinson, E. Hekimian, and C. T. Twentyman. 1984. "Unrealistic Expectations and Problem-Solving Ability in Maltreating and Comparison Mothers." *Journal of Consulting and Clinical Psychology* 52:687–691.

Azar, Sandra and Craig Twentyman. 1987. "An Evaluation of the Efficiency of Group Cognitive-Behavioral and Insight-Oriented Parent Training for Child Maltreatment." Manuscript.

Barone, V. J., B. F. Greene, and J. R. Lutzker. 1986. "Home Safety with Families Being Treated with Child Abuse and Neglect." *Behavior Modification* 10:93–114.

Barth, Richard, Betty Blythe, Steven Schinke, and Robert Schilling. 1983. "Self-Control Training with Maltreating Parent." *Child Welfare* 62:313–324.

Bayley, N. 1969. *The Bayley Scale of Infant Development.* Palo Alto, Calif.: Psychological Corporation.

Bauer, W. D. and C. T. Twentyman. 1985. "Abusing, Neglectful and Comparison Mothers' Responses to Child-Related and Non-Child-Related Stressors." *Journal of Consulting and Clinical Psychology* 53:335–343.

Behrman, Richard E. and Victor C. Vaughn III, eds. 1983. *Nelson Textbook of Pediatrics.* New York: W. B. Saunders.

Belsky, Jay. 1980. "Child Maltreatment: An Ecological Integration." *American Psychologist* 35:320–335.

Berrueta-Clement, J. R., L. J. Schweinhart, W. S. Barnett, A. S. Epstein, and D. P. Weikart, 1984. *Changed Lives: The Effects of the Perry Preschool Program on Youths Through Age 19.* Monographs on the High/Scope Educational Research Foundation, No. 8. Ypsilanti, Mich.: High/Scope.

Brown L., J. Oliver, and J. Klor de Alva, eds. 1985a. *A Resource Guide for Human Service Professionals: Sociocultural and Service Issues in Working with Hispanic American Clients.* Albany: Rockefeller College Press.

Brown, L., J. Oliver, and J. Klor de Alva, eds. 1985b. *A Resource Guide for Human Service Professionals: Sociocultural and Service Issues in Working with Afro-Americans.* Albany:Rockefeller College Press.

Burgess, Robert and Rand Conger. 1978. "Family Interactions in Abusive, Neglectful and Normal Families." *Child Development* 49:1163–1173.

Burgess, Robert L., Elaine A. Anderson, Cynthia J. Schellenbach, and Rand D. Conger. 1981. "A Social Interactional Approach to the Study of Abusive Families." John P. Vincent, ed. *Advances in Family Intervention, Assessment and Theory*, vol. 2, pp. 1–46. Greenwich, Conn.: JAI.

Burgess, Robert L. and L. Youngblade. 1987. "Social Incompetence and Intergenerational Transmission of Abusive Parental Practices." In R. J. Gelles, G. T. Hotaling, D. Finkelhor, and M. A. Straus, eds., *New Directions in Family Violence Research*, Newbury Park, Calif.: Sage.

Cadol, Roger V., Michael J. Fitch, Edward J. Goldson, Elaine K. Jackson, Darlene F. Swartz, and Theodore P. Wendel. 1976. *Prospective Study in Child Abuse: The Child Study Program.* Unpublished Final Report. Washington, D.C.: Office of Child Development, U.S. Department of Health, Education and Welfare.

Caldwell, Betty and Robert Bradley. 1979. *Home Observation for Measurement of the Environment.* Little Rock: University of Arkansas.

Campbell, Randy V., Shirley O'Brian, Alan D. Bickett, and John R. Lutzker. 1983. "In-Home Parent Training, Treatment of Migraine Headaches, and Marital Counseling as an Ecobehavioral Approach to Preventing Child Abuse." *Journal of Behavior Therapy and Experimental Psychiatry* 14:147–154.

Conger, R. D., R. Burgess, and C. Barret. 1979. "Child Abuse Related to Life Change and Perceptions of Illness: Some Preliminary Findings." *Family Coordinator* 28:73–78.

Crittenden, Patricia M. 1985. "Maltreated Infants: Vulnerability and Resistence." *Journal of Child Psychology and Psychiatry* 26:85–96.

Dangel, Richard F. and Richard A. Polster 1984. *Parent Training.* New York: Guilford.

Daro, Deborah and Anne H. Cohn. 1985. "A Decade of Child Maltreatment Evaluation Efforts: What We Have Learned." Paper presented at the 5th National Conference on Child Abuse and Neglect.

DeVore, W. 1981. *Ethnic Sensitive Social Work Practice.* St. Louis: C. L. Mosby.

Dumas, John and Robert G. Wahler, 1985. "Indiscriminate Mothering as a Contextual Factor in Aggressive-Oppositional Child Behavior: 'Damned If You Do, Damned If You Don't.' " *Journal of Abnormal Child Psychology* 13:1–17.

Edington, Alice, M. Hall, R. S. Rosser. 1980. "Neglectful Families: Measurement of Treatment Outcomes." Paper presented at the Tri-Regional Workshop of Social Workers in Maternal and Child Health.

Egeland, Byron. 1985. "The Consequences of Physical and Emotional Neglect on the Development of Young Children." Paper presented at the Symposium on Child Neglect, Chicago.

Egeland, Byron, M. Breitenbucher, and D. Rosenberg. 1980. "Prospective Study of the Significance of Life Stress in the Etiology of Child Abuse." *Journal of Consulting and Clinical Psychology* 48:195–205.

Egeland, Byron and L. A. Sroufe. 1981. "Attachment and Early Child Maltreatment." *Child Development* 55:753–771.

Elmer, Elizabeth. 1963. "Identification of Abused Children." *Children* 10:180–184.

Elmer, Elizabeth and G. Gregg. 1967. "Developmental Characteristics of Abused Children." *Pediatrics* 40:596–602.

Epstein, N., L. Baldwin, and D. Bishop. 1987. "McMaster Family Assessment Device." In K. Corcoran and J. Fischer, eds., *Measures for Clinical Practice: A Source Book*, p. 432. New York: Free Press.

Faller, Kathleen and Sally Russo. 1981. "Definition and Scope of the Problem of Child Maltreatment." In Kathleen Faller, ed. *Social Work with Abused and Neglected Children*, pp. 3–10. New York: Free Press.

Finkelhor, David. 1986. *Sourcebook on Child Sexual Abuse*. Beverly Hills, Calif.: Sage.

Finkelhor, David, Gerald T. Hotaling, and Kersti Yllo. 1988. *Stopping Family Violence: Research Priorities for the Coming Decade*. Newbury Park, Calif.: Sage.

Fontana, Vincent J. 1973. *Somewhere a Child Is Crying*. New York: Macmillan.

Frankenburg, William K., Josiah B. Dodds and Alma W. Fondal. 1968. *Denver Developmental Test Screening Manual*. San Francisco: Ladoca Publishing Foundation.

Frodi, A. M. and M. E. Lamb. 1980. "Child Abusers' Responses to Infant Smiles and Cries." *Child Development* 51:238–241.

Garbarino, James and Gwenn Gilliam. 1980. *Understanding Abusive Families*. Lexington, Mass.: Lexington Books.

Garmezy, N. 1983. "Stressors of Childhood." In N. Garmezy and Michael Rutter, ed., *Stress, Coping and Development in Children*, pp. 43–84. New York: McGraw-Hill.

Gelles, Richard J. 1973. "Child Abuse as Psychopathology: A Sociological Critique and Reformulation." *American Journal of Orthopsychiatry* 43:611–621.

Gil, David G. 1970. *Violence Against Children: Physical Child Abuse in the United States*. Cambridge: Harvard University Press.

Giovanonni, Jeanne and A. Billingsley. 1970. "Child Neglect Among the Poor: A Study of Parental Adequacy in Families of Three Ethnic Groups." *Child Welfare* 49:196–204.

Goldstein, Arnold P., Harold Keller, and Diane Erne. 1985. *Changing the Abusive Parent*. Champaign, Ill.: Research Press.

Gray, Jane D., Christy A. Cutler, Janet G. Dean, and C. Henry Kempe. 1977. "Prediction and Prevention of Child Abuse and Neglect." *Child Abuse and Neglect* 1:45–58.

Green, A. H. 1976. "A Psychodynamic Approach to the Study and Treatment of Child-Abusing Parents." *Journal of the Academy of Child Psychiatry* 22:231–237.

Green, A. H. 1978. "Child Abuse." In B. B. Wolman, J. Egan, and A. Ross, eds., *Handbook of Treatment of Mental Disorders of Childhood and Adolescence*, pp. 430–455. Englewood Cliffs, N.J.: Prentice-Hall.

Hampton, Robert L. and Eli H. Newberger. 1985. "Child Abuse Incidence and Reporting by Hospitals: Significance of Severity, Class and Race." *American Journal of Public Health* 75:56–60.

Hoffman-Plotkin, D. and C. T. Twentyman. 1984. "A Multimodal Assessment of Behavioral and Cognitive Deficits in Abused and Neglected Preschoolers." *Child Development* 55:794–802.

Hudson, Walter. 1982. *The Clinical Measurement Package: A Field Manual*. Chicago: Dorsey.

Ireton, Harold and Edward Thwing. 1974. *Manual for the Minnesota Child Development Inventory*. Minneapolis: Behavioral Science Systems.

**378** *Lynn Videka-Sherman*

Kadushin, Alfred. 1980. *Child Welfare Services*, 3d ed. New York: Macmillan.

Kaufman, Joan and Edward Zigler. 1987. "Do Abused Children Become Abusive Parents?" *American Journal of Orthopsychiatry* 57:186–192.

Kazdin, A. E., J. Moser, D. Colbus, and R. Bell. 1985. "Depressive Symptoms Among Physically Abused and Psychiatrically Disturbed Children." *Journal of Abnormal Psychology* 94:298–307.

Kelly, Jeffrey A. 1983. *Treating Abusive Families: Intervention Based on Skills Training Principles*. New York: Plenum.

Kempe, Charles H. 1973. "A Practical Approach to the Protection of the Abused Child and the Rehabilitation of the Abusing Parent." *Pediatrics* 51:804–812.

Kempe, Charles H. and Roy E. Helfer. 1972. *Helping the Battered Child and His Family*. Philadelphia: Lippincott.

Kempe, Charles H., F. N. Silverman, B. F. Steele, W. Droegenmueller, and H. K. Silver. 1962. "The Battered Child Syndrome." *Journal of the American Medical Association* 181:17–24.

Lahey, B. B., R. D. Conger, B. M. Atkeson, and F. A. Treiber. 1984. "Parenting Behavior and Emotional Status of Physically Abusive Mothers." *Journal of Consulting and Clinical Psychology* 52:1062–1071.

Laughlin, John and Myra Weiss. 1981. "An Outpatient Milieu Therapy Approach to Treatment of Child Abuse and Neglect Problems." *Social Casework* 62:106–109.

Levant, Ronald F. 1982. "An Evaluation of a Structured Approach to Treating Child Abuse." Unpublished ERIC document ED211865.

Light, Richard. 1973. "Abused and Neglected Children in America: A Study of Alternative Policies." *Harvard Educational Review* 43:556–598.

Locke, H. J. and K. M. Wallace. 1959. "Short Marital Adjustment and Prediction Tests: Their Reliability and Validity. *Marriage and Family Living* 21:251–255.

Loeber, R., W. Weissman, and J. Reid. 1983. "Family Interactions of Assaultive Adolescents, Stealers and Nondelinquents." *American Journal of Abnormal Child Psychology* 11:1–14.

Lorber, R., D. Felton, and J. B. Reid. 1984. "A Social Learning Approach to the Reduction of Coercive Processes in Child Abusive Families: A Molecular Analysis." *Advances in Behavior Research and Therapy* 6:29–45.

Lutzker, John D. 1984. "Project 12-Ways: Treating Child Abuse and Neglect from an Ecobehavioral Perspective." In Robert F. Dangel and Richard A. Polster, eds., *Parent Training*, New York: Guilford.

Maccoby, E. E. and J. A. Martin 1983. "Socialization in the Context of the Family: Parent–Child Interaction." In E. M. Hetherington, Ed., *Handbook of Child Psychology*, vol. 4, pp. 1–101. New York: Wiley.

Main, M. and C. George. 1985. "Responses of Abused and Disadvantaged Toddlers to Distress in Agemates: A Study in the Day Care Setting." *Developmental Psychology* 21:407–412.

Mash, E. J., C. Johnston, and K. Kovitz. 1983. "A Comparison of the Mother–Child Interactions of Physically Abused and Non-Abused Children During Play and Task Situations." *Journal of Clinical Child Psychology* 12:337–346.

McFarlane, Kee. 1986. *Sexual Abuse of Young Children: Evaluation and Treatment*. New York: Guilford Press.

Milner, Joel S. 1986. *The Child Abuse Potential Inventory Manual*, 2d ed. Webster, N.C.: Psytech.

Milner, Joel S. and R. C. Wemberly. 1980. "Prediction and Explanation of Child Abuse. *Journal of Clinical Psychology* 36:875–884.

Minuchin, Salvador and Charles H. Fishman. 1981. *Family Therapy Techniques*. Cambridge, Mass.: Harvard University Press.

Murphy, Sara. 1988. "A Five-Year Follow-Up of Child Maltreatment Victims: Psychological Findings." In E. James Anthony and Colette Chiland, eds., *The Child in His Family*, vol. 8:386–402 *Perilous Development: Child-Raising and Identity Formation Under Stress*, New York: Wiley.

Newberger, Carolyn Moore and Edward De Vos. 1988. "Abuse and Victimization: A Life-Span Developmental Perspective." *American Journal of Orthopsychiatry* 58:505–511.

O'Connor, Susan, Peter Vietze, Kathryn Sherrod, Howard Sandler, and William Altmeier. 1980. "Reduced Incidence of Parenting Inadequacy Following Rooming in." *Pediatrics* 66:176–182.

Oldershaw, L., G. C. Walter, and D. K. Hall. 1986. "Control Strategies and Noncompliance in Abusive Mother–Child Dyads: An Observational Study." *Child Development* 57:722–732.

Olds, David L., Charles R. Henderson, Robert Chamberlin, and Robert Tatelbaum. 1986. "Preventing Child Abuse and Neglect: A Randomized Trial of Nurse Home Visitation." *Pediatrics* 78:65–78.

Olsen, L. J. and W. M. Holmes. 1986. "Youth at Risk: Adolescents and Maltreatment." *Children and Youth Services Review* 8:13–35.

Parke, R. D. and C. W. Collmer. 1975. "Child Abuse: An Interdisciplinary Analysis." In E. M. Hetherington, ed., *Review of Child Development Research*, vol. 5. Chicago: University of Chicago Press.

Patterson, Gerald R. 1982. *Coercive Family Processes*. Eugene, Ore.: Castalia.

Pelton, Leroy H. 1978. "Child Abuse and Neglect: The Myth of Classlessness." *American Journal of Orthopsychiatry* 48:608–617.

Pianta, Robert C., Byron Egeland, and Amanda Hyatt. 1986. "Maternal Relationship History as an Indicator of Developmental Risk." *American Journal of Orthopsychiatry* 56:385–398.

Polansky, Norman A., Mary Ann Chalmers, Elizabeth Buttenwieser, and David P. Williams. 1981. *Damaged Parents*. Chicago: University of Chicago Press.

Price, Richard H., Emory L. Cowan, Raymond P. Lorion, and Julia Ramos-McKay. 1989. "The Search for Effective Prevention Programs: What We Have Learned Along the Way." *American Journal of Orthopsychiatry* 59:49–58.

Reuter, Jeanette and Laura Bickett. 1985. *The Kent Infant Development Scale* (KIDS) Kent, Ohio: Kent Development Metrics.

Rosenberg, M. S. and N. D. Rappucci. 1983. "Abusive Mothers: Perceptions of Their Own Children's Behavior." *Journal of Consulting and Clinical Psychology* 51:674–682.

Rutter, M. 1983. "Stress, Coping and Development: Some Issues and Some Questions." In N. Garmezy and M. Rutter, eds., *Stress, Coping and Development in Children*, pp. 1–41. New York: McGraw-Hill.

Schneider-Rosen, Karen and Dante Cicchetti. 1984. "The Relationship Between Affect and Cognition in Maltreated Infants: Quality of Attachment and the Development of Visual Self-Recognition." *Child Development* 55:648–658.

Seligman, Martin E. P. 1975. *Helplessness: On Depression, Development and Death*. San Francisco: Freeman.

Sgroi, Suzanne M., ed. 1988. *Vulnerable Populations: Evaluation and Treatment of Sexually Abused Children and Adult Survivors*. Lexington, Mass.: Lexington Books.

Sherman, Barry R. 1989. "Preventing Child Abuse and Neglect: Prenatal-Postnatal Paraprofessional Home Visitation for At-Risk Parenting Adolescents." Research in progress, New York State Department of Health.

Skinner, A. and R. Castle. 1969. *78 Battered Children*. London: National Society for Prevention of Cruelty to Children.

Smith, S. M., R. Hanson, and S. Noble. 1974. "Social Aspects of the Battered Baby Syndrome." *British Journal of Psychiatry* 125:568–582.

Spanier, G. 1987. "Scales for Assessing the Quality of Marriage and Similar Dyads." In K. Corcoran and S. Fischer, eds., *Measures for Clinical Practice: A Source Book*, p. 424. New York: Free Press.

Spinetta, J. J. 1978. "Parental Personality Factors in Child Abuse." *Journal of Consulting and Clinical Psychology* 46:1409–1414.

Spinetta, J. J. and D. Rigler. 1972. "The Child Abusing Parent: A Psychological Review." *Psychological Bulletin* 77:296–304.

Starr, Raymond H., Jr. 1982. "A Research-Based Approach to the Prediction of Child Abuse." In Raymond H. Starr, Jr., ed., *Child Abuse Prediction: Policy Implications*, pp. 105–134. Cambridge, Mass.: Ballinger.

Steele, B. J. and C. Pollack. 1968. "A Psychiatric Study of Parents Who Abuse Infants and Small Children." In R. Helfer and Charles H. Kempe, eds., *The Battered Child*, 86–102. Chicago: University of Chicago Press.

Stein, Theodore, Eileen Gambrill, and K. Wiltse. 1974. "Foster Care: The Rise of Contracts." *Public Welfare* 20–25.

Stevens-Long, J. E. 1973. "The Effect of Behavioral Context on Some Aspects of Adult Disciplinary Practice and Effort." *Child Development* 44: 476–484.

Straus, Murray and Richard J. Gelles. 1987. "Is Child Abuse Increasing? Evidence from the National Family Violence Resurvey." Paper presented at the 11th Annual Meeting of the American Association for Protecting Children, Austin, Texas.

Straus, Murray A., Richard J. Gelles, and S. Steinmetz. 1980. *Behind Closed Doors: Violence in the American Family*. Garden City, N.Y.: Doubleday/Anchor.

Sussman, E. J., P. K. Trickett, R. J. Ianotti, B. E. Hollenbeck, and C. Zahn-Wexler. 1985. "Child-Rearing Patterns in Depressed, Abusive and Normal Mothers." *American Journal of Orthopsychiatry* 55:237–251.

Tarter, R. E., A. E. Hegedus, N. E. Winsten, A. I. Alterman. 1984. "Neuropsychological, Personality and Familial Characteristics of Physically Abused Delinquents." *Journal of the American Academy of Child Psychiatry* 23:668–674.

Tertinger, Deborah A., Brandon F. Greene, and John R. Lutzker. 1984. "Home Safety: Development and Validation of One Component of an Ecobehavioral Treatment Program for Abused and Neglected Children." *Journal of Applied Behavior Analysis* 17:159–174.

U.S. HHS (U.S. Department of Health and Human Services). 1988. *Study Findings: Study of the National Incidence and Prevalence of Child Abuse and Neglect*. Washington, D.C.: U.S. HHS.

Uohara, Betsy. Undated. "Implementation and Maintenance of a High Risk Early Identification Project for Child Abuse Prevention." Unpublished manuscript, Honolulu, Hawaii.

Videka-Sherman, Lynn. 1989. *Effective Interventions for Child Abuse and Neglect*. Final Report to the National Center on Child Abuse and Neglect, unpublished.

Videka-Sherman, Lynn. In press. "Intervention for Child Neglect: The Empirical Knowledge Base." In H. Howerton, ed., *Current Issues in Child Neglect*. Rockville, Md.: Aspen Systems.

Wahler, R. G. and D. M. Hann. 1984. "The Communication Patterns of Troubled Mothers: In Search of a Keystone in the Generalization of Parenting Skills." *Education and Treatment of Children* 7:335–350.

Wauchope, Barbara A. and Murray Straus. 1987. "Age, Gender and Class Differences in Physical Punishment and Physical Abuse of American Children." Paper presented at the 3d National Conference on Family Violence Research, Durham, N.H.

Weiss, Heather B. 1989. "State Family Support and Education Programs: Lessons from the Pioneers." *American Journal of Orthopsychiatry* 59:32–48.

Weissbourd, B. and S. Kagan. 1989. "Family Support Programs: Catalysts for Change." *American Journal of Orthopsychiatry* 59:20–31.

Widom, Cathy Spatz. 1989. "Sampling Biases and Implications for Child Abuse Research." *American Journal of Orthopsychiatry* 58:260–270.

Wolfe, David. 1985. "Child Abusive Parents: An Empirical Review and Analysis." *Psychological Bulletin* 97:462–482.

Wolfe, David. 1987. *Child Abuse: Implications for Child Development and Psychopathology.* Newbury Park, Calif.: Sage.

Wolfe, David, Keith Kaufman, John Aragona, and Jack Sandler. 1981. *The Child Management Program for Abusive Parents.* Winter Park, Fla.: Anna.

Wolfe, David, Jack Sandler, and Keith Kaufman. 1981. "A Competency-Based Parent Training Program for Abusive Parents." *Journal of Consulting and Clinical Psychology* 49:633–640.

Wolfe, David A., J. Fairbank, J. A. Kelly, and A. S. Bradlyn. 1983. "Child Abusive Parents' Physiological Responses to Stressful and Nonstressful Behavior in Children." *Behavioral Assessment* 5:363–371.

Wood, Katherin M. and Ludwig Geismer. 1989. *Families at Risk: Treating the Multiproblem Family.* New York: Human Sciences Press.

Zigler, Edward and Kathryn B. Black. 1989. "America's Family Support Movement: Strengths and Limitations." *American Journal of Orthopsychiatry* 59:6–19.

Zuravin, Susan. 1985. "The Relationship Between the Various Types of Mental Illness and Child Neglect." Paper presented at the Child Neglect Symposium, Chicago.

# 12

## Children in Foster Care

▼

BRENDA G. MCGOWAN

EMILY STUTZ

From the earliest days of civilization, every society has had to develop some means of dealing with young children whose parents are unable or unwilling to provide adequate care. At various times in recorded history, children have been sold into slavery, donated to monasteries and convents under a process known as oblation, or left to die of exposure. Abandonment in public places was common from the days of imperial Rome until the end of the Middle Ages, when foundling hospitals were established in most European cities. Although this development marked a shift from reliance on the "kindness of strangers" to the allocation of responsibility to public institutions for the care of homeless children, the custom of abandoning children persisted. In Paris in the late eighteenth century, 20 to 30 percent of the recorded births resulted in abandonment (Boswell 1988). Thus, it is not surprising that we in the United States must still struggle with the task of finding appropriate solutions for children whose parents do not provide needed care.

Early social provisions for dependent children in this country derived from the English Poor Law tradition and relied heavily on a combination of poorhouses or orphanages for young children in urban areas and indenture or farming out for youth who could be taught a

This chapter is based in part on data collected for a study funded by the Foundation for Child Development. The authors also want to express their appreciation to Sister Mary Paul Janchill of the Center for Family Life in Sunset Park, New York. She is responsible for conceptualizing and developing the core-satellite foster care program described in the chapter as well as many other important innovations in child welfare practice.

trade. Although the number of orphanages expanded rapidly in the early nineteenth century, there was no significant change in the pattern of care for young children until Charles Loring Brace established the Children's Aid Society in New York in 1853. Concerned about the need to protect poor children from the evils of urban life, Brace recruited large numbers of free foster homes in Upstate New York and the Midwest and sent trainloads of homeless or destitute children to these localities. This program was closely paralleled by the Children's Home Society, first established by Martin Van Buren Van Arsdale in Illinois in 1883, and by the end of the century, free foster home care had become a well-established means of providing for dependent children. At the same time, many communities continued to place large numbers of children in orphanages or institutions, in part because of the concern of Roman Catholic and Jewish leaders about protecting children's religious heritage. Although most of the large children's residential institutions have been converted in recent years to smaller facilities with more specialized functions, these two traditions of foster family care and residential group care continue today as the primary societal mechanisms for caring for dependent children.

The term *foster care* is now commonly used to describe both family-based and congregate care settings, thus incorporating a wide range of substitute living arrangements for children whose parents are unable to provide adequate care temporarily or permanently. Foster care is customarily distinguished from other types of temporary substitute care for children by the fact that it involves a change of legal custody. It is distinguished from adoption by the fact that adoption involves a permanent change of legal guardianship as well as custody.

## PROBLEM DOMAIN

National data about children in foster care are limited because the federal government has made no effort in recent years to collect systematic data on this population or even to establish standard definitions and procedures for data collection so that state statistics can be readily aggregated. The best available data are gathered by the Voluntary Cooperative Information System (VCIS) for the American Public Welfare Association, which indicated that the states reported approximately 276,000 children in care at the end of fiscal year 1985.[1] A total of 460,000 were in care at some time that year, with an estimated 190,000 entering care and an estimated 184,000 being discharged during the year. The national prevalence rate for children in foster care was 3.7, meaning that for every 1,000 children in the country, 3.7 were in placement at the end of fiscal 1985 (Tatara 1988).

All available indicators suggest that the number entering care may have increased and the number leaving care decreased sharply since that time. For example, the number in care in New York City was expected to increase over 40 percent from the end of fiscal year 1985 to the end of 1989 (SSC 1989: Tables 1 and 3). Kamerman and Kahn (1989) reported that the respondents in their study indicated increasing numbers of young children entering care. And the Children's Defense Fund (1989:46) estimated that if current trends persisted, the total number of children and adolescents in care would increase to half a million by the year 2000.

Over half (58.9 percent) of the children who entered care in twenty-one reporting states in fiscal year 1985 had been placed because of child abuse or neglect; 16.4 percent had entered because of a parental condition or absence; 9.5 percent had been placed because of a status offense or delinquent behavior; and only 2.0 percent had entered care because of the child's disability (Tatara 1988). These findings indicate that foster care placements now occur primarily as a consequence of protective service investigation and that the vast majority enter care because of inadequacies in parental functioning, not because of their own behavioral problems or developmental needs.

Data from twenty-five reporting states indicate that one quarter of those who entered care in fiscal year 1985 were reentrants, meaning that they had been in care at least once during the previous year (Tartara 1988). Given the known trauma that repeated separations can create for children, this is a very troubling finding. No information is available about the proportion of children who may have had placements in previous years.

Well over half (65.3 percent) of the children who were discharged from care in fiscal year 1985 in thirty reporting states were reunited with parents or relatives; 8.8 percent were placed for adoption; 9.0 percent had reached the age of majority or had been emancipated; and 13.5 percent were discharged for other reasons, such as running away, death, incarceration, marriage, or transfer to another public agency. The median length of stay in foster care before discharge was 8.9 months (Tatara 1988). What is not known is the degree to which the problems that necessitated placement were resolved prior to discharge.

Table 12.1 presents selected demographic characteristics of the children in care at the end of fiscal year 1985 as reported by the Voluntary Cooperative Information Service. The picture that emerges from these data suggests that foster children are disproportionately

**TABLE 12.1.** Characteristics of Children in Foster Care at the End of FY 1985

Age ($N = 32$)[a]

| Under 1 Year | 1–5 Years | 6–12 Years | 13–18 Years |
|---|---|---|---|
| 3.4% | 22.4% | 28.7% | 42.4%[b] |

Sex ($N = 43$)

| Male | Female |
|---|---|
| 51.5% | 48.4% |

Race/Ethnicity ($N = 38$)

| White | Black | Hispanic | Other |
|---|---|---|---|
| 51.9% | 33.4% | 8.6% | 5.1% |

Living Arrangements ($N = 33$)

| Foster Home | Group Home | Child Care Facility |
|---|---|---|
| 65.4% | 6.1% | 13.2% |

Disabling Condition(s) ($N = 29$)

| One or More | None |
|---|---|
| 19.6% | 78.7% |

Total Number of Placements ($N = 23$)

| One | Two | Three/Four | Six or More |
|---|---|---|---|
| 51.3% | 22.2% | 20.3% | 5.8% |

Continuous Time in Placement ($N = 31$)

| 0–12 Months | 1–2 Years | 2–5 Years | 5 Years or More |
|---|---|---|---|
| 39.4% | 21.5% | 23.7% | 14.4% |

Permanency Planning Objective ($N = 29$)

| Discharge to Relatives | Adoption | Independent Living | Long-Term Foster care |
|---|---|---|---|
| 57.1% | 13.1% | 7.9% | 14.9% |

SOURCE: Toshio Tatara. 1988. *Characteristics of Children in Substitute and Adoptive Care* (July). Washington, D.C.: American Public Welfare Association.

[a] $N$ = Number of states reporting on each characteristic.

[b] Percentages do not add to 100 because unknowns and very small proportions have been eliminated.

adolescent minority-group members. Although most were placed because of inadequacies in parental functioning, one out of five had a disabling condition. One fourth of the children had had three or more placements, and well over one third had been in care longer than two years. These findings, together with the fact that one-fourth of those entering care had been in placement previously, raise a serious question about the amount of stability that foster care provides children.

Although foster care services developed as a solution to the needs of children who cannot remain with their own parents, the use of substitute care inevitably creates other problems. The term *foster care* itself has acquired a negative connotation for many foster children over the years because it implies a difference, and children do not like to be perceived as different. In a follow-up study of former foster children, Festinger (1983:273) reported that almost three out of five indicated there were times when they had not wanted to acknowledge that they were foster children. One of her respondents said, " 'Foster' sounds like a disease," and another commented, "you don't feel like an average kid." The discomfort that many foster children feel about their status has been compounded in recent years by changing attitudes regarding the viability of foster care as a solution for children who cannot be raised by their own parents.

As professional knowledge about the importance of the parent–child relationship and children's need for continuity and stability expanded and as the costs of maintaining children in foster care increased, public officials, researchers, and advocates alike began to criticize child welfare agencies for their tendency to allow foster care to drift in foster care, moving from one placement to another with no clear plan for discharge, either to their own families or to an adoptive home. The first real challenge to foster care in this country was posed in 1959 in Maas and Engler's study of children in foster care in nine communities. Their criticisms were echoed repeatedly and reached a crescendo in the late 1970s with the issuance of a number of influential reports (see, for example, Fanshel and Shinn 1972; TSCCW 1975; Vasaly 1976; Gruber 1978; Knitzer, Allen, and McGowan 1978; Persico 1979).

The purpose of foster care has since been redefined so that it is now commonly viewed, not as an open-ended option available until children reach majority, but as a temporary, planned service that should be used only when preventive services have failed and until more permanent living plans can be developed. Social work practice in foster care is now guided by the concept of *permanency planning,* which is defined as "a set of goal-directed activities designed to help children live in families that offer continuity of relationships with nurturing parents or caretakers and the opportunity to establish lifetime relationships" (Maluccio, Fein, and Olmstead 1986:5). This shift in perception of the purpose of foster care has been beneficial in forcing attention to the need for expanded services to biological parents and potential adoptive families, but it has also had the unfortunate effect of undermining the viability of long-term foster care as an appropriate option for selected youth and of conveying a pejorative view of the service to foster care, foster parents, and foster care workers alike.

As this changing perspective demonstrates, foster care is by definition a socially prescribed phenomenon and can be understood only in this context. The stresses in family functioning that bring children to the attention of child welfare authorities are a direct reflection of socioeconomic problems and racial and gender inequalities in the larger society. Moreover, the way children's needs are defined and the types of legal and service protections they are offered vary over time in accord with the prevailing norms of the communities in which they reside. Parents' and children's rights are both relative concepts, as are definitions of adequate parenting. Consequently, social service agencies and courts have great latitude and are heavily influenced by structural variables in determining when and under what circumstances children should enter and leave foster care. One need only read Billingsley and Giovannoni's history (1972) of child welfare services for black children in the United States to understand the ways in which racism has shaped service provision or Gordon's study (1988) of changing responses to family violence from 1880 to 1960 to understand how the politics of family life influence problem definition.

What has not changed significantly over time is the fact that foster care is essentially a service for poor children. Although the specific reasons for children's entering substitute care and types of care provided have varied throughout history, the problems necessitating placement have seldom been child-related. Instead, they have usually reflected inadequacies in parental functioning commonly associated with poverty. Thus, as Jenkins (1974) suggested, foster care must be understood in part as a class system that attempts to compensate for deficiencies in the social structure. Since there is little evidence that placement of children in foster care contributes to upward mobility for the children or their biological parents, foster care may actually contribute to maintaining the status quo. The very availability of substitute care resources deflects attention from the structural problems such as poverty, unemployment and homelessness that undermine parental capacity to provide adequate care.

At the same time, history suggests that society will always need some type of substitute care provision for children who cannot remain with their own parents. Although increased efforts to reduce socioeconomic deficits would undoubtedly decrease the number of children requiring foster care, structural changes alone cannot ensure equitable distribution of the emotional, cognitive, and physical resources also required for adequate parenting. Thus, some need for foster care services must be anticipated as long as the country maintains even minimal standards for child nurturance and protection. And because foster care *is* different and necessarily implies some deficit in family functioning, children in placement and their biological parents will always present special service needs.

## SOCIETAL CONTEXT

Although social workers have traditionally assumed primary responsibility for the administration and delivery of foster care services, their practice is structured in large measure by 1) social problems in the larger society that shape the size and nature of the population entering care and 2) federal and state laws and regulations governing the conditions under which children can or must be placed in foster care and the actions taken on their behalf.

As suggested above, poverty and minority ethnic status have long been recognized as variables that contribute disproportionately to the risk of children entering and remaining in foster care. In an effort to examine these associations in more detail, Jenkins and Diamond (1985) conducted an analysis of samples drawn from data sets compiled for the 1980 Office of Civil Rights Children and Youth Referral Survey and the 1980 United States Census. Their findings confirmed the general hypothesis that foster care as an institution reflects prevailing patterns of social and economic disorganization, demonstrating significant interactions among race, percentage of children in a county living in poverty, placement rate, and length of stay in foster care. They also discovered important differences in placement patterns between large cities and other areas, suggesting that urban foster care systems may experience special problems that disadvantage all children equally.

These patterns reflect longstanding structural problems in this country that influence the delivery of foster care services. However, it is also important for social workers to recognize the ways in which recent changes in social policy shape the service needs of children entering foster care and their parents. In the 1980s, low-income families across the country suffered the consequences of the Reagan administration's mean-spirited campaign to cripple and/or dismantle many of the federal programs established to strengthen family life and enhance child development. These efforts to strip families of needed resources have been widely documented and need not be repeated here. What is important to note is that the stresses of poverty contribute to the risk of family dysfunction and child placement. In families headed by young adults today, one in three children is poor. Poverty rates increased among children in all ethnic groups during the 1980s, and if present trends continue, all of the growth in the child population between now and the year 2000 will consist of poor children. There is a wider gap between the rich and poor today than at any time since the Census Bureau started gathering data in 1947 (CDF 1989:16–17). Thus, it is not surprising that the number of children in foster care has again started to increase.

Three problems associated with poverty—homelessness, maternal substance abuse, and AIDS—are also placing enormous demands on child welfare agencies today, especially in urban areas, and these stresses are expected to increase. These problems are of such recent origin that there are few systematic data available about their prevalence. However, the Select Committee on Children, Youth and Families of the U.S. House of Representatives has held hearings on each of these topics, and anecdotal evidence from across the country underscores the need for foster care agencies to anticipate serving increasing numbers of children exposed to one or more of these risks (see *The Crisis in Homelessness* 1987; *Continuing Jeopardy: Children and AIDS* 1988; and "Born Hooked: Confronting the Impact of Perinatal Substance Abuse" 1989). There are no ready solutions to any of these problems, nor does anyone really know their long-term consequences. Thus, child welfare workers in the 1990s must be prepared to deal with many unknowns and to "invent interventions" (Rosenfeld 1983) in order to address the needs of children and families exposed to these new hazards.

*Legal framework for service provision.* Unlike social workers in most other settings, those working with children in foster care have explicit legal responsibilities. These duties are imposed as a consequence of the transfer of legal custody from a child's biological parents to the local state authority. In making decisions and taking actions on behalf of a foster child, workers are acting as an agent of the state. Therefore, they must observe the laws and regulations set out to ensure that the state will fulfill its obligations under the doctrine of *parens patriae*, which gives the state the ultimate responsibility for protecting the welfare of all children.

State responsibilities for children are embodied in federal and state law, administrative regulations, and court decisions. All social workers in foster care must be familiar with the core components of two federal laws that set the basic framework for the current provisions of foster care services: Child Abuse Prevention and Treatment Act of 1974 (P.L. 93-247) and Adoption Assistance and Child Welfare Act of 1989 (P.L. 96-272).

Although protective services for children were initiated in the late nineteenth century with the establishment in a number of urban areas of Societies for the Prevention of Cruelty to Children, there were no federal laws guiding the provision of protective services until the passage of the Child Abuse Prevention and Treatment Act of 1974. A response to media exposés and agitation in the medical community about the newly identified "battered-child syndrome," this act established the National Center on Child Abuse and Neglect. It also provided limited funding for demonstration projects to states that comply with a series of regulations related to the establishment of statewide systems for reporting and investigating reports of suspected child abuse and neglect.

Although the title of this act implies legislative concern about prevention and treatment, the implementing regulations focus attention almost entirely on mandatory reporting and investigation. Moreover, the law fails to define precisely what is meant by *child abuse* and *neglect* or to specify the evidential standards for reporting. As a consequence, the primary effect of the law has been to enlarge the number of reports and investigations of child maltreatment, not to provide the resources or guidelines required for states to serve these cases more adequately.

Despite its limited scope and funding, this law has had a tremendous impact on the delivery of child welfare services across the country. All states have some type of mandatory reporting law that requires social workers as well as many other human service professionals to report suspected incidents of child abuse or neglect and that grants immunity from civil or criminal liability to those who make such reports. According to the American Association for Protecting Children, reports of suspected child maltreatment increased 158 percent from 1976 to 1984 (Daro 1988:13). There were approximately 2.2 million reports filed in 1986 (CDF 1989:47), and the numbers have been climbing.

Although not all reports of child abuse or neglect are substantiated (estimates of substantiation range from about 40 to 60 percent), enormous resources must be devoted simply to investigating these complaints. Consequently, public child welfare agencies across the country are increasingly preoccupied with their investigatory responsibilities. (*Child Abuse and Neglect in America* 1987). Based on a study of social services at twenty-two sites, Kamerman and Kahn noted, "Child protective services today constitute the core public child and family service, the fulcrum, and sometimes, in some places, the totality of the system" (1989:10). This shift in emphasis has obvious implications for the nature of social work practice in child welfare and the quality of service provision to children in foster care.

The Adoption Assistance and Child Welfare Act of 1980 (P.L. 96-272) was enacted after several years of congressional reform efforts aimed at addressing the well-documented problems in foster care mentioned above. Supported by a broad coalition of public officials, child advocates, child welfare professionals, and client organizations, this act amended Title IVB of the Social Security Law and replaced the Aid to Families with Dependent Children (AFDC) Foster Care Program with a new Title IVE, Foster Care and Adoption Assistance Program. It adopts what Allen and Knitzer have described as "a carrot-and-stick approach to redirect funds away from inappropriate, often costly, out-of-home care and toward alternatives to placement" (1983:120). Passage of this act made prevention of placement and permanency planning explicit objectives of federal child welfare policy. Moreover, by requiring states to establish standards and procedures consonant with the law in order to be eligible for federal funding, P.L. 96-272 ensures that these objectives will become the explicit policy of the state agencies responsible for the delivery of child welfare studies.

The standards established require the states to establish case review mechanisms—with judicial determination of need and opportunity for parental participation at specified intervals—to ensure that reasonable efforts are made to prevent placement, to arrange placement in the most appropriate setting, and to discharge children to permanent homes in a timely manner. Case planning must ensure that placement is arranged "in the last restrictive, most family-like setting available located in close proximity to the parents' home, consistent with the best interests and needs of the child." Also the law requires that the states establish statewide information systems.

There was great optimism surrounding the passage of this law, and a decline in the foster care population during the early 1980s pointed to its potential efficacy. However, numerous problems related to staff limitations and resource shortages—and perhaps even the viability of some of the assumptions underlying P.L. 96–272—have limited the capacity of the states to implement the intent of this legislation. (*Continuing Crisis in Foster Care* 1987).

Although social workers generally support the intent of this law, its implementation has created many strains for practitioners. One difficulty is that the increased demands for monitoring and accountability have resulted in an enormous expansion in reporting requirements. Many of the procedural protections designed to safeguard the interests of children and parents have been utilized in a *pro forma* way that increases workers' paperwork but does little to enhance the quality of the services they deliver. A second, related problem derives from the need for multiple administrative and court reviews of the status of children in care. These reviews inevitably press toward standardization of decision making, thereby decreasing workers' sense of professional autonomy and their capacity to develop carefully individualized intervention plans. Finally, in a system in which success is measured in part by reduction of foster care, not by reduction of the familial and social problems leading to placement, social workers are now confronted at times by situations in which they are ordered to implement discharge or adoption plans that they do not think are in the best interests of their clients.

## RISKS AND NEEDS OF POPULATION

All children in foster care, almost by definition, are children at risk. They generally come from low-income families with a high incidence of socioeconomic, physical, and emotional problems. They have frequently been exposed to repeated physical and sexual abuse and/or neglect. And many display serious developmental delays and behavioral problems. Compounding these disadvantages is the fact that these children have all been exposed to the trauma of at least one separation from a parent or parent figure and frequently more. Consequently, they often live in a state of limbo, uncertain about who is going to be caring for them or where they will live in the future.

In view of these enormous stresses, it is not surprising that former foster children tend to be overrepresented among runaways, prisoners, welfare recipients, and other "problem" groups. What is more remarkable is that repeated research has demonstrated that most current and former foster children function quite adequately, especially if they are compared to others from similarly troubled backgrounds. (for reviews of relevant research, see, for example, Fanshel and Shinn 1978; Festinger 1983; Kadushin and Martin 1988; Maluccio and Fein 1985).

However, most of the research on the impact of foster care was conducted on children who were in placement prior to passage of P.L. 96–272. As a consequence of the subsequent emphasis on permanency planning, child welfare agencies in recent years have made a strong effort to reunite children with their biological parents or place them in adoptive families as quickly as possible rather than allowing them to grow up in foster care. This trend poses some difficult questions about the comparative impact of these alternative placement outcomes. Several recent reviews of research on this topic have concluded that family reunification is not necessarily a permanent plan. Recidivism or replacement in foster care has increased with increased efforts to achieve early discharge (Rzepnicki 1987) and now occurs in approximately one quarter to one third of all cases (Seltzer and Bloksberg 1987:67). Moreover, a review of recent research on placement outcomes suggests that although family reunification may be most desirable from a value perspective, it is the option least likely to protect children from abuse and to promote developmental well-being (Barth and Berry 1987:82). These findings point clearly to the fact that former foster children who are reunited with their biological families continue to be very much at risk and in need of ongoing services.

Although adoption tends to be a much more stable plan for children who have been in foster care (Seltzer and Bloksberg 1987), in a large sample study in California, Barth (1988a) found a disruption rate of 10 percent in adoptions of children over the age of 3. As might be expected, the likelihood of disruption was higher if the children were older, had had a previous adoptive placement, had a number of problems, or were adopted by someone other than their foster parents. These findings again suggest that the risks for children in foster care do not end with implementation of a permanency plan and that follow-up services are needed, especially for those most likely to reenter foster care.

Unfortunately, because of the historic tendency to treat foster children as a unitary population, relatively little is known about the risks of various subgroups in care. All foster children are at somewhat higher risk of suffering abuse and/or neglect from their caretakers than are other children (Mushlin 1988). But the risk that they face more frequently is that of poor school performance. This educational deficit has been documented consistently in almost every study of the well-being of current and former foster children. Comparing a national random study of children in foster care to the national population in 1977, Gershenson and Kresh (1986:6) found that only 59 percent of children in foster care were at the modal age for their grade, compared to 80 percent of the general child population and 69 percent of those receiving child welfare services in their own homes.

A risk that has troubled child welfare experts for many years but is much harder to document relates to foster children's self-image and their capacity to handle the trauma of separation and to form other meaningful attachments. The first study of this topic (Weinstein 1960) concluded that foster children's understanding of their placement situation was an important predictor of well-being. More recent studies have highlighted the value of children who grow up in foster care retaining contact with their foster and birth parents (Barth 1986b). Unfortunately, there is much that the profession still does not understand about psychological development and how this may be affected by foster placement. As Fanshel and Shinn concluded, despite their finding that children who remain in care do not fare badly compared to those who are reunited with their families, "we are not sure that our procedures have captured the potential feeling of pain and impaired self-image that can be created by impermanent status in foster care" (1978:479).

The findings from a recent longitudinal study of children in long-term foster care in a large, voluntary agency provide some basis for beginning to identify subgroups that may be at particular risk. The authors (Fanshel, Finch, and Grundy 1989) found that the more volatility children entering care in this agency had experienced in their prior living arrangements (number of placements, number of foster parents, and number of returns to birth parents), the more hostile and oppositional they were at intake. Moreover, the degree of children's hostility at entry was the best predictor of their adjustment in care, and this, in turn, was the best predictor of their condition at discharge and subsequent adult adjustment. Few of children's other experiences prior to placement added any explanatory power. This finding raises a serious question about the current practice of searching endlessly for a permanency plan for children who are unlikely to be returned home or placed for adoption successfully and suggests instead that efforts should be directed toward stabilizing such children in long-term foster care. It also highlights the potential importance of early clinical intervention designed to reduce the anger and oppositional behavior of children who are hostile at intake.

## PROGRAMS AND SOCIAL WORK SERVICES

Foster care services are provided by both public and private child care agencies. Although any licensed agency can provide foster care for a child whose parents sign a voluntary placement agreement, court approval of the placement plan is required to secure public subsidy for the costs of placement. The local public department of social services or its equivalent is ordinarily responsible for determining whether involuntary placement is required and for securing the necessary court order. The public department may provide care directly through a foster home or group residence administered under its auspice, or it may contract for the provision of care with a licensed private agency. Since the vast majority of foster placements are ordered on an involuntary basis, it can be assumed that most placements are now arranged through a public agency. Moreover, all publicly financed foster placements are now subject to periodic administrative and court reviews. This recent shift in the legal framework has had a significant impact on the way foster care programs are organized.

Traditionally, the only service provided by many child welfare agencies was foster care. Starting in the 1920s, increasing numbers of these agencies began to offer adoption services, primarily for healthy white infants. Adoption services were expanded in the late 1960s as agencies began to seek adoptive homes for children formerly defined as "hard to place," i.e., older children, minority children, and those with physical handicaps or developmental disabilities. It was not until the 1970s that many child welfare agencies began to offer in-home services to families in which children were at risk of placement as well as to those whose children were in care.

P.L. 96–272 mandates that foster care today be viewed as part of a continuum of services to families in which parents need help in order to fulfill their basic role responsibilities. This service continuum includes supportive, supplementary, and substitute care services. Supportive services, often referred to as *preventive* or *home-based services*, are designed to strengthen parent and child functioning. They include various types of individual, family, and group counseling and education as well as a range of community advocacy efforts and concrete services.

Supplementary services are distinguished from supportive services by the fact that they are designed to fulfill at least part of parents' normal role responsibilities. Instead of aiming solely to strengthen the family, these services actually take some role in the family system (Kadushin and Martin 1988:143). The primary supplementary services are child care (full day and after-school programs) and home-maker–home help aides.

Substitute care services, which include both foster care and adoption, are designed to ensure that all parental responsibilities will be fulfilled in a setting apart from that of the birth parent(s). They include a wide range of placement options:

*Emergency Shelter:* Group residence where children may live up to thirty days until a more permanent placement can be arranged.

*Diagnostic Center:* Group residence where interdisciplinary staff conducts a full range of clinical evaluations and recommends appropriate treatment plan.

*Foster Boarding Home:* Licensed private family home in which parent(s) are paid a small per diem fee to provide care for up to six children in a "normal" family environment. (An adoptive family home prior to court approval of final adoption is technically one type of foster boarding home, but it is commonly referred to as a *preadoptive home.*)

*Agency-Operated Boarding Home:* Neighborhood-based home that provides care for up to six children in a familylike atmosphere in which the foster parents are paid a salary and the residence is maintained by the sponsoring agency.

*Group Home:* Neighborhood-based residence that provides care for six to twelve children in a group setting supervised by agency child care workers.

*Group Residence:* Neighborhood-based residence that provides care for thirteen to twenty-five youngsters in a group setting that is supervised by agency child care workers and ordinarily has social work and/or other clinical staff on site.

*Child Care Institution:* Residential facility that provides care for more than twenty-five children in a setting that is separated from the community and often maintains educational, medical, recreational, and social services on site.

*Residential Treatment Center:* Residential group facility with an interdisciplinary professional staff that provides care, education, and treatment on site for children who are emotionally disturbed or developmentally disabled.

Although a full continuum of services is required to fulfill the mandates of P.L. 96–272 and to ensure that an appropriate package of services will be offered to each child and family at risk, it is easier to conceptualize than to implement. Because of the vagaries of historical tradition and current funding patterns, few social agencies provide the required range of services. Instead, most administer one or a few specialized service programs. As a consequence families must often seek services from several agencies simultaneously and experience multiple changes of worker and agency as their service needs change over time. In this context, if often becomes increasingly difficult for foster care workers to provide the services required to effect family reunification in a timely manner, and parents tend to become increasingly distanced from their children in placement.

An innovative program designed to address these problems was initiated recently by a neighborhood family service center in New York City. Located in a low-income Hispanic community of about 90,000, the center was established in 1978 as a preventive service program designed to sustain children in their own homes. Open to all families with children under 19 who reside in the community, it offers a wide range of services, including individual, family, and group counseling; a number of activity groups for parents and children; an advocacy clinic; an emergency food program; a foster grandparent program; a summer day camp; after-school child care at two local elementary schools; a teen evening center; an infant–toddler stimulation program; a mother–young child activity group; an employment program for adults; and educational forums for parents.

Concerned about the difficulties the staff experienced in trying to work with other agencies to arrange appropriate, accessible foster placements for children who could not be maintained in their own homes, the center administrators decided to open a pilot neighborhood-based foster home program for children in the community. Called a *core-satellite model*, this program recruits foster homes in the neighborhood to serve children from the community who are in need of placement. The foster homes are conceptualized as satellites of the center, and all of its services are available to the foster children and their biological and foster parents. Frequent visiting is encouraged so that birth parents can fulfill as many of their traditional parental responsibilities as possible. For example, a mother might be encouraged to walk her child to school or to attend a parent–toddler play group with her child. Following reunification, the families can continue as clients of the center's family service program. The same social worker is responsible for arranging the placement and providing ongoing services to the foster and biological families during the placement and, if appropriate, after discharge.

The program was envisioned as offering several key advantages over the traditional pattern for foster care placements: 1) by placing children in close geographic proximity to their homes, frequent visiting can be encouraged, thus reducing the trauma of separation; 2) if large sibling groups cannot be placed together, they can at least be placed within easy walking distance of each other so that sibling ties are not disrupted; 3) children who are separated from their parents do not have to separate from their neighbors, friends, school, and other supportive aspects of their home environment; 4) the foster care worker can move quickly to initiate the full range of supportive and remedial services required to ensure that families will be reunited quickly; 5) the model is economical because it utilizes resources already available in the community and saves the time often spent in travel; 6) the potential for matching foster parents and biological parents along racial, ethnic, social class, and other lines is enhanced when they are members of the same community; 7) work with community institutions during the placement period (e.g., schools, health facilities, and day care) paves the way for better relationships with these institutions after discharge; and 8) there can be a natural transition from substitute to home care when parents are encouraged to assume increasing responsibility for their children in care, and continuity of service relationships is ensured during the critical early discharge period by linking the foster care and community-based service programs ("Shaping Foster Care as a Community Service" 1989:3–4).

This is a small program serving a total of thirty-six children in seventeen foster homes during its first year. Moreover, because of the intensity of the services offered and the complex, multiple demands it places on workers, it requires experienced, skilled professional staff and a low worker–client family ratio (maximum 1 to 7). However, the early results seem very promising, as will be illustrated in the case example presented below. What may be most important is that this pilot project demonstrates the feasibility of linking foster care and community-based services to promote a form of shared parenting (Gabinet 1983). This is quite different from the traditional foster care program, which removes children from their natural community, discourages informal contact between biological and foster parents, and carefully separates substitute care from the in-home services that could facilitate and sustain early discharge.

## DIFFERENTIAL CLINICAL ASSESSMENTS AND INTERVENTIONS

Children in foster care are not a homogeneous group, nor are the reasons for their placement or their experiences in care necessarily similar. Yet, in recent years, in response to increased judicial and administrative oversight, there have been increased efforts to standardize risk assessment and interventive planning for children entering foster care. This trend violates one of the core principles of social work practice, which is the need to individualize client service need, and it denies children the right to be known and cared for as unique individuals with different potentials, interests, and worries. At the same time, there are some common issues and themes that must be addressed to ensure that all children in foster care will receive equitable and appropriate treatment. Therefore, this section identifies the core questions that should be examined in assessing the different needs of children entering foster care and the principles that should guide ongoing practice with this population. These themes can be understood most easily if they are considered in relation to the major phases in the placement process.

A primary objective of child welfare services is to sustain children in their own homes and strengthen family functioning. Both by law and by professional mandate, social workers are expected to provide in-home services to families in which children are at risk of placement *prior* to considering foster care as a service option. The decision to place a child prior to provision of the services that might alleviate the need for foster care can be justified only if there is evidence that a child has been harmed or is at imminent risk of such harm (Stein and Rzepnicki 1983:273).

In assessing the service needs of families in which children are at risk, the worker will want to evaluate parental capacity:

- To provide a physical environment that protects the child's safety and health.
- To meet the child's instrumental needs for food, shelter, adequate sleeping arrangements, clothing and other essentials of life.
- To meet the child's emotional needs to be valued and to feel a sense of security and belonging.
- To set appropriate limits for the child and teach the values required to support moral development.
- To negotiate effectively with neighbors, friends, and community organizations to ensure that the child will have access to needed environmental supports.

In addition, the worker will need to identify the personal and environmental stresses that may inhibit parental capacity to fulfill one or more of these normal role expectations and the resources that may be available to support enhanced parental functioning. Finally, depending on the age and developmental level of the child, the worker must assess the degree to which some problem behavior or condition in the child is undermining parental capacity to function adequately, and what resources are required to alleviate this problem (Janchill 1981:37–39).

In addition to evaluating the risk of imminent harm to a child, Janchill (1983:40–41) suggested three critical questions that must be assessed before deciding whether foster placement is needed: 1) Is there sufficient parental desire to maintain the child at home? 2) If the child is old enough to express a preference, is the child willing to stay at home and try to work out areas of difficulty? 3) Are the resources required to sustain the child in the family available in the community? If the answer to any of these questions is negative, the worker may have to consider foster placement.

Once it has been decided that placement is essential, there are three tasks that the worker must address. First, the worker must select an appropriate placement site. As discussed earlier, federal law now requires that placement be arranged in the most familylike setting available in close geographic proximity to the biological parents that is consonant with the needs of the child. This means that foster families are normally considered the placement of choice, and group residences are selected only if the child cannot tolerate the intimacy of family life, requires specialized treatment that cannot be provided in a family home, or cannot be controlled in a community setting. If the child must be referred for group care, the worker should still attempt to locate a setting that is as close to the child's home as possible and that is no more restrictive or isolated from the community than necessary.

Other variables that should be considered in selecting a placement include 1) the desirability of placing sibling groups in the same setting or in as close geographic proximity as possible: 2) the anticipated length and stability of the placement; 3) the importance of matching the foster family as closely as possible with the child's own family in relation to language, race and ethnicity, religion, and other factors that influence a child's sense of identity; and 4) the degree to which the child's biological parents are likely to interact positively with the foster parents or the child care staff.

A second task that the worker should address early in the life of a case, and prior to placement if possible, is development of a comprehensive service plan. This plan should specify the anticipated duration of the placement, the changes that must occur before the child can return home (in specific, behavioral terms), the actions that will be taken by each of the involved parties (parents, child, agency worker, and foster parents), the role of other community agencies, tentative visiting arrangements, and a schedule for periodic assessment of progress (Blumenthal 1983). If the plan is developed in collaboration with the biological parent(s), as is desirable, it can be used as a basis for an ongoing clinical contract. In many situations, such a plan must now also be approved by the court ordering continued placement.

A third critical, early task for the worker is to provide supportive counseling and education and to facilitate ongoing contact in order to decrease the trauma and pain associated with separation. Even when the parent–child relationship is very conflicted or there has been serious abuse, parents and children tend to experience a terrible sense of loss after placement. Children often feel sad, abandoned, angry, and/or guilty and may act out these feelings in dysfunctional ways in the new foster home. Similarly, parents are likely to feel sad, guilty, fearful, and/or angry. Therefore, it is important that the worker view foster placement as a hazardous event that may precipitate a crisis response in the biological parent(s) and/or the child and plan accordingly. Drawing on the principles of crisis intervention theory, the worker can help both parents and children (if age-appropriate) to gain cognitive mastery of the situation by involving them actively in planning the placement, providing anticipatory guidance and rehearsal, and sharing as much information and decision-making responsibility as possible. A preplacement visit to the foster care setting can be helpful, as can the development of a written service plan that is distributed to all participants. One of the objectives throughout the planning process should be to give the participants a realistic sense of control and as much knowledge as possible about what is happening, why, and what can be anticipated in the future.

Once children enter placement, the worker should make continued efforts to diminish feelings of loss and separation by helping them understand what is happening and facilitating ongoing contact between the birth parents and the children. It is essential that children experience a sense of continuity in their lives. Frequent parental visiting not only helps to diminish fears of abandonment but is a strong predictor of early discharge (Fanshel and Shinn 1978). When contact is limited, parents begin to experience a sense of filial deprivation, and their attachment to their children gradually diminishes (Jenkins and Normal 1972).

Parental visits to the foster home and/or group residence can also be used by the worker as a means of assessing the parent–child bond, monitoring parents' behavior, and teaching improved parenting skills. If biological and foster parents are helped to develop a collaborative relationship, they can see themselves as working together to care for the child and can begin to share some parenting responsibilities, as is common with extended-family members. For example, a birth mother can be encouraged to feed and dress her infant in the foster home or to attend tutoring sessions with an older child or to accompany the child and the foster mother to a medical appointment. What is important is that the worker attempt to diminish the hostility and resentment that biological and foster parents often feel toward each other and to enable them to find ways to share their investment in the child's well-being. Even the most inadequate and abusive parents usually feel an attachment to their children that can be harnessed to work in the child's interests. Conversely, if the birth parents consistently refuse the invitation to remain involved in their child's life, the worker obtains valuable information about the feasibility of planning to reunite the family and data that can be used in court if termination of parental rights becomes necessary.

Although the worker's primary responsibility is to the child in foster care, it is important that the worker adopt a family-centered approach to practice. Repeated experience has demonstrated the futility of earlier efforts to "rescue" children from pathological family situations. Family ties are very powerful, and whether children live with their parents or not, they must deal with the fantasy and the reality of their family of origin.

Despite evidence that children who remain in long-term foster care or move into adoptive families may do as well as or better than some children who are reunited with their biological families, there is a strong social consensus in this country, now embodied in law, that children should grow up with their "natural" families whenever possible. Therefore, workers must view the biological family as the unit of attention and do everything possible to support that family system and enable the parent(s) and child(ren) to make the changes required to ensure that the family will be reunited. Thus, service plans for children in foster care may include parent education, individual and family treatment, remediation for children's developmental difficulties, vocational or educational counseling, coordination and advocacy with a range of community agencies, and/or efforts to strengthen the family's natural support network.

When foster care workers practice from a family-centered, ecosystems perspective, the therapeutic tasks they carry out may be very similar to those performed by workers providing services to at-risk families in their own homes. However, there are three important distinctions. One is the need discussed above to work specifically on issues related to separation. A second important difference is that foster care workers, by definition, must function as part of a service team, and they often carry lead responsibility for orchestrating the activities of various team members. No matter whether a foster child is placed in a foster home or a group residence, his or her well-being will be heavily influenced by the quality of care provided. Moreover, the attitudes and behavior of the foster parents or the child staff toward the birth parents can do much to enhance or undercut their willingness to participate in the service plan. Therefore, the social worker must actively monitor what is happening in the placement and work in a collegial manner with the foster parents and/or child care workers to enhance their transactions with the child and the biological parents. The worker's actual interventions in this context might include educating the child care staff about why a particular child is acting upset or defiant, arranging respite care or finding some special equipment for a foster parent, or mediating a conflict between the foster and birth mothers about appropriate discipline or visiting hours.

In addition to working with child care personnel, the foster care worker must consult with agency attorneys and testify at frequent court hearings. To work effectively with the courts, workers have to learn how to obtain the type of data that will be admitted in court, to document their own and clients' activities precisely, and to present their observations and recommendations persuasively. They must also learn to function comfortably in what can be an adversarial context and to answer questions that may be posed by the foster child's attorney or lay advocates in a factual, nondefensive manner. Rather than feeling like a pawn of the court, the competent worker will try to use court processes to enforce the service plan of greatest benefit to the child and the family.

The third and perhaps most critical difference between practice with or on behalf of children in the community and those in foster care is that in addition to serving the therapeutic and socialization functions frequently performed by community-based workers, the foster care worker must assume major case management and life-planning responsibilities. He or she must decide when and under what circumstances family reunification may be feasible and, if not, whether adoption may be a suitable alternative. Although final decision-making responsibility rests with the court, judges often rely heavily on the recommendation of the social worker. It is clearly much more stressful for the practitioner to be forced to take a position about what should happen to a child's life than it is for a worker to leave these decisions with the parents, emphasizing the importance of self-determination. Moreover, because of the awesome responsibilities that foster care workers assume, they are at much greater risk than social workers in other fields of practice of being held liable for a faulty decision or for failure to take an action that (only in retrospect) was essential to protect the life of a child or to preserve family unity.

Despite these pressures, the foster care worker must at some point decide whether it is realistic to continue to plan toward the child's eventual discharge to his or her own home or whether some alternative goal must be established. Although this decision should be made as quickly as possible, it must be made, except under extraordinary circumstances, prior to the mandated dispositional hearing scheduled within eighteen months of placement and periodically thereafter. Alternative planning options include placement with an extended-family member, adoption, legal guardianship, or long-term foster care, usually considered in that order. If efforts to move toward family reunification seem blocked, the worker must address two questions: 1) Should parental rights be terminated? 2) What would be the best legal status and living arrangement for this child or this sibling group?

Unless the parent(s) is willing to sign a voluntary surrender of parental rights, termination requires court action. However, the worker must decide whether to file a petition to terminate parental rights. If the parent has essentially abandoned the child, failing to visit and to make plans for discharge, this can be a relatively clear-cut recommendation. The practice dilemma arises when the parent continues to insist that he or she wants to resume care of the child but visits very sporadically and makes little effort to address the problems that necessitated placement or to develop realistic discharge plans. At that point, the worker, in consultation with the agency attorney and other involved agency staff and administration, must determine whether the parent's overt behavior gives sufficient evidence of his or her inability to fulfill normal parental role expectations. Maintenance of a specific service contract and carefully documented records of the parent's behavior can become invaluable at this time because they provide the evidence required for the agency and the court to make an informed and equitable decision.

The other issue that must be considered if a child cannot return home is what would be the best alternative. This decision will be influenced by the child's age and degree of attachment to the biological parents, the willingness of foster parents to consider adoption, the availability of extended-family members to care for the child, the child's readiness to form a meaningful attachment to other parental figures, the availability of potential adoptive parents, and, if the child is old enough, his or her own preferences.

There are no clear-cut criteria for making such a judgment and few hard data are available on which to base a prediction about the alternative likely to be most successful. What is known is that the older the child, the less likely he or she is to form a meaningful attachment to a new family, and that the child's adjustment to foster care is a good predictor of later adaptation. Also, there is now relatively strong evidence that children who grow up in stable long-term foster homes do relatively well, as do children who are adopted. It also seems clear that children can do as well in an "open" adoption, in which they retain some relationship with their birth parents, as they can in a long-term foster home setting, in which they maintain some links to their own parents. These latter findings are quite freeing for foster care workers because they suggest that there is no single "best" option for children in placement. The planning process requires real individualization of the child's developmental needs, family history, and circumstances.

No matter what the permanency goal, it must be emphasized that no service plan is necessarily permanent. Children are often returned to care after discharge home, adoptions are sometimes disrupted, and "long-term" foster care can be terminated. Therefore, it is essential that ongoing services be offered to the foster child and his or her "permanent" family—no matter whether this is the biological family, the extended family, the foster family, or the adoptive family—until it is certain that the child can grow up in this home with some degree of stability. Children need to know that there is at least one person committed to meeting their basic environmental needs until they are ready to live independently.

One final note: This essay emphasizes what is unique about the placement process, but children enter foster care because they themselves or their parents have one or more psychosocial problems that prevent them from living at home. For example, in recent years, child welfare agencies have observed increasing numbers of severely disturbed and violent adolescents entering care as well as a dramatic rise in the numbers of infants of drug-addicted mothers, multiply handicapped children, and children from homeless families referred for placement. Therefore, to be effective in providing foster care services, social workers must have the clinical knowledge required for practice with clients demonstrating the wide range of problems that may precipitate placement as well as the specific skills required to help children and parents deal successfully with the foster care experience.

## CASE ILLUSTRATION

Marcia Walters, a superviser at the city child–protective service agency, telephoned the neighborhood family service center described earlier to request a foster care placement for Cindy Davis, the 2-year-old interracial daughter of Susan Bissell, a 26-year-old single white woman of German background. Ms. Bissell had been in a relationship with Cindy's father for the past six years. Gabriel Davis is a 36-year-old black man who was reputed to have both a drinking problem and a history of beating Ms. Bissell while intoxicated. Cindy was being referred for foster care because she was ready to be discharged from the hospital following a 2½-week admission for treatment of an epidural hematoma. Because the protective service investigation had strongly implicated Ms. Bissell and Mr. Davis in Cindy's injury, their other daughter, Lisa, age 4, had been removed abruptly from Ms. Bissell the preceding week while she and her daughter were walking down the street together. (Ms. Bissell later said that her visual image of the removal was one of Lisa screaming for her as she was ushered into the protective service worker's car.)

Upon referring Cindy for foster care, Ms. Walters was surprised to hear that the center would not accept Cindy for placement unless Lisa was allowed to be moved to the same foster home with Cindy. However, Ms. Walters said that she recognized the logic in this, and she agreed to retrieve Lisa from the other agency so that she could be placed with Cindy.

At this point, the social worker at the center, Claire Shelton, began to address the tasks of preplacement assessment and planning. It was obvious to Ms. Shelton that this was a very high-risk family situation involving probable spouse and child abuse as well as alcoholism of at least one parent. Lisa had already been further traumatized by an abrupt separation from her remaining family, and Cindy was in a compromised, highly vulnerable medical state from which there could be lasting neurological effects. Ms. Walters had mentioned that both children were enrolled in a therapeutic nursery program about forty-five minutes out of the neighborhood, a program that was familiar to Ms. Shelton. Ms. Shelton called the program and reached the children's social worker, Suzanne Daly. Ms. Daly verified that the situation was extremely high-risk and that, while the children were "adorable, they were both severely language-delayed and accident-prone." Ms. Daly described the children's mother as an emotionally constricted woman who had difficulty expressing any affection or positive feeling to the girls. She also said that the girls had no behavior problems and suggested that they be placed with someone who was affectionate and nurturing rather than distant and discipline-oriented.

On the basis of this information, Ms. Shelton decided to place Lisa and Cindy in the home of Yolanda Nieves, a 36-year-old Puerto Rican single mother of four children ranging in age from 20 years to 3 months. Ms. Shelton knew Ms. Nieves well because she had completed the home study on this family herself. She was concerned about the lack of ethnic match but decided that the foster mother's capacity to meet the children's immediate emotional and developmental needs was more important, especially since she hoped this would be a brief placement. Ms. Nieves was chosen because she was highly motivated to be a good foster parent, and she had had special experience in raising her 9-year-old son, Robert, who is developmentally delayed and neurogically impaired. Also, she is a highly tolerant, accepting, flexible woman who disciplined her own children adequately but was not prone to rigid limit-setting.

Ms. Nieves agreed to accept the children and to meet with Ms. Shelton immediately. The foster mother began to inspect her home for possible hazards to Lisa and Cindy, who were scheduled to arrive shortly. Once the children's immediate safety was ensured, Ms. Shelton was able to focus her attention upon Susan Bissell, the girls' mother. She telephoned her to introduce herself, to explain that her children would be living in the neighborhood, and to offer a visit with the children. Ms. Bissell accepted a visit for the following day and agreed to meet with Ms. Shelton prior to the visit.

This first meeting and visit were of crucial importance in creating the right atmosphere for the ongoing work in the case. Ms. Bissell was encouraged to view Ms. Shelton and Yolanda Nieves as her potential allies, and Ms. Shelton was able to begin her assessment of Ms. Bissell's relationship with her children and their respective treatment needs.

During the initial encounter between Ms. Shelton and Ms. Bissell, Ms. Bissell presented as a profoundly angry, defensive woman who was nevertheless devoted to her children and concerned for their safety. Ms. Bissell seemed relieved by the worker's comment that her anger and upset were normal and could be expected of any mother in her situation who cared about her children. Ms. Bissell quickly volunteered that she had not caused Cindy's hematoma and postulated that it could have been caused either by Cindy's excessive headbanging, which was improbable, or else by a compilation of numerous head injuries that Cindy has sustained while in attendance at the therapeutic nursery program. This seemed more probable to the worker. Despite the fact that Ms. Bissell is an attractive, intelligent woman, Ms. Shelton sensed a pervasive, almost palpable sense of low self-esteem and feelings of worthlessness in her.

Immediately after the interview, Ms. Bissell had her first visit with Lisa and Cindy. Both girls appeared to be glad to see Ms. Bissell and ran to her eagerly when they entered the room. Lisa quickly settled in Ms. Bissell's lap and began talking to her, while Cindy scurried around the room looking for toys.

Initially, Ms. Bissell was reluctant to talk to the foster mother, but Ms. Shelton was able to facilitate an exchange of information between Ms. Bissell and Ms. Nieves about the children's basic eating and sleeping habits. This allowed them to converse in a factual, nonthreatening manner and set the tone for the cooperative relationship that would begin to develop between them and that would eventually contribute to the early discharge of the children.

Following the first interview and visit, Susan Bissell began to meet twice weekly with Ms. Shelton. Although she remained constricted and mistrustful, she was able to explore her lack of trust and the extreme anxiety and depression she was feeling about the children's placement. Gradually, as Ms. Bissell demonstrated her ability to keep frequent appointments and to use them as outlets to modify her hostility and mistrust, Ms. Shelton became convinced that if the necessary supportive services were put in place, Ms. Bissell might be able to utilize them to the extent that Lisa and Cindy could be returned home to her.

Another factor that contributed to the assessment that an early discharge might be feasible was the fact that both Lisa and Cindy continued to experience numerous head and bodily injuries while in the therapeutic nursery, despite the fact that there were no injuries in the foster home. This lent credence to Ms. Bissell's suggestion that Cindy's hematoma may have been caused by the injuries she sustained in the nursery program. For this reason, Ms. Shelton decided to remove the girls from the nursery and enroll them in programs in the local community. This would enable Ms. Shelton to monitor them more closely and would allow Ms. Bissell to become more involved in their education than she had been in the past. Ms. Shelton also thought that giving Ms. Bissell increased responsibilities for her children's needs while they were in care would provide a good indicator of how committed she would be to continuing remediation for Lisa and Cindy's language and developmental delays after their discharge home.

Ms. Bissell agreed to move Lisa to a neighborhood Head Start program and concurrently to enroll herself and Cindy in the center's parent–infant–toddler program. The Head Start program would provide Lisa with five-day-a-week, three-hour-a-day education and socialization, while the parent–infant–toddler program would offer both Ms. Bissell and Cindy a two-day-a-week, two-hour-a-day group experience. In this program, the parents met together for a counseling group in one room while the children had a play–stimulation group in an adjacent room.

During a joint meeting with Ms. Nieves and Ms. Bissell, it was agreed that Ms. Bissell would pick up Lisa and Cindy from the foster home in the morning, drop off Lisa at Head Start, and then continue with Cindy to the parent–infant–toddler group. Ms. Shelton clarified with both Ms. Bissell and the protective service supervisor that these responsibilities were being given to Ms. Bissell both to assess her level of responsibility to her children and to allow her to share more in the tasks of parenting with Ms. Nieves.

The intervention proved effective. Not only did Ms. Bissell succeed in keeping all of her individual and group counseling appointments and in transporting her children to their respective programs, she succeeded in convincing the children's father to accept Ms. Shelton's invitation to come in for an individual meeting. Mr. Davis eventually attended four individual counseling sessions, which were scheduled around the erratic demands of his job as a security guard. Although Mr. Davis denied being an alcoholic or ever hitting his children and minimized his physical assaults on Ms. Bissell, he was surprisingly willing to offer a detailed history of the emotional and physical abuse and neglect he had experienced as a child. In addition, although he also denied drinking currently, he gave a similarly detailed history of numerous episodes of binge drinking throughout his teen and adult years, which usually ended in blackouts and physical illness. About four weeks into the placement, as he began individual sessions, Mr. Davis began going with Ms. Bissell to visit the children. They were obviously glad to see him and physically affectionate with him.

By the inclusion of Mr. Davis as well as Ms. Bissell in the service plan, Ms. Shelton was able to gain a richer picture of the emotional deprivation and physical neglect and abuse in both of their backgrounds that had predisposed Ms. Bissell to the harsh treatment of her children and Mr. Davis to self-destructive behavior and violent behavior toward his family.

The foster mother, Yolanda Nieves, played a subtle but important role in ensuring a positive outcome of the placement. Ms. Nieves' accepting, nonjudgmental attitude toward Ms. Bissell and her calm, nonreactive demeanor, even when Ms. Bissell was explosively angry, served both to model more appropriate behavior and to reduce Ms. Bissell's mistrust in Ms. Nieves.

Eventually, Ms. Nieves allowed Ms. Bissell to visit Lisa and Cindy in her home, which further alleviated Ms. Bissell's mistrust of the foster care system. The experience of visiting in the foster home gave the client an additional impetus to explore the dynamics of developing trust in others, a task that was a precursor to her ability to work through the feelings of deprivation and abandonment that had plagued her throughout her life.

When Ms. Bissell and Mr. Davis went to their second court hearing almost 2½ months after the children had been placed, Ms. Shelton sent a letter to the judge saying that although some risk to the children would remain because of Ms. Bissell's history of physically punishing the children and Mr. Davis's difficulties with alcoholism and spouse abuse, she recommended that the children be returned home provided that the parents would agree to continue all counseling and educational services currently in place. In addition, Ms. Shelton suggested that Mr. Davis enroll in an alcoholism treatment program. The judge agreed with Ms. Shelton's recommendations but carried them one step further, ordering Mr. Davis either to receive alcoholism treatment services or else to move out of the home if his children were to return. Mr. Davis adamantly refused alcoholism treatment and angrily agreed to move out in order for Lisa and Cindy to be returned home to Ms. Bissell. Mr. Davis moved out of the home the next morning, and Lisa and Cindy returned home that afternoon.

It should be noted that Ms. Shelton did not agree with the judge's decision to order Mr. Davis out of the home because she believed that in the course of individual counseling, the issue of Mr. Davis' drinking problem would eventually become so overt that he would be forced to seek help. In addition, because the judge merely stated that Mr. Davis could not live with Ms. Bissell and his daughters and did not restrict his contact with them in any other way, the judge did not remove the threat of physical harm to the children and only disrupted the family's living arrangement against their will. Following Lisa and Cindy's return home, Mr. Davis attended two additional counseling sessions, during which he expressed tremendous anger at being court-ordered out of his home. He then dropped out of counseling entirely. About five months later, he began an alcoholic binge that resulted in the loss of his job and his housing, which reduced him to living on a street close to Ms. Bissell's apartment. Significantly, Ms. Bissell continued to remind Mr. Davis of the services available to him at the center.

Ms. Bissell and Lisa and Cindy continued to receive all the clinical and educational services initiated during the children's stay in foster care, and Ms. Shelton remained the family's social worker. Individual counseling sessions with Ms. Bissell continued to focus upon her need to explore the origins of her anger in a childhood that had been devoid of nurturance and to trace the ways in which that anger surfaced in her interactions with Lisa and Cindy and perpetuated itself in the physical and emotional abuse of her own children. Although the mystery of what had caused Cindy's epidural hematoma was never solved and the physical risks to her and Lisa were probably higher than they would have been if the children had remained in foster care, Ms. Bissell worked to replace physical punishments with behavioral consequences and to call either Ms. Shelton or other members of the parent–infant–toddler group if she felt herself losing control.

As Lisa and Cindy continued to attend Head Start and the parent–toddler program, respectively, they both made rapid gains in language development and socialization skills, to the extent that Lisa was attending a regular public kindergarten in the fall. Perhaps even more important is that during family sessions, Ms. Bissell was able to be more openly affectionate toward her children and more tolerant of their age-appropriate, rambunctious play. Ongoing work was planned to enable Ms. Bissell and Lisa and Cindy to improve their relationship and also to help Ms. Bissell to complete her enrollment in a community college where she planned to begin studies in zoology and to enroll Lisa and Cindy in the after-school and day care services available in the community. Ms. Bissell hoped eventually to obtain her bachelor's degree and to find a full-time job so that she would no longer need public assistance.

Ms. Shelton continued to be troubled about her inability to reengage the children's father after he had been court-ordered out of the home, and she remained available to work with him if he should reach the point where he was ready to address his drinking problem. What is most important, however, from the perspective of child and family functioning is that Ms. Bissell was able to separate sufficiently from Mr. Davis to set appropriate limits on his behavior, and that she began to build an independent life for herself and her children.

This case clearly illustrates the important work that can be accomplished by a skilled practitioner in a foster program designed to enhance parental capacities, normalize children's living arrangements, and sustain family life. If the social worker had not known that she could continue to monitor and support Ms. Bissell's parental functioning after the children were returned home, she might have been much more reluctant to effect an early discharge. And had Ms. Shelton not been able to form an early alliance with Ms. Bissell, to make a thoughtful assessment of her strengths and service needs, and to enable her to share parenting responsibilities with the foster mother, the case outcome would probably have been quite different. Unfortunately, the case also illustrates the ways in which court action may define and limit the practice objectives that can be achieved once children enter the foster care system.

Foster care as it is known today originated as a social invention of the mid-nineteenth century designed to ensure the well-being of children whose parents were unwilling or unable to provide adequate care. The early child welfare agencies established to deliver foster care services were important practice sites for the emerging profession of social work. Yet, little over a hundred years later, long-term foster care has been redefined as a social problem, and federal legislation now mandates the provision of services designed to prevent and/or limit foster care placement.

This societal reassessment of the value of foster care, together with the administrative and court review processes developed to monitor and regulate its use, have created new decision-making dilemmas and stresses for the many social workers who continue to work in this field of practice. But these changes have not eliminated the challenge and satisfaction inherent in providing effective services to children in foster care and their families. In fact, as the case illustration demonstrates, the need for professional leadership and creativity in child welfare practice may be greater now than ever before. Although children in foster care constitute a relatively small client population, they are one of the most vulnerable and disadvantaged groups in the country today. As such, they deserve attention from some of social work's most talented practitioners.

# Endnote

1. This figure includes children in 16 states who have returned home but are still receiving post-placement services and excludes children in pre-adoptive homes in 10 states. Correcting these figures to ensure comparability of data across states, the VCIS estimated an *adjusted* total in care at the end of the fiscal year of 265,000.

# REFERENCES

Allen, Mary and Jane Knitzer. 1983. "Child Welfare: Examining the Policy Framework." In Brenda G. McGowan and William Meezan, eds., *Child Welfare: Current Dilemmas, Future Directions*, pp. 93–141. Itasca, Ill.: F. E. Peacock.

Barth, Richard. 1988a. "Disruption in Older Child Adoptions." *Public Welfare* (Winter), 46:23–29.

Barth, Richard P. 1988b. *On Their Own: The Experiences of Youth After Foster Care.* Berkeley: Family Welfare Research Group, School of Social Welfare, University of California at Berkeley.

Barth, Richard P. and Marianne Berry. 1987. "Outcomes of Child Welfare Services Under Permanency Planning." *Social Service Review* (March), 61:71–90.

Billingsley, Andrew and Jeanne M. Giovannoni. 1972. *Children of the Storm: Black Children and American Child Welfare.* New York: Harcourt Brace Jovanovich.

Blumenthal, Karen. 1983. "Making Foster Care Responsive." In Brenda G. McGowan and William Meezan, eds., *Child Welfare: Current Dilemmas, Future Directions*, pp. 295–342. Itasca, Ill.: Peacock.

"Born Hooked: Confronting the Impact of Perinatal Substance Abuse." 1989. Summary of hearing before the Select Committee on Children, Youth and Families (April 27). U.S. House of Representatives, Washington, D.C.

Boswell, John. 1988. *The Kindness of Strangers.* New York: Pantheon.

*Child Abuse and Neglect in America: The Problem and the Response.* 1987. Hearing before the Select Committee on Children, Youth and Families (March 3). U. S. House of Representatives, 100th Congress, First Session, Washington, D.C.

CDF (Children's Defense Fund). 1989. *A Vision for America's Future.* Washington, D.C.: CDF.

*Continuing Crisis in Foster Care: Issues and Problems.* 1987. Hearing before the Select Committee on Children, Youth and Families (April 22). U.S. House of Representatives, 100th Congress, 1st Session, Washington, D.C.

*Continuing Jeopardy: Children and AIDS.* 1988. A Staff Report of the Select Committee on Children, Youth and Families (September). U.S. House of Representatives, 100th Congress, 2d Session, Washington, D.C.

*The Crisis in Homelessness: Effects on Children and Families.* 1987. Hearing before the Select Committee on Children, Youth and Families (February 24). U.S. House of Representatives, 100th Congress, 2d Session, Washington, D.C.

Daro, Deborah. 1988. *Confronting Child Abuse.* New York: Free Press.

Fanshel, David, Stephen J. Finch, and John F. Grundy. 1989. "Foster Children in Life Course Perspective: The Casey Family Program Experience." *Child Welfare* 63 (September/October):467–478.

Fanshel, David and Eugene Shinn. 1972. *Dollars and Sense in Foster Care.* New York: Child Welfare League of America.

Fanshel, David and Eugene Shinn. 1978. *Children in Foster Care: A Longitudinal Investigation.* New York: Columbia University Press.

Festinger, Trudy. 1983. *No One Ever Asked Us: A Postscript to Foster Care.* New York: Columbia University Press.

Gabinet, Laille. 1983. "Shared Parenting: A New Paradigm for the Treatment of Child Abuse." *Child Abuse and Neglect* 7:403–411.

Gershenson, Charles P. and Esther Kresh. 1986. "School Enrollment Status of Children Receiving Child Welfare Services at Home or in Foster Care." *Child Welfare Research Notes* (September), no. 15.

Gordon, Linda. 1988. *Heroes of Their Own Lives: The Politics and History of Family Violence.* New York: Penguin.

Gruber, Alan. 1978. *Children in Foster Care: Destitute, Neglected, Betrayed.* New York: Human Sciences Press.

Janchill, Sister Mary Paul. 1981. *Guidelines to Decision-Making in Child Welfare.* New York: Human Services Workshops.

Janchill, Sister Mary Paul. 1983. "Services for Special Populations of Children." In Brenda G. McGowan and William Meezan, eds., *Child Welfare: Current Dilemmas, Future Directions*, pp. 345–375. Itasca, Ill.: Peacock.

Jenkins, Shirley. 1974. "Child Welfare as a Class System." In Alvin Schorr, ed., *Children and Decent People*, pp. 3–24. New York: Basic Books.

Jenkins, Shirley and Beverly Diamond. 1985. "Ethnicity and Foster Care: Census Data as Predictors of Placement Variables." *American Journal of Orthopsychiatry* (April) 55:267–276.

Jenkins, Shirley and Elaine Norman. 1972. *Filial Deprivation and Foster Care.* New York: Columbia University Press.

Kadushin, Alfred and Judith A. Martin. 1988. *Child Welfare Services*, 4th ed. New York: Macmillan.

Kamerman, Sheila B. and Alfred J. Kahn. 1989. *Social Services for Children, Youth and Families in the U.S.* Greenwich, Conn.: Annie E. Casey Foundation.

Knitzer, Jane, Marylee Allen, and Brenda McGowan. 1978. *Children Without Homes.* Washington, D.C.: Children's Defense Fund.

Maas, Henry, and Richard Engler. 1959. *Children in Need of Parents.* New York: Columbia University.

Maluccio, Anthony N. and Edith Fein. 1985. "Growing Up in Foster Care." *Children and Youth Services Review*, 7:123–134.

Maluccio, Anthony N., Edith Fein, and Kathleen A. Olmstead. 1986. *Permanency Planning for Children: Concepts and Methods.* New York: Tavistock.

Maluccio, Anthony N. and James K. Whittaker. 1988. "Helping the Biological Families of Children in Out-of-Home Placement." In E. W. Nunnally, C. S. Chilman, and F. M. Cox, eds., *Troubled Relationships*, pp. 205–217. Beverly Hills, Calif.: Sage.

McFadden, Emily Jean. 1985. "Practice in Foster Care." In Joan Laird and Ann Hartman, eds., *A Handbook of Child Welfare*, pp. 585–616. New York: Free Press.

Mushlin, Michael B. 1988. "Unsafe Havens: The Case for Constitutional Protection of Foster Children from Abuse and Neglect." *Harvard Civil Rights–Civil Liberties Law Review* (Winter), 23:199–280.

Persico, Joseph. 1979. *Who Knows? Who Cares? Forgotten Children in Foster Care.* New York: National Commission on Children in Need of Parents.

Rest, Ellen Ryan and Kenneth Watson. 1984. "Growing Up in Foster Care." *Child Welfare* (July/August). 63:291–296.

Rosenfeld, Jona. 1983. "The Domain and Expertise of Social Work: A Conceptualization." *Social Work* (May/June), 28:186–192.

Rzepnicki, Tina L. 1987. "Recidivism of Foster Children Returned to Their Own Homes: A Review and New Directions for Research." *Social Service Review* (March). 61:56–69.

Seltzer, Marsha Mailick and Leonard M. Bloksberg. 1987. "Permanency Planning and Its Effects on Foster Children: A Review of the Literature." *Social Work* (January/February). 32:65–68.

"Shaping Foster Care as a Community Service: Early Findings." 1989. Brooklyn, N.Y.: Center for Family Life.

Shireman, Joan F. 1983. "Achieving Permanency After Placement." In Brenda G. McGowan and William Meezan, eds., *Child Welfare: Current Dilemmas, Future Directions*, pp. 377–421. Itasca, Ill., Peacock.

SSC (Special Services for Children). 1988. "Foster Care Expansion Plan for Fiscal Year 1989." New York: SSC.

Stein, Theodore J. and Tina L. Rzepnicki. 1983. "Decision-Making in Child Welfare." In Brenda C. McGowan and William Meezan, eds., *Child Welfare: Current Dilemmas, Future Directions*, pp. 259–292. Itasca, Ill.: Peacock.

Tatara, Toshio. 1988. *Characteristics of Children in Substitute and Adoptive Care: A Statistical Summary of the VCIS National Child Welfare Data Base* (July). Washington, D.C.: American Public Welfare Association.

TSCCW (Temporary State Commission on Child Welfare). 1975. *The Children and the State: A Time for a Chance.* Albany, N.Y.: TSCCW.

Vasaly, Shirley. 1976. *Foster Care in Five States.* Washington, D.C.: U.S. Department of Health, Education and Welfare.

Weinstein, David. 1960. *The Self-Image of the Foster Child.* New York: Russell Sage Foundation.

# 13

## Crime Victims

▼

ROSEMARY C. MASTERS

The United States Department of Justice (1986) estimated that in any given year, upwards of 34 million crimes are committed or attempted against individuals or households in this country. Of every 1,000 resident men and women over the age of 12, 28 are victims of violent crime (rape, robbery, and assault); 68 of every 1,000 resident Americans are victims of personal theft (crimes such as purse snatching and pick pocketing). Of every 1,000 residents, 10 have their car stolen. The homes of 170 of every 1,000 households are entered illegally. The President's Task Force on Victims of Crime (1982) estimated that a murder occurs in this country every twenty-three minutes and that a woman is raped every six minutes. Cumulatively, these numbers demonstrate that no citizen, of whatever economic class, is safe from crime.

Until the 1970s, victims of crime in this country were by and large ignored by the social welfare and criminal justice systems. Victims were treated primarily as fodder for the prosecutors' cases against defendants. Victims' complaints and testimony were a means to an end, the conviction of offenders. Their particular needs were unstudied and undocumented. The consequences of their victimization were left to be absorbed haphazardly by the social welfare, mental health, and health-care systems.

Beginning in the 1970s, a variety of voices began to comment on the impact of crime on the victims of crime. The women's movement drew public attention to the callous treatment often afforded victims of rape and domestic violence. Informal study of criminal justice practices at organizations such as the Vera Institute of Justice in New

**416**

York City identified widespread victim dissatisfaction resulting from contact with police and courts. By the late 1970s, a number of research studies had confirmed the economic, physical, and mental suffering that victimization imposes on the victims of crime (Bard and Sangrey 1986; Burgess and Holstrom 1977; Drapkin and Viano 1979; Kilpatrick, Veronen, and Resnick 1979; Knundten et al. 1976; McDonald 1976).

In 1976, social welfare and criminal justice personnel organized the National Organization for Victim Assistance (NOVA), an organization whose purpose is to promote the interests and concerns of victims of crime.

By the 1980s, there was a general societal recognition that victims of crime suffer from a specific complex of social, economic, physical, and mental health problems that require a coordinated societal response. Many large cities now have victim–witness assistance programs. Over thirty states have enacted crime victim compensation programs. As many as 4,000 agencies specializing in assisting crime victims now exist (U.S.D.J. 1988b).

Despite the increase in victim–witness assistance efforts, many localities lack such services altogether, and those with services often offer severely limited programs. Social workers whose jobs bring them into contact with victims of crime must be prepared to recognize the special problems such persons face and must be prepared to respond to their needs appropriately.

## PROBLEM DOMAIN

Elias (1986:72) observed that popular and scientific theories as to the reasons for crime and criminal victimization fall into four somewhat overlapping but nonetheless distinct categories of causation. Crime is variously attributed to 1) regulatory failure; 2) criminal characteristics; 3) victim precipitation; and 4) structural forces. Simplistically put, these theories, respectively, blame institutions, blame the offender, blame the victim, or blame society's politicoeconomic system. Each category calls for different strategies of prevention and response.

*Institution blaming* is used by those who insist that the police and the courts are "soft on crime." A high crime rate is attributed to insufficient numbers of arrests and convictions and to overly lenient or inconsistent sentences. Remedies are believed to include more police on the streets, greater professionalization of courts and prosecutors, and severe sentences. The problem with institution-blaming theories is that despite ever-increasing expenditures for law enforcement personnel, despite ever more sophisticated techniques of law enforcement, and despite doubling of prison terms since 1965, the crime rate has not declined (Elias 1986:75). Some other cause must therefore explain the high American crime rate.

Arguably, overregulation and underregulation by the criminal justice system may in part contribute to seriousness of crimes and to some forms of crime. The American failure to limit the right to own handguns may well add significantly to serious injuries and deaths incurred during commission of crime. On the other hand, criminalization of so-called victimless crimes (prostitution and sale of drugs) brings significantly greater numbers of people into the justice system than would be there were such activities legalized. Efforts by drug dealers and other criminal entrepreneurs to control the profits of illegal businesses may lead to violent acts against economic competitors. Still, it remains highly questionable whether greater regulation of weapons and decriminalization or lesser regulation of victimless crimes would significantly alter the basic crime rate.

*Offender blaming* attributes crime to fundamental deviant characteristics in those who commit crimes. Such theories ascribe criminal acts to persons who are genetically different, inherently evil, or morally unprincipled. The implication of such theories is that criminals are bad apples who need to be isolated and immobilized so that society can be protected from their "contamination." Of offender blaming theories, Elias observed:

> While some tiny fraction of crime might come from illnesses that provoke violent outbursts of crime, we have little evidence that crime results from inherent qualities, and many of the biological flaws we have discovered have no necessary relationship with crime or at best they describe only symptoms of deeper social causes. . . . Theories emphasizing personal choices and failure hold little more validity. . . . Social rules and values will be obeyed not merely because we thoroughly ingrain them but because we provide social circumstances that do not pervasively contradict them. (1986:81–82)

Ultimately, offender-blaming theories fail because they are too superficial. Such approaches merely affirm the obvious; criminals commit crimes. Offender-blaming theories do not adequately explain *why* the offenders commit crimes.

*Victim blaming*, as we will discuss later, is a natural defense; we all have against anxiety about being victimized. By attributing causation of a crime to the reckless or foolish behavior of the victim, we lull ourselves into thinking that we are safe from crime because *we* are smarter. Victim blaming was lent scientific credence by early victimology studies, which attributed to victim behavior or personality structure a substantial role in the victimization (Elias 1986:87). Freudian theory of unconscious motivation and fantasy doubtless lent further credence to ideas of victim blaming.

The problem with victim blaming as an explanation for victimizations is twofold. First, such theories overlook the fact that many victims have no choice but to live in close proximity to the criminal. A battered woman, for example, may lack the economic and social resources to remove herself from the batterer's household. Impoverished people cannot afford to move out of crime-ridden, dangerous public-housing high rises into security-conscious luxury condominiums. Second, even those victims who may in some way precipitate a crime (for example, by provoking a fight or selling drugs in a rival's territory) are ultimately products of the same social system that produces the criminal. Victims do not consciously or unconsciously *choose* their victimization; rather, they are caught up in social forces that *result* in their victimization. The more fundamental question is what factors led to the victim's lifestyle.

Finally, *structural theories* attribute crime and victimization to social, political, and economic conditions that lead people to commit crimes and that trap victims and criminals in the same violent milieu. A major source of victimization is held to be poverty and inequality:

> Poverty produces not merely little or no incomes, assets and property, but also poor health, housing, education, nutrition, unemployment, and other social maladies. . . . The manifestations and results of poverty and inequality may produce crime by creating needs and frustrations that crime might appear to satisfy, however illusionary. It may generate crime by limiting legitimate opportunities for improvement. . . . *In other words, poverty may help create crimes of accommodation, survival and resistance.* (Elias 1986:93; italics added)

Within a society as a whole, certain classes of people may be especially vulnerable to victimization because of cultural attitudes and inadequate economic and political power. Women, children and the elderly, for example, are particularly at risk because they lack the maturity, self-confidence, health or economic means to leave a violent household, and because they often do not receive police and court protection from criminally dangerous family members.

The structural theories of crime call for much more fundamental societal change than do other theories. What would be required to reduce crime and ameliorate victimization are economic and political reforms that distribute goods, services, and power more uniformly among the citizenry.

The current array of victim services reflects widely divergent theories of criminal causation. Many advocates of victim participation in the judicial process, for example, seem to be motivated by the perception that regulatory failure has led to the crime. Victim advocacy it is believed, will lead to a harsher sentence, greater deterrence, and therefore fewer crimes. Self-protection programs that teach "street smarts" or physical defense techniques are rooted to some extent in theories of victim incompetence. The vehement demands by some victim advocates for return to the death penalty seem to be ultimately rooted in the perception that the criminal is somehow uniquely different from other people, a "cancer" that should be cut out of the body of society. Finally, crime victim compensation and shelters for battered women draw their rationale from the idea that crime represents a structural inability on the part of society to prevent crime and to protect its citizens.

## SOCIETAL CONTEXT

At the outset, any discussion of services for crime victims raises several threshold questions. First of all, who is a crime victim, anyway? It seems obvious enough that a person who is raped, beaten up, or robbed at knife point is the victim of a crime. But what about the purchaser of an illegal drug or the client of a prostitute? Who is the victim here? Who is the victim of shoplifting? Is it the stockholders of the company that operates the store? Or is it the customers, who pay higher prices as a result of the thefts? Are persons who are injured by illegal chemical pollution crime victims? Even if a narrow definition of victimization is accepted—that is, if we limit the term *crime victim* to a person who suffers from unjustified bodily injury at the hands of another person or whose personal property is damaged or appropriated by another—how do we account for the fact that prior to the 1970s victims of such crimes were a well-nigh-invisible constituency, one that was left to fend for itself and for which no specific societal concerns or programs existed? Furthermore, what changes occurred in societal attitudes so that some, but not all, victims of crime became identified as a class of persons to whom redress and assistance should be afforded? The answers to these questions lie in the historical evolution of the criminal justice system and the interests that system came to represent.

In primitive societies, it was left to the individual and his or her family to enforce social behavior and redress wrongs done to persons and property. Victim retaliation (harm for harm or injury for injury) constituted the earliest form of social control. Where economic harm had been done (through theft of property or personal injury), victims, aided by friends and relatives, extracted economic compensation from the offender and the offender's relatives. (Elias 1986:10).

The problem with a system of social control based on victim self-help was that the offender and the offender's family and tribe might not necessarily agree that a wrong had been done or that the retribution inflicted was appropriate. An accused murderer might, for example, claim he had killed in self-defense. Retaliation by the victim or his family often led to counterretaliation by the offender's family, clan, or tribe. Unending cycles of vendettas, tribal warfare, and blood feuds resulted. As societies became more settled and complex, organized forms of social control were required to forestall chaos and anarchy. Systematic, written codes of laws that defined transgressions and provided for restitution to the victim and punishment of offenders were promulgated by monarchs or tribal lawgivers (examples include the Babylonian Code of Hammurabi and the Jewish Torah). Formal procedures were established by which the rights and wrongs in individual cases could be adjudicated. Individuals were designated to hear and resolve the competing claims of complainant and defendant. Retribution to the offender took the form either of the same injury for the injury inflicted (an eye for an eye or a hand for a hand) or, increasingly, of monetary compensation to the victim (Elias 1986:10).

Formal systems of law and judicial procedure had the advantage of clarifying what behaviors a given society expected from its citizens and of interposing impartial third parties between mutually antagonistic claimants, each of whom advocated his or her view of the dispute. Might, in theory, no longer made right. Inherently, from the outset, however, the criminal justice system was expected to achieve dual goals: redress to the victim on the one hand and social order on the other. These goals were not always compatible. For example, execution or exile of an offender would preclude further wrongdoing by that offender but might run counter to a victim's desire for economic restitution, since a dead or absent offender would be in no position to repay the victim for the victim's losses. Despite the conflicting aims of organized judicial systems, victim satisfaction and restitution continued to be a major aim of the justice system until well into the Middle Ages. Elaborate systems of negotiation between the families of the victim and of the offender, termed *composition*, were utilized. Composition provided for indemnification of the victim by the offender and his or her family. (Jacob 1977:45–51).

As strong central governments assumed ever-more-embracing control over human lives, the criminal justice system increasingly came to serve the purpose of maintaining the political and social authority of the state. Crimes were redefined as wrongs against the state rather than wrongs against individuals. Interests of the ruling classes were protected by ferocious penalties, including torture and death. Fines paid to the state took the place of restitution to the individual. Such fines ultimately became an important source of crown revenue (Ziegenhagen 1977).

The shift from a system that viewed the victim as the wronged party to one that regarded the state as the wronged party was reflected in an increasing displacement of the victim from the center to the periphery of the criminal justice process. Elias (1986:12) noted, for example, that in colonial America, the victim often personally arrested and prosecuted the offender. By the end of the eighteenth century, however, police and public prosecutors, salaried out of public monies, replaced victims as the persons responsible for the arrest, trial, and punishment of a criminal offender. The victim's role was reduced to that of witness for the prosecution. As such, he or she had no legal say in the charge levied, the evidence presented, and the sentence requested of the court.

Humanitarian reforms of the nineteenth century introduced still a third goal into the criminal justice system, that of rehabilitating offenders. These reforms had the paradoxical effect of further minimizing the victim's role. Sentences to the penitentiary were intended to educate criminals to a better way of life. They were imposed by judges on the recommendation of court-appointed probation officers. Parole was conceived of as a form of supervised reintroduction of the offender into society. The decision to parole was in the hands of state parole boards. Missing in these reform efforts was an opportunity for the victim to express concerns about the suitability of the sentence or the risks to the victim when the offender was released.

As the criminal law became progressively more an instrument of the state and its procedures became increasingly concerned with deterrence of crime and rehabilitation of the criminal, victims retained the theoretical right to sue the offender for restitution in the civil courts. This right proved to be more illusory than real. For one thing, civil court procedures, like those in the criminal courts, became increasingly technical. Legal counsel often was and is a prerequisite to bringing a lawsuit; frequently, legal costs outweigh whatever damages the courts award. Moreover, most criminal defendants are indigent, and civil courts lack the power to impose alternative penalties or to compel convicted offenders to work and thereby earn the income to pay victims for their injuries.

Although various theorists prior to the twentieth century argued that crime victims deserved special assistance from the state, it was not until the 1950s that the idea of state responsibility to victims of crime gained much currency. One of the most persuasive early advocates of victim assistance and restitution was an English social reformer, Mary Fry (1959), who advocated state-funded compensation for victims of crime. Her arguments were derived in part from the theories that underlie public assistance, workman's compensation, and other social welfare programs. Generally, such theories hold that the state has an obligation to protect the injured, the helpless, and the incompetent. More specifically, however, she contended that since the state has assumed the obligation to protect people from crime, a crime is "a failure to protect" on the part of the state, a failure for which the state should be obliged to compensate the victim.

Fry's proposal for compensation to crime victims gained widespread acceptance in the 1960s. Three mutually reinforcing trends appear to have contributed to acceptance of the idea of societal assistance to victims of crime. Smith and Freinkel (1988:16) believe that the dramatic expansion of the welfare state in this period led to a natural inclusion of crime victims in the group of disadvantaged toward whom it was felt government should play an enhanced role. Elias (1986:20) also credited the women's movement with drawing attention to the pervasive mistreatment of female victims by the criminal justice system. The failure of society to provide vigorous prosecution of rapists and batterers came to be seen as a glaring example of female inequality. Finally, the self-help movement, exemplified originally by Alcoholics Anonymous and similar grass-roots efforts, led to the formation of victim groups that challenged the conventional operations of society generally and of the criminal justice system in particular. Consciousness-raising feminist groups sponsoring "Take Back the Night" rallies; Mothers Against Drunk Driving (MADD) and Parents of Murdered Children are examples of mutually supportive grass-roots movements that challenge the criminal justice system's exclusion of victims from the process and that promote services for crime victims (Smith and Freinkel 1988:22). Besides monetary compensation, victims began to demand a greater role in the criminal justice process, including the right to recommend the sentence and to reject a defendant's offer to plead guilty to a lesser charge.

The first crime-victim-compensation bill was passed in California in 1966. Other states followed suit, until now over thirty states provide some reimbursement to crime victims for the medical costs and loss of wages incurred by victims of violent crimes. In 1984, Congress enacted the Victims of Crime Act (VOCA), which channels funds collected from federal criminal fines to victims' groups throughout the country. In 1986, $68 million was raised for crime victims. About a third of this money was allocated to crime victim compensation programs. The remainder was awarded to victim services. Priority was given to victims of sexual assault, child abuse, and spouse abuse. Courts in many jurisdictions now permit a victim to make a victim impact statement prior to the imposition of sentence.

The successes of the victims' rights movement thus far have resulted in part from an uneasy marriage of conservative and liberal interests. Conservative philosophy stresses concern for social order and individual responsibility. Conservatives regard the primary purpose of the criminal justice system to be deterrence of crime and preservation of the existing societal structure. Victim restitution and victim participation appeal to conservatives because they believe that these will lead to harsher treatment of criminals. Liberals, on the other hand, are concerned about giving the disadvantaged greater voice and power in the social system. Since the vast majority of crime victims are poor, programs of compensation and assistance to victims of crime are consistent with the liberal emphasis on government aid to those in need.

Over time, it is likely that the inherent contradictions in this liberal–conservative alliance will create barriers to continued expansion of crime victim services. Fiscal conservatism will place limits on the funds that can be provided to crime victims. To the extent that victim advocacy on behalf of women and minorities challenges the authority and prerogatives of the privileged and powerful, victim services risk curtailments. At present, victim services and crime victim compensation are directed primarily at crimes committed by poor and underclass perpetrators. Efforts to expand victim services and victim advocacy to victims of crimes by corporations—crimes such as air and water pollution or criminally negligent manufacture of unsafe products—may meet stiff resistance from established economic interests. On the other hand, to the extent that victim advocacy and participation lead to implementation of increasingly harsh penalties against lower-class and minority offenders, the victims' rights movement may face opposition from liberals and progressives concerned about the rights and needs of criminal defendants.

## RISKS AND NEEDS OF POPULATION

Victims of crime come from all walks of life, both sexes, all races, and all ethnic backgrounds. The myth of Robin Hood—robbing the rich to give to the poor—is exactly that, a myth, perhaps derived from our broader cultural myth of equal opportunity for all. Data gathered on 1986 crimes (U.S.D.J.) indicate that persons who earned less than $7,500 a year were 2.5 times more likely than persons earning over $50,000 to be victims of violent crime (49.3 per 1,000 resident population versus 20.1 per 1,000). Household crimes (burglary and illegal entry) against families earning less than $7,500 a year occurred at the rate of 201 per 1,000, whereas household crimes against families earning over $50,000 occurred in only 164 households per 1,000; thus, having less to steal provides no insurance against household theft (U.S.D.J. 1988a:3–6).

The popular perception that whites are victimized by minorities because of race is not supported by government statistics. Whites have about the same overall rates of victimization as blacks. An overwhelming majority of violent crimes are committed by offenders against members of their own race. In 1986, 80 percent of violent crimes against whites were committed by whites; 84 percent of violent crimes against blacks were committed by blacks. While it is true that 98 percent of offenses by white offenders were against whites and only 47 percent of the offenses by black offenders were against blacks, these latter statistics may reflect the fact that whites outnumber blacks in the overall population rather than an intentional victimization of whites by blacks (U.S.D.J. 1988a:7).

Victims of crime are disproportionately young and male. In 1986, young men aged 16 to 19 had an annual victimization rate for violent crime of 81 of a 1,000, nearly three times the national average. Young women aged 20 to 24 became victims of violent crime at a rate of 44 of 1,000. Divorced and separated women were another especially vulnerable group. Violent crimes were committed against such women at an annual rate of 54.2 per 1,000. In terms of marital status, only males who have never married are victimized at a higher rate (U.S.D.J. 1988a:3).

Another popular American myth, the unknown outlaw holding up the stage coach far out on the lonesome prairie, is belied by statistics on the identity of offenders and the locale of crimes. Of all violent crimes, 42 percent are committed by persons known to or related to the victim. Crime is quite literally a neighborhood problem. While residents of rural and suburban areas do fall victim to crime, a greater incidence of crimes occurs to residents of central cities (36.3 versus 23.8 per 1,000) (U.S. Justice 1986:6).

Overall, the statistics on criminal victimization in the United States reflect the vulnerability of the poor to the social disintegration and anarchy associated with inner-city ghetto life and with poverty in general. While crime affects all citizens, it is in the chaotic climate of poor neighborhoods that violence—whether in the form of gang fights, drug wars, robberies, burglaries, purse snatching, or auto theft— occurs most frequently and adds yet another stress to the over- whelming burdens of poor people.

For anyone who has never personally experienced a violent crime, it is difficult to comprehend the overwhelming impact of such an event on the victim. Even a crime that results in no physical harm can be extraordinarily upsetting because of the psychic and economic damage incurred. Specifically, some of the consequences of criminal victimization are as follows:

*Physical injury:* Bruises, cuts, gunshot and knife wounds, broken or lost teeth, fractured bones, and permanent disfigurement or dis- ability are not infrequent consequences of assault, rape, and robbery. For example, 32 percent of all robbery and assault victims sustain physical injury as a result of the crime (U.S. Justice 1986:8).

*Economic loss:* Victims of crime often bear multiple costs as a result of the crime. Medical and hospital expenses are rarely completely reimbursed by insurance. Indispensable property— eyeglasses, work tools, or a car for getting to and from work— must be repurchased. Broken locks and smashed windows de- mand immediate replacement. Time off from work for medical and hospital care can result in the loss of wages. If the victim chooses to report the crime and to cooperate in the prosecution of the perpetrator, the additional time off from work required may result in still more lost wages or loss of the job altogether.

*Inconvenience:* Documents lost because of a stolen purse or wallet may take days, sometimes months, to replace. Hours can be spent filling out insurance reports, standing in line for a new driver's license, or negotiating with credit card companies. Each effort to secure replacement and compensation takes time and energy out of a victim's life.

*Psychic trauma:* Most victims suffer from some degree of emotional distress. Intense rage, feelings of uneasiness, grief over injuries and lost cherished possessions, and anxiety about personal and family safety are common experiences of crime victims.

Where a crime results in physical injury and/or intense fear, or where the victim was especially vulnerable (an elderly person living alone, for example), a full-scale posttraumatic stress disorder can erupt. Symptoms include flashbacks of the incident during which the victim vividly reexperiences the original traumatizing event, nightmares, anxiety, restlessness, inability to concentrate, and feelings of numbing or detachment. Other symptoms include survivor guilt (if a fellow victim was killed or more seriously injured), memory loss, and avoidance of activities that arouse recollection of the traumatic events (APA 1980:236–237).

The problems listed above are common to victims of other types of major disasters, whether they are caused by humans, such as war, or by nature, such as floods, earthquakes, and tornadoes. A very particular consequence of criminal victimization, however, is the interaction the victim must endure with the criminal justice system.

Our society is governed by the rule of the law. Punishment of crime is meted out to defendants according to carefully delineated standards and by minutely detailed rules. The purpose of these rules is to ensure that each defendant will have a fair opportunity to refute the charges against him or her and that the evidence used to convict will be pertinent and reliable. For crime victims, a by-product of our legal system is that victims become caught up in a system that is, at best, repetitive and arcane and, at worst senseless, hostile, and even dangerous.

Victims are required to participate repeatedly in the preliminary stages of the criminal process: police lineup, grand jury proceedings, pretrial hearings, and the trial itself. Property belonging to the victim is often impounded as evidence.

On occasion, victim cooperation with the criminal justice system results in harassment, fear, further injury, or even death. Victims, defendants, and their respective families often sit and stand beside one another in police stations, court rooms, or courthouse corridors. Victims who agree to act as witnesses may be harassed by phone calls or in person (remember that 42 percent of all violent crimes are committed by persons known to the victims). In many jurisdictions, the defense attorney has the right to demand to know the home and work address of the victim in order to be able to gather evidence about the case or about the credibility of the victim. Intimidation threats and outright assault are often the result of these practices. In some instances, victims and other witnesses must literally flee for their lives. In so doing, they abandon home, possessions, and their entire support system of family and neighbors.

Prosecutors under our system have considerable discretion as to the severity of the charges they bring and as to whether or not to agree to a plea on a lesser charge by a defendant. For example, a defendant charged with attempted murder may be permitted to plead guilty to a crime carrying a lesser penalty, such as attempted assault. Such plea bargaining is necessitated by the fact that crowded court dockets make the trial of all cases impossible and because the quality of the evidence in a particular case may make conviction on a more serious charge doubtful. (Police and prosecutors typically "overcharge" at the time of arrest or indictment in order to preserve the state's right to try on a more serious offense.)

In some jurisdictions, prosecutors sensitive to the feelings of victims discuss a potential plea-bargain with a victim prior to acceptance. In other jurisdictions, victims learn of the acceptance of a plea to a lesser attempt after the fact, sometimes when they see a defendant on the street because her or his case has been dismissed or the sentence suspended. In any event, victims and their families have no say in how a case is tried and whether or not a case will be settled prior to trial. The mystification and sense of helplessness endured by victims and other witnesses often leave them dissatisfied and disgruntled, with a feeling that the defendant "got away with a slap on the wrist" or, worse still, "made a deal" with the district attorney or the judge.

Sentencing and parole of the convicted offender are advanced stages of the process, where a victim has even less right to participate or be informed. Some jurisdictions permit a defendant to make a victim impact statement. Such statements, either in writing or in person, inform the sentencing judge of the severity of the crime from the victim's perspective and of how the crime has affected the victim's life. In some jurisdictions, the victim may offer an opinion as to an appropriate sentence. Many jurisdictions, however, do not permit victim impact statements. Even in jurisdictions that do, the victim has no legal power to insist upon imposition of a particular sentence.

An offender who has served his or her minimum sentence may be released from prison prior to expiration of his or her sentence on condition of good behavior. This early release is what is meant by *parole*. Parole boards, the administrative bodies authorized to grant parole, may impose specific conditions on the parolee, such as place of residence or a requirement of employment. A victim is rarely informed that a parole hearing is pending and even more rarely is consulted about suitable terms of parole. At best, the failure to inform and consult a victim offends his or her sense of fairness, and at worst, it puts him or her in mortal danger. Particularly in domestic violence situations, there have been instances of parolees coming to the home of the victims to harass, injure, or kill the persons whose complaint sent them to jail in the first place. Some jurisdictions require that parole boards consult with the prosecutor of an offender prior to granting parole to that offender. Others do not. It is left to the prosecutor's discretion whether or not to consult with the victim or to warn the victim if the offender is paroled.

In summary, the victim of a crime suffers a complex and multiple trauma: physical injury, economic loss, personal inconvenience, psychic trauma, and repeated interactions with the criminal justice system, ongoing anxiety, anger, fear, and tension. In some instances, the victim and his or her family may lose everything: home, possessions, and even life itself. What has been said here applies not just to the victims of crime but also to those who witness a crime and agree to cooperate with police and prosecution. Indeed, it is fear of becoming victims themselves that often leads witnesses to decline to participate in criminal proceedings.

## PROGRAMS AND SOCIAL WORK SERVICES

Social work responses to the risks and needs of crime victims involve direct interventions on behalf of clients from the time a crime is committed through the arrest, trial, and sentencing of the perpetrator. Even after the offender has gone to jail or has been set free, issues may arise that require assistance from social work personnel.

Emergency information and referral at the time the crime is committed are usually offered over telephone hotlines, or sometimes at police stations and hospitals. Examples of the help offered include advice on where and how to report a crime, where to go for medical treatment, how to obtain counseling and economic assistance, and how to obtain information and assistance from police or court personnel.

Once a crime has been reported, the client then requires advocacy and assistance with police and the judicial system. Most crime victims benefit from basic information on the stages of a criminal case and the role of the various officials they will encounter. In addition, clients often require a variety of practical services to help them manage their role as victims or witness. Clients may need information on trial dates transportation to and from court, safe waiting areas at court, child care during court appearances, and information on the status of the case. If the defendant is convicted, the victim may need to be informed of his or her right to make a victim impact statement to the sentencing judge and may need assistance in preparing the statement. After trial, clients are helped to reclaim property held by police and prosecutors as evidence in the case.

Victim services programs also offer direct services aimed at protecting victims and witnesses from harassment by offenders and their associates. Such interventions may include advocacy with police, prosecutors, and judges to obtian police intervention and judicial orders of protection. Since police and prosecutors lack the personnel to provide twenty-four-hour surveilance in all but a handful of cases, victims known to the perpetrator of a crime may have no choice but to leave the neighborhood or even the community in which they live. In such cases, social workers provide referral to shelters and negotiate with departments of welfare and district attorneys' offices for funds to support such relocation. Workers may advocate on the client's behalf with judges to withhold the location of the victim's residence from the defendant.

Other direct services to victims include economic assistance, counseling and support groups. Clients may require help in applying for benefit programs such as crime victims' compensation, Supplemental Security Income, and public assistance. Sometimes, workers are called upon to advocate with landlords and employers to prevent eviction or termination of employment. Many victims require short-term or long-term help with the emotional and practical consequences of victimization. Support groups are a particularly effective method of helping victims formulate, normalize, and work through their experience.

Victim services programs provide indirect services to victims through education and sensitization of criminal justice personnel (including police, attorneys, and judges) as well as the staffs of other agencies and the general public to the impact of crime on the victim. Sensitization around issues of sexual abuse, rape, family violence, and the needs of child victims often requires special effort and intervention.

Social workers also advocate for legal and procedural change. Responses in this area include advocacy for administrative changes that reduce risks for and burdens on victims (for example, by simplifying procedures for returning property held as evidence or reducing the number of times a witness is called to court). Social workers also advocate with state and federal legislators for increased funding of services and economic support of crime victims as well as for changes in judicial codes so as to better protect the interests of crime victims.

Finally, victim service programs may intervene around issues of crime prevention. Among the services that can be offered are programs aimed at increasing security (such as emergency lock and window repair or street safety education), intervention in potentially violent domestic situations (for example, by offering counseling to violence-prone families), and conscienceness raising among high school students about societal attitudes that promote violence against women.

Services to crime victims are at present generally provided in the following settings:

1. *Government-funded victim–witness assistance programs.* Such programs, whether operating as arms of police and prosecutors' offices or as free-standing agencies, tend to have as a primary focus that of encouraging victims and witnesses to cooperate in the prosecution of a criminal case. Services afforded are usually time-limited and focus on criminal-justice-related issues. Among the most frequently provided interventions are a safe waiting area in the courthouse, information about the status of a case, notification of court appearances, transportation to and from court, retrieval of property held as evidence, and referral to agencies offering other services (e.g., welfare, mental health clinics, and crime victims' compensation programs). Social workers in these settings often have access to and thus an excellent opportunity of sensitizing personnel to the needs of crime victims. Victim–witness programs that are police- or court-based are less likely than independent victim services to offer long-term help such as counseling. Government-funded programs are also usually prohibited from lobbying for statutory change.

2. *Support and treatment services for specific victim subgroups.* A number of victim assistance programs for specific victim subgroups have grown up outside formal governmental agencies and community agencies. Such programs may offer telephone information and referral, counseling, and support groups to survivors of especially traumatic crimes such as rape, incest, and domestic violence; to families of homicide victims; and to especially vulnerable victims such as the elderly. Support and treatment services for special categories of victims can also operate within the structure of preexisting health and welfare agencies such as hospitals, mental health clinics, and community service agencies.

3. *Programs advocating changes in the law and criminal procedures.* Examples of such organizations include grass-roots groups supporting gun control, changes in laws governing sex crimes and domestic violence, and harsher penalties for offenders. Groups advocating harsher sentencing, especially capital punishment, however well intentioned, present ethical dilemmas for social workers because of the tendency of such efforts to dehumanize offenders and to stress simplistic solutions to complex social ills.

# DIFFERENTIAL CLINICAL ASSESSMENTS AND INTERVENTIONS

Given the frequency of crime in America, sooner or later virtually all practicing social workers are likely to confront a situation in which a client needs assistance with the problems that arise as a result of being a victim of or a witness to a crime. When such problems arise, they may be of an emergency nature. Skillful assessment of need and appropriate intervention begins, therefore, *prior* to client contact, with the worker informing herself or himself about the criminal justice system and the criminal-justice-related services in the locality of the worker's practice. Specifically, the worker should be familiar with the following information:

1. Does the local jurisdiction have a victim–witness assistance program? If so, who runs it—police, prosecutor's office, or another agency? Does the victim–witness program have a hotline? What is the number, and during what hours does it operate?

2. If the locale does not have a victim–witness service, who within the local police department and prosecutor's office is in a position to provide information about the status of a criminal case, emergency assistance to endangered victims, and knowledge about other resources in the jurisdiction?

3. What special services exist for victims and witnesses of crime? For example, is there a rape crisis program in a nearby hospital? Where are the nearest shelters for battered women? Does the state have a crime victims' compensation program? If so, what financial assistance is offered? Are there agencies or individual practitioners who treat posttraumatic stress disorder? What self-help and support groups exist for victims of rape, battered women, and families of homicide victims?

In working with crime victims, it is vital to bear in mind that the criminal justice process is a complex, multistage business. Different officials are likely to be responsible for each stage of the process. Sometimes, different officials handle the same stage of the process. The following is a simplified summary of the stages of the criminal justice process and the officials responsible for its operation.

Generally speaking, police officers take the victim's complaint, investigate the crime, collect evidence, and apprehend or arrest the suspected perpetrator of the crime. Following arrest, the police usually escort the suspect to court (or in lesser offenses, order the suspect to appear in court). At this point, the jurisdiction's prosecuting attorney (usually referred to as the *district attorney*) assumes responsibilty for the case.

The state or federal prosecutor, or more typically an attorney who assists the prosecutor, reviews the evidence collected by the police. If the prosecuting attorney believes the evidence is strong enough to convict the suspect, she or he presents the evidence to a grand jury, which formally indicts the suspect, who is thenceforth referred to as the *defendant*. Following indictment, the defendant is arraigned, that is, officially informed of the charges against him or her and required to plead guilty or not guilty.

A defendant who pleads guilty is sentenced at a subsequent hearing. If a not-guilty plead is entered, the defendant is ordered by the judge to stand trial. Prior to trial, a series of "discovery" hearings are usually held, during which prosecution and defense attorneys ask for one another's evidence and contend over whether various evidence may be used against or for the defendant. Ultimately, often months after the commission of the crime itself, the defendant is tried and found guilty or not guilty by a jury.

As noted previously, the vast majority of criminal cases are never brought to trial. Most are settled either by dismissal of the charges or by a plea bargain, that is, an arrangement between defense, prosecution, and the judge that the defendant will plead guilty to the charge or a lesser charge in return for a preagreed sentence. Sentence is imposed by the judge, who usually relies on an investigation and recommendation by the court probation department as the basis for the sentence.

Offenders who are sentenced are no longer the responsibility of the court or the district attorney. A new set of officials takes over, usually the state correction department, which is part of the administrative branch of government. In most cases, offenders are eligible for parole from prison prior to the expiration of their sentence. Whether or not offenders are paroled and on what terms is decided by a parole board, a body appointed by the governor in most states.

We have already observed how this immensely complex system invariably befuddles the victim, who, correctly, perceives it to be inconsistent and occasionally irrational. The more familiar a social worker is with the stages and purposes of the criminal process, and especially the more familiar he or she is with the officials responsible for a particular case, the more helpful he or she will be to the client.

Once a worker is actually faced with a client who has difficulties that result from having been a victim of crime, the following issues require assessment and, where appropriate, intervention:

1. *Physical security.* The first assessment to be made in any case of victimization is the physical security of the client. Where is the client at the time of contact? Is he or she telephoning from the street or an unsecured house? If the client is unsafe, appropriate interventions would include instructing the client to go to the nearest police precinct, a relative or neighbor's house, or a shelter. If the client's doors or windows have been damaged, it is appropriate to instruct the client to call a locksmith. If the client is in a threatening situation because of potential violence by the offender or the offender's associates, it is necessary to notify the prosecuting attorney, who can obtain a court order of protection. Where an order of protection is unlikely to be effective, the victim needs referral to a shelter or a safehome or assistance with relocation.

2. *Client's medical condition.* If the client has been raped or has received some other physical injury, he or she should be advised to seek medical attention at once. Such attention may be necessary not only to protect the client's health, but also to preserve evidence of the crime. Especially in rape cases, a proper physical examination by persons who are familiar with the evidence required in sexual assault cases may be essential if a later prosecution is to be successful. Semen samples, for example, not only prove sexual intercourse but may be genetically tested to establish the identity of the perpetrator. In cases of physical attack or abuse, photographs of the client's physical injuries substantiate assault charges. Wherever possible, clients should be referred to medical centers experienced in treating victims of crime.

3. *Status of the case against the perpetrator.* Often, clients request assistance with some aspect of the criminal case. They may wish to give information to the police. They may need to know or to request a change of the date and time of a court appearance. They may need protection from harassment by the defendant. They may wish to request return of property impounded as evidence. The worker should find out or instruct the client to find out to what stage of the process the case has proceeded. If possible, identifying case numbers should be obtained and recorded (typically, such numbers include complaint number, arrest number, and indictment number). The name of the officials who are handling or who have handled the victim's case should be obtained and recorded.

Clients are often intimidated by the justice system. The worker should, to the extent useful, explain to the client how the system works and should alert the client to the need to write down the case numbers and the names of responsible officials at each new stage of the process. The worker must stress to the client that he or she is entitled to consideration from criminal justice personnel and should encourage the client to seek the information and help required. Clients who have language difficulties or who are intimidated by criminal justice personnel may need the worker to make contact and negotiate for them.

4. *Economic problems resulting from victimization.* Often, a crime leaves the victim temporarily or permanently without the income needed to survive. For example, where a week's wages or the proceeds of a welfare check are stolen, the client may be unable to purchase food or pay rent. The client may need emergency food and shelter. If a client has been disabled, he or she may need to file for public assistance, social security, or (if the injury occurred as a result of a job-related activity) workman's compensation. The worker should be prepared to instruct clients where and how to apply for such entitlements and what documents the client will be required to produce to support the application.

In addition to loss of income, the client may have incurred crime-related expenses. Such costs may include replacing broken locks, installing security gates, and repurchasing personal items such as eyeglasses, dentures, and hearing aids. Where the crime was a violent one, additional medical and dental bills may require payment.

In many states, crime victim compensation programs reimburse victims for some crime-related expenses. Where loss of wages is due to physical injury (but not to work time lost while testifying about the crime), state programs may pay a portion of the income lost. Medical, dental, and funeral costs, if not otherwise reimbursed by private insurance, may also be repaid to the client.

In order to qualify for crime victim compensation, the victim must report the crime to the police within the time period designated by the statute. Most jurisdictions do not reimburse for losses incurred by persons where the victim's own criminal activities contributed to his or her injury (for example, a drug dealer injured in the course of a drug sale or a prostitute injured by a customer); consequently, compensation is granted only after consultation with police and prosecutors. Some states make emergency grants in situations where the victim or, in the case of a homicide, the victim's family clearly qualifies for compensation. Usually, however, several months are needed to investigate and process a claim.

Because most compensation programs do not pay to replace personal property, social workers may need to find creative ways to assist impoverished clients. Sometimes, the business community can be induced to contribute to a fund to replace locks, security gates, and eyeglasses for elderly or destitute crime victims. Other special programs that often attract community support are food, clothing, and furniture donations.

An economically related need of many clients is the necessity of replacing stolen documents such as medicaid cards, social security cards, driver's licenses, credit cards, and other identifying materials. The worker should review with the client what documents have been lost. If the stolen items include credit cards, savings account passbooks, checks, or other materials whose misuse could result in embezzlement or fraud, the client should be advised to contact her or his bank and/or companies issuing the credit cards. The client should also be informed how to replace government-issued documents such as welfare and social security cards or driver's license.

5. *The mental health consequences of the client's victimization.* Bard and Sangrey (1986), Ericson (1976), and Bettelheim (1980), among others, have observed that any major trauma, including criminal victimization, has a profoundly destabilizing effect on the mental health of a survivor. The central consequence of crime for the victim is the destruction of the narcissistic illusion of invulnerability with which most of us live in the world. Up to a point, this illusion constitutes healthy denial of unavoidable danger. Such defenses allow us to go though the day without dysfunctional anxiety. When these defenses are breached, the result is feelings of helplessness, panic, and a sense of shame.

Part of what ordinarily preserves our illusion of safety is the sense of security created by networks of supportive relationships, such as family, neighbors, community agencies, and government institutions. This network of support helps us "edit reality in such a way that [the culture's] perils are at least partially masked" (Ericson 1976:240). In many inner-city neighborhoods, the destruction or absence of a cohesive community means that the victim's sense of security is already compromised. Criminal victimization thus accentuates what is already an ongoing sense of vulnerability. Victimization also undermines the belief system that permits the victim to view the world as rational and just. A sense of despair, pessimism, or hopelessness thus often follows in the wake of a serious crime.

In initial contacts with crime victims, it is usually helpful to inform them that feelings of panic, rage, and depression as well as occasional flashbacks are a normal reaction to a shocking experience. The client should be told that such symptoms do not mean he or she is going crazy. The victim should be encouraged to talk about the experience as often as the need arises. Such talking out of the event permits a crime victim to integrate and achieve a sense of mastery over his or her experience.

Crime victims also benefit from interventions that help them gain a sense of control over their environment and a sense of reconnection to the society of which they are a member. Many of the interventions already suggested in previous sections have this effect. For example, a client who gains the respectful attention of a police officer or prosecutor or who receives crime victim compensation feels less powerless and, in addition, begins to regain some feeling of concern and protection from the society of which she or he is a part.

As Bard and Sangrey (1986:55–59) pointed out, many victims try to regain feelings of control by blaming themselves (e.g., "I shouldn't have gone out that night"). Such clients are not helped by assurances that they are not at fault, since the underlying dynamic for the guilt is the need to feel in control. They are better served by being offered more adaptive means of regaining a sense of mastery over their lives. For example, rape victims often benefit from a self-defense course. A dog, secure locks, or window gates also decrease real and imagined vulnerability. Often, suggestions as simple as avoiding unlit streets or rearranging the furniture of one's home help restore a sense of power to the victim.

Bettelheim observed that with respect to Holocaust survivors, the healthiest are those who integrate what has happened to them by fashioning a new belief system that provides a more adaptive response to their lives: "These are the survivors who tried to salvage something positive from their camp experience—horrible as it had been. This often made their lives more difficult than their old ones had been, also in some ways more complex, but possibly more meaningful" (1980:34).

Among the ways that crime victims arrive at integration of their experience and a more resilient belief system is by participation in self-help support groups or in formal group therapy. The group experience normalizes the victim's experience and can restore the sense of communality. In many parts of the country, there are groups for battered women, survivors of rape and child sexual abuse, and families of homicide victims. Social workers assisting crime victims should routinely mention the possibility of support groups since clients may become aware of the need for such help long after contact with the worker.

Many crime victims construct meaning out of their experience by finding ways to help other traumatized people or by participating in action efforts that address their own experience. Rape and battered-women hotlines, for example, are often operated by survivors of the same or similar crimes. Advocates of handgun control are often themselves victims of gun-related crimes.

For any client whose reaction to victimization seriously impairs functioning for more than a few days or is accompanied by suicidal ideation, a referral for psychiatric evaluation is definitely indicated. Where possible, referral should be to a clinic or a professional with expertise in posttraumatic stress disorder. Crime victims with a prior history of psychiatric illness should be considered especially vulnerable to recurrence of depression or psychosis. Referral for psychiatric evaluation should be routinely considered for such clients. Persons with character structures that leave them vulnerable to narcissistic injury are likely to need a good deal of support in integrating their victimization and should probably be encouraged to obtain counseling.

6. *Any special ethnic, cultural, or socioeconomic factors that put a client at particular risk and that require special intervention.* Obviously, clients who speak no English require more assistance to negotiate for their needs and concerns than do English-speaking clients. Foreign-born crime victims, even those fluent in English, may be wholly ignorant of American judicial procedure and may need detailed explanation of how our system operates. In addition, attitudes among some ethnic groups may pose special hazards for crime victims. For example, in some cultures, the victim of rape is considered irreparably soiled and damaged. Special efforts may be required to protect the identity of the victim from public knowledge and to educate the victim's family to the fact that rape is simply a violent crime for which the victim is in no way responsible.

In some religious and ethnic communities, it is unacceptable to seek redress from officials outside the community. These attitudes put victims of domestic violence at particular risk, since the victim may have no alternative but to stay in the household. Efforts to work with community leaders and to implement victim service programs from within the particular community may be required.

Poor and minority crime victims are usually very diffident about approaching prosecutors and public agencies for information or assistance. At best, they know they lack the technical vocabulary and social confidence required to deal with a public official and are pessimistic about their chances of success. At worst, they fear becoming suspects or defendants themselves. Victim advocates may need to walk such individuals through the system and negotiate on their behalf.

## CASE ILLUSTRATION

Mr. Smith called the hotline of his local victim–witness assistance agency shortly after midnight. Tearfully, he told the hotline worker that his 18-year-old son, Charlie, had been shot and killed during a dispute with a member of a local gang. His wife, Mrs. Smith, had been alerted to the fracas while it was going on in front of their house and had arrived at the door in time to see their son, mortally wounded, stagger up the front stoop and collapse at her feet in a pool of blood. Mr. Smith explained that his son's body was no longer in the hospital emergency room. He had no idea how to obtain it for burial. Moreover, he himself was disabled, living on workman's compensation, and unable to pay for the funeral. He wondered if there was "any government money to pay for this kind of thing." He also expressed worry that his other sons, 20-year-old Jim and 21-year-old Harry, were vowing vengeance against their brother's killer. Mr. Smith was fearful his family would be involved in further violence.

The hotline worker inquired whether the person who had shot Charlie had been arrested and whether there was any immediate likelihood of violence. Mr. Smith said the police had taken the man who had done the shooting into custody and things were quiet for the moment. The worker told Mr. Smith that Charlie's body had probably been taken to the morgue for autopsy and would be released to the family within a day or two. The worker also told Mr. Smith that crime victim compensation might pay for some of the funeral expenses. He told Mr. Smith that the victim-witness agency offered counseling services to families of homicide victims and suggested that Mr. Smith come to the agency in the morning to meet with a staff social worker to assess what help the family needed. He told Mr. Smith to call the local police precinct and find out the complaint number for the crime and the name of the police officers assigned to investigate the case.

The hotline worker's interventions have two primary aims: rapid assessment of risk to the client and clear advice and information on how and where to get help. The worker's style may seem dispassionate, perhaps almost cold. This stance is deliberate. People in crisis are best helped by precise, unambiguous directives and suppression of feelings until the moment of crisis is passed. The time for expression of overwhelming feelings will come later. Note, however, that the hotline worker ensures that follow-up contact will occur.

The next morning, Mr. Smith met with Miss Jones, the agency caseworker assigned to assist families of homicide victims. She gave Mr. Smith a crime victims' compensation application to fill out and suggested he take it immediately to the state crime victims' compensation office for processing as an emergency grant request. She cautioned him, however, that an emergency grant might not be issued because there might not be enough evidence to determine whether Charlie had been involved in some illegal activity that had led to his conflict with the perpetrator. Mr. Smith became very upset at learning this and insisted that Charlie was a "good boy who always kept out of trouble." Neighbors had told him that Charlie had been killed because he intervened to break up a fight between the gang member and his girlfriend. The worker suggested that Mr. Smith give this information to the crime victims' compensation office along with the names of witnesses to the crime and the police officers investigating the case. In Mr. Smith's presence, the worker called the coroner's office and learned that Charlie's body would be released to the family that afternoon. Miss Jones suggested to Mr. Smith that he contact his church for advice on a reputable funeral home. She also told Mr. Smith to get in touch with her in a few days to see what other needs the family might have.

At this early stage of client contact, the focus is still on direct, unambiguous advice on how to handle the immediate crisis. Note the explicitness of the worker's information. Highly traumatized persons often require step-by-step instructions because they are too numb and bewildered to think for themselves.

Miss Jones asked if Mr. Smith was still worried about further trouble between his sons and the gang members. Mr. Smith said he was. With Mr. Smith's permission, Miss Jones called the local police precinct and spoke with the commanding officer. She suggested that he or the officer investigating the case meet with the Smith children and urge them to let the police and prosecutors handle the case and to allow justice to take its course. The captain agreed to follow up on Miss Jones' suggestions.

The worker here serves as the victim's advocate with the police. She intervenes because it cannot be assumed that the officers assigned to the case are aware of the volatility of the situation or of the family's need for reassurance that the crime will be taken seriously by the criminal justice system.

Five days later, Mr. Smith called the worker. He had succeeded in getting crime victims' compensation. The family had been comforted by the funeral. Miss Jones inquired how he and his family were doing emotionally. He told her that his wife was in a "terrible state." She had been crying continuously, was unable to eat or sleep, and was scarcely able to speak. He had also been informed that a neighbor, Mrs. Brown, who had witnessed the homicide, had been threatened by friends of the perpetrator if she cooperated with the district attorney's office.

Miss Jones arranged for Mr. and Mrs. Smith to come in for an appointment. She also told Mr. Smith to have the witness contact her. Miss Jones called the district attorney's office. Initially, she contacted the office administrator and learned the name of the assistant district attorney who had been assigned to the case. She contacted this attorney and informed her that a witness had been threatened by friends of the defendant. The attorney agreed that Miss Jones' agency should assist the witness and offered to obtain an order of protection against the persons who had threatened the witness if the threats continued.

The worker here is careful to coordinate her efforts with the prosecutor's office. Attorneys prosecuting criminal cases often have justifiable concerns about vital or conflicting information being reported to the wrong persons. The worker, by contacting the attorney assigned to the case, makes clear her role and gives the attorney a chance to explain the legal concerns of her office.

Later that afternoon, Mrs. Brown, the witness, called the worker. After discussing various options, they agreed that Mrs. Brown should move in with her sister, who lived across town, until "things cooled down." The worker told the witness to call her if she had further trouble and told Mrs. Brown that she would probably be expected to testify at the grand jury hearing in a week or so. The worker told Mrs. Brown about the agency's witness alert program. If she needed information about when she would be required to testify, she could contact the agency personnel handling witness notifications. Ms. Jones also told Mrs. Brown that the agency had a safe waiting area at the courthouse. When the time came for her to testify, she could wait there so that she would not have to be near the defendant and his family. Miss Jones outlined for the witness the stages of the criminal justice system and when she would be expected to testify.

The worker educates the witness about the criminal justice system so that later, Mrs. Brown may feel less bewildered and pushed around by the many court appearances required of her.

Several days later, the worker met with Mr. and Mrs. Smith. Mrs. Smith appeared numb and confused. As she steadily cried, she told the worker that she kept having vivid recollections of her son's dying moments; these vivid flashbacks came back to her with all the reality of the original events. She had been unable to sleep since the murder. In response to Miss Jones' inquiry about prior emotional difficulties, Mrs. Smith reported an episode of depression ten years previously. Miss Jones asked Mr. Smith how he was doing. He told her that he too had trouble sleeping and was alternately numb and enraged.

With the defendant arrested and the immediate crisis somewhat cooled down, the worker now begins to give the clients a chance to explore and express their feelings. Mrs. Smith's prior history of depression alerts the worker to the fact that Mrs. Smith may be unable to cope with her grief and may need special help.

Miss Jones told the Smiths that many of their symptoms were the expectable reactions to a horrible experience. She suggested that Mrs. Smith consult her physician, who might recommend some medication to quell her anxiety and help reestablish her sleep pattern. Miss Jones warned that grief takes time and they could expect recurrent episodes of pain for at least a year. She also strongly recommended that the family join the agency's support group for families of homicide victims, which met at the agency every month. She recommended to Mr. Smith that he periodically get in touch with the prosecutor's office so that he could be informed of the progress of the case. She stressed that he was entitled to consideration from the prosecutor's office and that he should ask to be consulted if the prosecuting attorney wanted to plea-bargain the case.

The worker, while remaining responsive to Mrs. Smith's vulnerability to depression, helps normalize the clients' reactions and provides Mr. Smith with alternatives that may help him feel less powerless.

Over the next two years, the Smiths regularly attended the agency's support program. While Mr. Smith's mental state gradually improved, Mrs. Smith continued to be agitated, sleepless, and increasingly depressed. She felt unable to work and had recurrent thoughts of wanting to die. After two months, the worker who ran the support group referred Mrs. Smith to a psychiatrist who specialized in posttraumatic stress disorder. He diagnosed Mrs. Smith as suffering from clinical depression and prescribed antidepressant medication and some biofeedback exercises to assist her in blocking the recurrent troubling flashbacks.

The severity and duration of Mrs. Smith's reaction after two months indicate that her grief requires more intensive assistance.

Almost a year to the day after the murder of their son, the defendant came to trial. He had entered a plea of not guilty. His defense was that Charlie had threatened him and that he had killed Charlie in self-defense. The Smiths, their friends, and their family attended the trial every day. Midway through the trial, Mr. Smith called the worker who ran the support group and told her that the prosecution was considering accepting a plea of manslaughter. Mr. Smith was enraged and pained at this development. The prosecutor wanted to know what the family thought. After talking things over with the worker and, on her advice, with his wife and children, Mr. Smith told the prosecutor that he preferred that the case be sent to the jury for a verdict on the more serious charge of second-degree murder. The prosecutor agreed to follow their wishes but warned that an acquittal might be the result. Despite strong evidence by the prosecution witnesses, including Mrs. Brown, the jury found the defendant guilty of manslaughter, rather than second-degree homicide. This verdict meant that the defendant would receive far less than the life sentence the family had hoped for.

During the stress of the trial, the family received encouragement from their support group. The group shared their anger and dismay at the relatively light offense of which the defendant was convicted. Mrs. Smith experienced a revival of her posttraumatic stress symptoms. With the group worker's encouragement, she sought a further psychiatric consultation. The combination of additional medication and telephone reassurance from other group members brought her through this new episode within a few weeks.

Note that a full year after the homicide, the family is again in crisis and in need of assistance by the worker and the support group. Such recurrences of the original traumatic reaction are common as the offender's case moves through the system.

The group encouraged the Smiths to prepare a victim impact statement, which, with the cooperation of the prosecutor, they presented to the probation department. Based, in part, on this report, the judge sentenced the defendant to eight to twenty-five years in jail, the maximum the law permitted. The parents continued to participate in the support group. They now provided guidance and advice to new members and saw their participation as a way of "making sense out of what happened to Charlie."

The Smiths are attempting to integrate their tragedy into their lives by bringing something good and constructive to their situation. In Bettelheim's terms, they are trying to make something positive out of their experience.

Despite very major growth in services to crime victims since the mid-1970s, vast areas of this country offer only minimal services to crime victims or none at all. This remains so despite the fact that service to crime victims is one of the few programmatic areas that federal and state governments continued to fund during the conservative tide of the 1980s.

In general, where the needs of prosecutors and police coincide with the needs of crime victims (i.e., programs that facilitate victim–witness cooperation in the criminal justice process, such as notification of court appearances and transportation to court), funding is easiest to secure. Crime victims' compensation statutes (in the thirty-some states that offer it) alleviate some of the economic hardship caused by violent crime. Such programs reimburse victims for lost wages and medical expenses. As yet, however, there is little assistance to victims for losses from economic crimes such as theft, robbery, and other types of larceny.

Services to crime victims are still a relatively undeveloped area of social work practice. Workers must be prepared to use initiative and imagination in assisting clients. Advocacy for crime victims is likely to meet with support from sectors of government and society not usually noted for concern about social welfare issues. Police, prosecutors, judges, and other criminal justice personnel often prove willing to sponsor and cooperate with the development of programs for crime victims. Conservative politicians may find the needs of crime victims a more palatable cause than other human welfare problems. Volunteers are drawn to the plight of crime victims and can provide vital assistance and staffing. Many crisis hotlines, for example, are partially or fully staffed by volunteers, as are many safehomes for battered women. Overall, then, services to crime victims offer social workers unique opportunities for innovation and creative effort.

## REFERENCES

APA (American Psychiatric Association). 1980. *Diagnostic and Statistical Manual of Mental Disorders (DSM-III)*, 3d ed. Washington, D.C.: APA.

Bard, Morton and Sangrey, Dawn. 1986. *The Crime Victim's Book*, 2d ed. New York: Brunner/Mazel.

Bettelheim, Bruno. 1980. *Surviving and Other Essays*. New York: Vintage.

Drapkin, Israel and Viano, Emilio, eds. 1974. *Victimology: A New Focus*, vols. 1–5. Lexington, Mass.: D. C. Heath.

Elias, Robert. 1986. *The Politics of Victimization, Victims, Victimology and Human Rights*. New York: Oxford University Press.

Ericson, Kai. 1976. *Everything in Its Path, Destruction of Community in the Buffalo Creek Flood*. New York: Simon & Schuster.

Fry, Margaret. 1959. "Justice for Victims." *Journal of Public Law* 8:191–194.

Jacob, Bruce. 1977. "The Concept of Restitution: A Historical Overview." In J. Hudson and B. Galaway, eds., *Restitution in Criminal Justice: A Critical Assessment of Sanctions*, pp. 45–51. Lexington, Mass.: Lexington Books.

Kilpatrick, Dean, Lois Veronen, and Patricia Resnick. 1979. "The Aftermath of Rape: Recent Empirical Findings." *American Journal of Orthopsychiatry* 49:659–669.

Knudten, Richard D., et al. 1976. *Victims and Witnesses: The Impact of Crime and Their Experiences with the Criminal Justice System*. Milwaukee: Marquette University Center for Criminal Justice and Social Policy.

McDonald, W., ed. 1976. *Criminal Justice and the Victim*. Beverly Hills, Calif.: Sage.

Smith, Steven and Susan Freinkel. 1988. *Adjusting the Balance, Federal Policy and Victim Services*. New York: Geenwald.

United States. 1982. *President's Task Force on Victims of Crime, Final Report*. Washington, D.C.: GPO.

U.S. Justice (U.S. Department of Justice). 1986. *Criminal Victimization in the United States*. Washington D.C.: U.S. Department of Justice, Bureau of Justice Statistics.

U.S. Justice. 1988a. *Criminal Victimization in the United States*. Washington D.C.: U.S. Department of Justice, Bureau of Justice Statistics.

U.S. Justice. 1988b. *Research in Action* (August). Washington D.C.: National Institute of Justice.

Ziegenhagen, Eduard. 1977. *Victims, Crime and Social Control*. New York: Praeger.

# 14

## Death of a Child

▼

### BARBARA OBERHOFER DANE

Death, perhaps humanity's greatest mystery and source of fear, has from earliest recorded times been a chief focus of superstitions and beliefs about life and the world. Thoughts about death have influenced both philosophies and religions. Various cultures have devised strategies in dealing with the fact of death that have depended on the culture's religions, philosophies, legal and political institutions, and socioeconomic conditions. Whatever strategies or coping mechanisms society provides for the individual, the death of a loved one is a profound experience, disorienting and disturbing to one's physical and emotional balance.

The death of a loved one constitutes one of the most painful experiences we undergo in our lifetime. Death in old age or after a prolonged illness provides survivors with opportunities to do preparatory mourning and a chance to say good-bye. Sudden death such as by suicide, miscarriage, earthquake, or car accidents, is initially incomprehensible and takes a longer time to assimilate. Death out of turn, such as the sudden or accidental death of a child, is an excruciating experience for parents, given the implicit expectation that the parent will die before the child.

The integration and assimilation of a loved one's death are a slow process, and mourning is dependent upon the uniqueness of the individual's way of coping with stress and loss, the relationship to the bereaved, the manner of death, age, length of illness or suddenness of death, and the degree of change the survivors can bring about in their everyday life.

The specific focus of this essay is families who experience the unnatural death of a child—an untimely assault on the survivors. Loss of a nuclear family member takes its toll psychologically as well as physiologically. Loss of a child always extracts more severe forms of response. It take families by surprise. Suddenly, their world is turned upside down. Life will never be the same again. Because all this happened—striking like a tornado—leaving the family in shambles, there is no time for a careful accounting of resources. Helping families rebuild their lives after the loss of a child is a significant social work task.

## PROBLEM DOMAIN

Death threatens us with the abrogation of ourselves and all that we love and value. We are future-oriented, and to imagine a time in which there will be no future arouses anxiety. Even events associated with death, such as separation, loss, sleep, illness, loss of control, or saying good-bye can bring out this feeling. Each of us is continuously subject to the threat of death, and our most difficult experiences in life involve a loss of some kind, whether physical or symbolic. All of us are grievers, and themes of loss confront us over the life span. Death is the ultimate loss. As grievers, we can appreciate that an expenditure of physical and emotional energy is required.

Grief is a profound emotional crisis. It is enormously complex and is related to a wide array of circumstances. Bereavement, then, is not only a unique crisis but one of the stressful events in the life of an individual. Grief is a normal process, not a psychiatric disorder. The grief reaction itself carries with it elements that usually tend to produce their own healing (Margolis 1981).

The understanding of the grief phenomenon is connected to the different explanations of loss theories. Early studies of bereavement focused on the emotional reactions to loss and found that most persons tend to follow a particular sequence of reactions. In his paper "Mourning and Melancholia," Freud (1957) stressed that the bereaved person has to go through a period of mourning before giving up the loved person.

Lindemann (1944) stated that the duration of bereavement depends on the success of grief work. He described three phases that must be completed to successfully resolve grief: First, there is shock. Second, there is a period of intense grief characterized by periodic tears, a sense of disconnectedness, aimlessness, and an inability to comprehend the reality of the experience. For some, a numbness or absence of sensation exists. It is during this period that the survivor doubts the meaning and purpose of life and experiences the greatest sense of disorganization regarding the future and the value of striving. The third phase emerges when the death and all its social and emotional implications are usually acknowledged. The survivor begins to look outward, to pick up the pieces, and to focus on new and remaining relationships. Acceptance of the loss increases, though grieving and other expressions of mourning continue.

Bowlby (1961) advanced the concept of stages of mourning, based on a review of the works of Freud and other psychoanalysts. He noted three phases based on observations of young children's reaction to separation. The first of these phases, protest, which is characterized by weeping, anger, disappointment, or accusation, results from a strenuous effort, conscious or unconscious, to "recover the lost object." Second, despair, which is characterized by restlessness, an inability to sit still, and a lack of capacity to initiate and maintain organized patterns of behavior, represents a disorganization of behavior and the increased recognition of the lack of an object toward which to be organized. Third, detachment is a reorganization period where behavior directed toward the lost object persists but with gradual decline and increased ability on the part of the bereaved to discriminate between patterns that are no longer appropriate and those that can reasonably be maintained. While offering no time frame for such stages, Bowlby indicated that grief work could be considered ended when some form of more-or-less stable reorganization is beginning to occur.

The development of theory on the characteristic stages of grief does not explain the grief experience of families whose sorrow is not time-bound; by a twist of fate, a child dies, a teenager commits suicide, or war or an earthquake ends the life of a loved one. People who live with these experiences grieve differently; sometimes, their experience is described as *chronic sorrow* (Raphael 1983). The imposition of stage models on this experience distorts the experience and limits our understanding of the psychology of mourning. Stage theories generally presume a time-limited "natural" progress through the stages, which culminates in acceptance, reconciliation, or resolution.

Astute clinicians have observed that normal parental grief appears to approximate the commonly accepted descriptions of pathological mourning or unresolved grief. Research studies have documented that grief over the loss of a child is relatively more severe than grief over other losses (Clayton, 1980; Clayton, Desmarais, and Winokur, 1968; Sanders, 1979–80; Schwab et al. 1975; Shanfield and Swain 1984; Singh and Raphael 1981). The loss of a child has been found to be particularly complicated and long-lasting (Osterweis, Solomon, and

Green 1984) and to evidence major shifts in intensity over time, with symptoms frequently increasing following a decrease or absence of them previously (Fish and Whitty 1983; Rando 1983).

McClowry et al. (1987) interviewed forty-nine families in which children had died of cancer seven to nine years previously. They described three patterns of grieving that the families used: first, attempting to "get over it" by accepting the death as fate or God's will; second, attempting to "fill the emptiness" by keeping busy and adopting new goals; and third, "keeping the connection" by integrating the pain and loss into their lives. In most cases, the parents expressed pain and loss even after seven to nine years, and instead of "letting go" of the dead child, the families described the continuing presence of an "empty space" in their families.

Fish (1986) did a study of differences in grief intensity between grieving parents. The study involved seventy-seven women and thirty-five men who had been bereaved from one month to sixteen years. Fish argued that, unlike a "wound" which heals in time, the greiving process for parents is more like a "dismemberment," requiring adaptation to a loss that does not end. Klass and Marwit (1988–89) described this "metaphor of amputation" as the sense that a piece of the self has been cut out, that it is exaggerated in parental grief, and this sense of amputation does not diminish with time, that it is lifelong.

There are a number of factors that predispose bereaved parents to be exceptionally vulnerable to unresolved grief. The unique relationship of parental responsibility, child dependency, and intense types of psychological, social, and physical investment in the child in terms of hopes and dreams sets the stage for parental grief (Rando 1985). The child's significance to the parents in terms of meanings, the irreplaceability of the parental role, and the fact that parents are forced to grow up with the loss support the severity of the loss.

All bereaved people are somewhat socially stigmatized and may experience altered social relationships after being cast in a bereaved role. Parents whose children have died appear to experience more social stigma than do others. It is all too common for bereaved parents to experience feelings of abandonment, helplessness, and frustration in their experiences with other parents after the death of their child. They often complain that they feel like "social lepers." Frequently, they are avoided by other parents or find themselves the object of anger when their premorbid levels of activity and humor do not return quickly enough (Rando 1986).

Bereaved parents represent the worst fears of other parents, and consequently, they are subject to intense social ostracism and unrealistic expectations, as other parents attempt to ward off the anxieties generated within themselves. Clearly, other parents are made anxious by bereaved parents because of a recognition that this unnatural event could happen to them and their own children. Perhaps the "magical thinking" of childhood—the fear that if one thinks or says something it will come to pass in reality, or an unrealistic fear of "contagion"—is not restricted to the young child. This fear may account for the avoidance syndrome experienced by a majority of bereaved parents. Whatever the reason, bereaved parents are often left without many of the social and emotional supports desirable for coping with the grief process (Weizmann and Kamm 1988; Rando 1988).

## SOCIETAL CONTEXT

Every society cloaks death and the disposal of the dead body with social and religious rituals that may or may not be helpful to the survivors. Not only does the public recognition of the deceased heighten the reality of the death, but the ritual defines both implicitly and explicitly the process of acceptable emotional expression, a display of bereavement. Rituals and ceremonies provide support and give the family direction about how to be bereaved. All of this assists the bereaved person and gives some meaning, security, predictability, and control.

The elaborate arrangements—for burial service; a viewing of the body; selection of a coffin or urn, gravestone, or a cemetery site; and provision for care of the grave—allow adults to work through the reality of their own death by focusing on aspects of it over which they can have some control. The details of the funeral and the burial may not bring adults closer to an emotional acceptance of death, but they do give them some feeling of certainty about the events immediately following the death (Mitford 1978).

The expanded role of the funeral director and the funeral profession, coupled with societal changes, has had a substantial impact on the growth of their business. Some funeral directors place financial consideration above the needs of the survivors. At the same time, others are helpful during the death crisis and provide a source of knowledge and expertise in assisting the survivors.

There are practical demands with which the survivor has to deal. If the deceased is a family member, the sheer physical and social demands of religious and cultural rituals—like family gatherings, such as sitting *shivah* or participating in a wake—help one to cope with the loss. Within contemporary American society, much of this support system has been modified or eroded by change. As a result, acute grief is becoming more complex and its resolution more difficult.

Gorer (1965) observed that the decline in ritual is evidence of our death-denying society and may be responsible for a considerable amount of maladaptive behavior. It is not uncommon for those central to grieving, often the clergy, to attempt to keep deep feelings of grief restrained, and thus, mourners are left with the necessity of completing grieving during a sometime extended postfuneral period. A significant work focused on death (Barrett 1977) suggested that bereavement is less distressing in cultures that sanction elaborate public displays of grief. Since this country does not have nationally or culturally common mourning rituals, appropriate mourning behavior does not have a consensus of approval. The ambiguity with regard to proper mourning in the United States probably contributes to the difficulties of early widowhood (Wilcox and Sutton 1977). The funeral, therefore, is no longer an opportunity for the unrestrained exhibition of public grief.

Grief is a social process and is best dealt with in a social setting in which people can support and reinforce each other in their reactions to the loss. Three social conditions may give rise to complicated grief reactions (Lazare 1979). The first is a case in which the loss is socially unspeakable. This often happens in the case of suicidal death. When someone dies in this manner, particularly if the circumstances are somewhat ambiguous and no one wants to say whether it was suicide or an accident, there is a tendency for the family and friends to keep quiet about the circumstances surrounding the death. This conspiracy of silence causes great harm to the bereaved person, who may need to communicate with others to resolve his or her grief.

A second social factor that complicates a grief reaction results when the loss is socially negated, that is, when the person and those around her or him act as if the loss has not happened. This has been evidenced in the present AIDS epidemic. Parents have been shocked to learn of their adult child's sexual preferences and have refused to accept the illness and the resultant death or have chosen to hide the death from friends.

The absence of a social support network is a third social dimension that may cause complications. The kind of support matrix here includes people who knew the deceased and who can thus give each other support. In our society, people frequently move far away from friends and family members. Traditional relationships have changed as well. For example, there are more socially unsanctioned losses now with the increase in nontraditional relationships such as living together without being married or relationships between gay men or women. The high rate of remarriage, which blends stepfamilies, also brings difficult issues (Worden 1987).

Our increased technology means that we now have to deal with different types of death. Recently, there have been an increasing number of chemical disasters, as in Bhopal, India; and airplane crashes like the Pan Am tragedy in Lockerbie, Scotland. Parents whose children have died in these tragedies experience chronic sorrow and feelings of abandonment, helplessness, and frustration in their experiences.

In essence, societal developments have contributed to changing conditions for the bereaved. They have more dilemmas to cope with, fewer resources to help, fewer models to follow, and less experience to fall back on. Grief, then, is hard in our society and places additional stressful demands on the survivors.

## RISKS AND NEEDS OF POPULATION

Bereavement is viewed as a significant life event. Some aspects of grief are common to all bereaved people. After a loss, a family experiences a period of reorganization, which reflects their adaptive strategies to cope with the loss and its resultant stress.

While it's never easy to accept, the death of an older person, as when one loses a parent, although difficult, provides the satisfaction of a full life span. In addition, mourning the death of an older parent or spouse is a developmental task that is supported and accepted in this society. The death of a child is one of the most tragic events that can strike the average family. Barring the death of a spouse after a long marriage, no other type of loss even comes close to extracting the heavy outpouring of emotional anguish that child loss elicits. Although we know a good deal concerning the impact of death on adults, the death of a child takes on greater symbolic importance in terms of generativity and hope for the future.

In 1987 there were 70,239 children under the age of 19 who died from accidents, disease, suicide, or murder, leaving approximately 140,478 bereaved parents (National Center of Health Statistics). There were 16,597 deaths from accidents and injuries, the highest percentages between the ages of 15 to 19. Murders accounted for 4,530 deaths and suicide for about 3,273. Ages 5 and under have the highest death rate. One type of death that is particularly stressful is Sudden Infant Death Syndrome (SIDS), the leading cause of deaths of infants between one month and one year of age in the United States. Between 8,000 and 10,000 deaths annually are attributed to SIDS (Rendo 1988).

Although we live in a protected society in the sense that childhood death accounts for less than 5 percent of mortality in the United States, these statistics ensure that many of us will be touched more or less directly by this tragic event sometime in our lives. Each of these deaths has an impact with a tenacity that is difficult to comprehend. Years pass before some parents are able to resume their lives. Others never seem able to find their way out of the turmoil and disorganization of bereavement, embodying the real tragedies of childhood death in the collapse of the family and the psychological and emotional destruction of the parents.

In essence, a child's death affects many individuals, both the immediate and extended family and those outside the family, all of whom feel the impact of the loss. Often, there are siblings of the child who has died. Usually, the siblings, in their varying stages of development and maturation, must cope with and adapt to an event for which they are totally unprepared.

There has been much discussion in the literature about the importance of the child's age as a determinant in parental grief. Although researchers may argue about what the most critical age at which to lose a child is, the clinical evidence suggests that the question is meaningless to bereaved parents (Sanders 1979–80). It does not appear to make a difference whether one's child is 3, 13, or 30 when she or he dies. Regardless of the child's age, parents have lost their hopes, dreams, and expectations for that child; have lost parts of themselves and their future, and suffer the terrible ordeal of outliving their child (Pine and Brown 1986).

Thus, the "unnaturalness" is determined not by the age of the child, but by the role of the person who dies "out of turn." The "unnaturalness" of the event becomes a major stumbling block for the bereaved parent, who cannot comprehend why and can be offered no solace by being told that it was a predictable or expected event.

Much of parental identity centers on providing and doing for one's child, a basic function of the parent. Parents who have fulfilled the roles of provider, problem solver, protector, and adviser and who have been accustomed to being self-sufficient and in control must now confront the interruption of these roles and the severing of the relationship with the child. The death of a child robs parents of their ability to carry out their functional roles, leaving them with an overwhelming sense of failure and attacking their sense of power and ability. It assaults the sense of self to have these basic roles shattered and parental omnipotence over the child rendered useless and ineffective (Rando 1985).

Having a child die can have a devastating effect on a marriage. For couples with a history of good communication and for those able to develop these skills, a child's terminal illness or sudden death may strengthen the relationship. It is not uncommon, however, for marriages to break down under the strain imposed by a child's illness and death.

One factor that may exacerbate marital difficulties is the different styles of grieving among family members. In a study of 100 parents whose children died of cancer, Martinson et al. (1980) found that the fathers were nearly twice as likely as the mothers to reply that the most intense part of their bereavement was over within a few weeks to one month after the child's death, although their responses may have reflected the social expectation of fathers to "take it like a man." DeFrain et al. (1982) noted some variations in the responses of fathers and mothers: fathers reported more anger, fear, and loss of control than mothers, as well as a desire to keep their grieving private. The mothers responded with more sorrow and depression.

Women seem to be more vulnerable to the death of a child. In particular, the reactions of mothers to stillbirths and to perinatal and early infant deaths have received particular attention in recent years, and an extensive literature has arisen (Raphael 1980). Each of these types of loss has been shown to give rise to a great deal of distress for the mother. Depression, phobic overprotectiveness or neglect of other children, marital conflicts, infertility, and spontaneous miscarriages have all been reported as increased in frequency.

Survivor guilt runs rampant and may develop not only because one continues to exist after the death of one's child, but because of the feelings that one has "let the child down" by a failure to carry out the basic roles of parenthood. In no other role relationship are there so many inherently assumed and socially assigned responsibilities. This is a major reason why the resolution of parental grief is such a difficult task and why bereaved parents face so many more difficulties than other subpopulations (Rando 1988).

We cannot oversimplify the problem of bereavement. Although our first task may be to foster and strengthen the supports and mutual help that have always been available to the bereaved, there are a substantial number of people for whom this help will not be enough (Parkes 1988). Among this group, some will develop physical health problems, some will become mentally disturbed, and some will disturb the health and happiness of others. Understanding the grief experience when parents suffer the loss of a child will enable social workers to respond appropriately to the tragedy and focus attention on the special needs of the survivors.

## PROGRAMS AND SOCIAL WORK SERVICES

If we are to develop programs that assist bereaved persons when they most need it, we must understand the critical periods of this phenomenon. Bereavement services can be thought of as prevention. Interventions during the dying process and soon after death can be very helpful. Benoliel (1971) suggested that it is not enough for members of the health care team to recognize the signs of grieving and to respond in ways that facilitate the process. Clinicians must also be available to individuals at times when they are ready to use this kind of help, usually after the survivors are no longer in contact with the health care system. Prevention must also be considered for the caring health team members, since the multidisciplinary staff members experience grief.

Depending on the unique characteristics of the griever and the social and physical factors influencing the person's grief, professional help may be sought to help in the bereavement process. Family service agencies, mental health clinics, hospitals, community service programs, local funeral directors, and private practitioners are some resources that can be helpful in the bereavement process.

Professionals can consider *family counseling* as a preferred choice since the death of a child destroys the fabric of the family. Familial issues such as scapegoating, cutoff, blaming, and isolation emerge as responses to the loss. Generally, pressuring family members who are not yet prepared to deal with this highly charged issue can do more harm than good. Marital difficulties triggered by the child's death suggest the appropriateness of a couples modality.

Parents report that friends abandon them, family disappoint them, and no one understands their loneliness. To remove the bereaved family from isolation and alienation, a professionally led *mutual aid group* or a *self-help support group* in the community can become the vehicle of establishing new relationships.

The assumption that underlies mutual support bereavement groups, is that the person best qualified to understand and help with the problems of a bereaved person is another bereaved person (Parkes 1972). Mutual support or self-help groups can enhance one's sense of interpersonal confidence, increase self-worth and purpose, and restore meaning to life. These are groups of people who share the same problem, predicament, or life situation and who unite for the purpose of mutual aid. Postbereavement mutual support groups fall into two categories: first, those that help people deal with personal grief, with the problems resulting from bereavement, and with the reorganization of their lives around the new status of being a single person, and second, those that attempt to help survivors cope with a grief made particularly difficult by the circumstances of the death, e.g., suicide, homicide, or the death of a child.

Parents of Murdered Children; Mothers Against Drunk Driving; the Widow to Widow Program, the Compassionate Friends, and Kinder Mourn are examples of self-help groups. The Compassionate Friends was the first self-help group to be established in the United States that offers friendship and understanding to bereaved parents. The purpose of the group is to promote and aid parents in the positive resolution of the grief experienced upon the death of their child, and to foster the physical and emotional health of bereaved parents and their other children. The Compassionate Friends is open to parents who have experienced the death of a child, although other recently bereaved individuals also are permitted to attend the monthly meetings.

Parents of Murdered Children offers help to families cruelly bereaved. No one should have to endure the horror of a child's murder. Parents of Murdered Children provides continuous emotional support to parents by phone, by mail, in person on a one-to-one basis, in group meetings, and through literature. The purpose of the group is to serve as a link connecting any parent with others in the community who have survived their child's homicide. Like the Compassionate Friends, Parents of Murdered Children has no religious creed or affiliation and depends entirely on private donations to cover operating expenses.

Almost all groups have developed literature based on their own experiences, sometimes in collaboration with professionals, to educate others in similar circumstances, the general public, and health professionals. Many organizations have periodic newsletters that cover the types of services and benefits offered members; the grief process and its impact on the marriage and the family, including guidance for sibling grief; suggestions for the behavior of friends, relatives, and health professionals; community resources; reference lists and resource materials dealing with the latest scientific findings on causes and services; the personal experiences of survivors; and public policy issues.

# DIFFERENTIAL CLINICAL ASSESSMENTS AND INTERVENTIONS

Death of a loved one, like life itself, brings about an ecological process of transition involving the interplay of biological, social, cultural, psychological, temporal, and spatial forces. The grieving process does not proceed in a linear fashion.

Most significant losses occur within the context of a family unit. The distinctive person and environment assessments and interventions need to focus on the impact of a death on the entire family. A basic concept of family functioning is the notion of balance, homeostasis, or equilibrium. The loss of a significant person in the family group can unbalance this homeostasis and cause the family to feel deep pain and to seek help.

Knowledge of the total family configuration, the functioning position of the deceased person in the family, and the overall level of life adaptation is important for the worker who helps a family before, during, or after a death (Bowen 1978). It is not sufficient, therefore, to help each individual and his or her grief in relationship to the deceased without relating this help to the total family network.

Families vary in their ability to express and tolerate feelings. There is tremendous individual variation in a family's and an individual's reactions to the impact of a death. The degree of disruption is determined by the functioning level of emotional integration in the family. In addition, the importance of the person who has died influences the family's emotional equilibrium. One of the major stumbling blocks in resolving parental grief is the unnaturalness of a child's dying before a parent.

Preexisting personality variables, the nature of the bereaved person's prior relationship to the deceased, religious beliefs, culture, and the availability of supports are major determinants of assessments, ongoing counseling, and outcomes. All must be understood as fully as possible if the social worker is to be helpful to the bereaved person and the family members. Simultaneously, the emotional demands experienced by the worker can be exceedingly stressful. Coping with them requires continuous development of self-awareness in order to understand one's own feelings and responses to the bereaved and thus to control them in the service of the client.

To promote appropriate clinical interventions and therapeutic support for bereaved persons, professionals need to distinguish whether the family is seeking counseling for problems related to a recent or past death or is seeking help for some other problem in the family.

Even though the persisting symptoms may be related to the death, the family may not see the connection and therefore may not mention the death.

Whether a child's death is prolonged or sudden can have a different effect on the family (Herz 1980). With a prolonged death, the family has the opportunity to prepare for the death and to separate from the child, but the family undergoes a long period of stress. Watching a loved one die and not being able to do anything to prevent it is an emotionally draining experience. Sudden death, by contrast, involves a different source of stress because the survivors have little time for preparing, saying good-byes, or using other processes to help in separation.

The effects of loss are produced even when the death is of an unborn child. Families form emotional attachments to unborn children, and prebirth deaths, such as stillbirths, miscarriages, and abortions, can affect the family. After an initially intense grief reaction, the family may cover over the loss, and it may become a taboo topic that the family avoids mentioning (Herz 1980).

An example of the magnitude of the effects of a child's sudden death on the family is provided by sudden infant death syndrome (SIDS), or crib death, which creates an emotional crisis of enormous proportions for the surviving family (May and Breme 1982). Reported problems among surviving family members include disturbances in eating, sleeping, thinking, and working characteristic of depression; feelings of responsibility for the death; difficulties in conception for the grieving mothers, including higher than average rates of infertility and spontaneous abortion following the loss of the child (Mandell and Wolfe 1975); and severe stress on the surviving siblings, who have to deal both with their own irrational feelings of guilt and responsibility and with their parents' grief (May and Breme 1982).

Surviving siblings frequently become the focus of unconscious maneuvers designed to alleviate the guilt feelings of the parents and are used as a way to better control fate. One of the most difficult positions parents place a surviving sibling in is to be the substitute for the lost child. This often involves endowing the surviving child with qualities of the deceased. In some cases, the subsequent child is even given a similar or identical name. Some families cope with their feelings about the death of a child by suppressing the facts surrounding the loss so that the subsequent children may not know anything about their predecessors and, in some cases, do not even know there were predecessors at all. Clinical observations serve as a valuable source of insights, and an initial assessment task is to find out if any of these situations exist.

Four components may help the worker to ascertain the degree of threat, loss, or possible challenge experienced by the family: 1) obtaining a detailed description of the family's presenting problem(s); 2) taking a family history by using a genogram; 3) assessing the family's current functioning; and 4) observing family interaction patterns from the point of view of structural family theory (Minuchin 1974). If the clinician has worked with the family during the child's dying process, it may not always be necessary to do such an extensive or detailed assessment. The observations and clinical judgment of the social worker should prevail.

A variety of assessment techniques are useful in determining in a general way the extent and nature of the reactions and problems a family is confronting. Helping interventions are particularly salient to a bereaved family who are mourning the prolonged death of a child following many agonizing months of living with a chronic and/or terminal illness.

The social worker serves as a guide to the family, but primary healing takes place within the family system. Sometimes, family members may be seen in both individual and family sessions to grieve the loss individually, as a couple, and as a family. The worker follows his or her usual theoretical and technical preferences in working with the family. The most important task for the worker is to help the family talk openly about the death, about their emotional reactions to it, and about its impact on each member in the family unit.

Thorough assessments are important and begin during the intake call; they continue throughout as the social worker gathers new information and learns more about the family. Some families may be known to the worker, and to assess the current functioning of the family unit, it is helpful to ask for a description of the troubles they are currently experiencing. This inquiry helps the worker understand the present effects of grief on the family relationships. Families need to know they will survive, although they will not be the same.

Some bereaved families question their sanity, their lack of concentration, their irritability, and their preoccupation with images of the deceased child. Other parents express suicidal ideation, and the worker must determine whether the ideation reflects a wish to be less pained or actually to die. If a family member has a history of mental illness or is suicidal, referral to a psychiatrist is crucial.

Families need help to see that the age of the child is more-or-less inconsequential to the grieving process. Legitimizing the importance of the grief process for parents who have suffered miscarriage, stillbirth, or neonatal death is essential.

A genogram can provide important clinical information related to the family's ethnic, cultural, and religious background; losses in the past; and present role changes. Obtaining this information can have a therapeutic benefit. Unfulfilled or unresolved expectations of parents and/or surviving siblings of the deceased child may emerge, and the clinician attends to the preoccupation with these expectations while helping the members identify and gradually relinquish them.

When bereaved parents perceive difficulties in their attempt to continue to nurture the surviving children because of a preoccupation with the deceased child, helping them cope with this conflict is essential. Encouraging couples to give themselves permission to have a respite from their grief and to enjoy their other children, and to see this as pleasure and not as a betrayal of the deceased child is important. Suggesting they look at and renew other aspects of the lives they formerly enjoyed is helpful. Siblings' efforts to understand their feelings and responsibilities regarding the death of their brother or sister need exploration and support. Families may be helped to understand how to help their remaining children cope with sibling loss.

Focus on the impact on the marital relationship should not be omitted. Individual differences, open communication, and viewing problems as part of the grief process need to be encouraged. The worker helps the couple understand and work through the social conditioning that influences the expressions of grief in both sexes. Men need assistance in dealing with the socially conditioned responses that are antithetical to appropriate grief resolution: giving them permission to grieve and helping them to learn how to cry; encouraging discussion with other fathers; and supporting recognition of the fact that the father cannot "fix" everything despite his roles as protector, "macho man," emotionally controlled individual, provider, problem solver, and self-sufficient adult. Often, fathers attempt to protect their family from the effects of their own grief as well as from the grief experience of the family. This is an unrealistic and nontherapeutic goal. Physical activity can be suggested as a method to release anger, frustration, and other responses to the grief situation. Women should be helped to express their feelings of anger, which have traditionally been repressed. Women also need a perspective on the socially conditioned male response to grief so that they can understand it and not interpret it as a lack of love for them, the deceased child, or other family members (Rando 1985).

Supporting or enabling the family to maintain their normal routine and suggesting that mourning may not automatically decrease in a linear fashion with time are helpful. Families frequently question their progress. A helpful intervention is writing in a family journal. The process and the product of writing can serve as a form of family communication and allows each member to get more control of thoughts and feelings. Families can be encouraged to pour out feelings in the journal and chart their progress. This is an important skill of empowerment and a way to complete unfinished business.

Creating appropriate rituals for the expression of grief and referring parents to the nearest chapter of a self-help group of bereaved parents or a professionally led mutual aid group can be helpful. Through mutual sharing, support, modeling, and learning that they are not "going crazy," the mutual aid group process is particularly helpful for bereaved parents who lack emotional and social support for the expression and resolution of grief.

Helping the family accept the pain of loss is a major intervention. The pervasive, unrelenting feelings of sorrow, loss, and abandonment are overwhelming. The magnitude of the loss must be validated. Before the family can establish new relationships and behaviors, they must loosen the bond to the deceased child. Perhaps the single most important task for the social worker is to help the family to talk openly about the death, its impact on them, and their emotional reactions to it (Herz 1980). The social worker can help the family, when they are ready, to rehearse ways to create new relationships in this altered situation. Clinical intervention can help bereaved families prevent dysfunction and maladaptive behavior. Carefully balancing grief work with dealing with feelings and providing concrete information helps in the mastering of a stressful situation.

Social workers helping bereaved families must be aware of the factors that make family bereavement unique. Without an understanding of these special dynamics, the clinician will often misapply techniques, sustain inappropriate counseling expectations, or possibly miss valuable opportunities for intervention leading to the successful resolution of grief. The work of grieving entails mourning not only the person who has died but the hopes, wishes, dreams, fantasies, unfulfilled expectations, feelings, and needs one has for and with that person.

Many times, chronic sorrow is a way of coming to terms with a changed, sometimes suffering self. Social workers who view adjustment to sorrow as a time-bound process will view clients who experience repeated sorrow as dysfunctional. On the other hand, those who view "chronic" sorrow as a natural reaction to an ongoing tragic experience will offer a continuum of appropriate support services (Rosenblatt 1983).

## CASE ILLUSTRATION

Family ties are unlike any other. Members of a family are part of each other in ways that are so subtle, yet so intense, as to be almost beyond description. There is an interconnectedness among the members of a family that is so powerful that it accompanies us throughout all of our days. The influence of our families persists even beyond the time when we have close contact with them; indeed, it may persist even when families are no longer living.

Today, when families tend to be smaller, the death of a child exacts a particularly heavy toll. Parents invest so much in each one of their children that the loss of one of them is not easily overcome. In the following example, a family initiated help for their daughter after a call from the school's guidance counselor. It soon became clear that this family was coping with the recent loss of a family member.

Helen and John Romanelli, 37 and 39 years old, of Italian-American antecedent, lived in a middle-class suburb in Connecticut. They had been married for fourteen years and had two children: Rosalie, a vivacious, bright, red-haired 9-year-old, and Matthew, a 12-year-old son who three months before had been hit by a car as he was walking home from school. He was not killed instantly but had remained in a coma on a respirator, until his death one month before. The parents and both sets of grandparents had stood vigil at his bedside. Rosalie had not been permitted by the family to visit and had spent afternoons and evenings with her cousins and aunt. She had longed to see Matthew and, each evening upon her return home, would spend a few minutes in his bedroom playing the Nintendo game he had taught her. His absence had become apparent initially when Rosalie had no one to turn to for direction when she was stuck in freeing the Princess. Rosalie wrote letters to Matthew and drew pictures so he would suggest the next step she could take to free the Princess. Both Mr. and Mrs. Romanelli had taken the letters to the hospital. While Rosalie and her parents never discussed Matthew's condition at home, she had always believed Matthew would return. She also observed her mother's daily crying and her father's withdrawal. There were many evenings when he did not kiss Rosalie goodnight.

When hearing the news of Matthew's death, Rosalie felt very little emotion. She was in shock and denied that he would never return home. Since she had not been prepared for the loss and had had no time to mourn, her ways of attempting to cope with the stress of the loss included isolating herself and spending endless hours sleeping on the weekends.

Although the Romanellis were aware of Rosalie's behavior, they were immersed in their own grief. Rosalie's teacher informed them of her noticeably apathetic, sad, and lonely feelings and her withdrawn behavior. This was in sharp contrast to Rosalie's prior expressive and lively behavior. The Romanellis, with sustained support from the school's guidance counselor, thought counseling for Rosalie might be helpful. They recalled meeting a social worker in the intensive-care unit at the hospital on two occasions and called to make an appointment. She referred them to a family agency in a nearby town.

Assessment began during the initial telephone contact, and the worker suggested that the immediate family attend the first session. After the usual greeting rituals and introductions, the worker invited the family to present the troubles they were experiencing. Hearing each member's perception of the problem, the worker formalized a statement of what she heard their concerns to be and suggested that together they complete a genogram.

Since it was difficult for the family to tolerate discussion of the death, a genogram was used to uncover important clinical information from the past that had not been initially revealed. The process had a therapeutic effect, and several important historical issues were revealed.

In the process of completing the genogram, Mrs. Romanelli mentioned a miscarriage in her seventh month which had occurred about fourteen months prior to Matthew's birth. The worker then directed a series of questions to Mrs. Romanelli aimed at obtaining information about how she had coped with that earlier loss. Up to now, Mrs. Romanelli revealed, it had been a "family secret," and at the time, she had quickly immersed herself in work and had attempted to become pregnant again as soon as possible.

In the Italian culture, great importance is attached to the role of the eldest son. This was certainly the case with the Romanellis. The father, a lawyer who came from a family of lawyers, had looked forward to his eldest son's joining him in the family law firm and eventually taking it over. Mr. Romanelli tearfully faced his shattered hopes and dreams, and his wife suggested that he think of Rosalie as the family's future lawyer. The worker cautioned the couple about placing a burden on Rosalie to fulfill the expectations and yet avoiding the feelings attached to the son's death and the relinquishment of the family's hope.

The Catholic traditions of mourning, viewing the body, and funeral rituals supported the Romanellis in accepting the reality and the finality of the death. Although the family went through the traditional waking of the body, funeral mass, and burial rites, they were having a difficult time visiting the grave and making the necessary arrangements for a headstone. The worker was supportive, and in future sessions, they formulated a ritual that was "their own" and not bound by traditions of culture or religious beliefs.

Present and future work focused on attending to the father's reaction to the death of his son. He described a pattern of withdrawal, sadness, and low energy. He had previously been a man with a great zest for life, who had participated in the community both with his son at little league and in a number of church and legal societies. At present, it sounded as if his life was on hold. He said that his future was shattered and that his dreams and expectations could never be fulfilled. The social worker asked how Mrs. Romanelli was reacting to the death of her son. It appeared that some of her former coping had emerged, such as hoping for another child. One difference was her flight into activity in relation to her past withdrawal. The couple began to see how their relationship was mirrored in their daughter.

Rosalie was asked how she was feeling since Matthew's death. She burst into tears and was unable to talk. The worker and the parents comforted her and said how lonely she must feel without Matthew. Through her choked sobs, she said, "Daddy was to pick him up at school; it's his fault Matthew died." The parents tried to clarify this erroneous statement, but the worker redirected the interview to explore Rosalie's issues of fear of abandonment by her parents. This provided some beginning comfort, support, and reassurance that Rosalie was important and that their love for her had not changed. This issue was addressed each time the family met.

In the third and fourth interviews, the initial focus was on Blackie, the family's dog. Matthew had found the dog when he was 7 years old and was the dog's caretaker. The dog was a constant reminder of Matthew, and the family found his presence intolerable. In fact, there were some fights over who would assume responsibility for feeding him. They also mentioned Blackie's days and nights being spent in Matthew's room. The clinician used this subject to talk about the impact of the loss on the family and how and who would care for Blackie. Further focus was on exploring the anger they all might be feeling toward Matthew and giving permission to let out their feelings and to ask for support.

The worker focused on the family's going into Matthew's empty room in the fourth interview. Only Rosalie continued to spend some time there playing the computer game. Both parents stated that they walked past his room and tried not to think about the emptiness. The worker suggested that they think of a family ritual enabling them to go into Matthew's room and each take out an object that had special meaning between them and Matthew and recall the experience to the other family members. This served a twofold purpose: recalling positive memories in a life review and engaging in talking together about Matthew in recalling past memories and the present loss, rather than grieving silently.

After a number of family sessions, both parents reported that they had thought a great deal about what the worker had said about keeping their lives on hold and also feeling the support of normalizing this feeling. They recognized that they were stuck and felt they would like to begin to live again, recognizing they had another child who needed nurturing, support, and their emotional and physical availability. At the family's request, the eighth through the tenth sessions included both the maternal and the paternal grandparents, since they too were mourning the death of their grandson. During this time, Rosalie volunteered to care for Blackie, the family dog. She also described the extended families' visit to the cemetery and their placing flowers on the grave. At the last extended-family session, Rosalie was able to express her anger at her parents for not letting her visit Matthew in the hospital or spend a short time at the funeral home during the wake. She also showed her displeasure at her grandparents for not being available and helpful to her during Matthew's hospitalization.

The family was seen over a period of ten weeks. The initial phase focused on each family member's reaction to the death and the impact the loss was having on the family system. Earlier losses, hopes, and expectations were articulated, and the significance of these losses emerged but was not necessarily resolved. Patterns of coping and adapting to life losses became conscious, and numerous examples were used and related to present coping.

During the middle phase some acceptance of the loss began to emerge. Inclusion of extended-family members in treatment and the discussion of the family's pet were used as part of a life review and a thrust toward the future. A ritual designed by the family acted as a form of empowerment and helped them in their grief work.

The final counseling phase, although very painful, suggested the beginning of healing. Rosalie was able to express her anger at the family and gained permission to externalize her feelings to reduce the future pain she would experience. The family decided to stop counseling for a time but to return on a monthly basis.

Working with siblings' and parents' reactions to the death of a child is a complex and delicate task. Although the family's grieving is ongoing, they are able to talk about the "unspeakable." This case illustrates that the major purpose of family counseling following the death of a child is to prevent family symptoms and dysfunction from developing.

Herz (1980) suggested several important interventions: First, open, direct, clear, and factual language should be used, and euphemistic and technical language should be avoided. Second, the worker should combat the family's tendency to avoid issues related to the death by establishing at least one open relationship in the family. The death has to be discussed within the family. Third, the worker should remain calm. Families often seek help when their stress or tension level is high and they have been unable to reduce it. While the worker may experience strong emotions, if her or his interventions are determined by emotional reactivity, it can increase rather than decrease the stress level in the family. Fourth, the worker should encourage the family to mourn the death in ways consistent with their personal and religious customs, rituals, styles, and beliefs.

Successful intervention following the death of a child requires a combination of well-developed family assessments and counseling skills, a knowledge of issues related to death and dying, and the capacity to cope personally with the powerful emotions associated with the loss. Often, it is necessary for the worker to maintain a balance between having the family revisit the past to express unresolved feelings of grief and encouraging them to face the future so that family life can continue to develop.

As part of life, human beings have always struggled with the knowledge of personal death and coping with the death of a loved one. The overriding issue that faces us in all our determination to cope with loss and to help others cope with loss is the place accorded to death in our lives today. Mourning is not only normal, but essential.

The role of social work is vital in assisting bereaved families to cope with the death of a loved one. Because of the profession's holistic perspective and scope of responsibility, social workers are in a unique position to understand the dynamics involved in working with bereaved families. When a child dies, grief can be devastating.

Most bereaved families pass through a mourning process and resolve their grief and heal without suffering any long-term pathological effects. These families tend to have many resources, such as extended family, friends, neighbors, and religious activities available to them that help them cope with grief. Some families, without these resources, have the ability to reach out into the community when stressed and to seek professional help to aid them through this time of crisis. However, families who are socially isolated, have limited resources, and do not seek help are at risk.

In our society, grief reactions are often viewed with suspicion, and it is not long before the mourner is exhorted to "get on with it" and is assured that everything will be right again as soon as the mourner "stops feeling sorry for yourself." Negative attitudes such as these often encourage people to bury their grief. Consequently, they do not complete the tasks of mourning and never learn to accept their losses so they can move on.

Working with the family system is essential to enhance the homeostatic adaptation and family reorganization. The clinician judges the pace at which to proceed and is sensitive to individual issues. Once the family can express the grief that has been blocked, they will be able to place their dead loved one in the past and begin to resolve their grief.

Opportunities for the development of a supportive community can be provided by facilitating bonding among individuals who define themselves as permanently changed by recurrent sorrow. The mental and spiritual task of living without the loved one while coping with the inner reality of chronic sadness deepens our understanding of the complexity of the family's grief reactions. The caring, nonjudgmental social worker can provide an open environment where the bereaved does not need to be concerned about keeping up appearances. The needed open catharsis should be encouraged within the safety of a counseling relationship.

Understanding that some amount of guilt is normal in any death of a significant other and understanding the dynamics that compound guilt feelings for the bereaved can relieve some of the survivors' burden. Assurances by the social worker and others that they did not somehow cause the death or that it is not a punishment meted out to them can also help.

More than anything, the bereaved need help in rebuilding their lives. The social work role is to maintain and enhance family solidarity at a time of crisis. The social worker must remain especially sensitive to where the family is in this process. Professionals can give license to start anew, but they must also be very careful not to be perceived as pushing too hard or too fast before the necessary grieving has occurred. Generally, the decision to pursue future-oriented initiatives should come from the family, not the social worker.

## REFERENCES

Barrett, C. J. 1977. "Signs." *Journal of Women in Culture and Society* 2:858.

Benoliel, J. Q. and D. M. Crowley. 1974. "The Patient in Pain: New Concepts." In *Proceedings of the National Conference on Cancer Nursing*, pp. 191–203. New York: American Cancer Society.

Bishop, D. S. and N. Epstein. 1978. "The McMaster Model of Family Functioning." *Journal of Marriage and Family Counseling* 4:19–31.

Bowen, M. 1976. "Family Reaction to Death." In P. J. Guerin, ed., *Family Therapy: Theory and Practice*, pp. 335–348. New York: Gardner.

Bowen, M. 1978. *Family Therapy in Clinical Practice*. New York: Aronson.

Bowlby J. 1961. "Childhood Mourning and Its Implications for Psychiatry." *American Journal of Psychiatry*, 118:481–498.

Bowlby, J. 1962. "Processes of Mourning." *International Journal of Psycho-Analysis* 42:317–340.

Bristor, M. 1984. "The Birth of a Handicapped Child—A Holistic Model for Grieving." *Family Relations* (January), 33:25–32.

Cain, A. C. and B. S. Cain. 1964. "On Replacing a Child." *Journal of the American Academy of Child Psychiatry* 3:433–456.

Church, M. 1981. *When a Baby Dies*, booklet published for The Compassionate Friends, Inc., Oak Brook, Ill.

Clayton, P. J., L. Desmarais, and G. Winoker. 1968. "A Study of Normal Bereavement." *American Journal of Psychiatry* 125:168–178.

Clayton, P. J., J. A. Halikas, W. H. Maurice, and E. Robbins. 1973, "Anticipatory Grief and Widowhood." *British Journal of Psychiatry* 122:47–51.

DeFrain, J., J., Taylor, and L. Ernst. 1982. *Coping with Sudden Infant Death*. Lexington, Mass.: Lexington Books.

Engel, G. L. 1961. "Is Grief a Disease? A Challenge for Medical Research." *Psychosomatic Medicine* 23:18–22.

Fish, W. C. and S. M. Whitty. 1983. "Challenging Conventional Wisdom About Parental Bereavement." *Forum Newsletter–Forum for Death Education and Counseling*. 6(8):4.

Fish, W. 1986. "Differences of Grief Intensity in Bereaved Parents." In Therese Rando, ed., *Parental Loss of a Child*, pp. 415–428. Champaign, Ill.: Research Press.

Folta, J. R., and J. S. Deck. 1974. "Grief, the Funeral, and the Friend." Paper presented for the Foundation of Thanatology, New York, March.

Freud, S. 1957. *Mourning Melancholia*. London: Hogarth.

Furman, E. 1974. *A Child's Parent Dies: Studies in Childhood Bereavement.* New Haven, Conn.: Yale University Press.

Garfield, C. 1979. "A Child Dies." In Charles A. Garfield, ed., *Stress and Survival,* pp. 314–317. St. Louis: C. V. Mosby.

Gorer, G. 1965. *Death, Grief and Mourning.* New York: Doubleday.

Herz, F. 1989. "The Impact of Death and Serious Illness on the Family Life Cycle." In E. Carter and McGoldrick, eds., *The Family Life Cycle,* pp. 457–482. New York: Gardner

Hoagland, J. 1984. "Bereavement and Personal Constructs: Old Theories and New Concepts." *Death Education* 2–3:175–193.

Klass, D. and S. Marwit. 1988–89. "Toward a Model of Parental Grief." *Omega* 19(1):31–50.

Knapp, R. 1986. *Beyond Endurance When a Child Dies.* New York: Shocken.

Krant. M. J. 1973. 'Grief and Bereavement: An Unmet Medical Need." *Delaware Medical Journal* 45:282–290.

Lazare, A. 1979. "Unresolved Grief." In A. Lazare, ed., *Outpatient Psychiatry: Diagnosis and Treatment,* pp. 498–512. Baltimore: Williams & Wilkins.

Lindemann, E. 1944. "The Symptomatology and Management of Acute Grief." *American Journal of Psychiatry* 101:141–148.

Mandell, F. and L. C. Wolfe. 1975. "Sudden Infant Death Syndrome and Subsequent Pregnancy." *Pediatrics* 56:774–776.

Margolis, O. S. (ed.). 1981. *Acute Grief: Counseling the Bereaved.* New York: Columbia University Press.

Markusen, E., G. Owen, R. Fulton, and R. Bendiksen. 1977–78. "SIDS: The Survivor as Victim." *Omega* 8:277–284.

Martinson, I., D. Maldow, W. Henry. 1980. *Home Care for the Child with Cancer,* Washington, D.C.: National Cancer Institute.

May, H. J. and F. J. Breme. 1982–83. "SIDS Family Adjustment Scale: A Method of Assessing Family Adjustment to Sudden Infant Death Syndrome." *Omega* 13:59–74.

McClowry, S., E. B. Davies, K. A. May, E. J. Kulenkamp, and I. M. Martinson. 1987. "The Empty Space Phenomenon: The Process of Grief in the Bereaved Family." *Death Studies* 11:361–374.

Minuchin, S. 1974. *Families and Family Therapy.* Cambridge: Harvard University Press.

Mitford, J. 1963. *The American Way of Death.* New York: Simon & Schuster.

Momeyer, R. 1988. *Confronting Death.* Bloomington: Indiana University Press.

National Center for Health Statistics. 1987. *Monthly Vital Statistics Report.* U.S. Department of Health and Human Services, 38(9).

Osterweis, M., F. Solomon, and M. Green, eds. 1984, *Bereavement: Reactions, Consequences, and Care,* Washington, D.C.: National Academy Press.

Parkes, C. M. 1987–88. "Research: Bereavement." *Omega* 18(4):365–377.

Parkes, C. M. 1970. "The First Year of Bereavement." *Psychiatry* 33:444–467.

Parkes, C. M. 1972. *Bereavement: Studies of Grief in Adult Life.* New York: International Universities Press.

Parkes, C. M., and R. S. Weiss. 1983. *Recovery from Bereavement.* New York: Basic Books.

Parry, J. K. 1989. *Social Work Theory and Practice with the Terminally Ill.* New York: Haworth.

Peppers, L. G. and R. J. Knapp. 1980. *Motherhood and Mourning.* New York: Praeger.

Pine, V. and C. Brauer. 1986. "Parental Grief: A Synthesis of Theory, Research and Intervention." In Therese Rando, ed., *Parental Loss of a Child,* pp. 59–96. Champaign, Ill.: Research Press.

Rando, T. 1983. "The Particular Difficulties of Bereaved Parents: Unique Factors and Treatment Issues." *Forum Newsletter: Forum for Death Education and Counseling* 6:1–3.

Rando, T. 1984. *Grief, Dying and Death: Clinical Interventions for Caregivers.* Champaign, Ill.: Research Press.

Rando, T. 1985. "Bereaved Parents: Particular Difficulties, Unique Factors, and Treatment Issues." *Social Work 3(1):*19–23.

Rando, T. 1986. *Parental Loss of a Child.* Champaign, Ill.: Research Press.

Raphael, B. 1983. *The Anatomy of Bereavement.* New York: Basic Books.

Rosen, H. 1986. *Unspoken Grief: Coping with Childhood Sibling Loss.* Lexington, Mass.: Lexington Books.

Rosenblatt, P. C. 1983. *Bitter, Bitter Tears: Nineteenth-Century Diarists and Twentieth-Century Grief Theories.* Minneapolis: University of Minnesota Press.

Sakler, O., ed. 1978. *The Child and Death.* St. Louis: C. V. Mosby.

Sanders, C. 1980. "Comparison of Younger and Older Spouses in Bereavement Outcome." *Omega* 11(3):217–232.

Sanders, C. 1979–80. "A Comparison of Adult Bereavement in the Death of a Spouse, Child, and Parent." *Omega* 10(4):303–322.

Shanfield, S. B., and B. J. Swain. 1984. "Death of Adult Children in Traffic Accidents." *Journal of Nervous and Mental Disease* 172:533–538.

Singh, B. and B. Raphael. 1981. "Post-Disaster Morbidity of the Bereaved: A Possible Role for Preventive Psychiatry?" *Journal of Nervous and Mental Disease* 4(169):203–212.

Soricelli, B. and C. Utech. 1985. "Mourning the Death of a Child: The Family and Group Process." *Social Work* 3(5):429–434.

Spiegel, D. 1980. "The Recent Literature: Self-Help and Mutual Support Groups." *Community Mental Health Review* 15:15–25.

Tatelbaum, V. 1977. *The Courage to Grieve.* New York: Harper & Row.

Videka-Sherman, L. 1982. "Coping with the Death of a Child: A Study Over Time." *American Journal of Orthopsychiatry* 52:688–698.

Weenolsen, P. 1988. *Transcendence of Loss Over the Life Span.* New York: Hemisphere.

Weizman, S. and P. Kamm. 1985. *About Mourning: Support and Guidance for the Bereaved.* New York: Human Sciences Press.

Wilcox, S. G. and M. Sutton. 1977. *Understanding Death and Dying: An Interdisciplinary Approach.* New York: Alfred Press.

Worden, J. W. 1987. *Grief Counseling and Grief Therapy.* New York: Springer.

# 15

## Domestic Violence

▼

BONNIE E. CARLSON

The issue of domestic violence has been on the political and social agenda for barely fifteen years, brought to our attention largely through grass-roots efforts of the women's movement. The history of its "discovery" is thus quite different from that of child abuse, for example, which was identified as a social problem primarily by physicians. Recent research based on a nationally representative sample of married and cohabitating adults suggests that at least 1.6 million women are victimized by domestic violence yearly; a woman is battered by her partner approximately every eighteen seconds (Straus and Gelles 1986; Gelles and Straus 1988). These statistics lead to the conclusion that women are more likely to be assaulted in their homes, by a loved one, than in any other setting (Gelles and Straus 1988).

Insofar as social workers are very likely to come into contact with those affected by domestic violence in a variety of settings (Davis 1987), it is important that they be informed about both the nature of the problem and effective ways of ameliorating it. This is especially true insofar as there is evidence that the beliefs of social workers and other clinicians of both genders are often influenced by culturally based biases and stereotyping of women, ultimately contributing to victim blaming (Carmen 1981; Davis and Carlson 1981).

### PROBLEM DOMAIN

There are a variety of ways of looking at and defining the problem of domestic violence both within the social work profession and in the

**471**

larger community of helping professionals. These differing definitions have dramatic implications for how we think about the intervention process. The fact that the problem was brought to our attention by female victims themselves via the women's movement has been the most important influence on our definitions. From the beginning, the issue has been defined largely as a problem in which women are victimized by male partners. Initially, the problems was labeled *wife* or *woman abuse* or *battering*, with the victim generally referred to as a *battered woman* or *wife*. Many of those in the field prefer to avoid the term *wife*, since domestic violence is known to occur at about the same or a higher rate in cohabiting or common-law relationships (Yllo and Straus 1981). The terms *spouse abuse* and *domestic violence* are also used frequently, although they tend to shift the focus away from women as the most common victims of abuse.

Abuse, both physical and psychological, is also known to occur in both gay male and female couples, although the empirical research documenting such violence is very limited (Bologna, Waterman, and Dawson 1987; Brand and Kidd 1986; Kelly and Warshafsky 1987; Renzetti 1989). Furthermore, these researchers have found the prevalence and types of violence, dynamics, and consequences (except help seeking) to be more similar to than different from heterosexual couple violence.

Many in the field have relied on the definitions developed by Straus and his colleagues (Straus, Gelles, and Steinmetz 1980). These researchers have defined violence as consisting of aggressive behaviors, such as punching, slapping, or kicking, intentionally used to hurt another person. Abusive violence has been operationally defined as those behaviors likely to injure someone, such as hitting with a fist or beating up.

Feminist definitions, on the other hand, have focused more on power differentials between the partners and often go beyond aggressive behaviors (Bograd 1982). Schechter and Gray, for example, defined battering as an abuse of power in a relationship, a "pattern of coercive control that can take four forms: physical, emotional, sexual and economic" (1988:241). They acknowledged that every victim does not necessarily experience all forms of abuse.

The terms *violence* and *abuse* have often been used interchangeably and require definition and clarification. The term *violence* is used here to refer to those behaviors that are intended to hurt another person, including everything from slapping and shoving to beating up or using a weapon. *Abuse*, on the other hand, connotes a *pattern* of violent behaviors that are likely to hurt or injure someone. This distinction is fairly consistent with how these terms are used in the field, although there is no absolute consensus on these definitions or distinctions. Once physical abuse has been established, the other forms of abuse mentioned by Schechter and Gray (1988) are typically present as well, as the batterer strives to maintain dominance and reinforce the partner's submission. So the term *abuse* connotes a wider range of difficulties than just physically injurious violence.

What about husbands as victims, is there such a thing as battered husbands? It is known that husbands and male partners, too, can be physically abused by their wives or female partners, and reciprocal violence is known to be quite common (Straus, Gelles, and Steinmetz 1980). But the problem of husband *abuse* is far less common insofar as women are much less likely than men to have the superior power in a heterosexual relationship necessary to abuse someone physically and/or emotionally (Pagelow 1984).

The social work profession has gone through a variety of stages in how it has viewed the problem of domestic violence or battering according to Davis (1987). She analyzed thirty-three journal articles in the social work literature published between 1976 and 1984, concluding that there have been three stages in our understanding of this social problem. Initially, wife abuse was seen as a problem affecting large numbers of diverse kinds of women. It was thought to be caused largely by powerful social forces outside the individual, such as sexism and norms permitting men to physically abuse women, as well as current or past family environments. Little attention was paid to perpetrators at this early stage. The second stage saw wife battering as just one type of family violence, with some writers beginning to assert that the victims might be playing some role in their own victimization. Other writers at this stage began to devote attention to service delivery issues. The third stage of our understanding of the issue, as reflected in published articles, continued the change in focus from women to men, particularly services for men. Davis did not address the issue of husband battering as a controversy deflecting attention from battered women, perhaps because it was not reflected in the social work literature to as large an extent as it appears in the field of domestic violence more broadly defined.

Since the problem of domestic violence or battered women was discovered, it has become increasingly clear that it is an enormously complex issue that we are just beginning to understand, and one that is difficult to study. Many factors have hampered our ability to research this issue, not the least of which are the stigmatizing nature of the problem, norms about family privacy, and difficulties in generalizing from clinical samples. The nature of our understanding and the conclusions we draw about what causes domestic violence or wife battering have a direct effect on how we think about intervention. For example, if we conclude that sexism and sex-role socialization are the major causes of wife battering and its maintenance, then we should direct intervention efforts at the societal level, modifying social norms and ensuring that women will have equal opportunities in education and employment. However, if we instead locate the primary causes of the problem within the couple or the individual man or woman, our efforts should be directed primarily toward therapeutic interventions at the family and individual levels. If we adopt a multivariate approach to the contributing factors, as is recommended in this chapter, then it is incumbent upon us to conceptualize intervention broadly, spanning the societal, family, and individual levels.

## SOCIETAL CONTEXT

Several social and economic factors are related to domestic violence and, to some extent, illuminate the nature of the issue. First, we know that domestic violence is distributed across all social groupings. That is, wife battering can be found in all educational, economic, religious, and ethnic groups—though not necessary to an equal extent in all groups. The best research to date on the distribution of domestic violence comes from two surveys of nationally representative samples of American adults conducted by the Family Violence Research Laboratory at the University of New Hampshire (Straus, Gelles, and Steinmetz 1980; Gelles and Straus 1988; Straus and Gelles 1986). The most powerful demographic correlate of (and probably contributor to) wife beating is poverty and the stress it creates. Virtually every study examining the role of social class in family violence has found that low-income individuals are significantly more likely to engage in violence and abuse toward family members. This finding has dramatic social policy implications in that the amelioration of domestic violence is closely linked to the eradication of poverty.

Ethnicity has also been examined as a possible correlate of wife battering. Coley and Beckett (1988) reviewed literature examining the relationship between race and battering, finding only six studies. No consistent pattern was found in comparing rates of violence between whites and blacks, perhaps because some studies did not take social class into account. For example, the first national survey of family violence in 1975 found that rates of husband-to-wife violence were significantly higher among blacks and Hispanics than among whites (Straus, Gelles, and Steinmetz 1980). However, since no discussion of social class accompanied the presentation of the findings on ethnicity, it is reasonable to assume that social class was not controlled. Nor is there compelling evidence that minority women are any less likely to terminate violent relationships than white women (Coley and Beckett 1988). The most reasonable conclusion at this time is that ethnicity does not contribute independently to the incidence of domestic violence when social class is controlled. However, that does not mean that ethnic differences do not exist in the phenomenon or in how it is interpreted by the participants (Asbury 1987; Coley and Becket 1988).

For example, Torres (1987) compared the attitudes of twenty-five Hispanic and twenty-five non-Hispanic battered women from emergency shelters. She found more similarities than differences in their attitudes, but there were some important differences. The Hispanic women were less likely than non-Hispanic women to label verbal behaviors and hitting as abuse. They were also more likely to cite family reasons (e.g., presence of children) for not leaving the relationship, in contrast to the non-Hispanic women, who tended to say they loved the batterer or had nowhere else to go. Finally, the Hispanic women were more likely to have consulted a religious leader for help prior to seeking emergency shelter, especially folk healers, who are frequently used in the Hispanic community (Torres 1987).

Age is another factor associated with domestic violence. Both national surveys have found that younger couples, those under 30 in particular, are more likely to be violent (Gelles and Straus 1988; Straus, Gelles, and Steinmetz 1980). Perhaps the developmental stage of family life in which young couples find themselves is more stressful as a result of economic strains or the demands of young children in the home. This interpretation is consistent with research findings showing a relationship between violence and conflict related to both children and money. Conversely, it may also be true that a self-selection factor is operating; couples who have had violent relationships may separate and thus may not be found together as frequently after young adulthood (Straus, Gelles, and Steinmetz 1980).

Other societal factors contributing to wife battering include sexism and sex-role stereotyping, well established in Western culture for centuries. From the time that the first marriage laws were established by the Romans in 753 B.C. until the nineteenth century, wives were viewed as the rightful property of husbands. Although there was some regulation of what husbands could do legally to their wives, beating, unless it caused serious injury or death, was not only permitted but also expected for certain "infractions," such as infidelity (Dobash and Dobash 1981). Thus, it has been only fairly recently that men have been legally proscribed from using violence against their spouses.

Similarly, there have been different expectations for men and women in regard to their rights and privileges in all realms of society based on their socially derived sex roles. This situation, too, has been changing as women's rights have been expanded. However, equality with men has not yet been achieved, although equal rights are on the horizon in many domains.

The fact is that most men today were socialized in very traditional ways, and attitudinal changes may be more difficult to achieve than legal changes. Ironically, it might be argued that the changing norms for men and women, while they should lead to improvements for both men and women in the long run, are contributing to greater conflict, including violent conflict, in the short run as women demand better treatment and men resist such demands.

The final factor to be mentioned at the societal level is our general acceptance, or at least tolerance, of violence of all types. Although there is increased public concern about violence in the media, public schools, sports, and so forth, thus far this concern does not seem to be reflected in a demonstrable reduction of this violence. This tolerance of violence establishes a context for the acceptance of violence in intimate relationships (Carlson 1984).

## RISKS AND NEEDS OF POPULATION

Before the needs of those affected by domestic violence can be identified, it is essential for social workers to understand the dynamics that contribute to and support or maintain abuse in a couple relationship. As stated earlier, there is no one cause of domestic violence; rather, there is a complex, interacting set of contributors, not all of which necessarily operate in every case.

In addition to the factors identified above at the macrolevel, a number of potent contributing factors operate at the *family or couple level* of analysis. First, the family as a social group has some unique properties that contribute to the likelihood that high levels of conflict will exist. These include norms about privacy; involuntary membership; members of diverse ages, abilities, and needs; and expectations of behavior that are traditionally based on gender at a time when norms for role behaviors are in flux.

The sex-role norms discussed earlier manifest themselves powerfully at the couple level. Most men fully expect to be the dominant partner in a couple relationship, wielding power over their submissive wives. Many wives are willing to cooperate, but others cannot or will not subordinate themselves to their husbands. Any indications of autonomy or self-assertion may be perceived as threats to male dominance. This may be especially true when the husband lacks the resources (e.g., the education, job prestige, or earnings) to justify his superior position vis-à-vis his wife. A poignant example is the unemployed husband whose wife is employed, who continues to expect to control how money is spent in the family. In such circumstances, the husband may resort to what Allen and Straus (1980) called the "ultimate resource," namely, the threat or use of physical violence backed by his superior size and strength compared to his wife's. Thus, traditional sex roles can be considered a risk factor for violence.

Another way of analyzing couple dynamics in domestic violence situations is based on social exchange theory, which examines intimate relationships in terms of their costs and rewards. Simply put, family members hit one another because they can, meaning that the rewards for using violence outweigh the costs (Gelles 1983). This is especially true when someone who is more powerful—for example, the husband—abuses someone who is less powerful. This theory may also explain why a wife who is being abused does not end the relationship. A person will end a relationship whose costs outweigh its rewards, only if he or she also perceives the likelihood of forming an alternative relationship with higher rewards than the current relationship (Frisch and MacKenzie 1988; Pfouts 1978; Thibault and Kelley 1959).

Numerous risk factors operating at the *level of the individual* woman or man can also contribute to wife abuse. One of the most frequently cited factors is the family background of the husband or wife. Specifically, it has been observed by both clinicians and researchers that coming from a violent family increases the likelihood that one will become violent oneself. This is especially true if one had a violent parent of the same gender. Thus, if a man observed his father beat his mother, such a man is at increased risk of becoming abusive to his own wife (Gelles and Straus 1988; Straus, Gelles, and Steinmetz 1980). However, one must be cautious about assuming an inevitable relationship between exposure to family violence in childhood and becoming a perpetrator of violence against one's partner as an adult. Many men who observed violent fathers resolve to refrain from such behaviors with their own wives and succeed in being nonviolent. On the other hand, some men who never saw their fathers abuse their mothers go on to behave abusively toward their wives because of other factors, such as stress and alcoholism.

A variety of other risk factors pertaining to a man may encourage him to become violent or abusive toward his female partner. The connection between substance abuse and domestic violence is well established (Leonard and Jacob 1988). A recent review (Leonard and

James 1988) reported that the rate of alcohol problems in batterers ranges from 35 to 93 percent. It is difficult to determine the exact nature of the relationship between alcohol and battering because most of the studies are so poorly designed. Alcohol and drug use act as disinhibitors, removing the restraints that might otherwise be present to inhibit angry spouses from acting on the impulse to hurt their partner. Intoxication may also alter individuals' tolerance and judgment, thereby permitting them to behave in a way that they might otherwise avoid. The alcohol–violence connection is probably more complex than we recognize at this time and may not operate in the same way in all individuals. It has been observed that "there may be several subgroups among the alcoholics, those who never hit their spouses, those who hit their spouses whether they are sober or intoxicated, and those who hit their spouses only while intoxicated" (Leonard and Jacob 1988:391). The fact that some men abuse their wives whether intoxicated or not implies not that alcohol does not play a role, but that there are other factors operating as well.

Another risk factor for batterers is stress that overtaxes their coping abilities, especially stress emanating from the work setting, such as conflict with a supervisor or getting laid off (Bolton and Bolton 1987). Inability to resolve such stress at work can lead to displacement of anger and frustration onto family members.

Other male risk factors include low self-esteem, a high need for control, and irrational jealousy (Saunders 1982). Both abused wives and their batterers report extreme feelings of personal inadequacy and possessiveness on the part of the batterer. People who feel in control and secure in themselves and their relationships do not need to terrorize others or worry excessively about their partners' spending time with others. This jealousy frequently extends to the wife's family members and female friends and can lead to chronic, unresolved conflict. Often, women see the futility of resisting and over time become increasingly isolated from social contacts, ultimately contributing to unhealthy insularity in the couple's relationship.

Finally, batterers tend to have few close relationships beyond their partners, so that they are isolated and highly dependent, with few resources to support them through difficult times. Coupled with the last risk factor, a limited range of emotional expression, we see a profile of someone who is insecure and lacking in self-confidence, socially isolated, constricted and rigid emotionally, and lacking a repertoire of coping skills and a sense of personal control (Saunders 1982).

It is difficult to identify risk factors in the case of the battered woman insofar as much of what appears to distinguish them from other women when they appear for help is as likely to be an *outcome* of the violence as it is to be an *antecedent* to it. Two feminist authors have criticized the responses of helping professionals to battered women on exactly this issue: the confusion of effect with cause (Bograd 1982; Schechter and Gray 1988). Too often, clinicians have observed dysfunctionality in battered women and have assumed that is why they were abused, rather than seeing it as a consequence of the abuse (Schechter and Gray 1988).

However, there are some factors antecedent to a woman's abuse that might be considered risk factors. Anything about her circumstances that would tend to make it more difficult for her to leave a violent relationship could be described as a risk factor. These factors include 1) having children, especially very young children; 2) having little education; 3) not having marketable skills that would permit her to support herself and her children; 4) lacking social support; 5) feeling little self-worth, so that she doesn't feel she deserves to be treated well; 6) having high dependency needs (Dutton and Painter 1981); and 7) being ignorant of what her options are.

Domestic violence has potential consequences for all family members: wives, husbands, and children. Most of what we know about the consequences of domestic violence for wives comes from the clinical literature regarding women who request help from shelters or other counseling services as a result of battering. We should assume that this group is not a cross section of all battered women, but the most severely abused subgroup. Thus, we cannot generalize from these clinical samples to the larger population of abused women with regard to consequences.

However, the recent data from the Second National Survey of Family Violence (Gelles and Shaw 1988) address the consequences of violence and validate what clinicians have been reporting. An important finding from the Gelles and Straus (1988) research is that by no means all women who experience violence at the hands of their mate experience negative outcomes; in fact, fewer than half reported elevated levels of psychological symptoms. Another important finding is that the percentage of those reporting difficulties is directly related to the severity of the violence and abuse experienced: the worse the violence, the worse the symptoms.

Negative consequences are found in a number of areas. Obviously, one possible outcome is physical injury or even death. Separation or divorce and the accompanying feelings of loss are another possibility, which most battered women do not see as positive outcomes. But most of the outcomes identified are in the psychological and behavior realms and include the following:

1. *Anxiety* is experienced by almost half of those who reported being the victims of severe violence in the Gelles and Straus (1988) national data; others (Carmen 1981; Henson and Schinderman 1980; Rosewater 1988) have also reported the related symptoms of confusion and disorientation.

2. A combination of symptoms related to *depression* was reported by over one third of the Gelles and Straus severely abused sample, including pessimism, learned helplessness, a sense of powerlessness, extreme passivity, and hopelessness (Ball and Wyman 1977–78; Bolton and Bolton 1987; Brekke 1987; Carmen 1981; Douglas 1987; Gillman 1980; Hartman 1983; Henson and Schinderman 1980; Lewis 1983; Strube 1988; Walker 1980); thoughts of suicide and suicidal behavior have also been reported (Brekke 1987; Gelles and Straus 1988); and psychological entrapment, the sense that one has already invested too much in a relationship to leave, has been reported as well (Strube 1988).

3. *Stress*, emanating from financial problems, the partner's jealousy, constant conflict and violence, and the partner's substance abuse, leading to a sense of being overwhelmed and not being able to cope, is also commonly reported (Finn 1985; Gelles and Straus 1988).

4. *Social isolation*, or a lack of connectedness to others, is common (Hartman 1983; Henson and Schinderman 1980; Lewis 1983).

5. *Somatic problems*, such as extreme exhaustion, headaches, and loss of appetite, are reported (Gelles and Straus 1988).

6. *Low self-esteem, guilt, self-blame, feelings of worthlessness, and shame* are reported by many (Brekke 1987; Carmen 1981; Dutton and Painter 1981; Gillman 1980; Goodstein and Page 1981; Henson and Schinderman 1980; Lewis 1983).

7. *Aggression* toward both family members and nonfamily members has been identified (Brekke 1987; Gelles and Straus 1988; Gillman 1980).

8. Extreme *loyalty to the batterer* is not uncommon (Dutton and Painter 1981; Ferraro 1984; Goodstein and Page 1981).

9. *Anger and rage* and extreme ambivalence about their expression have been noted (Ball and Wyman 1977–78; Bolton and Bolton 1987; Carmen 1981; Gillman 1980; Henson and Schinderman 1980; Rosewater 1988).

10. Extreme *fear*, suspicion, and even paranoia are common (Ball and Wyman 1977–78; Henson and Schinderman 1980; Rosewater 1988).

Less work has been done on consequences for batterers. However, the major outcomes possible for batterers include loss of their wives through separation or divorce, which the vast majority do not want;

injury or death at the hands of a wife who decides to retaliate or defend herself aggressively; alienation from their children; guilt, shame, and loss of self-esteem; and a range of legal effects, including arrest, trial, and incarceration or other penalties.

Children who are exposed to interparental violence have been found to exhibit a broad range of reactions that appear to be affected by their gender and their developmental level. To the extent that most of the results pertain to children of mothers who have been sheltered, many of whom have also been victims of child abuse and/or neglect, the findings may be confounded by the effects of abuse or neglect on the children, which in fact are quite similar to the effects of witnessing spouse abuse.

In general, effects are seen in almost all areas of development. One common consequence is fear in children of all ages. Despite the best efforts of many parents, once violence and abuse have become a pattern it is almost impossible to shield children from its effects. Another possible effect on children who observe parental violence is that they may learn that this is an appropriate, or at least acceptable, way of resolving family disagreements (Wilson et al. 1989).

Previous research on preschool-aged children who have observed interparental violence has shown boys to be at higher risk for problems in the areas of aggression, somatic complaints, and social competence. Both boys and girls at this age were at elevated risk for behavior problems, and a majority of the girls studied were in the clinical range for depression (Davis and Carlson 1987).

Among school-aged children, girls were at especially high risk. Approximately half of those studied were in the clinical ranges for lack of social competence and aggression, and a majority were in the clinical range for behavior problems (88 percent) and depression (71 percent). School-aged boys were at elevated risk for lack of social competence and behavior problems (Davis and Carlson 1987).

Adolescents who have observed violence between their parents have not been as systematically studied, but they too are reported to exhibit problems such as aggressiveness and running away and, for girls, distrust of men (Hilberman and Munson 1977–78).

Negative consequences are also evident for the couple or the family as a system. Once violence becomes a pattern, a climate of fear, unpredictability, stifled emotions, and dysfunctional roles can be established in a family, affecting everyone (Star 1981). For the couple, the dependency relationships can become even more extreme and pathological, leading them to bond to each other in a very unhealthy way (Dutton and Painter 1981). One aspect is the extreme power imbalance that may have characterized the relationship prior to the abuse, which becomes even more extreme over time. Both of these may contribute to what Walker (1979) described as the "cycle of violence," wherein both partners become locked into a negative and self-perpetuating cycle that feels inevitable for both. Finally, mutual or reciprocal battering can occur, in which both partners use violence in the futile attempt to resolve conflict and to cope with frustration and stress (Felthous 1983).

Battered women have a variety of needs related to their life circumstances. Although there are similarities in their needs based on the impact of living in a chronically violent environment, each woman is unique and may have special needs based on her individual circumstances. As a group, battered women need the following kinds of services (Lynch and Norris 1977–78):

1. Crisis intervention.
2. Temporary emergency shelter.
3. Concrete services such as temporary financial assistance, food, and clothing.
4. Acceptance and understanding, validation that they are not crazy and that the abuse is not their fault.
5. Assurance that there are nonviolent alternatives and information about what those alternatives are.
6. Information about how to secure protection from the police and courts for themselves and their children.
7. Supportive services and programs that facilitate their independence, such as long-term housing, educational counseling, and job training.
8. Counseling, if they desire it, to address the consequences of being abused.

## PROGRAMS AND SOCIAL WORK SERVICES

Many, perhaps most, battered women do not seek assistance from professional helpers (Bowker 1984; Frisch and MacKenzie 1988). Instead, most seek help from informal sources such as family members and friends (Bowker 1984). However, increasingly, as services expand and are more widely publicized and the stigma attached to identifying oneself as battered decreases, abused women are approaching formal service providers for assistance.

The response of the social work profession to domestic violence is difficult to isolate from the broader societal response to the problem. Certainly, it is fair to say that the social work profession has not been in the forefront of developing programs and services for those affected by domestic violence. In fact, it could be argued that some social workers have impeded program development to the extent that their assumptions about the nature of the problem have placed responsibility for the abuse on the victim herself or reflect a systems perspective that assigns responsibility or blame equally to both partners. These perspectives are both eschewed by most working in the domestic violence field, and such views are seen as barriers to effective service delivery and amelioration of the problem.

Programs and services developed to address domestic violence have taken a variety of forms and often involve social workers in staff positions. These programs are described below. However, it should also be kept in mind that undoubtedly the most common avenue for social workers to encounter domestic violence is in a wide variety of agency settings (or private practice) that are not focused directly on family violence: family and mental health agencies, hospitals, schools, public welfare agencies, and so forth.

Specialized services for those affected by domestic violence were developed in response to the perceived lack of appropriate services in the community to address the problem of abuse in marital relationships. Domestic violence services can be divided into three categories: services for female victims; services for male batterers; and services for couples who wish to work together to eliminate the abuse and the circumstances leading to it.

## Services for Women

The primary site for services to battered women is the emergency shelter. Shelters began during the 1970s, often as safehomes initially rather than institutional shelters, and now number well over a hundred, with most major cities having a domestic violence shelter. Many are affiliated with existing community programs or agencies, such as the YWCA or the Salvation Army, whereas others are under independent auspices. Most are underfunded and rely heavily on volunteers and underpaid staff. Often, the staffing pattern consists largely of paraprofessionals, formerly battered women in particular. One study found that fewer than half of the shelters studied had a professional staff person such as a social worker or psychologist (Roberts 1984). This pattern may result from a combination of necessity, dictated by inadequate funding and low salaries, and ideological considerations wherein professionals may be regarded with distrust.

Shelters typically provide a range of critical services in addition to temporary, emergency housing for victims and their children. These include crisis intervention, twenty-four-hour hotlines, information and referral, child care, advocacy, group support and counseling, individual counseling, and, to a lesser extent, parent education and employment counseling. Some shelters also have a program for batterers, though these services are generally kept separate from the shelter program for women.

## Programs for Batterers

As of 1987, it was estimated that there were eighty-nine programs for batterers nationally (Gondolf 1987). Some are freestanding, whereas others are attached to an agency providing services to a broader population, such as a family service or mental health agency; still others may be sponsored by a shelter for abused women. Most are located in urban areas, have not been in existence for longer than a few years, and often have very unstable financial support, typically relying on volunteers to at least some extent for staffing. Many employ social workers as well as other helping professionals and, in some cases, reformed batterers.

Typically, there is an educational component in addition to counseling that addresses definitions and examples of abuse and the historical roots of male and female roles. Most often, counseling is based on cognitive-behavioral models of intervention. Treatment tends to be offered in groups, but many programs offer individual counseling as well. Groups are particularly useful in that the client can learn that he is not the only man with this problem, his denial can be confronted, and there is a natural means of acquiring social support.

Elements of treatment typically include assertiveness training; systematic desensitization and relaxation training to cope with stress and to reduce anger arousal; and anger control and cognitive restructuring to learn better ways of expressing anger. Modeling, rehearsal, and role playing are used throughout (Saunders 1982, 1984; Star 1983). Although batterers have reported therapy to be useful (Saunders 1984) little controlled research has been conducted on the effectiveness of these programs in assisting men in permanently stopping their violent behavior (Pirog-Good and Stets-Kealey 1985).

## Services for Couples

Programs for couples who wish to work conjointly on the problem of abuse in their relationship have been controversial. The controversy revolves around the assumptions, deriving from systems theory, typically made by marital and family therapists that if one is part of the system, one is, by definition, contributing to the problem in some way. Feminists and others in the domestic violence field have taken strong issue with that assumption and have tended to dismiss couples counseling or family counseling as a result (see Bograd 1984 for a well-reasoned feminist critique of the family systems approach to wife battering).

Others have noted that many battered women wish to remain with their partners if the partners can be assisted to refrain from further violence. That being the case, there is a need for marital and family counselors who are informed about domestic violence and who do not assume that violence is merely another symptom of a dysfunctional relationship, rather than the problem itself. These approaches need not assume that the victim has contributed to the problem and are discussed further below.

## DIFFERENTIAL CLINICAL ASSESSMENTS AND INTERVENTIONS

The wide variety of settings in which social workers can encounter battered women will in part determine the nature of the intervention or the range of possible interventions. One important issue that must be confronted immediately is whether the client is seeking help specifically because of the abuse, or whether the worker suspects or uncovers the existence of abuse in a client ostensibly seeking help for another problem. One needs to proceed somewhat differently in the latter case.

When seeing a client who presents with several of the risk factors identified above—or consequences, in the case of women—the worker should suspect the possibility of domestic violence in the home. The worker is advised to follow up cautiously on this suspicion, using the technique called *funneling* proposed by Brekke (1987) to detect family violence. Briefly, the technique involves focusing the interview on the issue of conflict in relationships, defining it, and establishing its universality in intimate relationships. The client should then be asked to discuss some areas of conflict in the relationship, including how disagreements are typically resolved. At this point, the worker can inquire directly about the use of violence as a means to resolve disagreements (Brekke 1987).

If, on the other hand, the client is seeking help specifically because of domestic violence, it is important to determine first if she is in a state of crisis as a result of a recent beating, which is often the precipitant of seeking professional assistance. Crisis intervention may be necessary to stabilize the client before beginning a systematic assessment and setting goals for intervention (Henson and Schinderman 1980).

The overarching goal of intervention, the goal articulated by most battered women, is finding a way to permanently end the violence. Since most seeking professional help have experienced chronic abuse and have made many previous attempts to stop the violence—all unsuccessful—finding a long-term solution may not be easy in most cases. Since battered women can be found in different stages of understanding of the violence and readiness for change (Hendricks-Matthews 1982), assessment is extremely important in determining what the client is seeking when the worker first sees her. Most shelters and counselors specializing in domestic violence work have found that battered women may need to seek help or leave a battering relationship several times before they are ready to make permanent decisions about their lives. This pattern appears normative for this population.

Hendricks-Matthews (1982) suggested evaluating the client's cognitive functioning to assess her readiness for change. Specifically, the worker should ask: To what extent does the client suffer from learned helplessness? Have these feelings of powerlessness generalized so that she feels her situation is hopeless? Is she using a great deal of denial, rationalization, and minimization about being abused? Does she feel she has any control over what happens to her? Most important, does she believe she has any control over her partner's violence? If the answer to the last question is yes, she may not yet be ready for real change because she still feels that there are things she can do (for instance, be a better wife or mother) that will induce the batterer to stop abusing her.

In light of the different stages of readiness for change that battered women experience, helping goals are perhaps best conceptualized on three levels: immediate, short-term, and long-term.

A variety of *immediate intervention goals* are appropriate for the typical battered woman, who may well be in a state of crisis when the social worker first sees her. The client in crisis is experiencing feelings of being overwhelmed, a state of disequilibrium, a sense of helplessness, and extreme emotional upset (Roberts 1984). Helping goals at this point should include:

1. Ensuring her personal safety and that of her children through creation of a safety or protection plan (Douglas 1987; Hartman 1983; Schechter and Gray 1988).

2. Identifying her strengths and resources (Goodstein and Page 1981; Carmen 1981).
3. Determining how she perceives the violence and modifying those views if necessary so that she recognizes that she cannot control his violence and it is not her fault that he is violent; helping her to see that the violence, while perhaps sporadic, is part of a continuing pattern and that it will recur, that is, breaking through her denial.
4. Obtaining other services she needs, such as a restraining order, emergency shelter, food, and clothing.
5. Identifying her alternatives for the future, such as shelter, legal services, and assistance with relocation.

*Assessment* is critical and should identify both internal and external factors that inhibit the client or can be mobilized on her behalf (Carmen 1981), as well as current needs. These include:

1. Her personal strengths and resources.
2. Her social network.
3. The lethality of the situation (how frequent and severe the violence has been, how longstanding, the presence of weapons in the home, and history of injuries).
4. Her perceptions and interpretations of the abuse (why it occurs and its consequences).
5. Her mental status or psychological state (she may be obviously in distress or even quite calm despite being in acute danger).
6. Her use of alcohol or drugs.
7. Her physical condition, especially the presence of injuries necessitating medical attention.
8. Her need for concrete services.
9. What she is seeking help with at this time.

Several worker roles and activities come into play to facilitate the accomplishment of the aforementioned goals once assessment has been completed: crisis intervention; providing support; providing information; referral; and advocacy.

Assistance with the development of a protection plan, an important aspect of empowerment, is essential to ensuring the safety of clients who will be returning to the home (Brekke 1987; Schechter and Gray 1988). In addition to having some obvious practical value, the plan will help create a sense of personal control for women who are unwilling or unable to leave the violent situation and will help forge a beginning relationship with the client. This protection plan should establish a way of the client and her children to escape in the event of another violent incident. It should include a place to stay temporarily, such as a shelter or the home of a friend or a family member, as well as access to a means of escape, such as a hidden car key or money for cab fare. Cues that signal that violence may be imminent should also be identified.

For many battered women, especially those seeking professional help for the first time, accomplishment of these immediate goals will be the most they can take on at this stage. It is important to understand, respect, and accept that. It is also important to communicate to the client at the end of treatment that the door is open to her in the future, should she decide to come back later to explore further treatment options.

For women who are ready to examine their own behavior and to begin to explore changes in themselves, numerous short-term or proximal goals can be undertaken, the accomplishment of which will facilitate the ultimate goal of freeing their lives of violence:

1. Development of trust and intimacy with another person via the helping relationship, following years of mistrust, suspicion, and betrayal (Henson and Schinderman 1980).
2. Increasing self-esteem and a positive sense of self-worth (Goodstein and Page 1981).
3. Decreasing dependency and learned helplessness and increasing personal autonomy (Ball and Wyman 1977–78; Cantoni 1981; Douglas 1987).
4. Increasing assertiveness and feelings of personal control or efficacy.
5. Addressing alcohol or drug use, legal as well as illegal, which are often used unsuccessfully by abused women to cope with the physical and emotional abuse.
6. Getting in touch with feelings, especially anger, which may be repressed because of a fear of being overwhelmed (Gillman 1980) (uncovering such feelings should be therapeutically approached with caution in working with women who are residing with the batterer).
7. Resolving the ambivalence in the relationship, including love/ hate and fear/anger toward the violent partner, as well as staying versus leaving (Walker 1979).
8. Decreasing social isolation through development or expansion of the client's social network.

An ideal way to accomplish these goals is through participation in a battered women's support group (Bolton and Bolton 1987; Fleming 1979; Hartman 1983; Lewis 1983; Roberts 1984), although some women may need individual work before they feel ready to handle a group and the admission of being abused to other members. Lewis (1983) and Hartman (1983) have described group counseling for battered women, a self-help model as well as a professionally led model. Groups are particularly well-suited to addressing feelings of stigma and self-blame, to reducing social isolation, and to increasing trust by providing an immediate support network of women with similar problems. Groups are also useful for providing a forum for development or enhancement of assertiveness, communication, and problem-solving and decision-making skills (Hartman 1983; Lewis 1983). A group can also be an excellent setting for discussion of why women remain in dangerous, violent situations. In sum, groups help to impart a sense of *empowerment* (Hartman 1983).

Working on proximal goals can also occur in the context of individual counseling. Some women prefer this, and in other cases, a group is not available. Worker roles and behaviors in support of these goals include:

1. Supporting and nurturing the client, as well as validating her inherent self-worth.
2. Reinforcing her strengths, such as loyality to her family, parenting skills, or previous attempts at ending the violence.
3. Helping the client to develop insight into the dynamics of battering specific to her own situation by analyzing what occurs prior to, during, and after violent incidents, including any role she may have played in precipitating the assault (if relevant), by offering appropriate interpretations.
4. Confronting the client about why she chooses to remain in the violent situation through discussion of the costs and benefits of the relationship as well as constraints that prevent her from leaving, if that is what she desires.

Ultimately, the two best *long-term* alternatives for a battered woman are to remain in the relationship if the abuse can be eliminated or to terminate the relationship and begin a new life if a nonviolent relationship is not possible. Most prefer the former and see the latter as a last resort. The purpose of the proximal treatment goals discussed previously is to move the client to the point where she can take steps to initiate an improved relationship or take steps to end it and get on with a life without physical and emotional abuse.

The challenge in pursuing the first course, an improved nonviolent relationship, is convincing the batterer to accept help. It is clear in many of these relationships that chronic violence has become a stable feature despite the wife's, and maybe even the husband's, attempts to eliminate the violence. Unless the batterer is willing to accept responsibility for his abusive behavior and seek help to eliminate this violence, things will continue as they have in the past.

The problem is that very few batterers are willing either to take responsibility for their behavior or to seek help voluntarily to change it. Most do not define the behavior as being a problem until forced to do so because their wives have taken the children and left and/or they encounter the criminal justice system via the arrest process (Bolton and Bolton 1987; Saunders 1982). Like the alcoholic, most will not seek help until the situation becomes a crisis and they are mandated to do so. In that most batterers are highly dependent on their wives and wish the relationship to continue, the wives are strongly advised to create leverage in getting their partners to change by temporarily separating from them and/or having them arrested after an assault. Unless the batterer experiences some aversive consequences as a result of his abuse, he is unlikely to change his behavior (Bolton and Bolton 1987; Schechter and Gray 1988). These recommendations are not made lightly, nor do they guarantee that the husband will accept responsibility for his violent behavior and seek help in changing it. Separation and arrest are seen as extreme measures, the only chance for change to occur by disrupting the equilibrium of the couple system and taking advantage of the husband's desire to maintain the relationship. If the husband will not agree to obtain counseling under these circumstances, there is little reason to believe he will change (Saunders 1982).

The ideal situation is for the wife to live separately from her partner and agree to reconcile only after an extended period of time without violence—for example, six to eight months—and with conjoint counseling. Having a court order to complete individual or group counseling for battering further increases the likelihood of completion of couples counseling. Attendance at a batterers' group prior to or concurrently with couples counseling, while the wife is in individual or group therapy, is the optimal arrangement.

Despite feminist reservations about couples or family therapy based on assumptions from family systems theory, it is possible to provide such counseling in a way that avoids assigning blame equally to both parties and that defines the violence as the problem itself rather than as a symptom of some other, underlying problem (Bograd 1984). As long as both parties agree to participate in the counseling and to refrain from all violent acts during the period of treatment, conjoint counseling is possible. Its goals should be the permanent cessation of all violence and other abusive behavior, the acquisition of understanding of the factors that led to and maintained the violence, and hopefully, an improvement in the overall quality of the relationship. The goal should *not* be to preserve the marriage at any cost. Substance abuse by either party should be addressed prior to conjoint therapy.

Several models have been developed for conjoint counseling of domestic violence (Deschner 1984; Neidig, Friedman, and Collins 1985; Taylor 1984; Weidman 1986). They have a number of features in common. All assume that violence is learned behavior that can be unlearned and replaced with less harmful, more effective methods of conflict resolution and anger management. All explore the roots of violence and why it is dysfunctional for families. Finally, all address general relationship enhancement. The reader is referred to the materials cited for further details on conducting conjoint treatment with couples experiencing violence.

When couples work is not successful in eliminating abusive behavior or when the batterer is unwilling to work toward ending his violent behavior, the abused wife may wish to end the relationship. Spouses separating under the best of circumstances tend to experience a variety of difficulties, especially if there are children (Weiss 1976). Wives emerging from violent homes can particularly benefit from supportive counseling. Many battered women are essentially indigent, even if their husbands are employed, since they may not have access to the husbands' income or their joint property. Thus, there are a number of areas where they can benefit from concrete assistance, such as obtaining public assistance or Aid to Families with Dependent Children and finding a new place to live. Many can benefit from educational counseling or job training as they strive to become self-supporting. Some can also benefit from parent education and supportive work with their children, who are likely to be quite distressed as a result of the history of violence as well as parental plans to separate.

Often, the decision to leave the marriage permanently puts the battered woman in grave danger as it precipitates a crisis in the batterer, who rarely supports this decision and may go to any lengths in his attempts to prevent his wife from leaving. Thus, a restraining order should be explored at this time, as well as an unlisted phone number. It may also be wise to avoid sharing the wife's new address, although this may be inconvenient in terms of child visitation.

Working with battered women is especially stressful and demanding for the worker. It may place the worker in danger, as irate husbands have been known to displace their anger onto helping professionals (Hartman 1983). In addition, violent incidents tend not to occur between nine and five on weekdays, and thus, one must be available for crisis and emergencies, which can occur frequently with this population (Bolton and Bolton 1987; Cantoni 1981). This can be exhausting.

At the outset of counseling, the worker may notice that he or she has to work especially hard at establishing a trusting relationship because of the client's history of mistrust and betrayal (Cantoni 1981) and because of her ambivalence about treatment (Goodstein and Page 1981). The battered woman may have had several previous, unsuccessful experiences with professionals who claimed to want to help her, and who, in the end, only blamed her or communicated that her situation was hopeless. It is particularly important to avoid pessimism about her circumstances (which may not be easy) because the client herself is likely to feel so hopeless and defeated at the outset. Understanding the dynamics of battering and being familiar with services that abused wives may need are helpful to the worker in avoiding the feeling of being overwhelmed by and discouraged about the situations of battered women.

Another potential issue is inadvertently fostering a transfer of the client's dependency from the batterer onto the worker. This can occur with clients who enter treatment in a highly passive state, apparently unable to make decisions or act on their own behalf, especially if the worker is inexperienced. If the client is to succeed in freeing her life of abuse, she must learn to become independent and take care of herself. Establishment of increased autonomy as an explicit helping goal may assist in preventing undue dependency on the worker.

It is difficult for many workers to understand and accept battered women's loyalty to, ambivalence about, and love for their batterers (Goodstein and Page 1981; Henson and Schinderman 1980). The client may choose to share only the batterer's bad points, such as his alcohol abuse and poor work history. But as soon as the worker makes a critical comment about him, such as, "He seems very immature and irresponsible," the client may become defensive and report what a good father he can be, leaving the worker confused about how the client really feels. It is important to remember that in most cases, the husband is violent, not all the time, but intermittently. He may have many other redeeming qualities that explain why the client loves him and wants to continue the relationship—but without the violence. If these issues are not thoroughly explored, the worker can easily become frustrated by and angry at the client, blaming her for not following through or being too ambivalent about her partner. At times like this, one needs to remind oneself about the importance of client self-determination. The client always has the right to make decisions about her own life, including returning to a violent partner, even if the worker does not approve or would not make the same decision. Nor should such a client be deprived of future services as a result of making such a decision.

## CASE ILLUSTRATION

Sharon W, a 29-year-old white woman, requested help from the local family and children's service agency because of her fear that she might seriously injure her youngest child, 4-year-old Anthony, Jr., in the course of disciplining him. She had two other children, 7-year-old Jessica and 12-year-old Jason, from her first marriage. Tony, her 26-year-old husband of five years, worked intermittently as a bricklayer, when he could get work. Sharon was not employed, although she wanted to look for a job since the family had trouble making ends meet. A constant source of friction for the couple was the fact that Sharon's ex-husband, whose whereabouts were unknown, had not paid any child support since the couple had divorced several years before. Thus, Tony supported all three children. Another chronic source of conflict revolved around Sharon's desire to work and Tony's opposition to her employment.

A week prior to her appointment at the agency, Sharon, who had been having difficulty with Anthony, Jr., had got so angry that she spanked him hard enough to bruise his buttocks; she discovered the bruises later that night while bathing him for bed. She had been feeling at her wits end with him because he had been sick so much lately, complaining of constant headaches and stomachaches; he had also been hard to control and aggressive. He was extremely uncooperative and would not mind. In addition, several mothers in the neighborhood had been complaining about his injuring their children when he played with them. Neither of her older children had behaved that way.

When asked about whether she had ever sought counseling before, Sharon reported that she had once gone to her parish priest for family problems and two months before had gone to her pediatrician because of Anthony's illnesses and behavior. He could find nothing physically wrong. His solution was to tell her that "boys will be be boys" and to give her a prescription for Valium.

Sharon's presenting affect was depressed and she was agitated throughout the interview. The preliminary assessment revealed that she had been sleeping poorly and often felt too "nervous" about Anthony to eat. She was quite thin and pale, and her appearance did not reflect much personal attention.

When asked about her current husband, Tony, Sharon reported that he was hard-working (when he could find work) but spent a lot of time away from home at a local bar when he was not working. Probing revealed that this appeared to be a means of escaping Sharon's complaints about not having any income and avoidance of the children's constant bickering. She also described Tony as very jealous, although she laughed about this and said it was his way of telling her how much he loved her since he wasn't very good at talking about his feelings. When asked if he would be willing to come with her for counseling, since some of the issues she had presented suggested the need for couples or family work, she replied that there was no possibility of his participation. In fact, he would be furious if he knew she was here now, since he believed family matters should be kept inside the family.

Several aspects of the case of Sharon W. suggested the possibility that she might be a victim of domestic violence. Sharon's depression, anxiety, and use of violence against her younger son suggested the possibility that she was being abused by Tony. Anthony's, Jr.'s difficulties (minor illnesses, unmanageability, and aggression toward peers) also suggested a possible reaction to witnessing violence between his parents. Finally, Sharon's description of Tony indicated several risk factors for abusive behavior, including intermittent blue-collar employment and financial problems, abuse of alcohol, excessive jealousy, and discomfort with discussion of feelings, even positive feelings. His reported refusal to enter counseling with Sharon as well as his anger if he were to find out that she was in counseling should also be regarded as risk factors. Finally, both spouses were young, under age 30.

During the assessment phase, the worker determined that Sharon was not in crisis but was physically and emotionally exhausted as well as depressed and anxious. During the first interview, the worker attempted to involve Sharon's husband in counseling by pointing out to Sharon that Anthony was his child, too, and that he needed to be involved in any efforts to address the child behavior problems. Sharon agreed to ask him to come to the next session but was not optimistic.

Because this client did not enter counseling with violence as the presenting problem, Brekke's (1987) funneling method was used as a means of determining if violence was present in this family. Assessment of the couple's means of conflict resolution and problem solving was thus a focus in the first session. Specific questions were formulated to determine how disagreements were resolved and what forms of aggression were used by the spouses and toward the children. The worker suspected that if Tony was abusing Sharon, he might also be using violence toward his stepchildren as well as his own young son.

The results of the funneling technique indicated the presence of intermittent marital violence, consisting of Tony's slapping, shoving, and once punching Sharon, as well as threatening to injure her seriously if she did not better control Anthony, Jr.'s behavior and force her ex-husband to pay child support. Sharon's protests that she didn't know where he was and would rather find a job herself led only to further abuse. All three children had at times witnessed these arguments, which also included much yelling, profanity, threats, and throwing of household objects. Sharon began to cry as she related this and admitted to being very frightened of Tony during these arguments. She also related that Tony had a very short temper with the children, especially the older ones and particularly when he had been drinking. On occasion, he had used excessive physical punishment but not to the point where any of the three had been injured.

Based on a preliminary assessment, Sharon appeared to be in a very early stage in her perceptions of the abuse, which she felt was a function of her own behavior and could be controlled largely by modification of her parenting and by contributing something economically to the support of her children. There were no indications that Sharon was considering a separation from her husband, permanent or temporary. However, she did indicate that she would like Tony to stop hitting her—it made her feel ashamed and bad about herself. The worker also learned that Sharon had never called the police because of the violence or left the home to avoid it. Nor had she been seriously injured during one of the attacks, although she had received a black eye when Tony punched her in the most recent fight. Following these violent arguments, most often Tony had stomped out of the house to cool off, returning after a few hours. Sometimes, he later acted as if nothing had happened, but more recently he had apologized, promising that he would never hit her again, and professing his love for her and the children.

Sharon left the first session somewhat relieved at having shared her difficulties and agreed to return the following week. In the second session, the worker's inquiries about Sharon's family of origin revealed that Sharon was somewhat close to her parents despite an earlier rift resulting from her getting pregnant and marrying at age 19. Her only sibling, a brother, lived in a distant state. She did not report violence between her parents, although their marriage was described as chronically unhappy and conflict-ridden, partly because of her father's intermittent heavy drinking. The worker concluded that Sharon's parents were potentially supportive (Sharon hadn't told them about the violence in her marriage) although they did not live nearby. Sharon's first marriage, while unhappy, was not described as abusive, although there had been many arguments.

Another focus of the second session was identification of Sharon's strengths and resources and a discussion of the need for a protection plan. The interview revealed that she had held jobs in the past and wished to find a job currently, both strengths, and had two close women friends, one in the neighborhood and one from a former job who lived in the same town. Only the neighbor knew of her current marital difficulties. For the most part, her parenting appeared to have been adequate, until the recent problems with Anthony, Jr. She recognized that her response to his unmanageable behavior was inappropriate and was highly motivated to learn more effective ways of dealing with him. Finally, she reported no illegal drug use, only occasional alcohol consumption, and no regular use of prescription drug medication. Thus, she demonstrated several important strengths, including past job experience and a desire to resume employment, basically good parenting, and some close relationships with family and friends.

The challenge of the second interview was to convince Sharon that her husband's violence was likely to continue, necessitating formulation of a safety plan and acquisition of information about her alternatives should the abuse continue. The worker told her that experience in working with women like her indicated that, over time, violence that began as relatively minor tended to recur, getting progressively more frequent and more severe as time went on. Although Sharon denied the likelihood that her husband would hit her again, she agreed to work on a safety plan.

The major focus of the third session was formulation of the safety plan. In the course of working together on the plan, the worker had the opportunity to tell Sharon that violence was not "normal" in marriage, something Sharon probably already knew since it had not occurred in her first marriage or her parents' marriage. But she also needed to hear that no matter how good or bad a wife or mother she was, she did not deserve to be hit. She also learned from the worker that marital violence is illegal and that she could call the police if things got worse in the future. They also discussed the circumstances that prevailed just before Tony "blew up" and hit her, and how they were different from the times when he got angry but didn't resort to violence. Unfortunately, it was very difficult to predict when he would get violent, except for the type of argument (kids' behavior and child support) and his drinking behavior, although even that wasn't consistent.

The plan they worked out consisted of having Sharon talk to her neighbor friend, who already knew about the violence, about going there temporarily with the children if they needed to get away; from there, she would call her parents, who lived about two hours away. This, in turn, led to the need to discuss the violence with her parents, who were retired, and getting them to agree to drive to the neighbor's home to pick up Sharon and the children. Although her parents were upset and disappointed when they learned that Sharon's second marriage had difficulties, they were basically supportive and agreed to the plan. The worker introduced the idea of a battered women's shelter, but Sharon didn't feel she wanted or needed to share her problems with strangers and said she would feel safer at her parents' home.

At the end of the third session, Sharon reiterated her need for help in finding a job and locating her ex-husband. She felt that her current husband would be more amenable to her getting a job if she took some action to find her former husband and to get him to contribute to the older children's support, thereby easing the family's financial strains. The worker agreed to assist with both of these tasks, suggesting that Sharon seek part-time employment as a compromise in the attempt to meet Tony's objections to her about being out of the home full time.

In the attempt to locate Sharon's ex-husband the worker introduced Sharon to the services of family court, but encouraged Sharon to follow through on the action herself to enhance her assertiveness, autonomy, and feelings of self-esteem. The worker agreed to intervene as an advocate on Sharon's behalf if she had difficulty or if there was a stalemate.

The worker had concerns about the psychosocial functioning of all three children and felt a report should be made to the child protective agency because of Sharon's reported loss of control and bruising of Anthony's buttocks while disciplining him. Once the worker had a beginning therapeutic relationship with Sharon, she felt better able to raise this issue with her. The worker began by building on Sharon's concern for her children's well-being and noting that witnessing marital violence can be harmful to children. Sharon admitted that the children did appear quite upset following the violent arguments and finally agreed to have the two older children come in for an assessment. The worker went on to note that if Sharon agreed to work voluntarily with child protective services, it would be a means of improving her ability to manage Anthony. Ultimately, she was referred to a structured parent education group for parents having difficulty with preschoolers.

Subsequent sessions were devoted to discussions of what type of job Sharon wanted, her limited skills and how she could upgrade them, and how to persuade Tony to change his views on her working. Role play and rehearsal were techniques used to help Sharon feel more confident in approaching him. The worker also made a referral to an employment counselor to have Sharon's skills evaluated and to determine what her current job options were. The worker also introduced the idea of day care, even if Sharon didn't get a job, to give her some relief during the day and to give Anthony the opportunity to develop social skills in a structured, supervised setting.

Sharon did succeed in convincing Tony that it was a good idea to have her work on a part-time basis, although he objected to Anthony, Jr.'s enrolling in day care. She followed through on the job-counseling referral and was assisted in finding a part-time entry-level job as a data-entry clerk, where she would learn some new skills and get some good benefits.

Since day-care was not an option, Tony agreed to watch Anthony when Sharon was at work, and Tony's mother agreed to baby-sit when Tony got work. Tony still was not working regularly, although he began to think about looking for a different line of work. Although Sharon's ex-husband could not be located, the tensions at home seemed to ease somewhat, and Sharon terminated counseling after seven sessions. Sharon was not able to persuade Tony to join her for counseling, although after a few sessions, she felt comfortable telling him that she was coming. Nor was the worker able to convince Sharon that she should join a battered women's support group, because Sharon didn't really consider herself a battered woman. Although violence did not occur during the course of counseling, it had not been a frequent occurrence prior to counseling and might well occur after counseling had ended. The worker was careful to let Sharon know that if she had difficulties in the future with this or other problems, she could return.

In this case, the worker was able to focus primarily on immediate goals because of where the client was when she began counseling. In the first session the worker determined that the client was upset (depressed, anxious, and exhausted) but not in a state of crisis. Using the funneling technique, she learned that minor marital violence had occurred and that the client mistakenly perceived it as being under her control. The violence had not progressed to the point where police intervention or leaving the home had occurred. In the second session, the worker explored the client's other possible experiences with domestic violence and use of alcohol and drugs, identified her strengths, and began to work on her perceptions of the violence. The third session was focused on development of a personal protection plan, discussion of a job-seeking strategy, and assessment of the children's functioning. Subsequent sessions were devoted to implementation of the safety plan via disclosure to the client's friend and parents and the introduction of the idea of day care for Anthony, Jr.

Proximal goals such as improving the client's self-esteem and assertiveness, decreasing her dependency, and expanding her social network, as well as more directly addressing her depression and anxiety, would have been targeted if termination had not occurred. But since the client was denying the future likelihood of violence, she did not appear ready to address these issues or her feelings of sadness, fear, and anger about the violence.

Domestic violence is a complex, difficult social problem with many contributing factors at the societal, family, and individual levels. It has widespread ramifications for all family members and society in general. Although its economic costs have not yet been documented, they are undoubtedly significant. Its human costs, on the other hand, have been amply demonstrated and are considerable.

Social workers are uniquely well trained among the human service professionals to both understand and intervene effectively in domestic violence situations. The ecological perspective, with which social workers are familiar and comfortable, provides a useful framework both for understanding contributing factors and organizing interventions. However, to be optimally effective, social workers need to be better informed about the nature of domestic violence, including its prevalence, causes, and consequences. The danger of being uninformed is that of making erroneous assumptions about this problem and blaming those who are already victimized, powerless, and stigmatized. This essay represents an attempt to provide information that will enable social work practitioners to be most effective in their efforts to ameliorate domestic violence and its pernicious effects.

## REFERENCES

Allen, C. M. and M. A. Straus. 1980. "Resources, Power, and Husband–Wife Violence." In M. A. Straus and G. T. Hotaling, eds., *The Social Causes of Husband–Wife Violence*, pp. 188–208. Minneapolis: University of Minnesota Press.

Asbury, J. 1987. "African-American Women in Violent Relationships: An Exploration of Cultural Differences." In R. L. Hampton, ed., *Violence in the Black Family: Correlates and Consequences*, pp. 89–105. Lexington, Mass.: Lexington Books.

Bagarozzi, D. A. and C. W. Giddings. 1983. "Conjugal Violence: A Critical Review of Current Research and Clinical Practices." *American Journal of Family Therapy* 11(3):3–15.

Ball, P. G. and E. Wyman. 1977–78. "Battered Wives and Powerlessness: What Can Counselors Do?" *Victimology* 2:545–552.

Bass, D. and J. Rice. 1979. "Agency Responses to the Abused Wife." *Social Casework* 60:338–342.

Bograd, M. 1982. "Battered Women, Cultural Myths and Clinical Interventions: A Feminist Analysis." *Women and Therapy* 1:69–77.

Bograd, M. 1984. "Family System Approaches to Wife Battering: A Feminist Critique." *American Journal of Orthopsychiatry* 54:558–568.

Bologna, M. J., C. K. Waterman, and L. J. Dawson. 1987. "Violence in Gay Male and Lesbian Relationships." Paper presented at the Third National Conference for Family Violence Researchers, Durham, NH.

Bolton, F. G. and S. R. Bolton. 1987. *Working with Violent Families: A Guide for Clinical and Legal Practitioners*. Newbury Park, Calif.: Sage.

Bowker, L. H. 1984. "Coping with Wife Abuse: Personal and Social Networks." In A. R. Roberts, ed., *Battered Women and Their Families*, pp. 168–191. New York: Springer.

Brand, P. A. and A. H. Kidd. 1986. "Frequency of Physical Aggression in Heterosexual and Female Homosexual Dyads." *Psychological Reports* 59:1307–1313.

Brekke, J. S. 1987. "Detecting Wife Abuse and Child Abuse in Clinical Settings." *Social Casework* 68:332–338.

Cantoni, L. 1981. "Clinical Issues in Domestic Violence." *Social Casework* 62:3–12.

Carlson, B. E. 1984. "Causes and Maintenance of Domestic Violence: An Ecological Analysis." *Social Service Review* 58:569–587.

Carmen, E. 1981. "Violence Against Wives: Treatment Dilemmas for Clinicians and Victims." *International Journal of Family Psychiatry* 2:353–367.

Coley, S. M. and J. O. Beckett. 1988. "Black Battered Women: A Review of Empirical Literature." *Journal of Counseling Development* 66:266–270.

Conroy, K. 1982. "Long-Term Treatment Issues with Battered Women." In J. Flanzer, ed., *The Many Faces of Family Violence*, pp. 24–33. Springfield, Ill: Charles C Thomas.

Davis, L. V. 1984. "Beliefs of Service Providers About Abused Women and Abusing Men." *Social Work* 29:243–250.

Davis, L. V. 1987. "Battered Women: The Transformation of a Social Problem." *Social Work* 32:306–311.

Davis. L. V. and B. E. Carlson. 1981. "Attitudes of Service Providers Toward Domestic Violence." *Social Work Research and Abstracts* 17:34–39.

Davis, L. V. and J. L. Hagen. 1988. "Services for Battered Women: The Public Policy Response." *Social Service Review* 62:649–667.

Deschner, J. P. 1984. *The Hitting Habit: Anger Control for Battering Couples.* New York: Free Press.

Dobash, R. P. and R. E. Dobash. 1981. "Community Response to Violence Against Wives: Charivari, Abstract Justice and Patriarchy." *Social Problems* 28:563–581.

Douglas, M. A. 1987. "The Battered Woman Syndrome." In D. J. Sonkin, ed., *Domestic Violence on Trial*, pp. 39–54. New York: Springer.

Dutton, D. and S. L. Painter. 1981. "Traumatic Bonding: The Development of Emotional Attachments in Battered Women and Other Relationships of Intermittent Abuse." *Victimology* 6:139–155.

Edleson, J. 1984. "Working with Men Who Batter." *Social Work* 29:237–242.

Felthouse, A. R. 1983. "Crisis Intervention in Interpartner Abuse." *Bulletin of the American Academy of Psychiatric Law* 11:249–260.

Ferraro, K. "Rationalizing Violence: How Battered Women Stay." *Victimology* 10:203–212.

Finn, J. 1985. "The Stresses and Coping Behavior of Battered Women." *Social Casework* 66:341–349.

Fleming, J. 1979. *Stopping Wife Abuse.* New York: Anchor/Doubleday.

Frisch, M. B. and C. J. MacKenzie. 1988. "A Comparison of Formerly and Chronically Battered Women on Cognitive and Situational Dimensions." Paper presented at the Annual Meeting of the Association for Advancement of Behavior Therapy, November.

Gelles, R. J. 1983. An exchange/social control theory. In D. Finkelhor, R. J. Gelles, G. T. Hotaling, and M. A. Straus (eds.), *The Dark Side of Families*, pp. 151–165. Beverly Hills, Calif.: Sage.

Gelles, R. J. and M. A. Straus 1988. *Intimate Violence: The Definitive Study of the Causes and Consequences of Abuse in the American Family.* New York: Simon & Schuster.

Gillman, I. S. 1980. "An Object-Relations Approach to the Phenomenon and Treatment of Battered Women." *Psychiatry* 43:346–358.

Gondolf, E. W. 1987. "Changing Men Who Batter: A Developmental Model for Integrated Interventions." *Journal of Family Violence* 2:335–349.

Goodstein, R. K. and A. W. Page. 1981. "Battered Wife Syndome: Overview of Dynamics and Treatment." *American Journal of Psychiatry* 138:1036–1044.

Hartman, S. 1983. "A Self-Help Group for Women in Abusive Relationships." *Social Work with Groups* 6:133–146.

Hendricks-Matthews, M. 1982. "The Battered Woman: Is She Ready for Help?" *Social Casework* 63:131–137.

Henson, D. M. and J. L. Schinderman. 1980. "Therapy with Battered Women." In A. Weick and S. T. Vandiver, eds., *Women, Power and Change*, pp. 27–37. Washington, D.C.: National Association of Social Workers.

Hilberman, E. and K. Munson 1977–78. "Sixty Battered Women." *Victimology* 2:460–470.

Kelly, E. E. and L. Warshafsky. 1987. "Partner Abuse in Gay Male and Lesbian Couples." Paper presented at the 3rd National Conference for Family Violence Researchers, Durham, N.H.

Leonard, K. E. and T. Jacob. 1988. "Alcohol, Alcoholism, and Family Violence." In

V. B. Van Hasselt, R. L. Morrison, A. S. Bellack, M. Hersen, eds., *Handbook of Family Violence*, pp. 383–406. New York: Plenum.

Lewis, E. 1983. "The Group Treatment of Battered Women." *Women and Therapy* 2:51–58.

Lynch, C. G. and T. Norris 1977–78. "Services for Battered Women: Looking for a Perspective." *Victimology* 2:553–562.

Neidig, P. H., D. H. Friedman, and B. S. Collins. 1985. "Domestic Conflict Containment: A Spouse Abuse Treatment Program." *Social Casework* 66:195–204.

Pagelow, M. D. 1984. *Family Violence*. New York: Praeger.

Pfouts, J. H. 1978. "Violent Families: Coping Responses of Abused Wives." *Child Welfare* 57:101–111.

Pirog-Good, M. and J. Stets-Kealey. 1985. "Male Batterers and Battering Prevention Programs: A National Survey." *Response* 8:8–12.

Renzetti, C. M. 1989. "Building a Second Closet: Third Party Responses to Victims of Lesbian Partner Abuse." *Family Relations* 38:157–163.

Roberts, A. R. 1984. "Crisis Intervention with Battered Women." In A. R. Roberts, ed., *Battered Women and Their Families*, pp. 65–83. New York: Springer.

Rosewater, L. B. 1988. "Battered or Schizophrenic? Psychological Tests Can't Tell." In K. Yllo and M. Bograd, eds., *Feminist Perspectives on Wife Abuse*, pp. 200–216. Newbury Park, Calif.: Sage.

Saunders, D. G. 1982. "Counseling the Violent Husband." In P. A. Keller and L. G. Ritt, eds., *Innovations in Clinical Practice: A Sourcebook*, pp. 16–29. Sarasota, Fla.: Professional Resource Exchange.

Saunders, D. G. 1984. "Helping Husbands Who Batter." *Social Casework* 65:347–353.

Schechter, S. and L. T. Gray. 1988. "A Framework for Understanding and Empowering Battered Women." In M. B. Straus, ed., *Abuse and Victimization Across the Life Span*, pp. 240–253. Baltimore: Johns Hopkins University Press.

Star, B. 1981. "The Impact of Violence on Families." *Conciliation Courts Review* 19:33–40.

Star, B. 1983. *Helping the Abuser: Intervening Effectively in Family Violence*. New York: Family Service Association of America.

Straus, M. A. and R. J. Gelles. 1986. "Societal Change in Family Violence from 1975 to 1985 as Revealed by Two National Surveys." *Journal of Marriage and the Family* 48:465–479.

Straus, M. B., R. J. Gelles, and S. K. Steinmetz. 1980. *Behind Closed Doors: Violence in the American Family*. Garden City, N.Y.: Anchor.

Strube, M. J. 1988. "The Decision to Leave an Abusive Relationship: Empirical Evidence and Theoretical Issues." *Psychological Bulletin* 104:236–250.

Taylor, J. W. 1984. "Structured Conjoint Therapy for Spouse Abuse Cases." *Social Casework* 65:11–18.

Thibault, J. W. and H. H. Kelley. 1959. *The Social Psychology of Groups*. New York: Wiley.

Torres, S. 1987. "Hispanic-American Battered Women: Why Consider Cultural Differences?" *Response* 10:20–21.

Walker, L. E. 1980. *The Battered Woman*. New York: Harper Colophon.

Weidman, A. 1986. "Family Therapy with Violent Couples." *Social Casework* 4:211–218.

Weiss, R. 1976. "The Emotional Impact of Marital Separation." *Journal of Social Issues* 32:135–145.

Wilson, S. K., S. Cameron, P. Jaffe, and D. Wolfe. 1989. "Children Exposed to Wife Abuse: An Intervention Model." *Social Casework* 70:180–184.

Yllo, K. and M. A. Straus. 1981. "Interpersonal Violence Among Married and Cohabitating Couples." *Family Relations* 30:339–347.

# 16

## Elderly in Need of Long-Term Care

▼

### TOBY BERMAN-ROSSI

The "graying of America" is more than a poetic image. It speaks of the dramatic increase in the absolute and relative number of older persons in the total population. Only 4 percent of the population at the beginning of this century, by 2050 the percentage of those over 65 will be 21.7 percent (Maldonado 1987; NIA, 1987). Fertility rates, decreased mortality, and migraton patterns have all contributed to the growth of the aged at a rate faster than that of any other population group (Cutler 1976). Concomitantly, there has been a striking increase in those over 75, and those above 85 have doubled each decade since 1940. By 2000, the projected proportion of the over-85 group will be 14.1 percent (Rosenwaike and Dolinsky 1987).

Sixty-five years, though still an arbitrary benchmark, no longer bespeaks the image of old age. It no longer evokes a homogeneous picture. Human development and human accomplishment increasingly defy established "stage"-related designations (Germain 1987). While there remains, for some, a homogeneous portrait with frailty as its premises, for others there is more vigorous representation. We now speak about the "young-old" and the "old-old" (Neugarten 1982a), the "healthy-aged" and the "frail-aged" (Mayer 1983). Some suggest

I am appreciative of discussion with Professor Irving Miller on the concept of frailty and its relationship to the aging field of practice and for his editorial suggestions.

My ideas about assessment have been influenced by the ideas of William Schwartz, particularly as expressed in his as-yet-unpublished book *Social Work with Groups: The Search for a Method.*

I am grateful to Margaret Frost for the case illustration, her written comments, and her ideas about practice. Ms. Frost is Assistant Director of Community Social Services, Jewish Home and Hospital for the Aged, New York City.

**503**

that an age entitlement marker of 75 be substituted as the age at which specialized services should be offered (FCA 1978). The very nature and meaning of *old* have been redefined.

Statistics inform us that, on the whole, the nation's elderly are enjoying the highest standard of living and the most satisfying lifestyle they have ever known. They are living longer; are more financially secure, better educated, more content with their lives; and are more politically active than ever (Neugarten 1982b). Less worried about financial matters, they are more likely to look forward to retirement, and those with the best retirement incomes often elect to retire earlier. This new status makes possible the development of new interests and a return to neglected pleasures.

While this life circumstance is true for many older persons, the statistics also reveal another story. It is a story of older persons who, for a variety of reasons, have become increasingly dependent upon others for assistance in managing their lives and sustaining a view that life is worth living. This segment of the older population also is not a homogeneous group. It includes those elderly who have, and have not, experienced major disadvantageous economic, physical, mental, and emotional conditions throughout their lives. The coping abilities of persons who are blind, developmentally disadvantaged, formerly hospitalized in psychiatric facilities, and experiencing long-term disabling conditions are further taxed by the stressors of aging (Feldstein 1985; Goodman 1985; Mailick Seltzer and Seltzer 1985; Trieschmann 1987). These elderly who are dependent upon others (i.e., those designated as "frail") are the fastest growing group in the elderly population (Brody and Brody 1987; Harel 1986; U.S. HHS, 1985–86). For them, the system has not worked nearly as well. The focus of this chapter is the poor lower- and middle-class group of older persons who need long-term care. This group is estimated to be 38 percent of the aged population (Hooyman and Lustbader 1986). These persons do not receive an adequate share of America's bounty. They live lives of unnecessary hardship resulting from a public policy that often provides insufficient income and services that are inadequate to sustain a meaningful life. A grudging response to their need becomes a powerful factor influencing the quality and nature of their lives.

Though the need for long-term care defies age, sex, culture, and economic class, older women and ethnic minorities are particularly disadvantaged in coping with their problems in living and in conducting the last part of their lives. A sexist, racist, class society, sharpened by ageism, imposes upon the older person a daunting and powerful combination of obstacles, and especially on those elderly who depend on formal and informal supports to maintain their lives either in the community or in long-term-care institutions.

The need to serve this group is pressing, because they are in fact most at-risk of increased morbidity, abuse, neglect, institutionalization, and death. These vulnerable elderly, and particularly women and ethnic minorities, are the specific populations to which social workers must attend. There is a pressing and clear need for leadership in social policy, planning and organization of services, and direct practice with this large and growing group of vulnerable persons.

## PROBLEM DOMAIN

The population of older persons in this chapter are often called the *frail elderly*. In the literature and in our mind's eye, *frail* conjures up a stereotype image—an elusive, vaguely generalized image, characteristic of the concept itself. At first glance, the most striking characteristic of the term is that it derives its meaning from the union of two concepts: frail and elderly. The term *frail* is used to suggest fragility, weakness, feebleness, infirmity, decrepitness, brittleness, perishableness, things easily broken, and a quality of being easily crushed, destroyed, or wanting in power (Funk and Wagnalls 1968; Longman 1986; Simpson and Weiner 1989; Webster 1951).

Though gerontologists try to define it operationally, the concept *frail elderly* contains a strong deficit orientation, centering on incapacity, i.e., what the older person is unable to do. These elderly are often viewed not in their wholeness as individuals, but in their limitations and dependence upon others. Consider, for example, the following definitions: "Older persons with mental, physical, and/or emotional disabilities that limit their independence and necessitate continuing assistance; persons 75 years or older" (Harris 1988:75), or "By frailty is meant reduction of physical and emotional capacities and loss of social-support systems to the extent that the elderly individual becomes unable to maintain a household or social contacts without continuing assistance from others" (FCA 1978:15).

These definitions of *frail elderly* suggest an individualistic, medical orientation as well as a linearity of approach. "Personal attributes" are viewed as primary factors in the older person's situation. The environment serves principally as a backdrop, rather than as as principal player in the creation of the "condition." "Disabilities" become intrinsic in the individual and not a function of social definition. Thus, the individual, not the environment, becomes the target for change. The logical outcome of a deficit medical model, focused on individual pathology, is a linear orientation to causality. As we shall see later, the medicalizing of aging underlies and dominates long-term-care services. This is epitomized by the fact that the Health Care Financing Administration funds and administers most federal long-term-care programs (Kane 1987). Such views are also consistent with a historical trend in which older persons gradually became viewed as a class —a class in need, a class embodying social problems. Eventually, the elderly have come to be equated with the social problems themselves (Dunkle 1984).

Characterizing older persons in terms of their limitations conflicts with our developing understanding of the ways in which a stable sense of self and a positive self-identification enable older persons, especially the very old, to age well (Gadow 1983; Kaufman 1986; Tobin 1988). In fact, describing oneself as aged and frail is associated with poorer mental health, a perceived external locus of control, and lowered physical and psychological health (Baum and Boxley 1983; Furstenberg 1989).

Our discussion of the "frail elderly" contrasts with current discussion of the needs of an entirely different population: busy business and professional persons "Too Many Chores? Help is at the Doorstep." 1989). These persons, many of whom use assistance to manage their households and personal lives, accrue status by virtue of their ability to purchase assistance. Need under these circumstances is quite acceptable. A comparison of these two groups suggests that it is neither need nor dependence that distinguishes them, but power. In this instance, power takes three forms: first, the power to define the situation in the manner most advantageous to the definer; second, the ability to command the necessary resources directly or through others; and third, the power of a strong voice, strong enough to resist forces tending to destroy. In short, deviance is a matter of definition, and the power of the definer to enforce that definition is required. Thus, frailty has to do with "delicacy of constitution, . . . liability to failure or destruction, . . . an incapacity for dealing with forces or powers opposed to it, or tending to destroy it . . . lack of power to resist," rather than any physical or mental impairment in itself (*Webster*'s 1951:882).

Taken together, these attributes of the "frail" suggest a complex interaction between older persons and their environment. "Frailty" is best understood by the context in which the older person must contend. The strength of the "forces tending to destroy" must be included in the discussion. When these elements in the environment are responsive to long-term need, the older person's strength will meet its demands. An unresponsive or menacing environment is one in which even greater strength is required to maintain the status quo, much less improve it. In such a situation, the capacity of the older person may not be equal to the tasks at hand. In such circumstances, needs increase and greater personal resources are required to maintain oneself. Thus, the balance in the transactions between the elderly and their environment is reflected in the character of their life experience. Frailty results not from attributes of the aged alone, but from a lack of congruence between their needs and capacities and the environment's demands and resources. What is defined as belonging to the individual more accurately belongs to the relationship between the individual and his or her environment. Institutionalization in a long-term-care facility is brought about by the interaction between social circumstances and the characteristics of the individual (Kane 1987).

Being dependent upon others in coping with chronic illness, chronic pain, and physical, emotional, and cognitive change, as well as economic and social losses, is at best very trying even when the relevant resources are available. Under the best of circumstances, this adaptive challenge consumes extraordinary personal capacities, capacities that are inevitably more and more difficult to replenish. Under the worst of circumstances, where capacities are modest and limited, extreme stress is inevitable. The diminishing of mental, physical, and social health creates the very condition that long-term care is designed to mitigate (Harel 1988). As noted before, a balance between the needs and capacities of the older person and the demands and resources of the environment is an outcome "devoutedly to be wished" and striven for by social workers.

## SOCIETAL CONTEXT

It is commonly assumed that the association between being over 65 and being frail embodies intrinsic truths. In fact, this perspective is socially constructed. This is not to suggest that hardship is not experienced by many with increased age, particularly those in need of long-term care. Rather, it is to suggest that the characterizing of an entire group in deficit terms derives from the complex interaction of social, economic, and political forces. Diverting attention from these forces perpetuates two powerful, but mistaken, beliefs: 1) older persons are responsible for their own difficulties, and 2) frailty is an inevitable outgrowth of the aging process.

There is perhaps no issue impinging more on the lives of those needing long-term care than the public policy that specifies need, creates the conditions under which need comes about, and sets up the service systems to meet the very need it has helped create. As an embodiment of values and philosophy, pubic policy expresses a point of view about the proper role of government in the lives of its citizens, about the varied beliefs and interests of those governed and the powerful groups that govern and create the social services. Thus, public policy is both proactive in creating the social context of older persons and reactive to the social context in which it finds itself.

The social context of public policy for the aged is not neutral. Maggie Kuhn, founder of the Gray Panthers, and recently deceased Claude Pepper, member of Congress from Florida, have given eloquent public testimony to the unmet needs of the elderly, particularly those most vulnerable. The term *ageism* was coined by Butler (1969) to convey a prejudiced social context that results in stereotyping and bias toward older persons. These biases have profound effects on how society behaves toward them.

Ageism is an insidious process that creeps into every aspect of private and public life. Within public life the most devastating and far-reaching effect of ageism is social policy that enacts the view that older persons constitute a class apart from the mainstream of society, where they are less worthy of social investment and less capable of acting in their own behalf. The needs of older persons, especially the vulnerable aged, are frequently counterposed to those of other groups, particularly children, who are viewed as a "better investment" (Monk 1981; Callahan 1987). Such a view assumes a utilitarian approach to the ethical question of the disposition of scarce resources. Services that are thought to achieve "little return" for the investment are valued less highly than services thought to offer a "higher return" (Monk and Abramson 1982). Negative views of the capacities of older persons support policies that diminish opportunities for the elderly to make even the most ordinary choices about their own lives. Forced retirement is a prime example of such a policy (Hooyman and Kiyak 1988). Devaluation of the older person and marginalization—i.e., ignoring or forgetting the older person (Monk, 1985)—also limit the creation of responsive social policy.

When ageism is internalized by the aged, as it is inevitably, the price paid is lowered self-esteem and a self-concept that often mirrors the definitions of others. Such self-perception insults a sense of oneself. An emotional state of helplessness and hopelessness can induce and maintain disease itself (Engel 1968; Mercer and Kane 1979). These feelings profoundly effect a person's level of assertiveness which is believed to be necessary to survival (Berman-Rossi 1986; Tobin and Lieberman 1976). The sense of oneself as potent has direct bearing upon the ability to cope successfully with life events over which older persons have diminished control as they age (Seligman and Elder 1986). Lieberman and Tobin (1983), in their study of differences among older persons in coping with the stress associated with a changing environment, found that adaptation was aided by a higher degree of perceived control between the preferred and the actual environment.

These effects of ageism are felt even more strongly by the vulnerable aged, who are struggling with the impact of chronic illness, lessened physical vigor, and an uncertain future. While all older persons are disadvantaged by stereotype policies and practices, those who need a high degree of instrumental and expressive support to survive in the community or in an institution are worse off. Handicapping conditions are always more disabling for those with the fewest personal and environmental resources. Those least powerful to resist are most negatively affected by "forces tending to destroy." In these circumstances, morbidity, abuse and neglect, institutionalization, and death are more likely to increase.

One policy debate that is of central importance is the question of whether old age, sex, and ethnicity as such are associated with the need for long-term care, or whether it is a consequence of social, political, and economic policies. In direct practice, how problems are defined and desired outcomes are specified influences what is to be done, as does a social policy that rests on a formulation or definition of the problem under discussion and embodies a vision of what is the social good. Those on either side of the dispute have very different recommendations to offer the aged and society. Needs versus age entitlement, as well as separatist versus integrated orientations, frame the bases for these differing recommendations.

Benitez (1976), Moon (1977), Estes (1979), and Neugarten (1982a) have been unequivocal that old age itself does not create the disadvantage. They believe that the problems faced by the elderly are the ones we create for them. Lifetime disadvantages in distribution of income, education, occupational skills, pension, and health care benefits, more than anything else, produce the troubles and trials experienced by older persons. Social definitions of the aged along with social and economic policies reinforcing and institutionalizing them are the problem. An incrementalist and individualistic public policy does little to mitigate inequities. The failure to correct past abuses limits the lives of older persons (Estes, Swan, and Gerard 1982) and frames the central challenge of social policy and planning for older persons.

Estes (1979) believes that economic policies, particularly those related to retirement, are central to the plight of the aged. This opinion is consistent with a universalist approach to social welfare, an approach that is viewed as least stigmatizing (Kohlert 1989). The common belief that dwindling abilities necessitate retirement is part of a socially created "truth" that serves to conceal the reality that retirement policies exist to regulate the labor market. That laws have been created to push workers out of the workplace is evidence of the power of the forces promoting such laws. Recent changes in mandatory retirement laws are more a function of market-needs assessments and shortages than of positive responses to the aging community.

The distribution of income overshadows all other policy decisions in the potency of its effects upon the lives of older persons. Income defines the degree of freedom available for problem solving and determines the degree to which individuals can partake of the country's growing standard of living (Benitez 1976). As income becomes restricted, and for some severely restricted, with retirement, and as the poverty of a lifetime is brought to advanced age, particularly for women and ethnic minorities, the ability to command the long-term-care resources necessary for a satisfying life is diminished. The elderly's dependence upon the "aging enterprise" (Estes 1979) and the dependence of the "aging enterprise" upon the elderly for their own existence generate a potent dialectic. This dialectic structures the meeting ground and influences the terms of engagement between the elderly and the aging service system. While this symbiosis potentially contains the elements necessary for a satisfying balance between older persons and their social institutions, social, political, and economic forces and inherent inequities in power act to distort this balance.

The central effect of the creation of a separate, "nonproductive," and therefore dependent class is the devaluation of an entire segment of society. Age-segregated policies stigmatize the aged. As the needs generated, for some, by the "normal dependencies of aging" (Blenkner 1977) are converted into social problems, older persons are moved further from the center of society. As we move toward structurally segregated, piecemeal policies, the aged are blamed for their needs and are viewed as a drain on society, especially by the young. Antagonistic perceptions of the aged support restrictive services. Recent discussion of the adequacy of the social security fund and rising health care costs are examples. Pitting the needs of one group against those of another, according to need entitlement proponents, becomes easier when an age entitlement orientation frames the formulation of social and economic policy. Age-based programs are also believed to increase the relative disadvantage of minority elderly. The higher mortality rates for minorities ensures that advanced age as a basis for entitlement will also ensure inequality of opportunity because the minority aged do not have an equal chance to reach advanced aged (Jacobson 1982).

In addition, because the aged are a heterogeneous group, age is increasingly a poor predictor of lifestyle or need. Thus, age provides a limited basis for formulating policies and programs. Chronological markers only serve to isolate the elderly and stand their needs apart from those of society (Neugarten 1982a).

The Federal Council on Aging (1978), in their position paper on pubic policy and the frail elderly, took an opposing stance. They are not prepared to abandon the present age-based social welfare structure and believe that, if the elderly are to receive more of their fair share of scarce resources, their needs must be singled out for attention. The council recommended continuing age as a determinant of benefits and suggested a second strata of age entitlement upon attainment of 75 years. The belief that advanced age correlates directly with increased functional impairment prompted this group to advance 75 and over as the necessary age entitlement for increased benefits. They offered the view that the inadequacies and uneven availability of services that normatively occur within the organization of social welfare become experienced more harshly by those who, because of increasing frailty, cannot adequately negotiate the important service systems in their lives. The lives of these elderly are thus further restricted by receiving limited services for both their normative and extraordinary needs. The use of an age designation, the council argued, would more widely ensure access to vital services. Mandated additional income for the normative increase in need and ensuring a significant person to assist the older person in managing his or her life would significantly increase the service base for those in need of long-term care who do not have access to service themselves and/or who do not have a significant other who can assist with such tasks. It is the council's belief that the separation of social services from income maintenance has been a failure for those elderly with "a weakened voice" who have difficulty negotiating their service environment. The need to integrate services and income maintenance is echoed by some within the social work profession (Wyers 1983).

These policy debates also have considerable importance for family, friends, and community persons. The freedom available to informal social supports is interdependent with the freedom accorded older persons in the form of income to purchase services or in the form of the quantity and quality of the services from which to choose. Society's value that children should care for parents, as well as the struggles of adult caregivers, can best be understood within this larger framework.

## RISKS AND NEEDS OF POPULATION

To understand the needs and risks of those requiring long-term care, sociodemographic, economic, health, physical, and mental health characteristics must be examined. Perhaps more than in any other age group, these elements are closely interdependent, and their combined effects constitute the aging experience. Coping with change in these areas becomes a dominant feature of growing old in America. The awareness that aging is affected not only by what occurs to those past 65 years, but also by experiences of a lifetime, makes knowledge of the effects of sex, race, and class upon older persons central to our understanding. Sex, race, and class determine the quantity and quality of economic and service resources available to the aged and inform our understanding of which elderly are most vulnerable and at risk.

### Sociodemographic Characteristics

The United States is currently experiencing a dramatic increase in the number and proportion of very old persons within the general population and within the population of elderly in general. By the year 2000, half the elderly are expected to be over 75. A sevenfold increase in those over 85 is expected by the mid-twenty-first century (U.S. HHS 1985–86). Of this group, the segment growing most rapidly is those over 75, particularly women and ethnic minorities (FCA 1978). Sex and minority status have emerged as critical variables in life expectancy. There is an eight-year difference for men and women (Maldonado 1987). A disadvantaged status in health care, social and economic conditions, preventive and health education services, and income contributes, if not causes, the shortened life expectancy of minority elderly (NYSOA 1989:25).

Within New York State, for example, which contains the second largest concentration of older persons in the nation (NYSOA 1987), in the ten years since the 1980 Census, the older Latino population was projected to increase by 86 percent, and the older African-American population by 41 percent (NYSOA 1989). The living arrangements of older persons are directly affected by life expectancy and marital and childbearing practices. One third of all widowed, divorced, or separated males and one half of all widowed, divorced, or separated females share a home with their children (Gratton and Wilson 1988). Of those over 75, 67 percent of women are widowed, while 67 percent of men are married; 42 percent of women live alone, and 19 percent of men live alone (U.S. HHS 1985–86). It should not be surprising that the majority of older persons living within nursing homes are widowed older women, with a high percentage of inhabitants childless or never married (Kane 1987; Neugarten 1982a). By 2018, 13.3 million elderly are expected to be living alone, 85 percent of whom will be female (CFC Kasper, 1988) Social isolation has been found to be positively correlated with increased age, a single or widowed status, few nearby informal supports, retirement, and decreased physical capacity (Shanas et al. 1968). Social isolation can lead to serious emotional, cognitive, and social difficulties (Bennett 1980). Associated poverty and decreased social supports clearly place this population of single women living alone most at risk of increased morbidity, neglect and abuse, institutionalization, and death. The small percentage of elderly men living alone with few social supports are also at risk. For those elderly living with families, a different set of needs is generated.

## Economic Characteristics

Over the last fifty years, there have been major gains in the economic status of older persons. A poverty rate for older persons of 75 percent in 1936 had been reduced to 18.6 percent by 1972 and to 12.4 percent by 1984 (U.S. HHS 1985–86). A rate of 50 percent total economic dependency on family in 1936 was reported as reduced to a rate of 1.5 percent in 1982 (Brody and Brody 1987). Between 1966 and 1982 the poverty rate decreased by 50 percent for the elderly while increasing slightly for all persons. In 1982, in-kind transfers reduced the poverty rate for all persons by 33 percent and for the elderly by 76 percent (Danziger 1987).

While the overall reduction in the poverty rate for older persons is encouraging, a more detailed analysis reveals considerable cause for concern, particularly for women and ethnic minorities. First, older persons are poorer than other adults. In 1985, the rate of elderly persons living within 150 percent of the poverty rate was 29.1 percent in comparison to 24.3 percent for all other adults (U.S. HHS 1985–86). Second, the poverty rate increases as one ages, with those over 85 experiencing nearly twice as much poverty as those aged 65 to 74 (U.S. HHS 1985–86). Third, older women are significantly poorer than older men. Poverty of a lifetime, minimum social security benefits as a result of a high degree of economic dependence upon men and lessened employment opportunities, a widowed status, and few other sources of income lock women into a position that they are unable to alter (Jones 1987). And finally, the poverty rates for older ethnic minorities, particularly women, are consistently higher than those for any other group in the nation. In 1984, 56.6 percent of elderly African-American women living alone were below the poverty level (U.S. HHS 1985–86), and two thirds of African-American women living alone lived at 125 percent of the poverty level (Brody and Brody 1987). Nationally, the figures for Latino elderly are only slightly improved (Maldonado 1987). Within New York State, 43 percent of the minority elderly live in marginal poverty or below the poverty level, with the statistics for Latino elderly slightly worse (47 percent) than those for African-Americans (45 percent). In 1985, the income for most Latino elderly within New York State clustered between $2,000 and $3,999. Poverty for these groups was expected to rise (NYSOA 1989).

Clearly, economic status controls the options available to older persons in need of long-term care and influences the degree of independence and hardship older persons have in managing their lives. An analysis of sources of income for the elderly indicates that poor older persons are highly dependent upon federal, state, and local programs for their minimum standard of living and have little opportunity to move beyond a poverty level through their own efforts. The inability to purchase services also increases the poor elderly's dependence upon family, public, and not-for-profit sources of support for the provision of long-term care. As a deterioration in the financial status of the elderly occurs, the pattern of reciprocity between the elderly and their informal support network also declines (Stone, Cafferata, and Sangle 1987).

While poor older persons are the most disadvantaged, lower- and middle-income persons in need of long-term care also experience handicapping economic conditions. The costs of long-term care that is provided by both the private and the not-for-profit sectors are so prohibitive that all lower- and middle-income elderly are at risk of impoverishment. In only one year, 90 percent of those needing daily home care would be impoverished under our present system, where all are required to "spend down" to a Medicaid level. Seventy percent of those needing nursing home care would be impoverished in only thirteen weeks (SCA 1987). The increasing pattern of spending limited dollars on fuel, rather than food (Maldonado 1987), further compromises many elderly already at risk because of their dependence upon others to plan meals, shop, and cook. Hospitalization and institutionalization are too frequently an outcome (Ludman and Newman 1986). As a result, most elderly will eventually have decreased possibilities of purchasing long-term care and will become more dependent upon programs for which they qualify as a result of financial eligibility. Fewer supportive and preventive programs will be used, as well, if older persons must choose between fuel and "luxuries," such as attendance at a senior service center.

## Health and Physical Characteristics

For obvious reasons, the health and physical status of older persons are of primary concern to them. The quality of their lives is intimately associated with their level of health and physical ability. Along with economic status, more than any other variable poor health can significantly decrease the older person's capacity for self-care and for a satisfying life. The resulting dependence upon informal and formal supports brings with it psychological and social consequences. To need others for one's very survival generates profound feeling that are always present.

While nearly half of the oldest old enjoy good health and have no serious physical disability, the likelihood of disability increases with age, particularly for those over 75 (Eustis, Greenberg, and Patten 1984; U.S. HHS 1985–86; Kane 1987). Though it is estimated that only 4 percent of the elderly are severely disabled (Hooyman and Kiyak 1988), 50 percent of those aged 75 to 84 and 60 percent of those over 85 experience significant limitations in functioning (Maldonado 1987). Chronic conditions, including arthritis, hypertension, hearing loss, heart conditions, visual and orthopedic impairments, and arteriosclerosis, rather than acute disease, tend to generate the limitations in self-care of greatest concern (Maldonado 1987). Disability associated with chronic health conditions is frequently increased for low-income persons owing to poorer housing, health care, and nutrition (Eustis, Greenberg, and Patten 1984). Reduced capacity for self-care becomes associated with chronic disease and is first in importance to the elderly and their informal and formal caregivers. A significant decrease in the capacity for self-care in the following areas increases the inevitability of long-term-care services: 1) *home management activities*, including preparing meals, shopping for personal items, managing money, using the telephone, doing light housework, and doing heavy housework; 2) *personal care activities*, including bathing, dressing, using the toilet, getting in and out of bed or a chair, and eating; 3) *mobility status;* and 4) *continence status* (NCHS 1989). Consistent with data on the double jeopardy of ethnicity and income, poor minority elderly also experience more difficulty in these respects than majority elderly (NCHS 1989).

The distinction between personal care tasks and household management tasks is important. Evidence suggests that the likelihood of institutionalization increases in accordance with increases in the degree of personal care tasks required (Gonyea 1987). The risk of neglect and abuse also increases as burdens rise, and little relief is in sight (Hooyman and Lustbader 1986). An emphasis upon what the older person can do, rather than the older person's diagnoses, is more instructive for service providers. Within New York State, in 1985, 42 percent of the elderly living within the community experienced activity limitations; 13 percent needed assistance to live at home, and 2 percent, or 40,000 older persons, were completely bedridden. While the bedridden were a small percentage of the state's total elderly, a very large, comprehensive, well-coordinated service program is required to serve such persons (NYSOA 1989). Further, chronic ailments have a demonstrable negative effect on social functioning. This is shown by a positive correlation between health and morale, social behavior, and leisure activity (Brody and Brody 1987). Decreased social functioning is thus another burden of many elderly.

Sex, ethnicity, and income join increased age as significant variables affecting health and physical status. Lifetime conditions of inadequate health care resources and limited access to health care, common among women, ethnic minorities, and the poor, exacerbate existing health problems and create new ones. In comparison to majority elderly, minority elderly report poorer health, experience greater functional disability, are restricted to bed more often, and at birth are expected to have a shorter life span (Manuel and Reid 1982). Older African-Americans are particularly disadvantaged and are thought to be placed in double jeopardy in health and income (Jackson, Kolody, and Wood 1982).

## Mental Health Characteristics

Though suicide rates for older persons had been gradually declining over the previous fifty years, the years from 1984 to 1989 saw an increase of 25 percent ("When Long Life is Too Much: Suicide Risk Among Elderly" 1989). This rise in a population already exhibiting the highest suicide rate for any age group in the nation (Butler and Lewis 1983) bespeaks enormous suffering. For these elderly and those who attempt suicide but are unsuccessful, life no longer contains enough elements to justify existence. Whether one believes that suicide is generated by rational decision making or by feelings of hopelessness and helplessness fueled by depression, there is no question that overpowering life conditions, circumstances, and events provide the energy for such a decision.

Who commits suicide among the elderly? The highest suicide rate is found among older white males, particularly those over 80 (Butler and Lewis 1983; Hooyman and Kiyak 1988). Of this group, older white males living alone have the highest suicide rate of all (Kalish 1985). Interestingly, older women—though poorer, at greater risk of health and physical problems, more likely to live alone, and more likely to be institutionalized—have a suicide rate that decreases with increasing age (Cox 1984). While elderly women attempt suicide three times more often than their male counterparts, elderly men are three times more successful (Reker and Wong 1985).

Loss of satisfying roles and relationships, lack of meaningful activity, conflicts around needing others and the resultant feelings of lessened self-esteem, depression, loneliness, and hopelessness may provide explanations for elderly suicide (Reker and Wong 1985). Financial limitations, a major loss of independence, a sudden decision to give away important possessions, and a general lack of interest in the physical and social environment should be listened to carefully (Hooyman and Kiyak 1988). For older men living alone, these authors believe that despair prompted by insurmountable losses is a more salient explanation. Another explanation posits that a state of psychological impotence is believed to develop when psychological or social devices used in the past are insufficient to cope with present changes (Engel 1968). Hopelessness can induce morbidity as well as death (Lieberman and Tobin 1983). The more hopeful the individual (Seligman and Elder 1986) and the greater the perceived control over a stressor (Schultz and Brenner 1977), the greater is the likelihood that negative events will not have aversive and harmful effects. The loss of personal resources increases the older person's sense of being at the mercy of the environment.

Hopefulness and perceived control over a stressor are especially difficult to achieve when far-reaching events occur and conditions arise over which little control can be exercised. Depression associated with the stress of loss (Rzetelny 1895), dementia, and paranoia, the three most prevalent later-life mental health conditions of concern, make hopefulness and a feeling of control difficult to sustain. Alzheimer's disease, the most common cause of irreversible dementia, estimated to affect 5 to 15 percent of those over 65 (Hooyman and Kiyak 1988), makes independent living an improbability. Decreases in attention span, learning, memory, language, judgment, and relational skills, coupled with a depressive reaction to the disease itself, increase the probability of institutionalization.

Hope, associated with predictablity and a locus of control within the self, is not easily achieved at a time in the life course characterized by enormous uncertainty. While functional limitations can be measured and quantified once they occur, they often cannot be foreseen. A calm of today can unpredictably explode under the power of tomorrow's life events. A broken hip, the death of a spouse, the loss of sight, the loss of an apartment, or the closing of a neighborhood store, for example, can dramatically change the lives of older persons who had once managed quite independently. Those who felt they had escaped the experience of needing others for instrumental assistance and expressive support discover the contrary. Intellectual acknowledgment of the possibility does not prepare one for the actuality. The need for informal and formal supports can arise instantaneously, propelling the individual into previously unexperienced role relationships with families, friends, neighbors, and formal service organizations.

In addition to the needs and risks we have defined, the necessity of long-term-care services produces its own set of complex tasks for the elderly. Gaining access to and negotiating service arrangements, as well as coordinating and monitoring care, become stressful demands, requiring a high degree of energy and physical, cognitive, and emotional capacity. A caring environment is required to lessen the possibilities of neglect, abuse, morbidity, institutionalization, and death. Whether older persons are able to maintain the assertive position required for survival, is directly affected by the nature of their environment. Power and influence are the best medicine for the hopeless, the helpless, and the despairing. Those elderly who have experienced little of such power and influence during their lives have even less reason to believe that they will live out this final period from a commanding position (Manuel 1982). "Learned helplessness" (Seligman and Elder 1986) is likely to predominate. Our discussion suggests that preventive, restorative, and supportive services that allow older persons to gain greater control over their lives would be most empowering.

## PROGRAMS AND SOCIAL WORK SERVICES

Historically, some elderly, with no other recourse, turned to "strangers" when family systems failed. Almshouses and public charity became the choices of last resort. Others—for example, African-Americans— learned early that public support was closed to them and that their survival was dependent upon the formation of informal mutual-aid societies. This longstanding pattern of depending on one's own in the face of hostility from "outside" was noted as early as 1914 by Dubois and Dill (Manuel 1982) and continues to this day. For many African-

Americans, the church remains an influential force in the development and sustaining of informal social supports and offers a salutary, buffering hub of social connections (Solomon 1976; Taylor and Chatters 1986).

Whether by choice, or by default, the elderly in need of long-term care cope with their lives through the use of a mixture of formal and informal supports. Understanding this pattern of use and factoring out the variables that influence the utilization of each system are exceedingly challenging. Most older persons learn quickly, as our analysis demonstrates, that formal supports are biased toward institutional care and that an adequate continuum of care if not available. To whom would the elderly turn, and for what, if the formal service system were accessible and their own financial and personal resources were adequate for securing, coordinating, and monitoring long-term care? What would the older person's preferred balance be between familial and organizational assistance? How does ethnicity, class, and sex influence the answers to these questions? The inadequacy of the formal service system compromises our ability to develop "pure" answers.

Though formal long-term-care services are commonly thought of as institutionally based, actually they are one among three categories of services provided: community-based, home-based, and congregate-residential- and institutional-based. Using an "impairment continuum," Tobin and Toseland (1985) highlighted thirty-seven different types of services and showed how services typically become segregated according to professional definitions of clients' capabilities. They noted that where clients are served has more to do with a patchwork response to the elderly than an overall plan about how needs can best be met. For example, there is no reason that mental health services for those with the greatest cognitive needs could not be integrated within community mental health centers, rather than segregated into medical and psychiatric day-care programs (FCA 1979). In contrast to an "impairment model," Hooyman (1983) developed a model around clients' problems in living and how community resources, both informal and formal, can be used to respond to these problems. For example, for persons needing assistance with person care, she suggested a variety of formal organizations providing such assistance, the possibility of student help where such help can be secured, and home sharing involving an exchange of assistance for room and board.

While many different types of programs exist, the services and the service system itself are woefully inadequate. Eight major problems with long-term care programs are repeatedly discussed in the literature: 1) persistence of unmet needs in the population; 2) bias toward institutionalization; 3) low levels of quality care; 4) geographical inequity and maldistribution of benefits; 5) excessive burdens placed on families; 6) rapidly rising public and private expenditures; 7) fragmentation among services and financing; and 8) lack of case management function (Bass 1980; Brody and Brody 1987; Callahan and Wallack 1981; Kane 1987; Monk 1985; Morris and Youket 1981; Tobin, Davidson, and Sack 1976; Tobin and Toseland 1985; Wilson 1984). The greater physical, psychological, and emotional energy and resolve required to transcend these deterrents to service use strain already strained personal resources.

Though all problems negatively influence the lives of vulnerable older persons, the bias toward institutional care has a direct influence on the creation of the remaining problems. The medicalizing of aging can be seen most clearly in the Congressional Budget Office's estimate that as of 1977, 90 percent of all public expenditures for long-term care were spent on nursing-home care (Morris and Youket 1981). Furthermore, 80 percent of these facilities and 75 percent of nursing-home beds are estimated to be operated by profit-making enterprises (Kane 1987). Thus, enormous sums of pubic money, made possible through Medicare and Medicaid, are funneled directly into private hands that operate facilities according to minimum federal standards, at best. Professional social workers have virtually no contact with thousands of older persons living in for-profit nursing homes. The few monthly hours of required "social work consultation" provide a negligible amount to the institution and nothing directly to its inhabitants. A social work presence is more likely to be felt in not-for-profit facilities, where concern for human need, rather than profit, is the guiding organizational priniciple. Paradoxically, if all facilities became not-for-profit, the profession would not have the personnel to staff the programs, not even at the rate of one social worker per facility. The privatization of services with limited public accountability is a major problem for the elderly. It also poses a particular dilemma for social workers who are concerned about the quality of care for the elderly in for-profit facilities yet may not wish to work in for-profit facilities.

The needs of the vulnerable aged do not support such a proliferation of institutional facilities, nor do they support the majority of available long-term-care funds being channeled to institutional settings. Admissions to long-term-care facilities have more to do with socially constructed definitions of need and social policy decisions than with qualities intrinsic in those in need of long-term care (Knight and Loiver Walker 1985). Estimates are that for each person institutionalized, there are two to three individuals with similar problems in living within the community (Kane 1987). Many who have been institutionalized could be better served in their homes or in other less restrictive environments (Kaye 1985). In truth, there are no long-term personal conditions that necessitate caring for older persons behind large institutional walls, if formal and informal supports are sufficient. Most older persons prefer to remain in their own homes and "accept" living with their children and in an institution as a last resort, only when there is no alternative (Tobin, Davidson, and Sack 1976). While the professional community may believe, not always with good documentation, that many older persons live fuller, better cared-for, less isolated lives in nursing homes (however well founded this belief may be) the choice is the older person's to make.

Paralleling the bias toward the institutional care have been simultaneous efforts to increase in-home and community-based alternative to institutional care. Social workers and older persons and their families have long advocated for a better continuum of long-term-care services. The quadrupling of skilled-nursing-facility costs from 1965 to 1985 prompted policymakers to join in a search for alternatives (Brody and Brody 1987).

The bias toward institutional care has taken its toll on the quantity and the quality of in-home and community-based care. Citation after citation attests to a historical disinclination to seriously develop and adequately fund such services. For example, Kay (1985), Lowy (1985), and Rathbone-McCuan and Coward (1985)—in discussions of home care, multitpurpose service centers and respite, and adult day care, respectively—have amply demonstrated how these services beneficially address the needs of the at-risk elderly at a lower level of cost yet receive low priority in the continuum of provided services. Nonmedical long-term-care services constitute the bulk of need for these at-risk elderly (Brody and Brody 1987). Medical prescription as the primary basis for most long-term-care services has conditioned the nature of the care provided, has limited access to services, and has made qualified social workers dependent upon physicians to prescribe nonmedical care. The options remain greater for those not dependent upon Medicaid, who can gain access to nonmedically based programs. The emphasis upon impairment and limitation once the condition has occurred means that the older person must fail before the service system is triggered. Supportive and preventive services, if available, are provided after the "functional impairment." The degrees of freedom available to the elderly, their families, and the social work profession are directly related to the funding, organization, and structure of long-term-care programs.

Social work services for the elderly in need of long-term care have developed sketchily. The aging field of practice has had to contend with external public policy, a funding environment with a "band-aid approach" to service development (Estes and Lee 1985), and the profession's own ageism and preference for other fields of practice. Even when some federal training funds were available in the 1960s and 1970s, social workers did not move into the aging field of practice, nor did the schools readily develop curricula in aging (Monk 1985). The reluctance of large numbers of social workers to work with older persons is particularly sad in light of the U.S. Labor Department's 1982 projection that by 1990 "geriatric social work" would be second only to industrial-robot engineering (quite a juxtaposition) in high-demand occupations. If social work jobs with vulnerable older persons currently go unfilled, how will we, as a profession, even make our contribution to serving the needs of this rapidly increasing population? The development of a national movement toward private, for-profit "geriatric care managers" and "fee-for-service" programs reflects the further movement of social workers away from the public and voluntary sectors and away from the vulnerable elderly.

Despite a seemingly baleful picture, there are some bright spots created by those social workers who labor long and hard with, and on behalf of, the elderly in need of long-term care. These efforts take place through age-segregated programs for older persons (e.g., nursing homes, multipurpose senior settings, meals on wheels, and sheltered residential facilities), as well as through age-integrated programs (e.g., acute hospitals, community mental health centers, and outpatient health services). Both demonstrate the flexibility and resourcefulness of social workers as they respond to the needs of older persons. The following programs are illustrative.

## Long-Term-Care Facilities

Social work's role in not-for-profit long-term-care facilities predates the consciousness of need and opportunities created through Medicare's financing of nursing homes in the 1960s. This role flows out of our longstanding interest in the relationship between persons and their environment (Getzel and Mellor 1982) and directs itself toward older persons, their families and friends, the interdisciplinary team, and the nursing-home milieu. In this setting, social workers provide a wide range of services aimed at helping residents with their life-transitional concerns, with the interpersonal tensions that normatively arise within a congregate setting, and with environmental obstacles to a more satisfying life. These problems in living can be addressed through individual, family, and group services (Brody 1974; Germain and Gitterman 1980). Group services decrease isolation, foster a sense of belonging and well-being, and mitigate feelings of loneliness and helplessness by increasing experiences in which control over the environment can be exercised (Berman-Rossi 1986; Berman-Rossi 1990; Miller and Solomon 1979). Families also do well in groups, where the pain brought on by the crisis of institutionalizing a loved one can be shared with others experiencing similar feelings, and families can use each others' strengths to assist in negotiating the nursing-home environment (Brubaker and Ward Schiefer 1987; Cox and Ephross 1989; Solomon 1982).

## Hospitals

Though commonly not thought of as a primary service setting for older persons in need of long-term care, the acute care hospital, in actuality, is inextricably linked to the future lives of the elderly. Diagnostic related group (DRG) treatment and discharge policies frame the organizational context in which social workers practice. Poised at this critical decision-making juncture, social workers provide a major contribution to the lives of the elderly by 1) helping patients and families cope with illness and hospitalization; 2) thinking through discharge options and arranging community supports; 3) educating the staff to the needs of older patients; and 4) providing support for others who work with these "low-status" clients (Blumenfield 1982). In addition to their direct practice role, social workers sometimes assume a leadership role in assisting medical centers to expand the definition of their domain to include a preventive and community medical orientation. Such a definition allows the institution to create services lacking in the community and to assist the elderly in securing services to which they are entitled (Lurie and Rich 1984). This same preventive role is actualized in hospital emergency rooms, where family members bring their relatives as a first step toward nursing-home placement (Shepard, Mayer, and Ryback 1987). These collective efforts decrease fragmentation of services and allow the older person and the social worker a wider range of options from which to choose. Without the buffering efforts of hospital social workers, it is likely that more older persons would fail or would require institutionalization.

## Rehabilitation Programs

Rehabilitation programs, whether attached to nursing homes or acute care hospitals, provide short-term rehabilitation care (Adelman et al. 1987; Seltzer and Charpentier 1982). These programs are designed to enable older persons to cope with specific medical traumas so that they have the option of returning to the community. The social worker provides service links during hospitalization and upon release and helps the older person and the family cope with the current medical trauma. Most important, the social worker holds, for all to see, a vision of the possibility of the older person's returning to the community.

## Sheltered Residential Facilities

For example, in New York State, enriched housing is a program regulated by the State Department of Social Services, with a fee-for-service monthly charge (Baker 1985). It is intended to offer, on a small scale, housing plus coordinated homemaker and housekeeper services. The social worker, who often administers the program, provides help with all problems experienced by the participants: familial and interpersonal concerns, financial matters, health worries, negotiation of the service environment, loss, and change. Group meetings for members provide a supportive medium in which members help each other with similar troubles. The strength of the program lies in the provision of a responsive physical environment, personal and household management care, and a social worker who provides an integrating force in residents' lives through the provision of all instrumental and expressive assistance.

## Adult Day Care

A more recent service option, adult day care has been developed for two purposes: to benefit the elderly through an alternative to institutionalization and to control the costs of nursing-home care (Goldstein 1982; Rathbone-McCuan and Coward 1985). Designed to serve those who wish to remain independent, adult day care tends to serve those elderly who often fall outside the "safety net" of other programs, i.e., those who are isolated and do not reach out to others and those with lessened mental and physical vigor. The social work, rehabilitation, recreational, transportation, nursing, and medical services combine to provide a comprehensive program that eliminates the splintering of services found elsewhere. As the older person improves and is meaningfully engaged during the day, families often feel less need of institutionalization.

## *Home Care Services*

Were it not for home care services, life in the community would not be possible for the homebound elderly, the elderly unable to manage on their own and without family, or the elderly with family whose long-term care needs exceed the family's resources. Administered by home care agencies, community agencies serving the aged, or institutions with community-based programs, home care services most often include assistance with personal care and home management activities. Social work's role in assisting clients with home care needs is of long standing and dates back to the 1920s (Kaye 1985). In executing this role, we are guided by our person-in-situation view. This vision enables us to understand the ways in which the need for home care services may be part of a total need for service. In this manner, a more holistic approach to service is developed.

If these services are not reflective of the dominant service delivery pattern for the elderly in need of long-term-care services, what enables the vulnerable aged to survive as well as they do? There is extensive evidence that, like persons of all ages, older persons turn first to family, friends, and neighbors (Hooyman 1983). The majority, perhaps 80 percent, of in-home long-term-care services are actually provided by informal social supports, particularly family (Coward 1987; Hooyman and Lustbader 1986). While some are pleased with this phenomenon from a financial standpoint, and others have visions of close ties between older persons and their families, a cautionary note is in order for social workers. Social workers must take care not to overtax already burdened families (Gratton and Wilson 1988) or to neglect demands upon policymakers and formal service organizations (Moody 1985). The notion that long-term care services should be organized "without eroding family care and the private purchase of help" (Kane 1987:61) is curious and merits suspicion. Family caregivers, particularly women—and working women—are especially burdened in this role (FCA 1984). Charting the proper role for the formal sector in supporting, while not abusing, efforts of informal caregivers is a major challenge for policymakers (Stone, Cafferata, and Sangle 1987) and practitioners alike. Increased survival rates and longer life spans, coupled with a declining number of descendants, make such an effort imperative (Treas 1977).

## DIFFERENTIAL CLINICAL ASSESSMENTS
## AND INTERVENTIONS

Hundreds of instruments have been developed for "assessing the elderly" in need of long-term-care services (Kane and Kane 1981; Kane 1985). These instruments include single-dimension tools measuring physical, mental, and social functioning, as well as multidimensional measures inquiring into more than one performance area. Assessment of need centers on the functional limitations of the elderly and their resulting dependence. These instruments quantify attributes located within the individual and believed stable enough to measure. In the main, these instruments represent a snapshot of the elderly—a moment frozen in time, extracted from a field of interacting forces.

It is not surprising that few of these instruments assess the environment or the congruity between client need and environmental resources. Geared toward geriatric rather than gerontological practice, they logically incorporate a view of aging as a medical experience and use a medical model of study, diagnosis, and treatment. In this quasi-linear approach, a manifest separation between assessor and assessed is established. The "greater knowledge" (and power) of the assessor, or diagnostician, is presumed. As in the case of medicine, "fixing" the older person is at the heart of the venture.

The point of these measurement instruments is to assist service providers to decide what type and amount of service to provide individual clients (Kane 1985). Kane believes that these tools have the potential to produce a functional computation that can serve as a reliable indicator for a service plan. Of course, how these tools actually guide the creation of a comprehensive service plan and how they are used in practice with older persons are the determining questions for practitioners. This is where the payoff lies. There is little discussion, however, of what the practitioner does, once armed with such an "indicator." It is as if the measurements themselves are the ends of their own utilization.

In social work, assessment and practice with older persons are better served by another tradition, a tradition in which the process of "knowing" and moving from "knowing to doing" is a complex, sometimes puzzling, often difficult, and nonlinear enterprise. Knowledge does not carry its own prescriptions for action (Millikan 1959; Schwartz 1962). The properties of individuals are not rigid and fixed but adapt and vary in interaction with the environment through a process of reciprocal adaptation (Germain and Gitterman 1980). Better suited to our work are the reciprocal (Schwartz 1971) and life (Germain and Gitterman 1987) models. These models suggest that the character of an entity is created by the interaction of its parts. To understand individuals, we must understand them in interaction with their environment. The tie between them is symbiotic (Schwartz 1961). Reciprocal and life models are appreciative of the ways in which older persons are changed in interaction with their environment. The older person's story is never finally written until death. Who the elderly are includes who they can still become. Each instance presents itself anew, affording the elderly the opportunity to create moments of their lives again and again. While certain functional measures can be achieved, the totality of an older person's life and its potentiality in a responsive environment do not hold still for easy measurement. It is this potentiality that social workers must understand as they work with the elderly.

The concept of *person–environment fit* has gained increasing prominence in our literature (Coulton 1979; French, Rodgers, and Cobb 1974; Germain 1979; Germain and Gitterman 1980; Kahana 1974, 1982) and is particularly useful in studying older persons and their ever-changing needs (Buffum 1987–88). For the elderly in need of long-term care, achieving an "internal steady state" (White 1974) is very difficult. Perhaps more than any other, this group is likely to experience a state of disequilibrium in which balance is thrown askew by three possible sources: the person, the environment, or the person-in-environment. The first includes those life conditions commonly attributed to the person, e.g., aphasia as a result of a stroke, a disease such as Alzheimer's, or loss of mobility because of arthritis. In these instances, individual attributes are relatively fixed and "knowable," independent of the external environment. The second source includes those life circumstances and events commonly defined as originating in the physical and social environment, e.g., the loss of a spouse, the loss of an apartment, or the discontinuation of income benefits as a result of changed eligibility requirements. In these instances, environmental factors are viewed as measurable and independent of the individual. It is understanding the third source of disequilibrium that poses the greatest challenge to the social worker. This source includes those events, situations, or circumstances where a clear separation between person and environment is difficult to establish. An example would be a decline in cognitive functioning precipitated by depression associated with social isolation and fewer orientation cues, or a weight loss instigated by ill-fitting dentures associated with poor health care benefits, or low benefit utilization associated with cognitive and physical loss. What is distinctive about this third factor is that the phenomenon is not "knowable" by measuring the person and the environment separately; rather it can best be understood through comprehension of the reciprocal interaction between the person and the environment. In these instances, the flow of energy and experience to and from, between the older person and his or her environment, actually creates the phenomenon itself. While the person, the environment, and the person-in-environment can each act as a primary trigger of a state of disequilibrium, it is the degree of congruity between the needs and capacities of the individual and the demands and resources of the environment that ultimately determines the nature of the consequences for the individual.

Each of the three categories provides pertinent data for practitioners from which to develop a working understanding of clients and their lives. Achieving such an understanding is difficult and challenging for social workers practicing with the elderly in long-term care. Complexity is a distinguishing feature of such an effort. The effects of quickly changing physical, social, economic, psychological, cognitive, and organizational forces make achieving an assessment of any particular phenomenon, no less an entire situation, difficult and subject to change.

Assessment in work with the elderly does not stand apart from practice with the elderly. From the initial moment of contact between worker and client, a strategy of how to proceed is required. Practice with the elderly begins with worker and client searching for a shared definition of the problem. This notion is important for three reasons. First, the concept of a shared definition immediately sets in place the idea that the worker–client relationship is one of a joint venture. Within this arrangement, the client becomes "coassessor" and, in whatever manner possible, director of his or her own life. Whether the "units of direction" be large or small, whether they entail where to live, what to wear, or what to eat, the older person must be placed, once again, in the director's chair. Ownership of the problem generates and releases energy for the tasks at hand. Second, agreement on what the problem is provides the driving force and guiding spirit in determining what data must be collected. The fullness of older persons' lives does not permit the gathering of a lifetime of information, yet the complexity of defining problems requires a breadth of knowledge. The press of current concerns militates against a leisurely, open-ended exploration of a life. Purposefulness strengthens physical and psychological energy, particularly when that energy is limited. And third, it is more possible to live in the here and now when the present, at least some of the time, is subject to one's own influence. Choice remains essential to maintaining or reestablishing a sense of oneself as competent (Lee 1983).

From the beginning of the working relationship, the worker fosters autonomy by providing information and helping clients arrive at their own direction, without coercion, even when other views are preferred by the worker (Monk and Abramson 1982). For the older person, highly dependent upon others, a perceived locus of control within the self encourages hope. These ideas about the interrelationship between assessment and practice are particularly fitting for the elderly in long-term care. Severely disenfranchised by our political, economic, and social system; severely discriminated against as a result of ageism; and coping with a wide range of disheartening life conditions, these elderly do not enter helping relationships imbued with their own power or a sense of competence. Their fear of being dominated by helpers is very real. A practice strategy that maximizes strengths, provides for choice, and encourages self-direction is the preferred strategy. This strategy applies even when the client, on the fact of it, seem to have "accepted" a high degree of dependence upon others. Not to encourage self-direction, where possible, is to deny the elderly the opportunity to exert influence.

The following *older-person-environment fit assessment tool* is proposed to practitioners. It allows salient data to be organized in keeping with the concepts of balance between the elderly and their environment and of the distinction between informal and formal social supports. Such a tool can be used by workers alone, or with clients. When the guide is used with clients, their perceptions of stress and environmental responsiveness can readily be identified. In addition, clients are invariably strengthened when they are an integral part of a search to understand the problem at hand and the resources that may diminish its potency.

This tool helps the worker to collect salient background information and information on significant life events, circumstances, conditions.

1. *Definition of the problem.* What is it? When and under what circumstances did it develop? How has the client dealt with the problem? What are his or her strengths and limitations in dealing with the problem? How much stress has been generated by it? What inferences can be made about the problem?

2. *Client's expectations of agency and worker.* Under what circumstances did the client's need come to the attention of the agency? Was the service sought, offered, or imposed? What are the client's expectations of the agency and the worker? What kinds of experiences has

the client previously had with social workers or organizational helpers? What inferences can be made about the client's expectations of the agency and the worker? How might past experiences with helpers influence the present?

3. *Client's strengths and limitations*. What are the client's strengths and limitations in dealing with the problem (consider physical, economic, social, psychological, cognitive, religious, and class dimensions)? How able is the client to negotiate organizational systems? What inferences can be made about the client's strengths and limitations in dealing with her or his problem(s) in the past and currently?

4. *Environmental Supports and Obstacles*. What is the client's physical environment, including the home, neighborhood, and organizational environment? What social supports are available, including informal supports (family, extended kin, friends, neighbors, and community associations) and formal supports (health and social welfare)? What inferences can be made about the client's environmental supports and obstacles?

5. *Degree of congruity between personal and environmental resources*. What forces promote and restrain problem resolution? What inferences can be made about the degree of congruity between personal and environmental resources?

6. *Case Direction*. Based upon your assessment, what additional data would be helpful? What will be your approach to the problem? What will you do to help?

Using this tool at at least three points in time captures change and strengthens evaluation and planning. *Time 1* records the state of the older-person–environment fit, in relation to the problem, at the beginning of contact between worker and client. *Time 2* records the state of the older-person–environment fit, with planned environmental changes designed to respond to the older person's unmet needs. *Time 3* records the state of the older-person–environment fit after a reasonable period of time has elapsed. The entire process would be reinitiated with a new event, condition, or circumstance. Social workers and clients are encouraged to think together about the ways in which changes in any one part of the older person's life can affect changes elsewhere.

Even when there is a high degree of congruence between older persons and their environment, an element of caution and a need for professional judgment obtain. Though positive value is commonly associated with a high degree of congruence, balance or homeostasis does not define the desirability of the state, or that all is well. Rather, it represents a statement that balance exists. The social worker must understand, and understand well, the basis of that state of congruence. For example, Kahana (1982) suggested that congruence models of person–environment interaction can be used to place older persons within particular environments. But what happens when this congruence is based upon a high degree of institutional authoritarianism and a lifetime of oppression, resulting in a low desire for assertion on the part of the older person? Should the client be placed in such an environment?

Helping strategies of "partnership," mutuality, and encouraging an internal locus of control, coupled with an understanding of the elderly in interaction with their environment, are equally important during the ongoing phase of work. It is during this phase that the worker becomes most tempted to "do for" clients, rather than painstakingly involving clients in their own lives. While the temptation to shortcut the process is understandable, doing so can only undermine clients' growing sense of confidence in their ability to influence those around them. When they are encouraged to make their own choices and are "lent a vision" of their own possibilities, then the potential of the helping relationship is being fulfilled. In a sense, it portends the clients' potential in other relationships as well. Who the client can become often begins with that relationship.

Of course, there are times when social workers must assume a protective role in work with older persons: situations where the elderly are unable to manage money, are unable to protect themselves against abuse and neglect, are unable to make decisions, and are without reliable personal relationships (Dunkle 1987). These times require the highest level of skill, lest our protective role inadvertently violate clients' rights and weaken their voices. Shulman's (1984) discussion of skills is helpful in highlighting how social workers strengthen clients' voices. Workers prepare to receive client communication by "tuning in" to the meaning of clients' struggles and their ambivalence about expressing strong sentiment, especially toward those on whom they are dependent. Elaborating skills help older persons tell their story by moving from the general to the specific, containing the worker's instinct to solve everything, reaching inside of silences, and asking questions to learn more. Empathic skills encourage clients to attach affect to the work at hand by reaching for feelings, displaying understanding of clients' feelings, and putting clients' feelings into words. The same set of values and principles that guide our "doing with" clients should guide our "doing for." These include the principle of the least restriction, a strategy of "partnership," and honoring the client's wishes, to the extent possible. Even persons with Alzheimer's disease can communicate preferences. It is we who must learn to listen well enough to hear and respond to such communications.

Ensuring the place of all elderly persons in the helping process demands a great deal of the social worker. The press of myriad demands pushes us quickly on and urges us to avoid attention to detail, to process, to feeling, to the complexity of the person-in-environment, to the worker–client relationship, and to the strength of the relationship that can develop when we and older persons work closely together. However, such avoidance fosters unnecessary dependency, stifles autonomy, and perpetuates the passivity associated with withdrawal and a failure to thrive.

## CASE ILLUSTRATION

Metro Home and Hospital for the Aged (MHHA) is a not-for-profit, long-term care facility with a 120-year history of serving older persons within the community and within the institution. Originally, MHHA served the aged who needed a residential facility. As funding priorities changed, and as ideas shifted toward serving the elderly in less restrictive environments, MHHA developed a wider range of community-based and in-home services. A broad range of programs and services, allowing older persons and their families a range of options, is one of MHHA's distinguishing features.

Mrs. Harper, an African-American widow who was 78 years old at the time of her application, was referred to MHHA's enriched-housing program by a community psychiatric-social-work team, working in a single-room-occupancy (SRO) Hotel. This program typified community outreach programs designed to provide personalized outreach to the isolated elderly who for a variety of reasons were hesitant to ask for help (Stuen 1985). These programs are designed to transcend organizational obstacles to service delivery by bringing service to the client. Mrs. Harper had been forced to relocate to the SRO two years prior when the building in which she had lived for 40 years was closed for renovation after being brought by a new owner. Her meager social security payments afforded no other choice. Moved out of her neighborhood, Mrs. Harper lost all ties to her church, her friends, and her community. She never became connected to her new neighborhood and never considered it "home." The forced nature of the relocation and the unpredictable quality of the new environment intensified the stress she experienced (Pastalan 1983). The social work team believed Mrs. Harper was increasingly depressed by and alienated from her environment. As the SRO became inhabited primarily by substance abusers, Mrs.

Harper's anxiety increased. She was afraid to leave her apartment and afraid to use the hall bathroom. The weaker she became, the more difficult it was for her to climb the stairs to her fifth-floor walk-up. She had one acquaintance in the building and was devastated when he moved. Her only relationships were with her social workers, who saw no hope of connecting her to her immediate environment. The social work team visited her two or three times weekly to ensure her safety, to provide food, and to help her cope with the enormous environmental obstacles and their impact on her sense of psychological well-being. Successful adaptation, which depends not only upon dealing with environmental demands but on controlling and influencing those demands, seemed tenuous at best (Mechanic 1974). When MHHA's enriched-housing program opened, the community social worker informed Mrs. Harper of this new housing-service option. Helped with the referral, Mrs. Harper was eager for the change.

Mrs. Harper had been born in New York City, the older of two children. She and her younger brother had not been in contact for several years. At the time of her application, there were no known relatives who could be located. Mrs. Harper described her early life with great bitterness. She stated that both she and her mother had been frequently beaten by her father, who favored her brother. She saw her mother as a sustaining force in her life and had been devastated by her death, to cancer, at an early age. Her marriage of ten years had dissolved shortly after her mother's death. She believed many of her difficulties had begun when her mother died. Though Mrs. Harper had enjoyed school, she left after sixth grade to work and assist her family financially. She vividly recalled hiding some of her money for her mother. Limited funds from public assistance never went far enough, especially when controlled by the father.

Though Mrs. Harper held many jobs in her early life, she had always dreamed of being a dancer. It was through this interest that she met and married her second husband. She worked as a domestic housekeeper for about twenty-five years, until age 71, when her husband of thirty-five years died. She stated that she had been too sad to work after his death, even though she was in even greater financial need. She felt that she and Mr. Harper had had a happy marriage. From the time of her husband's death, Mrs. Harper's problems in living greatly increased. About six months after her husband's death, Mrs. Harper suffered a stroke, from which there was some residual paresis. Her walking was impeded by the dragging of one leg. While she was in the hospital, all of her clothes and most of her belongings had been stolen. Though angry, she was somewhat philosophical, stating that she never had been able to hold onto things that mattered to her. While coping with her new status as widow, Mrs. Harper was suddenly required also to cope with being hospitalized and living with a handicapping condition.

Upon initially meeting Mrs. Harper, the enriched-housing social worker noted her "unkempt" physical appearance and speculated that her fear of the public bathroom, her physical limitations, and her depression had all contributed to this appearance. Despite being visited frequently by the hospital-outreach social-work team, Mrs. Harper had not been cared for medically. Owing to budget cuts, the local health clinic no longer made home visits. She had not seen a physician or another health professional for the last six months. Her long toenails made walking painful, and her lack of dentures made eating difficult. In addition, her uncorrected moderate to severe hearing loss increased the likelihood that she would misinterpret social cues. Despite all these medical problems, plus her ongoing need to have her cardiac condition monitored, Mrs. Harper refused to go to the hospital's clinic. Her Medicare had ended when she lost track of and failed to pay her premiums. She felt embarrassed when asked about her finances. Besides, she said, she had always mistrusted hospitals and held them responsible for her mother's death. She frequently stated that she didn't believe "her folk" were cared for well in hospitals.

Mrs. Harper needed assistance with all personal care and household management activities of daily living. She was accepted into the program. Mrs. Harper showed strength in her ability to establish a relationship with the worker, and in wanting to participate actively in becoming familiar with her new apartment. For the first time in months, she appeared energized. The community social worker, the enriched-housing social worker, and Mrs. Harper agreed that her former social worker would continue to visit until Mrs. Harper felt comfortable with the new worker. She would decide when to say good-bye.

The enriched-housing social worker's practice strategy was based upon her belief that Mrs. Harper had many strengths, strengths overwhelmed by insurmountable environmental problems. The resultant feelings of helplessness and despair, signs of oppression (Goldenberg 1978), were not, however, immutable. If Mrs. Harper could once again assume some control of her life, the worker reasoned, she would in fact be less oppressed and therefore better able to live a more satisfying life. Mrs. Harper spent the first month settling in.

What occurred for Mrs. Harper was different from most of what transpires for the elderly in need of long-term care. In Mrs. Harper's case, a skilled social worker, a responsive agency environment, and a partnership relationship with a client combined to mitigate most of the onerous effects of the "aging" service system. Service coordination and organizational responsiveness were the rule, not the exception.

With an emergency assistance grant to purchase furniture and donations from MHHA, Mrs. Harper was able to furnish her apartment. Though unable to do her own shopping, she gave the worker specific instructions about what she did and did not want. As she was not one to reach out to others, enriched-housing members reached out to her. Mr. Rodriquez checked on her each morning and accompanied her to dinner each evening. The members accepted her quietness at meals and remained cordial to her.

The worker's service priority included a medical assessment of Mrs. Harper's multiple health needs, evaluation by rehabilitation therapy about whether a walker would enhance mobility, and podiatry to attend to her toenails. Sturdy shoes and additional clothing were also important. Now that Mrs. Harper went out of her apartment, she felt embarrassed by her clothing. In time, the worker hoped that Mrs. Harper and her estranged brother would resume contact. In February, Mrs. Harper was devastated to learn, via the mail, that her only brother had died four months before. The loss of her last blood relative was like no other loss. Group members were supportive. The worker visited daily. Mrs. Harper rarely talked about how she felt. It was as if she did not trust anyone with such pain, not even the worker. The decline in Mrs. Harper's will to live was apparent to everyone.

Connecting Mrs. Harper to the health clinic proved difficult in unanticipated ways. Supplementary Security Insurance (SSI) was slow to process her application, and she had no money for shoes or a warm coat. The February cold demanded both. Despite all of the worker's skill, she could not speed up the application. Undaunted, the worker mediated between Mrs. Harper and MHHA, which lent Mrs. Harper some spending money. Unable to speak with her Spanish-speaking home attendant, she refused to go to the clinic without the worker. She trusted neither her own abilities nor the clinic to protect her interests. The worker was mindful that Mrs. Harper's growing strength was interdependent and intertwined with the worker's efforts. She sometimes worried that Mrs. Harper was becoming too dependent upon her, but she never denied service to Mrs. Harper as a result. She reminded herself that with older, vulnerable persons, autonomy and dependence were sometimes interconnected, and that autonomy depended upon self-determination, not independence from others. Interdependence, rather than independence, would more often be the case for older persons needing long-term care services. Nonetheless, the worker also worried whether Mrs. Harper was becoming too emotionally attached to her. She resolved to watch that Mrs. Harper's attachment to her did not preclude using others as well and to gently encourage her connections to the enriched-housing community. Community had been important to her earlier in her life, and perhaps it could be so again.

By the end of the fourth month, several important things were put into place. Mrs. Harper was pleased with her apartment and with receiving six-day four-hour-per-day home-attendant services, had attended the medical clinic, and was willing to be evaluated for a walker and possible physical therapy. Though she remained on the periphery of the enriched-housing group and watchful of all that went on, she maintained her friendship with Mr. Rodriquez. She seemed to take a small amount of pleasure from her life. Once, she remarked that it would be nice to sit outside in spring.

The stability of this period was abruptly altered. In mid-April, Mrs. Harper experienced severe back pain. Monday morning, the worker found her lying in a urine-soaked bed. She had not moved or eaten since the home attendant had left mid-Saturday. She quietly said, "I have no one." Her sense of being without family remained with her always, defining the worker's role. For the worker, working with Mrs. Harper meant accepting the fullness of their relationship, accepting the knowledge that with each day, with each interaction, she was becoming more and more important to Mrs. Harper. With the worker's assistance, an aide gently bathed Mrs. Harper, changed her linens, and put on fresh clothing. Through all of this, Mrs. Harper sobbed softly, saying that she missed her mother. Through this physical intimacy, the worker and Mrs. Harper became even closer. Mrs. Harper told the worker that she reminded her of her mother.

Their eyes met as the worker said thank you. Facing a weekend without home attendant assistance and possible renal failure, Mrs. Harper was hospitalized. She asked only only one thing: that she not be sent to the hospital where her mother and aunt had died. Though she thought the hospital was best for her, she seemed to give up.

The balance that Mrs. Harper had achieved was torn asunder by a three-month hospitalization. Renal insufficiency, secondary to dehydration, was worsened by her inconsistent eating and fluid intake. Acute renal failure hovered closeby. The worker continued to visit weekly and spoke with Mrs. Harper daily. The hospital social worker visited daily. Despite all efforts, Mrs. Harper appeared to be failing. Her will to live was faint. She said very little, keeping her most private thoughts to herself. It was as if she wondered why she should live. For whom and for what were questions she had difficulty answering. The hospital and enriched-housing social workers attempted to involve Mrs. Harper in her own care. They understood that assertion, not resignation, was required for survival. They offered her choices of food and decisions as to what to drink and when. Mrs. Harper exerted her control by refusing to "cooperate." If they did not discuss how and what she was doing, she was eager to see the worker and enjoyed hearing stories about her neighbors. She resisted anything that smacked of overt or covert coercion. She particularly brightened when the worker brought Mr. Rodriquez. The worker felt that there was nothing to do but to trust the process. To coerce Mrs. Harper was to destroy her will.

In early July, the worker arrived to find Mrs. Harper's hands bound to the bed and a nasal gastric tube in place. From the beginning, she complained about the tube and about the doctor. She stated, "I'm competent and the doctor had no right to impose medical care upon me." The worker said sadly, "I agree, but it is awfully hard for them not to do anything. Without hydration, you'll go into renal failure and may die." They were quiet for a moment. With trepidation, the worker said, "Is that what you want? To die?" They looked at each other for a long, long moment. Mrs. Harper said, "Don't worry; I'll get you off the hanger soon." She would not say what she meant. She said, "I'll tell you when I am ready." The worker, pressing and holding her hand, said, "I want you to come back to your apartment and . . . I don't want you to die." Mrs. Harper stared hard at the worker and, for the first time, despite ongoing talk of her apartment, said, "Do you mean I really still have my little apartment with the tree?" It was as if she suddenly believed in her own life, because she mattered to someone else.

Shortly after, Mrs. Harper was transferred to the rehabilitation unit of MHHA. Despite her initial vehement doubts, she understood that without mobility, she could not return home. Even if the worker could have arranged twenty-four-hour care, Mrs. Harper did not want anyone living with her. She made the choice.

Without this rehabilitation service and the worker's knowledge of the community Medicaid services to which Mrs. Harper was entitled, as well as how to mediate between Mrs. Harper and Medicaid, Mrs. Harper could not have returned to her apartment. Even if she were not in a hospital bed, she could not have negotiated the social service system without social work assistance. The worker continued as Mrs. Harper's social worker while she was at MHHA, mitigating the trauma that would have been felt with a new worker. The worker's presence at team meetings and her recommendations for a service plan were instrumental in Mrs. Harper's recovery. The worker made certain to speak about how Mrs. Harper lived in the world, with a sense of being oppressed by others, particularly by men, and how she did best when she felt in control. The invitation to Mrs. Harper to attend team meetings when her case was reviewed was received well by her. The team's willingness to place Mrs. Harper in charge of her service plan engaged her motivation and strengthened her will to live. This plan was not always easy to sustain. "Checking in" with Mrs. Harper was time-consuming and delayed decision making. Nonetheless, the team saw clearly that when they pressured Mrs. Harper, she withdrew. While most other rehabilitation residents had relatives, the team became Mrs. Harper's surrogate family.

Through one-to-one relationships with the physical therapist, the occupational therapist, the head nurse, and the physician, Mrs. Harper made major gains. She often commented on how much she enjoyed being cared for by all women. Nonetheless, her recovery was not always smooth. Coping with her medical problems taxed her strength, and sometimes her discouragement became an obstacle to her engagement.

Living across the street was ideal environmentally. Serving her within her home community decreased alienation from the environment and sustained her prior sense of community. Such continuity was unusual, as nursing homes often are not in communities of origin. The worker brought Mrs. Harper to her enriched-housing apartment for visits, to dinner meals, and to group meetings with other enriched-housing members. As Mrs. Harper progressed, she moved from a wheelchair to a walker. The encouragement of the team and her enriched-housing community was intimately intertwined with her own motivation. By the time of her discharge, she was well enough to need only six hours of care, six day per week. She had been away from her apartment for six months.

Mrs. Harper spent the remaining 2½ years of her life in her apartment, supported by the enriched-housing social worker and the community of residents. In nice weather, she could be found under her favorite tree. Those who knew her had no question that had she remained in the single-room-occupancy hotel, her life would have been filled with hardship and considerably shortened.

The case of Florence Harper vividly illustrates the way in which social policy, the planning and organization of services, and direct social work practice come together in a single life. It illustrates the harshness of life for poor African-American women and how that harshness continues into old age. At its core, it tells the story of an older woman, coping with a lifetime of oppression and an increasing need for the assistance of others, and a social worker, unable to correct past societal abuses, but nonetheless very much wanting to make this last period of Mrs. Harper's life as satisfying as possible.

Many important themes are illustrated by Mrs. Harper; some are about Mrs. Harper, some are about the environment, and the most important are about Mrs. Harper in her environment and the way the environment lived in Mrs. Harper. Mrs. Harper's life reflects themes that appear and reappear in the lives of older minority persons, particularly women, in need of long-term care. Much of the time, the environment was harsh in Mrs. Harper's life. From her earliest years, she had learned that the environmental forces against her would be greater than her capacity in relation to the environment. She blamed poverty and inadequate health care for her beloved mother's death. Limited education and employment consisting primarily of serving members of the majority culture took their toll and were carried into old age. Only her second marriage and her ties to her community had provided a respite that made life worth living.

As is common in old age, Mrs. Harper suffered greatly from events beyond her control. The death of her husband, her subsequent stroke, and her forced relocation to an inhospitable environment set loose a set of forces against which Mrs. Harper had little reserve. Her prior stroke had taxed much of her psychological and physical energy. The capacities that had been sufficient within her own apartment were not sufficient within her new, alien world. Except for the community social workers, there were no other physical or social supports. If, as Howell (1983) suggested, the self is defined affectively in relation to place, then it is unambiguously clear why Mrs. Harper increasingly defined herself negatively. Her world became circumscribed and confirmed to her that she would again suffer at the hands of the majority culture. Without adequate income to generate an adequate environment, Mrs. Harper had little to live for. The social workers represented, at best, a pleasant interlude in an altogether depressing life.

Mrs. Harper's strengths reappeared with the possibility of a more hospitable environment. Her life within her new apartment demonstrates the delicate balance between her ability to care for herself and her need for others to care for her as well. Moving into a new apartment provided Mrs. Harper with temporary relief from the belief that she did not matter to anyone. Living for herself had become most difficult with the devaluation and marginalization imposed upon her by society. Only at the brink of death, when she became convinced that she personally mattered to someone (in this instance, a member of the majority culture), and when she became convinced that she would be allowed, even encouraged, to take some control over her life, could she again live. Most striking is the way in which Mrs. Harper's life came alive again when she finally came to believe that her environment cared about her and would care for her. The intimacy she established with the enriched-housing program and with her social worker mediated her losses and helped her adapt to her new life (Powell 1988).

The enriched-housing social worker was clear that her practice strategy had to be directed toward establishing a more satisfying balance between Mrs. Harper's needs and capacities and the demands and resources of her environment. Two conditions stood out for her: the first was her understanding that Mrs. Harper had entered the program and their relationship with the experience of prejudice and discrimination at the hands of the majority culture, and the second was her understanding that their relationship was a microcosm of this phenomenon. Each act, each decision, each move, that took power away from Mrs. Harper moved their relationship toward being an oppressive one. Even the best motives would not suffice. The worker's role was to mediate between Mrs. Harper and her environment, to attend to the dialogue between them, and to help them communicate with each other with strong voices. Helping Mrs. Harper find an assertive voice would directly counter her sense of powerlessness and hopelessness.

Ultimately, Mrs. Harper survived because she was helped to find her voice: whether an angry voice, a depressed voice, a loving voice, a needy voice—no matter. The worker needed to hear it all, and Mrs. Harper needed to say it all. As the worker found her own voice in the hospital, Mrs. Harper heard it clearly. In this way, they came to know each other.

The tender, caring relationship that grew and developed between the worker and Mrs. Harper was nurtured by a caring environment. MHHA contained many distinctive organizational features that were vital to Mrs. Harper's life. The most important were a continuum of care and the ability of the enriched-housing social worker to remain as social worker throughout all points of Mrs. Harper's involvement with MHHA. MHHA's broad range of services ensured that in vital areas, she would not suffer from the fragmented organization of social services, as is so often the case for older persons. The institution's willingness to become a partner with Mrs. Harper in her own life was a critical variable in Mrs. Harper's growing belief that life could once again be worth living.

The subject of this essay is serving the elderly in need of long-term care. The demographies of aging provide a dramatic picture of the social, economic, and political context in which such older persons live. Social workers must heed this picture as they plan, organize, and deliver social services to a population made vulnerable by a public policy unresponsive to their needs. Of the elderly in need of long-term care, older women—particularly older minority women living alone —are especially disadvantaged by poverty. These older persons are most at risk of abuse and neglect, morbidity, institutionalization, and death. Older white men living alone are at risk of suicide. The notion that these persons are at risk because of personal attributes rather than society's failure is an example of societal ageism, in which the victims are blamed for their problems in living. Viewing the individual as independent of the environment is consistent with the medicalizing of aging. The transformation of older persons' needs into social problems pushes older persons further to the margins of society and pits their interests against the interests of others. Frailty (as in the "frail elderly") is socially defined and socially created. It comes about from the failure to provide the resources necessary for a satisfying life. The incongruity between older persons' needs and capacities, on one hand, and society's demands and resources, on the other, taxes diminishing and difficult-to-renew personal and environmental resources. Under such conditions, weakened voices are created. An unresponsive social context produces inadequate resources and fragmented services. It also produces isolating, age-segregated policies, the very situation long-term-care services are designed to mitigate.

The task for social workers is a difficult one. Though it is beyond our profession's ability or scope to bring about the redistribution of national resources, it is not beyond our purview to advocate for a responsive public policy centered on an adequate economic standard. Similarly, though it may be beyond our purview to integrate fragmented long-term care services, it is not unrealistic to undertake to plan integrative programs to serve the whole of our clients' lives by connecting them to services that our own agencies cannot provide. Moreover, though we can not ensure the responsiveness of others, we can bring the plight of the most vulnerable elderly to center stage in our own work and professional activities.

Practice with the elderly in need of long-term care requires a helping strategy directed toward assisting the elderly in making claim upon society through the strengthening of their voices. Placing older persons at the head of this effort, to whatever extent possible, maximizes their strengths and goes a long way toward reestablishing a sense of self consistent with potency. At least within our relationships, self-determination and a better balance of power should prevail.

However sanguine one may or may not feel about the overall picture, the efforts of social workers who work with the most vulnerable aged are often brave and creative. Their unflagging spirit, energy, and skill give reason for hope.

## REFERENCES

Adelman, R. D., K. Marron, L. Lebow, and R. Neufeld. 1987. "A Community-Oriented Geriatric Rehabilitation Unit in a Nursing Home." *The Gerontologist* 27(2):143–146.

Baker, R. 1985. "Housing for the Frail Elderly: A Model." *Journal of Gerontological Social Work* 8(3/4):257–264.

Bass, D. 1980. *The Continuum of Care for the Elderly: A Partnership Between the Consumer and the Provider.* U.S. Department of Health and Human Services, Office of Human Development Services, Office of Planning, Research and Evaluation.

Baum, S. K. and R. L. Boxley. 1983. "Age Identification in the Elderly." *The Gerontologist* 23(5):532–537.

Benitez, R. 1976. "Ethnicity, Social Policy and Aging." In Davis, R. H., ed., *Aging: Prospects and Issues*, pp. 164–177. Los Angeles: University of Southern California Press.

Bennett, R. 1980. "Summary and Concluding Remarks." In R. Bennett, ed., *Aging, Isolation and Resocialization*, pp. 197–207. New York: Van Nostrand Reinhold.

Berman-Rossi, T. 1986. "The Fight Against Hopelesssness and Despair: Institutionalized Aged." In A. Gitterman and L. Shulman, Eds., *Mutual Aid Groups and the Life Cycle,* pp. 333–358. Itasca, Ill.: Peacock.

Berman-Rossi, T. 1990. "Group Services for Older Persons." In A. Monk, ed., *Handbook of Gerontological Services,* New York: Columbia University Press.

Blumenfield, S. 1982. "The Hospital Center and Aging: A Challenge for the Social Worker." *Journal of Gerontological Social Work* 5(1/2):35–60.

Brody, E. M. 1974. *A Social Work Guide for Long-Term Care Facilities.* Rockville, Md.: National Institute of Mental Health.

Brody, E. M. and S. J. Brody. 1987. "Aged: Services." In *Encyclopedia of Social Work,* pp. 106–126. Silver Spring, Md.: National Association of Social Workers.

Brubaker, E. and A. Ward Schiefer. 1987. "Groups with Families of Elderly Long-Term Care Residents: Building Social Support Networks." *Journal of Gerontological Social Work* 10(1/2):167–175.

Buffum, W. E. 1987–88. "Measuring Person–Environment Fit in Nursing Home." *Journal of Social Service Research* 11(2/3):35–54.

Butler, R. N. 1969. "Ageism: Another Form of Bigotry." *The Gerontologist* 9(4):243–246.

Butler, R. N. and M. Lewis. 1983. *Aging and Mental Health.* New York: Plume, New American Library.

Callahan, D. 1987. *Setting Limits.* New York: Simon & Schuster.

Callahan, J. J., Jr., and S. S. Wallack. 1981. "Major Reforms in Long-Term Care." In J. J. Callahan, Jr., and S. S. Wallack, eds., *Reforming the Long-Term Care System,* pp. 3–10. Lexington, Mass.: Lexington Books, D. C. Heath.

Coulton, C. 1979. "A Study of Person–Environment Fit Among the Chronically Ill." *Social Work in Health Care* 5(1):5–17.

Coward R. T. 1987. "Factors Associated with the Configuration of the Helping Networks of Noninstitutionalized Elders." *Journal of Gerontological Social Work* 10(1/2):113–132.

Cox, C. and P. H. Ephross. 1989. "Group Work with Families of Nursing Home Residents: Its Socialization and Therapeutic Functions." *Journal of Gerontological Social Work* 13(3/4:61–73.

Cutler, N. E. 1976. "The Aging Population and Social Policy." In R. H. Davis, ed., *Aging: Prospects and Issues,* pp. 102–126. Los Angeles: University of Southern California Press.

Danziger, S. D. 1987. "Poverty." In *Encyclopedia of Social Work,* pp. 294–302. Washington, D.C.: National Association of Social Workers.

Dunkle, R. E. 1984. "An Historical Perspective on Social Service Delivery to the Elderly." *Journal of Gerontological Social Work* 7(3):5–18.

Dunkle, R. E. 1987. "Protective Services for the Aged." In *Encyclopedia of Social Work,* pp. 391–396. Silver Spring, Md.: National Association of Social Workers.

Engel, G. L. 1968. "A Life Setting Conducive to Illness: The Giving-Up–Given-Up Complex." *Bulletin of the Menninger Clinic* 32(6):355–365.

Estes, C. L. 1977. *The Aging Experience: A Critical Examination of Social Policies and Services for the Aged.* San Francisco: Jossey-Bass.

Estes, C. L. and P. R. Lee. 1985. "Social, Political, and Economic Background of Long Term Care Policy." In C. Harrington, R. J. Newcomer, C. L. Estes, and Associates, eds., *Long Term Care of the Elderly: Public Policy Issues,* pp. 17–39. Beverly Hills, Calif.: Sage.

Estes, C. L., J. S. Swan, and L. E. Gerard. 1982. "Dominant and Competing Paradigms in Gerontology: Towards a Political Economy of Ageing." *Ageing and Society* 2(2):151–164.

Eustis, N. N., J. N. Greenberg, and S. K. Patten. 1984. *Long-Term Care: A Policy Perspective.* Monterey, Calif.: Brooks/Cole.

FCA (Federal Council on the Aging). 1978. *Public Policy and the Frail Elderly.* Washington, D.C.: GPO.

FCA (Federal Council on Aging). 1979. *Mental Health and the Elderly: Recommendations for Action.* Washington, D.C.: GPO.

FCA (Federal Council on the Aging). 1984. *The Working Person as Caregiver: A Symposium on Increasing Support Services for the Frail Elderly.* Washington, D.C.: GPO.

Feldstein, D. 1985. "Permanent Patients: On Working with the Chronic Mentally Frail in the Community." *Journal of Gerontological Social Work* 8(3/4):121–140.

French, J. R. P., W. Rodgers, and S. Cobb. 1974. "Adjustment as Person–Environment Fit." In G. C. Coelho, D. A. Hamburg, and J. E. Adams, eds., *Coping and Adaptation,* pp. 316–333. New York: Basic Books.

*Funk and Wagnalls Modern Guide to Synonyms and Related Words.* 1968. New York: Funk & Wagnalls.

Furstenberg, A.-L. 1989. "Older People's Age Self-Concept." *Social Casework* 70(5):268–275.

Gadow, S. 1983. "Frailty and Strength: The Dialectic in Aging." *The Gerontologist* 23(2):144–147.

Germain, C. B. 1979. "Introduction: Ecology and Social Work." In Carel B. Germain, ed., *Social Work Practice: People and Environments, An Ecological Perspective,* pp. 1–22. New York: Columbia University Press.

Germain, C. B. 1987. "Human Development in Contemporary Environments." *Social Service Review* 61(4):565–580.

Germain, C. B. and A. Gitterman. 1980. *The Life Model of Social Work Practice.* New York: Columbia University Press.

Germain, C. B. and A. Gitterman. 1987. "Ecological Perspective." In *Encyclopedia of Social Work,* 17th ed., pp. 488–499. Washington, D.C.: National Association of Social Workers.

Getzel, G. S. and M. J. Mellor. 1982. "Introduction: Overview of Gerontological Social Work in Long-Term Care." *Journal of Gerontological Social Work* 5(1/2):1–6.

Goldenberg, I. 1978. *Oppression and Social Intervention.* Chicago: Nelson-Hall.

Goldstein, R. 1982. "Adult Day Care: Expanding Options for Service." *Journal of Gerontological Social Work* 5(1/2):157–168.

Gonyea, J. G. 1987. "The Family and Dependency: Factors Associated with Institutional Decision-Making." *Journal of Gerontological Social Work* 19(1/2):67–77.

Goodman, H. 1985. "Serving the Elderly Blind: A Generic Approach." *Journal of Gerontological Social Work* 8(3/4):153–168.

Gratton, B. and V. Wilson. 1988. "Family Support Systems and the Minority Elderly: A Cautionary Analysis." *Journal of Gerontological Social Work* 13(1/2):81–93.

Harel, Z. 1986. "Older Americans Act Related Homebound Aged: What Difference Does Racial Background Make?" *Journal of Gerontological Social Work* 9(1):133–143.

Harel, Z. 1988. "Coping with Extreme Stress and Aging." *Social Casework* 69(9):575–583.

Harris, D. K. 1988. *Dictionary of Gerontology.* New York: Greenwood Press.

Hooyman, N. R. 1983. "Social Support Networks in Services to the Elderly." In J. K. Whittaker, J. and J. Garbarino, eds., *Social Support Networks: Informal Helping in the Human Services,* pp. 133–164. New York: Aldine de Gruyter.

Hooyman, N. R. and H. Asuman Kiyak. 1988. *Social Gerontology.* Boston: Allyn & Bacon.

Hooyman, N. R. and W. Lustbader. 1986. *Taking Care: Supporting Older People and Their Families.* New York: Free Press.

Howell, S. C. 1983. "The Meaning of Place in Old Age." In G. D. Rowles and R. J. Ohta, eds., *Aging and Milieu*, pp. 97–107. New York: Academic Press.

Jackson, M., B. Kolody, and J. L. Wood. 1982. "To Be Old and Black: The Case for Double Jeopardy on Income and Health." In R. C. Manuel, ed., *Minority Aging: Sociological and Social Psychological Issues*, pp. 77–82. Westport, Conn.: Greenwood.

Jacobson, S. G. 1982. "Equity in the Use of Public Benefits by Minority Elderly." In R. C. Manuel, ed., *Minority Aging: Sociological and Social Psychological Issues*, pp. 161–170. Westport, Conn.: Greenwood.

Jones, L. E. 1987. "Women." In *Encyclopedia of Social Work*. pp. 872–881. Silver Spring, Md.: National Association of Social Workers.

Kahana, E. 1974. "Matching Environments to Needs of the Aged: A Conceptual Scheme." In J. F. Gubrium, ed., *Late Life: Communities and Environmental Policy*, pp. 201–214. Springfield, Ill.: Charles C Thomas.

Kahana, E. 1982. "A Congruence Model of Person–Environment Interaction." In M. P. Lawton, P. G. Windley, and T. O. Byerts, eds., *Aging and the Environment: Theoretical Approaches*, pp. 97–121. New York: Springer.

Kalish, R. A. 1985. "Services for the Dying." In A. Monk, ed., *Handbook of Gerontological Services*, pp. 531–546. New York: Van Nostrand Reinhold.

Kane, R. A. 1985. "Assessing the Elderly Client." In A. Monk, ed., *Handbook of Gerontological Services*, pp. 43–69. New York: Van Nostrand Reinhold.

Kane, R. A. 1987. "Long-Term Care." In *Encyclopedia of Social Work*, pp. 59–72. Silver Spring, Md.: National Association of Social Workers.

Kane, R. L. and R. A. Kane. 1981. *Assessing the Elderly*. Lexington, Mass.: Lexington Books, D. C. Heath.

Kasper, J. D. 1988. "Aging Alone: Profiles and Projections." Report of the Commonwealth Fund Commission on Elderly People Living Alone, Baltimore.

Kaufman, S. R. 1986. *The Ageless Self*. Madison: University of Wisconsin Press.

Kaye, L. W. 1985. "Homecare." In A. Monk, ed., *Handbook of Gerontological Services*, pp. 408–432. New York: Van Nostrand Reinhold.

Knight, B. and D. Loiver Walker. 1985. "Towards a Definition of Alternatives to Institutionalization for the Frail Elderly." *The Gerontologist* 25(4):358–363.

Kohlert, N. 1989. "Welfare Reform: A Historic Consensus." *Social Work* 34(4):303–306.

Lee, J. A. B. 1983. "The Group: A Chance at Human Connection for the Mentally Impaired Older Person." In Shura Saul, ed., *Group Work with the Frail Elderly. Social Work with Groups*. 5(2):43–55.

Lieberman, M. A. and S. S. Tobin. 1983. *The Experience of Old Age: Stress, Coping and Survival*. New York: Basic Books.

*Longman Synonym Dictionary*. 1986. Harlow Essex Great Britain: Robert Hartnoll, Bodmin.

Lowy, L. 1985. "Multipurpose Senior Centers." In A. Monk, ed., *Handbook of Gerontological Services*, pp. 274–301. New York: Van Nostrand Reinhold.

Ludman, E. K. and J. M. Newman. 1986. "Frail Elderly: Assessment of Nutritional Needs." *The Gerontologist* 26(2):198–202.

Lurie, A. and Rich, J. C. 1984. "The Medical Center's Impact in the Network to Sustain the Aged in the Community." *Journal of Gerontological Social Work* 7(3):65–73.

Mailick Seltzer, M. and G. B. Seltzer. 1985. "The Elderly Mentally Retarded: A Group in Need of Service." *Journal of Gerontological Social Work* 8(3):99–119.

Maldonado, David. 1987. "Aged." In *Encyclopedia of Social Work*, pp. 95–106. Silver Spring, Md.: National Association of Social Workers.

Manuel, R.C. 1982. "The Minority Aged: Providing a Conceptual Perspective." In

R. C. Manuel, ed., *Minority Aging: Sociological and Social Psychological Issues*, pp. 13–25. Westport, Conn.: Greenwood.

Manuel, R. C. and J. Reid. 1982. "A Comparative Demographic Profile of the Minority and Nonminority Aged." In R. C. Manuel, ed., *Minority Aging: Sociological and Social Psychological Issues*, pp. 31–52. Westport, Conn.: Greenwood.

Mayer, M. J. 1983. "Demographic Change and the Elderly Population." In Special Issue S. Saul, ed., *Group Work and the Frail Elderly. Social Work with Groups* 5(2):7–12.

Mechanic, D. 1974. "Social Structure and Personal Adaptation: Some Neglected Dimensions." In G. V. Coelho, D. Hamburg, and J. E. Adams, eds., *Coping and Adaptation*, pp. 32–44. New York: Basic Books.

Mercer, S. O. and R. A. Kane. 1979. "Helplessness and Hopelessness Among the Institutionalized Elderly: An Experiment." *Health and Social Work* 4(1):91–116.

Miller, I. and R. Solomon. 1979. "The Development of Group Services for the Elderly." In Carel B. Germain, ed., *Social Work Practice: People and Environments*, pp. 74–106. New York: Columbia University Press.

Millikan, M. 1959. "Inquiry and Policy: The Relation of Knowledge to Action." In D. Lerner, ed., *The Human Meaning of the Social Sciences*, pp. 158–180. New York: Meridian Books.

Monk, A. 1981. "Social Work with the Aged." *Social Work* 26(1):61–68.

Monk, A. 1985. "Gerontological Social Services: Theory and Practice." In A. Monk, ed., *Handbook of Gerontological Services*, pp. 3–23. New York: Van Nostrand Reinhold.

Monk, A. and M. Abramson. 1982. "Older People." In S. A. Yelaja, ed., *Ethical Issues in Social Work*, pp. 139–155. Springfield Ill.: Charles C Thomas.

Moody, H. R. 1985. "Book Review." *Journal of Gerontological Social Work* 9(1):1–5.

Moon, M. 1977. *The Measurement of Economic Welfare: Its Application to the Aged Poor*. New York: Academic Press.

Morris, R. and P. Youket. 1981. "The Long-Term Care Issues: Identifying the Problems and Potential Solution." In J. J. Callahan, Jr., and S. S. Wallack, eds., *Reforming the Long-Term-Care System*, pp. 11–28. Lexington, Mass.: Lexington Books, D. C. Heath.

NCHS (National Center for Health Statistics). 1989. *Vital and Health Statistics: Physical Functioning of the Aged, United States, 1984*. Hyattsville, Md.: U.S. Department of Health and Human Services.

NIA (National Institute on Aging). 1987. Established *Populations for Epidemiologic Studies of the Elderly*, eds. by J. Cornoni-Huntley, D. B. Breck, A. M. Qustfeld, J. D. Taylor, R. B. Wallace and M. Lafferty. Washington, D.C.: GPO.

Neugarten, B. L. 1982a. "Older People: A Profile." In B. L. Neugarten, ed., *Age or Need? Public Policies for Older People*, pp. 33–54. Beverley Hills, Calif.: Sage.

Neugarten, B. L. 1982b. "Policy for the 1980's: Age or Need Entitlement?" In B. L. Neugarten, ed., *Age or Need? Public Policies for Older People*, pp. 19–32. Beverley Hills, Calif.: Sage.

NYSOA (New York State Office for the Aging). 1987. *Annual Report*. New York: NYSOA.

NYSOA (New York State Office for the Aging). 1989. *Minority Elderly New Yorkers: The Social and Economic Status of a Rapidly Growing Population*. New York: NYSOA.

Pastalan, L. A. 1983. "Environmental Displacement: A Literature Reflectiing Old-Person–Environment Transactions." In G. D. Rowles and R. J. Ohta, eds., *Aging and Milieu*. pp. 171–186. New York: Academic Press.

Powell, W. E. 1988. "The 'Ties That Bind': Relationships in Life Transitions." *Social Casework* 69(9):556–562.

Rathbone-MaCuan, E. and R. T. Coward. 1985. "Respite and Adult Day-Care Service." In A. Monk, ed., *Handbook of Gerontological Services*, pp. 456–482. New York: Van Nostrand Reinhold.

Reker, G. T. and P. T. P. Wong. 1985. "Personal Optimism, Physical and Mental Health." In J. E. Birren and J. Livingston, eds., *Cognition, Stress, and Aging*, pp. 47–71. Englewood Cliffs, N.J.: Prentice-Hall.

Rosenwaike, I. and A. Dolinsky. 1987. "The Changing Demographic Determinants of the Growth of the Extreme Aged." *The Gerontologist* 27(3):275–280.

Rzetelny, H. 1985. "Emotional Stresses in Later Life." *Journal of Gerontological Social Work* 8(3/4):141–151.

Schultz, R. and G. Brenner. 1977. "Relocation of the Aged: A Review and Theoretical Analysis." *Journal of Gerontology* 32(3):323–333.

Schwartz, W. 1961. "The Social Worker in the Group." In *The Social Welfare Forum*, pp. 146–177. 1961 Proceedings of the National Conference on Social Welfare. New York: Columbia University Press.

Schwartz, W. 1962. "Toward a Strategy of Group Work Practice." *The Social Service Review* 36(3):268–279.

Schwartz, W. 1977. "Social Group Work: The Interactionist Approach." In *Encyclopedia of Social Work*, 17th ed., pp. 1328–1338. Washington, D.C.: National Association of Social Workers.

Schwartz, W. "Social Work with Groups: The Search for a Method." 1968. Unpublished.

SCA (Select Committee on Aging). 1987. "Long Term Care and Personal Impoverishment: Seven in Ten Elderly Living Alone Are At Risk." House of Representatives, Committee Publication Number 100-631. Washington, D.C.: GPO.

Seligman, M. and G. Elder, Jr. 1986. "Learned Helplessness and Life-Span Development." In A. B. Sorensen, F. E. Weinert, and L. R. Sherrod, eds., *Human Development and the Life Course: Multidisciplinary Perspectives*, pp. 377–428. Hillsdale, N.J.: Erlbaum.

Seltzer, G. B. and M. Charpentier. 1982. "Maximizing Independence for the Elderly: The Social Worker in the Rehabilitation Center." *Journal of Gerontological Social Work* 5(1/2):661–79.

Shanas, E., P. Townsend, D. Wedderburn, H. Friis, P. Milhos, and J. Stehouwar. 1968. *Old People in Three Industrial Societies*. New York: Atherton.

Shepard, P., J. B. Mayer, and R. Ryback. 1987. "Improving Emergency Care for the Elderly: Social Work Intervention." *Journal of Gerontological Social Work* 10(3/4):123–140.

Shulman, L. 1984. *The Skills of Helping Individual and Groups*. Itasca, Ill.: Peacock.

Simpson, J. A. and E. S. C. Weiner. 1989. *The Oxford English Dictionary*, 2d ed. Oxford: Clarendon Press.

Solomon, B. B. 1976. *Black Empowerment: Social Work in Oppressed Communities*. New York: Columbia University Press.

Solomon, R. 1982. "Serving Families of the Institutionalized Aged: The Four Crises." *Journal of Gerontological Social Work* 5(1/2):83–96.

Steinberg, R. M. 1985. "Access Assistance and Case Management." In A. Monk, ed., *Handbook of Gerontological Services*, pp. 109–141. New York: Van Nostrand Reinhold.

Stone, R., G. L. Cafferata, and J. Sangle. 1987. "Caregivers of the Frail Elderly: A National Profile." *The Gerontologist* 27(5):616–626.

Streib, G. F. 1983. "The Frail Elderly: Research Dilemmas and Research Opportunities." *The Gerontologist* 23(1):40–44.

Steun, C. 1985. "Outreach to the Elderly." *Journal of Gerontological Social Work* 8(3/4):85–96.

Taylor, R. J. and L. M. Chatters. 1986. "Church-based Informal Support Among Elderly Blacks." *The Gerontologist* 26(6):637–642.

Tobin, S. S. 1988. "Preservation of the Self in Old Age." *Social Casework* 69(9):550–555.

Tobin, S. S., S. M. Davidson, and A. Sack. 1976. *Effective Social Services for Older Americans.* Ann Arbor: Institute of Gerontology, University of Michigan–Wayne State University.

Tobin, S. S. and M. Lieberman. 1976. *Last Home for the Aged,* San Francisco: Jossey-Bass.

Tobin, S. S. and R. Toseland. 1985. "Models of Services for the Elderly." In A. Monk, ed., *Handbook of Gerontological Services,* pp. 549–567. New York: Van Nostrand Reinhold.

"Too Many Chores? Help Is at the Doorstep." 1989. *The New York Times* (June 21), Section C.

Treas, J. 1977. "Family Support Systems for the Aged." *The Gerontologist* 17(6):486–491.

Trieschmann, R. 1987. *Aging with a Disability.* New York: Demos.

U.S. HHS (U.S. Department of Health and Human Services). 1985–86. *Aging in America: Trends and Projections,* 1985–86 ed. Washington, D.C.: GPO.

*Webster's New Dictionary of Synonyms.* 1968. Springfield, Mass.: G. & C. Merriam.

"When Long Life and Is Too Much: Suicide Risk Among Elderly." 1989. *New York Times.* July 19, pp. 1 and 15.

White, R. W. 1974. "Strategies of Adaptation: An Attempt at Systematic Description." In G. V. Coelho, D. A. Hamburg, and J. E. Adams, eds. *Coping and Adaptation,* pp. 47–68. New York: Basic Books.

Wilson, A. J. E. 1984. *Social Services for Older Persons.* Boston: Little, Brown.

Wyers, N. L. 1983. "Income Maintenance and Social Work: A Broken Tie." *Social Work* 28(4):261–267.

# 17

# Family Caregivers of the Frail Elderly

▼

## RONALD W. TOSELAND
## GREGORY SMITH

There has been an increased awareness of the widespread nature of family caregiving and its importance to society, and the well-being of frail older persons. Numerous studies have documented how the stress of caregiving to frail older persons is associated with physical, psychological, social, and emotional problems. Recognition of these strains has led to the development of various supportive interventions. This essay describes the nature, prevalence, and impact of family caregiving; reviews the intervention programs that have been designed to support family caregivers; and presents guidelines for practice with this population.

## PROBLEM DOMAIN

The caregiving relationship "is defined by the existence of some degree of physical, mental, emotional, or economic impairment on the part of the older person which limites independence and necessitates ongoing assistance" (Horowitz 1985:195). Family caregiving arises out of needs created by chronic and acute functional disabilities. Especially in the early stages of chronic disease processes, the needs

Preparation of this essay was supported by a grant from the Health Sciences Research and Development Office of the Veterans' Administration. Research data reported in the essay were gathered through grants to the senior author from the Andrus foundation of the American Association of Retired Persons, the Prevention Research Branch of the National Institute of Mental Health, and the Veterans' Administration. The authors wish to acknowledge the contribution of Dr. Charles Rossiter to an early draft of this chapter.

of frail elderly family members are often episodic. Generally, the need for care increases over time, and although there may be some reduction in the physical demands of caregiving when a frail family member is hospitalized or institutionalized, the emotional demands of caregiving continue for as long as the family member lives. Thus, family caregiving frequently involves a long-term, open-ended commitment that wanes and waxes with the vicissitudes of the care receivers' condition.

Caregivers are confronted with many different tasks that vary depending on the problems experienced by their frail relative. Although caregiving is not characterized by any one type of assistance, emotional support, rather than physical or financial support, is the most common and most important type of assistance provided by family caregivers (Brody 1985; Horoowitz 1985). Other frequently provided types of assistance include transportation; shopping; doing household chores; coordinating assistance from social service and health care providers; routine health care such as administering and monitoring medications; personal care such as bathing, feeding, toileting, and dressing; supervision; financial management; financial assistance; and the sharing of a common household.

Caregiving is a rewarding, yet demanding and stressful, experience. Research findings suggest that family caregivers are motivated by three factors; "love and affection felt toward the individual, a sense of gratitude and desire to reciprocate caregiving or other help that was previously provided by the impaired elderly person to the spouse or the adult child, and allegiance to a more generalized societal norm of spousal or filial responsibility" (Doty 1986:46).

Social workers should be aware, however, that in certain situations, patterns of caregiving may exist that cause problems and jeopardize the well-being of the caregiver or the care receiver. Verbal or physical abuse may originate either with the caregiver or the care receiver. Patterns of neglect or enmeshment are also sometimes encountered. Dysfunctional caregiver or care-receiver relationships are often indicative of longstanding interpersonal conflicts, pathological codependence, or other psychopathology, rather than gratitude, love, or filial responsibility (Brody 1985).

Informal caregiving by family members is by far the most common means of providing long-term care to frail elderly persons (U.S. HHS 1982). Indeed, only one in five older persons with long-term-care needs is in a nursing home. Largely because of the assistance of family members, the remainder are able to live in the community despite severe disabilities.

Precise estimates of the number of individuals who provide care to frail elderly family members are unavailable, partly because a single caregiver may care for more than one family member, and several caregivers may provide different kinds of assistance to the same family member (Brody 1985). It is known, however, that 80 percent of persons 65 and older have at least one chronic disability (U.S. Senate 1987–88), and that nearly 5.1 million older persons living in the community require assistance with some aspect of personal care or home management in order to maintain independent living (AARP 1986). It is also known that nearly three quarters of the community-dwelling frail elderly rely solely on family and friends to meet their long-term-care needs, and that most of the remainder rely on a combination of family care and paid help (Doty 1986).

The commonly held belief that successive family cohorts are becoming less willing to care for frail elderly family members at home is not supported by the available data (Brody 1985; Horowitz 1985; Shanas 1979). Largely because of changing demographics, family caregiving is becoming increasingly common. There has been an increasing number of persons surviving to advanced old age in the United States, and this trend will continue for the next several decades. Between 1900 and 1970, the overall population increased 300 percent, but those 65 and older increased 700 percent. Today, approximately 11 percent of America's population is over 65, and by the year 2000 one in eight Americans will be 65 years of age or older. The growth rate of the "old-old," those who are 85 and older, is particularly pertinent to family caregiving because the old-old are much more likely to have some form of functional disability and three times as likely as those between 65 and 74 years to require some form of family assistance to remain in the community (Soldo and Manton 1985). The old-old are the fastest growing segment of the American population, and they are expected to nearly quadruple in size between 1980 and 2030 (U.S. Senate 1987–88).

The available data leave little question about the important role played by family caregivers. Frail old persons without family caregivers are much more likely to be found in nursing homes. Over 80 percent of nursing-home residents have no spouse, compared with 45 percent of the noninstitutionalized elderly. Similarly, compared with 81 percent of the noninstitutionalized elderly, only 63 percent of nursing-home residents have children (U.S. Senate 1987–88). But helping to prevent premature institutionalization is only one aspect of the contribution that family caregivers make to the quality of life of elderly people. At its best, the kind of high-quality, round-the-clock, personalized care that is provided by loving family members who are intimately familiar with the capacities, needs, and desires of frail family members cannot be duplicated even by the most dedicated and skilled of professional caregivers. Even when the health care needs of frail family members warrant professional intervention, including hospitalization or placement in a nursing home, family caregivers continue to play an important role in the family members' life.

The responsibility for the care of a frail elderly family member is rarely shared equally by all family members. Although some degree of shared responsibility is common, there is generally one primary caregiver in a family. It has been suggested that the decision about who will provide care follows a "principle of substitution," with one family member providing most of the care (Shanas 1968). If a spouse is available, he or she is most likely to provide care. If not, then an adult daughter is most likely to become the primary caregiver. In the absence of an adult daughter, a son or daughter-in-law is most likely to provide care. If none of these family members are available, other relatives, neighbors, and friends are the next most likely to provide care. Social workers should be aware that the differential sharing of caregiving responsibilities among family members can cause conflict, particularly among siblings, who may become angered by the lack of involvement of brothers or sisters in the care of a parent.

A national survey revealed some of the characteristics of family caregivers and care receivers (Stone, Cafferata, and Sangl 1987). Most caregivers were female. Their average age was 57.3, and most were between ages 40 and 65. Caregivers were typically wives (29 percent) or adult daughters (23 percent), and most were white, although a significant number were nonwhite. A majority (57 percent) of caregivers reported low or moderate incomes, and nearly a third (31.5 percent) reported income at poverty or near-poverty levels.

The average care receiver in the national survey was 78 years old. Sixty percent were female, and twenty percent were over age 85. Fifty-one percent of all care receivers were married, forty-one percent were widowed. They had a variety of chronic disabilities that limited their ability to perform instrumental activities of daily living. The vast majority lived with their spouses, with their children, or with other family members. Only 11 percent lived alone.

There is tremendous variability across the situations of different family caregivers. It has been said that "the caregiver may be a grandmother who is experiencing the decrements of aging or she may have young children at home" (Brody 1985:22). Caregivers differ considerably in such factors as health; marital, employment, and economic status; family constellation and dynamics; personality; coping styles; and the nature of the relationship with the care receiver. Caregiving situations also vary considerably depending on the nature, extent, and duration of the disabilities experienced by the care receiver, as well as each caregiver's unique response to the different responsibilities of an evolving caregiving situation. Recognition of this variability is essential in developing differential assessment and intervention strategies to best meet the needs of each caregiver who is served.

## SOCIETAL CONTEXT

Social workers and other helping professionals should be aware of a number of important social trends that influence family caregiving. One of the most striking is the changing role of female caregivers. Whereas women of all ages have been entering the job market in record numbers in recent years, U.S. Department of Labor statistics reveal that the greatest increase of new working women between 1950 and 1970 were those between the ages of 45 and 64 (Brody 1981). As previously mentioned, this is the age when family-caregiving responsibilities are most likely to arise.

Researchers disagree about whether working outside the home decreases the time devoted to caregiving (Doty 1986). Until recently, it was thought that the extra role demand of work contributed to the stress faced by women caregivers (Doty 1986), but work outside the home can also provide women with social contact and a needed respite from caregiving. Also, little is known about how the women's movement is affecting the thinking of younger women and men who will be expected to take on future family-caregiving responsibilities. It is clear, however, that the changing role of women means that social workers should make few assumptions about caregiving arrangements, and that a careful assessment of each situation is crucial.

There are also changes in family structure and function that are influencing who provides care and how much care is provided. Couples are having fewer children, thus making offspring less available to provide care in the future. Because of increased mobility, isolated nuclear families are more common than in the past. There are more single-parent families, more divorces and remarriages, and more women having their first child at a later age. Although the precise impact of these changes is unknonw, taken together the data suggest that changing family forms may have an adverse effect on family caregiving (Horowitz 1985). It is likely that there will be more people needing care in the future, and that they will be older and sicker. It also appears that even though more younger people will be providing care than in the past, the proportion of people needing family care, but not receiving it, is likely to increase (Gray 1983).

Another social trend influencing social work practice with family caregiving is the increasing longevity of care receivers. As the population ages, caregivers are being expected to care for increasingly aged family members who are likely to be in poorer health, to have more chronic disabilities, and to function less independently. This trend has been greatly accelerated by changing health care policies, which have shortened hospital stays for both physical and mental health problems and have resulted in the discharge of increasingly frail older people who are in greater need of intensive home health care than ever before.

As care receivers become older and more disabled, so to do their family caregivers. In fact, spousal caregivers may become so disabled themselves that they can no longer provide certain types of care, particularly care that requires lifting and other physical exertion. The aging of the population also means that the number of families comprising four and five generations will continue to expand. Increasingly, middle-aged relatives will become responsible either sequentially or simultaneously for the care of family members from two older generations. This situation prompted Brody (1985) to observe that for many individuals, family caregiving may become more like a career than a time-limited event in the life course.

Older persons from minority groups are a particularly rapidly growing group; nevertheless, relatively little attention has been paid to minority caregivers. The number of blacks aged 65 and over increased 34 percent between 1970 and 1980 (Watson 1982), and they are the most rapidly growing group of older Americans (Lockerly 1985). In the future, however, the growth of the Hispanic elderly may be the most dramatic because they are the fastest growing ethnic group in America, increasing 61 percent between 1970 and 1980, nearly six times the increase in the general population (Fitzpatrick 1983).

Not only are the numbers of minority elderly increasing rapidly, but their needs for service are greater than those of the majority (Watkins and Gonzales 1982). On most health status indicators, the black and Hispanic elderly are less healthy than the white elderly (Taylor and Taylor 1982). Nonwhites who are 65 and over have almost twice as many bed disability days and restrictive activity days as their white counterparts (Taylor and Taylor 1982). On other measures, the black and Hispanic elderly have less formal education and lower occupational status and are overrepresented in the lower socioeconomic strata of society (McAdoo 1988; Taylor and Taylor 1982).

In general, research findings have shown few differences to exist between the response of black and white family members to caregiving, but Hispanics appear to be more likely to reside in multigenerational households, to receive more direct services, and to have higher filial expectations and interactions than some other ethnic groups (Horowitz 1985). Little is known about how minority caregivers respond to specific stressors, or about whether intervention programs designed to alleviate caregiving stress are effective with minority populations (Gallagher 1985). Therefore, greater attention to the needs of minority family caregivers by social work practitioners and researchers is urgently needed.

Society has responded in many ways to the changing needs of family caregivers. To reduce the costs associated with the premature institutionalization of elderly persons, and to prevent future declines in family caregiving foreshadowed by the previously mentioned demographic trends, the following policy initiates have been considered by governmental agencies: 1) meeting intensive-care needs by increasing the availability of formal home care programs and case management services; 2) subsidizing formal services to supplement family care; 3) providing financial relief in the form of cash payments or expanded tax allowances; 4) compensating for the opportunity cost of foregone employment; and 5) providing respite and educational and counseling programs for caregivers (Doty 1986).

Several factors have come together to shape the current governmental response to the needs of family caregivers. Efforts to expand home health care and intensive case management programs have been impeded by fiscal concerns. Although evaluations of numerous home care demonstration programs have indicated that family members benefit from expanded home care coverage and that such programs do not reduce informal family caregiving, most programs have not proved to be cost-effective in regard to reducing health care costs for frail older persons (Kemper, Applebaum, and Harrigan 1987).

Another factor influencing the governmental response is that the motivations for family caregiving are primarily emotional (Doty 1986). Monetary incentives such as cash grants or tax allowances are unlikely to motivate families to provide home care that they would not otherwise provide. Doty (1986) suggested that public policy should emphasize programs aimed at alleviating the emotional stress associated with caregiving such as support groups, counseling, and respite services. Others have similarly noted that the emotional stresses of caregiving are more difficult for caregivers to cope with than are either the physical or the financial aspects of caregiving (Cantor 1983; George and Gwyther 1986; Horowitz 1985). In recent years, a wide array of religious, civic, and governmental health, mental health, and social service agencies have begun to offer programs of respite, support, and counseling for family caregivers.

The pervasiveness of family caregiving, combined with the high employment rate of females, has also begun to stimulate a response from employers. Realizing that caregiving responsibilities can affect morale and productivity, several large corporations have begun to provide programs of education and support through employee assistance programs, as well as flexible benefit packages that enable employees to continue to fulfill caregiving responsibilities (McCain 1986). These societal responses to the needs of caregivers are encouraging, and they suggest that there will continue to be an expanding role for social work practitioners in advocating for, developing, and implementing caregiver support programs.

## RISKS AND NEEDS OF POPULATION

Because it often involves a long-term commitment, caregiving can tax the resources of the caregiver. In their national survey of caregivers, Stone, Cafferata, and Sangl (1987) found that 20 percent had been providing care for five or more years, that 80 percent of caregivers provided care seven days a week, and that virtually all spousal caregivers reported giving care daily. The average caregiver was found to spend four hours a day providing care to a frail elderly family member.

In reviewing the literature on family caregiving to the elderly, Horowitz (1985) concluded that the specific type of assistance provided by family caregivers was a better predictor of stress than was the actual amount of effort expended. For example, personal care tasks such as toileting, bathing, lifting, and transferring are often thought to be extremely stressful because they require physical stamina from spousal caregivers and an uncomfortable degree of intimacy from adult children.

The type of impairment also makes a difference in the level of stress experienced by a caregiver. Horowitz suggested that it is "the appearance or worsening of mental, rather than physical, symptomology that is most stressful to families" (1985:215). Stress or burden is a function of the degree and kind of care provided, combined with the caregivers' expectations and resources, rather than the absolute amounts of care or impairment (Montgomery 1989). This viewpoint is clinically relevant because it implies that responses to caregiving are individually determined according to how each caregiver appraises his or her unique situation.

Although every caregiving situation is unique, there are nevertheless some universal themes faced by caregivers. The central issue confronting caregivers is their ability to understand, accept, and meet the dependency needs of care receivers (Brody 1985). Dependency needs may be perceived as particularly stressful when they are manifested in ways that are unpleasant or pathological. Dealing with a parent's incontinence, for example, is different from dealing with the incontinence of an infant. Also, it can be difficult to adjust to the shift in the balance of dependence and independence that occurs when a family member cares for someone upon whom they previously depended. The shift can also reactivate unresolved conflicts about dependency needs.

Caregiving also produces awareness both of the final separation from a loved family member and of the caregiver's own potential dependence and death. It is normative for caregivers to experience a partial loss because of the chronic illnesses and the increased frailties that often precede the death of a family member (Gallagher 1985). Although grief cannot be completely resolved until some time after the care receiver dies, social workers can help by validating anticipatory mourning as normative, and by striving to facilitate the caregiver's movement through the grief process.

Ironically, those who are emotionally closest to the care receiver are likely to experience the least stress (Horowitz 1985). Spouses tend to persevere in the caregiving role despite great personal costs and typically give up only when deterioration of their own health prohibits further caregiving. This often precipitates a crisis, sometimes necessitating the immediate response of adult protective services or some other community agency responsible for crisis intervention. In contrast, children appear to have a lower tolerance of the stress of caregiving and are more likely to consider nursing-home placement earlier than spouses (Doty 1986). Furthermore, adult children who are emotionally close to their elderly parents typically experience less stress than their counterparts who lack the same level of affection.

There is considerable evidence suggesting not only that females offer higher levels of assistance and more "hands-on" care than males, but also that they suffer higher levels of stress from caregiving (Horowitz 1985). Middle-aged women are particularly vulnerable to the stresses of caregiving (Brody 1981; Fengler and Goodrich 1979). In addition to the changing nature of their relationship with the care receiver, middle-aged women often have to respond to additional demands from work, family, and spouses. Many make adjustments in their work schedules to fulfill caregiving responsibilities. For example, Stone, Cafferata, and Sangl (1987) found that 9 percent of family caregivers quit their job to provide care, and over half said that the demands of caregiving had required them to reduce their work hours, rearrange their work schedules, or take time off without pay.

Practitioners should also be aware that individuals experience various stages of caregiving adaptation. This is particularly true when care receivers have illnesses such as Alzheimer's disease where there is often a long period of decline involving changes to which the caregiver must continually adjust. For example, accepting the initial diagnosis of Alzheimer's disease requires a different type of adaptation than eventually accepting the care receiver as a greatly changed person who will never again be the same.

Stress from caregiving can have a negative effect on the caregiver's emotional, social, and physical well-being. Symptoms of depression occur in as many as 52 percent of family caregivers (Stanford 1975), and clinical depression has been reported in about 27 percent of all caregivers (Coppel et al. 1985). Caregivers are also frequently troubled by anxiety, anger, interpersonal sensitivity, frustration, excessive guilt, and self-blame. When caregivers are asked what difficulties with caregiving trouble them the most, emotional problems are mentioned twice as frequently as any other type of problem (Toseland, Rossiter and Labrecque 1987b, Toseland, Rossiter and Labrecque 1989c).

The sources of emotional distress for caregivers are complex. Many feel guilty about not doing enough for a frail relative. Others feel guilty about feelings of anger, or about wishing for the care receivers' death. In addition, a general sense of anxiety and worry about the health of the care receiver may permeate the caregiving situation (Hasselkus 1988). Little changes, such as the development of a pain or the refusal to eat a meal, can be frightening, as any small change may be a signal of further decline in the care receivers' health. Spousal caregivers also often worry about their own health condition and whether they will continue to have the stamina to provide care.

Caregiving can contribute to social and interpersonal problems. Leisure and recreational activities are often restricted. Caregivers often feel trapped, isolated, and alone (Farkas 1980). Conflicts with family members about caregiving responsibilities are common (Cantor 1983). When caregivers become overwhelmed with the burden of caregiving, they are more likely to resent siblings who are less involved in caregiving. Adult children may encounter conflicts with their own children or spouse because of the demands that caregiving makes on their time and attention.

Physical problems such as disturbance of normal sleep patterns, problems with appetite, and psychosomatic difficulties are also common among family caregivers (Golodetz et al. 1969). Many caregivers have had little or no prior experience in meeting a care receivers' physical needs and are not aware of the most effective techniques. Lifting, toileting, transporting, and other physical demands of caregiving can be exhausting and may even cause back problems and other injuries.

Caregivers' subjective appraisal of the situation has a great deal to do with the level of stress they experience. Lawton, Brody, and Saperstein, for example, pointed out that "one's perception that caregiving has intruded upon one's social life, activities, work, and so on, is a subjective evaluation of one's life experience which may or may not agree with an externally measured assessment of impact" (1989:62).

Appraisal is a multifaceted process that includes many different types of subjective reactions to caregiving. Although the emphasis in the literature is often on the negative aspects of caregiving, it is likely that positive aspects of caregiving offset, to some degree, the previously mentioned negative aspects. For example, a 46-year-old daughter caring for her 72-year-old mother with terminal cancer explored with a social worker how she could use caregiving as an opportunity to communicate deep love to her mother, to express her religious values openly, and to serve as a role model for her teenage children. This positive focus of the work she and the practitioner did together enabled the caregiver to appraise some aspects of the situation, such as changing the dressing on an extremely unpleasant cancerous sore, as a means of demonstrating her love and concern.

A comprehensive review of studies of support groups for caregivers (Toseland and Rossiter 1989) revealed that six categories of needs are most frequently the focus of caregivers' attention: 1) understanding the elderly relative for whom they are caring; 2) making better use of informal and formal social supports; 3) improving their coping abilities; 4) taking better care of themselves by balancing the needs of others with their own needs; 5) improving problem relationships; and 6) improving home care and behavior management skills.

Gaining information about the processes of aging and the progression of specific ailments can sometimes help caregivers to improve their relationship with the frail relative for whom they are caring. Older people who need care are often distressed by their disabilities. Fears and frustrations brought about by increased dependence can evoke anxiety and anger, which are vented on the nearest available person, frequently the caregiver. When caregivers learn more about what the care receiver is going through both physically and emotionally, they often become more tolerant of the care receivers' behavior and more likely to attribute the care receivers' behavior to the situation rather than to deliberate malice (Smith and Sperbeck 1980). They also become less likely to take the care receivers' emotional outbursts and negative interactions personally and are able, therefore, to react with increased empathy and understanding. Also, understanding disease processes helps caregivers to anticipate and plan for future caregiving demands.

Sometimes, caregivers become overwhelmed because they do not get the help they need to continue caregiving. An important social work task is to help caregivers accurately assess the need for assistance and to encourage them to ask for and utilize any additional help that may be required. Some caregivers who need more assistance from relatives but are reluctant to ask because of past experiences can be encouraged to approach family members in new ways. For example, rather than making a vague request for help, caregivers can be encouraged to ask particular relatives to take on specific tasks for clearly delineated, regularly scheduled time periods.

Caregivers may also need to learn how to use formal sources of support more effectively. It has been argued that case management is the most important task of family caregivers (Lowy 1985), but caregivers are often unaware of important community resources or of whether their frail relatives are eligible to receive particular services. A demonstration project by Seltzer, Ivry, and Litchfield (1987) revealed that family members can be helped to increase their responsibility for the case management of services for frail elderly relatives.

Some caregivers need help to develop more effective coping strategies. It is known that a variety of different coping strategies are used by family caregivers (Quayhagen and Quayhagen 1988), and that coping strategies are not equally effective. For example, several investigators have found that passivity, fantasizing, self-blame, and escape–avoidance coping strategies are associated with health and mental health problems and that coping strategies such as problem solving, information seeking, and logical analysis are associated with emotional and physical well-being (Toseland and Smith 1989; Toseland, Smith, and Tobin 1989; Haley et al. 1987; Pratt et al. 1985; Quayhagen and Quayhagen 1988; Stephens et al. 1988).

Social workers should be aware that certain caregivers may favor particular coping strategies even though these may not be the most effective ones they could use. Young female caregivers, for example, tend to use escape–avoidance and distancing techniques more frequently than other caregivers, whereas spouses are more likely than other caregivers to become enmeshed in the caregiving role (Stephens et al. 1988; Johnson and Catalano 1983). When it is tailored to the needs of different caregivers, coping-skills training can be helpful in reducing stress and improving caregivers' emotional and physical well-being (Toseland et al. 1989b; Toseland and Smith in press).

Some caregivers also need to learn to take better care of themselves, and to balance their own needs with the needs of others. Caregivers frequently neglect their own needs to fulfill their caregiving, family, and work responsibilities. It can be helpful to remind caregivers of the importance of their own health and well-being, to themselves and to all those who depend upon them. Caregivers should be encouraged to set aside regularly scheduled time for themselves so that they can maintain their physical stamina and have some time to pursue social and recreational activities. Sometimes, this means helping caregivers to set new limits by informing the care receiver and other relatives that they will not be available for caregiving activities at certain times of the day. In one situation, for example, the social worker helped a caregiver who said, "I'm at the end of my rope" to tell her mother that the mother could no longer call her at work an average of six to ten times a day. The caregiver decided to limit her mother to one phone call, during the lunch hour. The social worker then proceeded to provide guidance, advice, and assistance with alternative caregiving arrangements. With the social worker's help, the caregiver was able to enroll her mother in a meals-on-wheels program and a telephone reassurance program that provided some beneficial alternative attention. Also, the caregiver decided to set aside two two-hour blocks of time each week to go swimming with a neighbor. A young women identified through the pastor of a local church was hired to watch her mother during these times. When they were visited six month later, both the caregiver and the care receiver appeared to be very satisfied with the new arrangements.

Some caregivers also need help in improving their home care and behavior management skills. Social workers can help by suggesting ways that the home environment can be better adapted to persons with physical or cognitive impairments. Telephones with large numerals, for example, can aid the vision-impaired, amplifiers connected to telephones can make telephoning easier for the hearing-impaired, and rearranging the household to minimize the need to climb stairs can make life easier for the physically impaired.

Social workers can also help by making referrals to community health nurses and other health care professionals to help caregivers learn about specific home care techniques. For example, there are right and wrong ways of lifting a bedridden person, but some caregivers do not know how to do so without risking injury to themselves or to their frail relative.

Because of organic brain syndromes and other physical and psychological problems, family caregivers can also benefit from training in behavior management skills (Haley 1983; Pinkston, Linsk, and Young 1988). For example, a 71-year-old male caregiver was troubled by interference, whenever he prepared meals, from his 68-year-old wife who had Alzheimer's disease. Although her intention was to be helpful and to maintain a sense of her former identity as a homemaker, her interference was a great source of stress for her husband. There was also the possibility that she would accidentally burn or cut herself. Her husband was taught how to engage her in, and praise her for, more acceptable behavior, and the disruptive behavior declined dramatically.

## PROGRAMS AND SOCIAL WORK SERVICES

For many years, the primary social work programmatic reponse to the needs of family caregivers was to provide support directly to frail older persons (see, for example, Blenkner et al. 1974). When family caregivers were actively involved in the care of a frail older person, they were not ignored, but they were rarely recognized as the target of intervention. Over the years, an increasing awareness of the importance of family caregivers has led to the development of programs targeted specifically at them. The current programmatic response, therefore, consists both of programs for frail elderly persons that indirectly benefit family caregivers, and of programs specifically designed to benefit family caregivers directly.

Many different programs have been developed to support family caregivers directly, and these can be categorized into 1) respite programs; 2) support group progams; 3) individual and family counseling programs; and 4) specialized educational and training programs. The programs are sponsored by a broad mix of public, voluntary, and private social service providers, and they may be delivered by paraprofessionals or professionals.

*Respite programs* are designed to provide periodic relief to family caregivers. Time off from the unrelenting demands of caregiving are believed to be directly therapeutic for the caregiver, and indirectly therapeutic for the care receiver (Lawton, Brody, and Saperstein 1989). However, relatively little is actually known about the effectiveness of respite services. In one of the few available studies, respite services produced caregiver satisfaction and enabled care receivers to remain in the community longer, but they were ineffective in reducing the caregivers' burdens or in improving the caregivers' mental health (Lawton, Brody, and Saperstein 1989). Also, there is some question about how receptive family caregivers are to using respite services (Montgomery and Borgota 1989), and whether the effectiveness of respite programs is sufficient to warrant government expenditures (Callahan 1989).

There are many types of respite programs, including temporary inpatient placement in residential facilities, nursing homes, or hospitals; in-home respite by paid homemakers or home health aides; and adult day care and adult day health programs (Gallagher 1985; Gallagher, Lovitt, and Zeiss 1989). Most of these programs do not provide psychotherapeutic intervention for the family member or the patient. Instead, they provide personal care for a fixed period of time, usually not exceeding a few weeks.

Different kinds of respite programs may be used in combination for various purposes, depending on the needs manifested in a particular situation. For example, a 52-year-old single daughter who lived alone with her frail 78-year-old mother paid homemakers to care for her parent while she was at work. The caregiver felt that this arrangement helped her to support herself and to get some relief from what she described as an "extremely close, sometimes too close, relationship with my mother." Twice a year, the daughter also arranged for in-patient respite care at a local nursing home so that she could enjoy vacations away from her job and her caregiving responsibilities.

There are also many different types of *support group programs* for family caregivers. Most mix education, discussion, and social activities in a warm, empathic atmosphere that emphasizes mutual sharing and mutual help, but some are more psychoeducationally oriented, focusing on the acquisition of specific problem-solving and coping skills. Groups may be short-term or long-term and may have closed or open membership policies. Support groups can prevent and alleviate stress in many ways: 1) providing caregivers with a respite from caregiving; 2) reducing isolation and loneliness; 3) encouraging the ventilation of pent-up emotions and the sharing of feelings and experiences; 4) validating, universalizing, and normalizing caregivers' experiences; 5) instilling hope and affirming the importance of the caregivers' role; 6) educating caregivers about the aging process, the effects of chronic disabilities, and community resources; 7) teaching effective problem-solving and coping strategies; and 8) helping caregivers to idenfify, develop, and implement effective action plans to resolve pressing problems related to caregiving (Toseland and Rossiter 1989; Toseland et al. in press b).

The clinical literature, which is largely based on case studies of individual groups, indicates that family caregivers find participation in support groups highly satisfying (Toseland and Rossiter 1989). Findings about other beneficial effects of groups are somewhat more equivocal, but recent studies that have utilized larger sample sizes and more rigorous research designs have indicated that groups can improve caregivers' mental and physical well-being, increase their knowledge of community resources and the size of their informal support networks, and alleviate pressing problems associated with caregiving (see, for example, Green and Monahan 1987; Montgomery and Borgotta 1989; Haley, Brown, and Levine 1987; Zarit, Anthony, and Boutselis 1987; Toseland et al. 1989a, 1989b, 1989c; Toseland in press).

There is much less information available about *individual and family-oriented counseling programs* for caregivers, perhaps because family caregivers often seek help through the regular, scheduled counseling programs of family service and community mental health agencies, where their problems are defined not as family care per se but as marital, family, or mental health problems.

The few studies of individual counseling programs for caregivers have yielded promising results. For example, Gallagher and her colleagues (Gallagher and Czirr 1984; Gallagher, Lovett, and Zerss 1989) found that individual therapy reduced depression among caregivers and helped them cope with anticipatory grief over the impending loss of a frail elderly caregiver. Toseland and Smith (1989) found that short-term individual counseling was effective in decreasing symptoms of psychological distress and in increasing feelings of competence and well-being. However, Zarit, Anthony, and Boutselis (1987) found that a program of individual and family counseling was no more effective than no treatment in reducing the burden and psychological problems associated with caregiving.

There is little doubt that caregiving is associated with increased family conflict and with heightened concerns and anxieties about neglecting other family members (see, for example, Horowitz 1985). However, despite the extensive attention that has been given to the impact of caregiving on marital and family relationships, the previously cited study by Zarit, Anthony, and Boutselis (1989) is the only one that has examined the benefits of family therapy for caregivers, and that study used "family meetings" only as a part of an individual counseling program. Most of the reports of family counseling for caregivers, therefore, are based on accumulated clinical practice experience and case examples. These sources indicate that when family members are willing to participate, family therapy can be a particularly effective modality for improving communication and reducing interpersonal conflict, for developing coordinated care plans, and for resolving specific problems that arise as the caregiving situation develops and evolves over time (see, for example, Lowy 1985; Carter and McGoldrick 1980; Herr and Weakland 1979).

Many *specialized education and training programs* have also been developed for family caregivers. Some are one-session community forums sponsored by religious, civic, and governmental agencies where service providers describe the available community programs and services, and caregivers are encouraged to ask questions and to find out how to apply for service. These programs particularly reach out to caregivers who might not otherwise learn about the programs and services available to help them care for a frail relative. Other educational programs provide weekly or monthly seminars that focus on different topics related to caregiving (see, for example, Reever 1984; Gray 1983). These programs are particularly appealing to caregivers who want to learn more about the effects of specific health problems, and about specific services and resources.

Specialized training programs have also been developed for family caregivers. The previously mentioned study by Seltzer, Ivry, and Litchfield (1987), for example, demonstrated that family caregivers can be trained to perform case management tasks on behalf of their elderly relatives. In an alternative approach, Pinkston, Linsk, and Young (1988) successfully trained caregivers to use operant learning principles to improve targeted behavior problems of care receivers. These programs are particularly exemplary because they demonstrate that a partnership can be forged between social workers and family caregivers, with social workers helping caregivers to maximize their abilities to provide high-quality care to frail family members.

The emotional commitment that family caregivers have to their frail elderly relatives means that any social service program that benefits frail older people has the potential to benefit family caregivers. In fact, some programs designed for frail older persons have been found to have at least as profound an effect on family caregivers as they have had on frail older persons (Kemper, Applebaum, and Harrigan 1987). Therefore, to be maximally effective when working with family caregivers, social workers should be familiar with all the community programs and services that are available for the elderly.

In most localities, the county department of aging, the area agency on aging, or the local community-planning agency have an up-to-date list of all the services that are available for older persons. Because frail older persons have most of the same needs as other older people, a general list of programs and services for older persons is indispensable for effective practice. It is usually best to begin with an existing directory of community services, focusing on program descriptions, contact persons, and eligibility requirements for the kinds of programs and services that are particularly likely to be helpful to frail older persons. In some communities, resource guides may have to be updated or expanded. They should include services for older persons in the following areas: 1) financial; 2) housing; 3) food; 4) day care; 5) home care; 6) health and mental health care; 7) residential and skilled nursing care; 8) social, recreational, and educational programs; 9) information and referral; 10) counseling; 11) employment; and 12) legal programs.

Social workers find that a combination of programs and services are often needed to effectively serve frail older persons and family caregivers. For example, a 52-year-old married daughter was willing and able to function as case manager for her 79-year-old father who lived by himself. After a careful assessment of the needs of the care receiver and the family member, the social worker helped them to arrange for meals on wheels, a part-time home health aide, and a twenty-four-hour medical emergency notification system made available by a local hospital. Also, a home energy assistance program, a reverse mortgage program, and a low-cost home repair program were all used to ensure that the elderly gentlemen would be able to remain in the home where he had lived for the past forty years.

## DIFFERENTIAL CLINICAL ASSESSMENTS AND INTERVENTIONS

Social work practice with family caregivers and their frail elders is similar to practice with other groups in that it is necessary to engage the client, to establish a therapeutic relationship, to assess needs, and to plan, implement, and monitor beneficial interventions. However, specific adaptations in these intervention processes are needed when working with family caregivers. Two sources are particularly useful for making these adaptations. Lazarus and Folkman's (1984) work on stress and coping provides a helpful theoretical orientation for practice with family caregivers. The life model's focus on adapatation to life transition problems such as family caregiving, its emphasis on people in the context of their social and physical environments, and its compatibility with a stress and coping theoretical orientation make it a particularly useful guide for practice with family caregivers (Germain and Gitterman 1980). Together, these two sources, as well as extensive clinical experience with family caregiveers, form the basis for the adaptations for practice with family caregivers described here.

Making initial contact with caregivers can be more difficult than with some other client groups. Caregivers tend to be reluctant to ask for help. Most believe that it is their filial responsibility to provide care, and that relinquishing the responsibility would be like abandoning the person for whom they are caring. Because of their perceived self-competence, and because many have never had to ask for help before, pride may also be an obstacle. The anticipation or actual experience of resistance or refusal of "outside help" by the frail older person, as well as the bewildering complexity of the social service and health care system, can present obstacles even for highly motivated caregivers.

Some active outreach efforts, which may be needed to engage family caregivers, are feature newspaper stories; personal or telephone contact with social service, health care, and religious organizations that frequently come into contact with frail older persons; public service announcements on radio and television; appearances on local radio and television programs; and educational forums sponsored by community agencies. Special recruitment efforts may be needed for Hispanic, Afro-American, and Asian minorities, who do not respond well to the recruitment methods just described (Toseland and Rossiter 1989). Extensive personal contact with religious and civic leaders, as well as networking with community organizations trusted in minority communities, is a more effective approach (Garcia-Preto 1982; Roberts 1987).

In practice with family caregivers, engagement may mean reaching out beyond the family caregiver. In some situations, caregivers clearly seek help only for themselves. They want to learn to cope more effectively and do not want the care receiver, or other family members, involved. In such situations, the caregivers' wishes should be respected. But when resistance is not a problem, it can be useful to take a broader perspective. Although the perceptions of the caregiver are extremely important, a direct assesssment of the care receiver, as well as one or more family meetings, can give the social worker a more complete understanding of the situation. The resulting information may also change the focus of the work. For example, instead of focusing exclusively on the caregiver, a family assessment may lead to additional service provision to the care receiver, or to other family members.

Once initial contact has been made, the worker should act as a supporter and an enabler. As a supporter, the social worker listens empathically to the caregivers' pent-up feelings and emotions. Many caregivers have not had the opportunity to express their feelings and welcome the opportunity. The worker validates and affirms the caregivers' experiences, applauding efforts by caregivers to take better care of themselves and to view their caregiving efforts more positively. As an enabler, the social worker provides hope and encouragement, helping caregivers to mobilize their coping resources and their motivation, so that they can begin the process of working on troubling problems and concerns.

There are two important characteristics of family caregivers that social workers should be aware of when conducting assessment and intervention planning. First, caregivers' are often reluctant to admit to difficulties, although they may be nearly overwhelmed by them. Instead of describing their emotional reactions, they tend to talk extensively about the care receiver and the circumstances surrounding the caregiving situation. They fear that their emotional reactions may be seen as complaining or uncaring. It is also characteristic of family caregivers to prefer talking about the care receiver and other family members rather than about their own role in the situation. To encourage caregivers to acknowledge and accept their own thoughts, feelings, and actions in the caregiving situation, attentive, focused, and empathic listening is essential.

To familiarize the social worker with the development and evolution of the caregiving situation, it is helpfuul to begin assessments by taking a fairly detailed history of family relationships and interactions. Once this is completed, the worker assesses the current physical, psychological, and social functioning of the caregiver and the care receiver, as well as the environment context in which care is provided.

Because of the importance of the physical capacities and limitations of both the caregiver and the care receiver, social workers need to assess this area carefully. If there are unmet health care needs, these should be addressed immediately. It may be helpful to obtain medical records, or to conduct a thorough assessment of the mental and physical health status of the care receiver. For a detailed discussion of assessment techniques for the frail elderly, see Kane (1985) or Kane and Kane (1981).

In many health care settings, the social worker may be expected to focus on the psychological, social, and environmental needs of caregivers. Information about the course of illnesses, the effects of medications, the physical abilities of the caregiver and the care receiver, and any other health problems and needs may be provided by doctors, nurses, and physical therapists. When a team approach is used, the social worker is also often called upon to coordinate input from other disciplines, developing a comprehensive helping plan based on a holistic view of the caregiver and the care receiver.

In the psychological realm, the worker assesses the caregivers' emotional reaction to the caregiving situation and their commonly used coping strategies. There is some evidence to suggest that individual counseling is more effective than group counseling in helping caregivers to improve coping skills in dealing with depression, anxiety, and other commonly experienced psychiatric symptoms (Toseland et al. 1989b; Toseland and Smith in press). Individual and group defenses against the expression of painful and highly personal emotions tend to prevent their expression in caregiver support groups (Schmidt and Keyes 1985; Toseland et al 1989, b, c).

In the social realm, assessment and intervention planning should focus on the quality of the relationship between the caregiver and the care receiver, on the impact of caregiving on family life, and on the adequacy of social supports for the caregiver and the care receiver.

Support groups should be considered the modality of choice when planning interventions for caregivers experiencing mild and moderate social and interpersonal problems (Toseland et al. 1989b). Because they put caregivers in contact with others experiencing similar problems and concerns, support groups are particularly useful in reducing feelings of loneliness and isolation, and in increasing social support (Gallagher et al. in press; Green and Monahan 1987; Toseland 1989). They are also particularly effective in helping caregivers to get feedback and suggestions about how to handle difficult interpersonal interactions.

For caregivers experiencing severe social and interpersonal problems, individual counseling should be considered. Severe social or interpersonal problems may make it difficult for a caregiver to benefit from participation in a support group. Also, the privacy of individual counseling encourages caregivers to discuss severe difficulties in marital relationships, longstanding emotionally charged interpersonal conflicts with family members, and other severe social problems that are not as likely to be shared in a support group (Toseland and Smith 1989; Toseland, Smith, & Tobin 1989).

The social worker should also carefully appraise the caregivers' environmental problems. Features of the physical environment are particularly important. Walkers, lifts, ramps, handrails, and other special modifications to the physical environment can make providing care easier and can contribute to the physical well-being of both the caregiver and the care receiver.

It is also important to assess whether caregivers are making use of the available community-based services. Sometimes, professional social workers forget how confusing the patchwork network of community services is for clients. One caregiver stated it well when she said, "I've been a high school math teacher for twenty-five years. I have a master's degree. I believe I am a fairly intelligent person. Do you know it took me nearly six months and endless phone calls to figure out how to get my mother the help she needed? Nobody seemed to know what anybody else was doing, and what's worse, a number of people gave me the wrong information. It was one of the most frustrating experiences I've ever had." Educational programs and resource guides that inform caregivers about available community services, the mutual sharing of information about community resources and services that takes place in a support group, and individual consultation, information, and referral can all be effective means of helping caregivers to make effective use of the available community services and resources. But because caregivers are often reluctant to reach out for services, social workers must follow up, making sure that caregivers receive the services they need. Also, when needed community services are unavailable, social workers should spend at least a portion of their time advocating for these services.

When intervening with family caregivers, social workers can act as consultants, coordinators, or case managers. Social workers adopt the consultant role in situations where the caregiver is functioning relatively well, has the necessary capacities and abilities to provide care, and desires only limited assistance. Before assuming a consultant role, social workers assess whether or not they can rely on the client to acknowledge a need and to request appropriate help. Ethical issues can arise when the worker's assessment suggests that the family caregiver needs more help than has been requested. In this situation, a general practice principal is that unless a caregivers or care receivers are in jeopardy of endangering themselves or some other third party, their request for autonomy should be respected.

When assuming a consultant role, the worker recognizes and acknowledges the caregivers' competency and expertise. The worker relies heavily on the caregivers' input during assessment and intervention planning and assumes that the caregiver will take day-to-day responsibility for the implementation and monitoring of any intervention plan that is developed. Generally, an intensive period of consultation is followed by occasional contact to ensure that the caregiver will be able to implement the agreed-upon plan of action. Workers may also respond on an "as-needed basis" to specific requests for information, advice, or other help.

As a consultant, the social worker may be asked to provide guidance on how to handle a wide variety of problems and concerns. Some of the most frequent are 1) nursing-home placement; 2) adjustments in living status, such as when a frail older person moves in with the caregiver; 3) behavioral and emotional problems; 4) resistance to some aspect of care that the caregiver believes to be in the best interests of the care receiver; 5) alcoholism; and 6) help in dealing with mental or physical impairments such as those arising from Alzheimer's disease (Tonti and Silverstone 1985).

As coordinators, social workers take on greater responsibility for implementing and monitoring intervention plans. The social worker may provide needed individual, family, or group counseling services directly to the caregiver or may see to it that these services are delivered in a timely and well-planned fashion. By being an enabler, a broker, and an advocate, the worker also helps the caregiver to arrange for needed services for the care receiver.

Once services are in place, the worker maintains regular contact with the caregiver. The caregiver is encouraged to take responsibility for the day-to-day implementation of the intervention plan. The worker's role is to ensure that any ongoing difficulties in implementing the plan will be resolved in a timely fashion, and to help the caregiver with needs that arise as care continues.

The case management role is assumed when social workers' assessments reveal that caregivers are unable, or unwilling, to fulfill the duties and responsibilities necessary to the care of a frail older family member. As a case manager, the worker involves the caregiver and the care receiver to whatever extent is possible in the development and implementation of an intervention plan. Generally, however, the worker helps the caregiver by removing some, or all, of the responsibility for the day-to-day care of the frail relative.

As a case manager, the worker 1) completes a comprehensive assessment of the needs of the caregiver and the care receiver without relying solely on information provided by the caregiver; 2) develops a comprehensive intervention plan that takes into consideration the needs of both the caregiver and the care receiver; 3) implements the plan by providing and coordinating the provision of health care and social services to meet the needs of the caregiver and the care receiver; and 4) maintains frequent and regular contact to monitor the day-to-day implementation of the plan and to ensure that the caregiver and the care receiver will continue to receive the appropriate services (Steinberg 1985; Steinberg and Carter 1983; Johnson and Rubin 1983).

In actual practice, social workers may be expected to perform all three roles. A typical case mix may require social workers to serve as consultants to some caregivers, and to provide case coordination and case management services for others. Also, a social worker may be called upon to perform multiple roles with the same caregiver. For example, a caregiver may need only consultation to resolve a particular concern but may need help with coordination to resolve other concerns. Also, the changing health status of the caregiver or the care receiver may necessitate a change in the social workers' role, such as moving from case coordination to case management. The choice of roles is guided by the wishes and desires of the caregiver and the care receiver, and by a careful assessment of the situation. The worker guards against the tendency to take over too much responsibility, thereby robbing the caregiver and the care receiver of their autonomy, and promoting the atrophy of their existing coping skills and resources.

## CASE ILLUSTRATION

Work with Mrs. Joan Dicks, age 52, the oldest of the two daughters and one son, illustrates some of the clinical social work practice processes that take place when working with family caregivers. A social worker at a family service agency, Mr. Dixon, first encountered Mrs. Dicks when she requested couple counseling, complaining primarily of marital problems that caused arguments leading to prolonged periods of silence, sleeplessness, lack of appetite, moodiness, heightened irritability, and tearfulness. During the intake interview, Mrs. Dicks also mentioned problems with her son, her sister, and her self-esteem. During the course of twelve individual and couple counseling sessions, Mr. Dixon helped Mrs. Dicks and her husband to make significant improvements in their marital relationship. Near the end of these sessions, the following interaction took place:

MRS. DICKS: Things are going really well with Ted [her husband] and me, but there's never any peace. Now I'm getting concerned about my mother and father. My dad is 77, and in the last few years, there's been a reversal in their roles. My mom has hardening of the arteries in her brain—at least, that's what her doctor says—and my dad has had to spend more and more time taking care of her. She can be really forgetful. *(Silence.)* She used to take care of him.

MR. DIXON. It's sad to see your parents decline, isn't it?

MRS. DICKS. Yeah. It's not only that. My dad has heart disease and his cardiologist just told him he's got to take it real easy. Caring for her is a big strain on him.

MR. DIXON. Well, I'm sorry your husband couldn't come today, but you are doing really well together. *(Mrs. Dicks nods.)* It gives us an opportunity to talk about your parents and what to do about them.

Already familiar with her psychosocial development from the previous work he had done with her and her husband, the worker encouraged Mrs. Dicks to talk about her current relationship with her parents, and about their abilities and disabilities. Mr. Dixon learned that Mrs. Dicks' relationship with her parents was much closer than her sister's relationship, and that she, rather than her sister, was called on by her parents when they needed assistance. He also learned that she anticipated being the primary caregiver when her father could no longer take care of her mother, and that a nursing home placement was not an option she would consider.

MR. DIXON. It sounds as if your mother's condition is worsening and you're worried because you don't know what the future will hold. You mentioned a family physician, but have you ever had your mother checked by a specialist who might be able to give you a clearer picture of what to expect in the future?

MRS. DICKS. No, Mom is very attached to her doctor. She's been going to him since I was a little kid, at least forty years, probably longer. He's almost as old as she is!

MR. DIXON. Well, you have to respect her wishes. It's too bad because there's a program in Troy for the assessment of individuals who have health problems—forgetfulness and confusion—like your mom's. It's staffed by an excellent geriatrician.

MRS. DICKS. I don't think Mom or Dad would go for that, but I'll ask. I wonder if there's a place I could go to learn more about my mother's condition.

MR. DIXON. Yes, as a matter of fact, there's an Alzheimer's disease support group that meets at St. Peter's Hospital. I think it's sponsored by the Alzheimer's Disease and Related Disorders Association, a self-help-oriented organization. Don't be put off by the name. It's really there to help anyone caring for a forgetful or confused older person; it doesn't matter whether or not your mom has Alzheimer's disease. I've heard really good things about it. I've referred a few people in the past couple of years, and they've all said how satisfied they were with the information and the support they received.

MRS. DICKS. What do they do, and when do they meet?

MR. DIXON. Let me look *(looking through a file box filled with cards with information about community agencies).* The president of the chapter is Mrs. Lot. You can contact her by calling 737-4445. I'll write that down for you. They have their meetings once a month in the main conference hall at St. Peter's, seven to nine in the evenings on Thursday. There's no charge. As for what they do, the format is that they have a speaker on a selected topic each month, and then there is a discussion. For example, they might invite a nurse to talk about home care techniques and resources, a social worker to talk about how to cope with stress, or a legal expert to talk about guardianships, wills, and so forth. I think a friend of mine spoke on nursing-home placement a couple of months ago.

MRS. DICKS. Sounds good. I'm free on Thursday evenings. I'll try it.

The first part of the record illustrates that individuals may seek service for other concerns and then gradually bring up problems related to family caregiving. It also reveals that by playing a consultant role, the worker recognized the caregiver's competence. He did not push the notion of a medical consultation, knowing that it would meet with resistance. Instead, he followed the client's lead, referring her to a resource targeted at caregivers. The transcript also illustrates the important connection between professional social workers and self-help organizations. The worker was not hesitant to refer the client to the self-help support group, and he gave it an enthusiastic recommendation.

After one additional session that both Mr. and Mrs. Dicks attended, Mr. Dixon and Mr. and Mrs. Dicks mutually decided to end their work together. Mr. Dixon did not see Mrs. Dicks again for almost two years; then, one day, he received a phone call from her, asking if she could see him again. When she came in, she explained that she and her husband were continuing to do much better together:

MRS. DICKS. Things are much better between us. I'm here because of my parents.

MR. DIXON. Your parents? Oh, yes. I recall. We talked about them briefly at the end of our sessions together, and you decided to go to the Alzheimer's support group at St. Peter's. How did that go?

MRS. DICKS. Well—I didn't go. I was going to call, but I'm really not sure if my mother has Alzheimer's disease. I remember you said it would be OK for me to go anyway, but I felt funny.

Had the practitioner followed up on the referral by suggesting that he and Mrs. Dicks talk about it by telephone a few weeks after their last session together, he might have prevented the failure of the referral. As the record continues, the interdependence of family members and the effects of caring for an increasingly frail older relative are revealed:

MR. DIXON. Well, why don't you tell me about what's going on?

MRS. DICKS. Since I saw you last, Mom has got worse. She is really forgetful. Sometimes, she can't remember where things are. She forgets people's names, neighbors she's known all her life. Recently, she left the stove on, and my father is afraid that she's going to burn the house down.

MR. DIXON. How is he doing?

MRS. DICKS. Well, that's just it. He's not doing well at all. His heart problems, combined with the arthritis in his hips and knees, make it difficult for him to keep up with the house, and with Mom. His cardiologist has told him he's a good candidate for bypass surgery, but Dad is avoiding that.

MR. DIXON. And you?

MRS. DICKS. I'm really worried about it. My dad can't handle the stress. My mom is a real handful. I'm over there constantly now, and I just don't know what to do. I've got a big place to care for myself—you remember my husband's job means he's out of town all the time—and my son is just returning from the army.

MR. DIXON. Oh yes, the one that was giving both of you all that trouble.

MRS. DICKS. Yeah, and I don't think the army made it any better. I think he will still be using drugs, and I just don't want him in my house under those conditions!

It was clear that Mrs. Dicks was feeling somewhat overwhelmed. Mr. Dixon and Mrs. Dicks continued to discuss the situation, and the topic of her sister and brother came up:

MR. DIXON. Yes, we'll have to talk about what you're going to do with him [the son], but first, should we focus on your parents? Sounds like you're really upset about them.

MRS. DICKS. Yes, my son won't be home from Germany for almost three months.

MR. DIXON. Good. Well, let's talk about what else I should know about the situation with your parents. How about your siblings?

MRS. DICKS. You mean Jean and Bob?

MR. DIXON. Yup.

MRS. DICKS. They're concerned about it, too, but that really is a problem, too.

MR. DIXON. A problem, too?

MRS. DICKS. Well, I've always been my parents' favorite, and Jean is resentful. I can understand that. They don't treat her right. But sometimes, her reactions are out of line. She takes it out on me. And Bob just isn't around much. He says he wants to help, but he never seems to come through. He's always got an excuse. So I get stuck with all of it. Not that I mind—I want to take care of my parents—but it's hard, especially now with my mother. I was going to go to the Alzheimer's meeting as you suggested, but I couldn't find the number, and I thought I'd give you a call.

This part of the transcript illustrates some of the complexities of the situation. Mrs. Dicks was struggling not only with how best to provide care for her frail elderly parents, but also with problems regarding her sister, her son, and her own emotional response to the situation. The worker did an effective job of helping to clarify what they would work on first. He also drew the client into the work by asking her to make a decision about what they should focus on first.

MR. DIXON. My father is frail, so I understand some of what you're going through. It's going to require a lot of work on your part, but if you follow through, I think you will feel less stressed than you do now.

MRS. DICKS. I know I'm going to have to do something. Even if they [her parents] are not agreeable to it.

Mr. Dixon and Mrs. Dicks spent the remainder of the session and the next session discussing the situation in depth, exploring options and alternative plans of action. At one point, Mr. Dixon suggested a plan of action that included a home visit by another agency.

MR. DIXON. Since you've told me that you don't have confidence in your mom's physician, and you really need some help in figuring out how best to help her, I suggest that you call Mrs. Eaton at the Capital District Psychiatric Center, and she will do a home visit. If she feels it is warranted, she can have your mother seen by the nurse or the doctor in the outpatient geriatric unit. They will help you get an accurate diagnosis of your mom's condition and will refer you to the appropriate resources. They also have a day treatment program.

MRS. DICKS. Day treatment?

MR. DIXON. Yes, a program for older people with memory impairments. Five days a week. They serve lunch, and there's a van service to transport all those who attend. *(Pause.)* Would you like me to call Mrs. Eaton right now?

MRS. DICKS. Yes. Oh, on second thought, let me tell Mom and Dad first. I'll tell them tonight and call myself tomorrow. Can I have her number.

MR. DIXON. Sure. But do you feel comfortable with this?

MRS. DICKS. Well, something has to be done. I'll definitely call.

MR. DIXON. I've met Mrs. Eaton on several occasions. She's really a lovely person. Really warm. She has a special gift when it comes to working with older people.

MRS. DICKS. I sure hope Mom doesn't do anything too crazy. She can really be nasty with strangers.

MR. DIXON. Mrs. Eaton is used to that, but let her know anyway. OK?

MRS. DICKS. Yes. I definitely have to do something.

MR. DIXON. It's almost time for us to stop. I'm looking forward to hearing how you make out. But before we end, I wanted to clarify how we will proceed. Let's let Mrs. Eaton help you with the plans for caring for your mom and dad. There are all kinds of options, like home health care and day care, and I bet she'll have some good ideas about home safety and your mom's care. I think it might be best for us to focus on how you're feeling about it all, and also about your relationship with your sister and your parents. OK?

MRS. DICKS. That would be fine. Maybe I'll try to have my sister come in with me. Would that be OK?

MR. DIXON. Sure.

MRS. DICKS. See you next week, and I'll let you know what happens when I call.

Mr. Dixon and Mrs. Dicks met the following week. She informed him that she had called Mrs. Eaton, who had made an appointment to come out to see her and her parents later in the week. She also told Mr. Dixon that she had invited her sister to come to the session, but that she had refused. However, she said that her sister was interested in what she and Mr. Dixon had talked about and would like to get together with her over "a cup of coffee to discuss it." Mrs. Dicks viewed this reaction quite positively, as she had been wanting an opportunity to have a "heart-to-heart talk" with her sister.

During the remainder of this session and six subsequent sessions, Mrs. Dicks and Mr. Dixon followed the plan they had agreed upon during the prior session, focusing primarily on Mrs. Dicks' relationship with her sister and her emotional reaction to the caregiving situation. The sessions also provided an opportunity to help Mrs. Dicks with her relationship with her son and provided Mr. Dixon with an opportunity to monitor the delivery of services to Mrs. Dicks' parents. At one point, when Mrs. Dicks complained that she was not being kept informed about her mother's enrollment in the day treatment program, Mr. Dixon called Mrs. Eaton and asked her to clarify the matter with Mrs. Dicks. This telephone contact proved helpful, because Mr. Dixon and Mrs. Eaton discussed their independent assessments and intervention goals and coordinated some of their efforts. During their last weekly meeting together, the following interaction took place between Mr. Dixon and Mrs. Dicks:

MRS. DICKS. I'm going to miss our sessions. You've really been helpful. When I opened up to my sister—I mean, when we both really talked about how we felt—it seemed we grew closer. Things are still not great between us, but they're much better. Mrs. Eaton's suggestion about asking my sister and brother to help out during specific times helped, too. My sister is happy to take care of my mother Saturday mornings, and my mother seems to be a little nicer to my sister these days. Between that and my brother's getting more involved—he comes over on Sundays now quite regularly—and I have more time, especially on the weekends when Ted is home, and I need it.

MR. DIXON. Wonderful!

MRS. DICKS. That program [day treatment] has been really good, too. My mom goes three times a week, and that gives Dad a real break. Also, I noticed she seems to be a little more with it. They do memory exercises and all. *(Pause.)* And I've been able to go back to that part-time bookkeeping job I had. I go two of the days my mom is at the program.

MR. DIXON. Good. Yes, they really have a good program. With your son coming home and the situation with your parents subject to change at any time, I think we should stay in contact, at least for the time being. How about planning to meet monthly, at least for a while, and so we can see how things continue to go?

MR. DICKS. That's fine. I also think I'm going to go to that support group you mentioned before. I have the number right here *(pointing to her handbag)*.

Mr. Dixon and Mrs. Dicks continued to meet monthly for the remainder of the year, and Mrs. Dicks began to attend the Alzheimer's support group on a regular basis. Her son's return did not present the problems she had anticipated, and her relationship with her sister continued to improve. Mrs. Eaton continued to help Mrs. Dicks with the care of her mother and father. A year after their last contact, and almost four years after they had first met, Mrs. Dicks wrote Mr. Dixon a letter, explaining that her mother had died two months before of a cerebral hemorrhage, and thanking him for all his help. She also explained that Mrs. Eaton was no longer working with her but had been helpful in getting her connected to a home health agency for assistance with her father, who was becoming increasingly frail.

Family caregivers play a vital role in maintaining the physical and emotional well-being of frail elderly people. Their role will almost certainly increase in importance as the numbers of frail older persons expands rapidly in the next few decades. Social workers and other helping professionals have a crucial role to play in supporting family caregivers, but until recently, this role was largely neglected. This essay describes the characteristics and needs of family caregivers, as well as what is known about ways to assist them. It is hoped that it will serve to stimulate additional interest in the development and implementation of public policies and intervention programs for the support family caregivers and frail older persons.

## REFERENCES

AARP (American Association of Retired Persons) 1986. *A Profile of Older Persons: 1986.* Washington, D.C.: AARP.

Blenkner, H., H. Bloom, M. Nielsen, and R. Weber. 1974. *Final Report—Protective Services for Older People: Findings from the Benjamin Rose Institute Study.* Cleveland: Benjamin Rose Institute.

Brody, E. M. 1981. "Women in the Middle and Family Help to Older People." *The Gerontologist* 21:471–480.

Brody, E. M. 1985. "Parent Care as a Normative Family Stress." *The Gerontologist* 25:19–29.

Callahan, J. J. 1989. "Play It Again Sam—There Is No Impact." *The Gerontologist* 29:5.

Cantor, M. H. 1983. "Strain Among Caregivers: A Study of Experience in the United States." *The Gerontologist* 23:597–604.

Carter, E. and H. McGoldrick, eds. 1980. *The Family Life Cycle*, New York: Gardner.

Coppell, D. B., C. Burton, J. Becker, and J. Fiore. 1985. "Relationships of Cognitions Associated with Coping Reactions to Depression in Spousal Caregivers of Alzheimer's Disease Patients." *Cognitive Therapy and Research* 9:253–266.

Doty, P. 1986. "Family Care of the Elderly: The Role of Public Policy." *The Milbank Quarterly* 64:34–75.

Farkas, S. 1980. "Impact of Chronic Illness on the Patient's Spouse." *Health and Social Work* 5:39–46.

Fengler, A. and N. Goodrich. 1979. "Wives of Elderly Disabled Men: The Hidden Patient." *The Gerontologist* 19:175–183.

Fitzpatrick, J. 1983. "Faith and Stability Among Hispanic Families." In W. D'Antonio and J. Andous, eds., *Families and Religions: Conflicts and Change in Modern Society*, Beverly Hills, Calif.: Sage.

Gallagher, D. E. 1985. "Intervention Strategies to Assist Caregivers of Frail Elders: Current Research Status and Future Research Directions." In C. Eisdorfer, M. P. Lawton, and G. Maddox, eds., *Annual Review of Gerontology and Geriatrics*, vol. 5, pp. 249–282, New York: Springer.

Gallagher, D. and R. Czirr. 1984. "Clinical Observations on the Effectiveness of Different Psychotherapeutic Approaches in the Treatment of Depressed Caregivers." Paper presented at the meeting of the Gerontological Society of America, San Antonio, Texas, November.

Gallagher, D., S. Lovett, and A. Zeiss. 1989. "Interventions with Caregivers of Frail Elderly Persons." In M. Ory and K. Bond, eds., *Aging and Health Care: Social Science and Policy Perspectives*, pp. 167–190. United Kingdom, London: Routledge.

Gallagher, D., J. Rose, P. Rivera, S. Lovett, and L. W. Thompson. In press. "Prevalence of Depression in Family Caregivers." *The Gerontologist*.

Garcia-Preto, D. 1982. "Puerto Rican Families." In M. McGoldrick, J. Pearce, and J. Giordino, Eds., *Ethnicity and Family Therapy*, pp. 164–186. New York: Guilford.

George, L. K. and L. Gwyther. 1986. "Caregiver Well-Being: A Multidimensional Examination of Family Caregivers of Demented Adults." *The Gerontologist* 26:253–259.

Germain, C. B. and A. Gitterman. 1980. *The Life Model of Social Work Practice.* New York: Columbia University Press.

Golodetz, A., R. Evans, G. Heinritz, and C. Gibson. 1969. "The Care of Chronic Illness: The Responsor Role." *Medical Care* 7:385–394.

Gray, V. K. 1983. "Providing Support for Home Caregivers." In M. A. Smyer and M. Gatz, Eds., *Mental Health and Aging*, Beverly Hills, Calif.: Sage, pp. 197–213.

Green, V. L. and D. J. Monahan. 1987. "The Effect of Professionally Guided Caregiver Support and Education Group on Institutionalization of Care Receivers." *The Gerontologist* 27:716–721.

Haley, W. E. 1983. "A Family-Behavioral Approach to the Treatment of the Cognitively Impaired Elderly." *The Gerontologist* 23:18–20.

Haley, W., L. Brown, and E. Levine. 1987. "Experimental Evaluation of the Effectiveness of Group Interventions for Dementia Caregivers." *The Gerontologist* 27:376–382.

Haley, W. E., E. G. Levine, S. C. Brown, and A. A. Bartolucci. 1987. "Stress Appraisal Coping and Social Support as Predictors of Adaptational Outcome Among Dementia Caregivers." *Psychology and Aging*, 2:323–330.

Hasselkus, B. R. 1988. "Meaning in Family Caregiving: Perspectives on Caregiver/ Professional Relationships." *The Gerontologist* 28:686–691.

Herr, J. J. and J. H. Weakland. 1979. *Counseling Elders and Their Families.* New York: Springer.

Horowitz, A. 1985. "Family Caregiving to the Frail Elderly." In C. Eisdorfer, M. P. Lawton, and G. L. Maddox, eds., *Annual Review of Gerontology and Geriatrics,* vol. 5, New York: Springer, pp. 194–246.

Johnson, C. L. and D. J. Catalano. 1983. "A Longitudinal Study of Family Supports to Impaired Elderly." *The Gerontologist* 23:612–618.

Johnson, P. J. and A. Rubin. 1983. "Case Management in Mental Health: A Social Work Domain." *Social Work* 28:49–55.

Kane, R. A. 1985. "Assessing the Elderly." In A. Monk, ed., *Handbook of Gerontological Services,* pp. 43–69. New York: Van Nostrand.

Kane, R. A. and R. L. Kane 1981. *Assessing the Elderly: A Practical Guide to Measurement.* New York: Lexington Books.

Kemper, P., R. Applebaum, and M. Harrigan. 1987. "Community Care Demonstrations: What Have We Learned?" *Health Care Financing Review* 8:87–100.

Lawton, M. P., E. M. Brody, and A. R. Saperstein. 1989. "A Controlled Study of Respite Service for Caregivers of Alzheimer's Patients." *The Gerontologist* 29:8–16.

Lazarus, R. S. and S. Folkman. 1984. *Stress, Appraisal, and Coping.* New York: Springer.

Lockerly, S. A. 1985. "Care in the Minority Family." *Generations* 10:27–29.

Lowy, L. 1985. *Social Work with the Aging: The Challenge and Promise of the Later Years,* 2d ed. New York: Longman.

McAdoo, H. P. 1988. *Black Families,* 2d ed. Newbury Park, Calif.: Sage.

McCain, N. 1986. "Corporate Help for the Caregivers." *The Boston Globe* (August 12),

Montgomery R. G. and E. Borgotta. "The Effects of Alternative Support Strategies on Family Caregiving." *The Gerontologist,* 29(4):457–464.

Montgomery, R. J. V. 1989. "Investigating Caregiver Burden." In K. S. Markides and C. L. Cooper, eds., *Aging Stress and Health,* pp. 201–218. New York: Wiley.

Pinkston, E. M., N. L. Linsk, and R. N. Young. 1988. "Home-Based Behavioral Family Treatment of the Impaired Elderly." *Behavior Therapy, 19:*331–344.

Pratt, C. C., V. C. Schmall, S. Wright, and M. Cleland. 1985. "Burden and Coping Strategies of Caregivers to Alzheimer's Patients." *Family Relations* 34:27–33.

Quayhagen, M. P. and M. Quayhagen. (1988). "Alzheimer's stress: Coping with the Caregiving Role." *The Gerontologist* 28:391–396.

Reever, K. E. 1984. "Self-Help Groups for Caregivers Coping with Alzheimer's Disease: The ACMA Model." *Pride Institute Journal of Long Term Health Care* 3:23–30.

Roberts, R. 1987. "The Epidemiology of Depression in Minorities." In P. Muehrer, ed., *Research Perspectives on Depression and Suicide in Minorities,* Washington, D.C.: U.S. Department of Health and Human Services, National Institute of Mental Health.

Sanford, K. A. 1975. "Tolerance of Debility in Elderly Dependents by Supporters at Home: Its Significance for Hospital Practice." *British Medical Journal* 3:471–473.

Schmidt, G. L. and B. Keyes. 1985. "Group Psychotherapy with Family Caregivers of Demented Patients." *The Gerontologist* 25:347–350.

Seltzer, M. M., J. Ivry, and L. C. Litchfield. 1987. Family Members as Case Managers: Partnership Between the Formal and Informal Support Networks." *The Gerontologist* 27:722–728.

Shanas, E. 1968. *Old People in Three Industrial Societies.* New York: Atherton.

Shanas, E. 1979. "The Family as a Social Support System in Old Age." *The Gerontologist* 19:169–174.

Smith, G. C. and D. J. Sperbeck. 1980. "Attributing Causality in Aging Families: Theoretical and Practical Implications of a Social-Psychological Perspective." Paper presented at the Annual Meeting of the Gerontological Society, San Diego, November.

Soldo, B. J. and K. G. Manton. 1985. "Health Status and Service Needs of the Oldest Old: Current Patterns and Future Trends." *The Milbank Quarterly,* 63:289–319.

Steinberg, R. M. 1985. "Access Assistance and Case Management." In A. Monk, ed., *Handbook of Gerontological Services,* pp. 211–239. New York: Van Nostrand.

Steinberg, R. M. and G. W. Carter. 1983. *Case Management and the Elderly.* Lexington, Mass.: Lexington Books.

Stephens, M. P. P., V. K. Norris, J. K. Kinney, S. W. Ritchie, and R. C. Grotz. 1988. "Stressful Situations in Caregiving: Relations Between Caregiver Coping and Well-Being." *Psychology and Aging* 3:208–209.

Stone, R., G. C. Cafferata, and J. Sangl. 1987. "Caregivers of the Frail Elderly: A National Profile." *The Gerontologist* 27:616–626.

Taylor, R. J. and W. H. Taylor. 1982. "The Social and Economic Status of the Black Elderly." *Phylon* 43:295–306.

Tonti, M. and B. Silverstone. 1985. "Services to Families of the Elderly." In A. Monk, ed., *Handbook of Gerontological Services,* pp. 211–239. New York: Van Nostrand.

Toseland, R. W. in press. "Long-term Effectiveness of Peer-Led and Professionally-Led Support Groups for Family Caregivers." *Social Service Review.*

Toseland, R. W. and C. M. Rossiter. 1989. "Group Intervention to Support Caregivers: A Review and Analysis." *The Gerontologist* 29(4):438–448.

Toseland, R. W., C. Rossiter, and M. Labrecque 1989a. "The Effectiveness of Peer-Led and Professionally-Led Groups to Support Family Caregivers." *The Gerontologist* 29(4):465–471.

Toseland, R. W., C. Rossiter, and M. Labrecque. 1989b. "The Effectiveness of Three Group Intervention Strategies to Support Caregivers." *American Journal of Orthopsychiatry* 59(3):420–429.

Toseland, R. W., C. Rossiter, and M. Labrecque. 1989c. "Effectiveness of Two Kinds of Support Groups for Caregivers." *Social Service Review.*

Toseland, R. W., C. Rossiter, T. Peak, and P. Hill. In press a. "Therapeutic Process in Support Groups for Caregivers." *International Journal of Group Psychotherapy.*

Toseland, R. W., C. Rossiter, T. Peak, and G. Smith. in press b. "The Comparative effectiveness of Individual and Group Interventions to Support Family Caregivers." *Social Work.*

Toseland, R. W., C. Rossiter, and S. Tobin. 1989. "Long-Term Effects of Two Types of Caregiver Support Groups on Care Receivers." Unpublished manuscript, State University of New York, Albany, Ringel Institute of Gerontology.

Toseland, R. W. and G. C. Smith. in press. "The Effectiveness of Individual Counseling by Professional and Peer Helpers for Family Caregivers of the Elderly." *Psychology and Aging.*

U.S. HHS U.S. Department of Health and Human Services, Assistant Secretary for Planning and Evaluation. 1982. "Working Papers on Long-Term Care Prepared for the 1980 Undersecretary's Task Force on Long-Term Care." Washington, D.C.: U.S. HHS.

U.S. Senate, Special Committee on Aging. 1987–88. *Aging in America.: Trends and Projections.* Washington, D.C.: U.S. Senate.

Watkins, T. R. and R. Gonzales. 1982. "Outreach to Mexican Americans." *Social Work* 21:68–73.

Watson, W. H. 1982. *Aging and Social Behavior: An Introduction to Social Gerontology*. Belmont, Calif.: Wadsworth.

Zarit, S., C. Anthony, and M. Boutselis. 1987. "Interventions with Caregivers of Dementia Patients: Comparison of Two Approaches." *Psychology and Aging* 2:225–234.

# 18

## Homeless People

### STEPHEN HOLLOWAY

Social and political changes in American life are often reflected by the emergence of new "classes" of affected people. The protest and unrest of the 1960s introduced us to the decade's dissidents. The civil rights activists, student protesters, and so-called flower children forced Americans in that era to acknowledge that there were many who felt profound anger about aspects of the society in which they lived. Similarly, in the 1970s, the returned Vietnam veterans represented a class of Americans who saw themselves as rejected patriots, shunned by a society that they felt they had served well. The Reagan years gave us the homeless, among other important changes.

Only a few years ago, most of us would not have believed that in this affluent society, homelessness would be a problem of any consequence. Yet, today, the problem is so pervasive and its evidence so compelling that there are few who do not acknowledge that, indeed, many Americans seem to have no place to live.

Homelessness is, of course, not a new phenomenon in this country. During the immigrations of the late nineteenth and early twentieth centuries, homeless people—frequently children—were common in urban centers. Again, in the 1930s, economic hardships associated with the Great Depression resulted in widespread homelessness. Homeless families, combing rural areas for work, and "hobos," camped

I gratefully acknowledge Mona Bergenfeld for her initial work in elaborating many of the assertions in the section on the risks of this population. I also wish to credit the staff of Columbia University Community Services for much of the practice insight offered in the section on clinical assessments and interventions. In particular, I acknowledge the contribution of Mona Bergenfeld, Jeanmarie Hargrave, Joyce Jackson, Julie Lorenzo, Suzanne Smith, and Andrea White.

on the outskirts of a small town and traveling the freight rails, are part of the imagery of that era. And of course, there is the skid-row alcoholic who has always been a feature of the urban landscape.

But today's homeless are far more diverse. Homeless people include immigrants, veterans, unemployed migrants, families, and seemingly able young men recently out of work, as well as the mentally ill, substance abusers, runaways, and the elderly. While most homeless people are alone, the number of families is significant. Homeless people are also much younger than in the past. The majority fall into the 20- to 40-year range. Most are white, but the percentage of minorities—upwards of 40 percent—is significantly greater than their proportional representation in the general population. (U.S. HUD 1984:7). Finally, homeless people are more highly educated than one would suppose. A recent California study, for example, suggested that the majority of those studied had completed high school and had a history of steady employment (Bishop 1989: A14).

The phenomenon has created a swirl of controversy. Advocates for the homeless assert that the problem is profound and growing rapidly (Baxter and Hopper 1981; Hopper and Hamberg 1984; Kozol 1988). The Reagan administration insisted that the problem was vastly exaggerated by advocates for the homeless and the popular media. In 1988, the president even went so far as to suggest that no one in the nation need be homeless and that therefore, those who were must be so by choice. Sectors of government debate the limits of their jurisdiction and responsibility in addressing aspects of the problem. Increasingly, the causes and extent of the problem are hotly debated in scholarly journals, the popular media, and the courts.

## PROBLEM DOMAIN

The controversies that typically frame discussions of homelessness in the professional literature, public documents, and the media have their antecedents partly in ideology and partly in the very real methodological problems that accompany the study of a social phenomenon like homelessness. The ideological dimension of the debate is probably best understood as an attack—and reactions to that attack—on the policies and belief systems of the Reagan approach to social issues which advocates for homeless people credit as having precipitated the homelessness of the 1980s.

But interacting with the ideological differences are the profound methodological problems that complicate research efforts that might otherwise assist us in understanding the real character and extent of the phenomenon. To begin with, defining homelessness is difficult. Beyond the so-called street people and shelter users who are typically included in the standard definitions are those who reside in halfway houses, long-term detoxification centers, or local jails, and who could well be on the street were they not temporarily "accommodated." Broader definitions of the homeless incorporate elements that are difficult to measure, such as those "lacking adequate shelter," "having insufficient resources to secure housing," or "lacking community ties." For many, homelessness is a periodic phenomenon. How does one count the "precariously housed" who have been homeless in the past and are likely to be so again? The absence of uniform definitions of the problem severely hampers a meaningful understanding of just what is being discussed or studied.

Definitional problems aside, measurement difficulties also cloud our ability to research the problem. Many homeless people are quite mobile and use their "invisibility" as a survival strategy in a dangerous urban environment. Developing sampling techniques that provide an accurate estimate of their numbers—let alone devising strategies to collect biographical and background information—is a daunting task. What we know is also severely limited by the lack of comparability between studies. As a result, significant distortions occur when one attempts to generalize findings across studies because their terms, definitions, and assumptions often lack sufficient commonality.

These and related measurement difficulties interact with the politically charged character of the problem in a way that significantly compromises our ability to specify with reasonable assurance the precise nature and extent of the problem. Perhaps the best example of this observation is the debate about the total number of homeless people in the nation. Advocates for the homeless insist that there are millions of homeless Americans. One such group produced data that suggest that the numbers may be as high as 3 million nationally (Hombs and Snyder 1982). In response, the Department of Housing and Urban Development (HUD) released a study placing the figure at 250,000 to 350,000 (U.S. HUD 1984). The HUD report, which was represented as being methodologically sophisticated and essentially accurate, was bitterly attacked by advocates for the homeless, who charged that the federal government had grossly misrepresented both the character and the extent of homelessness. Little progress has been made in unraveling these discrepancies, and depending upon the assumptions and methods of the investigator, recent work continues to reflect the disparities seen earlier (for example, see U.S. GAO 1988; Rossi et al. 1987).

The causes of homelessness and the character of the affected population are similarly contested. Advocates take the position that people are homeless as a consequence of public policies that have resulted in the elimination of low-income housing, slashed benefit programs, and increased poverty, thereby abandoning the society's most vulnerable to a life on the streets. The authors of one of the most thoughtful of these analyses, Hopper and Hamberg (1984), identified four areas of public policy that, they maintained, foreshadowed today's crisis. Federal withdrawal from developing low-income housing, along with local initiatives to redevelop marginal housing for middle- and upper-income use, Hopper and Hamburg argued, has resulted in a profound shortage of housing for the poor. They also asserted that the rise in unemployment and the reduction in benefit programs such as Supplemental Security Income (SSI) and in public welfare in the early Reagan years have made those on the lower end of the income scale increasingly poorer. Finally, they pointed to deinstitutionalization—the national trend in the 1960s and '70s to return long-term mental patients from the asylum back to their communities—as having resulted in vast numbers of chronically mentally ill people being left to fend for themselves in an underserviced and unresponsive urban environment. Hopper and Hamberg (1984) and others have substantiated this analysis with compelling data that document the policy and spending shifts over the 1980s that foreshadowed today's problem.

Many public officials and more conservative scholars have disputed the above analysis. Main (1986), for example, argued that, not only have the numbers of the homeless been vastly over estimated by their advocates, but the causes of the problem and the character of those affected have been distorted. Remarkably, he asserted that there is no intrinsic shortage of low-income housing (the primary tenet of the advocates' position) but simply a problem of overregulation by government, whereby standards regulating housing adequacy have prevented the open market from responding to the need. He suggested that these and related governmental regulations regarding low-income housing make it an unprofitable arena for the real estate industry. Main went on to assert that the core of the problem lies in the character of the homeless themselves. He observed that the homeless are a severely disabled population made up of substance abusers, the physically or mentally ill, and social deviants. He suggested that even with available housing, these are people who are not prepared to care for themselves. Advocates for the homeless have characterized this position as a classic case of blaming the victim.

While these disagreements abound in the literature, the popular media, and public documents, there is an emerging consensus about the broader parameters—if not the details and specifics—of the problem. By whatever count, it is clear that there are today several hundred thousand undomiciled Americans. Unlike in years past, when the vast majority of homeless individuals were unattached single, elderly white males, today's homeless are a more diverse group. Probably, not more than 65 percent of today's homeless are single men (U.S. HUD 1984: 19); 15 to 25 percent are women; and while their numbers have not been documented, perhaps 15 to 20 percent are family members (U.S. HHS 1984b:3).

The duration of homelessness varies significantly within the population. For many, the period is relatively short. Several studies suggest that over half of their samples had been homeless less than a year, and many of those less than a few months (Robertson et al. 1985:48; Roth and Bean 1986:7). For others, the experience is an episodic one where, depending on circumstances, they move between homelessness to precarious housing situations and back again. Finally, there is also a group of relatively long-term homeless. Struening (1986:x), for example, in a study of New York City public shelter users, reported that almost half of those studied had spent half, most, or all of the previous three years as shelter residents.

Disabilities among the homeless have been the source of much debate and investigation. The primary citations include substance abuse, mental illness, and physical illness. While studies report significant variations in the proportions, it is generally accepted that a significant percentage of the homeless population is chronically mentally ill. Two of the most comprehensive reviews of studies citing mental status data (Arce and Vergare 1984; U.S. GAO 1988) suggest that the percentage of homeless mentally ill people falls somewhere between 25 and 50 percent. Recently, the 30 to 35 percent figure seems to be receiving general acceptance as a working estimate of mental illness among homeless people.

While one might question whether substance abuse can be better understood as a response to the devastation of homelessness or its cause, it is clear that substance abuse is relatively common among homeless people. The two most frequently abused substances are alcohol and cocaine (typically in the form of "crack"), but the full range of street drugs is not uncommon within the population. Estimates of substance dependence among the homeless vary significantly but tend to cluster in the 30 to 40 percent range (e.g., Bassuk, Rubin, and Lauriat 1984: 1547; U.S. HUD, 1984:24; IOM 1988:60–65).

There are scant comparative data regarding the physical health of homeless people as compared to the domiciled population. Nonetheless, recent studies as well as the impressionistic reports of service providers suggest that homeless people are much more ill than the general population. To cite only three examples, studies report a rate of tuberculosis that is 100 to 200 times greater than in the general population; an incidence of disorders of the extremities (e.g., ulcers and edema) perhaps 15 times more common in homeless people; and respiratory disorders 4 to 5 times more common than in the general population (Wright 1987:157–158). The causes are understandable when one considers the conditions in which homeless people exist, on the one hand, and the difficulties they experience in accessing health care, on the other. In a recent survey of hospital emergency room and outpatient clinic services among the voluntary hospitals in New York City, health care providers readily acknowledged their ambivalence in serving homeless people. Many characterized them as "smelly, infested with lice and uncooperative in treatment encounters." For homeless people to receive effective medical care, the survey concluded, treatment protocols specifically designed for homeless people would have to be developed and institutions would need to make service delivery a specified priority (CUCS, 1988).

## SOCIETAL CONTEXT

Homelessness can be understood as a particularly compelling manifestation of extreme poverty. The extent of the problem must be associated to some degree with the social and political preoccupations of the late 1970s and the '80s. In stark contrast to the period that preceded it, this was an era of relative indifference to social issues.

The 1980s were dominated by conservative ideas and a preoccupation with individual gain. Political campaigns of the period emphasized traditional values, the resurrection of national pride, and the need to reassert our military might. It became fashionable for politicians to openly express skepticism about the effectiveness and appropriateness of social programs. These themes seemed to resonate with the national mood. During the Reagan era, public spending quickly reflected this shift in priorities. Military spending soared and benefit programs were cut. Restrictive eligibility criteria further curtailed their effectiveness. A kind of cynicism regarding the role of government in effecting social and economic redress became the vogue. The private sector was touted as the solution to social ills. A growing economy was associated with fuller employment; jobs, the ideology held, were the appropriate solution to poverty and social need. Stimulated by governmental policies particularly supportive of the corporate sector, tax relief, and accelerated deficit spending, the economy expanded, and eventually, unemployment dropped.

But poverty did not abate. The economic expansion was of little benefit to those with modest education and marginal skills. In fact, the proportion of people below the poverty line mushroomed during the era. But we seemed to have toughened. Reports on the worsening circumstances of the nation's poor received scant attention. These concerns had somehow passed from public debate.

It is difficult to find more graphic evidence of the failure of the conservative agenda to address the needs of the nation's poor than the explosion of homelessness during the 1980s. Unlike other social problems, this one shows a particularly public face. It was very difficult for us to escape awareness of the problem as we encountered increasing numbers of affected people in the course of our daily lives. As advocates for the homeless provided increasingly compelling evidence of the scope and severity of the problem, the debate described above regarding the extent, cause, and possible remedies for homelessness began to emerge.

The shape of this debate, the reluctance of sectors of government to intervene, and our lassitude in mobilizing a national initiative to address the problem meaningfully must be appreciated as a particularly clear reminder of the retreat from social concerns that characterized the Reagan era. Such ambivalence about grappling with this kind of extreme human misery would not have been tolerated during more socially progressive periods in our history. The relative indifference to the circumstances of others that so characterized the 1980s has unquestionably had the effect of delaying an effective response to the problem of homelessness.

## RISKS AND NEEDS OF THE POPULATION

Homelessness is a wretched condition. Because they are without resources, homeless people are urgently dependent on their environment; at the same time, they are shunned by that environment. Homeless people experience repeated and devastating loss. There is evidence that homeless people are much less likely to have active familial, spousal, or social ties. This is suggestive of repeated interpersonal loss. In addition, the process of becoming homeless is typically preceded by loss of economic independence. Finally, homelessness itself means loss of home, possessions, neighborhood, role and status, pride, and routine—losses that frequently trigger depression, anger, and diminished self-esteem. While many homeless people demonstrate significant strengths, one can quite safely assume that many of them have also been emotionally traumatized by the experience of becoming homeless.

A constant and crushing social reality for homeless people is the extent of their rejection by the dominant society. Most of us feel threatened by the degree of destitution reflected in the image of the homeless people whom we encounter. Sufficient numbers of homeless people are unclean and disorganized to reinforce the common impression that they all smell bad, are infested with lice, and are likely to behave in a bizarre ways. These impressions are enduring enough to result in dismissive and fearful responses toward the homeless person who seeks contact with others. Many people avoid looking at homeless people for fear of being approached or engaged, or simply to avoid the discomfort of momentarily sharing the experience of their helplessness. As a consequence, homeless people get few cues from their social environment and limited interpersonal feedback to guide their behavior or validate their self-worth. Considering the extent and frequency with which homeless people are shunned, it is not surprising that many isolate themselves in whatever ways are available to them and that when they do attempt to engage the social world, they do so in defensive and perhaps unconventional ways. Being homeless carries a profound stigma; the specter of that stigma dominates the social reality of all homeless people.

Homeless people are also dependent upon others for their survival. Given their social isolation, they tend to live from moment to moment, not knowing whether their basic needs will be met. Such constant uncertainty about where to sleep or when one will eat next inevitably results in high levels of stress. It also starkly reduces any sense of control or mastery that one might experience in relationship to the environment. This mix of rejection and dependence accounts in part for the often nomadic habits and bizarre and excessive strategies of survival that the homeless frequently adopt. Such environmental circumstances can be understood to reinforce any existing manipulative predispositions and to exacerbate dependent patterns of behavior, since conveying an image of extreme need may be the only available means of eliciting help.

Another aspect of the social world for homeless people is a total lack of privacy. We all need to shut a door at times and be alone. This option is not available to homeless people. The title of the groundbreaking study of homelessness aptly captured this circumstance: *Private Lives/Public Spaces* (Baxter and Hopper 1981). Living under these circumstances, homeless people understandably experience a loosening of the distinction between private and public behavior. Given the fact that virtually all their activities hold the potential for public scrutiny, it is little wonder that homeless people are often accused of evidencing "inappropriate behavior" in public. Behaviors such as expression of outrage, dressing, or attending to personal hygiene that are considered inappropriate in public are quite appropriate in private—a privacy, unfortunately, not available to homeless people.

The physical circumstances of being homeless are as profound as the social circumstances. Whether on the street, in welfare hotels, or in public shelters, homeless people live in constant fear for their physical safety. Recent surveys of public shelter users in large urban areas indicate the extreme nature of the physical threat. In one study, the respondents reported that during the past year, 26 percent had been robbed, 59 percent had had property stolen, 24 percent had been threatened with a gun or other weapon, and 18 percent had been physically beaten (Struening 1986: iv). When interviewed about what guides their decisions regarding where to sleep, homeless people cite safety as a primary concern.

## Homeless Singles: Adult Men, Women, and Youth

In aggregate, singles constitute the largest percentage of the homeless population. The majority are adult males. The available statistics suggest that 15 to 25 percent of the homeless single population are women (U.S. HHS 1984b; 19). There are probably several factors that account for the disproportionate numbers of adult males relative to adult women and youth. Despite the normative changes associated with changing roles of men and women in American society, adult males still experience more social mobility than women. It is more socially acceptable for men to "go it alone" than it is for women. Women who are experiencing extreme distress may well have access to more enduring social supports than would be available for "able-bodied" men, particularly when the elimination of such supports could lead to homelessness. It is no secret that homelessness is a dangerous existence. Given the greater vulnerability of homeless women to exploitation and physical harm, it is probable that women choose to endure more onerous living conditions than do men if the alternative is homelessness. Finally, under some circumstances, women may have relatively greater access to certain "supportive resources" than do men. The fact that women are more likely to retain custody of children than are men—particularly among those at the lower levels on the economic scale—means that they have access to public supports, Aid to Families with Dependent Children (AFDC), that enhance their ability to afford some form of marginal housing. Prostitution is also an available means of support for many impoverished younger women. Women may also select to live with a man who provides support and housing. While these options are open to some men, they are more characteristically utilized by women.

Some homeless women fit the stereotype of the urban "bag lady," dressed in layers of clothing and carrying their possessions with them in shopping bags. Many others do not. Like other homeless subpopulations, homeless women are a heterogeneous group. A study of homeless women in Columbia, South Carolina, is typical of an emerging pattern of data that suggest that homeless women constitute a more diverse group than the stereotypes suggest. The majority of the women in the study were under 40 years of age, were Caucasian, and had been long-time residents of South Carolina. Most were unemployed and lived on less than $3,000 per year. Dissatisfaction with their current lives, unemployment, separation from family, and nowhere to live were among the primary difficulties that they cited (Stoner 1983).

The consensus among service providers and researchers who have studied or worked with single homeless women is that in most respects, the backgrounds and circumstances of women are not significantly different than those of homeless men. The typical pattern is one of economic hardship and increasing disaffiliation. Many go to great lengths to maintain a clean and pleasant appearance and struggle to retain the independence and dignity that characterized their former lives. Some maintain contact with family and friends and move in and out of homelessness over time. Most have children of whom they no longer retain custody but with whom they maintain periodic contact and/or foster the hope of becoming reunited. Prior to becoming homeless, most lived in marginal circumstances such as single-room-occupancy hotels (SROs), boarding houses, or precarious situations in which they were not the primary tenant. As discussed above, mental illness and substance abuse constitute a significant problem for many.

At least one important difference between men and women also merits note. Homeless women in far greater proportions report histories of abuse and victimization. For some, the decision to leave an abusive relationship becomes the precipitating factor for their homelessness. This is most clearly the case for those who enter shelters and service facilities for battered women. For others, life on the streets or in marginal living circumstances is punctuated by episodes of victimization and exploitation. Many develop extreme defensive strategies to fend off assault. Such tactics as dressing unattractively, acting bizarrely, and maintain noxious body odors are not uncommon among homeless women. The functional aspects of these adaptations for them are often overlooked or misunderstood by those unfamiliar with the hazards that homelessness holds for the solitary female (Martin 1982).

Homeless youth—that is, those between the ages of 12 and 18—constitute a particularly vulnerable and exploited population. Estimates of their numbers are no more reliable than those for homeless adults. The Citizen's Committee for Children (1983:6) reported that a 1982 congressional study on the problem estimated the number to be between 250,000 and 500,000 nationally. Estimates have suggested that in New York City alone, the number may be as high as 20,000 (CCC 1983:6). Contrary to popular myth, the majority of homeless young people are not middle-class youth who have fled stable family situations in search of excitement and adventure. In New York State, for example, 64 percent of those studied would have required placement outside their home of origin, either because there really was no home or because that setting was too "dangerous" to sustain the young person's development (CCC 1983:11).

The portrait of New York's homeless youth is indeed grim. The overwhelming majority of those seeking assistance from social agencies are native to New York City, and it is clear that those not seeking assistance are even more likely to have grown up in the city. More than 80 percent are black or Hispanic, out of school, and possessing marginal or nonexistent personal and family ties. Substance abuse is endemic, and they are already embittered and cynical about their prospects for a productive adult life (CCC 1983:7).

Aspects of this picture, such as the extreme numbers of young people affected and their ethnicity, vary by geographic location, regional economic differences, and degree of urbanization. Nonetheless, the picture that emerges is one of rather resourceless individuals, typically coming from poor, deprived, or troubled home situations—or foster care—who, with significant disadvantages, are attempting to survive in a hostile urban environment. Survival options for these young people are extremely limited. They typically exclude legitimate employment and more commonly involve some combination of prostitution, criminal activity, and drug-related support.

## Homeless Families

Given the attention that family homelessness has received in the popular media, it is somewhat surprising that it has not been the subject of more systematic research. The few studies that have been conducted—chiefly in large urban areas, where family homelessness is particularly prevalent—cite highly disparate rates. Some researchers have reported relatively low percentages of families relative to the total homeless sample; for example, 5.2 percent in Minneapolis (Piliavin 1988) and 7 percent in several U.S. cities (Freeman and Hall 1986). Other researchers have reported much higher percentages. Sosin (1988) in Chicago and Morse, Shields, and Hanneke (1985) in St. Louis reported 36 percent and 30 percent, respectively. In 1988, the number of homeless family members temporarily housed by the City of New York (approximately 17,000 individuals, constituting slightly over 5,000 family units) was significantly in excess of the number of homeless singles housed in city facilities (approximately 11,000). The reasons for these discrepancies are probably complex and are important to investigate, since they may hold clues to the causes of and the remedies for the problem. It is generally assumed, however, that where the housing vacancy rate is low and the rates for available low-income housing exceed the welfare housing allowance, such as is the case in New York, Chicago, Los Angeles, and many other urban centers, the proportion of family homelessness is particularly high.

The typical homeless family consists of a young mother and two or three young children (Bassuk, Lauriat, and Rubin 1987:21). There is some evidence that this pattern varies from area to area and that the proportion of two-parent homeless families is higher in nonurban locations. Nevertheless, it is safe to assume that most homeless families are single-parent and female-headed, and that prior to becoming homeless they lived doubled up in cramped quarters with a parent or other relative. Conflicts with the primary tenant or homeowner are the most common reason reported for precipitating family homelessness in such situations. It is also the case in a significant minority of cases that the family was the primary tenant and the homelessness was precipitated by fire, domestic violence, eviction, or loss of benefits such as AFDC.

The key factor in understanding family homelessness is the relationship between the family's financial circumstances, on the one hand, and the lack of affordable housing, on the other. In no group is this more obvious than among public assistance recipients, who have experienced a consistent and growing gap between the welfare housing allowance and the cost of housing. It is generally accepted, for example, that households should not spend more than 25 to 30 percent of their income on rent. Yet, in New York City, where one third of all renters pay in excess of 40 percent of their income for rent, over 70 percent of welfare recipients must pay that amount of their income or more to secure housing (Dumpson 1987:44).

Researchers have attempted to distinguish between those families who become homeless and those in similar circumstances who seem able to maintain a permanent residence. These efforts have been initiated both to identify subpopulations for preventive intervention and to formulate effective remedial services. Remarkably, few differences have been substantiated. Some researchers have found marginal differences, including the fact that homeless families have histories of more frequent moves and have resided in more cramped quarters than otherwise similar nonhomeless families. After extensive efforts to differentiate the two groups, however, experts such as the administrators of New York's Human Resources Administration have concluded that the distinctions are obscure at best. The overwhelming reality is that when low-income housing is virtually unavailable relative to the demand, some percentage of families loses out (Main 1986:11). Further evidence for this conclusion is offered by a provocative study by the Settlement Housing Fund (1986), which followed several formerly homeless hotel families into public housing. While the study has some methodological problems associated with the lack of appropriate control groups, the researchers reported that nearly all the families who received decent housing adjusted to life in their new homes and were virtually indistinguishable from other public housing tenants after two years of residence. While there were understandable transitional issues in moving from hotel living to a permanent residence, the conclusion of the study is that the appropriate "treatment" for the homeless family is supplying affordable housing.

Family homelessness is a particularly stark tragedy because of the toll it takes on young children. The process of becoming homeless typically means loss of furniture and other domestic belongings. Owing to the availability of public assistance for families in the form of AFDC, the majority of homeless families reside in so-called emergency housing: hotels, motels, or family shelters that are accessed by public welfare officials.

In a provocative study, Jonathan Kozol (1988) compellingly documented the lives of homeless families in New York City's welfare hotels. His description of the hotel living conditions is chilling, yet unfortunately typical of the conditions that characterize emergency housing in large urban centers. These hotels are frequently located in the urban center—areas of high crime, prostitution, and drug activity. Family members are jammed into one room without benefit of refrigeration, cooking facilities, or even much light. Sanitary conditions are often inadequate, with malfunctioning plumbing and infestations of roaches and rodents constituting the norm. These facilities are threatening and dangerous environments for adults, let alone children. Drug traffic and violent behavior in hallways and stairwells is common. When children leave the bleak confines of their room and the threatening environment of the hotel common areas, they find themselves exposed to the harsh realities of the urban center.

## The Mentally Ill Homeless

The 1960s and '70s witnessed a profound shift in mental health policy in the United States. During that period, a confluence of factors, including the enormous costs of inpatient care, the development of psychotropic medication, and an increasing awareness of the inhumane nature of most mental hospital environments, led to the nationwide trend of adopting a treatment philosophy emphasizing the "least restrictive" method of treatment for the mentally ill. The result of this view was the rapid discharge of mental patients from hospitals to their communities of origin, a process that came to be referred to as *deinstitutionalization*. As a consequence, between 1955 and 1980, the census of the nation's mental hospitals dropped from approximately 560,000 to 132,000. Most of these patients were discharged to their natural families, adult homes, and single-room-occupancy hotels.

Deinstitutionalization was envisioned as including community-based care. The Community Mental Health Act of 1963 originally envisoned 2,000 community mental health centers throughout the country that would provide appropriate outpatient care for the mentally ill. In 1967, at the height of the community mental health movement, there were 650 such centers. The number declined significantly in subsequent years.

Thus, the mentally ill found themselves caught in a vicious squeeze. They had been discharged to their communities without adequate follow-up or outpatient care. In order to implement deinstitutionalization objectives, the admissions criteria for mental hospitals were profoundly tightened, thus preventing rehospitalization for all but the most violent of the population. As low-income housing became increasingly scarce, and without means to manage their chronic disabilities, the mentally ill found themselves living in the parks, shelters, and streets of their communities.

In contrast to such other subpopulations as homeless families, where distinctions between the homeless and their domiciled peers are obscure, the vagaries of mental illness can more easily be understood in the precipitation of homelessness. Chronic mental illness often engenders fear and suspicion in its victims. It also is frequently associated with bizarre and antisocial behavior. These factors usually result in increasing social isolation for the mentally ill. In response to their fears, they withdraw; in reaction to their behavior, they are shunned. When these symptoms precipitate disaffection from family or institutional supports, the mentally ill are often not able to negotiate the mechanics of competing for scarce housing. Unfortunately, without aggressive intervention, this process of isolation and disaffection continues unabated for the mentally ill. Without the normative influences of standard social encounters, the mentally ill withdraw further and further from reality, often losing the desire and the ability to care for themselves in conventional ways.

## The Rural Homeless

If our knowledge about the urban homeless is spotty and incomplete, we are essentially ignorant about the nature and extent of the problem in rural areas. The few existing studies suggest that numbers of homeless people can also be found throughout rural America. Some are single men who have no personal attachments; may suffer from alcoholism, mental illness, or physical disability; and have a history of inability to maintain employment or permanent residence. Others are intact families who might be characterized as belonging to the rural "working poor." When regional economic slumps occur, they are the most vulnerable. Unable to find work, they cannot sustain permanent residence. After moving in with family or friends for a brief time, they elect to travel in search of employment. As they travel, they sleep in abandoned dwellings or their automobiles, or they camp out. Many make use of public campgrounds. Patton (1988: 190) reported a study indicating that over half of those in one Maricopa County, Arizona, campground were homeless people seeking employment. Displaced farm families and seasonal farm workers also constitute a significant percentage of the rural homeless.

The composite picture of the rural homeless is one of intact families, most of whom are white, who have a working history, and who are without permanent residence because of economic adversity. They tend to be independent, struggling to find employment as best they can. Given the lack of social programs, shelters, and other emergency services in rural settings, the rural homeless constitute a vulnerable and hidden group (Patton 1988).

# PROGRAMS AND SOCIAL WORK SERVICES

The 1980s witnessed an enormous burgeoning of programs designed to assist homeless people. They began primarily in large urban areas, but soon, the development spread to towns and communities throughout the country. While these programs were clearly appropriate and far from sufficient relative to the need, their proliferation was nonetheless remarkable, occurring as they did in the 1980s.

The explanation for this relatively rapid development can be attributed in part to the public and compelling nature of the problem. But it also must be attributed to the tireless efforts of a network of sophisticated and committed advocates who were singularly effective in using the courts to force reluctant sectors of government to intervene, and in using the electronic and print media to bring the problem to the public eye. Before he left office, New York City's Mayor Koch, for example, boasted that his city spends more on programs for the homeless than any other municipality in the country. True enough, but only after numerous lawsuits brought by the New York Coalition for the Homeless, the Legal Aid Society, the Citizen's Committee for Children, and similar groups, which resulted in the courts' *mandating* programs and setting minimum service standards. Advocacy efforts in other parts of the country had similar outcomes.

While some social workers have been notable in their early role as advocates and service innovators for homeless people, professional social work services for the homeless have been a relatively recent development. This is perhaps an understandable occurrence in view of the organizational base of most social work practice with the poor. As municipalities and state governments began to develop programmatic responses, social workers came to fill these roles. With the increasing proliferation of such services, social workers have become more prominent as program innovators and service providers.

During the 1980s, programs not only increased in number and character but became more sophisticated with respect to their effectiveness in responding to the needs of homeless people. The first class of services—and very likely still the most common—were emergency services. These are soup kitchens, emergency shelters, and drop-in centers designed to respond to the immediate and basic needs of homeless people. Soon, various kinds of transitional programs began to appear. These tend to focus on specific subpopulations, such as women, families, or the mentally ill. Transitional services engage clients in their present circumstances and offer assistance in moving to a less difficult living circumstance, from the streets to temporary shelter, permanent housing, a treatment facility, or whatever. Third, there are supported housing programs—those that offer some form of permanent residence combined with relevant social services. Finally, there are housing development programs, efforts specifically designed to increase the supply of affordable housing for the benefit of homeless people. These program types are briefly detailed below. The reader should keep in mind that the "types" discussed are generic and not necessarily mutually exclusive. For example, it is quite possible for an emergency meal program to evolve over time in the direction of a transitional enterprise. Similarly, individual organizations and entities often mix and combine the individual program components identified here.

## Emergency Services

Perhaps the most common service, and surely the most responsive to the immediate circumstances of homeless people, is the emergency shelter. During the late 1970s and early 1980s, many municipalities opened large facilities that provided sleeping accommodations for homeless people. These shelters are typically located in large public buildings such as unused armories, schools, or hospitals. Sleeping cots are commonly arranged in rows in one large room, forming a barracks-type sleeping environment. Municipal shelters are usually open only during evening hours, and the shelter user is not allowed to remain in the facility during the day. The programs are either operated directly by municipalities or, sometimes, contracted to social service organizations to manage. Some facilities offer meals and some do not. Ancillary services are occasionally available, but they are the exception rather than the rule.

While minimum sanitary standards are usually maintained, these shelters are unpleasant and often unsafe. As one might expect, when large numbers of itinerant people are located in a common facility with minimum supervision, conflict and exploitation are inevitable. This form of temporary shelter has been severely criticized by advocates for the homeless. They object not only because of the limited amenities and cold environment but also because the service does not address the issue of permanent housing, which is, of course, the core client need.

There are also many forms of small temporary shelters. Most are operated by voluntary agencies, community groups, or religious organizations. These facilities typically offer a safer and more accepting alternative to the municipal shelter. A particularly popular model is the "church basement" program that is staffed by volunteers and offers safe quarters on a nightly basis to small groups of homeless people on a first come, first served basis.

Meals programs constitute the other most common form of emergency services for homeless people. Typically, they, too, are supported and run by voluntary agencies or religious organizations. Not unlike the so-called soup kitchens popularized during the depression years, these contemporary efforts provide a hearty midday or evening meal. Limited though they are, these programs constitute enormously important resources for impoverished homeless people.

In 1983, substantial private foundation money became available to fund emergency health care services in nineteen cities across the nation. As a result of this support, emergency medical screening, treatment, and referral services were established in selected communities. Sensitive to the fact that homeless people are often unable or unwilling to engage institutionally based services (e.g., hospital emergency rooms and outpatient clinics), the program design for this effort called for locating visiting health care teams in settings frequented by homeless people such as emergency shelters, soup kitchens, and outreach programs. The foundation funding terminated in 1989, but most programs have survived through a mix of public and voluntary support.

## *Transitional Services*

As service providers became more familiar with the needs and circumstances of homeless people, programs emerged that were designed to assist clients in making the transition from homelessness to permanent living, or, at the very least, to link clients to less accessible and needed services such as benefit programs and health or mental health care. Today, there are many varieties of transitional programs. For illustrative purposes, three are briefly described below: outreach programs, drop-in centers, and transitional housing.

With experience, service providers began to realize that many potential clients shunned the traditional forms of service provision. For many, the reasons were associated with repeated experiences in which these services failed to be of real help. For others, the reasons had to do with ignorance of what was available; exaggerated fear of contact, associated with mental illness; concern about their legal status, as would be the case with illegal aliens; or ignorance regarding the requisite procedures for accessing benefits such as public assistance and food stamps. In response to this observation, creative service providers commenced *outreach efforts* in the community, contacting homeless people where they stayed, in the street corners, public parks, and subways of their communities.

The basic strategy of these outreach services involves repeated and unobtrusive contacts with homeless people in community settings. Workers typically visit a homeless person offering a sandwich, small amounts of cash, or just a friendly chat. As much as possible, these visits are timed so that the homeless person can expect them on schedule, for example, returning to a street corner with a sandwich every day at noon or visiting an area in the park with hot soup every evening at dusk. Workers discovered that with time, clients came to expect the visits, and that with persistence, they were able to engage clients beyond the immediacy of the token of contact and commence the rudiments of a service relationship. Depending on client need and openness as well as the scope of the program in question, these services run the gamut from making simple referrals to other needed services—as well as providing the client transport and escort to, and perhaps advocacy with, the referral source—to engaging clients in more comprehensive programs or even residential options associated with the program's home base.

Outreach programs of the type described above represent an important component in the emerging network of services for homeless people. They acknowledge that institutionally based service efforts will simply not work for many homeless people and that if we are to serve them effectively, we must be creative and aggressive in our efforts. They also demonstrate that even in cases of extreme isolation, the "hard-to-reach" client can be assisted in receiving needed service.

The *drop-in center,* like the other service strategies described here, is not unique to work with the homeless. It is, however, particularly adapted to the needs and patterns of much of the population. Often linked with outreach efforts, drop-in centers provide a safe and warm environment for their clients. Many are equipped with sanitary facilities such as showers and washing machines—amenities of particular value to homeless clients. They usually offer a meal and a lounge setting in which clients may relax. Beyond the emergency services that these facilities provide, their unique character lies in the fact that trained staff are available who work to engage the clients in service activities focused on linking them to more stable living situations. The specific character of the work, of course, depends on client need and cooperation, but it includes the range of referral efforts, access to relevant benefit or treatment programs, and the attempt to secure permanent housing. These programs become enormously important in the lives of many homeless people, since they represent such an accepting and responsive alternative to the environment of the street or the emergency shelter.

*Transitional housing programs* constitute a particularly focused example of this category of services because they offer temporary residence to homeless people and engage clients in a comprehensive effort to secure permanent housing. They typically work with specific subpopulations, such as youth, families, battered women, or, in the case of treatment facilities, halfway houses for the mentally ill and residential treatment facilities for substance abusers. Given the residential nature of the program, the staff experience a maximum of opportunity to engage with clients in the service enterprise and, depending upon the needs and preferences of the client(s) and the barriers and opportunities associated with the case, to initiate appropriate problem-solving activities.

## Supported Housing

These programs represent a direct response to the core need of homeless people, which is, of course, decent and affordable permanent housing. They also acknowledge that for many, either because of mental illness or as a consequence of the traumas associated with protracted homelessness, on-going supportive services are a long-term necessity. In some cases, these programs are funded directly by states or municipalities, some by foundations and not-for-profit organizations. Whatever the source of support, they are most commonly operated directly by, or contracted to, social service organizations. The program model is far from new; essentially, it is that of the public housing project or settlement house that provides permanent housing and on-site or adjacent social services for residents.

Many supported housing programs specialize with one or another subpopulation, such as families, the aged, or the mentally ill. Others promote a "mixed-use" philosophy, which holds that permanent housing should integrate people of different backgrounds and needs. The service providers often assist in the process of selecting and placing the tenant population. Services vary and are adapted to the needs of the building or cluster of buildings. It is often the case that the service providers are active not only in assisting individuals or families with problems in living but in working with the entire tenancy of the building to foster within the building(s) a stable environment, supportive and harmonious relations, and a sense of community.

The rapid increase in supported housing represents a positive progression in the philosophy of service providers regarding appropriate responses to homelessness. With time, most of those who work with homeless people realize that service efforts that do not lead to permanent housing hold questionable long-term value for homeless people. Frustrated by the dearth of available housing alternatives for their clients, many such providers have moved from initially offering emergency or transitional services to becoming directly involved in rehabilitating or constructing housing and then operating the project for the benefit of their clients.

## Permanent Housing Development

While not technically a social service in the traditional sense, program models that are focused on the development of permanent housing are briefly mentioned here because of their critical importance in addressing the problem of homelessness. To date, the federal government has remained essentially unrelated to the effort to develop affordable housing for homeless people. But increasingly, municipalities and state governments are joining with social agencies, foundations, civic and community groups, and advocates for the homeless to sponsor projects that result in permanent housing units set aside for homeless people. The funding, sponsorship, and physical character of these projects vary greatly, but a few generalizations can be offered for illustrative purposes.

Municipalities and state governments have demonstrated increasing leadership in recent years. In 1985, for example, New York State's Governor Cuomo announced that the state would set aside $50 million over a five-year period to support local not-for-profit homeless housing-development efforts. Early in 1989, New York City announced a bold effort to empty its so-called welfare hotels and place those families in apartments that would be rehabilitated at city expense.

Another model involves public support or a combination of public and private support of a community group, a social agency, or a not-for-profit development corporation to sponsor a specific project. These projects usually involve the rehabilitation of a single building or, occasionally a set of buildings, in the urban neighborhood. Once completed, the facility is managed by the sponsoring organization or, occasionally, by a new entity specifically organized for that purpose.

A third model involves the formation of a not-for-profit housing development corporation that undertakes its own design, fund raising, and development. The more successful entities tend to "spin off" completed projects to independent management and focus their long-term efforts on new development rather than project management.

The economics of these efforts remains precarious. With the continuous increase in the cost of new construction and the leveling out of shelter allowances under various benefit programs, the rents that homeless people can pay will not generate a sufficient income stream even to sustain the not-for-profit developer without some kind of supplemental assistance. This comes in a variety of forms, including suspension of local or state taxes, construction grants, other direct aid, and rent subsidy programs. As a consequence, while the programs described here represent bold efforts to grapple with the tragedy of homelessness, relative to the need the new housing that they are generating is modest at best. The federal absence from these efforts is a national disgrace. Most housing experts agree that local efforts, no matter how aggressive, will not be sufficient to address the low-income housing crisis. Unless and until the federal government renews its commitment to the development of housing for the poor, the shame of homelessness will continue.

## DIFFERENTIAL CLINICAL ASSESSMENTS AND INTERVENTIONS

Reflecting on the heterogeneity of the homeless population, one might expect it to pose an unusually broad array of service needs. In one sense, this is true. Given the wide range of difference to be found among the homeless, as well as the uniqueness of each individual irrespective of "case similarities," the variety of service needs that might be identified is infinite. But it is not in their client's uniqueness or difference that those working with homeless people should find the key to effective service. Rather, it is in the commonality—the fact of being homeless—that the worker finds the primary service objective. What homeless people have in common more than any other need or characteristic is the fact that they do not have a permanent residence. As a population, what they need is a place to live.

Homeless people are quite articulate about their circumstances. When asked about their living conditions, all but the most severely impaired will detail the difficulties associated with being homeless and quickly acknowledge that, were it possible, their first priority would be to secure permanent housing. Indeed, it is often this issue that precipitates discord between the homeless and their would-be helpers in settings such as soup kitchens, drop-in centers, or the street. The provider offers help, and the homeless person states that he or she needs a place to live. "But this is a soup kitchen, we only provide . . ." The homeless person usually settles for whatever is offered but also remains clear about the primary need: a place to live.

The universality of permanent housing as a service objective provides a focus to work with homeless people and suggests a natural structure for the service relationship. Initial assessment largely relates to the identification of barriers to housing. Ongoing service activity involves joint work at securing resources, eliminating barriers, building capabilities, and progressing toward the housing objective. The effectiveness of this work always turns upon the goodness of fit between the client's specific housing needs and preferences, on the one hand, and the characteristics of the secured housing, on the other. A central challenge in this work relates to the accuracy of the assessment and the design of an appropriate housing match. Termination, depending upon the specifics of the case and the service setting, typically involves linking the client with necessary supports in the new setting to ensure that he or she will be able to sustain permanent residence.

The assertion that housing is always the ultimate service objective in work with the homeless is not meant to suggest that social work practice with homeless people is simpler or more predictable than might be the case with other populations. Quite the contrary. People are homeless for complex reasons. In addition, the trauma of protracted homelessness has often taken its toll. The lack of attachments and resources characteristic of the population significantly encumbers the placement process. The challenges of practice with homeless people are similar to those encountered with other populations at risk. But unlike work with other populations, in which the service objective is often varied or unfolds only after significant work, a unique aspect of work with homeless people is that the ultimate service objective is always clear and identifiable.

Most clinicians who are experienced in work with homeless people agree that to be able to offer effective service, one must work from a program base specializing in services to the population. In other words, it is not likely that a homeless person who visits an outpatient mental health clinic or some other program that provides generic social services will receive sufficient help to sustain the transition from homelessness to permanent housing. This is so for several reasons. Homeless people usually have access to few resources and present a broad range of needs. A typical case involves the need to effect medical referrals, mental health supports, and entitlement links, and to attend to issues of personal hygiene. Success is likely to depend on extensive skill building, problem solving, and aggressive work during and after the housing placement process. This kind of intensive work requires the development of a significant relationship with one's client, and most homeless people engage social workers with suspicion and ambivalence. The level of trust, cooperation, and work that is required to stabilize a homeless person in permanent housing usually develops only out of the kind of periodic and continuous contact that occurs in settings where clients spend significant amounts of time. Effective assessment, for example, requires extended observation of the client's functioning. Workers who are not attached to programs specializing in this kind of work typically lack the knowledge and referral resources to meet their client's needs. The demands of a particular case periodically transcend the ability of a given worker. The availability of a team to reinforce one's work is often essential. Building the necessary social skills or skills for daily living requires group and program settings in which clients can be assisted with focused activities. Ensuring that clients will follow through with various referrals requires escort services from trusted others. Thus, given the investment of effort and resources that effective work with this population requires, a programmatic base is likely to be a minimum prerequisite for success.

Assessments in work with the homeless are often complicated by the client's previous history. Homeless people frequently have experiences of past failure with service providers. Many have reasons such as immigration problems or criminal activity that lead them to hide information about themselves. Impairments such as mental illness, mental retardation, or substance abuse further complicate the worker's ability to quickly access relevant data about the client and his or her needs. As is the case with other distressed populations, assessments of homeless people are often protracted processes. Assessments begin with the initial contact but must occur over time, as clients gain greater comfort, confidence, and trust in their workers and as the workers discover new data that shape the character of the work together.

An early task in the assessment process involves determining the client's housing preferences and exploring the barriers that seem to preclude securing that housing. In order to do this effectively, workers must be knowledgeable about the range of the housing alternatives that exist for homeless people. Space does not permit a detailed discussion of these alternatives here, and in any case, they vary significantly from community to community. In order to be effective in work with homeless clients, however, providers must become thoroughly knowledgeable about the full range of the available resources. These typically include rooming houses, single-room-occupancy hotels (SROs), apartments, and other open-market options as well as service-related facilities such as group homes, serviced hotels and apartments, and health-related and/or treatment facilities. These housing options differ along many dimensions, including their eligibility criteria, imposed restrictions, available supports, and the nature of the setting in which they are located. These varying characteristics render specific housing alternatives more or less suitable to the particular needs of a given client.

As the client becomes articulate about his or her housing preferences, the worker can begin to explore the implications of that preference for the client's potential to sustain permanent living in such a setting. This exploration suggests a range of assessment categories that must be fully explored during the course of the client's and the worker's joint efforts. They include:

1. *History of housing and homelessness.* Rich information about clients and potential housing options can be derived from exploring the client's past history of housing and homelessness. Not only can past housing history inform judgments about suitable conditions for current living, but the exploration can offer revealing details of the clients' lives that provide meaningful material for additional exploration and discussion. Primary areas to investigate include independent housing, living with family or significant others, foster care, and psychiatric hospitalization or other institutional history, such as prison or a residential treatment facility. Clients' experiences and difficulties in their housing history should provide useful data in shaping future housing choices.

2. *Concrete supports.* The client's income and employment history are obviously of critical concern. The worker will also want to thoroughly investigate the possible income support programs for which the client may be eligible and what issues application to these programs may raise for the client (ambivalence about applying, lack of necessary documentation, etc.). Other relevant benefit programs for which the client may be eligible, such as food stamps of Medicaid, need to be identified and explored.

3. *Social functioning.* The worker evaluates how clients relate to others in different settings and situations. This constitutes a critical assessment issue, since the better the match between client characteristics and housing circumstances, the more likely is the client to be successful in sustaining permanent housing. Issues such as the client's comfort in group settings, the need or ability to sustain periods of social isolation, the client's interpersonal skills, and the extent, nature, and importance of his or her association network require full exploration. Data on such subjects, of course, come not only from

discussions between the client and worker, but from worker observation of the client in the program setting. Inconsistencies between client self-report and worker observation in this arena obviously merit attention and work.

4. *Mental status and psychiatric functioning.* Here, the worker attempts to assess the extent to which the client may be seriously disturbed or mentally ill and, if so, what import this condition holds for the quest for permanent housing. On the negative side, unmanaged symptomatology significantly reduces the likelihood that effective housing placement will occur. Such clients must be linked to appropriate treatment resources and assisted in learning the skills of mental illness management. On the positive side, however, mental illness offers housing and resource alternatives to clients. Housing programs specifically targeted for the mentally ill, as well as benefit programs such as SSI, become available and provide income support and other needed resources.

5. *Alcohol and substance abuse.* Client history and current use and abuse of substances hold important meaning in the placement process. Many housing providers require that clients not currently be using alcohol or drugs in order to be accepted for housing. Others are indifferent to use, and some even tolerate significant abuse. Gaining accurate information regarding substance use is often difficult and may require observation of the client over time as well as repeated discussion of the issue. The relationship of this topic to the client's ability to sustain permanent housing, however, frequently provides the worker with access and leverage in work on the issue.

6. *Skills for community and daily living.* This category refers to the range of skills that are necessary to sustain independent living in the community. They include personal hygiene, shopping, cooking, maintaining a proper diet, budgeting and prioritizing needs, management of one's living space, use of public transportation, ability to use a bank and keep records, and ability to negotiate benefit programs, landlords, and the like. Observing clients in a program setting as well as observing how they engage in the various tasks of seeking permanent housing such as applying for benefit programs, engaging health systems in order to receive service, etc., provides important data regarding these skills. As the worker and the client become clear on these skill levels, this information provides a useful agenda for the shaping of housing alternatives and the task of skill building as dictated by the client's housing aspirations.

7. *Medical factors.* Medical factors must be considered in evaluating a client's potential for housing. Homelessness is a dangerous circumstance, and many homeless people have developed acute or chronic

conditions during the period of their homelessness. Some medical conditions dictate particular housing options, such as a health-related facility. Others require special arrangements in the client's living setting.

Following the initial assessment, ongoing work with clients varies significantly in time and character depending upon the nature of the case. Some clients pose significant placement problems associated with conditions such as addiction or unmanaged mental illness. In such cases, the worker may discover that permanent placement is not possible unless the impairment in question is managed or abates. Clients who are resistant to assistance for such conditions require extensive work before they will agree to treatment. Some never will. Others require substantial work on the development of community and daily living skills before it is possible for them to sustain permanent residence. Structural barriers are also common in work with homeless people. Problems such as repeated denial of eligibility by benefit programs, problems associated with immigration or legal status, or difficulty in finding an appropriate residential site significantly protract the placement process.

As observed above, the activities of an ongoing program are most helpful in sustaining client motivation and providing a helpful environment during the course of the placement process. Day programs where clients have access to sanitary and laundry facilities, have a place to relax, are able to prepare and share meals together, and have access to their worker and other clients, both informally and in structured group settings, are an ideal context for work with homeless people. In addition to meeting the immediate and direct needs of clients, they offer a milieu that fosters support and mutual aid, the reinforcement of motivation, and the bolstering of attitudes helpful in facilitating the move from homelessness to permanent residence. With time, effort, and persistence, most clients who are served by such programs will be successful in the quest for a permanent resident.

Finally, as has also been suggested above, it is important to underscore the fact that effective practice with homeless people requires a proactive, directive, and orchestrating stance on the part of the worker—a stance that would be neither necessary nor appropriate under less compelling circumstances. The extent of the need, the dearth of resources, and the degree of impairment that is typically associated with protracted homelessness are seldom reversed without aggressive intervention. In the absence of independent supports and resources, the client is realistically dependent upon the worker for their provision. Remediating this disparity requires the lending of energy, strength, skill, and professional status until the client is once again ensconced in an environment that may reasonably be expected to sustain his or her needs.

## CASE ILLUSTRATION

Mrs. Ortiz was referred to Westside Community Services by a social worker in the New York City shelter system. Mrs. Ortiz had been staying at the shelter since her recent discharge from the inpatient psychiatric ward of a city hospital. The shelter worker indicated in a telephone conversation with the Westside worker that Mrs. Ortiz seemed highly motivated to move out of the shelter, but that her case was sufficiently complicated to preclude the ability of the shelter staff to offer effective assistance. The worker offered several details about the client's background.

Mrs. Ortiz was a 55-year-old native of the Dominican Republic who had come to New York with her husband in the 1950s. Her husband had been a day laborer, and Mrs. Ortiz had worked as a domestic until her husband's death approximately eighteen months before. Within a two-month period, it seems, this client had experienced devastating tragedy and loss. Her son, to whom she was very close, had been convicted of armed robbery and sentenced to prison in Upstate New York. Mr. Ortiz died suddenly from cardiac arrest. Soon after the husband's death, Mrs. Ortiz's other child—an 18-year-old daughter who Mrs. Ortiz suspected was using drugs—disappeared and had not been heard from since. In the months following these events, Mrs. Ortiz became severely depressed and was ultimately hospitalized following a psychotic break. During the period immediately preceding the hospitalization, Mrs. Ortiz had been unable to work and had fallen several months behind in her rent. When she went to the hospital, the landlord illegally rented her apartment, placing most of her belongings on the street save some clothing and a television set, which he held in the basement.

Mrs. Ortiz did not arrive for a morning appointment, which the Westside worker had confirmed with the shelter worker, but she did visit the center later that afternoon, asking for the worker by name. The worker rearranged some appointments and saw Mrs. Ortiz shortly after her arrival at the center. The client appeared withdrawn and tired. She indicated that she had come to obtain assistance in getting an apartment for herself and her son, but as the worker began to explore the client's background and circumstances, it became clear that information would not come easily. Mrs. Ortiz spoke English with a thick Hispanic accent. She answered questions politely but offered minimal information. It seemed to the worker that Mrs. Ortiz was still severely depressed.

The Westside program is a community-based service facility for homeless people. It operates service programs in several settings, including services to SROs and the drop-in center that Mrs. Ortiz was visiting. The drop-in center offers clients laundry and sanitary facilities, a place to spend the day, access to service staff, and program activities. It is a transitional service in that the aim is to assist clients in obtaining and sustaining permanent housing.

The worker indicated to Mrs. Ortiz that it would be useful for her to begin visiting the program during the day, since it would be necessary for them to work together over a period of time on the housing quest. In the meantime, the worker observed, the program would offer a pleasant alternative to the shelter day-room and convenient access to the worker. Mrs. Ortiz agreed but did not return to Westside until the worker personally visited the shelter and invited Mrs. Ortiz to come to the program "for lunch." It seemed that the formality of the invitation held special meaning for Mrs. Ortiz. With prodding by the worker, Mrs. Ortiz began to visit the program more frequently over the ensuing weeks.

Through repeated conversations and observations, it became clear that Mrs. Ortiz was severely depressed and defeated. She took personal responsibility for the dissolution of her family, implying that it reflected her lack of competence as a parent and a homemaker. She was very passive in her social relations, never initiating interaction. When engaged by others, she responded in a polite if distant fashion. When left alone, she sat all afternoon watching television or just staring blankly. Her domestic and housekeeping skills seemed to be intact, but unless prodded into action, she seemed to have no desire to participate in the activities of the day program. She was thin and had little appetite. As it turned out, she was an illegal alien, which meant that she was not eligible for entitlements.

The one spark for Mrs. Ortiz seemed to be the issue of her son. She expressed the desire to visit him in prison and continued to stress that the reason she wanted an apartment was to provide him with a home upon his release.

Over the next several weeks, the worker was able to convince Mrs. Ortiz to visit the outpatient mental health clinic at a nearby hospital with which Westside had an active relationship. It also became clear that it would be necessary for the worker to accompany Mrs. Ortiz to the facility if she were actually to keep the appointments. The psychiatrist confirmed the depression diagnosis, prescribed medication, and worked out a routine for the worker to assist Mrs. Ortiz in following the drug regimen. With the assistance of a cooperating Legal Aid lawyer, the worker and the client began the process of applying to legalize her immigration status. As it turned out, Mrs. Ortiz was eligible for a green card but had been unaware of this and had feared the possible negative consequences of contacting immigration officials to explore the issue. With her immigration status resolved, the client would become eligible for SSI. This would provide sufficient income to enable Mrs. Ortiz to obtain housing and to support herself. The worker began the arduous task of processing Mrs. Ortiz's application.

A major turning point for Mrs. Ortiz was a trip to the prison to visit her son. The worker determined that the prison was accessible by bus—a four-hour ride in each direction. The client had repeatedly expressed the desire to go but was clearly fearful and apprehensive about taking the bus trip. When the visit had been scheduled, she requested that the worker accompany her. The worker saw this as an opportunity to strengthen the relationship and agreed. The visit went very well. Mrs. Ortiz seemed energized and reassured by the experience.

As a consequence of her observations and dealings with Mrs. Ortiz, the worker felt apprehensive about the client's ability to sustain independent living in an apartment. While her depression had improved with medication, it was far from abating. The client's social isolation, lack of relatedness to events around her, and extreme passivity led the worker to fear that alone, Mrs. Ortiz might not be able to manage the tasks of supporting an independent household. The son would not come up for parole for another nine months, and the worker feared that the motivation posed by his possible release was too distant to sustain the client. She shared this judgment with Mrs. Ortiz suggesting that as a transitional measure, the client move into an SRO in which Westside had a social service team. In this setting, Mrs. Ortiz could be observed and encouraged to become more active.

The client resisted the option, stating that her son would not be able to join her there. This led to a difficult period during which Mrs. Ortiz became quite irregular in her visits to the program and expressed disillusionment with her worker. In part out of self-doubt regarding her assessment and in part to resolve the impasse, the worker challenged the client to move ahead with the search for an apartment, offering to join the effort and provide assistance. After several false starts, in which Mrs. Ortiz was not able to sustain the arduous task of visiting the grim neighborhoods in which there were units available within her price range, she proposed moving into the SRO on the condition that the worker would ultimately assist her in finding an apartment.

The move was completed with aid of the worker's car and included a somewhat traumatic trip to Mrs. Ortiz's old building to collect her clothing and television set. The worker visited her several times during the next couple of weeks, supporting her in the new setting and completing the transfer of the case to the hotel's service team. A year later, Mrs. Ortiz was still living in the hotel, having become an active member of the community. Her son's first parole application had been rejected, and the next hearing was not to be scheduled for several months.

The case of Mrs. Ortiz raises several issues pertinent to work with homeless people. The value of a program base into which the client can be integrated for purposes of assessment, support, and skill building is clear. So, too, is the fact that in the face of very scarce resources, minimal supports, and client impairment, it becomes necessary for the worker to assume an active and directing demeanor in assisting the client. Like other life crises, the task of overcoming homelessness is typically a developmental process involving incremental steps toward solving problems, accessing resources, developing links, tapping client strengths, and building or rebuilding client capability. In the case of Mrs. Ortiz, her depression and legal status required aggressive and proactive intervention. Initial success in these arenas enabled the client and the worker to process an application for income support— a critical prerequisite for permanent housing. The client's commitment to her son and her desire to reconstitute what remained of the family unit was the primary motivating factor that sustained her efforts with the worker. The support of the program and the continuous encouragement and active involvement of the worker were critical in assisting the client to negotiate the tasks of making the transition to independent living. The disagreement between the client and the worker as to the most appropriate initial setting for the client posed a challenge to the helping relationship but ultimately served a positive function in the transition process. It is clear that in the short run, Mrs. Ortiz needed the support of a serviced setting. Whether she remained in the SRO or ultimately moved to an apartment, she had succeeded in making the transition to permanent housing.

Social workers are not likely to bring an end to the national tragedy of homelessness. As a profession that has dedicated itself to promoting the interests of the society's have-nots, we must remember that our constituency stands quite outside the primary power arrangements that shape national policy. We can do much to raise important issues and to heighten public awareness of social injustice. We can advocate on behalf of our clients, inform and educate decision makers, and offer compelling moral appeals. Such efforts are important and must be undertaken with commitment and competence. But the policy and resource allocation decisions that will go to the roots of homelessness rest quite beyond the influence sphere of the social work profession. We have a very important role to play, but the kind of progressive policy that will fundamentally alter the circumstances of the nation's homeless requires a political consensus that is simply not possible for the social service community to engineer.

That having been said, homelessness does pose a major new challenge for social work. Advocates, as has been so clear in the recent past, must continue to use the courts, the media, and other public forums to heighten public awareness of the problem and to pressure reluctant sectors of government to intervene. Planners and administrators must continue to develop and refine service models that are responsive to the needs of the various subpopulations of homeless people. Beyond their clear need for housing, each group presents varying support and service requirements for which program responses must be developed. Similarly, a major role for direct practitioners is to elaborate services for the population, further developing and documenting the often creative and ingenious strategies they have adopted in order to assist them in the face of great need, on the one hand, and the dearth of available resources, on the other. Housing models appropriate for subpopulations must also be developed, and creative methods of financing devised. Finally, researchers have a vital role to play in our efforts to better appreciate and address the complex problems of homelessness. Insight into the causes and consequences of the problem will be critical in informing the evolving debate. So, too, research can assist us in the development and assessment of practice and program models focused on the needs of specific groups.

Tragically enough, homelessness may well be thought of as an emerging field of practice for social work. As such, it challenges us with all of the professional tasks, dilemmas, and opportunities that are associated with other practice arenas.

## REFERENCES

Arce, A. A. and M. J. Vergare. 1984. "Identifying and Characterizing the Mentally Ill Among the Homeless." In H. R. Lamb, ed., *The Homeless Mentally Ill*, Washington, D.C.: American Psychiatric Association, pp. 75–89.

Bassuk, Ellen L., Lenore Rubin, and Alison Lauriat. 1984. "Is Homelessness a Mental Health Problem?" *American Journal of Psychiatry* 141:1546–1550.

Bassuk, Ellen L., Lenore Rubin, and Alison Lauriat. 1986. "Characteristics of Sheltered Homeless Families." *American Journal of Public Health* 75(9):1097–1101.

Baxter, Ellen and Kim Hopper. 1981. *Private Lives/Public Spaces*. New York: Community Service Society.

Bishop, Katherine. 1989. "Tent Cities Becoming the Front Lines." *The New York Times* (September 11), p. B1.

CCC (Citizens' Committee for Children). 1983. *Homeless Youth in New York City: Nowhere to Turn*. New York: CCC.

CUCS (Columbia University Community Services). 1988. *Health Care and Homelessness*, ed. by Julie Bramnick. New York: CUCS.

Dumpson, James R. and David Dinkins. 1987. *Shelter Is Not a Home*. New York: Manhattan Borough President's Task Force on Housing for Homeless Families.

Freeman, Richard B. and Brian Hall. 1986. *Permanent Homelessness in America?* New York: National Bureau of Economic Research.

Hombs, Mary Ellen and Mitch Snyder. 1982. *Homelessness in America: A Forced March to Nowhere*. Washington, D.C.: Community for Creative Non-Violence.

Hopper, Kim and Jill Hamberg. 1984. *The Making of America's Homeless: From Skid Row to New Poor*. New York: Community Service Society.

IOM (Institute of Medicine). 1988. *Homelessness, Health, and Human Needs*. Washington, D.C.: National Academy Press.

Kozol, Johnathan. 1988. *Rachel and Her Children: Homeless Families in America*. New York: Fawcett Columbine.

Main, Thomas J. 1986. "What We Know About the Homeless." *Commentary* (May), pp. 26–31.

Martin, Marsha A. 1982. *Strategies of Adaptation: Coping Patterns of the Urban Transient Female*. Unpublished doctoral dissertation, Columbia University School of Social Work.

Morse, Gary, Nancy M. Shields, and Christina R. Hanneke. 1985. *Homeless People in St. Louis: A Mental Health Program Evaluation*. Jefferson City, Mo.: Department of Mental Health.

Patton, Larry T. 1988. "The Rural Homeless." Institute of Medicine. *Homelessness, Health, and Human Needs*. Washington D.C.: National Academy Press, pp. 183–217.

Piliavin, Irving. 1988. "Some Clues to the Dynamics of Homelessness." Paper presented at 90th Anniversary Conference of Columbia University School of Social Work, New York.

Robertson, Marjorie J., Ropers, R. and R. Boyer 1985. *The Homeless in Los Angeles County: An Empirical Assessment*. Los Angeles: University of California at Los Angeles School of Public Health.

Rossi, Peter H., et al. 1987. "The Urban Homeless: Estimating Composition and Size." *Science* (March), 235(3):1336–1341.

Roth, D. and G. J. Bean. 1986. "New Perspectives on Homelessness: Findings from a State-Wide Epidemiological Study." *Hospital and Community Psychiatry* 37:712–719.

SHF (Settlement Housing Fund). 1986. *Project Homeless: A Follow-Up Study for the New York City Housing Authority.* New York: SHF.

Sosin, Michael, Paul Colson, and Susan Grossman. 1988. *Homelessness in Chicago: Poverty and Pathology, Social Institutions, and Social Change.* Chicago: School of Social Service Administration, University of Chicago.

Stoner, Madeline R. 1983. "The Plight of Homeless Women." *Social Service Review* (December), 57:565–581.

Struening, Elmer L. 1986. *A Study of Residents of the New York City Shelter System.* New York: New York State Psychiatric Institute.

U.S. DHHS (U.S. Department of Health and Human Services). 1984a. *HHS Actions to Help the Homeless.* Washington, D.C.: U.S. HHS.

U.S. DHHS. 1984. *The Homeless: Background, Analysis and Options.* Washington, D.C.: U.S. HHS.

U.S. Department of Housing and Urban Development. 1984. *A Report to the Secretary on the Homeless and Emergency Shelters.* Washington, D.C.: U.S. HUD.

U.S. General Accounting Office. 1988. *Homeless Mentally Ill: Problems and Options in Estimating Numbers and Trends.* Washington, D.C.: GAO.

Wright, James D. 1987. "National Health Care for the Homeless Program." In Richard Bingham, Roy Green, amd Sammis White, eds., *The Homeless in Contemporary Society.* pp. 150–169. Newbury Park, Calif.: Sage.

# 19

## Immigrants and Refugees

DIANE DRACHMAN

ANGELA SHEN-RYAN

The movement of people across national borders is an international historical phenomenon. Historically, national states have had an interest in migration that is reflected in policies aimed at obtaining migrants such as contract labor programs, forced migration, and slavery, as well as policies aimed to control the exit and entry of people in their territories (Kritz 1987). The historical perspective is important for social work as it facilitates recognition that service to immigrant populations is an ongoing social work activity rather than a unique response to an unusual or temporary condition.

In recent years, there has been a major wave of migration to the United States. The newcomers, who range in age from children to older adults, have been seen by service providers in health, mental health and educational organizations, in family and children's service settings, and in the workplace. Although social work has historically been involved in service to immigrant populations,[1] the professional response to the recent wave of migration has been limited, as workers in the field have reported on the paucity of professionally trained personnel capable of understanding the different cultures of the newcomer groups, their different migration experiences, and the unique issues they face in the process of adjustment to living in the United States. In addition, few schools of social work have engaged in training students for service to immigrants and refugees. The lack of professional preparation has exacerbated a tendency for practitioners and service organizations to treat and classify Haitians as blacks,

Indochinese as Asians, and Soviets as Jews. Dominicans, Mexicans, Puerto Ricans, Salvadorans, Cubans, Ecuadorans, Columbians, Guatemalans, and Nicaraguans have been indistinguishable, as all have been considered Hispanic. Thus, the migration experiences, which have been traumatic for many; the special educational, social, and emotional needs; and the special strengths of each group, as well as their different views on health, mental health, and help-seeking behavior—all have been ignored or misunderstood.

The limited service response is partially the result of the view that population movements are atypical, isolated, temporary historical events rather than recurring phenomena (Stein 1986). The "temporal perspective" has led to an emergency ad hoc service-delivery pattern resulting in the development of new programs that surface and end. It has obscured consideration of commonalties in immigrant and refugee group experiences and behavior as well as lessons learned from past population movements and experiences that could inform present helping approaches and service delivery (Stein 1986).

## PROBLEM DOMAIN

According to the 1970 United States Census of Population, 9, 619,302 foreign-born individuals were residing in the United States. (Census 1970). By 1980, the Census reported 14,079,906 foreign-born individuals living in the United States (U.S. Census 1980). Thus, within a decade, the foreign-born population increased by 4.5 million, or 46 percent. Estimates of the number of undocumented aliens counted in the 1980 census report have varied widely. However, research on immigration statistics indicates that it is likely that no less than "1.5 million and no more than 3.5 million undocumented aliens were counted in the 1980 census report" (Hill 1985: 232). The continued rise in the immigrant population has been highlighted in labor force projections for the beginning of the twenty-first century. A recent labor report states that immigrants will represent the largest share of the increase in the population and in the work force since World War I (Johnston and Packer 1987).

In contrast to the mass migration that occurred early in the twentieth century, when most people came from Europe, the new immigrants are arriving mainly from Asia, the West Indies, Central America, the Middle East, and some from Africa and Eastern Europe. Although the countries of origin of immigrant groups may vary from wave to wave, immigration legislation and policy nonetheless determine the selection of populations permitted or refused entry into the

United States. The issues that underlie the selection process include foreign policy considerations, economic and labor force factors, racial and ethnic composition, humanitarian responses, and family reunification (Jenkins 1988; Briggs 1984). The different statuses of the foreign-born populations now residing in the United States are therefore related to immigration policy and reflect some of the above issues. The statuses also carry with them different entitlements to services that have implications for the adjustment and adaptation of the newly arrived groups. The statuses also have important practice implications.

The Immigration and Naturalization Service (INS), the federal agency assigned to carry out immigration law and policy, determines the status of aliens who enter the United States. The varied statuses include immigrants, refugees, entrants, asylees, parolees, temporary resident aliens, special agricultural workers, and undocumented aliens.

An immigrant is an alien lawfully granted the privilege of residing permanently in the United States. The individual seeking permanent resident alien status requires sponsorship by an individual or organization in the United States. Sponsorship is based on either kinship or occupation or employment.

Immigrants are entitled to many of the services available to citizens. However, some differences in eligibility affect service access and service utilization. For example, although entitled to federally funded means-tested income-support programs, an immigrant must account not only for his or her own income but the income of the sponsor in order to become eligible. Disincentives for the use of service programs or entitlements also exist. Although uncommon, an immigrant who becomes a public charge can legally be deported. Moreover, if an immigrant has received welfare funds and wishes to sponsor the immigration of a family member, it is likely that the sponsorship and immigration of the relative will be denied on the basis of the potential sponsor's having been a public charge. Health and education entitlements, however, appear to have fewer disincentives, as sponsors' income and resources are not considered unless they are contributed to the applicant.

The 1980 Refugee Reform Act defines a refugee as a person who is outside of and unable or unwilling to avail herself or himself of the protection of the home country because of persecution or a well-founded fear of persecution on account of race, religion, nationality, membership in a particular social group, or political opinion. The 1980 legislation mandated appropriations for refugee resettlement and service provision. As a result, refugees have become entitled to many of the programs and services available to citizens, such as Aid to Families with Dependent Children (AFDC), food stamps, Medicaid, and Supplemental Security Income (SSI). English-language training, employment and vocational counseling, and job placement are among the additional services offered, as they are consistent with the self-sufficiency emphasis of the service programs developed for refugees.

The individual who requests refugee status makes an application from abroad or from a country of asylum, which the INS accepts or rejects. Refugees are also exempt from some of the exclusionary criteria applied to individuals requesting permanent resident status, such as illiteracy, potential public charge, and lack of labor certification. After one year in the United States, the refugee may adjust the status to immigrant.

An asylee is essentially a refugee. The asylee, however, has arrived in the United States and applies for asylee status from United States territory.

The political debate over who is considered a refugee has affected both users and providers of service. The debate centers on the belief that decisions on asylum have been tailored to fit foreign policy goals or ideological preconceptions, despite the neutral stance on refugee policy established in 1980. Critics on both the right and the left of the political spectrum have engaged in the controversy: "Liberals say the I.N.S. has looked unfavorably on applications from Salvadorans because El Salvador is an ally. Conservatives complain bitterly about the rejection of Poles and other Eastern Europeans" (*New York Times*, March 15, 1987, p. A28).

In 1987, the U.S. Supreme Court decided that a "more generous standard" than the one used by the INS to determine eligibility for refugee/asylee status had been intended by Congress, and that aliens may be eligible for asylum if they can show that "persecution was a reasonable possibility." The individual's "subjective mental state" was considered a key factor (*New York Times*, March 15, 1987, p. A28). Although the Court's ruling made it easier for aliens to prove eligibility for asylum, many have remained in "uncertain status," and many have been considered economic migrants despite a reasonable possibility of persecution should they return to the native country. As a result, individuals and families have continued to live either in a legal limbo or anonymously and in hiding, being fearful of deportation. The controversy over who is considered a refugee has also placed workers and organizations in a conflict between the legal system and an individual's or a family's need for service.

The status of entrant was established by President Carter for Cubans and Haitians who entered the United States in boat lifts in 1980. The entrants received many but not all of the entitlements available to refugees. Although they were allowed to remain in the United States for a fixed period of time, they were ineligible to apply for permanent resident status until 1985 (Cubans) and 1986 (Haitians).

Under a 1981 federal policy designed to halt illegal immigration, the newly arriving Haitians requesting asylum were refused. They were viewed as economic migrants and consequently became undocumented aliens. Many were placed in detention centers upon arrival. As a result of a 1982 federal court decision they were released from detention. Haitians, however, have continued to arrive and seek asylum in the United States. The vacillating federal policy toward this group has affected their access to services.

A parolee is an individual admitted into the United States on an emergency basis. Admission is based on a "compelling reason" that is in the "public interest." A parolee has similar entitlements to those of refugees, asylees, and entrants. At present, few individuals enter the United States in this status.

Undocumented aliens are individuals who have no current authorization from the Immigration and Naturalization Service to be in the United States. This group consists of individuals who enter the country illegally. It also consists of individuals who enter legally in a nonimmigrant status for a temporary period of time, such as students or tourists, and whose visas expire while they remain in the United States. Others who enter legally may violate the terms of entry, by taking a job, for example. While federal authorities are required by law to prevent undocumented aliens from entering or remaining in the United States, which implies a view that undocumented aliens have no right to service, this view is in philosophical conflict with the service system, as service provision is based on need (particularly health and education) regardless of an individual's immigration status. Workers have reported that undocumented aliens tend to avoid service institutions because of fear of deportation. This impression has been supported by research on service utilization by this group (North 1982; Tienda and Jensen 1986; Jensen 1988).

In 1986, with the passage of the Immigration Reform and Control Act, an amnesty program was established for undocumented aliens. Two major conditions determined eligibility: arrival in the United States prior to January 1, 1982, and continued residence in the United States since that time. The legislation includes a provision forbidding employers to hire undocumented aliens. Individuals who have not applied or qualified for the amnesty program have remained as undocumented aliens. Those who qualified, however, are ineligible for a period of five years for AFDC, food stamps, and other federal assistance programs.

Although the amnesty program has been beneficial to many, numerous factors have diminished its effectiveness. The program has not reached the numbers of people it was designed to reach; it has created problems of separation among families, as some members have been ineligible for amnesty and could be deported; and as feared, it has led to discrimination in employment due to the requirement that employers review aliens' documentation of residence (*New York Times,* November 4, 1988, p. A1).

Several explanations have been suggested for the program's inability to reach those for whom it was designed. Many individuals had insufficient documentation of residency because of years of living anonymously. Many were wary of becoming involved in a system they had avoided for years. Deportation possibilities were increased if an individual was rejected for amnesty when the INS obtained information about the individual through the amnesty application. Employers were reluctant to provide documentation of residency, as many paid workers off the books, which raised concern about liability for back taxes. As a result, individuals who could qualify for amnesty have remained as undocumented aliens and have had limited or no access to the services they need.

## SOCIETAL CONTEXT

The United States has been described as a nation of immigrants, as historically, large populations from different countries have arrived and settled here. In fact, there have been points in United States history when the foreign-born population has outnumbered the native born in cities such as Chicago and New York (Rothman and Rothman 1975: 349). Thus, the history and tradition of acceptance of newcomers create a climate of social support for the newly arriving groups.

The heterogeneity of American society acts as a social support for newcomers, as many are able to find members of their group residing in the immigrant communities in the United States. These communities provide informal assistance, which is observable in neighborhoods where the spoken and written language of the groups and the habits of the cultures are expressed. There is added stress, however, for those who have come from a society and culture that is vastly different from those of the United States and where there has been no preestablished ethnic community.

The American tradition of voluntarism acts as a support, as private services have developed to assist newcomers. For example, the church-based Sanctuary movement provides assistance to Central Americans.

Legal services have developed, particularly for Central Americans who are requesting asylum. Community organizations in cities such as Los Angeles, San Francisco, Fresno, Miami, Houston, San Antonio, St. Paul, Portland, Boston, Chicago, and New York serve newcomer populations. Federal agencies provide assistance to refugees through contracts with voluntary agencies (VOLAGs) for resettlement services. State-administered resettlement programs for refugees also offer cash assistance and supportive services.

Adjustment is also influenced by the reception individuals experience in the United States. The reception has been stressful for many. Some reception issues affect all newcomers; others affect specific groups. The public debate that immigrants are a drain on the economy, that they absorb the jobs needed for citizens, and that they are on welfare is directed at all newcomer groups. Despite evidence that challenges these assumptions, specifically noting that immigrants contribute to the economy through sales and income tax more than they take (Simon 1980), and despite evidence that they are less likely than citizens to receive welfare (Tienda and Jensen 1986; Jensen 1988), the belief that they absorb more than they give persists. Thus, newcomers, although physically accepted, are predisposed to a situation of social marginality.

A significant proportion of the new arrivals are people of color. Although this group enters a multiracial society, it also enters a social context of race relations tension. The multiracial society acts as a support, but the status of newcomer, combined with the nonwhite minority status, diminishes acceptability.

Interethnic tensions are also part of the social context and are expressed in strained relations between Afro-Americans and the newly arriving Latino groups, English-speaking immigrants vs. the non-English-speaking Afro-Caribbeans vs. Afro-Americans, and the divisive comparison of all groups to the Asians—colloquially referred to as the model minority. The strained relations between Afro-Americans and Latinos have high visibility in Miami, as black parents raise concerns about the overcrowded conditions in schools created by the new arrivals and the non-English-speaking student population (*New York Times*, March 21, 1989, p. 1). Political pressure has been exerted in Congress among the English-speaking groups for legislation that would favor the entry of English-speaking people (*New York Times*, July 14, 1989, p. A1).

## RISKS AND NEEDS OF POPULATION

Many individuals who experience uprooting and migration adapt and cope as they build new lives and adjust to a new land. There are those, however, who have difficulty coping, as uprooting and migration entail considerable change—physical, social, and cultural (Shuval 1982). For some, there are massive personal, social, and economic losses. Others experience cumulative stress, beginning in the country of origin and at the point of departure, and continuing through the migratory passage and through years in the land of destination.

The present state of knowledge on migration and adaptation is inconclusive. Two research emphases appear in the epidemiological literature. The first is on the association between migration and mental illness (these studies generally use hospital admission as the operational definition of mental illness; Bagley 1968; Malzberg and Lee 1956, Odegaard 1936). This view has been challenged on the basis of differences in methodological procedures (Fabrega 1969; Vega, Kolody, and Valle 1987; Murphy 1965; Malzberg 1969; Kantor 1969); conceptual ambiguity and lack of consideration of variables in the culture of origin and destination; the varying social characteristics of the migrant; and the social psychological dimensions of the circumstances of migration.

The second and more recent research emphasis focuses on "how the many variables involved in the process of migration and culture change interact to affect different populations and individuals differentially" (Aronowitz 1984: 237). This second emphasis is useful for social work as it facilitates consideration of the multiple factors in the person and the environment within the context of migration. The following discussion of populations at risk illustrates the interaction of some of these factors.

The elderly immigrant population faces unique struggles created by the heavy demands for new learning, particularly of language, daily living skills, and differences in culture. These demands occur at a stage in life when individuals are less well equipped to meet them rapidly. Workers have reported that for some who have not developed sufficient language skills, fears of leaving the home or using public transportation have surfaced. These individuals have become confined to the home, spending days waiting for family members who may be working or going to school to assist them outside or on public transportation. Thus, the isolation that is frequently associated with advanced age among native-born individuals is increased for the foreign-born elderly who have limited language skills.

Cultural differences regarding attitudes and treatment of the elderly add complexity to the problem. Many of the foreign-born come from countries where the older individual is treated with special respect. As family members acculturate, expressions of respect may change or diminish. For some elders, the change has been experienced as a loss in status. The themes of helplessness, isolation, and loss of status that emerge in work with this population have additional meaning in the context of recent migration.

The experiences of immigrant women are also unique. Many head households alone. The struggles associated with the single-parent experience are compounded for immigrant women, as many need to master English, to find housing and work, to adjust to a new society, and to raise their children alone in an unfamiliar country. For married women who enter the labor force, other difficulties arise. Some obtain work more readily or receive higher salaries than their husbands—an experience that alters many marital and family role relationships.

The growing independence of immigrant women may lead to demands or expectations of their husbands that in their country of origin would be considered unacceptable. The shifts in roles and behavior have contributed to marital difficulties, and practitioners have reported the problem of separation or divorce even among those who have come from countries where marital dissolution is rare. Domestic violence has also been reported.

The vulnerability of some groups is increased by the interaction of migration with a high degree of cultural difference between the group's country of origin and the United States, significant difference in educational levels between the group and native Americans, limited transferability of the group's occupational skills, and the group's shift from a rural agricultural society to an urban technological society. The Hmong, for example, are tribal people from the mountains of Laos who fled during the war in Indochina and who have settled in different parts of this country. They are not literate in their own language and their occupational skills of fishing, farming, sewing, carpentry, healing, and religious activities have not been easily transferable to the United States. Many have not learned English. Their customs and habits, which are vastly different from those of Western society, have been misunderstood. The misunderstandings have led to conflict with landlords and the legal system in some communities and have created problems of eviction, shame, confusion, and eventual relocation (*New York Times*, February 10, 1988, p. B4). When relocation has been required, it has been exceptionally difficult, as this group has experienced years of involuntary uprootedness. Health and mental health clinics in contact with the Hmong have reported on problems of depression, psychophysiological symptoms, family difficulties, suspiciousness, social withdrawal, and suicide attempts (Westermeyer 1985; Kinzie 1986).

Children and adolescents who have arrived without their parents (unaccompanied minors) face special problems. Their experiences have been marked by discontinuity—broken bonds with parents, siblings, extended family, friends, environment, and culture. Educational and developmental delays have been reported, particularly for those who have had years of disruption either in flight and/or in refugee camps (Carlin 1986). Many have been placed in foster or adoptive homes. When the culture of the child and that of the foster or adoptive family are dissimilar, the adjustment process has had greater complexity, as issues of language, foods, customs, and past experiences have had to be managed, in addition to coping with the issues that are usually associated with a transition into a foster or adoptive home.

The long-lasting effects of terror and war have been experienced by some adults and children. Some have experienced torture and rape or have witnessed the death of family and friends by execution, disease, or starvation. Individuals with these experiences have been seen in clinics for problems of severe depression, somatic complaints, poor concentration, loss of appetite, and insomnia. Some have been diagnosed as suffering from posttraumatic stress disorder (Kinzie 1984; Mollica 1987).

## PROGRAMS AND SOCIAL WORK SERVICES

Historically, assistance to immigrants was provided either on an informal basis through self-help through religious organizations or voluntary associations. The resettlement houses that were part of the voluntary sector played a major role in the lives of immigrants. A similar tradition of service has continued, as self-help exists in the neighborhoods of the new immigrant communities; as religion-affiliated organizations, such as Catholic, Lutheran, and Jewish centers, provide assistance; and as community-based agencies offer services to the new arrivals. The multiple ethnic associations throughout the United States are a part of the voluntary sector that also offers services to the newly arrived groups. Some of these associations have had a long life, as they were formed by immigrants from previous waves of migration. There are also ethnic associations of recent origin. The newly developed groups represent the populations of recent arrivals. Some represent groups that have had no previous settlement in the United States, such as the Cambodians, the Laotians, and the Vietnamese.

Public social, health, and educational services are also offered to many categories of aliens: permanent resident aliens, refugees, asylees, parolees, and Cuban and Haitian entrants. The undocumented alien population, however, has limited rights to public service programs, although the right of undocumented alien children to public education has been upheld in the courts. While specific public services may be offered to different categories of aliens, their availability is often unknown to the consumer or the provider of service, as the eligibility criteria frequently change because of new legislation, new court decisions, and new readings of regulations and administrative directives (Bogen 1988).

Special programs for refugees have been established as a result of the Refugee Act of 1980. These include cash assistance for an eighteen-month period and services aimed at self-sufficiency and employment, such as job placement, vocational training, and language instruction, as well as other social supports. VOLAGs, which contract with the U.S. Department of State, also provide initial reception and placement services for refugees. Mutual-assistance associations (MAAs), which are refugee self-help groups, may also receive contracts from the state to "supplement local level service delivery, to identify and respond to gaps in locally available services, to act as a liaison between available resources and refugee families and to encourage local initiative in innovative program development" (Jenkins, Sauber, and Friedlander 1985: 17).

## DIFFERENTIAL CLINICAL ASSESSMENTS AND INTERVENTIONS

The assessment literature on immigrant groups is primarily located in the field of mental health and in the subspecialty of cross-cultural counseling. In the mental health field, immigrant groups are considered minority groups, and testing and mental and intellectual status are emphasized. There is also considerable debate in the literature regarding the cultural biases of the tests (Jackson 1975; A. R. Jensen 1980; Snowden and Todman 1982). A debate on the generalizability of Western notions of mental health and illness also exists in the cross-cultural counseling literature. However, culture-free assessment techniques are also emphasized, and the translation of assessment instruments through bilingual individuals and committees is one example of the methods used to correct for possible cross-cultural misunderstandings (William 1986).

In the authors' work with bicultural, bilingual workers and professionals drawn from refugee communities who were providing services to refugee client populations, a stage-of-migration framework was found to be a useful vehicle for assessment. The framework builds on the work of numerous writers in the field of migration who have examined the stages that individuals experience in the process of migration (Cox 1985; Gordon 1964; Keller 1975). The framework, which includes three stages in the migration process—premigration or departure, transit, and resettlement—is based on the following assumptions, which were outlined by Cox: "All immigrants have an experiential past; some experience abrupt departure while others experience a decision-making process and a period of preparation for a move; a physical move is always involved and finally resettlement and some type of adjustment to a new environment occurs" (Cox 1985: 75).

The stage framework has both generic and specific utility, as it can be applied to all immigrant groups and specific groups. It can be applied to the individual immigrant, as it offers a lens for assessment of the individual in the particular circumstance of migration. It enables workers and service organizations to consider and address the experiences and needs of the new arrivals as well as of future newcomers. It enables service providers to examine the relevance of previous immigrant group experiences and the attendant service delivery patterns to present-day experiences and present program responses.

Although the framework is emphasized, it is also assumed that variables of life stage, family composition, belief systems, social supports, and socioeconomic, educational, cultural, occupational, rural, and urban backgrounds interact with the migration process and color the individual or group experience in each of the migration stages. The following discussion on the premigration or departure, transit, and resettlement experiences of Soviets, Southeast Asians,[2] Cubans, Haitians, and Poles illustrates the applicability of the framework to different groups. The insights that are presented in this section were developed from contacts with bicultural personnel and professionals providing services to these populations.

## *Premigration and Departure Experiences*

The social, political, and economic factors surrounding the premigration and departure experiences are significant. The experiences in this phase are often evident in the reactions and behavior of individuals during the later stage of resettlement, when adjustment to the new country is required. Separation from family and friends, leaving a familiar environment, decisions regarding who is left behind, and life-threatening circumstances are some of the issues individuals face in this stage.

Sudden evacuation characterized the departure experiences of many Vietnamese during wartime conflict in Indochina. As a result, close family members were often left behind. The families of many were never reunited, as members either were lost in Vietnam or died during escape. These experiences have been associated with the survivor guilt and depression reflected in some unaccompanied minors and others who have arrived without families.

Many of the Chinese Vietnamese escaped by boats that were attacked by pirates. Some survivors experienced torture and repeated rape, while others witnessed family members being killed, raped, or taken away. The rape trauma has had added complexity for Southeast Asian women, as the Indochinese place high value on chastity and virginity and those who have been raped are no longer considered valuable or marriageable. Rape is also perceived as a disgrace to the family. The rape experience has therefore been a closely guarded secret to protect the future life of the individual and members of her family. To reveal the rape would also break a cultural tradition of emotional restraint. This information is valuable to service providers, as it sensitizes workers to a possible past trauma and offers insight into the cultural meaning attached to the experience. Since methods of helping are influenced by cultural interpretations of an experience, rape counseling for Southeast Asian women may entail different helping approaches than those used with American women.

The premigration and departure experiences of the Cambodians were traumatic. The Cambodians, who lived in a peaceful agricultural country, witnessed their family members and compatriots being killed during the Pol Pot regime. They witnessed family members dying of disease and starvation. They witnessed torture and executions and experienced forced labor. Many escaped in the midst of fear and crisis. When possible, they carried their children, spouses, and parents. Many family members died while escaping.

The severity of these premigration experiences has also been associated with the onset of posttraumatic stress disorder, as survivors have presented symptoms of conscious avoidance of remembering the past, panic attacks, startle reactions, uncontrollable intrusive thoughts, thoughts about suicide or killing members of one's own family, recurrent nightmares, insomnia, poor concentration, and emotional numbness. Practice implications therefore include an understanding of posttraumatic stress disorder, recognition of its symptoms, familiarity with appropriate methods of helping, and consideration of psychiatric referral or consultation.

According to those in contact with Polish émigrés, the sudden departure experiences of Poles contributed to their problems of adjustment in the United States. It has been reported that many exiled members of Solidarity were given forty-eight hours to leave Poland. These individuals had to make rapid decisions regarding who would or could accompany them in exile, and members of families were often left behind.

In contrast to the sudden departure experiences of the Vietnamese and other migrant populations, Soviet émigrés experienced a long wait before they were able to leave their country. The long wait was a by-product of the Soviet view that emigration was betrayal of one's country. Thus, an application to leave involved consequences such as loss of employment, uncertainty about departure possibilities, and years of waiting while unemployed.[3] In addition, individuals were expelled from the Communist Party and the Communist Fleet, a compulsory organization for those between the ages of 14 and 28. After expulsion, former coworkers and fellow students confronted, humiliated, and vilified the individual. Consent from both parents for permission to exit was also required, regardless of the individual's age or relationship to the parent, including situations where the biological parent had had limited or no contact with the individual. When parents provided consent, they, too, were viewed as "traitors" and they, too, were harassed. Some parents refused consent because it would have jeopardized their personal, social, and occupational lives. Therefore, the issue ruptured relationships in many families.

The negative attention that a departure application received in the Soviet Union, coupled with government attempts to hold onto potential émigrés and world press attention to the issue, fostered unrealistic expectations regarding one's reception and life in the new land. At the point of departure and during resettlement, there was also continued concern that the decision to emigrate would further jeopardize the welfare of relatives left behind.

The exodus from Haiti is due to two major forces: extreme poverty and fear of reprisal resulting from an individual's opposition to the government. The departure experiences of Haitians include a complex process of decision making, which revolves around the question of who in the Haitian family is the most appropriate member to leave. For rural Haitians, it can involve establishing temporary residence in Port-au-Prince while preparing the immigration papers. It involves considerable contact with a travel agent or other intermediary who assists his or her client in developing a strategy for visa eligibility. Remuneration for these services can absorb the total financial resources of the extended family. Other Haitians arrive in clandestine boats. A reservation on a boat often costs the individual his or her life savings. Some of the boats have capsized, and survivors have witnessed friends and family dying at sea.

Cuban migration experiences have differed according to the wave of migration with which Cubans have been associated. For example, the first group, which migrated to the United States between 1959 and 1962, included well-educated middle- and upper-middle-class white individuals and their families, who were mostly in business. Many in this group departed "voluntarily" with their capital assets.[4] The second group, which was composed of white, black, racially mixed, and Asian individuals and their families, was generally made up of professionals and tradespeople. These individuals departed with some capital assets, and many had contacts with individuals in the United States. This group, like the first, was driven by economic self-sufficiency. The third group (the Marielitos) migrated in the 1980s. Although the Marielitos included individuals from different socioeconomic and racial backgrounds, the group was comprised of two distinct migrating populations: "voluntary" migrants and those forced to leave the country. The thousands of voluntary migrants had grievances against the Cuban government that culminated in their taking over the Peruvian embassy. In response, the Cuban government allowed these people to leave through the Port of Mariel. At the same time, the government forced individuals whom they viewed as troublemakers to leave by placing them in boats departing from the Port of Mariel. This group included unaccompanied minors (mostly adolescents) and adults with histories of mental illness or prison records.

The premigration and departure circumstances of individuals from the different Cuban migrating groups have to be understood along the dimensions of the individual's socioeconomic class, race, education, and existing or nonexisting social networks in the United States. They have to be understood in terms of the degree of uprootedness experienced by the individual, which requires consideration of the voluntary or involuntary nature of the departure circumstances. In other words, the departure experiences and their aftereffects are likely to be different for a well-educated urban individual who makes the difficult decision to leave with his or her family and for a single adolescent with a mental illness who is physically placed on a boat that is leaving the country.

## Transit Experiences

In the transit phase, experiences may vary from a perilous sea journey on a fragile boat or an illegal border crossing to an uncomplicated arrangement for travel on a commercial flight. The duration of time may vary from years to hours. It could involve years of living in limbo in a refugee camp while awaiting a final destination. It could involve a long stay in a detention center while awaiting a receiving country's decision on entry or deportation. On the other hand, an individual may leave the country of origin and within hours connect with family or friends in the new country.

The transit experiences for many of the Southeast Asians have involved life in refugee camps. Thailand, for example, has been a first asylum country for many of the Cambodians, Laotians, Khmer, hill-tribe people, and Vietnamese. Many have remained in the Thai camps for years. The refugees in the Thai camps have arrived as homeless, starved, frightened people, many in poor physical health. Some died shortly after arrival. They arrived in the context of loss—loss of leaders, family, friends, possessions, community, and social, religious, and political organizations.

Despite humanitarian efforts, problems in the camps have included clothing shortages, inadequate water supply, and poor housing conditions. The competition for resources and services between the refugees and the local people has led to conflict among them—both in the camps and along the Thai borders. Thus, many refugees have encountered an unfriendly reception. The years of waiting in the camps prior to the resettlement in the United States (or another country) have been cited as a significant problem, as children have grown up in the camps; adolescents have become adults; and middle-aged individuals have grown old in the camps. Thus, a period of trauma has been followed by years of waiting for permission to relocate to begin a new life.

Knowledge of the behavior of Indochinese refugees during their stay in the camps is limited. However, the observations of a psychiatrist while working in Thai camps reveal stressful reactions and varied behavior:

> Refugees were guarded and unfriendly, indifferent and isolated, experienced as unreliable. Socially expected behavior diminished as thank you or friendly greetings were rarely heard. Emotional expression was restricted. More expressive individuals would cry when talking about their family. They would devour food or grasp rations while ignoring

spoken requests or signs. They had enormous tolerance for adversity and functioned well with major problems. They became depressed over minor problems and they were suspicious. (Sughandabhirom 1986: 88–89)

The transit experiences of the Soviets were generally orderly. Individuals departed from the Soviet Union by plan, leaving on planes or trains. They often went to Vienna, spending a week to two months there prior to proceeding to Rome. In Rome, they were housed in apartments while waiting for their papers to be processed for final relocation.

Polish émigrés generally arrived in West Germany, where they remained in a refugee camp for several weeks to a year. During their stay, they had access to multiple services, such as free medical and dental care, language and employment training, and education for the children. The availability of these services in West Germany and their relative inaccessibility in the United States led some refugees who relocated in the United States to return to West Germany.

Individuals departing from Haiti may arrive directly in the United States. Their initial experiences here may involve placement in a detention center, where they await a deportation decision or entry permission. Some have been moved from one detention center to another. Their detention center stays have ranged from weeks to over a year. Thus, after arrival, many Haitians have lived in a legal limbo and in isolation from the American community.

The transit experiences of Cubans have differed according to the wave of migration. The transit experiences of individuals migrating during the first and second waves were generally orderly, as people left by plan on boats or planes. Many of these arrivals had family or friends who offered homes and other help. The third wave included a rapid flow of refugees who arrived in overcrowded boats of all sizes and conditions. At the height of this wave, 2,100 persons a day arrived in Miami. Since thousands of people had no place to go, the U.S. government established several refugee camps as emergency housing. Many of the unaccompanied minors were initially mixed with adults in the refugee camps, where they experienced personal violence and were forced to defend themselves amidst explosive and terrifying riots (Szapocznik and Cohen 1986). To deal with the special needs of unaccompanied minors, a unique program for Cuban adolescents was developed and implemented with the objective of making life in the camp more comfortable and safe for the youths, while concurrently preparing them for life outside the camp (Szapocznik and Cohen 1986). Individual adults and unaccompanied minors remained in the camps up to six months before resettlement.

## *Resettlement*

As individuals resettle in the new country, cultural issues assume prominence. These issues include different views on health, mental health, education, help-seeking behavior, child-rearing practices, and the degree of cultural consonance or dissonance between the country of origin and the receiving country. Cultural factors also assume prominence in the interactions between service personnel and their clients. The reception offered by the host country, the extent of services available, the degree of cumulative stress experienced by the immigrant, and the discrepancy between the individual's expectations and the quality of actual life in the United States are issues that also surface in resettlement. Depression, suicidal ideation and suicide attempts, substance and chemical abuse, parent–child conflict, and wife and child abuse are among the commonly reported problems during the resettlement phase.

For the Soviets, there are unexpected difficulties in obtaining work or resuming an occupation for which they are trained. Many of the émigrés are well-educated, skilled individuals who experience lowered status as they shift from Soviet engineer, teacher, or musician to American street vendor. Some are unprepared for the multiple choices available to them in different aspects of U.S. life, and many are unprepared for the absence of services such as housing, employment, occupational training, and medical and dental care, which are the rights of citizens in the Soviet Union. These difficulties have led some to question or regret their decision to leave. Soviet émigré service professionals have suggested that the difficulties contribute to parent–child conflicts, depression, and chemical and alcohol abuse, which are the most commonly reported problems experienced by this group.

The problems experienced by the émigrés are often misunderstood by service personnel because of differences in cultural interpretations. Depression, for example, is perceived in the Soviet Union as a biological entity, and biochemical treatment is offered. A refugee client experiencing depression therefore expects to be treated with a pill. A service provider who attempts to deal with the depression through a commonly used method of talking therapy not only is perceived as strange but is also viewed as incompetent, as the client doesn't receive what he or she thinks is needed. This issue assumes greater complexity, as psychiatry has been used as a form of social control in the Soviet Union, and a service provider who initiates a talking therapeutic approach is likely to be received with suspicion.

Substance and chemical abuse among Russian adolescents has been reported by service organizations in contact with this population. It has been suggested that adolescents' vulnerability to drug use is associated with prior problems presented in school that have received relatively little parental attention because of the stresses of resettlement and because of cultural differences that revolve around the function and authority of the educational system. In the Soviet Union, schools assume considerable authority over the lives of children. Children attend school six days a week from 9:00 A.M. to 5:00 P.M. Schools also assume some socialization and recreational functions. The direction and management of a student's school problem in the Soviet Union is therefore viewed as being primarily within the jurisdiction of the school. The greater parental role in the direction and monitoring of children's education in the United States and the greater student autonomy have therefore been confusing to Russian parents and their children. As a result, some children have become lost in the school system, a circumstance reflected in truancy, dropping out, or continuing in school but avoiding classes. As these children enter adolescence, they have become prone to experimentation with drugs and, later, drug abuse.

Cultural factors have also complicated some parental responses to their children's involvement with drugs. Since it is common practice in the Soviet Union to become involved in the underground economy to increase one's wages, a child who does similarly here (i.e., one who brings home additional money through drugs) has been perceived by some parents as helping the family.

The resettlement of Haitians has been complicated by their reception in the United States, which has been influenced by the vacillating policy regarding their entry into the country; by the fear they are carriers of AIDS and other diseases; and by their being black. There is also a misbelief that Haitians are fluent in French, whereas most arrivals speak only Creole. According to Haitian service professionals, these factors have contributed to this population's difficulty and reticence in becoming involved in American society.

Cultural differences in authority over children have also complicated resettlement. A primary form of child discipline in Haiti is corporal punishment. Since Haitian schools are given major authority over children, they have the right to discipline, including the use of corporal punishment. In Haiti, parents are rarely consulted about a child's school problems, since they fall within the school's jurisdiction. When consultation with parents is requested by U.S. school personnel, Haitian parents may not attend, as the management of a school problem is not considered a parental issue. This cultural difference has resulted in a tendency for U.S. school and service personnel to label the Haitian parent as neglectful.

Child abuse among the Haitian population has also been reported. Cultural factors influence this problem, as the stresses of resettlement tend to increase the Haitian customary use of corporal punishment, and service personnel are unfamiliar with the extent of this child-rearing custom. Thus, informed assistance is minimized. Moreover, Haitians are wary of institutional services and authority because of the years of oppression during the Duvalier regimes. Assistance from service organizations is therefore rarely sought and reluctantly accepted.

A prominent concern in Cuban resettlement is the unaccompanied minor. These youths, who were abruptly disconnected from family and familiar environment, experienced migration as abandonment. Some were placed in foster care, and although correspondence with families in Cuba may have been maintained, when reunification occurred several years later family relationships were strained, as members experienced each other as strangers and parents lost their authority. Adaptational problems for the Marielito youths who were placed in prison rather than foster care have been another area of concern.

Resettlement for many Southeast Asians has been difficult because of significant differences in Eastern and Western ways of life and modes of thinking. These cultural differences have been more extreme for rural or hill-tribe people, as some have had little or no formal education in their home country. Limited contact outside the home environment has been one response to the culture shock. Service providers have reported that in families where this occurs, parents may not learn to speak English, creating greater isolation and reducing their sense of control over their environment. Children in these families have often developed competency in English, have adopted American ways, and have been called upon by their parents to translate for them or to perform functions ordinarily accomplished by the parents in their own country. The reversal of the roles of parent and child has been reported as a source of family stress, as parental roles and authority have become weakened. Moreover, parents have experienced their children as considering them less important here than in their home country. This is difficult for most Indochinese parents and elders to accept because, in their native society, they were revered and respected and their opinions were essential for any major family decision. Service providers need to be aware of this situation as a potential problem in the interview session if a child is used as a translator.

The role reversal of husband and wife has also been a source of difficulty. Some wives have found employment more easily than their husbands, as they have tended to accept lower paying and lower status jobs as housekeepers or garment workers. When the wife has become the wage earner, the husband may stay at home, care for the children, and do the housework—a situation considered intolerable by many Vietnamese and Cambodian men. Many have resorted to alcohol, spouse and child abuse, gambling, or joining a gang. Divorce, a rare phenomenon in Southeast Asia, has also begun to occur among this population.

Southeast Asian views on mental health differ significantly from Western concepts of mental health. Western-trained service providers often believe in intrapsychic influences on behavior. According to Southeast Asians, mental problems may be caused by organic disorders, genetic vulnerability, supernatural factors, physical or emotional exhaustion, metaphysical factors such as the imbalance between yin and yang, fatalism, and character weakness (Tung 1980, 1985; Kinzie 1985; Wong 1985; Nidorf 1985; Sugandabhirom 1986). To resolve a personal or interpersonal problem, the Indochinese in their home countries have relied on leaders in the community, elders in the family, religious leaders, and other community support mechanisms. What Americans view as professional interventions have appeared to many Southeast Asians as the meddling of an unwelcome stranger. Models of health care also differ. Scientism undergirds the Western model, whereas traditional and folk healing practices are common in Southeast Asia.

For more relevant and effective service delivery, providers therefore require knowledge of Southeast Asian views on health, mental health, and help-seeking behavior.

To summarize, all migrants go through stages in the migration process. Stress is universal. The experiences of loss and grief are common. Intergenerational conflicts are also common, as children generally move more rapidly than their parents into the new culture. Husband–wife conflicts are common as some women shift roles, becoming the primary wage earner. The social, political, and economic circumstances surrounding premigration and departure experiences are different. The transit experiences are also different. The different belief systems or value orientations of the varied migrant groups color each group's experiences in each phase. Thus, each group experience is different.

## CASE ILLUSTRATION

The following case of a Cambodian family seen in a community-based social service agency illustrates the role of indigenous personnel in the work. It illustrates specific cultural issues that enter the helping process. It portrays a problem common to many native-born Americans (i.e., family disruption and a child's school difficulty), but it also highlights the unique meaning attached to the family problem and its connection to the migration experience.

Mr. and Mrs. Bouhong were in their mid-30s at the time they were seen at the agency. They had four children, whose stated ages ranged from 3 to 12. The family had arrived from Cambodia two years prior to the referral. They were referred by the children's school because Sang, the oldest child, had become silent and withdrawn in class, although he had learned to speak English quite well. Sang had recently complained of stomach pains and headaches. Medical tests, however, were negative. Both parents worked. Mr. Bouhong was employed as a janitor, and Mrs. Bouhong did part-time sewing at home.

A Cambodian woman who had been a refugee was present at all interviews. She translated the sessions, offered cultural consultation to the worker, and acted as a cultural educator for Mr. and Mrs. Bouhong, explaining culturally relevant issues surrounding the work.

Initially, Mr. Bouhong maintained the position that there was nothing wrong with Sang—it was his character to be silent. Mrs. Bouhong offered few comments, but whenever questioned by the worker, she agreed with Mr. Bouhong. Sang's symptoms persisted for several months, culminating in his refusal to go to school. The parents then agreed that Sang should see the worker. Although initially uncommunicative, Sang, when he eventually talked, engaged in conversation about his hobbies and girls in his class. His interest in and discussion of the girls appeared to the worker to be developmentally beyond his stated age of 12 years. When this issue was pursued, Sang divulged his secret: he was actually 16 years old. He explained that when he was in the refugee camp, his father had made him younger because younger children had priority for food. He was concerned about discussing his secret, as his father was fearful that their welfare benefits would be curtailed or discontinued. When the worker allayed Sang's concern about this issue, the two of them agreed to discuss with his parents the problems he was experiencing because of the discrepancy between his stated and actual age. During the discussion with Mr. and Mrs. Bouhong, they were reassured that their welfare benefits would not be in jeopardy, and a plan was established by Sang, his parents, and eventually the school to advance Sang into a more age-appropriate class.

When Sang's symptoms subsided, Mr. and Mrs. Bouhong began to discuss their marital difficulties. Mrs. Bouhong indicated that she wanted her husband to leave the home. Mr. Bouhong stated that he had fallen in love with another woman in the refugee camp in Thailand. After the woman's arrival in the United States, she had moved into the Bouhong home with her two children. Mrs. Bouhong said that she had permitted this arrangement to please her husband, and although the woman had recently moved out, Mrs. Bouhong remained firm about wanting her husband to leave. Mr. Bouhong continued stating that he and Mrs. Bouhong had never been married. He was not the children's father. He was their uncle, as Mrs. Bouhong had been married to his brother. He explained that the family had escaped from Cambodia but his brother had gone back to assist others and had never returned. They assumed he was dead. In order for the entire family to gain entry into the United States, he had assumed the identity of the husband. Recently, they had heard that his brother might be alive in Cambodia.

Several issues predominated in the work: the couple's fear of deportation if their situation became publicly known; guilt about assuming the identity of her husband, particularly in light of recent information that the actual husband might be alive; their resolve to separate; their concern about Mr. Bouhong's relationship to the children; how to convey the situation to the children; and concern about losing face in the Cambodian community residing in the United States.

The Cambodian assistant was essential to the helping process. She informed the worker on significant issues, such as marital customs and marital role relationships, as the worker did not know if it was culturally normative for a husband to assume two wives or for two women and their respective children by one man to live together in the same household. The work assumed greater direction when the worker was informed that although a man may continue to have sexual relationships with other women while married, it is uncommon for two women and their children to reside in the same home. Mrs. Bouhong's silence in the interview sessions, her persistent agreement with Mr. Bouhong, and her permission for the other woman and children to move into their home became understandable when the worker was informed of the importance for wives to please their husbands and for women to assume a nurturing but background role.

The interpreter-consultant also explained to Mr. and Mrs. Bouhong differences in customs between Cambodia and the United States when dealing with school, parent–child, or marital difficulties, and she explained the practice for some of seeking or receiving professional help when such difficulties arise. The latter explanation was particularly important, as assistance on personal matters is customarily handled by the family, the elders, or religious leaders in the Cambodian community.

Although the interpreter-consultant assumed a central role in the work, several issues require consideration when working with indigenous personnel. Communication may be altered because of the interpreter's attitudes or views toward the client or the worker, or because the client's story may revive the interpreter's memories of his or her own experiences. This may take the form of substituting or omitting information to protect the client or his or her community from being presented in an unfavorable light, or a client's complaints may be censored for fear they will be construed as disrespectful of the worker. Misunderstandings may also occur because nonverbal communication is omitted in the translation, or there may be no corresponding translation because of differences in the internal structure of a language. To mitigate the problems cited above, the training of indigenous personnel is implied. When trained personnel are unavailable, it may be advisable for the worker to consult with the interpreter before and after sessions. Similarly, when working with a trained interpreter, consultation after a session may also be helpful in order to evaluate the content of the interview. For example, a worker may need to assess the cultural reasons for a client's attitude or belief or the acceptability of certain behavior in the client's culture.

Other cultural issues emerge in this case, in addition to those that became known through the interpreter-consultant. For example, Mr. Bouhong's response that Sang's silence was part of his character may be viewed as culturally normative, given that Southeast Asian societies rank organic or naturalistic phenomena as being among the important explanations of the causes of behavior (Tung 1980; Nguyen 1985).

Sang's physical complaints, which according to medical personnel had no physiological basis, may also be examined in the context of culture, as the tendency among Southeast Asians to somatize difficulties has been reported by practitioners and has been interpreted as a possible cultural phenomenon (Kinzie 1986; Lin 1986; Nguyen 1985).

At least two explanations have been offered of the tendency toward somatic complaints. One suggests that culturally shaped beliefs determine how distress is experienced, expressed, and interpreted (Kleinman 1977; Nguyen 1986). Another suggests that individuals from Southeast Asian societies place high value on interpersonal harmony; consequently, direct expression of feelings is discouraged (Tung 1980; Lin 1986).

The Bouhongs' concern about losing face in the U.S. Cambodian community may be tied to the cultural importance placed on belonging and maintaining honor for the family or kinship group. In contrast to the Western value placed on individual autonomy, self-determination, and independence, Southeast Asian societies place high value on community, kinship, and family. In keeping with the latter values, individual behavior is aimed at maintaining harmony for the group, and if one embarrasses the community, one is likely to lose face.

The case also illustrates the connection between the clients' problems and the migration process. Problems fostered by experiences during the premigration and transit phases surface in marital difficulties during resettlement. Experiences in the refugee camp contributed to Sang's school difficulty. In this case, as in others, the stage-of-migration framework previously discussed has implications for practice. With each stage in mind, a worker might consider a series of questions that could also apply to the Bouhong family. For example, the premigration-phase questions might include (Nidorf 1986): When did you leave your country? Can you tell me something about your escape? By what means? With whom? Who did you encounter along the way? Was anyone in your group hurt or lost? For the transit phase, the worker may ask the client to describe his or her life in the refugee camp, which may include such questions as: Could you describe your living quarters? With whom did you live? Was food available or scarce? What did a typical day look like? What were some of the problems people experienced in the camp? Were there any difficulties for you? For the resettlement phase, the worker may ask: How long have you been in the United States? With whom have you lived? Who are you living with now? A worker may also need to know if there was secondary migration, that is, a second move after initial resettlement in the United States.

The unique aspects of the case have been highlighted. The case also reflects common human problems that practitioners commonly address: parent–child, marital, and family relationships; relationships, or the lack of them, with one's community; stress related to massive and abrupt changes in one's life; and sadness due to loss. The management and adaptation related to these problems are unique to each individual, and social work knowledge and skills are suited to addressing unique individual reactions. However, knowledge of the cultural and migration variables can serve as a general field against which an individual client may be assessed and assisted.

The United States is in the midst of another major wave of immigration. The newcomers, who are diverse in their countries of origin, their languages, and their cultures, represent a new population with whom social workers will have increasing contact. Although many of the new arrivals have adapted well, there are those who have had difficulty coping, as uprooting and migration entail considerable change. For some, there have been significant losses: family, friends, home, community, familiar environment, and material possessions. Others have experienced severe trauma.

The task of addressing new populations is familiar to social work, as the profession has traditionally applied generic practice knowledge and skills, accompanied by the necessary specific information to respond to the new groups: "Attention to today's immigrant population requires exactly what has always been necessary—a framework for practice that allows one to learn about the particular needs and circumstances of the new population being served and the methodology and skills to be helpful" (Meyer 1984: 99).

The stage-of-migration framework outlined in the discussion is responsive to this practice task. It creates a vehicle for workers to obtain knowledge of the needs, experiences, and circumstances of the new immigrant groups. It facilitates understanding of the individual in the particular circumstance of migration. It has the utility for direct practice as well as program planning. It is based on the notion that migration is a recurring phenomenon rather than a temporary, unique historical event. Therefore, the framework can be applied to future newcomers. It enables practitioners and organizations to examine the similarities and differences in experiences, circumstances, and helping approaches of both past and present immigration groups. Thus, lessons learned from the past can inform present helping approaches.

## ENDNOTES

1. The term *immigrant* is used here in a generic sense, to refer to all foreign migrant populations in the United States unless specified otherwise.

2. The Southeast Asian population includes people from different countries who have different languages and cultures. It includes people from urban and rural societies, highly educated individuals, and individuals from societies with no writ-

ten language. However, part of this discussion is broad, as there is a comparison of Western and Southeast Asian views on health and mental health.

3. The premigration and departure experiences of individuals from the Soviet Union and Poland are now changing as a result of political shifts in that country. The receiving countries are also shifting their admission policies. The new and different circumstances are likely to create different experiences for the newly arriving groups. The framework presented in the discussion will therefore be useful in obtaining information about the more recent circumstances and experiences of the new arrivals.

4. The description of departure as "voluntary" may be misleading, as migrating individuals generally do not choose to leave their country of origin. Circumstances push them out. However, the departure circumstances and experiences of the voluntary migrant tend to be orderly and are different from the experiences associated with exile and sudden flight.

# REFERENCES

Aronowitz, M. 1984. "The Social and Emotional Adjustment of Immigrant Children: A Review of the Literature." *International Migration Review* 18(2):237–257.

Bagley, C. 1968. "Migration, Race and Mental Health: A Review of Some Recent Research." *Race* 9(3):343–356.

Bogen, E. 1989. "Interim Report on Immigrant Entitlements." Department of City Planning. City of New York Office of Immigrant Affairs.

Briggs, V. M. 1984. *Immigration Policy and the American Labor Force.* Baltimore: Johns Hopkins University Press.

Carlin, J. E. 1986. "Child and Adolescent Refugees: Psychiatric Assessment." In C. Williams and J. Westermeyer, eds., *Refugee Mental Health in Resettlement Countries*, pp. 131–139. Washington, D.C.: Hemisphere Publishing Corporation.

Cox, D. 1985. "Welfare Services for Migrants: Can They Be Better Planned?" *International Migration Review* 23(1):73–93.

Fabrega, H. 1969. "Social Psychiatric Aspects of Acculturation and Migration: A General Statement." *Comparative Psychiatry* 10:365–392.

Gordon, M. 1964. *Assimilation in American Life.* New York: Oxford University Press.

Hill, Kenneth. 1985. "Illegal Aliens: An Assessment." In B. Levine, K. Hill, and R. Warren, eds., *Immigration Statistics: A Story of Neglect*, pp. 225–250. Washington, D.C.: National Academy Press.

Jackson, G. D. 1975. "On the Report of the Ad Hoc Committee on Educational Uses of Tests with Disadvantaged Students: Another Psychological View from the Association of Black Psychologists." *American Psychology* 30:88–95.

Jenkins, S., M. Sauber, and E. Friedlander. 1985. *Ethnic Associations and Services to New Immigrants in New York City.* New York: Community Council of Greater New York.

Jenkins, S. 1988. "Immigration, Ethnic Associations and Social Services." In S. Jenkins, ed., *Ethnic Associations and the Welfare State: Services to Immigrants in Five Countries*, pp. 1–19. New York: Columbia University Press.

Jensen, A. R. 1980. *Bias in Mental Testing.* New York: Free Press.

Jensen, L. 1988. "Patterns of Immigration and Public Assistance Utilization 1970–80." *International Migration Review* 22(1):51–83.

Johnston, W. and A. Packer. 1987. *Workplace 2000: Work and Workers for the Twenty-first Century.* Indianapolis: Hudson Institute.

Kanton, M. B. 1969. "International Migration and Mental Illness." In S. Plog and R. Edgerton, eds., *Changing Perspectives in Mental Illness*, pp. 118–131. New York: Holt, Rinehart & Winston.

Keller, S. 1975 *Uprooting and Social Change: The Role of Refugees in Development*. Delhi: Manohar Book Service.

Kinzie, J. D., R. H. Fredrickson, R. Ben, J. Fleck, and W. Karls. 1984. "Posttraumatic Stress Disorder Among Survivors of Cambodian Concentration Camps." *American Journal of Psychiatry* 141(5):645–650.

Kinzie, J. D. 1985. "Overview of the Clinical Issues in the Treatment of Southeast Asian Refugees." In T. C. Owan, ed., *Southeast Asian Mental Health: Treatment, Prevention, Training and Research*, pp. 113–135. Washington, D.C.: U.S. Department of Health and Human Services.

Kinzie, J. D. 1986. "The Establishment of Outpatient Mental Health Services to Southeast Asian Refugees." In C. Williams and J. Westermeyer, eds., *Refugee Mental Health in Resettlement Countries*, pp. 217–231. Washington, D.C.: Hemisphere Publishing.

Kleinman, A. 1977. "Depression Somatization of the New Cross Cultural Psychiatry." *Social Science Medicine* 11:3–10.

Kritz, M. 1987. "International Migration Policies: Conceptual Problems." *International Migration Review* 21(4):947–964.

Lin, K. 1986. "Psychopathology and Social Disruption in Refugees." In C. Williams and J. Westermeyer, eds., *Refugee Mental Health in Resettlement Countries*, pp. 61–73. Washington, D.C.: Hemisphere Publishing.

Malzberg, B. 1969. "Are Immigrants Psychologically Disturbed?" In S. Plog and R. Edgerton, eds., *Changing Perspectives in Mental Illness*, pp. 43–56. New York: Holt, Rinehart & Winston.

Malzberg, B. and E. Lee. 1956. *Migration and Mental Disease: A Study of First Admissions to Hospitals for Mental Disease, New York 1939–1941*. New York: Social Service Research Council.

Meyer, C. 1984. "Working with New Immigrants." *Social Work* 29(2):99.

Mollica, R. 1987. "The Traumatic Story: The Psychiatric Care of Refugee Survivors of Violence and Torture." In F. Ochberg, ed., *Post-Traumatic Therapy and the Victim of Violence*, pp. 32–68. New York: Brunner/Mazel.

Murphy, H. B. 1965. "Migration and the Major Mental Disorders: A Reappraisal." In M. Kantor, ed., *Mobility and Mental Health*, pp. 5–29. Springfield, Ill.: Charles C. Thomas.

*New York Times*. 1987. March 15, p. A28.

*New York Times*. 1988. Feb. 10, p. B4; Nov. 4, p. A1.

*New York Times*. 1989. July 14, p. A1; March 21, p. A1.

Nguyen, S. D. 1985. "Mental Health Services for Refugees and Immigrants in Canada." In T. C. Owan, ed., *Southeast Asian Mental Health: Treatment, Prevention, Services, Training and Research*. pp. 261–281. Washington, D.C.: Department of Health and Human Services.

Nidorf, J. 1985. "Mental Health and Refugee Youths: A Model for Diagnostic Training." In T. C. Owan, ed., *Southeast Asian Mental Health: Treatment, Prevention, Services, Training and Research*, pp. 391–429. U.S. Department of Health and Human Services.

North, D. S. 1982. *Immigration and Income Transfer Policies in the United States: Analysis of a Non-Relationship*, 3d ed. Washington, D.C.: Center for Labor and Migration Studies, New TransCentury Foundation.

Odegaard, O. 1936. "Emigration and Mental Health." *Mental Hygiene* 20:546–553.

Rothman, D. and S. Rothman. 1975. *Sources of the American Social Tradition*. New York: Basic Books.

Simon, J. 1980. *What Immigrants Take from and Give to the Public Coffers*. Final

Report to the Select Commission on Immigration and Refugee Policy. Washington, D.C.: Refugee Policy Group.

Snowden, L. and P. A. Todman. 1982. "The Psychological Assessment of Blacks." In E. E. Jones and S. J. Korchin, eds. *Minority Mental Health*, pp. 117–130. New York: Praeger.

Stein, B. 1986. "The Experience of Being a Refugee: Insights from the Literature." In C. Williams and J. Westermeyer, eds., *Refugee Mental Health in Resettlement Countries*, pp. 5–23. Washington, D.C.: Hemisphere Publishing.

Sughandabhirom, B. 1986. "Experiences in a First Asylum Country: Thailand." In C. Williams and J. Westermeyer, eds., *Refugee Mental Health in Resettlement Countries*, pp. 81–96. Washington, D.C.: Hemisphere Publishing.

Szapocznik, J. and R. E. Cohen. 1986. "Mental Health Care for Rapidly Changing Environments: Emergency Relief to Unaccompanied Youths of the 1980 Cuban Refugee Wave." In C. Williams and J. Westermeyer, eds., *Refugee Mental Health in Resettlement Countries*, pp. 141–156. Washington, D.C.: Hemisphere Publishing.

Tienda, M. and L. Jensen. 1986. "Immigration and Public Assistance Participation: Dispelling the Myth of Dependency." *Social Science Research* 15:372–400.

Tung, T. M. 1980. *Indochinese Patients: Cultural Aspects of the Medical and Psychiatric Care of Indochinese Refugees*. Falls Church, Va.: Action for Southeast Asians.

Tung, T. M. 1985. "Psychiatric Care for Southeast Asians: How Different Is Different?" In T. C. Owan, ed., *Southeast Asian Mental Health: Treatment, Prevention, Services, Training and Research*, pp. 5–40. Washington, D.C.: U.S. Department of Health and Human Services.

U.S. Census (U.S. Bureau of the Census.) 1970. *Final Report PC(1)–C1*.

U.S. Census (U.S. Bureau of the Census). *Final Report PC 80-1-C1*.

Vega, W., B. Kolody, and J. R. Valle. 1987. "Migration and Mental Health: An Empirical Test of Depression, Risk Factors Among Immigrant Mexican Women." *International Migration Review* 21(3):512–529.

Westermeyer, J. 1985. "Mental Health of Southeast Asian Refugees: Observations Over Two Decades from Laos and the United States." In T. C. Owan, ed., *Southeast Asian Mental Health: Treatment, Prevention, Services, Training and Research*, pp. 65–89. Washington, D.C.: U.S. Department of Health and Human Services. pp. 65–89.

Williams, C. L. 1986. "Mental Health Assessment of Refugees." In C. Williams and J. Westermeyer, eds., *Refugee Mental Health in Resettlement Countries*, pp. 175–188. Washington, D.C.: Hemisphere Publishing.

Wong, H. 1985. "Training for Mental Health Service Providers to Southeast Asian Refugees: Models, Strategies, and Curricula." In T. C. Owan, ed., *Southeast Asian Mental Health: Treatment, Prevention, Services, Training and Research*. pp. 345–390. Washington, D.C.: U.S. Department of Health and Human Services.

# 20

## Imprisonment

▼

### BARBARA GRODD
### BARBARA SIMON

Imprisoned men and women, like the jails and prisons in which they are incarcerated, subsist far from the view and consciousness of the general public. They are people banished to a remote realm of punishment or, in the case of more than half the inmates of local jails, stored in confinement until they can be tried for the crimes for which they have been arrested.

Prisoners have been "put away" to protect the community from any further harm that they could inflict and to teach them the consequences of violating common standards of decency. They are confined purposefully "away from their loved ones, in very limited space and in stultifying routines" (Toch 1977: 5–6) in order to deter future criminal acts. Inmates are, in the public's mind, not only individual offenders, but also symbolic representatives of the breakdown of our social order. As such, they bear the brunt of communal rage for both their own particular criminal acts and for the entirety of crime in our culture. Consequently, the community, on the whole, remains uninterested in the welfare of inmates, seeking protection from them, not involvement with them. The prevailing conditions of prisons and jails and of the social services within them reflect this continuing disengagement.

### PROBLEM DOMAIN

Jails are local institutions run by counties, towns, or municipalities for keeping in confined custody four sorts of people: those arrested,

**647**

who are awaiting arraignment or trial; those convicted, who are sentenced to short terms of, usually, a year or less in that jail; those convicted and awaiting sentence; and state and federal prisoners, who have been transferred to local jails because of a shortage of space in prisons. Prisons, by contrast, are state or federal facilities to which convicted people are sent for terms usually of more than one year. Both jails and prisons, for the most part, succeed in confining those arrested, sentenced, and convicted. Regrettably, that is all they succeed in doing because that is all they are funded and officially assigned to do. Nonetheless, jails and prisons are expected by the public and its media to do much more: to protect the community, to control and deter crime, and to rehabilitate the offender (Irwin 1985). As an extreme measure for contending with soaring rates of crime, addiction, and violence, incarceration is assured of failure by virtue of the enormity of its charge: to counterbalance the absence of commitment in the United States to ensuring social welfare and its close correlate, crime prevention.

Over time, criminologists have justified imprisonment in four different ways. For many centuries and since the early 1980s, a retribution model has prevailed, a belief that jail exists to punish offenders, to make people pay in the coinage of pain and loss of freedom for violating the social contract (Blumstein 1989; Carney 1980). Quakers in the eighteenth century and many subsequent prison reformers introduced another approach to prisoners and prisons, the notion of rehabilitation, an idea in decline in the late twentieth century, discredited by a legacy of underfunded and undermined efforts to educate and restore. A third group of theorists, those from the deterrence school, have long argued that prison or jail is designed to prevent an offender from repeating his or her crime by making it too costly a venture to engage in again. At the same time, according to general deterrence theory, the imprisonment of criminals acts as a material and symbolic sanction that warns the rest of society to stay away from criminal activity, lest they be punished similarly. Finally, a fourth school of thought considers imprisonment a process of incapacitation, a way of preventing crime through the removal of offenders from the community in which they have been criminally active (Blumstein 1989; Carney 1980; Netherland 1987).

Imprisonment in the contemporary United States succeeds only in fulfilling the first claim, that of the theorists of retribution (Lipton, Martinson, and Wilks 1975). Prisons and jails do punish the imprisoned. The conditions in most contemporary prisons and jails and the reported experiences of the inmates who reside in them are, in the words of Hans Toch (1977) "noxious" (Bolduc 1985; Briar 1983; Netherland 1987; Toch, Adams, and Greene 1987). This noxiousness within prisons and jails takes many well-documented forms, among them overcrowding, violence, racial conflict, sodomy and rape, prevalent drug addiction, the loss of identity and self-esteem, suicide, self-mutilation, socialization into more hardened criminality, and the boredom and despair that result from the lack of meaningful work, training, education, and physical activity during imprisonment (Bowker 1982; Braswell, Dillingham, and Montgomery 1985; NYSDA 1985; Sherman and Hawkins 1981; Flanagan and Jamieson 1987; U.S. Justice 1988a).

Many implications flow from the primacy of the forces that regard imprisonment as punishment. First, jails and prisons are treated as arenas apart from the rest of society. Inmates are viewed not as people who will return to take their place in the community, but as people who must pay for their bad acts in an arena designed for punishment. Not surprisingly, conditions in jails and prisons directly mirror this viewpoint. Many reports from within and outside the criminal justice system document the grim, dingy, harsh, and overcrowded nature of jail and prison settings (Toch 1977). In some states, basic sanitation is inadequate within jail cells and sections. The prevalence of prison rape and assault is a matter of common knowledge, as well as of official tally (U.S. Justice 1988b). The sale and use of addictive drugs are widespread and even encouraged in some places. Brutality among inmates is compounded by harsh treatment by some correctional officers (NYSDA 1985). The absence in most jails and many prisons of educational resources, vocational training, meaningful work, and access to health and mental health care makes "doing time" a process without redeeming social value.

Service providers, of course, are directly limited in their work by conditions that can be difficult and by a shortage of space and resources that follows from the view that prison is a punitive payback. Mental health and health providers, chaplains, and educators have limited space, privacy, staff, institutional support, and funds with which to provide services. Burnout is a common phenomenon among social workers and other providers who work with populations with high recidivism rates, such as inmates of jails and prisons. Program directors often find it difficult to attract promising professionals and seasoned service providers to work in the confines of jails and prisons. In-service training is out of the question at many sites because of funding and staff shortages. Correctional officers and wardens often view human services within jails and prisons with fundamental suspicion, fearing that such services may interrupt and undermine the authority of criminal justice personnel and the climate of punishment. Morale among service providers is difficult to maintain in the face of the perennial scarcity of supports and resources, the recidivism of inmates, the scapegoating of human services for society's inability to control crime, and the invisibility of human service labor within jails and prisons.

The public at large pays heavily for the neglect of jails and prisons. Damaged and angry human beings exit from jails and prisons, usually without benefit of transitional planning or job counseling. A significant portion of inmates return to society with drug and alcohol addictions intact or intensified. Many reenter the community without educational or job skills that will assist them in anchoring and funding their existence outside jail. All leave jail and prison with a stigma that interferes with their finding jobs, training, and bank credit in all but the most enlightened of institutions.

The families of inmates also experience directly the consequences of retribution uninformed by compassion. The bonds between imprisoned parents and their children are usually severed partially or completely during the time of imprisonment. In only a few states—California, New York, and North Carolina among them—are imprisoned mothers permitted to keep their newborns with them during their first year of life. The parents and siblings of inmates usually take over child-raising responsibilities during the absence of the imprisoned family member. Family members share in the loss of income and the accrual of stigma that inmate status brings with it.

## SOCIETAL CONTEXT

The imbalance between the societal stress encountered by most offenders and ex-offenders and the societal support provided them before, during, and after incarceration is extreme. Even before the recent outbreak of the crack epidemic and the escalation of homelessness, the endemic issues of poverty, illiteracy, racism, sexism, abuse of children, alcoholism, and underemployment contributed relentlessly to the mounting rates of crime and imprisonment, particularly among teenagers and young adults in poverty, who witness daily the discrepancy between social classes and the immediate benefits of drug trafficking.

By the last decade of the twentieth century, two Reagan administrations have partially succeeded in dismantling a welfare state intended to provide sufficient social supports to prevent crime, malnutrition, and social disorder. Among the most eloquent anecdotal reports of the inadequacy of economic and social supports for the urban and rural poor are the intake narratives of several inmates at a large local jail, who reported that they had intentionally committed crimes to ensure their reincarceration because they found jail life preferable to that in the community (Grodd 1989). Social supports for potential offenders, offenders, and ex-offenders dwindle while the complex stressors of daily life, particularly in poor neighborhoods, multiply. Small wonder that the numbers of inmates, jails, and prisons multiply as well.

On June 30, 1986, one in every 648 adult residents of the United States was in a local jail, a rate more than double that of any Western European country and more than ten times that of Holland and Spain (Flanagan and Jamieson 1988; Kalish 1988; Netherland 1987). This strikingly high figure does not even take into account the additional 405,000 people incarcerated in state prisons and the 32,000 inmates in federal prisons (U.S. 1988a). Nor does it reflect the approximately 83,000 juveniles housed in juvenile facilities (U.S. Justice 1988b).

The number of incarcerated people in U.S. jails exploded upward during the 1980s. In the three-year period between 1983 (the year of the most recent full census of jails) and 1986, the population of U.S. inmates in jails increased by 23 percent, an annual average increase of approximately 8 percent (U.S. 1988a, 1988b). State and federal prison censuses have expanded in a similarly dramatic fashion since the early 1980s, as have the numbers of people on parole and probation. By 1986, more than 2.6 million adults in the United States were under some form of correctional care, custody, or supervision (U.S. 1988a).

Jail inmates, unlike those in prisons, include both convicted and unconvicted people. Convicted inmates include those awaiting sentencing, those serving a sentence, and those returned to jail because they have violated the terms of their probation or parole. Of the adult jail population in 1986, 47 percent were convicted inmates (Flanagan and Jamieson 1988). More than half of all jail inmates in 1986 (53 percent) were unconvicted. Included in this number were those people on trial, awaiting arraignment, or awaiting trial. By 1987 unconvicted inmates in jail had increased by a remarkable 25 percent since 1983, reflecting the rapid growth in arrest rates for robbery, burglary, and drug-related crimes (Flanagan and Jamieson 1988).

Predictably, the ranks of jail and prison inmates are made up of people from severely disadvantaged social and economic strata. Many inmates in the local jails of large cities are themselves the offspring of substance abusers and, as a result, may have been victims of persistent physical, sexual, or psychological abuse and neglect (Grodd and Wishart 1989; McDermott 1985). The level of formal education they have reached is far below that of the national average; over a third of the inmates entering many departments of corrections are functionally illiterate (Wilson and Herrnstein 1985). In 1980, in New York City jails, for example, fewer than half of all detained inmates had completed high school; 30 percent were high school dropouts; and 16 percent had attended only elementary school or had no formal education at all (Zanguillo 1981).

A staggering 45 percent of all jail inmates in the U.S. were unemployed at the time they entered jail in 1983, and 20 percent of adult felons reported never having worked for a formal wage or salary. Of all jail inmates in 1983, 22 percent were on welfare at the time of their arrest, and most inmates had been living at or below the poverty level during the year before their last arrest (U.S. Justice 1988a).

## RISKS AND NEEDS OF POPULATION

Who are contemporary jail inmates and prisoners? People imprisoned in the United States are, for the most part, men disproportionately drawn from the ranks of the young and of racial minorities. Men compromise 93 percent of jail inmates, 96 percent of state prisoners, and 95 percent of federal prisoners (U.S. Justice 1988a). Social workers in jails and prisons have noted two subgroups of men who are at particular risk while in jails and prisons. Those who have been in organized gangs before imprisonment are often expected to maintain loyalty to their gang during incarceration and after release. Such men are pressured to continue with the drug dealing and intergang warfare that they had participated in before jail or prison. Incarcerated gang members who seek to distance themselves from gang activities and alliances are, therefore, at particular risk of drug relapse, of becoming victim to assault or murder, or of becoming party to gang violence. Another subdivision of men—those who are slight of build, those who appear to be less physically rugged than others, those who are older than the average inmate, and those who are developmentally disabled—are, as Hollywood movies have so often depicted, at high risk of sexual assault and general harassment.

Two thirds of all jail and state prison inmates were ages 15 to 29 in 1980, though people in that age group made up only 27 percent of the overall population (U.S. Justice 1988a). Black male Americans are six times more likely than white Americans to be incarcerated at some time in their lives. By age 64, eighteen percent of black men have served time in a juvenile or adult correctional facility, compared with 3 percent of their white male counterparts (U.S. Justice 1988a; Netherland 1987). In 1984, blacks made up 12 percent of the U.S. population, 40 percent of the jail population, and 46 percent of state prison inmates (U.S. Justice 1988a). Hispanic American are also overrepresented in jails and prisons. They were 6 percent of the general population in 1984, but 13 percent of all male jail inmates and 11 percent of all female jail inmates in that year (U.S. Justice 1988a). Given the high rates of unemployment and of high school incompletion among racial minorities in the general population, social workers in jails and prisons identify minority men and women inmates as a category of clients for whom information, referrals, brokering, and advocacy concerning education and jobs are especially crucial. The social work function of linking clients with suitable resources and training cannot be overemphasized in work with inmates, in general, and with minority inmates, in particular.

Troubling rates of drug and alcohol abuse are found among inmates, rates that exceed markedly the disturbing rates of drug and drinking problems in the general U.S. population. A study of women in New York State's prison population revealed that 44 percent had discernible drug or alcohol problems (Applebome 1987). Jail and prison inmates are more than twice as likely as members of the general population to have used marijuana, amphetamines, and barbiturates and are more than ten times as likely to have used heroin (Innes 1988). When comparing the drinking habits of prisoners with those of the general population, one finds that 47 percent of the inmate population reported drinking one or more ounces of alcohol each day before entering jail or prison, while only 14 percent of the general population reported doing so (Innes 1988).

Many offenders report having been under the influence of drugs or alcohol at the time of their most recent offense. Roughly half of all convicted offenders incarcerated for a violent crime used alcohol before the crime; 40 percent of property offenders were under the influence of alcohol during their crime (Innes 1988). Drug and alcohol use contribute to crime and imprisonment in two ways: by loosening the behavioral restraints of offenders and by fueling their need to get money quickly, often illegally, to buy drugs. The New York City Department of Corrections has estimated that well over 60 percent of all prisoners in custody have a history of drug use prior to incarceration and were arrested and convicted of "money-seeking" crimes related to their drug use (MMC 1989). Since so many inmates have a history of drug use and abuse, social workers target certain subgroups of substance abusers as being the people in greatest jeopardy: Those who are polydrug abusers, those who have returned to jail two or more times on drug charges or crimes involved with obtaining drugs, those who are pregnant, and those who have overdosed in the past.

The high incidence of drug use among offenders puts them at especially high risk of contracting AIDS, hepatitis, other blood-related infections, and skin infections. Nutritional deficiencies are also disproportionately present among inmates who have been drug or alcohol abusers. Residents of jails and prisons also suffer from higher rates of venereal disease than the population at large (MMC 1989).

An informal survey carried out by the Montefiore Medical Center at the Rikers Island Correctional Facility in New York City in 1983 showed that approximately one half of the adolescents in custody had no family or other support systems in the community. Many had been in and out of foster care since birth (MMC 1987). It is not unusual for these youths to remain in custody for lengthy periods because of their inability to raise bails that are as little as $100 or less. Obviously, inmates with no kin or kith to whom they can turn upon release are at extreme risk of recidivism. Bloated jail censuses in major metropolitan areas, from surging rates of drug arrests during 1988 and 1989, may well force cities to expand pretrial release programs for people with low bail who are first-time youthful offenders (Bohlen 1989a). However, such programs will succeed only if they or related programs are equipped to provide first-time offenders with jobs, extensive counseling, detoxification, and education.

Female inmates enter confinement with special difficulties. They are sometimes pregnant upon admission. In New York City, for example, 8 percent of all females admitted into the custody of the New York City Department of Corrections were pregnant (Grodd and Wishart 1987b). Most (72 percent) of female inmates in New York City had dependent children for whom they bore primary responsibility. A few of these children of female inmates were placed in temporary custody with the Bureau of Child Welfare; most made caregiving arrangements in their families and neighborhoods (McDermott 1985). Though women make up fewer than 10 percent of jail and prison populations, their numbers have increased by 107 percent since 1976, a considerably faster rate of growth than for men. Most of the women who are in jail or prison (three of every four) are mothers (Flanagan and Jamieson 1988). Women in jails are at highest risk who have a history of drug abuse, mental illness, mental retardation, or prostitution. Those whose children have been removed from their custody and their family's custody are often subject to severe depression and require sustained supportive counseling.

The vast majority of both men and women who become inmates have, prior to their conviction and confinement, decades of exposure to the dynamics of poverty, institutional racism, and substance abuse. Not surprisingly, these toxic social and economic conditions result in major psychological damage for many inmates-to-be, damage that is then compounded by the jail or prison experience (NYSDA 1985). As two reporters succinctly put it, "Impulsiveness, insensitivity to social mores, a lack of deep and enduring emotional attachments to others, and an appetite for danger are among the temperamental characteristics of high-rate offenders" (Herrnstein and Wilson 1985).

Low self-esteem, a lack of self-discipline, low tolerance levels for frustration, the need for immediate gratification, and the tendency to place blame on others or on drugs or alcohol are common and costly attributes of inmates. Many have been marginal to mainstream society since childhood and, consequently, have developed unconventional values, beliefs, and behavioral patterns. Forced to endure disrupted and devalued lives as children and youth, they carry with them a chronic sense of loss. Many inmates respond with anger and antisocial attitudes, including overt hostility toward authority.

Having few material or emotional resources and being confined in a quasi-military setting, inmates need much. Among the most pressing of their needs are those for drug and alcohol rehabilitation, emotional constancy from a trusted other, literacy, education, vocational training and counseling, child care for their children, personal safety, health care, and assistance in obtaining decent housing, work, and income supports after release from jail or prison. Offenders encounter the same range of problems in living that other members of society do, and in addition, they must overcome the stigma and trauma of imprisonment. Therefore, their needs are compounded versions of those experienced by their nonimprisoned counterparts who spring from similar socioeconomic backgrounds of disadvantage. Those social workers who are effective in jails and prisons spend much of their time and talent as "couplers," as professionals who link their clients with the best of those resources to be found both during and after incarceration.

## PROGRAMS AND SOCIAL WORK SERVICES

Given the mushrooming of prison and jail populations since the early 1980s, municipal and state correctional authorities have concentrated primarily on acquiring more cell space for inmates, an acquisition that is usually made at the expense of programs within correctional facilities designed to address prisoners' educational, vocational, or recreational needs. Even the supply of health services for prisoners, the only form of service delivery mandated by federal, state, county, and municipal law, lags far behind the demand for health care generated by the soaring counts of inmates.

Jails in the United States have never had a mandate to rehabilitate inmates or to provide substantive programs in the vocational, therapeutic, or educational realms. The voting public and the legislatures continue to subscribe to the notion that prison is, plainly and simply, a "penalty box" for wrongdoing and to the correlative conceptualization of supportive services within jails and prisons as misguided humanitarianism that coddles miscreants. Nonetheless, despite the absence of external endorsement, departments of corrections do provide a variety of supportive programs for inmates, either because of prodding from watchdog agencies, community pressures, concern about departmental reputation in the face of rising recidivism, or, on occasion, enlightened leadership.

In prisons and jails, the survival and success of programs for inmates hinge upon the quality of the program staff's relationship with the correctional staff and management. Social work within prisons and jails is, essentially, a guest within the house of corrections. Consequently, it behooves the guest to treat the host with respectful attention and, when necessary, even deference. Though the goal and methods of therapeutic programs are antithetical to those of the training of correctional officers, careful and regular consultation initiated by social workers will reduce interprofessional rivalry and suspicion. Indeed, program staff who take the time to explain their program's purpose, rationale, and methodology and who continually update correctional officers concerning program successes and failures can turn the majority of custodial personnel into supportive allies. However, even with highly cooperative correctional staff, program activities are sometimes canceled if there is insufficient officer coverage or some form of institutional alarm or emergency.

Mental health programs have become common fixtures in jail and prison life since the early 1970's. The issuance of court-ordered minimum standards for medical and mental health services for inmates, the deinstitutionalization of state mental hospitals, and the use of more restrictive civil commitment standards are the key historical forces that have made local jails and state prisons and the sidewalks, rather than state mental hospitals, the prime repositories of the impoverished mentally ill of our culture.

In most municipal or state correctional systems, mental health services are lodged in forensic or mental observation units (MOs). Typically, mental health care in departments of corrections follows one of three usual formats: mental health care is offered on-site, within jails and prisons; inmates are sent to designated health services facilities for treatment; or prisoners are given access to forensic facilities within state mental hospitals.

Estimates vary widely concerning the percentage of the incarcerated population who are loosely described as "mentally disordered." For example, Coid (1984), using standardized criteria, claimed that major psychosis is no more common among offenders than in the general population (1984). By contrast, other researchers have suggested that the rise in the proportion of the mentally disordered in jails and prisons has outpaced that in the nonincarcerated population. Teplin (1983) and Briar (1983), among many others, have argued that mental illness has been criminalized since the deinstitutionalization of state mental hospitals in the mid-1960s, shifting the burden of responsibility for the chronically mentally ill to penal institutions. One study of inmates in North Carolina indicates that jail and prison inmates are mentally ill at approximately twice the rate for nonincarcerated people (Collins and Schlenger 1983). Within one category of mental illness, antisocial personality disorder, the rate of diagnosis was six to fourteen times higher than among the samples of those not imprisoned (Collins and Schlenger 1983; Mobley 1987).

For most mental observation units, management of mentally ill inmates, rather than treatment, is the focus of the work. High turnover among the incarcerated prevents mental health professionals from becoming involved in long-term treatment. Their chief task is to stabilize highly agitated or severely depressed persons who pose extreme risks of committing suicide or self-mutilation or attacking other inmates or jail staff. With this transient a population, mental health services must be rapid, effective, and appropriate. Medication is often called for to stabilize a patient quickly, provided that the patient agrees. Once medicated, patients may be treated while they remain in the MO and after they are returned to the general inmate population, or they may be admitted to an outside mental hospital. Medical professionals in jails and prisons may not give psychoactive medications without the inmate's permission, except in acute emergencies. Consequently, some agitated inmates who refuse medication must be isolated to prevent harm to the inmate in question or to others.

By 1989, jurisdictions within forty-six states had elaborated standards for mental health care to jail and prison inmates, ranging from those limited simply to concerns of safety and cleanliness to the most rigorous, such as those of the New York City Board of Correction. These Mental Health Minimum Standards require service goals that encompass crisis intervention, the management of acute psychiatric episodes, suicide prevention, the stabilization of mental illness, the alleviation of psychological deterioration in jail and prison settings, and elective therapeutic services and preventive treatment, resources permitting. The Minimum Standards also mandate the timely identification and detection of inmates who need psychiatric evaluation.

Furthermore, inmates whose behavior suggests that they are suffering from a mental or emotional disorder must receive prompt evaluation and appropriate referral. Inmates in need of emergency psychiatric care must be served immediately. According to the Mental Health Minimum Standards, inmates under the care of mental health services are entitled to the same rights and privileges as every other inmate. New York City jails are required to provide mental health care to inmates in an environment that facilitates care and treatment, provides for maximum observation, reduces the risk of suicide, and is minimally stressful. The Minimal Standards stipulate that medication must be employed as only one facet of an overall treatment plan and must not be used solely as a means of restraint or control. Physical restraints or the seclusion of inmates is not to be used as punishment, for the convenience of staff, or as a substitute for treatment programs. The Minimal Standards require that the principle of confidentiality regarding information about inmates obtained in the course of treatment be upheld. Finally, various services are to be coordinated within correctional facilities and between custodial and community-based services used after incarceration (NYCBC 1984).

At a major jail in New York City on any given day, approximately 450 inmates receive mental health care in specially designated mental health housing areas, 150 people are treated in psychiatric prison wards, and an unspecified percentage of jail residents obtain assistance in functioning with personality problems in the general jail population. Despite harsh conditions of overcrowding, drug trafficking within the jail by some correctional officers and inmates, and chronic shortages of social work and health care staff, this jail manages to maintain the ten key components of a competent on-site mental service unit. These components include 1) intake screening at booking; 2) psychological evaluation after initial screening; 3) assessment of competency to stand trial; 4) use of psychotropic medications; 5) counseling for substance abusers; 6) general short-term counseling; 7) inpatient mental health care; 8) external hospitalization when necessary; 9) a suicide prevention component; and 10) the formal linking of inmates with community mental health agencies following release from jail. This metropolitan jail's medical center, like other similar mental health services, reduces assaults, suicides, sexual assaults and harassment, and arson within the jail. However, no studies are yet available that evaluate the more long-term effects of intervention, such as the degree of stabilization of symptoms or the level of regular participation of former inmates in community mental health services.

Most mental health services in jails pay little attention to the mental health care needed in the community by inmates released from jail. Similarly, most community mental health care facilities spend few resources on forming links with jails and prisons. Meanwhile, few former inmates voluntarily seek treatment after release (Lamb and Grant 1982). Continuity of care for mentally disturbed people, whether imprisoned, institutionalized, or free, remains a community issue that most communities or states have yet to address. Until they do, the mental health staffs of jails and prisons will continue to constitute overworked isolates, rather than partners in a continuum of care that integrates the services of hospitals, penal institutions, and outpatient facilities.

Closely linked to the interventions of mental health units are the substance abuse prevention programs of jails and prisons. Both common knowledge and governmental statistics document the multiplying incidence of substance abuse in the general population, a trend that has resulted in rapidly expanding numbers of persons incarcerated for drug-related offenses or with serious addictions to drugs or alcohol. For example, in New York State, the Division of Substance Abuse Services found that 43 percent of the state's population in 1986 used addictive drugs nonmedically and that 10 percent of the state's population in that year were regular users of narcotic substances (Grodd and Wishart 1989).

Figures from the New York City Department of Correction provide a stark picture of the consequences for jails and prisons of this epidemic of drug abuse. Between 1981 and 1986, correctional facilities in New York City saw a 43 percent increase in the numbers of newly admitted inmates requiring detoxification from opiates. In 1987, 18,000 of 108,000 new inmates entering the correctional system in New York City required methadone detoxification, an alarming increase of 14 percent over the year before. At this point in history, roughly one of every five persons admitted to custody in the New York City Department of Correction is seriously addicted to heroine or other opiates, cocaine, or crack (CANY 1988).

A medical center that is located in a large urban jail and that is a satellite unit of a city hospital provides an example of the substance abuse prevention service that accompanies, in some cities and states, the on-site psychotherapeutic treatment programs for addicted or alcoholic inmates. This particular prevention effort, delivered through the school system in the jail, is designed to educate and counsel the inmates and thereby to prevent or delay the onset of drug and polydrug use by adolescents who may or may not yet be dependent on addictive drugs. The prevention program is also focused on preventing or delaying the transition from experimental to regular drug use, on preventing regular users from becoming "problem" users, and on preventing heavy users from deteriorating further in their everyday functioning.

To address these goals, this jail-based medical center created a substance abuse prevention curriculum that includes information on the physiological, psychological, and sociological aspects of drug and alcohol use. Another component of the curriculum explores decision-making and refusal skills, particularly in the context of peer pressure. The program also focuses on issues of self-esteem and self-concept in the adolescent and young adult phases of life.

The entire prevention curriculum is offered to all high school grade levels at the school serving the community surrounding the jail. In addition, the informational unit is taught at weekly classes in the adolescent reception detention center and at the correctional institution for women. Attempts are also made to hold at least one substance abuse prevention seminar each month for as many as 150 inmates. Requests to hold these large sessions, it should be noted, must be negotiated on a case-by-case basis with the correctional administration of each jail because of the department of correction's reluctance, for reasons of security, to bring large groups of inmates together. Leaders of each class and large session explain the counseling services of the substance abuse service's treatment team and enroll, on the spot, those members of the audience who express interest in and are eligible for participating in counseling, group work, vocational guidance, therapeutic communities within correctional facilities, and alternative placement services. This last option is a possibility only for detainees in jail who are awaiting disposition of their cases.

For social workers practicing in jails, the complex and satisfying process of matching substance-abusing detainees with the appropriate alternative placement, usually a residential treatment center, requires the worker to have a mastery of jail procedures and an up-to-date working knowledge of the capabilities and censuses at various community drug treatment centers. Applicants for alternative placements may be self-referred to recommended by the courts, attorneys, parole officials, correction officers, family members, or other educational or social service agencies that have worked with the candidates. The jail social worker begins the process of securing an applicant an alternative rehabilitative placement by conducting an intake assessment and as many follow-up counseling sessions as the next scheduled court date permits. Frequently, the worker, in conjunction with the applicant's attorney, requests an extension of the next court date to allow time to arrange for an alternative placement. The social worker then proceeds to contact the drug treatment centers with which she or he has familiarity and that have beds available. Most treatment agencies insist on a personal interview with the applicant, a process that the social worker makes possible at the jail. Once an applicant has been accepted, the worker informs the court and the attorney and, if necessary, pleads the case for placement. Ordinarily, if the preparatory work for placement is sound, the court supports placement in an alternative therapeutic setting.

At this point in the placement process, the judge wisely refuses, in most circumstances, to release an applicant on his or her own recognizance. Instead, escorts are needed to take the applicant from court to the treatment center, since neither the treatment center's nor the correctional facility's social service staff are large enough to meet their institution's heavy demands and also appear frequently in court. In some cities, escorts have come forward from agencies that are committed to placing detainees with substance abuse problems in rehabilitative treatment centers. Should a bed in a treatment facility not be available on the day the applicant is released from court, temporary supervised housing centers may be used, if the court approves. Unfortunately, in many communities, the process of making use of alternative placements is short-circuited by the scarcity of rehabilitative treatment center beds and the understaffing of social work teams within the mental health units of the correctional facilities.

Also scarce are therapeutic treatment communities within jails and prisons for substance abusers who are inmates in the midst of serving a sentence. New York State offers two examples of therapeutic programs within prison that merit mention, one an in-house therapeutic community for men and the other for women. To be eligible for these programs, an applicant must have a history of substance abuse or involvement with the drug culture, must demonstrate a history of "positive participation" in institutional and educational programs for at least the previous six months, and must be within two years of his or her normal parole board appearance. In addition, the applicant must have no history of severe mental illness, sex crimes, or escape attempts and must have no institutional infractions within the past eight months that involve physical violence. Unfortunately, these exemplary in-house centers, whose recidivism rates are lower than 10 percent, serve fewer than 100 inmates each year.

A cluster of other supports for inmates, in addition to prevention programs, mental health services, and alternative placements, have emerged during the past fifty years. One widely available program is work release, an option designed to help inmates keep jobs during and after incarceration, to provide them with marketable job experience and skills, and to socialize inmates who have poor work histories to develop work behaviors that will enable them to obtain and maintain legal paid employment after release. The eligibility criteria for work release programs tend to be strict. Only offenders nearing the end of their sentences whose records before and during imprisonment indicate that they pose little or no threat to society are granted work release opportunities. However, standards for work release eligibility may currently be softening in some jails that are particularly overcrowded (Bohlen 1989a).

The primary objective of vocational training, another program offered in some custodial facilities, echoes that of work release. Both programs attempt to reduce the unemployment rate of ex-offenders and thereby to reduce rates of recidivism. Alas, the success of vocational training in most penal institutions in meeting these goals is negligible. Inmates rarely perform the work after release that they do in jail. Most secure jobs after incarceration that do not require much prior training and are similar to those jobs they held before entering prison (NYSDA 1985; McDermott 1985). Opportunities for vocational training for women inmates are particularly limited, since they remain a small percentage of the correctional population.

Were political leaders, taxpayers, and the management of corrections to take vocational training for prisoners seriously, programs would be established that would incorporate meaningful education concerning the world of work, on-the-job training, careful counseling, job preparation workshops, and the tailored matching of inmates' abilities and skills with outside placements. As has already been done in some places, in-house, on-the-job training could be designed for such occupations as pipe fitting, child care, auto repair, pest control, retailing, sewing, computer programming, waitering and waitressing, and office and library work. Leaders of vocational training programs in jails and prisons of the future will have to be proactive in channeling inmates into training in a gender-neutral fashion to end the pervasive stereotyping by gender that has characterized past and present efforts to train and place offenders.

Social workers within corrections are accustomed to strained delivery systems, huge caseloads, and a programmatic vision that far outstrips institutional resources. Nonetheless, no one within social services in jails or prisons nor, for that matter, anyone within prison and jail top management could have been prepared for the sudden demands made by the AIDS epidemic since the first case was identified within correctional facilities in 1981. Responses within corrections to AIDS have ranged from total segregation for all those whose test results indicate that they are HIV-positive, as in Alabama, to the more integrative approach of states like New York, which, since 1987, has attempted to place inmates with AIDS, who have received medical clearance, in the general jail and prison population. New York State's response to inmates with AIDS is a useful example to explore since 51 percent of all inmate AIDS cases in the United States as of mid-1986 were found within that state's correctional facilities. The scope of the problem is startling: between 1984 and 1988, 499 inmates died from AIDS in New York State prisons and jails (Potter 1988). Among these dead, the typical female AIDS decedent had been a single mother with, on average, two children (Morse et al. 1987; Potter 1988).

In response to this escalating epidemic, New York State has created special AIDS units for inmates with AIDS who are acutely ill or in need of medical monitoring. Similarly, New York City has created a sixty-six-bed unit for those inmates with AIDS who require medical monitoring in a daily basis. From a medical point of view, health care staff see no reason to isolate this population from other infirmary patients and are awaiting a decision by the Department of Correction to proceed to mix the populations. It is not clear, from a mental health point of view, which is the better course.

At the present time, inmates who are no longer ambulatory are transferred to secured medical units in local hospitals. Most personnel who staff AIDS units within prisons and jails—doctors, nurses, social workers, pharmacists, and correctional personnel—have volunteered for this assignment. Patients in these units have filed relatively few and minor complaints about treatment in these special units. Indeed, several residents at the New York City AIDS units have deliberately committed an illegal act soon after discharge from the unit in order to return to it as quickly as possible and to avoid the alternatives that the street provides. Not surprisingly, in a system that lacks sufficient counselors and social workers for the general population, AIDS units in New York State, New York City, and throughout the country are understaffed in the extreme. One consequence of this shortage of staff is the necessity of sending inmates in AIDS dormitories who become acutely ill to a hospital after, roughly, a three-day period. By that point, staff find it difficult to calm other inmates, who, though initially supportive of the severely sick resident, become alarmed by symptoms and a condition that is so directly evocative of their own immediate fate.

Social work programming concerning AIDS in jails and prisons also involves sending AIDS educators throughout correctional systems in some states and cities. Furthermore, social workers have become active in calling for the development of statewide policies regarding housing and services for inmates with AIDS that are sufficiently flexible to respond to individual circumstances. These advocates within the ranks of social workers also lobby for the development of a plan that would ensure a continuum of health and mental health care for those inmates with AIDS who are released. Finally, social workers within jails and prisons are also pressing state legislatures to create uniform and appropriate mechanisms for granting early release to eligible inmate applicants who suffer from AIDS.

Social work's programmatic responses to inmates of prisons and jails are diverse, yet still minimal in most regions. Not only are professional staff few in number in most correctional facilities, but program supervision is inadequate, often focused exclusively on monitoring the numbers of people served and the proportion of clients who become recidivists. When refunding of human service programs in jails and prisons hinges primarily on the outcome measure of recidivism ratios, "creaming" results.

To avoid this weeding out of the most needy inmates and to develop program supervision of social work services that attends as carefully to the quality of service delivery as to the quantity of final consequences, programs for inmates require, at the very least, a phased plan for evaluating the efficacy of each incremental step in programming for inmates. Program evaluation is needed that will address the rates of participation in and the completion of employment, training, and treatment programs. Outcome measures would be expanded to incorporate rates of ex-offenders' reduction in arrests, jobs secured, money earned, and attendance in community-based mental health services and substance abuse programs.

Excellence in the professional supervision of social work programs for inmates depends as much upon fiscal, advocacy, and administrative skills as it does upon clinical skills. Given the pressures placed on program supervisors within correctional facilities to run cost-effective programs that process as many inmates as possible, it is advisable to develop a monitoring system involving a citizens' advisory committee comprised of representatives from agencies that have the professional expertise to evaluate the merits of prevention, treatment, and training components. Indeed, it would be wise in most circumstances to contract out supportive programs for inmates to civilian and community agencies that can assist offenders in securing employment, training, and housing both before and after release. Community agencies that are invited to create on-site prevention and treatment programs within jails and prisons are in a far better position to provide continuity of care to offenders who become ex-offenders that are jail-based programs.

## DIFFERENTIAL CLINICAL ASSESSMENTS AND INTERVENTIONS

Between 3 and 7 million inmates pass each year through jails, thirty times the number handled by all state and federal prisons (Flanagan and Jamieson 1988). Jails, unlike prisons, are locally administered and hold both convicted and unconvicted people, most of whom spend less than one year in jail. By contrast, prison inmates, all of whom are convicted, spend at least one year in confinement, constituting a relatively stable, long-term population with whom traditional therapeutic techniques can be used. The discussion that follows is confined to the subject of social work assessment and intervention in the correctional arena in which most clients are found: the local jail.

The environment in which jail inmates exist is one of continual flux. Inmates are added on a daily basis, and residents may be released with little warning on bail, on their own recognizance, or because their cases have been adjudicated. This incessant movement requires that jail counts be taken at least twice a day to check on the residents' whereabouts and numbers. During the counts, counseling, case management, group work, and all other access to inmates are stopped. The mission of jails is to detain people who are awaiting trial and to provide confinement, custody, and care for those with short-term sentences. Management-by-crisis prevails in jails, institutions that are forced to be reactive by the very nature of the process by which the courts and the parole systems supply and remove inmates. Jails have not been charged with providing rehabilitation; they are, nonetheless, expected by the public to prevent recidivism.

Obviously, inmates in jails do not stay long enough to participate in the full and complete treatment of substance abuse or of psychosocial problems and disorders. However, all those who enter jails with drug or alcohol habits necessarily undergo detoxification or "drying out" in jail and often require and desire attention during and after that difficult process. Some people are receptive at that time to the thought of a drug-free life. Others without drug or alcohol addictions find jail a time to rethink life patterns, daily routines, and plans for the future. Some of these inmates are also willing to invest in short-term counseling and training.

The distinctive assessment issues facing social workers in jails include, concomitantly, both questions concerning the client's willingness to change key behaviors and questions concerning the environment's—meaning both the jail's and the larger community's after jail—capacity to incorporate that client's participation into the work force, into school, and into community-based mental health treatment. In assessing an inmate's psychosocial needs, one considers all the factors ordinarily taken into account in such assessment processes: a psychosocial history of the individual within his or her family and community context, school and work record, absence or presence of drug or polydrug abuse, sexual history, personality profile, and configuration of current supports in the family, friendship network, and neighborhood. In addition, the social worker explores a client's capacity and willingness to identify and take responsibility for destructive patterns, relationships, choices, and activities; the degree of his or her desire to change self-destructive or illegal behaviors; his or her deficits and strengths in interpersonal, literacy, and vocational skills; his or her particular vulnerabilities to peer pressure and drugs within and outside of jail; his or her short-term goals within jail; his or her long-term goals in life; and his or her conception of the supports and dangers that await him or her after release.

In order to avoid making false promises to any inmate and to advocate for client needs in an informed fashion, the worker also continually assesses a jail's ability to provide rehabilitation for substance abuse, mental health counseling, schooling for adults and youth, meaningful work, vocational training, job placements and referrals to counseling and drug treatment programs after release, and physical exercise while in jail.

Counseling in jail is a process of habilitation, rather than rehabilitation. Most inmates have never experienced supportive nor steady family relationships and have not led productive lives. As a consequence, social work in jail, at its best, is a combination of counseling, socialization, education, and modified case management that assists with obtaining concrete services, housing, and jobs. The social worker combines intervention with prevention activities and focuses on clients' behavior and performance in jail. The work is highly time-limited, active, and directive, relying on many cognitive and behavioral techniques. Given that such a high proportion of inmates report that they have used addictive drugs recently, most social work in jail involves intensive exploration with clients of the role and consequences of drug and alcohol use in their lives.

In spite of inmates' general tendencies to put up a good front in an effort to impress others, low self-esteem is a pervasive attribute among offenders, a characteristic that social workers address in every therapeutic interaction. Patterns of denial, blaming, impetuosity, grandiosity, and exaggeration are also common among inmates. Many habitual substance abusers in jails are stalled in the maturation process and require assistance with issues of separation and individuation from parents, value formation, and developing socially responsible behavior. However, despite the prevalence of certain psychological patterns in jails, each inmate, like each client outside jail, has a particular configuration of strengths and deficits, one that requires an individualized plan and approach.

To maximize an offender's commitment to counseling, it is advisable for social workers to draw up a contract with each client who has completed the intake process. The contract articulates specific goals that the offender agrees to work toward achieving and may also specify a list of behaviors that need to be changed. The client then signs this form and a release-of-information form. At this point, a helping plan is drawn up that reflects careful negotiation with the client.

Resistance, as in any therapeutic project, surfaces around salient issues of the client's case, particularly at those points at which the worker starts to confront the client about certain inconsistencies and behaviors. For some residents, resistance takes the form of acting out in sessions or in daily living in jail, of denial, or of missing sessions. Because the confinement time is relatively short and counseling is often interrupted by clients' absenting themselves from sessions, social workers need to make use of spontaneous hallway contacts. In these circumstances, the worker reaches out and asks a nonthreatening question about the client's welfare. If some trust has developed previously, the resident usually responds with some request for assistance.

In the helping process, attentive listening, feedback, acceptance, and reassurance matter as much as timely confrontation. Contracted helping goals and purposes, rather than the etiology of problems, remain the central focus. Workers assist clients in identifying the immediate feelings and the sources of those feelings. Often, workers help residents recognize feelings by using language that is more specific than that used by the speakers.

Throughout the helping process, workers make a concerted effort to refrain from admonishing, moralizing, interrogating, or making light of inmates and their situations. Social workers also scrupulously avoid the role of "rescuer." Instead, social workers emphasize involving clients in solving their own problems and in remaining centered on the problem at hand. Assigning small tasks, such as writing a letter, calling a child, or researching outside employment, becomes part of the treatment process. Also helpful are graphic techniques that require clients to visualize complex feelings. For example, a resident may be asked to draw a pressure cooker pot into which he or she puts all feelings, positive and negative, that are present.

Once a client has developed a growing awareness of his or her own discomfort, vulnerability, and losses, he or she may be ready to consider serious behavioral change. At that point, some combination of ongoing individual counseling, group work, and peer counseling is in order. Later, life skill sessions and workshops are also introduced. Workshops on the communicative, interactive, and assertiveness skills needed in finding jobs, housing, food, and continuing treatment become significant and necessary complements to the intensive therapeutic work.

Multiple countertransferential issues emerge for the worker in sessions with clients who are substance abusers and perpetrators of violence and "con games." Careful clinical supervision is important in such settings, in which irresponsible, antisocial, and self-injuring behaviors occur on a regular basis. It is common for workers to begin to feel drained, used, disappointed, and angry. In jails, workers need professional goals that are extremely incremental and a large tolerance of failure with specific individual recidivists.

A worker must beware of becoming overly involved with the offender who is seeking someone to blame for his or her troubles. The worker also needs to be wary of the resident who claims to be a new person or a convert to a transformed way of being. This "convenient conversion syndrome" can delude both the worker and the client. Setting limits on client demands and behaviors is also critical with a population who persistently attempt to manipulate workers into performing many activities that they themselves feel they cannot do. A description of a case follows that illustrates the pace, constraints, frustrations, and opportunities that are embedded in social work performed in jails and prisons.

## CASE ILLUSTRATION

Tracey, a 38-year-old black woman inmate, worked as a typist for a department-of-corrections captain whose office was in the same area as the mental health offices in Coldwater Bay Correctional Facility, a pseudonym for an actual metropolitan jail. Noticing that some women offenders regularly saw a particular social worker, Tracey approached that worker diffidently, stating that she would like to talk to her. They agreed to meet at an appointed time.

Tracey kept her first appointment with the social worker, though she was late. She appeared nervous and hyperactive and seemed to have difficulty sitting still. She was a large woman with a bland, expressionless face marked by some scarring and a close-cropped hair style. She had the swollen hands and the general demeanor of a long-term heroin user. Tracey's overall affect was one of depression and anxiety. No other symptomatology was evident in the first session.

The worker began by asking, "How can I help you?" Tracey responded, "I don't know. You tell me." The worker answered, "Here, the main focus of our work is drug treatment and continuing community care. Do you want those things?" Tracey expressed her interest in these possibilities. The social worker proceeded to explain the drug-treatment and discharge-planning services that the program provides. As Tracey's anxiety diminished during the session, she expressed her need and desire for help in staying drug-free. Then the intake process began.

The worker learned that Tracey had an eighteen-year history of addiction. She used both cocaine and heroin intravenously and freebased and smoked marijuana. On two occasions, she had overdosed. Previously, Tracey had been in a fifteen-month treatment program, completing the program just five months prior to the intake interview. At one time, she had also been on a methadone maintenance program but did cocaine and marijuana along with the methadone. Tracey admitted to a $100-a-day habit, though the worker suspected that it was more severe an addiction than that.

Tracey reported no hospitalizations for psychiatric treatment or prior assignment to a mental observation unit during incarceration. She had seen a counselor when she was very young and had been committed to a home for girls for one month during adolescence on her mother's recommendation. Tracey claimed that from an early age, she had been identified as the black sheep in her family. Although she claimed to be estranged from her family, a sister was caring for her 7-year-old son in the large midwestern city from which she had come. Another sister, who, she reported, "had given up on her," lived in the same eastern city as Tracey.

Having earned a high school equivalency diploma and having majored in court stenography in a vocational institute, Tracey had, on several occasions, been able to obtain employment as a typist who types sixty-five words per minute. Her average length of employment was four months. Either she left jobs or was fired from them for drug-related reasons.

Not sure of the number of times she had been arrested, Tracey estimated that it was at least sixty times. The charges had been primarily sale and possession of drugs and petit larceny. Her major source of income was "boosting" (stealing).

Tracey was to be discharged two months from the date of the initial interview. Through the contracting process, Tracey and the social worker agreed to meet once a week for the next six weeks and twice a week for the two weeks prior to discharge. Tracey willingly agreed to attend the weekly drug groups, to consider returning to a community treatment center, to take an active role in reestablishing relationships with her family, and to participate in searches for employment and a support system. The worker agreed to work with her in sessions on her substance abuse problems and to provide Tracey with additional information on employment and supportive services.

In her assessment, the social worker wrote, "The client is depressed, but not clinically, has low impulse control and low self-esteem. She has lost control so many times she feels inadequate and incapable of change. Her inability to maintain abstinence and the resultant abandonment of her son has filled her with guilt and shame. Given the time constraints, the focus of the work will be to validate her strengths, to identify and help her manage her feelings, to teach her steps in problem solving, to connect her to the world around her, and to bypass any pathology."

At the first session following the intake interview, Tracey responded to the worker's questions in a forthright manner. She was open about her drug use, criminal history, and lesbianism. She admitted to being frightened, unsure of her ability to stop using drugs, friendless, and lonely. She felt that she had wasted much of her life, was conscious of getting older, and recognized that she needed and wanted help. Tracey was beginning to be aware that her discomfort with her present situation might be stronger than her need for drugs. She was insightful regarding her lack of self-esteem and identified feelings of loneliness and self-hatred as being triggers of her drug usage.

The work in the helping process centered upon Tracey's accepting and recognizing the need for continued drug treatment upon discharge. She began to attend in-house Narcotics Anonymous (NA) meetings and learned the locations of meetings and the name of a contact person in the outside NA community.

The helping process concurrently focused on assisting Tracey to accept herself as a worthwhile person. When she said, "I tried to keep my son with me, but I couldn't make it, and I sent him back to my mother," the worker responded, "You realized you weren't able to be the mother you felt your son deserved, that you had to solve your own problems before you could help someone else. So you did what was best for your son; you sent him back to a loving, stable environment. It was the caring thing to do." Continuing in this fashion, the social worker tried to relay to Tracey that she accepted Tracey as a valuable person and that Tracey had valid reasons for doing the same.

Having just completed a stay in a residential treatment center, Tracey resisted going back to one. She felt, instead, that NA, day or evening treatment, a job, and a place to live would help her sustain her abstinence. Within this framework, she began to set realistic goals for herself. She actively worked with the social worker in planning her discharge. The social worker would make one call to a community agency, and Tracey would make the next one, modeling her behavior on that of the worker. Role playing became a component part of the four final sessions, with both Tracey and the worker practicing talking to the sister in the nearby city. When Tracey actually made that phone call, the sister agreed to provide a place for Tracey to stay in her home as long as she remained drug-free. The worker's calls to a special employment program of the state department of labor elicited a commitment on the part of the director to "stick with her even if she slips."

Additional preemployment interviews were arranged by Tracey and the social worker. The worker also gave her information on a religiously affiliated support group for ex-offenders and a gay and lesbian support group. Tracey contacted both prior to her release. Arrangements were made for Tracey to participate in a day treatment program during her job search and, once employed, to join the program in the evenings.

The final sessions of the helping process constituted a review of the gains that Tracey had made. Both Tracey and the worker agreed that Tracey felt better about herself and was more aware of the "triggers" that usually preceded her return to drug use. She actively participated in arranging her own continuum of care and was more hopeful than in the past about her scheduled employment interviews and connections with the community to which she was about to return. The worker, in these final meetings, tried to convey to Tracey her belief that Tracey would succeed in achieving her goals if she were patient and persistent. The worker communicated that she cared that Tracey succeeded after release in staying drug-free and in meeting her own objectives. She also encouraged Tracey to call her for assistance, to give progress reports, or to just to talk after release.

The worker's final case note comment stated, "Tracey just might have a slim chance of staying free of criminal involvement." The case notes also reported that Tracey's hyperactivity had not abated and was still manifested in Tracey's inability to sit still and to stay centered for extended time periods. The worker also noted, "If there is an extended time frame prior to achieving her goals, and she meets with disappointment and frustration, Tracey probably will not be able to sustain her current determination to stay drug-free."

Three days after discharge, Tracey called the worker in an elevated mood. Things were working out with her sister, and Tracey had gone to NA, the drug treatment program, and two job interviews. In subsequent phone calls, Tracey said that she was also meeting with an ex-offender group and a lesbian support group. She noted that she found the groups helpful. Although she had not yet got a job, she had got on the civil service list.

However, the department of labor did not get her a job, nor did the director follow up on Tracey's case, as promised. Concerned, the prison social worker called the three employment centers at which Tracey had appointments. All claimed that they had sent her on interviews from which she had not got jobs. Each contact person promised to keep trying. The worker suspected that Tracey's appearance and, perhaps, her hyperactive tendencies were working against her.

Seven weeks after discharge, the worker called Tracey and discovered that she sounded different and had used cocaine a few times. Two and one half months after discharge, all contact was lost. Seven months after discharge, Tracey called and reported that she had gone back on drugs but had not lost total control. She had admitted herself into a detoxification program, then entered a methadone maintenance program, and was slowly reducing her level of methadone. Tracey viewed herself as working toward abstinence, was employed full time as a typist, and was again living with her sister. Some community resources, such as employment services, had failed Tracey. Others had remained committed to her, despite her relapse.

Tracey's case demonstrates the centrality of community supports and involvement in promoting the welfare of ex-offenders. The case study also reveals that concrete services and information about them are as important as traditional treatment for inmates and former inmates. Furthermore, Tracey's case documents the salience of the worker–client relationship in prison social work, as well as the potency of intensive short-term work with a motivated client. Finally, the case reveals the inch-by-inch quality of work with substance abusers in jails. Their repeated return to abusing drugs or alcohol after treatment may constitute failure. On the other hand, the helping process may eventually take effect, long after the fact.

Though social workers in jails and prisons appear, to the uninitiated, to work in intractable systems, they in fact report that they find significant opportunity over time to make innovations in the beleaguered criminal justice continuum. Social workers' continuing involvement with offenders and ex-offenders remain necessary along three fronts: improving services within jails and prisons, strengthening the social work profession's commitment to juvenile and adult offenders and to crime prevention, and helping to humanize and vitalize the neglected and archaic sector of public welfare.

Within jails and prisons, social workers can make an immediate contribution by conducting needs assessments and developing programs for inmates with mental retardation and learning disabilities. They are also needed to conduct training and screening for correctional officers who work on mental health and AIDS units.

Jail and prison social workers can enhance their profession by obtaining student stipends for prison field placements and by contributing to the institutionalization of the curricular components of social work with offenders and ex-offenders. They can also make much more audible and visible the satisfactions they obtain from conducting social work in jails and prisons.

In relation to the broad arena of criminal justice, social workers have much work to do as change agents, advocates, and program developers. Community-based, residential treatment services are needed for many categories of offenders and former offenders. The public must be made aware of the extreme consequences of the discontinuity between social services inside jails and the near void in supports that many people find after release. Social workers can help to reduce overcrowding in jails and prisons by working for the decriminalization of nonviolent first offenses, such as prostitution and drug use. They can also lobby for the expansion of prison and jail services for women inmates and for increases in the numbers of pretrial release services and alternatives to incarceration. In addition, social workers can redouble their ongoing efforts to obtain a proliferation of the prevention programs that are required to stanch the torrent of violence, abuse, and neglect in families and communities.

A century ago, Nietzsche made clear the impact of jails and prisons: "The broad effects which can be obtained by punishment are the increase of fear, the lack of trust, the sharpening of the senses and of cunning, and the mastery of the desires: so it is that punishment tames the person, but does not make him better" (1967: 71). The search for approaches that do "make him better" must be found if our society is to continue to cohere. Who is better equipped for the search than social workers?

## REFERENCES

Applebome, Peter. 1987. "Women in U.S. Prisons: Fast-Rising Population." *New York Times,* (June 16), p. A16.

Blumstein, Alfred. 1989. "Prison Crowding." U.S. Department of Justice, National Institute of Justice Crime File Study Guide. Washington, D.C.: GPO.

Bohlen, Celestine. 1989a. "Facing the Jail Crisis." *New York Times* (April 22), p. 31.

Bohlen, Celestine. 1989b. "$125 Million Jail Barge Is No Mere Ex-Troopship." *The New York Times* (March 22), p. B3.

Bolduc, Anne. 1985. "Jail Crowding." *The Annals of the American Academy of Political and Social Science* 478: 47–57.

Bowker, L. H. 1982. *Corrections: The Science and the Art.* New York: Macmillan.

Braswell, Michael, Steven Dillingham, and Reid Montgomery, eds. 1985. *Prison Violence in America.* Cincinnati: Anderson.

Briar, Katharine Hooper. 1983. "Jails: Neglected Asylums." *Social Casework,* 64:387–393.

Carney, Louis P. 1980. *Corrections: Treatment and Philosophy.* Englewood Cliffs, N.J.: Prentice-Hall.

Coid, J. 1984. "How Many Psychiatric Patients in Prison?" *British Journal of Psychiatry* 145:78–86.

Collins, J. J. and W. E. Schlenger. 1983. "The Prevalence of Psychiatric Disorder Among Admissions to Prison." Unpublished paper presented at the American Society of Criminology, Denver.

CANY (Correctional Association of New York). 1988. *News Bulletin* (December), no. 9. New york: CANY.

Engel, Kathleen C. and Katherine Gabel. 1987. "Female Offenders." In *Encyclopedia of Social Work,* New York: N.A.S.W. 18th ed., vol. 1, pp. 600–610.

Flanagan, Timothy J. and Katherine M. Jamieson, eds. 1988. *Sourcebook of Crimi-*

*nal Justice Statistics—1987.* U.S. Department of Justice, Bureau of Justice Statistics. Washington, D.C.: GPO.

Grodd, Barbara. 1989. "Notes on Practice." Unpublished notebook of Director of Substance Abuse Services, Montefiore Medical Center, Rikers Island Health Services, New York City.

Grodd, Barbara and Margaret Wishart. 1987a. "A Prevention, Education, and Diversion Program for Incarcerated Youth." Unpublished grant application, New York, Montefiore Medical Center, Rikers Island Health Services.

Grodd, Barbara and Margaret Wishart. 1987b. "A Proposal for the Provision of Substance Abuse Education and Diversion Services at the Rose M. Singer Center at the North Facility." Unpublished grant application, New York, Montefiore Medical Center, Riker's Island Health Services.

Herrnstein, R. J. and J. Q. Wilson. 1985. "Made or Born?" *New York Times Magazine* (August 4), pp. 31–33.

Innes, Christopher. 1988. "Drug Use and Crime." U.S. Department of Justice, Bureau of Justice Statistics Special Report (July). Washington, D.C.: GPO.

Irwin, J. 1985. *The Jail: Managing the Underclass in American Society.* Berkeley: University of California Press.

Kalish, Carol B. 1988. "International Crime Rates." U.S. Department of Justice, Bureau of Justice Statistics Special Report (May). Washington, D.C.: GPO.

Lamb, H. and R. Grant. 1982. "The Mentally Ill in an Urban Bounty Jail." *Archives of General Psychiatry* 91:17–22.

Lipton, D., R. Martinson, and J. Wilkes. 1975. *The Effectiveness of Correctional Treatment Evaluation Studies.* New York: Praeger.

McDermott, M. Joan. 1985. *Female Offenders in New York State* (November). Albany, N.Y.: New York State Division of Criminal Justice Services.

Mobley, Max J. 1987. "Psychotherapy with Criminal Offenders." In I. Weiner and A. Hess, eds., *Handbook of Forensic Psychology*, pp. 602–629. New York: Wiley.

MMC (Montefiore Medical Center, Substance Abuse Services). 1987–1989. Unpublished intake records, New York, Rikers Island Health Services.

Morse, D., J. Hanrahan, B. Truman, J. Feck, M. Woelfel, R. Broaddus, B. Maguire, J. Grabau, and C. Lawrence. 1987. "AIDS in New York State Prison Inmates." Albany: New York State Departments of Health and Correctional Services.

Netherland, W. 1987. "Corrections System: Adult." In *Encyclopedia of Social Work*, 18th ed., vol. 1, pp. 351–360. Silver Spring, Md.: National Association of Social Workers.

NYCBC (New York City Board of Correction). 1984. *Mental Health Standards for New York City Correctional Facilities.* New York: City of New York.

NYSDA (New York State Defenders Association). 1985. *What Prisons Do to People.* Albany: New York State Defenders Association.

Nietzsche, Friedrich. 1967. *The Genealogy of Morals*, trans. from the German by Walter Kaufman. New York: Random House.

Potter, C. 1988. "AIDS in Prison: A Crisis in New York State Corrections." Unpublished report to Correctional Association of New York State, (May).

Sherman, M. E. and G. E. Hawkins. 1981. *Imprisonment in America: Choosing the Future.* Chicago: University of Chicago Press.

Teplin, L. 1983. "The Criminalization of the Mentally Ill: Speculation in Search of Data." *Psychological Bulletin* 94:54–67.

Toch, Hans. 1977. *Living in Prison: The Ecology of Survival.* New York: Free Press.

Toch, Hans. Kenneth Adams, and Ronald Greene. 1987. "Ethnicity, Disruptiveness, and Emotional Disorder Among Prison Inmates." Criminal Justice and Behavior 14:93–109.

U.S. Justice (U.S. Department of Justice, Bureau of Justice Statistics). 1988a.

*Census of Local Jails, 1983*, vol. 5: *Selected Findings, Methodology, and Summary Tables.* Washington, D.C.: GPO.

U.S. Justice 1988b. *Technical Appendix to Report to the Nation on Crime and Justice*, 2nd ed. Washington, D.C.: GPO.

Weiner, Irving and Allen Hess, eds. 1987. *Handbook of Forensic Psychology.* New York: Wiley.

Zanguillo, P. 1981. "The New York City Male Detention Population." New York: New York City Criminal Justice Agency.

# 21

## Suicide and Suicidal Behavior

▼

### ANDRÉ IVANOFF

Suicide is the intentional taking of one's own life. What pain is so intense, what circumstance so desperate that it leads an individual to consider suicide? The questions surrounding suicide have provoked moral, political, religious, and social debate since the time of the Greek philosophers. The identification of risk and the prevention of suicide remain a source of study, speculation, and sleepless nights among those who make it their work and those who live with its consequences. Few social work practitioners specialize in working with suicidal clients; however, many practitioners are called upon to respond to a suicidal crisis in their work. The need to respond to this crisis immediately and accurately is a professional responsibility. The absence of appropriate and timely intervention may result in loss of life. Unfortunately, little training is provided within general social work curricula in the assessment of, intervention in, and prevention of suicidal behavior. Training available elsewhere is generally attended by those who *know* they need it, so that a large number of practitioners face the problem without benefit of training.

Crisis intervention theory and method provide the framework for dealing with suicidal crises. Competent knowledge and skill presuppose the ability to efficiently conduct a functional assessment, that is, an assessment focused on the actions within and the interactions between a client's individual, interpersonal, and environmental domains. Knowledge of client strengths as well as weaknesses is also necessary in developing intervention strategies. Not all suicidal be-

The author wishes to acknowledge Sandra Grochowski for her assistance and Mary Funnyé Goldson for her encouragement in the preparation of this chapter.

havior, however, is crisis in nature. There are some clients who think, talk, or act in suicidal ways as an ongoing means of coping with life distress. Vulnerabilities to suicide and suicidal behavior may originate within the individual, or within interpersonal or environmental domains. The clinical manifestation of these vulnerabilities, however, directly indicates that they affect other domains as well. This dynamic perspective has the highest potential of providing a comprehensive view of the problem to support the design of prevention and intervention strategies at the personal, program, and policy levels.

## PROBLEM DOMAIN

Suicide is a relatively rare event and is generally preceded by observable forms of nonfatal suicidal behavior. Practitioners are far more likely to encounter clients who are thinking about and talking about harming themselves in ways labeled as *suicidal*, than clients who actually go on to kill themselves. Attempted suicide and other nonfatal suicidal behaviors have been traditionally viewed as problems primarily because they carry with them an increased risk of suicide. More recently, however, nonfatal suicidal behaviors, including suicidal ideation and attempted suicide, have received some attention as problems in their own right. This change in approach is based on evidence that suicidal behavior does not lie along a continuum from least to most serious, but that individuals who engage in different suicidal behaviors may also possess other individual differences important in assessment and intervention (Linehan 1986).

The most frequently described nonfatal suicidal behaviors include suicidal ideation or thinking about suicide, suicide verbalization or talking about suicide, and suicide threats or informing others of plans to engage in an act of self-harm. The term *suicide gesture* refers coloquially to an act of self-harm in which the intention to die is judged as low. The lethality, or medical seriousness, of a suicide gesture is generally, but not always, also low. Attempted suicide is regarded as a failed effort to die. Based on our inability to reliably assess the intention of these acts after the fact, the term *parasuicide* has been suggested as a replacement for all categories of self-harm. Parasuicide is a deliberate, nonfatal act of self-harm; the term describes a suicide-like activity without inferring the actor's intent (Kreitman 1977). The terms *self-harm*, *parasuicide*, and *attempted suicide* are used synonomously in the literature (Hirsch, Walsh, and Draper 1982) and in this essay.

The lack of an agreed-upon definition of actual suicide is the major obstacle to the accurate collection of suicide statistics and research findings and the major obstacle to the development of theory about the nature and causes of suicide. Although an examination of the many classification systems of suicidal behavior underscores the complexity of defining suicide, it serves little utility in direct practice settings. In practice, there are two primary definitional questions: What *is* suicide? And how do I judge the *intention* to commit suicide?

The common *definition* of suicide is a simple one: "a human act of self-inflicted, self-intentional cessation" (Shneidman 1976: 5). The focus is on the intent of the actor and on the goal of the action. If this definition is broken down further, six factors are generally involved in defining suicide: the initiation of an act that leads to the death of the initiator; the willing of an act that leads to the death of the willer; the willing of self-destruction; the loss of will; the motivation to be dead or die; and the knowledge by an actor that the action is likely to produce death (Douglas 1967). These dimensions are important in determining whether a death is a suicide. Those responsible for making these determinations are concerned both with "false positives" (e.g., accidental overdoses ruled as suicides) and "false negatives" (e.g., a case in which evidence of suicide is concealed and the death is ruled as accidental).

Intent is an important concept in the assessment of suicide risk. Intent is how serious an individual is about ending his or her life (Beck, Schuyler, and Herman 1974). Judgments of low intent are frequently labeled as "less serious" or "manipulative" acts. Despite our best clinical efforts, there is little evidence suggesting that distinctions among levels of intent can be accurately or reliably made. Whether an individual truly wanted to die is simply too difficult to know after the fact.

Parasuicide may be used on the part of some severely distressed individuals to escape, cope with, or solve problems rather than to cause death. The ability to differentially assess intention plays an important role in choosing appropriate interventions and management strategies. Efforts to classify nonfatal suicidal behavior have been even less successful than those concerned with suicide. There is currently no widely accepted classification system in use.

*Theories* of suicide extend far back into recorded history. Early philosophical explanations and debates focused on individual rights, the rights of the community or state, and the morality of taking a life or the notion of higher right. Research into the causes of suicide is a more recent activity, formally beginning with Durkheim's *Le Suicide* in 1897. Although this iterative work was designed to illustrate the development of the sociological method, Durkheim's classification efforts resulted in three categories of suicide: 1) egoistic suicide, resulting from lack of or poor social integration into family, religious, or state communities; 2) altruistic suicide, resulting from excessive integration and identification, often identified with the "honorable" suicides of some Eastern cultures; and 3) anomic suicide, resulting from a loss of integration through trauma or catastrophe accompanied by alienation, social isolation, and loneliness (Durkheim 1897/1952).

Since Durkheim's work, there have been many classification systems describing the motives and intent of suicide. Common to the definitions used in most classification systems are the dimensions noted earlier: initiation; intent or motivation; and knowledge of the desired consequence (Douglas 1967). The current theories used to inform social work practice with suicidal individuals are based on the sociological, psychodynamic, biological, cognitive, and learning perspectives.

*Sociological theories* regard suicide as a function of an individual's role and status within social systems (Durkheim 1897 / 1952; Henry and Short 1954; Gibbs and Martin 1964; Douglas 1967; Braucht 1979). Originally, two characteristics of society—social regulation and social integration—were thought to determine social conditions and therefore the suicide rate. Social meaning, social norms and restraint, and the stability and durability of social relationships are now also regarded as important concepts and have contributed to the reformulation of these theories. Sociological theories are useful for predicting changes in suicide rates for total populations or subgroups; however, they are of limited utility for the practitioner because they are not useful in predicting individual behavior or in identifying strategies for change that can be implemented with individuals. Newer sociological theories, although still based on large group models, incorporate an interactionist perspective suggesting that suicide is the result of the interaction between types of individuals and the environment, rather than the result of the individual or the environment alone (Braucht 1979).

*Psychodynamic theories* view suicide as largely the product of internal, often unconscious, motives. Classic analytic theory defines suicide as an unconscious hostile impulse that is turned inward toward an introjected and ambivalently viewed love object. According to this theory, if this impulse is acted out against oneself, it will not be acted out against others. Menninger (1938) described three parts of this hostility: the wish to kill, the wish to be killed, and the wish to die. As part of Freud's evolving thoughts on suicide, factors in addition to aggression, such as maladaptive anxiety, guilt, dependency, and rage, are also acknowledged as potentially resulting in suicide-prone coping mechanisms. Rebirth, reunion with one's mother, identification with a lost object, and revenge are also suggested as motives. Feelings of abandonment and helplessness as well as hopelessness are also components of the psychodynamic formulation of suicide (Furst and Ostow 1979).

*Biological theories* suggest that either genetic predispositions or biochemical imbalances precipitate drives toward suicide. Although there is evidence of higher rates of suicide among male children of suicide victims (Stengel 1964), Wandrei (1985) found no evidence of higher rates among families of female suicides. A study of twin pairs in which one twin committed suicide did not find suicide in the other twin up to forty-nine years later (Kallman, et al. 1949). Despite evidence linking genetic factors to major affective and psychotic disorders, no clear relationship to suicide has been found (Motto 1986).

One of the most frequently replicated studies of biological indicators found low concentrations of a serotonin metabolite (5-HIAA) in the cerebrospinal fluid of suicide attempters and completers (Asberg, Thoren, and Traskman 1976). While these results are promising, they are not well established for two reasons. First, the numbers of participants in these studies was low, and second, we do not yet have information about normative levels of 5-HIAA in nonsuicidal populations (Motto 1986; Shaffer, et al. 1988). Currently, there is no biochemical indicator of suicidality useful in clinical work (Motto 1986).

*Cognitive theories* regard suicide and suicidal behavior as attempts to communicate or solve problems that cause intense interpersonal or environmental distress. The often-heard phrase "the cry for help" is used to convey the message contained in suicidal behavior (Farberow and Shneidman 1961).

Beck (1963) posited that suicidal behavior is caused by an individual's belief that current problems are insoluble. Hopelessness is strongly associated with suicidal behavior (Beck, Resnik, and Lettieri 1974; Kovacs, Beck, and Weissman 1975) and disordered patterns of thinking. Suicidal behavior has been conceptualized as a form of problem solving by several theorists (e.g., Applebaum 1963; Levenson and Neuringer 1971) and as an effort to get rid of, rather than cope with, problems through "manipulation" or death (Kovacs, Beck, and Weissman 1975; Olin 1976; Stengel 1964). Others have suggested that suicide attempts may be usefully regarded, in some individuals, as an attempt to cope with extremely difficult life situations (Linehan 1981, 1986; Maris 1971).

*Learning theories* define suicidal behavior as a function of two factors: 1) past responses in similar situations and 2) motivating, reinforcing and environmental conditions. Suicidal behavior is acquired through social learning methods and becomes part of the individual's repertoire of coping responses if it is supported and receives positive or desirable consequences from the environment. The probability of suicidal behavior is based on expectations of the act by the individual and others, on the opportunity to engage in the act, and on the presence or absence of preventive efforts by others (Diekstra 1973).

Linehan (1981) proposed a *social-behavioral model* of suicidal behavior integrating elements of the above models. This model, based on a review of empirical data on suicide and parasuicide, was originally an extension of the social-behavioral model of personality (Staats 1975). Although the original model has undergone some modification, its strength and its particular relevance to social work is that it articulates the interdependence of the dynamic interaction among an individual's cognitive, behavioral, and environmental systems. This conceptualization suggests that not only does the environment influence the individual, but individuals influence their environments. By cognitively acting on incoming information and by objectively changing outside influencing events, people can play a role in creating their own environment (Bowers 1973). The assessment and intervention methods that the model prescribes are based on the functional analyses of environmental as well as individual and interpersonal problems and resources.

## SOCIETAL CONTEXT

Suicide was the eighth leading cause of death in the United States in 1987, resulting in 30,980 deaths (12.7 per 100,000; NCHS, 1988a). The overall rates have remained relatively stable over the past 100 years with slight fluctuations. The reported rates were highest in the western states (Nevada, 24.1/100,000; Montana, 21.7/100,000; New Mexico, 19.3/100,000) and lowest in the Northeast (New York and New Jersey, 7.6/100,000; Massachusetts, 9.2/100,000) (NCHS 1988b).

Historically, suicide and suicidal behavior were judged primarily within religious contexts. More recently, social science and mental health research have altered the attitudes as well as the legal and religious responses to both. As evidence mounts correlating suicidal behavior and severe intrapersonal, interpersonal, and environmental stress, our attitudes and responses to the problem evolve. As we learn more about the multiple pathways to suicide, however, it becomes apparent that a permanent solution to or equation for explaining or preventing suicide is not likely to result. The social, psychological, and legal consequences of suicide are far-reaching.

It remains common to find reluctance to identify a death as suicide or to identify an act of self-harm as a suicide attempt. Several attitudes are responsible. The strong associations between mental illness (or more coloquially put, "being out of one's mind") and suicidal behavior possess negative social connotations that many victims and their families try hard to avoid. There are also still vestiges of religious sanction, longstanding beliefs that suicide is murder and a sin against God. Most churches, however, including the Catholic rites, no longer prohibit the burial of suicide victims in church cemeteries.

Since the late 1970s, we have witnessed an increase in the rates of suicide among young white men and in the attention paid to suicide among youth in the popular media. This attention has taken many forms, including movies, youth-oriented music, and heavy news coverage of youth suicides. Suicide is portrayed in highly romanticized fashion, with the victims often taking on folk hero status. Little or no acknowledgment is made of the individual mental-health or family-functioning problems that promote suicidal behavior, and the victims are presented as misunderstood but rational. Suicide is regarded as a reasonable solution to what are presented as the normal social pressures and problems of adolescence. The consequences have been two-fold: 1) the widespread perception among some youth that suicide is *not* tied to severely impaired functioning or psychiatric disorder (Shaffer et al. 1987) and 2) an increase in the rates of parasuicides and calls to suicide hotlines in the days following such portrayals (Gould and Shaffer 1986). Efforts are now being made to reduce the positive publicity given suicide. Or paramount importance in this effort is the message that suicidal behavior is not an effective means of solving life problems and that it is not chosen by rational and well-adjusted individuals as a way of solving problems.

## RISKS AND NEEDS OF POPULATION

A working knowledge of the risk factors associated with suicidal behavior is essential to identifying individuals at immediate and longer term risk. Risk factors are based on the characteristics of the populations in which rates of suicidal behavior are higher. They operate interactionally across the environmental, interpersonal, and individual domains. It is not at all clear how many, or which, risk factors place an individual at "high risk." Are more worse? Yes. Is not possessing one or even many of the characteristics a guarantee of low risk or insurance against suicidal behavior? Definitely not (Farberow and Mackinnon 1974; Lettieri 1974a, 1974b, Motto 1986).

Based on environmental and individual changes, one may move in and out of risk populations. Although many characteristics are shared by suicides and parasuicides or attempters, there are also differences between the two. There are also some risk factors about which information is available only for either suicide or parasuicide, but not both.

The *demographic risk factors* increasing the likelihood of suicide or suicidal behavior are sex, age, and race or ethnicity. Men commit suicide at rates nearly four times higher than women (NCHS 1988b). The overall suicide rates for both sexes are higher among those aged 65 and older. The suicide rates are almost twice as high among whites (13.9/100,000) as among blacks (6.5/100,000; NCHS 1988b). Among whites, the rates generally increase with age; males aged 80 to 84 have the highest reported rates (61.6/100,000). Among blacks and other racial minorities, however, the rates remain relatively constant in later life, peaking at 25 to 34 years (NCHS 1988b). Among youth aged 15 to 19, suicide is second only to accidents as a cause of death (NCHS 1988b). In contrast to patterns found in other age groups, the rate of suicide among males aged 15 to 24 has increased markedly since 1960.

The markedly higher suicide rates among elderly white men than among elderly black men have been examined from perspectives trying to explain each. Theories offer a variety of social, demographic, and individual factors as being responsible for these differences, such as the status and respect accorded the black elderly, the earlier exit of vulnerable black men from mainstream society because of homicide or incarceration, and the higher rates of alcoholism and depression among white men.

The lower suicide rates found among Mexican-Americans are hypothesized to be a function of differences from Anglo culture, including the supportive characteristics of family interaction (Hoppe and Martin 1986). The suicide rates among native Americans vary widely: they range from being similar to overall United States rates to being thirty times higher among some tribes (Hoppe and Martin 1986).

Attempted suicide is not recorded in any systematic fashion in the United States. Approximately 11 percent of admissions to some inpatient psychiatric units are reported to have been precipitated by suicide attempts (Wexler, Weissman, and Kasl 1978). Based on population statistics, this suggests a rate of 103 attempted suicides for every 100,000 people. The ratio of female to male attempters reported in the literature ranges from 1:1 to 5:1, although a ratio of 3:1 is most commonly cited. Attempted suicide or parasuicide rates decline with age. Black women attempt suicide less than their white counterparts (Baker 1984). It is suggested that the higher supports available within the black community for individuals alienated from the dominant society may be responsible for some of this difference (Poussaint 1975; Christian 1977; Davis 1979).

The literature on suicide and parasuicide suggests that the *social environments* linked to suicidal behavior have four characteristics: lack of social support, high negative stress, links to others or "models" of suicidal behavior, and possible positive consequences for suicidal behavior (Linehan 1981).

Unemployed or retired status is correlated with suicide. These individuals potentially lack the support and the social integration that a work setting provides. This is true for all groups except young employed professional women; rates of suicide in this group have recently been rising. The lack of social support in a suicidal person's life may also be due to immigrant status (Coombs and Miller 1975) or lack of shared social characteristics with neighbors (Braucht 1979). Living alone is linked both to those who commit suicide and to suicides with a history of parasuicide (Bagley, Jacobsen, and Rehin 1976; Shneidman, Farberow, and Litman 1970; Tuckman and Youngman 1968). Women attempters who later commit suicide are more isolated and may also receive less helpful care from service providers (Wandrei 1985). Unfortunately, little information exists to inform our clinical speculations about the quality of the social supports available to many suicidal individuals. There are some data suggesting that the relatives of attempters are hostile (Rosenbaum and Richman 1970), while successful suicides may lack even a hostile support system.

Suicidal behavior is widely regarded as a response to stressful, negative life events. Loss in general and patterns of negative life events distinguish suicide attempters and completers from other psychiatric inpatients (Birtchnell 1970; Levi et al. 1966). Suicide attempters report higher numbers of distressing, uncontrollable events than do nonsuicidal depressed individuals (Paykel 1979). Other studies have found that it is not the number or type of stressful life events involved that distinguishes suicidal individuals from others, but the perception of stressful negative events, i.e., a tendency for negative events to be regarded as more stressful by suicide attempters than by others (Linehan 1988a).

While most individuals with low social support and experiencing stressful life events do not go on to suicide or parasuicide, those who do may have suicidal behavior in their problem-solving response repertoires. Additionally, they may have positive expectations about the consequences of such action (Kreitman, Smith, and Tan 1970; Shaffer and Gould 1987; Chiles, Strosahl, and Linehan 1985).

Following a parasuicide, major environmental changes may occur in the direction desired by the attempter (Rubenstein, Moses, and Lidz 1958). These changes increase the positive expectations about suicidal behavior and may increase the risk of future attempts and of suicide (McCutcheon 1985).

Both observation and self-report of *interpersonal interaction patterns* suggest that suicidal and parasuicidal individuals may be lacking important social skills. Suicides and parasuicides exhibit low levels of social involvement and interaction. They are also less likely to ask for support or attention. There are some data suggesting that suidical individuals are less hostile and more passive and dependent than nonsuicidal individuals (Buglass and McCulloch 1970; Kreitman 1977).

Parasuicides are more likely to express dissatisfaction with treatment and to report discomfort around people in general (Cantor 1976). The interpersonal relationships of attempters are often characterized by high levels of conflict (Hawton and Catalan 1987; Linehan 1986); this finding is also well substantiated by clinical observation. In conjunction with interacting environmental factors, the above characteristics suggest a lack of mutually satisfying relationships, which may increase emotional pain, the perception of unmitigated stress, and the sense that help is unavailable.

*Individual risk factors* can be divided into three areas: cognitive, affective, and behavioral. As subsets of these, we discuss previous suicidal behavior and psychiatric disorder as correlates of increased risk.

*Cognitive risk factors* may be viewed as being of two kinds: those of cognitive style, or the processing, organization, and use of information, and those of cognitive content, or what an individual thinks about. The cognitive style most commonly linked to suicidal behavior is one of rigidity rather than reflectiveness (Patsiokas, Clum, and Luscomb 1979), impulsivity rather than deliberation (Farberow et al. 1970; Fox and Weissman 1975), field dependence rather than independence, and poor problem-solving ability (Levenson and Neuringer 1971; Linehan et al. 1987).

Hopelessness is generally regarded as the dominant cognitive feature of suicidal behavior (Beck 1963; Bedrosian and Beck 1979). Hopelessness is more strongly associated with current suicidal intent than is depression (Beck, Kovacs, and Weissman 1975; Kovacs, Beck, and Weissman 1975; Wetzel 1976). The available data make a case for the relationship between suicide and hopelessness, however, not between attempted suicide and hopelessness. Recent studies of attempted suicide have found mixed results concerning hopelessness, with higher levels of hopelessness among attempters found in some population samples (Paykel and Dienelt 1971; Wetzel 1976; Ivanoff under review), although not among teenaged minority female suicide attempters (Rotheram-Borus and Troutman 1988).

*Behavioral risk factors* are somewhat narrowly defined as those activities or physical states associated with increased risk. The single strongest risk factor for future suicidal behavior is a previous suicide attempt or parasuicide. The presence of a suicide note at the time of a previous parasuicide has also been linked to subsequent suicide. Highly disputed evidence exists linking the lethality of a prior attempt to subsequent suicide or parasuicide: some studies have found higher lethality in the prior attempts, while others have found no relationship between lethality and subsequent suicidal behavior (Linehan 1981).

Substance abuse and alcoholism are widely associated with an increased risk of suicide in both adults and adolescents. Up to 20 percent of all suicides are alcoholics (Roy and Linnoila 1986). Suicide attempters are significantly more likely to have used alcohol or drugs to alter their mood within the twenty-four hours preceding hospitalization than other psychiatric patients, even those thinking about suicide (Chiles, et al. 1986). Evidence of a criminal record is also associated with increased risk among young men (Lettieri 1974a, 1974b).

The presence of physical illness, whether terminal, chronic, or acute, is also linked to suicide and parasuicide. Efforts to obtain medical help are often made by those who are suicidal; most suicides and parasuicides have seen a physician within the six months prior to their act (Linehan 1981, 1988).

*Mental health or psychiatric disorders,* generally indicated by the presence of a psychiatric diagnosis, are also indicators of increased risk. Only a very small proportion of suicides among either adults or adolescents appear to be free of psychiatric symptoms (Shaffer et al. 1988). Adults diagnosed as schizophrenic are particularly vulnerable, especially if hopelessness is high (Beck, Kovacs, and Weissman 1975; Wetzel 1976). Among adult suicides, recurrent affective disorders (major depression and bipolar disorder) and schizophrenia are prevalent, while among repeated parasuicides, there is evidence that sociopathy is linked. Among adolescent suicides, less schizophrenia is reported, and the evidence on manic-depressive disorders is mixed; major depression is the most common diagnosis. In addition to depression, a variety of disorders labeled as psychiatric are found among teen-aged suicides, including antisocial behavior and learning disorders (Shaffer and Gould 1987).

## Consequences of Suicide and Suicidal Behavior

The consequences of suicide require discussion of the involved survivors. The experience of losing a parent, a child, a partner, or a close friend to suicide significantly marks a life. The reactions of guilt and anger coupled with profound loss can be extremely difficult to resolve without outside assistance. Unfortunately, the social sentiment toward suicide militates against survivors receiving adequate attention or support. Suicide remains a "shameful" death, generally regarded as best not discussed in detail. Ironically, one of the strongest needs among those attending suicide survivors' groups is to lay out, often in great detail, the immediate circumstances surrounding the suicide. Specifically, these may include finding the body, efforts to save the victim, and cleaning up any mess. Survivors not immediately present at the death may need to carefully describe the sequence of events as they understand it. Many report that they have had no opportunity to discuss these things before and experience great relief in doing so (Samaritans of the Capital District, personal communication, April 1987). Practical negative consequences may also ensue from a suicide, involving estate settlement, insurance claims, and worker compensation benefits. For a further discussion of the problems of survivors and the recommended interventions, see *Suicide and Its Aftermath* (Dunne, McIntosh, and Dunne-Maxim 1987).

Unfortunately, the circle of survivors extends far beyond the victim's immediate family and friends. Intervention with survivors may be needed in school, at work, or in religious communities. These interventions, sometimes referred to as *postvention*, are carried out in large and small groups, as well as in individual formats. As noted under "Societal Context," these situations must be carefully constructed with adolescents: postvention should be careful to convey the sadness associated with the loss, while not romanticizing the victim or the act, and while consistently maintaining that suicide is not a reasonable or good solution to problems.

The consequences of attempted suicide or parasuicide may be viewed as both positive and negative. For a desperate, distressed individual who is feeling that there is no place and no one to turn to, suicidal behavior may mobilize enough resources so that a solution to the immediate problem can be found. From a learning perspective, this is unfortunate for the individual, because the act has been effective; that is, it was successful in bringing about change in the desired direction. Interpersonally, attempted suicide may draw family and friends closer to the victim, as evidenced by such statements as "We had no idea how bad she was feeling until this happened," or may change the behavior of an estranged partner or spouse, who returns to the relationship following the other's parasuicide. Repeated parasuicide tends eventually to generate hostility and push others, even in primary significant relationships, away emotionally. When important social supports intentionally make themselves unavailable, further parasuicide, often of higher lethality, may occur as a way of trying to elicit a more caring response.

Systematically, nonfatal suicidal behaviors drain helping resources and place a chronic burden on the health care system, particularly on mental health and emergency services (Hawton and Catalan 1987; Kreitman 1977).

## PROGRAMS AND SOCIAL WORK SERVICES

The social worker plays an important role in the interdisciplinary programmatic response to suicide and suicidal behavior. Across all types and levels of service, including crisis intervention, case management, and primary intervention, social workers may have more contact with suicidal individuals and their families than most other professionals. In our communities, social workers often direct and coordinate crisis intervention services. In schools, preventive and postventive education is frequently a social work task. In health and mental health emergency settings, social workers are often the first to see suicidal individuals.

Crisis intervention or suicide prevention agencies may provide services such as telephone hotlines, walk-in counseling, and direct access to emergency medical and psychiatric services. Self-help groups dealing with surviving the loss due to suicide or coping with a suicidal loved one may also be offered through crisis intervention agencies. Most services of this types are locally run and are staffed by trained volunteers, often under the direction of a social worker. The types of specialized programs, the accessibility of the service, and the level of collaboration with other community agencies vary widely and should be known prior to client referral. Clients should also know whether crisis hotlines immediately notify police or mobile crisis units when suicide intent is expressed. For example, the Samaritans, an international organization with several branches in the eastern United States, do not initiate contact with medical authorities unless permission to obtain help is given by the caller (Hirsch 1981).

School-based prevention programs tend to be broadly based, focusing on suicide education as the primary interventive method. The rationale behind these programs is that increased knowledge and sensitivity will help identify and get help to at-risk adolescents. While this approach may make theoretical sense, it has been criticized as ineffective and inefficient. The only systematic controlled evaluation of school-based programs found no significant increase in appropriate attitudes or accurate knowledge about suicide, particularly its correlation with mental illness (Shaffer and Gould 1987). The group at highest risk, affectively disturbed young men, has not been successfully targeted by most school-based prevention programs (Shaffer et al. 1988). By defining the population at risk as all youth in the schools, we ignore much of what has been learned over the 1970s and 1980s about adolescent suicide, and we dilute prevention efforts.

Family service agencies, counseling services, mental health clinics, and even some psychiatric inpatient programs are beginning to respond more programmatically to the problems of suicide and suicidal behavior. In clinic or outpatient settings, clinician-led groups may be available that focus specifically on suicidal behavior (Linehan 1988) or on depression. In inpatient hospital settings, special programs have been designed to help the individual recover most quickly and to begin more adaptive problem solving. Detailed explanations of these programs are available in Hawton and Catalan (1987) and in Ivanoff (1984).

## DIFFERENTIAL CLINICAL ASSESSMENTS AND INTERVENTIONS

Social workers may encounter suicidal individuals in many service settings. There are several issues worth thought before one confronts a suicidal client. Nonfatal suicidal behaviors, including parasuicide, were noted earlier as sometimes being used as single or repetitive problem-solving or coping strategies by individuals who lack adequate skills or emotion regulation mechanisms. Suicidal behavior is a response to a problem the client views as unsolvable. Accordingly, it is regarded by the practitioner as problem solving in nature. An often used alternative is to describe the individual as a "manipulator": someone who probably does not really want to die but uses suicidal behavior to accomplish other means. The negative connotations tied to this view evoke hostility toward suicide attempters and may compromise a practitioner's ability to provide care. Parasuicides and repeated parasuicides are likely to receive less as well as lesser-quality care from service providers (Wandrei 1985).

Insofar as it is possible in the abstract, it is also worthwhile to consider one's own philosophy toward suicide: Under what circumstance does one believe in—and under what circumstances does one not believe in—preventing suicide? Is suicide an inalienable personal right? Those who argue that it is view all coercive forms of suicide prevention as maligning and disrespectful (Szasz 1986). The rational suicide movement also supports the right of individuals to choose suicide as an act of self-deliverance, most often in response to interminable physical pain and terminal illness. Based on clinical experience, however, there is also evidence that in many instances, suicidal intent may change dramatically within a few days. Providing control until the individual is able to regain self-management is regarded as humane and caring from this perspective.

From a legal perspective, agencies and individual practitioners alike worry about litigation and possible liability if suicide occurs. As a result, many agency policies require practitioners to enact restrictive means of prevention, such as involuntary hospitalization in all cases where the practitioner is not reasonably confident that clients will not harm themselves. In circumstances where no policy exists, workers must exercise greater self-awareness, risk assessment, and decision-making skills.

Finally, the need for ongoing consultation while working with suicidal clients cannot be overstated. The degree of judgment and the number and quality of decisions made require discussion with another professional, preferably one experienced in working with suicidal clients. The immediate and ongoing assessment of risk, the review of intervention strategies, and the exploration of other available prevention resources are three functions that this consultation can serve.

Another important reason to maintain close consultative contact during the period when a client is actively suicidal is to help maintain self-awareness and to help deal with one's personal responses engendered by the client's suicidal behavior. The possibility of losing a client to suicide and the consequent feelings of frustration, anger, and impotence are reasonable and normal; however, they can prevent a worker from being effective during this time. In cases of repeated parasuicide, consultation can be useful in helping maintain one's own problem-solving perspective and focus when feeling uncomfortably caught by the client's maladaptive efforts and in the assessment of further or increased risk.

Individual vulnerabilities such as psychiatric disorders, poor problem-solving abilities, or inadequate coping mechanisms that may increase vulnerability to suicidal behavior can be worsened by environmental stress. An ecological perspective assessing the interaction between individuals and their social and physical environments is important in acquiring an understanding of suicide risk. While the social worker practicing outside a mental health setting may have less occasion to assess suicide risk, nonetheless it remains necessary, given the possible consequence. In addition to mental health and counseling agencies, where one might typically find suicidal individuals, social workers also deal with clients at risk in public assistance or child welfare settings, in hospitals or health clinics, and particularly in institutional settings such as nursing homes, juvenile detention centers, jails, and prisons.

When seeing a client in an agency setting who presents several risk-population characteristics, it is best to ask directly about previous suicidal behavior. As part of a general assessment interview, the question can be incorporated into discussing ways in which the client has previously tried to cope with his or her problems, a standard component in social work assessment interviews (Hepworth and Larsen 1986). Contrary to myth, it is not advisable to avoid discussing suicide, nor is there any evidence that simply asking an adult about suicidal ideation or behavior plants the idea, i.e., "Well, no, I hadn't thought of it myself before, but that's not a bad idea!" In fact, clinical experience suggests that if clients are thinking about suicide, most feel relieved to be asked about it. Clients may be uncertain or fearful about the social worker's reaction to suicidal ideation and may hesitate to bring it up on their own; open talk about suicide and matter-of-fact questions can make discussion easier. A good question to begin with is "Have you ever thought about doing or done anything to hurt yourself?" The question should be asked directly, and the response should be explored immediately if the answer is affirmative.

Although most clients do not seek help for suicidal ideation, a client may seek help for problems of depression or hopelessness tied to a downward spiral in mood, feelings of self-worth, and success in solving or coping with life problems. Client comments that require further exploration include indirect statements of how others might be better off if the client were gone, comments such as "I can't stand it" or "I am at the end of my rope," or expressed wishes to be with dead relatives or pets. Such expressed wishes must be explored carefully in adolescents and adults for evidence of concrete thinking that may indicate a thought disorder. Direct statements of wanting to "end it all," "check out," or "go to sleep and never wake up" also require immediate follow-up with a question asking directly about ideation and self-harm.

Finally, social workers may see clients referred to them for ongoing individual or family intervention following a suicide attempt. In situations where the practitioner has prior knowledge that suicidal behavior has occurred in the recent past, it is important to establish quickly whether the ideation or intent remains. Whether the issue of suicide risk surfaces during the initial assessment or later, the social worker proceeds with the same follow-up questions.

The amelioration of the desire to die or permanently escape and the restoration of the desire to live are the broadly stated goals of intervention with suicidal individuals. Implicit in these goals are 1) the survival and protection of the individual during periods of crisis and 2) major shifts in cognitive, social, and environmental domains so that improved coping and problem solving may occur. However, in the words of one client, clients "just want to be happy and feel like there's something to live for!" The distance between the highly suicidal client expressing this plaintive goal and its achievement can seem enormous to the practitioner responsible for interventive planning.

In work with suicidal clients, the concept of breaking down large goals and selecting manageable units for immediate attention (i.e., partializing) is extremely useful. This is similar to social work practice with problems such as domestic violence and homelessness, where client problems are interactively lodged across individual, interpersonal, and environmental systems. Another element common to assessment and intervention in these problem areas is the timely recognition of and response to crises.

There are three goals of assessment in working with suicidal clients: 1) assessment of the long-term and immediate risks of suicide and suicidal behavior; 2) assessment of the actual suicidal responses across individual, interpersonal, and environmental systems; and 3) assessment of the problems that precipitated the suicidal behavior across individual, interpersonal, and environmental systems.

While high-risk characteristics provide information about the long-term risk, they do not precisely predict the likelihood of future suicide or parasuicide. Unknown are the combination and the number of risk characteristics necessary to place an individual at high risk. A number of suicide prediction scales have been developed to identify at-risk individuals. These scales alert the practitioner that a client is part of a risk population. However, individuals lacking one or many of the characteristics associated with suicide or parasuicide are not without risk, nor are they in any way immune to risk. Population risk characteristics are a useful indicator of increased risk, generally at some unspecified time in the future. They do not provide the information needed most by a practitioner about the likelihood of suicide or parasuicide in the next few days.

The assessment of suicide or parasuicide in the immediate or near future is indicated in several situations, including 1) when an individual possesses several risk-population indicators; 2) when a history of suicidal behavior becomes apparent during the course of an assessment interview; and 3) when a client communicates an intent to commit suicide, either in a crisis situation (e.g., in the middle of the night over the telephone) or during a regularly scheduled appointment.

Unfortunately, as in assessing long-term risk, no known set of factors can predict imminent risk. There are however, direct, indirect, and situational indicators (see table 21.1). These indicators discriminate suicidal or parasuicidal individuals from those who are not and describe circumstances associated with suicide or parasuicide within the next few days. This list of empirically derived indicators was originally compiled by Linehan (1981), but it has been updated for this purpose.

Assessment and intervention planning with a client manifesting suicidal behavior can be readily conceptualized in six topical areas:

1. *Suicidal behavior,* (includes all ideation, planning, threats, and parasuicide). Identification and description of suicidal behavior including dimensions (frequency, duration, intensity, and magnitude). Previous suicidal behavior of client and family. Preceding and consequent situational and behavioral events associated with suicidal behavior.

2. *Presenting and precipitant problems.* Client's description of problem leading up to suicidal behavior, including dimensions, history, and antecedent and consequent conditions of the situation and of the problems.

3. *Individual, interpersonal and environmental factors that increase and decrease risk.* Individual characteristics, including demographic, cognitive, affective, and behavioral risk factors. Environmental and interpersonal characteristics including social support, models for suicidal behavior, and consequences of suicidal behavior.

4. *Individual and environmental factors relevant to intervention.* Client's personal assets, such as aptitudes; cognitive, intellectual, and emotional abilities; skills; and cultural and religious values. Client's deficits or hindrances in the same areas. Char-

acteristics of the environment that may help or hinder intervention.

5. *Objectives for intervention.* Problem list with targets clearly specified. Outcome criteria and how progress will be measured.
6. *Planned interventions.* Immediate steps to reduce risk of suicidal behavior. List of intervention strategies with problem targets from above.

This assessment is based on the functional analysis interview model (Pomeranz and Goldfried 1970), adapted for suicidal behavior. It also incorporates components of the social-behavioral analysis of suicidal behavior (Linehan 1981).

---

TABLE 21.1. Factors Associated with Immediate Risk of Suicide or Parasuicide

---

I. Direct Indicators of Imminent Risk for Suicide or Parasuicide
  1. Suicide threats
  2. Suicide planning and/or preparations
  3. Parasuicide at anytime in the past
  4. Suicidal ideation
II. Indirect Indicators of Imminent Risk for Suicide or Parasuicide
  5. Client falls into suicide or parasuicide risk population
  6. Recent disruption or loss of interpersonal relationship; negative environmental changes in past month
  7. Indifference to or dissatisfaction with therapy; elopements and early pass returns by hospitalized patients
  8. Current hopelessness or anger, or both
  9. Recent medical care
  10. Indirect references to own death; arrangements for death
III. Circumstances Associated with Suicide and/or Parasuicide in the Next Several Hours or Days
  11. Alcohol consumption
  12. Suicide note written or in progress
  13. Methods available or easily obtained
  14. Isolation
  15. Precautions against discovery or intervention; deception and/ or concealment about timing, place, etc.

---

SOURCE: Adapted from M. M. Linehan. 1981. "A Social-Behavioral Analysis of Suicide and Parasuicide: Implications for Clinical Assessment and Treatment. In H. G. Glazer and J. F. Clarkin, eds., *Depression: Behavioral and Directive Intervention Strategies,* pp. 229–294. New York: Garland.

## *Short-Term Goals of Intervention*

To paraphrase a useful prioritizing expression, all forms of intervention are ineffective with a dead client (Mintz 1968). Crisis intervention is the social worker's front-line strategy with a client at immediate risk of suicidal behavior. The standard method of crisis intervention is described in detail elsewhere (Butcher and Maudal, 1976; Golan 1986). A summary of the recommended procedures is presented in table 21.2.

Once a worker determines that the client is at immediate risk through assessing the listed indicators, action must be taken to prevent further suicidal behavior. First of all, this means making certain that the client is physically safe: Does the client require hospitalization? Is there someone in the client's home environment willing and able to stay with the client until the crisis passes? Is this individual willing and able to call emergency services for assistance if the client

---

TABLE 21.2. General Crisis Management Procedures

---

1. Offer emotional support
2. Provide opportunity for catharsis
3. Communicate hope and optimism
4. Be interested and actively involved
5. Listen selectively; sift out material useful in bringing about change; leave defenses intact
6. Provide needed factual information
7. Formulate the problem situation; provide statement of problem to client
8. Be emphatic and to the point
9. Predict future consequences of various courses of action
10. Give advice and offer direct suggestions
11. Set limits; establish rules
12. Clarify and reinforce adaptive action and problem-solving
13. Confront the client's ideas or behavior directly
14. Terminate a session if the client is not at the point of working on his or her problems.
15. Place concrete demands or requirements on the client before the next contact
16. Work out an explicit, time-limited contract
17. Enlist the aid of significant others

---

SOURCE: Butcher and Maudal (1976).

appears unable to maintain control? A bias toward maintaining the client's sense of self-control and personal management whenever possible should be demonstrated in assessing how best to deal with a crisis.

The decision to hospitalize a client is generally made in conjunction with a physician or emergency room staff. The question to ask oneself when considering this decision is "Can I prevent a suicide now by hospitalization?" Some psychiatric disorders linked to increased suicide risk, such as delusional depression, schizophrenia, schizoaffective disorder, and panic disorder, are best treated in the hospital during their acute phases. In other cases, however, the negative consequences of hospitalization, including social stigma, loss of a feeling of control, and the unfavorable treatment received from hospital staff, are also considerations worth weighing. The more general question of whether hospitalization will prevent suicidal behavior from occurring in the future cannot be answered unequivocally, but hospitalization for this reason has found little positive endorsement.

The use of contracts, both verbal and written, is reported to be quite successful between suicidal individuals and practitioners. In this situation, the contract refers only to suicidal behavior, not other agreements for service that the client makes with the worker. Prior to leaving the social worker's office, the client is asked to agree not to commit suicide and, if feeling strong urges to do so, to contact the worker or some other stipulated service provider. If the client reports not feeling able to enter into this contract with the worker, a brief voluntary hospitalization may be discussed as a self-initiated method of regaining control.

If a suicide attempt has already been made or is in progress when the social worker is notified, it may be necessary to call the police or the emergency rescue squad for immediate action. If the worker knows that local emergency services are apt to be less than immediately responsive, an involved and supportive family member or friend may be called to go to the client and stay there until help arrives.

Ideally, the best way to manage a crisis is to predict and plan for it. If a client has experienced intermittent intense suicidal ideation or has acted on this ideation in the past, it is useful to acknowledge that the ideation will probably not end immediately after the first few sessions, that it may be useful to view it as a "habit," and that the client and the worker will together develop strategies for managing it in the future.

Based on the information about cognitive strengths and resources obtained in the assessment (e.g., important reasons for living, any positive hopes for the future, and acknowledgment that suicide is not an effective solution to problems), a plan for coping is developed. The product of this planning is kept on a "crisis card," a business-sized card containing the phone numbers of emergency contacts on one side and a list of coping strategies to help maintain control on the other. Carried in a wallet or pocketbook at all times, the card can be used as a self-instructional device for periods when the client is afraid of losing control.

## Intervention Methods and Strategies

An intervention plan is developed only after the client's problems have been identified. Vague presenting problems give an incomplete picture, without a precise specification of the problem determinants or a description of past and present coping resources. Accordingly, a contract or an explicit agreement between the worker and the client about the problems to be worked on is important. In addition to describing the problems, a contract should identify the desired changes in the problems so that both client and worker will know when the problem has been rectified or the goal accomplished. The individuals involved in the intervention plan should also be specified: the worker, the client, and any involved family members or significant others. Expectations that the client will attend sessions and work actively on the problems should be agreed upon. If family or others are involved, they should be clear about their role in intervention so that confusion does not result. The worker's role in helping the client work toward solutions to the problems and her or his response to any future suicidal behavior should also be made as clear as possible: the client has the right to know if the worker intends to encourage hospitalization or to speak to family members if the risk increases, or if there are circumstances in which the worker would pursue involuntary hospitalization. Finally, the practicalities of role expectations, the extent and limits of confidentiality, and the expected number of treatment sessions should be discussed as a part of the contract.

Direct focus on the suicidal behavior and active problem solving to ameliorate the problems and responses related to suicidal behavior are two hallmarks of the prescribed intervention programs (Clum, Patsiokas, and Luscomb 1979; Hawton and Catalan 1987; Linehan, 1981, 1988). Active problem-solving may involve training the client in problem-solving skills if these skills are deficient, encouraging and supporting the use of inhibited problem-solving skills, providing direct information when needed, and offering feedback about the efficacy of proposed problem-solving solutions.

Effective problem solving involves four separate tasks. Clients may experience difficulty in any one or more of these tasks. Identifying specific deficits or inhibitions can help target interventions. First, a problem must be recognized and accurately identified. Particularly among those who are depressed, there is a tendency to see only the negative aspects of any situation. After two weeks of an unsuccessful job search and frustrating interpersonal conflicts with family, a client came in presenting his problem as "not belonging in the world." While his feeling was understandable, his problems were not accurately described by his global statement.

Second, alternative ways of solving the problem must be generated; the more alternatives an individual can generate, the better the ability to move from one to another when necessary. The suicidal individual sees only one alternative to his or her problem; feeling trapped and seeing no way out represent a lack of ability to entertain alternative problem-solving strategies. Practitioners may hear, "But there is *no other* way!"

Third, the selection and implementation of the best solution occurs. Faulty choice and implementation may be the result of poor decision making or judgment, and of impulsiveness or not thinking through the consequences of an action.

Finally, once the solution is implemented, the effectiveness of the solution must be evaluated for learning and future action. Being able to sort out the lessons in successful as well as unsuccessful problem solving is important in further problem-solving skill development. For example, a client who had previously been unable to control outbursts of rage at her mother learned that with situational planning, a set of self-instructions developed for use when she was with her mother, and support from others afterward, she could, with practice over time, eliminate the feelings of severe self-recrimination that had led to suicidal ideation.

The role of the worker in the change process frequently includes three simultaneous activities. The first is to provide hope, in the absence of the client's own, that her or his problems can eventually be managed or solved. While providing hope is clearly important in the beginning phase of work, it is also common for the automatic "What's the use? I may as well give up" thoughts to return intermittently as problem solving becomes more difficult for the client. The practitioner should not be discomfited by the notion of lending his or her own hope to the client during the slow, gradual process of rebuilding the client's hope.

Second, the worker must model adaptive problem solving for the client through the worker's own behavior. This includes securing information and referrals for concrete services, generating alternatives when needed, accurately identifying problem situations, and consistently evaluating the effectiveness of problem-solving efforts.

Finally, the worker's response to the client's efforts should be supportive and encouraging, but also corrective. If a client persists in attempting to solve problems in an ineffective or maladaptive manner, change has not occurred, nor has the likelihood of future suicidal behavior decreased. Learning new ways of solving problems, however, is difficult. Each step toward adaptive problem solving should be verbally identified or even pointed out for clients, as they may not recognize the accomplishment. Warmth in responding to not-quite-right efforts, help in adjusting them, and encouragement of future efforts are frequently repeated worker tasks.

## CASE ILLUSTRATION

Elizabeth, a 22-year-old white unmarried woman, had previously attempted suicide three times. She initially came to the mental health clinic on a pass from the psychiatric unit of the local hospital, where she had been hospitalized for three weeks following a highly lethal overdose that she had acknowledged as an attempt to end her life. Her discharge from the hospital had been made contingent on beginning outpatient treatment. She presented as a very bright, depressed young woman and expressed amazement and ambivalence at still being alive. She acknowledged current suicidal ideation and at first insisted it was constant. However, upon closer questioning by the practitioner it appeared the ideation was more intermittent, occurring three or four times per day, usually when she was thinking about the "fucked-up mess my life is" and "this empty feeling inside me that makes me think there's no hope."

The second of five children, Beth had grown up in an upper-middle-class two-parent family in a western state. She described her physician father as caring but critical and her mother as distant and aloof. She reported no history of mental illness or emotional disorder among her parents or siblings and noted that her siblings were "wonderful and normal."

Her first suicide attempt was at age 16, while she was living at home. Following an argument with her parents, she ingested a potpourri of pills from the family's well-stocked medicine closet, became ill, and vomited. She received no medical attention and told no one of the incident at the time. Each of her attempts had been precipitated by a two- to three-month period of slowly deepening depression and lowered daily functioning. In addition, Beth reported that she had withdrawn from her few friendships and the activities that had provided satisfaction. She had increased her use of maladaptive coping methods, including alcohol and drug abuse, and spent long periods of time in bed.

The immediate precipitants of all the attempts had been interpersonal in nature, involving conflict or perceived or real rejection by an important other. The most recent attempt had been in response to a roommate and close friend's moving out of the apartment that the two were sharing and the news one week later that the clinician she had been seeing at another agency in town was leaving her position. Beth described how quickly life began to look empty and how thoughts of past relationship failures and feelings of being uncared for had crowded out all motivation to "keep my life together." Beth had had few long-term relationships, jobs, or avocational pursuits. Her strengths included her intellect, her ability to break down problems in living toward solving them (when not severely depressed), and her artistic abilities, most notably painting. She had been trained in art from an early age, and spending time painting afforded her a sense of self unavailable through other activities alone or with others. Her previous psychiatric diagnoses included both major depression and borderline personality disorder. Numerous problems with the use of psychiatric diagnoses have been described elsewhere in the social work literature (Kirk and Hutchins 1986), and it was not automatically assumed that these diagnoses were accurate or useful in providing social work intervention. The criteria for a diagnosis of major depression were consistent with the pattern of behavior, affect, and cognition that Beth described during each of the periods leading up to her parasuicides. The earlier diagnosis of borderline personality disorder was used as an indicator of previous practitioners' views of the severity and pervasiveness of Beth's inability to regulate her feelings when distressed and the possible forms and targets of her conflictual interpersonal style.

In assessing Beth's suicidal behavior and life situation, it became clear that her pattern of unsuccessful relationships and aborted occupational ventures had left her feeling quite hopeless about the future. While conveying strong sensitivity and empathy for how overwhelmed Beth felt, the practitioner told Beth she did not believe suicide was the best or only solution to Beth's problems. Beginning with the first contact, the practitioner let Beth know that although she understood Beth's feeling of desperation, she did not share Beth's feeling of hopelessness about her situation: she believed there *were* ways to work toward solving Beth's problems. The practitioner did believe that Beth's life could be improved, and she communicated this sincerely.

Initially, Beth was skeptical: "I know this is just your job! You don't really care! How could you know how to fix my life? What happens if I can't do it? What makes you think there's anything here worth saving?" The practitioner explained that she didn't *know* how to fix Beth's life, but that there were things they could do together to improve it. The worker frankly admitted that she didn't have the "right" answers but would help generate some alternatives during this time when Beth's capacity for solving problems was diminished by her depression and hopelessness. The practitioner went on to tell Beth that she regarded their work together as a collaborative enterprise, Beth's portion of which was, initially, to try to be honest about her feelings and to work toward her goals.

Initially, Beth was vague in describing what she wanted to change in her life. She defined her problems in global terms that contributed to her feeling overwhelmed by them. With the worker's help, she was able to identify two major areas that she wanted to work on: getting along better (with and without people) and finding work she was interested in doing. These goals were further broken down, as assessment indicated Beth's previous problem patterns in these areas.

Beth was willing to contract to come to every appointment and to be honest in discussing her feelings and in discussing her work toward the two goals. Beth expressed worry about lying to the worker about doing positive things when she hadn't really done them or, worse yet, being caught having agreed to do something particularly distasteful. For this reason, the worker and Beth initially agreed to individually negotiate and contract between-session tasks.

Contracting to avoid parasuicide, however, was somewhat more difficult. As Beth pointed out, "If I really want to do it, I'll do it, right? Just because I tell you I'll call someone if I feel like I want to knock myself off doesn't mean I have to do it, does it?" The worker, wishing to maximize Beth's sense of self-control, told Beth that she was absolutely correct, that the option to parasuicide was *not* being taken away from her by the contract. The practitioner described the contract as serving two purposes: to remind Beth of the purpose of their work together during periods when "automatic" suicide ideation may have taken over and to assure the practitioner that Beth felt confident enough in her own control to live at home. Possible scenarios were discussed: "What happens if . . . ?" "What if I forget until it's too late and call after I've taken something?" "If I screw up will you stop seeing me?" These questions, as well as when re-hospitalization might be considered, were discussed in detail. A problem-solving perspective was maintained, meaning that future suicidal behavior was regarded as an eventual probability, not to be punished (or praised via the practitioner's overattention), but to be *dealt with* as part of ongoing work. Beth made a verbal contract and following that, she and the practitioner made up a short written contract for six months which was signed by the two of them and placed in Beth's file. Beth was also given a copy to keep.

Each session initially began with a mini-functional analysis, similar to the one described in the assessment interview, discussing suicidal behavior since the last contact. Positive emphasis was placed on what Beth did to cope with the suicidal thoughts or urges to hurt herself. Less successful efforts at coping with suicidal thoughts were examined in view of how they could be strengthened. Together, the worker and Beth made up a one-page log, which Beth kept and brought in for review each week. The log detailed her thoughts about "giving up," the situation she was in at the time, how strong the urge to "do something" (negative) was on a 1–10 scale and how she coped with the situation. Beth managed to avoid further parasuicide, despite episodes of intense ideation which were almost every other day at first. By six months later these had decreased to approximately one episode a month.

Early on Beth confided that she kept a cache of psychotropic prescription drugs under her bed in case she decided she "couldn't take it any more." Sometimes Beth would get the box of pills out and take it out to the living room and play with it, counting out how many of each drug or drug combinations she would have to take to kill herself. She was highly conversant with lethal dosages of these medications. For some time after beginning work she found these thoughts comforting, a sort of "entertaining of options." She acknowledged that having the drugs represented an independence and sense of control for her. The practitioner told Beth she was uncomfortable with the risk posed by the accessibility of the drugs, although understood her feelings of lack of control and wish to attain it. Beth noted that times when she was most likely to get out the drugs were when she was depressed or when angry with the practitioner for "trying to make her live." As Beth had faithfully followed the terms of the suicidal behavior contract despite severe ideation and depression during this period, the worker was not certain hospitalization was the appropriate action. Following consultation with her immediate supervisor and another senior colleague, the worker did not suggest hospitalization at this time, identifying the sense of control Beth derived from the cache of drugs as important until it could be replaced by control gained through more adaptive means. (In retrospect, suggesting hospitalization *may* have enabled Beth to take adaptive control sooner.) Three months later Beth came in and announced she had flushed all the pills down the toilet, having decided it was "stupid to keep these things around the house anymore." This provided the impetus to review her progress and highly praise the adaptive efforts Beth was now making to maintain her sense of control over life.

Through discussion with the worker and information, testing and guidance from the Department of Vocational Rehabilitation, Beth went on to identify a new vocational pursuit, art restoration. While this work involved great technical knowledge and ability, the challenge for Beth was positive. A long apprenticeship followed months of study. During this time, many recurring doubts about the decision to study restoration plagued Beth, sometimes interrupting work. The focus in her work with the practitioner shifted to building a broader and more competent support system. Beth found a broader network of friends enabled her to manage periodic feelings of loss and rejection better. She learned to adaptively use others for "perception checks," and to buffer the stress of normal change and transition via comparing experiences. Episodes of severe depression continue, on an almost annual basis. These are not tied to suicide ideation, but regarded as "circuitry overload" and necessitate reflection, time out from everyday activities and occasional medication. Beth has learned ways to manage (or not manage, as she chooses) these episodes in such a way that the important sustaining structures of her career and friends are left intact.

Because of its person and situation perspective, social work is well suited to designing interventions, programs, and policies for working with the problems of suicide and nonfatal suicidal behavior. The similarities between suicidal individuals and the multiproblem clients seen in social service agencies are marked.

Although there have been no studies of professionals who work specifically with suicidal clients, social work appears to hold a considerable role in service provision. Given this role, social work should also take an active role in the development of intervention methods and models. To date, social work has contributed little to the literature that can help to inform prevention or intervention. With notable exceptions, most social work literature on suicidal behavior is reactive, examining the loss of a client to suicide rather than the effectiveness of intervention programs.

While the development of broad-based primary prevention programs that are focused on education about suicide does not appear to hold the answer (Shafer et al. 1988), the information available on risk factors can provide population and problem targets for designing interventions. Even though suicide cannot be predicted on a case-by-case basis, the evidence cited in this essay suggests that intervention models can be developed. This task involves the systematic description, application, and evaluation of specific intervention components. This work must necessarily take place through individual practitioners reporting their intervention results to others. The dual focus on suicide and nonfatal suicidal behavior is necessary both to reduce the suffering of individuals and their families and to improve the use of costly health care resources.

## REFERENCES

Applebaum, S. A. 1963. "The Problem-Solving Aspects of Suicide." *Journal of Projective Techniques* 27(1):259–268.

Asberg, M., P. Thoren, and L. Traskman. 1976. "Serotonin Depression: A Biochemical Subgroup Within the Affective Disorders?" *Science* 191:478–480.

Bagley, C., S. Jacobsen, and A. Rehin. 1976. "Completed Suicide: A Taxonomic Analysis of Clinical and Social Data." *Psychological Medicine* 6(3):429–438.

Baker, F. M. 1984. "Black Suicide Attempters in 1980: A Preventive Focus." *General Hospital Psychiatry* 6:131–137.

Beck, A. T. (1963). "Thinking and Depression: Idiosyncratic Content and Cognitive Distortions." *Archives of General Psychiatry* 9:324–333.

Beck, A. T. M. Kovacs, and A. Weissman. 1979. "Assessment of Suicide Intention: The Scale of Suicide Ideation." *Journal of Consulting and Clinical Psychology* 47(2):343–352.

Beck, A. T., M. Kovacs, and A. Weissman. 1975. "Hopelessness and Suicidal Behavior: An Overview." *Journal of the American Medical Association* 234:1146–1149.

Beck, A. T., H. L. P. Resnik, and D. J. Lettieri. 1974. *The Prediction of Suicide.* Bowie, Md.: Charles Press.

Beck, A. and A. Weissman. 1974. "The Measurement of Pessimism: The Hopelessness Scale." *Journal of Consulting and Clinical Psychology* 42(4):861–865.

Beck, A. T., D. Schuyler, I. Herman, 1974. "Development of Suicidal Scales." In A.

T. Beck, H. L. P. Resnick, D. J. Lettieri, eds., *The Prediction of Suicide*. Bowie, Md.: Charles Press.

Bedrosian, R. C. and A. T. Beck. 1979. "Cognitive Aspects of Suicidal Behavior." *Suicide and Life Threatening Behavior* 9:87–96.

Birtchnell, J. 1970. "The Relationship Between Attempted Suicide, Depression, and Parent Death." *British Journal of Psychiatry* 116:307–313.

Bowers, R. S. 1973. "Situationism in Psychology: An Analysis and a Critique." *Psychological Review* 80:307–336.

Braucht, G. N. 1979. "Interactional Analysis of Suicidal Behavior." *Journal of Consulting and Clinical Psychology* 47(532):653–669.

Brink, T. L. 1977. "Brief Psychotherapy: A Case Report Illustrating Its Potential Effectiveness." *Journal of the American Geriatric Society* 25:273–276.

Buglass, D. and J. W. McCulloch. 1970. "Further Suicidal Behavior: The Development and Validation of Predictive Scales." *British Journal of Psychiatry* 116:483–491.

Butcher, J. N. and G. R. Maudal. 1976. "Crisis Intervention." In I. B. Weiner, ed., *Clinical Methods of Psychology*. New York: Wiley.

Cantor, P. C. 1976. "Personality Characteristics Found Among Youthful Female Suicide Attempters." *Journal of Abnormal Psychology* 85:324–329.

Chiles, J. A., K. Strosahl, L. Cowden, R. Graham, and M. Linehan. 1986. "The 24 Hours Before Hospitalization: Factors Related to Suicide Attempting." *Suicide and Life Threatening Behavior* 16(3):335–342.

Chiles, J. A., K. D. Strosahl, L. McMurtray, and M. M. Linehan. 1985. "Modeling Effects on Suicidal Behavior." *Journal of Nervous and Mental Diseases* 8:477–481.

Christian, E. R. 1977. "Black Suicide." In C. L. Hatton, S. M. Valente, and A. Bink. eds., *Suicide: Assessment and Intervention*, pp. 143–159. New York: Appleton-Century-Crofts.

Coombs, D. and H. Miller. 1975. "The Scandinavian Suicide Phenomenon: Fact or Artifact? Another Look." *Psychology Reports* 37:1075–1078.

Clum, G. A., A. T. Patsiokas, and R. L. Luscomb. 1979. "Empirically Based Comprehensive Treatment Program for Parasuicide." *Journal of Consulting and Clinical Psychology* 47(5):937–945.

Davis, R. 1979. "Black Suicide in the Seventies: Current Trends." *Suicide and Life-Threatening Behaviors* 9:131–140.

Diekstra, R. 1973. "A Social Learning Theory Approach to the Prediction of Suicidal Behavior." Paper presented at the 7th Annual International Congress on Suicide Prevention, Amsterdam, The Netherlands.

Douglas, J. D. 1967. *The Social Meanings of Suicide*. Princeton, N.J.: Princeton University Press.

Dunne, E., J. McIntosh, and K. Dunne-Maxim, eds. 1987. *Suicide and Its Aftermath*. New York: W. W. Norton.

Durkheim, E. 1952. *Le Suicide* [Suicidal]. New York: Free Press of Glencoe. (Original work published 1897.)

Farberow, N. L. and D. MacKinnin. 1970. "Prediction of Suicidal in Neuropsychiatric Hospital Patients." In C. Neuringer, ed., *Psychological Assessment of Suicidal Risk*, Springfield, Ill.: Charles C Thomas.

Farberow, N. L. and E. S. Shneidman. eds. 1961. *The Cry for Help*. New York: McGraw-Hill.

Fox, K. and M. Weissman. 1975. "Suicide Attempts and Drugs: Contradiction Between Method and Intent. *Social Psychiatry* 10:31–38.

Furst, S. S. and M. Ostow. 1979. "The Psychodynamics of Suicide." In L. G. Hankoff and B. Einsidler, eds., *Suicide: Theory and Clinical Aspects*, pp. 165–178. Littleton, Mass.: P.S.G. Publishing.

Gibbs, J. P. and W. L. Martin. 1964. *Status Integration and Suicide: A Sociological Study.* Eugene: University of Oregon Press.

Golan, N. 1986. "Crisis Theory." In F. J. Turner, ed., *Social Work Treatment,* 3rd ed., pp. 296–340. New York: Free Press.

Gould, M. S. and D. Shaffer. 1986. "The Impact of Suicide in Television Movies: Evidence of Imitation." *The New England Journal of Medicine* 315:690–693.

Hawton, K. and J. Catalan. 1987. *Attempted Suicide: A Practical Guide to Its Nature and Management,* 2d ed. New York: Oxford University Press.

Henry, A. F. and J. F. Short. 1954. *Suicide and Homicide.* London: Free Press, Glencoe, Ill.: Collier-Macmillan.

Hepworth, P. H. and J. A. Larsen. 1986. *Direct Social Work Practice Theory and Skills,* 2d ed. Chicago: Dorsey.

Hirsch, S. 1981. "A Critique of Volunteer-Staffed Suicide Prevention Centers." *Canadian Journal of Psychiatry* 26:406–410.

Hirsch, S. R., C. Walsh and R. Draper. 1982. "Parasuicide: A Review of Treatment Interventions." *Journal of Affective Disorders* 4(4):299–311.

Hoppe, S. K. and H. W. Martin. 1986. "Patterns of Suicide Among Mexican Americans and Anglos." *Social Psychiatry* 21:83–88.

Ivanoff, A. and S. J. Jung. 1989. "Hopelessness, Suicidality and Social Desirability in a Prison Population." Unpublished manuscript, Columbia University.

Ivanoff, A M. 1984. "Inpatient Treatment for Suicide Attempters." Unpublished doctoral dissertation, University of Washington, Seattle.

Kallman, F. J., J. Deporte, E. Deporte, and L. Feingold. 1949. "Suicide in Twins and Only Children." *American Journal of Human Genetics* 1:113–126.

Kovacs, M., A. T. Beck, and A. Weissman. 1975. "Hopelessness: An Indicator of Suicidal Risk." *Suicide* 29(5):363–368.

Kreitman, N. 1977. *Parasuicide.* London: Wiley.

Kreitman, N., P. Smith, and E. Tan. 1970. "Attempted Suicide as a Language: An Empirical Study." *British Journal of Psychiatry* 116(534):465–473.

Kutchins, H. and S. A. Kirk. 1986. "The Reliability of DSM-III: A Critical Review," *Social Work Research and Abstracts* 22(4):3–12.

Lettieri, D. J. 1974a. "Research Issues in Developing Prediction Scales." In C. Neuringer, ed., *Psychological Assessment of Suicidal Risk.* Springfield, Ill.: Charles C Thomas.

Lettieri, D. J. 1974b. "Suicidal Death Prediction Scales." In A. T. Beck, H. C. P. Resnick, and D. J. Lettieri, eds., *The Prediction of Suicide,* pp. 163–192. Bowie, Md: Charles Press.

Levenson, M. and C. Neuringer. 1971. "Problem-Solving Behavior in Suicidal Adolescents." *Journal of Consulting and Clinical Psychology* 37(3):433–436.

Levi, D., C. Fales, M. Skin, and V. Sharp. 1966. "Separation and Attempted Suicide." *Archives of General Psychiatry* 15:158–164.

Linehan, M. M. 1981. "A Social-Behavioral Analysis of Suicide and Parasuicide: Implications for Clinical Assessment and Treatment." In H. Glazer and J. F. Clarkin, eds., *Depression: Behavioral and Directive Intervention Strategies,* pp. 147–169. New York: Garland.

Linehan, M. M. 1986. "Suicidal People." *Psychobiology of Suicidal Behavior. Annals of the New York Academy of Sciences* 487:16–33.

Linehan, M. M. 1988. "Dialectical Behavior Therapy: A Treatment for the Chronic Parasuicidal Client." *Journal of Personality Disorders* 1(4):328–333.

Linehan, M. M., P. Camper, J. A. Chiles, K. Strosahl, and E. Sheann. 1987. "Interpersonal Problem Solving and Parasuicide." *Cognitive Therapy and Research and Therapy* 11(1):1–12.

Linehan, M. M., J. A. Chiles, R. H. Devine, J. A. Laffaw, and K. J. Egan. 1986. "Presenting Problems of Parasuicides Versus Suicide Ideators and Nonsuicidal

Psychiatric Patients." *Journal of Consulting and Clinical Psychology* 54:880–881.

Maris, R. W. 1971. "Deviance as Therapy: The Paradox of the Self-Destructive Female." *Journal of Health and Social Behavior* 12:113–124.

Menninger, K. 1938. *Man Against Himself.* New York: Harcourt Brace.

Mintz, R. S. 1968. "Psychotherapy of the Suicide Patient." In H. L. P. Resnik, ed., *Suicidal Behaviors: Diagnosis and Management,* Boston: Little Brown.

Motto, J. A. 1986. "Clinical Considerations of Biological Correlates of Suicide." *Suicide and Life-Threatening Behavior* 16(2):83–102.

NCHS (National Center for Health Statistics). 1988a. "Annual Summary of Births, Marriages, Divorces and Deaths, United States, 1987." *Monthly Vital Statistics Report* 36(13). (DHHS Pub. No. (PHS) 88-1120). Hyattsville, Md: U.S. Public Health Service.

NCHS (National Center for Health Statistics). 1988b. *Vital Statistics of the United States, 1986,* vol. 2: Mortality, Part A. (DHSS Pub. No. (PHS) 88-1122). Washington, D.C.: GPO.

Olin, H. S. 1976. "Psychotherapy of the Chronically Suicidal Patient." *American Journal of Psychotherapy* 30:570–575.

Patsiokas, A., G. Clum, and R. Luscomb. 1979. "Cognitive Characteristics of Suicide Attempters." *Journal of Consulting and Clinical Psychology* 47(2):478–484.

Paykel, E. S. 1979. "Life Stress." In L. D. Hankoff and B. Einsidler, eds., *Suicide: Theory and Clinical Aspects.* Littleton, Mass.: P.S.G. Publishing, pp. 225–234.

Paykel, E. S., and M. N. Dienelt. 1971. "Suicide Attempts Following Acute Depression." *Journal of Nervous and Mental Disease* 153:234–243.

Pomeranz, D. M. and M. R. Goldfried. 1970. "An Intake Report Outline for Modification." *Psychological Reports* 26:447–450.

Poussaint, A. F. 1975. "Black Suicide." In R. A. Williams ed., *Textbook of Black-Related Diseases,* pp. 707–713. New York: McGraw-Hill.

Rosenbaum, M. and J. Richman. 1970. "Suicide: The Role of Hostility and Death Wishes from the Family and Significant Others." *American Journal of Psychiatry* 126:1652–1655.

Rotheram-Borus, M. J. and P. D. Trautman. 1988. "Hopelessness, Depression, and Suicidal Intent Among Adolescent Suicide Attempters." *Journal of the American Academy of Child and Adolescent Psychiatry* 27(6):700–704.

Roy, A. and M. Linnoila. 1986. "Alcoholism and Suicide." *Suicide and Life-Threatening Behavior* 16(2):244–273.

Rubenstein, R., R. Moses, and T. Lidz. 1958."On attempted Suicide." *American Medical Association Archives of Neurology and Psychiatry* 79:103–112.

Ruiz, M. R., V. Serrano, P. Padilla, and J. M. Pena. "The Public Image of Suicide: Attitudes Toward Suicide and Mental Illness." *Crisis: International Journal of Suicide* 7(2):84–88.

Shaffer, D. 1988. "The Epidemiology of Teen Suicide: An Examination of Risk Factors." *Journal of Clinical Psychiatry* 47(9):36–41.

Shaffer, D., A. Garland, M. Gould, P. Fisher, and P. Trautman. 1988. "Preventing Teenage Suicide: A Critical Review." *Journal of the American Academy of Child and Adolescent Psychiatry,* 27(6):675–687.

Shaffer, D. and M. Gould. 1987. "Study of Completed and Attempted Suicides in Adolescents. Unpublished Progress Report: National Institute of Mental Health."

Shearer, S. L., C. P. Peters, M. S. Quaytman, and B. E. Wadman. 1988. "Intent and Lethality of Suicide Attempts Among Female Borderline Inpatients." *American Journal of Psychiatry* 145(11):1424–1427.

Shneidman, E. S. 1976. "The Components of Suicide." *Psychiatric Annals* 6:51–66.

Shneidman, E. S., N. L. Farberow, and R. E. Litman, eds. 1970. *The Psychology of Suicide.* New York: Science House.

Staats, A. W. 1975. *Social Behaviorism.* New York: Dorsey.

Stengel, E. 1964. *Suicide and Attempted Suicide.* Baltimore: Penguin.

Szasz, T. 1986. "The Case Against Suicide Prevention." *American Psychologist* 41(7):806–812.

Tuckman, J. and W. F. Youngman. 1968. "Assessment of Suicide Risk in Attempted Suicides." In *Suicidal Behaviors: Diagnosis and Management,* pp. 190–197. Boston: Little Brown.

Wandrei, K. E. 1985. "Identifying Potential Suicides Among High-Risk Women." *Social Work* 30(6):511–517.

Wetzel, R. D. 1976. "Semantic Differential Ratings of Concepts and Suicide Intent." *Journal of Clinical Psychology* 32:11–12.

Wexler, L., M. M. Weissman, and S. V. Kasl. 1978. "Suicide Attempts 1970–75: Updating a United States Study and Comparisons with International Trends." *British Journal of Psychiatry* 132:180–185.

# 22

## Workers in Job Jeopardy

▼

BETH SILVERMAN

BARBARA SIMON

RICHARD WOODROW

Workers who enjoy job security in the United States are few in number and constitute a minor fraction of the overall work force. They are civil servants with considerable seniority in solvent polities, highly trained self-employed professionals and technicians, or tenured professors in universities with healthy endowments. Everyone else, more than 96 percent of the working population, is subject to temporary or long-term layoffs, to underemployment, to reductions in wages and benefits, and to the costly stress associated with fear of imminent or potential job loss (Briar 1987; U.S. Census 1987; U.S. Labor 1983). Job jeopardy, in short, takes many forms and is pandemic in a capitalist economy. Of these many kinds of job jeopardy, one sort, the menacing prospect of losing one's job, constitutes the focus of this discussion.

Social workers, some of whom are vulnerable themselves to job cutbacks, frequently have as clients employed individuals, couples, or groups of people with a strong likelihood of being laid off or fired. Whether working in family service agencies, mental health centers, child welfare agencies, hospitals, unions, corporations, rehabilitation programs, community centers, or schools, social workers encounter, both knowingly and unknowingly, many employees whose jobs are in a precarious state. The degree to which such professionals can become alert to the presence of threatened job loss and its impact on some of their clients affects the extent to which social workers can help people

710

who may themselves remain unaware of the corrosiveness of job jeopardy in their everyday lives.

Precariousness in employment comes about for many reasons, some environmental, some organizational, some interpersonal, and some intrapersonal. Ordinarily, an amalgam of varied causes places social work clients at risk of job loss. Similarly, the consequences of threatened or actual job loss contaminates many levels of an individual's family's, and community's existence. Responsive and responsible interventions by a social worker must be as multiform as is the threat to a given client's job security.

## PROBLEM DOMAIN

The threat of losing one's job contaminates every aspect of living (CPI 1982; Warr 1987). A worker's standard of living, economic security in the present and future, health care protections, and standing in the community and in the workplace all hinge on the predictability of steady employment (Garraty 1978). Equally at risk are an endangered worker's self-respect, relationships with family members, friendships, and general physical and mental welfare (Brenner 1984; Voydanoff and Majka 1988). Only the prospect of the death of a highly significant loved one takes as profound a toll as does the specter of the loss of one's job (Figley 1985; Warr 1987).

There are multiple sources of danger to clients' jobs, levels of experience that can trigger job loss and involve concomitantly the realms of the public and the private, the interpersonal and the intrapersonal, and the conscious and the unconscious. Exploration of environmental forces that threaten clients' jobs is our starting point.

### *Environmental Threats*

The "rustbelt" that stretches across western Pennsylvania, Ohio, Indiana, Illinois, and Michigan, like other concentrations of dislocated workers, is a direct consequence of two potent threats to job security: "runaway plants" and technological transformation (Bensman and Lynch 1988; Gill 1985; Perrucci et al. 1988). The international and competitive nature of postindustrial capitalism leads corporate decision makers to relocate production to areas of the United States and the Third World that offer cheap labor free of unionization (Buss and Redburn 1983; Perrucci et al. 1988). At the same time, robotics, other forms of automation, and the decline of the American manufacturing sector displace workers from their jobs in many parts of the United States (Hunt and Hunt 1983). Other workers, owners of small businesses and family farms in all sections of the country, each year confront job jeopardy; their assets may be sold on the auction block because of economies of scale, banking practices, and tax laws that place small entrepreneurs at a perennial disadvantage in relation to much larger competitors.

Those employees who work outdoors and in seasonal trades encounter layoffs in bad weather and in off-seasons. Occupational injuries and disease reduce the job security of thousands of other workers each year, most of whom, if the past forty years are any indication, have had severe difficulty in collecting recompense from their employers (Berman 1978).

In addition, some employees find their jobs or chances of obtaining jobs jeopardized because of their race, gender, age, sexual preference, disability, or religion. Discrimination in hiring, promotion, pay, and firing constitutes a well-documented barrier to achievement and an assault on job security that affects tens of millions of Americans (Arvey and Faley 1988; Berkowitz et al. 1988; BNA 1987; Jacobs 1989; Jenkins and Solomos 1987; Levine 1988; Reich 1981; Rose and Larwood 1988).

The inadequacy of societal supports for caregiving, together with the still-vital norm that relegates to women the primary responsibility for raising children and assisting physically and mentally dependent relatives, further jeopardizes the job security of many female workers. In most families, conflicts between work and family responsibilities remain a chronic problem for women to resolve, despite the encouraging increase in participation by some fathers, husbands, and sons. One prolonged health crisis in the life of an aged parent can threaten directly the reliability and reputation of a woman worker torn between paid labor and unpaid caregiving (Simon 1987). Gender-role definitions and expectations are indeed shifting in the late twentieth century, yet at a pace so glacial that only the most privileged of women can count on their spouses or lovers to share equally the dilemma of attempting to satisfy the demands of both job and family.

## *Organizational Threats*

Organizations, like people, are dynamic entities that continually change in response to internal and external imperatives, even when they have a generally stable structure and record of performance and productivity. Constant organizational flux is one major contributor to job jeopardy.

Employing organizations expand, contract, acquire, and merge. They accelerate, change direction, reconfigure central purposes, and form new alliances. Employers hire fresh personnel at all levels, relocate, retool, and reorganize. In the process, some jobs are done away with or are so transformed that the former fit between job and job occupant vanishes. In this near-Hobbesian state of affairs within contemporary American workplaces, in which only 19 percent of the work force is unionized, it is hardly surprising that some workers fear for their jobs (U.S. Census 1987).

The employees whose positions are at greatest risk because of organizational evolution are those in the following categories: the recently hired; those nearing retirement; those who skills were developed in an earlier era; those identified as especially loyal to a prior boss or minority faction within the organization; those with questionable verbal, mathematical, or computer literacy; and part-time employees. Because of the recency of entry into skilled and semiskilled positions of many individuals from racial and ethnic minority groups, women, people with disabilities, young adults, immigrants, and former inmates, the burden of job jeopardy falls disproportionately on these workers.

## Interpersonal Threats

Job insecurity can also spring from problem relationships on the job. Bosses, supervisors, colleagues, and supervisees are all crucial actors in the theater of the everyday workplace. Should people who work in the immediate environs of an employee choose to be punishing for some reason—to shun, harass, "gaslight," or undermine him or her or to withhold information, resources, or promotions—that worker would soon find his or her job to be in considerable danger. Employees with unusual or annoying interpersonal styles often encounter such punishment in the workplace, as do token members of groups that constitute minorities in a given setting or trade (Bunker and Wijnberg 1988; Kanter 1977a). Sexual harassment is a particularly omnipresent threat to job security, as is interpersonal racism in work relationships (Jenkins 1986; Rose and Larwood 1988; Smith et al. 1988).

## *Intrapersonal Threats*

The internal psychological troubles of some workers sabotage their own job security. Usually, such psychic difficulty, whether forged in childhood or adulthood, retards a person's acquisition of the skills and resources needed on the job. It also contributes to thorny and counterproductive work relationships and behaviors that eventually endanger the likelihood of keeping a job or securing a promotion. Unfortunately, self-knowledge about such intrapersonal scars is often generated only when an employee has reached an advanced state of job jeopardy.

Among the more common sorts of "troubled workers" are those people who characterologically resent supervision and direction; those who establish quarreling, cynicism, or passive resistance as a modus operandi; and those whose dependence on drugs or alcohol is severe (Middleman and Rhodes 1985). Behaviorally, such intrapersonal knots may surface in the form of absenteeism, tardiness, violation of work deadlines, skipping of team meetings or supervisory sessions, pugnacity, or inability to cooperate with other workers on the job.

Rarely do intrapersonal factors operate alone in endangering an employee's job. Nor do environmental, organizational, or interpersonal variables act separately to heighten the riskiness of someone's employment. Far more often, two, three, or four levels of forces combine to create a complex and interlocking cluster of immediate and middle-term threats to job security. Discerning the consonance and interactivity among these varied planes of danger is one job of a social worker whose client faces job jeopardy.

## SOCIETAL CONTEXT

Employees who encounter all or some of these four fundamental sources of job jeopardy do so within a cultural context whose implicit values exacerbate the pain of imminent job loss. A triad of cultural and political elements—inveterate individualism, a failure of community, and an ambivalent and perforated welfare state—serves to deepen the wounds incurred by people in job jeopardy (Bellah et al. 1984; Johnson 1987).

For more than a century, the ideological legacy of social Darwinism has left all but a small percentage of workers in the United States convinced that "good people get ahead" (Bellah et al. 1984). Correlatively, someone who is in danger of losing a job or who does not get a promotion must be lacking somehow in initiative, talent, or character. As simplistic and refutable as that notion is in the case of many people, self-blame for threatened or actual layoffs colors the conscious and unconscious feelings of significant numbers of employees whose jobs are in jeopardy (Bensman and Lynch 1988; Buss and Redburn 1988; Hutson and Jenkins 1989; Voydanoff and Majka 1988; Warr 1987).

Compounding the damage done by this proclivity toward self-blame among American workers is the absence for many of community life, with its organic and reciprocal bonds that formerly characterized town and village life. The cushioning of unexpected economic dislocation that community and extended-family members were once able to provide has deteriorated in many areas, except perhaps in some small towns and selected pockets of minority populations (Stack 1974). Supplanting communality is the ethos of "each family for itself," a premise that makes more isolated than in past centuries the situation of an endangered worker.

Having rejected the "cradle-to-grave" approach to social and economic security that characterizes some Common Market countries, the United States has chosen to heighten the vulnerability of workers whose jobs are in jeopardy by maintaining a fissured welfare state; there are major cracks through which can fall many an underemployed or unemployed individual and his or her family (Akabas and Kurzman 1982; Ford Foundation 1989; Johnson 1987; Kamerman and Kahn 1978; Kamerman and Kahn 1987; Richan 1988). Despite New Deal programs and more recent welfare legislation, in the 1990s social and economic insecurity await an employee whose job is terminated or whose health temporarily or permanently interrupts employment. The populations in our work force who are most likely to lose their jobs and to fall through the fissures in the social insurance system merit our immediate attention.

## RISKS AND NEEDS OF POPULATION

To identify, assess, and help high-risk populations, one must first define what is at risk. Within the "world of work" some people are at risk of inequitable access to rewards (lower salaries for women and fewer promotions to high-level positions for minorities) (Grubb and Wilson 1989). Others are vulnerable to punishments (sexual harassment buy supervisors). There are also risks inherent in work conditions, such as job-related stress. While these hazards are serious, this essay focuses on the most basic risk of not working, temporarily or permanently, by the threat of losing one's job and status as worker.

Work generates vital economic resources. For most people, work is necessary for survival; when work is in jeopardy, basic human needs are imperiled. Failure to work, or lack of access to reliable work, threatens the ability to purchase food, clothing, and housing. While societal programs are designed to cushion these vulnerabilities, they protect only a small segment of the population. Furthermore, many programs are subject to politically driven changes and seering stigma. It is not surprising that unemployment is related to homelessness and starvation (Briar 1978; Thompson 1985). People encountering job jeopardy may have to cope with these threatened possibilities.

In addition to remuneration, work can provide basic survival tools: insurance for health, life, and disability. Not working can imperil health and economic security for the worker and his or her family. The escalating costs of health care are creating class-related tiers of health provision (Raffel 1984; Woodrow 1986). People without jobs and insurance may have difficulty gaining access to health care or may encounter differences in treatment, including quality of care.

Work is also a source of status, reinforced by the social values of independence and self-reliance. One's work provides a measure of social class (Hall 1984; Terkel 1985) and a means of social interaction, partly framing one's choice of social network. Work further provides a measure of self-identity. The ability to work influences one's sense of achievement, mastery, and competence (White 1974). The work ethic is underpinned by a self-reliance ethic, and in a social-Darwinistic era, not working is often perceived as reflection of the person ("failure to work") rather than of the social structure. There is a devastating stigma to the threat of losing one's job and potentially being unemployed, unless it is through choice and accompanied by wealth. Thus, when work is in jeopardy, social and psychological risks are high. Job loss and unemployment have been related to such psychosocial phenomena as family stress, dissolution of family structure including divorce or placement of children, loss of social networks, depression, and suicide (O'Brien 1986).

The consequences of job jeopardy can be the loss of a particular job, eventually leading to another position in the same field or a comparable occupation, the need to relocate geographically or occupationally, or failure to find any meaningful work altogether. Thus, job jeopardy is conceptually and practically related to unemployment, a seering economic, political, personal, and social problem that affects many groups of people, including those whose jobs are in jeopardy. As of May 1989, 6,395,000 individuals in the United States were actively seeking work and were unable to secure it (*Monthly Labor Review* 1989). People in job jeopardy are at risk of entering into these statistics.

Sometimes job jeopardy imperils one or more occupational positions. At risk are both the employee and the work structure, as when workers and work organizations encounter plant closings, moves, retrenchments, mergers and acquisitions, and other dislocations. The employee experiences job insecurity and sometimes loss but usually is not defined as the cause of the problem, although self-blame can result. In other circumstances, the person holding a particular job, rather than the position itself, may be in jeopardy. At risk is the employee, whose role will be filled by someone else. Because this book is concerned with differential clinical assessment and interventions, we focus the remainder of this essay on helping employees in job jeopardy, whether or not the structural position itself is in danger. This emphasis in no way is intended to minimize critical and underplayed roles for social workers in assessing and intervening at organizational and policy levels, as in structural dislocations.

The greatest risk of job jeopardy is unemployment, temporary or permanent. Because the consequences of not working are so pervasive, it is possible that the longer one is not working (with the exception of personal choice), the more one is vulnerable. Time is one factor to consider in describing and assessing the populations at risk. Because not working limits the ability to master one's environment, control is another factor to consider. To identify and assess the populations at risk, several categories are suggested, according to time patterns and degree of choice.

The *chronically unemployed* are a class of people shut out of the world of work much of the time or altogether. Some populations lack the skills and abilities required to perform work in current technology, or they are perceived to lack these skills and are therefore denied access to employment. For example, people with developmental, physical, and psychological disabilities have historically encountered barriers to employment and have high rates of chronic unemployment (Eisenberg et al. 1982). Similarly, certain populations have been denied quality education and job preparation, encountering institutional racism and classicism. The unemployment rate of minority adolescents is illustrative: 34.7 percent of blacks aged 16 to 19, compared with 14.4 percent of whites aged 16 to 19, as of 1987 (U.S. Census 1988). These populations are often viewed with stigma and scorn and are defined as choosing not to work. Such definitions ignore social realities and social patterns, as well as social-psychological theories (Seligman 1975). Discouraged by the high odds of their failing to gain access to occupations that have been exclusionary historically and overwhelmed by attendant feelings of helplessness, some subgroups of the population may opt themselves out of the job market. Other groups have skills but lack the supports and resources required to enter employment; for example, parents without adequate child care often face untenable choices, particularly in single-parent families.

The chronically unemployed face pervasive problems associated with not working. They lack the economic and psychosocial resources that result from work, they drain the social welfare system, and they encounter severe social stigma. They often comprise populations served by public social service agencies. They generally do not face job jeopardy as explored in this chapter because they usually do not gain access to work. When they do, they are quite vulnerable to job jeopardy and are therefore particularly at risk.

The *seasonally unemployed* are people who periodically lose their jobs. We are not including those whose occupations are predictably seasonal and who maintain financial and psychological rewards during off-season (e.g., some athletes and teachers). Rather, we focus here on low-skilled laborers who are vulnerable to an economic market out of their control, and who cannot readily move to other work during layoffs. Workers in the garment and construction industries are illustrative.

These workers are vulnerable to economic, social, and psychological instability, as they go through a revolving door of employment and unemployment. Especially when the period of layoff is not predictable, or when jobs pay low wages and curtail benefits during layoffs, there is limited ability to plan. These workers are therefore likely to experience a pervasive lack of control, with associated difficulties in health care, family relationships, and social interactions (Kelvin and Jarrett 1985).

The *unexpectedly unemployed* are workers whose jobs are in jeopardy as specifically defined in this essay. They may have the requisite skills and supports, but they suddenly encounter unemployment or the threat of unemployment. Employment can be jeopardized by "nonwork" personal or family stresses, or by conditions in the work environment (changes in supervisor or the requisite technology, plant or company closings or relocation, abolition of positions or job shifts, or new policies regarding retirement age). One's job can be jeopardized by one's own behavior (problems in attendance, punctuality, or performance associated with addictions or psychological crises). This is the "troubled worker" (Akabas and Kurzman 1982). While we are defining these problems as located in the person, in fact the defining of the "troubled worker" may be a social phenomenon, reflecting the labeler and the work environment as well as (and sometimes rather than) the worker.

These displaced workers face sudden loss of employment and therefore often experience crisis. They are particularly vulnerable during the period just before or after being laid off. Before the actual layoff, the employee must cope with great uncertainty, rumors, and threats. She or he must somehow manage to maintain productivity while the job is tenuous, to wait it out, to sort facts through rumors, and to think about if not plan for the future, often without the time or resources to do so. Once the layoff occurs, the worker copes with the actual consequences. Because job jeopardy occurs within a relatively short and often unpredictable time, social work services must be accessible and keenly attuned to changes in the work environment. Therefore, work site programs have been particularly responsive to job jeopardy situations.

## PROGRAMS AND SOCIAL WORK SERVICES

In the 1980s, the general social service community's response to the growing needs of workers and their families expanded, but it lacks cohesion and comprehensive planning; the response to particular work problems such as job jeopardy tends to be secondary, fragmented, and difficult to document. Specialized programs sponsored by or targeted at workplace institutions, unions, and employers present a more patterned response to the needs and problems of work force participation, including job jeopardy.

### *General Social Service Responses*

Beyond the bounds of occupational social work, the general social service community has historically attempted to respond to the concerns of working people. These efforts tend to be sporadic and lack planful, unified, systematic programming. Nevertheless, moving through the life cycle and the specific populations of workers, one can discern a range of "work-related" practice activity, including programs that directly or indirectly serve people encountering job jeopardy.

Currently, there is concern about youth employment and unemployment, especially in minority communities. Policy analysts, legislators, and social work practitioners are involved in job-development and job-training programs; through career socialization activities, school social workers are trying to sensitize young people to the knowledge, values, and skills vital to adaptation to and coping in the workplace. These programs fortify young workers against job jeopardy.

Vocational training and rehabilitation have long been a subset of practice, although unfortunately viewed more in isolation than in the mainstream of social work activity. In the realm of the mental health and rehabilitation of the chronically mentally ill, several innovative program models use work as therapy, to improve adaptation, coping, and change; others emphasize skills training. These programs serve as buffers for job jeopardy, as they provide habilitation and rehabilitation, social supports, counseling, job placement, and job coaching.

With the dramatic demographic shifts in the labor force, primarily the significant presence of women (close to 50 percent), new work phenomena such as supermoms and commuter marriages have captured the imagination of the media (U.S. Census 1988). There has been progressive public awareness that the myth of separate worlds between work and family no longer holds true. Social agencies have expanded their programming to generate counseling and group services for such populations as dual-career couples and latchkey children.

Services for adult workers at risk of job jeopardy take particular forms with different populations or regions. In rural America, there is neither a significant not-for-profit voluntary sector nor an effectively distributed public sector. The absence of comprehensive mental health services for working men and women—or more often lately, unemployed men and women—means that they must rely on a single mental health facility, often as far as 100 miles from where they live. Some of these mental health facilities have developed a team of practitioners especially attuned to the biopsychosocial factors that affect and are affected by the presence or absence of work. They have used outreach efforts to link up with surrounding employers and worker collectives or organizations.

The farm crisis that hit the United States in the early 1980s dramatically linked job jeopardy and mental health concerns: there was a significant increase among farmers of serious depression and suicide as they were threatened with losing or actually lost their farms (Briar 1987). There is a growing trend, especially in communities in which a single industry, employer, or kind of work predominates, for the social service community to respond to crisis-inducing situations when employment conditions are drastically reduced or altered. Farm foreclosures, plant closings, and mass downsizing of staff lead to proactive and reactive programs (Briar 1983).

In an era of plant closings, mergers, and takeovers, working-class, middle-class, and upper-middle-class workers and their families have been forced to confront the psychosocial demons of unemployment, relocation, dislocation, retraining, and reemployment (Akabas and Kurzman 1982; Briar 1983). Some employers within the corporate community, as well as organized labor, have attempted to respond to the psychosocial needs of these at-risk workers and families, including by linking workers to community mental health and family service agencies. Even without formal agreements between work site and community agency, alterations in the workplace reverberate in the general social service community when work or its absence propels the request for help, or when it surfaces amidst other problems for which people seek help.

A heightened awareness of the saliency of work occurs at the end of the work cycle. The landscape of the American workplace has shifted with the rapid "graying" of America, and older workers are at risk of job jeopardy. There are 31 million Americans over the age of 65, and the most rapidly growing segment of our population is over the age of 85 (U.S. Census 1988). We now have the young-old (55–65), the old (65–75), and the old-old (75+). When a company is downsized, it is often the young-old worker who is encouraged or coerced to retire. Not everyone gets a "golden parachute" to cushion this exiting process. Even with an adequate financial package, it can be difficult to cope with the absence of the role-related rewards of being a worker in a particular position, including psychological meaning, purpose, and relationships. Voluntarism and hobbies are hardly adequate as universal replacements. The gerontological social service community has directed attention to the needs of older workers, including pre- and postretirement as foci for inquiry and intervention. Various community agencies have developed programs to respond to older workers facing retirement, although there has not been adequate attention to forced retirement and the need for valued work roles for older Americans.

## Specialized Work Program Responses

Work institutions have developed a range of clinical and programmatic responses targeting work force participants and their families, including workers in job jeopardy. Since the 1970s, the growth of employee assistance programs (EAPs) and labor-sponsored member assistance programs (MAPs) has been marked, reflecting a confluence of political, practical, and humanistic forces. In 1950, there were 50 EAPs in the United States. By 1979, 58 percent of the Fortune 500 companies had such a program; there are estimates that about 80 percent now have programs (BNA 1988). As a current national estimate, there are perhaps as many as 8,000 to 10,000 EAPs in America (Watkins 1987). These programs offer a variety of services, some targeted at the workers whose job is defined as being in jeopardy. Some programs focus on single problems, such as chemical dependency. Others introduce broadbrush services that encompass a range of behavioral, medical, and psychosocial problems. These programs are under the auspice of unions, management, or both. They may be proactive or reactive; they may provide individual or aggregate services in anticipation of a work-related stress or after the job-threatening situation has been identified. While services, staffing patterns, and intervention strategies may differ as a function of management or union auspices, the programs share a heightened awareness of the biopsychosocial and economic costs of sustaining a viable work force.

Practitioners provide assessment, information, referral, and, usually, short-term counseling for workers and their families regarding health, mental health, environmental, educational, and other human-service-related issues. Workshops and general information are provided to help workers balance work and family life; child care, elder care, sick or disabled family members, stress within and beyond the workplace, and wellness are common topics of interest. Within this spectrum, in an era of plant closings, takeovers, and mergers, as well as psychosocial problems that affect the work force, work site programs offer services that respond to the threat and the reality of job loss, relocation, retraining, and retirement.

Workplace sponsorship of human services since the 1970s has focused on the health and mental health problems that can trigger poor job performance and job jeopardy, most significantly chemical dependency. The employee assistance movement was propelled by workplace concerns with alcoholism and substance abuse. In an age of social, political, and legislative ferment regarding the need for a "drug-free workplace," both labor and management are devoting resources to developing relevant policies and programs. Other addictive and compulsive behaviors (e.g., gambling and eating disorders) are manifest in the workplace through poor job performance, and the work site has become a point of entry and access to services.

Work can also be jeopardized by illiteracy or the lack of a skill needed for a specific job task. Workplace sponsorship of literacy and job-training programs assist workers whose jobs are or may be in jeopardy, given the increasingly complex demands for technical and verbal proficiency in the workplace. For example, in 1989, a consortium of six labor unions in New York State had the largest basic literacy program funded by the New York State Department of Education.

If multiple environmental, organizational, interpersonal, and intrapersonal factors can thrust a worker into job jeopardy, the EAP or MAP is in a strategic position to respond immediately with a range of interventive activities. Along with the offer or service—although every worker in jeopardy has the right to refuse help—comes the opportunity for an employee to meet with a trained practitioner capable of assessing the individual worker and the conditions that inform his or her status as a worker in jeopardy. Following initial assessment, depending on the circumstances, the employee may continue working while obtaining needed services from the EAP practitioner or may be referred to appropriate community resources. Should it be determined that the locus of the problem is within the work organization or among coworkers, supervisors, management, or union personnel, it may also be possible for internal collaborative interventions to lead to problem solving at the workplace itself. Influencing the work environment is a challenging professional role that can be thornier than counseling the "troubled worker," particularly when the target is the employing organization, and it requires legitimacy and skill (Woodrow 1987). Some programs for workers in jeopardy are capable of intervening with both the person and the environment, some provide an assessment for the worker in jeopardy and make a referral to a community resource, and some are prepared to engage in structural alterations in the workplace itself.

It is assumed that availability of help so closely linked with the workplace can reduce the likelihood that workers in jeopardy will be prematurely disengaged from work itself. Even when, for reasons of health or mental health, a leave of absence is recommended, the presence of a network of social supports and a formal acknowledgment that a job will be held for a worker are significant preventive measures. They secure the right of a worker to maintain attachment to the job and the workplace.

While both labor and management sometimes provide a similar array of services, there are some important differences that shape the parameters of service delivery.

A union is a membership organization that generates for its constituency a philosophical and practical notion of entitlement and power. Members collectively bargain, vote, and pay dues. They can, if they choose, influence what and how services are delivered. *Union-based programs* tend to develop peer support models of intervention, including case advocacy, organizational and broader social change (e.g., representation at arbitration hearings, voter registration, and mobilization for national health insurance). Social work practitioners in such settings commonly try to mobilize peer support at the "shop" level to help members with personal problems (alcohol, drugs, family problems, and housing issues). They may also reach out to work sites to help employees identify work-related stress, land to encourage them to see the connections among workplace policies, social policies, and legislation.

*Management programs* tend to offer individual case assessment and referral services for a broad range of personal concerns. While they tend not to engage in the internal collectivist strategies of peer support that many union programs seek to develop, group services are often targeted at aspects of "wellness." This focus is linked with concerns about health-care cost-containment, so it is not uncommon for large companies to have programs for physical fitness, weight reduction, and smoking cessation. Management came to recognize in the 1980s that an ongoing investment in meeting workers' personal and work-related concerns is crucial to sustain a viable work force. Thus, workers in jeopardy of losing their jobs are now being linked with an array of services before being prematurely discharged from the workplace.

While many of the thousands of EAPs that exist today are sponsored by management, there are many varieties of models, based on location and auspices. Some are management EAPs, some are labor MAPs, and some are jointly sponsored; some are located at the workplace and some are off-site; some are public, some are private, some are subcontracted, and some are consortia.

All these workplace programs provide an opportunity to extend the social support network of workers whose jobs are in jeopardy. Because they build in a normative mechanism that creates access to help, these programs do not assume that a worker in jeopardy is a worker at fault. Thus, workers caught between the need to meet job demands and the need to meet personal requirements have a better opportunity for adaptation, coping, and even personal growth without losing the job, losing self-esteem, and losing wages and benefits.

While hardly a panacea for structural unemployment, major life-threatening illness, or severe disability, workplace services can mediate life circumstances and can provide conditions that allow some workers in jeopardy to sustain not only their livelihood but their sense of self-worth and dignity in the process. The workplace is, in essence, a functional community, but it is not a substitute for the larger sense of community so necessary to our sense of belonging.

## DIFFERENTIAL CLINICAL ASSESSMENTS AND INTERVENTIONS

The social worker often fulfills a mediating function between the worker in jeopardy and other critical workplace actors, constantly seeking an adaptive fit between the worker, the work, and the work environment. This function requires an awareness of client needs and resources, and of workplace demands and resources. The social worker is always assessing where to focus interventions: on the worker in jeopardy, on the workplace sponsor of the service, or on the collectivity of other workers—sometimes, on all of these. In most clinical settings external to the work site, it is the individual worker in jeopardy who is the client and the focus of attention. The other actors and systems are nevertheless crucial to assessment and interventive planning.

Job jeopardy can be a humiliating public experience, particularly for the "troubled worker" in work site programs. Job jeopardy can also be an "incognito problem" presented in other guises (alcoholism and substance abuse, marital and family problems, or depression), particularly in agencies outside work auspices. Social workers need to be curious about a client's work and, through exploration and engagement, to help clients cope with the humiliation or to speak the unspeakable, and to expose details about actual or threatened job loss. This section seeks to fortify that clinical curiosity.

### The Client as a Worker

To help people in job jeopardy, one must understand the impact of being a worker turned client, as well as the impact of job jeopardy on this person. Work and worker status can be used to engage a worker as client.

Client status implies some degree of dependency and powerlessness in relation to the helping agent or agency. Social work practice theorists have attempted to attenuate this power differential through professional values such as self-determination and empowerment, and through clinical processes such as contracting. However, the client role begins in a social and personal need that is sometimes externally defined and controlled, as in mandated services or offered services that are masked as mandated.

The worker role implies that someone else is in relative control and power. A worker has a generally accepted structural position in society, defined work tasks that require and imply mastery, and rewards for task performance including money, that are sources of power. Therefore, to some degree, the loss of a job is the loss of power. Client status can also imply the loss of power. In order to help clients whose jobs are in jeopardy, social workers must *sensitively engage the strengths and power of the client as a worker*. To do so, they must understand the vulnerability of "going public." In work settings, the client is usually introduced and defined as a "job jeopardy," so that public disclosure is neither the worker's choice nor under his or her control. Under nonwork auspices, people may already be clients, and the job problems can even go undetected and hidden beneath other presenting problems, such as family conflicts or substance abuse. The stigma of losing a job is great, even when it is not the worker's fault.

Interventions should be shaped to "normalize" the abnormal experience, for example, by providing statistics about job jeopardy, and by acknowledging the sense of shame and embarrassment; to acknowledge and understand the dimensions that define the clinician as a "worker" and to assess when, how, and if to use this knowledge with the client-worker in jeopardy; to search for areas in which the client has control, for example, by reframing what has led to the job jeopardy so the client is not a helpless victim but has work to do; and to focus on what can be done rather than solely on what has been done to jeopardize the job.

Workers whose jobs are in jeopardy can experience disaster and great time pressure. Even if there is uncertainty about the work future, as in the early stages of mergers and acquisitions or threatened cuts, time paradoxically seems pressurized while the client may feel helpless to take action. The social worker must be ready to *respond immediately and to be directive and direct, as in a crisis, in order to mobilize the client and the resources to action*. In addition, flexibility of time is required; for example, the client may need more frequent meetings in a compressed period of time, since job jeopardy can suddenly lead to job loss. The clinician must also be ready to withdraw when the job is no longer in jeopardy, or when the work goals have been reached. This is common practice in settings under work auspices or in community agencies that contract specifically for work-related problems, and it should be a viable option for nonwork mental health and family service agencies. Finally, unfortunately, job jeopardy can be a recurring problem. People must be able to return episodically, without being viewed as overly dependent.

The focus of the worker in jeopardy is work. Despite the sensitivity of potentially losing one's job, it is essential to understand the details of work in order to assess and intervene appropriately. Clinicians would not be satisfied with a parent-client's explanation that a child is "too demanding" without reaching for details (the child's behavior, the parent's definitions of "demanding," and the interaction of parent and child). Similarly, clinicians should not be satisfied with generalized feelings or explanations that there is trouble with a supervisor or job task performance or a plant closing. It is only *through the details of work that social workers can begin to pattern data and focus on salient issues for clinical intervention.*

In work site settings, the clinician has the benefit of multiple sources of work data, including observation and work personnel. In non-work-site settings, work information may be limited to a client's perceptions, without direct access to data. This does not imply that clients are unreliable sources of work data, but their information is limited by such factors as their structural position in an organization. It may be possible to meet with the client's family and to speak with work organization personnel to elaborate the data, with the caveat that an outside clinician's involvement may corroborate an employer's definition of a "troubled worker" and may therefore further imperil the job.

It may be helpful for assessment and intervention to think about collecting data regarding workers in jeopardy by *organizing work information into several broad categories related to the worker, the work environment, and their interaction* (Silverman 1988).

1. *The nature of work and work performance.* It is not enough to ask, "What do you do?" Curiosity about a client's work needs to extend to the nature of the tasks performed, the demands of these tasks, the client's ability to perform the work, and the way in which the client's time is organized. Inquiries of this sort about a client's work day can reveal particular stress points, such as difficulty in meeting expectations due to changing skill requirements or difficulty in arriving on time due to family obligations or pressures.

Attention should be paid to patterns of coping in the workplace, i.e., the client's thoughts, feelings, and behavior as they relate to job tasks, routines, and relationships. An employment history is useful to differentiate present difficulties from prior patterns of work, and strengths as well as conflicts.

2. *The organizational structure.* Practitioners should keep in mind

the formal and informal systems that exist in all organizations. What is the jeopardized worker's place in the system? Where is she or he in relationship to those with power and authority? Does the client have an understanding or awareness of these factors? What policies, procedures, and legislation influence the workplace (e.g., those of the Occupational Safety and Health Administration, Employment Retirement Income Security Act, the Rehabilitation Act of 1973, and Workers Compensation)? What rights, resources, and opportunities exist for a worker in the work setting? Is there a union, and if so, does the worker know the key actors (the shop steward and the union representative)? Does she or he know and how does she or he perceive other workplace actors (supervisors and managers)? Is she or he aware of grievance procedures or the stipulations of the work contract? These lines of inquiry can assist both practitioner and client in an illuminating review process, including a search for latent resources for intervention.

3. *The social environment of work.* What are the client's opportunities for communication and socialization with other workers? To what degree is the client isolated from a network of support? What is the degree of the client's participation in workplace decision making, and what are the client's attitudes about all of this? This line of inquiry suggests potential social networks and supports to help the client cope with job jeopardy.

4. *The physical environment of work.* Are there any special circumstances about light, heat, ventilation, space, equipment, or perceived threats to safety? This line of inquiry opens up questions of occupational safety and health that may contribute to job jeopardy.

5. *The psychological dimension of work.* This line of inquiry invites the client to review the meaning derived from work and its relationship to identity. It can include feelings and perceptions about autonomy; power; authority; control; feedback; work variety; task completion; level of stimulation; the impact of race, class, and gender; and perceptions of powerlessness or self-blame. These work variables can be discussed in relationship to the client's thoughts, feelings, and behaviors on the job. Job jeopardy involves loss and therefore anticipatory mourning; this inquiry helps one begin to cope with potential loss, or to fortify against loss, by considering its meaning to his or her life. Such inquiry can later help the client to consider the next steps if the job is lost.

The connection of work to other aspects of life has been conceptualized and documented (Kanter 1977a). The responsive practitioner *assesses and intervenes with an appreciation of the overlapping domains of work and family.* There is a reciprocal impact, as nonwork issues affect work role and performance, and as job jeopardy affects other realms.

Patterns of coping and conflict that appear in the workplace may carry over to outside or other primary relationships. However, one needs to be cautious about assuming that behavior from one domain (work or family) necessarily generalizes to another. Overgeneralization dilutes and distorts content about the specific worker and work context. What in the worker and in the workplace environment mobilizes or inhibits coping capacities?

Similarly, creative or myopic practitioners may be tempted to view job jeopardy only as a symptom of deeper personal or social problems to be treated. While job jeopardy can result from other personal problems, as when family stress or substance abuse interferes with job performance, arranging the problems hierarchically distorts the complexity of the interaction of the phenomena and blurs the potential for intervention. For example, threatened job loss or the ability to save one's job can be a powerful "lever" for dealing with denial and engaging clients in lifesaving alcoholism treatment. While job jeopardy can result from deep social dilemmas, such as economic factors related to plant closings, rarely is the clinician able to change these realities immediately or directly. This realization does not minimize the vital importance of social action, nor should it minimize the importance of clinical attention to individual workers who experience the devastating results of potentially losing their jobs.

Given the multiple triggers of job jeopardy, the multiple contributing factors, and the multiple consequences, it is easy to lose focus on the problem that needs attention. *The focus of job jeopardy is work.* When possible and appropriate to the particular client and situation, the clinical goal is to help the worker save the job. When not, the goal is to help the worker cope with potential and actual job loss and to consider options and next steps.

Clients in job jeopardy usually want to maintain or improve their job, or to return as soon as possible to a productive work role. Clinical activities should contribute to these work-related goals.

Job jeopardy thrusts people into the sense or actuality of losing control. Loss of control over events has been linked to learned helplessness and depression (Seligmman 1975), which can further spiral workers into job jeopardy. Work site changes beyond a worker's sense of control can precipitate psychosocial disequilibrium and self-blame (Lerner 1980). Interventions that *buttress a sense of mastery* in the present can mobilize the client to the action needed to attain goals. These interventions may include taking steps to alter the client's perceptions or others' perceptions of the client, putting the lack of control into perspective, developing appropriate strategies, and practicing alternative ways to respond at the work site. Change may be focused on the work environment (helping to influence a move to a new work unit and supervisor) and/or on the worker (acquiring a broader repertoire of workplace behaviors, and role playing how to assert oneself to an angry supervisor). Such activities focus on abilities and adaptive capacities, mastery, and competence. The client can thereby see herself or himself as capable of change, as an actor not only as a victim acted upon by others.

## The Work Organization as an Environment

Job jeopardy is intrinsically tied to the work environment. It is incumbent on clinicians to enrich assessment and, when advisable, to fortify interventions targeted on the work site. A job jeopardy situation is not only a seering personal experience for an individual worker, but a political problem for work organizations. It is often set off by organizational triggers (a plant closing or a decision by an employer about a worker's performance) and has reverberating social implications for the entire organization. The very word *jeopardy* connotes peril. Obviously, the worker whose job is in question is endangered. Once a job jeopardy situation has been defined, the pronouncement is threatening to many facets of the organization, including the social worker. The clinician needs to *be sensitive to job jeopardy as a charged political and organizational problem, as well as a deeply personal one.*

In a union, each job jeopardy situation challenges the union mission and threatens its success as a political member organization unless it can protect the position, if not the worker filling the position. The definition of job jeopardy sets the organization in political and sometimes adversarial gear. In an employing organization facing job jeopardy, the employer may need to justify decisions about termination; invariably, this need challenges policies of hiring, firing, and personnel practices. Again, the organization is primed for public scrutiny and potential adversity. Therefore, clinical activity related to job jeopardy is politicized. It is difficult for social work activity to remain private even if particular interventions are protected by confidentiality policies, because the worker's private pain has ramifications for public issues. Job jeopardy primes the setting for adversarial positioning, and the social worker has to be ready to operate within this politically charged environment.

The practitioner should assess rather than assume what the problem is. Particularly in work site programs, one must be cautious not to predetermine the problem by the auspices (i.e., to assume in a corporate EAP that a worker is troubled, or to assume in a union setting that an employer is abusive).

Given the potential for adversarial relationships, the social worker should *avoid the tempting peril of blame.* Job jeopardy situations can lead to blaming the client. This can happen overtly; for example, employees with recurrent work performance problems can exasperate others in a work environment: employers, union representatives, and coworkers, as well as social workers. It is easy to condemn the worker in order to maintain some semblance of control over one's own professional function. It is more likely that blame of client will take covert and subtle forms. For example, during a period of economic adversity and plant closings, it was popular for programs to offer assertiveness training to populations of workers when factories closed. While these workers needed help to find new jobs, the indirect implication was that were they only more assertive, they might have kept their jobs. Furthermore, a worker's job is defined as being in jeopardy by the work organization, often because of personal problems. Because of the political charge, there is a temptation to assume that the definition is correct. It is important to collect data and to develop inferences, including patterns of referrals, rather than to assume definitions imposed by others. For example, one social worker in a union setting noted that over a period of several months, several fragile young women with paranoid features had been referred from the same small garment shop. Each seemed to have florid delusional thinking with sexual content about the same supervisor. The social worker suggested to the union representative making the referrals that he investigate the work environment for problems of sexual harassment, rather than job performance. The social worker was correct.

On the other hand, it is tempting to blame the system. This can be a knee-jerk reaction of unions, which exist to protect the rights of and to advocate for the working class. Social workers who immediately assume that job jeopardy implies job inequities or a violation of workers' rights may bypass the needs of a particular worker or work site, and sometimes the potential to save that job.

The workplace is replete with natural helpers such as coworkers, shop stewards, union representatives, and supervisors. The social work community both within and outside the world of work needs to continue to work creatively with workers themselves to maximize the potential of natural helping networks in the workplace. To do so, practitioners must *understand the role and function of workplace personnel*—when, how, and if to mobilize them (Silverman 1988).

Collaboration may include dealing with the union organizer or business agent, or with an employer or supervisor in an EAP, to clarify the problem (what specifically is in jeopardy and when, why, and how—the worker's part, the union's part, and the employer's part), and to plan strategies that will move toward congruent goals rather than at cross-purposes. Always, the social worker strives to involve the worker, for collaboration rather than collusion.

With solid collaborative relationships, one can garner information more readily at a work site. For example, it helps to know just how slowly a "slow worker" is producing and when performance seems to slip, or to know detailed patterns of lateness for a "chronically late" worker, or to know which supervisors seem to set off rage in a "troubled, angry worker." Work site program intervention may include advising the supervisor or persuading the union to arrange a leave of absence for a worker in serious emotional crisis or a temporary change of work assignment to something less stressful; at the same time, the practitioner counsels the client, sometimes linking him or her to needed help and ongoing community supports.

Utilizing natural as well as other secondary helping systems can create helper gridlock. Collaboration (working together) is not automatic when a client deals with a union-sponsored social worker, union representatives, shop stewards, supervisors, and community-based professionals. Therefore, the social worker is advised to *negotiate (if not establish) the rules of collaboration, including the division of labor, within the norms of the particular organization.* Dealing with natural helpers in the work environment requires assessing the self-interests of the work organization personnel in the particular job jeopardy situation, understanding how social work intervention can meet these interests, and sometimes entering into the negotiating language and framework of a work organization. Similarly, if the client is involved with both community-based and work-site-based professionals, each needs to evolve a specific task or set of tasks that work together toward congruent goals.

Collaboration may also require establishing and protecting professional boundaries, such as confidentiality, without further jeopardizing the job. This is tricky in work site programs. As presented above, job jeopardy is a public issue of concern to the organization. Policies of confidentiality cannot always protect individuals from the perceptions and attitudes of the involved supervisors or union organizers. An artful social worker has to figure out how to use policies of confidentiality without turning a system against a client, and how to satisfy those involved that the client is improving without stigmatizing the worker or jeopardizing confidentiality. It is a delicate balance of public policy and public relations.

In carrying out these roles, it is important not to become case-bound. Social workers have been advised for many decades to move from case to cause; when work is in jeopardy, the case is often emblematic of a cause. While the practitioner may be faced by an individual in job jeopardy, a collective of people may have the same problem, as when several employees are affected by work conditions or job dislocation. Work site practitioners need to comprehend the cues that signal the conditions under which they should complement casework and case management with advocacy and organizing within the larger organizational system. This expansion of roles and broadening of focus would include trying to influence the organization by changing dysfunctional policies and procedures as well as developing new programs.

*Preventive, proactive means rather than solely reactive measures may mitigate the circumstances* that create workers in job jeopardy. The work site and workers' organizations are normative social contexts that people freely choose (usually, and relatively speaking). Therefore, there are implications for prevention in relation to health, mental health, family life, and many life transitional events. Access to information and services in a nonstigmatized arena fortifies an opportunity for both primary and secondary prevention. For example, potential work-stress points may provide a focus for social work services that will prevent job jeopardy: 1) alternations in work status: promotion, demotion, transfer, unemployment, lay-off, disability or medical leave, relocation, and retirement; and 2) rights-related concerns of workers in risk areas: discrimination by race, age, disability, sex, or sexual orientation, as well as sexual harrassment.

## CASE ILLUSTRATION

The agency is a social service department of a large urban labor union that represents over 100,000 public sector employees. The union members range in age, in ethnicity, and in job category from unskilled to professional. The union-sponsored members assistance program (MAP) provides broadbrush services for a range of problems, including job jeopardy. The services are part of a worker's entitlements for paying union dues. The social worker was a 32-year-old black professional who had been on staff at the MAP for three years.

The client was Mrs. Charlene Ames, a 38-year-old black woman who resided in a large urban community. She had been married for eighteen years and had two daughters, 10 and 12 years old. For the last five years Mrs. Ames had been employed as a clerical worker for a large bureaucracy that provides social services.

Mrs. Ames was born and raised on a southern farm. She was the eldest of six sisters and two brothers. Her father died in 1986 and her mother still lived in the South with her brothers and sisters. Mrs. Ames described her parents as loving, but very strict. She reported that even though the family were together all the time on the farm, she did not recall having a close relationship with any of them. Having been raised on a farm, she had had little opportunity to interact with other people besides her siblings and her parents. Mrs. Ames perceived that everyone had a designated role in the family and that these rigid roles had remained constant into her adulthood. Her father was viewed as both "prosecutor" and "judge," while her mother was described as the "nurturer" and "rock of the family."

After graduating from high school, Mrs. Ames left the South to follow her high school sweetheart and to pursue a life of her own. She had settled in this large northern urban community, had married, and later given birth to her two daughters.

Mrs. Ames described her husband in similar terms to her father: strong, authoritative, judgmental, and rather remote. She viewed with great respect his capacity for calmness when confronted by stressful situations, a quality she saw as lacking in herself. She believed that the emotional complementarity between them—his remote calm and her emotional sensitivity—explained their mutual attraction for one another and why they got along so well.

Before moving to the North, Mrs. Ames had worked as a dairy farmer with her family in the South. After moving north, she had remained a housewife until both her daughters began school. She claimed to have enjoyed this period of life because she did not have to answer to anyone or to interact with many others besides her family. She eventually found a job in a local insurance company as a claims clerk and simultaneously returned to school. After receiving a bachelor's degree in education, she had held a job as a teacher in the public schools for four years. She had left the school system because she did not feel the children were being fairly and adequately treated by the other teachers. She was outraged by her perception of racism within the school system but was afraid to speak up, lest she be forced to cope with repercussions. She subsequently took and passed the civil service exam to become a city employee, hoping that a new job might offer her "new experience" and additional material benefits.

Mrs. Ames came to the attention of the members assistance program when the intake social worker received a call from the union representative, who stated that Mrs. Ames' job was in jeopardy. He explained that earlier he had received a call from Mrs. Ames' supervisor. The supervisor was described as agitated, annoyed, and puzzled by what appeared to be Mrs. Ames' deteriorated job performance. She had developed an unexplained pattern of absenteeism and had received a poor work evaluation. A disciplinary action ensued, in which Mrs. Ames was told that her job would be in jeopardy if her performance did not improve. She was urged to seek help at the MAP. The aura surrounding the referral was rife with innuendo regarding Mrs. Ames' moodiness and absenteeism, hinting at possible substance abuse.

Mrs. Ames arrived at the intake interview early. Her face was drawn tight, and she did not look at the social worker for the first five minutes. Her behavior was similar to that described by the supervisor: she seemed remote and guarded, wrapping her arms tightly around herself, and crying uncontrollably as the worker began to explain her function (in retrospect, in a somewhat structured and formalized way that could have been seen as equally remote and threatening). Mrs. Ames appeared worn out and very sad. The worker then shifted her approach. She explained that she knew Mrs. Ames was worried about her job, and that she suspected that this was a very confusing and frightening time for Mrs. Ames, as it would be for any worker, to be told that her job was in jeopardy, and that to save it, she had to see a social worker. The worker tried to normalize and generalize the experience of what other workers in jeopardy felt when they first arrived at the MAP. Mrs. Ames began to sob, and in the next two interviews, she filled in the story of her work difficulties, as she perceived them.

At intake and in two following interviews, the following information was gather that elaborated the circumstances surrounding Mrs. Ames' life and behavior at the work site as well as at home:

1. Mrs. Ames reported that over the last six months, she had been unable to wake up in the morning in time for work because she was too tired. While at home, she recalled sleeping most of the day and barely rising to eat at all.

2. Mrs. Ames reported falling behind in her processing of the paperwork she was required to manage. New work was assigned on a monthly basis, and each worker was responsible for completing a batch for work before receiving a new load. Stressed by the awareness of how far behind she was falling in her work, she had started arriving at work one hour early and remaining two hours overtime. She said she had done this for the last three months, until she felt too exhausted to go in to work.

3. Mrs. Ames described the working conditions at her job as deplorable. Six months before, her work unit had relocated to a site that was shared by one of the city's shelters for homeless men. Even though her office was on a different floor with observable security, she often felt harassed by shelter residents as she either arrived at or departed from work. When she complained to her supervisor, she had been told that she was hypersensitive or exaggerating. She felt her complaints had simply been dismissed.

4. A few months before, Mrs. Ames had been assigned a new supervisor, and after a month of working together, Mrs. Ames had received a poor work evaluation for reasons she described as unfair. She reported that her supervisor would write her up when her work was incomplete or when errors were made. Mrs. Ames stated that it was common for workers to have incomplete work and that her errors were not as bad as her supervisor had stated. Mrs. Ames traced the increase in her absences to the arrival of her new supervisor. She felt that she was often embarrassed and humiliated publicly by her supervisor when he verbally abused her in front of her fellow employees. She reported that sometimes, he would literally throw work at her, which caused her to cry uncontrollably for hours at a time. She described feeling embarrassed and being unable to tell her supervisor how she felt when these incidents occurred.

5. Mrs. Ames reported that her behavior toward her family had also changed in the last several months. When she arrived home from work, she found herself taking her frustrations out on her daughters by yelling or giving unwarranted spankings. Her relationship with her husband, which she claimed had always been extremely positive, had become fraught with tension, conflict, and arguments. She found herself distancing herself from him, lest he find out what was happening at work. She feared that he would make her quit her job, something she did not feel prepared to do. Her withdrawal from her husband was

now both emotional and sexual. She attributed this to being too exhausted and preoccupied about work.

Mrs. Ames stated that in the last several weeks she had found herself crying uncontrollably at times. Her sleeping and eating patterns had changed as well. She had difficulty sleeping more than two or three hours a night and had very little appetite. She had little interest in the weekend outings that were part of her routine family life and had isolated herself from her friends. She feared the embarrassment and humuliation that she associated with having her friends witness her uncontrollable tears.

During the three interviews in which Mrs. Ames revealed this information, the worker tried to explore the problem sensitively, periodically shifting from the content to the process of what it was like for Mrs. Ames to have her job in jeopardy, to be referred to the MAP, and to face the "embarrassment and humiliation," in Mrs. Ames' words, of having her pain go public. The worker tried to define the service as part of any member's right and privilege of membership, yet she did not minimize how difficult it was for a private person to have to face the choice of airing her troubles or losing her job. While going public was a common concern when members first used the member assistance program, public humiliation seemed particularly upsetting to Mrs. Ames and alerted the clinician to a possible theme for attention. Through this kind of careful observation of behavior, occasional reaching for the meaning of nonverbal behavior, and clarifying perceptions of content, the practitioner began to understand when, how, and, to some degree, why Mrs. Ames sometimes suddenly became "absent" during the interviews, and perhaps at work as well, or else broke into uncontrollable tears. This withdrawing behavior became a signal that Mrs. Ames was upset about something in the interaction with the social worker or in the story she was telling. It also reflected a coping pattern in this woman's life: withdrawing when she felt criticized, or when she could not otherwise master a situation over which she had deep feelings but no apparent control.

Mrs. Ames was a competent adult who usually experienced a fair degree of mastery over situations in her life, despite dysfunctional areas. She had sustained a marriage, raised two daughters, earned a college degree, and still held a job, even under duress. She had until recently used a number of behaviors to "get her through." She thrived on success and positive feedback but had learned over the years to live (and sometimes through) criticism, distance, and remoteness from others on whom she depended: her father, her husband, her friends, and her supervisor. These coping strategies usually worked for her, although at a price. Through withdrawal, Mrs. Ames avoided conflict, dissension, and the feared repercussions of disagreement; but by withdrawing, she could not articulate her needs and sustained somewhat distancing relationships with the people from whom she craved closeness or at least approval.

Recent changes at the work site had made her normal behavior dysfunctional. She responded to criticism with long periods of crying at the work site, which only exacerbated the criticism. As she was literally withdrawing from conflict at work with her supervisor, her absenteeism and disorganization in the face of criticism jeopardized her work. Fearing further repercussions of unknown magnitude had further removed her from potential sources of support, including her husband, peers, and union representatives. The threat of losing her job had further immobilized Mrs. Ames, and she suffered from acute occupational stress and possibly clinical depression. The foundations of her sense of identity, competence, and control—work and family— appeared to be crumbling.

While the problem had been defined as job jeopardy, it was not lodged solely in Mrs. Ames' responses. The worker explored Mrs. Ames' perceptions of her work environment and corroborated them through several telephone calls to the shop steward, as well as a site visit to the job. Although viewed through a union perspective, the client's vision of her work realities did not seem blurred. The new physical environment was crowded and dismal, and the location was an added burden to Mrs. Ames. She was working in an environment in which she experienced considerable pressure from management and had caseloads beyond everyone's capacity, except through shortcuts that compromised the quality of task performance to which Mrs. Ames had been socialized by former supervisors. The change of supervisor and the critical edge of the new one were also difficult for other workers in the office. However, most people were not personally threatened by the supervisor, recognizing that he "had his ways" but that he usually "cooled off." Furthermore, his singling out Mrs. Ames had taken some of the pressure off the others, who felt sorry for her but were relieved that the supervisor was off their backs. The supervisor was a black male, new to his position and eager to do well. He adhered strictly to rules and regulations and could be quite harsh in his management style when he judged that there was a problem in someone's work performance. Because he knew the organization's concerns about drug testing, it was possible that he had interpreted Mrs. Ames' growing absenteeism and occasional eruptions of moodiness as evidence of substance abuse. Furthermore, the office had recently elected a new union shop steward, a popular but somewhat retiring person who had not reached out assertively to new employees or workers in jeopardy.

The interaction between Mrs. Ames and this work environment had caused problems. Mrs. Ames could not verbally express her anger or frustration at her boss or other people outside the work environment. Instead, she cried or suppressed these feelings or took them out on others in an indirect manner (scolding her daughters unnecessarily). This frustrated the others, who often misperceived the meaning and motivation of the behavior. Furthermore, Mrs. Ames had learned to structure her work behavior in a very organized (some would say rigid) way, and the recent changes had required new adaptations that were difficult for her. This had threatened her work performance, although she was usually a loyal and competent worker. She had been particularly uncomfortable working in a demanding environment in which there was need of great flexibility and response to feedback, including criticism, first as a teacher and now as an office associate. She appeared to have been happier working in a more independent environment in which she had relatively more authority and control, such as when she had been a housewife or a farm worker. There was some evidence of difficulty in dealing with people in authority, as she sought closeness through approval but distance to avoid disapproval. She was afraid of her current supervisor, who overtly criticized her, and she expressed having been afraid to confront the school administrators when she had a problem.

The precipitating event for referral was that Mrs. Ames' supervisor had allegedly called her "a stupid, incompetent bitch" and had thrown a case record at her in public, following which she had cried uncontrollably and left work for several days. (In later interviews, she revealed that her parents had used to humiliate her publicly, after which she would withdraw to her room, cry herself to sleep, and refuse to speak for days; years later, a fellow teacher had called her stupid in front of other faculty members, and she had left teaching.) Mrs. Ames was terrified of public humiliation, and the workplace was public.

Despite these problems, Mrs. Ames had had years of relative

success at work and in the home. She realized that she was in jeopardy of losing her source of income unless she untangled some of the knots at work. The work environment had potential supports in union shop stewards and peers. Despite his overt harshness, the supervisor was willing to speak with the social worker and wanted to perform his job well and be recognized by his superiors. It was difficult to assess the marital and family systems, as Mrs. Ames did not yet want the social worker to become involved for fear of further jeopardizing the situation.

This reluctance signaled the worker that she should direct her interventions to the immediate problems causing work stress and should help Mrs. Ames develop more effective ways of interacting with others in the work environment. According to Mrs. Ames, the goal was to save her job, but only if she could get back to work feeling less stressed and "accepted" as an effective worker. This goal required a dual focus on the worker and the work environment.

After two intake interviews, the following plan of action was developed. Mrs. Ames agreed to meet several times with the social worker, to focus on workplace issues, and specifically to figure out better ways to respond to the supervisor and other stressors at the work site. She also accepted a referral to a community mental health center, to be assessed for possible medication to help her sleep and for ongoing treatment. The psychiatrist would deal with nonwork issues and would explore some of the patterns in Mrs. Ames' life. The union social worker would arrange a three-way meeting between the union representative, Mrs. Ames, and herself. The purpose was to meet the union representative, to air workplace grievances, and to consider to what degree the union could negotiate work site changes, including changes in the supervisor. At this point, Mrs. Ames did not want her husband involved. The social worker agreed not to do anything against Mrs. Ames' wishes but said this would be important for them to consider as she started to feel stronger; to get that feeling of "acceptance" as an effective worker, others had to know just how effective and concerned she was. The worker further clarified that she could not "save" Mrs. Ames' job, that only union representatives were able to negotiate this, but that she could help clarify Mrs. Ames' wishes and needs and could connect her to people at the union or worksite or even speak with them herself.

Several steps followed in this woman's struggle with job jeopardy: referral to and consultation with a community mental health center; counseling around work and job performance; and consultation with the union and the supervisor.

Mrs. Ames demonstrated symptoms of clinical depression, and the social worker was concerned about the depth of depression. While Mrs. Ames was able to continue working during the period of the first two interviews, she continued to cry at the work site when criticized by her supervisor, to isolate herself, to take days off without permission, and to experience difficulties in sleeping and eating. The social worker explored the degree to which Mrs. Ames wanted to continue in her job. She was feeling overwhelmed and afraid of the supervisor and sometimes wanted to leave or to be fired; on the other hand, she realized that she had to work to survive financially and psychologically. The social worker explored the expressed ambivalence, asking Mrs. Ames what she would want to do if she could clear the problems with her supervisor. For an instant, Mrs. Ames came to life and said she wanted to work, that without work she didn't know what she would do.

It was important to help Mrs. Ames return to functioning as rapidly as possible, to save her job. Furthermore, the union would need to develop a strategy, and this was partly dependent on whether Mrs. Ames could continue to work in the current job, needed another position, or needed time off.

Mrs. Ames was scheduled for psychiatric evaluation several days after her second interview with the social worker. She was diagnosed as depressed and was prescribed Elavil. The psychiatrist recommended a three-month medical leave of absence, during which time the client would receive medication and individual treatment. Mrs. Ames was silent and tearful when the psychiatrist gave his recommendations. She said she had no questions but wanted to meet with the social worker.

She cried uncontrollably and could barely speak. Only with considerable sustaining and reaching did the social worker learn what had happened. Mrs. Ames was distraught over the recommendation that she take a leave, although she agreed she could not seem to work effectively and was perhaps too sick to continue for now. The social worker suggested that the two of them confer with the psychiatrist.

The psychiatrist explained his concern that Mrs. Ames was quite depressed and apparently unable to sustain herself at work and therefore would benefit from time off. The social worker agreed with the perception, but not the recommendation. She felt that removal from work would underline and deepen the problem. From her point of view, work was a goal as well as a healer, and she wondered if it wouldn't be more helpful for Mrs. Ames to take a week's vacation while she started medication, caught up on sleep, began psychiatric treatment, and continued to meet with the worker to figure out better ways of handling the work stress. The psychiatrist suggested that deeper problems needed to be addressed before Mrs. Ames would improve, and that this would take more than one week, but he agreed that they did not necessarily rule out working if the work stress could be reduced, and that there was no risk of suicide at this time.

Mrs. Ames agreed that the vacation would help, and she looked forward to having two different people to help with her problems after having to be alone for so long. However, she adamantly refused to take the medication. Discussion only deepened her conviction that she would conquer her problems without pills. It was the most forceful and assertive behavior she had demonstrated to either the social worker or the psychiatrist, and it suggested a reserve of strength (and a need for control) that could be tapped.

Mrs. Ames returned to see the social worker later that week. Without medication, she had slept a full night for the first time in a month, was visibly calmer, and said she wanted to get her job back. She was assured that she had not lost her job, as she had only taken a vacation. Mrs. Ames and the social worker agreed to meet weekly for two months. During this time, they would explore different ways for her to work in the best way possible. Meanwhile, she would begin biweekly meetings with her psychiatrist, around nonwork issues.

During the next two months, Mrs. Ames met six times with the social worker to facilitate her reentry to work and to stabilize the workplace. Mrs. Ames was able to use these meetings to recognize that she was running away from fear of humiliation and retaliation and was only getting the very reaction she most feared, her supervisor's rage. She began to see the social worker as someone who cared about work, and they discussed the details of her work day. The social worker learned that Mrs. Ames did not know who her shop steward was, nor most of her peers. The social worker introduced Mrs. Ames to the steward, who became an ally when the client was upset. Rather than cry in front of the supervisor, which only fueled the problem, she agreed and would call the social worker or the shop steward when she was upset. Furthermore, Mrs. Ames began to understand that she was isolating herself from another critical support, her husband, by not telling him about work. The social worker and Mrs. Ames discussed and then role-played her "greatest fear, being scorned and rejected" if she told her husband her job was in jeopardy. She recognized that the worst wasn't as bad as her fear of it and might not even be his response. Mrs. Ames did not speak with her husband, however, until several weeks later. One of the shortcomings and challenges in work site programs is difficulty in contacting the family, given the distinction of work and family that still exists in our social structure and norms.

After she returned to work, Mrs. Ames requested two additional unscheduled meetings with the social worker after a flare-up with the supervisor. In these meetings, role playing was used to identify her options and to practice alternative ways to respond to the supervisor. Mrs. Ames began to recognize that she was personalizing the supervisor's anger, and she mobilized her anger at the work site into action. She confronted the supervisor after he had humiliated her in front of other workers by accusing her of something she had not done. He continued to yell, but the other workers came to Mrs. Ames' support and told him he was harassing her. Mrs. Ames joined in and told the supervisor that he could criticize her but did not need to embarrass and humiliate her like this, that it was harassment. He then backed off. It was the first shift in the way they related to one another.

Early in the counseling, Mrs. Ames had agreed to meet with several people from the union. The social worker clarified that she could not directly protect Mrs. Ames' job nor investigate her problems with the supervisor, but that the union had several people whose job was to protect the workers. Mrs. Ames was afraid of the repercussions of being defined as a "troublemaker," or of being used as a "test case to make their political points." This was a common concern when members "went public" about work performance issues, and the social worker told Mrs. Ames so. She agreed that it was worse to be unprotected and was assured that the social worker would be with her throughout the process. In fact, Mrs. Ames experienced the union shop steward as a supporter and friend, someone she could turn to at the job when she felt afraid of the supervisor, rather than staying away or crying uncontrollably. She continued to cry, but as time went on, she did so more privately with the shop steward, rather than at her desk in front of the supervisor.

Several weeks into Mrs. Ames' contact with the social worker, the union representative explored in depth the work site situation and determined a "gray area" of possible harassment. The social worker called a three-way meeting with the representative and Mrs. Ames. At this time, Mrs. Ames asserted that she was afraid and did not want the union to proceed with her case. As the social worker knew that similar concerns about public humiliation had led to Mrs. Ames' leaving other jobs, she worked with the union representative on alternatives. He agreed to try to have Mrs. Ames moved to another work station, doing the same assignments but with a different supervisor. This move would take time, and Mrs. Ames and the social worker continued to work on her reactions to the current supervisor in the interim, and particularly in the event that the change might not be possible. Several weeks later, Mrs. Ames was moved.

At the same time, with the union's permission, the social worker met with the supervisor to "soften" the experience for him as well as for Mrs. Ames, in order to reduce the chance of the repercussions that Mrs. Ames so feared. At this meeting, the social worker attempted to define the problem as interactive, rather than blame Mrs. Ames or the supervisor. She learned that the supervisor thought Mrs. Ames was going to be his best worker, and that he was upset that her deterioration was going to reflect badly on him as well as her. His stake in her improving was thereby established, and he backed off a bit toward the end of Mrs. Ames' working with him. He specified which behaviors were a problem, and how his own responses might be tempered to improve her job performance, rather than fuel the interpersonal struggles.

Finally, Mrs. Ames agreed to join a union-sponsored work stress group that met for eight sessions. Run by union staff and another social worker, the group contributed to normalizing Mrs. Ames' concerns and reducing her fear of public humiliation. She saw that many workers experience stress, she developed new social supports, and she received some suggestions from other employees about how to respond to her supervisor.

It took several weeks to accomplish the transfer to a new work site. During this time, Mrs. Ames continued to work on putting her supervisor into realistic perspective, to respond somewhat differently to him, and to increase her supports at work. She began to understand that many people are work-stressed, including her supervisor. She cried, he screamed. While this didn't excuse his behavior, it helped her not to personalize and to understand that the supervisor's main goal in life was not to humiliate her.

It was agreed that her absenteeism had decreased dramatically. While she continued to cry occasionally at work and was slower than she needed to be, her job was no longer in jeopardy. She also continued to see the psychiatrist at the community mental health center, to deal with underlying issues that had surfaced through the job crisis. Longstanding patterns and an underlying depression compromised her social relations (including those with her husband, with her peers, and with people in authority). Mrs. Ames decided to continue at the community mental health center. She never took antidepressant medication, although the vegetative signs of her depression abated and did not return.

Mrs. Ames thought that she had been particularly helped through role play, whereby the social worker had taught her how to be assertive with her supervisor. She reported with pride that these skills and her gains at the work site had carryover to "her personal life," as she began to assert her rights in other spheres (e.g., demanding that money be returned by a local entrepreneur who had broken a signed contract).

Several weeks later, Mrs. Ames was transferred to a new work station. Her performance improved considerably, and she was defined as a competent, reliable worker by her supervisor. She developed an alliance with the shop steward and the union representative and periodically stopped by to see them. She continued to isolate herself from her coworkers and to withdraw when she was criticized. She no longer cried at the work site.

Mrs. Ames agreed to return to see her union social worker if she ever felt upset or afraid about work again. She also agreed that she wouldn't wait until her job was in trouble to do so.

Job jeopardy is a personally devastating, organizationally draining, and societally disturbing experience. It is a phenomenon with multiple causes and many avenues for intervention. As a profession, social work has developed some important specialized program responses to job jeopardy. As yet, we have not given organized and comprehensive thought to the phenomenon or to ways to respond as a profession or as professionals. It is a challenge that merits and impels attention.

## REFERENCES

Akabas, S., S. Bellinger, M. Fine, and R. Woodrow. 1981. "Confidentiality Issues in Workplace Settings: A Working Paper." New York: Industrial Social Welfare Center.

Akabas, S. and P. Kurzman, eds. 1982. *Work, Workers, and Work Organizations: A View from Social Work.* Englewood Cliffs, N.J.: Prentice-Hall.

Arvey, R. D. and R. H. Faley. 1988. *Fairness in Selecting Employees,* 2d ed. Reading, Mass.: Addison-Wesley.

Bellah, R., et al. 1984. *Habits of the Heart.* New York: Basic Books.

Bensman, D. and R. Lynch. 1988. *Rusted Dreams: Hard Times in a Steel Community.* Berkeley: University of California Press.

Berkowitz, M. et al. 1988. *The Older Worker.* Madison, Wis.: Industrial Relations Research Association.

Berman, D. M. 1978. *Death on the Job: Occupational Health and Safety Struggles in the United States.* New York: Monthly Review Press.

Borus, M. E., ed. 1988. *Older Worker: Research Volume.* Madison, Wis.: Industrial Relations Research Association.

Brenner, H. M. 1984. *Estimating the Effects of Economic Change on National Health and Social Well-Being.* Washington, D.C.: GPO.

Briar, K. H. 1978. *The Effect of Long-Term Unemployment on Workers and Their Families.* Saratoga, Calif.: R & E Publications.

Briar, K. H. 1983. "Unemployment: Toward a Social Work Agenda." *Social Work* (May/June) 28:3.

Briar, K. H. 1987. "Unemployment and Underemployment." In A. Minahan, ed., *Encyclopedia of Social Work,* 18th ed., vol. 2, pp. 778–788. Silver Spring, Md.: National Association of Social Workers.

Bunker, D. R. and M. H. Wijnberg. 1988. *Supervision and Performance.* San Francisco: Jossey-Bass.

B. N. A. (Bureau of National Affairs). 1988. *Employee Assistance Programs: Focusing on the Family.* Rockville, Md.: BNA.

BNA, 1987. *Older Americans in the Workforce: Challenges and Solutions.* Rockville, Md.: BNA.

Buss, T. F. and F. S. Redburn. 1983. *Mass Unemployment: Plant Closings and Community Mental Health.* Beverly Hills, Calif.: Sage.

Buss, T. F. and F. S. Redburn. 1988. *Hidden Unemployment: Discourages Workers and Public Policy.* New York: Praeger.

CPI (Committee on Psychiatry in Industry). 1982. *Job Loss: A Psychiatric Perspective.* New York: Mental Health Materials Center.

"Current Labor Statistics." 1989. *Monthly Labor Review* (July), 112(7): p. 62.

Eisenberg, M. G., et al. 1982. *Disabled People as Second-Class Citizens.* New York: Springer.

Figley, C. R., ed. 1985. *Trauma and Its Wake: The Study and Treatment of Post-Traumatic Stress Syndrome.* New York: Brunner/Mazel.

Ford Foundation. 1989. *The Common Good: Social Welfare and the American Future.* New York: Ford Foundation.

Garraty, J. A. 1978. *Unemployment in History.* New York: Harper & Row.

Gill, C. 1985. *Work, Unemployment, and the New Technology.* New York: Basil Blackwell.

Grubb, W. N. and R. H. Wilson. 1989. "Sources of Increasing Inequality in Wages and Salaries, 1960–80." *Monthly Labor Review* (April), 112(4): pp. 3–13.

Hall, R. H. 1984. *Dimensions of Work.* Beverly Hills, Calif.: Sage.

Hunt, H. A. and T. L. Hunt. 1983. *Human Resource Implications of Robotics.* Kalamazoo, Mich.: W. E. Upjohn Institute for Employment Research.

Hutson, S. and R. Jenkins. 1989. *Taking the Strain: Families, Unemployment, and the Transition to Adulthood.* Philadelphia: Open University Press.

Jacobs, J. A. 1989. *Revolving Doors: Sex Segregation and Women's Careers.* Stanford, Calif.: Stanford University Press.

Jenkins, R. 1986. *Racism and Recruitment: Managers, Organisations, and Equal Opportunity in the Labour Market.* New York: Cambridge University Press.

Jenkins, R. and J. Solomos. 1987. *Racism and Equal Opportunity in the 1980s.* New York: Cambridge University Press.

Johnson, N. 1987. *The Welfare State in Transition.* Amherst: Mass.: University of Massachusetts Press.

Kamerman, S., and A. Kahn, eds. 1978. *Family Policy: Government and Families in Fourteen Countries.* New York: Columbia University Press.

Kamerman, S., and A. Kahn. 1987. *The Responsive Workplace.* New York: Columbia University Press.

Kanter, R. 1977a. *Men and Women of the Corporation.* New York: Basic Books.

Kanter, R. 1977b. "Some Effects of Proportions on Group Life: Skewed Sex Ratios and Responses to Token Women." *American Journal of Sociology* 82:965–90.

Kelvin, P. and J. Jarrett. 1985. *Unemployment: Its Social Psychological Effects.* New York: Cambridge University Press.

Lerner, M. 1980. "Stress at the Workplace: The Approach of the Institute of Labor and Mental Health." *Catalyst* 2(4):75–82.

Levine, M. L. 1988. *Age Discrimination and the Mandatory Retirement Controversy.* Baltimore: Johns Hopkins University Press.

Middleman, R. R., and G. B. Rhodes. 1985. *Competent Supervision: Making Imaginative Judgments.* Englewood Cliffs, N.J.: Prentice-Hall.

Miller, I. and S. Akabas. 1978. *Industrial Social Welfare in the Generic Curriculum: Comments, Cases, Readings.* New York: Industrial Social Welfare Center.

O'Brien, G. E. 1986. *Psychology of Work and Unemployment.* New York: Wiley.

Perrucci, C. C., et al. 1988. *Plant Closings: International Context and Social Costs.* New York: A. de Gruyter.

Raffel, M., ed. 1984. *Comparative Health Systems: Descriptive Analyses of Fourteen National Health Systems.* State College: Pennsylvania State University Press.

Reich, M. 1981. *Racial Inequality: A Political-Economic Analysis.* Princeton, N.J.: Princeton University Press.

Richan, W. C. 1988. *Beyond Altruism: Social Welfare Policy in American Society.* New York: Haworth.

Rose, S. and L. Larwood, eds. 1988. *Women's Careers: Pathways and Pitfalls.* New York: Praeger.

Seligman, M. 1975. *Helplessness: On Depression, Development, and Death.* San Francisco: W. H. Freeman.

Silverman, B. 1988. "An Empirical Study of Practice in Industrial Social Work: Some Implications for Curriculum." D.S.W. dissertation, City University of New York.

Simon, B. L. 1987. *Never Married Women.* Philadelphia: Temple University Press.

Smith, J., et al. 1988. *Racism, Sexism, and the World-System.* New York: Greenwood.

Stack, C. 1974. *All Our Kin: Strategies for Survival in a Black Community.* New York: Harper.

Terkel, S. 1985. *Working.* New York: Ballantine.

Thompson, K., ed. 1985. *Work, Employment, and Unemployment: Perspectives on Work and Society.* Philadelphia: Taylor & Francis.

U.S. Census (U.S. Bureau of the Census) 1987. *Statistical Abstract of the United States: 1988,* 108th ed. Washington, D.C.: GPO.

U.S. Census (U.S. Bureau of the Census) 1988. *Statistical Abstract of the United States: 1989,* 109th ed. Washington, D.C.: GPO.

U.S. Labor. 1983. Handbook of Labor Statistics. Washington, D.C.: G.P.O.

Voydanoff, P. and L. C. Majka. 1988. *Families and Economic Distress: Coping Strategies and Social Policy.* Newbury Park, Calif.: Sage.

Warr, P. B. 1987. *Work, Unemployment, and Mental Health.* New York: Oxford University Press.

White, R. 1974. "Strategies of Adaptation: An Attempt at Systematic Description." In G. Coelho, D. Hamburg, and J. Adams, eds., *Coping and Adaptation,* New York: Basic Books.

Woodrow, R. 1986. "Social Work Practitioners in Health Care: A Population at Risk?" *Changes in Health Care Today: A Challenge to the Profession* (monograph). New York: Columbia University School of Social Work.

Woodrow, R. 1987. "Influence at Work." D.S.W. dissertation, New York: Columbia University School of Social Work.

# Author Index

▼

Abelson, Herbert I., 74
Abraham, K., 167
Abramson, M., 508, 529
Abuelo, D. N., 3
Adams, Gina, 10, 11, 325
Adams, J. E., 146, 148
Adams, Kenneth, 649
Adelman, Howard S., 242
Adelman, R. D., 524
Adler, G., 124
Akabas, Sheila H., 69, 715, 718, 721
Akers, Ronald L., 70, 71, 72, 75
Akiskal, H. S., 102
Alibhai, N., 211
Allegrante, J. P., 148
Allen, C. M., 477
Allen, M., 386, 391
Allon, N., 216
Altman, Dennis, 35
Altmeier, William A., 351
Andersen, R. M., 143
Anderson, Carol M., 118, 191, 298, 299, 304
Anderson, Gary B., 52
Anderson, Sandra C., 80
Andreasen, N., 290
Andrulonis, P. A., 3, 108, 109, 110, 111, 114
Aneshensel, C., 180
Annis, Helen M., 84, 88
Anthony C., 564
Apgar, V., 270

Applebaum, R., 555, 565
Applebaum, S. A., 681
Applebome, Peter, 653
Arce, A. A., 588
Arif, Awni, 73, 83
Aronowitz, M., 625
Arvey, R. D., 712
Asberg, M., 681
Asbury, J., 475
Asch, A., 138-39
Auerbach, Stephanie K., 331
Austin, Gregory A., 66-67
Averill, J. R., 148
Azar, Sandra, 349, 353

Bachrach, Leona, 297
Baekeland, Frederick, 76, 86
Bagley, C., 625, 685
Baker, F. M., 685
Baker, J. M., 274
Baker, P. K. S., 102, 107
Baker, R., 524
Baldwin, L., 174, 365
Balis, George U., 79, 84
Ball, P. G., 480, 488
Ballenger, J., 181
Bandura, Albert, 69, 85
Bank, Barbara J., 72
Barbanel, Josh, 65
Bard, Morton, 417, 436, 437
Baron, M., 179
Barone, V. J., 362

Barret, C., 351
Barrett, C. J., 451
Barth, Richrd P., 360, 393, 394
Bartman, E. R., 126
Bass, D., 520
Bassuk, Ellen L., 588, 595
Bateson, Mary Catherine, 36, 37
Battaglino, L., 183
Bauer, W. D., 353
Baum, S. K., 506
Baumohl, Jim, 72
Baxter, Ellen, 585, 591
Bayer, Ronald, 43, 51
Bayley, N., 365
Beach, S., 190
Bean, G. J., 588
Bean, Margaret H., 82
Beardslee, W., 175
Beattie, H., 208
Beck, A., 167, 170, 187, 190
Beck, A. T., 681, 686, 687, 679
Beck, J., 270
Becker, Howard S., 71
Beckett, J. O., 474, 475
Beckman, 187
Bedrosian, R. C., 686
Beels, C., 299, 303
Bellack, A., 190
Bellah, R., 714
Bellak, L. P., 109, 110, 293, 298
Belle, D., 180
Bellinger, Susan, 69
Belman, A. L., 270
Belsky, Jay, 349, 350
Bender, E., 221
Benitez, R., 509, 510
Bennet, P., 189
Bennett, R., 513
Benoliel, J. Q., 455
Bensman, D., 711, 715
Benson, R., 23
Bentler, P. M., 72, 73, 75
Berkowitz, Alan, 76
Berkowitz, M., 712
Berman, Allen, 243
Berman, D. M., 712
Berman-Rossi, T., 508, 523
Berne, E., 22
Bernheim, Kayla F., 182, 300
Berrueta-Clement, J. R., 357
Berry, Marianne, 393
Bertelsen, A., 172
Bettelheim, Bruno, 436, 437
Bibring, E., 167

Bickett, Laura, 365
Biddle, Bruce J., 72
Biernacki, Patrick, 69
Bifulco, A., 181
Biglan, A., 177, 190
Billings, A., 176, 177
Billingsley, Andrew, 351, 387
Birch, A., 237
Birley, L. T., 299
Birtchnell, J., 177, 685
Bishop, D., 174, 365, 376
Bishop, Katherine, 585
Black, Kathryn B., 183, 356
Black, R. B., 145, 148
Blaney, P., 170
Blazer, D., 180, 182
Blenkner, H., 510, 562
Bleuler, 289
Blevins, Gregory A., 78, 82
Bloksberg, Leonard M., 393
Bloom, Lois, 246
Blum, H. M., 121
Blum, K., 3
Blume, Sheila B., 77
Blumenfield, S., 523
Blumenthal, Karen, 400
Blumstein, Alfred, 648
Boche, H. Leonard, 67
Bogen, E., 628
Bograd, M., 472, 479, 485, 489
Bohlen, Celestine, 654, 662
Bohman, Michael, 3, 75
Bolduc, Anne, 648
Bologna, M. J., 472
Bolton, F. G., 478, 480, 488, 490, 492
Bolton, S. R., 478, 480, 488, 490, 492
Borgotta, E., 563, 564
Boskind-White, M., 221
Boswell, John, 382
Boutselis, M., 564
Bowe, F., 138, 143
Bowen, M., 457
Bowers, R. S., 682
Bowker, L. H., 482, 649
Bowlby, J., 448
Boxley, R. L., 506
Boyd, J., 11, 166, 178, 180, 187
Bradley, Robert, 366
Brager, G., 22
Brand, P. A., 472
Braswell, Michael, 649
Braucht, G. N., 680, 685
Brauer, C., 453
Brecher, Edward M., 67

Breier, A., 181
Breitenbucher, M., 351
Brekke, J. S., 480, 485, 487, 494
Breme, F. J., 458
Brenner, G., 517
Brenner, H. M., 711
Briar, Katharine Hooper, 648, 657, 716, 720, 721
Briggs, V. M., 620
Brill, Leon, 67
Brindis, Claire, 325
Brodoff, Ami, 304
Brody, E. M., 504, 513, 514, 516, 520, 521, 523, 550, 551, 552, 553, 554, 557, 559, 562, 563
Brody, S. J., 504, 513, 514, 516, 520, 521
Bromet, E., 177, 178
Brooks, N. A., 146, 147
Brown, Dale, 256
Brown, G., 176, 179, 180, 181
Brown, G. W., 299
Brown, L., 182, 194, 369, 564
Brown, S. S., 142
Brubaker, E., 523
Bruch, H., 208, 213, 217, 218, 219
Brunner, J., 21
Buchanan, Mary, 242
Buckingham, Stephan L., 47, 50
Buckley, Walter, 36
Buffum, W. E., 527
Buglass, D., 686
Buie, D., 124
Bulow, B., 182, 215
Bunker, D. R., 713
Burgess, 417
Burgess, Robert L., 351, 353, 365
Burke, Donald S., 43
Burns, D., 182
Burns, Thomas F., 71
Burov, Y., 3
Buss, T. F., 711, 715
Butcher, J. N., 696
Butler, R. N., 508, 516, 517

Cadol, Roger V., 360
Cadoret, Remi, 76
Caetano, Raul, 75
Cafferata, G., 11, 514, 525, 552, 556, 558
Cahalan, Don, 12, 72, 74, 75
Cahill, Kevin M., 35
Caldwell, Betty, 366
Callahan, D., 608

Callahan, J. J., Jr., 520, 543, 563
Calot, Gerard, 319
Campbell, Randy V., 362
Camus, Albert, 37
Cannon, Walter B., 36
Cantoni, L., 488, 492
Cantor, M. H., 555, 558
Cantor, P. C., 686
Cappell, Howard, 69
Caputo, Larry, 35, 52
Carlin, J. E., 627
Carlson, B. E., 471, 476, 481
Carmen, E., 471, 480, 487
Carney, Louis P., 648
Carpenter, William, 294
Carter, E., 565
Carter, G. W., 571
Castle, R., 9, 351
Catalan, J., 686, 689, 690, 698
Catalano, D. J., 561
Cermak, Timmen L., 87
Chackhes, Esther, 50
Chaney, Edmund F., 81, 90
Chapman, C., 187
Charpentier, M., 524
Chatters, L. M., 519
Chess, S., 237
Chessick, R. D., 124
Chi, Iris, 75
Child, Rachel, 51
Chiles, J. A., 686, 687
Chinn, P. C., 267
Christ, Grace, 48
Christian, E. R., 685
Cicchetti, Dante, 353
Clark, K., 7
Clark, Sam, 324
Clark, V., 180
Clark, Walter B., 73, 74, 75
Clayton, P. J., 448
Clements, Sam, 235
Cloninger, C. Robert, 3, 67, 75
Cloninger, R. S. T., 292
Cloward, Richard A., 69
Clum, G. A., 686, 698
Cobb, S., 527
Coelho, G. V., 146, 148
Cohen, D. J., 109
Cohen, David, 292
Cohen, H. J., 273
Cohen, M., 167
Cohen, R. E., 634
Cohen, Sheldon, 72
Coid, J., 657

Coley, S. M., 474, 475
Collard, Jean, 245
Collins, B. S., 491
Collins, J. J., 657
Collmer, C. W., 350
Conger, Rand D., 351, 353
Conn, Victoria S., 299
Connors, M., 221
Coombs, D., 685
Coombs, Robert H., 75, 76
Cooper, P., 210, 214, 215
Coppel, D. B., 558
Corbin, J. M., 143, 146, 147, 148
Cornelius, L. J., 143
Coryell, W., 187
Cotton, Nancy S., 74, 75, 76
Coulton, C., 527
Coward, R. T., 521, 524, 525
Cowdry, R. W., 115
Cox, C., 517, 523
Cox, D., 629
Coyne, J., 171
Crammond, J., 71
Crane, Rochelle, 253
Crisp, A., 214
Crittenden, Patricia M., 353
Cross, C., 166, 180
Crowell, B., 182
Cummings, B. H., 275
Cummings, Claudette, 84
Curran, James W., 40, 42
Cutler, N. E., 503
Czirr, R., 564

Dana, Robert Q., 78, 82
Dangel, Richard F., 359
Daniel, W., 217, 222
Danziger, S. D., 513
Daro, Deborah, 390
Darragh, P. M., 273
Davidson, S. M., 520, 521
Davis, Christine S., 84, 88
Davis, Donald I., 85
Davis, L. V., 471, 473, 481
Davis, R., 685
Dawson, L. J., 472
DeChillo, N., 215
DeFrain, J., 454
DeJong, G., 138
Deschner, J. P., 491
Desmarais, L., 448
DeVore, W., 369
Diamond, Barbara, 241
Diamond, Beverly, 388

Dickens, Bernard M., 43, 51
Dickerson, M. U., 3
DiClemente, Carlo C., 82
Diekstra, R., 682
Dienelt, M. N., 687
Dill, 518
Dillingham, Steven, 649
Dobash, R. E., 475
Dobash, R. P., 475
Dobson, K., 190
Dodds, Josiah B., 365
Dole, Vincent P., 67
Dolinsky, A., 503
Donovan, Dennis M., 81
Dornan, D. H., 148
Doty, P., 550, 551, 553, 555, 557
Douglas, J. D., 679, 680
Douglas, M. A., 480, 486, 488
Draper, R., 678
Drapkin, Israel, 417
Drew, C. J., 267
Drillien, C., 270
Druley, Keith A., 80
Drye, R. C., 103
Dubois, 518
Dubos, René, 37
Dumas, John, 351
Dumpson, James R., 595
Dunkle, R. E., 506, 531
Dunne, E., 688
Dunne-Maxim, K., 688
Dunner, D., 179
Durkheim, Emile, 679-80
Dussy, J., 22
Dutton, D., 479, 480, 481
D'Zurrilo, T., 22

Eagles, J., 179
Eaton, W. William, 295
Eckert, E., 210, 215
Eckman, T., 126
Eckrich, S., 102
Edgerton, Robert D., 69, 71
Edwards, Griffith, 82, 83
Egan, J. H., 115, 123
Egeland, Byron, 351, 353, 354, 355
Egeland, J., 172, 180
Eisenberg, M. G., 717
Elder, G., Jr., 509, 517, 518
Elias, Robert, 417-19, 421, 422, 423
Elkind, David, 320
Elliot, Stephen N., 238, 249
Ellis, A., 27
Elmer, Elizabeth, 352, 353

Elwood, J. H., 273
Emrick, Chad D., 80
Engel, G. L., 508, 517
Engler, Richard, 386
Englund, D. W., 107
Enright, Robert D., 249, 254
Ephross, P. H., 523
Epstein, N., 174, 365
Ericson, Kai, 436
Erikson, Erik H., 342
Erne, Diane, 359
Esman, A., 108
Estes, C. L., 510, 522, 509
Eustis, N. N., 515

Fabrega, H., 625
Faerstein, Leslie Morrison, 252
Fairburn, C., 210, 214, 215, 219
Faley, R. H., 712
Faller, Kathleen, 345
Fallon, A., 211
Faloon, Ian, 298, 300
Fanshel, David, 386, 392, 394, 401
Farberow, N. L., 681, 684, 685, 686
Farkas, S., 558
Fawzy, I., 75, 76
Featherstone, Helen, 256
Fein, Edith, 387, 392
Feingold, Ben, 239
Feinstein, A., 189
Feldman, Ronald, 3, 295
Feldstein, D., 504
Felthous, A. R., 482, 501
Felton, D., 353
Fengler, A., 557
Ferber, Jane, 80
Ferraro, K., 480, 501
Ferres, P., 299
Ferster, C., 170, 190
Festinger, Trudy, 386, 392
Figley, C. R., 711
Fimbres, Manuel, 35
Finch, Stephen J., 394
Fine, M., 69, 138-39
Fineberg, Harvey V., 35, 43
Fingarette, Herbert, 66
Finkelhor, David, 355, 358
Finn, J., 480
Fischer, A., 4
Fish, W. C., 449
Fishbach, M., 272
Fitzpatrick, 554
Flanagan, Timothy J., 649, 651, 654, 665

Fleming, J., 488
Foch, T., 3, 210
Folkman, S., 566
Fondal, Alma W., 365
Fontana, Vincent J., 353
Fossum, Merle A., 82
Foster, Andrew, 319
Fox, D. M., 139, 142
Fox, K., 686
Francell, Griffin Clair, 299
Frances, A. J., 114, 115, 116, 189
Frankenburg, William K., 365
Franklin, Deborah, 237
Fraser, Mark W., 86
Fredrichs, R., 180
Freed, A. O., 102
Freeman, Richard B., 595
Freinkel, Susan, 423
French, J. R. P., 527
Freud, Sigmund, 167
Friedland, Gerald H., 41, 44
Friedlander, E., 628
Friedman, A., 190
Friedman, D. H., 491
Friedman, Harold N., 119, 239
Friedman, J., 189
Frisch, M. B., 477, 482
Frodi, A. M., 353
Furnham, A., 211
Furst, S. S., 681
Furstenberg, A. L., 506

Gabinet, Laille, 398
Cadow, S., 506
Galanter, Marc, 86
Galizio, Mark, 70
Gallagher, D. E., 555, 557, 563, 564, 569
Gallo, Robert C., 42
Gallogoly, Virginia, 80
Gambe, Richard, 45, 51
Gambrill, Eileen, 367
Garbarino, James, 352
Garcia-Preto, D., 567
Gardner, D. L., 115
Garfinkel, P., 11, 12, 210, 213, 214
Garmezy, N., 355
Garner, D., 11, 12, 210, 212, 213, 214
Garraty, J. A., 711
Geismer, Ludwig, 348
Gelles, R. J., 5, 8, 346-47, 350, 356, 471, 472, 473, 474, 475, 477, 479, 480, 488
George, C., 354

George, L., 182
George, L. K., 555
Gerard, L. E., 509
Gerber, Barry, 75, 76
Gerhard, D., 180
Germain, C. B., 6, 15, 20, 21, 37, 66, 139, 218, 503, 523, 527, 567
Gershenson, Charles P., 393
Gershon, E., 3, 172
Gershon, Frank M., 238, 249
Getzel, George S., 35, 36, 42, 44, 45, 47, 48, 51, 522
Gibbs, J. P., 680
Gil, David G., 350, 356
Gilchrist, Lewayne, 332
Gill, C., 711
Gilliam, Gwenn, 352
Gillman, I. S., 480, 488
Ginzburg, Harold M., 66
Giovannoni, Jeanne M., 351, 387
Gitterman, Alex, 6, 15, 16, 20, 21, 37, 66, 139, 212, 218, 523, 527, 567
Gitterman, N. P., 244
Glaser, Frederick B., 77
Glatzer, H. T., 121
Glick, I., 191
Gliedman, J., 138
Glucksman, M. H., 210
Golan, N., 696
Gold, Mark S., 74
Goldberg, S. C., 114, 115
Goldenberg, I., 534
Goldfried, M., 22
Goldfried, M. R., 695
Goldsby, Richard, 36, 37
Goldstein, Arnold P., 359
Goldstein, E., 218
Goldstein, E. G., 102, 103, 108
Goldstein, Kurt, 235
Goldstein, R., 524
Goleman, Daniel, 237
Golodetz, A., 559
Goluke, Ulrich, 70
Gomberg, Edith S. Lisansky, 74
Gondolf, E. W., 484
Gonyea, J. G., 516
Gonzales, R., 554
Goode, Erich, 69
Goodman, H., 504
Goodrich, N., 557
Goodstein, R. K., 480, 487, 488, 492
Goodwin, Donald W., 3, 12, 75, 76
Gordon, Judith R., 69, 84, 85
Gordon, Linda, 387

Gordon, M., 629
Gorer, G., 451
Gotlib, I., 182
Gottheil, Edward A., 72, 80
Gottlieb, B., 6
Gould, C. L., 274
Gould, M. S., 683, 686, 688, 690
Gove, W., 180
Grant, R., 659
Gratton, B., 512, 525
Gray, D. Patricia, 299
Gray, Jane D., 358
Gray, L. T., 472, 473, 479, 486, 487, 490
Gray, V. K., 565
Graziano, R., 102
Greeley, Janet, 69
Green, A., 173
Green, A. H., 352
Green, Hanah, 286
Green, M., 448-49
Green, V. L., 564, 569
Greenberg, J. N., 515
Greene, Brandon F., 362
Greene, Ronald, 649
Greenly, Mike, 35
Gregg, G., 353
Gress, 289
Grinker, R., 102, 103, 108
Grobman, J., 121
Grodd, Barbara, 651, 654, 659
Gross, Mortimer D., 234, 235, 236, 251
Grosscup, S., 190
Grossman, H. J., 266
Grotstein, J. S., 106
Grubb, W. N., 715
Gruber, Alan, 386
Grundy, John F., 394
Grunebaum, H., 119
Guirguis, Waguih, 291
Gunderson, J. G., 102, 103, 107, 108, 109, 112, 123
Gust, Steven W., 66
Gwyther, L., 555

Haack, Mary R., 75
Haber, A., 270
Hagerman, P. J., 268
Hagerman, R. J., 268
Hagnell, O., 176
Hale, R., 80
Haley, Jay, 106, 118, 305
Haley, W. E., 560, 562, 564
Hall, A., 221

Hall, Brian, 595
Hall, D. K., 353
Hall, R. H., 716
Halmi, K. 207, 209, 214
Hamberg, Jill, 585, 587
Hamburg, D. A., 146, 148
Hampton, Robert L., 9, 353
Hann, D. M., 351
Hanneke, Christina R., 595
Hansen, Joel, 80
Hanson, Meredith, 70, 76, 81
Hanson, R., 352
Harding, Courtenay M., 297
Harding, P., 190
Hardy, Janet, 324
Harel, Z., 504, 507
Harford, Thomas C., 75
Harrigan, M., 555, 565
Harris, D. K., 505
Harris, Maxine, 302
Harris, T., 176, 179, 180, 181
Hartman, S., 480, 486, 488, 489, 491
Hartman, A., 22, 23
Hartocollis, P., 110
Hasselkus, B. R., 558
Hatfield, Agnes B., 148, 292
Hautzinger, M., 177
Hawkins, G. E., 649
Hawkins, J. David, 86
Hawton, K., 686, 689, 690, 698
Hayes, Cheryl, 9, 319, 324
Haynes, U., 270
Helfer, Roy E., 352
Helzer, John E., 65
Henderson, A., 176
Hendricks-Matthews, M., 486
Henry, A. F., 680
Henry, B., 175
Henson, D. M., 480, 486, 488, 492
Hepworth, P. H., 692
Herd, Denise, 74, 75
Herman, I., 679
Herman, J., 175
Herr, J. J., 565
Herrnstein, R. J., 10, 652, 655
Herson, M., 190
Herz, F., 458, 461, 466
Hester, Reid K., 78, 81, 85
Heyward, William, 40, 42
Hilberman, E., 481
Hill, Kenneth, 619
Himmelhoch, J., 190
Hinchcliffe, M., 177
Hirsch, J., 210

Hirsch, S., 678, 690
Hirschfeld, R., 166, 180
Hirschman, L., 175
Hobbs, N., 138, 139, 140, 141, 142, 143, 145
Hodgson, Ray, 83
Hodis, L., 102
Hoffman, N., 177
Hoffman-Plotkin, D., 354
Hogan, C., 208, 219
Hogarty, Gerald, 118, 298, 299, 304
Holden, Lynn, 256
Hollingshead, A., 4
Holloway, S., 22
Holmes, W. M., 9, 352
Holstrom, 417
Hombs, Mary Ellen, 586
Hooley, J., 178
Hooyman, N. R., 504, 508, 515, 516, 517, 519, 525
Hoppe, S. K., 684
Hopper, Kim, 585, 587, 591
Hops, H., 177, 190
Horn, John L., 82, 88
Horowitz, A., 11, 549, 550, 551, 553, 555, 556, 557, 564
Horwitz, L., 121, 122
Howell, S. C., 540
Howells, John G., 291
Hsu, L., 214
Huba, G. J., 72
Hudson, Walter, 365
Hughes, M., 180
Hull, J. T., 272
Humphrey, L., 209
Hunt, H. A., 712
Hunt, T. L., 712
Hunter, D., 300
Hutson, S., 715
Hyatt, Amanda, 351
Hyler, S., 189

Igoin-Apfelbaum, L., 215
Ilfield, F., 177
Innes, Christopher, 653
Iodice, Jody D., 298
Ireton, Harold, 365
Ireys, H. T., 138, 139, 140, 141, 142, 143, 145
Irwin, J., 648
Ito, J., 75
Ivanoff, A., 687, 690
Ivker, Barry, 301, 313
Ivry, J., 560, 565

Jackson, G. D., 628
Jackson, M., 516
Jackson, Sara C., 249, 254
Jacob, Bruce, 421
Jacob, M., 182, 183
Jacob, T., 477, 478
Jacobs, J. A., 712
Jacobsen, S., 685
Jacobson, N., 190
Jacobson, S. G., 511
Jahoda, G., 71
Jakobowski, P., 22
James, N., 187
Jamieson, Katherine M., 649, 651, 654, 665
Janchill, Sister Mary Paul, 399
Jarrett, J., 718
Jellinek, E. M., 66, 67
Jenkins, R., 712, 713, 715
Jenkins, Shirley, 387, 388, 401, 620, 628
Jensen, A. R., 628
Jensen, L., 622, 624
Jessor, Richard, 72
Jessor, Shirley L., 72
Jimenez, Mary A., 312
Johnson, Bruce D., 69
Johnson, C., 212, 214, 215, 221
Johnson, C. L., 561
Johnson, Doris J., 235
Johnson, Elsie, 72
Johnson, H. C., 102, 111, 118, 236, 254
Johnson, K. W., 142
Johnson, N., 714, 715
Johnson, P. J., 571
Johnson, Sharon, 241
Johnson, Vernon E., 82
Johnston, C., 353
Johnston, W., 619
Jones, D., 222
Jones, Elise, 321
Jones, L. E., 513
Joseph, Stanley, 41
Jourard, S., 212
Jung, Kenneth G., 3, 295

Kadushin, Alfred, 355, 392, 395
Kaestner, Elisabeth, 74
Kagan, J., 105
Kagan, S., 356, 381
Kahana, E., 527, 531
Kahn, Alfred J., 384, 391, 715
Kalish, Carol B., 651

Kalish, R. A., 517
Kallman, F. J., 681
Kalucy, R., 208, 214
Kamerman, Sheila B., 384, 391, 715
Kaminer, R. K., 273
Kamm, P., 450
Kandel, Denise B., 72, 73, 74
Kane, R. A., 11, 506, 507, 508, 513, 515, 520, 521, 525, 526, 568
Kane, R. L., 526, 568
Kanter, J., 178
Kanter, R., 713, 728
Kantner, John 324
Kanton, M. B., 625
Kaplan, Harold I., 289, 290, 293, 294
Karnes, M., 280
Karno, Marvin, 293
Kasl, S. V., 684
Kasper, J. D., 513
Katz, A., 221
Kaufman, Edward, 71
Kaufman, Keith, 360
Kaufman, S. R., 506
Kavanagh, James F., 247, 248, 249
Kaye, L. W., 521, 525
Kazdin, A. E., 354
Keller, Harold, 359
Keller, M., 187
Keller, S., 629
Kelley, H. H., 477
Kelly, E. E., 472
Kelly, Jeffrey A., 359
Kelvin, P., 718
Kempe, Charles H., 352
Kemper, P., 555, 565
Kennard, J., 177
Keogh, B., 274
Kerewsky, William, 323
Kermis, M. D., 142
Kernberg, Otto, 102-4, 110, 112, 121, 123, 124
Kernberg, Paulina, 106
Kessler, R., 172, 184
Kessler, Ronald C., 72
Kety, Seymour S., 3, 292
Keyes, B., 569
Kibel, H. D., 121
Kidd, A. H., 472
Kidd, K., 12, 180
Killner, Selma K., 253
Kilpatrick, Dean, 417
King, Barbara L., 82
Kinney, Jean, 77
Kinzie, J. D., 627, 638, 641

Kirk, S. A., 701
Kirk, Samuel, 235
Kirschenbaum, D., 209
Kissin, Benjamin, 66, 70, 80, 81
Kitano, Harry H. L., 75
Kiyak, H. Asuman, 508, 515, 517
Klass, D., 449
Klassen, Albert D., 77
Kleber, Herbert D., 76
Kleiman, Dena, 241
Klein, D., 185
Klein, D. F., 103, 109, 114, 115
Kleinfield, S., 143
Kleinman, A., 642
Klerman, G., 166, 174, 176, 190
Klotz, J., 179
Knight, B., 520
Knitzer, J., 386, 391
Knudten, Richard D., 417
Koenig, Michael, 325
Kohlert, N., 510
Kohut, Heinz, 68, 124
Kolata, Gina, 44
Kolody, B., 516, 625
Kornhaber, E., 217
Kornhaber, R., 217
Kosten, Thomas R., 76
Kovacs, M., 187, 681, 686, 687
Kovitz, K., 353
Kozol, Jonathan, 585, 596
Kraepelin, Emil, 289
Kramer, Larry, 35
Kreitman, N., 678, 686, 689
Kresh, Esther, 393
Kritz, M., 618
Kronick, Doreen, 249, 250, 256
Kurzman, P., 715, 718, 721
Kutchins, H., 701

Labrecque, M., 558
Lahey, B. B., 353
Lamb, H., 178, 659
Lamb, M. E., 353
Landeen, Robert, 70
Landis, K., 184
Lange, A., 22
Languetot, Roxanne, 304
Lanza-Kaduce, Lonn, 72
Larsen, J. A., 692
Larson, D., 180
Larson, Katherine A., 243
Larwood, L., 712, 713
Laughlin, John, 361-62, 366

Laumier, B., 21
Lauriat, Alison, 588, 595
Lavelle, N., 274
Lawton, M. P., 559, 562, 563
Lazare, A., 451
Lazarus, R. S., 21, 148, 566
Leary, Warren, 41
Leaton, Gwen, 77
Lee, E., 625
Lee, Felicia R., 8, 65
Lee, J. A. B., 529
Lee, P. R., 522
Lee-Benner, K., 221
Leete, Esso, 296
Leff, J., 178, 291, 300
Lefley, Harriet, 313
Lefstein, Leah, 323
Lehtinen, Laura, 235-36
Leigh, Gillian, 74
Lender, Mark E., 67
Leon, G., 211, 213
Leonard, K. E., 477-78
Lerner, Janet W., 235, 236, 237, 246, 249
Lerner, M., 729
Lettieri, D. J., 681, 684, 687
Leukefeld, Carl E., 35
Levant, Ronald F., 360-61
Levenson, M., 681, 686
Levi, D., 685
Levine, Baruch, 80
Levine, E., 564
Levine, Harry Gene, 66
Levine, M. L., 712
Lewert, George, 52
Lewinsohn, P., 170, 179, 180-81, 182, 190
Lewis, David C., 80
Lewis, E., 480, 488, 489
Lewis, Judith A., 78, 82
Lewis, M., 516, 517
Liberman, R. P., 126
Lidz, T., 686
Lieber, L. L., 274
Lieberman, M., 177, 180
Lieberman, M. A., 508, 509, 517
Liebowitz, M. R., 109, 115
Liem, J., 172
Liem, R., 172
Light, Richard, 351
Lin, K., 641, 642
Lindemann, E., 447
Linden, M., 177
Lindenthal, J., 172

Lineham, M. M., 120, 121, 124, 126, 678, 681, 682, 685, 686, 687, 690, 694, 695, 698
Links, P. S., 115
Linnoila, M., 687
Linsk, N. L., 562, 565
Lipton, D., 648
Litch, S., 268
Litchfield, L. C., 560, 565
Litman, R. E., 685
Locke, H. J., 365
Lockerly, S. A., 554
Loeber, R., 354
Loeper, C., 178
Logan, D. R., 267
Longabaugh, Richard, 80
Lopez, Diego J., 35, 36, 44, 45, 47
Lorber, R., 353
Lovett, S., 563, 564
Lowenkopf, E., 219
Lowry, M., 189
Lowy, L., 521, 560, 565
Lubben, James E., 75
Ludman, E. K., 514
Lukoff, Irving F., 12, 69, 73, 80
Lundwall, Lawrence, 76, 86
Lurie, A., 523
Luscomb, R. L., 686, 698
Lustbader, W., 504, 516, 525
Lutzker, John D., 362, 366
Lynch, C. G., 482
Lynch, R., 711, 715


Maas, Henry, 386
McAdoo, H. P., 554
MacAndrew, Charles, 69, 71
Macaskall, N. D., 121
McBogg, P., 268
McCain, N., 556
McCarthy, James J., 235
McCarthy, Joan F., 235
McClearn, G., 3, 76, 210
McClelland, David C., 68
McClowry, S., 449
McCollam, Janice B., 81
McCord, Joan, 68
McCord, William, 68
McCrady, Barbara S., 81
McCulloch, J. W., 686
McCutcheon, 686
McDermott, M. Joan, 651, 654, 662
McDonald, W., 416
McFarlane, Kee, 355

McGlashan, T. H., 124, 182, 289
McGoldrick, H., 565
McGowan, Brenda, 386
McIntosh, J., 688
McKenna, Thomas, 74
MacKenzie, C. J., 477, 482
MacKinnin, D., 684
McLellan, Thomas, 80
McMillin, Chandler Scott, 66
Maddahian, Ebrahim, 73, 75
Maggnuson, E., 8
Magruder-Habib, K., 189
Mahler, M. S., 106
Mahony, Kevin, 42, 51
Mailick Seltzer, M., 504
Main, M., 354
Main, Thomas J., 587, 596
Maisto, Stephen A., 70, 81
Majka, L. C., 711, 715
Maldonado, David, 503, 512, 514, 515
Malenbaum, R., 221
Maluccio, Anthony N., 24, 387, 392
Malzberg, B., 625
Mandell, F., 458
Mann, Jonathan M., 35, 40
Manton, K. G., 142, 551
Manuel, R. C., 518, 516
Margalit, Malka, 254
Margolis, O. S., 447
Margulies, Rebecca Z., 72
Maris, R. W., 681
Marlatt, G. Alan, 69, 81, 82, 84, 85, 90
Marlin, Marjorie M., 72
Marotta, J., 80
Marquez, C., 179
Marsiglio, William, 10, 322
Martin, H. W., 684
Martin, James K., 67
Martin, Judith A., 392, 395
Martin, Marsha A., 594
Martin, W. L., 680
Martinson, I., 454
Martinson, R., 648
Marwit, S., 449
Marziali, E., 121
Mash, E. J., 353
Mask, 353
Mason, Marilyn J., 82
Mass, Lawrence, 42
Masterson, J. F., 105-6, 123, 124
Mastria, Marie, 69
Matorin, Susan, 301
Matson, R. R., 146, 147
Maudal, G. R., 696

May, H. J., 458
Mayer, J., 24
Mayer, J. B., 523
Mayer, M. J., 503
Meadows, Dennis, 70
Mechanic, D., 533
Melges, F., 186
Meller, William H., 75
Mellor, M. J., 522
Mendelson, M., 213, 217
Mendelwicz, J., 3, 172, 179
Menninger, K., 680
Mercer, S. O., 508
Merikangas, K., 177, 178, 180
Meyer, C., 139, 643
Meyer-Kimling, E., 12
Meyers, J., 175, 179, 190
Michaelson, Arlene, 304
Midanik, Lorraine, 73, 74, 75
Middleman, R. R., 714
Miller, H., 685
Miller, I., 174, 523
Miller, J. D., 74
Miller, Peter M., 69
Miller, William R., 78, 81, 82, 84, 85
Millikan, M., 526
Milner, Joel S., 9, 366, 353
Milunsky, A., 268
Mintz, I., 208, 219, 223
Mintz, N., 222
Mintz, R. S., 696
Minuchin, Salvador, 118, 209, 305, 348, 459
Mitchell, C., 221
Mitchell, Faith, 325
Mitchell, J., 210, 215
Mitchell, R., 172
Mitford, J., 450
Mobley, Max J., 657
Molgaard, Craig A., 66
Mollica, R., 627
Monahan, D. J., 564, 569
Monk, A., 508, 520, 522, 529
Montagnier, Luc, 42
Montgomery, R. G., 563, 564
Montgomery, R. J. V., 556
Montgomery, Reid, 649
Moody, H. R., 525
Moon, M., 509
Mooney, J., 173
Moos, R., 172, 176, 177
Morgan, H. Wayne, 67
Morris, R., 520
Morrison, J., 188

Morse, D., 663
Morse, Gry A., 90, 595
Moses, R., 686
Mott, F., 10, 322, 325
Motto, J. A., 681, 684
Moynihan, Daniel, 293
Moynihan, Rosemary, 48
Mudrick, N. R., 140, 141
Mullner, R. M., 143
Munoz, R., 175
Munson, K., 481
Murdock, Jane Y., 249, 254
Murphy, H. B., 625
Mushlin, Michael B., 393
Musto, David F., 67
Myers, J., 172, 178
Myklebust, Helmer R., 235

Neidig, P. H., 491
Nelson, Judith C., 298, 364
Netherland, W., 648-49, 651, 652
Neugarten, B. L., 503, 504, 509, 511, 513
Neuringer, C., 681, 686
Newberger, Eli H., 9, 352
Newcomb, Michael D., 73, 75
Newman, J. M., 514
Nguyen, S. D., 641, 642
Nichols, Eve K., 35, 43
Nidorf, J., 638, 642
Nielsen, A., 190
Noble, S., 352
Noh, S., 182
Norman, Elaine, 401
Norris, T., 482
North, D. S., 622
Nyswanger, Marie, 67

O'Brien, G. E., 716
Ochroch, Ruth, 235
O'Connell, R., 176
Odegaard, O., 625
Ogborne, Alan C., 86
Ohlin, Lloyd E., 69
Oldershaw, L., 353
Olds, Dvid L., 357
O'Leary, K., 190
O'Leary, Michael R., 81, 90
Olin, H. S., 681
Oliver, 369
Olmstead, Kathleen A., 387
Olsen, L. J., 9, 352
O'Neal, Jeanine M., 289
Opton, E. M., 148

Orbach, S., 212
Ordman, A., 209
Orford, Jim, 66
Orley, J., 178
Orton, 235
Osterweis, M., 448–49
Ostow, M., 681
Overall, J., 175
Overmier, J., 170

Packer, A., 619
Page, A. W., 480, 487, 488, 492
Pagelow, M. D., 473
Painter, S. L., 479, 480, 481
Palacios-Jimenez, Luis, 36
Palmer, R., 208, 214
Palombo, J., 102, 103, 104, 107-8, 116
Paradise, Frank, 36
Parke, R. D., 350
Parker, G., 182, 194
Parkes, C. M., 454, 455
Parmelee, A. H., 270
Parry, G., 180
Passell, P., 6
Pastalan, L. A., 532
Patrick, C. H., 142
Patsiokas, A. T., 686, 698
Patten, S. K., 515
Patterson, Gerald R., 353, 354
Pattison, E. Mansell, 66, 78, 80
Patton, D., 177
Patton, Lary T., 598
Pauls, D., 180
Paykel, E. S., 174, 177, 181, 685, 687
Pearlin, L., 177, 180
Peele, Stanton, 66
Pelton, Leroy H., 352
Pepper, Bert, 297, 300
Pepper, M., 172
Perkins, H. Wesley, 76
Perrin, J. M., 138, 139, 140, 141, 142, 143, 145
Perrucci, C. C., 711
Persico, Joseph, 386
Peto, J., 181
Pettyjohn, 143
Pfohl, B., 187
Pfouts, J. H., 477
Pianta, Robert C., 351
Pickens, Roy, 74
Piliavin, Irving, 595
Pine, F., 106
Pine, V., 453
Pines, Maya, 237

Pinkerton, P., 138
Pinkston, E. M., 562, 565
Pirog-Good, M., 484
Pittman, Karen, 10, 11, 325
Pless, I. B., 138
Polansky, Norman A., 349, 351, 352, 366, 369
Pollock, C., 352
Polster, Richard A., 359
Pomeranz, D. M., 695
Pope, H., 223, 301
Post, R., 181
Potter, C., 663
Poussaint, A. F., 685
Powell, E., 7
Prather, R., 207
Pratt, C. C., 560
Price, Richard H., 356
Price, Richard W., 44
Prochaska, James O., 82
Prusoff, B., 12, 177, 180
Przybeck, Thoms R., 65, 73
Pyle, R., 210, 215

Quayhagen, M., 560, 581
Quayhagen, M. P., 560, 581
Quitkin, F., 109

Radloff, L., 179
Rado, Sandor, 68
Raffel, M., 716
Ragan, P., 182
Rainer, J., 3, 172
Rando, T., 449, 450, 452, 453, 454, 460
Raphael, B., 448, 454
Rappucci, N. D., 351
Rathbone-McCuan, E., 521, 524
Rauch, J., 4, 31
Ray, Oakley, 67
Redburn, F. S., 711, 715
Redfield, Robert R., 43
Redlich, F., 4
Reed, W., 25
Reever, K. E., 565
Regier, T., 175, 178, 179, 183, 195
Rehin, A., 685
Reich, J., 189
Reich, M., 712
Reich, Theodore, 76
Reid, J. B., 353, 354, 516
Reimherr, F. W., 111
Reiss, Douglas, 118, 298, 299, 304
Reker, G. T., 517
Renzetti, C. M., 472

Resnick, Patricia, 417
Resnik, H. L. P., 681
Reuter, Jeanette, 365
Rhodes, G. B., 714
Rice, D. P., 142
Rice, J., 175
Rich, J. C., 523
Richan, W. C., 715
Richman, J., 685
Rie, H., 275
Rifkin, A., 109
Rigler, D., 352
Rinsley, 105-6
Risse, Guenter B., 37
Ritter, David R., 249
Roberts, A. R., 483, 486, 488
Roberts, R., 567
Robertson, Marjorie J., 588
Robins, Lee N., 65, 71, 73
Rodgers, W., 527
Rodin, J., 211, 215
Rogers, David E., 35
Rogers, Ronald L., 66
Rolland, J. S., 143, 146
Ron, Aran, 35
Room, Robin, 12, 74
Rorhbaugh, M., 118
Rose, S., 712, 713
Rosen, Jacqueline, 331
Rosenbaum, M., 180-81, 685
Rosenberg, Charles E., 37
Rosenberg, D., 351
Rosenberg, M. S., 351
Rosenblatt, P. C., 461
Rosenfeld, Jona, 389
Rosenwaike, I., 503
Rosewater, L. B., 480
Rossi, Peter H., 586
Rossiter, C., 558, 559, 564, 567
Roth, D., 588
Roth, W., 138
Rothenberg, A., 210
Rotheram-Borus, M. J., 687
Rothgery, J., 186
Rothman, D., 623
Rothman, S., 623
Rounds, Kathleen A., 35
Rounsaville, B., 76, 177, 190
Roy, A., 181, 687
Roy-Byrne, P., 221
Rozin, P., 211
Rubenstein, R., 686
Rubin, A., 571
Rubin, Lenore, 588, 595

Rubinow, D., 181
Ruestow, P., 174
Runyan, D. K., 274
Ruocchio, Patricia J., 302
Rush, A., 187
Russell, G., 215, 223
Russell, M. B., 144
Russo, Sally, 345
Rutter, M., 181, 355
Ryan, Caitlin C., 36
Ryback, R., 523
Rzepnicki, Tina L., 393, 399
Rzetelny, H., 517


Sack, A., 520, 521
Salem, Deborah A., 301
Salisbury, J., 221
Saltz, C., 189
Sanders, C., 448, 453
Sandler, Jack, 360
Sandmaier, Marian, 74
Sangl, J., 11, 514, 525, 552, 556, 558
Sangrey, Dawn, 417, 436, 437
Saperstein, A. R., 559, 562, 563
Sauber, M., 628
Saunders, D. G., 478, 484, 490
Saunders, R., 211
Schechter, S., 472, 473, 479, 486, 487, 490
Scherer, Shawn E., 75, 76
Schiefer, A. Ward, 523
Schildkraut, J., 173
Schilling, Robert F., 256
Schinderman, J. L., 480, 486, 488, 492
Schinke, Stephen, 322, 332
Schlenger, W. E., 657
Schlesinger, 369
Schlesser, M., 189
Schmeck, H. M., Jr., 4
Schmidt, G. L., 569
Shneider-Rosen, Karen, 353
Schuckit, M., 190
Schultz, R., 517
Schulz, P. M., 118
Schulz, S. C., 109-10, 115
Schuster, Charles R., 74, 75
Schuyler, D., 679
Schwab-Bakman, N., 187
Schwartz, D., 212
Schwartz, Gary E., 81
Schwartz, M., 179
Schwartz, W., 526, 527
Scrimshaw, N. S., 273

Secord, P., 212
Segal, Steven P., 72
Seligman, M., 11, 170, 509, 517, 518, 717, 729
Sells, S. B., 80
Seltzer, G. B., 504, 524
Seltzer, Marsha Mailick, 393, 560, 565
Selvini-Palazzoli, M., 209
Selzer, Marvin L., 82
Senak, Mark, 43, 51
Sgroi, Suzanne M., 355
Shaffer, D., 681, 683, 686, 687, 688, 690, 705
Shah, Faridah, 324
Shanas, E., 513, 551, 552
Shanfield, S. B., 448
Shapiro, D., 180
Shapiro, R., 187
Sheehan, L., 286
Shepard, P., 523
Sherman, B., 189
Sherman, Barry R., 357
Sherman, M. E., 649
Shernoff, Michael, 36, 42
Shields, Nancy M., 595
Shiffman, Saul, 85
Shilts, Randy, 35
Shinn, Eugene, 386, 392, 394, 401
Shneidman, E. S., 679, 681, 685
Short, J. F., 680
Shulman, L., 221, 531
Shulman, Shmuel, 254
Siegel, R., 177
Sigvardsson, Soren, 3, 75
Silber, T., 214
Silberstein, L., 211, 215
Silver, Larry B., 234, 238, 239, 242, 246, 251, 253
Silverman, B., 727, 731
Silverstone, B., 571
Simon, B. L., 712
Simon, J., 624
Simpson, J. A., 505
Singh, B., 448
Skinner, A., 9, 351
Skinner, Harvey A., 82, 88
Small, Leonard, 234, 238, 239
Smith, G. C., 560, 561, 564, 569
Smith, J., 713
Smith, P., 686
Smith, S. M., 352
Smith, Sally L., 241, 250, 251
Smith, Steven, 423
Snowden, L., 628

Snyder, Mitch, 586
Sobell, Linda C., 66
Sobell, Mark B., 66
Soldo, B. J., 551
Soloff, P. H., 114, 115, 116
Solomon, B. B., 519
Solomon, F., 448-49
Solomon, R., 523
Solomon, Susan D., 80
Solomos, J., 712
Sonsel, George E., 36
Sontag, Susan, 35, 37
Sosin, Michael, 595
Spanier, G., 365
Spaniol, Leroy, 292
Sperbeck, D. J., 560
Spiegel, D., 182
Spiegler, Danielle L., 75
Spiker, D., 177, 178
Spinetta, J. J., 353, 352
Spring, G., 186
Sroufe, L. A., 353, 354
Staats, A. W., 682
Stack, C., 715
Stanford, 558
Stanton, M. Duncan, 81
Star, B., 481, 484
Starfield, B., 143
Stark, J., 271
Starr, Raymond H., Jr., 351, 353
Steele, B. J., 352
Stein, B., 619
Stein, Theodore, 367, 399
Steinberg, R. M., 571
Steiner, C. M., 22
Steiner, M., 115
Steinmetz, S. K., 346, 472, 473, 474, 475, 477
Stengel, E., 681
Stephens, M. P. P., 560, 561
Stets-Kealey, J., 484
Steun, C., 532
Stevens, E., 221
Stevens-Long, J. E., 353
Stiffman, Arlene Rubin, 3, 295
Stone, M. H., 101, 103, 108, 109, 112, 113, 114, 124, 125
Stone, R., 11, 514, 525, 552, 556, 558
Stoner, Madeline R., 593
Straus, Murray A., 5, 8, 346–47, 348, 350, 352, 356, 471, 472, 473, 475, 477, 479, 480
Strauss, A., 143, 146, 147, 148
Strauss, Alfred, 235-36

Straussner, Shulamith Lala Ashenberg, 77
Striegel-Moore, R., 211, 215
Strober, M., 209
Strole, L., 4
Strosahl, K. D., 686
Stroup, Stephen, 36
Strube, M. J., 480
Struening, Elmer L., 588, 592
Stuart, R., 221
Stuckey, M., 221
Stulberg, Ian, 50
Stunkard, A., 213, 216, 217
Style, C., 180
Sue, S., 75
Sughandabhirom, B., 638, 634
Sullivan, J., 190
Sullivan, Mercer, 321
Sussman, E. J., 353
Sutton, M., 451
Swain, B. J., 448
Swan, J. S., 509
Swenson, C., 23
Switalski, T., 182
Syme, S. Leonard, 72
Szapocznik, J., 634
Szasz, T., 691

Taintor, Z., 179
Tan, E., 686
Tarter, Ralph E., 73, 354
Tatara, Toshio, 384
Taylor, J. W., 491
Taylor, Linda, 242
Taylor, R. J., 519, 554
Taylor, W. H., 554
Teasdale, J., 178
Tennant, C., 176, 181
Teplin, L., 657
Terkel, S., 716
Terkelsen, K. G., 149, 150
Tertinger, Deborah A., 362
Teska, J., 280
Thibault, J. W., 477
Thoits, P., 180
Thomas, A., 237
Thomlison, R., 220
Thompson, K., 716
Thompson, M., 212
Thoren, P., 681
Thwing, Edward, 365
Tienda, M., 622, 624
Timms, N., 24

Tobin, S. S., 506, 508, 509, 517, 519, 520, 521, 560, 569
Toch, Hans, 647, 648, 649
Todman, P. A., 628
Tonti, M., 571
Topel, H., 3
Torgersen, S., 186
Torres, S., 475
Toseland, R. W., 519, 520, 558, 559, 560, 561, 564, 567, 569
Traskman, L., 681
Treas, J., 526
Trieschmann, R., 504
Troutman, P. D., 687
Truss, Tom J., 247, 248, 249
Tuckman, J., 685
Tung, T. M., 638, 641, 642
Tupling, H., 182, 194
Turkelson, Kenneth, 302
Turnbull, J., 177, 184, 190
Turner, R., 182
Twentyman, C. T., 353, 354

Uohara, Betsy, 358

Vaglum, P., 187
Vaglum, S., 187
Valle, J. R., 625
Vance, E., 12
VanGorp, Wilford G., 47
VanValkenberg, C., 182, 185, 186, 189
Varkof, A., 3
Vasaly, Shirley, 386
Vaughan, C., 178
Vega, W., 625
Vergare, M. J., 588
Veronen, Lois, 417
Viano, Emilio, 417
Videka-Sherman, Lynn, 349, 358-59
Volkan, V. D., 124
Voydanoff, P., 711, 715

Wahler, Robert G., 351
Waldinger, R. J., 101, 113, 122, 123, 124, 126
Walker, D. Loiver, 520
Walker, Gillian, 45, 50
Walker, L. E., 480, 488
Walkover, M., 139
Wallace, John, 3, 73, 76
Wallace, K. M.,, 365

Wallack, S. S., 520
Walsh, B., 223
Walsh, C., 678
Walsh, J. Michael, 66
Walsh, Joseph, 302, 303
Walter, G. C., 353
Walters, Leroy, 43
Wandrei, K. E., 681, 685, 691
Waring, E., 177
Warr, P. B., 711, 715
Warshafsky, L., 472
Washton, Arnold M., 74
Waterman, C. K., 472
Watkins, 722
Watkins, T. R., 554
Watson, W. H., 554
Wauchope, Barbara A., 346, 348, 352
Weakland, J. H., 565
Weibel, Joan Crofut, 75
Weidman, A., 491
Weiner, E. S. C., 505
Weiner, Lori, 48
Weiner, Z., 175
Weinstein, David, 394
Weismann, M., 177
Weiss, Heather B., 183, 356
Weiss, J. O., 145
Weiss, Myra, 361-62, 366
Weiss, R., 491
Weissbourd, B., 356
Weissman, A., 681, 687
Weissman, M., 11, 12, 166, 174, 175,
    177, 178, 179, 180, 187, 190, 684, 686
Weissman, W., 354
Weizmann, S., 450
Wemberly, R. C., 9, 351, 353
Wender, P., 3, 172
Wender, Paul H., 111, 246, 248, 252
Werble, B., 103
Westermeyer, J., 73, 627
Westoff, Charles, 319
Wetzel, R. D., 686, 687
Wexler, L., 684
Whalley, L., 179
White, R. W., 527, 716
White, W., 221
Whitty, S. M., 449
Widom, Cathy Spatz, 347
Wijnberg, M. H., 713
Wilcox, B., 177
Wilcox, S. G., 451
Wilhelm, S., 7
Wilkes, J., 648
Williams, C. L., 629

Williams, D. M., 270
Williams, Lena, 41
Williams, T., 190
Williamson, D., 207
Wills, Thomas Ashby, 85
Wilsnack, Richard W., 77
Wilsnack, Sharon C., 77
Wilson, A. J. E., 520
Wilson, C., 208, 219
Wilson, J. Q., 10, 652, 655
Wilson, R. H., 715
Wilson, S. K., 481
Wilson, V., 512, 525
Wilson, William C., 234, 235, 236, 251
Wilson, William Julius, 73
Wiltse, K., 367
Wing, J. K., 299
Winick, Charles, 74
Winokur, G., 74, 188, 189, 448
Wintersteen, Richard T., 312
Wishart, Margaret, 651, 654, 659
Wissler, T., 182
Wold, P., 209
Wolf, Joan S., 242
Wolfe, David, 352, 353, 354, 359, 360,
    367
Wolfe, L. C., 458
Wolman, B., 217
Wong, H., 638
Wong, P. T. P., 517
Wood, D. R., 111
Wood, J. L., 516
Wood, Katherin M., 348
Woodrow, R., 716, 723
Woodside, Migs, 76
Woodward, A., 175
Worden, J. W., 452
Wright, James D., 589
Wyers, N. L., 511
Wylie, Mary S., 72
Wyman, E., 480, 488

Yablonsky, Lewis, 79
Yager, J., 221
Yalom, I. D., 121
Yllo, K., 472
Youket, P., 520
Young, J. G., 109
Young, R. N., 562, 565
Youngman, W. F., 685
Yudkovitz, E., 222

Zabin, Laurie, 324
Zane, N., 75

Zanguillo, P., 652
Zarit, S., 564
Zeigler, Robert, 256
Zeiss, A., 563, 564
Zelnik, Melvin, 323, 324, 325
Zhukov, U., 3
Ziegenhagen, Eduard, 422

Zigler, Edward, 183, 350, 356
Zimmerman, M., 187
Zinberg, Norman E., 71
Zipple, Anthony M., 292
Zucker, Robert A., 71
Zuckerman, M., 72
Zung, W., 189

# Subject Index

▼

AA (Alcoholics Anonymous), 77-78
Abandoned children, 382
Absence of parents, and foster care, 384
Abstinence: in addiction, 68, 86, 87; obesity and, 221; sexual, 321
Abuse, definitions, 346, 472-73; see also Children, maltreatment of; Domestic violence
Abusive families, 9, 353-54; programs for, 359-61; see also Children, maltreatment of; Domestic violence
Abusive relationships: homelessness and, 593; in family caregiving, 550
Academic performance: adolescent pregnancy and, 320, 333; adolescent sexual activity and, 330; childhood maltreatment and, 354; of foster care children, 393
Acceptance of help, in chronic illness, 147
Accidental death of child, 452
Accountability issues, 26-27
Achondroplasia, 150-63
Acquired causes of mental retardation, 268-70
Acquired immune deficiency syndrome, see AIDS
Action, borderline personalities and, 122
Action methods of teaching, 23
Action tasks, in coping, 25-26

Acute care hospitals, AIDS patients in, 45-46
Adaptations, 533; in family caregiving, 558; of homeless women, 593-94
Adaptive functioning, 72
Adaptive mechanisms, slow, 250-51
Adaptive problem-solving, for suicidal persons, 699-700
Addiction, 10, 12, 65-100; and borderline personality, 101; and homelessness, 588, 610; of jail inmates, 665, 667; and job jeopardy, 714; of prison inmates, 659-61, 669-73; workplace programs for, 722; see also Alcoholism; Substance abuse
Adolescent mothers, 10, 332-33; child-maltreatment prevention, 356, 357
"Adolescent Pregnancy," Armstrong, 319-44
Adolescents, 11-12, 338; addicts, 71-73, 76-77; disabled, 159-60; disturbed, in foster care, 405; girls, eating disorders of, 208; interparental violence and, 481; learning disabled, 254, 255, 250, 259-60; minority, unemployment of, 717; obese, 210, 213, 216-17, 222-23; and parenthood, 341-42; prison inmates, 654; Russian immigrants, 636; sexuality of, adult attitudes toward, 321; suicide of, 687-88, 690
—pregnant, 10, 13, 319-44; and border-

Adolescents (*Continued*)
line personality, 101; and mental retardation of infant, 270
Adoption, 383, 393; decision factors, 404-5; of foster care children, 384; services, 395; studies, 210, 237
Adoption Assistance and Child Welfare Act (1980), 390, 391
Adoptive family homes, 396
Adult children, caregiving for parents, 557-58; *see also* Family caregivers
Adult day care, 521, 524-25
Adulthood, feared by anorexic girls, 208
Adult-onset obesity, 210
Adults: disabled, 140, 141, 143; learning-disabled, 242, 244, 250, 255-56
Advertising, and social problems, 8-9
Advice, from social workers, 24
Advocacy, 20; for adolescent parent, 328, 333, 341; for AIDS victims, 46; for battered women, 484, 487, 497; for crime victims, 420, 424, 429-30, 431, 438, 440-41, 444; for frail old people, 542; for homeless people, 599, 615
Aerosol pentamidine, 44
AFDC, *see* Aid to Families with Dependent Children
Affective dimension of depression, 165
Affective disorders, 16, 168-69; age of onset, 179; and borderline personality, 109, 110, 117, 124; and eating disorders, 209, 210; genetic factors, 172; and marital problems, 177-78; and suicide, 687; *see also* Depression
Affirmation stage of chronic illness, 147
Africa, HIV strain, 40
African-Americans, *see* Blacks
Age: of abused children, 347; and alcoholic relapse, 84; of child, and parental grief, 453; of child abusers, 348; and chronic illness, 142; and depression risk, 179, 180; and domestic violence, 475; of first sexual activity, 324; and job insecurity, 721; and major depressive disorder, 187; of mother, and mental retardation of infant, 270; and risk, 12; and substance abuse, 73-74; and suicide, 684-85; *see also* Age of on-

set; Adolescents; Frail old people; Old people
Age-based programs, 510, 522
Ageism, 508-11, 541
Agency-operated boarding homes, 396
Age of onset: of eating disorders, 214, 215; of mental retardation, 266; of schizophrenia, 294
Aggression: of children, interparental violence and, 481; domestic violence and, 480; medication for, 116
"Aging enterprise," 510
Aging of population, 554
"AIDS," Getzel, 35-64
AIDS (acquired immune deficiency syndrome), 7, 11, 35-36, 451; addiction and, 65-66; and adolescent pregnancy, 319; children with, 270; and child welfare, 389; clinical assessments and interventions, 46-53; genetic factors, 3; in prisons, 662-64; problem domain, 36-38; programs and services, 44-46; risks and needs of population, 40-44; service deficiencies, 139; societal context, 38-39
Aid to Families with Dependent Children (AFDC), 140, 319; and homelessness, 592-93; for refugees, 621
Airplane crashes, death of children, 452
Alabama, prison inmates with AIDS, 663
Alcohol Dependence Scale (ADS), 88
Alcoholics Anonymous (AA), 77-78
Alcoholism, 4, 12, 65-66; and child maltreatment, 352; and depression, 189, 190; and domestic violence, 9, 478, 488; and eating disorders, 206, 209, 210, 215; family history, 75-77; fetal effects, 269; genetic factors, 3; and homelessness, 588, 609; imprisonment and, 653-54; and job jeopardy, 729; and minor depressive disorders, 186; and obesity, 226, 227; of parent, and foster care, 405-6; problem domain, 66-70; risks and needs of population, 73-77; societal context, 71-72; and suicide, 687; workplace programs, 722; *see also* Addiction
"Alcoholism and Other Drug Addictions," Hanson, 65-100
Allergies, behavior and, 239

Almshouses, 518
Alternative placement for addicted jail inmates, 660-61
Alternatives: development of, 23; in problem-solving, 699, 702
Altruistic suicide, 680
Alzheimer's disease, 517, 531, 558, 562; genetic factors, 4; support group for caregivers, 573-74
Ambivalence in relationship, domestic violence and, 488, 492
American Association for Protecting Children, 390
American Association on Mental Deficiency, 265-66
American Human Association (AHA), child protective services reports, 346-48
American Public Welfare Association, 383
Amish people, depression among, 172
Amitriptyline (Elavil), 115
Amnestic disorders, 83
Amnesty program for undocumented aliens, 622-23
Amphetamines, borderline personality and, 109-10
Analytic theory, and suicide, 680
Anger: at AIDS diagnosis, 49; and child maltreatment, 352; depression and, 167; domestic violence and, 480, 488
Anhedonia, 184
Anhedonic alcoholics, 3
Anomic suicide, 680
Anorexia nervosa, 3, 9, 11, 205-12; assessments and interventions, 224-25; counseling for, 218-22; health problems, 217-18; hospitalization for, 223; medication for, 223; risk factors, 213-14
Anticipatory mourning of family caregivers, 557
Anticipatory planning by young parents, 340
Anticonvulsants, 115, 132
Antidepressant medication, 187-88; for borderline personality, 109; bulimia nervosa and, 223
Antidiscrimination laws, 140, 141
Antipsychotic drugs, 236
Antisocial behavior, learning disabilities and, 255
Antisocial personality disorders: alco-

holism and, 74; among prison inmates, 657
Anxiety, domestic violence and, 480
Apathy-futility syndrome, and child maltreatment, 352
Approach-avoidance response to AIDS diagnosis, 55
Armstrong, Bruce, "Adolescent Pregnancy," 319-44
Arrest for domestic violence, 490
Asia, HIV strain, 40
Asian-Americans, 75
Asphyxia, and birth defects, 269-70
Assertiveness: and domestic violence, 488; old people and, 508
Assertiveness training, 22, 187; for addicts, 81; and job jeopardy, 745; for terminated workers, 731
Assessments, 15-26; of addictions, 81-88; of adolescent pregnancy, 329-33; of AIDS patients, 46-53; of bereaved families, 457-61, 463; of borderline personality, 114-26; of child maltreatment, 363-69; of chronic illness and disability, 145-50; of crime victims, 432-38; of depression, 174, 184-91; of domestic violence, 485-95, 499; of eating disorders, 218, 224-26, 229; of family caregivers, 566-72; of foster care situation, 398-408; of frail old people, 526-32; of homeless people, 605-11; of immigrants, 628-38; of job jeopardy, 717, 725-33, 737-40; of learning disabilities, 244, 245-51; of mental retardation, 278-81; of prison inmates, 665-68, 670, 673; of schizophrenia, 301-6; of suicidal behavior, 677-78; of suicide risk, 679, 690-95, 703
Assistance for crime victims, 429-30
Assortative mating, 178, 180
Asylees, 621
Attachment disturbances in maltreating families, 353
Attempted suicide, 678, 683, 684-85; *see also* Parasuicide
Attention deficit disorders, 104, 110, 116, 238, 247; and borderline personality, 115; and learning disability, 254
Attitudes toward adolescent sexuality, 321
Attribution theory of depression, 171

Auditory perception, problems of, 247
Australia, HIV strain, 40
Autism, 236
Automobile accidents, 8
Autonomy: of AIDS victims, 56-57; of battered wives, 492-93, 497; borderline personality and, 122; of disabled child, 155-56; and domestic violence, 488; eating disorders and, 208; in family care for old people, 570, 572; learning disabilities and, 254; of old people, 528-29, 536; of women, men and, 476-77
Aversive conditioning, for addiction, 69
AZT (Azidodeoxythimidine), 44

Balance, problems with, 246
Basic skills: and adolescent parenthood, 325; and adolescent pregnancy, 320, 323; of maltreated child, 365
Battered husbands, 473
Battered women, 5, 8, 419, 471, 478-80, 482, 483-84; homeless, 593; *see also* Domestic violence
Bayley Scales of Infant Development, 266
Beauty, physical, standards of, 207, 211
Bedridden old people, 516; *see also* Family caregivers
Behavior: addictive, 81, 83; of borderline personality, 129-30; brain function and, 236-37; causing job jeopardy, 714; determinants, 235; of homeless people, 591-92; of learning disabled people, 247-48, 250-51; of prison inmates, 655; risk factors of parasuicide, 687; Southeast Asian views, 641
—change of: HIV avoidance, 42; jail inmates and, 668
—problems of: brain damage and, 236; childhood maltreatment and, 354; of children, interparental violence and, 481
Behavioral counseling: for anorexia, 219; for depression, 190; for obesity, 220, 226
Behavioral dyscontrol, 115-16
Behavior management skills, for family caregivers, 561-62

Behavior theory: of depression, 170; and group counseling for borderline personalities, 121
Behavior therapy: dialectical, 120; for suicidal behavior, 125
Beliefs, adolescent, about sex, 330
Benefit programs: for homeless people, 608, 613; for mentally ill people, 609
Benzodiazepines (Valium), 115
Bereavement groups, AIDS-related, 53
Bereavement, 166, 168, 186, 447-52; rituals of, 450-51
—of parents, 452-54; assessments and interventions, 457-61; case illustration, 462-67; counseling for, 455-56; programs and services for, 455-56
Berman-Rossi, Toby, "Elderly in Need of Long-Term Care," 503-48
Bias, toward old people, 508
Binge eating, 206, 225; *see also* Bulimia nervosa
Biochemical dysfunction, 239
Biological factors: in borderline personality, 104-5, 106, 108-10, 116-17, 118; in depression, 172-74, 187; in suicide, 681
Biology of AIDS, 42
Biopsychosocial approaches: to addictions, 70, 81, 92; to AIDS, 36-38; to depression, 173-76; to schizophrenia, 290
Bipolar disorder, 166, 168, 181; age of onset, 179; risk factors, 179-80; and suicide, 687; *see also* Depression
Birth, HIV transmission, 42
Birth control, 10; *see also* Contraception
Birth defects, 4, 269
Birth injuries, and mental retardation, 269
Birth rates, 11, 324
Bisexual men, HIV infections, 40
Black, Rita Beck, "Chronic Physical Illness and Disability," 137-64
Blacks: adolescent pregnancy, 322-25; affective disorders, 179; AIDS infections, 41; body weight, 216; chronic illnesses, 143; drug use patterns, 74-75; eating disorders, 214; elderly, 512, 514, 516, 532-41, 554; health problems, 7; homeless young people, 594; prison inmates, 10, 652-53; social supports, 518-19; and

suicide, 684, 685; unemployed, 7, 717

Blame, in job jeopardy, 731

Blood products, and HIV infection, 40-41, 42

Body fluid exchange, AIDS and, 42

Body image, 211-13; disturbed, 208-9, 217; eating disorders and, 210-11; obesity and, 213

Borderline personality, 3, 4, 101; assessments and interventions, 114-26; case illustration, 126-32; minor depressive disorders and, 187; problem domain, 102-11; programs and services, 113-14; risks and needs of population, 112-13; societal context, 111-12; and suicidal behavior, 701

"Borderline Personality," Johnson and Goguen, 101-36

Borderline Personality Disorder, DSM-III-R category, 103

Borderline Personality Organization, Kernberg, 103-4

Boys: and interparental violence, 481; self-esteem, 207; *see also* Males; Men

Brace, Charles Loring, 383

Brain damage, 239; behavior and, 236; and borderline personality, 110; from child abuse, 273-74; mental retardation and, 266

Brain function, behavior and, 235

Brantley, Dale M., "Mental Retardation," 265-85

Breast feeding, HIV transmission, 42

Broken homes, bulimia and, 215

Buddy programs: AIDS-related, 45, 53; for families of schizophrenics, 300

Bulimia nervosa, 3, 9, 11, 205-12, 218; assessments and interventions, 225; counseling for, 219, 221, 222; hospitalization for, 223; medication for, 223; risk factors, 214-15

Bureau of Child Welfare, 654

Burial ceremonies, 450

California, crime-victim-compensation bill, 423

Cambodian immigrants, 630, 639-43

Camus, Albert, *The Plague,* 61

Canada, HIV strain, 40

Cancer: death rates, 11; genetic factors, 4; poverty and, 7-8

Capitalism, and job insecurity, 711

Capital punishment, 420, 431

Carbamazepine (Tegretol), 115

Career counseling for adolescents, 327

Caregivers: for abused children, 347, 348; AIDS patients and, 52-53, 60-61; for chronic illness, 150; for frail old people, 11, 549-79

Care receivers (old people), 552; longevity of, 554; emotions of, 559-60

Caretaking abilities, support of, 145

Caring environment, for old people, 540

Carlson, Bonnie E., "Domestic Violence," 471-502

Carter, Jimmy, and immigrants, 621

Case illustrations, 26-27; addiction, 87-92; adolescent pregnancy, 333-41; AIDS, 46-47, 53-61; borderline personality, 126-32; child maltreatment, 369-75; chronic illness and disability, 150-63; crime victims, 439-44; death of child, 462-67; depression, 191-95; domestic violence, 493-99; eating disorders, 226-29; family care of frail old people, 572-79; foster care, 405-12; frail old people, 532-41; homelessness, 611-15; immigration, 639-43; job jeopardy, 733-45; learning disabilities, 257-60; mental retardation, 281-83; schizophrenia, 306-12; suicidal behavior, 700-4

Caseloads, AIDS effect on, 45

Case management: for adolescent parents, 328; for AIDS victims, 46; for child maltreatment, 368, 370, 374; by family caregivers, 560, 565-66; for family caregivers, 555; foster care, 403; for jail inmates, 666; for old people, 571-72

Case planning, foster care, 391, 400-5

Case status of criminal prosecution, 434-35

Catholic mourning traditions, 464

Causes: of crime, 417; of depression, 171; of domestic violence, perceptions of, 473-74; of homelessness, 587, 595; of learning disabilities, 238-39; of mental retardation, 268

Cell space for inmates, 655

Centers for Disease Control (CDC), AIDS estimates, 40

Central American immigrants, services for, 623-24

Central nervous system, delayed development, 239

Cerebral palsy, 270, 272

Change: battered women and, 486; stresses of, 15-16

Characteristics: of abusive persons, 478; of addict population, 67; of borderline personality, 101, 102, 103-4, 110; of bulimics, 215; of crime victims, 425; of depressed persons, 179-80, 187; of family caregivers, 552-53, 568; of foster care children, 385, 392; of learning disabilities, 247-48, 250; of maltreating families, 347-48, 352, 364; of obese persons, 213, 216-17; of prison inmates, 655; of suicidal persons, 686, 693-94; of wife-batterers, 494

Characterization by disease status, 139

Chemical dependency, *see* Addiction

Chemical imbalances, genetically induced, 3

Chestnut Lodge, therapy outcome study, 124-25

Child abuse: and borderline personality, 101; among Haitians, 637; prevention programs, 13; victim compensation, 424; *see also* Children, maltreatment of

"Child Abuse and Neglect," Videka-Sherman, 345-81

Child Abuse Potential Inventory (CAPI), 366

Child Abuse Prevention and Treatment Act (1974), 345, 390

Childbearing, age of, and child maltreatment, 352

Child care: for adolescent parents, 323, 328, 332; for battered women, 484; institutions, 396; personnel, 403; supplementary services, 395

Childhood development, psycholanalytic views, 235

Childhood trauma, depression and, 167, 181-82

Child neglect, 346, 348, 350-51, 359; *see also* Children, maltreatment of

Child Protective Services (CPS) reports, 346-47

Children: abandoned, 382; of adolescent mothers, 10; adult, home shared by parents, 512-13; assessment for welfare services, 399-400; chronically ill, 142, 143; death of, 447-68; of depressed parents, 175, 180; and domestic violence, 477, 479, 481, 491, 494-95, 497-98; of female prison inmates, 654; and foster care, 383-87, 392-412; handicapped, 140, 141, 271; HIV-infected, 41; hyperactive, 247-48, 251-52; immigrants, unaccompanied, 627; learning-disabled, 234-42, 249-50, 254-55; maltreated, 354, 364-65; obese, 216-17, 223, 226; poverty of, 6-7, 10-11, 13, 389; resilient to maltreatment, 355; of schizophrenic parents, 294-95; having siblings with AIDS, 45; undocumented aliens, 628

—maltreatment of, 8, 9, 345-75; domestic violence and, 481; and foster care, 384, 393, 405-6; and mental retardation, 273-74; reports of, 390-91; *see also* Domestic violence

"Children in Foster Care," McGowan and Stutz, 382-415

Children's Aid Society, New York, 383

Children's Defense Fund, 384

Children's Home Society, 383

Child welfare services, 399; AIDS-related, 52; early, 412; and learning disabilities, 244

Chromosomal abnormalities, 268

Chronic and intermittent depressive disorder, 166, 168

Chronic disabilities, of old people, 551, 552

Chronic dysphoria, 168, 186, 187

Chronic illness, 3, 137-63, 515, 516, 549-50; mental, 597-98, 657

"Chronic Physical Illness and Disability," Black and Weiss, 137-64

Chronic sorrow, 448, 461, 467

Chronic unemployment, 717-18

Chronic violence, 489-90

Church-based immigrant services, 623-24

Church basement programs, 601

Citizen's Committee for Children, 599

Civil courts, 422

Classes, new, 584

Classification systems: of addictions, 83; of suicide, 680

Clearinghouse on Child Abuse and Neglect Information, 347

Clients, workers as, 725-30
Client self-destruction, domestic violence and, 492-93
Clinical neurobiologists, 313
Clinical programs for depression, 182
Clinical services, effective, 87
Clinics, for adolescents, 326-27, 331
Cocaine, 65, 73, 74-75; and eating disorders, 206; fetal effects, 269; and homelessness, 588
Codependents, and addictions, 86
Coercive control, 472
Cognitive-behavioral counseling for eating disorders, 219, 224
Cognitive defects: attention disorders and, 238; learning disabilities, 251
Cognitive function of battered woman, 486
Cognitive psychotherapy: for addiction, 69; for depression, 187, 188, 190
Cognitive risk factors for suicidal behavior, 686
Cognitive strategies for depression, 193-94
Cognitive theories: of depression, 170; of suicide, 681
Cohabiting relationships; *see* Couple relationships
Cohesive groups, and borderline personalities, 122
Collaboration: in social work, 20; in workplace, 732
Colonial America: alcoholism, 66-67; crime victims, 422
Columbia, South Carolina, homeless women, 593
Common-law relationships, domestic violence in, 472
Communication patterns, analysis of, 22
Communication skills, teaching of, 23
Communication with immigrants, by interpreter, 640-41
Communities, of immigrants, 623, 627
Community assessment, for prevention of child maltreatment, 366
Community-based programs and services: for adolescents, 327-28; AIDS related, 44, 53-61; for chronic illness and disability, 144-45; for families of maltreated children, 355-63; family caregivers and, 570; for former prison inmates, 673; foster

care and, 398; for immigrants, 627, 639-43; for mental illness, 597; for old people, 521, 532; for prison inmates, 664-65; for schizophrenia, 293, 296, 300-1
Community dysfunctions, 4-5
Community living, skills for, 609
Community Mental Health Act (1963), 597
Community mental health care facilities, and former prison inmates, 659
Community organizations for immigrants, 624
Community supports: for former prison inmates, 673; and job insecurity, 715
Comorbidity, 189
Compassionate Friends, 456
Compensation for crime victims, 423, 439, 444; programs, 417, 420, 424, 435
Competence, professional, evaluation of, 26-27
Competition, mental retardation and, 271
Composition of crime, 421
Compulsive behaviors, workplace programs for, 722
Concrete supports of homeless people, 608
Concrete thinking, suicide and, 692
Condoms, 322
Confidentiality of information: about handicapped children, 271; and job jeopardy programs, 732-33
Conjoint counseling: for depression, 190; for domestic violence, 490-91
Consciousness-raising groups, 423
Consequences: of child maltreatment, 354-55; of domestic violence, 479-82; of early parenthood, 341-42; of suicidal behavior, 688-89; of violent crime, 426-27
Conservative politics: and homelessness, 589-90; and victims' rights, 424, 444
Consultants, social workers as, 570-71, 572, 574
Consultation by social workers, 191; for suicide prevention, 691
Content therapy for abusive families, 360-61

Contingency management for addiction, 69
Continuity, sense of, for children in foster care, 401
Contraception: access to, 321, 331; adolescent attitudes to, 330; information about, 322; used by adolescents, 321-22, 324, 338
Contracts: for alcoholism, 89-91; child maltreatment prevention, 367, 372, 374; foster care placement, 400-1; for job jeopardy, 725; for prison inmates, 667, 670; suicide prevention, 697, 698, 702-4
Control: of addictions, 66-67; coercive, in couples, 472; lack of, over eating, 206; need for, and domestic violence, 478; perceived, of old people, 517
—loss of: addiction as, 67-68, 81; job jeopardy and, 729
—sense of: AIDS and, 49, 55; and domestic violence, 488; victimization and, 436-37
Convenient conversion syndrome, 668
Convicted inmates, 651
Coordinators, social workers as, 571-72
Coping plan for suicidal person, 698
Coping skills, 6, 21, 23-26; for abusive parents, 359-60, 361, 363-64; for addiction, 80, 81, 85, 87, 89, 91-92; AIDS diagnosis and, 48, 49-50; for family caregivers, 569; illness related, 146, 147, 148, 153; of old people, 508-9; for women, 183
Coping strategies: and death of child, 465-67; of families of borderline personalities, 119; of family caregivers, 560-61; job jeopardy and, 737-38; suicidal behavior as, 678, 681-82, 690
Core interventions, for addiction, 79-80
Core-satellite foster care program, 397-98, 405-12
Correctional officers: socialworkers and, 656; training for, 673
Cortical dysfunction, 239
Costs: of addiction, 66; of adolescent pregnancies, 319; of AIDS care, 38-39; of chronic illness, 142; of depression, 175; of domestic violence, 499; of health care for old people, 555; of schizophrenia, 293-94

Counseling: for abusive parents, 411; for addiction, 80, 89-91; for borderline personalities, 118, 120-23; for chronic illness, 148-49; for crime victims, 430, 438; at death of child, 455, 464-68; for depression, 206; for eating disorders, 206, 218-24, 225, 229; for family caregivers, 564-65, 572-79; for family of learning-disabled child, 258-59; for family of mentally retarded child, 275, 276; for female prison inmates, 654; HIV tests and, 43; for jail inmates, 666-68; for job jeopardy, 720; for obesity, 226
—for adolescents, 327-28, 332; mothers, 341; pregnant, 326, 327
—for domestic violence, 484-85, 494-99; battered women, 482, 484, 488-89, 491-92; wife-batterers, 490-91
Couple relationships, violence in, 472-73, 476, 481-82; counseling for, 484-85, 490-91; *see also* Domestic violence
Court-mandated programs: child maltreatment services, 374; for homelessness, 599
Courts: and crime victims, 416; and domestic violence counseling, 490; and foster care, 403-4, 410, 412; orders of protection, 434
CPS (Child Protective Services) reports, 346-47
Crack addiction, 10, 65; and homelessness, 588; *see also* Addiction
Crib death, *see* SIDS
Crime, 5, 11-12; childhood maltreatment and, 354; economic status and, 10; victims of, 5, 8, 10, 416-45
Crime prevention, imprisonment as, 648
Crime-victim-compensation bills, 423-24
"Crime Victims," Masters, 416-45
Criminal justice system, 420-24, 432-33; and crime, 418; and female crime victims, 423; and learning disabilities, 244; and victimization, 427-30
Criminal procedure, advocacy of change, 431
Criminal record, and suicide risk, 687
Criminal sanctions against alcoholism, 67

Crippled Children's Services programs, 140
Crisis intervention: AIDS-related, 44-45, 53; for battered women, 482, 484, 486-87; foster placement, 401; suicide prevention, 677-78, 689, 696-97
Crisis phase of chronic illness, 146
Cross-cultural counseling, 628-38
Cuban-Americans, 75; immigrants, 621-22, 632, 634, 637
Cultural differences, immigrants and, 626-27
Cultural expectations, and adolescent pregnancy, 330
Cultural factors, 27; in addiction, 69, 71-73; in immigration, 630, 635-38, 640-43; in job insecurity, 714-15; in victimization, 419
Culture, AIDS epidemic and, 37, 38-39
Cuomo Mario, 604
Custodial care for mentally retarded persons, 280
Cycle of coercion in abusive families, 349, 354
Cycle of violence in couples, 482
Cyclothymia, 166, 168
Cyromegalovirus (CMV) infections during pregnancy, 269

Dane, Barbara Oberhofer, "Death of a Child," 446-70
Data organization, and communication problems, 17
Dating practices, and adolescent pregnancy, 331
Day programs for homeless people, 610
Death, 446-47; from AIDS, 41, 58-61; of child, 446-70; of loved one, 457; from pestilences, 37; suicide, 682-83
"Death of a Child," Dane, 446-70
Death penalty, 420, 431
Decision-making skills, addiction control, 85
Decriminalization of victimless crimes, 418
Deductive reasoning, 17-18
Defendants, criminal, 433
Definitions: addiction, 66-70; borderline personality, 102-3; child maltreatment, 345-46; chronic illness and disability, 138; depression, 173-74; domestic violence, 472; frail elderly, 505; homelessness, 586; learning disability, 237, 249; mental retardation, 265-66; schizophrenia, 289-90, 292; shared, worker-client, 528; suicide, 678-79
Deinstitutionalization, 5, 298; and homelessness, 587, 597-98; and prison populations, 656-57; schizophrenia and, 293-94
Delinquency: childhood maltreatment and, 354; learning disabilities and, 243
Dementia, 83, 517
Demographic risk factors of suicide, 684
Denial, as coping strategy, 50; in chronic illness, 146, 154; for learning disabilities, 253
Denmark, schizophrenia studies, 295
Department of Housing and Urban Development (HUD), homeless figures, 586
Departure experiences of migrants, 629-32
Dependency: in adolescence, 338; of battered wives, transfer to social worker, 492; and domestic violence, 478, 481-82, 488; economic, old age and, 513; of homelessness, 591; of old age, 504, 505, 510, 515, 526, 536, 557; and schizophrenia, 308; and suicidal behavior, 686
Dependent children, 382-83; of prison inmates, 654
Deportation of undocumented aliens, 623
Depression, 3, 4, 11, 12, 165-204; AIDS diagnosis and, 49, 54; alcoholism and, 74; and borderline personality, 101, 109, 117; childhood maltreatment and, 349, 354; of children, interparental violence and, 481; of crime victims, 438; domestic violence and, 480; and eating disorders, 205-6, 215; of family caregivers, 558; of immigrants, 630; job jeopardy and, 720, 729, 738-45; of neglectful parents, 362; and obesity, 207; in old age, 517; Soviet view, 635; and suicidal behavior, 687, 701-4
"Depression," Turnbull, 165-204
Depressive disorder diagnosis, 188-89
Depressive spectrum disorder, 189

Depressive symptoms, medication for, 115

Deprivation of necessities, child neglect, 348

Depth perception, problems of, 246

Descriptions of schizophrenia, 287-89, 296

Desipramine (Norpramine), 131

Destructive forces, in old age, 509

Detention centers, for immigrants, 634

Deterrence, imprisonment as, 648

Detoxification, 78-79, 84; of prison inmates, 659, 665

Devaluation of old people, 508

Developmentally Disabled Assistance Act, 140

Developmental problems, of maltreated children, 353, 354; assessment, 365

Developmental theories of schizophrenia, 290-91

Development of personality, 105-6

Diabetes, 7, 11; and mental retardation, 269

Diagnosis: of AIDS, reactions to, 48-49, 50, 54, 55; of borderline personality, 101, 103; of depression, 175, 185-91; of eating disorders, 206-7; of learning disabilities, 238; of mental retardation, 267, 268; of schizophrenia, 301, 308

Diagnostic and Statistical Manual of Mental Disorders (DSM-III, DSM-III-R), 83; depression, 185; borderline personality, 101, 103; eating disorders, 206-7; learning disabilities, 238, 247

Diagnostic centers for children, 396

Diagnostic classification of addictions, 83

Diagnostic quest, in chronic illness, 46

Diagnostic related groups (DRGs), 523

Dialectical behavior therapy, 120, 126

Diaries of eating patterns, 228-29

Didactic method of teaching, 21-22

Diet articles in magazines, 212

Dilantin, 132

Direct advice, 24

Disabilities: environments and, 4; of homeless people, 588; in old age, 515; physical, 137-63; supportive legislation, 240; *see also* Chronic illness; Learning disabilities

Disability Insurance (DI), 140

Disability rights movement, 138-39

Disabled people: children in foster care, 386; job insecurity of, 713

Disadvantaged social groups, 72-73

Disappointment reaction, 166, 168

Disasters, victims of, 427

Discharge-planning service, in prisons, 669, 671-72

Discovery hearings, 433

Discrimination: disabilities and, 138-39, 140, 141, 162; in employment, 712; laws against, 240, 276

Discussion method of teaching, 21

Disease: addiction as, 67-68, 70; elimination of, 36; prevention programs, 13; of prison inmates, 654; *see also* Chronic illness

Disease-oriented organizations, 145

Disequilibrium, of old age, 527-28

Disordered thinking: medication for, 115; schizophrenic, 289; and suicide, 681

Disorganization, learning disability and, 247

Distractible children, 248

District attorney, 432-33

Disulfiram, 80, 89, 91

Diurnal variation of depression, 184

Divorce: depression and, 177, 179; domestic violence and, 479; and mentally retarded child, 274

Divorced women, risk of victimization, 425

Documents, stolen, replacement of, 436

Domestic violence, 5, 8, 9-10, 11, 14, 347, 416, 471-502; addiction and, 65; and borderline personality, 101; and child maltreatment, 352; ethnic factors, 438; of immigrants, 626; prevention of, 13, 431; victim compensation, 424; *see also* Children, maltreatment of

"Domestic violence," Carlson, 471-502

Down syndrome, 268, 273

Doxepin (Sinequan), 131

Drachman, Diane, "Immigrants and Refugees," 618-46

Drop-in centers for homeless people, 602-3, 612

Drug abuse, 10, 12, 65-100; and adolescent pregnancy, 326; by adolescent Russian immigrants, 636; AIDS and, 48; and child maltreatment, 352; and domestic violence, 9, 488;

and eating disorders, 209; fetal effects, 269; and homelessness, 609; and imprisonment, 652, 653-54, 659-61; socioeconomic factors, 73-74; *see also* Addiction; Substance abuse
Drug-dependence scales, 82, 88
Drug-free social systems, 86
Drug-treatment programs in prisons, 669
Drug use, and addiction, 75
DSM-III, DSM-III-R, *see* Diagnostic and Statistical Manual of Mental Disorders
Dual-career couples, counseling for, 720
Dubos, René, 36
Due-process procedures for handicapped children, 271
Duration: of homelessness, 588; of services to prevent child abuse, 367-68
Dwarfism, 150-63
Dysfunctional relationships in family caregiving, 550
Dyslexia, 239
Dysphoria, 184
Dysthymia, 166, 168, 175, 186

EAPs, *see* Employee assistance programs
Early intervention programs: for child maltreatment, 357; for mental retardation, 277
Early onset of depression, 176
Early release from prison, for AIDS victims, 664
Eastern Europe, HIV strain, 40
Eating diaries, 228-29
Eating disorders, 9, 11, 12, 205-33; and borderline personality, 101; *see also* Anorexia nervosa; Bulimia nervosa; Obesity
"Eating Problems," Van Bulow, 205-33
Ecological approaches: to AIDS, 37; to child maltreatment, 349; to disabilities, 139; to domestic violence, 499-500; to eating disorders, 218
Ecomaps, 22-23
Economically disadvantaged neighborhoods, and adolescent pregnancy, 323
Economic assistance for crime victims, 430
Economic characteristics of old people, 513-15

Economic costs of AIDS care, 38-39
Economic factors: in adolescent parenthood, 322-23, 325; in child abuse, 348; in crime victimization, 425-26; in domestic violence, 9, 474; in family caregiving, 552; in foster care, 387-88; in health of old people, 515, 554; in victim compensation, 424
Economic policies, and problems of age, 509-10
Economic problems resulting from victimization, 435-36
Economic security, employment and, 711, 716
Economy, immigrants and, 624
Ecosystems perspective on social work, 2, 139; approach to foster care, 402-3
Education: addiction and, 68, 76, 77; adolescent pregnancy and, 325, 340-41; AIDS prevention, 41-42, 51; borderline personality intervention, 117-19; and child maltreatment, 352, 359-60; chronic illness and, 142, 162; of criminal justice personnel, 430; about depression, 169, 183; of homeless people, 585; of prison inmates, 651-52
—for children: chronically ill, 143; handicapped, 141, 237-38, 240-41, 271; undocumented aliens, 628
—programs and services: AIDS-related, 45; child maltreatment prevention, 356; for family caregivers, 565; for wife-batterers, 484
Educational neglect of child, 346
Education for All Handicapped Children Act (1975), 140, 240-41, 271
Education of Handicapped Act (1986), 241
Educator role of social worker, 20-26
Educators, and learning disabilities, 243
Effectiveness: of addiction services, 80; of borderline personality treatment, 125; of child maltreatment prevention, 358-59; of self-help groups, 77
Efficacy, sense of, and domestic violence, 488
Egocentric thinking of adolescence, 320
Egograms, 22
Egoistic suicide, 680
Elaborating skills of social workers, 531

Elavil (amitriptyline), 115
"Elderly in Need of Long-Term Care,"
Berman-Rossi, 503-48
Elderly people; *see* Frail old people;
Old people
Electroencephaligraphic abnormalities, 110; of borderline personality, 132
Embryonic development, and mental retardation, 269
Emergency services: for crime victims, 429, 435-36; for homeless people, 599-602; mental health systems, addiction and, 65; psychiatric care for prison inmates, 658
Emergency shelters: for battered women, 482, 483-84; for children, 396
Emotional abuse of child, 346
Emotional expression: in borderline families, 107; limited, and domestic violence, 478
Emotional liability, 250
Emotional neglect of child, 346
Emotional problems of prison inmates, 655
Emotional state, addiction and, 68, 84
Emotional stresses of family caregivers, 558
Emotional support for frail old people, 550
Emotions: at AIDS diagnosis, 48-49, 51; from crime victimization, 426-27; at death of child, 460, 466; of depression, 165; of family caregiving, 555-57; of homelessness, 590-91; of old people needing care, 559-60; of parents of mentally retarded child, 275; of stress, coping skills, 21; of suicide survivors, 688-89
Empathy: childhood maltreatment and, 354; social work skills, 531
Employee assistance programs (EAPs), 722-24; addiction services, 78; for alcoholism, 89, 90-91
Employment: and adolescent pregnancy, 322-23, 327; of borderline personalities, 112-13; and care for old people, 558; chronic illness and, 162; of disabled persons, 143; of former prison inmates, 662; mental retardation and, 276; need for, 716; problems of, 710-48; and suicide, 685; of undocumented aliens, 622-23

Employment counseling, for refugees, 621
Empowerment of clients, 20-21, 725; addiction control, 81, 86; battered women, 487, 489; disabled persons, 145-46
Enabler role of social worker, 19-20, 568
Enactive learning, 21
Encephalitis, and borderline personality, 110
Endogenomorphic depression, 187
Endogenous depression, 184-85, 187-88
English-language training for refugees, 621
English Poor Laws, and dependent children, 382-83
English-speaking immigrants, 624
Enriched-housing program, 532, 533-41; for old people, 524
Entitlements: AIDS-related, 53; of old age, 509, 510-11; of refugees, 620
Environment: of poverty, 7; and social function, 5; and stress, 18-20
Environmental agents, and genetic factors, 4
Environmental change programs, 13, 15
Environmental demands, response to, 72
Environmental factors, 4, 16, 26; in addition, 80-81, 87; in adolescent pregnancy, 321, 330, 338; in borderline personality, 104, 106, 108, 111-12, 117, 127; in child maltreatment, 351, 364; in depression, 172, 182, 186; in job jeopardy, 711-12, 730-33, 738-39; in old age problems, 506-7, 526-27, 541, 561, 569; in schizophrenia, 290, 293, 295; in suicidal behavior, 682, 685, 692
Environmental pollutants, and learning disabilities, 239
Epidemics, 37
Epilepsy, and borderline personality, 110
Escape-avoidance coping strategy, 560
Ethical issues: AIDS-related, 43, 51; in child maltreatment, 368-69; in family care for old people, 570
Ethnic associations, immigrant services, 627-28
Ethnicity: addiction and, 74-75; and adolescent pregnancy, 324-25; and

child abuse, 348; of crime victims, 438; and depression, 179; and domestic violence, 474-75; and eating disorders, 214; and family caregiving, 554; and foster care, 388; and immigration problems, 624; obesity and, 216; and old age, 504-5, 516; and risk, 11; and schizophrenia, 308

Evaluation: of learning disabilities, 245; of programs for prison inmates, 664; of stresses, 21

Expectations, inappropriate, and child maltreatment, 352-53

Experiential factors: in chronic illness, 147; in therapy, 124

Expressed emotion: depression and, 178; and schizophrenia, 291, 299-300, 305

Expressive support for depression, 176

Extended families: and death of child, 465-66; foster care, 404

Eye dysfunctions, learning disabilities and, 239

Facilitator role of social workers, 20

Families, 12; and adolescent pregnancy, 330-34; and AIDS, 48-49, 50-52, 54, 56, 58-59, 61; and alcoholism, 74, 90; assessment for child welfare, 399-400; assessment tools, 365-66; black, 7; and body image of women, 212; of borderline personalities, 127; care for old people, 525, 549-79; child-maltreating, 347-66; and chronic illness, 142, 143, 147-50, 151-63; and death of child, 449-67; and depression, 175-76, 178, 181-83, 188, 190-92, 194; and domestic violence, 477, 481-82; dysfunction, 4-5; and eating disorders, 208, 209, 212, 226-27; of foster care children, 392, 393, 401-2; homeless, 585, 588, 594-97, 598; of homicide victims, 439-40; of intravenous drug users, 51-52; and job jeopardy, 728-29, 734, 736-37; and learning disabilities, 253-54, 256, 257-61; and mental retardation, 274-75, 278-83; nurse-visited, 357-58; of nursing home residents, 551; and obese children, 217; of prison inmates, 650; resettlement stresses, 637-38; and schizophrenia, 295-96, 298-300, 303-6, 307-13; and temperament of

child, 237; and violence, 476; *see also* Family caregivers; Family history

Family caregivers: AIDS and, 52-53; for frail old people, 525, 549-79; job insecurity, 712

"Family Caregivers of the Frail Elderly," Toseland and Smith, 549-83

Family-centered ecosystems approach to foster care, 402-3

Family counseling: for addiction, 77; AIDS-related, 45; for borderline personalities, 105, 118-19; for caregivers, 564-65; at death of child, 455, 464-68; for depression, 169; for domestic violence, 485, 490; for eating disorders, 222-26; for neglectful parents, 362; for parents of mentally retarded child, 283; for schizophrenia, 303, 304, 308-10

Family history: and addiction, 75-77; and bulimia, 215; and depression, 180, 187, 188-89, 192-93; and domestic violence, 496; and learning disability, 243; and mental retardation, 273; and violent behavior, 8

Family laws, child maltreatment, 345

Family-planning services, 331

Family sculpture, 23

Family support programs: for mental retardation, 277-78; for prevention of child maltreatment, 356, 357-58

Family systems theories: of borderline personality, 106-8; of child maltreatment, 348; of depression, 171; of schizophrenia, 291-92

Family training programs for mental retardation, 277

Family violence, *see* Domestic violence

Family Violence Research Laboratory, 474

Farm crisis, mental health concerns, 720-21

Fathers: adolescent, 332, 333; of bulimics, 209; and death of child, 454, 460, 464; of mentally retarded children, 274-75

Fear, domestic violence and, 480, 481

Federal agencies for refugees, 624

Federal Council on Aging, 511

Federal government: and homelessness, 587, 605; and immigration, 619-20; and learning disabilities, 237-42; longterm-care programs,

Federal government (*Continued*)
506; and rights of handicapped
children, 271; services for disabled
people, 140; subsidies for mental
retardation, 276
—laws: child protection, 390-91; education of handicapped children,
140, 240-41, 271; foster care regulation, 390-92
Federally funded programs: for child
care, 323; and employment discrimination, 140
Federal prosecutors, 433
Feedback, coping skills, 25
Fee-for-service programs, for geriatric
care, 522
Female inequality, and victimization,
423
Females: abused children, 347; borderline personality, 110, 112; eating
disorders, 207, 213-14; *see also* Adolescents, pregnant; Women
Femininity, concerns with, 208
Feminism, 183; and child maltreat-
ment 356; and disability rights,
138-39; and domestic violence, 485
Fetal alcohol or drug syndromes, 4, 77,
273
Financial stress, and domestic vio-
lence, 480
Fines, for crimes, 422
First-time offenders, pretrial release
programs, 654
5-HIAA, 681
Fixations, in borderline personality,
105
Folk healers, 475, 638
Food programs for homeless people,
601
Food Stamps, 319; for refugees, 621
Forced retirement, 508, 721
Foreign-born people, 619, 620; crime
victims, 438; *see also* Immigrants;
Refugees
Foreign policy, and immigration, 619
Formal service systems for old people,
519
Former prison inmates: job insecurity,
713; and mental health care, 659;
services for, 673; *see also* Prison in-
mates
For-profit nursing homes, 520, 522
Foster boarding homes, 396
Foster care, 7, 382-412; and adolescent

pregnancy, 326; and imprisonment,
654
Foster Care and Adoption Assistance
Program, 391
Foster grandparents, 328
Foster parents: relationship with birth
parents, 401-2; social workers and,
403-4
Foundations, private, services for
homeless people, 601
Foundling hospitals, 382
Fragile X syndrome, 268
Frail old people, 504-5; assessments
and interventions for, 526-32; case
illustration, 532-41; family caregiv-
ing, 549-83; problem domain, 505-
7; programs and services, 518-26;
risks and needs of population, 512-
18; services for, 565-66; societal
context, 507-11; *see also* Old people
Frailty, 541-42
Freud, Sigmund, 291, 447; and suicide,
680-81
Friends of AIDS victims, 48-49, 51
Frustration tolerance, and child maltreatment, 352
Fry, Mary, 423
Functional disorders, and mental retardation, 272-73
Functional family of AIDS victim, 50
Funding sources: for crime victim programs, 444; disability services, 139-
40; for handicapped education programs, 241; for mental retardation
services, 278
Funerals, 450-51; crime victim compensation, 439
Funneling technique to detect domestic violence, 485, 494-95, 499

Galactosemia, 268
Game patterns, recognition of, 22
Gang members, prison inmates, 652
Gay couples, and AIDS diagnosis, 51
Gay men, HIV infections, 40
Gay Men's Health Crisis, 44
Gemmill, Patsy A., "Mental Retarda-
tion," 265-85
Gender: of abused children, 347; and
addiction, 74; and alcoholic re-
lapse, 84; and borderline personal-
ity, 110; and depression, 179-80;
and job insecurity, 712; and mental

retardation, 268, 272; and old age, 512; and risk, 11

Generalizations, 17

Genetic factors, 3-4, 27; in achondro-plasia, 150-51; in addiction, 67, 76; in behavior, 237; in crime, 418; in depression, 172-73, 188-89; in eating disorders, 209-10; in learning disabilities, 239, 243; in mental retardation, 268, 273; in obesity, 210; in schizophrenia, 290, 292, 294-96, 307; in suicide, 681; in temperament, 237

Genograms, 22; of bereaved families, 459, 463, 499-60; of schizophrenia, 308

Geriatric social work, 522

Getzel, George S., "AIDS," 35-64

Girls: and interparental violence, 481; obese, 213, 216; self-esteem of, 207; *see also* Adolescents, pregnant; Females; Women

Gitterman, Alex, "Social Work Practice with Vulnerable Populations," 1-32

Gitterman, Naomi Pines, "Learning Disabilities," 234-64

Goals: of depression interventions, 190; of domestic violence interventions, 486-89; of job jeopardy interventions, 729; of schizophrenia interventions, 308-9; of social workers in jails, 668; of suicide interventions, 693, 696-98, 702

Goguen, Dennis E., "Borderline Personality," 101-36

Government, role of, 508

Government agencies: and family caregivers, 555; and housing development, 604; *see also* Federal government

Government-funded victim-witness assistance programs, 431

Grandparents of disabled child, 153

Graphic presentations, teaching method, 22

Graphic therapy techniques, 668

Gray Panthers, 508

Grief, 186, 447-52, 461; AIDS patients and, 49, 60; in chronic illness, 147; at death of child, 452-61; of family caregivers, 557; for learning-disabled child, 253; at mental retardation of child, 275; resolution of, 467

Grodd, Barbara, "Imprisonment," 647-76

Gross motor coordination problems, 246

Group counseling: for addiction, 77, 80; for adolescent parents, 328; for adolescents, 327; for alcoholism, 89-90; for battered women, 489; of borderline personalities, 120-23; for eating disorders, 220-22, 226; for families of schizophrenics, 299, 304; for family caregivers, 569; for wife-batterers, 484; *see also* Mutual aid groups; Support groups

Group residences, foster care, 396, 400

Group services, for old people, 523

Group training of abusive parents, 360

Guilt feelings, 166; of addicts, 82; at AIDS diagnosis, 49; at death of child, 467-68; in depression, 184; domestic violence and, 480

Gunshot wounds, 8

Haiti, immigrants from, 631-32, 634; entry status, 621-22; resettlement problems, 636-37

Haldol (haloperidol), 115

Halfway houses, 79; for addicts, 78-79; for borderline personality, 128-29; for schizophrenia, 296

Hallucinations of schizophrenia, 289

Hallucinogens, 83

Haloperidol (Haldol), 115, 116

Handguns, and crime, 418

Handicapped people, 138-39; and mental retardation, 267-68; *see also* Chronic illness; Disabilities

—children: education for, 237-38, 271; in foster care, 405

Hanson, Meredith, "Alcoholism and Other Addictions," 65-100

Harassment, in prison, 652

Head injuries: and borderline personality, 116-17; and mental retardation, 273

Head Start programs, 276, 357, 408, 411

Health: of family caregivers, 561; of homeless people, 588-89; of old people, 515-16

Health care: for chronic illness, 140-41; employment and, 711, 716; for homeless people, 601; for prison in-

Health care (*Continued*)
mates, 655-56; public policy, and family caregiving, 554
Health Care Financing Administration, 506
Health care personnel, grief at death of child, 455
Health insurance, chronic illness and, 162
Health problems: addictions, 65; adolescent pregnancy and, 325; and child maltreatment, 352; coping strategies and, 560; eating disorders, 207, 218; of maltreated children, 353; maternal, and mental retardation, 270; of old age, 535; poverty and, 7
Health programs, 13, 14-15; in schools, 327
Help, acceptance of, in chronic illness, 147
Helping activities: for adolescent parents, 332; for frail old people, 531, 542; for prison inmates, 667-68, 671-72; at prolonged death of child, 459
Helping relationships: AIDS and, 57; for learning disabilities, 252-53; for mental illness, 176; in workplace, 731-32
Helplessness, feelings of, 6, 10-11; in depression, 165, 167, 170-71; eating disorders and, 208; of old people, 508
Heroin addiction, 67, 73; of prison inmates, 653; relapse, 84; Vietnam veterans and, 71
Heterogenous developmental course, and borderline personality, 104
Heterosexual contact, and HIV infections, 40-41
Hierarchical intervention model for depression, 190
High-risk situations: for alcohol use, 88; for drug use, 84-85
Hispanics: adolescent pregnancy, 324-25; AIDS infections, 41; birth rates, 11; drug use patterns, 74-75; eating disorders, 214; elderly, 512, 514, 554; family caregiving for old people, 555; homeless young people, 594; and prenatal care, 142; prison inmates, 653; women, and domestic violence, 475

HIV (human immunodeficiency virus), 37, 40-44, 47-48; fear of, 51; *see also* AIDS
Hmong people, 626-27
Holding environment: counseling as, 123-24, 126; for schizophrenia, 292
Holloway, Stephen, "Homeless People," 584-617
Holocaust survivors, 437
Home-based services, 395
Home care: for frail old people, 521, 525-26, 555; techniques, 656-62
Homeless children, 382; foster care, 405
Homelessness, 5, 10, 584-615; addiction and, 65; and adolescent pregnancy, 323-24, 326; AIDS and, 46; and child welfare, 389; and mental illness, 289, 292, 293; and unemployment, 716
"Homeless People," Holloway, 584-617
Home maintenance of mentally retarded persons, 278-79
Homemaker–home help aides, 395
Home management assistance, needed by old people, 551
Home visits: for adolescent parents, 328; prevention of child maltreatment, 357-58, 360, 373
Homicide victims, counseling for families, 439-40
Homocystinuria, 268
Homosexual couples, domestic violence, 472
Homosexuality: AIDS and, 48; and HIV infections, 40; prejudice against, 39
Hope, AIDS victims and, 49-50
Hopelessness, 6; childhood maltreatment and, 354; of old people, 508, 517-18; and suicidal behavior, 686-87; and suicide, 681, 699
Hospice programs for AIDS victims, 45
Hospital-based social workers, 144
Hospitalization: of borderline personality, 110, 124-32; of chronically ill children, 160-61; for depression, 191; for eating disorders, 223-26; for schizophrenia, 287-88, 296, 298, 308; of suicidal persons, 696-97, 698
Hospitals: addiction services, 78; adolescent pregnancy programs, 326; AIDS units, 663; fear of, 534; and homeless people, 589; mental ill-

ness programs, 182-83; social work for old people, 523

Hostility: depression and, 195; of foster care children, 394; of prison inmates, 655; repressed, 167

Hotlines: for battered women, 484; for crime victims, 439-40, 444-45; suicide prevention, 689-90

Household crimes, risk of victimization, 425

Household management tasks, age and, 515-16

Housing: for adolescent parents, 323-24, 327; for homeless people, 603-5, 607-8, 615

Housing costs, and homelessness, 595-96

Housing development programs, 600, 604-5

Husbands, battered, 473

Hyperactivity, 247-48; medication for, 251-52

Hyperaroused alcoholics, 3

Hyperkenesis, 236

Hypertension, 11; blacks and, 7-8

Hypoactivity, 248

Hypochrondria, 251

Hypomania, 166, 168; medication for, 115

Iconic learning, 21

Identification of crime victims, 420

Identity: chronic illness and, 148-49; job jeopardy and, 738; parental, and death of child, 453

Identity transformations, of addicts, 79

Idiographic treatment issues for child maltreatment, 366-39

Illegal aliens, 416, 622; homeless, 612-13

Illinois, program for neglectful families, 362

Illiteracy of prison inmates, 652

Illness: chronic, 3, 137-63, 515, 516, 549-50; and secondary depression, 189-90; *see also* Disabilities; Disease

Illusion of invulnerability, 436

Imipramine (Tofranil), 109, 115

Immaturity, social, and learning disability, 249

Immediate intervention for domestic violence, 486-88, 499

Immigrants, 13, 618-46; job insecurity

of, 713; suicide of, 685; use of term, 643*n*

"Immigrants and Refugees," Drachman and Shen-Ryan, 618-46

Immigration and Naturalization Service (INS), 620

Immigration Reform and Control Act (1986), 622

Imminent risk of suicide, 694-95

Immune system, collapse of, 42

Impairment type, family caregivers and, 556

Impotence, psychological, and suicide, 517

Impoverishment of old people, 514

"Imprisonment," Grodd and Simon, 647-76

Impulse control, stimulant medication and, 111

Impulsivity, 115-16, 248, 254; and suicidal behavior, 686

Inadequacy feelings, and domestic violence, 478

Inattention, problems with, 248

Incapacitation, imprisonment as, 648

Incest: and borderline personality, 108; depression and, 175

Incidence rates: of adolescent pregnancy, 319; of child death, 452-54; of child maltreatment, 346-48; of chronic illness and disability, 142-43; of crime, 416, 425; of depression, 178-79; of domestic violence, 471, 474; of eating disorders, 213-14; of foster care, 383-86; of learning disabilities, 242-43; of mental retardation, 272; of schizophrenia, 293, 294

Income: for borderline personalities, 112; of family caregivers, 552; for homeless people, 608, 613; for old people, 510, 511, 514

Incontinence, of old people, 557

Inconvenience from crime victimization, 426

Indenture of dependent children, 382-83

Independence: of disabled children, 156-58; of immigrant women, 626; mental retardation and, 266

Indians, *see* Native Americans

Indictment of suspects, 433

Individual counseling: for abusive parents, 411; for adolescent parents,

Individual counseling (*Continued*) 328; for adolescents, 327; for alcoholism, 89; for battered women, 489; for borderline personalities, 120-23; for eating disorders, 218-20, 224; for family caregivers, 564, 569, 572-79; for obesity, 226, 227; for schizophrenia, 302

Individualism, 369; and job insecurity, 714

Individuality: of AIDS victims, 46-48; of battered women, 482; of caregiving situations, 557; of children, 398; of eating disordered clients, 229; of jail inmates, 667; of schizophrenia patient, 302

Individualized education plan (IEP), 271

Individualized services for addiction, 81, 87, 91

Indochinese refugees, 633-34; resettlement problems, 637-38

Inductive reasoning, 17

Industrialized cultures, and schizophrenia, 296

Ineffectiveness, sense of, eating disorders and, 208

Inequalities: crime and, 419; in workplace, 715

*I Never Promised You A Rose Garden*, 286

Infantilism, and child maltreatment, 352

Infants: HIV-infected, 40-41; of addicted mothers, 77, 405; death of, 7, 11, 454; stimulation programs, 276; *see also* Children

Infections during pregnancy, and mental retardation, 269

Inferences, development of, 17

Infertility, 4

Informal family caregiving, 550

Informal social supports of old people, 525

Information, relevant for coping, 23-24; for battered women, 482, 484, 487, 497; about criminal justice system, 432-33; for chronic illness assistance, 149; about chronic illness course, 147-48, 153; for families of schizophrenics, 304; for family caregivers, 559-60, 570; about troubled workers, 727-28, 735-37; to prevent unplanned pregnancy, 330

In-home care, for old people, 521, 532-41; long-term, 525

In-kind contributions, of adolescent fathers, 332

Inmates; *see also* Prison inmates

Inner-city communities, 10, 39; black, 72-73; children, 8; crime, 426

Inner resources, and stress, 18-19

Inpatient mental health services for borderline patients, 113

Inpatient rehabilitation facilities for addicts, 78-79

INS (Immigration and Naturalization Service), 620

Insight therapy: borderline personalities and, 125, 126; chronic dysphoria and, 187; and depression, 193, 194-95; for suicidal behavior, 125

Institute of Living, Hartford, Connecticut, 110

Institutionalization: of frail old people, 516, 517, 520-21, 551-52; long-term, 507; of mentally retarded people, 278-80

Institution-blaming crime theories, 417-18

Institutions, and social problems, 6

Instrumental support, 176

Insurance, employment and, 716

Integration, social, and suicide, 680

Integration stage of chronic illness, 147

Intellectual development factors, 267

Intelligence, and achondroplasia, 150; *see also* IQ scores

Intensive counseling for borderline personalities, 122-23

Intent, in suicide risk assessment, 679

Interactional theories: of borderline personality, 108-11; of suicide, 680

Interaction patterns, in maltreating families, 353-54

Interdependence, of old people, 536

Intergenerational conflicts of immigrants, 638

Intergenerational transmission of child maltreatment, 352

Intermittent depressive disorder, 166

Internal advocates, 20

Internalization of interpersonal relations, 105

Internal mediators, 20

Internal steady state, for old people, 527
Interpersonal harmony, somatic complaints and, 642
Interpersonal relationships: borderline personality and, 108, 113; communication problems, 16-26; depression and, 167, 171-72, 177-78; internalization of, 105; of schizophrenia, 290; and suicidal behavior, 686, 701
—conflicts: and addiction relapses, 84; and alcoholism, 88; coping skills, 89-90; of family caregivers, 558, 569; and job jeopardy, 713, 738-45
Interpersonal therapy for depression, 190
Interpretations offered by social worker, 24-25; to borderline personalities, 123
Interpreters, for immigrants, 640-41
Interventions, 15-26; for addiction, 68-70, 77, 79-87, 89-92; for adolescent pregnancy, 327, 329-33, 338-41; for AIDS patients, 46-53, 55; for bereaved families, 455, 457-61, 466; for borderline personality, 114-26; for child maltreatment, 349, 350-51, 355, 366-69; for chronic illness and disability, 145-50; for crime victims, 429, 432-38; for depression, 169, 186-91; for domestic violence, 474, 485-93, 498-99; for eating disorders, 224-26; for family caregivers, 566-72; for foster care children, 398-405; for frail old people, 526-32; for homeless people, 605-11; for immigrants, 628-38; for job jeopardy, 725-33; for learning disabilities, 251-56, 261; for mental retardation, 278-81; for prison inmates, 665-68; for schizophrenia, 301-6; for suicidal behavior, 690-700, 705; for suicide survivors, 688
Intimacy: AIDS patients and, 60; and depression, 177-78; and domestic violence, 488
Intrapersonal threats to job security, 714
Intravenous drug users, and AIDS, 39, 42
—HIV infected, 40-41, families of, 51-52
Investigation of child maltreatment reports, 390-91

Involuntary foster care placement, 395
Involuntary immigrants, Cuban, 632
IQ scores: childhood maltreatment and, 354; of mental retardation, 266-67; and therapy outcome, 124
Ireland, schizophrenia in, 295
Isolation: physical, of prison inmates, 657, 658
—social: of adolescent parents, 320; of AIDS victims, 48-54; and child maltreatment, 375; at death of child, 455; domestic violence and, 478, 480, 488-89; of elderly immigrants, 625-26; of homelessness, 591; job insecurity and, 715; mental illness and, 598; of old age, 513, 532-33; in schizophrenia, 290; of suicidal women, 685
*Is There No Place on Earth for Me?*, 286
Ivanoff, André, "Suicide and Suicidal Behavior," 677-709

Jails, 647-48, 656, 665-68; inmates, 651, 652; mental health services, 658-59; substance abuse prevention programs, 660-61
Japan, eating disorders, 214
Japanese-Americans, 75
Jealousy, and domestic violence, 478, 480
Job development programs for addicts, 70
Job jeopardy, 710-11; and addiction, 82, 87-91; assessments and interventions, 725-33; case illustration, 733-45; problem domain, 711-14; risks and needs of population, 715-19; societal context, 714-15
Job placement for refugees, 621
Job-training programs, 187, 723
Johnson, Harriette C., "Borderline Personality," 101-36
Journal writing, therapeutic, at death of child, 460-61
Judicial process, victim participation, 420; *see also* Criminal justice system
Juvenile-onset obesity, 210, 216-17

Kernberg, Otto, 106
Kindling hypothesis, 181
Koch, Edward, 599
Korean-Americans, 75
Kuhn, Maggie, 508

Lability, emotional, 250
Labor market, and adolescent pregnancy, 322-23
Labor-sponsored member assistance programs (MAPs), 722-24, 733-45
Language: developmental problems, 245-46; of Haitian immigrants, 636; and immigration problems, 624, 625; speech therapy, 251
Laotian immigrants, 626-27
Latchkey children, counseling for, 720
Latin America, HIV strain, 40
Latinos, *see* Hispanics
Laudanum, addiction to, 67
Laws, 421; advocacy of change, 431; child maltreatment, 345; disability services, 239-42, 139-40; education for handicapped children, 237-38; foster care, 390-92
Learned behavior: addiction as, 69; domestic violence as, 5; drug use as, 71, 72; violence as, 491
Learned helplessness, 10; antidepressant medication and, 187-88; depression model, 169, 170-71; and domestic violence, 488; and job jeopardy, 729; in old age, 518
Learning disabilities, 3, 234-64; and borderline personality, 101, 110; young maternal age and, 325
"Learning Disabilities," Gitterman, 234-64
Learning process, 21, 235, 237
Learning theories of suicide, 681-82
Least restrictive environment: for education of handicapped, 240, 241; for mental illness treatment, 293, 597
Legal Aid Society, 599
Legal approaches to addiction, 66-67
Legal aspects: of foster care, 389-90, 395, 403, 404; of suicide prevention, 691
Legal services, for immigrants, 624
Legislation, *see* Laws
Levels of mental retardation, 266
Liberal politics, and victims' rights, 424
Life companions of AIDS victims, 51
Life conditions: borderline personality and, 101, 108; grief, 447; old age, 527; suicide and, 681, 685
Life cycle events: AIDS victims and, 52; and depression, 180-81, 191-92;

of old age, 527; stressful, coping skills, 23-26
Life-cycle family-support programs, 356, 357-58
Life expectancy, 36, 512, 516
Life management skill, and child maltreatment, 364
Life model, stress and coping, 566-67
Life-planning decisions of foster care, 403-4
Life skills counseling: for adolescents, 332; for homeless people, 609, 610; for jail inmates, 668
Life space interviewing of adolescents, 333
Life-styles: and addiction, 80, 87; of old people, 504
Life transitions, problems in, 15-16
Literacy programs, 722-23
Lithium carbonate, 116, 130, 131
Living alone, and suicide, 685
Living arrangements of old people, 512-13
Living conditions: in prisons, 649; in welfare hotels, 596-97
Living standards, 6; and job security, 711
Longevity of care receivers, 554
Long-term alternatives for domestic violence, 489
Long-term care: costs of, 514; foster care, 394, 404-5, 412; need for, 504, 509
—for frail old people, 507, 515-16, 518; assessment of need, 526-32; case history, 532-41; facilities, 522-23; programs, 519-26
Long-term homelessness, 588
Long-term memory, 247
Los Angeles AIDS Project, 44
Losses: of homelessness, 590; of migration, 643; suicide and, 685
Loss of control: addiction as, 67-68, 81; job jeopardy and, 729
Loss of job, threats of, 711-14
Loss of parents, and depression, 181-82
Loss theories, 447-48
Loved one, death of, 446, 457
Low birth weight, 239, 325-26; and learning disability, 243; and mental retardation, 270
Low-cost housing, 587; and homelessness, 595-96

Low-dose neuroleptics, 115, 116
Low mood, and depression, 167, 184
Loxapine (Loxitane), 127, 288
Loyalty, domestic violence and, 480, 492
Lung cancer, blacks and, 7

McGowan, Brenda G., "Children in Foster Care," 382-415
Magazines, diet articles, 212
Magical thinking: AIDS-related, 43, 49; and death of child, 450
Major affective disorders, 168-69
Major depressive disorder, 166, 179-80, 185, 187-91; case illustration, 192-95; genetic factors, 173; *see also* Depression
Major physical injury, child abuse, 348
Maladaptive interpersonal processes, 16-26
Males: abused children, 347; addicts, 67; adolescent, 11; and adolescent pregnancy, 321-22; black, unemployed, 7; borderline personality, 110; eating disorders, 213; learning disabilities, 243; mentally-retarded, 268, 272; risk of victimization, 425; young, 12; *see also* Boys; Men
Malnutrition: fetal effects, 269; and mental retardation, 273
Maltreatment of children, 345-81; and foster care, 393, 405-6; domestic violence and, 481; *see also* Child abuse
Management-by-crisis, in jails, 665
Management of stress, 23
Management programs, for employees, 724
Mania, 168
Manic-depressive disorder, 166, 168, 185; *see also* Depression
Manipulation, suicidal behavior as, 690
MAOIs (monoamine oxidase inhibitors), 115
Maple syrup urine disease, 268
MAPs (Labor-sponsored member assistance programs), 722-24, 733-45
Marginalization of old people, 508
Marielitos, 632, 637
Marijuana, 74, 83; and eating disorders, 206

Marital counseling, 572; and addiction, 77
Marital relationship: assessment of, 365; and death of child, 453-54, 460; of immigrants, 626
—difficulties in: adolescent pregnancy and, 334; death of child and, 454, 455; depression and, 175, 177-78, 190-91, 193-94; and domestic violence, 475, 478, 493; of immigrants, 640; job jeopardy and, 736-37; and learning-disabled child, 256; and mentally retarded child, 274, 282-83; obesity and, 227-28; schizophrenia and, 307
Marital status: and depression, 179; and risk of victimization, 425
Marital therapists, and domestic violence, 485
Marital therapy for depression, 169
Marker variables for child maltreatment, 352
Mass deaths, 37
Mass media, 8-9; AIDS epidemic, 38; and ideal female figure, 212; and suicide of young people, 683; and teenage pregnancy, 321, 322
Masters, Rosemary C. "Crime Victims," 416-45
Maternal factors in mental retardation, 270
Maternal substance abuse, and child welfare, 389
Maternity residences, 332
Matorin, Susan, "Schizophrenia," 286-316
Maturational lag, 239
MBD, *see* Minimal brain dysfunction
Meals programs, for homeless people, 601
Measurements of depression, 173
Media, *see* Mass media
Meditating role of social workers, 20, 725
Medicaid, 7, 140, 276, 319, 514, 520; for pregnant adolescents, 332, 334-35; for refugees, 621
Medical care: for HIV infections, 43-44; for homeless people, 589
Medical emergencies, addiction and, 65
Medical evaluation: of crime victim, 434; of eating disorders, 224

Medical factors in homelessness, 609-10

Medicalization of aging, 520, 541

Medical social workers, and eating problems, 217

Medical students, reproductive health counseling, 328

Medicare, 140, 520

Medications: for borderline personality, 104-5, 109-11, 114-16, 127; for depression, 169, 187-88, 194; for eating disorders, 223; for learning disabilities, 244, 251-52; for mentally ill prison inmates, 657, 658; and minimal brain dysfunction, 236; for schizophrenia, 288-89, 296-97, 301-2, 309

Melancholic depression, 187-88

Mellaril (thioridazine), 127, 131

Memory disability, 246

Men, 11-12; alcoholic relapses, 84; black, health problems, 7; and death of child, 460; dominance in couples, 476; drinking practices, 73-74; elderly, 512-13; HIV-infected, 40; homeless, 588, 592-93, 598; obese, 216; prison inmates, 652; substance abuse by, 74; suicide of, 517, 683, 684; wife-battering, 477-78, 480-81, 484; *see also* Males

Menstrual irregularities, and eating disorders, 215

Mental disorders, alcoholism and, 74

Mental health: coping strategies and, 560; of immigrants, assessment of, 628-29; of old people, 516-18; of Russian immigrants, 635; of Southeast Asian immigrants, 635; of Southeast Asian immigrants, 638; and suicidal behavior, 687-88; and victimization, 436-37, 442-44; *see also* Mental illness

Mental health center, 597

Mental Health Minimum Standards, 657-58

Mental health professionals, and families of schizophrenics, 298-300, 303-6

Mental health services, 297; addiction and, 65; for borderline patients, 113; and child maltreatment, 349; and job jeopardy, 720-21; for old people, 519; for prison inmates, 656-59

Mental illness, 165; continuity of care, 659; families and, 182; and homelessness, 588, 593, 597-98, 609, 610, 611-15; immigration and, 625, 627; of prison inmates, 657-59; social factors, 4; and suicidal behavior, 683; *see also* Depression; Schizophrenia

Mental impairment, family caregivers and, 556

Mental observation units in prisons, 656-57

Mental patients, deinstitutionalization, 587

Mental retardation, 4, 265-85; and child maltreatment, 370-74; genetic factors, 3

"Mental Retardation," Brantley and Gemmill, 265-85

Metabolic disorders, and mental retardation, 268

Methadone, 68, 80

Methylphenidate (Ritalin), 110-11, 115

Mexican-Americans: and alcoholism, 75; suicide rate, 684

Mexico, HIV strain, 40

Microorganisms, and disease, 36-37

Middle-aged women, and care of old people, 557-58

Migrations, 618-19

Mild mental retardation, 266, 267, 272, 273, 283

Minimal brain dysfunction (MBD), 116, 235, 236-37, 249, 250; and borderline personality, 110

Minor depressive disorders, 166, 168-69, 186-87

Minority groups: and child abuse, 347-48; and chronic illness, 142; elderly, 510-11, 512, 514, 516, 539, 541, 554; family caregivers, 555, 567; homeless, 585; job inequities, 715; job insecurity, 713; legislation for, 239-40; and old age, 504-5; prison inmates, 652-53; suicide rates, 684; unemployment of, 717

Minor physical injury, child abuse, 348

Minor tranquilizers, 115

Miscarriage, grief at, 459

Misinformation, 23, 24

Miss America Pageant, 212

Moderate mental retardation, 266, 267, 272, 280

Monitoring of prison inmate programs, 664

Monoamine oxidase inhibitors (MAOIs), 115; for bulimia, 223

Montefiore Medical Center, 654

Mood stabilizers, 115, 116

Mood-swings, 166

Moral definitions of addiction, 66-67

Mothering, inadequate, and mental retardation, 273

Mothers: adolescent, 10, 332-33, 356, 357; and body image of daughters, 212; and borderline personality, 106-8; of bulimics, 209; and child maltreatment, 349, 350, 357; and death of child, 454, 458, 460, 464; and depression of daughters, 181-82, 192, 194; of mentally retarded children, 275; psychoanalytic views, 235; relationship with daughters, 208, 209

Motivational dimension of depression, 165

Motivations: for addiction assistance, 82; for drug use, 72; for family caregiving, 550, 555; to avoid pregnancy, 330

Motor coordination, problems of, 246

Mourning, 446, 447-52, 467; at death of child, 460-61; rituals of, 464

"Mourning and Melancholia," Freud, 447

Multidisciplinary interventions: in child maltreatment, 355; for chronic illness and disability, 144; for learning disabilities, 244

Multiple family groups, 191

Multiply handicapped children, in foster care, 405

Multiracial society, immigrants and, 624

Murder, 8, 416; of children, 4452, 456

Mutual aid groups, 145; for bereaved parents, 455-56, 461; for eating disorders, 221; families of learning-disabled children, 244; for schizophrenia, 301; *see also* Self-help groups; Support groups

Mutual-aid societies: African-American, 518-19; for refugees, 628

Mutual battering, 482

Narcissistic persons in group counseling, 121

Narcotics Anonymous (NA), 77, 670-71

Nardil (phenelzine), 115

National Advisory Committee on Handicapped Children, 237

National Alliance for the Mentally Ill, 119, 306

National Association of Social Workers (NASW), 46

National Center of Child Abuse and Neglect (NCCAN), 346-47, 361, 390

National Incidence Study (NIS) of child maltreatment, 346-48

National Institute of Mental Health, 313; child maltreatment studies, 347; epidemiological study, 65

National Joint Committee on Learning Disabilities, 238

National Organization for Victim Assistance (NOVA), 417

National Urban League, and adolescent pregnancy, 321

Nations, and migration, 618

Native Americans: and alcoholism, 75; suicide rates, 684

Natural helpers: and chronic illness, 149; for mental illness, 176; in workplace, 731-32

Navane (thiothixene), 115

Needs of populations, 9-12; addicts, 73-77; AIDS victims, 40-44; battered women, 476-82; borderline personalities, 112-13; and child maltreatment, 352-55; children, for foster care, 387, 392-94; chronic illness and disability, 143; crime victims, 425-29; at death of child, 452-54; depression, 178-82; eating disorders, 213-17; family caregivers, 559-62; homeless people, 590-98, 606-7; immigrants, 625-27; job insecurity, 716-19; learning disabilities, 242-43; mental retardation, retardation, 272-76, 284; old people, 508, 509, 512-18; pregnant adolescents, 324-26; prison inmates, 652-55; schizophrenics, 294-97; suicide survivors, 688-89

Negative cognitive schemata, 170

Negative emotional states, and addiction relapses, 84

Negative life events, depression and, 180-81

Negative outcomes: of domestic violence, 479-82; of schizophrenia, 297

Negative self-image, AIDS and, 48-49
Negative symptoms of schizophrenia, 289-90
Neglectful families, 346, 348, 353-54; case illustration, 369-75; programs for, 361-63; studies of, 359; *see also* Children, maltreatment of
Neighborhoods, and child maltreatment, 351
Neitzsche, Friedrich, 674
Neonatal death, grief at, 459
Networks, *see* Social networks
Neurochemical predispositions, 3
Neuroendocrine deficiency, and depression, 172-73
Neuroleptic drugs, 116, 131; for borderline personality, 115
Neurological abnormalities of borderline personality, 110, 116-17, 132
Neurologists, and learning disabilities, 244
Neurotic depression, 166, 168, 186
New populations, 643
New York City: child care program, 397-98; children in foster care, 384; Gay Men's Health Crisis, 44; homelessness, 10, 594, 595-97, 599; housing for homeless people, 604; jail inmates, 652, 657-59; poverty, 7
New York Coalition for the Homeless, 599
New York State: addicted prison inmates, programs for, 661; enriched housing program, 524; female prison inmates, 653; homeless housing development, 604; literacy programs, 723; old people in, 512, 516; prison inmates with AIDS, 663
New York State Psychiatric Institute, borderline personality study, 125
New Zealand, HIV strain, 40
Nicotine withdrawal, and appetite, 206
Nineteenth century: drug addiction, 67; protective services for children, 390
NIS (National Incidence Study) of child maltreatment, 346-48
Nonadaptive transactions, recognition of, 22
Nondrinkers, 75
Nonfatal suicidal behavior, 678, 690, 705; *see also* Parasuicide

Nonindustrialized countries, schizophrenia in, 296
Nonmarital childbearing, 325, 322; *see also* Adolescents, pregnant
Nonmedical long-term care services, 521
Nonspecialized addiction services, 77
Nontraditional relationships, and grief experience, 451-52
Nonwhites: addiction patterns, 75; elderly, health of, 554; immigrants, 624; *see also* Minority groups
Norpramine (Desipramine), 131
North Africa, HIV strain, 40
North Carolina, prison inmates, 657
Not-for-profit enterprises: housing development corporations, 604-5; long-term-care facilities, 522; nursing homes, 520
NOVA (National Organization for Victim Assistance), 417
Nuclear families, 553
Nurse home visits, to prevent child maltreatment, 357-58
Nursing-home care, 513, 520-21, 550, 551; costs of, 514
Nurturing adults, and maltreated children, 355
Nutritional deficiencies of prison inmates, 654

Obesity, 205, 207, 210-13; assessments and interventions, 225-26; bulimia and, 215; counseling for, 219-23; genetic factors, 3, 210; health problems, 218; hospitalization for, 223-24; and medication, 223; psychological effects, 213; risk factors, 215-17
Object relations theories: of borderline personality, 105-6; of child maltreatment, 349; of eating disorders, 208-9
Observation of learning disabilities, 245
Obsessive-compulsive neuroses, eating disorders as, 210
Occupational hazards and job security, 712
Offender-blaming crime theories, 418
Office of Civil Rights Children and Youth Referral Survey (1980), 388
Older-person-environment fit assessment tool, 529-30

Old-old people, 551
Old people, 503-5; care of, 11; death of, 452; immigrants, 625-26; job insecurity, 721; suicide of, 11, 684; *see also* Frail old people
Open adoption, 404-5
Opiate addicts, 67, 75; alcoholic, 76; social network, 86; therapeutic communities, 79
Opoids, 3
Opportunistic infections, AIDS and, 42, 44
Organic brain disorder, 104; and addiction, 83
Organizational threats to job security, 712-13, 717
Organizer role of social worker, 20
Orphanages, 382-83
Outcomes: of borderline personality treatments, 124-25; of domestic violence, 479; evaluation of, 26-27; of foster care placement, 393; of schizophrenia, 297
—measures of: for depression, 174; for prison inmate programs, 664
Outpatient services: for addiction, 79; AIDS-related, 46; for borderline patients, 113
Outreach programs: for family caregivers, 567; for homeless people, 601-2; for isolated old people, 532, 535
Overeaters Anonymous, 221, 226

PA (Pills Anonymous), 77
Pacific, HIV strain, 40
Panic disorders, medication for, 115
Paranoia: domestic violence and, 480; in old age, 517
Parasuicide, 678, 679; assessments and interventions, 690-700; consequences of, 688-89; mass media and, 683; risk factors, 683-88; societal context, 682-83; *see also* Suicide
*Parens patriae* doctrine, 389-90
Parental grief, 449, 454, 462-67; *see also* Death, of child
Parental rights, termination of, 404
Parental role reversals in Southeast Asian immigrant families, 637-38
Parent-child attachment, disturbances of, 353

Parent education, and child maltreatment, 359-60
Parent-infant-toddler program, 408-9, 411
Parenting skills, 329; for abusive parents, 361; for adolescent mothers, 337; teaching of, 328-29, 372-73, 375
Parents: abusive, 9, 352, 363-64; and addictions, 72, 76; adolescent, 320, 327-28, 331, 332-33, 340, 341-42; and adolescent sexuality, 321; bereaved, 452-61; and borderline personality, 107-8; of bulimics, 209; and child maltreatment, 351; depressed, children of, 180; and depression, 181-82; and disabled child, 151-58, 160; and foster care, 384-86, 387, 401-2, 407-11; of learning-disabled child, 244, 252-54, 256; of mentally retarded child, 274-75, 282-83; of obese children, 217; and pregnancy of adolescent child, 331-33; schizophrenic, children of, 294-95
Parents Anonymous, 356
Parents of Murdered Children, 456
Parole, 422, 428-29, 433
Parolees, 622
Partializing of goals, 693
Pathological ego structure, 103-4
PCP infections, treatment for, 44
Peer relationships: childhood maltreatment and, 354, 365; and drug use, 72
Peer-support parents, 155
Penitentiary sentences, 422
Pepper, Claude, 508
Perceived self-efficacy, and addiction, 85, 90, 91
Perceptions of environment, 5
Perinatal deaths, reactions to, 454, 458, 459
Perinatal factors in mental retardation, 269-70, 273
Permanency planning, in foster care, 386-87, 392-94, 405
Permanent housing, need for, 604-6
Permanent resident alien status, 620-22
Perphenazine (Trilafon), 115
Perscription drugs, abuse of, 74
Perseveration, 250

Personal advocacy skills for chronic illness, 150

Personal appraisals: of chronic illness, 148; of disability, 151

Personal care of old people, 515-16, 551, 556

Personal costs of teenage pregnancy, 319, 320

Personal fable of adolescence, 320

Personal histories of violence, and child maltreatment, 352

Personality: addiction and, 68; borderline structure, 103-4; and child maltreatment, 352; development of, 105-6; genetic factors, 237; of obese people, 216-17

Personal problems, and job jeopardy, 729

Personal strengths of battered women, 487

Person-environment fit, 18-19; for frail old people, 527-30, 540-41; prevention of adolescent pregnancy, 329; schizophrenia interventions, 301-6

Person-in-situation view of home care services, 525

Personnel of workplace, helping networks, 731-32

Phases of chronic illness, 146

Phencyclidine, 83

Phenelzine (Nardil), 115

Phenylketonuria, 268

Philosophy of suicide prevention, 691

Phobic anxiety, and borderline personality, 109

Physical assessment of maltreated child, 364-65

Physical abuse, 473; of child, 346, 359; *see also* Children, maltreatment of; Domestic violence

Physical beauty standards, 207, 211

Physical characteristics of old people, 515-16

Physical illness, and suicide, 687

Physical impairments, environmental adaptations for, 561

Physical injury, from crime, 426, 434

Physical neglect of child, 346

Physical problems of family caregivers, 559

Physical restraint of prison inmates, 658

Physical safety: of crime victims, 434; of suicidal person, 696-97

Physical violence in couple relationships, 477

Physicians, relationships with AIDS patients, 59

Physiological dysfunction, 239

Pills Anonymous (PA), 77

Placement options for children, 395-96, 400

*The Plague*, Camus, 61

Plagues, social effects, 37

Planning for actions, 25-26; depression interventions, 189

Plant closings, and job loss, 711, 717

*Playboy* magazine, 212

Plea bargaining, 428, 433

Police officers, 432

Polish émigrés, 631, 634, 644n

Political factors: in homelessness, 585, 586-87, 589-90, 615; in job jeopardy, 714-15, 730-33; in old age, 541-42; in refugee status, 621; in victims' rights movement, 424

Polydrug abusers, 653

Poor impulse control, 248

Population: foreign-born, 619-20; old people in, 503, 512, 551, 554; of prisons, 651

Positive aspects of family caregiving, 559

Positive expectations of suicidal behavior, 685-86, 688-89

Positive HIV test, reactions to, 43

Possessiveness, and domestic violence, 478

Postbereavement mutual support groups, 455-56

Postnatal factors in mental retardation, 270, 273

Posttest counseling, HIV tests, 43

Posttraumatic stress disorder: of children, 8; of crime victims, 427, 438, 443; of immigrants, 627, 630-31

Postventions, 688

Poverty, 5, 6-7, 9, 10-12, 27-28; and adolescent pregnancy, 320, 323, 329; AIDS and, 46; of battered women, 491; and child maltreatment, 348, 352, 369; children in, 10-11, 13; and chronic illness, 142-43; and crime, 419, 426; and domestic violence, 474; family caregivers and, 552; and foster care, 387-89; and homelessness, 589-90; and imprisonment, 650-51, 652, 654; and mental retardation, 271, 273; and old age, 510, 513-15, 532, 534-35, 541; and single parenthood, 325; and victimization, 438

Power: addiction and, 68; in couple relationships, 472, 476-77, 481-82; and status, 506; work and, 726

Powerlessness of AIDS victims, 39, 49

Practice outcomes, 26-27

Preadoptive homes, 396

Prebirth deaths, reactions to, 458

Precariously housed people, 586

Precipitating factors in depression, 173, 180-81

Predisposing factors: in depression, 173, 181-82; in obesity, 217

Pregnancy: in adolescence, 10, 13, 101, 270, 319-41; child maltreatment prevention programs, 357; and substance abuse, 77; unplanned, 4-5

Pregnant prison inmates, 653, 654

Prejudice: and AIDS epidemic, 39; disabilities and, 138-39, 141; *see also* Discrimination

Prematurity, and mental retardation, 270

Premigration experiences, 629-32, 642

Prenatal care, 142; for adolescents, 325, 338

Prenatal factors in mental retardation, 269, 273

Prenatal programs to prevent child maltreatment, 357, 358

Preparation planning, 25-26

Preschool-aged children, and interparental violence, 481

Preschool programs for mental retardation, 277

Prescription drug abuse, 77

President's Task Force on Victims of Crime, 416

Pretest counseling, HIV tests, 43

Pretrial release programs, 654, 674

Prevention: of child maltreatment, 349, 350; of crime, social workers and, 430-31; of mental retardation, 284

Preventive programs, 674; for child maltreatment, 355-63; for drug abuse by prison inmates, 659-61; to avoid foster placement, 395, 397-98; for job jeopardy, 733

Previous housing history of homeless people, 608

Primary caregivers for old people, 552

Primary prevention programs, 12-15; child maltreatment, 355-56; suicide, 705

Primitive societies, crime victims, 420

Prison inmates, 10, 11-12, 647-74

Prisons, 648, 665

Privacy, lacking in homelessness, 591-92

Private foundations, services for homeless people, 601

Private institutions: for mental retardation, 280; schools for learning disabilities, 243

Problem-analysis, addiction control, 85

Problem domains, 2-6; addiction, 66-70; adolescent pregnancy, 320-22; AIDS, 36-38; borderline personality, 102-111; child maltreatment, 345-51; chronic physical illness and disability, 138-39; crime victims, 417-20; death of child, 447-50; depression, 167-76; domestic violence, 471-74; eating problems, 205-11; family caregivers for frail old people, 549-53; foster care, 383-88; frail old people, 505-7; homelessness, 585-89; immigrants and refugees, 619-23; job jeopardy, 711-14; learning disabilities, 235-39; mental retardation, 265-71; prison inmates, 647-50; schizophrenia, 287-92; suicide, 678

Problems: definitions of, 66; social, 1-2

Problems-in-living, data organization, 17

Problems solving skills, 22; borderline personalities and, 119-20; delinquency and, 243; social, and learning disability, 249; for suicidal persons, 698-700, 702; suicide as, 681, 685, 690

Professional caregivers, in chronic illness, 150

Professional competence, evaluation of, 26-27

Profound mental retardation, 266, 267-68, 272

Programs and services, 12-15; addiction control, 77-81; for adolescent pregnancy, 326-29, 332, 334-42; AIDS related, 44-46; for battered women, 482-85; for bereaved parents, 455-56; for borderline person-

Programs and services (*Continued*) ality, 112-14; for child maltreatment, 355-63; for chronic illness and disability, 143-45; for crime victims, 420, 429-31, 444-45; for depression, 182-83; for domestic violence, 482-85; for eating disorders, 217-24; for family caregivers, 556, 562-66; foster care services, 394-98; for frail old people, 508, 511, 516, 518-26, 656-66; for handicapped people, 140; for homeless people, 599-607; for immigrants, 620, 627-28; for job jeopardy, 719-25; for learning disabilities, 243-45; for mental retardation, 276-78, 284; for prison inmates, 655-65, 673; for refugees, 621; for schizophrenia, 293-94, 297, 298-301, 311-12; for suicide prevention, 689-90
Project 12-Ways, 362
Prolonged death of child, families and, 458, 459
Propranolol, 116
Prosecuting attorneys, 432-33, 441-42
Prostitution, 593; criminalization of, 418
Protection, court ordered, 434
Protection plans for battered women, 486, 487-88
Protection programs, 13-14; for children, 390; for crime victims, 430
Protective factors in childhood maltreatment, 355
Proximal goals for domestic violence intervention, 488-89, 499
Prozac, 223
Psychiatric disorders: and homelessness, 609; of immigrants, 627, 638; overlapping populations, 109; and suicidal populations, 109; and suicidal behavior, 687-88, 697, 701
Psychiatric evaluation of crime victims, 438
Psychiatric social workers, and eating disorders, 218
Psychiatrists, and learning disabilities, 244
Psychiatry, Russian view, 635
Psychic effects of victimization, 426-27, 436-37, 442-44
Psychoactive substance abuse, 83
Psychoanalysis, for eating disorders, 219-20

Psychodynamic counseling for obesity, 226
Psychodynamic theories: of addiction, 68; of child maltreatment, 348-49; of depression, 167-69; and group counseling for borderline personalities, 121; of suicide, 680-81
Psychoeducational support, 120-23; for adolescents, 327; for borderline personalities, 117-19; for families of depressed persons, 182-83, 191; for families of schizophrenics, 298-300, 304; for family caregivers, 563; for schizophrenia, 309, 311, 312
Psychogenic views of borderline personality, 104, 105-8
Psychological entrapment, 480
Psychological factors: in child maltreatment, 352, 411; in depression, 173-74; in family caregiving, 558, 564-65; in foster care, 394; in imprisonment, 655; in job security, 714; in obesity, 213
Psychological theories: of addiction, 70; of eating disorders, 208
Psychological therapies for depression, 169
Psychoneurological learning disability, 235
Psychopathology, 106: borderline personality, 102-3; and child maltreatment, 352; drug abuse and, 71; ecological perspective, 218; family-systems view, 106; systems interpretations, 108
*Psychopathology and Education of the Brain-Injured Child*, Straus and Lehtinen, 235-36
Psychosocial effects: of AIDS diagnosis, 48; of unemployment, 716
Psychosocial factors: in depression, 189; in mental retardation, 273
Psychosocial needs of jail inmates, 666-68
Psychotherapy: borderline personality and, 113, 125-26; and endogenous depression, 188; for learning disabilities, 252; for wife-batterers, 484
Puberty, and eating disorders, 208-9
Public agencies foster care placements, 395
Public assistance, 518; for adolescent mothers, 332; borderline personalities and, 112; for immigrants, 628

Public health services: and addiction, 76; for child maltreatment, 355
Public policy: and family caregivers, 555; and homelessness, 587, 615; and immigration, 619-20; and old age, 507-11
Public schools, and learning disabilities, 243
Public welfare recipients, and homelessness, 595-96
Puerto Ricans, 75
Punishment, imprisonment as, 648-50
Purging behavior, 225

Quakers, view of prison, 648
Quality of life, mental retardation and, 271

Race relations, immigrants and, 624
Racial factors: in child abuse, 347-48; in crime victimization, 425; in depression, 179; in health status, 143
Racism, 8; and imprisonment, 654; and job security, 713
Radiation exposure, 4; and learning disabilities, 239
Rage: at AIDS diagnosis, 49, 57; domestic violence and, 480
Rape, 8, 416; of Asian immigrants, 630; ethnic factors in, 438; medical examination, 434; victim compensation, 424
Rational suicide movement, 691
Rats, alcoholism experiments, 3
Reactive depression, 166-67, 168, 185-86, 189
Reception of immigrants, 624
Reciprocal adaptation, 527
Reciprocal battering, 482
Referrals: for adolescent parents, 328; for battered women, 487; for domestic violence, 498; for eating disorders, 207; for family caregivers, 561-62, 576-77; for homeless people, 602; for pregnant adolescents, 335, 339, 341
Reforms of criminal justice system, 422
Reformulated model of depression, 171
Refugee camps, 633
Refugee Reform Act (1980), 620, 621, 628
Refugees, 620-24, assessments and interventions, 629-38; Indochinese, 633-34; programs and services, 628
Regression, in depression, 189
Regulation of foster care, 388, 389-92, 395, 400, 412
Rehabilitation: of child-maltreating families, 358-63; for frail old people, 524, 538; imprisonment as, 648; of offenders, 422; programs, 144, 720
Rehabilitation Act (1973), 138, 140, 240
Relapses, in addictions, 84
Relationships, 22; abusive, 472, 477; anorexics and, 220; of borderline personalities, 121; caregiving, 549-50; and depression, 176-78; and eating disorders, 226-27; family ties, 462; and job security, 711, 713-14; learning disabilities and, 238; problems of, 16-26; supportive, for schizophrenia, 302-3; unstable, and child maltreatment, 351; *see also* Support groups
—social worker-client: AIDS victims, 57-58; borderline personalities, 101, 122-24; depressed people, 194-95; frail old people, 536-38, 540-41; homeless people, 606-7; in prisons, 673
Relatives of family caregivers, help from, 560
Relaxation, stress management, 23; training for abusive parents, 360
Religion: and obesity, 216; and schizophrenia, 308; and suicide, 682-83
Religious groups: foster care, 383; homeless services, 600-1; immigrant services, 627
Relocation: of crime victims, 434; in old age, 532-33
Repeated foster care placement, 384, 386, 393
Repeated imprisonment, drugs and, 653
Repeated suicide attempts, 689, 691
Reporting requirements: AIDS-related, 51; child maltreatment, 390-91
Reports of child maltreatment, 347; requirements, 390-91
Reproductive behaviors, 329
Research: on child maltreatment, 349-51, 358-59; on HIV, 42-43; on schizophrenia, 293-94; *see also* Studies

Resettlement houses, 627
Resettlement of immigrants, 635-38
Residential facilities, 79, 383, 396; for addicts, 78-79; for adolescent parents, 327-28; for mental retardation, 277
Resilient children to childhood maltreatment, 355
Resistance to help: by frail old people, 567; of jail inmates, 667
Resolve to recover from addiction, 82
Resources, personal: of battered women, 487, 496; and grief resolution, 467; of homeless people, 606; of suicidal people, 697-98
Respiratory disorders of homeless people, 589
Respite care: for adolescent parents, 328; for AIDS caregivers, 52-53; for family caregivers of old people, 562-63; for family of mentally retarded person, 277
Responses: to AIDS, understanding of, 53; to stress, 21
Responsibility: avoidance by borderline personality, 129; for care of old people, 552, 567; social, mental retardation and, 266
Restrictive in-patient care for schizophrenia, 297
Retaliation for crimes, 420-21
Retirement, 504, 510, 721; and suicide, 685
Retribution model of imprisonment, 648-50
Reunification of family, foster care alternatives, 404
Rewards for work, inequitable, 715
Rights, foster care issues, 387
Rigidity, and suicidal behavior, 686
Risk indications, 9-12; addiction, 73-77, 81; adolescent pregnancy, 324-26, 329-30; AIDS, 40-44; borderline personality, 112; child maltreatment, 352-55; chronic illness and disability, 142-43; crime victimization, 425-29; death of child, 452-54; depression, 178-82; domestic violence, 476-82; eating disorders, 213-17; foster care need, 392-94; family caregiving, 556-62; frail old age, 512-18; homelessness, 590-98; immigrants, 625-27; imprisonment, 652-55; job jeopardy, 715-19; learning disabilities, 242-43; mental retardation, 272-76; schizophrenia, 294-97; suicide, 683-89, 705
Ritalin (Methylphenidate), 110-11, 115
Rituals of death, 450-51, 464, 461
Robbery, and physical injury, 426
Role play teaching method, 23; coping skills for addiction, 90
Roles of social work, 19-26
Rubella, 269
Runaways, adolescent pregnancy and, 325-26
Rural areas: homelessness in, 598; mental health services, 720
Russian immigrants, 644n

Sadness, chronic, 467
Safehomes for battered women, 483
Safer sex, education for, 42, 45, 51
Safety: of battered women, 486, 487-88, 496-97, 499; of homeless people, 592; illusion of, 436
Sale of drugs, criminalization of, 418
Samaritans (suicide prevention organization), 689-90
Sanctuary movement, 623
San Francisco, AIDS project, 44
Schizophrenia, 4, 12, 286-312; family systems view, 106; genetic factors, 3; psychoeducational family therapy, 118-19; racial factors, 179; and suicide, 687
"Schizophrenia," Matorin, 286-316
Schizophrenogenic mother theory, 107
Schizotypal characteristics, and borderline personality, 109-10
School-aged children, interparental violence and, 481
Schools: and adolescent pregnancy, 323; employment programs, 720; health programs, 327; and hyperactivity, 248; immigrants and, 636-37; for mentally retarded children, 277; performance of maltreated child, 365; sex education, 322; suicide prevention programs, 690
Scientific knowledge about HIV, 42-43
Secondary depression, 189-90
Secondary emotional problems of learning disability, 251
Secondary prevention of child maltreatment, 356, 357-58
Second National Survey of Family Violence, 479

Security of employment, 710; threats to, 711-14; *see also* Job jeopardy

Seizure disorders, 272; and learning disabilities, 243

Select Committee on Children, Youth and Families, 389

Selective abstraction, 170

Self-assertion of women, men and, 476-77

Self-blame: by crime victims, 437; domestic violence and, 480; for job insecurity, 715; for unemployment, 717

Self-care, chronic disease and, 515

Self-concept: obesity and, 210-11; of old people, 508

Self-control, development of, 122; for abusive parents, 360

Self-defeating behavior: advice to discourage, 24; of poor blacks, 8

Self-destructive behavior, 23; counseling for, 122, 123; treatment effectiveness, 125-26

Self-determination issues, 369, 725

Self-discipline of prison inmates, 655

Self-efficacy, perceived, and addiction, 85, 90, 91

Self-esteem, 207; addiction and, 68; and adolescent pregnancy, 340; ageism and, 508; of anorexics, 220; and body image, 212; of borderline personalities, 121; childhood maltreatment and, 354; chronic illness and, 148; disabilities and, 154; domestic violence and, 478, 480, 488; learning disabilities and, 251, 260; low, 8, 166; of prison inmates, 655, 666-67, 670

Self-harm, 678; *see also* Parasuicide

Self-help groups: addicts, 77-78, 80, 86, 89, 91; battered women, 489; bereaved parents, 455-56, 461; child-abuse prevention, 356; crime victims, 423, 437; depressed people, 182; disease-oriented, 145, 150; eating disorders, 221-22; families with mentally ill members, 183, 300-1; immigrants, 627; obesity, 226, 227; refugees, 628; schizophrenics, 292, 306; social workers and, 574; suicide survivors, 689; *see also* Mutual aid groups; Support groups

Self-identity: and ageing, 506; employment and, 716

Self-image: AIDS and, 48-49; chronic illness and, 148; of foster care children, 394

Self-protection programs, 420

Self psychology, view of borderline personality, 104

Self-respect, and job security, 711

Self-treatment of depression, 182

Self-worth, and domestic violence, 488

Sensitization, to victim issues, 430, 431

Sensory deprivation, and mental retardation, 271

Sentencing of criminals, 428, 433

Separation, in marriage: and depression, 179; domestic violence and, 479, 490, 491; and risk of victimization, 425; young children and, 448

Separation-individuation process in women, 208; anorexia and, 222

Serotonin, and alcoholism, 3

Services, *see* Programs and services

Severe chronic illness, 138; of children, 142

Severe mental retardation, 266, 267-68, 272, 273, 280

Severity of addiction, 82-83; and type of help, 84

Sex differences, *see* Gender

Sex education, in schools, 322

Sex-role stereotyping, and wife-battering, 475-77

Sexual abuse of child, 346, 348

Sexual activity, 10; adolescent, 324, 330-31; and HIV transmission, 42; first occurrence, 323, 324; media and, 8-9; obesity and, 216

Sexual assault: in prison, 652; victim compensation, 424

Sexual development, chronic disorders and, 159

Sexual freedom, AIDS and, 39

Sexual harassment, and job security, 713, 715

Sexuality of adolescents, attitudes toward, 321

Shame: bulimia and, 207; domestic violence and, 480; of addicts, 82

Shanti Project, San Francisco, 44

Shared definitions, worker-client, 528

Shared parenting, foster care, 398, 401-2, 407-10, 412

Sharing of family caregiving, 552

Sheltered facilities: residential, for old people, 524; workshops for mentally retarded children, 277

Shelters: for battered women, 482, 483-84; for crime victims, 430; for homeless people, 600-1; users of, 586, 588, 592

Shen-Ryan, Angela, "Immigrants and Refugees," 618-46

Short-term interventions for domestic violence, 488-89, 499

Short-term memory, 247

Siblings: with AIDS, 45; of chronically ill children, 143, 145; death of, 453, 458, 460, 462-66; of disabled children, 158-59; of family caregivers, 576, 577-79; foster placement, 400; of learning-disabled children, 256; of obese children, 217; of pregnant adolescents, 334-36, 339, 341; of schizophrenics, 309, 311

Side effects of schizophrenia medication, 301

SIDS (Sudden Infant Death Syndrome), 452, 458

Silverman, Beth, "Workers in Job Jeopardy," 710-48

Simon, Barbara, "Imprisonment," 647-76; "Worker in Job Jeopardy," 710-48

Sinequan (doxepin), 13

Single homeless people, 592-94; men, 588

Single mothers, 325; programs to prevent child maltreatment, 357

Single old people, 512-13

Single-parent families, 6-7, 553; and adolescent pregnancy, 323; chronic illness and, 162; homeless, 595; immigrant, 626; with mentally retarded child, 275; and unemployment, 718

Situational assessment of alcoholism, 88

Situational Confidence Questionnaire (SCQ), 88-89

Situational interventions in addictions, 85

Skills: for abusive parents, 360; for neglectful parents, 372-73

—social: and child maltreatment, 351; for community living, 609; for jail inmates, 668; and learning disabilities, 249-50, 254, 255, 258-59; lacking in suicidal persons, 686

Skills development interventions, for addiction, 69, 85

Slow adaptive mechanisms, 250-51

Small motor coordination problems, 246

Smith, Gregory, "Family Caregivers of the Frail Elderly," 549-83

Social adjustment, mental retardation and, 267

Social attitudes to grief, 467

Social-behavioral model of suicidal behavior, 682, 695

Social change: and adolescent pregnancy, 322-23; and domestic violence, 476; and grief experience, 451-52; new classes, 584

Social class: and body weight, 211, 216; and depression, 179; and domestic violence, 474; and mental illness, 4

Social competence of children, interparental violence and, 481

Social construction of disability, 138-39

Social control, organized, 421

Social costs of teenage pregnancy, 319-20

Social Darwinism, 714-15; unemployment and, 716

Social development, obesity and, 216

Social dysfunction, addiction as, 69-70

Social exchange theory of domestic violence, 477

Social factors: in addictions, 71-73, 86; in adolescent pregnancy, 322; in depression, 172, 173-74, 176; in domestic violence, 474; in eating disorders, 211-12, 215-16; in imprisonment, 654-55; in old age needs, 509

Social function: of homeless people, 608-9; in old age, 516; in schizophrenia, 289

Social interventions for young addicts, 77

Socialization: of men, and domestic violence, 476; women, and depression, 194

Social learning approach to child maltreatment, 348-49, 352-53

Social needs, of schizophrenia, 296

Social-network maps, 23

Social networks: and addictions, 86; and domestic violence, 488-89; illness-related, 158; *see also* Support networks

Social organizations for addicts, 86

Social pathology, 13-14

Social policy: ageism in, 508-11; and foster care, 388-89

Social pressures: and addiction relapses, 84; and alcoholism, 88, 90

Social process, grief as, 451

Social relationships, childhood maltreatment and, 354

Social responses to homelessness, 591

Social responsibility, mental retardation and, 266

Social-role therapy for schizophrenia, 298

Social Security, 140, 141

Social skills: and child maltreatment, 351; for jail inmates, 668; and learning disabilities, 249-50, 254, 255, 258-59; lacking in suicidal persons, 686

Social support, 9-10; and adaptive functioning, 72; for addicts, 81; of adolescent prison inmates, 654; and child maltreatment, 351; chronic illness and, 149-50; and depression, 169, 176-77; for family of mentally retarded child, 281; grief and, 712, 724; and suicide, 685, 450-51; and homelessness, 592; for immigrants, 623; and job insecurity

Social values, Southeast Asian, 642

Social welfare, inequities of, 511

Social work, 12-15, 19-20

Social workers, 1-2, 15-26, 28; and addicts, 78-92; and adolescent pregnancy, 329-42; and AIDS, 35-36, 41-42, 45-60; and bereaved parents, 454-68; and borderline personalities, 116-32; and child maltreatment, 363-75; and child protection laws, 391-92; and chronic illness and disability, 144-63; and crime victims, 429-45; and depression, 165, 182-96; and domestic violence, 471, 473-74, 476, 482-500; and eating disorders, 205, 207, 217-29; and employment stresses, 710-11; and family caregivers, 553, 559-79; and

foster care, 387-90, 398-412; and frail old people, 522-42; and homeless people, 605-17; and immigrants, 618-19, 622, 628-44; in jails, 660; and job insecurity, 717, 719-45; and learning disabilities, 234, 243-45, 252-61; and mental retardation, 265, 275-84; and nursing home care, 520; in prisons, 649-50, 653, 655, 656, 662-74; and schizophrenia, 286-87, 291-92, 298-313; and suicidal behavior, 677, 689-705

Societal contexts, 6-9; addictions, 70-73; adolescent pregnancy, 322-24; AIDS, 38-39; borderline personality, 111-12; child maltreatment, 351; chronic physical illness and disability, 139-41; crime victims, 420-24; death of child, 450-52; depression, 176-78; domestic violence, 474-76; eating disorders, 211-13; family care for old people, 553-56; foster care, 388-92; frail old age, 507-11; homelessness, 589-90; immigration, 623-24; imprisonment, 650-52; job insecurity, 714-15; learning disabilities, 239-42; mental retardation, 271; schizophrenia, 292-94; suicidal behavior, 682-83

Societal expectations, and child maltreatment, 366-67

Societies for the Prevention of Cruelty to Children, 390

Society: AIDS epidemic and, 37, 38-39; and child maltreatment, 349-50, 356; and chronic illness, 162-63; dysfunctions of, 4-5

Sociodemographic characteristics: of child maltreatment, 352; of frail old people, 512-13

Socioeconomic factors: and child maltreatment, 350, 352; in Cuban immigration, 632; in drug abuse, 73; and eating disorders, 213-16; ethnicity and, 75; in foster care, 387-89, 392, 400; in imprisonment, 651-53; and learning disabilities, 243, 244-45; in mental retardation, 271, 273, 274-75; in old age, 554; in schizophrenia, 295; in service needs, 76

Sociograms, 23

Sociological theories: of child mal-

Sociological theories (*Continued*) treatment, 348; of schizophrenia, 290; of suicide, 680

Sociopathy, and suicidal behavior, 687

Somatic problems: domestic violence and, 480, 481; of Southeast Asians, 641-42

Sorrow, chronic, 448, 461, 467

South Carolina, homeless women, 593

Southeast Asian immigrants, 633-34, 643-44$n$; departure experiences, 630; resettlement problems, 637-38

Soviet émigés, 631; resettlement problems, 635-36; transit experiences, 634

Specialized addiction services, 77-78

Specification of action tasks, 25

Specific Development Disorders, 238

Specific protection programs, 13-14

Speech therapy, 251, 258

Splitting, in borderline personality, 105

Sponsorship of immigrants, 620

Sporadic depressive disorder, 189

Spousal caregivers, 554, 556-58; coping strategies, 560-61

Spouse abuse, *see* Domestic violence

Spouses of AIDS victims, 51

Stage-of-migration framework, 629-38, 642-43

Stage theories of mourning, 448

Standardization, of foster care, 398-99

Standard of living, of old people, 504

Standards of mental health for prison inmates, 657-58

Stanford-Binet Intelligence Scale, 266

Starvation, unemployment and, 716

State: crimes against, 422; responsibility to crime victims, 423-24

State prison inmates, 652

State prosecutors, 433

States: child maltreatment definitions, 345; mental health standards for prison inmates, 657-58; responsibilities for children, 389-91; schools for mentally retarded, 279-80

Status, employment and, 716

Status of case against crime perpetrator, 434-35

Stelazine (trifluoperazine), 115, 131

Stereotypes of old age, 508-9

Stigma, social: of AIDS, 39, 53; of bereavement, 449-50; of domestic violence, 473; of homelessness, 591; of

imprisonment, 650; of unemployment, 716, 717, 718, 726

Still-birth, grief at, 459

Stimulant medications: for borderline personality, 110-11; for hyperactivity, 251-52

Stolen documents, replacement of, 436

Street people, 586

Strengths, personal: of battered women, 496, 487; of old people, 534-35, 540; of suicidal person, 697-98

Stress, 16, 18-20, 23; and addictions, 81; and borderline personality, 108, 123; and child maltreatment, 351, 353, 363, 364; coping skills, 21; from death of child, 458, 466; and depression, 176, 180-81, 193-94; and domestic violence, 474-75, 478, 480; of family caregiving, 555-57, 556-64; of family with mentally retarded child, 274; of foster care children, 392; of homelessness, 591; of immigrants, 623, 638; job-related, 710, 715, 739-40; from life transitions, 15-16; of old age, 504, 517-18; of parents, 399; and schizophrenia, 293, 308; and suicidal behavior, 685, 692

Structural theories of crime, 419

Structured programs for learning disabilities, 244

Studies: of child maltreatment, 346-48, 352-55, 358-59; of depression, 173-75; of homelessness, 586, 594-95; of schizophrenia, 294-95

Stutz, Emily, "Children in Foster Care," 382-415

Subaverage intelligence, 266

Subjective appraisal of caregiver situation, 559

Subpopulations, identification of, 14

Substance abuse, 8, 12; by adolescent Russian immigrants, 636; and child welfare, 389; crime and, 653-64; depressed parents and, 180; and domestic violence, 477-78, 480, 491; and eating disorders, 206; homelessness and, 588, 593, 594, 609; and imprisonment, 651, 654, 669-73; and job jeopardy, 729; prevention programs for prison inmates, 659-60; and suicidal behavior, 687;

workplace programs, 722; *see also* Alcoholism; Drug abuse
Substitute care services, 395-96; for chronic illness and disability, 145
Success of treatment for addiction, 77
Sudden death, 446; of child, 458
Sudden evacuation of immigrants, 630
Sudden Infant Death Syndrome (SIDS), 452, 458
Suicidal behavior, 122-23, 677-78; case illustrations, 126-32, 700-4; depression and, 175; effectiveness of interventions, 125-26; grief and, 451; imminent risk, 694-95; job insecurity and, 720; medication for, 115; problem domain, 678; *see also* Parasuicide; Suicide
Suicide, 8, 11, 12; and borderline, 274; of old people, 516-17; risk factors, 684; schizophrenia and, 294; theories of, 679-82; thoughts of, 166, 184, 480, 678
"Suicide and Suicidal Behavior," Ivanoff, 677-709
Suicide gestures, 678; *see also* Parasuicide
Suicide prevention agencies, 689
Supplemental Security Income (SSI), 140, 276; for refugees, 621
Supplementary services: for addiction, 80; for chronic illness and disability, 145; to families, 395
Support, social: and adaptive functioning, 72; for addicts, 81; chronic illness and, 149-50; and depression, 169, 176-77; for family of mentally retarded child, 281; and grief, 450-51; for job-insecure workers, 724
Support groups: for adolescent parents, 328, 339-40; AIDS-related, 45, 51, 52, 53, 55-61; for Alzheimer's disease caregivers, 573-74; for battered women, 484, 488-89; for bereaved parents, 455-56; for chronic disorders, 150, 151; for crime victims, 430, 437, 442-44; for families of borderline personalities, 119; for family caregivers, 563-64, 569-70; for former prison inmates, 671-72; for minor depressive disorders, 187; for parents of disabled children, 155, 156-58; for schizophrenia, 303, 306; *see also* Mutual aid groups; Self-help groups

Supportive counseling: for battered women, 491-92; for chronic illness, 148-49; for depression, 188, 192
Supportive environments, borderline personality and, 111-12
Supportive relationships for schizophrenia, 302
Support networks: for addicts, 80, 86, 91; of adolescent prison inmates, 654; informal, of old people, 514; of social workers, 46
Support programs and services: for battered women, 482, 487; to families, 395; and foster care, 400-1, 408-9; for homeless people, 608; for mental illness, 183; for parents of mentally retarded child, 275; for prison inmates, 656, 661-62; *see also* Programs and services
Supreme Court, and alien eligibility for asylum, 621
Survivor guilt: and death of child, 454; of immigrants, 630
Survivors, 5; of multiple AIDS losses, 45; of suicides, 688-89
Symbolic learning, 21
Symptom models of addiction, 68
Systematic desensitization stress management, 23
Systems theories of borderline personality, 104, 108-11

Take Off Pounds Sensibly (TOPS), 221
Talking about suicide, 678, 692; *see also* Parasuicide; Suicidal behavior
Tardive dyskinesia, 116
Task formulation, specific, 25
Teaching methods, 21-22
Technological change, and job insecurity, 711
Teenage pregnancy, *see* Adolescents, pregnant
Tegretol (carbamazepine), 115
Temperament, 237; and child maltreatment, 353
Temporary shelters: for battered women, 488; for homeless people, 600-601
Terminal phase of chronic illness, 146
Termination: of abusive relationship, 475, 477, 489, 491; of parental rights, 404
Tertiary prevention of child maltreatment, 356, 358-63

Tests: for HIV infection, 43, 51; of learning disabilities, 244, 245

Thailand, refugee camps, 633-34

Theories: of addiction, 66-70; of child maltreatment, 348-49; of criminal behavior, 417-19; of depression, 167-76; of schizophrenia, 290-92; of suicide, 679-82

Therapeutic communities: for addicts, 70, 77, 78-79; in prisons, 661

Thinness, 211-12

Thioridazine (Mellaril), 127, 131

Thiothixene (Navane), 115

Threats of suicide, 678; *see also* Parasuicide

Threats to job security, 711-14

Thyroid deficiency, during pregnancy, 269

Time line, of schizophrenia, 308

Tobacco, fetal effects, 269

Tofranil (imipramine), 115

Tolerance, social, of violence, 476

TOPS (Take Off Pounds Sensibly), 221

Toseland, Ronald W., "Family Caregivers of the Frail Elderly," 549-83

Toxemia, 269

Toxic substances: and genetic factors, 4; and mental retardation, 269

Toxoplasmosis, 269

Training: for family caregiving, 565; for suicide prevention, 677

Trajectory of chronic illness, 146-47

Transference regression, 121

Transit experiences of immigrants, 633-34, 642

Transitional services for homeless people, 599-603, 614-15

Transitional stresses, 15-16

Transmission of AIDS and HIV, 40-41, 42

Traumas of migration, 630-31, 643

Treatments: of borderline personality, 104-5; for depression, 186, 195-96; medical, of HIV infections, 43-44; for schizophrenia, 296-97

Treatment outcomes of addiction services, 80

Tricyclic antidepressants, 115, 131; for bulimia, 223

Trifluoperazine (Stelazine), 115, 131

Trilafon (perphenazine), 115

Troubled workers, 714, 718-19; assessments and interventions, 725-33

Trust, development of, and domestic violence, 488, 492

Tuberculosis, among homeless people, 589

Turnbull, Joanne E., "Depression," 165-204

Twin studies, 3, 237; depression rates, 172; eating disorders, 210; schizophrenia, 294; suicide rates, 681

Two-parent families, homeless, 595

Ultimate resource, physical violence as, 477

Unaccompanied minor immigrants, 627; Cuban, 632, 634, 637; psychic problems, 630

Unborn child, death of, 458

Unconvicted jail inmates, 651

Understanding, for battered women, 482

Undocumented aliens, 619, 622-23; services for, 628

Unemployment, 5, 7, 710, 716-17; and child maltreatment, 352; and domestic violence, 10, 477; imprisonment and, 652; and suicide, 685; unexpected, 718-19

Unions, 723-24; and job jeopardy, 730-33; literacy programs, 723; member assistance programs, 722, 724, 733-45

Unipolar depressive disorder, 166, 168; age of onset, 179

Uniqueness of caregiving situations, 557

United States: attitudes toward adolescent sexuality, 321; drug use in, 70-71; HIV strain, 40; migration to, 618-19; prison population, 651

United States Census (1980), 388

United States House of Representatives, Select Committee on Children, Youth and Families, 389

Universalist approach to age problems, 509-10

University of New Hampshire, Family Violence Research Laboratory, 474

Unplanned pregnancy, 4-5, 342; *see also* Adolescents, pregnant

Unprotected intercourse, 320, 329

Unresolved grief, 186; of parents, 449

Unsubstantiated reports of child maltreatment, 347

Urban areas: adolescent sexual activity, 324; crime in, 425-26; depression in, 180; foster care systems, 388-89; and mental retardation, 273; schizophrenia in, 293, 295

Valium (Benzodiazepines), 115
Values, social: and child maltreatment, 368-69; communication of, 72; of prison inmates, 655; Southeast Asian, 642
Van Arsdale, Martin Van Buren, 383
Van Bulow, Barbara, "Eating Problems," 205-33
Variability in caregiving situations, 552-53
Variables in child maltreatment, 352
VCIS (Voluntary Cooperative Information System), 383, 384
Vegetative dimension of depression, 166
Venereal disease of prison inmates, 654
Vera Institute of Justice, 416-17
Verbal abuse of child, 346
Victim-blaming theories: of crime, 418-19; of domestic violence, 471, 483
Victim impact statements, 424, 428, 429-30, 444
Victimless crimes, 418
Victims, 5; of domestic violence, 8, 471; *see also* Battered women; Children, maltreatment of
—of crime, 5, 8, 10, 416-17; assessments and interventions, 432-38; case illustrations, 439-44; problem domain, 417-20; programs and services, 429-31; risks and needs of population, 425-29; societal context, 420-24
Victims of Crime Act (VOCA), 424
Victim-witness assistance programs, 417, 439-40; government-funded, 431
Videka-Sherman, Lynn, "Child Abuse and Neglect," 345-81
Vietnamese, departure experiences, 630
Vietnam veterans, drug use, 71
Violence, 8, 10, 472; and child maltreatment, 350; domestic, 471-502;

poverty and, 9; social tolerance of, 476
Violent crime, 11-12, 416; consequences of, 426-27; risk of victimization, 425; substance abuse and, 653
Visual methods of teaching, 22-23
Visual perception, problems of, 246-47
VOCA (Victims of Crime Act), 424
Vocational counseling: for adolescents, 327; for refugees, 621
Vocational rehabilitation services for mental retardation, 277
Vocational training programs, 720; for addicts, 70; for prison inmates, 662
Voluntary agencies: for crime victims, 444-45; disease-oriented, 144-45; for homeless people, 600-1; immigrant services, 623-24, 627
Voluntary Cooperative Information System (VCIS), 383, 384
Voluntary foster care placement, 394-95
Voluntary hospitals, and homeless people, 589
Voluntary migration, 644n
Volunteer work, AIDS-related, 45, 53
Vulnerability factors for depression, 179, 181

Wage-replacement programs, 141
Wechsler Intelligence Scale for Children-Revised (WISC-R), 266-67
Weight Watchers, 221, 226
Weiss, Joan O., "Chronic Physical Illness and Disability," 137-64
Welfare hotels, 596-97
Welfare state: and crime victim compensation, 423; and job insecurity, 715
Wellness, 14; programs for, 724
Western culture: and body weight, 211-12; and wife abuse, 475
Western Europe. HIV strain, 40
West Germany, immigration services, 634
Whites: adolescent pregnancy, 325; adolescent sexual activity, 324; drug use patterns, 74-75; suicide of, 11, 683, 684-85
Widowhood, 512-13; and mourning, 451

Wife-battering, 9, 14, 480-81, 489-90; programs or, 484; views of, 473-74; *see also* Domestic violence

Withdrawal: from addiction, 83, 84 —social: as coping strategy, 737-38; learning disability and, 251

Witnesses of crime, 429; programs for, 431, 441-42

Women: addicts, 67, 74, 77; alcohol use, 74; battered, 5, 8, 419, 471, 478-80, 482, 483-84, 593; body image, 211-12; child maltreatment research and, 350; and death of child, 454, 460; depression of, 11, 179, 180, 182, 186-87, 189, 190, 194; disabled, 141; dominance by men, 476-77; eating disorders, 213-14; elderly, 504-5, 512-14, 516, 539, 541; family caregivers, 525, 552, 553, 557-58, 560; HIV-infected, 39, 40-41, 45, 663; homeless, 588, 592-94; immigrant, 626; job inequities, 715; job insecurity, 712, 713; nondrinkers, 75; obese, 216; prison inmates, 653, 654, 662, 663, 668-74; risks of, 11, 425; suicidal behavior, 126, 700-4; suicide, 517, 685; suicide attempts, 684-85; in work force, 553, 720; *see also* Adolescents, pregnant; Females

Women's movement: and crime victims, 416, 423; and domestic violence, 471, 472, 476; and family caregiving roles, 553

Woodrow, Richard, "Workers in Job Jeopardy," 710-48

Work, need for, 716

Workers, as social work clients, 725-30

"Workers in Job Jeopardy," Silverman, Simon, Woodrow, 710-48

Work force: foreign-born, 619; shifts in, 720; women in, 553, 720

Work organization, as environment, 730-33

Workplace stress, and domestic violence, 478

Work reentry contract, 90-91

Work release programs for prison inmates, 662

Work site programs, 722-24; for drug prevention, 70; for job jeopardy, 719, 730-33

World Health Organization, HIV infection estimates, 40

Worthlessness, feelings of, 166, 184; domestic violence and, 480

X-linked mental retardation, 268

Xanax, 115, 131

Young people: addiction service needs, 76-77; alcoholic relapses, 84; employment programs, 719-20; homeless, 594; job insecurity, 713; risks of, 12, 425; substance abuse, 73-74; suicide of, 683, 684, 687-88, 690; *see also* Adolescents; Children

Young teens: babies born to, 325; pregnancy rate, 324; *see also* Adolescents, pregnant

Yugoslavia, schizophrenia, 295